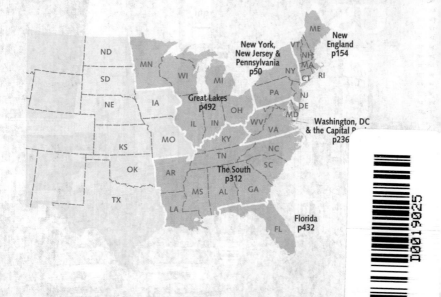

New England p154

New York, New Jersey & Pennsylvania p50

Great Lakes p492

Washington, DC & the Capital R... p236

The South p312

Florida p432

THIS EDITION WRITTEN AND RESEARCHED BY
Karla Zimmerman
Glenda Bendure, Jeff Campbell, Ned Friary,
Michael Grosberg, Emily Matchar, Kevin Raub, Regis St Louis

welcome to Eastern USA

Mighty Metropolises

New York, New York is top of the heap, as Frank Sinatra famously crooned. Brimming with 8.3 million people, the megalopolis looms like an alien mother-ship over the East, offering a mind-blowing array of culture, cuisine and entertainment. Cloud-poking Chicago; power-brokering Washington, DC; and fiery, Latin-fused Miami rise up close on its heels as one-of-a-kind cityscapes. Look deeper, and you'll find the captivating old quarters of New Orleans, still rising up from waterlogged ashes, and raw-edged Detroit, where young do-it-yourselfers are flocking to transform the abandoned city.

Beaches & Back Roads

The East Coast is where America gets its beach on, from the wild dunes and whale-rich waters of Cape Cod, to the taffy-shop-lined boardwalks of Ocean City, to the coral reefs of the Florida Keys. Inland, nature puts on a show in the swampy Florida Everglades, wolf-howling Boundary Waters, mist-tipped Appalachian Mountains and, in New England's forests which blaze red, orange and yellow each autumn. Slowpoke byways unfurl throughout so you can soak up the landscapes, along with historic Civil War battlefields and kitschy roadside attractions of the giant fiberglass-spaceman ilk.

Flanked by mega-cities New York City and Chicago; landscaped with dune-backed beaches, smoky mountains and gator swamps; and steeped in musical roots, the East rolls out a sweet trip.

(left) Times Square (p71), New York City
(below) Fall foliage, New Hampshire (p214)

Chowhounds' Smorgasbord

Good eatin' reaches epic proportions in the region, and belt loosening becomes a necessity. On the menu: hulking steamed lobsters with melted butter in Maine's seafood shacks, bagels and lox in Manhattan's delis, saucy barbecue ribs in Memphis' roadhouses, butter-smothered biscuits in North Carolina's diners, hot-spiced gumbo in New Orleans' cafes and – for dessert – thick slices of berry pie in the Midwest's supper clubs. You'll certainly work up a thirst. That's when the region's sweet white wines, microbrewed beers and home-grown bourbon do their slaking.

Cultural Cradle

The museums here are the nation's greatest hits – the Smithsonian, housing everything but the kitchen sink; the Metropolitan Museum of Art, a city-state of treasures; and the Art Institute of Chicago, hanging Impressionists by the roomful. Musically speaking, the Eastern USA birthed the blues, jazz and rock and roll. Explore the roots at Sun Studio in Memphis, where Elvis got his groove on; Cleveland's Rock and Roll Hall of Fame, for artifacts like Jimi Hendrix' Stratocaster; and the juke joints of Clarksdale, where the blues' slide guitar first pierced the air. For sky-high designs, Chicago and New York are drawing boards for the modern era's great architects.

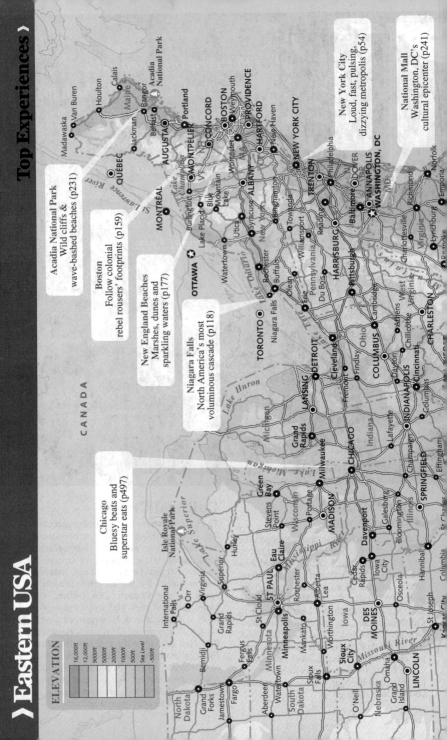

› Eastern USA

Top Experiences ›

Acadia National Park
Wild cliffs &
wave-bashed beaches (p231)

Boston
Follow colonial
rebel rousers' footprints (p159)

New England Beaches
Marshes, dunes and
sparkling waters (p177)

Niagara Falls
North America's most
voluminous cascade (p118)

Chicago
Bluesy beats and
superstar eats (p497)

New York City
Loud, fast, pulsing,
dizzying metropolis (p54)

National Mall
Washington, DC's
cultural epicenter (p241)

ELEVATION
16,000ft
12,000ft
9000ft
5000ft
2000ft
1000ft
500ft
Sea Level
-500ft

Appalachian Trail
Trek from
Georgia to Maine (p301)

Blue Ridge Parkway
Sublime drive through
the Appalachians (p304)

Great Smoky Mountains
Misty, forested,
most-visited park (p330)

Walt Disney World
The world's
greatest theme park (p485)

Miami
Chic, sexy,
Latin-spiced culture (p437)

Florida Keys
Coral reefs and
a helluva party (p458)

Everglades National Park
Seek alligators
in the swamp (p455)

New Orleans
Sazerac-soaked
Cajun banquet (p402)

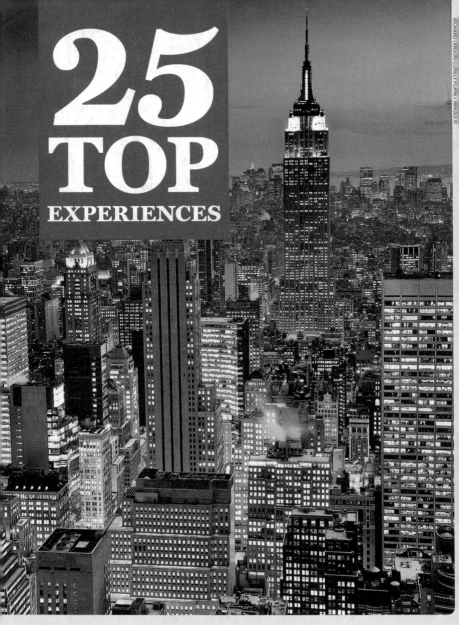

25 TOP EXPERIENCES

New York City

1 Home to striving artists, hedge-fund moguls and immigrants from every corner of the globe, New York City (p54) is constantly reinventing itself. It remains one of the world centers of fashion, theater, food, music, publishing, advertising and finance. A staggering number of museums, parks and ethnic neighborhoods are scattered through the five boroughs. Do as every New Yorker does: hit the streets. Every block reflects the character and history of this dizzying kaleidoscope, and on even a short walk you can cross continents.

National Mall

2 Nearly two miles long and lined with iconic monuments and hallowed marble buildings, the National Mall (p241) is the epicenter of Washington, DC's, political and cultural life. In the summer, massive music and food festivals are staged here, while year-round visitors wander the halls of America's finest museums lining the green. For exploring American history, there's no better place to ruminate, whether tracing your hand along the Vietnam War Memorial or ascending the steps of Lincoln Memorial (p247), where Martin Luther King Jr gave his famous 'I Have a Dream' speech.
Lincoln Memorial

Walt Disney World

3 Want to set the bar high? Call yourself 'The Happiest Place on Earth.' Walt Disney World (p485) does, and then pulls out all the stops to deliver the exhilarating sensation that you are the most important character in the show. Despite all the frantic rides, entertainment and nostalgia, the magic is watching your own child swell with belief after they have made Goofy laugh, been curtsied to by Cinderella, guarded the galaxy with Buzz Lightyear, and battled Darth Maul like your very own Jedi knight.

Chicago

4 The Windy City (p497) will blow you away with its architecture, lakefront beaches and world-class museums. But its true mojo is its blend of high culture and earthy pleasures. Is there another metropolis that dresses its Picasso sculpture in local sports team gear, or where residents queue for hot dogs and to dine in North America's top restaurant in equal measure? While the winters are long, come summer, Chicago fetes the arrival of warm days with a huge array of food and music festivals that make fine use of its waterfront. *Crown Fountain* (p499), by Jaume Plensa

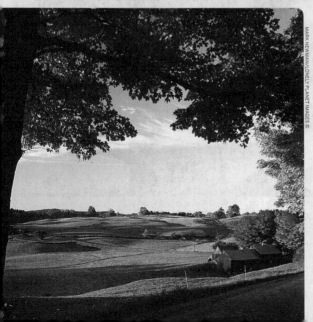

Fall Foliage in New England

5 It's a major event, and one approaching epic proportions in New England (p154): watching the leaves change color. You can do it anywhere – all you need is one brilliant tree. But if you're most people, you want lots of trees. From the Lichfield Hills in Connecticut and the Berkshires in Massachusetts to Stowe in northern Vermont, entire hillsides blaze in brilliant crimsons, oranges and yellows. Covered bridges and white-steeple churches with abundant maple trees put Vermont and New Hampshire in the forefront of leaf-peeping heaven. Vermont (p204)

6 Snaking across the nation's belly, this fragile ribbon of concrete was the USA's original road trip (p526), connecting Chicago with Los Angeles in 1926. True, most of the Mother Road unfurls through the western part of the country, but the 300-mile section in Illinois offers a classic, time-warped stretch to tap into. Fork into thick slabs of pie in small-town diners; snap photos of roadside attractions like the Gemini Giant, a sky-high fiberglass spaceman; and motor on past neon signs, drive-in movie theaters and other Americana.

New Orleans

7 While the rest of us eat to live, New Orleanians live to eat. The French, Spanish, Sicilians, Filipinos, Haitians, Germans and Lord knows who else have all contributed to the gastro-amalgamation here, making New Orleans (p402) the most foodcentric city in the USA. Sure, there's unique history, gorgeous architecture and amazing music, but, in the end, a visit here inevitably turns out to be all about the food. Get out of the French Quarter and eat with the locals in Riverbend, Uptown, Faubourg Maringy and the Bywater for the true taste of N'awlins. Beignets, Cafe du Monde (p414)

Blue Ridge Parkway

8 In the southern Appalachian Mountains of Virginia and North Carolina, you can take in sublime sunsets, watch for wildlife and lose all sense of the present day while staring off at the vast wilderness surrounding this 469-mile roadway (p304). Dozens of great hikes take you deeper into nature, from easy trails along lakes and streams to challenging scrambles up to eagles' nest heights. Camp or spend the night at forest lodges, and don't miss the great bluegrass and mountain music scene of nearby towns.

BONNIEBMAY/DREAMSTIME ©

KEVIN TAVARES/SHUTTERSTOCK ©

Niagara Falls

9 Crowded? Cheesy? Well, yes. Niagara (p118) is short, too – it barely cracks the top 500 worldwide for height. But c'mon, when those great muscular bands of water arch over the precipice like liquid glass, roaring into the void below, and when you sail toward it in a misty little boat, Niagara Falls impresses big time. In terms of sheer volume, nowhere in North America beats its thundering cascade, with more than one million bathtubs of water plummeting over the edge every second.

Civil War Sites

10 Sites scatter over swathes of the eastern USA, from Pennsylvania to Louisiana. Renowned places to connect with America's darkest hours are at Antietam (p278), Maryland (site of the bloodiest day in American history, where 23,000 soldiers died); Gettysburg (p145), Pennsylvania (the battlefield and cemetery, where President Lincoln delivered his 'Four score...' address); and Vicksburg (p398), Mississippi (a must for history buffs, with a 16-mile driving tour through the areas General Grant besieged for 47 days). In summer, many sites host battle re-enactments.
National Military Park, Vicksburg

OLIVER STREWE/LONELY PLANET IMAGES ©

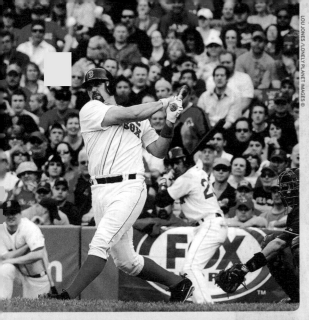

Boston

11 From cobbled colonial lanes to crazed sports fans, Boston (p159) brews a colorful scene. It is arguably the USA's most historic city – site of the Boston Tea Party, Paul Revere's ride and the first battle of the Revolutionary War – all of which you can trace on the 2.5-mile, redbrick Freedom Trail. Harvard University's campus lets you do a little rebel-rousing yourself at its famed music clubs. Boston's oyster houses, cafes and trattorias (especially thick in the Italian North End) fortify you for the exploits. Boston Red Sox, Fenway Park (p174)

Antebelum South

12 Steeped in history and regional pride, the Antebelum South is about grand homes and cotton plantations, moss-draped trees and azalea-choked gardens. Absorb the vibe in Charleston (p332), with strolling, admiring the architecture and lingering over dinners on the verandah. Fall under the spell of Savannah's (p383) live oaks, shady boulevards, seafood and humid nights. Or ogle the mansions of genteel Natchez (p400), the oldest town on the Mississippi River, where you'll be hard-pressed to see more sweeping staircases per square mile. Charleston

Florida Keys

14 This island chain (p458) drifts as far south as you can get in the continental USA. Except for drinking and partying (more on that below), people come to the Keys to do stuff: fish, snorkel, dive, kayak, hike, cycle, fish some more, snorkel again, swim with dolphins. North America's best coral reefs percolate under the jade-green water and provide brag-worthy expeditions. Then there's Key West, the gloriously unkempt, bawdy, freak-loving exclamation point at the end of the line. Hippies, fire-jugglers, artists and other free spirits converge on its carnival atmosphere after dark. Islamorada (p459)

Musical Roots

13 Name the genre, and it probably began here. The Mississippi Delta birthed the blues, while New Orleans opened the door to jazz. Rock and roll arrived the day Elvis Presley walked into Sun Studio (p346) in Memphis. And country made its way from fiddle-and-banjo Appalachian hamlets to Nashville's Grand Ole Opry (p354). The Mississippi River took the music north, where Chicago and Detroit riffed into the electric blues and Motown sound, respectively. It all translates into great live music wherever you are in the region. Trumpeter, New Orleans

Miami

15 Miami (p437) bubbles with a swank mayhem of Latin-world expectations, and indeed, the city moves to a rhythm different from anywhere else in the USA. In cigar-filled dancehalls, Havana expats dance to son and boleros, while in exclusive nightclubs stiletto-heeled, fiery-eyed Brazilian models shake to Latin hip-hop. Improve your love life in a Haitian botanica, watch old men clack dominos in the park, and then let the flavors of the Caribbean, Cuba, Argentina, Spain and more – from street vendor to gastronomic temple – send your palate into ecstasy. Calle Ocho Festival, Carnaval Miami (p445)

Boardwalk Empire

16 Strolling along the beach boardwalk is a rite of passage, be it in Ocean City (p277), Maryland; Rehoboth Beach (p280), Delaware; Virginia Beach (p296), Virginia; or Atlantic City (p124), New Jersey. It doesn't matter where. The point is to enjoy the all-star roster of summer indulgence that inevitably lines the walkway: funnel cakes, go-karts, pizza shacks, glow-in-the-dark mini-golf, saltwater taffy shops. Parents push strollers, tots lick ice-cream cones, and teenagers check each other out. Don't get so caught up you forget to take in the sea views! Rehoboth Beach

Along the Mississippi River

17 If you trace Old Man River (p571) from its Northwoods beginning in Minnesota to its palmetto-fringed end in Louisiana, it meanders past eagles' nests and juke joints, pine forests and plantations. Covering more than 2000 miles, it churns through major cities like Minneapolis, Memphis and New Orleans. There are still riverboats, as in Mark Twain's heyday, but they're more likely to be casinos or tour vessels now. Road trippers heed the call of the mythic Great River Road as it edges the waterway throughout its duration.

MARK NEWMAN/LONELY PLANET IMAGES ©

Appalachian Trail

18 The country's longest footpath (p235) is over 2100 miles long, crosses six national parks and slices through 14 states from Georgia to Maine. Deep woods, alpine peaks, cow-dotted farms and foraging bears are all part of the landscape. It's estimated two to three million people trek a portion of the trail every year, inhaling the fresh air and admiring the spectacular scenery. Less than 600 hikers persevere all the way through. Got six months and fortitude to spare? The reward is sublime. That's true for shorter stretches, too.

HAVESEEN/SHUTTERSTOCK ©

Everglades National Park

19 The Everglades (p455) unnerve. They don't reach majestically skyward or fill your heart with the aching beauty of a glacier-carved valley. They ooze, flat and watery, a river of grass mottled by hammocks, cypress domes and mangroves. You can't hike them, not really. To properly explore the Everglades – and meet its prehistoric residents, like the snaggle-toothed crocodile, up close – you must leave the safety of land. You must push a canoe off a muddy bank, tamp down your fear, and explore the waterways on the Everglades' own, unforgettable terms.

New England Beaches

20 Summer in New England is humid, so the region's population flocks to the coast for cool ocean breezes. In Massachusetts, beaches ring the island of Martha's Vineyard (p187). At nearby Cape Cod National Seashore (p182), salt marshes and wild dunes steep the landscape, while humpback whales spout offshore. Unspoiled Block Island (p198) offers simple pleasures – rolling farms, uncrowded beaches and quiet hiking and cycling trails – a short float from Rhode Island. Cape Cod National Seashore

JEFF GREENBERG/GETTY ©

Acadia National Park

21 Acadia National Park (p231) is where the mountains meet the sea. Miles of rocky coastline and even more miles of hiking and biking trails make this wonderland Maine's most popular destination, and deservedly so. The high point (literally) is Cadillac Mountain, the 1530ft peak that can be accessed by foot, bicycle or vehicle. Early risers can catch the country's first sunrise from this celebrated summit. Later in the day, after working up an appetite on the trails and beaches, indulge in tea and popovers at Jordan Pond.

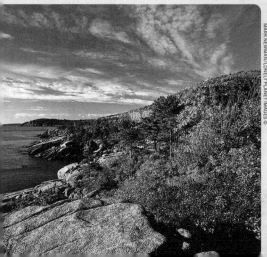

MARK NEWMAN/LONELY PLANET IMAGES ©

Great Smoky Mountains

22 Named after the heather-colored mist that hangs over the peaks, the Smokies (p330) comprise a national park that receives more visitors than any other. The pocket of deep Appalachian woods straddles Tennessee and North Carolina and protects thickly forested ridges where black bears, white-tailed deer, antlered elk, wild turkeys and over 1600 kinds of flowers find sanctuary. Ten million people a year come to hike, camp, ride horses, cycle, raft and fly fish, though it's easy to lose the crowds if you're willing to walk or paddle. Mountain Farm Museum (p330)

JOHN ELK III/LONELY PLANET IMAGES ©

Awesome Art

23 Start with the big guns – New York's Metropolitan Museum of Art (p75) and the Art Institute of Chicago (p503) – behemoths you could spend days at. Pittsburgh has the Andy Warhol Museum (p148), an eerie funhouse of pop art and bizarre films, while the mind-blowing Dalí Museum (p477), designed by HOK architects, adds a surreal splash to St Petersburg, Florida. But art isn't confined to the cities. Jet setters head to the hills of New York's Lower Hudson Valley for the hulking mod pieces at Storm King Art Center (p108) and Dia Beacon (p109). Dalí Museum, St Petersburg, Florida

JONAS KALTENBACH/LONELY PLANET IMAGES ©

Great Lakes

25 There are five Great Lakes (p492) – Superior, Michigan, Huron, Ontario and Erie – and together they possess about 20% of the earth's fresh water and 95% of America's. They offer miles of beaches, dunes, resort towns and lighthouse-dotted scenery. Add in wave-bashed cliffs, islands freckling the shore, and freighters chugging in to busy ports, and you can see how the region earned its 'Third Coast' nickname. Anglers, kayakers and even surfers will find their sweet spot here. Lake Michigan (p557)

SHARPLY DONE/ISTOCKPHOTO ©

Amish Country

24 Life slows waaay down in the Amish communities of northeast Ohio (p540), southeast Pennsylvania (p143) and northern Indiana (p534) – the USA's three largest clusters, in that order. Little boys in straw hats steer horse-drawn buggies, long-bearded men hand-plow the tidy fields, and primly dressed ladies carry shoofly pies to market. The 'Plain People', as they're known, are a centuries-old sect who live a simple life sans electricity, telephones or motorized vehicles. Berlin, Ohio, Lancaster, Pennsylvania, and Middlebury, Indiana, are good places to immerse and turn back the clock.

need to know

Currency
» US dollar ($)

Language
» English

When to Go

Boston
GO Apr-Oct

Chicago
GO May-Sep

New York City
GO May-Sep

Washington DC
GO Mar-Apr &
Sep-Oct

New Orleans
GO Feb-May

Miami
GO Dec-Apr

Tropical climate
Dry climate
Warm to hot summers, mild winters
Mild to hot summers, cold winters

High Season
(Jun–Aug)

» Warm sunny days across the region, with generally high temperatures

» Busiest season, with bigger crowds and higher accommodation prices

Shoulder Season
(Oct & Apr–May)

» Milder temperatures, fewer crowds

» Blooming spring flowers (April); fiery autumn colors (October), especially New England

Low Season
(Nov–Mar)

» Dark, wintry days, with snowfall in the north, and heavier rains in some regions

» Lowest prices for accommodation (aside from ski resorts and warmer getaway destinations like Florida)

Your Daily Budget

Budget Less than
$100

» Dorm beds: $20–30; campgrounds: around $15–30; budget motels: from $60

» Free activities (concerts, museums)

» Travel off-season; avoid resort areas

Midrange
$100–200

» Double room in midrange hotel: $100–200

» Dinner in decent restaurants: $50–80 for two

» Car hire from $30 per day

Top End More Than
$200

» Lodging resort from $250

» Dining in top restaurants: $60–100 per person

» Big nights out (plays, concerts): $60–200

Money

» ATMs widely available. Credits cards accepted at most hotels, restaurants and shops.

Visas

» Visitors from Canada, UK, Australia, New Zealand, Japan and many EU countries do not need visas for 90-day stays (see http://travel.state.gov).

Cell Phones

» Europe and Asia's GSM 900/1800 standard does not work in the USA. It's better to buy a cheap phone with a pay-as-you-go plan.

Driving

» Drive on the right; steering wheel is on the left side of the car.

Websites

» **Lonely Planet** (www.lonelyplanet.com/usa) Destination information, hotel bookings, travel forum, photos.

» **Away.com** (www.away.com) Boundless ideas for outdoor and urban adventure travel across the 50 states.

» **Festivals.com** (www.festivals.com) Find America's best celebrations: live-music, food, drink, dance and more.

» **Roadside America** (www.roadsideamerica.com) For all things weird and wacky.

Exchange Rates

Australia	A$1	$1.00
Canada	C$1	$0.97
Europe	€1	$1.34
Japan	¥100	$1.29
UK	UK£1	$1.57

For current exchange rates see www.xe.com.

Important Numbers

To call any regular number, dial the area code, followed by the seven-digit number.

Country code	☎1
International access code	☎011
Emergency	☎911
Directory assistance	☎411
International directory assistance	☎00

Arriving in Eastern USA

» **JFK, New York**
Airtrain to Jamaica Station, then LIRR to Penn Station: $12 to $14 (45 minutes)
Taxi to Manhattan: $45, (45 minutes)

» **Chicago O'Hare**
CTA Blue Line train to downtown: $2.25 (45 minutes)
Airport Express shuttle van: $29 (35 minutes)
Taxi to downtown: $45 (25 minutes)

» **Miami International**
Airport Flyer Express Bus 150 to South Beach: $2.35 (36 minutes)
Taxi to Miami Beach: $32 (25 minutes)

National Parks

Visiting a national park costs anywhere from nothing to $25 per vehicle for a seven-day pass. You pay at the park entrance station, but some accept cash only, so be sure to have greenbacks on hand. If you're going to be visiting several parks, consider the **America the Beautiful Pass** (www.nps.gov/findapark/passes.htm; per year $80), which covers all national park entrance fees, as well as those for all other federally managed lands, such as wildlife refuges and forests. You can buy the pass online in advance, or on site at any park.

National park lodges and campgrounds book up far in advance; for summer vacations, reserve six months to one year ahead. For overnight backpacking and some day hikes, you'll need a wilderness permit – the number of permits is often subject to quotas, so apply in advance.

if you like...

Big Cities

They're the East's dominant feature, doing the melting-pot thing for better or worse, richer or poorer.

New York City You can't get any bigger than Gotham, 8.3 million people strong and loud, fast, pulsing with energy, symphonic, exhausting and always evolving (p54)

Chicago The nation's third-largest city (behind New York and Los Angeles) is a tremendous cultural stew of skyscrapers, public art, vast museums, indie clubs, free festivals and a delirious number of eats (p497)

Baltimore The gritty port city has morphed into a hip beauty, sporting world-class museums, trendy shops, ethnic restaurants and boutique hotels (p263)

Philadelphia History is everywhere in the USA's first capital, but Philly's urbane side comes out in its energetic food, music and arts scenes (p126)

Detroit The Motor City is a case study of how metropolises rise and fall, and maybe – just maybe – rise again (p547)

National Parks

A bevy of beauties pops up throughout the East, from New England's wind-whipped shores to the coral reefs of south Florida.

Great Smoky Mountains Heather-colored mist clings to the peaks, while black bears, antlered elk and wild turkeys roam the sublime woodlands of the USA's most-visited parkland (p330)

Acadia Maine's unspoiled wilderness of surging coastal mountains, towering sea cliffs, surf-pounded beaches and quiet ponds provides a playground for adrenaline junkies and leisurely outdoors-folk alike (p231)

Shenandoah Spectacular vistas unfurl along the Blue Ridge Mountains, with great hiking and camping, including along the Appalachian Trail (p301)

Everglades Home to snaggle-toothed crocodiles, stealthy panthers, pink flamingos and mellow manatees, South Florida's Caribbean bays and 'rivers of grass' attract wildlife watchers (p455)

Isle Royale The forested land-mass floats in Lake Superior's midst, devoid of roads, cars and crowds, so the wolves and moose have room to prowl (p563)

Fabulous Food

The East piles up a juicy plate, spanning Maine lobster, Philly cheesesteaks, Memphis barbecue and Wisconsin cheddar among the regional bites.

New York City Whether you crave steak frites, linguini con vongole, sushi, chicken tikka masala or gourmet hot dogs, globe-trotting Gotham has you covered (p89)

Alinea At the continent's best restaurant, located in Chicago, superstar chef Grant Achatz serves 24 courses of space-age cuisine (p517)

New Orleans Loosen the belt and bring on the Cajun-Creole fare: shrimp remoulade, crabmeat ravigote, crawfish étouffée, fresh-shucked oysters, bourbon-soaked bread pudding and chicory-spiced coffee. And that's just day one... (p413)

Providence What? You haven't heard of Providence, Rhode Island, as chowhound heaven? It is indeed, with Italian fare and off-the-boat seafood setting the table (p194)

Madison An impressive locavore scene has cooked here for 30 years, along with food trucks, ethnic eats and one of the nation's hugest farmers markets (p568)

If you like... Wine
More than 65 vineyards stripe the Finger Lakes region in upstate New York, known for ice wines (p110)

Architecture

'Think big' has been the mantra of designers in the East from the get-go. Cloud-poking cityscapes and aesthetic head-turners in smaller towns prevail throughout the region.

Chicago It's the birthplace of the skyscraper and home of the nation's tallest building. The Chicago Architecture Foundation brings it all in focus with cool tours (p504)

Fallingwater A few hours from Pittsburgh, this 1939 Frank Lloyd Wright masterpiece blends into the forested landscape and the waterfall over which the house is built (p153)

Miami Miami's art-deco district is a Technicolor dream come to life – and the largest collection of deco buildings found anywhere in the world (p439)

Taliesin Another one for Frank Lloyd Wright fans: Taliesin was the site of his home and influential school, well worth the pilgrimage to Spring Green, Wisconsin (p571)

Columbus Believe it: there's big architecture in small Columbus, Indiana, thanks to the town's forward-thinking industrialists (p541)

Museums

The East's museums serve up a mix of the classic, the avant-garde and the down-right indescribable.

Smithsonian Institution If America was a quirky grandfather, the Smithsonian would be his attic. Rockets, dinosaurs, Rodin sculptures, Tibetan thangkas and diamonds stuff the place. It's actually a group of museums and get this: they're all free (p244)

Metropolitan Museum of Art The top-draw attraction in NYC is like a cultural city-state, boasting a treasure trove of two million artworks (p75)

Art Institute of Chicago The nation's second-largest art museum (after the Met) hangs masterpieces aplenty, especially Impressionist and Post-Impressionist paintings (p503)

Andy Warhol Museum The big-spectacled king of pop art bestows Pittsburgh with far-out works (p148)

Salvador Dalí Museum A magnificent collection of the Surrealist's oil paintings makes its odd home in St Petersburg, Florida (p477)

Theme Parks

America's theme parks come in many varieties – from old-fashioned cotton candy and rollercoaster fun to multiday immersions in Peter-Pan-style make-believe. Many parks are impressive enough to plan a whole itinerary around.

Walt Disney World Immerse yourself into the enchanting, fairytale world of 'The Happiest Place on Earth' and get swept up in miles of nostalgia and thrill rides (p485)

Dollywood It's a paean to the much-loved country singer Dolly Parton, with Appalachian-themed rides and attractions in the hills of Tennessee (p362)

Cedar Point The Valhalla of roller coasters rises up near Sandusky, Ohio. Masochists line up for 17 screamers, such as the Top Thrill Dragster, one of the world's highest and fastest coasters (p539)

Universal Orlando Resort Want to be in the movies? Here's your chance. Universal brings on super heroes, Harry Potter, the Simpsons and more via its massive complex of action-filled theme parks (p481)

If you like... Beer
In Durham, NC, Fullsteam Brewery goes wildly Southern with sweet potato beer, kudzu beer and more (p325)

Outdoor Activities

Lace up the shoes, wax the board, and get those paddles ready: the East is ready to boost your adrenaline.

Appalachian Trail Even if you choose not to walk all 2100 miles of this 'mother of all trails' as it slices across the Eastern US, hop on for a mile or two to experience the sublime scenery (p624)

Boundary Waters Canoe deep into Minnesota's northern wilderness, where wolves and black bears roam, to camp under a blanket of stars and maybe glimpse the aurora borealis (p588)

New River Gorge National River Legendary white water froths in West Virginia, ripping through a primeval forest gorge that's utterly Eden-like (p310)

Long Island Surf's up in New York, from Montauk's Ditch Plains to Nassau County's Long Beach, the newest stop on surfing's pro tour (p106)

Stowe Mountain Vermont invented snowboarding, and the state's premier crag is the place to shred (p210)

History

The north has Colonial and Revolutionary hot spots, while the mid-Atlantic and south hold the majority of Civil War battlefields.

Independence National Historic Park Known as America's most historic square mile, highlights include the Liberty Bell and Independence Hall, where the founding fathers signed the Constitution (p127)

Boston's Freedom Trail Walk by Paul Revere's former home, the graveyard where 18th-century patriots lie buried, and 14 other famous Revolutionary sites along the 2.5-mile path (p166)

Henry Ford Museum/Greenfield Village The adjacent museums hold history's greatest hits: Rosa Parks' bus, Lincoln's assassination chair, the Wright Brothers' airplane workshop and more (p554)

Washington, DC Visit the theater where John Wilkes Booth shot America's favorite president, the steps of Lincoln Memorial where Martin Luther King Jr gave his 'I have a dream' speech and the infamous Watergate Hotel (p241)

Vicksburg It's ground zero for Civil War buffs, with a 16-mile driving tour through the Mississippi area that General Grant besieged for 47 days (p398)

Nightlife

When the sun goes down, the music cranks up across the region, from swanky urban clubs to beer-and-a-shot juke joints.

New Orleans Bourbon St gets the press, but the nightlife is better in the neighborhoods beyond where Sazerac swirls in glasses, and jazz, Dixieland and zydeco spill out of clubs (p415)

New York City It's the city that doesn't sleep, as Sinatra sang, and the drinkeries of the Lower East Side, East Village, Greenwich Village and Meatpacking District continue to do him proud (p98)

Athens, Georgia The compact little college town plugs in a mighty music scene that launched the B-52s, REM and Widespread Panic amid all the beer drinking (p381)

Minneapolis Everyone's in a band, and there are bars and banged-up clubs aplenty to let them plug into (p580)

Memphis Par-tee on Beale St, a round-the-clock carnival of bars, to-go beer counters and live, fret-bending blues and rock music (p345)

» Fallingwater (p153), Frank Lloyd Wright

Offbeat America

When you tire of traipsing through museums and ticking off well-known sights (perhaps because some guidebook suggested you shouldn't miss it), throw yourself into the strange world of American kitsch.

Foamhenge A magnificent homage to Styrofoam, this is Stonehenge redux, done to scale and appropriately tranquil around sunset – there's even a resident wizard watching over the proceedings (p304)

NashTrash Tours Nashville's tall-haired 'Jugg Sisters' take visitors on a deliciously tacky journey through the city's spicier side (p355)

Spam Museum Chat up staff (aka 'spambassadors') and try your hand at canning the sweet pork magic in Austin, Minnesota, the blue-tinned meat's revered birthplace (p585)

Interstate Mullet Toss Locals gather on the Florida-Alabama border at Perdido Key and throw mullets (a one-pound indigenous fish) as far as they can across the state line. Perhaps not surprisingly, a pub organizes the raucous beach event (p457)

Theater

New York City and Chicago are the stars, while smaller cities such as Minneapolis and Louisville give voice to emerging talents.

Broadway Theater District It doesn't get more iconic than the bright lights and glittery marquees along a certain road in Midtown Manhattan – the apex of the theater world (p71)

Steppenwolf Theatre John Malkovich, Gary Sinise and other now-famous actors launched Chicago's scene here nearly four decades ago; quality dramas remain the hallmark (p520)

Guthrie Theater Minneapolis has so many theaters it's nicknamed 'Mini Apple,' and foremost among them is the uber-cool, Tony Award-winning Guthrie (p580)

Hudson Valley Shakespeare Festival See the Bard's plays staged under the stars, set against the backdrop of the magical Boscobel estate, high on a bluff overlooking the Hudson River (p109)

Grand Ole Opry Oh, it's more than country music under the lights here; it's a full-fledged, foot-stompin' variety show (p358)

Beaches

Coastlines edging the Atlantic, Gulf of Mexico and Great Lakes present tough choices for beach-lovers.

South Beach Famous the world over, South Beach is less about wave frolicking than taking in the passing people parade crossing Miami's favorite playground (p439)

Cape Cod National Seashore Massive sand dunes, picturesque lighthouses and cool forests invite endless exploring on the famous Massachusetts cape (p182)

Montauk Past Fire Island and the Hamptons, at the eastern tip of Long Island lies windswept Montauk, with pretty shoreline, beach camping and an 18th-century (still functioning) lighthouse (p107)

Michigan's Gold Coast Endless stretches of sand, dunes, wineries, orchards and B&B-filled towns coat the state's western shoreline along Lake Michigan (p557)

Outer Banks North Carolina's isolated barrier islands offer fragile ribbons of sand; some are populist with sandals 'n' sunblock shops, while others are remote where wild ponies run free (p317)

month by month

January

The New Year starts off with a shiver, as snowfall blankets large swaths in northern regions. Ski resorts kick into high gear, while sun-lovers seek refuge in warmer climes (especially Florida).

Mummers Parade

Philadelphia's biggest event is this brilliant parade, where local clubs spend months creating costumes and mobile scenery in order to win top honors on New Year's Day. String bands and clowns add to the all-round good cheer (www.phillymummers.com).

Chinese New Year

In late January or early February, you'll find colorful celebrations and feasting anywhere there's a China-town. NYC and Chicago each ring-in the occasion with a parade, floats, fire-crackers, bands and plenty of merriment.

St Paul Winter Carnival

Is it cold in Minnesota in late January? You betcha. That doesn't stop denizens from bundling up in parkas and snow boots to partake in 10 days of ice sculptures, ice skating and ice fishing (www.winter-carnival.com).

February

Aside from mountain getaways, many Americans dread February with its long dark nights and frozen days. For foreign visitors, this can be the cheapest time to travel, with ultra-discount rates for flights and hotels.

Mardi Gras

Held in late February or early March, on the day before Ash Wednesday, Mardi Gras (Fat Tuesday) is the finale of Carnival. New Orleans' celebrations are legendary as colorful parades, masquerade balls, feasting and plenty of hedonism rule the day.

March

The first blossoms of spring arrive (at least in the south – the north still shivers in the chill). In New England's mountains, it's still ski season. Meanwhile, the Spring Break masses descend on Florida.

☆ Baseball Spring Training

Throughout March, Florida hosts MLB's spring training 'Grapefruit League': 13 pro baseball teams train and play exhibition games, drawing fans to the Orlando, the Tampa Bay and the southeast (www.floridagrapefruitleague.com) areas.

St Patrick's Day

On the 17th, the patron saint of Ireland is honored with brass bands and ever-flowing pints of Guinness; huge parades occur in New York, Boston and Chicago (which goes all-out by dyeing the Chicago River green).

National Cherry Blossom Festival

The brilliant blooms of Japanese cherry blossoms around DC's Tidal Basin are celebrated with concerts, parades, taiko drumming, kite-flying and 90 other events during the five-week fest. More than one million people attend each year, so don't forget to book ahead (www.nationalcherry blossomfestival.org).

🍴 Maple Syrup Tasting

Vermont's maple syrup producers invite the public to their 'sugarhouses' to see the sweet stuff being made during the Vermont Maple Open House Weekend (www.vermontmaple.org) in late March. Maine producers do the same, the last Sunday of the month.

April

The weather is warming up, but April can still be unpredictable with chilly weather mixed with a few, teasingly warm days up north. Down south, it's a fine time to travel.

🏃 Boston Marathon

At the country's 'longest running' marathon, tens of thousands of spectators watch runners cross the finish line at Copley Sq on Patriots Day, a Massachusetts holiday held the third Monday of April (www.baa.org).

✨ New Orleans Jazz Fest

The Big Easy hosts the country's best jazz jam for 10 days late-month, with top-notch horn blowers and ivory ticklers. Almost better than the music is the food: soft-shell crab po' boys, Cajun rice-and-pork sausage and white-chocolate bread pudding (www.nojazzfest.com).

✨ Tribeca Film Festival

Robert DeNiro co-organizes this NYC soiree showcasing documentaries and narrative features, held during 12 days in late April. It has quickly risen in stature since its 2002 inception (www.tribecafilmfestival.com).

May

May is true spring and one of the loveliest times to travel, with blooming wildflowers and generally mild sunny weather. Summer crowds and high prices have yet to arrive.

⭐ Kentucky Derby

On the first Saturday of the month, a who's who of upper crust America puts on their pinstripe suits and most flamboyant hats and descends on Louisville for the horserace known as the 'greatest two minutes in sports' (www.kentucky derby.com).

✨ Movement Electronic Music Festival

The world's largest electronic music festival packs Detroit's Hart Plaza over Memorial Day weekend. You'll find both up-and-comers and the big names in the biz, such as Fatboy Slim, Carl Craig and Felix da Housecat at the dance-loving extravaganza (www.movement.us).

✨ Spoleto USA

Charleston's 17-day performing arts festival in late May/early June carries big-time prestige. It stages operas, dramas and musicals across the city, while artisans and food vendors line the streets (www.spoleto usa.org).

June

Summer is here. Americans spend more time at outdoor cafes and restaurants, and head to the shore or to national parks. School is out; vacationers fill the highways and resorts bringing higher prices.

✨ Goombay Festival

In Miami's Coconut Grove, this massive four-day, early-June street party draws over 300,000 to celebrate the city's Bahaman culture with music, dancing and parades; it's one of America's largest black culture festivals (www.goombayfestival coconutgrove.com).

✨ Chicago Blues Festival

It's the globe's biggest free blues fest, with three days of the electrified music that made Chicago famous. More than a half million people unfurl blankets by the multiple stages that take over Grant Park in early June (www.chicago bluesfestival.us).

✨ CMA Music Festival

Legions of country music fans don their cowboy boots and unite in Nashville for the chance to hear the genre's top crooners. Over 400 artists perform at stages on Riverfront Park and LP Field (www.cmaworld.com).

✨ Mermaid Parade

In Brooklyn, Coney Island celebrates summer's steamy arrival with a kitsch-loving parade. Skimpily attired but brilliantly imaginative mermaids and horn-blowing mermen march through Coney Island. Afterwards, everyone (at least those not afraid of NY Harbor Water) takes a dip in the ocean.

Summerfest
Milwaukee lets loose with a heckuva music fest for 11 days in late June/early July with hundreds of big-name rock, blues, jazz, country and alternative bands swarming 10 lakefront stages. Local beer, brats and cheese accompany the proceedings (www.summerfest.com).

July
With summer in full swing, Americans break out the backyard barbecues or head for the beach. The prices are high and the crowds can be fierce, but it's one of the liveliest times to visit.

Independence Day
The nation celebrates its birthday with a fireworks-filled bang on the 4th. In Philadelphia, descendents of the Declaration of Independence signatories ring the Liberty Bell. Chicago, Washington DC, New York and Boston are also great spots to enjoy the fun.

National Black Arts Festival
Artists converge on Atlanta for this 10-day event celebrating African American music, theater, literature and film. Maya Angelou, Wynton Marsalis, Spike Lee and Youssou N'Dour are among those who've

strutted their stuff (www.nbaf.org).

Newport Folk Festival
Newport, RI, a summer haunt of the well-heeled, hosts this high-energy music fest in late July. Top folk artists from every corner of America take to the storied stage, best remembered as the venue where Bob Dylan went electric (www.newportfolkfest.net).

August
Expect blasting heat in August, with temperatures and humidity less bearable the further south you go. You'll find people-packed beaches, high prices and empty cities on weekends, when residents escape to the nearest waterfront.

Lollapalooza
Once upon a time, this mondo rock fest traveled city to city; now its permanent home is in Chicago. It's a raucous event, with 130 bands – including many A-listers – spilling off eight stages in Grant Park the first Friday-to-Sunday in August (www.lollapalooza.com).

Maine Lobster Festival
If you love lobster like Maine loves lobster, why not indulge in this feeding frenzy held in Rockland in early August? King Neptune and the Sea Goddess oversee a week full of events and, of course, as much crustacean as you can eat (www.mainelobsterfestival.com).

September
With the end of summer, cooler days arrive, making for pleasant outings regionwide. The kids are back in school, and concert halls, gallery spaces and performing arts venues kick off a new season.

New York Film Festival
One of several big film fests in NYC (Tribeca Film Fest in late April is another), this one features world premiers from across the globe, plus Q&As with indie- and prominent directors alike. Lincoln Center plays host (www.filmlinc.com).

October
Temperatures are falling, as autumn brings fiery colors to northern climes. It's high season where the leaves are most brilliant (New England); elsewhere expect lower prices and fewer crowds.

Halloween
It's not just for kids; adults celebrate Halloween at masquerade parties. In NYC, you can don a costume and join the Halloween parade up Sixth Avenue. Chicago does a cultural take with skeleton-rich Day of the Dead events at the National Museum of Mexican Art.

Fantasy Fest
Key West's answer to Mardi Gras brings more than 100,000 revelers to the subtropical enclave on the week leading up to

Halloween. Expect parades, colorful floats, costume parties, the selecting of a conch king and queen and plenty of alcohol-fueled merriment (www.fantasyfest.net).

🏃 Head of the Charles Regatta

Thousands of rowers and thousands more spectators gather for gliding on Boston's River Charles the third weekend in October. It's the world's largest rowing event and offers lots of Ivy League flair (www.hocr.org).

🏃 Championship Outhouse Races

Bizarre but true: in Mountain View, Arkansas, crowds cheer on their favorite 'people-powered potty' as it races to the finish line. The event usually takes place around the last week in October.

November

No matter where you go, this is generally low season, with cold winds discouraging visitors and lower prices (although airfares skyrocket around Thanksgiving). There's much happening culturally in the main cities.

🍴 Thanksgiving

On the fourth Thursday of November, Americans gather with family and friends over daylong feasts – roast turkey, sweet potatoes, cranberry sauce, wine, pumpkin pie and loads of other dishes. New York City hosts a huge parade, and there's pro football on TV.

(above) Independence Day fireworks, National Mall (p240), Washington, DC
(below) Lion dance performance, Chinese New Year, Philadelphia (p126)

December

Winter arrives (though skiing conditions in Eastern USA usually aren't ideal until January). Christmas lights and holiday fairs make the region come alive during the festive season.

Art Basel

This massive arts fest is four days of cutting-edge art, film, architecture and design. Over 250 major galleries from across the globe come to the event, with works by some 2000 artists; plus much hobnobbing with a glitterati crowd in Miami Beach (www.art baselmiamibeach.com).

New Year's Eve

Americans are of two minds when it comes to ringing in the New Year. Some join festive crowds to celebrate; others plot a getaway to escape the mayhem. Whichever you choose, plan well in advance. Expect high prices (especially in NYC).

itineraries

Whether you've got six days or 60, these itineraries provide a starting point for the trip of a lifetime. Want more inspiration? Head online to lonelyplanet.com/thorntree to chat with other travelers.

Three Weeks
Down the Coast

> It's 1800 miles from Maine to Miami, plenty of time to breathe in the sea air. Start at rock-ripped **Acadia National Park** and spend a few days hiking, cycling the carriage roads and cracking into fresh lobster. Roll into **Boston** for two days of historic sightseeing, dining in the North End and pub-hopping in Cambridge. Drop by **Newport** to ogle outlandish, old-money mansions atop wave-battered cliffs, then set a course for **New York City**. Spend three days blending touristy must-dos – Top of the Rock viewpoint, Upper East Side art museums, Central Park rambling – with vibrant nightlife and dining adventures, perhaps in the East Village. Head onward to **Washington, DC**, and its dizzying array of sights, plus great dining (crab feasts, global fare) after the museums close.

Stick to the coast as you drive south during the next 10 days. Make time for the **Outer Banks**, a ribbon of barrier islands, dunes and local wild ponies. Take in the antebellum allure of **Charleston** and **Savannah** and the cobblestoned history of **St Augustine** before immersing in **Walt Disney World**. The swank mayhem of **Miami** will seem tame by comparison.

One Month
Eastern Grand Tour

Talk about a road trip: this one loops around the East through towns big and small. Start in **New York City** (but hire a car in cheaper New Jersey) and hit the pavement for week one. Head west toward **Lancaster** to explore the idyllic back roads of Pennsylvania Dutch Country. Next is **Pittsburgh**, a surprising town of picturesque bridges and green spaces, cutting-edge museums and lively neighborhoods. Enter Ohio by interstate, but quickly step back in time amid the horses, buggies and byways of **Amish Country**. See the skyscrapers rising on the horizon? That's big-shouldered **Chicago**. Hang out for a few days to stroll or bike the lakefront, marvel at famous artworks and steely architecture, and take a culinary journey through the city's celebrated restaurant scene.

For week two, motor south from Chicago on old Route 66, at least for a few time-warped, pie-filled miles. **Memphis** is the next destination, a mecca for Elvis fans, barbecue connoisseurs, civil rights students and blues music buffs alike. Follow the Great River Rd south from here through juke-jointed **Clarksdale**, the Civil War battlegrounds of **Vicksburg** and antebellum mansion-splashed **Natchez**. It's not far now to **New Orleans**, where Katrina be damned, you can still hear live jazz, drink Sazerac cocktails, consult with a voodoo priestess or even ride a steamboat on the Mississippi River.

Begin journeying back east for week three. Wheel along the Gulf Coast to the azalea-lined boulevards of **Mobile** (mo-*beel*), then inland to **Montgomery**, where museums honor civil rights pioneers like Rosa Parks, who refused to give up her seat to a white man on a city bus. Fall under the spell of **Savannah's** live oaks and **Charleston's** pastel architecture and decadent food. Take your pick of **Durham** or **Chapel Hill**, side-by-side university towns offering groovy nightlife.

Begin week four brushing up on your history in Virginia. Outside Richmond visit **Jamestown**, where Pocahontas helped the New World's first English settlement survive. Then wander through the 18th century at nearby **Williamsburg**. A pair of big cities completes the route: **Washington, DC**, is a museum free-for-all (literally free at the Smithsonian Institution's 19 venues), while **Philadelphia** fires up the Liberty Bell, Ben Franklin and the mighty, meaty cheesesteak. Finally, it's back to the neon lights of NYC.

» (above) Statue of Elvis Presley by sculptor Eric Parks, Memphis (p343)
» (left) Lou Mitchell's restaurant (p516), Chicago, at the start of Route 66

Bright Lights, Big Cities

For big, brawny, bold metropolises, the East is your place. Begin with a few days in history-rich **Boston**. Walk the Freedom Trail past Paul Revere's house and the Revolutionary War's first battleground. Hang out in Harvard Square's cafes and bookshops, and chow down in North End trattorias and oyster houses. Then catch the train to **New York City**. With four days, you can indulge in iconic Manhattan and beyond. Stroll Central Park, walk the canyons of Wall Street, go bohemian in Greenwich Village and catch a ferry to the Statue of Liberty. For a more local scene, join residents on the High Line, in NoLita's stylish shops and in Brooklyn's cool cafes.

Next hop a train to **Philadelphia**, which is practically down the block from NYC. Philly was the birthplace of American independence, and has the Liberty Bell and Declaration artifacts to prove it. Spend a few days touring the historic sites and indulging in foodie neighborhoods like Manayunk. Now you can't leave the northeast without spending a few days in **Washington, DC**, a quick trip by bus or train. Beyond the insane number of free museums and monuments – the Air and Space Museum, Lincoln Memorial, Martin Luther King Jr Memorial and Hirshhorn Sculpture Garden among them – the US capital has rich dining and drinking veins in Georgetown, Adams Morgan and Dupont Circle. Who knows what politico might be swirling a Scotch next to you.

It's a long haul to **Miami** (flying is the easy way to go), so allocate four days to get your money's worth exploring the exotic museums and galleries, the art-deco district, Little Havana and sexy, sultry South Beach. For a change of pace, day-trip to the **Everglades** and commune with alligators. Keep the Southern thing going in jazz-loving **New Orleans**, with a soundtrack of smokin' hot funk brass bands and the sizzle of Cajun and Creole food. Three days of heavy eating with locals in Riverbend, Uptown, Faubourg Marigny and the Bywater should do it.

Last, but not least, **Chicago** leaps up; the *City of New Orleans* train is a scenic way to arrive. Bike to the beach, see mod art in Millennium Park, sip martinis in Al Capone's gin joint and plug into the blues. Chicago rocks, like the rest of the East's big cities.

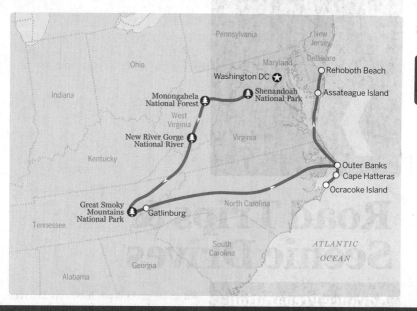

The Great Outdoors

This trip is for those who like their nature ancient and wild. **Shenandoah National Park** rolls out the welcome mat. This sliver of gorgeousness straddles the Blue Ridge Mountains, so-named for their color when glimpsed in the hazy cerulean distance. Besides scenic drives, hiking is the big to-do. Five hundred miles of paths – including 100 miles of the Appalachian Trail – wind by spring wildflowers, summer waterfalls and fiery autumn leaves. More activities await a few hours west at **Monongahela National Forest**, where you can strap on boots for Snowshoe Mountain, ropes for Seneca Rocks and a bicycle helmet for the Greenbrier River Trail. Adventure sports enthusiasts will find their wet-and-wild bliss nearby at **New River Gorge National River**. Outfitters provide white-water rafting gear for the infamous class V rapids.

Next up: **Great Smoky Mountains National Park**. True, it is the USA's most popular patch of parkland, but you can leave most of the 10 million annual visitors behind if you're willing to hike or paddle. Studies have shown that 95% of tourists never venture further than 100 yards from their cars! Of course, after a day spent in the wilderness surrounded by lush, heather-colored peaks, there's nothing quite like arriving in **Gatlinburg**, the park's kitschy base. Prepare for hillbilly-themed mini-golf, Ripley's Believe It or Not oddities and moonshine distilleries.

So goes the first week. Now it's time to fuel up for the twisty drive through the mountains and across to the coast, where the **Outer Banks** pay off big. Laid-back beach towns full of locally owned ice-cream shops and mom-and-pop motels dot the windswept barrier islands. Check out **Cape Hatteras** with its unspoiled dunes, marshes and woodlands, or catch the ferry to remote **Ocracoke Island** where the wild ponies run. Speaking of which: more wild horses roam **Assateague Island**, which floats to the north between Virginia and Maryland. It, too, offers brilliant, secluded beaches and a landscape ripe for birding, kayaking, crabbing and fishing.

Still craving surf and sand? Family-friendly, gay-friendly **Rehoboth Beach** bestows traditional gingerbread houses, kiddie amusements and a big ol' boardwalk along the oceanfront.

Road Trips & Scenic Drives

Advance Preparation

Join an automobile club (p636) that provides 24-hour emergency roadside assistance and discounts on lodging and attractions.

Some international clubs have reciprocal agreements with US automobile associations, so check first and bring your member card from home.

International travelers might want to review the USA's road rules (p637) and common road hazards (p637).

What to Pack

Make sure your vehicle has a spare tire, tool kit (eg jack, jumper cables, ice scraper, tire pressure gauge) and emergency equipment (eg flashers).

Bring good maps, especially if you're touring off-road or away from highways; don't rely on a GPS unit – they can malfunction, and in remote areas they may not even work.

Always carry your driver's license (p636) and proof of insurance (p636).

Fill up the gas tank and buckle up. Everyone knows road tripping is the ultimate way to see America. You can pick a highway and forge your own path. Or you can set out on one of the region's renowned, slowpoke byways. Dawdle in diners along the Lincoln Hwy, marvel at plantation mansions on the Natchez Trace, climb through the Appalachians on the Blue Ridge Parkway or swing into bluesy joints along the Great River Rd. The local experience is about so many things – bluegrass and beaches, Cajun food and farmers markets, rolling vineyards and hardwood forests, and big cities and small towns in which to retreat after days well spent beneath the wide-open skies. There's no better way to get a taste for the East in all its complexity and with all its contradictions than by setting off on a classic four-wheeled journey.

For more road-tripping ideas, turn to the Itineraries chapter (p29).

Blue Ridge Parkway

Snaking for some 469 miles through the southern Appalachian Mountains, the Blue Ridge Parkway is the land of great hiking and wildlife watching, old-fashioned music and captivating mountainous scenery – all of which make for a memorable and easily accessible road trip.

Construction on the parkway began in 1935 under President Franklin D Roosevelt

● 1	Blue Ridge Parkway
● 2	Great River Road
● 3	Lincoln Highway
● 4	Natchez Trace Parkway

PLAN YOUR TRIP ROAD TRIPS & SCENIC DRIVES

and it was one of the great New Deal projects that helped put people back to work. This massive effort took over 52 years to complete, with the final section laid in 1987.

Why Go

Watch the sun set over this vast wilderness of forest and mountain, tranquil streams and blissful silence – and you might feel like you've gone back a few centuries. Although it skirts dozens of small towns and a few metropolitan areas, the Blue Ridge Parkway feels far removed from modern-day America. Here, rustic log cabins with creaky rocking chairs on the front porches still dot the hillsides, while signs for folk-art shops and live bluegrass music joints entice travelers onto meandering side roads. History seems to permeate the air of these rolling backwoods – once home to Cherokee tribal people and later to early colonial homesteads and Civil War battlefields.

There are great places to sleep and eat along the way. Early-20th-century mountain and lakeside resorts still welcome families like old friends, while log-cabin diners dish up heaping piles of buckwheat pancakes with blackberry preserves and a side of country ham.

When you need to work off all that good Southern cooking, over 100 hiking trails can be accessed along the Blue Ridge Parkway, from gentle nature walks and easily summited peaks to rough-and-ready tramps along the legendary Appalachian Trail. Or clamber on a horse and ride off into the refreshingly shady forests. Then go canoeing, kayaking or inner tubing along rushing rivers, or dangle a fishing line over the side of a rowboat on petite lakes. And who says you even have to drive? The parkway makes an epic trip for long-distance cyclists, too.

The Route

The bucolic byway connects Virginia's Shenandoah National Park with Great Smoky Mountains National Park, straddling the North Carolina–Tennessee border. Towns along the way include Boone and Asheville in North Carolina and Galax and Roanoke in Virginia, with Charlottesville, VA, also a short drive away. Bigger cities within range of the parkway include Washington, DC (140 miles), and Richmond, VA (95 miles).

Many road trippers also add Skyline Dr onto their Blue Ridge route. The bendy, 105-mile Skyline connects to the parkway's northern end and ups the scenic ante by doling out mind-blowing mountain vistas on its ramble through Shenandoah National Park.

BEFORE YOU HIT THE ROAD

A few things to remember to ensure your road trip is as happy-go-lucky as possible:

» Join an automobile club (p636) that provides members with 24-hour emergency roadside assistance and discounts on lodging and attractions; some international clubs have reciprocal agreements with US automobile associations, so check first and bring your member card from home.

» Check the spare tire, tool kit (eg jack, jumper cables, ice scraper, tire pressure gauge) and emergency equipment (eg flashers) in your car; if you're renting a vehicle and these essential safety items are not provided, consider buying them.

» Bring good maps, especially if you're touring off-road or away from highways; don't rely on a GPS unit – they can malfunction, and in remote areas such as deep canyons or thick forests they may not even work.

» Always carry your driver's license (p636) and proof of insurance (p636).

» If you're an international traveler, review the USA's road rules (p637) and common road hazards (p637).

» Fill up the tank often, because gas stations can be few and far between on the East's scenic byways.

When to Go

Keep in mind that the weather can vary greatly, depending on your elevation. While mountain peaks are snowed in during winter, the valleys can still be invitingly warm. Most visitor services along the parkway are only open from April through October. May is best for wildflowers, although most people come for leaf-peeping during fall. Spring and fall are both good times for bird-watching, with nearly 160 species having been spotted in the skies over the parkway. Expect big crowds if you go during the summer or early autumn.

Resources

Hiking the Blue Ridge Parkway by Randy Johnson offers in-depth trail descriptions, topographic trail maps and other essential info for hikes both short and long (including overnight treks).

Blue Ridge Parkway (www.blueridgeparkway. org) Maps, activities and places to stay along the way. Also offers the free *Blue Ridge Parkway Travel Planner* download.

Recreation.gov (www.recreation.gov) Some campsites can be reserved through this site.

Time & Mileage

Time: It's possible to drive the parkway in two days, but allow five days to do it right; it's slow going on the steep, curvy mountain roads, plus you'll want to pit stop for hiking, eating and sightseeing

Mileage: 469 miles

Great River Rd

Established in the late 1930s, the Great River Rd is an epic, 2000-mile journey from the Mississippi's headwaters in the northern lakes of Minnesota, floating downstream all the way to the river's mouth on the Gulf of Mexico near New Orleans. For a look at America across cultural divides – north-south, urban-rural, Baptist-bohemian – this is the road trip to make.

Why Go

You'll be awed by the sweeping scenery as you meander alongside America's longest river, from the rolling plains of the north down to the sun-baked cotton fields of the Mississippi Delta. Wind-hewn bluffs, dense forests, flower-filled meadows and steamy swamps are all part of the backdrop – along with smokestacks, riverboat casinos and urban sprawl: this is the good, the bad and the ugly of life on the Mississippi. The portrait though isn't complete without mentioning the great music, lip-smacking food and down-home welcome at towns well off the beaten path along this waterfront itinerary.

Small towns provide a glimpse into varying facets of American culture: there's Brainerd, MN, as seen in the Coen Brothers' film *Fargo;* La Crosse, WI, where the world's largest six-pack pops its top; and Nauvoo, IL, a pilgrimage site for Mormons, complete with gleaming white temple.

The southern section of the route traces American musical history, from rock and roll in Memphis to blues in the Mississippi Delta to jazz in New Orleans. You won't go hungry either, with retro Midwestern diners, Southern barbecue joints and smokehouses, and Cajun taverns and dance halls in Louisiana.

The Route

Despite the name, the Great River Rd is not a single highway, but a series of linked federal, state and county roads that follow the Mississippi River as it flows through 10 different states. Major urban areas that provide easy access to the road include New Orleans, Memphis, St Louis and Minneapolis.

When to Go

The best time to travel is from May to October, when the weather is warmest. Avoid going in the winter (or else stick to the deep south) when you'll have to contend with snowstorms.

Resources

'Ten states, one river' is the slogan for the official site of **Mississippi River Travel** (www.experiencemississippiriver.com), which is a great resource for history, outdoor recreation, live music and more.

Time & Mileage

Time: You'll need at least six days to drive the road from north to south; 10 days enables a more comfortable, realistic pace
Mileage: About 2000 miles

Lincoln Hwy

America's first transcontinental roadway – begun in 1913 and paved to completion by 1925 – rambles from New York City to San Francisco. Its 1000-mile eastern portion traces a distinctive path through the nation's heartland, leaving giant coffee-pot statues, fried-chicken diners, jellybean murals and other Americana in its wake. And who knows? You might be so inspired by the time you reach the Eastern USA's edge that you decide to keep on rolling all the way west.

Why Go

The Lincoln Hwy is authentic road tripping, sans much of the hype and commercialization of other famous byways. While the route navigates some of the East's prominent cities – NYC and Philadelphia among them – it also steers well off the tourist path in genuine back-road style. You'll tick off seven states along the way: New York, New Jersey, Pennsylvania, West Virginia, Ohio, Indiana and Illinois.

The Route

Between New York City and Fulton, IL, the roadway cuts across the middle Atlantic and Midwestern regions. Note the Lincoln Hwy doesn't appear on most maps, because it's no longer an official road, but rather a patchwork of federal and state highways. A good, detailed tourist guide (see p39) will help you follow the course.

The journey begins at Times Square, where the bright lights of Broadway provide an epic send-off. From there it's on

---

DOWNLOADS: BLUEGRASS SOUNDS

If you can't catch a live show at Virginia's **Blue Ridge Music Center** (www.blueridgemusiccenter.org), open from May through October, then load up your Mp3 player with some beloved 'mountain music' classics:

» 'Blue Moon of Kentucky' – Bill Monroe and the Blue Grass Boys

» 'Foggy Mountain Breakdown' – Earl Scruggs

» 'Orange Blossom Special' – Rouse Brothers

» 'Rocky Top' – Osborne Brothers

» 'Windy Mountain' – Lonesome Pine Fiddlers

» 'Flame of Love' – Jim and Jesse

» 'I'm a Man of Constant Sorrow' – Stanley Brothers

» 'Every Time You Say Goodbye' – Alison Krauss and Union Station

» 'Like a Hurricane' – The Dillards

» (above) Natchez Trace Parkway
» (left) The Coffee Pot, Pennsylvania

Kitschy, time-warped and just plain odd roadside attractions? Here are a few Lincoln Hwy landmarks to get you started:

» Big-eared curios at **Mr Ed's Elephant Museum** (www.mistereds.com; Ortanna, PA)

» Ronald Reagan portrait made from 14,000 jellybeans at the **Dixon Historic Center** (www.dixonhistoriccenter.org; Dixon, IL)

» Boot-shaped, 48ft **Shoe House** (www.shoehouse.us; York, PA)

» Giant **Coffee Pot** (www.lhhc.org/coffeepot.asp; Bedford, PA)

» Ghosts at the **Mansfield Reformatory** (www.mrps.org; Mansfield, OH)

to New Jersey and Princeton, the natty Ivy League university town. Pennsylvania rolls up next, offering the Liberty Bell and Independence Hall in Philadelphia; quilts and clip-clopping horses in the Amish communities near Lancaster; the Civil War super-site of Gettysburg; and river-tastic, pop-art-rich Pittsburgh. Cornfields and haunted prisons flash by in Ohio. Indiana's pit stops include more Amish areas and the town of South Bend, home to a vintage Studebaker car museum and the football-crazed university of Notre Dame. In Illinois, the route swipes Chicago's suburbs, then sets a course through small farming communities pressed flat against the horizon. After that, the Lincoln Hwy heads over the Mississippi River and onward west through Iowa, Nebraska, Colorado, Wyoming, Utah, Nevada and California, before pulling up at the Pacific Ocean.

Cities that provide easy access to the road include New York City, Philadelphia, Pittsburgh and Chicago.

When to Go

April through October is the best time to travel. Snowy roads in winter detract from the fun, plus many of the smaller attractions reduce their hours or shut down entirely between November and March.

Resources

The official **Lincoln Highway Association** (www.lincolnhighwayassoc.org) provides lots of free info online. It also sells driving maps that are the definitive source for turn-by-turn directions.

The Lincoln Highway (2007) by Michael Wallis is a coffee-table book filled with gorgeous photos and the lowdown on route hot-spots.

Time & Mileage

Time: You could drive it in 2½ days without stopping much, but four or five days lets you soak up the highway's essence

Mileage: About 1000 miles for the eastern portion

Natchez Trace Parkway

With emerald mounds, jade swamps, hiking trails, opulent mansions, riverside saloons and layer upon layer of American history, the Natchez Trace Parkway is the richest drive in the South. It winds 444 gorgeously wooded miles from Nashville to Natchez in southern Mississippi.

Why Go

When we say history, we're talking 10,000 years' worth. The Old Trace was a natural corridor from the southern Appalachian foothills in Tennessee to the lower Mississippi River, and the Natchez, Chickasaw and Choctaw nations had long used it to travel across their traditional homelands. In the late 1700s and early 1800s, more people began using the rough path as the USA began expanding west, and these new travelers soon beat it into a clearly marked trail. In 1801, President Thomas Jefferson named the Trace as the official route for mail delivery between Nashville and Natchez, and the road was on its way to prominence.

Think about this as you set out: you'll be following the same path as a who's who of historic figures, including Andrew Jackson (7th president of the US and face of the $20 bill), Jefferson Davis (president of the Confederacy), James Audubon (naturalist and painter), Meriwether Lewis (famous explorer who died on the Trace in 1809), Ulysses S Grant (18th president of the US) and – wait for it – a young Elvis Presley. The drive meanders by various cultural and historic sites that let you learn more about each man.

The Route

Nashville is the easiest place to access the parkway, and for country-music fans and wannabe songwriters all over the world, a trip to the city is the ultimate pilgrimage. There are boot-stomping honky-tonks, the Country Music Hall of Fame and a sweet historic district to explore. There's also good eatin' at local cafeterias, the ultimate way to indulge in everything from barbecue chicken and pig's feet to turnip greens and baked apples.

About 10 miles beyond Nashville, the road swings by one of the Civil War's bloodiest battlefields at Franklin, where 20,000 Confederates and 17,000 Union soldiers fought on November 30, 1864. Further along are confederate gravesites for unknown soldiers. Several centuries-old indigenous burial mounds likewise rise up along the way. Emerald Mound, near Natchez, is one of the nation's largest, and the massive grassy pyramid still buzzes with ancient energy.

Other highlights en route include the town of Tupelo, where you can visit the humble house where Elvis grew up, learned to play the guitar and dreamed big; and tree-shaded, milky-green Cypress Swamp, filled with alligators. Natchez itself is a living antebellum museum, all sweeping spiral staircases,

ALSO WORTH A SPIN

So far we've described just a few of the great road trips that the Eastern USA has to offer. But there are scores of other scenic byways, country roads and blue-line highways webbing across the region. For more faves, see the following table and also look for the Scenic Drive boxed texts scattered throughout the destination chapters. Lonely Planet's *Trips* series of guidebooks covers a wide assortment of road trips throughout the US from the small to the epic.

ROUTE	STATE	START/END	SIGHTS & ACTIVITIES	BEST TIMES	MORE INFO
Rte 28	NY	Stony Hollow/Arkville	Catskills mountains, lakes, rivers; hiking, leaf-peeping, tubing	May-Sep	p111
Old Kings Hwy	MA	Sagamore/ Provincetown	Historic districts, period homes, coastal scenery	Apr-Oct	p181
Hwy 13	WI	Bayfield/Superior	Lakeside beaches, forests, farmlands; nature walks	May-Sep	p573
Hwy 61	MN	Duluth/Canadian Border	State parks, waterfalls, quaint towns; hiking	May-Sep	p587
VT 100	VT	Stamford/Newport	Rolling pastures, green mountains; hiking, skiing	Jun-Sep	p210
Kancamagus Hwy	VT	Conway/Lincoln	Craggy mountains, streams, waterfalls; camping, hiking, swimming	May-Sep	p217
Hwy 12	NC	Corolla/Sealevel	Beaches, lighthouses, ferry rides, Wright Brothers launching site	Apr-Oct	p317
Overseas Hwy	FL	Key Largo/Key West	Beaches, protected coral reefs, plates of conch fritters, key lime pie	Dec-Apr	p458

ROUTE 66

For a classic American road trip, nothing beats good ol' Route 66. Nicknamed the 'Mother Road' by novelist John Steinbeck, this string of small-town main streets and country byways first connected big-shouldered Chicago with the waving palm trees of Los Angeles in 1926.

Most of the Mother Road unfurls through the western part of the country, but Illinois' 300-mile portion offers classic, time-warped moseying. Fork into thick slabs of pie in neon-lit diners; snap photos of roadside attractions like the Gemini Giant, a sky-high fiberglass spaceman; and motor on past drive-in movie theaters, mom-and-pop motels and other Americana. For details, see p526.

Road trippers with a couple of extra weeks to spare can keep on truckin'. The route's remaining 2100 miles wind by singular sensations such as frozen custard stands in Missouri, a totem pole park in Oklahoma, a barbed wire museum in Texas, the Grand Canyon in Arizona and wild and crazy Santa Monica Pier in California. See **Historic Route 66** (www.historic66.com) for more.

chandeliers and thick column houses. If you've ever wanted to make like Scarlett O'Hara and collapse into the luxurious shade of your verandah, the town's historic plantations turned boutique hotels can accommodate.

When to Go

The weather is best from April to June and from September to November. Summer can be hotter than hot.

Resources

Natchez Trace Parkway (www.nps.gov/natr) The National Park Service maintains the byway, and its website provides road construction and closure updates, plus information on local activities and historic sites.

Natchez Trace Compact (www.scenictrace. com) The state tourism bureaus of Tennessee, Alabama and Mississippi band together to offer route itineraries, maps and event info.

Time & Mileage

Time: Allot three days for the trip, though you could do it in two; travel times aren't exactly speedy, as this is a two-lane road with a 50m/h speed limit most of the way.
Mileage: 444 miles

Travel with Children

Best Regions for Kids in the Eastern USA

New York, New Jersey & Pennsylvania

New York City offers adventure, such as row-boating in Central Park and kid-friendly museums. Head to the Jersey shore for boardwalk fun and to Pennsylvania for Amish Country horse-and-buggy rides.

New England

Boston's waterfront is a gateway to adventure with an aquarium, an 18th-century warship and whale-watching cruises. Plimoth Plantation, with its recreated Wampanoag and Pilgrim villages is good family fun.

Washington, DC, & the Capital Region

Washington is alluring for families, with staggering kid-focused museums, a panda-loving zoo, and a carousel on the Mall. Virginia's Williamsburg is a slice of 18th-century USA with fanciful activities (witch trials, ghost walks).

Florida

Orlando's Walt Disney World, the largest theme park on earth, is well worth planning a vacation around. Afterwards, hit the state's beautiful beaches.

The Eastern USA generally welcomes families with young travelers. From north to south, you'll find superb attractions for all ages: bucket-and-spade fun at the beach, amusement parks, zoos, eye-popping aquariums and natural history exhibits, hands-on science museums, camping adventures, battlefields, leisurely bike rides through serene countryside (easygoing and challenging alike) and plenty of other activities likely to wow the young ones. The great outdoors is a good place to start: most national and state parks gear at least some exhibits, trails and programs (junior ranger activities and the like) towards families with kids.

The Eastern USA for Kids

Dining with Children

The local restaurant industry seems built on family-style service: children are not just accepted at most places, but are often encouraged by special children's menus with smaller portions and lower prices. In some restaurants children under a certain age even eat for free. Restaurants usually provide high chairs and booster seats. Some restaurants may also offer children crayons and puzzles, and occasionally live performances by cartoon-like characters.

Restaurants without children's menus don't necessarily discourage kids, though higher-end restaurants might; even at

To find family-oriented sights and activities, accommodations, restaurants and entertainment throughout this guide, just look for the child-friendly icon (🔅).

When to Go

» Peak travel season is June to August, when schools are out and the weather is warmest. Expect high prices and abundant crowds – meaning long lines at amusement and water parks, fully booked resorts and heavy traffic on the roads; book well in advance for popular destinations.

» High season for winter resorts (in the Catskills and White Mountains) runs from January to March.

Need to Know

» Many public toilets have a baby-changing table (sometimes in men's toilets, too), and gender-neutral 'family' facilities appear in airports.

» Medical services and facilities in America are of a high standard. See p625 for more on health and health insurance.

» Items such as baby food, formula and disposable nappies are widely available – including organic options – in supermarkets across the country.

» Single parents or guardians traveling with anyone under 18 should carry proof of legal custody or a notarized letter from the nonaccompanying parent(s) authorizing the trip. This isn't required, but it can help avoid potential problems entering the USA.

Helpful Resources

For more information and advice, check out Lonely Planet's *Travel with Children*. For outdoor advice, read *Kids in the Wild: a Family Guide to Outdoor Recreation* by Cindy Ross and Todd Gladfelter or Alice Cary's *Parents' Guide to Hiking & Camping*.

Family Travel Files (www.thefamilytravelfiles.com) Ready-made vacation ideas, destination profiles and travel tips.

Go City Kids (www.gocitykids.com) Excellent coverage of kid-centric activities and entertainment in over 50 US cities.

Kids.gov (www.kids.gov) Enormous, eclectic national resource; download songs and activities or even link to the CIA Kids' Page.

the nicer places, however, if you show up early enough (right at dinner time opening hours), you can usually eat without too much stress – and you'll likely be joined by other foodie couples with kids. You can ask if the kitchen will make a smaller order of a dish, or if they will split a normal-size main dish between two plates for the kids. Chinese, Mexican and Italian restaurants seem to be the best bet for finicky young eaters.

Farmers markets are growing in popularity in the region, and every sizeable town has at least one a week. This is a good place to assemble a first-rate picnic, sample the local specialties and support independent growers in the process.

Accommodations

Motels and hotels typically have rooms with two beds, which are ideal for families. Some also have roll-away beds or cribs that can be brought into the room for an extra charge – but keep in mind these are usually Pack 'n' Plays, which not all children sleep well in. Some hotels offer 'kids stay free' programs for children up to 12 or sometimes 18 years old. Be wary of B&Bs, as many don't allow children.

Babysitting

Resort hotels may have on-call babysitting services; otherwise, ask the front-desk staff or concierge to help you make arrangements. Always ask if babysitters are licensed and bonded, what they charge per hour per child, whether there's a minimum fee, and if they charge extra for transportation or meals. Most tourist bureaus list local resources for childcare and recreation facilities, medical services and so on.

EASTERN LIT FOR KIDS

» *Little Women* (1868) is Louisa May Alcott's wonderful book about girls growing up in 19th-century Concord.

» Henry Wadsworth Longfellow combined history, poetry and suspense in his classic *Paul Revere's Ride* (1861).

» Six-year-old *Eloise* (1955) lives in the Plaza Hotel in NYC, a prime place to launch into all sorts of mischief.

» Tween sleuths solve a mystery involving ghosts, treasure and Frank Lloyd Wright's Robie House in Chicago in *The Wright 3* (2006) by Blue Balliett.

Driving & Flying

Every car rental agency should be able to provide an appropriate child seat, since these are required in every state, but you need to request it when booking and expect to pay around $10 more per day.

Domestic airlines don't charge for children under two. Those two years and up must have a seat, and discounts are unlikely. Very rarely, some resort areas (like Disneyland) offer a 'kids fly free' promotion. Amtrak and other train operators occasionally run similar deals (ie kids under 15 free).

Discounts for Children

Child concessions often apply for tours, admission fees and transport, with some discounts as high as 50% off the adult rate. However, the definition of 'child' can vary from under 12 to under 16 years. Some popular sights also have discount rates for families, which can save a few dollars. Most sights also give free admission to children under two years.

Children's Highlights
Outdoor Adventure

» Kayak, canoe or join guided walks in the Florida Everglades.

» Go white-water rafting in the New River Gorge National Park, WV.

» Spot humpbacks on a whale-watch tour out of Boston or Provincetown, MA.

» Take an underground boat ride through Lost River Cave in central Kentucky.

Theme Parks & Zoos

» Immerse in the king of them all: Walt Disney World, where four action-packed parks spread across 20,000 Florida acres.

» Hop the subway from Manhattan to one of the USA's best zoos at Bronx Wildlife Conservation Park, NY.

» Drive among 900 wild creatures roaming the Lion Country Safari in West Palm Beach, FL.

» Splash it up at the Wisconsin Dells' 21 water parks and water-skiing thrill shows.

Traveling in Time

» Don 18th-century garb and mingle with costumed interpreters in the history-rich settings of Plimoth, Williamsburg, Yorktown or Jamestown.

» Plug your ears as costumed soldiers fire muskets and cannons at Fort Mackinac, MI.

» Go on a walking tour of Boston's Freedom Trail with Ben Franklin (or at least his 21st-century lookalike).

» Stroll in the footsteps of one of America's greatest presidents at the Lincoln Presidential Museum in Springfield, IL.

Rainy-Day Activities

» Inspire budding aviators at the National Air & Space Museum, Washington, DC, with rockets, spacecraft, old-fashioned biplanes and ride simulators.

» Discover the massive planetarium, immense dinosaur skeletons and 30 million other artifacts at New York's American Museum of Natural History.

» Roam three stories of adventure and (cleverly disguised) learning, including an Egyptian tomb, farmers market, train, art studio and physics stations at Baltimore's Port Discovery Museum.

Eating

» Get messy eating scrumptious Maryland blue crabs at open-air restaurants along Chesapeake Bay.

» Turn the clock back a few generations at the retro 1950s Ellen's Stardust Diner in NYC.

» Heft a slice of deep-dish pizza (and scrawl your name on the wall) at Gino's East in Chicago.

regions at a glance

New York City is the East's hub. More than eight million inhabitants pile into the megacity, a world center for fashion, food, arts and finance. The crowd thins out in neighboring New Jersey and Pennsylvania, where beaches, mountains and literal horse-and-buggy hamlets join the landscape. New England arches north to rocky shores, clapboard fishing villages and Ivy League universities. The Capital Region begins the march south through voluptuous valleys and a slew of historic sites. By the time you reach the true South, the pace has slowed, pecan pie tempts on the table and bluesy tunes drift from juke joints. Surreal Florida brings on mermaids, manatees, Mickey Mouse and Miami, while the sensible Great Lakes region prefers burgers and beer with its natural attractions.

New York, New Jersey & Pennsylvania

Arts & Culture ✓✓✓
History ✓✓
Outdoors ✓✓

Mega-Culture

Home to the MET, MOMA and Broadway – and that's just NYC. Buffalo, Philadelphia and Pittsburgh have their fair share of world-renowned cultural institutions, too, as well as burgeoning bohemian enclaves with live music scenes.

Liberty Bell & Beyond

From spectacularly preserved Gilded Age mansions in the Hudson Valley, Independence National Historic Park in Philadelphia, and sites dedicated to formative moments in the nation's founding, the region provides a top-flight interactive education.

Al Fresco Activities

The great outdoors lurks just beyond the city's gaze, with great hiking in the Adirondacks and Catskills, rafting trips down the Delaware River, and Atlantic Ocean frolics along the Jersey Shore or in the Hamptons.

p50

New England

Food & Drink ✓✓
History ✓✓✓
Beaches ✓✓✓

Seafood
New England is justifiably famous for its fresh seafood. Seaside eateries pepper the coast, where you can shuck and suck oysters, crack lobster claws (and dab 'em in butter) and spoon into creamy clam chowder while watching day-boats haul in the next meal's catch.

Colonial Tales
From the Pilgrims landing in Plymouth and the witch hysteria in Salem to Paul Revere's revolutionary ride and the Boston Tea Party dumping grounds, New England has shaped American history.

Beachy Keen
Cape Cod, Martha's Vineyard and Block Island – New England is a summer mecca for sand and sea worshippers. The region's scores of beaches run the gamut from kid-friendly tidal flats to gnarly open-ocean surf.

p154

Washington, DC & the Capital Region

Arts & Culture ✓✓✓
History ✓✓✓
Food & Drink ✓✓

Museums & Music
Washington has a superb collection of museums and galleries, plus free summer concerts and world-class performances at big venues. You'll also find down-home mountain music on Virginia's Crooked Road, famous regional theaters, and edgy art in Baltimore.

Times Past
For historical lore, Jamestown, Williamsburg and Yorktown offer windows into Colonial America, while Civil War battlefields stud the Virginia countryside. There are also fascinating presidential estates like Mount Vernon and Monticello, plus history-rich charmers like Annapolis and Lewes.

Fork In
Decadent feasts await: Maryland blue crabs, oysters and seafood platters; international restaurants in DC; and farm-to-table dining rooms in Baltimore, Charlottesville, Staunton, Rehoboth and other towns.

p236

The South

Food & Drink ✓✓✓
Music ✓✓✓
Southern Charm ✓✓✓

Biscuits & Barbecue
Slow-cooked barbecue, fried chicken and catfish, butter-smothered biscuits, corn bread, grits and spicy Cajun-Creole dishes make the South a magnificent (if artery-clogging) place to fill up a plate.

Big Notes
There is nowhere on earth that has a soundtrack as influential as the American South. Head to music meccas for the authentic experience: country in Nashville, blues in Memphis and big-band jazz in New Orleans – with plenty of fusions and alternative sounds all across the region.

Southern Charm
Picture-book towns like Charleston and Savannah, among others, have long captivated visitors with their historic tree-lined streets, antebellum architecture and friendly down-home welcome. Other southern belles include Chapel Hill, Oxford, Chattanooga and Natchez.

p312

Florida

Arts & Culture ✓✓
Outdoors ✓✓✓
Beaches ✓✓✓

Coat of Many Colors
Florida has a complicated soul: it's the home of Miami's colorful art-deco district and Little Havana, plus historical attractions in St Augustine, massive theme parks in Orlando and museums and island heritage in Key West.

Wildlife Watching
Florida is the place to immerse yourself in aquatic life on a snorkeling or diving trip. For bigger beasts, head off on a whale-watching cruise or try to spy alligators – along with egrets, eagles, manatees and other wildlife – on an Everglades excursion.

Shades of Sand
You'll find a heady array of sandy shores from steamy South Beach to upscale Palm Beach, island allure on Sanibel and Captiva, and panhandle rowdiness in Pensacola.

p432

Great Lakes

Food & Drink ✓✓✓
Music ✓✓
Roadside Attractions ✓✓

Chowhound Heaven
From JBF–award-winning restaurants in Chicago and Minneapolis to fresh-from-the-dairy cheeses to roadside diners wafting a rack full of pie, the Midwest's farms, orchards and breweries satisfy the palate.

Rockin'
Home to the Rock and Roll Hall of Fame, blowout fests like Lollapalooza, Dylan, techno music and thrashing clubs in all the cities, the region knows how to turn up the volume.

Outsider Art?
A big ball of twine, a mustard museum, a cow-dung throwing contest: the quirks rise from the Midwest's backyards and back roads, wherever there are folks with passion, imagination and maybe a little too much time on their hands.

p492

Look out for these icons:

 TOP CHOICE Our author's recommendation

 A green or sustainable option

FREE No payment required

See the Index for a full list of destinations covered in this book.

On the Road

New York, New Jersey & Pennsylvania

Includes »

Why Go?

Where else could you visit an Amish family's farm, camp on a mountaintop, read the Declaration of Independence and view New York, New York from the 86th floor of an art-deco landmark - all in a few days? Even though it's the most densely populated part of the US, it's full of places where jaded city dwellers escape to seek simple lives, where artists retreat for inspiration, and pretty houses line main streets in small towns set amid stunning scenery.

Urban adventures in NYC, historic and lively Philadelphia and river-rich Pittsburgh are a must. Miles and miles of glorious beaches are within reach, from glamorous Long Island to the Jersey Shore – the latter ranges from stately to kitschy. The mountain wilderness of the Adirondacks reaches skyward just a day's drive north of New York City, a journey that perfectly encapsulates this region's heady character.

Best Places to Eat

- » Blue Hill (p92)
- » Morimoto (p137)
- » The Breslin (p92)
- » Anchor Bar (p117)
- » Primanti Bros (p151)

Best Places to Stay

- » Bowery Hotel (p86)
- » Mohonk Mountain House (p109)
- » Saugerties Lighthouse (p110)
- » Morris House Hotel (p136)
- » Caribbean Motel (p125)

When to Go

New York City

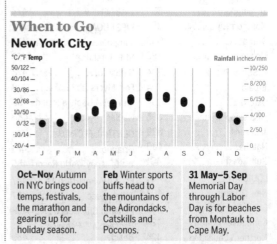

Oct–Nov Autumn in NYC brings cool temps, festivals, the marathon and gearing up for holiday season.

Feb Winter sports buffs head to the mountains of the Adirondacks, Catskills and Poconos.

31 May–5 Sep Memorial Day through Labor Day is for beaches from Montauk to Cape May.

Transportation

The big cities all have airports, but New York's John F Kennedy is the region's major international gateway. Alternatives include Newark Liberty International Airport and La Guardia, in Queens, with mostly domestic flights. Philadelphia and Pittsburgh also have small international airports.

Greyhound buses serve main cities and towns, while Peter Pan Bus Lines and Adirondack Trailways are two regional bus lines. Amtrak provides rail services linking New York with much of New Jersey, as well as Philadelphia and Pittsburgh. Most popular day trips, at least from New York City, are easily accessible by one of the three commuter-rail lines. If you're driving, the main north–south highway is the I-95.

NATIONAL & STATE PARKS

Parklands and recreation areas are in big supply here, as is wildlife, which is at first surprising to many who associate these states only with large urban areas. Black bears, bobcats and even elk can be found in forested parts of the states; more common are various species of deer. Falcons, eagles, hawks and migrating species of birds stop over in the region, some even within only a few miles of New York City.

In New York alone, you'll find hundreds of state parks, ranging from waterfalls around Ithaca to wilderness in the Adirondacks. In New Jersey, float down the Delaware River, grab some sun at the Cape May beach and hike the forested Kittatinny Valley in the north. Pennsylvania includes a huge array of thick forests, rolling parklands and a significant portion of the Appalachian National Scenic Trail, a 2175-mile footpath that snakes its way from Maine to Georgia.

Top Five Scenic Drives

» **Catskills, New York – Rte 23A to 214 to 28**: This takes you past forested hills, rushing rivers and spectacular falls.

» **North Central, Pennsylvania – Rte 6**: A drive through this rugged stretch of mountains and woodlands includes gushing creeks, wildlife and state forests.

» **Lake Cayuga, New York – Rte 80**: Head north from Ithaca above the lake past dozens of wineries.

» **Delaware Water Gap, New Jersey – Old Mine Rd**: One of the oldest roads in the US past beautiful vistas of the Delaware River and rural countryside.

» **Brandywine Valley, Pennsylvania – Rte 100, 52 and 163**: Only 25 miles through rolling horse country and lovely farmland.

THE HIGH LINE

Originally built in the 1930s to lift freight trains off Manhattan's streets, the High Line is now a brilliantly designed elevated park that embraces the natural and industrial, from the Meatpacking District to Chelsea.

Fast Facts

» Hub cities: New York City (population 8,175,000), Philadelphia (population 1,526,000)

» New York to Philadelphia: 97 miles

» New York to Niagara Falls: 408 miles

» Time zone: Eastern Standard

» Number of politicians resigned or jailed after scandal: enough to fill the legislature

Did You Know?

From November to April harbor seals, as well as other seal species, migrate to the waters of the Jersey Shore, Long Island Sound and NYC, from Staten Island to beaches in the Bronx.

Resources

» New York State Tourism (www.iloveny.com) Info, maps, travel advice available by phone.

» New Jersey Travel & Tourism (www.visitnj.org) Statewide tips on sights, accommodations and festivals.

» Pennsylvania Travel and Tourism (www.visitpa.com) Maps, videos and suggested itineraries.

New York, New Jersey & Pennsylvania Highlights

1 Traveling round the world without ever leaving the kaleidoscope of neighborhoods and cultures that is **New York City** (p54)

2 Enjoying the kitsch and calm of the **Jersey Shore** (p122)

3 Absorbing the story of the birth of the nation in Philadelphia's **Independence National Historic Park** (p127)

4 Walking the densely forested paths of the unspoiled **Catskills** (p110)

5 Exploring the impressive wilderness beauty of the **Adirondacks** (p114)

6 Camping along the shores of the St Lawrence River in the **Thousand Islands** (p115)

7 Bar-hopping on the Strip in **Pittsburgh** (p147)

8 Wine tasting on Long Island's **North Fork** (p108)

9 Cycling the back roads of **Pennsylvania Dutch Country** (p143)

10 0 Floating past bucolic scenery in the **Delaware Water Gap** (p121)

NEW YORK CITY

Loud and fast and pulsing with energy, New York City is symphonic, exhausting and always evolving. Maybe only a Walt Whitman poem cataloguing typical city scenes, from the humblest hole-in-the-wall to grand buildings, could begin to do the city justice. It remains one of the world centers of fashion, theater, food, music, publishing, advertising and even, in light of the late-naughts financial collapse, finance. And as Groucho Marx once said, 'When it's 9:30 in New York, it's 1937 in Los Angeles.' Coming here for the first time from anywhere else is like stepping into a movie, one you've probably been unknowingly writing, one that contains all imagined possibilities. From the middle of Times Square to the most obscure corner of the Bronx, you'll find extremes. From Brooklyn's Russian enclave in Brighton Beach to the mini South America in Queens, virtually every country in the world has a bustling proxy community in the city. You can experience a little bit of everything on a visit here, as long as you take care to travel with a loose itinerary and an open mind.

History

After Henry Hudson first claimed this land in 1609 for his Dutch East India Company sponsors, he reported it to be 'as beautiful a land as one can hope to tread upon.' Soon after it was named 'Manhattan,' derived from local Munsee Native American words and meaning 'Island of Hills.'

By 1625 a colony, soon called New Amsterdam, was established, and the island was bought from the Munsee Indians by Peter Minuit. George Washington was sworn in here as the republic's first president in 1789, and when the Civil War broke out, New York City, which supplied a significant contingent of volunteers to defend the Union, became an organizing center for the movement to emancipate slaves.

Throughout the 19th century successive waves of immigrants – Irish, German, English, Scandinavian, Slavic, Italian, Greek and central European Jewish – led to a swift population increase, followed by the building of empires in industry and finance, and a golden age of skyscrapers.

After WWII New York City was the premier city in the world, but it suffered from a new phenomenon: 'white flight' to the suburbs. By the 1970s the graffiti-ridden subway system had become a symbol of New York's civic and economic decline. But NYC regained much of its swagger in the 1980s, led by colorful three-term mayor Ed Koch. The city elected its first African American mayor, David Dinkins, in 1989, but ousted him after a single term in favor of Republican Rudolph Giuliani (a 2008 primary candidate for US president). It was during Giuliani's reign that catastrophe struck on September 11, 2001, when the 110-story twin towers of the World Trade Center were struck by hijacked commercial airlines, became engulfed in balls of fire and then collapsed, killing 3000 people, the result of a now-infamous terrorist attack.

In 2001 New York elected its 108th mayor, Republican Michael Bloomberg. Reelected for a second term in November 2005, Bloomberg won a third term in 2009 after the passage of a highly controversial amendment that allowed him to run. Bloomberg

DON'T MISS

ICONIC NYC

Recognizing that any New York City highlights list is inevitably abbreviated, necessary shorthand for a city with so much to do and see, the following offers a few sights not to miss on a short visit:

» **Museums** – The massive and exceptional **Metropolitan Museum of Art** (p75) can occupy your entire visit. Take in the iconic works at the **Museum of Modern Art** (p67) on a weekday morning to avoid the gridlock.

» **Views** – The open-air observation deck of the **Top of the Rock** (p71) offers an unparalleled perspective. On a nighttime stroll, stop midway across the **Brooklyn Bridge** (p55) for one of the more romantic sights the city has to offer.

» **Green Space** – Whatever the season, a walk through **Central Park** (p74) is the quintessential New York experience. To get a sense of how much of the city lives, head out to Brooklyn's **Prospect Park** (p80) for a weekend picnic.

One Week

Start off with a gentle introduction in **Philadelphia**, birthplace of American independence. After a day of touring the historic sites and a night of sampling the hoppin' nightlife, head into New Jersey for a bucolic night in **Cape May**. Sample another beachtown like **Wildwood** or **Atlantic City** further north along the **Jersey Shore**, landing in **New York City** the following day. Spend the rest of your visit here, blending touristy mustdos – such as the **Top of the Rock** and **Central Park** – with vibrant nightlife and eclectic dining adventures, perhaps in the city's bustling **East Village**.

Two Weeks

Begin with several days in **New York City**, then a night somewhere in the **Hudson Valley**, before reaching the **Catskills**. After touring this bucolic region, head further north to **Saratoga Springs** and **Lake George**. The outdoor-minded will want to explore the forested **Adirondack Mountains** before looping back south and west with a night in college-town **Ithaca**. From here you can head to **Buffalo** and **Niagara Falls** or south to the **Poconos** of northern Pennsylvania. The southern portion of the state has loads of historic sites as well as **Lancaster County** where you can stay on a working Amish farm. From here it's a short jaunt to **Philadelphia**, which deserves at least a couple of nights. Follow it up with a stay at a quaint B&B in **Cape May**, a day of boardwalk amusements in **Wildwood** and casino fun in **Atlantic City**.

---

is known as an independent political pragmatist, and his administration has earned both raves and criticism for its dual pursuit of environmental and development goals (the citywide nonsmoking law has proved popular, while congestion pricing to combat gridlock failed to get approval).

◉ Sights

LOWER MANHATTAN

TOP
CHOICE **Brooklyn Bridge**   BRIDGE
(Map p58) Marianne Moore's description of the world's first suspension bridge – which inspired poets from Walt Whitman to Jack Kerouac even before its completion – as a 'climatic ornament, a double rainbow' is perhaps most evocative. Walking across the grand Brooklyn Bridge is a rite of passage for New Yorkers and visitors alike – with this in mind, walk no more than two abreast or else you're in danger of colliding with runners and speeding cyclists. With an unprecedented span of 1596ft, it remains a compelling symbol of US achievement and a superbly graceful structure, despite the fact that its construction was plagued by budget overruns and the death of 20 workers. Among the casualties was designer John Roebling, who was knocked off a pier in 1869 while scouting a site for the western bridge tower and later died of tetanus poisoning. The bridge and the smooth pedestrian/cyclist path, beginning just east of City Hall, affords wonderful views of Lower Manhattan and Brooklyn. Observation points under the two stone support towers have illustrations showing panoramas of the waterfront at various points in New York's history. On the Brooklyn side, the ever-expanding **Brooklyn Bridge Park** and restaurants of **Dumbo** are excellent end points for your stroll.

Statue of Liberty   MONUMENT
(Map p56; ☎212-363-3200; www.nps.gov/stli; New York Harbor, Liberty Island; ☺9:30am-5pm) In a city full of American icons, the Statue of Liberty is perhaps the most famous. Conceived as early as 1865 by French intellectual Edouard Laboulaye as a monument to the republican principals shared by France and the USA, it's still generally recognized as a symbol for at least the ideals of opportunity and freedom to many. French sculptor Frédéric-Auguste Bartholdi traveled to New York in 1871 to select the site, then spent more than 10 years in Paris designing and making the 151ft-tall figure *Liberty Enlightening the World*. It was then shipped to New York, erected on a small island in the harbor and unveiled in 1886. Structurally, it consists of an iron skeleton (designed by Gustave Eiffel) with a copper skin attached to it by stiff but flexible metal bars.

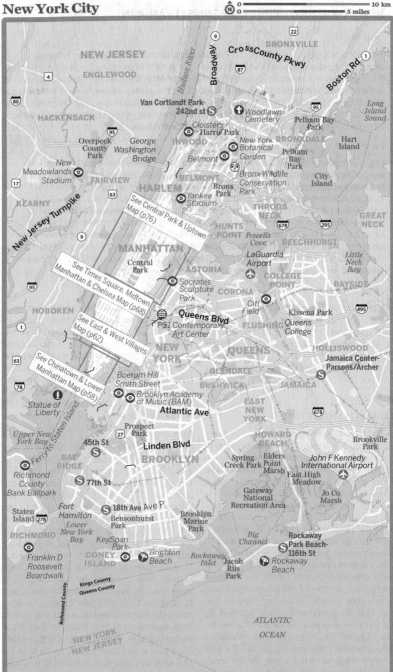

0   10 km
0   5 miles

NEW JERSEY
ENGLEWOOD
BRONXVILLE
CrossCounty Pkwy
Boston Rd
Hudson River
Broadway
Van Cortlandt Park-242nd st
Woodlawn Cemetery
Pelham Bay Park
Long Island Sound
HACKENSACK
Overpeck County Park
George Washington Bridge
Cloisters
Harris Park
INWOOD
New York Botanical Garden
BRONXDALE
Hart Island
New Meadowlands Stadium
FAIRVIEW
Belmont
BELMONT
Bronx Wildlife Conservation Park
Pelham Bay Park
City Island
KEARNY
HARLEM
Yankee Stadium
Bronx Park
THROGS NECK
GREAT NECK
New Jersey Turnpike
See Central Park & Uptown Map (p76)
HUNTS POINT
Powells Cove
BEECHHURST
MANHATTAN
Central Park
ASTORIA
LaGuardia Airport
Little Neck Bay
BAYSIDE
HOBOKEN
See Times Square, Midtown Manhattan & Chelsea Map (p68)
Socrates Sculpture Park
COLLEGE POINT
CORONA
Citi Field
Kissena Park
Queens College
See East & West Villages Map (p62)
Queens Blvd
PS1 Contemporary Art Center
NEW YORK
FLUSHING
QUEENS
HOLLISWOOD
Jamaica Center-Parsons/Archer
See Chinatown & Lower Manhattan Map (p59)
Boerum Hill
Smith Street
Brooklyn Academy of Music (BAM)
Atlantic Ave
GLENDALE
BUSHWICK
JAMAICA
Statue of Liberty
EAST NEW YORK
Upper New York Bay
Prospect Park
Linden Blvd
HOWARD BEACH
Brookville Park
45th St
BROOKLYN
Spring Creek Park
Elders Point Marsh
John F Kennedy International Airport
Richmond County Bank Ballpark
77th St
East High Meadow
Staten Island
Fort Hamilton
18th Ave Ave P
Bensonhurst Park
Brooklyn Marine Park
Gateway National Recreation Area
Jo Co Marsh
Lower New York Bay
KeySpan Park
Big Channel
Rockaway Park Beach-116th St
RICHMOND
Franklin D Roosevelt Boardwalk
CONEY ISLAND
Brighton Beach
Rockaway Inlet
Jacob Riis Park
Rockaway Beach
Kings County
Queens County
ATLANTIC OCEAN
NEW YORK
NEW JERSEY

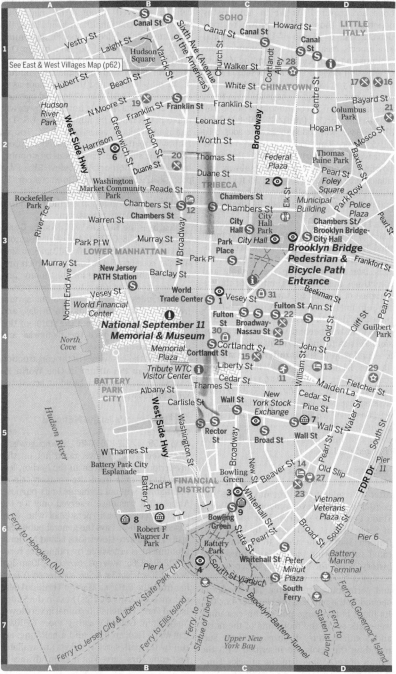

See East & West Villages Map (p62)

The crown is again open to the public – numbers are limited, however, so reservations are required, as far in advance as possible. For those without crown reservations, a visit to Statue of Liberty National Monument means you can wander the grounds and enjoy the view from the 16-story observation deck; a specially designed glass ceiling lets you look up into the statue's striking interior. The trip to its island, via ferry, is usually visited in conjunction with nearby Ellis Island. **Ferries** (Map p58; 201-604-2800, 877-523-9849; www.statuecruises.com; adult/child $13/5; every 30min 9am-5pm, extended summer hr) leave from Battery Park. South Ferry and Bowling Green are the closest subway stations. Ferry tickets (additional $3 for crown admission) include admission to both sights and reservations can be made in advance.

Ellis Island   MUSEUM

The way-station from 1892 to 1954 for more than 12 million immigrants who were hoping to make new lives in the United States, Ellis Island conjures up the humble and sometimes miserable beginnings of the experience of coming to America – as well as the fulfillment of dreams. More than three thousand died in the island's hospital and more than two percent were denied admission. Ferries to the Statue of Liberty make a second stop at the **immigration station** on Ellis Island (Map p56). The handsome main building has been restored as the **Immigration Museum** (212-363-3200; www.ellisisland.org; New York Harbor; audio guide $8; 9:30am-5pm), with fascinating exhibits and a film about immigrant experiences, the processing of immigrants and how the influx changed the USA.

National September 11
Memorial & Museum   MEMORIAL

After a decade of cost overruns, delays and politicking the redevelopment of the World Trade Center site destroyed by the attacks of September 11, 2001 is finally coming to fruition. Half of the area's 16 acres is dedicated to honoring victims and preserving history, while the remaining space will be occupied by office towers, a transport hub and performing arts center. The Memorial opened to the public on September 12, 2011. Its focus is two large pools with cascading waterfalls set in the footprints of the north and south towers. Bronze parapets surrounding the pools are inscribed with the names of those killed in the attacks. Hundreds of swamp whitewood trees will provide shade to the site. Visitor passes (free) can be reserved through the memorial's website (www.national911memorial.org; the museum is scheduled to open in September 2012). Construction of the $3.2 billion One World Trade Center, formerly known as the Freedom Tower and the signature building of the site, has reached the 65th floor as of the summer of 2011 (the scheduled opening is for 2014); at 1776ft its antenna tower will make it the tallest building in the US. The Santiago Calatrava-designed WTC Transit Hub will open in 2014. You can check progress on the site or reserve passes by stopping by the **9/11 Memorial Preview Site** (Map p58; 212-267-2047; www.911memorial.org; 20 Vesey St; 10am-7pm, to 6pm Sun), which has exhibits and information on the rebuilding or go to www.wtcprogress.com.

Nearby is the **Tribute WTC Visitor Center** (Map p58; 866-737-1184; www.tributewtc.org; 120 Liberty St; admission $10; 10am-6pm Mon, Wed-Sat, noon-6pm Tue, to 5pm Sun), which provides exhibits, first-person testimony and **walking tours** of the site ($15 per person and includes museum admission, several from 11am to 3pm Sunday to Friday, and to 4pm Saturday); though the status of this center is unclear once the memorial and museum are open.

Some of the best views of the construction site are from the atrium in One World Financial Center, an office building across the West Side Hwy.

FREE Governor's Island National
Monument   PARK

(Map p56; 212-825-3045; www.nps.gov/gois) Most New Yorkers have gazed out on this mysterious path of green in the harbor, less than half a mile from the southern tip of Manhattan, without a clue as to its purpose. Although it was once reserved only for the army or coast guard personnel who were based here, these days the general public can visit. The 22-acre Governor's Island National Monument is accessible by riding the **ferry** (212-514-8285; www.nps.gov/gois; 10am-3pm Wed-Fri, 10am-5pm Sat & Sun, summer only) leaving from the **Battery Marine Terminal** (Map p58; cnr South & Whitehall Sts) next to the Staten Island Ferry Whitehall Terminal in very lower Manhattan. Guided **walking tours** (10am-1pm Wed & Thu), an hour and a half long, are run by the park service; tickets are available first-come, first-served an hour in advance at the Battery Marine Terminal. Highlights include two 19th-century fortifications – Fort Jay and the three-tiered, sandstone Castle Williams – plus open lawns, massive shade trees and unsurpassed city views.

South Street Seaport NEIGHBORHOOD
Known more for the large commercial mall jutting out over the East River on Pier 17, this 11-block enclave of cobblestoned streets and restored historic buildings has been revitalized into an area worthy of a walk. The Fulton Fish Market is long gone but a combination of residents and tourists mix in a handful of bars and restaurants housed in restored mid-19th-century buildings. When in the area it's worth considering hopping on the Ikea water taxi (Map p58; ⊙every 40min 2-6:40pm Mon-Fri, 11am-7:40pm Sat & Sun) operated by the Swedish furniture store from Pier 11 (six blocks south of South Street Seaport) to its store in Red Hook, Brooklyn. Besides offering the chance to get out on the water and take in breathtaking views of the city, it's free for customers (free for all Saturday and Sunday, otherwise $5).

Bowling Green Park & Around PARK
(Map p58; cnr State & Whitehall Sts) At Bowling Green Park, British residents relaxed with quiet games in the late 17th century. The large **bronze bull** here is a tourist photo stop. The National Museum of the American Indian (Map p58; ☎212-514-3700; www.nmai.si.edu; 1 Bowling Green; admission free; ⊙10am-5pm, to 8pm Thu), housed in the gorgeous and historic Alexander Hamilton US Customs House, has quite an extensive collection of Native American arts, crafts and exhibits, plus a library and a great gift shop. Just up Broadway from here is the African Burial Ground (Map p58; ☎212-637-2019; www.nps.gov/afbg; Ted Weiss Federal Bldg, 1st fl, 290 Broadway, btwn Duane & Reade Sts; admission free; ⊙10am-4pm Tue-Sat), where the skeletal remains of more than 400 free and enslaved African men and women were discovered during preliminary construction of a downtown office building in 1991.

WALL STREET & THE FINANCIAL DISTRICT
Of course once-venerable banks including Lehman Brothers and Bear Stearns have shuttered and thousands of jobs were lost in the worldwide economic crash of late 2007/early 2008, however the neighborhood and financial industry have rebounded. Still, these days, in the mind of Main St, Wall

Street is synonymous with shortsighted greed and decadent irresponsibility. Both an actual street and the metaphorical home of US commerce, its etymological origin is the wooden barrier built by Dutch settlers in 1653 to protect Nieuw Amsterdam from Native Americans and the British. A comprehensive overview, warts and all, of the US economy is explained in fascinating up-to-date exhibits at the **Museum of American Finance** (Map p58; ☎212-908-4110; www.moaf.org; 48 Wall St; adult/child $8/free; ◎10am-4pm Tue-Sat) housed in the venerable former home of the Bank of New York. To get an up-close and personal view of what makes the world go round, sign up for an hour-plus tour of the **Federal Reserve** (Map p58; ☎212-825-6990; www.nps.gov/feha; 26 Wall St; admission free; ◎9am-5pm).

Battery Park & Around   NEIGHBORHOOD
The southwestern tip of Manhattan Island has been extended with landfill over the years to form Battery Park, so named for the gun batteries that used to be housed at the bulkheads. **Castle Clinton**, a fortification

built in 1811 to protect Manhattan from the British, was originally 900ft offshore but is now at the edge of Battery Park, with only its walls remaining. Come summertime, it's transformed into a gorgeous outdoor concert arena. The **Museum of Jewish Heritage** (Map p58; ☎646-437-4200; www.mjhnyc.org; 36 Battery Pl; adult/child $12/free; ◎10am-5:45pm Sun-Tue & Thu, to 8pm Wed, to 5pm Fri) depicts aspects of New York Jewish history and culture, and includes a holocaust memorial. Also worth a look, the **Skyscraper Museum** (Map p58; ☎212-968-1961; www.skyscraper.org; 39 Battery Pl; adult/child $5/2.50; ◎noon-6pm Wed-Sun) housed in a ground-floor space of the Ritz-Carlton Hotel features rotating exhibits plus a permanent study of high-rise history. Finally, Battery Place is the start of the stunning **Hudson River Park** (www.hudsonriverpar.org), which incorporates renovated piers, grassy spaces, gardens, basketball courts, a trapeze school, food concessions and, best of all, a ribbon of a bike/skate/running path that stretches 5 miles up to 59th St.

TRIBECA & SOHO

The 'TRIangle BElow CAnal St,' bordered roughly by Broadway to the east and Chambers St to the south, is the more downtown of these two sister 'hoods. It has old warehouses, very expensive loft apartments and chichi restaurants. On the historic side, the **Harrison Street town houses** (Map p58; Harrison St) west of Greenwich St, were built between 1804 and 1828 and are New York's largest remaining collection of Federal architecture.

SoHo has nothing to do with its London counterpart, but instead, like Tribeca, takes its name from its geographical placement: SOuth of HOuston St. SoHo is filled with block upon block of cast-iron industrial buildings that date to the period just after the Civil War, when this was the city's leading commercial district. It had a Bohemian/artsy heyday that had ended by the 1980s, and now this super-gentrified area is a major shopping destination, home to chain stores and boutiques alike and to hordes of consumers, especially on weekends.

SoHo's hip cup overfloweth to the northern side of Houston St and east side of Lafayette St, where two small areas, NoHo ('north of Houston') and NoLita ('north of Little Italy'), respectively, are known for excellent shopping – lots of small, independent and stylish clothing boutiques for women – and dining. Add them to SoHo and Tribeca for a great experience of strolling, window-shopping and cafe-hopping, and you'll have quite a lovely afternoon.

CHINATOWN & LITTLE ITALY

More than 150,000 Chinese-speaking residents live in cramped tenements and crowded apartments in Chinatown, the largest Chinese community that exists outside of Asia (though there are two other major Chinatowns in the city – Sunset Park in Brooklyn and Flushing, in Queens). In the 1990s, the neighborhood also attracted a growing number of Vietnamese immigrants, who set up their own shops and opened inexpensive restaurants here; depending on what street you're on, you'll often notice more of a Vietnamese than Chinese presence.

The best reason to visit Chinatown is to experience a feast for the senses – it's the only spot in the city where you can simultaneously see whole roasted pigs hanging in butcher-shop windows, get whiffs of fresh fish and hear the twangs of Cantonese and

Vietnamese rise over the calls of knock-off-Prada-bag hawkers on Canal St.

Museum of Chinese in America MUSEUM
(Map p62; ☎212-619-4785; www.mocanyc.org; 215 Centre St; adult/child $7/free; ⊙11am-5pm Mon, to 9pm Thu, 10am-5pm Fri-Sun) Strikingly designed and cutting edge interactive exhibits trace the history and cultural impact of Chinese communities in the US. Lectures, film series and walking tours as well.

Little Italy NEIGHBORHOOD
Once known as a truly authentic pocket of Italian people, culture and eateries, Little Italy is a barely-there remnant that's constantly shrinking (Chinatown keeps encroaching). Still, loyal Italian Americans, mostly from the suburbs, flock here to gather around red-and-white-checked tablecloths at one of a handful of long-time red-sauce restaurants. Join them for a stroll along **Mulberry Street**, and take a peek at the **Old St Patrick's Cathedral** (Map p62; 263 Mulberry St), which became the city's first Roman Catholic cathedral in 1809 and remained so until 1878, when its more famous uptown successor was completed. The former **Ravenite Social Club** (Map p62; 247 Mulberry St), now a fancy shoe shop, is a reminder of the not-so-long-ago days when mobsters ran the neighborhood. Originally known as the Alto Knights Social Club, where big hitters like Lucky Luciano spent time, the Ravenite was a favorite hangout of John Gotti (and the FBI) before his arrest and life sentencing in 1992.

LOWER EAST SIDE

First came the Jews, then the Latinos, and now, of course, the hipsters. Today the place, once the densest neighborhood in the world, is focused on being cool – by cramming into low-lit lounges, live-music clubs and trendy bistros. Luxury high-rise condominiums and boutique hotels coexist with public housing projects (read Richard Price's novel *Lush Life* for entertaining insight into this class conflict). Nevertheless, 40% of residents are still immigrants and two-thirds speak a language other than English at home.

Eldridge Street Synagogue RELIGIOUS
(Map p58; ☎212-219-0302; www.eldridgestreet.org; 12 Eldridge St, btwn Canal & Division Sts) Built in 1887 with Moorish and Romanesque ornamental work, this synagogue attracted as many as 1000 worshippers on the High Holidays at the turn of the 20th century. But

membership dwindled in the 1920s with restricted immigration laws, and by the 1950s the temple closed altogether. A 20-year restoration project was finally completed in 2007 and now the synagogue holds Friday-evening and Saturday-morning worship services, hosts weddings and offers **tours** (adult/child $10/6; ⊙10am-5pm Sun-Thu, on the half-hour) of the building. Perhaps the most breathtaking aspect of the interior is the new massive circular **stained-glass window** above the ark (space where torahs are kept). The synagogue helps organize the early-June **Egg Cream and Egg Roll Festival**, a celebration of Jewish and Chinese cultural and gastronomic traditions.

Lower East Side Tenement Museum TOUR
(Map p62; ☎212-982-8420; www.tenement.org; 90 Orchard St, at Broome St; tours $17; ⊙visitor center 10am-5:30pm, tours 10:15am-5pm) To keep the humble past in perspective, this museum puts the neighborhood's heartbreaking heritage on full display in several reconstructed tenements. Plans call for a reconstruction of a butcher shop and saloon on the ground floor. Visits are available only as part of variously themed scheduled tours, which typically operate every 40 or 50 minutes.

EAST VILLAGE

Bordered roughly by 14th St, Lafayette St, E Houston St and the East River, the East Village has gentrified in the last decade or so, much to the horror of longtime tenants and punk-kid squatters, who have been around for decades. These days real-estate developers have the upper hand – although the 'hood has not yet shaken its image as an edgy, radical, be-yourself kind of place.

Tompkins Square Park PARK
This park between Seventh and Tenth Sts and Aves A and B is an unofficial border between the East Village (to the west) and Alphabet City (to the east). It was once an Eastern European immigrant area; you'll

East & West Villages

still see old Ukrainians and Poles in the park, but they'll be alongside punks, students, panhandlers and a slew of dog-walking yuppies.

New Museum of Contemporary Art

MUSEUM

(Map p62; ☎212-219-1222; www.newmuseum. org; 235 Bowery, at Prince St; adult/child $12/ free; ☺11am-6pm Wed, Fri, Sat & Sun, to 9pm Thu) Housed in an architecturally ambitious building on a formerly gritty Bowery strip, this is the city's sole museum dedicated to contemporary art. There's the added treat of a city viewing platform, which provides a unique perspective on the constantly changing neighborhood landscape.

Russian & Turkish Baths

SPA

(Map p62; ☎212-505-0665; www.russianturkish baths.com; 268 E 10th St; admission $30; ☺noon-10pm Mon, Tue, Thu & Fri, from 9am Sat, 8am-1pm Sun) The historic bathhouse is a great place to work out your stress in one of the four

hot rooms; traditional massages are also offered. It's authentic and somewhat grungy, and you're as likely to share a sauna with a downtown couple on a date, a well-known actor looking for a time-out or an actual Russian.

Astor Place & Around

NEIGHBORHOOD

(Map p62) At the west end of St Mark's Pl, Astor Place was once an elite neighborhood and some of its impressive original Greek Revival residences remain. These days a large Starbucks anchors one corner and a K-Mart another, while a tall glass condominium dominates the skyline across the street. The landmark rotating sculpture – 'the Cube' – remains, as do the young skateboarders who congregate here.

Cooper Union

HISTORIC BUILDING

(Map p62; www.cooper.edu; 51 Astor Pl) The large brownstone Cooper Union is a public college founded by glue millionaire Peter Cooper in 1859. Abraham Lincoln gave his 'Right

East & West Villages

Makes Might' speech condemning slavery before his election to the White House in the college's Great Hall.

WEST (GREENWICH) VILLAGE

Once a symbol for all things artistic, outlandish and Bohemian, this storied and popular neighborhood – the birthplace of the gay-rights movement as well as former home of Beat poets and important artists – feels worlds away from busy Broadway, and in fact almost European. Known by most visitors as 'Greenwich Village,' although that term is not used by locals, it has narrow streets lined with well-groomed and high-priced real estate, as well as cafes and restaurants, making it an ideal place to wander.

Washington Square Park & Around   PARK
(Map p62) This park began as a 'potter's field' – a burial ground for the penniless – and its status as a cemetery protected it from development. It is now a completely renovated and incredibly well-used park, especially on the weekend. Children use the playground, NYU students catch some rays and friends meet 'under the arch,' the renovated landmark on the park's northern edge, designed in 1889 by society architect Stanford White. Dominating a huge swath of property in the middle of the Village, New York University, one of the largest in the country, defines the area around the park and beyond architecturally and demographically. The undersized basketball court, the Cage (cnr Sixth Ave & W 3rd St), considered one of the more competitive playgrounds in the city, draws onlookers and top ballers – the more people-watching, the more showboating.

Christopher Street Pier (Pier 45)   PLAZA
(Map p58; Christopher St, at the Hudson River; ⊙closes 1am) Developers of the Hudson River Park Project paid special attention to this prime waterfront spot, adding a lawn and flower bed, wooden deck, tented shade shelters, benches and a grand stone fountain at its entrance.

Sheridan Square & Around   NEIGHBORHOOD
The western edge of the Village is home to Sheridan Square, a small, triangular park where life-size white statues by George Segal honor the gay community and gay pride movement that began in the nearby renovated Stonewall Inn sitting just across the street from the square. A block further east, an appropriately bent street is officially named Gay St. Although gay social scenes have in many ways moved further uptown to Chelsea, Christopher Street is still the center of gay life in the Village.

MEATPACKING DISTRICT

Nestled between the far West Village and the southern border of Chelsea is the gentrified and now inappropriately named Meatpacking District. The neighborhood was once home to 250 slaughterhouses – today only eight butchers remain – and was best known for its groups of tranny hookers, racy S&M sex clubs and, of course, its sides of beef. These days the hugely popular High Line park has only intensified an every increasing proliferation of trendy wine bars, eateries, nightclubs, high-end designer clothing stores, chic hotels and high-rent condos.

TOP CHOICE High Line   PARK
(Map p58; www.thehighline.org; ⊙7am-10pm) With the completion of the High Line, a 30ft-high abandoned stretch of elevated railroad track transformed into a long ribbon of parkland (from Gansevoort St to W 34th St; entrances are at Gansevoort, 14th, 16th, 18th, 20th and 30th Sts; elevator access at all but 18th St), there's finally some greenery amid the asphalt jungle. Only three stories above the streetscape, this thoughtfully and carefully designed mix of contemporary, industrial and natural elements is nevertheless a refuge and escape from the ordinary. A glass-front **amphitheater** with bleacher-like seating sits just above 10th Ave – bring some food and join local workers on their lunch break. Rising on concrete stilts over the High Line, the Standard is one of the celebrated destinations of the moment, with two choice drinking spots and a grill (plus hotel rooms where high-paying guests sometimes expose themselves in front of their floor-to-ceiling windows in a towel – or less). The second phase, a half-mile stretch from 20th to 30th Sts, the northern end not far from Penn Station, opened in the summer of 2011. The **Whitney Museum of American Art** (long located on the Upper East Side), has broken ground on construction of its new meatpacking district home on Gansevoort St scheduled for a 2015 opening.

CHELSEA

This 'hood is popular for two main attractions: one, the parade of gorgeous gay men (known affectionately as 'Chelsea boys') who roam Eighth Ave, darting from gyms to trendy happy hours; and two, it's one of the

START **5**
CHRISTOPHER ST
FINISH FIFTH AVE &
WAVERLY PL
DISTANCE ½ MILE
DURATION 30 MINUTES

West Village

Greenwich Village

New York University

Washington Sq Park

Waking Tour

Manhattan's most unruly maze of streets can be found in Greenwich Village, historically a hotbed for upstarts, radicals, Bohemians, poets, folk singers, feminists and freedom-seeking gays and lesbians. To begin, disembark the subway at Christopher St and stop at tiny **1 Christopher Park**, where two white, life-size statues of same-sex couples (Gay Liberation, 1992) stand guard. On its north side is the legendary **2 Stonewall Inn**, where a clutch of fed-up drag queens rioted for their civil rights in 1969, signaling the start of the gay revolution. Cross Seventh Ave South and continue west along Christopher St, still known as the pulse of gay life here. Turn left onto quaint Bedford St; stop and peer into **3 Chumley's**, the site of a prohibition-dodging socialist-run speakeasy. Continue along Bedford St for several blocks, make a left on Downing St and cross Sixth Ave. Continue east on the crooked Minetta St, home to the unremarkable Panchito's Mexican Restaurant which recently painted over the faded sign for the **4 Fat Black**

Pussycat – called The Commons in 1962, when a young Bob Dylan wrote and first performed 'Blowin' in the Wind' here. Turn right on Minetta Lane and right on MacDougal St to find the historic **5 Minetta Tavern**, which opened as a speakeasy in 1922, its walls now lined with photos of celebs who have visited. Also on this block is the former site of the **6 Folklore Center**, where Izzy Young established a hangout for folk artists including Dylan, who found his first audience at the music venue **7 Cafe Wha?**. Double back along MacDougal to the current Research Fellows & Scholars Office of the NYU School of Law, the former site of the **8 Liberal Club**, a meeting place for free thinkers, including Jack London and Upton Sinclair, founded in 1913. Beyond here is the southwest entrance to **9 Washington Square Park**, which has a long history as a magnet for radicals. Wrap up the tour by leaving the park at the iconic arch and head up Fifth Ave.

hubs of the city's art-gallery scene – it's currently home to nearly 200 modern-art exhibition spaces, most of which are clustered west of Tenth Ave. Find specific galleries at www.westchelseaarts.com.

Rubin Museum of Art
MUSEUM

(Map p68; ☏212-620-5000; www.rmanyc.org; 150 W 17th St at Seventh Ave; adult/child $10/free; ◷11am-5pm Mon & Thu, to 7pm Wed, to 10pm Fri, to 6pm Sat & Sun) Dedicated to art of the Himalayas and surrounding regions, this museum's impressive collections include embroidered textiles from China, metal sculptures from Tibet, intricate Bhutanese paintings, as well as ritual objects and dance masks from various Tibetan regions, spanning from the 2nd to the 19th centuries.

Chelsea Piers
HEALTH & FITNESS

(Map p68; ☏212-336-6666; www.chelseapiers. com; W 23rd St, at Hudson River) A waterfront sports center that caters to the athlete in everyone. It's got a four-level driving range, indoor ice rink, jazzy bowling alley, Hoop City for basketball, a sailing school for kids, batting cages, a huge gym, indoor rock-climbing walls – the works.

FLATIRON DISTRICT
At the intersection of Broadway, Fifth Ave and 23rd St, the famous (and absolutely gorgeous) 1902 Flatiron Building has a distinctive triangular shape to match its site. It was New York's first iron-frame high-rise, and the world's tallest building until 1909. Its surrounding district is a fashionable area of boutiques, loft apartments and a growing high-tech corridor, the city's answer to Silicon Valley between here and neighboring Chelsea. Peaceful Madison Square Park bordered by 23rd and 26th Sts, and Fifth and Madison Aves, has an active dog run, rotating outdoor sculptures, shaded park benches and a popular burger joint. Several blocks to the east is the Museum of Sex (Map p68; ☏212-689-6337; www.museumof sex.com; 233 Fifth Ave, at W 27th St; admission $18; ◷10am-8pm Sun-Thu, to 9m Fri & Sat), a somewhat intellectualized homage to intercourse. Only 18 and over admitted.

UNION SQUARE
A true town square, albeit one with a grassy interior, Union Square is a hive of activity with all manner of New Yorkers rubbing elbows, sharing hacky sacks and eyeing each other. A major renovation has brought a showpiece playground and public toilets to the northern end while the steps of the southern end are the place for antiwar and other liberal-leaning demonstrators.

Greenmarket Farmers Market
FOOD MARKET

(Map p68; ☏212-788-7476; www.grownyc.org; 17th St, btwn Broadway & Park Ave S; ◷8am-6pm Mon, Wed, Fri & Sat) On most days, Union Square's north end hosts the most popular of the nearly 50 greenmarkets throughout the five boroughs, where even celebrity chefs come for just-picked rarities including fiddlehead ferns, heirloom tomatoes and fresh curry leaves.

GRAMERCY PARK
This area, loosely comprising the 20s east of Madison Ave, is named after one of New York's loveliest parks; it's for residents only, though, and you need a key to get in! If you're strolling by, peer through the gates and get a good look at what you're missing.

Theodore Roosevelt's Birthplace
HISTORIC SITE

(Map p68; ☏212-668-2251; www.nps.gov/thrb; 28 E 20th St, btwn Park Ave & Broadway; admission $3; ◷9am-5pm Tue-Sat) A National Historic Site; however, this building is simply a re-creation – the actual house where the 26th president was born was demolished in his lifetime.

MIDTOWN
The classic NYC fantasy – shiny skyscrapers, teeming mobs of worker bees, Fifth Ave store windows, taxi traffic – and some of the city's most popular attractions can be found here. Long ago when print ruled and newspaper and magazines were the cultural currency of the day, Midtown was actually also the literary district – the prime movers and shakers used to meet at the Algonquin Hotel. Major media companies such as the *New York Times* are still based here.

Museum of Modern Art
MUSEUM

(MoMA; Map p68; ☏212-708-9400; www.moma.org; 11 W 53rd St, btwn Fifth & Sixth Aves; adult/child $20/free, free 4-8pm Fri; ◷10:30am-5:30pm, to 8pm Fri, closed Tue) A veritable art universe of more than 100,000 pieces, the 75-year old Museum of Modern Art houses one of the more significant collections of works in the world. A controversial renovation project designed by the architect Yoshio Taniguchi doubled the museum's capacity to 630,000 sq ft on six floors. Most of the big hitters – Matisse,

0   500 m
0   0.25 miles

See Central Park & Uptown Map (p76)

57th St
E 57th St
80
E 55th St
Museum of
Modern Art
Lexington
Ave-53rd St
Fifth Ave-
53rd St
10
E 53rd St
Roosevelt
Island
51st St
31
E 51st St
FDR Dr
Top of the Rock
70   12   21
20
St Patrick's
Cathedral
E 49th St
2   54
47th-50th Sts-
Rockefeller Center
E 47th St
THE DIAMOND DISTRICT
51
46
E 45th St
17
8   42nd St-
Bryant Park
5th Ave
Grand Central
Station
3
E 42nd St
Queens-Midtown Tunnel
Bryant
Park
New York
Public Library
42nd St-
Grand Central
E 40th St
E 38th St
11
E 36th St
St Vartan
Park
HERALD
SQUARE
34th St-
Herald Sq   5
44
53
E 34th St
E 33rd St
New York
University
Medical
Center
33rd St
45
23
E 30th St
East River
28th St   9   29
LITTLE
INDIA
28th St
39
E 28th St
Bellevue
Hospital
Center
E 26th St
FLATIRON
DISTRICT
Madison
Square
Park
30
42   50
6   23rd St   23rd St
E 23rd St
24th
St Park
FDR Dr
23rd St
Peter Cooper Rd
E 21st St
15
Gramercy
Park
E 19th St
78
E 17th St
STUYVESANT
TOWN
John
Murphy
Park
26
UNION
SQUARE
37   7
Union
Square
65
Stuyvesant
Square
16
6th Ave-
14th St
14th St-Union Sq
E 14th St
3rd Ave
1st Ave
See East &
West Villages Map (p62)

Times Square, Midtown Manhattan & Chelsea

Picasso, Cézanne, Rothko, Pollock and many others – are housed in the central five-story atrium. Be prepared for long entrance lines and crowds.

Times Square & Theater District NEIGHBORHOOD

(Map p68) There are few images more universally iconic than the glittering orb dropping from Times Square on New Year's Eve – the first one descended 100 years ago. Smack in the middle of Midtown Manhattan, this area around the intersection of Broadway and Seventh Ave, with its gaudy billboards and glittery marquees, has become so intertwined with New York City in the minds of non-New Yorkers that regardless of how Disneyfied it has become, it's still considered quintessential New York. Once again 'the Crossroads of the World' and unrecognizable from its '70s-era seediness of strip clubs, hookers and pickpockets, the square draws 35 million visitors annually. Massive chains like American Eagle and themed stores like Hershey's pull in folks and multiplex theaters draw crowds with large screens and stadium seating. In an effort to make the area more pedestrian-friendly and diminish the perpetual gridlock, Broadway from 47th to 42nd St was turned into a vehicle-free zone.

The Times Square area is at least equally famous as New York's official Theater District, with dozens of Broadway and off-Broadway theaters located in an area that stretches from 41st to 54th Sts, between Sixth and Ninth Aves. The Times Square branch of New York City & Company (☎212-763-1560; www.timessquarenyc.org; 1560 Broadway, btwn 46th & 47th Sts; ◷9am-7pm Mon-Fri, 8am-8pm Sun) sits smack in the middle of this famous crossroads, inside the beautifully restored landmark Embassy Theater. Broadway, the road, once ran all the way to the state capitol in Albany.

Rockefeller Center HISTORIC BUILDING, TOUR

(Map p68) It was built during the height of the Great Depression in the 1930s, and construction of the 22-acre Rockefeller Center, including the landmark art-deco skyscraper gave jobs to 70,000 workers over nine years and was the first project to combine retail, entertainment and office space in what is often referred to as a 'city within a city.' The 360-degree views from the tri-level observation deck of the Top of the Rock (☎212-698-

2000; www.topoftherocknyc.com; main entrance 50th St, btwn Fifth & Sixth Aves; adult/child $22/15; ◷8am-midnight) are absolutely stunning and should not be missed; on a clear day you can see quite a distance across the river into New Jersey. The 67th and 69th floors have outdoor terraces. In winter the ground floor outdoor space is abuzz with ice-skaters and Christmas-tree gawkers. Within the complex is the 1932, 6000-seat Radio City Music Hall (☎212-247-4777; www.radiocity.com; 1260 Sixth Ave; tours adult/child $22.50/16; ◷tours 11am-3pm Mon-Sun). To get an inside look at this former movie palace and protected landmark that's been gorgeously restored in all its art-deco grandeur join one of the frequent guided tours that leave the lobby every half-hour. Fans of the NBC TV show 30 Rock will recognize the 70-story GE Building as the network headquarters. Tours of the NBC studios, (☎212-664-3700; www.nbcstudiotour.com; 30 Rockefeller Plaza; adult/child $20/17; ◷8:30am-5:30pm Mon-Sat, to 6:30pm Fri & Sat, 9:15am-4:30pm Sun) leave from the lobby of the GE Building every 15 minutes; note that children under six are not admitted. The Today Show broadcasts live 7am to 11am daily from a glass-enclosed street-level studio near the fountain.

FREE New York Public Library LIBRARY, MUSEUM

(Map p68; ☎212-340-0833; www.nypl.org; Fifth Ave, at 42nd St; ◷10am-6pm Tue-Sat) Flanked by two huge marble lions nicknamed 'Patience' and 'Fortitude' by former mayor Fiorello La-Guardia, the stairway leading up to the New York Public Library is a grand entrance. The massive, superb beaux-arts building stands as testament to the value of learning and culture in the city, as well as to the wealth of the philanthropists who made its founding possible. A magnificent 3rd-floor reading room has a painted ceiling and bountiful natural light – rows of long wooden tables are occupied by students, writers and the general public working away at laptops. This, the main branch of the entire city library system, has galleries of manuscripts on display, as well as fascinating temporary exhibits. Immediately behind the library is beautifully maintained Bryant Park, a grassy expanse furnished with tables and chairs, and even a lending library, chessboards and Ping Pong tables in warm weather (free wi-fi too), as well as an ice-skating rink in winter.

Empire State Building
HISTORIC BUILDING

(Map p68; ☑212-736-3100; www.esbnyc.org; 350 Fifth Ave, at E 34th St; adult/child $20/15; ⊙8am-2am) Catapulted to Hollywood stardom both as the planned meeting spot for Cary Grant and Deborah Kerr in *An Affair to Remember*, and the vertical perch that helped to topple King Kong, the classic Empire State Building is one of New York's most famous members of the skyline. It's a limestone classic built in just 410 days, or seven million man-hours, during the depths of the Depression at a cost of $41 million. On the site of the original Waldorf-Astoria Hotel, the 102-story, 1472ft (to the top of the antenna) Empire State Building opened in 1931 after 10 million bricks were laid, 6400 windows installed and 328,000 sq ft of marble laid. Today you can ride the elevator to observatories on the 86th and 102nd floors (for the latter it's an additional $17), but be prepared for crowds; try to come very early or very late (and purchase your tickets ahead of time, online or pony up for more expensive 'express passes') for an optimal experience.

Grand Central Station
HISTORIC BUILDING

(Map p68; www.grandcentralterminal.com; 42nd St, at Fifth Ave) Built in 1913 as a prestigious terminal by New York Central and Hudson River Railroad, Grand Central Station is no longer a romantic place to begin a cross-country journey, as it's now the terminus for Metro North commuter trains to the northern suburbs and Connecticut. But even if you're not boarding a train to the 'burbs, it's worth exploring the grand, vaulted main concourse and gazing up at the restored ceiling, decorated with a star map that is actually a 'God's-eye' image of the night sky. There's a high-end food market and the lower level houses a truly excellent array of eateries, while the balcony has a cozy '20s-era salon kind of bar called the Campbell Apartment.

Fifth Avenue & Around
NEIGHBORHOOD

Immortalized in both film and song, Fifth Ave first developed its high-class reputation in the early 20th century, when it was considered desirable for its 'country' air and open spaces. The series of mansions called Millionaire's Row extended right up to 130th St, though most of the heirs to the millionaire mansions on Fifth Ave above 59th St sold them for demolition or converted them to the cultural institutions that now make up Museum Mile.

The avenue's Midtown stretch still boasts upmarket shops and hotels, including Trump Tower (725 Fifth Ave, at 56th St) and the Plaza (cnr Fifth Ave and Central Park South). While a number of the more exclusive boutiques have migrated to Madison Ave – leaving outposts of Gap and H&M in their wake – several superstars still reign over Fifth Ave above 50th St, including the famous Tiffany & Co.

Pierpont Morgan Library
MUSEUM

(Map p68; ☑212-685-0008; www.morganlibrary.org; 29 E 36th St at Madison Ave; adult/child $15/10; ⊙10:30am-5pm Tue-Thu, to 9pm Fri, 10am-6pm Sat & Sun) The beautifully renovated library is part of the 45-room mansion once owned by steel magnate JP Morgan. His collection features a phenomenal array of manuscripts, tapestries and books, a study filled with Italian Renaissance artwork, a marble rotunda and the three-tiered East Room main library.

United Nations Headquarters
TOUR

(Map p68; ☑212-963-8687; www.un.org/tours; First Ave, btwn 42nd & 48th Sts; tours adult/child $16/9; ⊙tours 9:45am-4:45pm) The UN is technically on a section of international territory overlooking the East River. Take a guided 45-minute tour of the facility and you'll get to see the General Assembly, where the annual fall convocation of member nations takes place, the Security Council Chamber (depending on schedules) and also the Economic & Social Council Chamber. There is a park to the south of the complex which is home to several sculptures with a peace theme. English-language tours of the UN complex depart frequently; limited tours in several other languages are also available.

Paley Center for Media
MUSEUM

(Map p68; ☑212-621-6800; www.paleycenter.org; 25 W 52nd St; adult/child $10/5, theater $6; ⊙noon-6pm Fri-Wed, to 8pm Thu) TV fanatics who spent their childhood glued to the tube and proudly claim instant recall of all of Fonzi's *Happy Days* exploits can hold their heads high. This is the 'museum' for them. Search through a catalogue of more than 100,000 US TV and radio programs and advertisements and a click of the mouse will play your selection on one of the library's computer screens. A comfy theater shows some great specials on broadcasting history, and there are frequent events and screenings.

Intrepid Sea, Air & Space Museum
MUSEUM

(Map p68; ☑212-245-0072; www.intrepidmuseum.org; Pier 86, Twelfth Ave at 46th St; adult/child $24/12; ☺10am-5pm, to 6pm Sat & Sun) The USS Intrepid, a hulking aircraft carrier that survived both a WWII bomb and kamikaze attacks has been transformed into a military museum with high-tech exhibits and fighter planes and helicopters for view on the outdoor flight deck. The pier area contains the guided-missile submarine *Growler,* a decommissioned Concorde and in 2012 the *Enterprise* space shuttle.

International Center of Photography
MUSEUM

(Map p68; ☑212-857-0000; www.icp.org; 1133 Sixth Ave, at 43rd St; adult/child $12/free; ☺10am-6pm Tue-Sun, to 8pm Fri) The city's most important showcase for major photographers, especially photojournalists. Its past exhibitions have included work by Henri Cartier-Bresson, Matthew Brady and Robert Capa.

Herald Square & Around
NEIGHBORHOOD

This crowded convergence of Broadway, Sixth Ave and 34th St is best known as the home of **Macy's** department store, where you can still ride some of the remaining original wooden elevators to floors ranging from home furnishings to lingerie. But the busy square gets its name from a long-defunct newspaper, the *Herald,* and the small, leafy park here bustles during business hours. (The indoor mall south of Macy's on Sixth Ave houses the standard array of suburban chain stores.) In order to cut down on some of the area gridlock, Broadway, from 33rd to 35th St has been closed to traffic and turned into a pedestrian plaza.

West of Herald Sq, the **Garment District** has most of New York's fashion design offices, and while not much clothing is actually made here anymore, for anyone into pawing through dreamy selections of fabrics, buttons, sequins, lace and zippers it is the place to shop.

From 31st St to 36th St, between Broadway and Fifth Ave, **Koreatown** is an interesting and lively neighborhood with an expanding number of good restaurants and authentic karaoke spots.

Hell's Kitchen (Clinton)
NEIGHBORHOOD

For years, the far west side of Midtown was a working-class district of tenements and food warehouses known as Hell's Kitchen – supposedly its name was muttered by a cop in reaction to a riot in the neighborhood in 1881. A 1990s economic boom seriously altered the character and developers reverted to using the cleaned-up name Clinton, a moniker originating from the 1950s; locals are split on usage. New restaurants exploded along Ninth and Tenth Aves between about 37th and 55th Sts, and now it's a great place to grab a pre- or post-theater meal. Antique-lovers should visit the **Hell's Kitchen Flea Market** (Map p68; ☑212-243-5343; www.hellskitchenfleamarket.com; W 39th St, btwn Ninth & Tenth Aves; ☺7am-5pm Sat & Sun), boasting 170 vendors of vintage clothing, antique jewelry, period furniture and many more treasures.

Museum of Arts and Design
MUSEUM

(Map p76; ☑212-299-7777; www.madmuseum.org; 2 Columbus Circle; adult/child $15/free; ☺11am-6pm Tue-Sun, to 9pm Thu) On the southern side of the circle, exhibiting a diverse international collection of modern, folk, craft and fine art pieces. The plush and trippy design of the 9th floor **restaurant** complements fantastic views of Central Park.

Chrysler Building
HISTORIC BUILDING

(Map p68; 405 Lexington Ave) Just east of Grand Central Station, the Chrysler Building, an art-deco masterpiece that's adorned with motorcar motifs, was completed in 1930 to be the headquarters for Walter P Chrysler and his automobile empire. Luckily, because visitors can't go up in the building (it's full of offices), it's most magnificent when viewed from a distance.

ⓘ SOLD!

Even if your idea of a significant art purchase is a Van Gogh postcard, the adrenalin-pumping thrill of an art auction combines the best of museum-going and high-end shopping. Both **Christie's** (☑212-636-2000; www.christies.com; 20 Rockefeller Plaza) and **Sotheby's** (☑212-606-7000; www.sothebys.com; 1334 York Ave, at 72nd St), two of the city's and world's most prominent auction houses are open to the public. Whether it's a collection of Warhol canvases or old European masterworks, the prices remain generally stratospheric – keep your hands down or else your casual twitch will be taken for a bid and you could be on the hook for tens of millions of dollars.

UPPER WEST SIDE

Shorthand for liberal, progressive and intellectual New York – think Woody Allen movies (although he lives on the Upper East Side) and Seinfeld – this neighborhood comprising the west side of Manhattan from Central Park to the Hudson River, and from Columbus Circle to 110th St, is no longer as colorful as it once was. Upper Broadway has been taken over by banks, pharmacies and national retail chain stores and many of the mom-and-pop shops and bookstores are long gone. You'll still find massive, ornate apartments and a diverse mix of stable, upwardly mobile folks (with many actors and classical musicians sprinkled throughout), and some lovely green spaces – Riverside Park stretches for 4 miles between W 72nd St and W 158th St along the Hudson River, and is a great place for strolling, running, cycling or simply gazing at the sun as it sets over the Hudson River.

Central Park PARK

(Map p76; ☑212-310-6600; www.centralparknyc.org; btwn 57th & 110th Sts & Fifth Ave & Central Park; ☻) It's hard to imagine what the city would be like without this refuge from the claustrophobia, from the teeming sidewalks and clogged roadways. This enormous wonderland of a park, sitting right in the middle of Manhattan, provides both metaphorical and spiritual oxygen to its residents. The park's 843 acres were set aside in 1856 on the marshy northern fringe of the city. The landscaping (the first in a US public park), by Frederick Law Olmsted and Calvert Vaux, was innovative in its naturalistic style, with forested groves, meandering paths and informal ponds. Highlights include Sheep Meadow (mid-park from 66th to 69th Sts), where tens of thousands of people lounge and play on warm weather weekends; Strawberry Fields at 72nd St, dedicated to John Lennon, who lived at (and was murdered in front of) the Dakota apartment building across the street; the sparkling Jacqueline Kennedy Onassis Reservoir, encircled by joggers daily; Central Park Zoo (☑212-439-6500; www.wcs.org; 64th St, at Fifth Ave; adult/child $10/5; ☻10am-5pm Mon-Fri, to 5:30pm Sat & Sun); the formal, tree-lined promenade called the Mall, which culminates at the elegant Bethesda Fountain; and the Ramble, a rest stop for nearly 250 migratory species of birdlife – early morning is best for sightings. A favorite tourist activity is to rent a horse-drawn carriage (Map p76; 30min tour $35 plus generous tip) at 59th St (Central Park South) or hop in a pedicab (30min tours $30); the latter congregate at Central Park West and 72nd St. For more information while you're strolling, visit the Dairy Building visitor centre (Map p76; ☑212-794-6564; Central Park, at 65th St; ☻10am-5pm Tue-Sat) in the southern section of the park.

Lincoln Center ARTS CENTER

(Map p76; ☑212-875-5456; www.lincolncenter.org; cnr Columbus Ave & Broadway) Only a few unfinished elements remain to complete the billion-dollar-plus redevelopment of the world's largest performing arts center. The dramatically redesigned Alice Tully Hall anchors one end of the property and other stunning venues surround a massive fountain; public spaces, including the roof lawn of the North Plaza (an upscale restaurant is underneath), have been upgraded. The lavishly designed Metropolitan Opera House (MET), the largest opera house in the world, seats 3900 people. Fascinating one-hour tours (☑212-875-5350; adult/child $15/8) of the complex leave from the lobby of Avery Fisher Hall from 10:30am to 4:30pm daily; these vary from architectural to backstage tours. Free wi-fi is available on the property as well as at the _____ (Broadway, btwn 62nd & 63rd Sts), a modern public space featuring a lounge area, cafe, information desk and a ticket center offering day-of discounts to Lincoln Center performances.

TOP CHOICE **American Museum of Natural History** MUSEUM

(Map p76; ☑212-769-5100; www.amnh.org; Central Park West, at 79th St; suggested admission adult/child $16/9, extra for space shows, IMAX shows & special exhibits; ☻10am-5:45pm; ☻) Founded in 1869, this museum includes more than 30 million artifacts, interactive exhibits and loads of taxidermy. It's most famous for its three large dinosaur halls, an enormous (fake) blue whale that hangs from the ceiling above the Hall of Ocean Life and the elaborate Rose Center for Earth & Space. Just gazing at its facade – a massive glass box that contains a silver globe, home to space-show theaters and the planetarium – is mesmerizing, especially at night, when all of its otherworldly features are aglow.

New York Historical Society MUSEUM

(Map p76; ☑212-873-3400; www.nyhistory.org; 170 Central Park W, at 77th St; adult/child $10/6;

10am-6pm Tue-Sun) This museum, founded in 1804 and widely credited with being the city's oldest, received a full-scale makeover in 2011. The quirky and wide-ranging permanent collection, including original watercolors from John James Audubon's *Birds of America* will be housed in a spruced-up contemporary exhibition space; there's a new auditorium, library and restaurant as well.

MORNINGSIDE HEIGHTS

The Upper West Side's northern neighbor, comprises the area of Broadway and west up to about 125th St. Dominating the neighborhood is Columbia University, the highly rated Ivy League college, which features a spacious, grassy central quadrangle.

Cathedral of St John the Divine
CHURCH

(Map p76; 212-316-7540; 1047 Amsterdam Ave, at 112th St; 7am-6pm, to 7pm Sun) A decades-long restoration of this Episcopal cathedral, the largest place of worship in the USA, is a truly stunning accomplishment. High Mass, held at 11am Sunday, often with sermons by well-known intellectuals.

UPPER EAST SIDE

The Upper East Side (UES) is home to New York's greatest concentration of cultural centers, including the grand dame that is the Metropolitan Museum of Art (see below), and many refer to Fifth Ave above 57th St as Museum Mile. The real estate, at least along Fifth, Madison and Park Aves, is some of the most expensive in the world. Home to ladies who lunch as well as frat boys who drink, the neighborhood becomes decidedly less chichi the further east you go.

Metropolitan Museum of Art
MUSEUM

(Map p76; 212-535-7710; www.metmuseum.org; 1000 Fifth Ave, at 82nd St; suggested donation $25, children free; 9:30am-5:30pm Tue-Thu & Sun, to 9pm Fri & Sat) With more than five million visitors a year, the Met is New York's most popular single-site tourist attraction, with one of the richest coffers in the arts world. The Met is a self-contained cultural city-state, with two million individual objects in its collection and an annual budget of over $120 million; its 19th-century European paintings and sculpture galleries have been greatly expanded and refurbished.

Highlight rooms here include Egyptian Art, American Paintings and Sculpture, Arms and Armor, Modern Art, Greek and Roman Art, European Paintings and the gorgeous rooftop, which offers bar service and spectacular views throughout the summer. Note that the suggested donation (which is, truly, a *suggestion*) includes same-day admission to the Cloisters.

[TOP CHOICE] Frick Collection
MUSEUM

(Map p76; 212-288-0700; www.frick.org; 1 E 70th St; admission $18; 10am-6pm Tue-Sat, 11am-5pm Sun) This spectacular art collection sits in a mansion built by Henry Clay Frick in 1914; it's a shame that the 2nd floor of the residence isn't open for viewing. The 12 richly furnished rooms on the ground floor display paintings by Titian, Vermeer, El Greco, Goya and other masters. Perhaps the best asset here is that it's rarely crowded, providing a welcome break from the swarms of gawkers at larger museums, especially on weekends.

Solomon R Guggenheim Museum
MUSEUM

(Map p76; 212-423-3500; www.guggenheim. org; 1071 Fifth Ave; adult/child $18/free; 10am-5:45pm Sat-Wed, to 7:45pm Fri) The inspired work of Frank Lloyd Wright, and its sweeping spiral of a staircase is a superb sculpture, holding 20th-century paintings by Picasso, Pollock, Chagall and Kandinsky.

Neue Galerie
MUSEUM

(Map p76; 212-628-6200; www.neuegalerie.org; 1048 Fifth Ave, at 86th St; adult $15, children under 12 not admitted; 11am-6pm Thu-Mon) Housed in a stately and elegant Fifth Ave mansion, the Neue showcases German and Austrian artists, with impressive works by Gustav Klimt and Egon Schiele. Café Sabarsky, on the ground floor, is alone worth a visit for its fin de siécle European vibe, rich desserts (apple strudel $8) and cabaret performances on Thursday nights ($45).

Whitney Museum of American Art
MUSEUM

(Map p76; 212-570-3600; www.whitney.org; 945 Madison Ave, at 75th St; admission $18; 11am-6pm Wed, Thu, Sat & Sun, to 9pm Fri) One of the few museums that concentrates on American works of art, specializing in 20th-century and contemporary art, with works by Hopper, Pollock and Rothko, as well as special shows, such as the much-ballyhooed Biennial. The Whitney is moving in 2015 to Gansevoort St in the Meatpacking District.

Jewish Museum
MUSEUM

(Map p76; 212-423-3200; www.jewishmuseum. org; 1109 Fifth Ave at 92nd St; adult/child $12/free; 11am-5:45pm Sat-Tue, to 8pm Thu, to 4pm Fri)

Central Park & Uptown

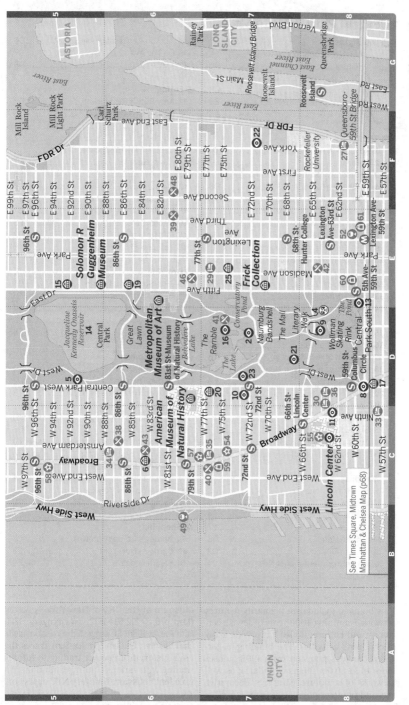

ASTORIA

LONG ISLAND CITY

UNION CITY

East River

Mill Rock Island

Mill Rock Light Park

Carl Schurz Park

East River

Rainey Park

Roosevelt Island Bridge

Vernon Blvd

East Channel East River

Queensbridge Park

Roosevelt Island

Main St

Roosevelt Island

Queensboro-59th St Bridge

West Rd

East Rd

FDR Dr

FDR Dr

East End Ave

E 99th St
E 97th St
E 96th St
E 94th St
E 92nd St
E 90th St
E 88th St
E 86th St
E 84th St
E 82nd St
E 80th St
E 79th St
E 77th St
E 75th St
E 72nd St
E 70th St
E 68th St
E 65th St
E 62nd St
E 59th St
E 57th St

York Ave

22

First Ave

Rockefeller University

27

96th St

Park Ave

Second Ave

48

Third Ave

39

Lexington Ave

Lexington Ave

77th St

Park Ave

Solomon R Guggenheim Museum

86th St

19

15

East Dr

Jacqueline Kennedy Onassis Reservoir 14

Central Park

Great Lawn

Metropolitan Museum of Art

81st St-Museum of Natural History

46
29
25

Frick Collection

Madison Ave

Fifth Ave

Belvedere Lake

The Ramble 16

Conservatory Pond

Naumburg Bandshell

The Mall

Literary Walk

9

60

59th St-5th Ave

4

Hunter College

68th St-Hunter College

Lexington Ave-63rd St

52

61

Lexington Ave

42

The Lake

41

2

21

23

Wollman Skating Rink

The Pond

Central Park South 13

59th St-Columbus Circle

West Dr

West Dr

West End Ave

W 96th St
W 94th St
W 92nd St
W 90th St
W 88th St
W 85th St

Central Park West 5

86th St

W 81st St

American Museum of Natural History

43

6

38

34

W 97th St

W 96th St

96th St 58

Amsterdam Ave

Broadway

West End Ave

Broadway

W 79th St

W 77th St

W 75th St

W 72nd St

W 70th St

66th St-Lincoln Center

W 66th St

W 62nd St

W 60th St

W 57th St

57
40
59
35
54

20
10

72nd St

72nd St

Lincoln Center

55

11

36

30

8
17

33

49

Riverside Dr

Ninth Ave

West Side Hwy

West Side Hwy

5

6

7

8

A B C D E F G

See Times Square, Midtown
Manhattan & Chelsea Map (p68)

Central Park & Uptown

This homage to Judaism primarily features artwork examining 4000 years of Jewish ceremony and culture; it also has a wide array of children's activities. The building, a gorgeous banker's mansion from 1908, houses more than 30,000 items of Judaica, as well as works of sculpture, paintings, decorative arts and photography.

Museum of the City of New York   MUSEUM
(Map p76; ☎212-534-1672; www.mcny.org; 1220 Fifth Ave, at 103rd St; suggested admission adult/child $10/free; ☺10am-5pm Tue-Sun) Traces the city's history from beaver trading to futures trading with various cultural exhibitions. An excellent bookstore for every NYC obsession.

El Museo del Barrio
MUSEUM

(☎212-831-7272; www.elmuseo.org; 1230 Fifth Ave, at 104th St; adult/child $9/free; ⊙11am-6pm Tue-Sun) The Latino cultural institution houses a collection of Latin American and Caribbean art with a special focus on the Puerto Rican and Dominican communities. There's also an attractive street-side cafe.

HARLEM
The heart of African American culture has been beating in Harlem since its emergence as a black enclave in the 1920s. This neighborhood north of Central Park has been the setting for extraordinary accomplishments in art, music, dance, education and letters from the likes of Frederick Douglass, Paul Robeson, Thurgood Marshall, James Baldwin, Alvin Ailey, Billie Holiday, Jessie Jackson and many other African American luminaries. After steady decline from the 1960s to early '90s, Harlem is today experiencing something of a second renaissance in the form of million-dollar brownstones and condos for sale next door to neglected tenement buildings and the presence of big box national chain stores all along 125th St.

For a traditional view of Harlem, visit on Sunday morning, when well-dressed locals flock to neighborhood churches. Just be respectful of the fact that these people are attending a religious service (rather than being on display for tourists). Unless you're invited by a member of a small congregation, stick to the bigger churches.

Abyssinian Baptist Church
RELIGIOUS

(Map p76; ☎212-862-7474; www.abyssinian.org; 132 W 138th St) Has a superb choir and a charismatic pastor, Calvin O Butts, who welcomes tourists and prays for them. Sunday services start at 9am and 11am – the later one is *very* well attended.

Apollo Theater
ARTS CENTER

(Map p76; ☎212-531-5300; www.apollotheater.com; 253 W 125th St) Not just a mythical legend but a living theater. Head here for concerts (Prince performed here in 2009) and its famous (if very touristy) amateur night ($19 to $29), 'where stars are born and legends are made.'

Studio Museum in Harlem
MUSEUM

(Map p76; ☎212-864-4500; www.studiomuseum.org; 144 W 125th St; suggested donation $7; ⊙noon-9pm Thu & Fri, to 6pm Sat & Sun) One of the pre-

mier showcases for African American artists; look for excellent rotating exhibits from painters, sculptors, illustrators and other installation artists.

WASHINGTON HEIGHTS
Near the northern tip of Manhattan (above 155th St), Washington Heights takes its name from the first US president, who set up a Continental Army fort here during the Revolutionary War. An isolated spot until the end of the 19th century, it attracted lots of new blood as New Yorkers sniffed out affordable rents. Still, this neighborhood manages to retain its Latino – mainly Dominican – flavor, and is an interesting mix of blocks that alternate between former downtowners and longtime residents who operate within a tight, warm community.

TOP CHOICE Cloisters
MUSEUM

(Map p56; ☎212-923-3700; www.metmuseum.org/cloisters; Fort Tryon Park, at 190th St; suggested admission adult/child $20/free; ⊙9:30am-4:45pm Tue-Sun Nov-Feb, to 5:15pm Mar-Oct) Most visitors to Washington Heights come here, a branch of the Metropolitan Museum of Art. Constructed in the 1930s using stones and fragments from several French and Spanish medieval monasteries, the romantic, castle-like creation houses medieval frescoes, tapestries, courtyards, gardens and paintings, and has commanding views of the Hudson. The walk from the subway stop to the museum through Fort Tryon Park offers stupendous views of the Hudson River; rock climbers head here for practice.

WORTH A TRIP

THE LITTLE RED LIGHTHOUSE

Manhattan's last remaining lighthouse acquired its affectionate nickname from the 1942 classic children's book, *The Little Red Lighthouse and the Great Grey Bridge*. Decommissioned after the construction of the GW Bridge, which looms massively overhead, the lighthouse was saved from demolition by an outpouring of public support. To visit, cross the pedestrian bridge over the Henry Hudson Parkway at the end of 181st St and follow the winding path down to the park at the edge of the water.

BROOKLYN

Brooklyn is a world in and of itself; residents sometimes don't go into Manhattan for days or even weeks at a time. With 2.5 million people and growing, from well-to-do new parents seeking stately brownstones in Carroll Gardens to young band members wanting cheap rents near gigs in Williamsburg, this outer borough has long succeeded Manhattan in the cool and livability factors in many people's minds. From sandy beaches and breezy boardwalks at one end to foodie destinations at the other, and with a massive range of ethnic enclaves, world-class entertainment, stately architecture and endless shopping strips in between, Brooklyn is a rival to Manhattan's attractions. The **Brooklyn Tourism & Visitors Center** (☑718-802-3846; www.brooklyntourism. org; 209 Borough Hall, Joralemon St; ◎10am-6pm Mon-Fri), in Brooklyn Heights, is an informative place to begin.

TOP CHOICE Coney Island &
Brighton Beach   NEIGHBORHOOD

About 50 minutes by subway from Midtown, this popular pair of beach neighborhoods makes for a great day trip. The wide sandy beach of Coney Island has retained its nostalgic, kitschy and slightly sleazy charms, wood-plank boardwalk and famous 1927 Cyclone roller coaster despite the recent makeover of the amusement park area (a handful of adrenalin-pumping thrill rides are a recent addition) and plans for developers to transform the area into a sleek residential city complete with high-rise hotels. The **New York Aquarium** (☑718-741-1818; www.nyaquarium.com; Surf Ave, btwn 5th & W 8th Sts; adult/child $15/11; ◎10am-6pm Mon-Fri, to 7pm Sat & Sun; ☜) is a big hit with kids, as is taking in an early evening baseball game at **KeySpan Park** (☑718-449-8497; 1904 Surf Ave), the waterfront stadium for the minor league Brooklyn Cyclones.

A five-minute stroll north along the boardwalk past handball courts where some of the best in the world compete brings you to **Brighton Beach** ('Little Odessa'), where old-timers play chess and locals enjoy pierogies (boiled dumplings filled with meat or vegetables) and vodka shots in the sun at several boardwalk eateries. Then head into the heart of the 'hood, busy Brighton Beach Ave, to hit the many Russian shops, bakeries and restaurants.

Park Slope & Prospect Heights   NEIGHBORHOOD

The Park Slope neighborhood is known for its classic brownstones, tons of great eateries and boutiques (especially along Fifth Ave, which is more cutting edge than the other major strip, Seventh Ave), lesbian residents and stroller-pushing couples who resemble those on the Upper West Side (but have a backyard attached to their apartment). The 585-acre Prospect Park, created in 1866, is considered the greatest achievement of landscape designers Olmsted and Vaux, who also designed Central Park. Wander along its forested pathways, go for a run along its 3-plus-mile loop or jump on a boat that tours its 60-acre lake from May to October; a new skating rink is open in winter. Next door is the excellent 52-acre **Brooklyn Botanic Garden** (☑718-623-7200; www.bbg.org; 1000 Washington Ave; adult/child $8/free, free Tue; ◎8am-6pm Tue-Fri, from 10am Sat & Sun), which features impressive cherry-tree blossoms in spring. Beside the garden is the **Brooklyn Museum** (☑718-638-5000; www.brooklynmuseum.org; 200 Eastern Pkwy; suggested admission $10; ◎11am-6pm Wed, Sat & Sun, to 10pm Thu & Fri) with comprehensive collections of African, Islamic and Asian art, plus the Elizabeth A Sackler Center for Feminist Art.

Downtown Brooklyn   NEIGHBORHOOD

When Robert Fulton's steam ferries started regular services across the East River in the early 19th century, well-to-do Manhattanites began building stellar houses – Victorian Gothic, Romanesque, neo-Greco, Italianate and others – in Brooklyn Heights. Strolling along the tree-lined streets to gaze at them now is a lovely afternoon activity; don't miss the 1881 Queen Anne–style landmark building that houses the **Brooklyn Historical Society** (☑718-222-4111; www.brooklynhistory. org; 128 Pierrepont St; admission $6; ◎noon-5pm Wed-Fri & Sun, 10am-5pm Sat), which features a library (with some 33,000 grainy digitized photos from decades past), auditorium and museum devoted to the borough. The society also leads several walking tours.

Follow **Montague St**, the Heights' main commercial avenue, down to the waterfront until you hit the **Brooklyn Heights Promenade**, which juts out over the Brooklyn–Queens Expwy to offer stunning views of Lower Manhattan. Underneath the Expwy is the **Brooklyn Bridge Park**, an 85-acre development of landscaped green space and pathways, built on piers stretching from the Brooklyn Bridge south to Atlantic Ave.

The 1848 beaux-arts **Brooklyn Borough Hall** (209 Joralemon St) straddles both Brooklyn Heights and downtown Brooklyn, characterized by its various courts. The small but fascinating **New York Transit Museum** (☎718-694-1600; www.mta.info/mta/museum; Boerum Pl, at Schermerhorn St; adult/child $5/3; ☺10am-4pm Tue-Fri, noon-5pm Sat & Sun) has an amazing collection of original subway cars and transit memorabilia dating back more than a century. Construction of the long-delayed and controversial **Barclay's Center**, future home to the NBA's New Jersey Nets, is finally progressing apace across the street from the Atlantic Center shopping mall in downtown Brooklyn. The surrounding neighborhoods expect change, as well as a worsening of the already terrible traffic, after the team moves here in 2012.

Dumbo
NEIGHBORHOOD

Dumbo's nickname is an acronym for its location: 'Down Under the Manhattan–Brooklyn Bridge Overpass,' and while this north Brooklyn slice of waterfront used to be strictly for industry, it's now the domain of high-end condos, furniture shops and art galleries. Several highly regarded performing arts spaces are located in the cobblestone streets and the **Empire-Fulton Ferry State Park** hugs the waterfront and offers picture postcard Manhattan views.

Boerum Hill, Cobble Hill, Carroll Gardens & Red Hook
NEIGHBORHOOD

These neighborhoods, home to a mix of families, mostly Italian, who have lived here for generations, and former Manhattanites looking for a real life after the city, are full of tree-lined streets with rows of attractively restored brownstones. **Smith St** and **Court St** are the two main arteries connecting to the most southerly area of the three, Carroll Gardens. The former is known as 'restaurant row,' while the latter has more of the old-school groceries, bakeries and red-sauce restaurants. A block west of here is **Cobble Hill Park**, a manicured patch of green with benches and picnic tables where locals hang. Even further west (and south) is **Red Hook**, a waterfront area with cobblestoned streets and hulking industrial buildings. Though it's a bit of a hike from the subway line, the formerly gritty area is now home to a handful of bars and eateries, as well as a massive waterfront branch of **Fairway** (☎718-694-6868; 480 Van Brunt St), a beloved gourmet grocery with breathtaking **views** of NY harbor and the Statue of Liberty. Also here is the Swedish furniture megastore Ikea (see p59 for information on the free water taxi to downtown Manhattan), which has transformed the neighboring waterfront into attractive green spaces and lounging areas.

Williamsburg, Greenpoint & Bushwick
NEIGHBORHOOD

There is a definite Williamsburg look: skinny jeans, multiple tattoos, a discreet body piercing, shaggy hair for men, maybe some kind of retro head covering for a woman. Denizens of this raggedy and rowdy neighborhood across the East River on the L train seem to have time and money to slouch in cafes and party all night in bars; a fair share of older – early 30s – transplants from Manhattan and Europe qualify as elders. The main artery is **Bedford Ave** between N 10th St and Metropolitan Ave, where there are boutiques, cafes, bars and cheap eateries. But cool spots have also sprouted along N 6th St and Berry St, and perhaps a sign of the times is that the uber-hip consider Williamsburg over and have long-since moved on to colonizing next door **Greenpoint**, a traditionally Polish neighborhood as well as the former warehouse buildings further out in **Bushwick**. The **Brooklyn Brewery** (☎718-486-7422; www.brooklynbrewery.com; 79 N 11th St; admission free; ☺6-11pm Fri, noon-5pm Sat) hosts weekend tours (on the hour from noon to 6pm), special events and pub nights.

Fort Greene
NEIGHBORHOOD

This residential neighborhood of late-19th-century brownstones and gospel churches is home to a racially diverse group of young professionals and working-class families. Its gem is the **Brooklyn Academy of Music** (Map p62; ☎718-636-4100; www.bam.org; 30 Lafayette Ave), a highly respected performing arts complex and cinema. A well-regarded art and architecture school, the **Pratt Institute** calls the neighborhood home. Unbeknownst to the majority of dog walkers and sunbathers, over 11,000 prisoners of war from the Revolutionary War's Continental Army are buried underneath the grassy mounds of **Fort Greene Park**.

THE BRONX

Brooklyn's fierce northern rival is this 42-sq-mile borough, which has several claims to fame: the Yankees, fondly known as the

Bronx Bombers, who can be seen in all their pinstriped glory at the new **Yankee Stadium** (Map p56; www.yankees.com; 161st St, at River Ave) in spring and summer; the 'real' Little Italy, or **Belmont** (Map p56; www.arthuravenuebronx.com), bustling stretches of Arthur and Belmont Aves that burst with Italian gourmet markets and eateries; and a super-sized attitude that's been mythologized in Hollywood movies from *The Godfather* to *Rumble in the Bronx*.

But it's also got some cool surprises up its sleeve: a quarter of the Bronx is parkland, including the city beach of Pelham Bay Park.

Also up in these parts is the magical City Island, a little slice of New England in the Bronx.

TOP CHOICE **New York Botanical Garden** GARDENS
(Map p56; ☎718-817-8700; www.nybg.org; Bronx River Pkwy, at Fordham Rd; grounds only adult/child $6/3, all-gardens adult/child $20/8; ◷10am-6pm Tue-Sun; ▣) There are 250 acres, with old-growth forest, a wetlands trail, nearly 3000 roses and tens of thousands of newly planted azalea plants.

Bronx Wildlife Conservation Park ZOO
(Map p56; ☎718-220-5100; www.bronxzoo.com; Bronx River Pkwy, at Fordham Rd; adult/child $16/12; ◷10am-5pm Apr-Oct; ▣) Otherwise known as the Bronx Zoo, this is one of the biggest, best and most progressive zoos anywhere.

Woodlawn Cemetery CEMETERY
(Map p56; ☎718-920-0500; www.thewoodlawncemetery.org; Webster Ave, at 233rd St) Famous, historic and fascinating, 400-acre burial ground of many notable Americans, including Irving Berlin and Herman Melville.

QUEENS

There is no longer any typical Queens accent. Think Archie and Edith Bunker in *All in the Family* and you're as likely to hear Bengali and Spanish – 170 languages are spoken – in this, the largest (282 sq miles) and most ethnically diverse county in the country. There are few of the tree-lined brownstone streets you find in Brooklyn, and the majority of the neighborhoods, architecturally speaking at least, are unbefitting of this borough's grand name. However, because close to half its 2.3 million residents were born abroad, parts of Queens are endlessly reconstituting themselves, creating a vibrant and heady

CITY ISLAND

Only 15 miles from midtown but a complete world away is the surprising neighborhood of **City Island**, a 1.5-mile-long fishing community that's filled with boat slips, yacht clubs, waterfront seafood eateries and windswept little spits of sand. Lovely Victorian clapboard houses look more New England than the Bronx.

alternative universe to Manhattan. It's also home to two major airports, the Mets, a hip modern-art scene, miles of excellent beaches in the **Rockaways** and walking trails in the **Gateway National Recreation Area** (Map p56; www.nps.gov/gate), a wildlife refuge in Jamaica Bay only minutes from JFK airport. The **Queens Historical Society** (☎718-939-0647; www.queenshistoricalsociety.org) offers tours on many areas of the massive borough.

Astoria NEIGHBORHOOD
Home to the largest Greek community outside of Greece, this is obviously the place to find amazing Greek bakeries, restaurants and gourmet shops, mainly along Broad . An influx of Eastern European, Middle Eastern (Steinway Ave, known as 'Little Egypt,' is the place for falafel, kebabs and hookah pipes) and Latino immigrants have created a rich and diverse mix. Young bohemian types have also migrated here, making the area Queens' answer to Williamsburg. A reminder that moviemaking started in Astoria in the 1920s, the newly renovated **American Museum of the Moving Image** (☎718-777-6888; www.ammi.org; 36-01 35th Ave, at 36th St; admission $7; ◷10am-5pm Tue-Fri) exposes some of the mysteries of the craft with amazing exhibits and screenings in its recently renovated ornate theater. In summer, cool off at the **Astoria Pool** (19th St, at 23rd Dr), the city's largest and oldest. Much of the neighborhood, as well as curious Manhattanites, can be found at the **Bohemian Hall & Beer Garden** (2919 24th Ave, Astoria; ◷5pm-1am Mon-Thu, to 3am Fri & Sat) during warm afternoons and evenings.

Long Island City NEIGHBORHOOD
Neighboring Long Island City has several high-rise condominiums lining the riverfront with fantastic views of Manhattan. The area has also become a hub of art museums.

PS 1 Contemporary Art Center (☎718-784-2084; www.ps1.org; 22-25 Jackson Ave, at 46th Ave; suggested donation $10; ☺noon-6pm Thu-Mon) is dedicated solely to new, cutting-edge works. On Saturdays (admission $15, open 2pm to 9pm) from early July through September, the center's outdoor courtyard is transformed into an installation art space and crammed with the highest concentration of hipsters this side of the Mississippi. If the weather is pleasant, don't miss the waterside Socrates Sculpture Park (☎718-956-1819; www.socratessculpturepark.org; Broadway, at Vernon Blvd; admission free; ☺10am-dusk) with its outdoor exhibits of massive, climbable sculptures by greats including Mark di Suvero, who founded the space.

Flushing & Corona   NEIGHBORHOOD
The intersection of Main St and Roosevelt Ave, downtown Flushing, can feel like the Times Square of a city a world away from NYC. Immigrants from all over Asia, primarily Chinese and Korean, make up this neighborhood bursting at the seams with markets and restaurants filled with delicious and cheap delicacies. The Long Island Rail Road station and terminal for the 7 train see around 100,000 people pass through daily. Flushing Meadows Corona Park, meanwhile, is the home of Citi Field, the USTA National Tennis Center (the US Open is held here every August) and many lakes, ball fields, bike paths and grassy expanses, and was used for the 1939 and 1964 World's Fairs, of which there are quite a few faded leftovers – including Queens' most famous landmark, the stainless steel Unisphere, standing 120ft high and weighing 380 tons. Kids can learn about science and technology through fun hands-on exhibits at the New York Hall of Science (☎718-699-0005; www.nysci.org; adult/child $11/8; ☺9:30am-2pm Mon-Thu, to 5pm Fri, to 6pm Sat & Sun; ⊞); a quirky mini-golf course is on the site. Also within this massive park is the Queens Museum of Art (☎718-592-9700; www.queensmuseum.org; New York City Bldg, Flushing Meadows Corona Park; suggested donation $5; ☺noon-6pm Wed-Sun).

Jackson Heights   NEIGHBORHOOD
A fascinating mix of Indian (74th St) and South American (Roosevelt Ave) cultures, this is the place to purchase saris and 22-karat gold, dine on South Indian *masala dosas* – huge, paper-thin rice crepes folded around flavorful mixtures of masala pota-

toes, peas, cilantro and other earthy treats – and continue on with a plate of Colombian arepas (corn pancakes), a bite of Argentine empanadas and a cocktail at one of several Latin gay and lesbian bars, several of which line the main drag of Broadway.

STATEN ISLAND
While many New Yorkers will say that Staten Island has more in common with its neighbor, New Jersey, because of its suburban house and car cultures, there are some undoubtedly compelling reasons to count this borough in your urban explorations. First and foremost is the free Staten Island Ferry (☎718-876-8441; www.siferry.com; ☺24hr; 25min), which shuttles blasé commuters to work while offering breathtaking views of the Statue of Liberty and the Manhattan skyline. Not far from the ferry station on the Staten Island side is the Richmond County Bank Ballpark (Map p56; www.siyanks.com; Richmond Terrace), home to the minor-league Staten Island Yankees, as well as the hipper-than-ever neighborhood of St George.

🏃 Activities
Cycling
Hundreds of miles of designated bike lanes have been added throughout the city by Mayor Bloomberg's very pro-cycling City Hall, sometimes despite objections. However, unless you're an experienced urban cyclist, pedaling through the streets can be a high-risk activity, as bike lanes are often blocked by trucks, taxis and double-parked cars. More than 28-miles of mostly riverfront have been integrated into the Manhattan Waterfront Greenway, a patchwork of park pathways, overpasses and a few city streets that circle the entire island of Manhattan. The mostly uninterrupted 10-mile stretch from the GW Bridge to Battery Park, including Hudson River Park, is perhaps the most spectacular. Of course Central Park and Brooklyn's Prospect Park have lovely cycling paths and the beautiful Franklin D Roosevelt Boardwalk (cnr Father Capadanno Blvd & Sand Lane) along South Beach in Staten Island, hugs 4 miles of unspoiled beaches.

For cycling tips and weekend trips, contact Five Borough Bicycle Club (☎347-688-2925; www.5bbc.org). Transportation Alternatives (☎212-629-8080; www.transalt. org), a nonprofit bicycle-lobbying group, is also a good source of information. Gay cycling enthusiasts should check the website of Fast & Fabulous (www.fastnfab.org), a gay cycling club that organizes long weekend rides. For bike rentals, try Central Park's **Loeb Boathouse** or locate a rental shop on the comprehensive website **Bike New York** (www.bikenewyork.org). The Bloomberg administration is planning its own large-scale bike-sharing program throughout the city.

Water Sports

This is an island, after all, and as such there are plenty of opportunities for boating and kayaking. The **Downtown Boathouse** (Map p62; www.downtownboathouse.org; Pier 40, near Houston St; ⊙9am-6pm Sat & Sun May 15-Oct 15) offers free 20-minute kayaking (including equipment) in the protected embayment of the Hudson River. Other locations include Pier 96 and 72nd St.

In Central Park, **Loeb Boathouse** (Map p76; ☑212-517-2233; www.thecentralparkboathouse. com; Central Park, btwn 74th & 75th Sts; per hr $12; ⊙10am-dusk Mar-Oct) rents rowboats for romantic trysts, and even fills Venice-style gondolas in summer ($30 for 30 minutes). For a sailing adventure, hop aboard the *Schooner Adirondack* at **Chelsea Piers** (Map p68).

If you'd rather get all wet, check out the cool new **Floating Pool Lady** (www.floating pool.org), a 25m swimming pool on top of a massive barge that moves around the Hudson and docks in various city locations. Admission is free but limited to 175 people, so expect to wait on hot days.

Surfers may be surprised to find a tight group of wave worshippers within city limits, at Queens' **Rockaway Beach** at 90th St, where you can hang ten after only a 45-minute ride on the A train from midtown.

New York for Children

Contrary to popular belief, New York can be a pretty child-friendly city. Cutting edge playgrounds have proliferated from Union Square to Battery Park and of course the city's major parks, including **Central Park's Safari Playground** (Map p76), have them in abundance. There are at least as many attractions that would appeal to toddlers and tweens as there are for adults, from the two children's museums – **Children's Museum of Manhattan** (Map p76; ☑212-721-1223; www.cmom.org; 212 W 83rd St, btwn Broadway & Amsterdam Ave; admission $10; ⊙10am-5pm Tue-Sun) and the **Brooklyn Children's Museum** (☑718-735-4400; www.brooklynkids.org; 145 Brooklyn Ave, Prospect Heights; admission $7.50; ⊙11am-5pm Wed-Fri, from 10am Sat & Sun) – to the Central Park and Bronx zoos to the Coney Island aquarium.

Times Square's themed megastores and their neighboring kid-friendly restaurants are easy options. Check out the weekend Arts section of the *New York Times* for kid-themed events and performances.

☞ Tours

The following is just a sample:

Big Onion Walking Tours WALKING
(☑212-439-1090; www.bigonion.com; tours $15) Popular and quirky guided tours specializing in ethnic and neighborhood tours.

Circle Line BOAT
(Map p68; ☑212-563-3200; www.circleline42. com; Pier 83, W 42nd St; tickets $16-34) Ferry boat tours, from semicircle to a full island cruise with guided commentary.

Gray Line Sightseeing BUS
(☑212-445-0848; www.coachusa.com/newyork sights; 49 W 45th St; adult/child from $42/$32) Hop-on, hop-off double-decker multilingual guided bus tours of all the boroughs (except Staten Island).

Jetty Jumpers BOAT
(☑917-734-9919; www.jettyjumpers.com; tours $275) Offers guided jet-ski tours of NYC waterways.

Municipal Art Society WALKING
(☑212-935-3960; www.mas.org; 457 Madison Ave; tours adult $15) Various scheduled tours focusing on architecture and history.

New York City Audubon WALKING
(☑212-691-7483; www.nycaudubon.org; tours $8-100) Expert instructors and guides lead trips including birding in Central Park and the Bronx and ecology cruises of the Jamaica Bay Wildlife Refuge.

On Location Tours WALKING
(☑212-209-3370; www.screentours.com; tours $15-45) A *Gossip Girl* tour is the latest addition to the list of tours available for fulfilling your Carrie Bradshaw or Tony Soprano fantasies.

★ Festivals & Events

Festivities never cease in New York. From cultural street fairs to foodie events and outdoor concerts, you are bound to find something that will excite you, no matter the time of year. There's almost too much to digest in summer, when outdoor celebrations proliferate.

Restaurant Week FOOD
(☑212-484-1222; www.nycgo.com) Dine at top restaurants for $20 and $30 deals – first in February and again in July.

Armory Show
CULTURAL

(212-645-6440; www.thearmoryshow.com; Piers 92 & 94, West Side Hwy at 52nd & 54th Sts) New York's biggest contemporary art fair sweeps the city in March, showcasing the new work of thousands of artists from around the world.

Tribeca Film Festival
FILM

(212-941-2400; www.tribecafilmfestival.com) Robert De Niro co-organizes this local downtown film fest, held in late April and early May, that's quickly rising in prestige on the circuit.

Fleet Week
NAVAL

(212-245-0072) Annual convocation of sailors and their naval ships and air rescue teams, who descend upon the city in their formal whites every May.

Lesbian, Gay, Bisexual & Transgender Pride
CULTURAL

(212-807-7433; www.nycpride.org) Pride month, in June, with a packed calendar of parties and events, culminates with a major march down Fifth Ave on the last Sunday of the month.

Mermaid Parade
CULTURAL

(www.coneyisland.com/mermaid) Something of Mardi Gras on the boardwalk, Surf Ave on Coney Island in Brooklyn turns into an artistic, crazy and fun free-expression zone in late June.

New York Film Festival
FILM

(www.filmlinc.com) Major world premieres from prominent directors at this Lincoln Center event, held in late September.

New Yorker Festival
CULTURAL

(www.newyorker.com) A mid-October line-up of interviews, talks and tours from some of the most prominent literary and cultural figures in the world.

🛏 Sleeping

Keep in mind that prices change depending on the value of the euro, yen and other worldwide currencies, as well as the general drift of the global economic climate, not to mention the day of the week and the season, with spring and fall being most expensive. Tax adds an additional 13.25% per night. For longer stays, an apartment rental or sublet can be the best option (there's no tax on rentals), secured with the help of an agency like City Sonnet (212-614-3034; www.west villagebb.com; apt from $135 per night). A cluster of national chains, including Sheraton,

Ramada and Holiday Inn, have affordably priced rooms in hotels within a few blocks of one another around 39th Ave in Long Island City, Queens, a quick N, Q or R train into midtown Manhattan directly across the river.

LOWER MANHATTAN

Gild Hall Wall Street
BOUTIQUE HOTEL $$$

(Map p58; 212-232-7700; www.wallstreetdistrict. com; 15 Gold St; r from $225; ✳@🛜) Part of the Thompson line of fabulous NYC hotels, Gild Hall sports a funky English-hunting-lodge lobby. All the rooms, including the small and simple standards, have oversized leather headboards and notably comfortable beds. Only a few blocks from Wall St and several subway lines, you won't feel stranded.

Wall Street Inn
LUXURY HOTEL $$$

(Map p58; 212-747-1500; www.thewallstreetinn. com; 9 S William St; r incl breakfast from $275; ✳🛜) Lehman Brothers, the failed bank, once occupied this classic limestone building and, while the mood of the hotel is very early American banker, there's little risk in a stay here. Old-fashioned and warm rather than stuffy, the rooms, with luxurious marble baths, are slightly over-furnished for their size.

TRIBECA & SOHO

Soho Grand Hotel
BOUTIQUE HOTEL $$$

(Map p62; 212-965-3000; www.sohogrand.com; 310 W Broadway; d $195-450; ✳@🛜) The original boutique hotel of the 'hood still reigns, with its striking glass-and-cast-iron lobby stairway, and 367 rooms with cool, clean lines plus Frette linens, plasma flat-screen TVs and Kiehl's grooming products. The lobby's Grand Lounge buzzes with action.

Sixty Thompson
BOUTIQUE HOTEL $$$

(Map p62; 212-431-0400; www.60thompson. com; 60 Thompson St, btwn Broome & Spring Sts; s/d $360/425; ✳@🛜) Another minimalist charmer. Rooms here have down duvets, flat-screen TVs and cozy tweed sofas. The rooftop Thom Bar is a stunning place to see and be seen.

Cosmopolitan Hotel
HOTEL $$$

(Map p58; 212-566-1900; www.cosmohotel.com; 95 W Broadway, at Chambers St; d from $200; ✳🛜) Don't let the name fool you – rather than being urbane and sophisticated, the Cosmopolitan is more akin to the average Main St USA hotel. Clean, carpeted, though decidedly cramped, it's an affordable downtown option with a cafe serving crepes attached.

TOP CHOICE Lita SoHo
HOTEL $$$

(Map p62; ☎212-925-3600; www.solitasohotel. com; 159 Grand St, at Lafayette St; r from $220; ❋❄) Part of the Clarion chain, the SoLita is a clean, functional alternative with boutique-style furnishings close to Little Italy, Chinatown, Soho and the Lower East Side. Lower winter rates.

Hotel Azure
HOTEL $$$

(Map p62; ☎212-925-4378; www.hotelazure.com; 120 Lafayette St; r from $220; ❋❄) Another choice only a block away. Also good deals in winter.

LOWER EAST SIDE & EAST VILLAGE

Bowery Hotel
BOUTIQUE HOTEL $$$

(Map p62; ☎212-505-9100; www.theboweryhotel. com; 335 Bowery, btwn E 2nd & 3rd Sts; r from $325; ❋@❄) Perhaps as far as you can get from the Bowery's gritty flophouse history, this stunningly stylish hotel is all 19th-century elegance. Rooms come equipped with lots of light and sleek furnishings mixed with antiques. The baroque-style lobby bar attracts the young and chic and on-site restaurant Gemma serves upscale Italian.

Hotel on Rivington
BOUTIQUE HOTEL $$

(Map p62; ☎212-475-2600; www.hotelonrivington. com; 107 Rivington St, btwn Essex & Ludlow Sts; r from $160; ❋@❄) This shimmering 20-floor tower looms large over Lower East Side tenement buildings, its glass-enclosed rooms offering stunning views of the East River and downtown's spread. Rooms vary quite a bit – some have balconies, some have hanging flat-screen TVs – and the ground-floor restaurant is a scenester hot spot.

Gem Hotel
BOUTIQUE HOTEL $$

(Map p62; ☎212-358-8844; www.thegemhotel.com; 135 Houston St, at Forsyth St; r from $180; ❋@❄) The Gem still has the plain, boxy exterior of the Howard Johnson hotel that once occupied the site, however the small cheerful rooms have plush bedding, small desks and flat-screen TVs. Expect some street noise.

East Village Bed & Coffee
B&B $$

(Map p62; ☎212-533-4175; www.bedandcoffee. com; 110 Ave C, btwn 7th & 8th Sts; r with shared bath from $115; ❋❄) The 10 airy rooms sport different well-executed themes – Mexican (with a bright-yellow wall and pressed-tin doodads), Zen (with a small Buddha and icy tones) and so on – and common areas are lovely, from the high-ceilinged kitchen to the leafy back garden.

WEST (GREENWICH) VILLAGE

Abingdon Guest House
B&B $$

(Map p62; ☎212-243-5384; www.abingdonguest house.com; 21 Eighth Ave, at Jane St; r from $159; ❋@❄) Don't look out the window and you'll swear you've landed in a New England B&B. Elegant, comfortable rooms feature four-poster beds, (nonworking) fireplaces, scads of exposed brick, and billowing curtains. Plus a lovely little garden out back.

Larchmont Hotel
HOTEL $$

(Map p62; ☎212-989-9333; www.larchmontho tel.com; 27 W 11th St, btwn Fifth & Sixth Aves; s/d with shared bath & breakfast from $90/119; ❋❄) Housed in a prewar building that blends in with the other fine brownstones on the block, a stay at the Larchmont is about location. The carpeted rooms are basic and in need of updating, as are the communal baths, but it's not a bad deal for the price.

Jane Hotel
HOTEL $$

(Map p62; ☎212-924-6700; www.thejanenyc.com; 113 Jane St; r with shared bath from $100; ❋❄) Originally built for sailors (which is obvious after one look at the cabin-sized rooms), then a temporary refuge for survivors of the *Titanic*, a YMCA and rock-and-roll venue, the single bunk rooms feature flat-screen TVs and the communal showers are more than adequate.

MEATPACKING DISTRICT & CHELSEA

Hotel Gansevoort
LUXURY HOTEL $$$

(Map p62; ☎212-206-6700; www.hotelgansevoort. com; 18 Ninth Ave, at 13th St; r from $395; ❋@❄❄) This 187-room luxury hotel in the trendy Meatpacking District has been a hit for its 400-thread-count linens, hypoallergenic down duvets, plasma TVs, chic basement spa and rooftop bar with fabulous views. Down-to-earth types, beware: it's on the nauseatingly trendy side of things.

Ace Hotel New York City
BOUTIQUE HOTEL $$

(Map p68; ☎212-679-2222; www.acehotel.com/ newyork; 20 W 29th St; r from $99-369; ❋❄) This outpost of a hip Pacific northwest chain is on the northern edge of Chelsea. Clever touches such as vintage turntables and handwritten welcome notes elevate the Ace beyond the standard. However, prison-issued bunk beds in one of the room styles are missteps. Juice, coffee and croissants are available in the morning.

Chelsea Lodge
B&B $$

(Map p68; ☎212-243-4499; www.chelsealodge. com; 318 W 20th St, at Eighth Ave; s/d $124/134;

❁) Housed in a landmark brownstone, the European-style 20-room Chelsea Lodge has homey, well-kept, though tight, rooms. There are showers and sinks in rooms, but toilets are down the hall. Six suite rooms have private bathrooms, and two come with private garden access. Wi-fi in the lobby.

Chelsea International Hostel   HOSTEL $

(Map p68; ☎212-243-3700; www.chelseahostel. com; 222 W 20th St, btwn Seventh & Eighth Aves; dm with/without bath $70/65, s/d with shared bath $70/155; ❁@🖳🛜) This well-located hostel draws an international crowd accustomed to partying and bunking down for a few hours. No doubt you'll make friends in the communal kitchen.

UNION SQUARE, FLATIRON DISTRICT & GRAMERCY PARK

Marcel   BOUTIQUE HOTEL $$

(Map p68; ☎212-696-3800; www.nychotels.com; 201 E 24th St, at Third Ave; d from $175; ❁🛜) Minimalist with earth-tone touches, this 97-room inn is a poor-man's chic boutique and that's not a bad thing. Modernist rooms on the avenue have great views, and the sleek lounge is a great place to unwind from a day of touring. Visit its website for other classy affordable inns within the Amsterdam Hospitality group.

Chelsea Inn   B&B $$

(Map p68; ☎212-645-8989; www.chelseainn.com; 46 W 17th St, near Sixth Ave; r from $100; ❁🛜) This funky-charming hideaway made up of two adjoining 19th-century four-story walk-up townhouses has small but comfortable rooms that look like they were furnished entirely from flea markets or grandma's attic. Most of the rooms have private baths; the two rooms that go for the lowest prices share a bathroom.

Gershwin Hotel   HOTEL $$

(Map p68; ☎212-545-8000; www.gershwinho tel.com; 7 E 27th St, at Fifth Ave; dm/d/ste from $45/109/299; ❁@🛜) This popular and funky spot is half youth hostel, half hotel, and buzzes with original pop art, touring bands and a young and artsy European clientele.

MIDTOWN

Hudson   HOTEL $$$

(Map p76; ☎212-554-6000; www.hudsonhotel. com; 356 W 58th St, btwn Eighth & Ninth Aves; r from $240; ❁@🛜) This delicious marriage between designer Phillipe Starck and hotelier Ian Schrager is an absolute jewel – if you're not aching for quiet, that is. Part hotel and part nightclub, this beauty has several lounge bars that are always jammin', and the teensy rooms are highly stylized, with lots of glass, bright wood and gossamer scrims.

Room-Mate Grace   BOUTIQUE HOTEL $$

(Map p68; ☎212-354-2323; www.room-matehotels. com; 125 W 45th St; r incl breakfast from $185; ❁🛜🛁) Part of a Spanish chain, this ultra-hip hotel is good value when you consider you're steps from the midtown action. Like other hotels of the same genre, space is at a premium and sleekness is prized over warmth. A steam room, sauna and lively pool-bar are reasons to choose the Mate over others.

Pod Hotel   HOTEL $$

(Map p68; ☎212-355-0300; www.thepodhotel.com; 230 E 51st St, btwn Second & Third Aves; r from $129; ❁@🛜) A dream come true for folks who'd like to live inside their iPod – or at least curl up and sleep with it – this afford-able hot spot has a range of room types, most barely big enough for the bed. 'Pods' have bright bedding, tight workspaces, flat-screen TVs, iPod docking stations and 'rain' showerheads.

414 Hotel   HOTEL $$

(Map p68; ☎212-399-0006; www.414hotel.com; 414 W 46th St, btwn Ninth & Tenth Aves; r incl break-fast from $200; ❁🛜) More like a guesthouse than a hotel and only a couple of blocks west of Times Square. All rooms are well-kept and attractively furnished and there's a small courtyard between the townhouse's two buildings; a small kitchen for guests to use.

Yotel   HOTEL $$

(Map p68; ☎646-449-7700; www.yotel.com; 570 Tenth Ave, at 41st St; r from $150; ❁🛜) Sci-fi meets boutique meets airport terminal at this newest outpost of an international chain. Super helpful staff (crew) and a cool bar, lounge and restaurant – plus a robot (mechanical arm) will store your luggage.

Broadway Rooms   HOTEL $$

(Map p68; ☎212-397-9686; www.broadwayrooms. com; 337 W 55th St, btwn Eighth & Ninth Aves; r with shared bath $107-220; ❁@) Though the name has changed (formerly 1291 B&B), this hostel-hotel is still rough around the edges, with cramped private rooms and shared rooms with a bunk bed and two single beds, best for small groups.

Big Apple Hostel
HOSTEL $

(Map p68; ☑212-302-2603; www.bigapplehostel.com; 119 W 45thSt, btwn Sixth & Seventh Aves; dm/r $44/135; ✳@🛜) Dreary rooms with exposed pipes, windows open onto fire escapes, but at least there's a small outdoor patio for fresh air.

UPPER WEST SIDE

Empire Hotel
HOTEL $$$

(Map p76; ☑212-265-7400; www.empirehotelnyc.com; 44 W 63rd St; r from $225; ✳@🛜≋) An uptown version of the W, the Empire is a chic hotel directly across the street from the Lincoln Center. The decor is all classy earth tones and rooms are a decent size – for NYC. There's a rooftop pool deck with fabulous views and, when not closed for private functions, it's a nighttime hot spot.

On the Ave
BOUTIQUE HOTEL $$$

(Map p76; ☑212-362-1100; www.ontheave.com; 2178 Broadway, at W 77th St; r from $225; ✳@🛜) A more welcoming feel and larger rooms make On the Ave a cut above the average sleek boutique hotel. And it's a good deal considering the high-concept design, stainless steel and marble baths, featherbeds, flat-screen TVs and original artwork. It's near the Lincoln Center, Central Park and a slew of good eats.

HOSTEL $$

(Map p76; ☑212-912-2600; www.ymca.com; 5 W 63rd St at Central Park West; r from $100; ✳@) Just steps from Central Park, this grand art-deco building has several floors – 8th to the 13th – of basic, but clean, rooms. Guests have access to extensive, but old-school, gym, racquet ball courts, pool and sauna. Wi-fi on the ground floor. Other locations on the Upper East Side and Harlem.

Jazz on Amsterdam Ave
HOSTEL $

(Map p76; ☑646-490-7348; www.jazzhostels.com; 201 W 87th St at Amsterdam Ave; dm $44, r $100; ✳@) Only a short walk to Central Park, this hostel chain's Upper West Side branch has clean rooms, both private and two- to six-bed dorms. Free wi-fi in the lobby. Other branches in Harlem and Chelsea.

Hostelling International-New York
HOSTEL $

(Map p76; ☑212-932-2300; www.hinewyork.org; 891 Amsterdam Ave, at 103rd St; dm $32-40, d from $135; ✳@🛜) It's got clean, safe and air-conditioned dorm rooms in a gorgeous landmark building, with a sprawling and shady patio and a super-friendly vibe.

UPPER EAST SIDE

Carlyle
LUXURY HOTEL $$$

(Map p76; ☑212-744-1600; www.thecarlyle.com; 35 E 76th St, btwn Madison & Park Aves; r from $450; ✳🛜) This legendary New York classic, the epitome of old-fashioned luxury hosts foreign dignitaries and celebrities alike. Opulence reigns from the hushed lobby with glossy marble floors to framed English country scenes or Audubon prints in the rooms; some have terraces and baby grand pianos.

Bentley
BOUTIQUE HOTEL $$$

(Map p76; ☑888-664-6835; www.nychotels.com; 500 E 62nd St, at York Ave; r from $200; ✳🛜) Featuring great East River views, the Bentley overlooks FDR Dr, as far east as you can go. Formerly an office building, the hotel has shed its utilitarian past in the form of chic boutique-hotel styling, a swanky lobby and sleek rooms.

Bubba & Bean Lodges
B&B $$

(Map p76; ☑917-345-7914; www.bblodges.com; 1598 Lexington Ave, btwn 101st & 102nd Sts; r from $180; ✳🛜) Hardwood floors, crisp white walls and pretty navy bedspreads make the rooms at this nifty B&B feel spacious, modern and youthful. The rooms are really more like full apartments (some fit up to six people). Good winter rates.

HARLEM

102 Brownstone
HOTEL $$

(Map p76; ☑212-662-4223; www.102brownstone.com; 102 W 118th St, btwn Malcolm X & Adam Clayton Powell Blvds; r from $120; ✳🛜) A wonderfully redone Greek Revival row house on a beautiful residential street; room styles, all with plush bedding, range from Zen to classy boudoir.

710 Guest Suites
APARTMENT $$

(☑212-491-5622; www.710guestsuites.com; 710 St Nicholas Ave, at 146th St; ste from $174; ✳🛜) Three fabulously chic suites with high ceilings, contemporary furnishings and wood floors in a brownstone. Three-night minimum and lower rates from January through March make this exceptional good value.

Harlem Flophouse
INN $$

(Map p76; ☑347-632-1960; www.harlemflophouse.com; 242 W 123rd St, btwn Adam Clayton Powell & Frederick Douglass Blvds; r with shared bath from $125) The four attractive bedrooms have antique light fixtures, glossed-wood floors and big beds, plus classic tin ceilings and wooden shutters. Cat on the premises.

BROOKLYN

TOP CHOICE New York Loft Hostel   HOSTEL **$**
(☑718-366-1351; 248 Varet St; dm/r incl breakfast $65/90; ✹☎) Live like a Williamsburg or more accurately Bushwick hipster in this renovated loft building. Brick walls, high ceilings, a beautiful kitchen and rooftop Jacuzzi make Manhattan hostels seem like tenements. Closest subway is Morgan Ave L stop.

Nu Hotel   HOTEL **$$$**
(☑718-852-8585; www.nuhotelbrooklyn.com; 85 Smith St; d incl breakfast from $199; ✹@☎) This location, only blocks from Brooklyn Heights and a nexus of attractive brownstone neighborhoods, is absolutely ideal – except for the fact that it's across the street from the Brooklyn House of Detention. It has a chic minimalist vibe and the clean, all-white rooms are comfortable.

Hotel Le Bleu   HOTEL **$$**
(☑718-625-1500; www.hotelbleu.com; 370 4th Ave; d incl breakfast $169-349; P✹@☎) On a busy avenue with belching trucks and auto body shops, however, welcoming and busy Park Slope is a short walk away. Boutique styling: sleek, white, minimalistic – king-sized beds and balconies with good views of Manhattan.

3B   B&B **$$**
(☑347-762-2632; www.3bbrooklyn.com; 136 Lawrence St; dm/r incl breakfast $40/120; ✹☎) The 3rd floor unity of this downtown Brooklyn brownstone has been turned into a bright and contemporary four-room B&B.

✖ Eating

In a city with nearly 19,000 restaurants, and new ones opening every single day, where are you supposed to begin? From Little Albania to Little Uzbekistan, your choice of ethnic eats is only a short subway ride away. A hotbed of buzz-worthy culinary invention and trends like artisanal doughnuts, farm-to-table pork sandwiches and *haute cuisine* reinterpretations of fried chicken, pizza and good ol' burgers and fries, NYC's restaurant scene, like the city is constantly reinventing itself. The latest foodie obsession is the flotilla of roving, tweeting food trucks, the 21st-century equivalent of the classic pushcart, selling gourmet cupcakes, dumplings and Jamaican curry goat and everything in between.

A, B, C   89

Those letter grades you see posted in the windows of every NYC restaurant aren't the report cards of the owner's kids. They're issued by the NYC health department after an inspection of each establishment's hygiene standards. A is best and C worst – anything lower, well, you probably wouldn't want to eat there anyway.

LOWER MANHATTAN

Bridge Café   MODERN AMERICAN **$$**
(Map p58; 279 Water St; mains $23; ☺11:45am-11pm) Serving downtown since 1794, this unassuming cozy restaurant is widely credited with being the oldest in the city. There's nothing stodgy or Revolutionary War-era about the modern meat and seafood menu sourced with seasonal ingredients and the banana chocolate bread-pudding dessert is a satisfying coda to the meal.

Smorgas Chef Wall St   SCANDINAVIAN **$$**
(Map p58; 53 Stone St; mains $9-24; ☺10:30am-10:30pm) Located on quaint and narrow Stone St (the colony of New Amsterdam's first paved roadway), this fine bistro serves Scandinavian fare such as Swedish meatballs as well as lighter fare like fish and salads. During the summer months, Smorgas Chef and neighboring restaurants put tables outside, turning the street into one big block party.

Table Tales   SANDWICHES **$**
(Map p58; 243 Water St; mains $9; ☺11:30am-10pm Mon-Sat) Take a break from the tourist mobbed, chain-saturated South St Seaport area at this precious and cozy nook, run by a catering company, where you'll find a chill vibe along with both filling cafe items and full-on dinner mains.

Ruben's Empanadas   ARGENTINE, FAST FOOD **$**
(Map p58; 76 Nassau St, at John St; empanadas $4; ☺9am-7pm) Refuel with one of this Argentine chain's filling, greaseless empanadas in endless varieties, from chicken to apple or spicy tofu. Two other locations in the neighborhood.

Zaitstaff   BURGERS **$**
(Map p58; 72 Nassau St; mains $9; ☺9:30am-9:30pm, 10:30am-1pm Sat & Sun) A loyal following packs this little restaurant amid blocks full of delis and fast-food chains for

its Kobe Beef burgers (turkey and veggie as well).

Alfanoose
MIDDLE EASTERN $
(Map p58; 8 Maiden Lane, btwn Broadway & Nassau; mains $6; ☺11:30am-9:30pm Mon-Sat) Syrian-Lebanese specialties, as many vegetarian as meat and a few not found on the typical falafel-joint menu.

TRIBECA, SOHO & NOHO

Mooncake Foods
ASIAN, SANDWICHES $
(Map p62; 28 Watts St, at Broome; mains $8; ☺10am-11pm Mon-Fri, 9am-11pm Sat & Sun) This unpretentious family-run restaurant serves some of the best sandwiches in the neighborhood, nay city. Try the smoked white-fish salad sandwich or Vietnamese pork meatball hero. Another location in Chelsea and uptown in Hell's Kitchen.

Edward's
AMERICAN $$
(Map p58; 136 W Broadway, btwn Thomas & Duane Sts; mains $13; ☺9am-midnight) Located on a busy block in Tribeca, Edward's has the feel of a casual European bistro – high ceilings, mirrored walls and darkwood booths. The menu offers everything from pasta to burgers.

La Esquina Taqueria
MEXICAN $
(Map p62; 114 Kenmare St, at Cleveland Pl; mains $6; ☺8am-1:45am, from noon Sat & Sun) This Mexican hot spot, whose only marking is a huge neon sign that blares 'The Corner' (hence *la esquina*), bustles night and day for good reason. Delectable, authentic treats are served at the counter or in the mellow cafe around the corner.

Bubby's Pie Company
AMERICAN $$
(Map p58; 120 Hudson St, at N Moore St; mains $12-25; ☺1am-noon Mon, 8am-midnight Tue, 24hr Wed-Sun) This kid-friendly Tribeca standby is *the* place for simple, big, delicious food: slow-cooked BBQ, grits, matzo-ball soup, buttermilk potato salad, fried okra and big fat breakfasts, all melt-in-your-mouth good.

CHINATOWN, LITTLE ITALY & NOLITA

Peasant
ITALIAN $$$
(Map p62; ☎212-965-9511; 194 Elizabeth St, btwn Spring & Prince Sts; mains $20-30; ☺6-11pm Tue-Sat, to 10pm Sun) A warm dining area of bare oak tables is structured around a brick hearth and open kitchen, which lovingly turns out hearty, pan-Italian, mostly meat-based fare. Solid stunners include gnocchi with wild mushrooms and oven-baked rabbit. After dinner, head downstairs to the dark and cozy cellar wine bar.

Ruby's
AMERICAN $$
(Map p62; 219 Mulberry St; mains $12; ☺10am-11pm) Tuck in those elbows for a seat at one of the picnic tables at this unpretentious tiny nook serving healthy salads, paninis and apparently Aussie burgers (ground beef mixed with onions and peppers and topped with fried eggs, beets and roasted pineapple).

Torrisi Italian Specialties
ITALIAN $
(Map p62; 250 Mulberry St, at Prince; sandwiches $8; ☺11am-10pm) By day, an unassuming grocery-restaurant with meat hanging in the windows and sandwiches like chicken parm and lasagna. At night, Torrisi serves a prix fixe feast ($45) of inventive, haute versions of Italian-American favorites with local and seasonal ingredients.

Focolare
ITALIAN $$
(Map p62; 115 Mulberry St, btwn Canal & Hester; mains $15; ☺11am-10pm) If you're bent on a Little Italy dinner experience, this is a fine choice, at least as much for its cozy interior as the classic dishes.

Bánh Mí Saigon Bakery
VIETNAMESE $
(Map p62; 198 Grand St; mains $5; ☺10am-7pm) This no-frills storefront doles out some of

---

EATING NYC: CHINATOWN

With hundreds of restaurants, from holes-in-the-wall to banquet-sized dining rooms, Chinatown is wonderful for exploring cheap eats on an empty stomach. One of the best places to lunch for Cantonese cuisine is Amazing 66 (Map p58; 66 Mott St, at Canal St; mains $7; ☺11am-11pm). The best of the dumpling joints is Vanessa's Dumpling House (Map p62; 118 Eldridge St, at Broome St; 4 dumplings $1; ☺7:30am-10:30pm). Head to Big Wong King (Map p58; 67 Mott St, at Canal; mains $5-20; ☺7am-9:30pm) for chopped meat over rice and reliable congee (sweet or savory soft rice soup). Always busy Joe's Shanghai (Map p58; 9 Pell St; mains $10; ☺11am-11pm) is tourist-friendly and does good noodle and soup dishes. And finally, the Egg Custard King (Map p62; Natalie Bakery Inc; 271 Grand St; custards $1; ☺7am-9:30pm) is the place for the eponymous dessert.

the best *bánh mì* – Vietnamese roast-pork sandwiches served on fat baguettes – in town.

Fonda Nolita
MEXICAN $

(Map p62; 267 Elizabeth St, near Houston St; mains $4; ☺8am-midnight) Hearty tacos (try the chorizo breakfast one) served out of a VW wagon parked inside.

LOWER EAST SIDE

Spitzer's Corner
MODERN AMERICAN $$

(Map p62; ☑212-228-0027; 101 Rivington St; mains $9-19; ☺noon-4am Mon-Sat, 10am-midnight Sun) The corner location offers an open-air gastropub experience with a concise menu designed by a Michelin-starred chef, and more than 40 different beers on tap. Large communal tables and a lengthy counter facing the street encourage socializing.

Katz's Delicatessen
DELI $$

(Map p62; 205 E Houston St; sandwiches $13; ☺8am-9:45pm Mon & Tue, to 10:45pm Wed, Thu & Sun, to 2:45am Fri & Sat) One of the few remaining Jewish delicatessens in the city, Katz's attracts locals, tourists and celebrities whose photos line the walls. Massive pastrami, corned beef, brisket and tongue sandwiches are throwbacks, as is the payment system: hold on to the ticket you're handed when you walk in and pay cash only.

Kuma Inn
ASIAN $$

(Map p62; ☑212-353-8866; 113 Ludlow St, btwn Delancey & Rivington; mains $11; ☺6-11pm) Reservations are a must at this strikingly popular spot, in a secretive 2nd-floor location that feels like a reconfigured apartment. Filipino- and Thai-inspired tapas run the gamut, from vegetarian summer rolls to an oyster omelet and grilled salmon with mung beans and pickled onions.

Fat Radish
MODERN AMERICAN $$$

(Map p62; 17 Orchard St; mains $21; ☺8am-midnight, from 11am Sat & Sun, closed Mon) Young and fashionable pack in to this dimly lit dining room with exposed white brick and industrial touches. There's a loud buzz and people checking each other out but the entrees, typical of the local-seasonal-haute pub fare fad are worth your attention.

Economy Candy
CANDY $

(Map p62; 108 Rivington St; candies from $4; ☺9am-6pm Sun-Fri, 10am-5pm Sat) Fancy any of the myriad crazy, nostalgic candies you consumed as a kid? Whatever it is, as long as it contains sugar, it's probably crammed or stacked in this hole-in-the-wall candy purveyor.

Russ & Daughters
DELI $

(Map p62; 179 E Houston St; mains $5; ☺8am-8pm Mon-Fri, to 7pm Sat, to 5:30pm Sun) Evocative of a bygone era, this landmark establishment serves up Eastern European Jewish delicacies like caviar, herring and lox, and of course a smear of cream cheese on a bagel.

Souvlaki GR
GREEK $

(Map p62; 116 Stanton St, near Essex St; mains $5; ☺11am-midnight) Owners of a food truck have opened this little restaurant that looks like a soundstage for a film set on a Greek isle.

Donut Plant
DESSERT $

(Map p62; 379 Grand St, at Norfolk; doughnuts $2.75; ☺6:30am-6:30pm) Inventively flavored (eg peanut butter and jelly) doughnuts with all-natural ingredients. Another location in the Chelsea Hotel at 222 W 23rd St.

EAST VILLAGE

Every cuisine and style is represented in the East Village, though even the very best places are certainly more casual than stuffy. St Marks Place and around, from Third to Second Ave, has turned into a little Tokyo with loads of Japanese sushi and grill restaurants. Cookie-cutter Indian restaurants line Sixth St between First and Second Ave.

TOP CHOICE Momofuku Noodle Bar
JAPANESE $$

(Map p62; 171 First Ave, at 11th St; mains $9-16; ☺noon-4pm & 5:30-11pm Sun-Thu, to midnight Fri & Sat) Ramen and steamed buns are the name of the game at this infinitely creative Japanese eatery, part of the growing David Chang empire. Seating is on stools at a long bar or at communal tables. Momofuku's famous steamed chicken and pork buns ($9 for two) are recommended.

Counter
VEGETARIAN $$

(Map p62; ☑212-982-5870; 105 First Ave, btwn E 6th & 7th Sts; mains $15-25; ☺5pm-midnight Mon-Thu, to 1am Fri, 11am-1am Sat, to 4pm Sun; ☑) This unique eatery manages to mix infused-vodka martinis and organic vegetarian cuisine with outlandish success. Credit the futuristic, backlit dining room, fabulous large-scale artwork and innovative dishes like cauliflower 'risotto.'

Il Bagatto
ITALIAN $$

(Map p62; ☑212-228-0977; 192 E 2nd St, near Ave B; mains $18; ☺5:30pm-midnight, closed Mon) A bustling yet romantic little nook, this spot has thoroughly delicious Italian creations at exceptionally reasonable prices – plus an excellent wine list.

Xi'an Famous Foods
CHINESE $

(Map p62; 81 St Mark's Pl, at First Ave; mains $6; ⊙24hr) This Flushing, Queens, original is a sliver of a restaurant with an interesting menu specializing in spicy noodle and soup dishes. Two other locations in Chinatown.

Veselka
EASTERN EUROPEAN $$

(Map p62; 144 Second Ave, at 9th St; mains $12; ⊙24hr) Generations of East Villagers have been coming to this bustling institution for blintzes and breakfast regardless of the late hour.

WEST (GREENWICH) VILLAGE

Blue Hill
MODERN AMERICAN $$$

(Map p62; ☎212-539-1776; 75 Washington Pl, btwn Sixth Ave & MacDougal St; mains $22-50; ⊙5:30-11pm Mon-Sat, to 10pm Sun) A place for high-rolling Slow Food junkies, Blue Hill is a low-key, high-class dining spot where you can be certain that everything on your plate is fresh and seasonal. Expect barely seasoned veggies as centerpieces for dishes with poultry and fish. The below-street-level space is sophisticated and serene.

Olivette
FRENCH $$

(Map p62; 42 Grove St; mains $12; ⊙8am-2am Mon-Fri, 11am-2am Sat & Sun) Cramped or cozy depending on your mood, this romantically lit bistro serves up miniaturized versions of inspired tapas-like dishes such as house-cured salt cod whipped with olive oil. Meat, cheeses and tartines on offer as well.

Snack Taverna
GREEK $$

(Map p62; 63 Bedford St; mains $15-25; ⊙noon-11pm Mon-Sat, to 10pm Sun) If you can't make it out to the Greek restaurants in Astoria, Queens, try this West Village place. The menu goes beyond the standard gyro and moussaka – the small plates like the smoked trout with barley rusks, tomato, cheese and balsamic vinaigrette are excellent.

Perilla
MODERN AMERICAN $$

(Map p62; ☎212-929-6868; 9 Jones St; mains $22-27; ⊙5:30-11pm Mon-Thu, to 11:30pm Fri & Sat, 11am-10pm Sun) Run by popular reality-TV show Top Chef, Perilla is an extremely creative yet well-grounded American bistro. The spicy duck meatballs and roasted main

sardines are both good ways to start off a meal.

Thelewala
INDIAN $$

(Map p62; 112 MacDougal St, near Minetta Lane; mains $5; ⊙11:30am-2am Sun-Thu, to 5am Fri & Sat) Located on a food strip with high turnover, the delicious 'Calcutta rolls' and 'street food' at this tiny and sleek eatery should guarantee a long stay.

Taïm
MIDDLE EASTERN $

(Map p62; 222 Waverly Pl, btwn Perry & W 11th Sts; mains $7-9; ⊙noon-10pm) This tiny little falafel joint serves smoothies, salads and tasty falafel, which ranges from the traditional to those spiced up with roasted red pepper or hot harissa.

CHELSEA, UNION SQUARE, FLATIRON DISTRICT & GRAMERCY PARK

TOP CHOICE The Breslin
MODERN AMERICAN $$

(Map p68; 16 West 29th St; mains $18; ⊙7am-midnight) It might be hard to hear yourself think and the hipster overflow from the attached uber-trendy Ace Hotel can rub some the wrong way... However, what really matters is the pub-influenced meat heavy menu by widely celebrated chef April Bloomfield's doesn't disappoint. Big groups can occupy the single large table fronting the open kitchen for the whole roasted suckling pig extravaganza (per person $65 with sides, salad and desserts). No reservations, so expect a wait.

Eataly
ITALIAN $

(Map p68; www.eataly.com; 200 Fifth Ave at 23rd St; mains $7; ⊙noon-10pm) The Macy's of food courts, celebrity-chef Mario Batali's NYC empire now has a footprint to match his ambitions. With a handful of specialty dining halls, all with a different focus (pizza, fish, vegetables, meat, pasta) and the pièce de résistance, a rooftop beer garden, not to mention a coffee shop, gelateria and grocery, there's enough choice to overwhelm even a blogging gourmand.

Co.
PIZZERIA $$

(Map p68; 230 Ninth Ave, at 24th St; pizza $16; ⊙5-11pm) Unsurprisingly, because the chef/owner of this contemporary pizzeria is first and foremost a baker, the paper-thin crust is arguably the best in the city. Go with a group to sample a number of pies with a combination of fresh and inventive toppings.

Chat N' Chew

AMERICAN **$$**

(Map p58; 10 E 16th St; mains $12-20; ⊙11am-midnight Mon-Fri, 10am-midnight Sat, 10am-11pm Sun) It's all down-home comfort food, though of a generally high quality, like macaroni and cheese, mashed potatoes and fried chicken; the onion ring loaf should be divided by a minimum of four people – who don't suffer from heart disease.

Blossom

VEGAN **$$$**

(Map p58; ☎212-627-1144; 187 Ninth Ave, btwn 21st & 22nd Sts; mains $25-35; ⊙noon-10:30pm Fri, Sat & Sun, 5-10pm Mon-Thu; ☝) A creative and elegant vegan spot, housed in a Chelsea town house, where menu items span the globe and enliven the taste buds. Try the flaky seitan empanada, mojo-marinated tempeh or portobello stuffed with cashew-tahini sauce.

The Highliner

DINER **$$**

(Map p68; 210 Tenth Ave, at 22nd St; mains $12; ⊙11am-11pm) Former space of beloved Empire Diner, this new spot, regardless of the quality of its fancy diner fare, will draw in High Line roving crowds.

Shake Shack

BURGERS **$**

(Map p68; Madison Ave, at E 23rd St; burgers from $4; ⊙11am-11pm) Tourists line up in droves for the hamburgers and shakes at this Madison Square Park counter-window-serving institution.

Chennai Garden

INDIAN **$$**

(Map p68; 129 E 27th St, btwn Park & Lexington Aves; mains $9-15; ⊙noon-10pm) Come for South Indian faves such as paper-thin dosas (rice-flour pancakes) stuffed with spicy mixtures of potatoes and peas, and a range of more expected curries.

Chelsea Market

MARKET **$$**

(Map p68; www.chelseamarket.com; 75 Ninth Ave, btwn W 15th & 16th Sts; ⊙7am-10pm Mon-Sat, 7am-10pm Mon-Sat, 8am-8pm Sun) Will thrill gourmet food fans with its 800ft-long shopping concourse.

MIDTOWN

TOP
CHOICE **Kum Gang San**

KOREAN **$$**

(Map p68; 49 W 32nd St, at Broadway; mains $12-26; ⊙24hr) One of Koreatown's larger and more extravagant restaurants, Kum Gang San serves standout barbecue – you do it at your table. As in most Korean restaurants, the side dishes that accompany the mains are delicious meals in themselves. Large, loud and kind of kitschy, it's still a reliable introduction to Koreatown.

Pietrasanta

ITALIAN **$$**

(Map p68; ☎212-265-9471; 683 9th Ave, at 47th St; mains $16-24; ⊙noon-10:30pm Mon-Thu & Sun, to midnight Fri & Sat) The best of the many Italian restaurants within several blocks from here, Pietrasanta welcomes as many neighborhood regulars as tourists in the city for a night of theater. The pumpkin ravioli is a favorite, as are the hummus and flavored butter spreads.

Café Edison

DELI **$**

(Map p68; 228 W 47th St, btwn Broadway & Eighth Ave; mains from $6; ⊙6am-9:30pm Mon-Sat, to 7:30pm Sun) Where else can you get a bologna sandwich? This landmark New York spot has been in business since the 1930s, serving up American diner classics like grilled cheese, hot corned beef, open-faced turkey sandwiches and cheese blintzes. Cash only.

Ellen's Stardust Diner

DINER **$$**

(Map p68; 1650 Broadway, at 51st St; mains $15; ⊙7am-midnight Mon-Thu, to 1am Fri & Sat, to 11pm Sun) No New Yorker would be caught dead here, but this '50s theme diner/dinner theater is a super-fun place to head after a show. When the talented waitstaff belt out show tunes and pop songs while picking up your checks, you can't help but applaud.

44 & X

MODERN AMERICAN **$$**

(Map p68; 622 Tenth Ave, at W 44th St; mains $16-30; ⊙5:30pm-midnight Mon-Fri, 11:30am-midnight Sat, to 10:30pm Sun) Worth venturing this far west for, this sleek and airy dining room serves a little something for everyone, from macaroni and cheese to grilled braised short ribs.

Mandoo Bar

KOREAN **$$**

(Map p68; 2 W 32nd St, near Fifth Ave; mains $10; ⊙11:30am-11pm) Handmade in the street-side window, the Korean dumplings served at this narrow eatery are a nice change from all the BBQ places on the block.

Mechango Tei

JAPANESE **$$**

(Map p68; 45th St, btwn Lexington & Third Aves; mains $11; ⊙11:30am-11:30pm) Slurp down a bowl of the signature dish at this bona fide noodle house. The photo-heavy menu helps put novices at ease. Another location on 55th St between Fifth and Sixth Aves.

Poseidon Bakery

BAKERY **$**

(Map p68; 629 Ninth Ave, at W 44th St; pastries from $2; ⊙9am-7pm Tue-Sat). Family-owned Greek bakery serving handmade baklava (pastry made with walnuts and almonds) and spanakopita (feta cheese and spinach wrapped in phyllo pastry) are delicious.

Sophie's　　　　　　　　CUBAN $
(Map p68; 21 W 45th St, btwn Fifth & Sixth Ave; mains from $6; ⏱10am-8pm Mon-Fri, to 6pm Sat) Bustling lunchtime spot, beef and oxtail stew, grilled chicken, beans and rice, meat patties to go ($2); seven other locations throughout the city.

Daisy May's BBQ　　　　BARBECUE $$
(Map p68; 626 Eleventh Ave, at 46th St; mains $12; ⏱11am-10pm) A convenient stop on your way to the Intrepid or Hudson River Park and one of the better BBQ places in the city with Memphis-style ribs.

Patsy's　　　　　　　　ITALIAN $$$
(Map p68; 236 W 56th St, btwn Broadway & Eight Ave; mains $23; ⏱noon-9:30pm) Sinatra used to eat at this old-school Italian restaurant.

UPPER WEST SIDE & MORNINGSIDE HEIGHTS

Big Nick's　　　　　　　DINER $
(Map p76; 2175 Broadway at 77th St; mains $8; ⏱24hr) Looking something like the mess hall of a Cold War-era submarine with a menu the size of the NYC phonebook (these still exist), a meal at Big Nick's is a nostalgia-filled trip down a greasy memory lane. That's not to say the food, including the 1lb sumo burger, gyros, hot dogs, quesadillas, ribs, tofu pizza, challah Monte Cristo, to name only a few choices, is not good. It is generally, but that you just don't find places like this any more.

Barney Greengrass　　　　DELI $$
(Map p76; 541 Amsterdam Ave, at W 86th St; mains $8-17; ⏱8:30am-4pm Tue-Fri, to 5pm Sat & Sun) Old-school Upper Westsiders and pilgrims from other neighborhoods crowd this century-old 'sturgeon king' on weekends. It serves a long list of traditional if pricey Jewish delicacies, from bagels and lox to sturgeon scrambled with eggs and onions.

Hungarian Pastry Shop　　BAKERY $
(Map p76; 1030 Amsterdam Ave, btwn W 110th & 111th Sts; pastries $2-4; ⏱7:30am-11:30pm, to 10:30pm Sun) Bring a dog-eared copy of Kierkegaard to blend in with the intensely serious Columbia University students working in front of steaming laptops and cooling coffee. Excellent pastries and cakes are available.

Flor de Mayo　CHINESE, SOUTH AMERICAN $$
(Map p76; 484 Amsterdam Ave, at 83rd St; mains $9-14; ⏱noon-midnight) One of a handful of unpretentious NYC restaurants combining Peruvian and Chinese cuisine. It's somewhat hectic at dinnertime, but it's the place for choosing between egg foo young and *ceviche de pescado*.

UPPER EAST SIDE

Daniel　　　　　　　　FRENCH $$$
(Map p76; ☎212-288-0033; 60 E 65th St, btwn Madison & Park Aves; 3-course prix fixe dinners $105; ⏱Mon-Sat 5:30-11pm) This chichi French palace features floral arrangements and wide-eyed foodies who gawk over plates of peekytoe crab and celery-root salad, foie gras terrine with gala apples and black truffle-crusted lobster – and that's just the first course. There's an all-veggie menu, too.

**Central Park Boathouse
Restaurant**　　　　　　　AMERICAN $$$
(Map p76; ☎212-517-2233; Central Park Lake, enter Fifth Ave, at 72nd St; mains $15-40; ⏱noon-9:30pm) The historic Loeb Boathouse, perched on the shores of the park's lake, is one of the city's more incredible settings for a serene and romantic meal. Food is top-notch, too – reserve early and aim for an outdoor table.

Beyoglu　　　　　　　　TURKISH $$
(Map p76; ☎212-650-0850; 1431 Third Ave at 81st St; mains $15; ⏱noon-10:30pm) A loungey space that's just a short stroll away from the Met, serving traditional small plates, such as yogurt soup, doner kebabs and eggplant puree. Down a shot or two of the traditional, anisette-flavored raki as an after-meal spirit.

Totonno's　　　　　　　ITALIAN $$
(Map p76; 1544 Second Ave; mains $14; ⏱noon-4pm Mon-Fri) The Manhattan branch of a Coney Island classic New York pizza joint.

Nectar Café　　　　　　DINER $$
(Map p76; 1022 Madison Ave at 79th St; mains $13; ⏱6am-9pm) Only a few blocks from several major museums, this standard diner's prices are only justified by its location – but still for this 'hood it's not bad value.

HARLEM

Red Rooster　　　MODERN AMERICAN $$$
(Map p76; ☎212-792-9001; 310 Lenox Ave, near 125th St; mains $14-32; ⏱11:30am-10:30pm) Something of a pioneer, chef Marcus Samuelson's sophisticated uptown venture steps from the 2 or 3 train stop has a downtown bistro vibe. A variety of southern, soul and new American cooking, the kitchen does blackened catfish, meatballs with mashed potatoes and ligonberries and creative sand-

wiches. The front bar area and breakfast nook has pastries, biscuits and coffee.

Amy Ruth's Restaurant
SOUTHERN $$

(Map p76; 113 W 116th St, btwn Malcolm X & Adam Clayton Powell Jr Blvds; mains $10-16; ⊙11:30am-11pm Mon, from 8:30am Tue-Thu & Sun, to 5:30pm Fri & Sat) Tourists flock here for the specialty waffles; choose from sweet (chocolate, strawberry, blueberry, smothered in sautéed apples) or savory (paired with fried chicken, rib-eye or catfish). Smoked ham, chicken and dumplings are favorites as well.

Londel's Supper Club
CAJUN $$

(Map p76; ✆212-234-6114; 2620 Frederick Douglass Blvd; mains $12-24; ⊙11:30am-11pm Tue-Sat, to 5pm Sun) The wall photos of famous patrons are testament to this elegant restaurant's status and popularity. Londel's menu combines Cajun and continental flavors and live jazz Friday and Saturday nights.

BROOKLYN

Of course it's impossible to begin to do justice to Brooklyn's eating options – it's as much a foodie's paradise as Manhattan. Virtually every ethnic cuisine has a significant presence somewhere in this area. As far as neighborhoods close to Manhattan go: Williamsburg is chockablock with eateries, as are Fifth and Seventh Aves in Park Slope. Smith St is 'Restaurant Row' in the Carroll Gardens and Cobble Hill neighborhoods. Atlantic Ave, near Court St, has a number of excellent Middle Eastern restaurants and groceries.

TOP CHOICE Frankies 457
ITALIAN $$

(457 Court St, Carroll Gardens; mains $15; ⊙11am-11pm Sun-Thu, to midnight Fri & Sat) A Carroll Garden's favorite packing in regulars night after night, Frankies feels both homey and romantic. Dark and candlelit at night, it has an attractive backyard garden for warm weather brunches. Small cheese plates, crostinis and veggie side dishes can be shared by the table.

Blue Ribbon Brasserie
SEAFOOD, AMERICAN $$$

(✆718-840-0404; 280 5th Ave, btwn 1st St & Garfield Pl, Park Slope; mains $15-27; ⊙5pm-midnight Mon-Thu & Sun, to 2am Fri & Sat) This restaurant in the heart of Park Slope has something for everyone: an incredible raw bar, pork ribs, matzo-ball soup, paella, fried chicken and chocolate-chip bread pudding. It's open late but doesn't take reservations for parties fewer than six.

Farm on Adderly
MODERN AMERICAN $$

(✆718-287-3101; 1108 Cortelyou Rd, Ditmas Park; dinner mains $18; ⊙11:30am-11pm) This is the sort of farm-to-table place where waiters know the life story of the fish, poultry and meat on your plate – if pressed they might be able to supply names. Dine in the patio out back but whatever you do try the Cascadia cocktail (pear brandy, gin, absinthe, honey and tonic) and the salted chocolate mousse for dessert.

Peter Luger
STEAKHOUSE $$$

(✆718-387-7400; 178 Broadway, Williamsburg; lunch mains $5-20, dinner mains $30-32; ⊙11:45am-9:45pm Mon-Thu, to 10:45pm Fri & Sat, 12:45-9:45pm Sun) The aged porterhouse at this venerable 100-year-old German steakhouse at the foot of the Williamsburg Bridge is often regarded as one of the best steaks in the country. Reservations required and cash and debit cards only.

Tom's Restaurant
DINER $

(782 Washington Ave, at Sterling Ave, Prospect Heights; mains $6; ⊙6am-4pm) Inspiration for the eponymously named Suzanne Vega song, this old-school soda fountain diner's specialty is its variety of pancakes (eg mango walnut). Coffee and cookies are served to those waiting in the line that invariably snakes out the door on weekend mornings.

Bar Tabac
FRENCH $$

(128 Smith St, at Dean, Cobble Hill; mains $15; ⊙11am-2am) No better place for weekend brunch at one of this bistro's sidewalk tables while the jazz band plays inside.

Roberta's
PIZZERIA $$

(261 Moore St, near Bogart, Bushwick; pizzas $14; ⊙noon-midnight) Worth the trip to a gritty Bushwick block, this pizzeria does Neapolitan pies with creative topping combinations.

Yemen Café
MIDDLE EASTERN $$

(176 Atlantic Ave, Brooklyn Heights; mains $9; ⊙10am-10:30pm) This welcoming authentic Yemeni cafeteria-style place is above a barbershop.

🍷 Drinking

Watering holes come in many forms in this city: sleek lounges, cozy pubs and booze-soaked dives – no smoke, though, thanks to city law. The majority are open to 4am, though closing (and opening) times do vary. Here's a highly selective sampling.

DOWNTOWN

Decibel
SAKE BAR

(Map p62; 240 E 9th St; ⊙6pm-3am) Just nod your head and sip. Hearing is a challenge even when you're crammed in a corner touching knees. Nevertheless, this cozy and dark downstairs hideaway feels like an authentic Tokyo dive, from the sake varieties to the delicious snacks.

KGB Bar
BAR

(Map p62; ✆212-505-3360; 85 E 4th St, at 2nd Ave; ⊙7pm-3:30am) The East Village's own grungy Algonquin roundtable has been drawing literary types to its regular readings since the early 1990s. Even when there's no artist in residence the heavily worn wood bar is good for kicking back.

Mayahuel
TEQUILA BAR

(Map p62; 304 E 6th St, at Second Ave; ⊙6pm-2am) About as far from your typical spring break tequila bar as you can get – more like the cellar of a monastery. Devotees of the fermented agave can seriously indulge themselves experimenting with dozens of varieties (all cocktails $13).

McSorley's Old Ale House
BAR

(Map p62; 15 E 7th St, btwn Second & Third Aves; ⊙11am-1am) Around since 1854 – it has the cobwebs and sawdust floors to prove it McSorley's feels far removed from the East Village veneer of cool: you're more likely to drink with firefighters, Wall St refugees and a few tourists.

Fat Cat
BAR

(Map p62; 75 Christopher St, at Seventh Ave; cover up to $3; ⊙2pm-5am Mon-Thu, from noon Fri-Sun; ☎) Evocative of a fantasy fraternity basement, this gaming paradise has Ping-Pong, billiards, chess, even shuffleboard, cheap beer and live music every night.

Fresh Salt
BAR

(Map p58; 146 Beekman St; ⊙10am-4am) Only steps from a beautiful pier on the East River, and close to the financial district, Fresh Salt manages to avoid the boisterous feel of the after-work Wall St crowd. This small and rustic bar has board games (Boggle, chess etc) and a great hummus plate.

Mulberry Project
COCKTAIL BAR

(Map p62; ✆646-448-4536; 149 Mulberry St, near Grand St; ⊙7pm-4am) This Little Italy bar has a 2nd floor outdoor patio, a great place to sip a custom-crafted cocktail made by mixologists – not bartenders.

Henrietta Hudson
LESBIAN

(Map p62; 438 Hudson St, at Morton St; ⊙5pm-4am Wed-Sun, to 2am Mon & Tue) All sorts of cute young women storm this long-running lesbian spot, a former pool-and-pint joint that's now a sleek lounge with varied DJs.

Welcome to the Johnsons
BAR

(Map p62; 123 Rivington St; ⊙3pm-4am) Looking like a set from *The Brady Bunch* or *That '70s Show,* this Lower East Side theme bar can be enjoyed with or without irony. Wash down the free Doritos with a Jack Daniel's and root beer.

Schiller's Liquor Bar
BAR

(Map p62; 131 Rivington St, at Norfolk St; ⊙11am-1am Mon-Wed, to 2am Thu, to 3am Fri, 10am-3am Sat, 10am-1am Sun) This trendy spot serves cocktails as delicious as its food (mains $12 to $25).

Ulysses
COCKTAIL BAR

(Map p58; 58 Stone St; ⊙11am-4am) Big with old-school financial types, Ulysses is an Irish-modern hybrid, with a long bar and a kitchen serving oysters and sandwiches and picnic tables out on cobbled Stone St.

MIDTOWN

Russian Vodka Room
BAR
TOP
CHOICE

(Map p68; 265 W 52nd St, btwn 8th Ave & Broadway; ⊙4pm-2am) Actual Russians aren't uncommon at this swanky and welcoming bar. The lighting is dark and the corner booths intimate, but more importantly the dozens of flavored vodkas, from cranberry to horseradish, are fun to experiment with. Eastern European dishes such as latkes, smoked fish and schnitzel can tame a rumbling stomach.

Rudy's Bar & Grill
DIVE BAR

(Map p68; 627 Ninth Ave; ⊙8am-4am) This semi-dive bar – neighborhood newcomers and professional types rub beer-soaked shoulders with hard-core drinkers – is a good place for cheap beer and even greasy hot dogs, if you don't mind not being able to hear yourself think. A backyard garden with makeshift furniture and artificial turf is open in the summer months.

Morrell Wine Bar & Café
WINE BAR

(Map p68; 1 Rockefeller Plaza, W 48th St, btwn Fifth & Sixth Aves; ⊙11:30am-midnight Mon-Sat, noon-6pm Sun) The list of vinos at this pioneering New York City wine bar is over 2000 long, with a whopping 150 available by the glass. And the airy, split-level room, right across from the famous skating rink, is equally as intoxicating.

Therapy
GAY

(Map p68; 348 W 52nd St, btwn Eighth & Ninth Aves; ⊙5pm-2am, to 4am Fri & Sat) Multileveled, airy and sleekly contemporary, Therapy is a long-standing gay Hell's Kitchen hot spot. Theme nights abound, from stand-up comedy to musical shows.

Réunion Surf Bar
BAR

(Map p68; 357 W 44th St at Ninth Ave; ⊙5:30pm-2am, to 4am Thu-Sat) Swanky Tiki-themed bar and restaurant serving delicious French South Pacific cuisine, eg banana-leaf-steamed mahi mahi.

Mé Bar
ROOFTOP BAR

(Map p68; 14th fl, 17 W 32nd St near Fifth Ave; ⊙5:30pm-2am Sun-Tue, to 4am Wed-Sat) The small rooftop deck of the budget La Quinta hotel in Koreatown feels like a secret, though one with great views of the Empire State Building.

On the Rocks
COCKTAIL BAR

(Map p68; 696 Tenth Ave, btwn 48th & 49th Sts; ⊙5pm-4am) Whisky nerds will delight at this cubbyhole-sized space.

Rum House
COCKTAIL BAR

(Map p68; 228 W 47th St, btwn Broadway & Eighth Ave; ⊙11am-4am) Once a no-frills regulars bar in the Edison Hotel, now renovated with wood-paneling, leather banquets and mixologists.

UPTOWN

79th Street Boat Basin
BAR

(Map p76; W 79th St, in Riverside Park; ⊙noon-11pm) A covered, open-sided party spot under the ancient arches of a park overpass, this is an Upper West Side favorite once spring hits. Order a pitcher, some snacks and enjoy the sunset view over the Hudson River.

Subway Inn
BAR

(Map p76; 143 E 60th St, btwn Lexington & Third Aves; ⊙11am-4am) An old-geezer watering hole with cheap drinks and loads of authenticity. The entire scene – from the vintage neon sign outside to the well-worn red booths and old guys huddled inside – is truly reminiscent of bygone days.

Lenox Lounge
COCKTAIL BAR

(Map p76; ☎212-427-0253; 288 Malcolm X Blvd (Lenox Ave), btwn 124th & 125th Sts; ⊙noon-4am) The classic art-deco Lounge, which once hosted the likes of Billie Holiday and Miles

Davis and is an old favorite of local jazz cats, is still going strong. The luxe Zebra Room in back is a beautiful and historic setting to hear top-flight musicians. Cover charge can be pricey.

Bemelman's Bar
BAR

(Map p76; Carlyle Hotel, 35 E 76th St, at Madison Ave; ⊙11am-1am) Waiters wear white jackets, a baby grand piano is always being played and Ludwig Bemelman's *Madeline* murals surround you. It's a classic spot for a serious cocktail – the kind of place that could easily turn up in a Woody Allen film.

Ding Dong Lounge
BAR

(Map p76; 929 Columbus Ave, btwn 105th & 106th Sts; ⊙4pm-4am) This former crack den turned punk bar is a small slice of downtown for streams of Columbia students and nearby hostel guests. There's a pool table and some cuckoo clocks, and the DJ dips into kept-real R&B.

BROOKLYN

Brooklyn Social
BAR

(335 Smith St, at Carroll St, Carroll Gardens; ⊙5pm-2am, to 4am Fri & Sat) Typical of this genre of bar, signage is a no-no and discretion an asset. Young neighborhood types cozy up to the bar or one of the barely lit corner lounges.

Iona Bar
BAR

(180 Grand St; ⊙1pm-4am) Hipsters infiltrate this Scottish-Irish bar on weekend nights; other nights it's a less American Apparel crowd enjoying happy hour (beer $4). Meat and veggie pies play second fiddle in summer when the barbecue in the backyard garden turns out hamburgers and hot dogs.

Turkey's Nest
BAR

(94 Bedford Ave, at N 12th St; ⊙10am-4am) The eclectic crowd at the Nest in Williamsburg loves the huge Styrofoam containers of cheap beer and cocktails served in plastic cups. Watch the Yankees or the Mets or play the hunting video game in the back. Whatever you do, wear a hazmat suit when you use the toilet.

Union Hall
BAR

(702 Union St, at Fifth Ave; ⊙4pm-4am, from noon Sat & Sun) In Park Slope, head to this creatively idiosyncratic bar – leather chairs à la a snooty London social club, walls lined with bookshelves and two bocce courts, plus live music downstairs and an outdoor patio.

Weather Up　　　BAR

(589 Vanderbilt Ave; ⊙7pm-3am, closed Mon) No signage marks the exterior of this dark and shadowy Prospect Heights cocktail-centric speakeasy-like neighborhood favorite.

Radegast Hall & Biergarten　　　BEER HALL

(113 N 3rd St; ⊙4pm-4am) Rowdy Williamsburg spot with excellent veal schnitzel.

Henry Public　　　BAR

(329 Henry St, at Atlantic Ave; ⊙5pm-2am, Fri to 4am, from noon Sat & Sun) Part of the Brooklyn saloon-style revival, Henry Public has a handsome zinc-tipped bar and excellent turkey-leg sandwich.

☆ Entertainment

Those with unlimited fuel and appetites can gorge themselves on a seemingly infinite number of entertainments – from Broadway shows to performance art in someone's Brooklyn living room, and everything in between. *New York* magazine and the weekend editions of the *New York Times* are great guides for what's on once you arrive.

NIGHTCLUBS

Most nightclubs are open from 10pm to 4am but some open earlier.

SOBs　　　CLUB

(Map p62; ☑212-243-4940; www.sobs.com; 204 Varick St, at W Houston) Brazilian bossa nova, samba and other Latin vibes draw a mix of those who know how to move smooth and sensually and those who like to watch.

Santos Party House　　　CLUB

(Map p58; ☑212-584-5492; www.santospartyhouse; 96 Lafayette St; cover $5-15) Shaggy rocker Andrew WK created this bi-level 8000-sq-ft cavernous bare-bones dance club. Devoted to good times and good vibes, this place requires that you check your attitude at the door – funk to electronica, and WK spins some nights.

Beauty & Essex　　　CLUB

(Map p62; ☑212-614-0146; www.beautyandessex. com; 146 Essex St) This newcomer's glamour is concealed behind a pawnshop front space and memories of its former incarnation as a furniture store. Now, there's 10,000-sq-ft of sleek lounge space filled with a mix of well-dressed twenty- and thirty-somethings.

Sullivan Room　　　CLUB

(Map p62; ☑212-505-1703; www.sullivanroom.com; 218 Sullivan St, btwn Bleecker & W 3rd Sts; ⊙Wed-

Sun) An eclectic downtown mix and top-flight DJs make Sullivan Room one of the best places to dance the night away. There's nothing pretentious – no need for high heels or cheesy leather jackets.

Cielo　　　CLUB

(Map p62; ☑212-645-5700; www.cieloclub.com; 18 Little W 12th St, btwn Ninth Ave & Washington St; cover $5-20) Known for its intimate space and kick-ass sound system, this space-age-looking Meatpacking District staple packs in a fashionable, multiculti crowd nightly for its blend of tribal, old-school house and soulful grooves.

Pacha　　　CLUB

(Map p68; ☑212-209-7500; www.pachanyc.com; 618 W 46th St, btwn Eleventh Ave & West Side Hwy) A massive and spectacular place, this is 30,000 sq ft and four levels of glowing, sleek spaces and cozy seating nooks that rise up to surround the main dance-floor atrium. Big-name DJs are always on tap.

M2 Ultra Lounge　　　CLUB

(Map p68; ☑212-629-9000; www.m2ultralounge. com; 530 W 28th St, btwn Tenth & Eleventh Aves; admission $20; ⊙Thu-Sat) This megaclub will blow out your ear drums and your wallet – drinks are expensive ($15). In some ways this is the classic big club – long lines, opulent booths, bottle service and sexy go-go dancers.

LIVE MUSIC

Maybe less indie-dominated than music scenes in Austin or Seattle, NYC does of course still boast an enormous number of venues varying greatly in size, crowd and genre of music.

Le Poisson Rouge　　　LIVE MUSIC

(Map p62; ☑212-796-0741; www.lepoissonrouge. com; 158 Bleecker St, at Sullivan St) This Bleecker St basement club is one of the premier venues for experimental contemporary, from classical to indie rock to electro-acoustic.

Joe's Pub　　　LIVE MUSIC

(Map p62; ☑212-967-7555; www.joespub.com; Public Theater, 425 Lafayette St, btwn Astor Pl & E 4th St) Part cabaret theater, part rock and new-indie venue, this small and lovely supper club has hosts a wonderful variety of styles, voices and talent.

BB King Blues Club & Grill　　　LIVE MUSIC

(Map p68; ☑212-997-4144; www.bbkingblues.com; 237 W 42nd St) In the heart of Times Square

JAZZ

Second only to New Orleans, Harlem was an early home to a flourishing jazz scene and one of its principal beating hearts. The neighborhood fostered greats like Duke Ellington, Charlie Parker, John Coltrane and Thelonius Monk. From bebop to free improvisation, in classic art-deco clubs and at intimate jam sessions, Harlem and other important venues scattered throughout the city, especially around the Village, continue to foster old-timers and talented newcomers alike. Tune in to **WKCR** (89.9 FM) for jazz and especially from 8:20am to 9:30am Monday through Friday for Phil Schaap's 27-year-old program in which he dazzles listeners with his encyclopedic knowledge and appreciation for the art form. The **National Jazz Museum in Harlem** (☎212-348-8300; www.jazzmuseumin harlem.org; 104 E 126th St, Suite 2D; admission free; ◷10am-4pm Mon-Fri) has a collection of books, CDs and photos for passionate fans.

Smalls (Map p62; ☎212-252-5091; www.smallsjazzclub.com; 183 W 4th St; cover $20) is a subterranean jazz dungeon that rivals the world-famous **Village Vanguard** (Map p62; ☎212-255-4037; www.villagevanguard.com; 178 Seventh Ave, at W 11th St) in terms of sheer talent. Of course, the latter has hosted every major star of the past 50 years; there's a two-drink minimum and a serious no-talking policy.

Heading uptown, **Dizzy's Club Coca-Cola: Jazz at the Lincoln Center** (Map p76; ☎212-258-9595; www.jalc.org/dccc; 5th fl, Time Warner Bldg, Broadway, at W 60th St), one of Lincoln Center's three jazz venues, has stunning views overlooking Central Park and nightly shows featuring top lineups. Further north on the Upper West Side, check out the **Smoke Jazz & Supper Club-Lounge** (Map p76; ☎212-864-6662; www.smokejazz.com; 2751 Broadway, btwn W 105th & 106th Sts), which gets crowded on weekends.

offers old-school blues along with rock, folk and reggae acts.

Barge Music CLASSICAL MUSIC
(☎718-624-2083; www.bargemusic.org; Fulton Ferry Landing) Exceptionally talented classical musicians perform in this intimate space, a decommissioned barge docked under the Brooklyn Bridge.

Highline Ballroom LIVE MUSIC
(Map p68; ☎212-414-5994; www.highlineballroom. com; 431 W 16th St, btwn Ninth & Tenth Aves) A classy Chelsea venue with an eclectic lineup, from Mandy Moore to Moby.

Beacon Theatre CONCERT VENUE
(Map p76; ☎212-465-6500; www.beacontheatre. com; 2124 Broadway, btwn W 74th & 75th Sts) This Upper West Side venue hosts big acts for folks who want to see shows in an environment that's more intimate than that of a big concert arena.

Madison Square Garden CONCERT VENUE
(Map p68; ☎212-465-5800; www.thegarden.com; Seventh Ave, btwn W 31st & W 33rd Sts) For the biggest acts like Green Day and Andrea Bocelli, this place draws stadium-sized crowds.

Radio City Music Hall CONCERT VENUE
(Map p68; ☎212-247-4777; www.radiocity.com; Sixth Ave, at W 50th St) In the middle of Mid-town, the architecturally grand concert hall hosts the likes of Barry Manilow and Cirque de Soleil and of course the famous Christmas spectacular.

Mercury Lounge LIVE MUSIC
(Map p62; ☎212-260-4700; www.mercurylounge nyc.com; 217 E Houston St)

Delancey Lounge LIVE MUSIC
(Map p62; ☎212-254-9920; www.thedelancey. com; 168 Delancey St, at Clinton St) Great indie-band bookings.

Webster Hall CONCERT VENUE
(Map p62; ☎212-353-1600; www.websterhall.com; 125 E 11th St, at 3rd Ave)

Irving Plaza CONCERT VENUE
(Map p68; ☎212-777-6800; www.irvingplaza.com; 17 Irving Pl)

Terminal 5 CONCERT VENUE
(Map p68; ☎212-260-4700; www.terminal5nyc. com; 610 W 56th St, at 11th Ave) All book big and quality acts.

Southpaw LIVE MUSIC
(☎718-230-0236; www.spsounds.com; 125 5th Ave) In Park Slope, Brooklyn, head here for a nightly lineup.

THEATER

In general, 'Broadway' productions are staged in the lavish, early-20th-century theaters surrounding Times Square. You'll choose your theater based on its production – *The Book of Mormon, Spider-Man: Turn off the Dark, Lion King*. Evening performances begin at 8pm.

'Off Broadway' simply refers to shows performed in smaller spaces (500 seats or fewer), which is why you'll find many just around the corner from Broadway venues, as well as elsewhere in town. 'Off-off Broadway' events include readings, experimental and cutting-edge performances and improvisations held in spaces with fewer than 100 seats; these venues are primarily downtown. Some of the world's best theater happens in these more intimate venues before moving to Broadway. Some distinguished theaters include:

Public Theater THEATER
(Map p62; ☏212-539-8500; www.publictheater. org; 425 Lafayette St, btwn Astor Pl & E 4th St)

St Ann's Warehouse THEATER
(☏718-254-8779; www.stannswarehouse.org; 38 Water St)

PS 122 THEATER
(Map p62; ☏212-477-5288; www.ps122.org; 150 First Ave, at E 9th St)

Playwrights Horizon THEATER
(Map p68; ☏212-564-1235; www.playwrightshori zon.org; 416 W 42nd St, btwn Ninth & Tenth Aves)

New York Theater Workshop THEATER
(Map p62; ☏212-780-9037; www.nytw.org; 79 E 4th St, btwn Second & Third Aves)

Ontological Theater THEATER
(Map p62; ☏212-420-1916; www.ontological.com; 131 E 10th St)

Choose from current shows by checking print publications, or a website such as **Theater Mania** (www.theatermania.com). You can purchase tickets through **Telecharge** (☏212-239-6200; www.telecharge.com) and **Ticketmaster** (www.ticketmaster.com) for standard ticket sales, or **TKTS ticket booths** (www.tkts.com; Downtown Map p58; Front St, at John St, South St Seaport; ☉11am-6pm; Midtown Map p68; under the red steps, 47th St, at Broadway; ☉3-8pm) for same-day tickets to Broadway and off-Broadway musicals at up to 50% off regular prices.

COMEDY

From lowbrow prop comics to experimental conceptual humor, there's a venue for every taste and budget. More-established ones push the alcohol with drink minimums.

Upright Citizens Brigade Theatre COMEDY
(Map p68; ☏212-366-9176; www.ucbtheatre. com; 307 W 26th St) Improv venue featuring well-known, emerging and probably-won't-emerge comedians in this small basement theater nightly.

Village Lantern COMEDY
(Map p62; ☏212-260-7993; www.villagelantern. com; 167 Bleecker St) Nightly alternative comedy underneath a bar of the same name.

Caroline's on Broadway COMEDY
(Map p68; ☏212-956-0101; www.carolines.com; 1626 Broadway) One of the best-known places in the city, and host to the biggest names on the circuit.

Gotham Comedy Club COMEDY
(Map p68; ☏212-367-9000; www.gothamcom edyclub.com; 208 W 23rd St, btwn Seventh & Eighth Aves) A plush venue featuring mostly mainstream-style comedy.

Stand-Up New York COMEDY
(Map p76; ☏212-595-0850; www.standupny.com; 236 W 78th St; tickets $5-12) Gets surprise appearances from star comedians.

CINEMAS

Long lines in the evenings and on weekends are the norm. It's recommended that you call and buy your tickets in advance (unless it's midweek, midday or for a film that's been out for months already). Most cinemas are handled either through **Movie Fone** (☏212-777-3456; www.moviefone.com) or **Fandango** (www.fandango.com). You'll have to pay an extra $1.25 more per ticket, but it's worth it. Large chain theaters with stadium seating are scattered throughout the city including several in the Times Square and Union Square areas. During the summer months free outdoor screenings blossom throughout the city on rooftops and park spaces.

IFC Center CINEMA
(Map p62; ☏212-924-7771; www.ifccenter.com; 323 Sixth Ave, at 3rd St) Formerly the Waverly, is a three-screen art-house cinema showing new indies, cult classics and foreign films – and the popcorn is organic.

Landmark Sunshine Cinema CINEMA
(Map p62; ☏212-358-7709; www.landmarkthe atres.com; 143 E Houston St) Housed in a former Yiddish theater; shows first-run indies.

Anthology Film Archives CINEMA
(Map p62; ☏212-505-5181; www.anthologyfil marchives.org; 32 Second Ave, at E 2nd St) Film studies majors head to this schoolhouse-

like building, for independent and avant-garde cinema.

Brooklyn Academy of Music Rose Cinemas CINEMA

(BAM; ☑718-636-4100; www.bam.org; 30 Lafayette Ave) In Brooklyn, and comfortable as well as popular for its new-release indies and special festival screenings.

Film Forum CINEMA

(Map p62; ☑212-627-2035; www.filmforum.org; 209 W Houston St) The long and narrow theaters can't dent cineastes' love for this institution showing revivals, classics and documentaries.

Ziegfeld CINEMA

(Map p68; ☑212-307-1862; www.clearviewcinemas.com; 141 W 54th St) A regal old-school holdout with over a thousand seats, crystal chandeliers and Hollywood blockbusters on its single screen.

PERFORMING ARTS

World-class performers and venues mean the city is a year-round mecca for arts-lovers.

Every top-end genre has a stage at the massive Lincoln Center complex. Its Avery Fisher Hall is the showplace of the New York Philharmonic, while recently redesigned Alice Tully Hall houses the Chamber Music Society of Lincoln Center, and the New York State Theater is home to the New York City Ballet (the New York City Opera decided to decamp in 2011). Great drama is found at both the Mitzi E Newhouse and Vivian Beaumont theaters; and frequent concerts at the Juilliard School. But the biggest draw is the Metropolitan Opera House, home to the Metropolitan Opera and American Ballet Theater.

Carnegie Hall CONCERT VENUE

(Map p68; ☑212-247-7800; www.carnegiehall.org; 154 W 57th St, at Seventh Ave) Since 1891, the historic Carnegie Hall has hosted performances by the likes of Tchaikovsky, Mahler and Prokofiev and more recently Stevie Wonder, Sting and Tony Bennett. Today its three halls host visiting philharmonics, the New York Pops orchestra and various world-class musicians (mostly closed in July and August). Before or after a performance, check out the recently remade Rose Museum for a history of the institution.

Symphony Space PERFORMING ARTS

(Map p76; ☑212-864-5400; www.symphonyspace.org; 2537 Broadway, at W 95th St) A multigenre

space with several facilities in one. This Upper West Side gem is home to many performance series as well as theater, cabaret, comedy, dance and world-music concerts throughout the week.

Brooklyn Academy of Music PERFORMING ARTS

(BAM; ☑718-636-4100; www.bam.org; 30 Lafayette Ave) Sort of a Brooklyn version of the Lincoln Center – in its all-inclusiveness rather than its vibe, which is much edgier – the spectacular academy also hosts everything from modern dance to opera, cutting-edge theater and music concerts.

SPORTS

In 2009 the city's two major-league baseball teams, the uber-successful New York Yankees (www.yankees.com), who play at Yankee Stadium (Map p56; cnr 161st St & River Ave, the Bronx), and the more historically beleaguered New York Mets (www.mets.com), who play at Citi Field (Map p56; 126th St, at Roosevelt Ave, Flushing, Queens), inaugurated long-anticipated brand-new stadiums. For less-grand settings but no-less-pleasant outings, check out the minor-league Staten Island Yankees (www.siyanks.com) at Richmond County Bank Ballpark (Map p56; 75 Richmond Terrace, Staten Island) or the Brooklyn Cyclones (www.brooklyncyclones.com) at KeySpan Park (Map p56; cnr Surf Ave & W 17th St, Coney Island).

For basketball, you can get courtside with the NBA's New York Knicks (www.nba.com/knicks) at Madison Square Garden (btwn Seventh Ave & 33rd St), called the 'mecca of basketball'; the Knicks have been rejuvenated by the acquisition of stars Carmelo Anthony and Amar'e Stoudemire. The cross-river rivals, New Jersey Nets (www.nba.com/nets) are scheduled to move to the Atlantic Yards, a large complex in downtown Brooklyn some time in 2012. Also playing at Madison Square Garden, the women's WNBA league team New York Liberty (www.wnba.com/liberty) provides a more laid-back time.

New York City's NFL (pro-football) teams, the Giants (www.giants.com) and Jets (www.newyorkjets.com), share the New Meadowlands Stadium in East Rutherford, New Jersey.

🔒 Shopping

While chain stores have proliferated, turning once-idiosyncratic blocks into versions of generic strip malls, NYC is still the best American city for shopping. It's not unusual for shops – especially downtown boutiques – to stay open until 10pm or 11pm.

DOWNTOWN

Lower Manhattan is where you'll find across-the-board bargains, as well as more of the small, stylish boutiques. Downtown's coolest offerings are in NoLita (just east of SoHo), the East Village and the Lower East Side. SoHo has more expensive though no less fashionable stores, while Broadway from Union Sq to Canal St is lined with big retailers like H&M and Urban Outfitters, as well as dozens of jeans and shoe stores – the museum-like Prada NYC flagship is also here. The streets of Chinatown are filled with knock-off designer handbags, jewelry, perfume and watches.

For coveted designer labels stroll through the Meatpacking District around 14th St and Ninth Ave.

TOP CHOICE **Strand Bookstore**   BOOKS
(Map p62; 828 Broadway, at E 12th St; ☺9:30am-10:30pm Mon-Sat, from 11am Sun) The city's preeminent bibliophile warehouse, selling new and used books.

Century 21   DEPARTMENT STORE
(Map p58; 22 Cortlandt St, at Church St) A four-level department store loved by New Yorkers of every income, is shorthand for designer bargains.

J&R Music & Computer World   ELECTRONICS
(Map p58; 15-23 Park Row) Every electronic need, especially computer and camera related, can be satisfied here. Takes up a full city block.

Eastern Mountain Sports   OUTDOOR EQUIPMENT
(Map p62; 530 Broadway, at Spring St) A high-quality outdoor emporium outfitting every imaginable adventure and the staff is extremely knowledgeable and friendly.

Bloomingdale's SoHo   DEPARTMENT STORE
(Map p62; 504 Broadway) The smaller, younger outpost of the Upper East Side legend focuses on designer fashion.

Topshop   WOMEN'S CLOTHING
(Map p62; 478 Broadway, at Broome St) The trendy British superstore for women; where to go for shiny spandex and disco tops.

Uniqlo   CLOTHING
(Map p62; 546 Broadway) Japanese retailer with moderately priced men's and women's fashions.

McNally Jackson Books   BOOKS

(Map p62; ☎212-274-1160; 52 Prince St; ☺10am-10pm Mon-Sat, to 9pm Sun) A NoLita refuge containing a nice cafe and regular author readings.

Idlewild Books   BOOKSTORE
(Map p68; ☎212-414-8888; 12 W 19th St; ☺11:30am-8pm Mon-Fri, noon-7pm Sat & Sun) Near Union Square. Fiction and nonfiction are uniquely organized by country and regions of the world.

Apple Store   ELECTRONICS
(Map p58; 401 W Fourteenth St, at Ninth Ave) Pilgrims flock here for shiny new gadgets.

MIDTOWN & UPTOWN

Midtown's Fifth Ave and the Upper East Side's Madison Ave have the famous high-end fashion and clothing by international designers. Times Square has many super-sized stores, though they're all chains. Chelsea has more unique boutiques, though it too has been colonized by banks, drugstores and big-box retailers.

Tiffany & Co   JEWELRY
(Map p68; 727 Fifth Ave) Has become synonymous with NYC luxury. This famous jeweler, with the trademark clock-hoisting Atlas over the door, carries fine diamond rings, watches, necklaces etc, as well as crystal and glassware.

Macy's   DEPARTMENT STORE
(Map p68; 151 W 34th St) The grande dame of midtown department stores sells everything from jeans to kitchen appliances.

Bloomingdale's   DEPARTMENT STORE
(Map p76; 1000 3rd Ave, at E 59th St) Uptown, the sprawling, overwhelming Bloomingdale's is akin to the Metropolitan Museum of Art for shoppers.

Barney's Co-op   CLOTHING
(Downtown Map p68; 236 W 18th St; Uptown Map p76; 2151 Broadway) Offers hipper, less-expensive versions of high-end fashion.

ℹ Information

Internet Access

There are many wi-fi access hot spots around the city, including Lincoln Center uptown, Bryant Park in midtown, Union Square downtown and the entire Dumbo neighborhood in Brooklyn; summer 2011 plans call for a total of 20 NYC parks to offer free wi-fi in the near future. The hourly fee for surfing the web at internet cafes ranges from $3 to $12. If you have a laptop, you won't have to go far to find a coffee shop or restaurant with free wi-fi and of course there are more than 200 Starbucks and a handful of Barnes & Nobles with free wi-fi as well.

Cybercafe Times Square (250 W 49th St, btwn Broadway & 8th Ave; per 30min $7; ⊙8am-11pm Mon-Fri, from 11am Sat & Sun)

Netzone Internet Cafe (28 W 32nd St, 5th fl; per hr $5; ⊙9am-5am)

New York Public Library (⌨212-930-0800; www.nypl.org/branch/local; E 42nd St, at Fifth Ave) Offers free half-hour internet access; more than 80 other local branches also have free access.

Media

Daily News (www.nydailynews.com) A daily tabloid, leans toward the sensational – archrivals of the *New York Post*.

New York (www.newyorkmagazine.com) Weekly featuring nationally oriented reporting as well as NYC-centric news and listings for the arts and culture-oriented reader.

New York Post (www.nypost.com) Famous for spicy headlines, celebrity scandal-laden Page Six and good sports coverage.

New York Times (www.nytimes.com) The 'Gray Lady' is the newspaper of record for readers throughout the US and much of the English-speaking world.

NY1 An excellent source of local news, this is the city's all-day news station on Time Warner cable's Channel 1.

Onion (www.onion.com) Weekly fake news and satire website; the print edition has real and extensive listings for goings-on about town, especially comedy.

Village Voice (www.villagevoice.com) The weekly tabloid is still a good resource for events, clubs and music listings.

WFUV-90.7FM The area's best alternative-music radio station is run by the Bronx's Fordham University.

WNYC 820am or 93.9FM National Public Radio's local affiliate.

Medical Services

Big retail pharmacies are everywhere and some stay open late.

Interchurch Center Medical Office (⌨212-870-3053; www.interchurch-center.org; 475 Riverside Dr) Upper West Side office open to general public. Recommended for reasonably priced travel immunizations; offers expert consultation as well.

New York University Langone Medical Center (⌨212-263-7300; 550 First Ave; ⊙24hr)

Travel MD (⌨212-737-1212; www.travelmd.com) A 24-hour house-call service for travelers and residents.

Telephone

There are thousands of pay telephones lining the streets, but many are out of order. Manhattan's telephone area codes are ⌨212, ⌨646, ⌨917 and the newest ⌨929; in the four other boroughs they're ⌨718 and ⌨347. You must dial 1 + the area code, even if you're calling from a borough that uses the same one you're calling to.

The city's wonderful ⌨311 service allows you to dial from anywhere within the city for info or help with any city agency, from the parking-ticket bureau to the noise complaint department.

Tourist Information

New York City & Company (Map p68; ⌨212-484-1222; www.nycgo.com; 810 Seventh Ave, at 53rd St; ⊙8:30am-6pm Mon-Fri, 9am-5pm Sat & Sun) The official information service of the Convention & Visitors Bureau, it has helpful multilingual staff. Other branches include Chinatown (Map p58; cnr Canal, Walker & Baxter Sts; ⊙10am-6pm Mon-Fri, to 7pm Sat); Harlem (Map p76; 144 W 125th St btwn Adam Clayton Powell & Malcolm X Blvds; ⊙noon-6pm Mon-Fri, 10am-6pm Sat & Sun); Lower Manhattan (Map p58; City Hall Park at Broadway; ⊙9am-6pm Mon-Fri, 10am-5pm Sat & Sun); Times Square (Map p68; 1560 Broadway, btwn 46th & 47th Sts; ⊙8am-8pm Mon-Sun).

ⓘ Getting There & Away

Air

Three major airports serve New York City. The biggest is **John F Kennedy International Airport** (JFK; www.panynj.gov/aviation/jfk frame), in the borough of Queens, which is also home to **La Guardia Airport** (LGA; www.panynj.gov/avia tion/lgaframe). **Newark Liberty International Airport** (EWR; www.panynj.com), across the Hudson River in Newark, NJ, is another option. While using online booking websites, search 'NYC' rather than a specific airport, which will allow most sites to search all three spots at once. **Long Island MacArthur Airport** (ISP; www.ma carthurairport.com), in Islip, is a money-saving (though time-consuming) alternative, but may make sense if a visit to the Hamptons or other parts of Long Island are in your plans.

Bus

The massive and confusing **Port Authority Bus Terminal** (Map p68; 625 Eighth Ave, btwn 40th & 42nd St) is the gateway for buses into and out of Manhattan. **Short Line** (www.shortlinebus.com) runs numerous buses to towns in northern New Jersey and upstate New York, while **New Jersey Transit** (www.njtransit.state.nj.us) buses serve all of New Jersey.

A number of comfortable and reliably safe bus companies with midtown locations, including **Bolt Bus** (www.boltbus.com) and **Megabus** (www.megabus.com), link NYC to Philadelphia ($10, two hours), Boston ($25, four hours 15 minutes) and Washington, DC ($25, four hours 30 minutes); most offer free wi-fi. Those bus companies running from Chinatown have seriously spotty safety records.

Car & Motorcycle

See p635 for information about vehicle rentals. Note that renting a car in the city is expensive, starting at about $75 a day for a midsize car – before extra charges like the 13.25% tax and various insurance costs.

Ferry

Seastreak (www.seastreak.com; round-trip $43) to Sandy Hook, New Jersey and **New York Waterway** (www.nywaterway.com) leave from Pier 11 on the East River near Wall St and the World Financial Center on the Hudson for Hoboken, Jersey City and other destinations.

Train

Penn Station (Map p68; 33rd St, btwn Seventh & Eighth Aves), not to be confused with the Penn Station in Newark, NJ, is the departure point for all **Amtrak** (www.amtrak.com) trains, including the speedy Acela Express service to Boston (three hours 45 minutes) and Washington, DC (two hours 52 minutes). All fares and durations vary based on the day of the week and the time of day you want to travel. Also arriving into Penn Station (NYC), as well as points in Brooklyn and Queens, is the **Long Island Rail Road** (LIRR; www.mta.nyc.ny.us/lirr), which serves several hundred-thousand commuters each day. **New Jersey Transit** (www.njtransit.com) also operates trains from Penn Station (NYC), with services to the suburbs and the Jersey Shore. Another option for getting into New Jersey, but strictly to points north of the city such as Hoboken and Newark, is the **New Jersey PATH** (www.pathrail.com), which runs trains on a separate-fare system ($1.75) along the length of Sixth Ave, with stops at 34th, 23rd, 14th, 9th and Christopher Sts, and the reopened World Trade Center station.

The only train line that still departs from Grand Central Station, Park Ave at 42nd St, is the **Metro-North Railroad** (www.mnr.org), which serves the northern city suburbs, Connecticut and locations throughout the Hudson Valley.

ⓘ Getting Around

To & From the Airport

All major airports have on-site car-rental agencies. It's a hassle to drive into NYC, though, and many folks take taxis, shelling out the $45 taxi flat rate (plus toll and tip) from JFK and Newark or a metered fare of about $35 to Midtown from La Guardia.

A cheaper and pretty easy option to/from JFK is the **AirTrain** ($5 one way), which connects to subway lines into the city ($2.25; coming from the city, take the Far Rockaway-bound A train) or to the LIRR (about $7 one way) at Jamaica Station in Queens (this is probably the quickest route to Penn Station in the city).

To/from Newark, the AirTrain links all terminals to a New Jersey Transit train station, which connects to Penn Station in NYC ($12.50 one way combined NJ Transit/Airtrain ticket).

For La Guardia, a reliable option to consider if you allow plenty of time is the M60 bus ($2.25), which heads to/from Manhattan across 125th St in Harlem and makes stops along Broadway on the Upper West Side.

All three airports are also served by express buses ($12 to $15) and shuttle vans ($20); such companies include the **New York Airport Service Express Bus** (www.nyairportservice.com), which leaves every 15 minutes for Port Authority, Penn Station (NYC) and Grand Central Station; and **Super Shuttle Manhattan** (www.supershuttle.com), which picks you (and others) up anywhere, on demand, with a reservation.

Car & Motorcycle

Even for the most spiritually centered, road rage is an inevitable byproduct of driving within the city. Traffic is a perpetual problem and topic of conversation.

If you are driving out or in, however, know that the worst part is joining the masses as they try to squeeze through tunnels and over bridges to traverse the various waterways that surround Manhattan. Be aware of local laws, such as the fact that you can't make a right on red (like you can in the rest of the state) and also the fact that every other street is one way.

Ferry

An East River ferry service (one way $4, every 20 minutes) connecting spots in Brooklyn (Greenpoint, North and South Williamsburg and Dumbo) and Queens (Long Island City) with Manhattan (Pier 11 at Wall St and E 34th St) was inaugurated in June 2011.

Public Transportation

The **Metropolitan Transport Authority** (MTA; www.mta.info) runs both the subway and bus systems. Depending on the train line, time of day and whether the door slams in your face or not, New York City's 100-year-old round-the-clock subway system (per ride $2.25) is your best friend or worst enemy. The 656-mile system can be intimidating at first, but regardless of its faults it's an incredible resource and achievement, linking the most disparate neighborhoods in a continually pulsating network. Maps should be available for the taking at every stop. To board, you must purchase a MetroCard, available at windows and self-serve machines, which accept change, dollars or credit/debit cards; purchasing many rides at once works out cheaper per trip.

If you're not in a big hurry, consider taking the bus (per ride $2.25). You get to see the world go by, they run 24/7 and they're easy to navigate – going crosstown at all the major street byways (14th, 23rd, 34th, 42nd, 72nd Sts and all the others that are two-way roads) and uptown or downtown, depending which avenue they serve. You can pay with a MetroCard or exact change but not bills. Transfers from one line to another are free, as are transfers to or from the subway.

Taxi

The classic NYC yellow cab is no longer a boxy gas-guzzling behemoth but rather a streamlined hybrid model, outfitted with mini-TVs and credit-card machines. No matter the make or year of the car, however, expect a herky-jerky, somewhat out-of-control ride. Current fares are $2.50 for the initial charge (first one-fifth mile), 40¢ each additional one-fifth mile, as well as per 60 seconds of being stopped in traffic, $1 peak surcharge (weekdays 4pm to 8pm), and 50¢ night surcharge (8pm to 6am daily). Tips are expected to be 10% to 15%; minivan cabs can hold five to six passengers. You can only hail a cab that has a lit light on its roof. Also know that it can be difficult to score a taxi in the rain, at rush hour and at around 4pm, when many drivers end their shifts.

Pedicabs – human-powered taxis, basically cycle rickshaws – roam around Central Park South and other heavily touristy areas. Rides cost around $10 to $20 but fares are negotiable.

NEW YORK STATE

There's upstate and downstate and never the twain shall meet. The two have about as much in common as NYC's Upper East Side and the Bronx. And yet everyone shares the same governor and dysfunctional legislature in the capital, Albany. While this incompatibility produces legislative gridlock and downright operatic drama, it's a blessing for those who cherish quiet and pastoral idylls as much as Lower East Side bars and the subway. Defined largely by its inland waterways – the Hudson River, the 524-mile Erie Canal connecting Albany to Buffalo, and the St Lawrence River – New York stretches to the Canadian border at world-famous Niagara Falls and under-the-radar Thousand Islands. Buffalo is a cheap foodies' paradise and wine aficionados can pick their favorite vintage from around the state, but especially in the Finger Lakes region close to the col-

lege town of Ithaca. From wilderness trails with backcountry camping to small-town Americana and miles and miles of sandy beaches, from the historic, grand estates and artists colonies in the Hudson Valley and Catskills to the rugged and remote Adirondacks, it's easy to understand why so many people leave the city, never to return.

❶ Information

New York State Office of Parks, Recreation and Historic Preservation (☎518-474-0456, 800-456-2267; www.nysparks.com) Camping,

NEW YORK FACTS

» **Nicknames** Empire State, Excelsior State, Knickerbocker State

» **Population** 19.5 million

» **Area** 47,214 sq miles

» **Capital city** Albany (population 94,000)

» **Other cities** Buffalo (population 261,000)

» **Sales tax** 4%, plus additional county and state taxes (total approximately 8%)

» **Birthplace of** Poet Walt Whitman (1819–92), President Theodore Roosevelt (1858–1919), President Franklin D Roosevelt (1882–1945), first lady Eleanor Roosevelt (1884–1962), painter Edward Hopper (1882–1967), movie star Humphrey Bogart (1899–1957), comic Lucille Ball (1911–89), filmmaker Woody Allen (b 1935), actor Tom Cruise (b 1962), pro athlete Michael Jordan (b 1963), pop star Jennifer Lopez (b 1969)

» **Home of** Six Nations of the Iroquois Confederacy, first US cattle ranch (1747, in Montauk, Long Island), US women's suffrage movement (1872), Erie Canal (1825)

» **Politics** popular Democratic governor Mario Cuomo, NYC overwhelmingly Democratic, upstate more conservative

» **Famous for** Niagara Falls (half of it), the Hamptons, Cornell University, Hudson River

» **Unusual river** Genesee River is one of the few rivers in the world that flows south–north, from south central New York into Lake Ontario at Rochester

» **Driving distances** NYC to Albany 160 miles, NYC to Buffalo 375 miles lodging and general info on all state parks. Reservations can be made up to nine months in advance.

511 New York: Traffic, Travel & Transit Info (www.511ny.org) Weather advisories, road information and more.

Uncork New York (☑585-394-3620; www.newyorkwines.org) One-stop shop for statewide wine info.

Long Island

Private-school blazers, nightmare commutes, strip malls colonized by national chains, cookie-cutter suburbia, moneyed resorts, windswept dunes and magnificent beaches – and those accents. Long Island, a long peninsula contiguous with the boroughs of Brooklyn and Queens, has all of these things, which explains its somewhat complicated reputation. The site of small European whaling and fishing ports from as early as 1640, Levittown, just 25 miles east of Manhattan in Nassau County, is where builders first perfected the art of mass-producing homes. But visions of suburban dystopia aside, Long Island has wide ocean and bay beaches, important historic sites, renowned vineyards, rural regions and of course the Hamptons, in all their luxuriously sunbaked glory.

NORTH SHORE

Outside the suburban town of Port Washington, Sands Point Preserve (☑516-571-7900; www.sandspointpreserve.org; 127 Middleneck Rd; admission per car $5, free Thu; ◎9am-4:30pm) includes forested trails and a beautiful sandy bayfront beach worth a stroll; it's also home to the 1923 Falaise (admission $6; ◎tours hourly noon-3pm Thu-Sun Jun-Oct), one of the few remaining Gold Coast mansions and now a museum. East of there is the bucolic town of Oyster Bay, home to Sagamore Hill (☑516-922-4788; www.nps.gov/sahi; adult/child $5/free; ◎10am-4pm Wed-Sun), where Theodore Roosevelt vacationed during his presidency. Spring and summer months mean long waits for guided tours. A nature trail leading from behind the excellent museum (admission free) ends at a picturesque waterfront beach.

SOUTH SHORE

Despite the periodic roar of over-flying jets, Long Beach, the closest beach to the city and most accessible by train, has a main town strip with ice-cream shops, bars and eateries, a lively surfers' scene and pale trendy city types mixing with suntanned locals.

On summer weekends the mob scene on the 6-mile stretch of pretty Jones Beach is a microcosm of the city's diversity, attracting surfers, wild city folk, local teens, nudists, staid families, gay and lesbian people and plenty of old-timers. The Long Island Rail Road (LIRR) service to Wantagh has a bus connection to Jones Beach.

Further east, just off the southern shore, is a separate barrier island. Fire Island includes Fire Island National Seashore (☑631-289-4810; www.nps.gov) and several summer-only villages accessible by ferry from Long Island. The Fire Island Pines and Cherry Grove (both car-free) comprise a historic, gay bacchanalia that attracts men and women in droves from New York City, while villages on the west end cater to straight singles and families. There are limited places to stay, and booking in advance is strongly advised (check www.fireisland.com for accommodations information). Beach camping is allowed in Watch Hill (☑631-567-6664; www.watchhillfi.com; campsites $25; ◎early May-late Oct), though mosquitoes can be fierce and reservations are a must. At the western end of Fire Island, Robert Moses State Park is the only spot accessible by car. Fire Island Ferries (☑631-665-3600; www.fireislandferries.com) runs services to Fire Island beaches and the national seashore; the terminals are close to LIRR stations at Bayshore, Sayville and Patchogue (round-trip adult/child $17/7.50, May to November).

THE HAMPTONS

Attitudes about the Hamptons are about as varied as the number of Maseratis and Land Rovers cruising the perfectly landscaped streets, however no amount of attitudinizing can detract from the sheer beauty of the beaches and what's left of the picturesque farms and woodland. If you can bury the envy, a pleasurable day of sightseeing can be had simply driving past the homes of the extravagantly wealthy, ranging from cutting-edge modernist to faux-castle monstrosities. However, many summertime residents are partying the weekends away in much more modest group rentals and at the revolving doors of clubs. While each Hampton is not geographically far from every other, traffic can be a nightmare. Check out long-time

Hamptons resident and publisher of local paper Dan Rattiner's *In the Hamptons* for stories of the area's famous characters.

Southampton

Though the village of Southampton appears blemish-free as if it has been Botoxed, it gets a face-lift at night when raucous clubgoers let their hair down. Its beaches – only Coopers Beach (per day $40) and Road D (free) offer parking to non-residents May 31 to Sep 15 – are sweeping and gorgeous, and the **Parrish Art Museum** (☑631-283-2118; www.parrishart.org; 25 Jobs Lane; adult/child $5/3; ☺11am-5pm, daily Jun–mid-Sep) is an impressive regional institution. At the edge of the village is a small Native American reservation, home to the Shinnecock Nation, which runs a tiny **museum** (☑631-287-4923; 45 Montauk Hwy; adult/child $5/3; ☺11am-4pm Thu-Sat, from noon Sun); a decades-long effort to build a large casino on Shinnecock land continues to make its way through a jumble of legal and other obstacles. For a quick and reasonable meal try **Golden Pear** (99 Main St; sandwiches $9; ☺7:30am- 5pm), which serves delicious soups, salads and wraps.

Bridgehampton & Sag Harbor

Moving east, Bridgehampton has a more modest-looking drag, but has its fair share of trendy boutiques and fine restaurants. The modest low-slung **Enclave Inn** (☑631-537-2900; www.enclaveinnn.com; 2668 Montauk Hwy; r from $99; ❀❂❂), just a few blocks from the heart of the village, is one of the better value accommodation options; there are four other locations elsewhere in the Hamptons. Old-fashioned diner **Candy Kitchen** (☑646-537-9885; Main St; mains $5-12; ☺7am-6pm) has a luncheonette counter serving filling breakfasts, burgers and sandwiches.

Seven miles north, on Peconic Bay, is the lovely old whaling town of Sag Harbor; ferries to Shelter Island leave a few miles north of here. Check out its **Whaling & Historical Museum** (☑631-725-0770; www.sagharborwhalingmuseum.org; adult/child $5/1; ☺10am-5pm May-Oct), or simply stroll up and down its narrow, Cape Cod–like streets. Get gourmet sustenance at **Provisions** (☑631-725-3636; cnr Bay & Division Sts; sandwiches $9; ☺8:30am-8pm), a natural foods market with delicious take-out wraps, burritos and sandwiches.

East Hampton

Don't be fooled by the oh-so-casual-looking summer attire, heavy on pastels and sweaters tied around the neck – the sunglasses alone are probably equal to a month's rent. Some of the highest profile boldface celebrities have homes here. Catch readings, theater and art exhibits at **Guild Hall** (☑631-324-0806; www.guildhall.org; 158 Main St). East of town on the way to Bridgehampton is the **Townline BBQ** (3593 Montauk Hwy; mains $9; ☺11:30am-9pm Sun, Mon & Thu, to 10pm Fri & Sat), a down-to-earth roadside restaurant churning out smoky ribs and barbecue sandwiches. Just to the west toward Amagansett is **La Fondita** (74 Montauk Hwy; mains $9; ☺11:30am-8pm Wed, Thu & Sun, to 9pm Fri & Sat), the place to go for reasonably priced Mexican fare. Nightclubs come and go with the seasons. A word to the wise: strike the phrase 'bottle service' from your vocabulary.

Montauk & Around

More Jersey Shore, less polo club, Montauk is the humble stepsister of the Hamptons, though its beaches are equally beautiful. There's a slew of relatively reasonable restaurants and a louder bar scene. At the very eastern, wind-whipped tip of the South Fork is **Montauk Point State Park**, with its impressive, 1796 **Montauk Point Lighthouse** (www.montauklighthouse.com; adult/child $9/4; ☺10:30am-5:30pm, hours vary), the fourth oldest still-active lighthouse in the US. You can camp a few miles west of town at the dune-swept **Hither Hills State Park** (☑631-668-2554; www.nysparks.com; New York residents/nonresidents Mon-Fri $28/56, higher prices Sat & Sun; ☺Apr-Nov), right on the beach; just reserve early during summer months. Several miles to the north is the Montauk harbor, with dockside restaurants and hundreds of boats in the marinas.

You'll find a string of standard motels near the entrance to the town beach, including the **Ocean Resort Inn** (☑631-668-2300; www.oceanresortinn.com; 96 S Emerson Ave; r $105-165; ❀❂). A few miles west, just across the street from the beach, is **Sunrise Guesthouse** (☑631-668-7286; www.sunrisebnb.com; 681 Old Montauk Hwy; r $115-145; ❀), a modest and comfortable B&B.

Two great places to wind down the day (from May to October) with drinks and hearty, fresh seafood are the roadside restaurants **Clam Bar** (2025 Montauk Hwy; mains 7-$22; ☺noon-8pm) and **Lobster Roll** (1980 Montauk Hwy; mains $11-26; ☺11:30am-9:30pm) aka 'Lunch', now in its fifth decade, both on the highway between Amagansett and Montauk.

Mainly, the North Fork is known for its unspoiled farmland and wineries – there are close to 30 vineyards, clustered mainly around the towns of Jamesport, Cutchogue and Southold – and the Long Island Wine Council (☑631-722-2220; www.liwines.com) provides details of the local wine trail, which runs along Rte 25 north of Peconic Bay. One of the nicer outdoor settings for a tasting is the Peconic Bay Winery (☑631-734-7361; www.peconicbaywinery.com; 31320 Main Rd/Rte 25, Cutchogue); this also means it's popular with bus and limo-loads of partiers. Beforehand, stop at popular Love Lane Kitchen (240 Love Lane; mains $10; ⊙7am-9:30pm, to 6pm Mon-Tue) in Matituck for a meal, especially weekend brunch.

The main North Fork town and the place for ferries to Shelter Island, Greenport is a charming laid-back place lined with restaurants and cafes, including family-owned Claudio's Clam Bar (111 Main St; mains $15; ⊙11:30am-9pm) with a wraparound deck perched over the marina. Or grab sandwiches and a cupcake at Butta' Cakes Café (119 Main St; sandwiches $9; ⊙8am-9:30pm) for a picnic at the Harbor Front Park where you can take a spin on the historic carousel.

Between the North and South Forks, , accessible by ferry from North Haven to the south and Greenport to the north (vehicle and driver $9, 10 minutes, every 15 to 20 minutes), is a low-key microcosm of beautiful Hamptons real estate and the Mashomack Nature Preserve (☑631-749-1001; www.nature.org/mashomack; ⊙9am-5pm, closed Tue except Jul & Aug) covering over 2000 acres of the southern part of the island. It's a great spot for hiking or kayaking (no cycling).

On Shelter Island, just down the road from Crescent Beach and nestled on a prime piece of property surrounded by woods fronting the bay, Pridwin Beach Hotel & Cottages (☑631-749-0476; www. pridwin.com; r & cottages from $159-199; P❋☀) has standard hotel rooms as well as private water-view cottages, some in high-designer style.

❶ Getting There & Around

The most direct driving route is along the I-495, aka the LIE (Long Island Expwy), though be sure to avoid rush hour, when it's commuter hell. Once in the Hamptons, there is one main road to the end, Montauk Hwy. The Long Island Rail Road (LIRR; www.mta.nyc.ny.us/lirr) serves all regions of Long Island, including the Hamptons ($25 one way, two hours 45 minutes), from Penn Station (NYC), Brooklyn and Queens. The Hampton Jitney (www.hamptonjitney.com; one way Tue-Thu $26, Fri-Mon $30) and Hampton Luxury Liner (www.hamptonluxuryliner.com; one way $40) bus services connect Manhattan's midtown and Upper East Side to various Hamptons villages; the former also has services to/ from various spots in Brooklyn.

Hudson Valley

Immediately north of New York City, green becomes the dominant color and the vistas of the Hudson River and the mountains breathe life into your urban-weary body. The region was home to the Hudson River School of painting in the 19th century and its history is preserved in the many grand estates and picturesque villages. The Lower Valley and Middle Valley are more populated and suburban, while the Upper Valley has a rural feel, with hills leading into the Catskills mountain region. For area-wide information, check out the Hudson Valley Network (www.hvnet.com).

LOWER HUDSON VALLEY

A pristine forested wilderness with miles of hiking trails is available just 40 miles north of New York City; (☑845-786-2701) covers 72 sq miles and offers swimming, hiking and camping; adjacent Bear Mountain State Park (☑845-786-2701; ⊙8am-dusk) offers great views from its 1305ft peak, with the Manhattan skyline looming beyond the river and surrounding greenery; and there's a restaurant and lodging at the inn on Hessian Lake. In both parks there are several scenic roads snaking their way past secluded lakes with gorgeous vistas.

Several magnificent homes and gardens can be found near Tarrytown and Sleepy Hollow, on the east side of the Hudson. Kykuit, one of the properties of the Rockefeller family, has an impressive array of Asian and European artwork and immaculately kept gardens with breathtaking views. Lyndhurst is the estate of railroad tycoon Jay Gould and Sunnyside is the home of author Washington Irving. Go to the Historic Hudson Valley (www.hudsonvalley.org) website for info on these and other historic attractions.

West of Rte 9W and 50 miles north of New York City, the Storm King Art Center (☑845-534-3115; www.stormking.org; Old Pleasant

Rd, Mountainville; adult/child $12/free; ⊙10am-5:30pm Wed-Sun Apr-Nov) is a 500-acre outdoor sculpture park with rolling hills that showcases stunning avant-garde sculpture by well-known artists; a free tram gives tours of the grounds. Nearby **West Point** (☑845-938-2638; ⊙9am-5pm), open to visitors on **guided tours** (☑845-446-4724; www.westpointtours.com; adult/child $12/9), was a strategic fort before becoming the US Military Academy in 1802. Not far from here, the large, strip mall filled town of Newburgh is the site of **Washington's Headquarters State Historic Site** (☑845-562-1195; Liberty St, at Washington St; donations accepted; ⊙10am-5pm Wed-Sat, from 1pm Sun, Apr-Oct), General George's longest-lasting base during the Revolutionary War; there's a museum, galleries and maps.

Across the river, near the town of Cold Spring, the **Hudson Valley Shakespeare Festival** (☑845-265-9575; www.hvshakespeare.org) takes place between mid-June and early September, staging impressive open-air productions at the Boscobel estate, a magnificent piece of property.

At Beacon, a fairly nondescript town east of Rte 9W, fashionable regulars of the international art scene stop for **Dia Beacon** (☑845-440-0100; www.diaart.org; adult/child $10/free; ⊙11am-6pm Thu-Mon mid-Apr–mid-Oct, call for other hr), which features a renowned collection from 1960 to the present, and enormous sculptures and installation pieces.

MIDDLE & UPPER HUDSON VALLEY

On the western side of the Hudson is **New Paltz**, home of a campus of the State University of New York, natural food stores and a liberal ecofriendly vibe. In the distance behind the town the ridge of the Shawangunk (Shon-gum or just the 'Gunks') mountains rises more than 2000ft above sea level. More than two-dozen miles of nature trails and some of the best rock climbing in the Eastern US is found in the **Mohonk Mountain Preserve** (☑845-255-0919; www.mohonkpreserve.org; day pass for hikers/climbers & cyclists $12/17). Nearby **Minnewaska State Park Preserve** has 12,000 acres of wild landscape, the centerpiece of which is a usually ice-cold mountain lake. Contact **Alpine Adventures** (☑877-486-5769; www.alpineendeavors.com) for climbing instruction and equipment.

The iconic **Mohonk Mountain House** (☑845-255-1000; www.mohonk.com; 1000 Mountain Rest Rd; r $320-2500; ✴❄✸) looks like it's straight out of a fairy tale: a rustic castle

perched magnificently over a dark lake. It's an all-inclusive resort where guests can gorge on elaborate five-course meals, stroll through gardens, hike miles of trails, canoe, swim etc. A luxury spa center is there to work out the kinks. Nonovernight guests can visit the grounds (adult/child per day $25/20, less on weekdays) – well worth the price of admission.

On the eastern side of the river is **Hudson** – a beautiful town with a hip, gay-friendly community of artists, writers and performers who fled the city. Warren St, the main roadway through town, is lined with antiques shops, high-end furniture stores, galleries and cafes. A historic Greek Revival home c 1830, the **Union Street Guest House** (☑518-828-0958; www.unionstreetguesthouse; 345-349 Union St; r from $125; ✴❄) has been transformed into a cozy boutique-style inn.

Further south is **Rhinebeck**, with a charming main street, inns, farms and wineries. There's also an **Aerodrome Museum** (☑845-752-3200; www.oldrhinebeck.org; ⊙10am-5pm mid-Jun–mid-Oct) and the destination bistro, worth the trip in itself, **Terrapin** (☑845-876-3330; 6426 Montgomery St; lunch sandwiches $7, dinner mains from $19; ⊙11:30am-11:30pm). Another good choice is the **Bread Alone Bakery** (45 E Market St; mains $9; ⊙7am-7pm, 8am-3pm), which serves lunch specialties like a brisket panini and spinach and feta quiche.

Just south of Rhinebeck is **Hyde Park**, long associated with the Roosevelts, a prominent family since the 19th century. The estate of 1520 acres, formerly a working farm, includes the **Franklin D Roosevelt Library & Museum** (☑800-337-8474; www.fdrlibrary.marist.edu; 511 Albany Post Rd/Rte 9; admission $14; ⊙9am-6pm May-Oct, to 5pm Nov-Apr), which details important achievements in FDR's presidency; a visit usually includes a guided tour of FDR's lifelong home where he delivered his fireside chats. First Lady Eleanor Roosevelt's peaceful cottage, **Val-Kill** (☑877-444-6777; www.nps.gov/elro; admission $8; ⊙9am-5pm), was her retreat from Hyde Park, FDR's mother and FDR himself. Across the street from the entrance to the library and museum is the **Hyde Park Drive-In Movie Theater** (☑845-229-4738; 4114 Albany Post Rd/Rte 9). Just north of here is the 54-room **Vanderbilt Mansion** (☑877-559-6777; www.nps.gov/vama; Rte 9; admission $8; ⊙9am-5pm), a Gilded Age spectacle of lavish beaux-arts design; nearly all of the original furnishings imported from European castles and villas remain in this country house – the smallest of any of the Vanderbilt family's! Hudson River views are best from the gardens and the Bard Rock trail on the property.

Hyde Park's famous **Culinary Institute of America** (☑845-471-6608; www.ciachef. edu; 1964 Campus Dr) trains future chefs and can satisfy absolutely anyone's gastronomic cravings; the **Apple Pie Café** (mains $10; ⏱7:30am-5pm), one of the student-staffed eateries looks out onto a tranquil courtyard and serves up gourmet sandwiches as well as specialty pastries (these go fast and the selection is slim at the end of the day). If you're between tours in Hyde Park, the **Eveready Diner** (4189 Albany Post Rd/Rte 9; mains $10; ⏱5am-1am Sun-Thu, 24hr Fri & Sat), a modernized version of the classic soda fountain restaurant might be more convenient.

A little further south of here is **Poughkeepsie** (puh-*kip*-see), the largest town on the Hudson's east bank famous for **Vassar**, a private liberal-arts college that until 1969 only admitted women. Worth a stroll for its breathtaking views is the **Walkway Over the Hudson** (www.walkway.org; ⏱7am-sunset); formerly the Highland-Poughkeepsie railroad bridge and since 2009 the world's longest pedestrian bridge and the state's newest park. Cheap motel chains are clustered along Rte 9, south of the Mid-Hudson Bridge, but try the **Copper Penny Inn** (☑845-452-3045; www.copperpennyinn.com; 2406 Hackensack Rd; r incl breakfast $140-230; ❋), a charming and cheerful B&B set on 12 wooded acres.

Catskills

The introduction of fine cuisine and cute boutiques has yet to overwhelm the pastoral atmosphere and small-town charm of the Catskills. For some out-of-staters this bucolic region of undulating, forest-covered mountains and picturesque farmland is still synonymous with Borscht-belt family resorts. However, that era is long past, and after some economically tough times the Catskills, though having a lower profile than the Hamptons, have become a popular choice for sophisticated city dwellers seeking second-home getaways.

WOODSTOCK & AROUND
Shorthand for free love, free expression and the political ferment of the 1960s, world-famous **Woodstock** today still wears its counterculture tie-dye in the form of healing centers, art galleries, cafes and an eclectic mix of aging hippies and young Phish-fan types. The famous 1969 Woodstock music festival, though, actually occurred in Bethel, a town over 40 miles southwest. Overlooking Woodstock's town square, actually in front of the bus stop, is the **Village Green B&B** (☑845-679-0313; 12 Tinker St; r incl breakfast $135; ❋🐾), a three-story Victorian with comfortable rooms. Housed in an elegantly-restored farmhouse half a mile southeast of the town square, **Cucina** (☑845-679-9800; 109 Mill Hill Rd; mains $18; ⏱5am-late, from 11am Sat & Sun) does sophisticated seasonal Italian fare and thin crust pizzas.

Saugerties, just 7 miles east of Woodstock, is not nearly as quaint and feels by comparison like the big city, but the **Saugerties Lighthouse** (☑845-247-0656; www.saugertieslighthouse.com; r incl breakfast $200; ⏱Thu-Sun, closed Feb) offers a truly romantic and unique place to lay your head. The picturesque 1869 landmark is located on a small island in the Esopus Creek, accessible by boat or more commonly by a half-mile-long trail from the parking lot. Rooms are booked far in advance but a walk to the lighthouse is highly recommended regardless.

Having a car is near essential in these parts. **Adirondack Trailways** (www.trailways ny.com) operates daily buses from NYC to Kingston (one way $25, two hours), the Catskills' gateway town, as well as to Catskills and Woodstock (one way $27, two hours 30 minutes). Buses leave from NYC's Port Authority. The commuter rail line **Metro-North** (www.mta.info/mnr) makes stops through the Lower and Middle Hudson Valleys.

Finger Lakes Region

A bird's-eye view of this region of rolling hills and 11 long narrow lakes – the eponymous fingers – reveals an outdoor paradise stretching all the way from Albany to far-western New York. Of course there's boating, fishing, cycling, hiking and cross-country skiing, but this is also the state's premier wine-growing region, with more than 65 vineyards, enough for the most discerning oenophile.

One sign that you've crossed into the Catskills is when the unending asphalt gives way to dense greenery crowding the snaking roadway as you exit the I-87 and turn onto Rte 28. As you drive through the heart of the region, the vistas open up and the mountains (around 35 peaks are above 3500ft) take on stunning coloring depending on the season and time of day. Esopus Creek winds its way through the area and **Ashokan Reservoir** is a nice place for a walk or drive.

Emerson Spa Resort (☑877-688-2828; www.emersonresort.com; 5340 Rte 28, Mt Tremper; r at lodge/inn from $159/199; ❄@⚲≋) offers a full-service base for Catskills adventures whatever time of year. From luxurious Asian-inspired suites to rustic-chic rooms in the log-cabin-style lodge, Emerson aims to please; staff can help arrange trips from skiing to kayaking. The Phoenix restaurant (mains $15 to $30) is probably the best in the region and the Catamount, popular with locals, has pub fare (mains $10) including burgers and BBQ ribs and live music and dancing Monday nights. The world's largest kaleidoscope and kaleidoscope boutique, selling sculpture quality pieces, is attached, as well as a coffee-sandwich shop.

Only a few miles further west is the one-lane town of **Phoenicia**. It's a pleasant place to stop for a meal and a tube – **Town Tinker Tube Rental** (☑845-688-5553; www.towntinker.com; 10 Bridge St; tubes per day $15) can hook you up for repeated forays down the Esopus rapids. The refreshing water of Pine Hill Lake at nearby **Belleayre Beach** (☑845-254-5600; www.belleayre.com; ⛟) is the summertime place to cool off (or ski in the winter). Continuing on Rte 28 takes you past the town of Fleischmann's, where you can stop for the night at the **River Run B&B** (☑845-254-4884; www.riverrunbedandbreakfast.com; 882 Main St; r from $89-135; ❄@⚲), a professionally run Victorian inn.

In nearby Arkville, you can take a scenic ride on the historic **Delaware & Ulster Rail Line** (☑845-586-3877; www.durr.org; Hwy 28; adult/child $12/7; ⚘11am & 2pm, Sat & Sun Jun-Nov, additional trips Thu & Fri Jul-Sep; ⛟). In the winter, skiers should head further north, where Rtes 23 and 23A lead you to **Hunter Mountain Ski Bowl** (☑518-263-4223; www.huntermtn.com), a year-round resort with challenging runs and a 1600ft vertical drop.

From here you can carry on to the **Roxbury** (☑607-326-7200; www.theroxburymotel.com; 2258 County Hwy 41; r $100-335; ❄⚲), in the tiny village of the same name, a wonderfully creative gem of a place with luxuriously designed and whimsically named rooms, each inspired by a particular '60s- or '70s-era TV show; a spa is attached and a cool cocktail lounge is across the street (open Wednesday to Sunday).

West of Roxbury is the 26-mile-long **Catskill Scenic Trail** (a good map is available at www.catskillsscenictrail.org), a mostly flat path built on top of a former rail bed, ideal for cycling, hiking and cross-country skiing in the winter. For rougher hikes through dense forest, the **Utsayantha Trail System** intersects at several points around the town of Stamford.

ITHACA & AROUND

An idyllic home for college students and older generations of hippies who cherish elements of the traditional collegiate lifestyle – laid-back vibe, cafe poetry readings, art-house cinemas, green quads, good eats – Ithaca is perched above Cayuga Lake. Besides being a destination in itself, it is also a convenient halfway point between New York City and Niagara Falls. For tourist information, head to the **Visit Ithaca Information Center** (☑607-272-1313; www.visitithaca.com; 904 E Shore Dr; ⚘9am-5pm Mon-Fri, from 10am Sat).

Founded in 1865, **Cornell University** boasts a lovely campus, mixing traditional and contemporary architecture, and sits high on a hill overlooking the picturesque town below. The modern **Herbert F Johnson Museum of Fine Art** (☑607-255-6464; www.museum.cornell.edu; University Ave; admission free; ⚘10am-5pm Tue-Sun), designed by IM Pei, has a major Asian collection, plus pre-Columbian, American and European exhibits. Just east of the center of the campus is **Cornell Plantations** (☑607-255-2400; www.cornellplantations.org; Plantations Rd; admission free; ⚘dawn-dusk), an expertly curated herb and flower garden, arboretum. Kids can go interactive-wild at the extremely hands-on **Sciencenter** (✆607-272-0600; www.sciencecenter.org; 601 First St; adult/child $7/5; ◎10am-5pm Tue-Sat, from noon Sun; ☒). On several weekends from July through August Tony Simons, a professor at Cornell's School of Hotel Administration turns his attention to teaching beginners how to **firewalk** (www.ithacafirewalks.com; per person $75) – in the very least it's an exercise in motivation.

The area around Ithaca is known for its waterfalls, gorges and gorgeous parks. However, downtown has its very own, **Cascadilla Gorge**, starting several blocks from Ithaca Commons and ending, after a steep and stunning vertical climb, at the Performing Arts Center of Cornell. Eight miles north on Rte 89, the spectacular **Taughannock Falls** spills 215ft into the steep gorge below; **Taughannock Falls State Park** (✆607-387-6739; www.taughannock.com; Rte 89) has two major hiking trails, craggy gorges, tent-trailer sites and cabins. **Buttermilk Falls Park** (✆summer 607-273-5761, winter 607-273-3440; Rte 13) has a popular swimming hole at the foot of the falls, as does **Robert Treman Park** (✆607-273-3440; 105 Enfield Falls Rd), a few miles further out of town. **Filmore Glen Park** (✆315-497-0130; 1686 Rte 38) 20 miles to the northeast of Ithaca outside the town of Moravia offers more wooded hiking trails.

Dozens of wineries line the shores of Cayuga Lake, Lake Seneca and Lake Keuka. Two recommended Cayuga Lake wineries are **Sheldrake Point** (✆607-532-9401; www.sheldrakepoint.com; 7448 County Rd), which has lake views and award-winning whites and **Americana Vineyards** (✆607-387-6801; www.americanavineyards.com; 4367 E Covert Rd) whose **Crystal Lake Café** (mains $11; ◎noon-8pm Thu-Sun) farm-to-table menu is highly recommended by locals. Also on Rte 89 near the village of Interlaken is the **Creamery** (◎11am-8pm), a roadside restaurant that in addition to conventional ice-cream sundaes serves buzz-inducing wine-infused sorbet ($4).

Around 44 miles to the southwest is the charming town of Corning, home to Corning Glass Works and the hugely popular **Corning Museum of Glass** (✆800-732-6845; www.cmog.org; adult/child $14/free; ◎9am-8pm; ☒). The massive complex is home to fascinating exhibits on glassmaking arts, complete with demonstrations and interactive items for kids.

🛏 Sleeping

TOP CHOICE / **William Henry**

Miller Inn   B&B $$
(✆607-256-4553; www.millerinn.com; 303 N Aurora St, Ithaca; r incl breakfast $115-215; ☒☒☒) Gracious and grand, only a few steps from the commons, is a completely restored historic home with luxuriously designed rooms – three have Jacuzzis – and a gourmet breakfast.

Inn on Columbia   INN $$
(✆607-272-0204; www.columbiabb.com; 228 Columbia St, Ithaca; d $150; ☒☒) Also recommended; a modern, contemporary home on a quiet residential street.

Climbing Vine Cottage   HUT $$
(✆607-564-7410; www.climbingvinecottage.com; 257 Piper Rd, Newfield; d $150; ☒☒) Rather a fully furnished yurt with mod-cons in a beautifully landscaped garden setting off Rte 34 south of Ithaca.

Buttonwood Grove Winery   CABIN $$
(✆607-869-9760; www.buttonwoodgrove.com; 5986 Rte 89; r $135) Has four fully furnished log cabins nestled in the hills above Lake Cayuga (open April to December); free wine tasting included.

🍴 Eating

A half-dozen restaurants, including Japanese, Middle Eastern, Mexican and Spanish tapas, with outdoor seating line North Aurora St between East State and East Seneca Sts at the east end of the Commons. Relatively upscale **Mercato** (108 N Aurora St; mains $20; ◎5-9pm Mon-Thu, to 10pm Fri & Sat) is one of the best. **Ithaca's Farmers Market** (Third St; www.ithacamarket.com; ◎Apr-Dec) is considered one of the region's best; local wines and cheeses are highlights; check the website for operating hours.

Glenwood Pines   BURGERS $
(burgers $5; ◎11am-9:30pm Sun-Thu, to 10:30pm Fri & Sat) According to locals in the know this modest roadside restaurant, overlooking Lake Cayuga on Rte 89 and 4 miles north of Ithaca, serves the best burger.

Moosewood Restaurant   VEGETARIAN $$
(215 N Cayuga St; mains $8-18; ◎11:30am-8:30pm) Famous for its creative and constantly changing vegetarian menu and recipe books by founder Mollie Katzen.

Yerba Maté Factor Café & Juice Bar   SANDWICHES $
(143 The Commons; mains $8; ◎9am-9pm Mon-Thu, to 3pm Fri, from noon Sun) Run by

members of a fairly obscure religious organization, this large restaurant, housed in a converted historic building on the Ithaca commons, is good for Belgian waffles, sandwiches and coffee.

Hazelnut Kitchen AMERICAN **$$**
(📞607-387-4433; 53 East Main St, Trumansburg; ⏰dinner only) The menu here is inspired by local ingredients and changes monthly. It is 12 miles north of Ithaca.

ⓘ Getting There & Away

Shortline Bus (www.coachusa.com) has frequent departures to New York City ($53, four hours). Delta Airlines has direct flights from the **Ithaca Tompkins Regional Airport** (ITH; www.flyithaca.com) to Detroit, Newark and Philadelphia.

Capital Region

ALBANY

Synonymous with legislative dysfunction as much as legislative power, Albany (or 'Smallbany' to jaded locals) remains a tourism backwater. It became New York State's capital in 1797 because of its geographic centrality to local colonies and its strategic importance in the fur trade. Several blocks from the city center and the ostentatiously modern government buildings in the 98-acre Empire State Plaza, stately brownstones give way to derelict and neglected streets and a general feeling of malaise. **Lark St**, north and uphill of downtown, has several restaurants and bars popular with university students when school is in session.

East of the plaza is the **Albany Institute of History & Art** (📞518-463-4478; www.alba nyinstitute.org; 125 Washington Ave; adult/child $10/6; ⏰10am-5pm Wed-Sat, noon-5pm Sun), which houses decorative arts and works by Hudson River School painters.

There are a handful of chain hotels downtown, however **74 State** (📞518-434-7410; www.74state.com; 74 State St; r incl breakfast from $180; ❇️🛜), a high-end boutique hotel in the heart of downtown is a better choice.

A number of restaurants are located along Pearl St and Lark St and a strip of bars and clubs on North Pearl St downtown gets hopping when workers spill out of the nearby government buildings. To experience Albany in all its elegant and back-room-dealing clubby glory try **Jack's Oyster House** (📞518-465-8854; 42 State St;

mains $19-25; ⏰11:30am-10pm), serving porterhouse steaks and seafood with a French twist; its lunchtime menu has burgers and sandwiches ($10). **Albany Pump Station** (19 Quackenbush Sq; mains $12; ⏰11:30am-10pm) has its own microbrewery and large varied menu while **Justin's** (📞518-436-7008; www. justinsonlark.com; 301 Lark St; ⏰11am-1am) has live jazz every night of the week, dinner and drinks.

SARATOGA SPRINGS

When 'taking the waters' was equivalent to a trip to the hospital, this settlement north of Albany was world famous in its heyday in the early 1800s – Joseph Bonaparte, Napoleon's older brother and King of Spain, took his medicine here once. Despite the encroachment of large-scale retail chains, Saratoga Springs' main commercial street retains something of the artsy, laid-back feel of a college town and it's rightly famous for its performing arts, horse racing and the liberal-arts Skidmore College.

The only remaining bathhouse – the first was built in 1784 – is the **Roosevelt Baths and Spa** (📞866-925-0622; www.rooseveltbath sandspa.com; 40min spa $25; ⏰9am-7pm) in the 2300-acre **Saratoga Spa State Park** (📞518-584-2535; www.saratogaspastatepark.org; 19 Roosevelt Dr; per car $4; ⏰sunrise-sunset). The mineral- and gas-infused waters are pumped underground from Lincoln Springs over a mile away. These days very hot tap water is added to the mix, though purists insist on going cold. Park grounds include golf courses, picnic areas, an Olympic-sized pool complex, multiuse trails, ice rinks and world-famous **Saratoga Performing Arts Center** (📞518-587-3330; www.spac.org; 108 Ave of the Pines), with orchestra, jazz, pop, rock and dance performances. From late July to September, horse-racing fans flock to **Saratoga Race Course** (📞518-584-6200; www. saratogaracetrack.com; 267 Union Ave; admission/ clubhouse $3/5), the country's oldest thoroughbred track.

There are more campsites around Lake George further north; however, the **Rustic Barn Campground** (📞518-654-6588; www. rusticbarncampground.com; 4748 Rte 9; campsites/ cabins $26/160), on a wooded property with a pond and hiking trails about 9 miles north in Corinth, is an option. There are plenty of inns and B&Bs in town; impossible to overlook is the four-story ornately designed facade of the landmark 19th-century **Adelphi Hotel** (📞518-587-4688; www.adelphihotel.

com; 365 Broadway; r/ste incl breakfast from $130/170; ❄🛜🐾); rooms are individually and idiosyncratically decorated (open May to October).

Restaurants and cafes line Broadway and the intimate side streets, including cozy **Mrs London's** (464 Broadway; mains $10; 🕖7am-6pm, to 9pm Fri & Sat, closed Mon),which serves satisfying pastries as well as vegetarian paninis, soups and salads. With prices and decor from a bygone era, there's no more old-school place than the basic diner **Compton's** (457 Broadway; mains $4; 🕖4am-2:45pm). A few miles south of town is **PJ's Bar-B-Q** (Rte 9; mains $6; 🕚11am-9pm), a honky-tonk style roadhouse eatery that serves up slow-cooked ribs (six for $12) and smoked brisket, chicken and pork sandwiches.

❶ Getting There & Around

Adirondacks Trailways (www.trailwaysny.com) and **Greyhound** (www.greyhound.com) head to/from New York City (one way $45, four hours). Amtrak stops out of New York City ($52 one way, four hours), and several major airlines fly into **Albany International Airport** (ALB; www.albanyairport.com) about 10 miles north from downtown.

COOPERSTOWN

For sports fans, , 50 miles west of Albany, is instantly recognized as the home of the shrine for the national sport (baseball). But the small-town atmosphere and stunning views of the countryside around beautiful Ostego Lake make it worth visiting even for those who don't know the difference between ERA and RBI.

The **National Baseball Hall of Fame & Museum** (☎888-425-5633; 25 Main St; www.baseballhall.org; adult/child $19.50/7; 🕘9am-5pm, to 9pm summer; 👔) has exhibits, a theater, a library and an interactive statistical database. The old stone **Fenimore Art Museum** (☎888-547-1450; www.fenimoreartmuseum.org; 5798 Lake Rd/Hwy 80; adult/child $12/free; 🕙10am-5pm) has an outstanding collection of Americana.

Several affordable low-slung motels line Rte 80 alongside the lake outside of town. The **Inn at Cooperstown** (☎607-547-5756; www.innatcooperstown.com; 16 Chestnut St; r incl breakfast from $110; ❄🛜) is a beautifully restored country home located just blocks from Main St. The tiny **Cooperstown Diner** (136½ Main St; mains $8; 🕕6am-8pm) does burgers and comfort food.

The Adirondacks

Majestic and wild, the Adirondacks, a mountain range with 42 peaks over 4000ft high, rival any of the nation's wilderness areas for sheer awe-inspiring beauty. The 9375 sq miles of park and forest preserve that climb from central New York State to the Canadian border include towns, mountains, lakes, rivers and more than 2000 miles of hiking trails. There's good trout, salmon and pike fishing, along with excellent camping spots. The Adirondack Forest Preserve covers 40% of the park, preserving the area's pristine integrity. In colonial times settlers exploited the forests for beaver fur, timber and hemlock bark, but by the 19th century 'log cabin' wilderness retreats, both in the form of hotels and grand estates, became fashionable.

LAKE GEORGE, LAKE PLACID & SARANAC LAKE

Maybe it's a blessing that the primary gateway to the Adirondacks, the village of **Lake George**, is a kitsch tourist town full of cotton candy, arcades and cheap souvenirs. The real reason for coming is the 32-mile-long lake itself, with its crystalline waters and forested shoreline, and once you leave the town behind the contrast is only more striking. Paddlewheel boat cruises, parasailing, kayaking and fishing trips are popular.

The state maintains wonderfully remote **campgrounds** (☎800-456-2267; www.dec.ny.gov/outdoor; tent sites $25) on Lake George's islands, and one of several places for wilderness information is the **Adirondack Mountain Club** (☎518-668-4447; www.adk.org; 814 Goggins Rd). Small motels line the main street of Lake George toward the northern end of town. Two with lake views that can be recommended are **Georgian Lakeside Resort** (☎518-668-5401; www.georgianresort.com; r incl breakfast from $99; ❄🛜🐾) and newly renovated **Surfside on the Lake** (☎518-668-2442; www.surfsideonthelake.com; r from $50; ❄🛜🐾). Dozens more hotels, inns and cabins extend north on either side of Rte 9 to the village of **Bolton Landing**.

It's something of a stretch to imagine this small mountain resort was once at the center of the world's attention – well, twice. In 1932 and 1980, **Lake Placid** hosted the Winter Olympics and the facilities and infrastructure remain; elite athletes still train here. Parts of the **Olympic sports centers** (☎518-523-1420; www.whitefacelakeplacid.com) are open to visitors, including ice arenas, a

BUGS

Come May swarms of black flies can be enough of a scourge to discourage some people from traveling to the Adirondacks. Through much of June the problem of these gnat-like flying insects can be such a sanity-challenging nuisance that residents stay indoors and when outdoors experiment with all manner of home remedies to keep the bites at bay.

ski-jumping complex and a chance to **bobsled** (per day $70; ☺10am-4pm Thu-Mon Jun-Jul) with a professional driver. Hotels, restaurants, bookstores and shops line the frontier-like main street in town, which actually fronts Mirror Lake. Skiers should head to nearby **Whiteface Mountain** (www.whiteface. com), with 80 trails and a serious 3400ft vertical drop.

South of Lake Placid town, **Adirondack Loj** (☑518-523-3441; www.adk.org; dm/r incl breakfast $55/160), run by the Adirondack Mountain Club (ADK), is a rustic retreat surrounded by mountains on the shore of peaceful Heart Lake. Wilderness campsites, lean-tos and cabins are also available.

Further north is the **Saranac Lake** region, where you'll find even more secluded wilderness areas – small lakes and ponds, ancient forests and wetlands. The town of Saranac Lake itself, once a center for tuberculosis treatments, feels a little down on its luck. However, the nearby **Porcupine Inn** (☑518-891-5160; www.theporcupine.com; 350 Park Ave; r incl breakfast $155-252; ❇☞), housed in a classic Adirondacks-style lodge house, is run with loving care and perfection. A hike up to nearby Moody Pond and Baker Mountain affords excellent views of the area.

❶ Getting There & Around

Both **Greyhound** (www.greyhound.com) and **Adirondack Trailways** (www.trailwaysny.com) serve various towns in the region. A car is really essential for exploring the region.

Thousand Islands Region

Virtually unknown to downstate New Yorkers, in part because of its relative inaccessibility, this region of over 1800 islands – from tiny outcroppings just large enough to lie down on to larger islands with roads and towns – is a scenic wonderland separating the US from Canada. From its source in the Atlantic Ocean far to the north, the wide and deceptively fast-moving St Lawrence River East empties into Lake Ontario at Cape Vincent. This portion of the river was once a summer playground for the very rich, who built large, stately homes here. It is still a popular vacation area known for its boating, camping and even shipwreck scuba diving.

Sackets Harbor was the site of a major battle during the War of 1812. While it is on Lake Ontario and not technically part of the Thousand Islands, it is a convenient starting point for touring the region. Several inviting restaurants line the street that runs down to the harbor front with waterside patio seating.

The relaxing, French-heritage village of **Cape Vincent** is at the western end of the river where it meets the lake. Drive out to the **Tibbetts Point Lighthouse** for stunning lake views; an attractive **hostel** (☑315-654-3450; www.hihostels.com; dm/r $18/40) shares the property. Nearby **Burnham Point State Park** (☑315-654-2522; Rte 12E; campsites $25) has wooded, lakeside campsites.

Clayton, 15 miles to the east along the Seaway Trail (Rte 12), has more than a dozen marinas and a few good eating choices in an area generally bereft of them. **TI Adventures** (☑315-686-2500; www.tiadventures.com; 1011 State St; half-day kayak rental $30) rents kayaks and runs white-water rafting trips down the Black River. Such activities are also organized by several companies in Watertown, a sizable city half an hour's drive to the south.

Lyric Coffee House (246 James St, Clayton; ☺8am-8pm, 9am-4pm Sun; ☞), surprisingly contemporary for this town, serves specialty coffee drinks, gelato, pastries and specials such as lasagna for lunch.

Further east, **Alexandria Bay** (Alex Bay), an early-20th-century resort town, is still the center of tourism on the American side – its sister city is Gananoque in Canada. While it is run-down and tacky, there's enough around to keep you occupied: go-karts, mini-golf and a **drive-in movie theater** (www. baydrivein.com; adult/child $5/2; ☻) are only minutes away. It's also the departure point for ferries to Heart Island, where **Boldt Castle** (☑315-482-2501; www.boldtcastle.com; adult/child $6.50/4; ☺10am-6:30pm mid-May–mid-Oct) marks the love story of a rags-to-riches New York hotelier who built the castle for his beloved wife. Sadly, she died before its completion. The same hotelier once asked his chef to create a new salad dressing, which was popularized as 'Thousand Island' – an unfortunate blend of ketchup, mayonnaise and relish. **Uncle Sam's Boat Tours** (☑315-482-2611; www.usboattours.com, 45 James St; 2-nation tour adult/child $18.50/9.25; ●) has several departures daily for its recommended two-nation cruise (visiting both the US and Canadian sides of the river), which allows you to stop at Boldt Castle and ride back on one of its half-hourly ferries for free.

Wellesley Island State Park (☑518-482-2722; www.nysparks.com; campsites from $15) offers camping, which is probably the best accommodations option even for the raccoon-averse. Many sites are almost directly on the riverfront and some have their own 'private' beaches. The island is only accessible by crossing a toll portion ($2.50) of the Thousand Islands Bridge.

There are several supposedly upscale resorts around Alex Bay, though none is especially good value. Probably the best mid-range choice is **Capt Thomson's Resort** (☑315-482-9961; www.captthomsons.com; 45 James St; d from $80; ❄🐾🏊) on the waterfront next to the office for Uncle Sam's Boat Tours.

Jet Blue (www.jetblue.com) has regular daily flights to Hancock International Airport (SYR) in Syracuse, an hour and a half south. Several major car-rental agencies have offices in the airport. Cyclists will enjoy the mostly flat Scenic Byway Trail.

Western New York

Still trying to find their feet after hemorrhaging industries and population for over a decade, most of the cities in this region live in the shadow of Niagara Falls, a natural wonder that attracts upward of 12 million visitors from around the world per year. Buffalo was once a booming industrial center and the terminus of the Erie Canal, which used to serve as the transportation lifeline connecting the Great Lakes and the Atlantic Ocean; it now boasts an indigenous culinary scene and Bohemian enclaves. Syracuse and Rochester are both home to big universities.

BUFFALO

This often maligned working-class city does have long, cold winters and its fair share of abandoned industrial buildings, but Buffalo also has a vibrant community of college students and thirty-somethings living well in cheap real estate and gorging on this city's unique and tasty cuisine. Settled by the French in 1758 – its name is believed to derive from *beau fleuve* (beautiful river) – the city's illustrious past as a former trading post and later a booming manufacturing center and terminus of the Erie Canal means there's a certain nostalgia and hopefulness to the continuing limbo of ambitious revitalization plans (the latest calls for a massive expansion and relocation of the University of Buffalo medical school to downtown). Buffalo is about an eight-hour trip from New York City and less than an hour south of Niagara Falls.

The helpful **Buffalo Niagara Convention & Visitors Bureau** (☑716-218-2922; www.visitbuffaloniagara.com; 617 Main St; ◷10am-4pm Mon-Fri, 10am-2pm Sat) has good walking-tour pamphlets and a great website.

◉ Sights & Activities

Architecture buffs will enjoy the city (for details check out www.walkbuffalo.com). North of downtown, sprawling Delaware Park was designed by Frederick Law Olmsted. The **Elmwood** neighborhood, stretching along Elmwood Ave between Allen St and Delaware Park, is dotted with hip cafes, restaurants, boutiques and bookstores. Hertle Ave, designated as 'Little Italy' in North Buffalo also has several good restaurants and cafes.

This is a hard-core sports town and locals live and die with the **NFL Buffalo Bills** (www.buffalobills.com) football team and the **Buffalo Sabres** (www.sabres.com), the city's NHL ice-hockey team. A lower-key, no less recommended, option to rub elbow's with local sports fanatics is to catch the **Buffalo Bisons** (www.bisons.com), the AAA affiliate of the major-league baseball team, the New York Mets, in their trendy-traditional downtown ballpark.

Albright-Knox Art Gallery   MUSEUM
(☑716-882-8700; www.albrightknox.org; 1285 Elmwood Ave; adult/child $12/5; ◷10am-5pm Tue-Sun, to 10pm first Fri) A sizable museum, including some of the best French Impressionists and American masters.

Burchfield Penney   MUSEUM
(☑716-878-6011; www.burchfieldpenney.org; 1300 Elmwood Ave; adult/child $9/5; ◷10am-5pm Tue, Wed, Fri & Sat, to 9pm Thu, 11am-5pm Sun) Modern building housing works, mostly American and western New York artists, from the late 19th century to contemporary.

Frank Lloyd Wright Darwin
Martin House TOUR
(☎716-856-3858; www.darwinmartinhouse.org; 125 Jewett Pkwy; tours $15-40) Tours of the 1904 Prairie-style home and neighboring **Barton House** (118 Summit Ave) begin with a video and exhibits at the next-door visitor center. The $50 million restoration, which began in 1992, is nearing completion; the iconic pergola was only rebuilt in 2007.

Theodore Roosevelt Inaugural
National Historic Site MUSEUM
(☎716-884-0095; www.trsite.org; 641 Delaware Ave; adult/child $10/5; ⊙9am-5pm Mon-Fri, noon-5pm Sat & Sun) Partly guided tours of the Ansley-Wilcox house examine the tale of Teddy's emergency swearing-in here following the assassination of William McKinley in 1901. Interactive exhibits for the attention deficient.

🛏 Sleeping

Standard chains line the highways around the city. Depending on the weather and time of day, downtown can feel like a ghost town. However, it's a geographically convenient base and the **Hamptons Inn & Suites** (☎716-855-2223; www.hamptoninn.com; 220 Delaware Ave; r incl breakfast from $150; P❋@🛜🏊) can be recommended for its large rooms and excellent breakfast.

Mansion on Delaware
Avenue B&B $$
(☎716-886-3300; www.mansionondelaware. com; 414 Delaware Ave; r incl breakfast from $175; ❋🛜) For truly luxurious accommodations and flawless service, head to this very special and grand mansion.

Beau Fleuve B&B $$
(☎800-278-0245; www.beaufleuve.com; 242 Linwood Ave; s/d incl breakfast from $120/135; ❋) A historic B&B in the Linwood neighborhood.

Hostelling International –
Buffalo Niagara HOSTEL $
(☎716-852-5222; www.hostelbuffalo.com; 667 Main St; dm/r $25/60; ❋@) For budget travelers.

🍴 Eating

Buffalo is curiously blessed with an abundance of eateries serving unique, tasty and cheap dishes.

TOP CHOICE Anchor Bar PUB $$
(☎716-883-1134; 1047 Main St; 10 wings $11; ⊙10am-11pm Mon-Thu, 10am-1am Fri & Sat) For the famous deep-fried chicken wings covered in a spicy sauce, head to this landmark bar, which claims credit for inventing the 'delicacy.' Sandwiches, burgers, seafood, pizza and pasta are also on the menu. Motorcycles and other random paraphernalia line the walls and live music Thursday through Saturday nights.

Ulrich's GERMAN $$
(☎716-8; 674 Ellicott St; mains $15; ⊙11:15am-late Mon-Sat) One of Buffalo's oldest taverns has warped floors and dark wood walls. Try the gut-busting German fish fry, which comes with red cabbage, sauerkraut, potatoes and vegetables. Homemade potato pancakes ($7), liverwurst and red onions on rye ($11) are also recommended.

Left Bank FRENCH $$
(☎716-882-3509; 511 Rhode Island St; mains $10-19; ⊙5-11pm Mon-Thu, to midnight Fri & Sat, 11am-10pm Sun) Housed in an attractive 100-year-old building, Left Bank is an atmospheric restaurant serving large portions of homemade ravioli, grilled meat and good wine.

Betty's MODERN AMERICAN $$
(☎716-362-0633; 370 Virginia St; mains $12; ⊙8am-9pm Tue, 8am-10pm Wed-Fri, 9am-10pm Sat, 9am-3pm Sun) For slightly more upscale eats. In the neighborhood of Allentown, Betty's does interpretations of American comfort food.

Also recommended:

Duff's PUB $
(☎716-834-6234; 3651 Sheridan Dr, Amherst; 10 wings $8; ⊙11am-11pm) Locals in the know say the wings here are the best.

Bob & John's
La Hacienda SANDWICHES, PIZZA $
(☎716-836-5411; 1545 Hertel Ave; sandwiches $5, 10 wings $9; ⊙11am-11pm) Serves sandwiches, buffalo wings and, according to some, the best pizza in Buffalo.

Ted's FAST FOOD $
(☎716-834-6287; Sheridan Ave; hot dogs $2; ⊙10:30am-11pm Mon-Sun) Fast-food specialty is hot dogs, foot-longs, any way you like 'em.

Chef's ITALIAN $$
(☎716-856-9187; 291 Seneca St; mains $15; ⊙11am-9pm Mon-Sat) In business for 85 years, this is a Buffalo landmark doling out classic red-sauce Italian dishes.

🍷 Drinking & Entertainment

Bars along Chippewa St (aka Chip Strip) are open until 4am and cater primarily to the frat-boy crowd. More eclectic neighborhoods such as Elmwood, Linwood and Allentown have more than their fair share of late-night options. From June through August a **summer concert series** (☑716-856-3150; www.buffaloplace.com) draws an eclectic mix of new and established artists to outdoor spaces in downtown.

Several gay bars are clustered around the south end of Elmwood.

Nietzches   DIVE BAR
(☑716-886-8539; 248 Allen St; ⊙1pm-2am) A legendary dive bar with live music.

Allen Street Hardware Cafe   LIVE MUSIC
(☑716-882-8843; 245 Allen St; ⊙5pm-midnight, to 1am Fri & Sat) Where the best local musicians play to regularly packed houses. Full food menu as well.

Eddie Brady's   BAR
(97 Genesee St; ⊙5pm-2am) Neighborhood tavern in a rehabilitated downtown building (c 1863).

ⓘ Getting There & Around
Buffalo Niagara International Airport (BUF; www.buffaloairport.com), about 16 miles east of downtown, is a regional hub. Jet Blue Airways offers affordable round-trip fares from New York City. Buses arrive and depart from the **Greyhound terminal** (181 Ellicott St). **NFTA** (www.nfta.com) local bus 40 goes to the transit center on the American side of Niagara Falls ($1.75, one hour). From the downtown **Amtrak train station** (75 Exchange St), you can catch trains to major cities (to NYC is $55, eight hours; to Albany $43, six hours; to Syracuse $24, 2½ hours). The Exchange Street station can feel dodgy, especially at night; locals recommend the Buffalo-Depew station (55 Dick Rd), 6 miles east.

NIAGARA FALLS & AROUND
It's a tale of two cities and two falls, though either side of this international border affords views of an undeniably dramatic natural wonder. There are honeymooners and heart-shaped Jacuzzis, arcades, tacky shops and kitsch boardwalk-like sights, but as long as your attention is focused nothing can detract from the majestic sight. The closer to the falls you get the more impressive they seem and the wetter you become. For good reason, the Canadian side is where almost everyone visits, though it's easy to stroll back and forth between the two. The New York side is dominated by the purple, glass-covered Seneca Niagara Casino & Hotel, which towers over the surrounding derelict blocks.

◉ Sights & Activities
The falls are in two separate towns: Niagara Falls, New York (USA) and Niagara Falls, Ontario (Canada). The towns face each other across the Niagara River, spanned by the Rainbow Bridge, which is accessible for cars and pedestrians. Famous landscape architect Frederick Law Olmstead helped rescue and preserve the New York side which by the 1870s was dominated by industry and gaudy signs. You can see views of the **American Falls** and their western portion, the **Bridal Veil Falls**, which drop 180ft from the **Prospect Point Observation Tower** (admission $1; ⊙9:30am-5pm Mon-Thu, to 7pm Fri & Sat, to 6pm Sun). Cross the small bridge to **Goat Island** for close-up viewpoints, including Terrapin Point, which has a fine view of Horseshoe Falls and pedestrian bridges to the Three Sisters Islands in the upper rapids. From the north corner of Goat Island, an elevator descends to the **Cave of the Winds** (☑716-278-1730; adult/child $6/4; ⊙9am-5pm), where walkways go within 25ft of the cataracts (raincoats provided). The **Maid of the Mist** (☑716-284-8897; www.maidofthemist.com; tours adult/child $13.50/8; ⊙10am-5pm Mon-Fri, to 6pm Sat & Sun May-Sep; ⊛) boat trip around the bottom of the falls has been a major attraction since 1846 and is highly recommended. Boats leave from the base of the Prospect Park Observation Tower on the US side and from the bottom of Clifton Hill on the Canadian side.

For those seeking more of an adrenaline rush, check out **Whirlpool Jet Boat Tours** (☑888-438-4444; www.whirlpooljet.com; 1 hr adult/child $50/42), which leave from **Lewiston**, a charming town with several good eateries 8 miles north of Niagara Falls. Shoppers can head to the **Tanger Outlet stores** a few miles west of town for designer-wear deals.

Northeast of Niagara Falls is the town of **Lockport**, the western terminus of the Erie Canal. There's an excellent visitors center and **museum** and **boat tours** during the summer months.

🛏 Sleeping & Eating
Some of the national hotel chains are represented – Ramada Inn, Howard Johnson, Holiday Inn, however the pickings are slim compared to the Canadian side. There are a few restaurants near the bridge area, including several Indian takeaway places.

TOP CHOICE ✦ **The Giacomo**   BOUTIQUE HOTEL $$
(☑716-299-0200; www.thegiacomo.com; 220 First St; r from $150; P❋☎) The equal of any Canadi-

an-side lodging in terms of stylish comfort, the Giacomo occupies a renovated 1929 art-deco office tower. While the majority of floors are taken up by high-end condos, the three dozen spacious rooms are luxuriously appointed and the 19th-floor lounge offers spectacular falls views. Considering the fact that it sleeps eight comfortably, the platinum suite, suitable for a season of *Real Life Niagara Falls,* is a good deal ($500, two-night minimum).

ⓘ Information

On the US side, the **Niagara Tourism & Convention Corporation** (☑716-282-8992; www.niagara-usa.com; 10 Rainbow Blvd; ☺9am-7pm Jun-Sep 15, to 5pm Sep 16-May 31) has all sorts of guides; its Canadian counterpart is located near the base of the **Skylon Tower** (☑905-356-6061; www.niagarafallstourism.com; 5400 Robinson St; ☺9am-5pm).

ⓘ Getting There & Around

NFTA (Niagara Frontier Transportation Authority; www.nfta.com) has seven daily buses from the Buffalo Airport to Niagara Falls; look for the 210 Metro Link Express ($3, 50 minutes). The stop in Niagara Falls is at First and Rainbow Blvd (there's no reason to go to the terminal at Main and Pine Sts). Taxis run around $75. For downtown Buffalo bus 40 leaves from Third St and Old Falls Blvd ($1.75, one hour). The **Amtrak train station** (27th St, at Lockport Rd) is about 2 miles northeast of downtown. From Niagara Falls, daily trains go to Buffalo ($12, 35 minutes), Toronto ($38, three hours) and New York City ($60, nine hours). **Greyhound** (303 Rainbow Blvd) buses are run out of the Daredevil Museum.

Parking costs $5 to $10 a day on either side of the falls. Most of the midrange hotels offer complimentary parking to guests, while upscale hotels (on the Canadian side) tend to charge $10 to $20 a day for the privilege.

Crossing the Rainbow Bridge to Canada and return costs US$3.25/1 per car/pedestrian. There are customs and immigration stations at each end – US citizens are required to have their passport or an enhanced driver's license (see p632). Driving a rental car from the US over the border should not be a problem (see p630 and p633) but check with your rental company before you depart.

NEW JERSEY

There are McMansions, à la the *Real Housewives of New Jersey* (NJ), guys who speak with thick Jersey accents like characters from a TV crime drama, and guidos and guidettes who spend their days GTL'ing (gym, tan and laundry) on the Shore. However, the state is at least as well defined by high-tech and banking headquarters and sophisticated, progressive people living in charming towns. Get off the exits, flee the malls and you are privy to a beautiful side of the state: a quarter is farmland and it has 127 miles of beautiful beaches and charming and fun beachside towns, as well, of course, as two of New York City's greatest icons: the Statue of Liberty and Ellis Island.

ⓘ Information

NJ.com (www.nj.com) Statewide news from all the major dailies including the Newark Star-Leger and Hudson County's Jersey Journal.

New Jersey Monthly (www.njmonthly.com) Monthly glossy with features on attractions and other stories relevant to visitors.

NEW JERSEY FACTS

» **Nickname** Garden State

» **Population** 8.8 million

» **Area** 8722 sq miles

» **Capital city** Trenton (population 85,000)

» **Other cities** Newark (population 277,000)

» **Sales tax** 7%

» **Birthplace of** musician Count Basie (1904–84), singer Frank Sinatra (1915–98), actor Meryl Streep (b 1949), musician Bruce Springsteen (b 1949), actor John Travolta (b 1954), musician Jon Bon Jovi (b 1962), rapper Queen Latifah (b 1970), pop band Jonas Brothers: Kevin (b 1987), Joseph (b 1989), Nicolas (b 1992)

» **Home of** the first movie (1889), first professional baseball game (1896), first drive-in theater (1933), the Statue of Liberty

» **Politics** Republican governor Chris Christie though strong traditionally Democratic legislature

» **Famous for** The Jersey Shore (the real thing and MTV reality show), the setting for The Sopranos, Bruce Springsteen's musical beginnings

» **Number of** wineries 36

» **Driving distances** Newark to NYC 11 miles, Atlantic City to NYC 135 miles

New Jersey Department of Environmental Protection (www.state.nj.us/dep/parksandforests) Comprehensive information on all state parks, including camping and historic sites.

❶ Getting There & Away

Though NJ is made up of folks who love their cars, there are other transportation options:

New Jersey PATH train (www.panynj.gov/path) Connects lower Manhattan to Hoboken, Jersey City and Newark.

New Jersey Transit (www.njtransit.com) Operates buses out of NYC's Port Authority and trains out of Penn Station, NYC.

New York Waterway (www.nywaterway.com) Ferries to northern New Jersey.

Northern New Jersey

Stay east and you'll experience the Jersey urban jungle. Go west to find its opposite: the peaceful, refreshing landscape of the Delaware Water Gap and rolling Kittatinny Mountains.

HOBOKEN & JERSEY CITY

A sort of TV-land version of a cityscape, Hoboken is a cute little urban pocket just across the Hudson River from New York City – and, because of cheaper rents that lured pioneers over a decade ago, a sort of sixth city borough, too. On weekends the bars and live-music venues come alive – especially the legendary **Maxwell's** (☎201-653-1703; www.maxwellsnj.com; 1039 Washington St), which

has featured up-and-coming rock bands since 1978. But the town also has loads of restaurants lining commercial Washington St, some lovely residential lanes and a leafy, revitalized waterfront – a far cry from when the gritty *On the Waterfront* was filmed here.

Perhaps there's no clearer symbol for this transformation than the crowds that line up every morning to glimpse the spectacular confections made by Bartolo Jr 'Buddy' Valastro of reality TV show *Cake Boss* at **Carlo's City Hall Bake Shop** (☎201-659-3671; www.carlosbakery.com; 95 Washington St; ⊙7am-7:30pm Mon-Wed & Sun, to 9pm Thu-Sat).

High-rise buildings housing condominiums and the offices of financial firms seeking lower rents have transformed **Jersey City** for better or worse from a primarily blue-collar and immigrant neighborhood into a 'restored' area for the upwardly mobile. Its biggest draw is the 1200-acre **Liberty State Park** (☎201-915-3440; www.libertystatepark.org; ⊙6am-10pm), which hosts outdoor concerts with the Manhattan skyline as a backdrop and has a great bike trail, and also operates **ferries** (☎877-523-9849; www.statuecruises.com) to Ellis Island and the Statue of Liberty. Also in the park and great for kids – virtually every exhibit is interactive – is the expansive and modern **Science Center** (☎201-200-1000; www.lsc.org; adult/child $15.75/11.50, extra for IMAX & special exhibits; ⊙9am-5pm; 🖬).

BORDER CROSSING: CANADIAN NIAGARA FALLS

When people say they are visiting the falls they usually mean the Canadian side, which is naturally blessed with superior views. Canada's **Horseshoe Falls** are wider and especially photogenic from Queen Victoria Park; at night they're illuminated with a colored light show. The **Journey Behind the Falls** (adult/child US$15/7; ⊙9am-8:30pm Mon-Fri) gives access to a spray-soaked viewing area beneath the falls. **Niagara on the Lake**, 15km to the north, is a small town full of elegant B&Bs and a famous summertime theater festival.

Virtually every major hotel chain has at least several locations on the Canadian side of the falls. Backpackers can head to the somewhat messy **HI Niagara Falls Hostel** (☎905-357-0770; www.hostellingniagara.com; 4549 Cataract Ave; dm/r incl breakfast US$30/60; 🕸🛜). **Skyline Inn** (☎905-374-4444; www.skylineinnniagarafalls.com; 4800 Bender St; r from US$70; 🅿🕸@🛜) is a good choice if you're seeking a budget place away from the noise and there's a walkway to the **indoor waterpark** across the street. River Rd is lined with B&Bs but **Chestnut Inn** (☎905-374-7623; www.chestnutinnbb.com; 4983 River Rd; r from US$90; 🕸), a tastefully decorated colonial home with a wrap-around porch, stands above the rest.

Obvious tourist-trap restaurants are a dime a dozen in and around Clifton Hill. American fare and chains dominate the culinary scene. The Lundy's Lane area has tons of cheap eats.

NEWARK

Though many NYC-bound travelers fly into Newark Liberty International Airport, few stick around to see the city they've landed in. Long mired in images of the 1960s race riots that made it off-limits to many for so long, Newark has been on a long road to recovery. Cory Booker, the city's young, high-profile ambitious mayor, who took office in 2006, is only the city's third mayor since 1970. Crime, endemic poverty and dwindling finances all continue to mar the city's reputation though downtown streets bustle with shoppers and office workers during the daytime in warmer months.

Brazilian, Portuguese and Spanish restaurants line the streets of the thriving Ironbound District (www.goironbound.com) only a few blocks from the city's neoclassic Penn Station (accessible from NYC's same-named station via NJ Transit). Down some sangria and the seafood combo for two ($41) at the fortress-like Iberia Peninsula (63-69 Ferry St; mains $15; ⊙11am-2am). Not far from here is the Newark Museum (☎973-596-6550; www.newarkmuseum.org; 49 Washington St; suggested donation $10; ⊙noon-5pm Wed-Fri, 10am-5pm Sat & Sun), which has a renowned Tibetan collection and hosts the annual Newark Black Film Festival in June. Some 2700 cherry trees blossom in April in the 400-acre Frederick Law Olmstead-designed Branch Brook Park. The New Jersey Performing Arts Center (☎888-466-5722; www.njpac.org; 1 Center St) is the city's crowning jewel, hosting national orchestras, operas, dance, jazz and other performances. The Prudential Center (www.prucenter.com), aka 'The Rock' has become the focal point for sports, home to the New Jersey Devils hockey team, plus basketball games and concerts.

DELAWARE WATER GAP

The Delaware River meanders in a tight S-curve through the ridge of NJ's Kittatinny Mountains, and its beauteous image turned this region into a resort area, beginning in the 19th century. The Delaware Water Gap National Recreation Area (☎570-426-2452; www.nps.gov/dewa), which comprises land in both New Jersey and Pennsylvania, was established as a protected area in 1965, and today it's still an unspoiled place to swim, boat, fish, camp, hike and see wildlife – just 70 miles east of New York City.

The 3348-acre Kittatinny Valley State Park (☎973-786-6445; admission free) is home to lakes with boat launches, lime outcroppings, and campsites, plus former railroads that have been converted into hiking and cycling trails. North of here, High Point State Park (☎973-875-1471; vehicle weekdays/weekends $5/10), which is also great for camping and hiking, has a monument that, at 1803ft above sea level, affords wonderful views of surrounding lakes, hills and farmland. The nearby town of Milford across the border in Pennsylvania is a charming place with several good restaurants.

Princeton & Around

Central New Jersey, otherwise known as 'the armpit' (only for how it looks on a map, of course), is home to a string of beautiful, wealthy communities including Princeton, at the eastern border of Pennsylvania as well as the state capital of Trenton.

Settled by an English Quaker missionary, the tiny town of Princeton is filled with lovely architecture and several noteworthy sites, number one of which is its Ivy League Princeton University (www.princeton.edu), which was built in the mid-1700s and soon became one of the largest structures in the early colonies. The town's Palmer Square, built in 1936, is a lovely place to shop and stroll. The Historical Society of Princeton (☎609-921-6748; www.princetonhistory.org; 158 Nassau St; tours adult/child $7/4) leads historical walking tours of the town on Sundays at 2pm, and the Orange Key Guide Service & Campus Information Office (☎609-258-3060; www.princeton.edu/orangekey) offers free university tours.

Accommodations are expensive and hard to find during graduation time in May and June, but beyond that it should be easy to arrange for a stay at one of several atmospheric inns, including the traditionally furnished Nassau Inn (☎609-921-7500; www.nassauinn.com; 10 Palmer Sq; r incl breakfast from $169; ❋@🖜) and the Inn at Glencairn (☎609-497-1737; www.innatglencairn.com; 3301 Lawrenceville Rd; r incl breakfast from $195; ❋🖜), a renovated Georgian manor with old-world style and modern amenities.

It may not be the most beautiful place, but New Jersey's capital, Trenton, has several historic sites, a museum and farmers market worth stopping in on – especially if you can pair it up with a trip to Philly or Atlantic City.

Perhaps the most famous and revered feature of New Jersey is its sparkling shore, stretching from Sandy Hook to Cape May and studded with resort towns from tacky to classy (www.visitthejerseyshore.com). You'll find as many mothers pushing strollers as throngs proudly clutching souvenir beer bongs. Though it's mobbed during summer weekends, you could find yourself wonderfully alone on the sand come early fall. Beach access varies across communities, though the majority charge reasonably priced fees for the day. Putting up a tent in a state park or private campground is a low cost alternative during the summer months when finding good-value accommodations is nearly as difficult as locating un-tattooed skin.

SANDY HOOK & AROUND

At the northernmost tip of the Jersey Shore is the Sandy Hook Gateway National Recreation Area (☏732-872-5970; www.nps.gov/gate; off Rte 36; parking per car $10; ☺7am-10pm), a 7-mile-long sandy barrier beach at the entrance to New York Harbor. You can see the city skyline from your beach blanket on clear days, which only heightens the sense of pleasure and feeling of dislocation. The ocean side of the peninsula has wide, sandy beaches (including a nude beach, the only legal one in NJ, at Gunnison Beach) edged by an extensive system of bike trails, while the bay side is great for fishing or wading. The brick buildings of the abandoned coast-guard station, Fort Hancock (☺1-5pm Sat & Sun) houses a small museum. The Sandy Hook Lighthouse, which offers guided tours, is the oldest in the country. Bug spray is recommended as biting flies can be a nuisance at dusk.

The town next door, the Highlands, has a few seafood restaurants on the water and an outpost of the famous Brooklyn pizzeria Grimaldi's (☏732-291-1711; 123 Bay Ave; small pizza $14; ☺3-10pm, from noon Sat & Sun), whose coal-fired brick-oven pies are the equal of the original. A fast ferry service Seastreak (☏800-262-8743; www.seastreak.com; round-trip adult/child $43/16, 1hr), runs between Sandy Hook (and the Highlands) and Pier 11 in downtown Manhattan or East 35th St, NYC.

About 10 miles inland is the artsy town of Red Bank, with a hoppin' main strip of shops, galleries and cafes, plus a sizable Mexican population (and plenty of authentic Mexican-food eateries. New Jersey Transit stops here.

LONG BRANCH, ASBURY PARK & OCEAN GROVE

Sanitized and slightly generic compared to other shore locations, Long Branch is the first major beach town south of the Highlands. A mall-like food-and-shopping complex by the ocean packs 'em in for everything from Greek dinners to swimwear shopping. Just a bit inland from here is the famed Monmouth Park Race Track (☏732-222-5100; www.monmouthpark.com; grandstand/clubhouse $3/5; ☺11:30am-6pm May-Aug), where you can see thoroughbred racing in a gracious, historic setting.

Just south of Long Branch massive homes the size of museums in the community of Deal are worth a look simply to gawk at. However, once you cross over Deal Lake into Asbury Park, luxury gives way to abandoned row houses and potholed streets. The town though, which experienced passing prominence in the 1970s when Bruce Springsteen 'arrived' at the Stone Pony (☏732-502-0600; www.stoneponyonline.com; 913 Ocean Ave) nightclub and then a major decline, is being revitalized. Led by wealthy gay men from NYC who snapped up blocks of forgotten Victorian homes and storefronts to refurbish, the downtown (one of the liveliest on the shore), which includes several blocks of Cookman Ave, is lined with charming shops, cafes and restaurants. The sprawling Antique Emporium of Asbury Park (☏732-774-8230; 646 Cookman Ave; ☺11am-5pm Mon-Sat & noon-5pm Sun) has two levels of amazing finds, while trendy Restaurant Plan B (☏732-807-4710; 705 Cookman Ave; mains $10-25; ☺4:30-9pm Tue-Thu & Sun, to 10pm Fri, to 11pm Sat) serves excellent weekend brunch. On the southern end of the boardwalk, the grand looking renovated art-deco Paramount Theatre (☏732-897-8810; www.apboardwalk.com/venues; 1300 Ocean Ave) hosts live theater and music performances.

The town immediately to the south, Ocean Grove, is a fascinating place to wander. Founded by Methodists in the 19th century, the place retains what's left of a post–Civil War Tent City revival camp – now a historic site with 114 cottage-like canvas tents clustered together that are used for summer homes. The town has dazzling ornate well-preserved Victorian architecture and a 6500-seat wooden auditorium, and there are many beautiful, big-porched Victorian inns to choose from for a stay; visit www.ocean grovenj.com for guidance. A few miles inland just off the Garden State Pkwy is a very utilitarian-looking Premium outlet store mall.

BRADLEY BEACH TO SPRING LAKE

Bradley Beach has row after row of adorable summer cottages and a beautiful stretch of shore. Belmar's beach is equally inviting and has a boardwalk with a few food shacks and a handful of restaurants and busy bars on the oceanfront road. The New Jersey Sandcastle Contest (www.njsandcastle.com) is held here in mid-July.

South of here is Spring Lake, a wealthy community once known as the 'Irish Riviera,' with meticulously manicured lawns, grand oceanfront Victorian houses, a gorgeous beach and elegant accommodations. If you're interested in a low-key quiet base – a stay here is about as far from the typical shore boardwalk experience as you can get – try the bright and airy Grand Victorian at Spring Lake (☑449-5327; www.grandvictorianspringlake.com; 1505 Ocean Ave; r from $79; ✱ ⑦).

Only 5 miles inland from Spring Lake is quirky Historic Village at Allaire (☑732-919-3500; www.allairevillage.org; adult/child $3/2; ☺noon-4pm Wed-Sun late May-early Sep, check for other times), the remains of what was a thriving 19th-century village called Howell Works. You can still visit various 'shops,' all run by folks in period costume.

OCEAN COUNTY BEACHES

Just south of the Manasquan River is Point Pleasant, whose northern end of the boardwalk is backed by small, idiosyncratic vacation homes only feet from the beach-going hordes. The southern half, called Jenkinson's Boardwalk has the usual salt-water taffy shops, eateries, amusement rides, as well as an aquarium good for kids and an enormous bar and restaurant for adults jutting out over the beach. A few seafood restaurants with outdoor patios built over the water can be found on a marina and inlet of the river – one worth a try is the Shrimp Box (75 Inlet Dr; sandwiches $10, mains $17; ☺noon-10:30pm). Just north of here in Manasquan, Inlet Beach has the Shore's most reliable year-round waves for surfers.

Just below there, the narrow Barnegat Peninsula barrier island extends some 22 miles south from Point Pleasant. In its center, Seaside Heights of MTV reality-show *Jersey Shore* fame sucks in the raucous twenty-something summer crowds with

two amusement piers and an above-average number of boardwalk bars. Because the beach is relatively narrow, this is not the place to go for privacy or quiet. Grab a seat – and a drink and tortilla chips – at the 2nd floor terrace of Spicy Cantina (500 Boardwalk; mains $11; ☺11am-midnight) for a front-row seat of the human parade below. Or better yet ride the chair lift running from the Casino Pier to the northern end of the boardwalk. If the ocean is not to your taste, beat the heat on the lazy river at the Breakwater Beach Waterpark (www.casinopiernj.com/breakwaterbeach; admission $25; ☺10am-7pm May-Aug; ⊛). To witness guidos and guidettes in all of their fist-bumping glory check out Karma (401 Blvd; ☺Thu-Sun), the nightclub of choice for Snooki, Sitch and the gang. There isn't much to recommend about a stay at one of the crash pads on the neglected sun-baked streets inland from the boardwalk. Camping at Surf & Stream Campground (☑732-349-8919; www.surfnstream.com; 1801 Ridgeway Rd/Rte 571, Toms River; campsites $45) is a convenient option.

Occupying the southern third of Barnegat Peninsula is Island Beach State Park (☑732-793-0506; www.islandbeachnj.org; per car weekday/weekend $6/10; ☺8am-dusk), a 10-mile barrier island that's pure, untouched dunes and wetlands. Although the very southern tip of the park is within throwing distance of Long Beach Island just across a narrow inlet to the bay south of here, to reach this long sliver of an island with beautiful beaches and impressive summer homes you have to backtrack all the way to Seaside Heights and travel along Rte 9 or the Garden State Pkwy. The landmark Barnegat Lighthouse State Park (☑609-494-2016; www.njparksandforests.org; off Long Beach Blvd; ☺8am-4pm) offers panoramic views at the top and fishermen cast off from a jetty extending 2000ft along the Atlantic Ocean. A few miles south of Rte 72 that bisects Long Beach Island is Daddy O (☑609-361-5100; www.daddyohotel.com; 4401 Long Beach Blvd; r $195-375; ✱ ⑦), a sleek boutique hotel and restaurant near the ocean.

South Jersey

When folks from Philly say they're heading to the Shore, they're more often than not referring to this slice of the coastline. A mixture of kitsch and country, the state's southern region – represents the best of New Jersey's extremes.

PINE BARRENS

Locals call this region the Pinelands – and like to carry on the lore about the one million acres of pine forest being home to a mythical beast known as the 'Jersey Devil.' Containing several state parks and forests, the area is a haven for bird-watchers, hikers, campers, canoeists and all-round nature enthusiasts. Inland is the **Wharton State Forest** (☑609-561-0024; www.state.nj.us), one of the good places to canoe – as well as hike and picnic. A good outfitter is **Micks Pine Barrens Canoe and Kayak Rental** (☑609-726-1515; www.mickscanoerental.com; 3107 Rte 563, Chatsworth; per day kayak $43, canoe $55), which has maps and other details about boating trips in the area. Further south along the coast is the **Edwin B Forsythe National Wildlife Refuge** (☑609-652-1665; www.forsythe.fws.gov; per vehicle $4), 40,000 acres of bays, coves, forests, marshes, swamps, and barrier beaches and a paradise for bird-watchers.

ATLANTIC CITY

It's not exactly Vegas, but for many a trip to AC conjures *Hangover*-like scenes of debauchery. And while you might spot bachelors and bachelorettes, gray-haired retirees and vacationing families are at least as accurate as a cross section of typical visitors. Inside the casinos that never see the light of day, it's easy to forget there's a wide white-sand beach just outside and boarded-up shop windows a few blocks in the other direction. The 'AC', known throughout the late 19th and early 20th century for its grand boardwalk and Oceanside amusement pier and the glamorously corrupt one of the HBO series *Boardwalk Empire* set in 1920 Prohibition-era AC, has been thoroughly overturned. Since 1977 when the state approved gambling casinos in the hope of revitalizing this fading resort, it has been on a bumpy ride. An ever expanding number of mostly Native American–owned casinos throughout Pennsylvania and New York are challenging AC's gambling hegemony and raison d'être. A slew of nightclubs and hotel-casinos like the massive Borgata have brought glitz and glamour, the **Pier at Caesars**, a spiffy shopping mall jutting out into the Atlantic, a steady stream of overseas visitors and an express train service from NYC have kept AC from hemorrhaging too many visitors. If gambling isn't your thing, the boardwalk offers up an all-star roster of summer indulgence, from funnel cakes to go-karts to cheesy gift shops. The small **Atlantic City**

Historical Museum (☑609-347-5839; www.acmuseum.org; cnr Boardwalk & New Jersey Aves; admission free; ☺10am-4pm) provides a quirky look at AC's past.

🛏 Sleeping & Eating

A handful of motor inns and cheap motels line Pacific Ave, a block inland from the boardwalk. The best in-casino dining is to be had at the Borgata. Good (and more affordable) food can be found in the 'real' part of downtown, too.

Chelsea BOUTIQUE HOTEL $
(☑800-548-3030; www.thechelsea-ac.com; 111 S Chelsea Ave; r from $80; P🅿❄@🛜🏊) Non-casino, trendy with art-deco-style furnishings. Rooms in the attached annex are less expensive. Also houses a retro diner, steakhouse and cabana club.

Water Club & Spa BOUTIQUE HOTEL $$
(☑609-317-8888; www.thewaterclubhotel.com; 1 Renaissance Way; r from $119; P❄@🛜🏊) This club is 43-story boutique-style chic.

Borgata CASINO $$
(☑866-692-6742; www.theborgata.com; r $149-400; P❄🛜🏊) An enormous Las Vegas-like resort with high-style rooms, a full-service spa, major concert hall, four five-star restaurants and, of course, a grand casino in the Marina District.

Reddings SOUTHERN $
(1545 Pacific Ave; mains $10; ☺11am-10pm Mon-Thu, 7am-midnight Fri & Sat) One of the most satisfying noncasino meals in AC. The chef-owner, a Harlem transplant, serves fine Southern-style cooking, like chicken dumplings and turkey chops, in a large and comfortable dining room.

Kelsey & Kim's Café BARBECUE $
(201 Melrose Ave; mains $9; ☺7am-10pm) Excellent southern comfort food like fried whiting, pulled BBQ beef brisket sandwich and fried chicken.

🍷 Drinking & Entertainment

It's the casinos, as you may have guessed, that are the biggest draw here. Inside they're all basically the same: nonstop clanging, flashing and miles of blackjack, poker, baccarat and craps tables.

Beyond the casino walls you'll find the wide, oceanfront **boardwalk**, the first in the world; enjoy a walk or a hand-pushed rolling-chair ride (there's a price chart posted inside each chair).

Check out the calendar at the Borgata, which has a comedy club, an intimate concert hall and a massive music venue that hosts big acts.

❶ Information

The **Atlantic City Convention & Visitors Bureau** (📞609-348-7100; www.atlanticcitynj.com; 2314 Pacific Ave; ⏱9am-5pm) has a location in the middle of the Atlantic City Expwy and another right on the boardwalk at Mississippi Ave. **Atlantic City Weekly** (www.atlanticcity weekly.com) has useful info on events, clubs and eateries.

❶ Getting There & Away

Air Tran and Spirit Airlines fly into the small **Atlantic City International Airport** (ACY; www. acairport.com), a 20-minute drive from the center of Atlantic City and a great option for reaching any part of South Jersey or Philadelphia.

There are a busload of bus options to AC, including NJ Transit (one way $36, 2½ hours) and Greyhound (one way $25, 2½ hours), both leaving from New York's Port Authority. A casino will often refund much of the fare (in chips, coins or coupons) if you get a bus directly to its door.

New Jersey Transit (www.njtransit.com) trains only go to Atlantic City from Philadelphia (one way $10, 1½ hours). A double-decker train service, **ACES** (Atlantic City Express Train Service; www.acestrain.com; ⏱Fri-Sun) connects AC to Penn Station, NYC (from $29, two hours 40 minutes).

OCEAN CITY & THE WILDWOODS

South of Atlantic City, Ocean City is an old-fashioned family holiday spot, home to dune-swept beaches and a number of child-centric arcades and themed playlands along its lively boardwalk. Motels are plentiful, relatively cheap and old-fashioned, as are the myriad crab shacks and seafood joints. Around 25 miles southwest of Ocean City down a long country road is the family-run **Frontier Campground** (📞609-390-3649; www.frontiercampground.com; campsites $35); sites are surrounded by blossoming pink and white mountain laurel flowers.

Further south on the way to Cape May, the three towns of **North Wildwood**, **Wildwood** and **Wildwood Crest** are an archaeological find – whitewashed motels with flashing neon signs, turquoise curtains and pink doors, especially in Wildwood Crest, a kitsch slice of 1950s Americana. Check out eye-catching motel signs like the **Lollipop** at 23rd and Atlantic Aves. Wildwood, a party town popular with teens, twenty-somethings and the young primarily Eastern Europeans who staff the restaurants and shops, is the main social focus. The width of the beach (all three beaches are free), more than 1000ft in parts making it the widest in NJ, means there's never a lack of space. Several massive piers are host to **water parks** and **amusement parks** – easily the rival of any Six Flags Great Adventure – with roller coasters and rides best suited to aspiring astronauts anchoring the 2 mile-long Grand Daddy of Jersey Shore boardwalks. Glow-in-the-dark 3D mini-golf is a good example of the Wildwood boardwalk ethos – take it far, then one step further. Maybe the best ride of all, and one that doesn't induce nausea, is the **tram** (one way $2.50; ⏱9am-1am) running the length of the boardwalk from Wildwood Crest to North Wildwood. There's always a line for a table at Jersey Shore staple pizzeria **Mack & Manco's** on the boardwalk (it has other shore boardwalk locations).

About 250 small motels – no corporate chains here – offer rooms for $50 to $250, however, it makes sense to narrow your search to the more salubrious area of Wildwood Crest. The Day Glo-colored ultra-retro **Caribbean Motel** (📞609-522-8292; www. caribbeanmotel.com; 5600 Ocean Ave; r from $65; ❄🛜🏊) has been painstakingly and lovingly renovated – think of a cross between the TV shows *Happy Days* and *The Jetsons*. Another recommended place is the **Pan American Hotel** (📞609-522-6936; www.panamericanhotel. com; 5901 Ocean Ave; r from $100; ❄🛜🏊).

CAPE MAY

Founded in 1620, Cape May – the only place in the state where the sun both rises and sets over the water – is on the state's southern tip and is the country's oldest seashore resort. Its sweeping beaches get crowded in summer, but the stunning Victorian architecture is attractive year-round.

In addition to 600 gingerbread-style houses, the city boasts antique shops and places for dolphin-, whale- (May to December) and bird-watching, and is just outside the **Cape May Point State Park** and its 157ft **Cape May Lighthouse** (📞609-884-5404; www. capemaymac.org; adult/child $7/3; ⏱10am-8pm Jun-Sep); there's an excellent visitors center and museum with exhibits on wildlife in the area. A mile-long loop of the nearby **Cape May Bird Observatory** (📞609-884-2736; www.birdcapemay.org; Sunset Blvd; admission $5; ⏱9:30am-4:30pm, closed Tue) is a pleasant stroll through preserved wetlands. The wide sandy **beach** at the park (free) or the one in town is the main attraction in summer months. **Aqua Trails** (📞609-884-5600;

www.aquatrails.com) offers kayak tours of the coastal wetlands.

Cape May's B&B options are endless, though the majority lean toward overstuffed and chintzy; check out www.capemaytimes for an up-to-date listing. The classic, sprawling **Congress Hall** (☑609-884-8422; www.congresshall.com; 251 Beach Ave; r $100-465; ❋🛜❋) has a range of beautiful quarters overlooking the ocean, plus there's a cool on-site restaurant and bar; the affiliated **Beach Shack** (www.beachshack.com) and **Star Inn** (www.thestarinn.net) offer a variety of accommodations for various budgets.

The size (and decor) of a high-school cafeteria from the 1950s, **Uncle Bill's Pancake House** (Beach Ave at Perry St; mains $7; ⊘6:30am-2pm) has been drawing in crowds for its flapjacks for 50 years. Otherwise head to the Washington Street Mall, a cobblestone street lined with shops and more than a half-dozen restaurants.

To continue your journey further south without having to backtrack north and far inland, the **Cape May-Lewes Ferry** (www.cmlf.com; car/passenger $44/8; 1½hr) crosses the bay to Lewes, Delaware near Rehoboth Beach.

PENNSYLVANIA

In a state so large it's unsurprising that geography in part determines identity. The further west you go the closer you are to the rest of America. Philadelphia, once the heart of the British colonial empire and the intellectual and spiritual motor of its demise, is firmly ensconced culturally in the East Coast. Residents of Pittsburgh and western Pennsylvania (PA), on the other hand, are proud to identify themselves as part of the city or immediate region, relishing their distinctiveness from East Coasters and their blue-collar reputation. Moving east to west, the terrain becomes more rugged and you begin to appreciate the sheer size and diversity of this one state. Philly's Independence Park and historic district offer an ideal opportunity to come to some understanding of this nation's origins. Nearby, the battle sites of Gettysburg and Valley Forge provide another chance to travel back in time. But the city and state offer more than the clichés associated with school field trips. Stunning natural forests and mountain areas including the Poconos and Allegheny National Forest provide endless outdoor adventures. Both Philly and Pittsburgh are vibrant university cities with thriving music, performance and art scenes. Frank Lloyd Wright's architectural masterpiece, Fallingwater, and Amish country, not to mention the region's small, artsy towns, are perfect for weekend getaways.

History

William Penn, a Quaker, founded his colony in 1681, making Philadelphia its capital. His 'holy experiment' respected religious freedom (a stance that attracted other minority religious sects, including the well-known Mennonite and Amish communities), liberal government and even indigenous inhabitants. But it didn't take long for European settlers to displace those communities, thus giving rise to Pennsylvania's status as the richest and most populous British colony in North America. It had great influence on the independence movement and, much later, became an economic leader through its major supply of coal, iron and timber, followed by raw materials and labor during WWI and WWII. In the postwar period its industrial importance gradually declined. Urban-renewal programs and the growth of service, high-tech and health-care industries have boosted the economy, most notably in Philadelphia and Pittsburgh.

Philadelphia

Although it may seem like a little sibling to NYC, which is less than 90 miles away, Philadelphia is more representative of what East Coast city living is like. And in the minds of many, it offers every upside of urban life – burgeoning food, music and art scenes, neighborhoods with distinct personalities, copious parkland and maybe equally importantly, relatively affordable real estate. The older, preserved buildings in historic Philadelphia provide a picture of what colonial American cities once looked like – based on a grid with wide streets and public squares.

For a time the second-largest city in the British Empire (after London), Philadelphia became a center for opposition to British colonial policy. It was the new nation's capital at the start of the Revolutionary War and again after the war until 1790, when Washington, DC, took over. By the 19th century, New York City had superseded Philadelphia as the nation's cultural, commercial and industrial center. Though urban renewal has been going on for decades, some parts of the city formerly populated by industrial work-

PENNSYLVANIA FACTS

» **Nicknames** Keystone State, Quaker State

» **Population** 12.4 million

» **Area** 46,058 sq miles

» **Capital city** Harrisburg (population 53,000)

» **Other cities** Philadelphia (population 1.45 million), Pittsburgh (population 313,000), Erie (population 102,000)

» **Sales tax** 6%

» **Birthplace of** Writer Louisa May Alcott (1832–88), dancer Martha Graham (1878–1948), artist Andy Warhol (1928–87), movie star Grace Kelly (1929–82), comic Bill Cosby (b 1937)

» **Home of** US Constitution, the Liberty Bell, first daily newspaper (1784), first auto service station (1913), first computer (1946)

» **Politics** 'Swing state,' Republican Governor, progressive Philly and blue collar Democrats elsewhere

» **Famous for** soft pretzels, Amish people, Philadelphia cheesesteak, Pittsburgh steel mills

» **Wildlife** home of the largest herd of wild elk east of the Mississippi

» **Driving distances** Philadelphia to NYC 100 miles, Philadelphia to Pittsburgh 306 miles

ers are blighted and worlds away from the carefully manicured lawns and park-service-glutted historic district around the Liberty Bell and Independence Hall.

◉ Sights & Activities

Philadelphia is easy to navigate. Most sights and accommodations are within walking distance of each other, or a short bus ride away. East–west streets are named; north–south streets are numbered, except for Broad and Front Sts.

Historic Philadelphia includes Independence National Historic Park and Old City, which extends east to the waterfront. West of the historic district is Center City, home to Penn Sq and City Hall. The Delaware and Schuylkill (*skoo*-kill) Rivers border South Philadelphia, which features the colorful Italian Market, restaurants and bars. West of the Schuylkill, University City has two important campuses as well as a major museum. Northwest Philadelphia includes the genteel suburbs of Chestnut Hill and Germantown, plus Manayunk, with plenty of bustling pubs and hip eateries. The South St area, between S 2nd, 10th, Pine and Fitzwater Sts, has Bohemian boutiques, bars, eateries and music venues. Northern Liberties is a burgeoning neighborhood with eclectic cafes and restaurants.

Independence National Historic Park HISTORIC SITE
(☎215-597-1785; www.nps.gov/inde) This L-shaped 45-acre park, along with Old City, has been dubbed 'America's most historic square mile.' Once the backbone of the United States government, today it is the backbone of Philadelphia's tourist trade. Stroll around and you'll see storied buildings in which the seeds for the Revolutionary War were planted and the US government came into bloom. You'll also find beautiful, shaded urban lawns dotted with large groups of schoolchildren and costumed actors. Most sites are open every day from 9am to 5pm, and some are closed Monday. Note that you must call or stop in to the **Independence Visitor Center** to make a timed reservation before visiting the high-volume Independence Hall, and beware that lines for the Liberty Bell can be extremely long.

Liberty Bell Center
(Map p132; 6th & Market Sts) Philadelphia's top tourist attraction was commissioned to commemorate the 50th anniversary of the Charter of Privileges (Pennsylvania's constitution, enacted in 1701 by William Penn). The 2080lb bronze bell was made in London's East End by the Whitechapel Bell Foundry in 1751. The bell's inscription, from Leviticus 25:10, reads: 'Proclaim liberty through all the land, to all the inhabitants thereof.' The bell was secured in the belfry of the Pennsylvania State House (now Independence Hall) and tolled on important occasions, most notably the first public reading of the Declaration of Independence in Independence Sq. The bell became badly cracked during the 19th century; despite initial repairs it became unusable in 1846 after tolling for George Washington's birthday.

National Constitution Center
(Map p132; ☎215-409-6700; www.constitutioncenter.org; 525 Arch St; adult/child $12/8; ◷9:30am-5pm Mon-Fri, to 6pm Sat, noon-5pm

NEW YORK, NEW JERSEY & PENNSYLVANIA PENNSYLVANIA

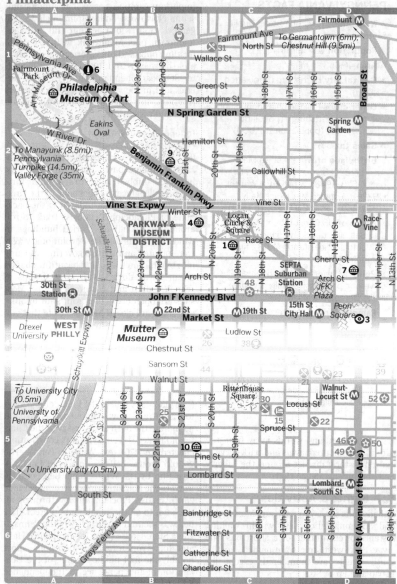

Sun; ⌂) Highly recommended, next to the visitor center, makes the United States Constitution interesting for a general audience through theater-in-the-round re-enactments. There are exhibits, including interactive voting booths and Signer's Hall,

which contains lifelike bronze statues of the signers in action.

Independence Hall

(Map p132; Chestnut St, btwn 5th & 6th Sts) The 'birthplace of American government,' where

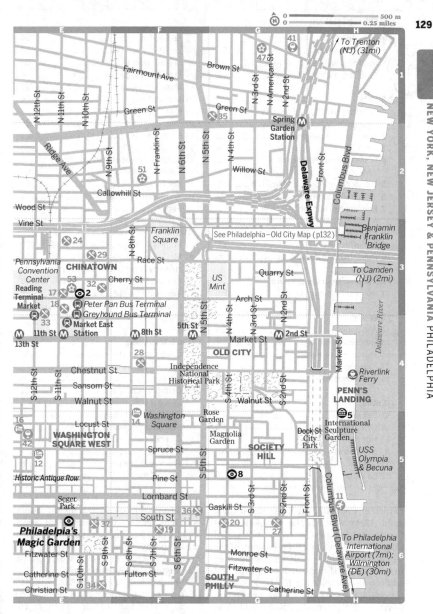

0 500 m
0 0.25 miles

To Trenton (NJ) (31mi)

Fairmount Ave

Brown St

Green St

Green St

N 12th St
N 11th St
N 10th St

Ridge Ave

N 9th St

N Franklin St

N 6th St

N 5th St

N 4th St

N 3rd St

N American St

N 2nd St

Spring Garden Station

Columbus Blvd

Delaware Expwy

Front St

Willow St

Callowhill St

Wood St
Vine St

Franklin Square

See Philadelphia–Old City Map (p132)

Benjamin Franklin Bridge

Pennsylvania Convention Center

CHINATOWN

Cherry St

Race St

Quarry St

US Mint

Arch St

To Camden (NJ) (2mi)

Delaware River

Reading Terminal Market

Peter Pan Bus Terminal
Greyhound Bus Terminal
Market East Station

11th St Station
13th St

8th St

5th St

Market St

OLD CITY

8th St

2nd St

Market St

Riverlink Ferry

Chestnut St

Sansom St

Walnut St

Independence National Historical Park

Walnut St

PENN'S LANDING

International Sculpture Garden

Washington Square

Rose Garden

Magnolia Garden

Dock St City Park

USS Olympia & Becuna

WASHINGTON SQUARE WEST

Spruce St

SOCIETY HILL

Historic Antique Row

Pine St

Lombard St

Seger Park

South St

Gaskill St

Columbus Blvd (Delaware Ave)

Philadelpia's Magic Garden

Fitzwater St

Catherine St

Christian St

Fulton St

Monroe St

Fitzwater St

SOUTH PHILLY

Catherine St

To Philadelphia International Airport (7mi); Wilmington (DE) (30mi)

delegates from the 13 colonies approved the Declaration of Independence on July 4, 1776. A great example of Georgian architecture, it sports understated lines that reveal Philadelphia's Quaker heritage. Behind is **Independence Square**, where the Declaration of Independence was first read in public.

Other Attractions

Other attractions in this historic park include: **Carpenters' Hall**, owned by the

Philadelphia

Carpenter Company, the USA's oldest trade guild (1724), which is the site of the First Continental Congress in 1774; **Library Hall** (Map p132), where you'll find a copy of the Declaration of Independence, handwritten in a letter by Thomas Jefferson, plus first editions of Darwin's *On the Origin of the Species* and Lewis and Clark's field notes; **Congress Hall** (Map p132; S 6th & Chestnut Sts), the meeting place for US Congress when Philly was the nation's capital; and **Old City Hall** (Map p132), finished in 1791, which was home to the US Supreme Court until 1800. The **Franklin Court** (Map p132) complex, a row of restored tenements, pays tribute to Benjamin Franklin with a clever underground museum displaying his inventions, as well as details on his many other contributions (as statesman, author and journalist) to society. **Christ Church** (Map p132; N 2nd St), completed in 1744, is where George Washington and Franklin worshipped.

Philosophical Hall (Map p132; ☎215-440-3400; www.apsmuseum.org; 104 S 5th St; admission $1; ☺10am-4pm Thu-Sun), south of Old City Hall, is the headquarters of the American Philosophical Society, founded in 1743 by Benjamin Franklin. Past members have included Thomas Jefferson, Marie Curie, Thomas Edison, Charles Darwin and Albert Einstein.

Second Bank of the US (Map p132; Chestnut St, btwn 4th & 5th Sts), modeled after the Greek Parthenon, is an 1824 marble-faced Greek Revival masterpiece that was home to the world's most powerful financial institution until President Andrew Jackson dissolved its charter in 1836. The building then became the Philadelphia Customs House until 1935, when it became a museum. Today it's home to the **National Portrait Gallery** (Map p132; Chestnut St; admission free; 30min free guided tours noon, 3pm & 4pm Sat & Sun), housing many paintings by Charles Willson Peale, America's top portrait artist at the time of the American Revolution.

OLD CITY

Old City – the area bounded by Walnut, Vine, Front and 6th Sts – picks up where Independence National Historical Park leaves off. And, along with Society Hill, Old City was early Philadelphia. The 1970s saw revitalization, with many warehouses converted into apartments, galleries and small businesses. Today it's a quaint and fascinating place for a stroll. Check out the 9ft-tall **Ben Franklin sculpture** at Fourth and Arch Sts.

Elfreth's Alley   STREET
(Map p132; off 2nd St, btwn Arch & Race Sts) The tiny, cobblestoned alley is believed to be the oldest continuously occupied street in the USA. Its 32 well-preserved brick row houses are still inhabited with real live Philadelphians, so be considerate as you stroll along, and be sure to stop into **Elfreth's Alley Museum** (Map p132; ☑215-574-0560; www.elfrethsalley.org; No 126; guided tours $5; ☺10am-5pm Tue-Sat, from noon Sun), which was built in 1755 by blacksmith and alley namesake Jeremiah Elfreth; it's been restored and furnished to its 1790 appearance.

National Museum of American Jewish History   MUSEUM
(Map p132; ☑215-923-3811; www.nmajh.org; 55 N 5th St; adult/child $12/free; ☺10am-5pm Tue-Fri, to 5:30pm Sat & Sun) The distinctly translucent facade of the museum houses state-of-the-art exhibits that examine the historical role of Jews in the USA.

Betsy Ross House   HISTORIC BUILDING
(Map p132; ☑215-686-1252; www.betsyrosshouse.org; 239 Arch St; suggested donation adult/child $4/3; ☺10am-5pm) Where it is believed that Betsy Griscom Ross (1752–1836), upholsterer and seamstress, may have sewn the first US flag.

FREE **Clay Studio**   GALLERY
(Map p132; ☑215-925-3453; www.theclaystudio.org; 139 N 2nd St; ☺11am-7pm Tue-Sat, noon-6pm Sun) Staid exhibits as well as oddball works in ceramic; it's been in Old City since 1974 and is partially responsible for the development of the area's burgeoning gallery scene.

FREE **US Mint**   TOUR
(Map p132; ☑215-408-0110; www.usmint.gov; Arch St, btwn 4th & 5th Sts; ☺tours 9am-3pm Mon-Fri) You can line up for same-day, self-guided tours that last about 45 minutes.

Arch Street Meeting House   RELIGIOUS
(Map p132; ☑215-627-2667; www.archstreetfriends.org; 320 Arch St; ☺9am-5pm Mon-Sat, 1-5pm Sun) The USA's largest Quaker meeting house.

SOCIETY HILL

Architecture from the 18th and 19th centuries dominates the lovely residential neighborhood of Society Hill, bound by Front and 8th Sts from east to west, and Walnut and Lombard Sts north and south. Along the cobblestoned streets you'll see mainly 18th- and 19th-century brick row houses, mixed in with the occasional modern highrise, like the **Society Hill Towers** designed by IM Pei, but **Washington Square** was conceived as part of William Penn's original city plan, and offers a peaceful respite from sightseeing.

Physick House   HISTORIC BUILDING
(Map p128; ☑215-925-7866; 321 S 4th St, at Delancey St; adult/child $5/free; ☺noon-4pm Thu-Sat, 1-4pm Sun) The home of surgeon Philip Syng Physick was built in 1786 by Henry Hill – a wine importer who kept City Tavern well stocked – and is the only freestanding, Federal-style mansion remaining in Society Hill.

Powel House   HISTORIC BUILDING
(Map p132; ☑215-627-0364; 244 S 3rd St; adult/child $5/free; ☺noon-4pm Thu-Sat, 1-4pm Sun) The 18th-century house was home to Samuel Powel, a mayor of Philadelphia during colonial times.

CENTER CITY, RITTENHOUSE SQUARE & AROUND

Philadelphia's center of creativity, commerce, culture and just about everything else, this region is the engine that drives the city. It contains the city's tallest buildings, the financial district, big hotels, museums, concert halls, shops and restaurants.

The leafy **Rittenhouse Square**, with its wading pool and fine statues, is the best known of William Penn's city squares.

City Hall HISTORIC BUILDING
(Map p128; ☎215-686-2840; www.phila.gov; cnr Broad & Market Sts) The majestic City Hall, completed in 1901, stands 548ft tall in Penn Sq. It's the world's tallest masonry construction without a steel frame, and it's topped by a 27-ton bronze statue of William Penn. Just below that is an **observation deck** (admis-

sion $5; ☺9:30am-4:15pm), where you can get a bird's-eye view of the city.

Mutter Museum MUSEUM
(Map p128; ☎215-563-3737; www.collphyphil.org; 19 S 22nd St; adult/child $14/10; ☺10am-5pm) Skip med school and visit the seriously twisted to learn all about the history of medicine in the US.

Rosenbach Museum & Library MUSEUM
(Map p128; ☎215-732-1600; www.rosenbach.org; 2010 Delancey Pl; adult/child $10/5; ☺noon-5pm Tue & Fri, to 8pm Wed & Thu, to 6pm Sat & Sun) For bibliophiles, as it features rare

books and manuscripts, including James Joyce's *Ulysses,* and special exhibits.

BENJAMIN FRANKLIN PARKWAY & MUSEUM DISTRICT

Modeled after the Champs Elysées in Paris, the parkway is a center of museums and other landmarks.

TOP CHOICE Philadelphia Museum of Art
MUSEUM

(Map p128; ☎215-763-8100; www.philamuseum. org; cnr Benjamin Franklin Pkwy & 26th St; adult/ child $16/free; ◎10am-5pm Tue-Sun, to 8:45pm Fri) This is the area's highlight and is one of the nation's largest and most important museums, featuring some excellent collections of Asian art, Renaissance masterpieces, postimpressionist works and modern pieces by Picasso, Duchamp and Matisse. The grand stairway at its entrance was immortalized when Sylvester Stallone ran up the steps in the 1976 flick *Rocky.* You can enjoy music, food and wine on Friday nights.

Pennsylvania Academy of the Fine Arts
MUSEUM

(Map p128; ☎215-972-7600; www.pafa.org; 118 N Broad St; adult/child $15/free; ◎10am-5pm Tue-Sat, from 11am Sun) A prestigious academy that has a museum with works by Ameri-

can painters, including Charles Willson Peale and Thomas Eakins.

Franklin Institute Science Museum
MUSEUM

(Map p128; ☎215-448-1200; www2.fi.edu; 222 N 20th St; adult/child $15.50/12; ◎9:30am-5pm; ♠) Where hands-on science displays were pioneered; a highlight is the kids-oriented interactive sports center.

Academy of Natural Sciences Museum
MUSEUM

(Map p128; ☎215-299-1000; www.ansp.org; 1900 Benjamin Franklin Pkwy; adult/child $12/10; ◎10am-4:30pm Mon-Fri, to 5pm Sat & Sun) Features a terrific dinosaur exhibition where you can dig for fossils on weekends.

Rodin Museum
MUSEUM

(Map p128; ☎215-568-6026; www.rodinmuseum. org; Benjamin Franklin Pkwy & N 22nd St; suggested donation $5; ◎10am-5pm Tue-Sun) You'll find Rodin's great works *The Thinker* and *Burghers of Calais* here.

SOUTH STREET

Sort of a Greenwich Village of Philly, South Street is where one goes to find record shops, art-supply stores, tiny cheapskate eateries and college favorites such as head shops, T-shirt stores and the teenage goth chicks who populate them.

Philadelphia's Magic Garden
GARDENS

(Map p128; ☎215-733-0390; www.philadelphias magicgardens.org; 1020 South St; adult/child $5/2; ⏱11am-6pm, to 8pm Fri & Sat) A hidden gem worth seeking out is this mystical, art-filled pocket of land that's the passion of mosaic muralist Isaiah Zagar.

SOUTH PHILADELPHIA

Italian Market
MARKET

(www.italianmarketphilly.org; S 9th St, btwn Wharton & Fitzwater Sts; ⏱9am-5pm Tue-Sat, to 2pm Sun) A highlight of South Philadelphia. One of the country's largest outdoor markets, it's where butchers and artisans hawk produce and cheese, homemade pastas, incredible pastries and freshly slaughtered fish and meats, from lamb to pheasant. A great time to experience it in all its glory is in mid-May, for the annual South Ninth Street Italian Market Festival.

Mummers Museum
MUSEUM

(☎215-336-3050; www.mummersmuseum.com; 1100 S 2nd St; adult/child $3.50/2.50; ⏱9:30am-4:30pm Wed, Fri & Sat, to 9:30pm Thu) Celebrating the tradition of disguise and masquerade. It has an integral role in the famed Mummers Parade, which takes place here every New Year's Day.

CHINATOWN & AROUND

The fourth-largest Chinatown in the USA, Philly's version has existed since the 1860s. Chinese immigrants who built America's transcontinental railroads started out west and worked their way here. Today's Chinatown remains a center for immigrants, though now many of the neighborhood's residents come from Malaysia, Thailand and Vietnam in addition to every province in China. Though it does hold a few residents, the tone of Chinatown is thoroughly commercial.

African American Museum in Philadelphia
MUSEUM

(Map p132; ☎215-574-0380; www.aampmuseum. org; 701 Arch St; adult/child $10/8; ⏱10am-5pm Tue-Sat, from noon Sun) Housed in a foreboding concrete building, it contains excellent collections on African American history and culture.

Chinese Friendship Gate
LANDMARK

(Map p128; N 10th St, btwn Cherry & Arch Sts) A decorative arch built in 1984 as a joint project between Philadelphia and its Chinese sister city, Tianjin. The multicolored, four-story gate is Chinatown's most conspicuous landmark.

PENN'S LANDING

Back in its heyday Penn's Landing – the waterfront area along the Delaware River between Market and Lombard Sts – was a very active port area. Eventually those transactions moved further south down the Delaware, and today most of the excitement is about boarding boats, like the Riverboat Queen (Map p132; ☎215-923-2628; www.riverboatqueenfleet.com; tours from $15) or Spirit of Philadelphia (Map p128; ☎866-394-8439; www.spiritcruises.com; tours from $40), for booze cruises, or simply strolling along the water's edge. The 1.8-mile Benjamin Franklin Bridge, the world's largest suspension bridge when completed in 1926, spans the Delaware River and dominates the view.

Independence Seaport Museum
MUSEUM

(Map p128; ☎215-413-8655; www.phillyseaport.org; 211 S Columbus Blvd; adult/child $12/7; ⏱10am-5pm) The museum highlights Philadelphia's role as an immigration hub; its shipyard closed in 1995 after 200 years. Nearby is a grassy sculpture garden.

UNIVERSITY CITY

This neighborhood, separated from downtown Philly by the Schuylkill River, feels like one big college town. That's because it's home to both Drexel University and the Ivy League (commonly called 'U Penn'), founded in 1740. The leafy, bustling campus makes for a pleasant afternoon stroll, and it's got two museums definitely worth a visit.

University Museum of Archaeology & Anthropology
MUSEUM

(☎215-898-4000; www.pennmuseum.org; 3260 South St; adult/child $10/6; ⏱10am-5pm Tue & Thu-Sun, to 8pm Wed) Contains archaeological treasures from ancient Egypt, Mesopotamia, Mesoamerica, Greece, Rome and North America.

FREE Institute of Contemporary Art
MUSEUM

(☎215-898-7108; www.icaphila.org; 118 S 36th St; ⏱11am-8pm Wed, to 6pm Thu & Fri, to 5pm Sat & Sun) An excellent place to catch shows by folks making a big splash at the cutting edge of the art world.

30th St Station
LANDMARK

(☎215-349-2153; 30th St, at Market St) Whether you're catching a train or not, be sure to pop your head into this romantic, neoclassical station while you're in the 'hood.

FAIRMOUNT PARK

The snaking Schuylkill River bisects this 9200-acre green space that's bigger than New York's Central Park and, in fact, the largest city park in the country. From the earliest days of spring every corner is thrumming with activity – ball games, runners, picnickers, you name it. Runners will love the tree-lined, riverside trails, which range from 2 miles to 10 miles in length. Park trails are also great for cycling. Stop by **Fairmount Bicycles** (☑267-507-9370; www.fairmountbicycles.com; 2015 Fairmount Ave) for rentals (full/half-day $18/30) and information.

Boathouse Row   HOUSE

On the east bank, Boathouse Row has Victorian-era rowing-club buildings that lend a lovely old-fashioned flavor to this stretch. Across the park are a number of **early American houses** (adult/child $5/2) that are open to the public.

Shofuso Japanese
House and Garden   HOUSE, GARDEN

(☑215-878-5097; www.shofuso.com; adult/child $6/3; ⊙10am-4pm Wed-Fri, 11am-5pm Sat & Sun May-Sep) A picturesque home and teahouse constructed in the traditional 16th-century style. Scattered all throughout the park are some notable monuments, including one, at the far east end, for **Joan of Arc**.

Philadelphia Zoo   ZOO

(☑215-243-1100; www.philadelphiazoo.org; 3400 Girard Ave; adult/child $18/15; ⊙9:30am-5pm) The country's oldest zoo, which has tigers, pumas, polar bears – you name it – in naturalistic habitats.

MANAYUNK

A compact residential neighborhood northwest of the city, with steep hills and Victorian row houses, Manayunk, from a Native American expression meaning 'where we go to drink,' is a lovely place for an afternoon and evening. Just be aware that thousands of others have the same idea on weekend nights, when this otherwise peaceful area overlooking the Schuylkill River has the feel of a raucous frat party. As well as drinking, visitors are also permitted to eat and shop. Parking is near impossible to come by here on weekends, so cycling is a good option – there's a towpath that runs alongside the neighborhood.

GERMANTOWN & CHESTNUT HILL

An odd mix of blight and preserved grandeur, the Germantown historic district – a good 20-minute drive or ride north on the Septa 23 from central downtown Philly – has a handful of tiny museums and notable homes worth checking out.

Wissahickon Valley Park   PARK

(☑215-247-0417; www.fow.org) One of the best places to go for a run in the city is this long and narrow park, part of the Fairmount Park system; essentially a steep forested gorge with 57 miles of trails.

Cliveden of
the National Trust   HISTORIC BUILDING

(☑215-848-1777; www.cliveden1767.wordpress.com; 6401 Germantown Ave; admission $10; ⊙noon-4pm Thu-Sun) The summer home of wealthy Benjamin Chew was built in 1760 and was used as a de facto stronghold in the Battle of Germantown during the Revolutionary War in 1777.

Chestnut Hill   NEIGHBORHOOD

(www.chestnuthillpa.com) Located just north of Germantown, with its quaint, small-town-like main strip of shops and eateries, and huge and historic residential homes and mansions.

Johnson House   HISTORIC BUILDING

(☑215-438-1768; www.johnsonhouse.org; 6306 Germantown Ave; adult/child $8/4; ⊙10am-4pm Thu & Fri, from 1pm Sat) Tours of the site of a 1768 station house for the Underground Railroad.

☞ Tours

Ed Mauger's Philadelphia on Foot   WALKING

(☑215-627-8680; www.ushistory.org/more/mauger; per person $20) Historian and author Ed Mauger offers walking tours with a wide variety of themes, including Exercise Your Rights (Conservatives Tour), Exercise Your Lefts (Liberals Tour) and Women in the Colony.

Mural Tours   TROLLEY

(☑215-389-8687; www.muralarts.org/tours; tours free to $30) Guided trolley tour of the city's diverse and colorful outdoor murals, the largest collection in the country.

Philadelphia Trolley Works &
76 Carriage Company   TROLLEY

(☑215-389-8687; www.phillytour.com; adult/child from $25/10) Tour part of the city or just about every last corner, either on a narrated trolley ride or quieter horse-drawn carriage.

✨ Festivals & Events

Mummers' Parade
CULTURAL

(www.mummers.com) A very Philly parade, this is an elaborate celebration of costumes every New Year's Day (January 1).

Manayunk Arts Festival
CULTURAL

(www.manayunk.com) It's the largest outdoor arts and crafts show in the Delaware Valley, with more than 250 artists from across the country each June.

Philadelphia Live
Arts Festival & Philly Fringe
CULTURAL

(www.livearts-fringe.org) Catch the latest in cutting-edge performance each September.

🛏 Sleeping

Though the majority of places are found in and around Center City, alternatives are sprinkled throughout other neighborhoods. There's certainly no shortage of places to stay, but it's primarily national chains or B&Bs. The Lowes, Sofitel and Westin can all be recommended. Note that most hotels offer some kind of parking service, usually costing about $20 to $45 per day.

Morris House Hotel
BOUTIQUE HOTEL $$$

(Map p128; 215-922-2446; www.morrishouse hotel.com; 225 S 8th St; r incl breakfast from $189; ❄ 🛜) If Benjamin Franklin were a hotelier he would have designed a place exactly like the Morris House Hotel. Upscale colonial-era boutique, this Federal-era building has the friendly charm and intimacy of an elegant B&B and the professionalism and good taste of a designer-run 21st-century establishment.

Hotel Palomar
BOUTIQUE HOTEL $$

(Map p128; 888-725-1778; www.hotelpalomar-philadelphia.com; 117 S 17th St; r from $149; ❄🛜) Part of the Kimpton chain, the Palomar, occupying a former office building a few blocks from Rittenhouse Square is the new kid on Philly's boutique block. Marble and dark wood accents add warmth to the hip and stylish room furnishings. On offer are wine and snacks, hot chocolate (in winter), a gym and an attached restaurant.

The Independent
Philadelphia
BOUTIQUE HOTEL $$

(Map p128; 215-772-1440; www.theindependent hotel.com; 1234 Locust St; r incl breakfast from $150; ❄🛜) Another good Center City option housed in a handsome brick Georgian-Revival building with a four-story atrium. The wood-floored rooms are cozy and bright and the complimentary off-site gym pass and wine and cheese every evening sweeten the deal.

Rittenhouse 1715
BOUTIQUE HOTEL $$$

(Map p128; 215-546-6500; www.rittenhouse1715. com; 1715 Rittenhouse Sq; r from $206; ❄🛜) Just steps from Rittenhouse Sq, this is an elegant, top-notch choice. Housed in a 1911 mansion and infused with old-world sophistication, it's brimming with modern amenities – iPod docking stations, plasma TVs and rain showerheads. The friendly and efficient staff is also worth noting.

Penn's View Hotel
HOTEL $$

(Map p132; 215-922-7600; www.pennsviewhotel. com; 14 N Front St, at Market St; r from $155; ❄🛜) Housed in three early-19th-century buildings overlooking the Delaware waterfront, Penn's View is ideal for exploring the Old City district. Quaint and full of character, but not overly nostalgic, the rooms have marble baths and modern conveniences.

Alexander Inn
HOTEL $$

(Map p128; 215-923-1004; www.alexanderinn. com; 12th & Spruce Sts; s/d incl breakfast from $120/130; ❄🛜) Exceptionally good value for its Center City location and for the professionalism and helpfulness of its staff. While the room decor is fairly standard you wouldn't expect a fitness room or breakfast at this price.

Apple Hostels of Philadelphia
HOSTEL $

(Map p132; 215-922-0222; www.applehostels. com; 32 S Bank St; dm $37, r from $90; @🛜) Sparkling clean and in a safe neighborhood just a short walk from major sights, there's no competition in this price bracket. Everything looks like it's straight out of an Ikea catalogue – not a bad thing. Friendly and helpful staff and events such as walking tours and movie nights with free beer (Tuesday).

Chamounix Mansion Hostel
HOSTEL $

(215-878-3676; www.philahostel.org; 3250 Chamounix Dr, West Fairmount Park; dm $23; ❄@) Looking more like a B&B than hostel, the Chamounix really should only be considered by those with use of a car. It's in a lovely wooded area in Fairmount Park north of the city on the way to Manayunk. Despite the 19th-century-style parlor and large communal rooms, the dorms themselves are basic but clean.

✖️ Eating

Philly is deservedly known for its cheese-steaks – you shouldn't leave without a sampling – the city's dining scene has grown exponentially, in part due to the contributions of the Starr and Garces groups, which have added a range of quality international eateries. Because of Pennsylvania's arcane liquor laws, many restaurants are Bring Your Own Bottle (BYOB).

OLD CITY

Amada
SPANISH $$

(Map p132; ☑215-625-2450; 217 Chestnut St; tapas $6-20; ◷11:30am-10pm Mon-Thu, to midnight Fri, 5pm-midnight Sat, 4-10pm Sun) Weekend dinner reservations at this Spanish tapas place, the first of renowned restaurateur Jose Garce's Philly eateries, are still hard to come by. The long communal tables foster a happening and loud atmosphere and the combination of bold and traditionally flavored dishes are phenomenal.

Cuba Libre
CUBAN $$

(Map p132; ☑215-627-0666; 10 S 2nd St; dinner $13-31; ◷11:30am-10pm Mon-Fri, from 10:30am Sat & Sun, to 11:30pm Fri & Sat) Colonial America couldn't feel further away at this festive, multistoried Cuban eatery and rum bar. The creative and inspired menu includes Cuban sandwiches, guava-spiced BBQ, and savory black beans and salads tossed with smoked fish.

La Locanda del Ghiottone
ITALIAN $$

(Map p132; ☑215-829-1465; 130 N Third St; mains $17; ◷5-11pm Tue-Sun) The name means 'the Place of the Glutton,' and Chef Giussepe and Joe the head waiter encourage overeating. Unlike other nearby trendy spots, this place is small and modestly designed. The gnocchi, mushroom crepes and mussels are recommended. BYOB.

Silk City Diner
DINER $$

(Map p128; 435 Spring Garden St; mains $13; ◷4pm-1am, from 10am Sat & Sun) Cocktails have replaced milkshakes at this classic-looking diner on the edge of the Old City and Northern Liberties. It's worth noting Silk City is as much a late night dance spot – Jerseyites come in for Saturday DJ nights. Outdoor beer garden in summer.

Franklin Fountain
DESSERTS $

(Map p132; 116 Market St; ◷11am-midnight) One of the more romantic date spots in the city, especially on weekend nights, this very-old-school ice-cream parlor features locally grown fruit and top-flight sundaes.

Zahav
MIDDLE EASTERN $$

(Map p132; ☑215-625-8800; 237 St James Pl; mains $11; ◷5-10pm Sun-Thu, to 11pm Fri & Sat) Small plates of sophisticated and modern Israeli and North African cuisine on Society Hill towers grounds.

CENTER CITY & AROUND

🏆 Morimoto
TOP CHOICE
JAPANESE $$$

(Map p128; ☑215-413-9070; 723 Chestnut St; mains $25; ◷11:30am-10pm Mon-Fri, to midnight Fri & Sat) High concept and heavily stylized from the dining room that looks like a futuristic aquarium to a menu of globe-spanning influence and eclectic combinations, a meal at this *Iron Chef* regular's restaurant is a theatrical experience.

Le Bec-Fin
FRENCH $$$

(Map p128; ☑215-567-1000; 1523 Walnut St; prix fixe dinners $80-185; ◷11:30am-10:30pm Mon-Fri, from 5:30pm Sat) Totally over-the-top in its old-world snooty splendor, Le Bec-Fin is rated by many gourmets as the country's best restaurant for its setting, service and superb French food. Expect top-notch service, stuffy diners and rich and sophisticated meat and seafood dishes. The five-course lunch menu at $55 is good value.

Reading Terminal Market
MARKET $

(Map p128; cnr 12th & Arch Sts; dishes $3-10; ◷8am-6pm Mon-Sat, 9am-5pm Sun) At the budget end, this huge indoor market is the best you'll find. Take your pick, from fresh Amish cheeses and Thai desserts, to falafel, cheesesteaks, salad bars, sushi, Peking duck, great Mexican and cups of fresh-roasted java.

Supper
MODERN AMERICAN $$

(Map p128; ☑215-592-8180; South St; mains $24; ◷6pm-11:30pm) Truly farm-to-table, supplied with fresh seasonal produce by its very own farm, Supper epitomizes the current culinary spirit which weds the rural with the urban. Entrees are inventive and tasty creations like crispy confit duck leg with pecan waffles.

La Viola
ITALIAN $$

(Map p128; ☑215-735-8630; 253 S 16th St, at Spruce St; mains $13; ◷11am-10pm Tue-Sat, 4-10pm Sun) Facing off across the street from one another are the old and new La Violas – both BYOB. The former is a cramped and unpretentious dining room, while the latter is larger and more modern; the cuisine at both, however, is fresh and reasonably priced.

Parc Brasserie
FRENCH $$$

(Map p128; 215-545-2262; 227 S 18th St; mains from $23; 7:30am-11pm, to midnight Fri & Sat) This enormous polished Rittenhouse Sq prime people-watching bistro hits all the right notes. Brunch and lunch menus are good value.

Mama Palmas
PIZZERIA $$

(Map p128; 215-735-7357; 2229 Spruce St; pizzas $10; 4-10pm Tue-Fri, 11am-11pm Sat, 2-10pm Sun) Just off Rittenhouse Sq, this small BYOB place serves up some of the best thin-slice brick-oven pizza in the city.

Continental
DINER $$

(Map p132; 138 Market St; mains $15; 11:30am-11pm, to midnight Thu-Sat, from 10am Sat & Sun) Stylish Stephen Starr joint housed in the shell of a classic diner – Korean pork tacos and tofu tempura mean the cuisine is not stuck in the past.

Mama's Vegetarian
FALAFEL $

(Map p128; 18 S 20th St; sandwiches $6; 11am-9pm Mon-Thu, to 3pm Fri, noon-7pm Sun;) An always bustling kosher Middle Eastern eatery, serves heaping falafel north of the city center.

Joe's
PIZZERIA $

(Map p128; 122 S 16th St; slices $2.25) Some of the best pizza by the slice in the whole neighborhood.

Philly Flavors
ICE CREAM $

(Map p128; 2004 Fairmount Ave, at 20th St; ices $2.50; 11am-11pm Sun-Thu, to midnight Fri & Sat) Some say this is the best place for Italian ices in the city.

SOUTH STREET

Jim's Steaks
SANDWICHES $

(Map p128; 400 South St, at 4th St; steak sandwiches $6-8; 10am-1am Mon-Thu, to 3am Fri & Sat, 11am-10pm Sun) If you can brave the long lines you'll be in for a treat at this Philly institution, which serves mouthwatering cheesesteaks and hoagies (plus soups, salads and breakfasts).

Horizons
VEGAN $$

(Map p128; 215-923-6117; 611 S 7th St; mains $15-20; 6-10pm Tue-Thu, 6-11pm Fri & Sat;) One of the few restaurants in Philly to satisfy the vegan gourmand, Horizons serves healthy, guilt-free dishes made of soy and veggies.

Maoz Vegetarian
FALAFEL $

(Map p128; 248 South St; dishes $6; 11am-10pm Sun-Thu, to 3am Fri & Sat) This tiny storefront, an outpost of an international chain is always packed and known for its fresh falafel sandwiches.

CHINATOWN

Rangoon
ASIAN $$

(Map p128; 112 N 9th St; mains $6-15; 11:30am-9pm Sun-Thu, to 10pm Fri & Sat) Try this Burmese spot in Chinatown, offering a huge array of tantalizing specialties from spicy red-bean shrimp and curried chicken with egg noodles to coconut tofu.

Han Dynasty
CHINESE $$

(Map p132; 108 Chestnut St; mains $15; 11:30am-11:30pm) Innovative and burn-your-tongue spicy soups and noodle dishes in a more upscale dining room.

Dim Sum Garden
CHINESE $

(Map p128; 59 N 11th St, mains $6; 11:30am-10pm) Overall, not the most salubrious looking hole-in-the-wall near the bus station but some of the tastiest steamed buns in the city.

Nanzhou Handdrawn Noodle House
CHINESE $

(Map p128; 927 Race St; mains $6; 11:30am-10pm) Serves satisfying and inexpensive meat noodle soups.

Banana Leaf
ASIAN $

(Map p128; 1009 Arch St; mains $8; 11am-1am) Specializes in Malaysian and Japanese cuisine.

Lee How Fook
CHINESE $$

(Map p128; 219 N 11th St; mains $9-13; 11:30am-10pm Tue-Sun) Has excellent contemporary Chinese.

SOUTH PHILADELPHIA & ITALIAN MARKET

Local aficionados debate the relative merits of this city's legendary cheesesteak shops as if they are biblical scholars parsing the meaning of Deuteronomy.

The area around the corner of Washington and 11th Sts is chockablock with tasty family-owned Vietnamese restaurants.

Paradiso
ITALIAN $$$

(215-271-2066; 1627 E Passyunk Ave; mains $18-26; 11:30am-10pm Mon-Thu, Fri & Sat to midnight) An elegant airy part of South Philly's Restaurant Row, Paradiso turns out upscale Italian feasts such as pistachio-crusted lamb chops, homemade gnocchi and New York strip steak glazed with anchovy butter.

Fond AMERICAN $$$
(☎212-551-5000; 1617 E Passyunk Ave; mains $25; ☺5:30-10pm) Tired of the neighborhood sandwich shops? Head to this upscale fine dining restaurant whose young chefs turn out creatively conceived fish, meat and chicken dishes with French accents and seasonal ingredients.

Pat's King of Steaks SANDWICHES $
(1237 E Passyunk Ave, at S 9th St; sandwiches $7; ☺24hr) Considered classic Philly, frequented as much by tourists and inebriated patrons, possibly unaware of the level of grease they're ingesting, as diehard locals.

Tony Luke's Old Philly Style Sandwiches SANDWICHES $
(39 E Oregon Ave; sandwiches $7; ☺6am-midnight Mon-Thu, to 2am Fri & Sat) Some swear by Tony Luke's, especially the roast pork or roast beef with hot peppers; it's by the sports stadiums with picnic tables and an ordering window.

South Street Souvlaki GREEK $
(Map p128; 507 South St; mains $9; ☺noon-9:30pm Tue-Thu, to 10pm Fri & Sat, to 9pm Sun) One of the best places for Greek food in the city.

Sabrina's Cafe AMERICAN $
(Map p128; 910 Christian St; mains $9; ☺8am-10pm Tue-Sat, to 4pm Sun & Mon) An extremely popular brunch spot.

UNIVERSITY CITY

🌱 **White Dog Cafe** MODERN AMERICAN $$$
(☑215-386-9224; 3420 Sansom St; dinner mains $27; ☺11:30am-9:15pm Mon-Thu, to 10pm Fri & Sat, from 10:30am Sat & Sun) This 27-year-old institution is the kind of funky-yet-upscale place that college students get their visiting parents to take them to for special dinners or brunch ($11). The local, largely organic menu offers creative interpretations of meat and fish dishes.

Pod ASIAN $$$
(☑215-387-1803; 3636 Sansom St; dinner mains $14-29; ☺11:30am-11pm Mon-Thu, to midnight Fri, 5pm-midnight Sat, to 10pm Sun) Part of restaurateur Stephen Starr's empire, this space-age-looking theme restaurant has pan-Asian treats including dumplings and some of the best sushi in Philly, plus plenty of quirky cocktails and original desserts.

Satellite Coffee Shop CAFE $
(701 S 50th St; sandwiches $5; ☺7am-10pm) This Cedar Park vegetarian-friendly cafe is a boho meeting ground – try the kale smoothie and vegan wraps.

Abyssinia Ethiopian Restaurant ETHIOPIAN $
(229 S 45th St; mains $9; ☺9am-midnight) Excellent foul madamas (bean dip) and good brunch with a recommended bar upstairs.

Fu-Wah Mini Market SANDWICHES $
(819 S 47th St; mains $4.50; ☺9am-9pm) Serves up tofu hoagies and Vietnamese chicken sandwiches.

Lee's Hoagie House SANDWICHES $
(4034 Walnut St; sandwiches $7; ☺10am-10pm Mon-Sat, 10:30am-9pm Sun) For meat and chicken sandwiches, definitely the best in area.

Koreana KOREAN $
(3801 Chestnut St; mains $7; ☺11:30am-10pm, closed Mon) Satisfies students and others interested in good, inexpensive Korean fare; enter from the parking lot in the back of the shopping plaza.

Distrito MEXICAN $$
(3945 Chestnut St; mains $9-30; ☺11:30am-11pm Mon-Fri, 5-11pm Sat, to 10pm Sun) The vibrant pink and lime decor doesn't drown out the taste of the contemporary Mexican fare.

Green Line Café CAFE $
(4239 Baltimore St; mains $4; ☺7am-11pm, 8am-8pm Sun) One of the better spots for coffee.

MANAYUNK & AROUND

Trolley Car Diner DINER $$
(7619 Germantown Ave; dinner mains $9-20; ☺7am-9pm Mon-Thu, to 10pm Fri & Sat) Housed in a classic art-deco diner, this old-fashioned, family-style diner serves all the comfort food: club sandwiches, patty melts, fried shrimp, salads and a homemade, white-bean 'peanut butter' sandwich.

Dalessandro's Steaks SANDWICHES $
(600 Wendover St, Roxborough; mains $6.50; ☺11am-midnight Mon-Sat, to 9pm Sun) Cheesesteak snobs rave about this place.

Chubby's SANDWICHES $
(5826 Henry Ave; mains $6.50; ☺11am-1am Mon-Thu, to 2am Fri & Sat, to 11pm Sun) Has the better chicken sandwiches.

Mama's Pizzeria PIZZA, SANDWICHES $
(426 Belmont Ave, Bala Cynwyd; sandwiches $10; ☺11am-9pm) Another contestant in the cheesesteaks sweepstakes – certainly Mama's are right up there in size.

Kildare's Irish Pub PUB $
(4417 Main St; mains $9; ☺11am-2am Mon-Sat, from 10am Sun) The place for chicken wings – grilled, fried and baked.

Drinking & Entertainment

Bars & Nightclubs

McGillin's Olde Ale House
PUB

(Map p128; 1310 Drury St; ⊙11am-2am) Philadelphia's oldest continually operated tavern (since 1860) has great buffalo wings (Tuesday is a special wing night) and karaoke on Wednesdays and Fridays.

Standard Tap
PUB

(Map p128; cnr 2nd & Poplar Sts; ⊙4pm-2am) One of the pioneers in the gastropub movement, this Northern Liberties bar offers a great selection of local brews on tap, as well as burgers and steaks.

Urban Saloon
PUB

(Map p128; 2120 Fairmount Ave; ⊙5pm-2am Mon-Fri, 11am-2am Sat & Sun) This Fairmount bar has a neighborhood feel. Dancing Friday nights, and a kid-friendly brunch Sundays (the peanut burger is recommended).

Shampoo
NIGHTCLUB

(Map p128; ☑215-922-7500; www.shampooonline.com; Willow St, btwn N 7th & 8th Sts; cover $7-12; ⊙9pm-2am) Home to foam parties, hot tubs and velvet seating, this giant nightclub's weekly repertoire includes an immensely popular gay night on Fridays and a conventional free-for-all on Saturdays.

BAR

(45th & Locust St; ⊙6pm-2am) Tiny spot above the Abyssinia Ethiopian restaurant in West Philly. Live music Thursday through Sunday.

Brasil's
NIGHTCLUB

(Map p132; ☑215-413-1700; www.brasilsnightclub-philly.com; 112 Chestnut St; cover $10; ⊙10pm-2am Wed-Sat) The place to bump and grind to Latin, Brazilian and Caribbean sounds, with DJ John Rockwell.

Elena's Soul
BAR, LIVE MUSIC

(⊙215-724-3043; 4912 Baltimore Ave; ⊙3pm-2am) Live blues, jazz, drinks, food, place to dance – all rolled into one West Philly spot.

Village Whiskey
BAR

(Map p128; 118 S 20th St; ⊙11:30am-11:30pm, to 1am Fri & Sat) Cool vibe, long whiskey menu and creative cuisine.

Franklin Mortgage & Investment Co
COCKTAIL BAR

(Map p128; 112 S 18th St; ⊙5pm-2am) Expertly made rye, whiskey and gin drinks in a classy setting.

Local 44
BAR

(4333 Spruce St; ⊙11:30am-midnight) Good pub grub and beer selection.

Gojjo Bar & Restaurant
BAR

(4540 Baltimore Ave; ⊙4pm-2am) Great back patio at this Ethiopian place.

Other places to recommend in the burgeoning brewpub scene:

Earth Bread & Brewery
BREWERY

(7136 Germantown Ave; ⊙4:30pm-midnight, closed Mon)

Nodding Head Brewery
BREWERY

(Map p128; 1516 Sansom St; ⊙11:30am-2am) An area that lies between Broad and 12th Sts and Walnut and Pine Sts, unofficially called 'gayborhood,' was dubbed Midtown Village and permanently decked out with rainbow-flag-festooned street signs during a special ceremony. Because nights and venues change frequently, check out www.phillygaycalendar.com.

Tavern on Camac
GAY

(Map p128; ☑215-545-0900; 243 S Camac St; ☑4pm-2am) Show tunes and other old-school fun reign in the downstairs piano bar; one of the older gay bars in Philly, while a small upstairs dance floor gets packed with dance-happy folks.

LESBIAN

(Map p128; ☑215-735-0735; www.sistersnightclub.com; 1320 Chancellor St; ⊙5pm-2am Tue-Sat, from noon Sun) A huge nightclub and restaurant for the ladies.

Dock Street Brewery & Restaurant
BREWERY

(701 S 50th St; ⊙3pm-11pm, to 1am Fri & Sat) Artisan beer and brick oven pizza in West Philly.

Live Music

Chris' Jazz Club
JAZZ

(Map p128; ☑215-568-3131; www.chrisjazzcafe.com; 1421 Sansom St; cover $10-20) Showcasing local talent along with national greats, this intimate space features a four o'clock piano happy-hour Tuesday through Friday and good bands Monday through Saturday nights.

Ortlieb's Jazzhaus
JAZZ

(Map p128; ☑215-922-1035; www.ortliebsjazzhaus.com; 847 N 3rd St; cover Tue-Thu, $10 Fri, $15 Sat, $3 Sun) A respectable jazz lineup with a house band jamming every Tuesday night and Cajun cuisine on the menu (mains $20).

World Cafe Live
LIVE MUSIC

(Map p128; ☑215-222-1400; www.worldcafelive.com; 3025 Walnut St; cover $10-40) Located on the eastern edge of University City, World Cafe Live has upstairs and downstairs performance spaces featuring a restaurant and bar and is home to the radio station WXPN. It hosts an eclectic variety of live acts.

Theater & Culture

Kimmel Center for the Performing Arts
PERFORMING ARTS

(Map p128; ☑215-790-5800; www.kimmelcenter.org; cnr Broad & Spruce Sts) Philadelphia's most active center for fine music, the Kimmel Center organizes a vast array of performances, including those for many of the companies following.

Philadelphia Theatre Company
THEATER

(Map p128; ☑215-985-0420; www.philadelphiatheatrecompany.org; Suzanne Roberts Theatre, 480 S Broad St, at Lombard St) This company, which produces quality contemporary plays by regional actors, has a high-end home in the heart of the arts district.

Pennsylvania Ballet
DANCE

(Map p128; ☑215-551-7000; www.paballet.org; 1819 John F Kennedy Blvd) An excellent dance company that performs in the beautiful Academy of Music and the next-door Merriam Theater.

Philadelphia Dance Company
DANCE

(☑215-387-8200; www.philadanco.org; 9 N Preston St) For almost 40 years this company has been providing top-shelf exhibitions of dance, blending ballet and modern as the resident company at the Kimmel Center.

Philadelphia Orchestra
CLASSICAL MUSIC

(Map p128; ☑215-893-1999; www.philorch.org; cnr Broad & Spruce Sts) The city's orchestra, founded in 1900, is going through tough financial times. After filing for bankruptcy in April, 2011 its future is in flux.

Trocadero Theater
PERFORMING ARTS

(Map p128; ☑215-922-6888; www.thetroc.com; 1003 Arch St; cover up to $12) An arts and culture showcase in Chinatown housed in a 19th- century Victorian theater. Monday night is movie night with a hodgepodge of musicians, spoken-word artists and comedians other nights.

Sports

Football is all about the Philadelphia Eagles (www.philadelphiaeagles.com), who play at state-of-the-art Lincoln Financial Field (S

11th St) from August through January, usually twice a month, on Sunday. The baseball team is the National League Philadelphia Phillies (www.phillies.mlb.com), who play 81 home games at Citizen's Bank Park from April to October. Finally, basketball comes courtesy of the Philadelphia 76ers (www.nba.com/sixers) at Wells Fargo Center (3601 S Broad St).

❶ Information

Media

Philadelphia Daily News (www.philly.com/dailynews) A tabloid-style daily.

Philadelphia Magazine (www.phillymag.com) A monthly glossy.

Philadelphia Weekly (www.philadelphiaweekly.com) Free alternative available at street boxes around town.

Philly.com (www.philly.com) News, listings and more, courtesy of the *Philadelphia Inquirer.*

WHYY 91-FM (www.whyy.org) Local National Public Radio affiliate.

Medical Services

Pennsylvania Hospital (☑215-829-3000; www.pennhealth.com/hup; 800 Spruce St; ⊘24hr)

Tourist Information

Greater Philadelphia Tourism Marketing Corp (www.visitphilly.com; 6th St, at Market St) The highly developed, nonprofit visitors bureau has comprehensive visitor information. Its welcome center shares space with the NPS center.

Independence Visitor Center (☑800-537-7676; www.independencevisitorcenter.com; 6th St, at Market St; ⊘8:30am-5:30pm) Run by the NPS, the center distributes useful visitor guides and maps, and sells tickets for the various official tours that depart from nearby locations.

❶ Getting There & Away

Air

Philadelphia International Airport (PHL; www.phl.org; 8000 Essington Ave), 7 miles south of Center City, is served by direct international flights; domestically, it has flights to over 100 destinations in the USA.

Bus

Greyhound (www.greyhound.com; 1001 Filbert St) and **Peter Pan Bus Lines** (www.peterpanbus.com; 1001 Filbert St) are the major bus carriers; **Bolt Bus** (www.boltbus.com) and **Mega Bus** (www.us.megabus.com) are popular and comfortable competitors. Greyhound connects Philadelphia with hundreds of cities nationwide, while Peter Pan and the others concentrate on the northeast. When booked online a round-trip fare to New York City can be as low as $18 (2½ hours one way), to Atlantic City it's $20 (1½ hours) and to Washington, DC, it's $28 (4½ hours). **NJ Transit** (www.njtransit.com) carries you from Philly to various points in New Jersey.

Car

Several interstate highways lead through and around Philadelphia. From the north and south, the I-95 (Delaware Expwy) follows the eastern edge of the city beside the Delaware River, with several exits for Center City. The I-276 (Pennsylvania Turnpike) runs east across the northern part of the city and over the river to connect with the New Jersey Turnpike.

Train

Beautiful 30th St Station is one of the biggest train hubs in the country. **Amtrak** (www.amtrak.com) provides service from here to Boston (regional and Acela express service one way $87 to $206, five to 5¾ hours) and Pittsburgh (regional service from $47, 7¼ hours). A cheaper (not compared to the bus) but longer and more complicated way to get to NYC is to take the Septa R7 suburban train to Trenton in New Jersey. From there you can connect with **NJ Transit** (www.njtransit.state.nj.us) to Newark's Penn Station, then continue on NJ Transit to New York City's Penn Station.

🛈 Getting Around

The fare for a taxi to Center City from the airport is a flat fee of $25. The airport is also served by Septa's regional service using the R1 line. The R1 ($7) will drop you off in University City or in numerous stops in Center City.

Downtown distances are short enough to let you see most places on foot, and a train, bus or taxi can get you to places further out relatively easily.

Septa (www.septa.org) operates Philadelphia's municipal buses, plus two subway lines and a trolley service. Though extensive and reliable, the web of bus lines (120 routes servicing 159 sq miles) is difficult to make sense of. The one-way fare on most routes is $2, for which you'll need exact change or a token. Many subway stations and transit stores sell discounted packages of two tokens for $3.10.

Cabs, especially around City Center, are easy to hail. The flag drop or fare upon entry is $2.70, then $2.30 per mile or portion thereof. All licensed taxis have GPS and most accept credit cards.

The **Phlash** (www.phillyphlash.com; ☺9:30am-6pm) shuttle bus looks like an old-school trolley and loops between Penn's Landing and the Philadelphia Museum of Art (one way/

all day $2/5). It runs approximately every 15 minutes.

Around Philadelphia
BRANDYWINE VALLEY

Straddling the Pennsylvania–Delaware border southwest of Philadelphia, the Brandywine Valley is a patchwork of rolling, wooded countryside, historic villages, gardens, mansions and museums. The spectacular Longwood Gardens (☏610-388-1000; www.longwoodgardens.org; Rte 1; adult/child $18/free; ☺9am-5pm, to 6pm Apr-Aug; 🚻) near Kennett Sq has 1050 acres, 20 indoor gardens and 11,000 kinds of plants, with something always in bloom. There's also a Children's Garden with a maze, fireworks and illuminated fountains in summer, and festive lights at Christmas. The Brandywine Valley Wine Trail (www.bvwinetrail.com), meanwhile, is a lovely conduit between a handful of vineyards, all with tasting rooms.

A showcase of American artwork, the Brandywine River Museum (☏610-388-2700; www.brandywinemuseum.org; cnr Hwy 1 & Rte 100; adult/child $10/6; ☺9:30am-4:30pm), at Chadd's Ford, includes the work of the Brandywine School – Howard Pyle, NC Wyeths and Maxfield Parrish. One of the valley's most famous attractions, though, is ??terthur (☏302-888-4600; www.winterthur.org; 5105 Kennett Pike/Rte 52, Winterthur, DE; adult/child $18/5; ☺10am-5pm Tue-Sun), actually in Delaware, an important museum of American furniture and decorative arts that was the country estate of Henry Francis du Pont until he opened it to the public in 1951.

VALLEY FORGE

After being defeated at the Battle of Brandywine Creek and the British occupation of Philadelphia in 1777, General Washington and 12,000 continental troops withdrew to Valley Forge. Today, Valley Forge symbolizes Washington's endurance and leadership. The Valley Forge National Historic Park (☏610-783-1099; www.nps.gov/vafo; cnr N Gulph Rd & Rte 23; admission free; ☺park grounds 7am-dark, welcome center & Washington's Headquarters 9am-5pm) contains 5½ sq miles of scenic beauty and open space 20 miles northwest of downtown Philadelphia – a remembrance of where 2000 of George Washington's 12,000 troops perished from freezing temperatures, hunger and disease, while many others returned home. A 22-mile cycling path along the Schuylkill River connects Valley Forge to Philadelphia.

NEW HOPE & LAMBERTVILLE

New Hope, about 40 miles north of Philadelphia and its sister town Lambertville, across the Delaware River in NJ, sit equidistant from Philadelphia and New York City, and are a pair of quaint, artsy little towns. Both are edged with long and peaceful towpaths, perfect for runners, cyclists and strollers, and a bridge with a walking lane lets you crisscross between the two with ease. The towns draw a large number of gay folk; rainbow flags hanging outside various businesses demonstrate the town's gay-friendliness.

The **Golden Nugget Antique Market** (☎609-397-0811; www.gnmarket.com; 1850 River Rd; ⊙6am-4pm Wed, Sat & Sun), 1 mile south of Lambertville, has all sorts of finds, from furniture to clothing, from a variety of dealers. Or spend a few picturesque hours gliding downstream in a canoe, kayak, raft or tube, courtesy of **Bucks County River Country** (☎215-297-5000; www.rivercountry.net; 2 Walters Lane, Point Pleasant; ⊙rental 9am-2:30pm, return by 5pm), about 8 miles north of New Hope on Rte 32.

Both towns have a plethora of cute B&Bs, if you decide to make a weekend out of it. Try the **York Street House Bed & Breakfast** (☎609-397-3007; www.yorkstreethouse.com; 42 York St, Lambertville; r incl breakfast $125-260; ❋🐾), a 1909 mansion with cozy rooms and big breakfasts.

For a meal in a divinely renovated former church try the **Marsha Brown Creole Kitchen and Lounge** (15 S Main St, New Hope; mains $15-22; ⊙5-10pm) in New Hope serving catfish, steaks and lobster. Or head 4 miles north to the town of Stockton to **Meil's Restaurant** (cnr Main & Bridge Sts; mains $10-15; ⊙8am-9pm Sun-Thu, to 10pm Fri & Sat) for large portions of satisfying comfort food.

Pennsylvania Dutch Country

The core of Pennsylvania Dutch Country lies in the southeast region of Pennsylvania, in an area about 20 miles by 15 miles, east of Lancaster. The Amish (*ah*-mish), Mennonite and Brethren religious communities are collectively known as the 'Plain People.' All are Anabaptist sects, who were persecuted in their native Switzerland, and from the early 1700s settled in tolerant Pennsylvania. Speaking German dialects, they became known as 'Dutch' (from 'Deutsch'). Most Pennsylvania Dutch live on farms and their beliefs vary from sect to sect. Many do not use electricity, and most opt for horse-drawn buggies – a delightful sight, and sound, in the area. The strictest believers, the Old Order Amish, wear dark, plain clothing, and live a simple, Bible-centered life – but have, ironically, become a major tourist attraction, thus bringing busloads of gawkers and the requisite strip malls, chain restaurants and hotels that lend this entire area an oxymoronic quality, to say the least. Because there is so much commercial development – fast-food restaurants, mini-malls, big-box chain stores, tract housing – continually encroaching on multigenerational family farms, it takes some doing to appreciate the unique nature of the area. Try to find your way through a series of back roads snaking their way through rural countryside between Intercourse and Strasburg.

◉ Sights & Activities

On the western edge of Amish country, the city of Lancaster – a mix of art galleries, well-preserved brick row houses and somewhat

---

IF YOU HAVE A FEW MORE DAYS

The town of Bethlehem, from its initial founding by a small religious community to heavy industry center to its current incarnation as a gambling destination, retains a charming historic quality. The massive casino built on the site of the former Bethlehem Steel factory takes design cues from its utilitarian past.

The town of Easton, home to Lafayette College, is in the Lehigh Valley, just over the New Jersey border and on the banks of the Delaware River, only 70 miles or so from both Philadelphia and New York City. Kids can get silly with the hands-on exhibits at the Crayola Factory (☎610-515-8000; www.crayola.com/factory; 30 Centre Sq; admission incl National Canal Museum $9.75; ⊙11am-5pm Memorial Day-Labor Day; ♿). If you want to make an evening of it, grab a cozy room at the Lafayette Inn (☎610-253-4500; www.lafayetteinn.com; 525 W Monroe St; r incl breakfast $125-175; P🐾) and dinner at sophisticated Tuscan trattoria Sette Luna (219 Ferry St; mains $15; ⊙11:30am-10pm) a few blocks from the center of town.

derelict blocks – was briefly the US capital in September 1777, when Congress stopped here overnight. The monthly **First Friday** (www.lancasterarts.com) celebration brings out a friendly local crowd for gallery hops along artsy Prince St.

Probably named for its crossroads location, **Intercourse** has heavily touristy shops selling clothing, quilts, candles, furniture, fudge and, of course, souvenirs with off-color jokes. The **Tanger Outlet stores** on Rte 30 draw tourists with their 21st-century designer clothes.

FREE **Heritage Center Museum** MUSEUM
(☏717-299-6440; www.lancasterheritage.com; 13 W King St, Lancaster; ◉9am-5pm Mon-Sat, 10am-3pm Sun) Has a collection of 18th- and 19th-century paintings and period furniture, and gives an excellent overview of Amish culture.

Aaron & Jessica's Buggy Rides TOUR
(☏717-768-8828; 3121 Old Philadelphia Pike; ◉9am-5pm Mon-Sat; adult/child $10/6; 🚼) Does a fun 2-mile tour narrated by an Amish driver.

Turkey Hill Experience TOUR
(☏888-986-8784; www.turkeyhillexperience. com; 301 Linden St, Columbia; adult/child $14/11; ◉10am-5pm) This brand name's interactive homage to cows and ice cream a la Hershey's Chocolate World.

Sturgis Pretzel House TOUR
(☏717-626-4354; www.juliusssturgis.com; 219 E Main St, Lititz; admission $3; ◉9am-5pm Mon-Sat) Twist your own dough at the USA's first pretzel factory.

Ephrata Cloister HISTORIC SITE
(☏717-733-6600; www.ephratacloister.org; 632 W Main St, Ephrata; adult/child $9/6; ◉9am-5pm Mon-Sat, from noon Sun) Gives tours of its collection of surviving restored buildings at one of the country's earliest religious communities.

🛏 Sleeping

There's a slew of inns and B&Bs in Amish country, and you will find cheap motels along the southeastern portion of Rte 462/ Rte 30. Farm homes rent rooms for $50 to $100 – they welcome kids, provide home-cooked meals and offer a unique opportunity to experience farm life.

Fulton Steamboat Inn HOTEL **$$**
(☏717-299-9999; 1 Hartman Bridge Rd; r from $100; ❄🛜🏊) A nautically themed hotel in land-locked Amish country seems like a gimmick even if the inventor of the steamboat was born nearby. The slight kitsch works however – from shiny brass old-timey light fixtures and painterly wall-paper – the hotel's interior is rather elegant and rooms are spacious and comfy. It's located at a crossroads convenient for trips to farm country or Lancaster.

Red Caboose Motel & Restaurant MOTEL **$$**
(☏888-687-5005; www.redcaboosemotel.com; 312 Paradise Lane, Ronks; r from $120; ❄🛜🚼) There's nothing very hobo-esque about a night's sleep in one of these 25-ton cabooses – TVs and mini-fridges included – though the basic furnishings aren't the draw. Even if spaces are narrow – the width of a train car – the novelty appeals to adults as well as kids. Set on a beautiful rural lane surrounded by picturesque countryside with a small petting zoo and silo to climb with views.

Cork Factory BOUTIQUE HOTEL **$$**
(☏717-735-2075; www.corkfactoryhotel.com; 480 New Holland Ave; r incl breakfast from $125; ❄🛜) An abandoned brick behemoth now houses a stylishly up-to-date hotel only a few miles northeast of the Lancaster city center. Sunday brunch at the hotel's restaurant is a fusion of seasonal new American and down-home comfort cooking.

Beacon Hollow Farm HOMESTAY **$**
(☏717-768-8218; 130 Centreville Rd; r incl breakfast $95) A dairy farm in Gordonville, has a cozy cottage with two bedrooms, provides a country breakfast and lets you milk the cows.

Landis Farm HOMESTAY **$$**
(☏717-898-7028; www.landisfarm.com; 2048 Gochlan Rd, Manheim; r incl breakfast $100) A slightly more upscale and modern (complete with cable TV) experience can be had at this 200-year-old stone home with pinewood floors.

🍴 Eating

To sample one of the famous family-style restaurants and hearty dishes of Amish country, get prepared to rub elbows with lots of tourists. Stop by the **Dutch Haven** (2857 Lincoln Hwy/Rte 30, Ronks; 6-inch pies $7) for a sticky-sweet shoofly pie.

TOP CHOICE **Bird-in-Hand Farmers Market** MARKET **$**
(☏717-393-9674; 2710 Old Philadelphia Pike, Bird-in-Hand; ◉8:30am-5:30pm Wed-Sat Jul-Oct, call for

other times of year) Great deals on tasty locally made jams, cheeses, pretzels, beef jerky and more; two lunch counters serve meals.

Good 'N Plenty Restaurant
AMERICAN $$

(Rte 896, Smoketown; mains $11; ⏰11:30am-8pm Mon-Sat, closed Jan) Sure, you'll be dining with busloads of tourists and your cardiologist might not approve, but hunkering down at one of the picnic tables for a family-style meal ($21) is a lot of fun. Besides the main dining room, which is the size of a football field, there are a couple of other mini-areas where you can order from an à la carte menu.

Miller's
BUFFET $$

(Rte 30, Ronks; mains $11; ⏰7am-8pm Mon-Sat) To smorgasbord ($23) or not to smorgasbord there's no question. Otherwise, the alternative menu of diner-style dishes is fairly ordinary. The anchor of a touristy complex of shops, this pavilion-size restaurant draws crowds for the buffet featuring Amish-style entrees and desserts.

Family Cupboard Restaurant & Buffet
BUFFET $$

(3029 Old Philadelphia Pike; mains $11; ⏰11am-8pm Mon-Thu, 7am-8pm Fri & Sat) To avoid the tour-bus crush, try this place in Bird-in-Hand, for mouthwatering specials such as ham loaf (yes, that's right) and chicken in gravy over waffles.

Lancaster Brewing Co
PUB $$

(302 N Plum St, Lancaster; mains $9-22; ⏰11:30am-10pm) Just down the street from the Cork Factory Hotel in Lancaster, the bar here draws young neighborhood regulars and the menu is a big step-up from standard pub fare – rack of wild boar and cranberry sausage is an example – but you can't beat specials like 35¢-wing night.

Central Market
MARKET $

(23 N Market St, Lancaster; ⏰6am-4pm Tue & Fri, to 2pm Sat) The bustling market offers local produce, cheese, meats and Amish baked goods and crafts.

ⓘ Information

Use a map to navigate the back roads, avoiding main Rtes 30 and 340, or simply visit in winter when tourism is down. Even better, rent a bicycle from **Rails to Trail Bicycle Shop** (☎717-367-7000; www.railstotrail.com; 1010 Hershey Rd, Elizabethtown; rental per day $25; ⏰10am-6pm) between Hershey and Lancaster, pack some food and hit the road. The **Dutch Country Visi**tors Center (☎800-723-8824; www.padutchcountry.com; ⏰9am-6pm Mon-Sat, to 4pm Sun), off Rte 30 in Lancaster, offers comprehensive information.

ⓘ Getting There & Around

RRTA (www.redrosetransit.com) local buses link the main towns, but a car is much more convenient for sightseeing. The **Capitol Trailways & Greyhound terminal** (Lancaster train station) has buses to Philadelphia ($15, two hours 40 minutes) and Pittsburgh ($71, eight hours). The **Amtrak train station** (53 McGovern Ave, Lancaster) has trains to and from Philadelphia ($15, 70 minutes) and Pittsburgh ($48, six hours).

South Central Pennsylvania

HERSHEY

Less than two hours from Philly is the fabled kids' favorite Hershey (www.hersheypa.com), home to a collection of attractions that detail, hype and, of course, hawk, the many trappings of Milton Hershey's chocolate empire. The pièce de résistance is Hershey Park (☎800-437-7439; www.hersheypark.com; 100 W Hersheypark Dr; adult/child $54/33; ⏰10am-10pm Jun-Aug, days & times vary other months; ♿), an amusement park with more than 60 thrill rides, a zoo, water park plus various performances and frequent fireworks displays. Don a hairnet and apron and punch in a few choices on a computer screen and then *voilà*, watch your very own chocolate bar roll down a conveyor belt at the Create Your Own Candy Bar ($15) attraction, part of Hershey's Chocolate World, a mock factory and massive candy store with overstimulating features like singing characters and free chocolate galore. For a more low-key informational visit, try the Hershey Story, The Museum on Chocolate Avenue (☎717-534-3439; www.hersheymuseum.org; 111 W Chocolate Ave; adult/child $10/7.50; ⏰9am-7pm summer, to 5:30pm other times), which explores the life and fascinating legacy of Mr Hershey through interactive history exhibits; try molding your own candy in the hands-on 'Chocolate Lab.'

GETTYSBURG

This tranquil, compact and history-laden town, 145 miles west of Philadelphia, saw one of the Civil War's most decisive and bloody battles. It's also where Lincoln delivered his Gettysburg Address. The area is anchored by the 8-sq-mile Gettysburg National Military

Park (☏717-334-1124; www.nps.gov/gett; 1195 Baltimore Pike (Rte 97); park admission free; ◷6am-10pm Apr-Oct, to 7pm Nov-Mar), with a great **museum and visitor center** (☏877-874-2578; www.gettysburgfoundation.org; adult/child $10.50/6.50 ◷8am-6pm). Here you can pick up a map that details a self-guided auto tour, with somber sights including the Wheatfield, which was strewn with more than 4000 dead and wounded after battle.

The annual **Civil War Battle Reenactment** (☏717-338-1525; www.gettysburgreenactment.com), a festival taking place the first weekend of July, features living-history encampments and battle reenactments drawing aficionados from near and wide.

For accommodations, try the stately three-story Victorian **Brickhouse Inn** (☏717-338-9337; www.brickhouseinn.com; 452 Baltimore St; r $115-165; ❊❀), built c 1898, a wonderful B&B with charming rooms and an outdoor patio. For a meal in Gettysburg's oldest home, built in 1776, head to **Dobbin House Tavern** (☏717-334-2100; 89 Steinwehr Ave; mains $8-25; ◷11:30am-9pm), which serves heaping sandwiches and more elaborate meat and fish meals in kitschy themed dining rooms.

Northeastern

Occupying the northeast corner of Pennsylvania is the famed **Poconos** (☏800-762-6667; www.800poconos.com) region, containing 2400 sq miles of mountains, streams, waterfalls, lakes and forests, making it a beautifully natural getaway at any time during the four seasons. Among the quaint (as well as tacky) towns is adorable **Milford**, home to the lovingly and luxuriously restored **Hotel Fauchere** (☏570-409-1212; www.hotelfauchere.com; 401 Broad St; r incl breakfast from $215; ❊❀); the hotel's stylish **Bar Louis** (mains $21, sandwiches $11) has seasonally inspired fare. The menu at **Muir House** (☏570-296-6373; 102 State St; mains $21; ◷from 5:30pm Wed-Sun) includes a stuffed lamburger ($19) and bulgogi in a lettuce wrap ($12).

For river fun, contact **Adventure Sports** (☏570-223-0505; www.adventuresport.com; Rte 209; per day canoe/kayak $40/44; ◷9am-6pm May-Oct) in Marshalls Creek, Pennsylvania. There are several different put-in and take-out points that allow a variety of itineraries, from quick half-day trips to leisurely multi-day adventures. Camping is allowed at many

PENNSYLVANIA WILDS

Commonly and appropriately referred to as the Pennsylvania Wilds, this little-visited part of Central Pennsylvania includes the largest free-roaming elk herd east of the Mississippi – **Elk State Forest** (www.elkcountryvisitors center.com); an official dark sky park and the best place in the northeastern US for stargazing – **Cherry Springs State Park** (www.dcnr.state.pa.us/state parks/parks/cheerysprings); the **Kizua Bridge Skywalk** (www.visitanf.com) part of the Allegheny National Forest; and overlooks and waterfalls around **Pine Creek Gorge** (www.visittiogapa. com/canyon) in the Tioga State Forest.

points along the way and is a great way to experience the beauty of the area.

A little further west in a tucked-away valley is **Jim Thorpe** (named for an athletic hero of the early 1900s who was buried here – but likely never visited – after town officials decided they needed a signature tourism sight; one of Thorpe's sons recently sued the town to have the remains moved to Oklahoma, his father's home state), which offers a slew of mountain-biking trails and rafting runs (as well as the requisite outfitters).

North of here, where the Delaware River swings west, marking the border between Pennsylvania and New York, and not far from the Catskills, are a number of small, primarily blue-collar towns with the occasional bistro that caters to weekending downstaters. **Lander's River Trips** (☏800-252-3925; www.landersrivertrips.com; per day canoe/kayak/tube $39/45/26) in Callicoon, NY, and in Narrowsburg, NY, further down the river, rents canoes, kayaks and tubes. The rocks at nearby **Skinners Falls** is a great place to spend the day.

Pittsburgh

Famous as an industrial center during the 19th century, to many Americans Pittsburgh still conjures stark images of billowing clouds emanating from steel and coal factories. Today's city, however, despite continuing economic challenges, has a well-earned reputation for being one of the more livable metropolitan areas in the country. The city sits at the point where the Monongahela and Allegheny Rivers join the Ohio River, spreads out over the waterways and has hilly neighborhoods connected by picturesque bridges (all with footpaths), more than any other city in the US. Teeming with students from the many universities in town, it's a surprisingly hip and cultured city with top-notch museums, abundant greenery and several bustling neighborhoods with lively restaurant and bar scenes.

Scottish-born immigrant Andrew Carnegie made his fortune here by modernizing steel production, and his legacy is still synonymous with the city and its many cultural and educational institutions. Production dipped during the Great Depression but rose again because of mass-produced automobiles in the 1930s. When the economy and local steel industry took another major hit in the 1970s, the city's pride was buoyed by its local NFL football team: the Steelers achieved a remarkable run of four Super Bowl championships, a feat whose importance to the continuing psyche of some Pittsburghers can't be underestimated. After the steel industry's demise, Pittsburgh's economy has refocused on health care, technology and education and the city is home to several notable Fortune 500 companies, including Alcoa and Heinz.

◉ Sights & Activities

Points of interest in Pittsburgh are scattered everywhere, and the city's spread-out nature makes it a difficult place to cover thoroughly on foot. Driving can also be troublesome, due to the oddly laid-out streets, which confuse even locals. Public buses, luckily, are quite reliable. University of Pittsburgh, Carnegie-Mellon University, Duquesne University and several other smaller colleges are all large presences in town, with sprawling campuses and bustling academic crowds.

The mystical-sounding Golden Triangle, between the converging Monongahela and Allegheny Rivers, is Pittsburgh's renovated downtown. Just northeast of here, the Strip offers warehouses, ethnic food stores and nightclubs and a little further north is gallery-filled up-and-coming Lawrenceville. Across the Allegheny River, the North Side has big sports stadiums plus several museums. Across the Monongahela River is the South Side, whose Slopes rise up to Mt Washington; at the Flats, E Carson St bustles with clubs and restaurants. East of

downtown is Oakland, the university area, and beyond that Squirrel Hill and Shadyside, residential neighborhoods with an elegant, small-town feel.

Pittsburgh Parks Conservancy   PARK
(☑412-682-7275; www.pittsburghparks.org) For pretty much any outdoor pursuit, the best option is the elaborate, 1700-acre system of the Pittsburgh Parks Conservancy, which comprises Schenley Park (with ball fields, a public swimming pool and golf course), Highland Park (with swimming pool, tennis courts and cycling track), Riverview Park (sporting ball fields and horseback riding trails) and Frick Park (with hiking trails, clay courts and a bowling green), all with beautiful running, cycling and in-line skating trails. Check out Golden Triangle Bike Rental (☑412-600-0675; www.goldentriangle bikenblade.com; 600 First Ave; rental per hr/day $8/30) for rentals and tours of the city; there's even a continuous trail all the way to Washington, DC called the Great Allegheny Passage (www.gaptrail.org). Another prime source for info on cycling, hiking and kayaking in the city's parks and around the area is Venture Outdoors (☑412-255-0564; www.wpfi.org; 304 Forbes Ave).

DOWNTOWN
This area is referred to as the 'Golden Triangle' only in official tourist brochures.

Point State Park   PARK
At the triangle's tip is the renovated and beautified waterfront, which is popular during summer with strollers, cyclists, loungers and runners; for a longer run, head to the 11-mile gravel-paved Montour Trail (www.montourtrail.org), accessible by crossing the 6th St Bridge and catching the paved path at the Carnegie Science Center. The park's renovated Fort Pitt Museum (☑412-281-9285; www.heinzhistorycenter.org; 101 Commonwealth Pl; adult/child $5/free; ☺10am-5pm) commemorates the historic heritage of the French and Indian War.

Senator John Heinz Pittsburgh
Regional History Center   MUSEUM
(☑412-454-6000; www.heinzhistorycenter.org; 1212 Smallman St; adult/child incl Sports Museum $10/5; ☺10am-5pm) The remodeled brick warehouse offers a good take on the region's past, with exhibits on the French and Indian War, early settlers, immigrants, steel and the glass industry; it's also home to the Western Pennsylvania Sports Museum (☺10am-5pm; 🚹), focusing on champs from

Pittsburgh. Fun interactive exhibits for kids and adults who refuse to admit their shot at professional sports has passed them by.

August Wilson Center for African American Culture
ARTS CENTER

(☑412-258-2700; www.augustwilsoncenter.org; 980 Liberty Ave) Named after an award-winning playwright and Pittsburgh native son, this contemporary institution focuses on African American arts, performance and culture.

SOUTH SIDE & MT WASHINGTON

Youthful, funky and bustling like NYC's East Village, the South Side is bursting with shops, eateries and drinking spots. In the 10 blocks between the 10th St Bridge and Birmingham Bridge there are dozens of bars, including a bunch of hole-in-the-wall joints.

TOP CHOICE Monongahela & Duquesne Incline
TRAM

(one way adult/child $2.25/1.10; ⊗5:30am-12:45am Mon-Sat, from 7am Sun) The historic funicular railroads (c 1877) that run up and down Mt Washington's steep slopes afford great city views, especially at night. At the start of the Duquesne Incline is Station Square (Station Sq Dr, at Fort Pitt Bridge), a group of beautiful, renovated railway buildings that now comprise what is essentially a big ol' mall. Rising up from the bustling South Side valley is the neighborhood called the South Side Slopes, a fascinating community of houses that seem perilously perched on the edge of cliffs, accessible via steep, winding roads and hundreds of stairs.

FREE Society for Contemporary Art
ARTS CENTER

(☑412-261-7003; www.contemporarycraft.org; 2100 Smallman St; ⊗10am-5pm Mon-Sat) For cutting-edge crafts and other art exhibitions.

NORTH SIDE

While this part of town feels most populated when its PNC Park is filled with sports fans for a Pittsburgh Steelers game, rest assured that its many museums are hopping, too.

TOP CHOICE Andy Warhol Museum
MUSEUM

(☑412-237-8300; www.warhol.org; 117 Sandusky St; adult/child $15/8; ⊗10am-5pm Tue-Thu, Sat & Sun, to 10pm Fri) Celebrates Pittsburgh's coolest native son, who became famous for his pop art, avant-garde movies, celebrity connections and Velvet Underground spectaculars. Exhibits include celebrity portraits, while the museum's theater hosts frequent film screenings and quirky performers. Friday-night cocktails at the museum are popular with Pittsburgh's gay community.

Carnegie Science Center
MUSEUM

(☑412-237-3400; www.carnegiesciencecenter.org; 1 Allegheny Ave; adult/child $18/10, IMAX & special exhibits extra; ⊗10am-5pm Sun-Fri, to 7pm Sat; ♠) Great for kids and a cut above the average hands-on science museum, with innovative exhibits on subjects ranging from outer space to candy.

Children's Museum of Pittsburgh
MUSEUM

(☑412-322-5058; www.pittsburghkids.org; Allegheny Sq; adult/child $11/10; ⊗10am-5pm Mon-Sat, noon-5pm Sun; ♠) Features loads of interactive exhibits, including a chance for kids to get under the hood of real cars and some child-friendly Warhol works.

Mexican War Streets
NEIGHBORHOOD

Nearby in the northwest is the Mexican War Streets neighborhood, named after battles and soldiers of the 1846 Mexican War. The carefully restored row houses, with Greek Revival doorways and Gothic turrets lining the quiet streets, make for a peaceful, post museum stroll.

National Aviary
ZOO

(☑412-323-7235; www.aviary.org; 700 Arch St, Allegheny Sq; adult/child $13/11; ⊗10am-5pm; ♠) Another treat, with more than 600 exotic and endangered birds.

Mattress Factory
ARTS CENTER

(☑412-231-3169; www.mattress.org; 500 Sampsonia Way; adult/child $10/free; ⊗10am-5pm Tue-Sat, 1-5pm Sun) Hosting unique large-scale installation art and frequent performances.

OAKLAND & AROUND

The University of Pittsburgh and Carnegie Mellon University are here, and the surrounding streets are packed with cheap eateries, cafes, shops and student homes.

Carnegie Museums
MUSEUM

(☑412-622-3131; www.carnegiemuseums.org; 4400 Forbes Ave; adult/child to both $15/11; ⊗10am-5pm Tue-Sat, from noon Sun) The Carnegie Museum of Art (www.cmoa.org), with terrific exhibits of architecture, impressionist, postimpressionist and modern American paintings; and the Carnegie Museum of Natural History (www.carnegiemnh.org) featuring a complete Tyrannosaurus skeleton and exhibits on Pennsylvania geology and Inuit prehistory.

FREE Frick Art & Historical Center   MUSEUM
(✆412-371-0600; www.frickart.org; 7227 Reynolds St; ⏱10am-5pm, closed Mon) East of Oakland, in Point Breeze, is this wonderful center, which displays some of Henry Clay Frick's Flemish, French and Italian paintings in its Art Museum; assorted classics in the Car & Carriage Museum; more than five acres of grounds and gardens; and Clayton (tours $10), the restored 1872 Frick mansion.

🖌 Phipps Conservatory   GARDENS
(✆412-622-6914; www.phipps.conservatory.org; One Schenley Park; adult/child $12/9; ⏱9:30am-5pm, to 10pm Fri) An impressive steel and glass greenhouse with beautifully designed and curated gardens.

FREE Cathedral of Learning   TOWER
(✆412-624-6000; 4200 Fifth Ave; tours $3; ⏱9am-3pm Mon-Sat, from 11am Sun) Rising up from the center of the U Pitt campus, a grand, 42-story Gothic tower which, at 535ft, is the second-tallest education building in the world. It houses the elegant **Nationality Classrooms**, each representing a different style and period; most are accessible only with a guided tour.

SQUIRREL HILL & SHADYSIDE

These upscale neighborhoods feature wide streets, excellent restaurants, chain stores and independent boutiques and bakeries (try the burnt-almond tortes, a classic Pittsburgh dessert). Squirrel Hill is home to Pittsburgh's large Jewish community, the city's best kosher eateries, butchers and Judaica shops; apartment buildings, duplexes and more modest housing are almost as common as the grand mansions the neighborhood is known for.

In Shadyside, Walnut St is the bustling main strip. The leafy campus of **Chatham University**, located between the two neighborhoods, is a nice place to stroll.

GREATER PITTSBURGH

Formerly gritty **Lawrenceville** has become the city's **Interior Design District**, comprising the stretch on and around Butler St from 16th to 62nd Sts. It's a long and spotty strip of shops, galleries, studios, bars and eateries that's on every hipster's radar, and runs into the gentrifying **Garfield** neighborhood, a good place for cheap ethnic eats. **Bloomfield**, a really little Little Italy, is a strip of groceries, Italian eateries and, of all things, a landmark Polish restaurant, the Bloom-field Bridge Tavern. The Pittsburgh zoo and aquarium and a waterpark are nearby.

Tour-Ed Mine   MINE
(✆724-224-4720; www.tour-edmine.com; 748 Bull Creek Rd, Tarentum; adult/child $7.50/6.50; ⏱10am-4pm, closed Tue, Jun-Sep) To experience something of the claustrophobia and learn about the working lives of coal miners, take this tour 160ft below the earth's surface.

Kennywood Amusement Park   AMUSEMENT PARK
(✆412-461-0500; 4800 Kennywood Blvd, West Mifflin; www.kennywood.com; adult/child $37/24; ⏱10:30am-10pm Jun-Aug) A nationally historic landmarked amusement park 12 miles southeast of downtown with four old wooden roller coasters.

👉 Tours

TOP CHOICE Alan Irvine Storyteller Tours   WALKING
(✆412-521-6406; www.alanirvine.com; tours $10-15) This historian brings the city's past to life in a journey through several different neighborhoods.

'Burgh Bits & Bites Food Tour   WALKING
(✆800-979-3370; www.burghfoodtour.com; tours $35) Wonderful way to discover the city's unique ethnic eats.

Pittsburgh History & Landmarks Foundation   WALKING
(✆412-471-5808; www.phlf.org; Station Sq; some tours free, others from $5) Specialized historic, architectural or cultural tours by foot or motor coach.

✨ Festivals & Events

Hothouse   CULTURAL
(www.sproutfund.org/hothouse) Annual summertime night of eclectic performance, art and music supports Pittsburgh's creative side.

Three Rivers Art Festival   CULTURAL
(www.3riversartsfes.org) Showcasing the city's cultural credentials, this 10-day blowout in June features free concerts and outdoor visual and performance arts in Point State Park.

🛏 Sleeping

Straight-up chain hotels, especially around Oakland, dominate the city's lodging options. The Omni Penn Hotel towers over the downtown district. For more character, check in with the **Pittsburgh Bed & Breakfast Association** (www.pittsburghbnb.com).

Inn on Negley
INN $$

(☏412-661-0631; www.innonnegley.com; 703 Negley Ave; r $180-240; P❀🐾) Formerly a pair of Shadyside inns, these two Victorian houses have been combined into one newly refurbished gem with a clean-line aesthetic that still bursts with romance. It features four-poster beds, handsome furniture and fireplaces, large windows and, in some rooms, hot tubs.

The Priory
INN $$

(☏412-231-3338; www.thepriory.com; 614 Pressley St; r incl breakfast from $140; P❀🐾) Housed in a former Catholic monastery on the North Side just over the Veterans Bridge, the Priory is a mix of old-fashion furnishings with contemporary design touches. There's a parlor with a fireplace and interior courtyard good for drinks in warm months. A new wing with rooms was added in 2011. Attached is the magnificent Grand Hall, a former church, now host to weddings and events.

Inn on the Mexican War Streets
INN $$

(☏412-231-6544; www.innonthemexicanwarstreets.com; 604 W North Ave; r incl breakfast $139-189; P❀🐾) This historic, gay-owned mansion on the North Side is near the museums and right on the bus line that takes you downtown. Expect hearty homemade breakfasts, charming hosts, stunning antique furnishings and an elegant porch, plus a martini lounge and the four-star restaurant Acanthus.

The Parador Inn
B&B $$

(☏412-231-4800; www.theparadorinn.com; 939 Western Ave; r incl breakfast $150; P❀🐾) This lovingly restored mansion on the North Side not far from the National Aviary and Heinz Field is a charming hodgepodge of aesthetic influence – from Victorian to Caribbean and everything in between. The owner is on hand to answer any questions and there are public rooms and a garden to relax in.

Sunnyledge
HOTEL $$$

(☏412-683-5014; www.sunnyledge.com; 5124 Fifth Ave; r/ste $189/275; ❀) Though it refers to itself as a 'boutique hotel,' it would be more accurate to describe the Sunnyledge as a 'historic' one. Housed in an 1886 mansion in Shadyside, the atmosphere is one of traditional elegance that's overwrought at times.

Morning Glory Inn
INN $$$

(☏412-431-1707; www.gloryinn.com; 2119 Sarah St; r incl breakfast $145-190, ste $175-450; ❀🐾) An Italianate-style Victorian brick townhouse in the heart of the busy South Side. The overall decor is slightly chintzy but you can relax in the charming backyard patio, and delicious breakfasts are a major plus.

✕ Eating

The highest concentration and majority of restaurants are located on the South Side on and around Carson St. The Italian shops in the Strip district are where local chefs go to shop for meat and cheese.

Southside

Cafe du Jour
MEDITERRANEAN $$$

(1107 E Carson St; mains $15-35; ⏱11:30am-10pm Mon-Sat) Part of the raucous South Side 'hood, Cafe du Jour has a constantly changing menu of Mediterranean dishes. It does especially good soups and salads for lunch; try to get a seat in the small outside courtyard. It's BYOB.

Dish Osteria Bar
MEDITERRANEAN $$

(☏412-390-2012; 128 S 17th St; mains $18; ⏱5pm-2am Mon-Sat) A tucked-away, intimate locals' fave. The simple wood tables and floors belie the at-times extravagant Mediterranean creations, which range from fresh sardines with caramelized onions to fettuccine with lamb *ragù*.

Gypsy Café
MEDITERRANEAN $$

(☏412-381-4977; 1330 Bingham St; mains $15; ⏱11:30am-midnight) The purple floors and walls and brightly colored rugs make loyal patrons here as happy as the fresh, seasonal fare. Sample menu items include a smoked trout plate and a stew of shrimp, scallop and feta. Hours are changeable so call ahead.

Café Zenith
VEGETARIAN $$

(86 S 26th St; mains $10; ⏱11am-9pm Thu-Sat, 11am-3pm Sun) A meal at this Southside restaurant is like eating in an antique shop and everything from the formica tables and up, is for sale. Regardless, the Sunday brunch ($10) and lengthy tea menu are up to date.

City Grill
AMERICAN $$

(2019 E Carson St; mains $10-25; ⏱11am-11pm Mon-Thu, to midnight Fri & Sat, 4-10pm Sun) On the South Side; known for mouthwatering burgers, considered one of the best in the city.

Kessab's
MIDDLE EASTERN $

(1207 Carson St; mains $6; ☺10:30am-10pm
Mon-Thu, to 11pm Fri & Sat) This Lebanese restaurant on the South Side serves splendid
baba ghanoush.

Double Wide Grill
AMERICAN $$

(2339 E Carson St; mains $16; ☺11am-10pm Mon-
Wed, to midnight Thu-Sat, 10am-10pm Sun) Does
barbecue as well as interesting veggie op-
tions like pulled seitan and coconut tofu.

Other Neighborhoods

Dinette
PIZZERIA $$

(☑412-362-0202; 5996 Penn Circle South; pizzas $14; ☺6-11ppm, to midnight Fri & Sat) James
Beard award-semi finalist two years running,
Sonja Finn has elevated this casual Shadyside eatery into a destination for Yinzer
foodies. The individual gourmet thin-crust
pizzas are topped with locally sourced meat
and produce and an excellent wine selection.

Primanti Bros
SANDWICHES $

(18th St, at Smallman St; sandwiches $6; ☺24hr) A
Pittsburgh institution on the Strip, this always packed place specializes in greasy and
delicious hot sandwiches – from knockwurst
and cheese to the 'Pitts-burger cheesesteak.'
Other outlets are in Oakland, downtown
and South Side.

Essie's Original Hot Dog Shop
FAST FOOD $

(3901 Forbes Ave; meals $3; ☺10am-3:30am Mon-
Thu, to 5am Fri & Sat) Affectionately nicknamed
'dirty Os' or 'the O' by locals, this Oakland
favorite is known for its cheap dogs and
mounds of crispy fries – especially after a
night at the bars.

Quiet Storm Coffeehouse &
Restaurant
VEGETARIAN $

(5430 Penn Ave; mains $8; ☺8am-7pm Mon-Thu,
to 10pm Fri, 10am-10pm Sat, 10am-4pm Sun; ☑)
This hipster-filled, multiuse cafe in Garfield specializes in veggie and vegan cuisine
and hosts frequent readings and musical
performances.

Pamela's Diner
DINER $

(3703 Forbes Ave; mains $6; ☺7:30am-4pm)
Locals – and President Obama, who said the
crepe-style pancakes were his favorite – swear
by the breakfast at this Oakland spot. Other
locations in the Strip, Shadyside and Squirrel
Hill.

Ritter's Diner
DINER $

(5221 Baum Blvd; mains $7; ☺24hr) A classic
greasy spoon where locals of the Bloom-
field neighborhood head for a pierogi after

a long night out. Each table has its own
jukebox.

Pho Minh
VIETNAMESE $

(4917 Penn Ave; mains $7; ☺noon-9pm Wed, Thu
& Sun, to 10pm Fri & Sat) Tiny and popular
in Bloomfield; does excellent Vietnamese
noodle, soup and tofu dishes.

🍷 Drinking & Entertainment
BARS & NIGHTCLUBS

Most nightlife is centered on the South Side
and the Strip. Carson St is ground zero for
bar-hopping. You'll find several big, frenzied
dance clubs, known 'meatmarkets,' clustered
at the edge of the Strip district. Most gay bars
are in a concentrated stretch of Liberty Ave
downtown. They're hoppin' and plentiful.

Bloomfield Bridge Tavern
PUB

(4412 Liberty Ave; ☺5:30pm-2am Tue-Sat) The
only Polish restaurant in Lil' Italy, is a
gritty pub that serves beers with excellent
sides of pierogi and the occasional indie
rock band.

Church Brew Works
BREWERY

(3525 Liberty Ave; ☺10:30am-10pm) Serving
handcrafted beers in a massive former
church space, this brewery is a standout
in Lawrenceville.

Hofbräuhaus
BEER HALL

(2705 S Water St; ☺11am-11pm, to 2am Fri & Sat)
An imitation of the famous Munich beer
hall and only a block off Carson.

Gooski
BAR

(3117 Brereton St; ☺3pm-2am) Hipster bar
in Polish Hill neighborhood with cheap
drinks and jukebox.

Brillo Box Bar
BAR

(4104 Penn Ave; ☺11am-2am Tue-Sat, from 6pm
Sun) Live music, excellent menu and a
good Sunday brunch at this popular spot
in Lawrenceville.

Dee's Cafe
BAR

(1314 E Carson St; ☺noon-2am Mon-Sat, from
2pm Sun) The Southside bar for billiards
with Pabst on tap.

Smokin' Joe's
BAR

(2001 E Carson St; ☺11am-2am) Good for its
huge beer selection.

LIVE MUSIC

Shadow Lounge
LIVE MUSIC

(☑412-363-8277; www.shadowlounge.net; 5972
Baum Blvd) Two venues for catching hot

hip-hop and house DJs, plus indie bands, readings and open-mic nights.

Rex Theater CONCERT VENUE
(☎412-381-6811; www.rextheater.com; 1602 E Carson St) This is a favorite South Side venue, a converted movie theater, for touring jazz, rock and indie bands; everyone from Edgar Winter to Ani DiFranco.

Manchester Craftsman Guild LIVE MUSIC
(☎412-322-0800; www.mcgjazz.org; 1815 Metropolitan St) Live concerts and recordings of top jazz musicians are held here, on the north side of the city.

Club Café LIVE MUSIC
(☎412-431-4950; www.clubcafelive.com; 56-58 S 12th St) On the South Side, has live music nightly, mostly of the singer-songwriter type.

THEATER & CULTURE

Pittsburgh Cultural Trust PERFORMING ARTS
(☎412-471-6070; www.pgharts.org; 803 Liberty Ave) Promotes all downtown arts, from the Pittsburgh Dance Council and PNC Broadway in Pittsburgh to visual art and opera; the website has links to all main arts venues.

Gist Street Readings PERFORMING ARTS
(www.giststreet.org; 3rd fl, 305 Gist St; readings $10) Holds monthly readings from local and well-known national literary figures. Best to get there when doors open at 7:15pm, since turnout is typically large. Bring your own refreshments.

Harris Theater CINEMA
(☎412-682-4111; www.pghfilmmakers.org; 809 Liberty Ave) The restored theater screens a wide variety of art-house films, often part of film festivals. Operated by the Pittsburgh Filmmakers organization.

SPORTS

Pittsburgh is a big-time sports city. Fans will tell you they bleed black and gold, the colors of the hometown NFL franchise the Steelers who play at Heinz Field (www.pittsburghsteelers.com). Also on the North Side, just by the Allegheny River, is PNC Park (www.pirateball.com), where the Pittsburgh Pirates major-league baseball team bases itself. Mellon Arena (www.penguins.nhl.com), just east of downtown, is where the NHL Pittsburgh Penguins drop the puck. The University of Pittsburgh basketball team, the Pitt Panthers (www.pittsburghpanthers.com), is a perennial top-ranked team with a rabid fan base.

ⓘ Information

Media

Pittsburgh City Paper (www.pghcitypaper.com) Free alternative weekly with extensive arts listings.

Pittsburgh Post-Gazette (www.post-gazette.com) A major daily.

Pittsburgh Tribune-Review (www.pittsburghlive.com) Another major daily.

Pittsburgh's Out (www.outonline.com) Free monthly gay newspaper.

WQED-FM: 90.5 Local National Public Radio affiliate.

WYEP-FM: 91.3 Local independent station with eclectic music.

Medical Services

Allegheny County Health Department
(☎412-687-2243; 3333 Forbes Ave) Has a walk-in medical center.

University of Pittsburgh Medical Center
(☎412-647-8762; 200 Lothrop St; ☻24hr) Emergency, high-ranking medical care.

Tourist Information

Greater Pittsburgh Convention & Visitors Bureau Main Branch (☎412-281-7711; www.visitpittsburgh.com; Suite 2800, 120 Fifth Ave; ☻10am-6pm Mon-Fri, to 4pm Sat, to 3pm Sun) Publishes the *Official Visitors Guide* and provides maps and tourist advice.

Websites

Citysearch (pittsburgh.citysearch.com) Nightlife, restaurant and shopping listings.

Pittsburgh.net (www.pittsburgh.net) Listings, neighborhoods and events.

Pop City (www.popcitymedia.com) Weekly e-magazine highlighting arts and cultural events.

ⓘ Getting There & Away

Air

Pittsburgh International Airport (PIT; www.pitairport.com), 18 miles west from downtown, has direct connections to Europe, Canada and major US cities via a slew of airlines.

Bus

Arriving in its station near the Strip, **Greyhound** (cnr 11th St & Liberty Ave) has frequent buses to Philadelphia ($46, seven hours), New York ($54, 11 hours) and Chicago, IL ($62, 10 to 14 hours).

Car

Pittsburgh is easily accessible via major highways, from the north or south on the I-76 or I-79, from the west on Rte 22 and from the east on the I-70. It's about an eight-hour drive from New York City and about three hours from Buffalo.

Train

Amtrak (1100 Liberty Ave) is behind the magnificent original train station, with trains heading to cities including Philadelphia (from $47, seven to eight hours) and New York (from $63, nine to 11 hours).

ⓘ Getting Around

The excellent **28X Airport Flyer** (www.port authority.org/PAAC.com; one way $2.60) public bus makes runs from the airport to Oakland and downtown every 20 minutes. Taxis are readily available and cost about $40 (not including tip) to downtown. Various shuttles also make downtown runs and cost $15 to $20 per person one way.

Driving around Pittsburgh can be extremely frustrating – roads end with no warning, one-way streets can take you in circles and there are various bridges to contend with.

Port Authority Transit (www.portauthority. org) operates an extensive bus system and a limited light-rail system, the 'T,' which is useful for going from downtown to the South Side. Bus and T fares range from free to $3, depending on the zone in which you're traveling.

For taxis, call **Yellow Cab Co of Pittsburgh** (☑412-321-8100), which charges by zone.

Around Pittsburgh

A Frank Lloyd Wright masterpiece, **Fallingwater** (☑724-329-8501; www.fallingwater. org; adult/child $18/12; ☺10am-4pm, closed Wed, check for detailed schedule) is south of Pittsburgh on Rte 381. Completed in 1939 as a weekend retreat for the Kaufmanns, owners of the Pittsburgh department store, the building blends seamlessly with its natural setting. To see inside you must take one of the hourly guided tours, and reservations are recommended. A more intensive two-hour tour, with photography permitted, is offered ($55; times vary depending on day and month, reservations required). The rather attractive forested grounds open at 8:30am.

Much less visited is **Kentuck Knob** (☑724-329-1901; www.kentuckknob.com; adult/child $16/10; ☺10am-5pm Tue-Sun, from noon Wed), another Frank Lloyd Wright house (designed in 1953), built into the side of a rolling hill. It's noted for its natural materials, hexagonal design and honeycomb skylights. House tours last about an hour and include a jaunt through the onsite sculpture garden, with works by Andy Goldsworthy, Ray Smith and others.

To spend a night or two in the area, opt for the historic mountaintop **Summit Inn** (☑724-438-8594; www.summitinnresort. com; 101 Skyline Dr; r from $120; ❋☎❋) or the swank **Nemacolin Woodlands Resort & Spa** (☑724-329-8555; www.nemacolin.com; 1001 Lafayette Dr; r from $200), with a spa, golf course and dining rooms. Both are in Farmington.

New England

Includes »

Best Places to Eat

» Simon Pearce (p209)

» Mezze Bistro + Bar (p193)

» Frank Pepe's (p200)

» Costantino's Venda Ravioli (p194)

» Black Trumpet Bistro (p215)

Best Places to Stay

» Omni Parker House (p167)

» Carpe Diem (p184)

» Willard Street Inn (p213)

» Ale House Inn (p215)

» Providence Biltmore (p194)

Why Go?

New England may look small on a map, but don't let that fool you. Yes, you could drive from one end to the other in a day but really, why would you want to? There are simply too many enticements along the way. The cities offer a vibrant mix of historical sites, chef-driven restaurants and Ivy League campuses. On the coast you'll find age-old fishing villages and sandy beaches begging a dip. Or head inland, where the northern states are as rural and rugged as the mountains that run up their spines. So take it slow. Crack open a lobster and let the sweet juices run down your fingers. Hike quiet trails. Or just get lost on a scenic back road and count the covered bridges. And if you're lucky enough to be here in autumn, you'll be rewarded with the most brilliant fall foliage you'll ever see.

When to Go
Boston

May–Jun Uncrowded sights and lightly trodden trails. Whale-watching begins.

Jul–Aug Top tourist season with summer festivals, warm ocean water and beach parties.

Fall New England's blazing foliage peaks from mid-September to mid-October.

Getting There & Around

Getting to New England is easy, but once you arrive you'll need a car if you want to explore the region thoroughly. The coastal I-95 and the inland I-91, the main north–south highways, transverse New England from Connecticut to Canada. Public transportation is fine between major cities but scarce in the countryside. **Greyhound** (www.greyhound.com) operates the most extensive bus service.

Amtrak's (www.amtrak.com) Northeast Corridor service connects Boston, Providence, Hartford and New Haven with New York City; smaller regional services operate elsewhere in New England.

Boston's **Logan International Airport** (BOS) is New England's main hub. **TF Green Airport** (PVD) in Providence, Rhode Island, and **Manchester Airport** (MHT) in New Hampshire – both about an hour's drive from Boston – are growing 'minihubs' boasting less congestion and cheaper fares.

NEW ENGLAND PARKS

Acadia National Park (p231), on the rugged, northeastern coast of Maine, is the region's only national park but numerous other large tracts of New England's forest, mountains and shoreline are set aside for preservation and recreation.

The **White Mountain National Forest** (p218), a vast 800,000-acre expanse of New Hampshire and Maine, offers a wonderland of scenic drives, hiking trails, campgrounds and ski slopes. Vermont's **Green Mountain National Forest** (p208) covers 400,000 acres of unspoiled forest that's crossed by the Appalachian Trail. Another gem of nationally preserved lands is the **Cape Cod National Seashore** (p182), a 44,600-acre stretch of rolling dunes and stunning beaches that's perfect for swimming, cycling and seaside hikes.

State parks are plentiful throughout New England, ranging from green niches in urban locations to the remote, untamed wilderness of **Baxter State Park** (p235) in northern Maine.

Seafood Specialties

» **Clam chowder** Or, as Bostonians say, *chow-dah,* combines chopped clams, potatoes and clam juice in a milk base

» **Oysters** Served raw on the half-shell or, for the less intrepid, broiled; sweetest are Wellfleet oysters from Cape Cod

» **Steamers** Soft-shelled clams steamed and served in a bucket of briny broth

» **Clambake** A meal of steamed lobster, clams and corn on the cob

DON'T MISS

You can't leave New England without cracking open a steamed lobster at a beachside seafood shack, such as the Lobster Dock in Boothbay Harbor.

Fast Facts

» Hub cities: Boston (population 617,600), Providence (population 178,000)

» Boston to Acadia National Park: 310 miles

» Time zone: Eastern

» States covered in this chapter: Massachusetts, Rhode Island, Connecticut, Vermont, New Hampshire, Maine

Did You Know?

Four of the six US states that have legalized gay marriage are in New England.

Resources

» Discover New England (www.discovernewengland. org) links to destinations throughout New England.

» Yankee Magazine's fall foliage guide (www.yankee foliage.com) gives foliage forecasts and scenic drives.

New England Highlights

❶ Following in the footsteps of Colonial rebel rousers along **Boston's Freedom Trail** (p166)

❷ Romping across the dunes at **Cape Cod National Seashore** (p182)

❸ Ogling the palatial mansions and basking in music at folk and jazz festivals in **Newport** (p195)

❹ Wandering the cobbled Moby Dick–era streets of **Nantucket** (p186)

❺ Driving the scenic **Kancamagus Highway** (p217) across the craggy White Mountains

❻ Hiking and cycling the carriage roads of **Acadia National Park** (p231)

7 Working off an organic lunch at one of **Burlington's** (p212) green cafes with a paddle around Lake Champlain

8 Stretching your quads on a hike in the **Green Mountains** (p208)

9 Treating yourself to dazzling fall foliage in the **Berkshires** (p191) and **Litchfield Hills** (p204)

History

When the first European settlers arrived, New England was inhabited by native Algonquians who lived in small tribes, raising corn and beans, hunting game and harvesting the rich coastal waters.

English captain Bartholomew Gosnold landed at Cape Cod and sailed north to Maine in 1602 but it wasn't until 1614 that Captain John Smith, who charted the region's coastline for King James I, christened the land 'New England.' With the arrival of the Pilgrims at Plymouth in 1620, European settlement began in earnest. Over the next century the colonies expanded, often at the expense of the indigenous people.

Although subjects of the British crown, New Englanders governed themselves with their own legislative councils and they came to view their affairs as separate from those of England. In the 1770s King George III instituted policies intent on reining in the colonists' free-wheeling spirits and he imposed a series of costly taxes. The colonists, unrepresented in the English Parliament, revolted under the slogan 'no taxation without representation.' Attempts to squash the revolt resulted in the battles of Lexington and Concord, setting off the American Revolution that gave birth to the USA in 1776.

Following independence, New England became an economic powerhouse, its harbors booming centers for shipbuilding, fishing and trade. New England's famed Yankee Clippers plied ports from China to South America. The USA's first water-powered cotton-spinning mill was established in Rhode Island in 1793. In the years that followed New England's swift rivers became the engines of vast mills turning out clothing, shoes and machinery.

But no boom lasts forever. By the early 20th century many of the mills had moved south. Today education, finance, biotechnology and tourism are linchpins of the regional economy.

Local Culture

New Englanders tend to be reserved by nature, with a Yankee thriftiness of speech, which stands in marked contrast to the casual outgoing nature of, say, Californians. This taciturn quality shouldn't be confused with unfriendliness, as it's simply a more formal regional style.

Particularly in rural areas you'll notice the pride folks take in their ingenuity and self-sufficient character. These New Englanders remain fiercely independent, from the fishing boat crews who brave Atlantic storms to the small Vermont farmers who fight to keep operating independently within America's gobble-up agribusiness economy.

Fortunately for the farmers and fishers, buy-local and go-organic movements have grown by leaps and bounds throughout New England. From bistros in Boston to small towns in the far north the menus are greening.

One place you won't find that ol' Yankee reserve is at the ball field. New Englanders are absolutely fanatical about sports. Attending a Red Sox game is as close as you'll come to a modern-day gladiators-at-the-coliseum scene – wild cheers and nasty jeers galore.

Generally regarded as a liberal enclave, New England's in the forefront on pro-

---

NEW ENGLAND IN...

One Week

Start in **Boston**, cruising the **Freedom Trail**, dining at a cozy **North End bistro** and exploring the city's highlights. Next, tramp through the mansions in **Newport**, then hit the beaches on **Cape Cod** and hop a ferry for a day trip to **Nantucket** or **Martha's Vineyard**. End the week with a jaunt north to New Hampshire's **White Mountains**, circling back down the **Maine coast**.

Two Weeks

Now you've got time for serious exploring. Visit the lively burgs of **Providence**, **Portland** and **Burlington**, get a taste of maritime history in **Mystic** and take a leisurely drive through the **Litchfield Hills** and the **Berkshires**. Kayak along the shores of **Acadia National Park**. Wrap it up in Maine's vast wilderness, where you can work up a sweat on a hike up the northernmost peak of the **Appalachian Trail** and take an adrenaline-pumping ride down the **Kennebec River**.

gressive political issues from gay rights to health-care reform. Indeed the universal health insurance program in Massachusetts became the model for President Obama's national plan.

MASSACHUSETTS

New England's most populous state packs in appealing variety from the woodsy hills of the Berkshires to the sandy beaches of Cape Cod. Massachusetts' rich history oozes from almost every quarter: you can explore Plymouth, 'America's hometown;' walk the Freedom Trail in Boston, where the first shots of the American Revolution rang out; and hit the cobbled streets of the old whaling village of Nantucket. University-laden Boston offers all the accoutrements – from world-class museums to edgy nightlife – you'd expect of a great college town. Provincetown's a gay-extravaganza whirl like no other, Northampton's got the coolest cafe scene this side of New York, and Martha's Vineyard offers the perfect family vacation – just ask the Obamas and Clintons.

History

Massachusetts has played a leading role in American politics since the arrival of the first colonists. In the 18th century, spurred by a booming maritime trade, Massachusetts colonists revolted against trade restrictions imposed by Great Britain. British attempts to put down the revolt resulted in the 1770 Boston Massacre, which became a rallying cry to action. In 1773, angered by a new British-imposed tax on tea, colonists raided three British merchant ships and dumped their cargo of tea into Boston Harbor. Known as the Boston Tea Party, this tax revolt against the crown set the stage for the battles that started the American Revolution.

In the 19th century Massachusetts became the center of the world's whaling industry, bringing unprecedented wealth to the islands of Nantucket and Martha's Vineyard, whose ports are still lined with grand sea captains' homes.

ⓘ Information
Boston Globe (www.boston.com) The region's main newspaper has a great online site.
Massachusetts Dept of Conservation and Recreation (☑877-422-6762; www.mass.gov/dcr/recreate/camping.htm) Offers camping in 29 state parks.

MASSACHUSETTS FACTS

» **Nickname** Bay State

» **Population** 6.5 million

» **Area** 7840 sq miles

» **Capital city** Boston (population 617,600)

» **Other cities** Worcester (population 181,000), Springfield (population 153,000)

» **Sales tax** 6.25%

» **Birthplace of** inventor Benjamin Franklin (1706–90), five presidents including John F Kennedy (1917–63), authors Jack Kerouac (1922–69) and Henry David Thoreau (1817–62)

» **Home of** Harvard University, Boston Marathon, Plymouth Rock

» **Politics** New England's most liberal state

» **Famous for** Boston Tea Party, first state to legalize gay marriage

» **Most parodied accent** Bostonians' pahk the cah in Hahvahd Yahd

» **Driving distances** Boston to Provincetown 145 miles, Boston to Northampton 98 miles

Massachusetts Office of Travel & Tourism (☑617-973-8500; www.massvacation.com) Provides information on the entire state.

Boston

One of America's oldest cities is also one of its youngest. A score of colleges and universities add a fresh face to this historic capital and feed a thriving arts and entertainment scene. But don't think for a minute that Boston is all about the literati. Grab a seat in the bleachers at Fenway Park and join the fanatical fans cheering on the Red Sox. Wicked pissah (super cool), as they say here in the Hub.

History

When the Massachusetts Bay Colony was established by England in 1630, Boston became its capital. It's a city of firsts: Boston Latin School, the first public school in the USA, was founded in 1635, followed a year later by Harvard, the nation's first university. The first newspaper in the colonies was printed here in 1704, America's first labor union organized here in 1795 and the country's first subway system opened in Boston in 1897.

Not only were the first battles of the American Revolution fought here, but Boston was also home to the first African American regiment to fight in the US Civil War. Waves of immigrants, especially Irish in the mid-18th century and Italians in the early 20th, have infused the city with European influences.

Today Boston remains at the forefront of higher learning and its universities have spawned world-renowned industries in biotechnology, medicine and finance.

◎ Sights & Activities

Boston retains an intimate scale that's best experienced on foot. Most of Boston's main attractions are found in or near the city center, making it easy to ramble from one to the next.

Begin at Boston Common, where you'll find the tourist office and the start of the Freedom Trail. Everything radiates out from the Common, with historic sites, graceful parks and promenades around every corner.

BOSTON COMMON & PUBLIC GARDEN

Boston Common   PARK
(Map p168) The heart of Boston since 1634, the 50-acre common, bordered by Tremont, Beacon and Charles Sts, was the nation's first public park. In years past it was a pasture for cattle grazing, a staging ground for soldiers of the American Revolution and the site of chastising pillory-and-stocks for those who

dared defy Puritan mores. These days it's a gloriously carefree scene, especially at the **Frog Pond**, where waders cool off on hot summer days and ice-skaters frolic in winter.

Public Garden   GARDENS
(Map p168) Adjoining the Common, the 24-acre Public Garden provides an inviting oasis of bountiful flowers and shady trees. Its centerpiece, a tranquil lagoon with old-fashioned pedal-powered **Swan Boats** (www.swanboats.com; adult/child $2.75/1.50; ◎10am-4pm or 5pm mid-Apr–mid-Sep; ☉), has been delighting children for generations.

BEACON HILL & DOWNTOWN

Rising above Boston Common is Beacon Hill, Boston's most historic and affluent neighborhood. To the east is the city's downtown, with a curious mix of Colonial-era sights and modern office buildings.

FREE State House   HISTORIC BUILDING
(Map p168; ☎617-727-3676; Beacon St, at Park St; ◎8am-5pm Mon-Fri) Crowning Beacon Hill is the golden-domed capitol building, the seat of Massachusetts' government since 1798. Volunteers lead free 40-minute tours from 10am to 3:30pm.

Granary Burying Ground   CEMETERY
(Map p168; cnr Tremont & Park Sts) Tons of history lie buried at this Colonial graveyard, which dates to 1660 and holds the bones of influential Bostonians, including Revolutionary heroes Paul Revere, Samuel Adams and John Hancock.

BOSTON IN...

Two Days

Follow in the footsteps of America's revolutionary founders on the **Freedom Trail**, stopping to imbibe a little history at the **Bell in Hand Tavern**, the oldest tavern in the USA. Wrap up your first day with a scrumptious meal in the **North End**, Boston's 'Little Italy.'

Your mother always wanted you to go to Harvard, right? Begin day two in **Cambridge** poking around Harvard Sq and cruising the campus sights. End the day gallery browsing and schmoozing with the beautiful people on **Newbury St**.

Four Days

Start day three at one of the city's stellar museums – for classic American art, head to the **Museum of Fine Arts** or for cutting edge, the **Institute of Contemporary Art**. For a sumptuous city view, take an elevator up 50 floors to the **Prudential Center Skywalk**.

On your final day, head west to **Lexington** and **Concord** if you have a literary inclination, or spend the day at kid-friendly **Plimoth Plantation**. When you get back into town, take in a **play** at one of Boston's renowned theaters or head to Fenway Park to catch a **Red Sox** game.

Faneuil Hall HISTORIC SITE

(Map p168; Congress St) This landmark red-brick hall, topped with its famed grasshopper weathervane, has been a market and public meeting place since 1740. Today the hall, Quincy Market and North and South Market buildings make up the Faneuil Hall Marketplace chock-full of small shops and eateries.

Museum of Afro-American History MUSEUM

(Map p168; www.afroammuseum.org; 46 Joy St; adult/child $5/3; ⊙10am-4pm Mon-Sat) Illustrating the accomplishments of Boston's African American community, this museum includes the adjacent African Meeting House, where former slave Frederick Douglass recruited African American soldiers to fight in the Civil War.

Old South Meeting House HISTORIC BUILDING

(Map p168; www.oldsouthmeetinghouse.org; 310 Washington St; adult/child $6/1; ⊙9:30am-5pm) In 1773 Colonists met here for a rousing debate on taxation before throwing the Boston Tea Party.

Old State House HISTORIC BUILDING

(Map p168; www.bostonhistory.org; 206 Washington St; adult/child $7.50/3; ⊙9am-5pm) Boston's oldest public building, erected in 1713, has simple displays depicting the American Revolution.

NORTH END & CHARLESTOWN

An old-world warren of narrow streets, the Italian North End offers visitors an irresistible mix of colorful period buildings and mouthwatering eateries. Colonial sights spill across the river into Charlestown, home to America's oldest battleship.

Paul Revere House HISTORIC BUILDING

(Map p168; www.paulreverehouse.org; 19 North Sq; adult/child $3.50/1; ⊙9:30am-5:15pm) The oldest (1680) house still standing in Boston. Even more significantly, it's the former home of Paul Revere, a leader of the colonial militia the Minutemen, so named for their ability to deploy rapidly. It was Revere who jumped on his horse and rode through the streets shouting the warning 'the British are coming.'

Old North Church CHURCH

(Map p168; www.oldnorth.com; 193 Salem St; ⊙9am-6pm Jun-Oct, 9am-5pm Nov-May) It was at this church, built c 1723, that two lanterns were hung in the steeple on that pivotal night of April 18, 1775, signaling to a waiting

The hulking highway that once tore across the center of the city has morphed into a ribbon of green stretching from Chinatown to the North End. Known as the Rose Kennedy Greenway in honor of JFK's mother, this meandering green space reclaims land that was until a few years back the elevated section of I-93.

Completed in late 2008, the interconnecting pocket parks that comprise the greenway offer shady respites from the city bustle, replete with water fountains, artwork and sculpture gardens.

Incidentally, if you're wondering what happened to the highway, it's now buried in tunnels running beneath the city, thanks to the 'Big Dig,' the costliest highway project in US history.

Paul Revere that British forces were setting out by sea ('one if by land, two if by sea').

FREE USS Constitution BATTLESHIP

(Map p162; www.history.navy.mil/ussconstitution; Charlestown Navy Yard; ⊙10am-6pm Tue-Sun Apr-Oct, 10am-4pm Thu-Sun Nov-Mar; ⊛) Clamber the decks of this legendary warship, built in 1797. Its oak-timbered hull is so thick that cannonballs literally bounced off it, earning it the nickname 'Old Ironsides.' Families: don't miss the museum, which has sailor garb that kids can don for photo ops.

FREE Bunker Hill Monument MONUMENT

(Map p162; www.nps.gov/bost; Monument Sq; ⊙9am-5pm) This 221ft granite obelisk commemorates the American Revolution's first major battle and offers a fine vista for those willing to climb 294 stairs (huff, huff).

BACK BAY

Extending west from Boston Common this well-groomed neighborhood boasts graceful brownstone residences, grand edifices and the tony shopping mecca of Newbury St.

Copley Square PLAZA

(Map p162) Here you'll find a cluster of handsome historic buildings, including the ornate French-Romanesque Trinity Church (www.trinitychurchboston.org; cnr Boylston & Clarendon Sts; adult/child $7/free; ⊙9am-5pm Mon-Sat, 1-6pm Sun), the masterwork of architect

HH Richardson. Across the street, the classic **Boston Public Library** (www.blp.org; 700 Boylston St; ☉9am-9pm Mon-Thu, 9am-5pm Fri & Sat; ☎), America's first municipal library, lends credence to Boston's reputation as the 'Athens of America.' Pick up a self-guided tour brochure and wander around, noting gems like the murals by John Singer Sargent and sculpture by Augustus Saint-Gaudens.

Prudential Center Skywalk VIEWPOINT
(Map p162; ☎617-859-0648; 800 Boylston St; adult/child $12/8; ☉10am-10pm) For a stunning 360-degree bird's-eye view of the city, head to this tower's 50th-floor observation deck.

WATERFRONT & SEAPORT DISTRICT
Boston's waterfront offers an ever-growing list of attractions, all connected by the Harborwalk, a dedicated pedestrian path.

Institute of Contemporary Art MUSEUM
(off Map p168; ☎617-478-3100; www.icaboston.org; 100 Northern Ave; adult/child $15/free; ☉10am-5pm Tue, Wed, Sat & Sun, 10am-9pm Thu & Fri) This dazzling museum snags rave exhibits by the likes of street artist Shepard Fairey. The building's striking cantilevered architecture defines modern, and its floor-to-ceiling glass walls pop with Boston's most dramatic harbor view. Admission's free after 5pm Thursday.

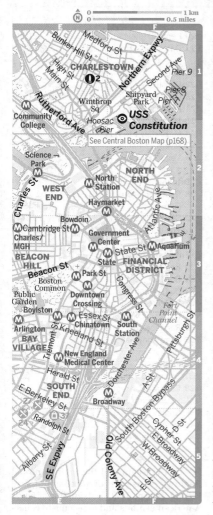

See Central Boston Map (p168)

Compact and easy to stroll, Chinatown offers up enticing Asian eateries cheek-by-jowl, while the adjacent Theater District is clustered with performing-arts venues. The sprawling South End boasts one of America's largest concentrations of Victorian row houses, a burgeoning art scene and terrific neighborhood cafes.

FENWAY & KENMORE SQUARE

With world-class museums and America's oldest ballpark, the Fenway neighborhood is a destination in itself.

Museum of Fine Arts MUSEUM

(MFA; Map p162; ☎617-267-9300; www.mfa.org; 465 Huntington Ave; adult/child $20/7.50; ⊙10am-4:45pm Sat-Tue, 10am-9:45pm Wed-Fri) One of the country's finest art museums just got better with the opening of its spectacular new Art of the Americas wing, whose 53 galleries showcase everything from pre-Columbian art to Paul Revere silver and Winslow Homer paintings. The MFA also has a solid French Impressionist collection, Egyptian mummies and much more. Admission is free for everyone after 4pm on Wednesdays and for children after 3pm weekdays, all day weekends and daily in summer.

Isabella Stewart Gardner Museum MUSEUM

(Map p162; ☎617-566-1401; www.gardnermuseum. org; 280 The Fenway; adult/child $12/free; ⊙11am-5pm Tue-Sun) Gardner assembled her vast collection – which ranges from Rembrandts to portraits by Bostonian John Singer Sargent – a century ago and lived in the magnificent Venetian-style palazzo that houses it all. Seeing the mansion itself, with its garden courtyard, is alone worth the price of admission. And if your name's Isabella, the ticket is free!

CAMBRIDGE

On the north side of the Charles River lies politically progressive Cambridge, home to academic heavyweights Harvard University and Massachusetts Institute of Technology (MIT). Some 30,000 students make for a diverse, lively scene. Its central Harvard Square (Map p162) overflows with cafes, bookstores and street performers.

Harvard University COLLEGE CAMPUS

(Map p162) Along Massachusetts Ave, opposite the Harvard T station, lies the leafy campus of Harvard University. Dozens of Nobel laureates and eight US presidents

New England Aquarium AQUARIUM

(Map p168; ☎617-973-5200; www.neaq.org; Central Wharf; adult/child $22/14; ⊙9am-5pm Mon-Fri, 9am-6pm Sat & Sun; ☝) Centering on a four-story tank teeming with sharks and tropical fish, this aquarium is a magnet for kids. The cool penguin pool is a big hit. Also popular are the aquarium's whale-watching cruises (adult/child $40/32; ⊙Apr-Oct), led by naturalists. The cruises head 30 miles out to Stellwagen Bank National Marine Sanctuary, a massive underwater plateau off Cape Cod's northern point, where you can see humpback whales doing their acrobatics.

Boston

are among its graduates – for other chewy tidbits join a free student-led campus tour at the **Harvard University Information Center** (☏617-495-1573; www.harvard.edu/visitors; 1350 Massachusetts Ave; ⊙1hr tours 10am, noon & 2pm Mon-Sat).

Harvard Art Museums   MUSEUM
(Map p162; ☏617-495-9400; www.harvardartmuseum.org; 485 Broadway; adult/child $9/free; ⊙10am-5pm Tue-Sat) It should come as no surprise that the nation's oldest (1636) and wealthiest university has amassed incredible art collections, with works covering a broad gamut from Picasso to Islamic art.

**Harvard Museum of
Natural History**   MUSEUM
(Map p162; ☏617-495-3045; www.hmnh.harvard.edu; 26 Oxford St; adult/child $9/6; ⊙9am-5pm;

⊞) This museum and the interconnected **Peabody Museum of Archaeology & Ethnology** present outstanding Native American exhibits and an exquisite collection of 4000 hand-blown glass flowers. The admission price gets you through the doors of both attractions.

**Massachusetts Institute
of Technology**   COLLEGE CAMPUS
(MIT; Map p162) Nerds rule ever so proudly at America's foremost tech campus. Stop at the **MIT Information Center** (Map p162; ☏617-253-4795; www.mit.edu; 77 Massachusetts Ave; ⊙free 90min tours 11am & 3pm Mon-Fri) for the scoop on where to see campus art, including Henry Moore bronzes and cutting-edge architecture by the likes of Frank Gehry.

MIT Museum
MUSEUM

(Map p162; www.mit.edu/museum; 265 Massachusetts Ave, adult/child $7.50/3; ⊙10am-5pm) Packed with wow-'em exhibits like the world's largest holography collection, robots from MIT's Artificial Intelligence Laboratory and cool kinetic sculptures. Swing by between 10am and noon on Sundays and admission is free.

GREATER BOSTON

Museum of Science
MUSEUM

(Map p168; ☎617-723-2500; www.mos.org; Charles River Dam; adult/child $21/18; ⊙9am-5pm Sat-Thu, 9am-9pm Fri, longer hr Jul-Aug; 🚼) At this state-of-the-art museum, a short hop from MIT, hundreds of interactive displays explore the latest tech trends. Clamber around a full-scale space capsule, explore nanotechnology and more. Kids will find plenty of hands-on fun. A fresh multimillion-dollar upgrade of the museum's **planetarium** adds another dimension.

John F Kennedy Library & Museum MUSEUM
(off Map p162; ☎617-514-1600; www.jfklibrary.org; Columbia Point; adult/child $12/free; ⊙9am-5pm) In a striking IM Pei–designed building overlooking Boston Harbor, this museum provides an ode to all things Kennedy. Theaters and multimedia displays replay key historical events such as the Cuban missile crisis. Take the T's Red Line to JFK/UMass, then hop on a free 'JFK' shuttle bus.

☞ Tours

Boston Duck Tours
ADVENTURE

(Map p162; ☎617-723-3825; www.bostonducktours. com; adult/child $32/22; ⊙9am-dusk mid-Mar–mid-Nov; 🚼) Ridiculously popular tours using WWII amphibious vehicles that cruise the downtown streets before splashing into the Charles River. Tours leave from the Prudential Center and the Museum of Science.

Boston By Foot
WALKING

(☎617-367-2345; www.bostonbyfoot.org; adult/child $12/8; ⊙May-Oct) Knowledgeable guides lead a variety of city tours, including Freedom Trail walks that uncover fun tidbits like the hidden crypts under the King's Chapel. Other tours focus on architecture, literary landmarks and the Italian-centric North End. Departure points vary.

Freedom Trail Foundation
WALKING

(Map p168; ☎617-357-8300; www.thefreedom trail.org; adult/child $12/6; ⊙10:30am-5pm; 🚼) Guides dressed in Colonial garb – think Ben

WHAT THE...?

Ever had a hankering to walk across the entire planet? The Christian Science Church's **Mapparium** (Map p162; www. marybakereddylibrary.org; 200 Massachusetts Ave; adult/child $6/4; ⊙10am-4pm Tue-Sun; 🚼), an enormous stained-glass globe with a bridge through its center, provides the easiest route.

Franklin – lead 90-minute walking tours of the Freedom Trail, departing from the visitor center on the Boston Common. They also do a Freedom Trail pub crawl on Tuesday evenings.

Segway Experience
SEGWAY

(Map p168; ☎617-723-2500; www.mos.org; 1hr tour $65; ⊙10am-1pm) Satisfy your inner geek on a Segway tour from the Museum of Science to the MIT campus, taking in lots of cool sights. Participants must be aged 14 or older and weigh 100 pounds to 260 pounds.

Urban Adventours
BICYCLE

(Map p168; ☎617-670-0637; www.urbanadven tours.com; 103 Atlantic Ave; tour $50; ⊙9:30am-4:30pm) Cyclists can pedal the Freedom Trail, take in a brewery or bike Boston at night.

FREE **Boston National Historical Park Visitors Center**
WALKING

(Map p168; ☎617-242-5642; www.nps.gov/bost; 15 State St; ⊙9am-5pm) Park rangers lead walking tours of the Freedom Trail.

★☆ Festivals & Events

Boston Marathon
RUNNING EVENT

(www.baa.org) One of the country's most prestigious marathons takes runners on a 26.2-mile course ending at Copley Sq on Patriots Day, a Massachusetts holiday on the third Monday in April.

Fourth of July
PATRIOTIC FESTIVAL

(www.july4th.org) Boston hosts one of the biggest Independence Day bashes in the USA, with a free Boston Pops concert on the Esplanade and a fireworks display that's televised nationally.

Patron Saints' Feasts
RELIGIOUS FESTIVAL

(www.northendboston.com) In the North End, Italian patron saints are celebrated with food and music events on weekends in July and August.

Walking Tour
Freedom Trail

❭ Trace America's revolutionary birth along the Freedom Trail, which covers Boston's key Colonial sites. The well-trodden route, marked by a double row of red bricks, starts at the ❶ **Boston Common**, America's oldest public park. Follow the trail north to the gold-domed ❷ **State House**, designed by Charles Bulfinch, Colonial Boston's best-known architect. Rounding Park St onto Tremont St takes you past the Colonial-era ❸ **Park Street Church**; the ❹ **Granary Burying Ground**, where victims of the Boston Massacre lie buried; and ❺ **King's Chapel**, topped with one of Paul Revere's bells. Continue down School St, past the site of ❻ **Boston's first public school**, built in 1635, and the ❼ **Old Corner Bookstore**, a 19th-century haunt of literary geniuses Hawthorne and Emerson.

A minute's detour south from the corner of School and Washington Sts leads to the ❽ **Old South Meeting House**, where the nitty-gritty on the Boston Tea Party is proudly displayed. True diehards will find more Revolutionary exhibits at the ❾ **Old State House**. Nearby, a ring of cobblestones at the intersection of State, Devonshire and Congress Sts marks the ❿ **Boston Massacre site**, where the first victims of the American Revolution died. Next up is ⓫ **Faneuil Hall**, a public market since Colonial times.

Walk north on Union St and up Hanover St, the trattoria-rich heart of Boston's Italian enclave. Treat yourself to lunch before continuing to North Sq, where you can tour the ⓬ **Paul Revere House**, the Revolutionary hero's former home. Follow the trail to the ⓭ **Old North Church**, where a lookout in the steeple signaled to Revere that the British were coming, setting off his famous midnight gallop.

Continue northwest on Hull St, where you'll find more Colonial graves at ⓮ **Copp's Hill Burying Ground** before crossing the Charlestown Bridge to reach the ⓯ **USS Constitution**, the world's oldest commissioned warship. To the north lies ⓰ **Bunker Hill Monument**, the site of the first battle fought in the American Revolution.

Head of the Charles Regatta ROWING RACE
(www.hocr.org) Spectators line the banks
of the Charles River on a weekend in
mid-October to watch the world's largest
rowing event.

🛏 Sleeping

Boston has a reputation for high hotel prices, but online discounts can lessen the sting
at even high-end places. You'll typically find
the best deals on weekends. The majority
of hotels are in the downtown area and the
Back Bay, both convenient to public transportation and sightseeing.

For places that book solely through agencies, try **Bed & Breakfast Associates Bay
Colony** (☑617-720-0522, www.bnbboston.com; r
from $100), which handles B&Bs, rooms and
apartments.

TOP CHOICE Omni Parker House HISTORIC HOTEL **$$**
(Map p168; ☑617-227-8600; www.omniparkerhouse.
com; 60 School St; r $219-419; ✳🛇🖗🏄) If the walls
could talk, this historic hotel overlooking the
Freedom Trail would fill volumes. Employees
have included Malcolm X and Ho Chi Minh,
the guest list Charles Dickens and JFK. De-
spite its well-polished elegance, dark woods
and chandeliers, there's nothing stodgy
about the place – you can be as comfortable
here in a T-shirt as in a suit and tie. And you
couldn't be more in the thick of things; it's
just a stroll to many of Boston's top sights.

🍃 Harding House B&B **$**
(Map p162; ☑617-876-2888; www.cambridgeinns.
com/harding; 288 Harvard St; r incl breakfast
$165-265; ✳🛇🏄) A classic Victorian, blend-
ing comfort and artistry in spacious, bright
rooms. Old wooden floors toss back a warm
glow and lovely antique furnishings com-
plete the inviting atmosphere. Perks include
museum passes and a breakfast table replete
with organic delights.

Charlesmark Hotel BOUTIQUE HOTEL **$$**
(Map p162; ☑617-247-1212; www.thecharlesmark.
com; 655 Boylston St; r incl breakfast $189-219;
✳🛇🛇) This smart boutique hotel packs it
all from an unbeatable Copley Sq location to
cheery rooms graced with artwork, Italian
tile and high-tech amenities. Runners, take
note: the Boston Marathon finish line is just
outside the front door.

Harborside Inn HOTEL **$$$**
(Map p168; ☑617-723-7500; www.harborsideinn
boston.com; 185 State St; r $189-269; ✳🛇🛇)

ℹ **DOWNLOADABLE
WALKING TOURS**

If you're traveling with an MP3 player,
you can be your own guide by down-
loading a free walking tour of Cam-
bridge at www.cambridge-usa.org and
of the Harborwalk at www.bostonhar-
borwalk.com.

This renovated 19th-century warehouse-
turned-inn offers cozy rooms just steps
from Faneuil Hall and Boston's waterfront.
No two rooms are alike but period ambi-
ence, from the exposed brick walls to the
hardwood floors, prevails throughout. Light
sleepers should request an inside atrium
room.

Chandler Inn BOUTIQUE HOTEL **$$**
(Map p162; ☑617-482-3450; www.chandlerinn.com;
26 Chandler St; r $149-179; ✳🛇) For a delectable
taste of the hip South End, book a room at
this European-style boutique hotel within
roaming range of some of Boston's hottest
nightspots. The staff is friendly, the rooms
small but tidy, and the price a fraction of any
faceless chain hotel.

Hotel Buckminster HOTEL **$$**
(Map p162; ☑617-236-7050; www.bostonhotelbuck
minster.com; 645 Beacon St; r $149-189; ✳🏄)
Built in 1897 by renowned architect Stan-
ford White, this Kenmore Sq hotel is a mere
baseball's toss from Fenway Park. Don't ex-
pect anything fancy – it's a faded dame, but
the rooms are adequate and sport money-
saving conveniences such as microwaves
and refrigerators.

HI Boston Hostel HOSTEL **$**
(Map p162; ☑617-536-9455; www.bostonhostel.
org; 12 Hemenway St; dm incl breakfast $31-48,
r incl breakfast $73-132; @🛇) This terrific year-
round Back Bay hostel offers dorm rooms
with just four to six beds and lots of perks,
from free use of linens to organized tours. It
fills quickly, especially in summer, so book
early.

Kendall Hotel BOUTIQUE HOTEL **$$**
(Map p162; ☑617-577-1300; www.kendallhotel.
com; 350 Main St; r incl breakfast $129-199; ✳🛇)
Unique, reasonably priced and on the
doorstep of the MIT campus, this former
brick firehouse retains a firefighter riff,
without a whiff of 'cutesy.'

Central Boston

500 m
0.25 miles

EAST CAMBRIDGE

Monsignor O'Brien Hwy

Memorial Dr

Charles River Bridge

East St

Science Park

Museum of Science

Charles River

Charles River Bike Path

Longfellow Bridge

The Esplanade

Nashua St

Martha Rd

Wm Cardinal Way

O'Connell Way

WEST END

Blossom St

Blossom St

Parkman St

Fruit St

Massachusetts General Hospital

31

Charles/MGH

Revere St

Phillips St

Anderson St

Garden St

Irving St

S Russell St

Myrtle St

Hancock St

Ridgeway La

Temple St

Derne St

Somerset St

Cambridge St

Bowdoin St

Bowdoin

5

Science Park

North Station

Stanford St

Causeway St

New Chardon St

Congress St

Portland St

Friend St

Canal St

Valenti Way

Beverly St

Lovejoy Ave

Lovejoy Wharf

Charlestown Bridge

Zakim Bridge

Paul Revere Park

N Washington St

Haymarket

GOVERNMENT CENTER

City Hall Plaza

16

Government Center

Cornhill St

Cambridge St

Hanover St

Endicott St

Margin St

N Margin St

Cross St

Salem St

Old North Church

Charter St

Charter St

Commercial St

Hull St

Snowhill St

Sheafe St

Tileston St

Prince St

N Bennet St

Cooper St

NORTH END

NORTH SQUARE

Paul Revere House

Fleet St

Richmond St

Fulton St

N Bennet St

Parmenter St

S Wales St

North End Park

Salt La

North St

Congress St

Chatham St

Clinton St

Atlantic Ave

WATERFRONT

John F Fitzgerald Expwy

New Sudbury St

28

24

23

21

22

19

34

30

32

3

35

17

27

20

Summer Tunnel (toll)

Callahan Tunnel (toll)

US Coast Guard Piers

MBTA Water Shuttle

Constitution Wharf

Battery Wharf

Fire Boat Dock

Battery St

Battery St

North St

Commercial St

Clark St

Union Wharf

Sargents Wharf

Lewis Wharf

Commercial Wharf

Commercial Wharf

Boston Inner Harbor

Long Wharf

Ferry to Boston Harbor Islands National Recreation Area

Aquarium

11

Central Boston

◉ Irving House
B&B **$$**

(Map p162; ☎617-547-4600; www.irvinghouse.com; 24 Irving St; r incl breakfast with shared/private bath $135/170; ❄@⑨⚑） Minutes from Harvard University and a convenient base for exploring Cambridge. With 44 rooms it's a cross between a hotel and a B&B.

Oasis Guest House
B&B **$$**

(Map p162; ☎617-267-2262; www.oasisgh.com; 22 Edgerly Rd; s/d with shared bath $99/129, r with private bath $179; ❄@⑨) Just beyond bustling Mass Ave, Oasis offers straightforward rooms simply furnished but comfortable enough. One caveat: noise can be an issue.

HI Fenway Summer Hostel
HOSTEL **$**

(Map p162; ☎617-267-8599; www.bostonhostel.org/fenway.shtml; 575 Commonwealth Ave; dm/r incl breakfast $38/100; ⊙Jun-Aug; @） A Boston University dormitory in winter, this Kenmore Sq hostel has dorms with just three beds each. Good dining and nightlife options are close at hand.

✗ Eating

No matter what your taste, Boston will tantalize your buds. Head to Chinatown for affordable Asian fare, to the South End for the cafe scene. And when the sun sets, there's no place like the Italian North End, whose narrow streets are thick with trattorias and ristorantes.

BEACON HILL & DOWNTOWN

Ye Olde Union Oyster House SEAFOOD **$$$**

(Map p168; ☎617-227-2750; www.unionoysterhouse.com; 41 Union St; mains $16-28; ⊙11am-9:30pm) Slurp up fresh-shucked oysters and a heaping of history at Boston's oldest (1826) restaurant. It's been a haunt of many prominent Bostonians including JFK, who had his own booth in the upstairs dining room. Forget the meat dishes – this place is all about seafood.

Durgin Park
AMERICAN **$$**

(Map p168; ☎617-227-2038; 340 Faneuil Hall Marketplace; lunch mains $9-30; ⏰11:30am-10pm Mon-Sat, 11:30am-9pm Sun; 👶) Climb the stairs to this storied eatery for a taste of good ole Colonial fare. Durgin Park's been dishing out New England staples like Yankee pot roast, Indian pudding and slow-cooked Boston baked beans since 1827.

Paramount
AMERICAN **$**

(Map p168; www.paramountboston.com; 44 Charles St; mains $5-18; ⏰8am-10pm) Beacon Hill's top neighborhood eatery, with fruity pancakes, meaty sandwiches and a loyal following.

Quincy Market
FOOD COURT **$**

(Map p168; off Congress & North Sts; ⏰10am-9pm Mon-Sat, noon-6pm Sun; 👶👶) For a quick eat along the Freedom Trail, stop at this storied market lined with stalls selling everything from Chinese food to New England clam chowder.

NORTH END

📋 Pomodoro
ITALIAN **$$**

(Map p168; ☎617-367-4348; www.pomodorobos ton.com; 319 Hanover St; mains $15-25; ⏰3-11pm Tue-Fri, 11am-11pm Sat & Sun) This cozy place is one romantic setting for homestyle Italian cuisine. The food is simply but perfectly prepared: snag a table and order the most

delectable seafood *fra diavolo* in the entire North End. Reserve ahead or be prepared to wait.

171

Modern Pastry Shop
BAKERY **$**

(Map p168; www.modernpastry.com; 257 Hanover St; snacks $2-4; ⏰8am-10pm Sun-Fri, 7am-midnight Sat) Not the biggest bakery on Hanover St, but certainly the best. Chocolate ganache and decadent cannoli filled to order in front of your eyes...oh so sweet!

Neptune Oyster
SEAFOOD **$$$**

(Map p168; ☎617-742-3474; www.neptuneoyster. com; 63 Salem St; mains $20-32; ⏰11:30am-11pm) Barely bigger than a clam, this snappy place has the North End's best raw bar and good Italian-style seafood. You *will* want to start with the oysters.

Regina Pizzeria
PIZZA **$$**

(Map p168; www.pizzeriaregina.com; 11 Thatcher St; pizzas $12-18; ⏰11:30am-11:30pm) The North End's finest thin-crust pizza by the slice or pie.

WATERFRONT & SEAPORT DISTRICT

🌿 Flour Bakery & Cafe
BAKERY **$**

(Map p168; www.flourbakery.com; 12 Farnsworth St; light eats $3-10; ⏰7am-7pm Mon-Fri, 8am-6pm Sat, 9am-4pm Sun; 👶) Certified green and scrumptiously affordable, this bakery makes awesome pecan sticky buns and wildly innovative sandwiches and pizzas. Their motto is 'make life sweeter...eat dessert first.' No argument here.

BOSTON FOR CHILDREN

Boston is a family-friendly destination. Changing stations are ubiquitous in public restrooms and many restaurants offer children's menus and high chairs.

You'll have no trouble taking your kid's stroller on the T. Boston's crowded old streets and sidewalks present more of a challenge. Curbs are not always cut for easy rolling, so keep this in mind if you'll be pushing a stroller.

Boston's small scale makes it easy for families to explore. A good place to start is the **Public Garden**, where fans of Robert McCloskey's classic Boston tale *Make Way for Ducklings* can visit bronze **statues** (Map p168) of the famous mallards and paddle the lagoon in one of the Swan Boats. Across the street at the **Boston Common** (p168), kids can cool their toes in the Frog Pond and romp on playground swings and jungle gyms.

Boston Children's Museum (Map p168; ☎617-426-6500; www.bostonchildrensmuseum.org; 300 Congress St; admission $12; ⏰10am-5pm Sat-Thu, 10am-9pm Fri) offers oodles of fun for the younger ones, while the **Museum of Science** (p173) thrills kids of all ages. Hits at the **New England Aquarium** (p171) include petting cool creatures at the touch pool, watching seals being fed and hopping aboard a whale-watching tour.

Boston By Little Feet (Map p168; ☎617-367-2345; www.bostonbyfoot.org; 1hr tour $8), departing from Faneuil Hall and designed for kids aged six to 12, offers a fun slice of the Freedom Trail from a child's perspective. And those quirky, quacky **Boston Duck Tours** (p173) are always a hit.

FARMERS MARKETS

Boston has several neighborhood farmers markets that truck seasonal fruits and vegetables into the city from mid-May to November. The ultimate bonanza of ripe and ready produce is the Haymarket (Map p168; Blackstone & Hanover Sts; ⊙7am-5pm Fri & Sat), where more than 100 vendors line up along the street.

Other markets:

City Hall Plaza (Map p168; City Hall Plaza; ⊙11am-6pm Mon & Wed)

Copley Square (Map p162; St James Ave; ⊙11am-6pm Tue & Fri)

South Station (Map p168; Dewey Sq; ⊙11:30am-6:30pm Tue & Thu)

Barking Crab   SEAFOOD $$

(Map p168; ☑617-426-2722; www.thebarkingcrab. com; 88 Sleeper St; mains $12-34; ⊙11:30am-10pm; ⏺) A waterfront landmark, this brightly painted and ever-bustling seafood shack serves big buckets of steaming crabs, authentic New England clambakes and good ol' beer-battered fish and chips.

Legal Sea Foods   SEAFOOD $$$

(Map p168; ☑617-227-3115; www.legalseafoods. com; 255 State St; mains $15-32; ⊙11am-10:30pm Mon-Sat, 11am-10pm Sun) Running with the motto 'If it isn't fresh, it isn't Legal,' this waterfront establishment indeed serves top-of-the-line seafood – broiled, grilled or fried – and invariably draws a satisfied crowd.

CHINATOWN, THEATER DISTRICT & SOUTH END

TOP CHOICE **Myers + Chang**   ASIAN FUSION $$

(Map p162; ☑617-542-5200; www.myersandchang. com; 1145 Washington St; mains $10-18; ⊙11:30am-10pm Sun-Wed, 11:30am-11pm Thu-Sat) A marriage of two South End top chefs, this smokin' multiethnic joint dishes up eclectic taste treats, blending Thai, Chinese and Vietnamese influences with an urban New England tweak. Think shiitake-basil spring rolls, wok-roasted mussels and tea-smoked spareribs. No matter what you order, the spicy, fresh herbs carry the day. The food's local whenever possible, the scene's hip and casual.

New Jumbo Seafood   CHINESE $$

(Map p168; www.newjumboseafoodrestaurant.com; 5 Hudson St; mains $6-30; ⊙11am-1am Sun-Thu, 11am-4am Fri & Sat) A wall of tanks crawling with lobster, crabs and eels constitute the decor at this Chinatown classic renowned for its fresh seafood and Cantonese cuisine. Lunch specials ($5) offered weekdays until 3pm are a bargain.

Montien   THAI $$

(Map p168; ☑617-338-5600; www.montien-boston. com; 63 Stuart St; mains $10-16; ⊙11:30am-10:30pm Mon-Sat, 4:30-10pm Sun; ⏺) For a tasty meal before the opening curtain, head to this Thai restaurant in the midst of the theater district. Montien has wonderfully fragrant curries and other spicy counterparts, including scores of vegetarian options. The food's the real deal, so let the server know how much heat you can handle.

Franklin Café   AMERICAN $$

(Map p162; ☑617-350-0010; www.franklincafe. com; 278 Shawmut Ave; mains $16-20; ⊙5:30pm-1:30am) Search out this tiny South End haunt for New American comfort food with a gourmet twist. Everyone orders the roasted turkey meatloaf with cinnamon fig gravy and chive mashed potatoes – arguably the most famous meal in the South End. Just a half-dozen booths and a line of bar stools, so get there early.

CAMBRIDGE

Veggie Planet   VEGETARIAN $

(☑617-661-1513; www.veggieplanet.net; Club Passim, 47 Palmer St; mains $6-12; ⊙11:30am-10:30pm; ☑⏺) The crunchy granola crowd gravitates to this cafe, a block northwest of Harvard Square, for all things vegetarian. Creativity knows no bounds – vegans favor the coconut curry tofu pizza. Big organic salads and delicious homemade soups too.

Mr Bartley's Burger Cottage   BURGERS $

(Map p162; www.mrbartley.com; 1246 Massachusetts Ave; burgers $10-12; ⊙11am-9pm Mon-Sat; ⏺) Join the Ivy Leaguers at this landmark joint serving juicy hamburgers with quirky names, like the Yuppie Burger topped with boursin cheese and bacon. The onion rings and sweet potato fries score an A-plus too.

Casablanca   MEDITERRANEAN $$

(☑617-876-0999; www.casablanca-restaurant. com; 40 Brattle St; mains $10-24; ⊙11:30am-11:30pm) A colorful mural depicting Rick's Café sets the stage for innovative Mediterranean delights at this Harvard Sq hangout of film fans and other arty types.

Miracle of Science Bar & Grill   PUB $$
(Map p162; www.miracleofscience.us; 321 Massachusetts Ave; mains $6-14; ⏱7am-1am Mon-Fri, 9am-1pm Sat & Sun) With all the decor of your high-school science lab, this bar and grill is still pretty hip, and is popular among MIT students.

🍷 Drinking

Alibi   LOUNGE
(Map p168; www.alibiboston.com; 215 Charles St) The quirkiest place to have a drink in Boston is in the former Charles Street Jail, now renovated into the upscale Liberty Hotel. The lounge decor features slammin' remnants of its former life, such as iron cell bars.

Cask 'n' Flagon   SPORTS BAR
(Map p162; www.casknflagon.com; 62 Brookline Ave) Sports bars pepper the neighborhood around Fenway Park, including this venerable place, which is wallpapered with classic Red Sox memorabilia and frenzied fans.

Bell in Hand Tavern   PUB
(Map p168; www.bellinhand.com; 45 Union St) A gaggle of bars lines historic Union St, just north of Faneuil Hall, including this one, which opened in 1795, making it the oldest tavern in the USA.

Cheers   BAR
(Map p168; www.cheersboston.com; 84 Beacon St) Only the exterior of this landmark bar appeared in the opening scenes of the *Cheers* sitcom and it serves so many tourists that nobody knows anybody's name, but what the heck.

Top of the Hub   LOUNGE
(Map p162; www.topofthehub.net; 800 Boylston St) A head-spinning city view is on tap at this chic restaurant-lounge on the 52nd floor of the Prudential Center.

Sonsie   CAFE
(Map p162; www.sonsieboston.com; 327 Newbury St) Overlooking the action on trendy Newbury St, Sonsie is where the beautiful people go to see and be seen. Lemontini, anyone?

Shays   PUB
(www.shayspubandwinebar.com; 58 John F Kennedy St, Cambridge) Harvard's favorite student bar, three blocks south of Harvard Sq. It's crowded, cozy and cheap – what's not to love?

☆ Entertainment
Boston's entertainment scene offers something for everyone. For up-to-the-minute listings, grab a copy of the free *Boston Phoenix*.

Nightclubs & Live Music

Club Passim   FOLK
(☎617-492-7679; www.clubpassim.org; 47 Palmer St) Folkies flock to this venerable Cambridge club, which has been a haunt of up-and-coming folk singers since the days of Dylan and Baez. It's just a couple of minutes walk northwest of the Harvard Sq metro stop.

Paradise Rock Club   ROCK
(off Map p162; ☎617-562-8800; www.thedise.com; 967 Commonwealth Ave) Top bands – like U2, whose first gig in the USA was on this stage – rock at this edgy landmark club.

Great Scott   ROCK
(off Map p162; ☎617-566-9014; www.greatscottboston.com; 1222 Commonwealth Ave) The 'it' place for rock and indie, this cavernous club rarely gets uncomfortably crowded.

House of Blues   ROCK
(Map p162; ☎888-693-2583; www.hob.com/boston; 15 Lansdowne St) Big venue with big-name regional acts like J Geils Band, the Cars and My Chemical Romance.

GAY & LESBIAN BOSTON
Naturally, the hub city of the first state to legalize gay marriage embraces gay travelers. You'll find openly gay communities throughout Boston and Cambridge, but the pulse of the action beats from Boston's South End.

The stalwart of the gay and lesbian scene is Club Café (Map p168; www.clubcafe.com; 209 Columbus Ave), a convivial South End bar and entertainment venue. Another gay landmark is Fritz (Map p162; www.fritzboston.com; 26 Chandler St), a bustling, hustling watering hole in the South End that proudly proclaims itself 'Boston's gay sports bar.'

You'll find other LGBT gathering spots, as well as events and entertainment listings, at Bay Windows (www.baywindows.com), a weekly serving the gay and lesbian community, and Edge Boston (www.edgeboston.com). The city's biggest gay and lesbian event, Boston Pride (www.bostonpride.org), includes a parade, a festival and block parties in mid-June.

Berklee Performance Center
ECLECTIC
(Map p162; ☑617-747-2261; www.berkleebpc. com; 136 Massachusetts Ave) One of America's premier music schools hosts concerts by famed alumni and other renowned artists.

Theater & Culture

Hatch Memorial Shell
BANDSTAND
(Map p168; Charles River Esplanade; ☐) Free summer concerts take place at this outdoor bandstand on the banks of the Charles River. The highlight is the Boston Pops' July 4 concert and fireworks, the biggest annual music event in Boston.

Club Oberon
EXPERIMENTAL THEATER
(Map p162; ☑866-811-4111; www.cluboberon. com; 2 Arrow St, Cambridge) Part theater, part nightclub, with a versatile space that allows the stage to be anywhere and everywhere as the actors interact with the audience.

Wang Theatre
THEATER, DANCE
(Map p168; ☑617-482-9393; www.citicenter. org; 270 Tremont St) One of New England's largest theaters, this lavish 1925 landmark hosts top dance and theater performances.

Symphony Hall
MUSIC
(Map p162; ☑888-266-1200; www.bso.org; 301 Massachusetts Ave) The celebrated Boston Symphony Orchestra and Boston Pops perform here.

Opera House
THEATER
(Map p168; ☑617-880-2442; http://bostonopera houseonline.com; 539 Washington St) Restored to its 1920s grandeur, this extravagant theater hosts Broadway productions.

Sports

Boston is a huge sports city with top-rated pro teams. From April to September join the fans cheering on the Boston Red Sox (☑617-267-1700; www.redsox.com), at Fenway Park (Map p162), major-league baseball's oldest (1912) and most storied ballpark.

CHEAP SEATS

Half-price tickets to same-day theater and concerts in Boston are sold at the BosTix kiosks (www.bostix.org; ⊙10am-6pm Tue-Sat, 11am-4pm Sun) Faneuil Hall (Map p168; Congress St); Copley Sq (Map p162; cnr Dartmouth & Boylston Sts). No plastic– these deals are cash only.

TD Garden
BASKETBALL, HOCKEY
(Map p168; 150 Causeway St) From October to April, the NBA Boston Celtics (☑617-523-3030; www.celtics.com) play basketball, and the 2011 Stanley Cup–winning Boston Bruins (☑617-624-2327; www.bostonbruins.com) play ice hockey here.

Gillette Stadium
FOOTBALL, SOCCER
In Foxboro, 25 miles south of Boston, the NFL New England Patriots (☑800-543-1776; www.patriots.com) play football from August to January and the MLS New England Revolution (☑877-438-7387; www.revolutionsoccer. net) plays soccer from April to October.

🛍 Shopping

Head to Newbury St for the most interesting shopping stroll. Starting on its highbrow east end it's all Armani, Brooks Brothers and Cartier, but by the time you reach the west end you'll find offbeat shops and funky bookstores.

Copley Place (Map p162; www.shopcopley place.com; 100 Huntington Ave) and the Prudential Center (Map p162; www.prudentialcenter. com; 800 Boylston St), both in Back Bay, are the city's main indoor malls.

Jake's House
CLOTHING
(Map p162; www.lifeisgood.com; 285 Newbury St; ☐) Life *is* good for this locally designed brand of T-shirts and backpacks in fun-loving styles.

Coop
CLOTHING
(thecoop.com; 1400 Massachusetts Ave, Cambridge) Harvard Sq institution selling sweatshirts and all sorts of souvenirs emblazoned with the Harvard logo, as well as regional books and music.

Cambridge Artists' Cooperative
ARTS & CRAFTS
(Map p162; www.cambridgeartistscoop.com; 59a Church St, Cambridge) Wide range of arts and crafts at this multifloor Harvard Sq gallery operated by Cambridge artists.

Bromfield Art Gallery
ARTS & CRAFTS
(Map p162; www.bromfieldgallery.com; 450 Harrison Ave) Browse for arts and crafts at Boston's oldest cooperative.

ⓘ Information

Internet Access
Boston Public Library (Map p162; www.bpl. org; 700 Boylston St; ⊙9am-9pm Mon-Thu, 9am-5pm Fri & Sat) Free for 15 minutes, or get a visitor card at the circulation desk and sign up for longer terminal time.

Tech Superpowers & Internet Café (www.techsuperpowers.com; 252 Newbury St; per 15min/1hr $3/5; ☺9am-7pm Mon-Fri, 11am-4pm Sat & Sun) Provides online computers, but if you have your own device wi-fi access is free throughout Newbury St.

Media
Boston Globe (www.boston.com) New England's major daily newspaper provides a wealth of information online.

Boston Phoenix (www.thephoenix.com) Free alternative weekly with solid arts and entertainment coverage.

Improper Bostonian (www.improper.com) A sassy biweekly distributed free from sidewalk dispenser boxes.

Medical Services
CVS Pharmacy (☎617-437-8414; www.cvs.com; 587 Boylston St; ☺24hr) Opposite the public library.

Massachusetts General Hospital (☎617-726-2000; www.mgh.org; 55 Fruit St; ☺24hr) At the west side of the city center.

Money
You'll find ATMs throughout the city, including at most subway stations. Foreign currency can be exchanged at **Citizens Bank** (www.citizensbank.com); State St (53 State St); Boylston St (607 Boylston St).

Post
Main post office (Map p168; www.usps.com; 25 Dorchester Ave; ☺6am-midnight) One block southeast of South Station. There are other post offices around central Boston and near Harvard Sq.

Tourist Information
Cambridge Visitor Information Booth (☎617-497-1630; www.cambridge-usa.org; Harvard Sq; ☺9am-5pm) This kiosk right on the square has the nitty-gritty on Cambridge.

Greater Boston Convention & Visitors Bureau (www.bostonusa.com) Has visitor centers at Boston Common (Map p168; ☎617-426-3115; 148 Tremont St; ☺8:30am-5pm Mon-Fri, 9am-5pm Sat & Sun) and the Prudential Center (Map p162; 800 Boylston St; ☺9am-5pm).

Websites
www.bostoncentral.com A solid resource for families, with listings for activities good for kids.

www.cityofboston.gov Official website of Boston city government with links to visitor services.

❶ Getting There & Away

Getting in and out of Boston is easy. The train and bus stations are conveniently side by side, and the airport is a short subway ride away.

AIR Logan International Airport (BOS; www.massport.com/logan), just across Boston Harbor from the city center, is served by major US and foreign airlines and has full services.

BUS South Station (Map p168; 700 Atlantic Ave) is the terminal for an extensive network of long-distance buses operated by **Greyhound** (www.greyhound.com). In addition, **Fung Wah Bus Company** (www.fungwahbus.com) runs buses between South Station and New York City for just $15 each way.

TRAIN MBTA Commuter Rail (www.mbta.com) trains connect Boston's North Station (Map p168) with Concord and Salem and Boston's South Station (Map p168) with Plymouth and Providence; fares vary with the distance, maxing out at $8.25.

The **Amtrak** (www.amtrak.com) terminal is at South Station; trains to New York cost $67 (4¼ hours) or $99 on the speedier *Acela Express* (3½ hours).

❶ Getting Around

TO/FROM THE AIRPORT Downtown Boston is just a few miles from Logan International Airport and is accessible by subway.

CAR Major car-rental companies have offices at the airport, and many have locations around the city. Bear in mind that driving in Boston is utterly confusing with lots of one-way streets and archaic traffic patterns. It's best to stick to public transportation within the city. If you're traveling onward by rental car, pick up your car at the end of your Boston visit.

SUBWAY The **MBTA** (www.mbta.com; single ride $2, day/week pass $9/15; ☺5:30am-12:30am) operates the USA's oldest subway (the 'T'), built in 1897. Five color-coded lines – Red, Blue, Green, Orange and Silver – radiate from the downtown stations of Park St, Downtown Crossing and Government Center. 'Inbound' trains are headed for one of these stations, 'outbound' trains away from them.

GRAB A BIKE

In the summer of 2011 Boston launched Hubway (www.thehubway.com), a new bike sharing program with 600 bicycles stationed at 60 kiosks throughout the city. The program is expected to grow tenfold in the next couple of years. The good: it's cheap and convenient – $5 unlocks a bike for you to use all day; you can pick it up at one kiosk and drop it back at another. The bad: roads are narrow, bike lanes few and Boston traffic aggressive. Want to test the waters? The first 30 minutes are free.

TAXI Taxis are plentiful; expect to pay between $10 and $25 between two points within the city limits. Flag taxis on the street, find them at major hotels or call **Metro Cab** (617-242-8000) or **Independent** (617-426-8700).

Around Boston

The historic towns rimming Boston make for fine day-tripping. If you don't have your own transportation, you can reach these places by MBTA (p175) buses and rail.

LEXINGTON & CONCORD

In 1775 the Colonial town of Lexington, 15 miles northwest of Boston, was the site of the first battle of the American Revolution. Following the battle, the British redcoats marched 10 miles west to Concord where they fought the American Minutemen at the town's North Bridge – the first American victory. You can revisit this momentous bit of history at **Minute Man National Historic Park** (978-369-6993; www.nps.gov/mima; 174 Liberty St, Concord; admission free; 9am-5pm) and along the 5.5-mile **Battle Road Trail**, which is open to cyclists as well as hikers.

In the 19th century, Concord harbored a vibrant literary community. Next to the Old North Bridge is the Old Manse (978-369-3909; 269 Monument St; adult/child $8/5), former home of author Nathaniel Hawthorne. Within a mile of the town center are the **Ralph Waldo Emerson house** (978-369-2236; 28 Cambridge Turnpike; adult/child $8/6), Louisa May Alcott's **Orchard House** (978-369-4118; 399 Lexington Rd; adult/child $9/5) and the **Wayside** (978-369-6993; 455 Lexington Rd; adult/child $5/free), where Alcott's *Little Women* was set.

Walden Pond, where Henry David Thoreau lived and wrote *Walden,* is 3 miles south of the town center; you can visit his cabin site and take an inspiring hike around the pond. All these authors are laid to rest in **Sleepy Hollow Cemetery** (Bedford St) in the town center. Admission is free to Walden Pond and the cemetery. **Concord Chamber of Commerce** (978-369-3120; www.concordchamberofcommerce.org; 58 Main St; 10am-4pm) has full details on sites, including opening hours for the homes, which vary with the season.

SALEM

Salem, 20 miles northeast of Boston, burned itself an infamous place in history with the 1692 hysteria that put innocent people to death for witchcraft. The tragedy has proven a boon for operators of numerous Salem witch attractions, some serious, others just milking witchy-wacky-woo for all it's worth. **Destination Salem** (877-725-3662; www.salem.org; 2 New Liberty St; 9am-5pm) has full information on town sights.

The exceptional **Peabody Essex Museum** (978-745-9500; www.pem.org; East India Sq; adult/child $15/free; 10am-5pm Tue-Sun) reflects Salem's rich maritime history. The museum was founded upon the art, artifacts and curios collected by Salem traders during their early expeditions to the Far East. As the exhibits attest, they had deep pockets and refined taste. In addition to world-class Chinese and Pacific Island displays, the museum boasts an excellent Native American collection.

Salem was the center of a thriving clippership trade with China and its preeminent trader, Elias Derby, became America's first millionaire. For a sense of those glory days,

---

WITCH HUNTS

In early 1692 a group of Salem girls began to act strangely. The work of the devil? The girls, pressured to blame someone, accused a slave named Tituba of witchcraft. Under torture, Tituba accused others and soon accusations were flying thick and fast. By September, 55 had pleaded guilty and 19 who wouldn't 'confess' to witchcraft were hanged. The frenzy finally died down when the accusers pointed at the governor's wife.

The most poignant site in Salem is the **Witch Trials Memorial** (Charter St), a quiet park behind the Peabody Essex Museum, where simple stones are inscribed with the names and final words of the victims, decrying the injustice befallen them.

Best of Salem's other 'witchy' sites is the **Witch House** (www.witchhouse.info; 310 Essex St; adult/child $10.25/6.25; 10am-5pm), the home of the magistrate who presided over the trials. To dig deeper, read Arthur Miller's *The Crucible,* which doubles as a parable to the 1950s anticommunist 'witch hunts' in the US Senate that resulted in Miller's own blacklisting.

NEW BEDFORD, 'THE WHALING CITY'

At the height of the whaling era, New Bedford was the largest whaling port on earth. Among the thousands finding work on the ships was author Herman Melville, who roamed the harborfront before setting off on the adventure that inspired *Moby-Dick*. Indeed, the opening scenes of the novel are set in New Bedford. With its gas lamps and cobbled stone streets, the town center looks much as it did in 1841 when Melville crewed up on the whaler *Acushnet*. The old port, which extends four blocks inland from the harbor, is now preserved as **New Bedford National Historical Park**. Start at the **Park Visitor Center** (☎508-996-4095; www.nps.gpv/nebe; 33 Williams St; ☺9am-5pm), where you can pick up a map and watch a short film that'll make the perfect introduction to your sightseeing.

Within a stone's throw of the visitor center lies the **Seaman's Bethel**, the chapel where Melville and crewmates attended services before setting sail for the Pacific whaling grounds. Nearby at the terrific **New Bedford Whaling Museum** (☎508-997-0046; www.whalingmuseum.org; 18 Johnny Cake Hill; adult/child $10/6; ☺9am-5pm) you'll gape at full-size whale skeletons, clamber aboard a half-size replica of a whaling schooner and find evocative exhibits. Search for the one on Frederick Douglass, the former slave who landed a job as a dockworker here at age 21 and left three years later as one of America's leading abolitionists. (New Bedford in the 19th century was one of the most integrated places in America.)

Today New Bedford still looks to the sea and lays claim to being New England's largest fishing port. For the best briny delights in town make your way to **Antonio's** (☎508-990-3636; www.antoniosnewbedford.com; 267 Coggeshall St; meals $10-18; ☺11:30am-9:30pm), where fresh catch melds with New Bedford's Portuguese heritage; the delicious paella, brimming with lobster and shellfish, will sate any appetite.

To get to New Bedford take I-195 to MA 18 south; take the Elm St exit. Park at the municipal parking garage, a block up Elm St. The national park visitor center is one short block to the south.

take a walk along Derby St and out to Derby Wharf, now the center of the **Salem Maritime National Historic Site**.

PLYMOUTH

Proclaiming itself 'America's hometown,' Plymouth celebrates its heritage as the region's first permanent European settlement. **Plymouth Rock**, a weather-worn chunk of granite on the harborfront, is said to mark the place the Pilgrims came ashore in 1620. Don't expect anything monumental; the rock upon which America was built is indeed small – so diminutive that most visitors have to take a second look.

These days, people make their pilgrimage to **Plimoth Plantation** (☎508-746-1622; www.plimoth.org; MA 3A; adult/child $29.50/19; ☺9am-5pm mid-Mar–Nov; ♿), an authentically recreated 1627 Pilgrim village. Everything – the houses, the crops, the food cooked over wood stoves and even the vocabulary used by the costumed interpreters – is meticulously true to the period. Equally insightful are the home sites of the Wampanoag tribe, who helped the Pilgrims through their first difficult winter. If you're traveling with kids, or you're a history buff, don't miss it. The admission price includes entry to the *Mayflower II,* a replica of the Pilgrims' ship, at Plymouth Harbor.

Destination Plymouth (☎508-747-7533; www.visit-plymouth.com; 134 Court St; ☺8am-4pm), has details on all sights. When hunger strikes, you'll find good seafood restaurants right at the harbor.

Cape Cod

Clambering across the National Seashore dunes, cycling the Cape Cod Rail Trail, eating oysters at Wellfleet Harbor – this sandy peninsula serves up a bounty of local flavor. Fringed with 400 miles of sparkling shoreline, 'the Cape,' as it's called by Cape Codders, rates as New England's top beach destination. But there's a lot more than just beaches here. When you've had your fill of sun and sand, get out and explore artist enclaves, take a cruise, or join the free-spirited street scene in Provincetown.

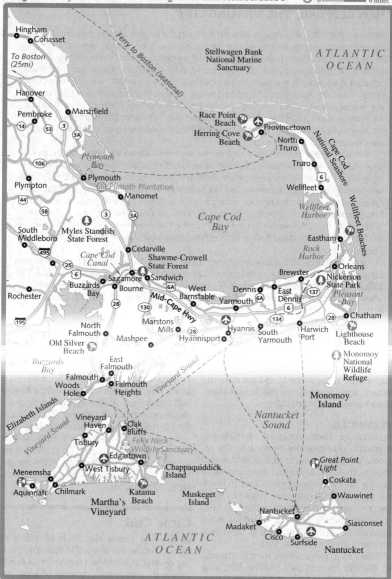

Cape Cod, Martha's Vineyard & Nantucket

0 ──── 10 km
0 ──── 6 miles

Hingham
Cohasset
To Boston (25mi)
Hanover
Pembroke (14) (53) (3)
Marshfield
(3A)
(106)
Plympton
Plymouth
(44)
Plimoth Plantation
Manomet
South Middleboro (58)
Myles Standish State Forest (3) (3A)
(495)
Cape Cod Canal (25)
Cedarville
Shawme-Crowell State Forest
Rochester
Buzzards Bay
Sagamore Sandwich
Bourne (6A)
(28)
Mid-Cape Hwy
West Barnstable
(130)
Marstons Mills (28)
North Falmouth
Old Silver Beach
Mashpee
Hyannisport
Hyannis
Dennis
Yarmouth
East Dennis (6A)
(6)
South Yarmouth (134)
Buzzards Bay
East Falmouth
Falmouth
Woods Hole
Falmouth Heights
Vineyard Sound
Elizabeth Islands
Vineyard Sound
Vineyard Haven
Oak Bluffs
Tisbury
Felix Neck Wildlife Sanctuary
Menemsha
West Tisbury
Edgartown
Chappaquiddick Island
Aquinnah Chilmark
Katama Beach
Martha's Vineyard
Muskeget Island
ATLANTIC OCEAN
Nantucket Sound
Monomoy Island
Monomoy National Wildlife Refuge
Lighthouse Beach
Chatham (28)
Harwich Port
Pleasant Bay
Brewster
Orleans
Nickerson State Park (137)
Eastham
Rock Harbor
Wellfleet
Wellfleet Harbor
Wellfleet Beaches
Truro
North Truro
Provincetown
Race Point Beach
Herring Cove Beach
Cape Cod National Seashore
(6)
Cape Cod Bay
Stellwagen Bank National Marine Sanctuary
ATLANTIC OCEAN
Plymouth Bay
Plouth Plantation
Ferry to Boston (seasonal)
Great Point Light
Coskata
Wauwinet
Siasconset
Nantucket
Madaket
Cisco
Surfside
Nantucket

Cape Cod Chamber of Commerce (📞508-362-3225; www.capecodchamber.org; MA 132 at US 6, Hyannis; ⏰10am-5pm) has info.

SANDWICH

The Cape's oldest village wraps its historic center around a picturesque swan pond with a grist mill (c 1654) and several small museums.

◉ Sights & Activities

If you're ready for salt spray, head to **Sandy Neck Beach** (Sandy Neck Rd), off MA 6A, a 6-mile dune-backed strand (parking $15) ideal for beachcombing and a bracing swim.

Sandwich Glass Museum · MUSEUM
(508-888-0251; www.sandwichglassmuseum.org; 129 Main St; adult/child $5/1.25; 9:30am-5pm) Artfully displayed here is the town's 19th-century glass-making heritage. Glass-blowing demonstrations are given on the hour.

Heritage Museums & Gardens · MUSEUM
(508-888-3300; www.heritagemuseumsandgardens.org; cnr Grove & Pine Sts; adult/child $12/6; 10am-5pm;) The 76-acre site sports a terrific **vintage automobile collection**, folk-art exhibits and one of the finest **rhododendron gardens** in America. Kids will love riding the classic 1912 **carousel**.

Hoxie House · HISTORIC HOUSE
(508-888-1173; 18 Water St; adult/child $3/2; 10am-5pm Mon-Sat, 1-5pm Sun) The Cape's oldest house (c 1640).

Cape Cod Canal · BIKE PATH
A 6-mile path perfect for cycling and in-line skating runs along the south side of the Cape Cod Canal starting at Sandwich Harbor.

Sleeping & Eating

Belfry Inne & Bistro · B&B $$
(508-888-8550; www.belfryinn.com; 8 Jarves St; r incl breakfast $189-255;) Ever fall asleep in church? Then you'll love the rooms, some with the original stained-glass windows, in this creatively restored former church, now an upmarket B&B. If, however, having the angel Gabriel watching over you in bed seems a bit too quirky, Belfry has two adjacent inns with more conventional rooms.

Shawme-Crowell State Forest · CAMPGROUND $
(508-888-0351; www.reserveamerica.com; MA 130; campsites $14) You'll find 285 shady campsites in this 700-acre woodland, near MA 6A.

Brown Jug · CAFE $
(www.thebrownjug.com; 155 Main St; mains $6-10; 9am-5pm Tue-Sat, noon-4pm Sun) A great sandwich in Sandwich? Natch. This smart wine shop/cafe makes fab salads, sandwiches and cheese plates. Or step up to the deli and stock your picnic basket with truffle mousse pâté, caviar and artisanal breads for a romantic outing.

Seafood Sam's · SEAFOOD $$
(www.seafoodsams.com; 6 Coast Guard Rd; mains $10-20; 11am-9pm;) Sam's is a good family choice for fish and chips, clams and lobster. Dine at picnic tables overlooking Cape Cod Canal and watch the fishing boats sail by.

FALMOUTH
Fantastic beaches and a seaside bike trail highlight the Cape's second-largest town.

Sights & Activities

TOP CHOICE **Shining Sea Bikeway** · BIKE TRAIL
Cyclists won't want to miss this 10.7-mile beaut that runs along the entire west coast of Falmouth, offering unspoiled views of salt ponds and seascapes. The route is flat, making it well suited as a family outing. **Corner Cycle** (508-540-4195; www.cyclecorner.com; 115 Palmer Ave; per day $17; 9am-6pm) rents bicycles near the trail.

Old Silver Beach · BEACH
(off MA 28A, North Falmouth; parking $20;) Deeply indented Falmouth has 70 miles of coastline, none finer than this long, sandy stretch with calm water. A rock jetty, sandbars and tidal pools provide lots of fun diversions for kids.

Sleeping & Eating

Falmouth Heights Motor Lodge · MOTEL $$
(508-548-3623; www.falmouthheightsresort.com; 146 Falmouth Heights Rd; r incl breakfast from $149;) Don't be fooled by the name. This tidy family-run operation is no drive-up motor lodge – it's not even on the highway. All 28 rooms are a cut above the competition. The beach and Vineyard ferry are minutes away.

Casino Wharf FX · SEAFOOD $$
(508-540-6160; www.casinowharf.weebly.com; 286 Grand Ave; mains $10-30; 11:30am-10:30pm) This place is so close to the water that you could cast a fishing pole from the deck. But

NEW ENGLAND CAPE COD

WHAT THE...?

Lobster mania takes a new twist at **Ben & Bill's Chocolate Emporium** (209 Main St, Falmouth; cones $5; 9am-11pm) where the crustacean has crawled onto the ice-cream menu. Forget plain vanilla. Step up to the counter and order a scoop of lobster ice cream. Now there's one you won't find with the old 31 flavors folks.

why bother? Just grab a deck table and let the feast begin. Music, often live and lively, on weekends.

Clam Shack SEAFOOD $
(227 Clinton Ave; items $5-15; ⊙11:30am-7:30pm) A classic of the genre, right on Falmouth Harbor. It's tiny, with picnic tables on the back deck and lots of fried seafood. The clams, huge juicy bellies cooked to a perfect crisp, are the place to start.

HYANNIS

Cape Cod's commercial hub, Hyannis is best known to visitors as the summer home of the Kennedy clan and a jumping-off point for ferries to Nantucket and Martha's Vineyard.

⊙ Sights & Activities

The town's mile-long Main St is fun to stroll and the place for dining, drinking and shopping. **Kalmus Beach** (Ocean St) is popular for windsurfing, while **Craigville Beach** (Craigville Beach Rd) is where the college set goes; parking at either costs $15.

John F Kennedy Hyannis Museum MUSEUM
(☎508-790-3077; http://jfkhyannismuseum.org; 397 Main St; adult/child $5/2.50; ⊙9am-5pm Mon-Sat, noon-5pm Sun) Celebrates the USA's 35th president with photos, videos and exhibits.

Hy-Line Cruises HARBOR CRUISE
(☎508-790-0696; www.hylinecruises.com; Ocean St Dock; adult/child $16/8; ⊙mid-Apr–Oct) Offers an hour-long harbor cruise aboard an old-fashioned steamer that circles past the compound of Kennedy family homes.

🛏 Sleeping

TOP CHOICE Anchor-In HOTEL $$
(☎508-775-0357; www.anchorin.com; 1 South St; r incl breakfast $139-259; ❄@🕸❄) Bright airy rooms with harbor-view balconies separate this family-run, boutique hotel from all the chains back on the highway. And if you're planning a day trip to Nantucket, the ferry is just a stroll away.

HI-Hyannis HOSTEL $
(☎508-775-7990; http://capecod.hiusa.org; 111 Ocean St; dm/private r incl breakfast $32/99; @❄) Overlooking the harbor, this shiny new hostel is within walking distance of the Main St scene, beaches and ferries. Just 44 beds, so book early.

SeaCoast Inn MOTEL $$
(☎508-775-3828; www.seacoastcapecod.com; 33 Ocean St; r incl breakfast $108-158; ❄@❄) The rates are a bargain, but it's no Plain Jane. Rooms are spacious with perks aplenty, from free wi-fi to kitchenettes, and the central location is just minutes from everything in town.

🍴 Eating

Raw Bar SEAFOOD $$
(www.therawbar.com; 230 Ocean St; lobster rolls $18-25; ⊙11am-7pm) Come here for the mother of all lobster rolls – it's like eating an entire lobster in a bun. The view overlooking Hyannis Harbor isn't hard to swallow either.

Brazilian Grill BRAZILIAN $$
(680 Main St; lunch/dinner buffet $15/28; ⊙11:30am-10pm) Celebrate Hyannis' Brazil-

---

WORTH A TRIP

WOODS HOLE

The tiny village of Woods Hole is home to the largest oceanographic institution in the US. Research at the Woods Hole Oceanographic Institution (WHOI, pronounced 'hooey') has covered the gamut from exploring the sunken *Titanic* to global warming studies.

For the skinny, join one of the free tours departing from the **WHOI information office** (☎508-289-2252; www.whoi.edu; 93 Water St; ⊙75-min tours 10:30am & 1:30pm Mon-Fri Jul & Aug). You'll also gain insights into scientists' work at the **WHOI Ocean Science Exhibit Center** (15 School St; admission free; ⊙10am-4:30pm Mon-Sat).

Woods Hole Science Aquarium (http://aquarium.nefsc.noaa.gov; 166 Water St; admission free; ⊙11am-4pm Tue-Sat; 🚸) has little flash and dazzle, but you'll find unusual sea life specimens, local fish and the *Homarus americanus* (aka lobster). Kids will enjoy the touch-tank creatures. Coolest time to come is at 11am or 4pm when the seals are fed.

Keeping with the nautical theme, head over to the drawbridge where you'll find **Fishmonger Café** (56 Water St; mains $10-25; ⊙7am-9:30pm), with water views in every direction and an eclectic menu emphasizing fresh seafood.

To get to Woods Hole from Falmouth center take Woods Hole Rd south from MA28.

SCENIC DRIVE: MA 6A

When exploring the Cape, eschew the speedy Mid-Cape Hwy (US 6) and follow instead the Old King's Hwy (MA 6A), which snakes along Cape Cod Bay. The longest continuous stretch of historic district in the USA, it's lined with gracious period homes, antique shops and art galleries, all of which makes for good browsing en route.

ian side at this real-deal *rodízio*, a feast that pairs a splendid buffet with *churrasco* (barbecued meats on skewers) brought to your table by hunky gauchos in traditional garb.

La Petite France Café   CAFE $
(www.lapetitefrancecafe.com; 349 Main St; sandwiches $7; ⊙7am-3pm Mon-Sat) The star of the Hyannis cafe scene makes flaky croissants, superb baguette sandwiches and homemade soups.

BREWSTER

Woodsy Brewster, on the Cape's bay side, makes a good base for outdoorsy types. The Cape Cod Rail Trail cuts clear across town and there are excellent options for camping, hiking and water activities.

⦿ Sights & Activities

FREE **Nickerson State Park**   STATE PARK
(☑508-896-3491; 3488 MA 6A; ⊙dawn-dusk) Miles of cycling and walking trails and eight ponds with sandy beaches highlight this 2000-acre oasis.

Jack's Boat Rental
(☑508-349-9808; www.jacksboatrental.com; rentals per hr $20-40; ⊙9am-6pm) Rents canoes, kayaks, stand-up paddleboards and sailboats in the park.

Barbara's Bike
(☑508-896-7231; www.barbsbikeshop.com; rental per day $24; ⊙9am-6pm) Rents bicycles by the park entrance.

**Cape Cod Museum of
Natural History**   MUSEUM
(☑508-896-3867; www.ccmnh.org; 869 MA 6A; adult/child $8/3.50; ⊙9:30am-4pm; ⓓ) Come here for exhibits on the Cape's creatures and a cool boardwalk trail that tromps across a saltmarsh to a remote beach.

🛏 Sleeping

Old Sea Pines Inn   B&B $$
(☑508-896-6114; www.oldseapinesinn.com; 2553 MA 6A; r incl breakfast $85-165; @🛜) A former girls' school dating to 1840, the inn's 21 rooms retain a simple yesteryear look. It's a bit like staying at grandma's house: antique fittings, sepia photographs, clawfoot bathtubs. No TV, but rocking chairs await on the porch.

Nickerson State Park   CAMPGROUND $
(☑877-422-6762;   www.reserveamerica.com; campsites $17) Head here for Cape Cod's best camping with 418 wooded campsites; it often fills, so reserve your spot early.

🛏 Eating

TOP CHOICE **Brewster Fish House**   SEAFOOD $$
(www.brewsterfish.com; 2208 MA 6A; mains $12-30; ⊙11:30am-3pm & 5-9:30pm) Not an eye-catcher from the outside but inside you'll find some of the best seafood on the Cape. Start with the lobster bisque, naturally sweet with chunks of fresh lobster. From there it's safe to cast your net in any direction. Just 11 tables, and no reservations, so think lunch or early dinner to avoid long waits.

Cobie's   CLAM SHACK $$
(3256 MA 6A; takeout $8-23; ⊙10:30am-9pm) Conveniently located near Nickerson State Park, this roadside clam shack dishes out fried seafood that you can crunch and munch at outdoor picnic tables.

CHATHAM

Upscale inns and tony shops are a hallmark of the Cape's most genteel town, but some of Chatham's finest pleasures come free for the taking. Start your exploring on Main St, with its old sea captains' houses and cool art galleries.

At **Chatham Fish Pier** (Shore Rd) watch fishermen unload their catch and spot seals basking on nearby shoals. A mile south on Shore Rd is **Lighthouse Beach**, an endless expanse of sea and sandbars that offers some of the finest beach strolling on Cape Cod. The 7600-acre **Monomoy National Wildlife Refuge** (www.fws.gov/northeast/monomoy) covers two uninhabited islands thick with shorebirds; to see it up close take the 1½-hour boat tour with **Monomoy Island Excursions** (☑508-430-7772; www.monomoysealcruise.com; 702 MA 28, Harwich Port; adult/child $35/30).

🛏 Sleeping & Eating

Bow Roof House
B&B $$

(☎508-945-1346; 59 Queen Anne Rd; r incl breakfast $100-115) This homey, six-room, c 1780 house is delightfully old-fashioned in price and offerings, and within walking distance of the town center and beach. Except for a few later-day conveniences like the addition of private bathrooms, the house looks nearly the same as it did in colonial times.

Chatham Squire
PUB $$

(www.thesquire.com; 487 Main St; mains $8-22; ⊙11:30am-10pm) This perky pub is the busiest place in town. The menu's piled high with Monomoy steamers, raw oysters and other briny local delights. How fresh is the seafood? Just take one look at the fishermen hanging at the bar.

CAPE COD NATIONAL SEASHORE

Cape Cod National Seashore (www.nps.gov/caco) extends some 40 miles around the curve of the Outer Cape and encompasses most of the shoreline from Eastham to Provincetown. It's a treasure-trove of unspoiled beaches, dunes, salt marshes and forests. Thanks to President John F Kennedy, this vast area was set aside for preservation in the 1960s, just before a building boom hit the rest of his native Cape Cod. The Salt (☎508-255-3421; cnr US 6 & Nauset Rd, Eastham; admission free; ⊙9am-5pm) is the place to start and has a great view to boot. Here you will find exhibits and films about the area's ecology and the scoop on the park's numerous cycling and hiking trails, some of which begin right at the center.

You brought your board, didn't you? Coast Guard Beach, just down the road from the visitor center, is a stunner that attracts everyone from surfers to beachcombers. And the view of untouched Nauset Marsh from the dunes above the beach is nothing short of spectacular. Nauset Light Beach, running north from Coast Guard Beach, takes its name from the lighthouse perched above it; three other classic lighthouses are nearby. Summertime beach parking passes cost $15/45 per day/season and are valid at all Cape Cod National Seashore beaches including Provincetown.

WELLFLEET

Art galleries, primo beaches and those famous Wellfleet oysters lure visitors to this little seaside town.

👁 Sights & Activities

Wellfleet Beaches
BEACHES

Marconi Beach has a monument to Guglielmo Marconi, who sent the first wireless transmission across the Atlantic from this site, and a beach backed by undulating dunes. The adjacent White Crest Beach and Cahoon Hollow Beach offer high-octane surfing. SickDay Surf Shop (☎508-214-4158; www.sickdaysurf.com; 361 Main St; half-/full day $18/25; ⊙9am-9pm Mon-Sat) rents surfboards.

🍃 Wellfleet Bay Wildlife Sanctuary
WILDLIFE SANCTUARY

(☎508-349-2615; www.massaudubon.org; West Rd, off US 6; adult/child $5/3; ⊙8:30am-dusk; 🖈) Birders flock to Mass Audubon's 1100-acre sanctuary, where trails cross tidal creeks, salt marshes and sandy beaches.

🎉 Festivals & Events

Wellfleet OysterFest
FOOD

(www.wellfleetoysterfest.org) Held in mid-October the town hall parking lot morphs into a wildly popular festival with a beer garden, oyster shucking contest and, of course, bellybusters of the blessed bivalves.

🛏 Sleeping & Eating

B&B $$

(☎508-349-9565; www.stonelioncapecod.com; 130 Commercial St; r incl breakfast $150-220; ❄️🎍) Historic without being cloying, this 1871 Victorian is the finest place in Wellfleet to tuck

---

CYCLING THE RAIL TRAIL

A poster child for the rails-to-trail movement, the Cape Cod Rail Trail follows a former railroad track for 22 glorious miles past cranberry bogs and along sandy ponds ideal for a dip. It's one of the finest cycling trails in all New England. There's a hefty dose of Olde Cape Cod scenery en route and you can detour into quiet villages for lunch or sightseeing. The path begins in Dennis on MA 134 and continues all the way to South Wellfleet. If you have time to do only part of the trail, begin at Nickerson State Park in Brewster and head for the Cape Cod National Seashore in Eastham. Bicycle rentals are available at the trailhead in Dennis, at Nickerson State Park and opposite the National Seashore's Salt Pond Visitor Center.

in. Pine floors, antique decor and handcrafted furnishings set the tone. The location is handy for exploring town on foot.

Mac's Seafood Market CLAM SHACK **$$**
(www.macsseafood.com; Wellfleet Town Pier, takeout $6-20; ⊙7:30am-11pm) Head here for market-fresh seafood at bargain prices. Fried-fish standards are paired with snappy-fresh oysters harvested from nearby flats. Order at a window and chow down at picnic tables overlooking Wellfleet Harbor.

Mac's Shack SEAFOOD **$$**
(☑508-349-6333; 91 Commercial St; mains $15-30; ⊙4:30-9:45pm) Fancier, full-service version of Mac's Seafood Market.

PB Boulangerie & Bistro FRENCH BAKERY **$**
(www.pbboulangeriebistro.com; 15 Lecount Hollow Rd; ⊙7am-7pm Wed-Sun) Incredible pastries and artisanal breads.

🍷 Drinking & Entertainment

TOP CHOICE Beachcomber DANCE CLUB
(☑508-349-6055; www.thebeachcomber.com; 1120 Cahoon Hollow Rd) 'Da Coma' is the coolest summertime hangout on the entire Cape. Set in a former lifesaving station right on Cahoon Hollow Beach, you can enjoy the surf action till the sun goes down. And at night some really hot bands – like the Wailers and the Lemonheads – take to the stage.

Wellfleet Harbor Actors Theater THEATER
(WHAT; ☑508-349-9428; www.what.org; 2357 US 6) This acclaimed theater produces edgy contemporary plays.

Wellfleet Drive-In DRIVE-IN
(☑508-349-7176; www.wellfleetcinemas.com; US 6; 🔊) Enjoy an evening of nostalgia at this old-fashioned drive-in theater.

TRURO

Squeezed between Cape Cod Bay on the west and the open Atlantic on the east, narrow Truro abounds with water views and beaches.

🔘 Sights

Cape Cod Highland Light LIGHTHOUSE
(www.capecodlight.org; Light House Rd; admission $4; ⊙10am-5:30pm) Dating to 1797, this lighthouse casts the brightest light on the New England coastline and offers a sweeping view.

🛏 Sleeping

Hostelling International Truro HOSTEL **$**
(☑508-349-3889; http://capecod.hiusa.org; N Pamet Rd; dm incl breakfast $32-42; ☺) Budget digs

don't get more atmospheric than at this former coast guard station dramatically sited amid beach dunes. Book early.

PROVINCETOWN

This is it: as far as you can go on the Cape, and more than just geographically. The draw is irresistible. Fringe writers and artists began making a summer haven in Provincetown a century ago. Today this sandy outpost has morphed into the hottest gay and lesbian destination in the Northeast. Flamboyant street scenes, brilliant art galleries and unbridled nightlife paint the town center. But that's only half the show. Provincetown's untamed coastline and vast beaches also beg exploring. Sail off on a whale-watch, cruise the night away, get lost in the dunes – but whatever you do, don't miss this unique corner of New England.

🔘 Sights & Activities

Cape Cod National Seashore NATIONAL SEASHORE
The **Province Lands Visitor Center** (www.nps.gov/caco; Race Point Rd; admission free; ⊙9am-5pm) has displays on dune ecology and a rooftop observation deck with a 360-degree view of the outermost reaches of Cape Cod. The deck stays open to midnight, offering stellar stargazing.

The nearby **Race Point Beach** is a breathtaking stretch of sand with crashing surf and undulating dunes as far as the eye can see. Swimmers favor the calmer though equally brisk waters of **Herring Cove Beach**; nude (though illegal) sunbathers head to the left, families to the right. Herring Cove faces west, making for spectacular sunsets.

TOP CHOICE Whale-Watching WHALE-WATCHING
Provincetown is the perfect launch point for whale-watching, since it's the closest port to Stellwagen Bank National Marine Sanctuary, a summer feeding ground for humpback whales. These awesome creatures with a flair for acrobatic breaching come surprisingly close to the boats, offering great photo ops. Many of the 300 remaining North Atlantic right whales, the world's most endangered whale species, also frequent these waters.

Dolphin Fleet Whale Watch WHALE-WATCHING
(☑508-240-3636; www.whalewatch.com; MacMillan Wharf; adult/child $39/31; ⊙Apr-Oct; 🔊) Offers up to nine tours daily in peak season, each lasting three to four hours.

Pilgrim Monument

MUSEUM

(www.pilgrim-monument.org; High Pole Rd; adult/child $7/3.50; ⊙9am-5pm) Climb to the top of the USA's tallest all-granite structure, 253ft high, for a sweeping view of town and the surrounding coast. The monument and its interesting museum commemorate the *Mayflower* Pilgrims, who landed in Provincetown in 1620 before moving on to Plymouth.

Provincetown Art Association & Museum

MUSEUM

(PAAM; www.paam.org; 460 Commercial St; adult/child $7/free; ⊙11am-8pm Mon-Thu, 11am-10pm Fri, 11am-5pm Sat & Sun) Established in 1914 to celebrate the town's thriving art community, this superb museum displays the works of artists who have found inspiration in Provincetown over the past century. On Friday evenings, admission is free.

Cycling

CYCLING

Eight exhilarating miles of bike trails crisscross the forest and undulating dunes of the Cape Cod National Seashore and lead to Herring Cove and Race Point Beaches.

The best place to rent bicycles is at **Ptown Bikes** (☎508-487-8735; www.ptownbikes.com; 42 Bradford St; per day $22; ⊙9am-6pm) though you'll also find rental shops in the center of town on Commercial St.

Art's Dune Tours

TOURS

(☎508-487-1950; www.artsdunetours.com; 4 Standish St; adult/child $26/17) Hour-long 4WD tours through the dunes.

Whydah Pirate Museum

MUSEUM

(www.whydah.org; MacMillan Wharf; adult/child $10/8; ⊙10am-5pm) See the salvaged booty from a pirate ship that sank off Cape Cod in 1717.

★ Festivals & Events

Carnival Week

CARNIVAL PARADE

(www.ptown.org/carnival.asp; mid-Aug) Mardi Gras, drag queens, flowery floats – this is the ultimate gay party event in this gay party town, attracting tens of thousands of revelers.

🛏 Sleeping

Provincetown offers nearly 100 guesthouses without a single chain hotel to mar the view. In summer it's wise to book ahead, doubly so on weekends. If you arrive without a booking, the chamber of commerce keeps tabs on available rooms.

GALLERY BROWSING

Provincetown hosts scores of art galleries. For the best browsing begin at PAAM and walk southwest along waterfront Commercial St. Over the next few blocks every second storefront harbors a gallery worth a peek.

TOP CHOICE Carpe Diem

INN $$$

(☎508-487-4242; www.carpediemguesthouse.com; 12 Johnson St; r incl breakfast $175-359; ❋@🛜) Sophisticated and relaxed, with smiling buddhas, orchid sprays and a European-style spa. Each room's decor is inspired by a different gay literary genius; the room themed on poet Raj Rao, for example, has sumptuous embroidered fabrics and hand-carved Native American furniture.

Christopher's by the Bay

B&B $$

(☎508-487-9263; www.christophersbythebay.com; 8 Johnson St; r with shared/private bath from $105/155; ❋🛜) Tucked away on a quiet side street, this welcoming inn is top value. The 2nd-floor rooms are the largest and snazziest, but the 3rd-floor rooms, which share a bathroom, get the ocean view.

Cape Codder

GUESTHOUSE $

(☎508-487-0131; www.capecodderguests.com; 570 Commercial St; r with shared bath $60-85; 🛜) The cheaper rooms are small, there are no TVs or phones, but it's clean, and heck, for these prices in this town it's a deal. The 14 rooms share just four baths, so time yourself accordingly.

Race Point Lighthouse

LIGHTHOUSE INN $$

(☎508-487-9930; www.racepointlighthouse.net; Race Point; r $155-185) Shack up at a 19th-century lighthouse amid the dunes.

Moffett House

GUESTHOUSE $$

(☎508-487-6615; www.moffetthouse.com; 296a Commercial St; r with shared bath $90-174; ❋🛜) A quiet guesthouse with a bonus: free bicycles for your entire stay.

Pilgrim House Hotel

BOUTIQUE HOTEL $$

(☎508-487-6424; www.thepilgrimhouse.com; 336 Commercial St; r $159-250; ❋🛜) Fresh arty decor and a party-central location directly above Vixen nightclub.

Dunes' Edge Campground

CAMPGROUND $

(☎508-487-9815; www.dunes-edge.com; 386 US 6; campsites $40; 🖵) Camp amid the dunes at this family-friendly place.

✕ Eating

Every third building on Commercial St houses some sort of eatery, so that's the place to start.

Mews Restaurant & Café   BISTRO $$
(☎508-487-1500; www.mews.com; 429 Commercial St; mains $12-18; ☺6-10pm) Want affordable gourmet? Skip the excellent but pricey restaurant and go upstairs to the bar for a fab view, great martinis and scrumptious bistro fare. Perhaps the Angus gorgonzola burger?

Fanizzi's by the Sea   FAMILY RESTAURANT $$
(☎508-487-1964; www.fanizzisrestaurant.com; 539 Commercial St; mains $10-25; ☺11:30am-10pm; ♣) Consistent food, an amazing water view and reasonable prices make this restaurant at the east end of Provincetown a sure winner. The extensive menu has something for everyone, from fresh seafood to salads and fajitas.

Purple Feather   CAFE $
(www.thepurplefeather.com; 334 Commercial St; snacks $3-10; ☺8am-midnight; ☎) Head to this stylish cafe for killer panini sandwiches, blueberry gelato and decadent desserts all made from scratch. No better place in town for light eats.

Lobster Pot   SEAFOOD $$$
(☎508-487-0842; www.ptownlobsterpot.com; 321 Commercial St; mains $20-35; ☺11:30am-10pm) True to its name, this bustling fish house overlooking the ocean is *the* place for lobster. Service can be s-l-o-w. Best way to beat the crowd is to come in mid-afternoon.

Portuguese Bakery   BAKERY $
(299 Commercial St; snacks $2-5; ☺7am-11pm) Old-school bakery serving up linguica sandwiches and Portuguese pastries.

Karoo Kafe   SOUTH AFRICAN $$
(www.karookafe.com; 338 Commercial St; mains $8-16; ☺11am-9pm; ☑) Authentic home-style cooking from South Africa. The ostrich satay's a favorite.

Spiritus Pizza   PIZZERIA $
(www.spirituspizza.com; 190 Commercial St; pizza slice $3; ☺11:30am-2am) A favorite spot for a late-night bite and cruising after the clubs close.

� Drinking & Entertainment

BARS

Patio   CAFE
(www.ptownpatio.com; 328 Commercial St) Grab yourself a sidewalk table and order up a ginger-lime cosmo at this umbrella-shaded cafe hugging the pulsating center of Commercial St.

Ross' Grill   BISTRO
(www.rossgrille.com; 237 Commercial St) A fab water view and 75 different wines by the glass.

NIGHTCLUBS

Provincetown is awash with gay clubs, drag shows and cabarets. And don't be shy if you're straight – everyone's welcome.

Crown & Anchor   NIGHTCLUB
(www.onlyatthecrown.com; 247 Commercial St) The queen of the scene, this multiwing complex has a nightclub, a leather bar and a steamy cabaret that takes it to the limit.

Vixen   NIGHTCLUB
(www.ptownvixen.com; 336 Commercial St) A favorite lesbian hangout, with everything from an intimate wine bar to comedy shows and dancing.

A-House   DANCE CLUB
(www.ahouse.com; 4 Masonic Pl) A hot weekend dance spot for gay men.

THEATER

Provincetown boasts a rich theater history. Eugene O'Neill began his writing career here and several stars including Marlon Brando and Richard Gere performed on Provincetown stages before they hit the big screen.

Provincetown Theater   THEATER
(☎508-487-7487; www.provincetowntheater.org; 238 Bradford St) Provincetown's leading theater

---

WHAT THE...?

In a town of quirky attractions the **Provincetown Public Library** (356 Commercial St; ☎) might be the last place you'd expect to find a hidden treasure. Erected in 1860 as a church, it was turned into a museum a century later, complete with a replica of Provincetown's race-winning schooner *Rose Dorothea*. When the museum went bust, the town converted the building to a library. One catch: the boat, which occupies the building's upper deck, was too big to remove. So it's still there, with bookshelves built around it. Pop upstairs and take a look.

troupe, the New Provincetown Players, takes the stage here.

🛍 Shopping

Shops lining Commercial St sell everything from kitsch and tourist T-shirts to quality crafts and edgy clothing.

Shop Therapy
SEX TOYS

(www.shoptherapy.com; 346 Commercial St) Downstairs it's tie-dye clothing and X-rated bumper stickers. But everyone gravitates upstairs, where the sex toys are wild enough to make an Amsterdam madam blush. Parents, use discretion: your teenagers *will* want to go inside.

Womencrafts
CRAFTS

(www.womencrafts.com; 376 Commercial St) The name says it all: jewelry, pottery, books and music by female artists from across America.

ℹ Information

Post office (www.usps.com; 219 Commercial St)
Provincetown Business Guild (www.ptown. org) Website that is oriented towards the gay community.
Provincetown Chamber of Commerce (☎508-487-3424; www.ptownchamber.com; 307 Commercial St; ⊙9am-5pm) The town's helpful tourist office is located at MacMillan Wharf.
Provincetown on the Web (www.provincetown. com) Online guide with the entertainment scoop.
Seamen's Bank (221 Commercial St) Has a 24-hour ATM.
Wired Puppy (www.wiredpuppy.com; 379 Commercial St; ⊙6:30am-10pm; 🛜) Free online computers for the price of an espresso.

ℹ Getting There & Away

Plymouth & Brockton buses (www.p-b.com) connect Boston and Provincetown ($35, 3½ hours). From mid-May to mid-October, **Bay State Cruise Company** (☎877-783-3779; www. baystatecruises.com) runs a ferry (round-trip $79, 1½ hours) between Boston's World Trade Center Pier and MacMillan Wharf.

Nantucket

Once home port to the world's largest whaling fleet, Nantucket's storied past is reflected in its period homes and cobbled streets. When whaling went bust in the mid-19th century the town plunged from riches to rags. The population dwindled, and its grand old houses sat idle until wealthy urbanites discovered Nantucket made a fine place to summer. High-end tourism has been Nantucket's mainstay ever since.

👁 Sights & Activities

Step off the boat and you're in the only place in the USA where the entire town is a National Historic Landmark. It's a bit like stepping into a museum – wander around, soak up the atmosphere. Start your explorations by strolling up Main St, where you'll find the grandest whaling-era mansions lined up in a row.

Nantucket Whaling Museum
MUSEUM

(www.nha.org; 13 Broad St; adult/child $17/8; ⊙10am-5pm) A top sight is this evocative museum in a former spermaceti (whale-oil) candle factory.

Nantucket Beaches
BEACHES

If you have young 'uns head to **Children's Beach**, right in Nantucket town, where the water's calm and there's a playground. **Surfside Beach**, 2 miles to the south, is where the college crowd heads for an active scene and bodysurfing waves. The best place to catch the sunset is Madaket Beach, 5.5 miles west of town.

Cycling
CYCLING

No destination on the island is more than 8 miles from town and thanks to Nantucket's relatively flat terrain and dedicated bike trails, cycling is an easy way to explore. For a fun outing, cycle to the picturesque village of **Siasconset** ('Sconset), known for its rose-covered cottages. A couple of companies rent bikes ($30 a day) right at the ferry docks.

🛏 Sleeping

Pineapple Inn
B&B $$$

(☎508-228-9992; www.pineappleinn.com; 10 Hussey St; r incl breakfast $200-375; ✳@🛜) The 12 guest rooms at this 1838 whaling captain's house have been completely restored with understated elegance. Run by restaurateurs, the inn is justifiably famous for its breakfast. Everything, including the oversized beds with goose-down comforters, spells complete romance.

Nesbitt Inn
B&B $$

(☎508-228-0156; nesbittinn@comcast.net; 21 Broad St; s incl breakfast $105, d $125-170) Operating as an inn since 1872, Nesbitt's a bit faded but it has damn good prices and plenty of old-fashioned character. The finest room, the Captain's Quarters, has a bay window overlooking bustling Broad St and a cavernous bathroom with a real-deal clawfoot tub. Most other guest rooms share bathrooms.

HI Nantucket HOSTEL $

(📞508-228-0433; http://capecod.hiusa.org; 31 Western Ave; dm incl breakfast $32-42; @) Known locally as Star of the Sea, this atmospheric hostel in an 1873 lifesaving station has a million-dollar setting at Surfside Beach. As Nantucket's sole nod to the budget traveler, it books up well in advance.

✖ Eating

Centre Street Bistro CAFE $$

(www.nantucketbistro.com; 29 Centre St; lunch $7-12, dinner $20-30; ⊘11:30am-9:30pm; 🖉) Settle in at a parasol-shaded sidewalk table and watch the traffic trickle by at this relaxed cafe. The chef-owners make everything from scratch from the breakfast granola to the warm goat's cheese tarts.

Brotherhood of Thieves PUB $$

(www.brotherhoodofthieves.com; 23 Broad St; mains $7-25; ⊘11:30am-1am) Nantucketers come here for the friendly tavern atmosphere – all brick and dark woods – and the island's best burgers. Good fresh seafood too, including sweet Nantucket scallops.

Black-Eyed Susan's CAFE $$

(www.black-eyedsusans.com; 10 India St; mains $8-30; ⊘7am-1pm daily & 6-10pm Mon-Sat) Snag a seat on the back patio and try the sourdough French toast topped with caramelized pecans and Jack Daniels butter. At dinner the fish of the day with black-eyed peas takes top honors.

❶ Information

Visitor Services (📞508-228-0925; www.nantucket-ma.gov/visitor; 25 Federal St; ⊘9am-5pm) has tourist information and maintains a kiosk at the ferry dock.

❶ Getting There & Around

AIR Cape Air (www.flycapeair.com) flies from Boston, Hyannis, Martha's Vineyard and Providence to Nantucket Memorial Airport (ACK).

BOAT The Steamship Authority (📞508-477-8600; www.steamshipauthority.com; round-trip adult/child slow ferry $35/18, fast ferry $67/34) runs ferries throughout the day between Hyannis and Nantucket. The fast ferry

takes an hour; the slow ferry 2¼ hours. The slow ferry takes cars, but the $400 round-trip fare aims to discourage visitors from adding to traffic congestion on Nantucket's narrow streets.

BUS Getting around Nantucket is a snap. The **NRTA Shuttle** (www.shuttlenantucket.com; rides $1-2, day pass $7; ⊘late May-Sep) operates buses around town and to 'Sconset, Madaket and the beaches. Buses have bike racks, so cyclists can bus one way and pedal back.

Martha's Vineyard

New England's largest island is a world unto itself. Home to 15,500 year-round residents, its population swells to 100,000 in summer. The towns are charming, the beaches good, the restaurants chef-driven. And there's something for every mood here – fine-dine in gentrified Edgartown one day and hit the cotton candy and carousel scene in Oak Bluffs the next.

Martha's Vineyard Chamber of Commerce (📞508-693-0085; www.mvy.com; 24 Beach Rd, Vineyard Haven; ⊘9am-5pm Mon-Fri) has visitor information. There are also summertime visitor kiosks at the ferry terminals.

OAK BLUFFS

Odds are this ferry-port town, where the lion's share of boats arrive, will be your introduction to the island. Welcome to the Vineyard's summer fun mecca – a place to wander with an ice-cream cone in hand, poke around honky-tonk sights and go clubbing into the night.

◉ Sights & Activities

Campgrounds & Tabernacle GINGERBREAD HOUSES

Oak Bluffs started out in the mid-19th century as a summer retreat by a revivalist church, whose members enjoyed a day at the beach as much as a gospel service. They built around 300 cottages, each adorned with whimsical gingerbread trim. These brightly painted cottages – known today as the Campgrounds – surround **Trinity Park** and its open-air **Tabernacle** (1879), a venue for community sing-alongs, festivals and concerts.

Flying Horses Carousel HISTORIC SITE

(www.mvpreservation.org; cnr Lake & Circuit Aves; rides $2; ⊘10am-10pm; 🖼) Take a nostalgic ride on the USA's oldest merry-go-round, which has been captivating kids of all ages since 1876. The antique horses have manes of real horse hair and if you stare into their glass eyes you'll see neat little silver animals inside.

Bike Trail
CYCLING

A scenic bike trail runs along the coast connecting Oak Bluffs, Vineyard Haven and Edgartown – it's largely flat so makes a good pedal for families. Rent bicycles at **Anderson's Bike Rental** (☎508-693-9346; 1 Circuit Ave Extension; per day $18; ⊙9am-6pm) near the ferry terminal.

⊨ Sleeping

Nashua House
HOTEL $$

(☎508-693-0043; www.nashuahouse.com; 30 Kennebec Ave; r with shared bath $69-219; ❋☎) The Vineyard the way it used to be – no phones, no TV, no in-room bath. Instead you'll find suitably simple and spotlessly clean accommodations at this small inn right in the center of town.

Narragansett House
B&B $$

(☎508-693-3627; www.narragansetthouse.com; 46 Narragansett Ave; r incl breakfast $140-275; ❋☎) On a quiet residential street, this B&B occupies two adjacent Victorian gingerbread-trimmed houses. It's old-fashioned without being cloying and unlike other places in this price range all rooms have private baths.

✕ Eating

Slice of Life
CAFE $$

(www.sliceoflifemv.com; 50 Circuit Ave; mains $8-20; ⊙8am-9pm Tue-Sat; ☑) The look is casual, the fare is gourmet: portobello mushroom omelets, roasted cod with sun-dried tomatoes and luscious desserts.

Giordano's
ITALIAN $$

(www.giosmv.com; cnr Circuit & Lake Aves; mains $10-20; ⊙11:30am-10:30pm) Established in 1930, this family-friendly eatery is famous for its fried clams and also serves good hand-tossed pizzas.

MV Bakery
BAKERY $

(5 Post Office Sq; baked goods $1-3; ⊙7am-5pm) Inexpensive coffee, famous apple fritters and cannoli are served all day, but best time to swing by is from 9pm to midnight, when folks line up at the back door to buy hot doughnuts straight from the baker.

● Drinking & Entertainment

Offshore Ale Co
MICROBREWERY

(www.offshoreale.com; 30 Kennebec Ave) This popular microbrewery is the place to enjoy a pint of Vineyard ale while soaking up live jazz and Irish music on weekday nights.

Lampost
DANCE CLUB

(www.lampostmv.com; Circuit Ave) Head to this combo bar and nightclub for the hottest dance scene on the island. In the unlikely event you don't find what you're looking for here, keep cruising Circuit Ave where you'll stumble across several dive bars (one actually named the Dive Bar, another the Ritz), both dirty and nice.

VINEYARD HAVEN

A harbor full of classic wooden sailboats, and streets lined with eye-catching restaurants and shops, lures visitors to this appealing town.

⊨ Sleeping & Eating

HI Martha's Vineyard
HOSTEL $

(☎508-693-2665; http://capecod.hiusa.org; Edgartown-West Tisbury Rd, West Tisbury; dm $32-42; ◎) Reserve early for one of the 72 beds at this popular purpose-built hostel 8 miles from Vineyard Haven. The public bus stops out front and it's right on the bike path.

🍃 Art Cliff Diner
CAFE $$

(☎508-693-1224; 39 Beach Rd; mains $7-15; ⊙7am-2pm Thu-Tue) *The* place for breakfast and lunch. Chef-owner Gina Stanley, a grad of the prestigious Culinary Institute of America, adds flair to everything she touches from the lemon crepes to the fresh-fish tacos. Expect a line – it's worth the wait.

EDGARTOWN

Perched on a fine natural harbor, Edgartown has a rich maritime history and a patrician air. At the height of the whaling era it was home to more than 100 sea captains whose fortunes built the grand old homes that line the streets today.

Stroll along Main St where you'll find several historic buildings, some of which open to visitors during the summer.

◉ Sights

Katama Beach
BEACH

(Katama Rd) One of the Vineyard's best beaches is just 4 miles south of Edgartown center. Also called South Beach, Katama stretches for three magnificent miles. Rough surf is the norm on the ocean side but there are protected salt ponds on the inland side.

⊨ Sleeping & Eating

Edgartown Inn
GUESTHOUSE $$

(☎508-627-4794; www.edgartowninn.com; 56 N Water St; r with shared bath $100-125, with private bath $150-300; ❋) The inn's the best bargain

Known as **Up-Island**, the rural western half of Martha's Vineyard is a patchwork of rolling hills, small farms and open fields frequented by wild turkeys and deer. Feast your eyes and your belly at the picturesque fishing village of **Menemsha**, where you'll find seafood shacks with food so fresh the boats unload their catch at the back door. They'll shuck you an oyster and steam you a lobster while you watch and you can eat al fresco on a harbor-side bench.

The coastal **Aquinnah Cliffs**, also known as the Gay Head Cliffs, are so special they're a National Natural Landmark. These 150ft-high cliffs glow with an amazing array of colors that can be best appreciated in the late-afternoon light. You can hang out at **Aquinnah Beach**, just below the multihued cliffs, or walk a mile north along the shore to an area that's popular with nude sunbathers.

Cedar Tree Neck Sanctuary (www.sheriffsmeadow.org; Indian Hill Rd, West Tisbury; admission free; ⊙8:30am-5:30pm), off State Rd, has an inviting 2.5-mile hike across native bogs and forest to a coastal bluff with views of Cape Cod. The Massachusetts Audubon Society's **Felix Neck Wildlife Sanctuary** (www.massaudubon.org; Edgartown-Vineyard Haven Rd; adult/child $4/3; ⊙dawn-dusk) is a birder's paradise with 4 miles of trails skirting marshes and ponds.

in town with straightforward rooms spread across three adjacent buildings. The oldest dates to 1798 and claims Nathaniel Hawthorne and Daniel Webster among its early guests!

Détente   FRENCH $$$
(☎508-627-8810; www.detentemv.com; 3 Nevin Sq; mains $28-40; ⊙5-10pm) Détente's French-inspired fare includes a rave rendition of ahi tuna tartare served with vanilla-lychee puree. Local organic greens, island-raised chicken and Nantucket bay scallops get plenty of billing on the innovative menu.

Among the Flowers Café   CAFE $$
(17 Mayhew Lane; mains $7-20; ⊙8am-4pm; ☑) Join the townies on the garden patio for crepes, homemade soups and sandwiches. Although everything's served on paper plates, it's still kinda chichi. In July and August it also serves dinner.

❶ Getting There & Around

Boat

Frequent ferries operated by the **Steamship Authority** (☎508-477-8600; www.steam shipauthority.com; round-trip adult/child/car $16/8.50/135) link Woods Hole to both Vineyard Haven and Oak Bluffs, a 45-minute voyage. If you're bringing a car, book well in advance.

From Falmouth Harbor, the passenger-only ferry **Island Queen** (☎508-548-4800; www. islandqueen.com; 75 Falmouth Heights Rd; round-trip adult/child $18/9) sails to Oak Bluffs several times daily in summer.

From Hyannis, **Hy-Line Cruises** (☎508-778-2600; www.hylinecruises.com; Ocean St Dock; round-trip adult/child slow ferry $45/free, fast ferry $71/48) operates a slow ferry (1½ hours) once daily to Oak Bluffs and a high-speed ferry (55 minutes) five times daily.

Bus

Martha's Vineyard Regional Transit Authority (www.vineyardtransit.com; 1-/3-day pass $7/15) operates a bus network with frequent service between towns. It's a practical way to get around and you can even reach out-of-the-way destinations like the Aquinnah Cliffs.

Central Massachusetts

Poking around this central swath of Massachusetts, between big-city Boston and the fashionable Berkshires, provides a taste of the less-touristed stretch of the state. But it's no sleeper, thanks largely to a score of colleges that infuse a youthful spirit to the region.

The **Central Massachusetts Convention & Visitors Bureau** (☎508-755-7400; www.centralmass.org) and the **Greater Springfield Convention & Visitors Bureau** (☎413-787-1548; www.valleyvisitor.com) provide regional visitor information.

WORCESTER

The state's second-largest city had its glory days in the 19th century. The industries that made the town rich went bust but the old barons left a legacy in Worcester's fine museums. The first-rate **Worcester Art Museum**

DON'T MISS

WORCESTER DINERS

Worcester nurtured a great American icon: the diner. Here, in this rustbelt city, you'll find a dozen of them tucked behind warehouses, underneath old train trestles, or steps from dicey bars. Miss Worcester Diner (300 Southbridge St; meals $5-8; ⊙6am-2pm) is a classic of the genre. Built in 1948, it was a showroom diner of Worcester Lunch Car Company, who produced 650 diners at its factory right across the street. Harleys parked on the sidewalk and Red Sox paraphernalia on the walls set the tone. Enticing selections like banana bread French toast compete with the usual greasy spoon menu of chili dogs and biscuits with gravy. It's one tasty slice of Americana.

(☎508-799-4406; www.worcesterart.org; 55 Salisbury St; adult/child $14/free; ⊙11am-5pm Wed-Fr & Sun, 10am-5pm Sat) showcases works by luminary French Impressionists and American masters like Whistler. The amazing Higgins Armory Museum (☎508-853-6015; www.higgins.org; 100 Barber Ave; adult/child $10/7; ⊙10am-4pm Tue-Sat, noon-4pm Sun) is a military buff's heaven. It started as the private collection of a local steel tycoon who built a fanciful art-deco armory to house thousands of military collectibles including Corinthian helmets from ancient Greece and more than 100 full suits of armor.

SPRINGFIELD

Workaday Springfield's top claim to fame is as the birthplace of the all-American game of basketball. The Naismith Basketball Hall of Fame (☎413-781-6500, www.hoophall.com; 1000 W Columbus Ave; adult/child $17/12; ⊙10am-5pm; ☒), south of I-91, celebrates the sport with exhibits and memorabilia from all the big hoop stars.

It's also the hometown of Theodor Seuss Geisel, aka children's author Dr Seuss. You'll find life-size bronze sculpture of the Cat in the Hat and other wonky characters at the Dr Seuss National Memorial Sculpture Garden (cnr State & Chestnut Sts; admission free).

NORTHAMPTON

The region's best dining, hottest nightlife and most interesting street scenes all await in this uber-hip burg known for its liberal politics and outspoken lesbian community. Easy to explore on foot, the eclectic town center is chockablock with cafes, funky shops and art galleries. Greater Northampton Chamber of Commerce (☎413-584-1900; www.explorenorthampton.com; 99 Pleasant St; ⊙9am-5pm Mon-Fri) is information central.

The Smith College (www.smith.edu) campus, covering 127 acres with lovely gardens, is well worth a stroll. Don't miss the Smith College Museum of Art (☎413-585-2760; Elm St at Bedford Tce; adult/child $5/2; ⊙10am-4pm Tue-Sat, noon-4pm Sun), which boasts an impressive collection of 19th- and 20th-century European and North American paintings, including works by John Singleton Copley, Eastman Johnson and Claude Monet.

🛏 Sleeping

Hotel Northampton　　　HISTORIC HOTEL $$
(☎413-584-3100; www.hotelnorthampton.com; 36 King St; r from $180; ☒☒) Northampton's most upscale sleep since 1927, this 100-room hotel in the town center features period decor and well-appointed rooms.

Autumn Inn　　　MOTEL $$
(☎413-584-7660; www.hampshirehospitality.com; 259 Elm St/MA 9; r incl breakfast $99-169; @☒☒) Despite its motel-like layout, this two-story place near Smith College sports an agreeable inn-like ambience and large, comfy rooms.

🍴 Eating

Sylvester's　　　FAMILY DINING $
(www.sylvestersrestaurant.com; 111 Pleasant St; mains $5-10; ⊙7am-3pm) Follow the locals to this unassuming eatery for the best breakfast in town. Forget mixes – everything is from scratch, real maple syrup tops the pancakes, the home fries are loaded with sautéed onions and the omelets are however you like them.

Paul & Elizabeth's　　　CAFE $$
(www.paulandelizabeths.com; 150 Main St; mains $8-16; ⊙11:30am-9:15pm; ☒) Fresh, local and organic ingredients highlight the menu at this stellar natural food cafe serving innovative vegetarian fare and Japanese-style fish dishes.

Green Bean　　　CAFE $
(241 Main St; mains $6-8; ⊙7am-3pm) Pioneer Valley farmers stock the kitchen at this cute eatery that dishes up organic eggs at breakfast and juicy hormone-free beef burgers at lunch.

Northampton Brewery   BREWPUB
(www.northamptonbrewery.com; 11 Brewster Ct)
On a sunny day you'll find half of Northampton chugging ales on the rooftop beer garden at New England's oldest microbrewery.

Calvin Theatre   CONCERT VENUE
(☎413-584-0610; www.iheg.com; 19 King St) The venue for big-name performances for everything from hot rock and indie bands to comedy shows.

Diva's   CLUB
(www.divasofnoho.com; 492 Pleasant St) The city's main gay-centric dance club keeps patrons sweaty with a steady diet of thumping house music.

Iron Horse Music Hall   CONCERT VENUE
(☎413-584-0610; www.iheg.com; 20 Center St) Nationally acclaimed folk and jazz artists line up to play in this intimate setting.

Haymarket Café   CAFE
(www.haymarketcafe.com; 185 Main St; ☎) Northampton's coolest hangout for bohemians and caffeine addicts.

AMHERST

This college town, a short drive from Northampton, is built around the mega **University of Massachusetts** (www.umass.edu) and two small colleges, the liberal **Hampshire College** (www.hampshire.edu) and the prestigious **Amherst College** (www.amherst.edu). Contact them for campus tours and event information; there's always something happening. If hunger strikes, you'll find the usual bevy of college-town eateries radiating out from Main St in the town center.

The lifelong home of poet Emily Dickinson (1830–86), the 'belle of Amherst', is open to the public as the **Emily Dickinson Museum** (☎413-542-8161; www.emilydickinson museum.org; 280 Main St; adult/child $8/4; ☎11am-4pm Wed-Sun). Admission includes a 40-minute tour.

The Berkshires

Tranquil towns and a wealth of cultural attractions are nestled in these cool green hills. For more than a century the Berkshires have been a favored retreat for wealthy Bostonians and New Yorkers. And we're not just talking Rockefellers – the entire Boston symphony summers here as well. The **Berkshire Visitors Bureau** (☎413-743-4500; www.berk shires.org; 3 Hoosac St, Adams; ☎10am-5pm) can provide information on the entire region.

GREAT BARRINGTON

Hands-down the best place in the Berkshires to be at mealtime. Head straight to the intersection of Main (US 7) and Railroad Sts in the town center where you'll find an artful mix of galleries and eateries serving mouth-watering food – everything from bakeries to ethnic cuisines.

For wholesome Berkshire-grown meals on a budget, go to **Eastern Mountain Cafe** (www.berkshire.coop; 42 Bridge St; meals $6-10; ☎8am-7pm Mon-Sat, 10am-5pm Sun; ☎) inside the Berkshire Co-op Market. Families will love **Baba Louie's** (www.babalouiespizza.com; 286 Main St; pizzas $12-18; ☎11:30am-9:30pm; ☎) for its organic wood-fired pizzas and $6 kids specials. For fine dining, **Allium** (☎413-528-2118; www.alliumberkshires.com; 42 Railroad St; mains $15-28; ☎5-9:30pm) offers innovative New American cuisine in a stylish setting.

STOCKBRIDGE

This timeless New England town, sans even a single traffic light, looks like something straight out of a Norman Rockwell drawing. Oh wait…it is! Rockwell (1894–1978), the most popular illustrator in US history, lived on Main St and used the town and its residents as subjects. At the evocative **Norman Rockwell Museum** (☎413-298-4100; www. nrm.org; 9 Glendale Rd/MA 183; adult/child $15/5; ☎10am-5pm), Rockwell's slice-of-Americana paintings come to life when examined up close.

LENOX

The cultural heart of the Berkshires, the refined village of Lenox hosts one of the country's premier music series, the open-air **Tanglewood Music Festival** (☎413-637-5165; www.tanglewood.org; ☎late Jun-early Sep), featuring the Boston Symphony Orchestra and guest artists like James Taylor and Yo-Yo Ma. Buy a lawn ticket, spread a blanket, uncork a bottle of wine and enjoy the quintessential Berkshires experience.

Shakespeare&Company (☎413-637-1199; www.shakespeare.org; 70 Kemble St) performs the Bard's work throughout the summer. The renowned **Jacob's Pillow Dance Festival** (☎413-243-9919; www.jacobspillow.org; 385 George Carter Rd; ☎Jun-Aug), 10 miles east of Lenox in Becket, stages contemporary dance performances.

The **Mount** (☑413-551-5111; www.edithwhar ton.org; 2 Plunkett St, at US 7; adult/child $16/free; ⏱10am-5pm May-Oct), novelist Edith Wharton's former estate, offers hour-long tours of her mansion and inspirational gardens.

Charming period inns abound in Lenox. The senior of them, **Birchwood Inn** (☑413-637-2600; www.birchwood-inn.com; 7 Hubbard St; r incl breakfast $175-335; ☎), registered its first guest in 1767 and continues to offer warm hospitality today.

Spread across three historic houses, **Cornell in Lenox** (☑413-637-4800; www.cor nellbandb.com; 203 Main St; r incl breakfast $150-200; @☎) offers good value in a high-priced town.

You'll find stylish bistros along Church St in the town center, including **Bistro Zinc** (☑413-637-8800; www.bistrozinc.com; 56 Church St; mains $15-30; ⏱11:30am-3pm & 5:30-10pm) with hot postmodern decor and French-inspired New American fare. For family fare at honest prices visit **Olde Heritage Tavern** (12 Housatonic St; mains $6-15; ⏱8am-10pm), an upbeat pub whose menu ranges from waffles to steaks.

PITTSFIELD

Just west of the town of Pittsfield is Hancock Shaker Village (☑413-443-0188; www.hancock shakervillage.org; US 20; adult/child $17/4; ⏱10am-5pm May-Oct), a fascinating museum illustrating the lives of the Shakers, the religious sect that founded the village in 1783. The Shakers believed in communal ownership, the sanctity of work and celibacy, the latter of which proved to be their demise. Their handiwork – graceful in its simplicity – includes wooden furnishings and 20 buildings, the most famous of which is the round stone barn.

WILLIAMSTOWN & NORTH ADAMS

Cradled by the Berkshire's rolling hills, Williamstown is a picture-perfect New England college town revolving around the leafy campus of Williams College. Williamstown and neighboring North Adams boast three outstanding art museums, each a worthy destination in itself.

◉ Sights & Activities

TOP CHOICE Clark Art Institute MUSEUM
(☑413-458-2303; www.clarkart.edu; 225 South St, Williamstown; adult/child Jun-Oct $15/free, Nov-May free to all; ⏱10am-5pm, closed Mon Sep-Jun) Focuses on 19th-century paintings with oodles of Renoirs and other French impressionists as well as a solid collection of American paintings by Winslow Homer, John Singer Sargent and others.

FREE Williams College Museum of Art MUSEUM
(☑413-597-2429; www.wcma.org; 15 Lawrence Hall Dr, Williamstown; ⏱10am-5pm Tue-Sat, 1-5pm Sun) Showcases works by American luminaries such as Mary Cassett, Edward Hopper and Georgia O'Keeffe.

Mass MoCA MUSEUM
(☑413-662-2111; www.massmoca.org; 87 Marshall St, North Adams; adult/child $15/5; ⏱10am-6pm Jul & Aug, 11am-5pm Wed-Mon Sep-Jun; ☎) This contemporary art museum sprawls across an amazing 222,000 sq ft, making it the USA's largest. Bring your walking shoes! In addition to description-defying installation pieces, MoCA is a venue for cutting-edge theater and dance.

🖊Mt Greylock State Reservation PARK
(☑413-499-4262; www.mass.gov/dcr/parks/mt Greylock; 30 Rockwell Rd, Lanesborough) Just south of North Adams, this park has trails up to Massachusetts' highest peak (3491ft), where there's a panoramic view of several ranges and, on a clear day, five different states. The park offers camping, backpack shelters and a rustic lodge; see its website for details.

🎎 Festivals & Events

Williamstown Theatre Festival THEATER
(☑413-597-3400; www.wtfestival.org; 1000 Main St, Williamstown) This first-rate festival stages contemporary and classic plays in July and August, often with notable casts.

🛌 Sleeping & Eating

River Bend Farm B&B $$
(☑413-458-3121; www.windsorsofstonington.com/ RBF; 643 US 7; r incl breakfast with shared bath $120) Step back to the 18th century in this Georgian Colonial B&B furnished with real-deal antiques and boasting five fireplaces.

Porches B&B $$
(☑413-664-0400; www.porches.com; 231 River St; r incl breakfast $180-250; ❇☎🖥) Across the street from MASS MoCA, the artsy rooms here combine well-considered color palettes, ample lighting and French doors.

TOP CHOICE Mezze Bistro + Bar FUSION $$$
(☑413-458-0123; www.mezzerestaurant.com; 777 US 7; mains $18-27; ⏱5-10pm) East meets West

at this chic restaurant where chef Joji Sumi masterfully blends contemporary American cuisine with classic French and Japanese influences. The seasonal farm-to-table menu, utilizes organic meats, cheeses and produce.

Tunnel City Coffee CAFE $
(www.tunnelcitycoffee.com; 100 Spring St; snacks $2-6; ☺6am-6pm; 🐀) Come to this student haunt near Williams College campus for potent espressos, light eats and sugar-laced desserts.

RHODE ISLAND

America's smallest state packs a lot into a compact package, more than making up for its lack of land with 400 miles of craggy coastline, deeply indented bays and lovely beaches. The state's engaging capital, Providence, is small enough to be friendly but big enough to offer top-notch dining and attractions. Newport, a summer haunt of the well-heeled, brims with opulent mansions, pretty yachts and world-class music festivals. Should you want to take it further afield, hopping on a ferry to Block Island makes a perfect day-trip.

RHODE ISLAND FACTS

» **Nicknames** Ocean State, Little Rhody

» **Population** 1,053,000

» **Area** 1045 sq miles

» **Capital city** Providence (population 178,000)

» **Other city** Newport (population 24,700)

» **Sales tax** 7%

» **Birthplace of** Broadway composer George M Cohan (1878–1942) and toy icon Mr Potato Head (b 1952)

» **Home of** the first US tennis championships

» **Politics** majority vote Democrat

» **Famous for** being the smallest state

» **Official state bird** A chicken? Why not? The Rhode Island Red revolutionized the poultry industry

» **Driving distances** Providence to Newport 37 miles, Providence to Boston 50 miles

---

History

The name Roger Williams (1603–83) gave to the community he founded in 1636 – nothing less than Providence! – spoke to the optimism his followers shared. A religious outcast from Puritanical Boston, Williams established the colony on the principle that all people were entitled to freedom of conscience. He was an early advocate of separation of religion and government, a concept that later became a foundation of the US Constitution. Progressive little Rhode Island became the first American colony to abolish slavery (1774) and the first to declare independence from Britain in 1776.

❶ Information

Providence Journal (www.projo.com) The state's largest daily newspaper.

Rhode Island Parks (www.riparks.com) Offers camping in five state parks.

Rhode Island Tourism Division (☑800-250-7384; www.visitrhodeisland.com) Distributes visitor information on the whole state.

Providence

The revitalization of Providence has turned this once-dreary capital into one of the finest small cities in the Northeast. Not only has it been infused with an artsy edge, but it's the only city in the USA to have its entire downtown on the National Register of Historic Places. From the period buildings in the city center to the cafe-laden streets embracing Brown University, everything about this town invites a closer look.

◉ Sights & Activities

Exit 22 off I-95 deposits you downtown. The university area is a short walk to the east. The colorful Italian enclave of Federal Hill centers on Atwells Ave, a mile west of the city center.

Museum of Art MUSEUM
(☑401-454-6500; www.risdmuseum.org; 224 Benefit St; adult/child $10/3; ☺10am-5pm Tue-Sun) Wonderfully eclectic, the Rhode Island School of Design's art museum showcases everything from ancient Greek art to 20th-century American paintings and decorative arts. Pop in before 1pm Sunday and admission is free.

FREE **State House** HISTORIC BUILDING
(☑401-222-3983; 82 Smith St; ☺8:30am-4:30pm Mon-Fri, free tours 9am, 10am & 11am) Providence's

WHAT THE...?

Move over, Christo. Providence has blazed onto the public art installation scene with WaterFire (www.waterfire. org), set on the river that meanders through the city center. Nearly 100 braziers poke above the water, each supporting a bonfire that roars after dark. Flames dance off the water, music plays, black-clad gondoliers glide by, and party-goers pack the riverbanks. A captivating blend of art and entertainment, WaterFire takes place about a dozen times between May and September, mostly on Saturday, from sunset to 1am.

focal point is crowned with one of the world's largest self-supporting marble domes. Check out the Gilbert Stuart portrait of George Washington, then compare it to the $1 bill in your wallet.

FREE **Roger Williams Park** PARK
(1000 Elmwood Ave; ⊕) With so many Victorian-era touches, such as its classic carousel, it's been cited by the National Trust for Historic Preservation as one of America's top urban parks. Among its varied sights are flowery botanical gardens and a zoo (☎401-785-3510; www.rogerwilliamsparkzoo.org; adult/child $12/8; ⊗9am-4pm; ⊕) with snow leopards and elephants. From downtown, take I-95 south to exit 17.

Culinary Archives & Museum MUSEUM
(☎401-598-2805; www.culinary.org; 315 Harborside Blvd; adult/child $7/2; ⊗10am-5pm Tue-Sun) This offbeat museum contains half-a-million items devoted to the history of dining – everything from ancient cookbooks to early-20th-century dining cars. It's at Johnson & Wales University; take I-95 exit 18, turn right on Allens Ave and follow the signs.

Brown University COLLEGE CAMPUS
(www.brown.edu; 71 George St) On the hillside above the Rhode Island School of Design lies the eminently strollable Brown University campus awash in Ivy League charm.

🛏 Sleeping

TOP
CHOICE **Providence Biltmore** HISTORIC HOTEL $$
(☎401-421-0700; www.providencebiltmore.com; 11 Dorrance St; r/ste from $159/199; ❄ 🞰) Entering the chandeliered lobby of this historic

downtown hotel is like stepping back into the 1920s. The classic appeal continues in the rooms fitted with damask upholstered chairs, gilt mirrors and king beds.

Edgewood Manor INN $$
(☎401-781-0099; www.providence-lodging.com; 232 Norwood Ave; r incl breakfast $139-299; 🞰) If you're in the mood for pampering, book a room in this elegant Greek Revival B&B bordering Roger Williams Park. The lavish lobby drips with museum-quality antiques, while the rooms boast four-poster mahogany beds and marble baths.

Christopher Dodge House B&B $$
(☎401-351-6111; www.providence-hotel.com; 11 W Park St; r incl breakfast $149-190; @) Cozy quilts and gas fireplaces add a warm glow at this inviting B&B overlooking the State House. If it's full, ask about its sister inn, the Mowry-Nicholson House, just a block away.

🍴 Eating

Providence abounds with superb eateries. For the 'Little Italy' immersion, stroll the trattorias lining Atwells Ave on Federal Hill. For the cafe scene head to Thayer St, on the hill above Brown University.

TOP
CHOICE **Costantino's Venda Ravioli** DELI $
(www.vendaravioli.com; 265 Atwells Ave; meals $6-14; ⊗8:30am-6pm Mon-Sat, 8:30am-5pm Sun) Grab one of the small tables lining this bustling deli for the most amazing dining experience on Federal Hill. Hanging salamis, crispy breads, every imaginable antipasto, real gelato – you'll think you're in Italy.

Meeting Street Café CAFE $$
(www.meetingstreetcafe.com; 220 Meeting St; mains $8-15; ⊗8am-11pm) For thick sandwiches and luscious desserts head to this perky cafe near Brown University. The meats are hormone-free, the veggies fresh and the servings so big that most everything feeds two.

Cassarino's ITALIAN $$
(☎401-751-3333; www.cassarinosri.com; 177 Atwells Ave; mains $15-20; ⊗11:30am-10pm Mon-Fri, noon-11pm Sat) Good Italian fare at moderate prices in a Federal Hill setting that would make Tony Soprano feel at home. Excellent $10 lunch deals before 3pm Monday to Friday.

Caserta Pizzeria PIZZERIA $$
(☎401-621-3618; www.casertapizzeria.com; 121 Spruce St; pizza $7-19; ⊗9:30am-10:30pm)

Spartan eatery on the back side of Federal Hill serving the best Sicilian pizza in all Rhode Island. The secret: a sauce so spicy it'll make your mouth sing.

East Side Pockets   MEDITERRANEAN $
(www.eastsidepocket.com; 278 Thayer St; mains $4-7; ☻10am-1am Mon-Sat, 10am-10pm Sun; ☝) Fabulous falafels and baklava at student-friendly prices.

🍷 Drinking & Entertainment

Providence Performing Arts Center   PERFORMING ARTS
(☎401-421-2787; www.ppacri.org; 220 Weybosset St) Concerts, comedy and Broadway musicals take the stage at this beautifully restored 1928 art-deco theater.

Lupo's Heartbreak Hotel   MUSIC
(☎401-331-5876; www.lupos.com; 79 Washington St) Providence's legendary music venue features top rock bands and indie acts.

Trinity Brewhouse   MICROBREWERY
(☎401-453-2337; www.trinitybrewhouse.com; 186 Fountain St; ☻11:30am-1am Sun-Thu, noon-2am Fri & Sat) This microbrewery in the entertainment district brews terrific British-style beers. Don't miss the stouts.

AS220   CLUB
(☎401-831-9327; www.as220.org; 115 Empire St; ☻5pm-1am) An alternative space abuzz with experimental bands, offbeat films, poetry slams – you never know what you'll find here.

🛍 Shopping

Boutiques and funky collegian shops can be found along Thayer St near Brown University. For urban shopping, **Providence Place** (www.providenceplace.com; 1 Providence Place) in the city center is Rhode Island's largest mall.

ℹ Information

Post office (www.usps.com; 2 Exchange Tce)
Providence Visitor Information Center (☎401-751-1177; www.goprovidence.com; Rhode Island Convention Center, 1 Sabin St; ☻9am-5pm Mon-Sat)

ℹ Getting There & Away

TF Green Airport (PVD; www.pvdairport.com; I-95, exit 13, Warwick), 20 minutes south of downtown Providence, is served by major US airlines and car-rental companies.

  Peter Pan Bus Lines (www.peterpanbus.com) connects Providence with Boston ($8, 1¼ hours) and New York ($37, 3½ hours). **Amtrak** (www.

amtrak.com) trains also link cities in the Northeast with Providence.

  The **Rhode Island Public Transit Authority** (RIPTA; www.ripta.com; one way $2, day pass $6) runs old-fashioned, trolley-style buses throughout the city from its downtown Kennedy Plaza hub; other RIPTA buses link Providence with Newport.

Newport

The town's very name conjures up images of Great Gatsby mansions and unbridled wealth. In the 1890s Newport became *the* place for rich New Yorkers to summer. They built opulent seaside mansions, each successive one attempting to outdo the neighbors. These mansions – dubbed 'summer cottages' – are so dazzling that people still flock to Newport today just to ogle them. Newport is also famous for its legendary music festivals and its active yachting scene.

◉ Sights & Activities

Preservation Society of Newport County   MANSIONS
(☎401-847-1000; www.newportmansions.org; 424 Bellevue Ave; all 5 sites adult/child $31/10, Breakers alone $16.50/4, Breakers plus 1 other mansion $24/6) Five of Newport's grandest mansions are managed by this society. Each mansion takes about 90 minutes to tour. From April to mid-October, the Breakers is open from 9am to 5pm and the other mansions from 10am to 5pm. Off-season hours vary – call ahead.

Breakers
(44 Ochre Point Ave) If you have time for only one Newport mansion, make it this extravagant 70-room, 1895 Italian Renaissance mega-palace built for Cornelius Vanderbilt II, patriarch of America's then-richest family.

Rosecliff
(548 Bellevue Ave) A 1902 masterpiece of architect Stanford White, Rosecliff resembles the Grand Trianon at Versailles. Its immense ballroom had a starring role in Robert Redford's *The Great Gatsby*.

Marble House
(596 Bellevue Ave) The Palace of Versailles also inspired this 1892 mansion, posh with Louis XIV–style furnishings.

Elms
(367 Bellevue Ave) Built in 1901, the Elms is nearly identical to the Château d'Asnières near Paris.

NEW ENGLAND RHODE ISLAND

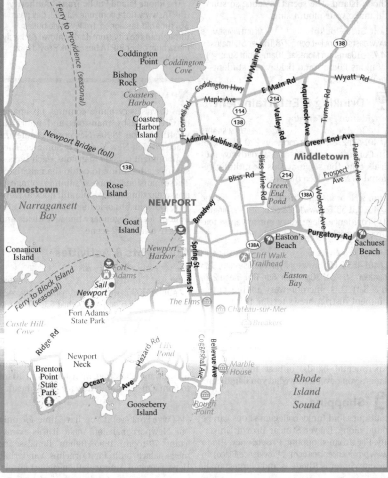

Chateau-sur-Mer

(474 Bellevue Ave) This Victorian mansion, built in 1852, was the first of Newport's palatial 'summer cottages.'

Rough Point   MANSION

(www.newportrestoration.com; 680 Bellevue Ave; admission $25; ⊙9:45am-5pm Tue-Sat) Once called the 'richest little girl in the world,' Doris Duke (1912–1993) was just 13 years old when she inherited this English manor estate from her father. Duke had a passion for travel and art collecting; Rough Point houses many of her holdings, from Ming dynasty ceramics to Renoir paintings. The grounds are equally impressive.

FREE **Cliff Walk**   WALKING

For a glorious hike take the 3.5-mile Cliff Walk, which hugs the coast along the back side of the mansions. You will not only enjoy the same dramatic ocean views that were once reserved for the filthy rich, but you will get to gawk at their mansions along the way. The Cliff Walk stretches from Memorial Blvd to Bailey's Beach; a scenic place to start is at Ruggles Ave near the Breakers.

International Tennis Hall of Fame
MUSEUM

(☑401-849-3990; www.tennisfame.com; 194 Bellevue Ave; adult/child $11/free; ⊘9:30am-5pm) The world's largest tennis museum is housed in the club where America's first tennis championships took place in 1881. For $90 you can jump into your whites and play a game on those classic grass courts.

FREE Fort Adams State Park
PARK

(www.riparks.com; Harrison Ave; ⊘sunrise-sunset) Site of the largest coastal fortification (c 1824) in the USA, Fort Adams borders Newport Harbor with expansive lawns ideal for picnicking. Swimming is OK at Fort Adams, but **Easton's Beach** (Memorial Blvd), also known as 'First Beach,' and **Sachuest (Second) Beach** (Purgatory Rd) are better.

Touro Synagogue National Historic Site
SYNAGOGUE

(☑401-847-4794; www.tourosynagogue.org; 85 Touro St; adult/child $5/free; ⊘noon-2pm Sun-Fri) Tour the oldest synagogue (c 1763) in the USA, an architectural gem that treads the line between austere and lavish.

Sail Newport
SAILING

(☑401-846-1983; www.sailnewport.org; 60 Fort Adams Rd; sailboat rental per 3hr $64-121; ⊘9am-7pm) As you'd expect in the hometown of the prestigious America's Cup, the sailing in breezy Newport is phenomenal.

Adirondack II
CRUISE

(☑401-847-0000; www.sail-newport.com; 1½hr cruise $27-35; ⊘11am-7pm) This schooner sails from Bowen's Wharf five times a day.

⚑ Festivals & Events

Newport's summer music events draw large crowds, so plan ahead.

TOP CHOICE Newport Folk Festival
MUSIC

(www.newportfolkfest.com; Fort Adams State Park; admission $69-77) Everybody who's anybody in the folk world has taken the stage at this hallmark festival, held the last weekend in July.

Newport Jazz Festival
MUSIC

(www.newportjazzfest.net; Fort Adams State Park; admission $40-100) The roster reads like a who's who of jazz, with the likes of Dave Brubeck and Wynton Marsalis, on a weekend in early August.

Newport Music Festival
MUSIC

(www.newportmusic.org; admission $20-40) A class act, with 17 days of chamber music held at various mansions in July.

🛏 Sleeping

Stella Maris Inn
INN $$

(☑401-849-2862; www.stellamarisinn.com; 91 Washington St; r incl breakfast $125-195; 🛜) Grab a rocking chair on the porch and watch the sailboats breeze by at this comfortably old-fashioned inn occupying a former convent. High ceilings and heaps of dark wood set the mood. In a quiet neighborhood and just a stroll to the city center.

Ivy Lodge
INN $$$

(☑401-849-6865; www.ivylodge.com; 12 Clay St; r incl breakfast $169-379; ❄🛜) Treat yourself to the good life at this grand Victorian inn mere steps from Newport's sumptuous mansions. All rooms have antique furnishings, most have fireplaces, and if you need more romance, some have Jacuzzis.

Admiral Fitzroy Inn
INN $$

(☑401-848-8000; www.admiralfitzroy.com; 398 Thames St; r $145-300; ❄🛜) Named for the admiral who sailed with Darwin, the atmosphere is fittingly nautical. The inn fronts bustling Thames St near the harbor. While noise from emptying bars can be disruptive, the rooftop terrace makes up for it with sweeping water views.

Newport International Hostel
HOSTEL $

(☑401-369-0243; www.newporthostel.com; 16 Howard St; dm with shared bath incl breakfast $35-89; @) This central hostel in a period home has just a handful of beds, so book ahead. The friendly manager has tips aplenty for having a great time in Newport without breaking the bank.

🍴 Eating

TOP CHOICE Mooring
SEAFOOD $$

(☑401-846-2260; www.mooringrestaurant.com; Sayer's Wharf; mains $10-36; ⊘11:30am-10pm) A harborfront setting and a menu brimming with fresh seafood make this an unbeatable combination for seaside dining. Tip: if it's packed, take the side entrance to the bar, grab a stool and order the meaty clam chowder and a 'bag of doughnuts' (tangy lobster fritters).

Salvation Café
CAFE $$

(☑401-847-2620; www.salvationcafe.com; 140 Broadway; mains $14-25; ⊘5-10pm) A funky, eclectic decor and brilliant food are in store at this bohemian cafe. The multiethnic menu ranges far and wide, from pad Thai to Moroccan spiced lamb, but seldom misses the mark.

Mamma Luisa ITALIAN $$

(401-848-5257; www.mammaluisa.com; 673 Thames St; mains $14-25; 5-10pm Thu-Tue) Escape the Newport crowds at this cozy restaurant serving classic pasta dishes (cheese ravioli with fava beans, spaghetti *alle vongole*), as well as meat and fish entrees. Upstairs feels like eating at grandma's house.

Gary's Handy Lunch DINER $

(462 Thames St; mains $4-8; 5am-3pm, to 8pm Fri) Newport's working folk kick-start their day over coffee and simple breakfast fare at this old-school diner.

Wharf Pub PUB $$

(401-846-9233; Bowen's Wharf; mains $10-18; 11:30am-11pm) Reasonable prices, good portions and fast service. Think sandwiches, fried calamari and burgers. Wash it down with a Newport Storm ale.

Drinking & Entertainment

Newport Blues Café CLUB

(401-841-5510; www.newportblues.com; 286 Thames St) Intimate atmosphere and one of the best blues and R&B scenes this side of New York City.

Fastnet BAR

(www.thefastnetpub.com; 1 Broadway) This friendly pub serves a fine selection of Irish beers on tap, decent pub grub and live-feed rugby.

Information

Citizens Bank (401-847-4411; 8 Washington Sq)

Newport Gateway Transportation & Visitors Center (800-976-5122; www.gonewport. com; 23 America's Cup Ave; 9am-5pm) Newport's tourist office distributes a handy guide and tracks accommodation vacancies.

Post office (www.usps.com; 320 Thames St)

Getting There & Away

Peter Pan Bus Lines (www.peterpanbus. com) has several buses daily to Boston ($27, 1¾ hours). State-run **RIPTA** (www.ripta.com) operates frequent buses (one way $2, day pass $6) from the visitor bureau to the mansions, beaches and Providence.

Scooter World (401-619-1349; Christie's Landing; per day $30; 9am-7pm) rents bicycles.

Rhode Island Beaches

If you're up for a day at the beach, Rhode Island's southwestern coastal towns fit the bill. It is the Ocean State, after all.

The mile-long **Narragansett Town Beach** in Narragansett is the place to go for surfing. The nearby **Scarborough State Beach** is among Rhode Island's finest, with a wide beach, a glorious pavilion and inviting boardwalks. **Watch Hill** at the state's

---

IF YOU HAVE A FEW MORE DAYS

Unspoiled **Block Island**, separated from the rest of Rhode Island by 12 miles of open ocean, offers simple pleasures: rolling farms, uncrowded beaches and miles of quiet hiking and cycling trails.

Ferries dock at Old Harbor, the main town, which has changed little since its gingerbread houses were built in the late 19th century. The beaches begin right at the north side of town. If you continue north 2 miles you'll come to the **Clay Head Nature Trail**, which follows high clay bluffs above the beach offering good bird-watching along the way. **Rodman Hollow**, a 100-acre wildlife refuge at the island's south end, is also laced with interesting trails.

A mere 7 miles long, Block Island begs to be explored by bicycle; several places near the ferry dock rent them for $25 a day. The **Block Island Chamber of Commerce** (800-383-2474; www.blockislandchamber.com), at the ferry dock, can help with accommodations, but be aware the island's four-dozen inns typically book out in summer and many require minimum stays.

The **Block Island Ferry** (866-783-7996; www.blockislandferry.com; adult round-trip slow/high-speed $26/36) operates high-speed (30 minutes) and slow-speed (55 minutes) ferries from Galilee State Pier in Point Judith, each four to eight times a day, as well as once-daily slow ferries (two hours, July and August) from Fort Adams State Park in Newport. Children pay half price; bring a bicycle along for $6 round-trip. Schedules are convenient for day-trippers, thanks to morning departures and late-afternoon returns.

southwestern tip is a wonderful place to turn back the clock, with its Flying Horse Carousel and Victorian setting. The **South County Tourism Council** (☎800-548-4662; www.southcountyri.com) has details on the entire area.

CONNECTICUT

Sandwiched between sexy New York City and northerly New England's quainter quarters, Connecticut typically gets short shrift by travelers. Sure the brawny I-95 coastal corridor is largely industrial, but take a closer look and you're in for pleasant surprises. Seaside Mystic, with its nautical attractions, and the time-honored towns bordering the Connecticut River are a whole other world, and the Litchfield Hills, in the state's northwestern corner, are as charmingly rural as any place in New England.

Incidentally, the Connecticut River, which slices clear across Connecticut, gives the state its name. The word comes from the Mohegan mouthful *quinnehtukqut,* which means 'place of the long river.'

History
In 1633 the Dutch built a small settlement at current-day Hartford, but it was the English, arriving en masse in the following years, that shaped Connecticut.

Thanks to the industriousness of the citizenry, the Connecticut Yankee peddler became a fixture in early American society, traveling by wagon from town to town selling clocks and other manufactured gadgets. Connecticut etched a leading role in the Industrial Revolution when Eli Whitney built a New Haven factory in 1798 to produce firearms with interchangeable parts – the beginning of modern mass production.

In 1810 America's first insurance company opened in Hartford and by the 1870s the city boasted the highest per capita income in the USA. Two of America's leading literary figures, Harriet Beecher Stowe (1811–96) and Mark Twain (1835–1910), were Hartford neighbors for 17 years.

❶ Information
There are welcome centers at the Hartford airport and on I-95 and I-84 when entering the state by car.
Connecticut Tourism Division (www.ctvisit. com) Distributes visitor information for the entire state.

» **Nicknames** Constitution State, Nutmeg State

» **Population** 3.6 million

» **Area** 4845 sq miles

» **Capital city** Hartford (population 124,775)

» **Sales tax** 6%

» **Birthplace of** abolitionist John Brown (1800–59), circus man PT Barnum (1810–91), actress Katharine Hepburn (1909–2003)

» **Home of** the first written constitution in the US; the first lollipop, Frisbee and helicopter

» **Politics** Democrat-leaning state

» **Famous for** starting the US insurance biz and building the first nuclear submarine

» **Quirkiest state song lyrics** *Yankee Doodle,* which entwines patriotism with doodles, feathers and macaroni

» **Driving distances** Hartford to New Haven 40 miles, Hartford to Providence 75 miles

Hartford Courant (www.courant.com) The state's largest newspaper with online entertainment listings.

Connecticut Coast

The Connecticut coast is not all of a piece. The western end is largely a bedroom community connected by commuter rail to New York City. By the time you get to New Haven, Connecticut's artsier side shines through. Maritime Mystic, at the eastern end of the state, spotlights tall ships and the siren call of the sea.

NEW HAVEN
For visitors New Haven is all about Yale. Head straight to New Haven Green, graced by old Colonial churches and Yale's hallowed ivy-covered walls. The city's top museums and best restaurants are all within a few blocks of the Green. The oldest planned city in America (1638), New Haven (population 129,800) is laid out in orderly blocks spreading out from the Green, making it a cinch to get around. **INFO New Haven** (☎20 3-773-9494; www.infonewhaven.com; 1000 Chapel

St; ⊙10am-9pm Mon-Sat, noon-5pm Sun) is the city's helpful tourist office.

◉ Sights & Activities

Yale University COLLEGE CAMPUS
Not only is it the prestigious alma mater of five US presidents but it's one cool campus thick with Gothic buildings. Most impressive of the spires is **Harkness Tower**, from which a carillon peals at measured moments throughout the day. For campus tours or to pick up a campus map, drop by Yale's **visitor center** (☑203-432-2300; www. yale.edu/visitor; 149 Elm St; ⊙9am-4:30pm Mon-Fri, 11am-4pm Sat & Sun) on the north side of the Green. There are free one-hour tours at 10:30am and 2pm weekdays, and at 1:30pm on weekends.

FREE **Yale University Art Gallery** MUSEUM
(☑203-432-0600; artgallery.yale.edu; 1111 Chapel St; ⊙10am-5pm Tue-Sat, 1-6pm Sun) America's oldest university art museum boasts American masterworks by Winslow Homer, Edward Hopper and Jackson Pollock, as well as a superb European collection that includes Vincent van Gogh's *The Night Café*.

Peabody Museum of Natural History MUSEUM
(☑203-432-5050; www.yale.edu/peabody; 170 Whitney Ave; adult/child $9/5; ⊙10am-5pm Mon-Sat, noon-5pm Sun; ♠) Wannabe paleontologists will be thrilled by the dinosaurs here.

FREE **Yale Center for British Art** MUSEUM
(☑203-432-2800; ycba.yale.edu; 1080 Chapel St; ⊙10am-5pm Tue-Sat, noon-5pm Sun) The most comprehensive British art collection outside the UK.

⌂ Sleeping

Study at Yale HOTEL $$$
(☑203-503-3900; www.studyhotels.com; 1157 Chapel St; r from $219; ❄❂) Ready for an Ivy League splurge? This sleek boutique hotel right in the midst of the campus offers 124 ultra-mod rooms with featherbeds, soft leather chairs, flat-screen TVs and iPod docking stations.

Touch of Ireland Guest House B&B $$
(☑203-787-7997; www.touchofirelandguesthouse. com; 670 Whitney Ave; r incl breakfast $135-150; ❄❂) Share tips with fellow travelers in the fireplaced den at this friendly B&B on the north side of the city. The four guest rooms sport an Irish theme and comfy down-home decor.

✕ Eating

TOP CHOICE **Frank Pepe's** PIZZERIA $$
(☑203-865-5762; www.pepespizzeria.com; 157 Wooster St; pizza $7-20; ⊙11:30am-10pm) New Haven's most famous eatery takes its name from the Italian immigrant who tossed America's first pizza a century ago. You'd best believe they've got the recipe down pat. For the ultimate, order Pepe's signature white pizza topped with garlicky fresh clams.

Miya's Sushi JAPANESE $$
(☑203-777-9760; www.miyassushi.com; 68 Howe St; meals $18-40; ⊙Tue-Sat 12:30-11pm; ✎) Tokyo meets Yale at this fun restaurant serving superb sushi, an amazing sake selection and tasty vegetarian offerings. Miya's menu focuses on sustainable species, earning it a top award from the Monterey Bay Aquarium. The menu is broad and inventive – start with the pumpkin miso soup.

Louis' Lunch BURGERS $
(www.louislunch.com; 261 Crown St; hamburgers $5.25; ⊙11am-3:45pm Tue & Wed, noon-2am Thu-Sat) New Haven's classic hamburger joint invented America's iconic fast food in 1900 and it still broils burgers in the original cast-iron vertical grills. Some things have changed over the century – but you won't find them here. Don't even think of asking for ketchup.

Sally's Apizza PIZZERIA $$
(☑203-624-5271; www.sallysapizza.com; 237 Wooster St; pizza $7-16; ⊙5-10:30pm Tue-Sun) If Pepe's is packed, as it often is, try this place nearby, a breakaway started by a relative of Pepe's in 1938. Like Pepe's, Sally's also specializes in terrific wood-fired thin-crust pizza.

✕ Entertainment

New Haven has a first-rate theater scene. The free weekly *New Haven Advocate* (www.newhavenadvocate.com) lists current entertainment happenings.

Toad's Place MUSIC
(☑203-624-8623; www.toadsplace.com; 300 York St) The hottest music scene this side of New York City. Everyone from Count Basie to Bob Dylan and U2 have taken the stage at this legendary venue.

Shubert Theater THEATER
(☑203-562-5666; www.shubert.com; 247 College St) Catch a hit before it happens at the vener-

able Shubert, which has been hosting Broadway musicals on their trial runs since 1914.

Yale Repertory Theatre — THEATER

(☑203-432-1234; www.yale.edu/yalerep; 1120 Chapel St)

Long Wharf Theatre — THEATER

(☑203-787-4282; www.longwharf.org; 222 Sargent Dr)

❶ Getting There & Away

By train from New York City skip Amtrak and take **Metro North** (www.mta.info; one way $14-19), which has near-hourly services and the lowest fares. **Greyhound Bus Lines** (www.greyhound.com) connects New Haven to scores of cities including Hartford ($18, one hour) and Boston ($37, four hours).

MYSTIC & AROUND

A centuries-old seaport, Mystic boasts a top-notch nautical museum, a stellar aquarium and attractive period accommodations. Yes, it gets inundated with summer tourists, but there's a good reason why everyone stops here (including fans of the 1988 film *Mystic Pizza*), so get off the highway and check it out. Swing by on a weekday to avoid the worst of the crowds. The **Greater Mystic Chamber of Commerce** (☑860-572-1102; www.mysticchamber.org; 2 Roosevelt Ave; ⊙9am-4:30pm), at the old train station, has visitor information.

◉ Sights & Activities

Mystic Seaport — MUSEUM

(☑860-572-5315; www.mysticseaport.org; 75 Greenmanville Ave/CT 27; adult/child $24/15; ⊙9am-5pm; ⊞) America's maritime history springs to life as costumed interpreters ply their trades at this sprawling re-created 19th-century seaport village. You can scurry aboard several historic sailing vessels, including the *Charles W Morgan* (built in 1841), the last surviving wooden whaling ship in the world. If you want to experience a little voyage yourself, the **Sabino**, a 1908 steamboat, departs hourly ($5.50) on jaunts up the Mystic River.

Mystic Aquarium — AQUARIUM

(☑860-572-5955; www.mysticaquarium.org; 55 Coogan Blvd; adult/child $26/19; ⊙9am-6pm; ⊞) Home to all manner of interesting sea creatures, and we're not talking just fish. The residents include penguins, sea lions and even a beluga whale! And where else can a kid pet a cownose ray?

Foxwoods Resort & Casino — CASINO

(☑800-369-9663; www.foxwoods.com; CT 2, Ledyard) Feeling lucky? In nearby Ledyard, the Mashantucket Pequot tribe operates this mega-splash casino, the largest gambling venue this side of Vegas.

Mashantucket Pequot Museum & Research Center — MUSEUM

(☑800-411-9671; www.pequotmuseum.org; 110 Pequot Trail, off CT 214, Mashantucket; adult/child $15/10; ⊙10am-4pm Wed-Sat) This extensive center, funded by the casino, features a re-constructed 16th-century Native American village.

🛏 Sleeping

Old Mystic Inn — B&B $$

(☑860-572-9422; www.oldmysticinn.com; 52 Main St, Old Mystic; r incl breakfast $165-215; 🛜) Canopy beds, cozy fireplaces and gourmet breakfasts set the tone at this romantic 1784 Colonial inn near the head of the Mystic River. Formerly a bookstore, its rooms are themed after American authors like Henry David Thoreau and Mark Twain.

Whaler's Inn — INN $$

(☑860-536-1506; www.whalersinnmystic.com; 20 E Main St; r $139-259; ❇@🛜) By the drawbridge in the center of Mystic, this place offers a variety of comfy accommodations from traditionally decorated rooms in an 1865 Victorian house to modern rooms in motel-style buildings. It's an ideal location for walking to just about everything.

🍴 Eating & Drinking

S&P Oyster Co — SEAFOOD $$

(☑860-536-2674; www.sp-oyster.com; 1 Holmes St; mains $10-25; ⊙11:30am-10pm) On a summer day, there's nothing better than dining on the waterfront. This reliable seafood eatery, famous for oysters on the half shell and hefty portions of fish and chips, is in the town center at the east side of the drawbridge.

Harp & Hound — PUB $$

(☑860-572-7778; www.harpandhound.com; 4 Pearl St; mains $8-15; ⊙11:30am-1pm) This pub, in a historic building on the west side of the drawbridge, is the late-night place to grab a pint of Irish ale; decent pub grub and English football on the telly too.

Mystic Drawbridge Ice Cream — ICE CREAM $

(www.mysticdrawbridgeicecream.com; 2 W Main St; cones $4; ⊙9am-11pm) Strolling through town is best done with an ice-cream cone in your hand. In addition to cool flavors of homemade ice cream, this perpetually buzzing parlor also serves sandwiches, salads and baked goods.

Lower Connecticut River Valley

Several Colonial-era towns grace the banks of the Connecticut River, offering up their rural charm at an unhurried pace. The **River Valley Tourism District** (☎860-787-9640; www.visitctriver.com) provides information on the region.

ESSEX

The genteel riverside town of Essex, established in 1635, makes a good starting point for exploring the valley. The streets are lined with handsome Federal-period houses, the legacy of rum and tobacco fortunes made in the 19th century.

The **Connecticut River Museum** (☎860-767-8269; www.ctrivermuseum.org; 67 Main St; adult/child $8/5; ◷10am-5pm Tue-Sun) exhibits regional history and includes a reproduction of the world's first submarine, a hand-propelled vessel built at this site in 1776.

The best way to see the river valley is hopping aboard the **Essex Steam Train & Riverboat** (☎860-767-0103; www.essexsteamtrain.com; 1 Railroad Ave; adult/child $17/9, with cruise $26/17; ◷departure times vary; ⚓), an antique steam locomotive that runs 6 scenic miles to Deep River, where you can cruise on a Mississippi-style riverboat before returning by train.

The landmark **Griswold Inn** (☎860-767-1776; www.griswoldinn.com; 36 Main St; r incl breakfast $110-305; ✴☎), in the town center, has been providing cozy Colonial comfort since 1776, making it one of the oldest inns in America. It's also a favorite place to dine on traditional New England cuisine in a historic setting.

OLD LYME

Set near the mouth of the Connecticut River, Old Lyme was home to some 60 sea captains in the 19th century. Today its claim to fame is its art community. In the early 1900s art patron Florence Griswold opened her estate to visiting artists, many of whom offered paintings in lieu of rent. Her Georgian mansion, now the **Florence Griswold Museum** (☎860-434-5542; www.flogris.org; 96 Lyme St; adult/child $9/free; ◷10am-5pm Tue-Sat, 1-5pm Sun), exhibits 6000 works with solid collections of American Impressionist paintings, sculpture and decorative arts.

The prettiest place to lay your head is the classy **Bee & Thistle Inn** (☎860-434-1667; www.beeandthistleinn.com; 100 Lyme St; r $180-275; ☎), a 1756 Dutch Colonial farmhouse with antique-filled rooms and four-poster beds.

EAST HADDAM

Two intriguing attractions mark this small town on the east bank of the Connecticut River. The medieval-style **Gillette Castle** (☎860-526-2336; 67 River Rd; adult/child $10/4; ◷10am-4:30pm late May–mid-Oct) is a wildly eccentric stone-turreted mansion built in 1919 by actor William Hooker Gillette, who made his fortune playing Sherlock Holmes. The classic **Goodspeed Opera House** (☎860-873-8668; www.goodspeed.org; 6 Main St), an 1876 Victorian music hall known as 'the birthplace of the American musical,' still produces a full schedule of musicals.

Hartford

Connecticut's capital is best known as the hometown of America's insurance industry – not exactly a 'let's-rush-to-see-the-place' endorsement. But look beyond its backbone of office buildings and you'll find some worthwhile sights offering unique slices of Americana. The **Greater Hartford Welcome**

WHAT THE...?

Jaded museum browsers, don't turn your nose up at this one. Garbage goes green at the curious **Trash Museum** (☎860-757-7765, 211 Murphy Rd, Hartford; admission free; ◷noon-4pm Wed-Fri Sep-Jun, 10am-2pm Tue, 10am-4pm Wed-Fri Jul-Aug) smack in the midst of a trash facility. Run by the Connecticut Resources Recovery Authority (CRRA), it enlightens visitors on earth-friendly recycling techniques. A viewing platform overlooking the sorting operation takes center stage while cool sculptures made from trash and wormy composting displays plug the green side of it all. You'll also get the scoop on CRRA's trash-to-energy program that fuels a billion kilowatts of green electric power annually. To get to the museum take I-91 to exit 27, which dumps you right at the site.

Center (☎860-244-0253; www.enjoyhartford.com; 31 Pratt St; ⏰9am-5pm Mon-Fri) distributes tourist information.

◉ Sights & Activities

Mark Twain House & Museum   MUSEUM
(☎860-247-0998; www.marktwainhouse.org; 351 Farmington Ave; adult/child $16/10; ⏰9:30am-5:30pm Mon-Sat, noon-5:30pm Sun) It was at this former home of Samuel Langhorne Clemens, aka Mark Twain, that the legendary author penned many of his greatest works, including *A Connecticut Yankee in King Arthur's Court*. The house itself, a Victorian Gothic with fanciful turrets and gables, reflects Twain's quirky character.

Harriet Beecher Stowe House   MUSEUM
(☎860-522-9258; www.harrietbeecherstowe.org; 77 Forest St; adult/child $9/6; ⏰9:30am-4:30pm Tue-Sat, noon-4:30pm Sun) Next door to the Twain house is the former home of Harriet Beecher Stowe, who wrote *Uncle Tom's Cabin*. The book so rallied Americans against slavery that Abraham Lincoln once credited Stowe with starting the US Civil War.

Wadsworth Atheneum   MUSEUM
(☎860-278-2670; www.wadsworthatheneum.org; 600 Main St; adult/child $10/free; ⏰11am-5pm Wed-Fri, 10am-5pm Sat & Sun) America's oldest art museum showcases outstanding collections of Hudson River School paintings and sculptures by renowned Connecticut artist Alexander Calder (1898–1976).

FREE State Capitol   HISTORIC BUILDING
(☎860-240-0222; cnr Capitol Ave & Trinity St; ⏰9am-3pm Mon-Fri) You can tour the state capitol, built in 1879 in such a hodgepodge of styles that it's sometimes dubbed 'the most beautiful ugly building in the world.' Below the capitol grounds, the 37-acre Bushnell Park features a working 1914 carousel, lovely gardens and summer concerts.

Old State House   HISTORIC BUILDING
(☎860-522-6766; www.ctosh.org; 800 Main St; adult/child $6/3; ⏰10am-5pm Tue-Sat) The real prize of Connecticut's public buildings, designed by famed Colonial architect Charles Bulfinch. Erected in 1796, it's one of the oldest capitol buildings in the USA.

🛏 Sleeping & Eating

Hilton Hartford   HOTEL $$
(☎860-728-5151; www.hilton.com; 315 Trumbull St; r $100-189; ❈@☲) Within walking distance

of the city's central sights, this is Hartford's most conveniently located hotel. The rooms are dated but comfortable, and amenities include state-of-the-art fitness facilities. On weekends, when the lowest rates are offered, it's a deal.

Vaughan's Public House   PUB $$
(☎860-882-1560; www.irishpublichouse.com; 59 Pratt St; pub fare $9-16; ⏰11:30am-1am) This friendly Irish pub serves a full menu ranging from hearty sandwiches and salads to perfect beer-battered cod and chips. A river of Guinness flows, with good happy hour deals from 3pm to 7pm.

Mo's Midtown Restaurant   DINER $
(☎860-236-7741; 25 Whitney St; meals $3-7; ⏰7am-2:30pm Mon-Fri, 8am-1:30pm Sat & Sun) Head to this classic diner for fab breakfast fare on a shoestring. The grill is heaped with home-fried potatoes, served alongside stacks of whole-wheat pancakes loaded with seasonal fruit. Awesome huevos rancheros too.

❶ Getting There & Away

The conveniently central **Union Station** (www.amtrak.com; 1 Union Pl) links Hartford by train to cities throughout the Northeast, including New Haven (one way $17, one hour) and New York City (one way $52, three hours).

Litchfield Hills

Laced with lakes, woodlands and vineyards, the rolling hill country of northwestern Connecticut provides rich opportunities for quiet escapes. The **Litchfield Hills Connecticut Visitors Bureau** (www.litchfieldhills.com) has information on the entire region.

LITCHFIELD

Founded in 1719, Litchfield prospered from the commerce brought by stagecoaches traveling between Hartford and Albany, and its many handsome period buildings are a testimony to that era. Stroll along North and South Sts to see the finest homes, including the 1773 **Tapping Reeve House & Law School** (☎860-567-4501; www.litchfieldhistoricalsociety.org; 82 South St; adult/child $5/free; ⏰11am-5pm Tue-Sat, 1-5pm Sun), the USA's first law school, which trained 129 members of Congress. Included in the admission fee is the **Litchfield History Museum** (7 South St).

Haight-Brown Vineyard (☎860-567-4045; www.haightvineyards.com; 29 Chestnut Hill Rd, off CT 118; ⏰noon-5pm), the state's first winery, offers tours, tastings and self-guided vineyard walks.

If you're ready for a hike, Connecticut's largest wildlife preserve, the **White Memorial Conservation Center** (☑860-567-0857; www.whitememorialcc.org; US 202; admission free; ☉sunrise-sunset), 2.5 miles west of town, has 35 miles of inviting trails with good bird-watching.

LAKE WARAMAUG

The most beautiful of the dozens of lakes and ponds in the Litchfield Hills is Lake Waramaug. As you make your way around the northern shore on North Shore Rd, stop at **Hopkins Vineyard** (☑860-868-7954; www.hopkinsvineyard.com; 25 Hopkins Rd; ☉10am-5pm Mon-Sat, 11am-5pm Sun) for wine tastings. It's next to the 19th-century **Hopkins Inn** (☑860-868-7295; www.thehopkinsinn.com; 22 Hopkins Rd, Warren; r from $130; ❋☎), which has lake-view accommodations and a well-regarded restaurant with Austrian-influenced country fare. **Lake Waramaug State Park** (☑860-868-0220; 30 Lake Waramaug Rd; sites $17-$27) has lakeside campsites, but book well in advance.

VERMONT

Artisanal cheeses, buckets of maple syrup, Ben & Jerry's ice cream...just try to get out of this state without gaining 10 pounds. Fortunately, there are plenty of ways to work it off: hike the trails of the Green Mountains, paddle a kayak on Lake Champlain or hit Vermont's snowy slopes.

Vermont gives true meaning to the word rural. Its capital would barely rate as a small town in other states and even its largest city, Burlington, has just 42,500 content souls. The countryside is a blanket of rolling green, with 80% of the state forested and most of the rest given over to some of the prettiest farms you'll ever see. So take your time, meander down quiet side roads, stop in those picturesque villages, and sample a taste of the good life.

History

Frenchman Samuel de Champlain explored Vermont in 1609 and in his ever-humble manner lent his name to Vermont's largest lake.

Vermont played a key role in the American Revolution in 1775 when Ethan Allen led a local militia, the Green Mountain Boys,

VERMONT FACTS

» **Nickname** Green Mountain State

» **Population** 625,740

» **Area** 9250 sq miles

» **Capital city** Montpelier (population 8050)

» **Other cities** Burlington (population 42,500)

» **Sales tax** 6%

» **Birthplace of** Mormon leader Brigham Young (1801–77), President Calvin Coolidge (1872–1933)

» **Home of** more than 100 covered bridges

» **Politics** independent streak, leaning Democrat

» **Famous for** Ben & Jerry's ice cream

» **Sudsiest state** most microbreweries per capita in the USA

» **Driving distances** Burlington to Bennington 116 miles, Burlington to Portland, Maine 194 miles

to Fort Ticonderoga, capturing it from the British. In later years Allen took a friendlier stance toward the British, and considered petitioning the crown to make Vermont an independent British state. In 1791, two years after Allen's death, Vermont was finally admitted to the USA.

The state's independent streak is as long and deep as a vein of Vermont marble. Long a land of dairy farmers, Vermont is still largely agricultural and has the lowest population of any New England state.

❶ Information

Vermont Dept of Tourism (www.vermontvacation.com) Online information by region, season and other user-friendly categories.

Vermont State Parks (www.vtstateparks.com) Operates 40 state parks with camping.

Southern Vermont

The southern swath of Vermont holds its oldest towns, the cool trails of the Green Mountain National Forest and plenty of scenic back roads just aching to be explored.

BRATTLEBORO

Ever wonder where the 1960s counter-culture went? It's alive and well in this riverside burg overflowing with craft shops and more tie-dye per capita than any other place in New England.

◉ Sights & Activities

Begin at Main St, which is lined with period buildings, including the handsome art-deco Latchis Building, which houses a hotel and theater.

Windham County, surrounding Brattleboro, boasts several **covered bridges**. Pick up a driving guide to them at the **Brattleboro Area Chamber of Commerce** (✆802-254-4565; www.brattleborochamber.org; 180 Main St; ☉9am-5pm Mon-Fri).

Brattleboro Museum & Art Center   MUSEUM

(www.brattleboromuseum.org; 10 Vernon St; adult/child $6/free; ☉11am-5pm Thu-Mon) Showcases the multimedia works of regional artists.

🛏 Sleeping

Forty Putney Road B&B   B&B $$

(✆802-254-6268; www.fortyputneyroad.com; 192 Putney Rd; r incl breakfast $179-269; @☎) This estate-home-turned-B&B is one sweet spot: classy rooms, beautiful grounds, river views, hot tub, billiards and a gourmet breakfast. The 'beer geek' owners even have a pint-size pub perfect for sampling Vermont brews.

Vermont & New Hampshire

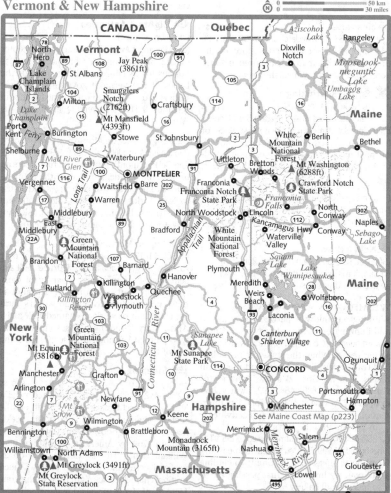

VERMONT FRESH NETWORK

Locavore food dominates in Vermont, and the state has its own label: the farm and chef partnership **Vermont Fresh Network** identifies restaurants that focus on sustainable, locally sourced food. Just look for the green-and-white square sticker with a plate and silverware drawn in it – it's an easy way of knowing that the eatery probably got its eggs from a neighboring farm. For a full listing of restaurants with this label, visit www.vermontfresh.net.

Latchis Hotel
HOTEL $$
(☑802-254-6300; www.latchis.com; 50 Main St; r $95-160; ☎) You couldn't be more in the thick of things than at this restored art-deco hotel with 30 simply furnished rooms.

✖ Eating & Drinking

Amy's Bakery Arts Café
CAFE $
(113 Main St; dishes $3-10; ⊙8am-5pm Mon-Fri, 10am-5pm Sat, 9am-5pm Sun) The best place for lunch. The baked goods are terrific but it's the healthy fare – tapenade mozzarella sandwiches and salads – that rake in the crowds.

Brattleboro Food Co-op
DELI $
(2 Main St; ⊙8am-9pm Mon-Sat, 9am-9pm Sun) Naturally this town has a big-league health-food store, with all the fixings for a locavore picnic.

McNeill's Brewery
PUB $
(90 Elliot St; ⊙5pm-2am Mon-Thu, 2pm-2am Fri-Sun) This friendly brewpub flows with award-winning suds.

WILMINGTON & MT SNOW

Wilmington, midway between Brattleboro and Bennington, is the gateway to **Mt Snow** (www.mountsnow.com; VT100), a family-oriented skiing resort. When the snow melts, its lifts and trail system draw hikers and mountain bikers. The **Mt Snow Valley Chamber of Commerce** (☑802-464-8092; www.visitver mont.com; 21 W Main St; ⊙10am-5pm) has information on accommodations and activities.

In Wilmington the **Nutmeg Country Inn** (☑802-464-7400; www.nutmeginn.com; 153 VT 9; r incl breakfast $99-205; ❀☎), an 18th-century farmhouse, offers local hospitality including a full country breakfast. Just passing by? It also has a small bakery.

BENNINGTON

A measure of how rural southern Vermont really is, cozy Bennington, with just 15,000 inhabitants, ranks as the region's largest town. You'll find an interesting mix of cafes and shops downtown along Main St, while the hillside area known as Old Bennington boasts age-old Colonial homes and a trio of covered bridges. A hilltop granite obelisk commemorating the 1777 Battle of Bennington towers above it all, making Bennington visible from miles around.

The **Bennington Area Chamber of Commerce** (☑802-447-3311; www.bennington. com; US 7; ⊙9am-5pm Mon-Fri, 10am-4pm Sat & Sun), a mile north of downtown, provides visitor information.

◉ Sights & Activities

Old First Church
HISTORIC SITE
(cnr Monument Ave & VT 9) Gracing the center of Old Bennington, this historic church is famous for its churchyard, which holds the bones of five Vermont governors and poet Robert Frost, who is buried beneath the inscription 'I Had a Lover's Quarrel with the World.'

Bennington Battle Monument
HISTORIC SITE
(Monument Ave; adult/child $3/1; ⊙9am-5pm mid-Apr–Oct) Vermont's loftiest structure offers an unbeatable 360-degree view of the countryside with peeks at covered bridges and across to New York. And you won't have to strain hamstrings climbing this 306ft obelisk – an elevator whisks you painlessly to the top.

Bennington Museum
MUSEUM
(☑802-447-1571; www.benningtonmuseum.com; 75 Main St/VT 9; adult/child $10/free; ⊙10am-5pm Thu-Tue) Showcasing an array of early Americana crafts, Bennington Museum is most notable for having the world's largest collection of works by famed folk artist Anna Mary 'Grandma' Moses (1860–1961), who painted Vermont farm scenes until the age of 100.

⬛ Sleeping

Henry House
B&B $$
(☑802-442-7045; www.henryhouseinn.com; 1338 Murphy Rd; r incl breakfast $90-145) Sit on the rocking chair and watch the traffic trickle across a covered bridge at this Colonial home built in 1769 by American Revolution hero William Henry. This is the real deal on 25 peaceful acres and dripping with so much original character you might expect long-gone Lieutenant Henry to walk down the hall.

Paradise Inn MOTEL $$
(☑802-442-8351; www.theparadisemotorinn.com; 141 W Main St; r $85-145; ❊🔊☒) Attractive rooms, a quiet yet central setting and a heated outdoor pool add up to good bang for the buck. Spend the extra for a premier room and enjoy your own little sauna and a Jacuzzi.

🍴 Eating & Drinking

TOP CHOICE **Blue Benn Diner** DINER $
(☑802-442-5140; 314 North St; mains $5-12; ⊙6am-4:45pm Mon-Fri, 7am-3:45pm Sat & Sun) It may be a classic 1950s-era diner, but it's no greasy spoon. The extensive menu includes breakfast all day and a healthy mix of American, Asian and Mexican fare – even vegetarian. Scrambled tofu with shiitake mushrooms, or perhaps the chocolate chip raspberry pancakes?

Izabella's CAFE $
(☑802-447-4949; 351 W Main St; mains $6-10; ⊙8:30am-3pm Tue-Fri, 8:30am-4pm Sat) This hip cafe in the center of town adds an innovative twist to American standards. The locavore menu changes with the season. If you're lucky, the baked apple and cheddar scones or the zesty Senegalese peanut soup will be on offer.

Madison Brewing Co PUB $$
(☑802-442-7397; www.madisonbrewingco.com; 428 Main St; mains $9-20; ⊙11:30am-9:30pm; 🚸) A family-style microbrewery? Yep, this perky pub-restaurant brews homemade root beer as well as heady malt ales. The food ranges from veggie burgers to juicy steaks and there's even a kids menu.

🛍 Shopping

Bennington Potters POTTERY
(www.benningtonpotters.com; 324 County St) Bennington pottery is a popular souvenir. Tour

the workshop where the distinctively mottled-design stoneware has been made for more than a half-century, and follow with a visit to the on-site shop.

MANCHESTER

Sitting in the shadow of Mt Equinox, Manchester's been a fashionable summer retreat since the 19th century. The mountain scenery, the agreeable climate and the Batten Kill River – Vermont's best trout stream – continue to draw vacationers today.

The town has two faces, both likable. Manchester Center, at the north end, sports cafes and upscale outlet stores. To the south lies dignified Manchester Village, lined with marble sidewalks, stately homes and the posh Equinox hotel.

The **Manchester & the Mountains Regional Chamber of Commerce** (☑800-362-4144; www.manchestervermont.net; 5046 Main St, Manchester Center; ⊙9am-5pm Mon-Fri, 10am-5pm Sat) provides visitor information.

🔘 Sights & Activities

The **Appalachian Trail**, which overlaps the **Long Trail** in Vermont, passes just east of Manchester. For trail maps as well as details on shorter day hikes, stop by the **Green Mountain National Forest office** (☑802-362-2307; 2538 Depot St, Manchester Center; ⊙8am-4:30pm Mon-Fri).

For a view from the top, drive to the summit of **Mt Equinox** (3816ft). Take VT 7A south of Manchester to **Skyline Drive** (☑802-362-1114; car & driver $12, additional passenger $2; ⊙9am-sunset May-Oct), a private 5-mile toll road.

Hildene HISTORIC SITE
(☑802-362-1788; www.hildene.org; 1005 Hildene Rd/VT 7A; adult/child $13/5; ⊙9:30am-4:30pm) Just south of Manchester, this 24-room Georgian Revival mansion was the country estate

---

SCENIC DRIVE: COVERED BRIDGES

A 30-minute detour from Bennington takes you across three picture-perfect covered bridges spanning the Wallomsac River at the rural north side of town. To get started turn west onto VT 67A just north of the tourist office and continue 3.5 miles, turning left on Murphy Rd at the **Burt Henry Covered Bridge**. Exhale, slow down: you're back in horse and buggy days. As you pop out the back side of this 117ft-long bridge dating to 1840, curve to the left. Murphy Rd soon loops through the **Paper Mill Bridge**, which takes its name from the 1790 mill that once sat beneath the bridge (look along the river for the old gear works). Next turn right onto VT 67A, go half a mile and turn right onto Silk Rd where you'll soon cross the **Silk Road Bridge** (c 1840). If you continue along Silk Rd for 2 miles, bearing to the left at each turn, you'll reach the **Bennington Battle Monument**.

of Robert Todd Lincoln, son of President Abraham Lincoln. You can tour the mansion decorated with original Lincoln family furnishings and stroll its lovely gardens, though don't expect much to be in bloom before June.

American Museum of Fly Fishing MUSEUM
(www.amff.com; 4104 VT 7A; adult/child $5/3; ⊙10am-4pm Tue-Sat) Anglers make pilgrimages to Manchester to visit this museum, where rods used by Ernest Hemingway and other famed fishers are displayed; to shop at the adjacent Orvis flagship store, which is dedicated to outfitting fisher-folk; and to fly-fish for trout in the Batten Kill River.

BattenKill Canoe BOATING
(☑802-362-2800; www.battenkill.com; 6328 VT 7A, Arlington; rentals per day $40-70; ⊙9:30am-5:30pm May-Oct) Located 5 miles south of Manchester, rents canoes and kayaks for paddling the Batten Kill River.

🛏 Sleeping

Aspen Motel MOTEL $
(☑802-362-2450; www.theaspenatmanchester. com, 5669 Main St/VT 7A; r $80-115; 🅿🛜🎿) An affordable standout, this family-run hotel set back serenely from the road has 25 comfortable rooms and a convenient location within walking distance of Manchester Center.

Equinox RESORT $$$
(☑802-362-4700; www.equinoxresort.com; 3567 Main St; r $289-689; 🅿🏊) Manchester's grande dame since 1769 boasts 195 rooms, its own 18-hole golf course, two pools, restaurants and a luxury spa. Despite modern upgrades its handsome period character prevails.

✗ Eating

TOP CHOICE Up for Breakfast BREAKFAST $
(☑802-362-4204; 4935 Main St; mains $6-14; ⊙7am-12:30pm Mon-Fri, 7am-1:30pm Sat & Sun) Search out this hole-in-the-wall 2nd-floor restaurant in Manchester Center for the best breakfast in town, anything from good ol' blueberry pancakes to smoked-salmon-and-caper omelets.

Ye Olde Tavern AMERICAN $$$
(☑802-362-0611; www.yeoldetavern.net; 5183 Main St; mains $17-28; ⊙5-9:30pm) Hearthside dining enhances the experience at this gracious 1790s inn. The menu ranges from colonial favorites like Yankee pot roast to a delectable roast duck in a port wine reduction sauce.

Spiral Press Café CAFE $
(cnr VT 11 & 7A; mains $6-10; ⊙7am-6:30pm; 🛜) Stop at this Manchester Center cafe attached to Northshire Bookstore for flaky croissants and delicious panini sandwiches. Good lattes too.

Central Vermont

Nestled in the Green Mountains, central Vermont is classic small-town, big-country-side New England. Its time-honored villages and ski resorts have been luring travelers for generations.

WOODSTOCK & QUECHEE

The archetypal Vermont town, Woodstock has streets lined with graceful Federal- and Georgian-style houses. The Ottauquechee River, spanned by a covered bridge, meanders right through the heart of town. Quechee (*kwee*-chee), Woodstock's smaller cousin 7 miles to the northeast, abounds in rural scenery. The whole area invites you to slow down. The Woodstock Area Chamber of Commerce (☑802-457-3555; www. woodstockvt.com; 61 Central St; ⊙8:30am-4:30pm Mon-Fri) provides visitor information.

👁 Sights & Activities

Quechee Gorge, an impressive 170ft-deep gash cut by the Ottauquechee River, can be viewed from above or along walking trails that skirt the 3000ft-long chasm. Begin at the Quechee Gorge Visitor Center (☑802-295-6852; US 4, Quechee; ⊙9am-5pm May-Oct, 10am-4pm Nov-Apr), at the east side of the gorge, where you can pick up a trail map.

FREE **Marsh-Billings-Rockefeller National Historical Park** PARK
(☑802-457-3368; www.nps.gov/mabi) Occupying a former Rockefeller family estate, this is the only national park to tell the story of America's conservation history and land stewardship. The 550-acre park is crisscrossed with shady trails that beg a stroll and it's just a mile north of Woodstock center.

🍃 **VINS Nature Center** RAPTOR CENTER
(☑802-359-5000; www.vinsweb.org; US 4, Quechee; adult/child $10.50/8.50; ⊙10am-5:30pm; 🚸) A mile west of the gorge, rehabilitates injured bald eagles and other raptors. Get a close-up look at these magnificent birds, then enjoy a nature walk on the center's 47 acres.

Billings Farm & Museum   FARM
(☑802-457-2355; www.billingsfarm.org; VT 12, at River Rd; adult/child $12/6; ☺10am-5pm May-Oct; 🐾) See what 19th-century farm life was all about at this living-history museum and functioning dairy farm adjacent to the Marsh-Billings-Rockefeller National Historical Park.

🛏 Sleeping

Ardmore Inn   B&B $$
(☑802-457-3887; www.ardmoreinn.com; 23 Pleasant St, Woodstock; r incl breakfast $130-205; ❄🖥) This congenial inn, just a five-minute walk from Woodstock town center, occupies a stately 1867 Greek Revival building and features five antique-laden rooms with marble baths. The home-cooked multicourse breakfast seals the deal.

Shire Riverview Motel   MOTEL $$
(☑802-457-2211; www.shiremotel.com; 46 Pleasant St/US 4; r $98-188; ❄🖥) The best motel value in Woodstock center. The colonial decor is agreeable, the manager helpful and the view of the Ottauquechee River, which runs along the motel's back side, is second to none.

Quechee State Park   CAMPGROUND $
(☑888-409-7579; www.vtstateparks.com; 5800 US 4, Quechee; campsites/lean-tos $20/27) Campers will find 45 pine-shaded campsites and seven lean-tos in this 600-acre park bordering Quechee Gorge.

🍴 Eating

TOP CHOICE Simon Pearce   NEW AMERICAN $$
(☑802-295-1470; www.simonpearce.com; 1760 Main St, Quechee; lunch mains $13-17, dinner mains $25-32; ☺11:30am-2:45pm & 6-9pm) Not only is Simon Pearce an unbeatable choice for an upscale meal but lunch is surprisingly affordable. Start by watching the artisans hand-blowing glass and throwing pottery in the basement workshops, then go upstairs and enjoy creative New American fare served on their handiwork. Very cool place – it even generates its own electricity from the waterfall the restaurant overlooks.

Prince & the Pauper   AMERICAN $$$
(☑802-457-1818; www.princeandpauper.com; 24 Elm St; bistro mains $14-22, prix-fixe menu $49; ☺6-9pm) The boneless lamb in puff pastry is a rave at this classic New England restaurant in the center of Woodstock. If you're not up for the hearty three-course fixed-price dinner, there's also a bistro menu with lighter fare and enticing options.

Osteria Pane e Salute   ITALIAN $$
(☑802-457-4882; www.osteriapanesalute.com; 61 Central St; mains $14-21; ☺6-10pm Thu-Mon) Come here for superb thin-crust Tuscan-style pizzas and traditional Italian fare the way mama used to make it...well, if your mama was Italian. Think slow food, boutique Italian wines and aromatic spices.

KILLINGTON

An hour's drive west of Woodstock, **Killington Resort** (www.killington.com) is New England's answer to Vail, boasting 200 runs on seven mountains, a vertical drop of 3150ft and more than 30 lifts. And thanks to the world's most extensive snowmaking system, Killington has one of the longest seasons in the east. Come summer when the snow melts, mountain bikers and hikers claim the slopes.

There are more than a hundred places to stay in the Killington area, from cozy ski lodges to chain hotels. Most are along Killington Rd, the 6-mile road that heads up the mountain from US 4. The **Killington Chamber of Commerce** (☑802-773-4181; www.killingtonchamber.com; US 4; ☺10am-4:30pm Mon-Sat) has all the nitty-gritty.

MIDDLEBURY

This former factory town has converted its old water-driven mills into enticing riverside restaurants and galleries. Add the verdant campus of Middlebury College and you've got yourself a fine place to while away an afternoon. The small but diverse **Middlebury College Museum of Art** (☑802-443-5007; S Main St; admission free; ☺10am-5pm Tue-Fri, noon-5pm Sat & Sun) takes you on a world twirl beginning with an Egyptian sarcophagus and ending with Andy Warhol. The **Addison County Chamber of Commerce** (☑802-388-7951; www.addisoncounty.com; 93 Court St; ☺9am-5pm Mon-Fri) has area information.

On the National Register of Historic Places, the gracious, 1803 Federal-style **Inn on the Green** (☑802-388-7512; www.innonthegreen.com; 71 S Pleasant St; r incl breakfast $149-269; @🖥) has 11 attractive rooms that overlook the town green. Talk about pampering – they'll even serve you breakfast in bed.

For a slice of retro Americana, stop at the **A&W Drive-In** (1557 US 7; mains $3-6; ☺11am-8pm) where carhops – some on roller skates – deliver root beer floats, cheeseburgers, onion rings and other artery-clogging goodness directly to your car window.

For a fine river view and good food at honest prices make your way to **Storm Cafe** (www.thestormcafe.com; 3 Mill St; mains $5-22; ☺11am-6pm Tue-Sat), which serves up a standard cafe menu of soups, salads and sandwiches at lunch and fancier fare at dinner.

WARREN & WAITSFIELD

The towns of Warren and Waitsfield boast two significant ski areas: **Sugarbush** (www.sugarbush.com) and **Mad River Glen** (madriver.glen.com), in the mountains west of VT 100. Opportunities abound for cycling, canoeing, horseback riding, kayaking, gliding and other activities. Stop at the **Mad River Valley Chamber of Commerce** (☏802-496-3409; www.madrivervalley.com; VT 100, Waitsfield; ☺9am-5pm Mon-Fri) for a mountain of details; brochures and restrooms are available 24/7 in the chamber's lobby.

Northern Vermont

The lushly green northern region of Vermont cradles the fetching state capital of Montpelier, the ski mecca of Stowe, the vibrant college town of Burlington and the state's highest mountains. It has some of the prettiest landscapes in the Northeast.

MONTPELIER

America's smallest capital, Montpelier is a thoroughly likable town full of period build-ings and backed by verdant hills. It speaks to its village nature that you can walk in the front door of the gold-domed **State House** (www.vtstatehouse.org; 115 State St; admission free; ☺tours 10am-3:30pm Mon-Fri, 11am-2:30pm Sat Jul–mid-Oct), built c 1836, and exit out the back onto a forested trail. Tours run on the half hour. The **Central Vermont Chamber of Commerce** (www.centralvt.com) has tourist information on Montpelier.

If you come through at mealtime, head for the intersection of State and Main Sts, where you'll find several restaurants. Don't even think junk food – Montpelier prides itself on being the only state capital in the USA without a McDonald's! The bakery-cafe **La Brioche** (89 Main St; snacks $2-7; ☺6:30am-5pm Mon-Fri, 7am-5pm Sat), run by students from Montpelier's New England Culinary Institute, gets an A-plus for its innovative sandwiches and flaky French pastries. Or make your way over to **Hunger Mountain Co-op** (☏802-223-8000; 623 Stone Cutters Way; buffet $8; ☺8am-7:30pm), a terrific health-food store and deli with cafe tables perched above a river.

STOWE & AROUND

With Vermont's highest peak, Mt Mansfield (4393ft), as its backdrop, Stowe ranks as Vermont's classiest ski destination. It packs all the Alpine thrills you could ask for – both cross-country and downhill skiing, with gentle runs for novices and challenging drops for pros. Cycling, hiking and kayaking take center stage in the summer. Lodgings and eateries are thick along VT 108 (Mountain Rd), which continues northwest from Stowe center to the ski resorts. The **Stowe Visitors Center** (☏802-253-7321; www.gostowe.com; 51 Main St; ☺9am-5pm Mon-Sat) provides information.

◉ Sights & Activities

The 5.5-mile **Stowe Recreation Path**, a greenway running along the West Branch River northwest from the village center, is a great place for walking, jogging, cycling and skating.

Vermont's **Long Trail**, which passes through Stowe, follows the crest of the Green Mountains and runs the entire length of Vermont with rustic cabins, lean-tos and campsites along the way. Its caretaker, the **Green Mountain Club** (☏802-244-7037; www.greenmountainclub.org; 4711 Waterbury-Stowe Rd, VT 100), has full details on the Long Trail and shorter day hikes around Stowe.

SCENIC DRIVE: VT 100

Running up the rugged backbone of Vermont, VT 100 meanders through the rural heart of the state. This quintessential country road rambles past rolling pastures speckled with cows, through tiny villages with white-steepled churches and along green mountains crossed with hiking trails and ski slopes. It's the perfect sidetrip for those who want to slow down, inhale pine-scented air and soak up the bucolic country life that forms the very soul of Vermont. Think farm stands, century-old farmhouses converted to small inns, pottery shops, country stores and home-style cafes. The road runs north to south all the way from Massachusetts to Canada. It has some tranquil moments but never a dull one – jump on for a taste of it at any point.

If the snow has cleared, be sure to take a drive through dramatic **Smugglers Notch**, northwest of Stowe on VT 108 (the road's closed in winter). This narrow pass slices through mountains with 1000ft cliffs on either side, and there are plenty of places where you can stop along the way to ooh and aah or take a short walk.

Ben & Jerry's Ice Cream Factory   TOUR
(☎802-882-1240; www.benjerrys.com; 1281 VT 100, Waterbury; adult/child $3/free; ☺9am-5:30pm, with longer summer hr; ♿) Get the inside scoop, where tours and a moo-vie about the hippie founders are topped off with a taste tease of the latest flavor.

Stowe Mountain Resort   SKIING
(☎802-253-3000; www.stowe.com; 5781 Mountain Rd) Wintertime's action-central, this twin-peak resort has a variety of terrains with ski runs suitable for all levels.

AJ's Ski & Sports   SPORTS RENTALS
(☎802-253-4593; www.ajssportinggoods.com; 350 Mountain Rd; ☺10am-6pm) Next to the Stowe Recreation Path, rents skis and snowboards for $29 per day and bikes for $27 per day.

Umiak Outdoor Outfitters   BOATING
(☎802-253-2317; www.umiak.com; 849 S Main St; ☺9am-6pm) Rents canoes ($50 per day) and kayaks ($40) and offers two-hour guided river trips ($45).

🛏 Sleeping

Fiddler's Green Inn   INN $$
(☎802-253-8124; www.fiddlersgreeninn.com; 4859 Mountain Rd; r incl breakfast $125; ❄) This 1820s farmhouse near Stowe's ski lifts has rustic appeal with a fieldstone fireplace that roars on nippy nights and seven straightforward guest rooms geared to outdoor enthusiasts.

Trapp Family Lodge   LODGE $$$
(☎802-253-8511; www.trappfamily.com; 700 Trapp Hill Rd; r from $270; @🛜🏊) If the *Sound of Music* is one of your favorite things, then you'll love this Austrian-style mountain lodge built by the Von Trapp family and offering cross-country skiing, snowshoeing and hiking.

Best Western Waterbury-Stowe   MOTEL $$
(☎802-244-7822; www.bestwesternwaterburys towe.com; VT 100, I-89 exit 10; r incl breakfast $109-149; ❄@🛜🏊♿) Family-friendly, this convenient hotel has a playground, a sunny atrium pool and fitness facilities a notch above the usual standards. And it's just a short drive from Ben & Jerry's.

(☎802-253-4014; 6443 Mountain Rd; campsites/ lean-tos $20/27; ☺mid-May–mid-Oct) Camp at the base of Mt Mansfield, 9 miles northwest of downtown Stowe on VT 108.

✗ Eating

TOP CHOICE **Hen of the Wood**   AMERICAN $$$
(☎802-244-7300; www.henofthewood.com; 92 Stowe St, Woodbury; mains $18-32; ☺5-10pm Tue-Sat) Arguably the finest dining in northern Vermont, this chef-driven restaurant gets rave reviews for its innovative farm-to-table cuisine. Set in a historic grist mill, the ambience is as fine as the food, which features densely flavored dishes like smoked duck breast and sheep's milk gnocchi.

Pie-casso   PIZZERIA $$
(☎802-253-4411; www.piecasso.com; 1899 Mountain Rd; mains $9-22; ☺11am-9pm) This pizzeria goes far beyond the simple pie: organic arugula chicken salad, portobello paninis and hand-tossed pesto pizzas are just part of the menu. There's a bar and live music too.

Harvest Market   MARKET $
(1031 Mountain Rd; ☺7am-5:30pm) Stop at this gourmet market for morning coffee and delicious pastries, Vermont cheeses and sandwiches before you head for the hills.

Burlington

This hip college town on the shores of scenic Lake Champlain is one of those places that makes you think, wouldn't it be great to live here? The cafe and club scene is on par with a much bigger city, while the slow, friendly pace is pure small town. And where else can you walk to the end of Main St and paddle off in a kayak?

◉ Sights

Vermont's largest city is a manageable place with most of its cafes and pubs on or near Church St Marketplace, a brick-lined pedestrian mall, where half of Burlington hangs on a sunny day. The mall sits midway between the University of Vermont and Lake Champlain.

Fleming Museum   MUSEUM
(☎802-656-2090; www.uvm.edu/~fleming; 61 Colchester Ave; adult/child $5/3; ☺noon-4pm Tue-Fri, 1-5pm Sat & Sun May-Aug, longer hr Sep-Apr) The

WHAT THE...?

Packrats, take note. The **world's tallest filing cabinet** – a 50ft-high shrine to dead letters – sits in a roadside field midway between downtown and Magic Hat Brewery. Turn west onto Flynn Ave off US 7/Shelburne Rd and go 700 yards; it's on the right, adjacent to 208 Flynn Ave.

University of Vermont's (UVM) beautiful beaux-arts-style museum houses a 2000-item Native American gallery and works by American artists ranging from John James Audubon to Andy Warhol.

Magic Hat Brewery BREWERY
(802-658-2739; www.magichat.net; 5 Bartlett Bay Rd, South Burlington; 10am-6pm Mon-Sat, noon-5pm Sun) This insanely popular brewery, off US 7, offers free tours of its brew operation – and of course they'll tip the tap to let you sample the art. Perhaps the coolest brewery you'll ever see.

Shelburne Museum MUSEUM
(802-985-3346; www.shelburnemuseum.org; US 7, Shelburne; adult/child $20/10; 10am-5pm Mon-Sat, noon-5pm Sun mid-May–Oct) On a 45-acre estate, 7 miles south of Burlington in Shelburne, this museum boasts a stellar collection of American folk art, New England architecture and, well, just about everything. The wildly eclectic collection ranges from an early American sawmill to the Lake Champlain side-wheeler steamship *Ticonderoga*. How's that for lawn decor?

Shelburne Farms FARM
(802-985-8686; www.shelburnefarms.org; 1611 Harbor Rd, Shelburne; adult/child $8/5; 9am-5pm) You can get a taste of Vermont farm life at this classic 1400-acre farm laid out by Frederick Law Olmsted, America's premier 19th-century landscape architect. Try your hand at milking a cow, feed the chickens, or hike the extensive nature trails through pastures and along Lake Champlain.

ECHO Lake Aquarium & Science Center AQUARIUM
(802-864-1848; www.echovermont.org; 1 College St; adult/child $10.50/8.50; 10am-5pm;) On the waterfront, ECHO will delight youngsters with its aquatic habitats wriggling with creatures and hands-on interactive exhibits illuminating Lake Champlain's ecological wonders.

Oakledge Park PARK
(Flynn Ave) Near the south end of the Burlington Bike Path, this park has a beach, an awesome **tree house** at its south end and the **Burlington Earth Clock**, a cool Stonehenge-wannabe sun clock, at its north end.

Activities

Ready for outdoor adventures? Head to the waterfront, where options include boating on Lake Champlain and cycling, in-line skating and walking on the 9-mile shorefront Burlington Bike Path. Jump-off points and equipment rentals for all these activities are within a block of each other near the waterfront end of Main St.

Local Motion BICYCLE RENTAL
(802-652-2453; www.localmotion.org; 1 Steele St; bikes per day $30; 10am-6pm) Rents quality bikes.

Waterfront Boat Rentals BOAT RENTAL
(802-864-4858; www.waterfrontboatrentals.com; Perkins Pier; rentals per hr $10-16; 10am-6pm) Rents canoes, kayaks and rowboats.

Lake Champlain Cruises CRUISE
(802-864-7669; www.lakechamplaincruises.com; 1 King St; 1½-hr trip adult/child $15/6) For an inexpensive cruise of the lake, hop aboard the 115ft *Northern Lights,* a replicated 19th-century steamboat.

Sleeping

TOP CHOICE **Willard Street Inn** INN $$
(802-651-8710; www.willardstreetinn.com; 349 S Willard St; r incl breakfast $145-235;) With marble floors and a solarium dining room, this gracious inn, a short walk from UVM, is a class act. The 14 rooms are comfy, some with lake views and gas fireplaces, and the gourmet breakfast will start your day in style.

Inn at Shelburne Farms INN $$$
(802-985-8498; www.shelburnefarms.org; 1611 Harbor Rd, Shelburne; r with shared bath $155, private bath $260-465) Vacation like a millionaire at this lakefront manor-house-turned-inn at Shelburne Farms. On the National Register of Historic Places, this former summer residence of the Vanderbilts has 24 antique-filled bedrooms and the air of a bygone era.

Lang House
B&B **$$**

(802-652-2500; www.langhouse.com; 360 Main St; r incl breakfast $145-245;) Little extras like cozy bathrobes and a home-cooked breakfast add to the appeal of this friendly Victorian inn. Situated between downtown and the university, it makes an ideal base for exploring Burlington.

Burlington Hostel
HOSTEL **$**

(802-540-3043; www.theburlingtonhostel.com; 53 Main St; dm incl breakfast $30;) Just minutes from the action centers of Church St and Lake Champlain, Burlington's hostel accommodates up to 48 guests and offers both mixed and women-only dorms.

North Beach Campground
CAMPGROUND **$**

(802-862-0942; www.enjoyburlington.com; 60 Institute Rd; campsites $26;) This choice lakeside campground skirts the Burlington Bike Path and has a sandy beach with kayak and canoe rentals.

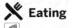 Eating

Magnolia Bistro
CAFE **$$**

(802-846-7446; www.magnoliabistro.com; 1 Lawson Lane; mains $7-12; 7am-3pm Mon-Fri, 8am-3pm Sat & Sun;) Magnolia utilizes sustainable local ingredients from range-fed beef to leafy green salads, and is certified by the Green Restaurant Association. Specialties include the house-cured organic salmon and the Vermont maple sausage omelet.

Penny Cluse Café
CAFE **$**

(www.pennycluse.com; 169 Cherry St; mains $7-10; 6:45am-3pm Mon-Fri, 8am-3pm Sat & Sun) One block east of Church St Marketplace, Penny Cluse packs a perky college crowd with its southwestern accented dishes like ranchero-style omelets, fish tacos and freshly squeezed juices. Forget weekends, however, when the wait just for a table can be more than an hour.

L'Amante
ITALIAN **$$$**

(802-863-5200; www.lamante.com; 126 College St; mains $23-30; 5-10pm Mon-Sat) Sleek yet engagingly informal, L'Amante serves upscale northern Italian cuisine such as squash-blossom fritters with truffle oil, and swordfish with saffron-encrusted risotto. Perfect for a memorable night out.

Stone Soup
CAFE **$**

(www.stonesoupvt.com; 211 College St; mains $5-10; 7am-9pm Mon-Fri, 9am-9pm Sat;) Don't let the bargain prices fool you. The food at this laid-back cafe is hearty and healthy, most of it vegetarian, much of it organic. Sandwiches, soups and a buffet bar of fresh salads and hot dishes shore up the menu.

August First Bakery & Cafe
BAKERY **$**

(www.augustfirstvt.com; 149 S Champlain St; sandwiches $5-9; 7:30am-5pm Mon-Fri, 8am-3pm Sat) Thickly stacked sandwiches on homebaked organic bread and sinful pastries are in store at this bakery-cafe a block from the waterfront.

Muddy Waters
CAFE **$**

(184 Main St; snacks $3-6; 7:30am-6pm Mon, 7:30am-11pm Tue-Sun;) As much a chill-out spot as eatery, this arty student haunt offers light eats like vegan chili and a full array of drinks from espressos and smoothies to Vermont-brewed beers.

Burlington Farmers Market
MARKET **$**

(www.burlingtonfarmersmarket.org; cnr St Paul & Cottage Sts; 8:30am-2pm Sat) Fruits and veggies don't get any fresher than at this outdoor market a block south of Church St Marketplace that's run by local farmers.

Drinking & Entertainment

Nectar's
CLUB

(www.liveatnectars.com; 188 Main St) This is the place where the jam band Phish got its start; aspiring bands still take the stage at Nectar's hoping to be the next big thing. Maybe you'll catch a rising star.

Radio Bean
COFFEEHOUSE

(www.radiobean.com; 8 N Winooski Ave; 8am-2am;) A social hub for the music scene, this bohemian coffeehouse serves fair-trade coffee by day and transforms after dark into an intimate venue for jazz and indie bands.

Vermont Pub & Brewery
MICROBREWERY

(www.vermontbrewery.com; 144 College St; 11:30am-1am Sun-Wed, 11:30am-2am Thu-Sat) Vermont's oldest microbrewery attracts a crowd with its bustling outdoor beer garden and burly ales. Try the Dogbite Bitter and howl at the moon.

Red Square
CLUB

(www.redsquarevt.com; 136 Church St) With a stylish Soho-like ambience, this is where the club crowd hangs to listen to Burlington's best roadhouse music, which spills onto the outdoor patio on warm nights.

Splash at the Boathouse
BAR

(0 College St; 11:30am-2am) Head to this floating boathouse at the foot of College

St for a fabulous view of Lake Champlain. *The* place to enjoy a sunset drink.

🛍 Shopping

You'll find boutiques and smart craft shops along Church St Marketplace. Don't miss the **Frog Hollow Craft Center** (www.froghollow. org; 85 Church St), a collective featuring some of the finest work in Burlington.

ℹ Information

Fletcher Allen Health Care (☎802-847-0000; 111 Colchester Ave; ⏰24hr) Vermont's largest hospital.

Lake Champlain Regional Chamber of Commerce (☎802-863-3489; www.vermont. org; 60 Main St; ⏰8am-5pm Mon-Fri) Also maintains a 24-hour visitor kiosk on Church St Marketplace.

Post office (www.usps.com; 11 Elmwood Ave)

Seven Days (www.7dvt.com) Free weekly with event and entertainment listings.

ℹ Getting There & Away

Lake Champlain Ferries (☎802-864-9804; www.ferries.com; King St Dock; adult/child/car $4.95/2.20/17.50) runs ferries several times a day from mid-June to mid-October across the lake to Port Kent, NY (one hour).

NEW HAMPSHIRE

You're gonna like the scale of things in the Granite State: the towns are small and personable, the mountains majestic and rugged. The heart of New Hampshire is unquestionably the granite peaks of the White Mountain National Forest. Outdoor enthusiasts of all stripes flock to New England's highest range (6288ft at Mt Washington) for cold-weather skiing, summer hiking and brilliant fall foliage scenery. Oh, and don't be fooled by that politically conservative label that people stick on the state. The state mantra, 'Live Free or Die,' indeed rings from every automobile license plate, but truth be told residents here pride themselves on their independent spirit more than right-wing politics.

History

Named in 1629 after the English county of Hampshire, New Hampshire was one of the first American colonies to declare its independence from England in 1776. During the 19th-century industrialization boom, the state's leading city, Manchester, became such a powerhouse that its textile mills were the world's largest.

New Hampshire played a high-profile role in 1944 when president Franklin D Roosevelt gathered leaders from 44 Allied nations to remote Bretton Woods for a conference to rebuild global capitalism. It was at the Bretton Woods Conference that the World Bank and the International Monetary Fund emerged.

In 1963 New Hampshire, long famed for its antitax sentiments, found another way to raise revenue – by becoming the first state in the USA to have a legal lottery.

ℹ Information

Welcome centers are situated at major state border crossings, including one at the south end of I-93 that's open 24/7.

New Hampshire Division of Parks and Recreation (☎877-647-2757; www.nhstateparks.org) Offers camping in 19 state parks.

New Hampshire Division of Travel & Tourism Development (☎603-271-2665; www.visitnh. gov) Distributes visitor information on the state, as do the welcome centers.

Union Leader (www.unionleader.com) The state's largest newspaper.

NEW HAMPSHIRE FACTS

» **Nicknames** Granite State, White Mountain State

» **Population** 1.3 million

» **Area** 8968 sq miles

» **Capital city** Concord (population 42,700)

» **Other cities** Manchester (population 109,600)

» **Sales tax** none

» **Birthplace of** America's first astronaut Alan Shepard (1923–98), *The Da Vinci Code* author Dan Brown (b 1964)

» **Home of** the highest mountains in northeastern USA

» **Politics** New England's most Republican state

» **Famous for** being the first to vote in US presidential primaries, which gives the state enormous political influence for its size

» **Most extreme state motto** 'Live Free or Die'

» **Driving distances** Boston to Portsmouth 60 miles, Concord to Hanover 66 miles

Portsmouth

America's third-oldest city (1623), Portsmouth wears its history on its sleeve. Its roots are in shipbuilding, but New Hampshire's sole coastal city also has a hip, youthful energy. The old maritime warehouses along the harbor now house cafes and boutiques. Elegant period homes built by shipbuilding tycoons have been converted into B&Bs.

◉ Sights & Activities

Strawbery Banke Museum   MUSEUM
(☑603-433-1100; www.strawberybanke.org; cnr Hancock & Marcy Sts; adult/child $15/10; ⊘10am-5pm May-Oct) Encompassing an entire neighborhood of 40 period buildings, Strawbery Banke is an eclectic living-history museum depicting the town's multilayered past. Visit the old general store, watch the potter throw his clay then treat yourself to a scoop of homemade ice cream.

USS Albacore   MUSEUM
(☑603-436-3680; http://ussalbacore.org; 600 Market St; adult/child $5/3; ⊘9:30am-5pm Jun–mid-Oct, 9:30am-4pm Thu-Mon mid-Oct–May) Like a fish out of water, this 205ft-long submarine is now a beached museum on a grassy lawn. Launched from Portsmouth Naval Shipyard in 1953, the Albacore was once the world's fastest submarine.

Isles of Shoals Steamship Company   CRUISE
(☑603-431-5500; www.islesofshoals.com; 315 Market St; adult/child $28/18; ▣) From May to September you can hop aboard a replica 1900s ferry for a leisurely harbor cruise that takes in three lighthouses, nine islands and countless harbor sights. On Fridays the cruise includes a lobster clambake (adult/child $58/27).

🛌 Sleeping

TOP CHOICE Ale House Inn   INN $$
(☑603-431-7760; www.alehouseinn.com; 121 Bow St; r $140-239, ✴🛜) Portsmouth's snazziest boutique inn occupies an atmospheric brewery (c 1880). The building's period character of brick and wood fuses flawlessly with the rooms' clean contemporary design. Perks like in-room iPads, guest bicycles and free tickets to the adjacent repertory theater add to the appeal.

Inn at Strawbery Banke   B&B $$
(☑603-436-7242; www.innatstrawberybanke.com; 314 Court St; r incl breakfast $160-170) Friendly innkeepers, cozy rooms and a delicious homemade breakfast are the hallmarks of this Colonial-era B&B convenient to both the Strawbery Banke Museum and the city center.

✕ Eating & Drinking

Head to the intersection of Market and Congress Sts, where restaurants and cafes are thick on the ground.

TOP CHOICE Black Trumpet Bistro   INTERNATIONAL $$$
(☑603-431-0887; www.blacktrumpetbistro.com; 29 Ceres St; mains $17-35; ⊘5:30-9pm) Chef-driven and oozing sophisticated ambience, Portsmouth's top bistro whips up inventive dishes like baharat-crusted dayboat scallops over whipped parsnips and olive oil cake with tiramisu and brandy espresso. Fab food, high energy and high-decibel levels.

Jumpin' Jay's Fish Café   SEAFOOD $$$
(☑603-766-3474; www.jumpinjays.com; 150 Congress St; mains $20-26; ⊘5:30-10pm) Fish-fanciers book tables at this sleek contemporary seafooder, which features a wide range of fresh pan-seared fish spiced with delicious sauces. Other briny delights include a raw bar with regional oysters.

Breaking New Grounds   CAFE $
(14 Market St; snacks $2-5; ⊘6:30am-11pm; 🛜) Get your caffeine fix at this cafe smack in the heart of town. Plump muffins, crispy croissants and outdoor tables perfect for people-watching.

Friendly Toast   DINER $
(113 Congress St; mains $7-10; ⊘7am-10pm Sun-Thu, 7am-2am Fri & Sat; 🛜🍴) Whimsical furnishings set the scene for filling omelets, Tex-Mex and vegetarian fare at this retro diner serving breakfast all day.

Portsmouth Brewery   MICROBREWERY $
(www.portsmouthbrewery.com; 56 Market St; light eats $7-12; 🛜) This lively microbrewery serves specialty beers like Smuttynose Portsmouth Lager along with light eats, including the best fish sandwich in town.

❶ Information

Greater Portsmouth Chamber of Commerce
(☑603-436-3988; www.portsmouthchamber. org; 500 Market St; ⊘8:30am-5pm Mon-Fri, lobby 24hr) Provides visitor information.

Monadnock State Park

The 3165ft **Mt Monadnock** (www.nhstate parks.org; NH 124; adult/child $4/2), in the southwestern corner of the state, is the most hiked summit in New England. 'Mountain That Stands Alone' in Algonquian, Monadnock is relatively isolated from other peaks, which means hikers who make the 5-mile round-trip to the summit are rewarded with unspoiled views of three states.

Manchester

A couple of colleges and an art school give this old mill town fresh vitality. New Hampshire's largest city, Manchester became a manufacturing powerhouse in the 19th century by harnessing the ripping Merrimack River. The brick **Amoskeag Mills** (1838), which stretch along the Commercial St riverbanks for more than a mile, now house software companies and other 21st-century backbones of the city's economy.

Head to Elm St near the town green where you'll find the tourist office and the lion's share of eateries and pubs. The **Greater Manchester Chamber of Commerce** (603-666-6600; www.manchester-chamber.org; 889 Elm St; 9am-5pm) has visitor information.

The city's highlight, the **Currier Museum of Art** (603-669-6144; www.currier.org; 201 Myrtle Way; adult/child $10/free, Sat morning free; 11am-5pm Sun, Mon & Wed-Fri, 10am-5pm Sat), showcases works by American artists Georgia O'Keeffe and Andrew Wyeth. It also operates the 1950 **Zimmerman House** (tours $15), the only home in New England designed by famed American architect Frank Lloyd Wright (1867–1959) open to the public.

I-93, US 3 and NH 101 all pass through Manchester. The **Manchester Airport** (MHT; www.flymanchester.com) is served by major US airlines, including discounter Southwest Airlines. **Greyhound** (www.greyhound.com) provides bus services between Manchester and other New England cities.

Concord

History-laden Concord makes a refreshing break. Don't let the fact that it's a state capital throw you – think of it as a laid-back little town that just happens to have a capitol building gracing Main St, the way other communities this size would have a town hall. Everything radiates out from the State House – you'll find several delis and restaurants nearby.

The gold-domed, eagle-topped **State House** (107 N Main St; admission free; 8am-4:30pm Mon-Fri), built in 1819 of New Hampshire granite, houses the oldest legislative chamber in the US. Forget heavy-handed security, this is a remarkably relaxed affair – you can walk right in, check out the intriguing lobby display of battle-tattered Civil War flags, then head up to the 2nd floor to visit the chamber. The **Museum of New Hampshire History** (603-228-6688; www.nhhistory.org; 6 Eagle Sq; adult/child $5.50/3; 9:30am-5pm Mon-Sat, noon-5pm Sun, closed Mon Jan-Jun), opposite the State House, chronicles the history of the Granite State in more depth. **Pierce Manse** (603-225-4555; www.pierce manse.org; 14 Horseshoe Pond Lane; adult/child $7/3; 11am-3pm Tue-Sat mid-Jun–mid-Sep), the home of Franklin Pierce (1804–69), the only

WORTH A TRIP

CANTERBURY SHAKER VILLAGE

A traditional Shaker community from 1792, **Canterbury Shaker Village** (603-783-9511; www.shakers.org; 288 Shaker Rd, Canterbury; adult/child $17/8; 10am-5pm mid-May–Oct) maintains the Shaker heritage as a living-history museum. Interpreters demonstrate the Shakers' daily lives, artisans create Shaker crafts, and walking trails invite pond-side strolls. The greening of America has deep roots here – for more than two centuries the Shakers' abundant gardens have been turning out vegetables, medicinal herbs and bountiful flowers the organic way. If you're ready for a soulful diversion you could easily spend half a day here on the farm, which covers nearly 700 acres. Take a little wholesomeness home with you – there's a store selling Shaker handicrafts, a farm stand and a superb restaurant serving the kind of food grandma used to make using heirloom veggies fresh picked from the garden. The village is 15 miles north of Concord; take I-93 to exit 18 and follow the signs.

One of New England's finest, the 35-mile Kancamagus Hwy (NH 112) is a beauty of a road cutting through the White Mountain National Forest between Conway and Lincoln. Laced with excellent hiking trails, scenic lookouts and swimmable streams, this is as natural as it gets. There's absolutely no development along the entire highway, which reaches its highest point at Kancamagus Pass (2868ft).

You can pick up brochures and hiking maps at the Saco Ranger District Office (☑603-447-5448; 33 Kancamagus Hwy; ◷8am-4:30pm) at the eastern end of the highway near Conway.

Coming from Conway, 6.5 miles west of the Saco ranger station, you'll see Lower Falls on the north side of the road – stop here for the view and a swim. No trip along this highway is complete without taking the 20-minute hike to the breathtaking cascade of Sabbaday Falls; the trail begins at Mile 15 on the south side of the road. The best place to spot moose is along the shores of Lily Pond; stop at the roadside overview at Mile 18. At the Lincoln Woods ranger station, which is near the Mile 29 marker, cross the suspension footbridge over the river and hike 3 miles to Franconia Falls, the finest swimming hole in the entire national forest, complete with a natural rock slide. Parking anywhere along the highway costs $3 per day (honor system) or $5 per week; just fill out an envelope at any of the parking areas.

The White Mountain National Forest is ideal for campers, and you'll find several campgrounds run by the forest service accessible from the Kancamagus Hwy. Most are on a first-come, first-served basis; pick up a list at the Saco ranger station.

US president to hail from New Hampshire, can be toured in summer. The Greater Concord Chamber of Commerce (☑603-224-2508; www.concordnhchamber.com; 40 Commercial St; ◷9am-5pm Mon-Fri, 9am-3pm Sat) maintains a tourist information kiosk on the sidewalk in front of the State House.

Lake Winnipesaukee

A popular summer retreat for families looking for a break from the city, New Hampshire's largest lake stretches 28 miles in length, contains 274 islands and offers abundant opportunities for swimming, boating and fishing.

WEIRS BEACH

This lakeside town dishes up a curious slice of honky-tonk Americana with its celebrated video arcades, mini-golf courses and go-cart tracks. The Lakes Region Chamber of Commerce (☑603-524-5531; www.lakesregionchamber.org; 383 S Main St, Laconia; ◷8:30am-4:30pm Mon-Fri) supplies information on the area.

Mount Washington Cruises (☑603-366-5531; www.cruisenh.com; cruises $27-43) operates scenic lake cruises, the pricier ones with champagne brunch, from Weirs Beach aboard the old-fashioned MS *Mount Washington*. For a unique experience hop aboard the MV *Sophie C*, the oldest floating post

office in the USA, on its two-hour cruise (adult/child $24/12) to deliver mail to the lake islands.

Winnipesaukee Scenic Railroad (☑603-279-5253; www.hoborr.com; adult/child $15/11) offers train rides along the shore of Lake Winnipesaukee.

WOLFEBORO

On the opposite side of Lake Winnipesaukee, and a world away from the ticky-tacky commercialism of Weirs Beach, sits genteel Wolfeboro. Anointing itself 'the oldest summer resort in America,' the town's awash with graceful period buildings, including several that are open to the public. The Wolfeboro Chamber of Commerce (☑603-569-2200; www.wolfeborochamber.com; 32 Central Ave; ◷10am-5pm Mon-Sat, 11am-2pm Sun), in the old train station, has the scoop on everything from boat rentals to lakeside beaches.

Wolfeboro is home to the Great Waters Music Festival (☑603-569-7710; www.greatwaters.org; Brewster Academy, NH 28; ◷Jul & Aug), featuring folk, jazz and blues artists at venues throughout town.

Off NH 28, about 4 miles north of town, is lakeside Wolfeboro Campground (☑603-569-9881; www.wolfeborocampground.com; 61 Haines Hill Rd; campsites $30) with 50 wooded campsites.

The classic stay is the Wolfeboro Inn (☎603-569-3016; www.wolfeboroinn.com; 90 N Main St; r incl breakfast $179-259), the town's principal lodging since 1812. Some of the rooms have balconies overlooking the lake. The inn's cozy pub, Wolfe's Tavern (90 N Main St; mains $10-24; ☺8am-10pm), offers a varied menu ranging from pizza to seafood. The old-school Wolfeboro Diner (5 N Main St; mains $5-10; ☺7am-2pm) hits the mark with juicy cheeseburgers and straightforward breakfast fare at honest prices.

White Mountains

What the Rockies are to Colorado the White Mountains are to New Hampshire. New England's loftiest mountain range is a magnet for adventurers, with boundless opportunities for everything from hiking and kayaking to skiing. Those who prefer to take it in from the comfort of a car seat won't be disappointed either, as scenic drives wind over rugged mountains ripping with waterfalls, sheer rock faces and sharply cut gorges.

You'll find information on the White Mountains at ranger stations throughout the White Mountain National Forest (www. fs.fed.us/r9/white) and chambers of commerce in the towns along the way.

WATERVILLE VALLEY

In the shadow of Mt Tecumseh, Waterville Valley was developed as a resort community during the latter half of the 20th century, when hotels, condos, golf courses and ski trails were all laid out. It's very much a planned community and arguably a bit too groomed but there's plenty to do, including tennis, indoor ice skating, cycling and other family fun. The Waterville Valley Region Chamber of Commerce (☎603-726-3804; www.watervillevalleyregion.com; 12 Vintinner Rd, Campton; ☺9am-5pm), off I-93 exit 28, has all the details.

Like many New England ski mountains, the Waterville Valley ski area (www.water ville.com) is open in the summer for mountain biking and hiking.

MT WASHINGTON VALLEY

Stretching north from the eastern terminus of the Kancamagus Hwy, Mt Washington Valley includes the towns of Conway, North Conway, Intervale, Glen, Jackson and Bartlett. Every conceivable outdoor activity is available. The area's hub and biggest town, North Conway, is also a center for outlet shopping, including some earthy stores like LL Bean.

◉ Sights & Activities

Conway Scenic Railroad RAILROAD
(☎603-356-5251; www.conwayscenic.com; NH 16, North Conway; adult $15-65, child $10-50; ☺daily May-Oct, Sat & Sun Apr & Nov; ⊕) Nostalgia at its finest, this antique steam train operates a variety of excursions from North Conway through Mt Washington Valley and dramatic Crawford Notch. It's a real stunner, especially during the fall foliage season.

Echo Lake State Park PARK
(www.nhstateparks.org; River Rd; adult/child $4/2) Two miles west of North Conway off US 302, this park rests at the foot of a sheer rock wall called White Horse Ledge. Come here for lakeside hiking, swimming and the road up to 700ft-high Cathedral Ledge for panoramic views.

Saco Bound BOATING
(☎603-447-2177; www.sacobound.com; 2561 E Main/US 302, Conway; rental per day $26) If you're up for a water adventure, Saco Bound rents canoes and kayaks and also offers guided tours ranging from placid lake paddles to day-long white-water outings.

Attitash SKI RESORT
(☎603-374-2368; www.attitash.com; US 302, Bartlett) This ski resort 5 miles west of Glen also operates America's longest alpine slide in summer.

Black Mountain Ski Area SKI RESORT
(☎603-383-4490; www.blackmt.com; NH 16B, Jackson) Cross-country skiing mecca with summertime horseback riding.

⨋ Sleeping

North Conway in particular is thick with sleeping options from resort hotels to cozy inns.

TOP CHOICE Wildflowers Inn B&B $$
(☎603-356-7567; www.wildflowersinn.com; 3486 White Mountain Hwy, North Conway; r incl breakfast $99-269; ❀ ☎) Start your day with a three-course gourmet breakfast at this elegant Victorian-style inn. Other pluses: pretty rooms with comfy beds and fireplaces, a living room with a pool table and a huge deck with huge views. The higher-priced rooms are large suites with two-person Jacuzzis.

Cranmore Inn B&B $$
(☎603-356-5502; www.cranmoreinn.com; 80 Kearsarge St, North Conway; r incl breakfast $89-149;

✱🛜📶) With a convenient location, this North Conway landmark has been operating as a country inn since 1863 and good-value, home-style comfort is its key to success.

North Conway Grand Hotel   HOTEL $$
(☑603-356-9300; www.northconwaygrand.com; NH 16, Settlers' Green, North Conway; r $99-229; ✱🛏🐾) If you're looking for all the trappings of a resort hotel, this family-friendly place has commodious rooms with full amenities and extras like a free DVD library and children's programs.

White Mountains Hostel   HOSTEL $
(☑603-447-1001; www.whitemountainshostel.com; 36 Washington St, Conway; dm/r $23/58; 🛜) Perched on the edge of the White Mountain National Forest, off NH 16, this 45-bed hostel in a converted farmhouse is well situated for outdoor adventurers.

Saco River Camping Area   CAMPGROUND $
(☑603-356-3360; www.sacorivercampingarea.com; 1550 NH 16, North Conway; campsites $32; 🛜📶) On the Saco River, with canoe and kayak rentals and a heated pool.

✖ Eating & Drinking

🔝CHOICE Peach's   CAFE $
(www.peachesnorthconway.com; 2506 White Mountain Hwy, North Conway; mains $6-10; ⊙7am-2:30pm) This peachy place, a half-mile south of the chamber of commerce, really captures a small-town feel. Who can resist fruit-smothered waffles, hearty omelets and homemade soups served in somebody's cozy living room?

🖊 Flatbread Company   PIZZERIA $$
(☑603-356-4470; www.flatbreadcompany.com; 2760 White Mountain Hwy, North Conway; pizzas $11-20; ⊙11:30am-10pm) A socially conscious pizzeria, Flatbread uses organic veggies and nitrate-free meats, and dishes up a portion of its profits to local environmental causes. The deliciously crispy pizzas are cooked in front of your eyes in a wood-fired clay oven built into the dining room.

Moat Mountain Smoke House & Brewing Co   PUB $$
(☑603-356-6381; www.moatmountain.com; 3378 White Mountain Hwy; mains $8-22; ⊙11:30am-11pm) Barbecued ribs and juicy burgers are mainstays at this watering hole restaurant, which brews its own ales on site.

Café Noche   MEXICAN $$
(www.cafenoche.net; 147 Main St, Conway; meals $10-15; ⊙11:30am-9pm) Tex-Mex fare topped with real-deal salsas at this festive central Conway spot. The margaritas, in a head-spinning variety of flavors, will rev up the appetite.

ℹ Information
Mt Washington Valley Chamber of Commerce
(☑603-356-5701; www.mtwashingtonvalley.org; 2617 White Mountain Hwy, North Conway; ⊙9am-5pm) Information on the entire region.

NORTH WOODSTOCK & LINCOLN
You'll pass right through the twin towns of Lincoln and North Woodstock on your way between the Kancamagus Hwy and Franconia Notch State Park, so it's a handy place to break for a bite or a bed. The towns straddle the Pemigewasset River at the intersection of NH 112 and US 3. If you're ready for some action, **Loon Mountain** (☑603-745-8111; www.loonmtn.com; Kancamagus Hwy, Lincoln) offers winter skiing and snowboarding, and in summer has mountain-bike trails, climbing walls and New Hampshire's longest gondola ride. Or ratchet the adrenaline up a notch by zipping 2000ft down a hillside while strapped to just a cable with **Alpine Adventures** (☑603-745-9911; www.alpinezipline.com; 41 Main St, Lincoln; zips $89; ⊙9am-4pm) treetop zip line.

🛏 Sleeping
Woodstock Inn   INN $$
(☑603-745-3951; www.woodstockinnnh.com; US 3, North Woodstock; r incl breakfast with shared bath $78-129, with private bath $99-229; ✱🛜) Spread across five historic houses in the heart of North Woodstock, this inn offers a variety of comfortable rooms, many furnished with antiques, some with fireplaces and Jacuzzi baths.

Wilderness Inn   B&B $$
(☑603-745-3890; www.thewildernessinn.com; cnr US 3 & NH 112; r incl breakfast $85-165; ✱🛜) Gather round the fireplace with other guests at this century-old B&B with hardwood floors and country-style decor. Or if you want your own private space, swing for the cottage ($175) with a gas fireplace and oversized Jacuzzi tub. The multicourse breakfasts are marvelous.

✖ Eating
🔝CHOICE Cascade Coffee House   CAFE $
(115 Main St, North Woodstock; mains $4-9; ⊙7am-3pm Mon-Fri, 7am-5pm Sat & Sun; 🛜) This creative place in the center of town serves

up luscious pastries, fresh smoothies and micro-roaster coffees. At lunch, you'll also find crispy panini sandwiches and innovative salads.

Woodstock Inn Station & Brewery PUB $$
(☑603-745-3951; US 3, North Woodstock; mains $9-23; ☉11:30am-10pm) If your family can't settle on what to eat, this brewpub satisfies an amazing range of food cravings with pub grub, steaks, pizza and Mexican fare. There's live entertainment on weekends in summer and frothy microbrewed ales year-round.

❶ Information

Lincoln-Woodstock Chamber of Commerce
(☑603-745-6621; www.lincolnwoodstock.com; Main St/NH 112, Lincoln; ☉9am-5pm Mon-Fri)

FRANCONIA NOTCH STATE PARK

Franconia Notch is the most celebrated mountain pass in New England, a narrow gorge shaped over the eons by a rushing stream slicing through the craggy granite. I-93, in places feeling more like a country road than a highway, runs straight through the state park. The Franconia Notch State Park visitor center (☑603-745-8391; www.franconianotchstatepark.com; I-93, exit 34A), 4 miles north of North Woodstock, can give you details on hikes in the park, which range from short nature walks to day-long treks.

❂ Sights & Activities

Flume Gorge HIKING
(www.flumegorge.com; adult/child $13/10; ☉9am-5pm May-Oct) A 2-mile self-guided walk beginning at the park visitor center takes you right through this awesome cleft in the granite bedrock, which narrows to a mere 12ft, as water rushes at your feet. The rock walls tower 90ft above you. One cool walk on a hot day.

Frost Place HISTORIC SITE
(☑603-823-5510; www.frostplace.org; 158 Ridge Rd, Franconia; adult/child $5/3; ☉1-5pm Sat & Sun late May-Jun, 1-5pm Wed-Mon Jul–mid-Oct) A few miles north of Franconia Notch lies the farm where poet Robert Frost (1874–1963) wrote his most famous poems, 'The Road Not Taken' and 'Stopping by Woods on a Snowy Evening.' The farmhouse retains the simplicity and inspiration of Frost's day.

Cannon Mountain Aerial Tramway TRAM
(☑603-823-8800; www.cannonmt.com; I-93, exit 34B; round-trip adult/child $13/10; ☉9am-5pm late May–mid-Oct; ☝) This tram whisks you to a

4080ft summit, where you're rewarded with breathtaking views of Franconia Notch and the White Mountains.

Basin Trail HIKING
For an enjoyable 20-minute stroll, stop at the Basin pull-off, between exits 34A and 34B, where a half-mile trail runs along a pretty stream to a glacier-carved granite pool.

Echo Lake BEACH
(☑603-823-8800; I-93, exit 34C; adult/child $4/2; ☉10am-5:30pm) A swimming lake just off the highway where you can also rent kayaks and canoes.

🛏 Sleeping

Lafayette Place Campground CAMPGROUND $
(☑603-271-3628; www.reserveamerica.com; campsites $25) Franconia Notch State Park's popular campground is a hub for hikers. The 97 wooded campsites fill up early in summer, so it's best to reserve in advance.

BRETTON WOODS & CRAWFORD NOTCH

Before 1944, Bretton Woods was known primarily as a low-key retreat for wealthy visitors who patronized the majestic Mt Washington Hotel. After President Roosevelt chose the hotel for the historic conference that established a new post-WWII economic order, the town's name took on worldwide recognition. The countryside, with Mt Washington looming above it, is as magnificent today as it was back then. The Twin Mountain-Bretton Woods Chamber of Commerce (☑800-245-8946; www.twinmountain.org; cnr US 302 & US 3, Twin Mountain) has details on the area.

The region's largest ski area, Bretton Woods ski station (☑603-278-3320; www.brettonwoods.com; US 302) offers downhill and cross-country skiing as well as a zipline.

US 302 heads south from Bretton Woods to Crawford Notch (1773ft) through stunning mountain scenery ripe with towering cascades. Crawford Notch State Park (☑603-374-2272; www.nhstateparks.org; adult/child $4/2) maintains an extensive system of hiking trails, including short hikes around a pond and to a waterfall, and a longer trek up Mt Washington.

🛏 Sleeping

Mt Washington Hotel HOTEL $$$
(☑603-278-1000; www.mountwashingtonresort.com; US 302; r $149-600; @🛜🏊) If walls could

talk, the ones here could spin quite a tale. Opened in 1902, this grande dame of New England mountain resorts boasts 2600 acres of grounds, 27 holes of golf, 12 clay tennis courts, a pair of heated pools and an equestrian center.

Dry River Campground CAMPGROUND $
(☎603-271-3628; www.reserveamerica.org; US 302; campsites $25; ⊗late May-Sep) Inside Crawford Notch State Park, this campground has 33 quiet sites and good facilities.

MT WASHINGTON
From Pinkham Notch (2032ft), on NH 16 about 11 miles north of North Conway, a system of hiking trails provides access to the natural beauties of the Presidential Range, including lofty **Mt Washington** (6288ft), the highest mountain east of the Mississippi and north of the Smoky Mountains. Hikers need to be prepared: Mt Washington's weather is notoriously severe and can turn on a dime. Dress warmly – not only does the mountain register New England's coldest temperatures (in summer, the average at the summit is 45°F) but unrelenting winds make it feel colder than the thermometer reading. In fact, Mt Washington holds the record for the USA's strongest wind gust – 231mph!

One of the most popular trails up Mt Washington begins at the AMC's Pinkham Notch Visitor Center and runs 4.2 strenuous miles to the summit, taking four to five hours to reach the top and a bit less on the way down.

If your quads aren't up for a workout, the **Mt Washington Auto Road** (☎603-466-3988; www.mountwashingtonautoroad.com; car & driver $25, extra adult/child $8/6; ⊗mid-May–mid-Oct) offers easier summit access, weather permitting.

While purists walk, and the out-of-shape drive, the quaintest way to reach the summit is to take the **Mt Washington Cog Railway** (☎603-278-5404; www.thecog.com; adult/child $62/39, ⊗May-Oct). Since 1869, coal-fired steam-powered locomotives have followed a 3.5-mile track up a steep mountainside trestle for a jaw-dropping excursion.

The **Pinkham Notch Visitor Center** (☎603-466-2727; www.outdoors.org; NH 16; ⊗6:30am-10pm), run by the Appalachian Mountain Club (AMC), is the area's informational nexus for like-minded adventurers and a good place to buy hiking necessities, including topographic trail maps and the handy *AMC White Mountain Guide.*

The AMC runs the adjacent **Joe Dodge Lodge** (☎603-466-2727; r incl breakfast & dinner $75). **Dolly Copp Campground** (☎603-466-2713; www.campsnh.com; NH 16; campsites $20), a USFS campground 6 miles north of the AMC's Pinkham Notch facilities, has 176 simple campsites.

Hanover

The archetypal New England college town, Hanover has a town green that is bordered on all four sides by the handsome brick edifices of Dartmouth College. Virtually the whole town is given over to this Ivy League school; chartered in 1769, Dartmouth is the nation's ninth-oldest college.

Main St, rolling down from the green, is surrounded by perky pubs, shops and cafes that cater to the collegian crowd.

◉ Sights & Activities

Dartmouth College COLLEGE CAMPUS
Hanover is all about Dartmouth College, so hit the campus. Join a free student-guided **campus walking tour** (☎603-646-2875; www.dartmouth.edu) or just pick up a map at the admissions office and head off on your own. Don't miss the **Baker-Berry Library,** splashed with the grand *Epic of American Civilization,* painted by the outspoken Mexican muralist José Clemente Orozco (1883–1949), who taught at Dartmouth in the 1930s.

FREE **Hood Museum of Art** MUSEUM
(☎603-646-2808; Wheelock St; ⊗10am-5pm Tue-Sat, to 9pm Wed, noon-5pm Sun) The collections here cover a wide swath from Assyrian stone reliefs that date back to 883 BC to contemporary American art by heavyweights Jackson Pollock and Edward Hopper.

🛏 Sleeping & Eating

Chieftain Motor Inn MOTEL $$
(☎603-643-2550; www.chieftaininn.com; 84 Lyme Rd/NH 10; r $119-140; ❋⊛⊠) In a riverfront setting on the north side of town, this rustic inn offers complimentary use of canoes, making it a good spot to combine an outing with a night's sleep.

🍴 **Canoe Club Bistro** CAFE $$
(☎603-643-9660; www.canoeclub.us; 27 S Main St; mains $10-23; ⊗11:30am-11:30pm) This smart cafe does a fine job with grilled food – not

just burgers and steaks, but also tasty treats like duck breast with fig port glaze. There's also live entertainment nightly – anything from acoustic to jazz.

Lou's DINER $
(lousrestaurant.net; 30 S Main St; mains $5-10; ⏰6am-3pm Mon-Fri, 7am-3pm Sat & Sun) A student haunt since 1947, Lou's has good sandwiches and pastries, but everybody comes to this simple diner for the hearty breakfasts served until closing.

🍷 Drinking & Entertainment

Murphy's on the Green PUB
(www.murphysonthegreen.com; 11 S Main St) At this classic Irish pub, students and faculty discuss weighty matters over pints of Irish ale.

Hopkins Center for the Arts PERFORMING ARTS
(☑603-646-2422; www.hop.dartmouth.edu; Lebanon St) The 'Hop' is Dartmouth's refined venue for string quartets, modern dance and plays.

ⓘ Information

Hanover Area Chamber of Commerce (☑603-643-3115; www.hanoverchamber.org; 53 S Main St; ⏰9am-4pm Mon-Fri) Good place to start your visit.

MAINE

Maine is New England's frontier – a land so vast it could swallow the region's five other states with scarcely a gulp. The sea looms large with mile after mile of sandy beaches, craggy sea cliffs and quiet harbors. While time-honored fishing villages and seaside lobster joints are the fame of Maine, inland travel also offers ample reward. Maine's rugged interior is given over to rushing rivers, dense forests and lofty mountains just aching to be explored.

As a traveler in Maine, your choices are as spectacularly varied as the landscape. You can opt to sail serenely along the coast on a graceful schooner or rip through white-water rapids on a river raft, spend the night in an old sea captain's home-turned-B&B, or camp among the moose on a backwoods lake.

History

It's estimated that 20,000 Native Americans from tribes known collectively as Wabanaki ('People of the Dawn') inhabited Maine when the first Europeans arrived. The French and

MAINE FACTS

» **Nickname** Pine Tree State
» **Population** 1.3 million
» **Area** 35,387 sq miles
» **Capital city** Augusta (population 18,600)
» **Other cities** Portland (population 66,200)
» **Sales tax** 5%
» **Birthplace of** poet Henry Wadsworth Longfellow (1807–82)
» **Home of** horror novelist Stephen King
» **Politics** split between Democrats and Republicans
» **Famous for** lobster, moose, blueberries, LL Bean
» **State drink** Maine gave the world Moxie, America's first (1884) and spunkiest soft drink
» **Driving distances** Portland to Acadia National Park 160 miles, Portland to Boston 150 miles

English vied to establish colonies in Maine during the 1600s, but, deterred by the harsh winters, these settlements failed.

In 1652 Massachusetts annexed the territory of Maine to provide a front line of defense against potential attacks during the French and Indian Wars. And indeed Maine at times did become a battlefield between English colonists in New England and French forces in Canada. In the early 19th century, in an attempt to settle sparsely populated Maine, 100-acre homesteads were offered free to settlers willing to farm the land. In 1820 Maine broke from Massachusetts and entered the Union as a state.

In 1851 Maine became the first state to ban the sale of alcoholic beverages, the start of a temperance movement that eventually took hold throughout the United States. It wasn't until 1934 that Prohibition was finally lifted.

ⓘ Information

If you're entering the state on I-95 heading north, stop at the well-stocked visitor information center on the highway.
Maine Bureau of Parks and Land (☑800-332-1501; www.maine.gov/doc/parks) Offers camping in 12 state parks.

Maine Coast

50 km
30 miles

N

CANADA

Nova Scotia

CANADA

ATLANTIC OCEAN

Bay of Fundy

Grand Manan Island

St George

Calais

Border Crossing

Mooshorn National Wildlife Refuge

Eastport

Lubec

Quoddy Head State Park

Jonesport

Machias

Beals

Great Wass Island

Schoodic Peninsula

Downeast Maine

Bar Harbor

Cadillac Mountain (1530ft)

Acadia National Park

Bangor

Ellsworth

Trenton

Blue Hill

Bucksport

Mt Desert Island

Deer Isle

Stonington

Isle au Haut

Acadia National Park

To Baxter State Park (50mi)

Belfast

Lincolnville

Camden Hills State Park

Camden

Rockland

Penobscot Bay

Waldoboro

Damariscotta

Pemaquid Peninsula

Port Clyde

New Harbor

Ferry

Monhegan Island

Skowhegan

Waterville

AUGUSTA

Kennebec R.

Bath

Boothbay Harbor

Ferry

Casco Bay

To Caratunk (7mi);
The Forks (9mi)

Longfellow Mountains

Sugarloaf Mtn (4237ft)

Rangeley

Brunswick

Sabbathday Lake

Freeport

Portland

Cape Elizabeth

Kennebunkport

New Hampshire

Colebrook

Aziscohos Lake

Errol

Grafton Notch State Park

Bethel

Appalachian Trail

Sunday River Ski Resort

White Mountain National Forest

See Vermont & New Hampshire Map (205)

Naples

Sebago Lake

Sebago Lake

Lake Winnipesaukee

Laconia

CONCORD

Rochester

Ogunquit

Kittery

Portsmouth

Maine Turnpike

Maine Office of Tourism (☑888-624-6345; www.visitmaine.com) Will send out a handy magazine on Maine destinations.

Southern Maine Coast

Maine's most touristed quarter, this seaside region lures visitors with its sandy beaches, resort towns and outlet shopping. The best place to stop for the latter is the southernmost town of Kittery, which is chockablock with outlet stores.

OGUNQUIT

Aptly named, Ogunquit means 'Beautiful Place by the Sea' in the native Abenaki tongue, and its 3-mile beach has long been a magnet for summer visitors. Ogunquit Beach, a sandy barrier beach, separates the Ogunquit River from the Atlantic Ocean, offering beachgoers the appealing option to swim in cool ocean surf or in the warmer, calmer cove.

As a New England beach destination, Ogunquit is second only to Provincetown for the number of gay travelers who vacation here. Most of the town lies along Main St (US 1), lined with restaurants, shops and motels. For waterfront dining and boating activities head to Perkins Cove at the south end of town.

Sights & Activities

A highlight is walking the scenic 1.5-mile Marginal Way, the coastal footpath that skirts the 'margin' of the sea from Shore Rd, near the center of town, to Perkins Cove. A sublime stretch of family-friendly coastline, Ogunquit Beach, also called Main Beach by locals, begins right in the town center at the end of Beach St.

Ogunquit Playhouse THEATER
(☑207-646-5511; www.ogunquitplayhouse.org; 10 Main St; 👶) First opened in 1933, presents both showy Broadway musicals and children's theater each summer.

Finestkind Scenic Cruises CRUISE
(☑207-646-5227; www.finestkindcruises.com; Perkins Cove; adult/child from $16/8; 👶) Offers several boat cruises, including cool 50-minute voyages to pull up lobster traps.

Sleeping

TOP CHOICE **Gazebo Inn** B&B $$
(☑207-646-3733; www.gazeboinnogt.com; 572 Main St; r incl breakfast $109-239; ❉🅿🐾) Attentive innkeepers, a hearty breakfast and rustic-chic touches make this a top choice

with returning guests. Occupying a restored farmhouse that's been converted into a 14-room B&B, the rooms have exposed wood beams, gas fireplaces and lots of space.

Ogunquit Beach Inn B&B $$
(☑207-646-1112; www.ogunquitbeachinn.com; 67 School St; r incl breakfast $139-179; ❉🅿) A favorite among Ogunquit's gay visitors, this pleasant B&B in the town center is close to both Main St and the beach. The accommodating hosts supply little extras like complimentary use of beach chairs and a movie library.

Pinederosa Camping CAMPGROUND $
(☑207-646-2492; www.pinederosa.com; 128 North Village Rd, Wells; campsites $30; 🅿) The nearest camping is off US 1, a mile north of Ogunquit's center.

Eating

You'll find Ogunquit's restaurants on the south side of town at Perkins Cove and in the town center along Main St.

Bread & Roses BAKERY $
(www.breadandrosesbakery.com; 246 Main St; snacks $3-9; ⏱7am-7pm; 🅿) The kind of bakery that most small towns only dream about – the raspberry croissants are heavenly, the salads healthy, the panini sandwiches grilled to perfection. It's takeout, but there are cafe tables outside.

Lobster Shack SEAFOOD $$
(110 Perkins Cove Rd; mains $10-25; ⏱11am-8pm) If you want good seafood and aren't particular about the view, this reliable joint serves lobster in all its various incarnations from lobster rolls to lobster in the shell.

Barnacle Billy's SEAFOOD $$$
(☑207-646-5575; www.barnbilly.com; 183 Shore Rd; mains $12-35; ⏱11am-9pm) For lobsters with a view, this landmark restaurant overlooking Perkins Cove is the one. The lobster prices depend on the weight you choose but expect to pay $25 to $30 on average.

Information

Ogunquit Chamber of Commerce (☑207-646-2939; www.ogunquit.org; 36 Main St; ⏱9am-5pm Mon-Fri, 10am-3pm Sat & Sun)

KENNEBUNKPORT

On the Kennebunk River, Kennebunkport fills with tourists in summer who come to stroll the streets, admire the century-old mansions and get their fill of sea views. Be sure to take a drive along Ocean Ave, which runs along the east side of the Kennebunk River and then follows a scenic stretch of the Atlantic that holds some of Kennebunkport's finest estates, including the summer home of former president George Bush Snr.

Three public beaches extend along the west side of the Kennebunk River and are known collectively as **Kennebunk Beach**. The center of town spreads out from Dock Sq, which is along ME 9 (Western Ave) at the east side of the Kennebunk River bridge. The **Kennebunk/Kennebunkport Chamber of Commerce** (☑207-967-0857; www.visit thekennebunks.com; 17 Western Ave; ☺10am-5pm Mon-Fri year-round, 10am-3pm Sat & Sun Jun-Sep) has tourist information.

🛌 Sleeping

Franciscan Guest House GUESTHOUSE **$$**
(☑207-967-4865; www.franciscanguesthouse.com; 26 Beach Ave; r incl breakfast $89-159; ✳@🛜🏊) Serenity awaits at this suitably simple, but perfectly comfortable, 50-room guesthouse on the grounds of St Anthony's Monastery. Enjoy the outdoor saltwater pool and 60 acres of wooded walking trails.

Colony Hotel HOTEL **$$**
(☑207-967-3331; www.thecolonyhotel.com; 140 Ocean Ave; r incl breakfast $129-299; ✳🛜🏊) Built in 1914, this grand dame of a summer resort evokes the splendor of bygone days. The 124 old-fashioned rooms have vintage cabbage-rose wallpaper and authentically creaky floors. Be aware they're anything but sound-proof – upper floor rooms are quietest.

Green Heron Inn INN **$$$**
(☑207-967-3315; www.greenheroninn.com; 126 Ocean Ave; r incl breakfast $190-225; ✳@🛜) In a fine neighborhood, overlooking a picturesque cove, this engaging inn has 10 cozy rooms and is within walking distance of a sandy beach and several restaurants. Breakfast is a multicourse event.

🍴 Eating

🍃 **Bandaloop** BISTRO **$$$**
(☑207-967-4994; www.bandaloop.biz; 2 Dock Sq; mains $17-27; ☺5-9:30pm; 🌱) Local, organic and deliciously innovative, running the gamut from grilled ribeye steak to baked tofu with hemp-seed crust. For the perfect starter order the skillet steamed Casco Bay mussels and a Peak's organic ale.

Hurricane AMERICAN **$$$**
(☑207-967-9111; www.hurricanerestaurant.com; 29 Dock Sq; mains $10-45; ☺11:30am-9:30pm) Right

on the water with good food and a wonderful sense of place. If you're not whizzing through and have time for a leisurely lunch, order the handpicked Maine crabmeat sandwich on sourdough, a glass of wine and enjoy the view.

Clam Shack SEAFOOD **$$**
(2 Western Ave; mains $7-20; ☺11am-9:30pm) By the bridge at the west side of the Kennebunk River, this simple joint is justifiably famous for its fried clams, but the lobster roll overflowing with succulent chunks of lobster is the ultimate prize here.

Portland

The 18th-century poet Henry Wadsworth Longfellow referred to his childhood city as the 'jewel by the sea,' and thanks to a hefty revitalization effort, Portland once again sparkles. Its lively waterfront, burgeoning gallery scene and manageable size add up to great exploring. Foodies, rev up your taste buds: cutting-edge cafes and chef-driven restaurants have turned Portland into the hottest dining scene north of Boston.

Portland sits on a hilly peninsula surrounded on three sides by water: Back Cove, Casco Bay and the Fore River. It's easy to find your way around. Commercial St (US 1A) runs along the waterfront through the Old Port, while the parallel Congress St is the main thoroughfare through downtown.

👁 Sights

Old Port NEIGHBORHOOD
Portland's heart thumps from the Old Port, where salt-scented breezes, brick sidewalks and gas-lamp-lit streets just beg for poking about. This restored waterfront district centers on the handsome 19th-century buildings lining Commercial St and the narrow side streets extending a few blocks inland. Once home to the brawny warehouses and merchant quarters of a bustling port, the focus has shifted from shipping to shopping. What to do here? Eat some wicked fresh seafood, down a local microbrew and peruse the numerous galleries.

Portland Museum of Art MUSEUM
(☑207-775-6148; www.portlandmuseum.org; 7 Congress Sq; adult/child $10/4, 5-9pm Fri free; ☺10am-5pm Sat-Thu, 10am-9pm Fri, closed Mon mid-Oct–May) Works of Maine painters Winslow Homer, Edward Hopper and Andrew Wyeth are showcased here. Maine's finest art

museum also boasts solid contemporary collections; post-Impressionist works by Picasso, Monet and Renoir; and a brilliant collection of Portland art glass. If you enjoy period homes, be sure to stroll through the restored 1801 McLellan House, entered through the museum and included in the ticket price.

Fort Williams Park LIGHTHOUSE
(admission free; ⊙sunrise-sunset) Up for a picnic in an unbeatable setting? Head 4 miles south of central Portland to Cape Elizabeth and this 90-acre park where you'll find Portland Head Light (☎207-799-2661; www.port landheadlight.com; 1000 Shore Rd, Cape Elizabeth; lighthouse museum adult/child $2/1; ⊙10am-4pm Jun-Oct), New England's most photographed lighthouse and the oldest (1791) of Maine's more than 60 lighthouses.

Portland Observatory Museum HISTORIC SITE
(☎207-774-5561; www.portlandlandmarks.org; 138 Congress St; adult/child $8/5; ⊙10am-5pm late May-early Oct) History buffs won't want to miss this hilltop museum, built in 1807 as a maritime signal station to direct ships entering the bustling harbor. Its function was roughly on par with that of an airport traffic control tower today. From the top of this observatory, the last of its kind remaining in the USA, you'll be rewarded with a sweeping view of Casco Bay.

Longfellow House HISTORIC BUILDING
(☎207-879-0427; www.mainehistory.org; 489 Congress St; adult/child $12/3; ⊙10am-5pm Mon-Sat, noon-5pm Sun May-Oct) The childhood home of Henry Wadsworth Longfellow (1807–82) retains its original character, complete with the poet's family furnishings. Admission includes entry to the adjacent Maine Historical Society Museum, which has exhibits on the state's history.

Children's Museum of Maine MUSEUM
(☎207-828-1234; www.childrensmuseumofme. org; 142 Free St; admission $9; ⊙10am-5pm Mon-Sat, noon-5pm Sun, closed Mon Sep-May; ⊕) Folks with children in tow should head to this house of fun, next to the Portland Museum of Art.

Maine Narrow Gauge Railroad Co & Museum RAILROAD
(☎207-828-0814; www.mngrr.org; 58 Fore St; adult/child $10/6; ⊙10am-4pm mid-May–Oct, shorter hr off-season; ⊕) Ride antique steam trains along Casco Bay; journeys depart on the hour.

⚡ Activities

For a whole different angle on Portland and Casco Bay, hop one of the boats offering narrated scenic cruises out of Portland Harbor.

Casco Bay Lines CRUISE
(☎207-774-7871; www.cascobaylines.com; 56 Commercial St; adult $13-24, child $7-11) This outfit tours the Portland coast and Casco Bay islands on a variety of cruises that last from 1¾ to six hours.

Maine Island Kayak Company KAYAKING
(☎207-766-2373; www.maineislandkayak.com; 70 Luther St, Peaks Island; tour $70; ⊙May-Nov) You can have Casco Bay Lines drop you off at Peaks Island and then hook up with this outfit for a half-day kayak tour of the bay.

Portland Schooner Company CRUISE
(☎207-776-2500; www.portlandschooner.com; 56 Commercial St; adult/child $35/10; ⊙May-Oct) Let the wind carry you away on a two-hour sail aboard an elegant century-old wooden schooner.

🛏 Sleeping

In addition to in-town choices, there are several chain hotels south of the city near the airport.

B&B $$
(☎207-774-6900; www.morrillmansion.com; 249 Vaughan St; r incl breakfast $149-239; ❋⊛) The former home of Charles Morrill, who founded B&M baked beans, this B&B has seven handsome guest rooms furnished in a trim, classic style. Little extras like a generous home-cooked breakfast and afternoon cookies add a welcoming touch. Ask about last-minute discounts.

Inn at St John INN $$
(☎207-773-6481; www.innatstjohn.com; 939 Congress St; r incl breakfast $79-169; ❋@⊛) Built in 1897 to accommodate train passengers arriving at the old Union Station, this Victorian hotel retains its period character with style. One caveat: the location opposite the bus station and hospital can be noisy. Light sleepers should request a room away from Congress St.

La Quinta Inn HOTEL $$
(☎207-871-0611; www.laquinta.com; 340 Park St; r incl breakfast $75-149; ❋@⊛≋) Best value among the chains, La Quinta has well-maintained rooms and a convenient location opposite the ballpark of the Portland Sea Dogs, a Boston Red Sox–affiliate team.

Portland Harbor Hotel
HOTEL $$$

(☎207-775-9090; www.portlandharborhotel.com; 468 Fore St; r from $269; ☞) Portland's finest hotel radiates period appeal from the coiffed lobby to the classically fitted rooms with sunny gold walls and pert blue toile bedspreads.

✖ Eating

TOP CHOICE Green Elephant
VEGETARIAN $$

(☎207-347-3111; www.greenelephantmaine.com; 608 Congress St; mains $9-13; ☉11:30am-2:30pm Tue-Sat & 5-9:30pm Tue-Sun; ✐) Even carnivores shouldn't miss the brilliant vegetarian fare at this Zen-chic, Thai-inspired cafe. Start with the crispy spinach wontons, then move on to one of the exotic soy creations like gingered 'duck' with shiitake mushrooms. Save room for the incredible chocolate orange mousse pie.

Hugo's
FUSION $$$

(☎207-774-8538; www.hugos.net; 88 Middle St; mains $24-30; ☉5:30-9pm Tue-Sat) James Beard award-winning chef Rob Evans presides over this temple of molecular gastronomy. Trained at Napa Valley's elite restaurant French Laundry, Evans masterfully fuses California influences with fresh New England ingredients. Pistachio-encrusted lobster anyone?

Great Lost Bear
PUB $$

(www.greatlostbear.com; 540 Forest Ave; mains $8-16; ☉noon-11pm; ☞) Decked out in flea-market kitsch, this boisterous cave of a bar and restaurant is a Portland institution. You'll find dozens of regional brews on tap, big juicy burgers and all the usual pub grub. Skip the bland Tex-Mex offerings.

Standard Baking Co
BAKERY $

(75 Commercial St; snacks $2-4; ☉7am-6pm Mon-Fri, 7am-5pm Sat & Sun) For a sweet breakfast treat, wander around to this Old Port bakery and order a blueberry cream scone and a chocolate croissant. Portland's best organic rustic breads are also made here.

Portland Lobster Co
SEAFOOD $$

(www.portlandlobstercompany.com; 180 Commercial St; mains $10-23; ☉11am-9pm) Lobster stew, lobster rolls and lobster dinners shore up the menu at this harborfront shack. Take your meal to the deck and watch the boats pull up as you get crackin'.

J's Oyster
SEAFOOD $$

(www.jsoyster.com; 5 Portland Pier; mains $6-24; ☉11:30am-11:30pm Mon-Sat, noon-10:30pm Sun) This well-loved joint has the cheapest raw oysters in town. Eat 'em on the deck overlooking the pier. The oyster-averse have sandwiches and seafood mains to choose from.

🍷 Drinking & Entertainment

Gritty McDuff's
BREWPUB

(www.grittys.com; 396 Fore St; ☉11am-1am) This Old Port brewpub has it all: harbor views, high energy, good pub grub and award-winning ales. Order up a robust pint of Black Fly stout and join the crowd.

Big Easy Blues Club
CLUB

(www.bigeasyportland.com; 55 Market St) There's live music nightly at this intimate music club featuring a lineup of rock, jazz and blues bands.

Blackstone's
BAR

(www.blackstones.com; 6 Pine St) Portland's oldest gay bar is still a fine place for a drink.

🛍 Shopping

Go to Exchange and Fore Sts for gallery row.

Edgecomb Potters
FINE ART

(www.edgecombpotters.com; 49 Exchange St) Where contemporary pottery, glass and sculpture rules.

Abacus
CRAFTS

(www.abacusgallery.com; 44 Exchange St) For jewelry, glass and colorful gift items.

Maine Potters Market
POTTERY

(www.mainepottermarket.com; 376 Fore St) A collective of top Maine potters.

ℹ Information

Greater Portland Convention & Visitors Bureau (☎207-772-5800; www.visitportland. com; 14 Ocean Gateway Pier; ☉9am-5pm Mon-Fri year-round, 9am-4pm Sat & Sun Jul & Aug) Pick up a free Portland guide here.

Maine Medical Center (☎207-662-0111; 22 Bramhall St; ☉24hr)

Portland Phoenix (www.thephoenix.com/portland) Free alternative weekly newspaper, covering events and entertainment.

Portland Public Library (www.portlandlibrary. com; 5 Monument Sq; ☉10am-7pm Mon-Thu, 10am-6pm Fri, 10am-5pm Sat; @☞) Free internet access.

Post office (www.usps.com; 400 Congress St; ☉8am-7pm Mon-Fri, 9am-1pm Sat)

Getting There & Around

Portland International Jetport (PWM; www.portlandjetport.org) has nonstop flights to cities in the eastern US.

Greyhound (www.greyhound.com) buses and **Amtrak** (☑800-872-7245; www.amtrak.com) trains connect Portland and Boston; both take about 2½ hours and charge $20 to $24 one way.

The local bus **Metro** (www.gpmetrobus.com; fares $1.50), which runs throughout the city, has its main terminus at Monument Sq, the intersection of Elm and Congress Sts.

Central Maine Coast

Midcoast Maine is where the mountains meet the sea. You'll find craggy peninsulas jutting deep into the Atlantic, alluring seaside villages and endless opportunities for hiking, sailing and kayaking.

FREEPORT

The fame and fortune of Freeport, 16 miles northeast of Portland, began a century ago when Leon Leonwood Bean opened a shop to sell equipment to hunters and fishers heading north into the Maine wilderness. Bean's good value earned him loyal customers, and over the years the LL Bean store (www.llbean.com; Main St; ☑24hr) has expanded to add sportswear to its outdoor gear. Although a hundred other stores have joined the pack, the wildly popular LL Bean is still the epicenter of town.

Ironically, this former stopover for hardy outdoor types is now devoted entirely to city-style shopping, consisting of a mile-long Main St (US 1) lined with outlet stores that sell everything from dinnerware to shoes. **Freeport Merchants Association** (☑207-865-1212; www.freeportusa.com; 23 Depot St; ☑9am-5pm Mon-Fri) provides information.

Although 'shop till you drop' may be the town's motto, there's no need to stay on your feet all night – this town has some two dozen inns.

The Victorian-era **White Cedar Inn** (☑207-865-9099; www.whitecedarinn.com; 178 Main St; r incl breakfast $150-185; ☑) is conveniently located within walking distance of the shops. The former home of Arctic explorer Donald MacMillan, it has seven atmospheric rooms, with brass beds and working fireplaces.

A favorite with shoppers, **Lobster Cooker** (☑207-865-4349; www.lobstercooker.net; 39 Main St; mains $9-22; ☑11am-7pm), just south of LL Bean, has generous fish sandwiches, homemade chowders and steamed lobsters.

For the best atmosphere, head to the casual, harbor-side **Harraseeket Lunch & Lobster Co** (☑207-865-4888; www.harraseeketlunchandlobster.com; 36 Main St, South Freeport; mains $10-25; ☑11am-7:45pm, to 8:45pm Jul & Aug), 3 miles south of Freeport center, for its popular lobster dinners, steamers and fried seafood. Feast at picnic tables within spitting distance of the bay.

BATH

Bath has been renowned for shipbuilding since Colonial times and that remains the raison d'être for the town today. **Bath Iron Works**, one of the largest shipyards in the USA, builds steel frigates and other ships for the US Navy. The substantial **Maine Maritime Museum** (☑207-443-1316; www.mainemaritimemuseum.org; 243 Washington St; adult/child $12/9; ☑9:30am-5pm), south of the ironworks on the Kennebec River, showcases the town's centuries-old maritime history, which included construction of the six-mast schooner *Wyoming*, the largest wooden vessel ever built in the USA.

BOOTHBAY HARBOR

On a fjord-like harbor, this achingly picturesque fishing village with narrow, winding streets is thick with tourists in the summer. Other than eating lobster, the main activity here is hopping on boats.

Cruises (☑207-633-2284; www.balmydayscruises.com; Pier 8) runs one-hour harbor tours (adult/child $15/8) and day trips to Monhegan Island (adult/child $32/18). **Cap'n Fish's Boat Trips** (☑207-633-3244; www.mainewhales.com; Pier 1; ⊡) offers four-hour whale-watching trips (adult/child $38/25). **Tidal Transit** (☑207-633-7140; www.kayakboothbay.com; 18 Granary Way) leads three-hour kayak tours ($45 to $50) up coastal waters where wildlife abounds. The **Boothbay Harbor Region Chamber of Commerce** (☑207-633-2353; www.boothbayharbor.com; 192 Townsend Ave; ☑8am-5pm Mon-Fri) provides visitor information.

Sleeping & Eating

Tugboat Inn   HOTEL **$$**
(☑207-633-4434; www.tugboatinn.com; 80 Commercial St; r incl breakfast $100-240; ❄@☑) Wings of this hotel, literally hanging over the water, are on piers, offering the most amazing water views you'll ever experience without being on a boat. You could cast a fishing pole from your front door. The rooms themselves are straightforward, nothing fancy – this is all about the setting.

Adorning the southernmost tip of the Pemaquid Peninsula, **Pemaquid Point** is one of the most wildly beautiful places in Maine, with its tortured igneous rock formations pounded by treacherous seas. Perched atop the rocks in the 7-acre **Lighthouse Park** (☎207-677-2494; www.bristolparks.org; Pemaquid Point; adult/child $2/free; ☉sunrise-sunset) is the 11,000 candle power Pemaquid Light, built in 1827. A climb to the top will reward you with a fine coastal view. A star of the 61 surviving lighthouses along the Maine coast, you may well be carrying an image of Pemaquid Light in your pocket without knowing it – it's the beauty featured on the back of the Maine state quarter. The keeper's house now serves as the **Fishermen's Museum** (☉9am-5:15pm mid-May–mid-Oct) displaying period photos, old fishing gear and lighthouse paraphernalia. Admission is included in the park fee. Pemaquid Peninsula is 15 miles south of US 1 via ME 130.

Topside Inn B&B **$$**
(☎207-633-5404; www.topsideinn.com; 60 McKown St; r incl breakfast $155-275) Perched on a hilltop, this 19th-century sea captain's house turned B&B has 21 comfortable rooms, hospitable owners and a quiet location. Request an upper-floor room in the main house for a stunning panorama.

Gray Homestead CAMPGROUND **$**
(☎207-633-4612; www.graysoceancamping.com; 21 Homestead Rd, Southport; campsites $37) Fall asleep to the lull of the surf at this oceanside campground 4 miles south of Boothbay Harbor via ME 27 and 238.

Lobster Dock SEAFOOD **$$**
(www.thelobsterdock.com; 49 Atlantic Ave; mains $10-25; ☉11:30am-8:30pm) Boothbay Harbor crawls with lobster eateries. This is one of the best and cheapest. From chunky lobster stew to boiled lobster in the shell, this seaside place perfects everything that can be done with Maine's signature shellfish.

Blue Moon Cafe CAFE **$**
(54 Commercial St; mains $5-8 ☉7:30am-2:30pm) Get a $5 breakfast with a million-dollar view on the waterfront deck of this family-run cafe serving omelets, blueberry pancakes and sandwiches.

MONHEGAN ISLAND

This small granite island with high cliffs and crashing surf, 9 miles off the Maine coast, attracts summer day-trippers, artists and nature-lovers who find inspiration in the dramatic views and agreeable isolation. Tidy and manageable, Monhegan is just 1.5 miles long and a half-mile wide. The online **Monhegan Island Visitor's Guide** (www.monheganwelcome.com) has information and accommodation links. Rooms typically book

out in summer, so plan ahead if you're not just visiting on a day trip.

In addition to its 17 miles of walking trails, there's an 1824 **lighthouse** with a small museum in the former keeper's house and several artists' studios that you can poke your head into.

The 28 rooms in the 1870 **Monhegan House** (☎207-594-7983; www.monheganhouse.com; s/d incl breakfast $87/155; ☎) have shared baths but offer cheery ocean and lighthouse views. The cafe at the Monhegan House sells pizza, sandwiches and ice cream.

Departing from Port Clyde, the **Monhegan Boat Line** (☎207-372-8848; www.monheganboat.com; round-trip adult/child $32/18) runs three trips daily to Monhegan from late May to mid-October, once a day for the rest of the year. The **MV Hardy III** (☎800-278-3346; www.hardyboat.com; round-trip adult/child $32/18; ☉mid-Jun–Sep) departs for Monhegan twice daily from New Harbor, on the east side of the Pemaquid Peninsula. Both boats take approximately one hour and both have early morning departures and late-afternoon returns, perfect for day-tripping.

CAMDEN

With rolling hills as a backdrop and a harbor full of sailboats, Camden is a gem. Home to Maine's justly famed fleet of windjammers, it attracts nautical-minded souls.

You can get a superb view of pretty Camden and its surroundings by taking the 45-minute climb up Mt Battie in **Camden Hills State Park** (☎207-236-3109; 280 Belfast Rd/US 1; adult/child $4.50/1; ☉7am-sunset) at the north side of Camden.

Lobster fanatics (and who isn't!) won't want to miss the **Maine Lobster Festival** (www.mainelobsterfestival.com), New England's ultimate homage to the crusty crustacean,

HOIST THE SAILS

Feel the wind in your hair and history at your side aboard the gracious, multimasted sailing ships known as windjammers. The sailing ships, both historic and replicas, gather in the harbors at Camden and neighboring Rockland to take passengers out on day trips and overnight sails.

Day sails cruise for two hours in Penobscot Bay from June to October for around $35 and you can usually book your place on the day. On the Camden waterfront, look for the 86ft wooden tall-ship **Appledore** (☎207-236-8353; www.appledore2.com) and the two-masted schooner **Olad** (☎207-236-2323; www.maineschooners.com).

Other schooners make two- to six-day cruises, offer memorable wildlife viewing (seals, whales and puffins) and typically include stops at Acadia National Park, small coastal towns and offshore islands for a lobster picnic.

You can get full details on several glorious options in one fell swoop through the **Maine Windjammer Association** (☎800-807-9463; www.sailmainecoast.com), which represents 13 traditional tall ships, several of which have been designated National Historic Landmarks. Among them is the granddaddy of the schooner trade, the *Lewis R French*, America's oldest (1871) windjammer. Rates range from $400 for a two-day cruise to $1000 for a six-day voyage and are a bargain when you consider they include meals and accommodation. Reservations for the overnight sails are a must. Prices are highest in midsummer. June offers long days, uncrowded harbors and lower rates, though the weather can be cool. Late September, when the foliage takes on autumn colors, captures the scenery at its finest.

held near the beginning of August in nearby Rockland.

The Camden-Rockport-Lincolnville Chamber of Commerce (☎207-236-4404; www.camdenme.org; 2 Public Landing; ⊙9am-5pm), near the harbor, provides visitor information on the region.

⌂ Sleeping

Camden Maine Stay Inn   B&B **$$**
(☎207-236-9636; www.camdenmainestay.com; 22 High St; r incl breakfast $135-270; 🖱) This stately 1802 home has lovely gardens, an agreeable period ambience and a fine location, just a couple blocks from restaurants and the waterfront. The friendly owners offer eight nicely appointed rooms and can share a wealth of insights on the area.

Whitehall Inn   INN **$$**
(☎207-236-3391; www.whitehall-inn.com; 52 High St; r incl breakfast $119-219; ⊙May-Oct; 🖱) Camden-raised poet Edna St Vincent Millay got her start reciting poetry to guests at this century-old summer hotel. The 45 rooms have a vintage boarding-house character, some with in-room pedestal sinks and claw-foot tubs.

Captain Swift Inn   B&B **$$**
(☎207-236-8113; www.swiftinn.com; 72 Elm St; r incl breakfast $119-245; ❋🖱) Crème brûlée French toast? That gives you just a taste of what

you're in for at this pampering B&B. Occupying an 1810 Federal-style home, the eight comfortable rooms vary, but think hardwood floors, four-poster beds and a warm fireplace.

Camden Hills State Park   CAMPGROUND **$**
(☎207-624-9950; www.campwithme.com; 280 Belfast Rd/US 1; campsites $27; ⊙mid-May–mid-Oct) This popular park has 107 forested campsites and 30 miles of scenic hiking trails; reservations advised in midsummer.

✗ Eating

Camden Deli   DELI **$**
(www.camdendeli.com; 37 Main St; mains $6-10; ⊙7am-10pm) Family-run Camden Deli has a rooftop deck overlooking Camden Harbor and everything from Maine blueberry pancakes to Italian sub sandwiches piled high with salami and hot peppers. Come between 4pm and 7pm for free appetizers and $3 draft beers.

Cappy's   SEAFOOD **$$**
(www.cappyschowder.com; 1 Main St; mains $8-15; ⊙11am-11pm; 🖱) The star of Cappy's is the award-winning clam chowder, sold by the cup, bowl or pint. You can also order burgers, fresh fish sandwiches and lobster rolls but definitely start off with the rich, creamy chowder. Good bakery items too.

Waterfront   SEAFOOD **$$**

(☑207-236-3747; www.waterfrontcamden.com; 40 Bayview St; mains $10-28; ☺11:30am-9pm) Perched smack on the water, this harborfront eatery specializes in seafood with a twist. Local rock crab and artichoke fondue, blackened haddock, lobster risotto – yowza!

BLUE HILL

Graced with period houses, Blue Hill is a charming coastal town that's home to artists and craftspeople. Start your exploration at Main St and the adjoining Union St, where you'll find several quality galleries selling Blue Hill pottery, sculptures and paintings.

Since 1902 the **Kneisel Hall Chamber Music Festival** (☑207-374-2203; www.kneisel.org; Pleasant St/ME 15; tickets $20-30; ☺Fri-Sun late Jun-Aug) has attracted visitors from far and wide to its summer concert series. The **Blue Hill Peninsula Chamber of Commerce** (☑207-374-3242; www.bluehillpeninsula.org; 107 Main St; ☺10am-4pm Mon-Fri) has visitor information.

Evening hors d'oeuvres by the fireplace and a gourmet breakfast are just two of the perks at **Blue Hill Inn** (☑207-374-2844; www.bluehillinn.com; 40 Union St; r incl breakfast $145-225; ✲◉☺), the town's landmark B&B since 1840.

Every artists' enclave needs a top-notch natural food store, and in these hills it's the **Blue Hill Co-op** (http://bluehill.coop; 4 Ellsworth Rd; mains $5-8; ☺7am-7pm), which also serves good cafe fare including crunchy granola, falafels and organic coffee.

Acadia National Park

The only national park in New England, Acadia encompasses an unspoiled wilderness of undulating coastal mountains, towering sea cliffs, surf-pounded beaches and quiet ponds. The dramatic landscape offers a plethora of activities for both leisurely hikers and adrenaline junkies.

The park was established in 1919 on land that John D Rockefeller donated to the national parks system to save from encroaching lumber interests. Today you can hike and bike along the same carriage roads that Rockefeller once rode his horse and buggy on. The park covers over 62 sq miles, including most of mountainous Mount Desert Island and tracts of land on the Schoodic Peninsula and Isle au Haut, and holds a wide

diversity of wildlife including moose, puffins and bald eagles.

❶ Information

Granite mountains and coastal vistas greet you upon entering **Acadia National Park** (www.nps.gov/acad). The park is open year-round, though Park Loop Rd and most facilities are closed in winter. An admission fee is charged from May 1 to October 31. The fee, which is valid for seven consecutive days, is $20 per vehicle between mid-June and early October, $10 at other times, and $5 on bike or foot.

Start your exploration at **Hulls Cove Visitor Center** (☑207-288-3338; ME 3; ☺8am-4:30pm mid-Apr–mid-Jun & Oct, 8am-6pm mid-Jun–Aug, 8am-5pm Sep), from where the 20-mile **Park Loop Rd** circumnavigates the eastern portion of the park.

◉ Sights & Activities

PARK LOOP ROAD

Park Loop Rd, the main sightseeing jaunt through the park, takes you to several of Acadia's highlights. If you're up for a bracing swim or just want to stroll Acadia's longest beach, stop at **Sand Beach**. About a mile beyond Sand Beach you'll come to **Thunder Hole**, where wild Atlantic waves crash into a deep narrow chasm with such force that it creates a thundering boom, loudest during incoming tides. Look to the south to see **Otter Cliffs**, a favorite rock-climbing spot that rises vertically from the sea. At **Jordan Pond** choose from a 1-mile nature trail loop around the south side of the pond or a 3.5-mile trail that skirts the entire pond perimeter. After you've worked up an appetite, reward yourself with a relaxing afternoon tea on the lawn of Jordan Pond House. Near the end of Park Loop Rd a side road leads up to Cadillac Mountain.

CADILLAC MOUNTAIN

The majestic centerpiece of Acadia National Park is Cadillac Mountain (1530ft), the highest coastal peak in the eastern US, reached by a 3.5-mile spur road off Park Loop Rd. Four **trails** lead to the summit from four directions should you prefer hiking boots to rubber tires. The panoramic 360-degree view of ocean, islands and mountains is a winner any time of the day, but it's truly magical at dawn when hardy souls flock to the top to watch the sun rise over Frenchman Bay.

OTHER ACTIVITIES

Some 125 miles of **hiking trails** crisscross Acadia National Park, from easy half-mile nature walks and level rambles to mountain treks up steep and rocky terrain. A standout is the 3-mile round-trip Ocean Trail, which runs between Sand Beach and Otter Cliffs and takes in the most interesting coastal scenery in the park. Pick up a guide describing all the trails at the visitor center.

The park's 45 miles of carriage roads are the prime attraction for cycling. You can rent quality mountain bikes, replaced new at the start of each season, at Acadia Bike (☎207-288-9605; www.acadiabike.com; 48 Cottage St, Bar Harbor; per day $22; ☺8am-8pm).

Rock climbing on the park's sea cliffs and mountains is breathtaking. Gear up with Acadia Mountain Guides (☎207-288-8186; www.acadiamountainguides.com; 228 Main St, Bar Harbor; half-day outing $75-140; ☺May-Oct); rates include a guide, instruction and equipment.

Scores of ranger-led programs, including nature walks, birding talks and kids' field trips, are available in the park. Check the schedule at the visitor center. For information on kayaking and other activities see Bar Harbor.

🛏 Sleeping & Eating

The park has two campgrounds, both wooded and with running water, showers and barbecue pits. If these are full several commercial campgrounds can be found just outside Acadia National Park.

There are scores of restaurants, inns and hotels in Bar Harbor, just a mile beyond the park.

Blackwoods Campground CAMPGROUND $
(☎877-444-6677; www.recreation.gov; ME 3; campsites $20; ☺year-round) This 279-site campground, 5 miles south of Bar Harbor, accepts advance reservations for all its sites.

Seawall Campground CAMPGROUND $
(www.recreation.gov; ME 102A; campsites $14-20; ☺late May-Sep) This 210-site campground, 4 miles south of Southwest Harbor, operates mostly on a first-come, first-served basis but accepts some advance reservations.

Jordan Pond House AMERICAN $$
(☎207-276-3316; www.thejordanpondhouse.com; afternoon tea $9, mains $10-25; ☺11:30am-9pm mid-May-Oct) For a memorable afternoon break sit on the lawn overlooking the pond and order afternoon tea served with warm popovers and homemade strawberry jam. The park's sole restaurant also has lobster rolls at lunchtime and prime rib dinners.

🛈 Getting There & Around

The convenient Island Explorer (www.exploreacadia.com; rides free; ☺late Jun-early Oct) runs eight shuttle bus routes throughout Acadia National Park and to adjacent Bar Harbor, linking trailheads, campgrounds and accommodations.

Bar Harbor

Set on the doorstep of Acadia National Park, this alluring coastal town once rivaled Newport, RI, as a trendy summer destination for wealthy Americans. Today many of the old mansions have been turned into inviting inns and the town has become a magnet for outdoor enthusiasts. The Bar Harbor Chamber of Commerce (☎207-288-5103; www.barharbormaine.com; 1201 Bar Harbor Rd/ME 3, Trenton; ☺8am-6pm late May-mid-Oct, 8am-5pm Mon-Fri mid-Oct-late May) has a convenient welcome center just before the bridge onto Mount Desert Island.

⊙ Sights & Activities

Abbe Museum MUSEUM
(☎207-288-3519; www.abbemuseum.com; 26 Mount Desert St; adult/child $6/2; ☺10am-5pm) Abbe has fascinating presentations on the Native American tribes that hail from this region and thousands of artifacts ranging from pottery dating back more than a millennium to contemporary woodcarvings and baskets.

Bar Harbor Whale Watch CRUISE
(☎207-288-2386; www.barharborwhales.com; 1 West St; adult $32-62, child $20-32; ☺mid-May-Oct; ⊕) This outfit has a wide variety of sightseeing cruises, including whale-watching and puffin trips. It also offers a ranger-led tour to Baker Island, a 130-acre island that's part of Acadia National Park but reachable only by boat.

Coastal Kayaking Tours KAYAKING
(☎207-288-9605; www.acadiafun.com; 48 Cottage St; 2½/4hr tours $38/48; ☺8am-8pm) Kayaking tours generally go to the islands in Frenchman Bay or the west side of Mount Desert Island, depending on which way the wind's blowing. This outfit offers personalized tours, taking out a maximum of six kayaks at a time.

Downeast Windjammer Cruises CRUISE
(☎207-288-4585; www.downeastwindjammer.com; 27 Main St; adult/child $38/28) For a cruise in style, hop aboard the four-mast

schooner *Margaret Todd,* which sets sail three times a day.

Acadian Nature Cruises   CRUISE

(☑207-288-2386; www.acadiannaturecruises.com; 1 West St; adult/child $27/16; ☉mid-May–Oct) See bald eagles, seals and coastal sights on these narrated two-hour nature cruises.

🛏 Sleeping

There's no shortage of sleeping options in Bar Harbor, ranging from period B&Bs to the usual chain hotels.

Holland Inn   B&B $$

(☑207-288-4804; www.hollandinn.com; 35 Holland Ave; r incl breakfast $95-175; ❄🐾🛜) Nine cheery rooms with frill-free decor, a hearty breakfast and innkeepers who make you feel at home are in store at this inn just a short stroll from the town center and waterfront.

Anne's White Columns Inn   B&B $$

(☑207-288-5357; www.anneswhitecolumns.com; 57 Mount Desert St; r incl breakfast $75-165; ❄) Once a Christian Scientist church, this B&B's name refers to its dramatic columned entrance. Rooms have a quirky Victorian charm, with plenty of florals and bric-a-brac. Get here in time for the afternoon wine and cheese reception.

Aysgarth Station Inn   B&B $$

(☑207-288-9655; 20 Roberts Ave; www.aysgarth.com; r incl breakfast $115-155; ❄) On a quiet side street, this 1895 B&B has six cozy rooms with homey touches. Request the Tan Hill room, which is on the 3rd floor, for a view of Cadillac Mountain.

Acadia Park Inn   MOTEL $$

(☑207-288-5823; www.acadiaparkinn.com; ME 3; r incl breakfast $109-169; ❄🐾🛜) A good base for exploring the national park, this motel has comfy renovated rooms just 2 miles north of the park's main entrance.

Aurora Inn   MOTEL $$

(☑207-288-3771; www.aurorainn.com; 51 Holland Ave; r $89-169; ❄🛜) Retro motor lodge with 10 simple rooms and a convenient in-town location.

🍴 Eating & Drinking

TOP CHOICE Cafe This Way   AMERICAN $$

(☑207-288-4483; www.cafethisway.com; 14½ Mount Desert St; mains breakfast $6-9, dinner $15-24; ☉7-11:30am Mon-Sat, 8am-1pm Sun, 5:30-9pm nightly; 🐾) *The* place in Bar Harbor for breakfast. Vegans will love the scrambled tofu

chock-full of veggies, old-schoolers the eggs Benedict with smoked salmon. Solid seafood menu at dinner.

🌿 McKays   AMERICAN $$

(☑207-288-2002; www.mckayspublichouse.com; 231 Main St; mains $10-20; ☉4:30-9:30pm Tue-Sun) One of Maine's buy-local and organic-when-possible restaurants, this pub-style eatery dishes up Maine crab cakes, farm-raised chicken and good ol' beer-battered fish and chips.

Trenton Bridge Lobster Pound   SEAFOOD $$

(ME 3, Ellsworth; lobsters $10-15; ☉10:30am-8pm Mon-Sat) Sit at a picnic table and crack open a boiled lobster at this traditional lobster pound bordering the causeway that connects Mount Desert Island to mainland Maine.

🌿 Finback Alehouse   BISTRO $$

(☑207-288-0233; www.finbackalehouseme.com; 30 Cottage St; mains $10-20; ☉11am-1am) Creative Maine-centric fare featuring locally caught seafood and juicy grass-fed sirloin burgers. Live music on weekends.

2 Cats   CAFE $$

(☑207-288-2808; www.2catsbarharbor.com; 130 Cottage St; mains $8-17; ☉7am-1pm; 🐾) The perfect place for scones and tea on drizzly day. Awesome lobster omelets too

🌿 Havana   LATIN $$$

(☑207-288-2822; www.havanamaine.com; 318 Main St; mains $19-29; ☉5-10pm) Maine goes Latin at this elegant dinner restaurant presenting seafood with a Cuban twist. Award-winning wine list.

Downeast Maine

The 900-plus miles of coastline running northeast from Bar Harbor are sparsely populated, slower-paced and foggier than southern and western Maine. Highlights include the **Schoodic Peninsula**, whose tip is a noncontiguous part of Acadia National Park; the lobster fishing villages of **Jonesport** and **Beals**; and **Great Wass Island**, a nature preserve with walking paths and good bird-watching, including the chance to see puffins.

Machias, with a branch of the University of Maine, is the center of commerce along this stretch of coast. **Lubec** is about as far east as you can go and still be in the USA;

like to watch the sun rise at nearby ...dy Head State Park so they can say ...ey were the first in the country to catch the sun's rays.

Calais (*ka*-lus), at the northern end of US 1, is a twin town to St Stephen in New Brunswick, Canada. Southwest of Calais is the **Moosehorn National Wildlife Refuge** (moosehorn.fws.gov; US 1, Baring; admission free; ☺sunrise-sunset), which has hiking trails and offers opportunities to spot bald eagles, America's national bird.

Interior Maine

Sparsely populated northern and western Maine is rugged outdoor country. River rafting, hiking trails up Maine's highest mountain and the ski town of Bethel make the region a magnet for adventurers.

AUGUSTA

In 1827 Augusta became Maine's capital, but it's small and, truth be told, not terribly interesting. The **Kennebec Valley Chamber of Commerce** (☏207-623-4559; www.augustamaine.com; 21 University Dr; ☺8:30am-5pm Mon-Fri) provides information on Augusta. If you're passing through, take a gander at the granite **State House** (1829), then stop at the adjacent (☏207-287-2301; www.mainestatemuseum.org; State House Complex, State St; adult/child $2/1; ☺9am-5pm Tue-Fri, 10am-4pm Sat; ⌨), a treasure trove of fascinating exhibits tracing the state's natural and cultural history.

BANGOR

A boomtown during Maine's 19th-century lumbering prosperity, Bangor was destroyed by a sweeping fire in 1911. Today it's a modern, workaday town, perhaps most famous as the hometown of horror novelist Stephen King (look for his mansion – complete with bat-and-spider-web gate – among the grand houses along West Broadway). Can't miss the **Bangor Region Chamber of Commerce** (☏207-947-0307; www.bangorregion.com; 519 Main St; ☺9am-5pm Mon-Fri) in the shadow of a 31-foot-tall (yikes!) Paul Bunyan statue.

SABBATHDAY LAKE

The nation's only active Shaker community is at Sabbathday Lake, 25 miles north of Portland. Founded in the early 18th century, a handful of devotees keep the Shaker tradition of simple living, hard work and fine artistry alive. You can tour several of their buildings on a visit to the **Shaker Museum** (☏207-926-4597; www.shaker.lib.me.us; adult/child $6.50/2; ☺10am-4:30pm Mon-Sat late May–mid-Oct). To get there, take exit 63 off the Maine Turnpike and continue north for 8 miles on ME 26.

BETHEL

The rural community of Bethel, nestled in the rolling Maine woods 12 miles east of New Hampshire on ME 26, offers an engaging combination of mountain scenery, outdoor escapades and good-value accommodations. **Bethel Area Chamber of Commerce** (☏207-824-2282; www.bethelmaine.com; 8 Station Pl; ☺9am-5pm Mon-Fri) provides information for visitors.

🏃 Activities

Bethel Outdoor Adventure   KAYAKING
(☏207-824-4224; www.betheloutdooradventure.com; 121 Mayville Rd/US 2; per day kayak/canoe $45/65; ☺8am-6pm) Right beside the banks of the Androscoggin River, this outfitter rents canoes and kayaks; rates include a shuttle upriver allowing you to paddle back at your own pace. It also rents bicycles, can set you up for fly-fishing and offers on-site camping.

Grafton Notch State Park   HIKING
(☏207-824-2912; ME 26) If you're ready for a hike, head to this park north of Bethel for pretty mountain scenery, waterfalls and lots of trails of varying lengths.

Sunday River Ski Resort   SKIING
(☏800-543-2754; www.sundayriver.com; ME 26; ⌨) Located 6 miles north of Bethel, Sunday River is one of the best family-oriented ski centers in the region, with eight interconnected mountain peaks and 120 trails.

🛏 Sleeping & Eating

Chapman Inn   B&B $
(☏207-824-2657; www.chapmaninn.com; 2 Church St; incl breakfast dm $35, r $89-129; ❀@⊛) A great place to share notes with fellow travelers, this friendly, central 1865 B&B has 10 country-style rooms as well as hostel-style dorm beds. A gourmet breakfast, billiards, two saunas and free bicycles add to the fun.

Sudbury Inn & Suds Pub   INN $$
(☏207-824-2174; www.sudburyinn.com; 151 Main St; r incl breakfast $99-159; ❀) The choice place to stay in downtown Bethel, this historic inn has 17 rooms, a pub with 29 beers on tap, pizza and live weekend entertainment. It

also has an excellent dinner restaurant serving Maine-centric fare (mains $18 to $26).

White Mountain
National Forest CAMPGROUND $
(☑877-444-6777; www.recreation.gov; campsites $18) The Maine portion of this national forest has several basic campgrounds near Bethel.

CARATUNK & THE FORKS

For white-water rafting at its best, head to the Kennebec River, below the Harris Dam, where the water shoots through a dramatic 12-mile gorge. With rapid names like White-washer and Magic Falls, you know you're in for an adrenaline rush.

The adjoining villages of Caratunk and The Forks, on US 201 south of Jackman, are at the center of the Kennebec River rafting operations. The options range from rolling rapids and heart-stopping drops to calmer waters where children as young as seven can join in. Rates range from $75 to $130 per person for a day-long outing. Multiday packages, with camping or cabin accommodations, can also be arranged.

Reliable operators include the following:

Crab Apple Whitewater RAFTING
(☑800-553-7238; www.crabapplewhitewater.com)

Three Rivers Whitewater RAFTING
(☑877-846-7238; www.threeriverswhitewater.com)

Northern Outdoors RAFTING
(☑800-765-7238; www.northernoutdoors.com)

BAXTER STATE PARK

Set in the remote forests of northern Maine, Baxter State Park (☑207-723-5140; www.baxterstateparkauthority.com; per car $14) centers on Mt Katahdin (5267ft), Maine's tallest mountain and the northern terminus of the 2175-mile Appalachian Trail (www.nps.gov/appa). This vast 209,500-acre park is maintained in a wilderness state – no electricity and no running water (bring your own or plan on purifying stream water) – and there's a good chance you'll see moose, deer and black bear. Baxter has extensive hiking trails, several leading to the top of Mt Katahdin, which can be hiked round-trip in a day as long as you're in good shape and get an early start.

Baxter's 10 campgrounds contain 1200 campsites ($30 per day) but they do fill up, so it's best to book in advance.

At Millinocket, south of Baxter State Park, there are motels, campgrounds, restaurants and outfitters that specialize in white-water rafting and kayaking on the Penobscot River. Get information from the Katahdin Area Chamber of Commerce (☑207-723-4443; www.katahdinmaine.com; 1029 Central St, Millinocket).

Washington, DC & the Capital Region

Best Places to Eat

» Minibar at Café Atlantico (p256)

» Blue Hill Tavern (p270)

» Robert Morris Inn (p276)

» Fat Canary (p293)

» Local (p300)

Best Places to Stay

» Hay-Adams (p253)

» Bellmoor Inn & Spa (p281)

» Colonial Williamsburg Historic Lodging (p292)

» Martha Washington Inn (p306)

» Greenbrier (p311)

Why Go?

No matter your politics, it's hard not to fall for the nation's capital. Iconic monuments, vast (and free) museums and venerable restaurants serving cuisine from around the globe: this is just the beginning of the great DC experience. There's much to discover: leafy cobblestoned neighborhoods, sprawling markets, heady multicultural nightspots and verdant parks – not to mention the corridors of power where visionaries and demagogues still roam.

Beyond the Beltway, the diverse landscapes of Maryland, Virginia, West Virginia and Delaware offer potent enticement to travel beyond the marble city. Craggy mountains, rushing rivers, vast nature reserves (including islands where wild horses run), sparkling beaches, historic villages and the magnificent Chesapeake Bay form the backdrop to memorable adventures: sailing, hiking, rafting, camping or simply sitting on a pretty stretch of shoreline, planning the next seafood feast. It's a place where traditions run deep – from the nation's birthplace to Virginia's still-thriving bluegrass scene.

When to Go
Washington, DC

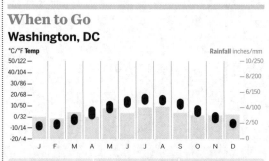

Mar-Apr Cherry blossoms bring crowds to the city in bloom during DC's most popular festival.

Jun-Aug Beaches and resorts heave; prices high and accommodations scarce.

Sep-Oct Fewer crowds and lower prices, but pleasant temperatures and fiery fall scenery.

Transportation

The region is served by three major airports: Washington Dulles International Airport (IAD), Ronald Reagan Washington National Airport (DCA) and Baltimore/Washington International Thurgood Marshall Airport (BWI). Norfolk International Airport (ORF) and Richmond International Airport (RIC) are smaller regional hubs.

Traveling by train is possible in some areas, with service provided by Amtrak (www.amtrak.com). Key towns connected by rail from DC include Baltimore, MD; Wilmington, DE; Harpers Ferry, WV; and in VA: Manassas, Fredericksburg, Richmond, Williamsburg, Newport News and Charlottesville.

TIPS ON VISITING WASHINGTON, DC

DC has a lot of great museums, but there's no way to see them all – even if you spend two weeks in the capital. Some sights – like the Washington Monument, US Holocaust Memorial Museum and Ford's Theatre – have limited admittance; if they're high on your list, go early to ensure you get a spot.

Aside from the Museum of the American Indian, which has a great restaurant, dining is limited along the Mall. One strategy: hit Eastern Market first to assemble a picnic for later in the day (on the Mall or around the Tidal Basin).

If possible, leave the car at home. The Metro is excellent, and driving in the city can get pricey – with overnight lots charging upward of $25 a night.

Best National Parks

» The New River Gorge National River (p310) is utterly Eden-like and home to white-tailed deer and black bears. It also has world-class white-water rafting.

» Shenandoah National Park (p301) provides spectacular scenery along the Blue Ridge Mountains, with great hiking and camping, including along the Appalachian Trail.

» Assateague Island National Seashore (p277) and Chincoteague (p298) are beautiful coastal environments with great blue herons, ospreys, blue crabs and wild horses.

» George Washington and Jefferson national forests (p302) protect more than 1500 sq miles of forests and alpine scenery bordering the Shenandoah Valley.

» Virginia's famous battlefields are also part of the park system. Good places to reconnect with America's darkest hours are Antietam (p278) and Manassas (p287).

DON'T MISS

With Chesapeake Bay at its doorstep, this region is pure heaven for seafood-lovers. The Maine Avenue Fish Market (p256) in DC is legendary. In Baltimore, Annapolis and all along Maryland's Eastern Shore, you'll also find top-notch seafood.

Fast Facts

» Population: 622,000 (Baltimore), 602,000 (Washington, DC), 440,000 (Virginia Beach)

» Distances from DC: Baltimore (40 miles), Williamsburg (152 miles), Abingdon (362 miles)

» Time Zone: Eastern

» States covered in this chapter: Washington, DC, Maryland, Delaware, Virginia, West Virginia

Did You Know?

» Thomas Jefferson was one of many Virginians to make wine in the state in the past 400 years. Now, Virginia has over 192 wineries and earns high marks at international awards shows.

Resources

» Washington (www.washington.org) lists upcoming events and loads of DC details.

» The Crooked Road (www.thecrookedroad.org) is the gateway to Virginia's heritage music trail.

» Virginia Wine (www.virginiawine.org) is essential for planning a route through wine country.

Washington, DC & the Capital Region Highlights

① Visit Washington's **Smithsonian Institution museums** (p244), then watch the sunset over **Lincoln Memorial** (p247).

② Trace America's roots at the living-history museum of **Colonial Williamsburg** (p291).

③ Explore the region's nautical past with a pub crawl through the cobblestoned port-town neighborhood of **Fells Point** (p268), Baltimore.

④ Take a Sunday drive along **Skyline Drive** (p301), followed by hiking and camping under the stars in **Shenandoah National Park** (p301).

5 Marvel at Thomas Jefferson's masterpieces of **Monticello** (p298) and the **University of Virginia** (p299) in historic Charlottesville.

6 Stroll the boardwalk in the family- and gay-friendly resort of **Rehoboth Beach** (p280).

7 Tackle the rapids of **New River Gorge National River** (p310) in Fayetteville.

8 Feel the beat of the clog dancers at a jamboree in **Floyd, VA** (p306).

History

Native Americans populated this region long before European settlers arrived. Many of the area's geographic landmarks are still known by their Indian names, such as Chesapeake, Shenandoah, Appalachian and Potomac. In 1607 a group of 108 English colonists established the first permanent European settlement in the New World: Jamestown. During the early years, colonists battled harsh winters, starvation, disease and occasionally hostile Native Americans.

Jamestown survived, and the Royal Colony of Virginia came into being in 1624. Ten years later, fleeing the English Civil War, Lord Baltimore established the Catholic colony of Maryland at St Mary's City, where a Spanish-Jewish doctor treated a town council that included a black Portuguese sailor and Margaret Brent, the first woman to vote in North American politics. Delaware was settled as a Dutch whaling colony in 1631, practically wiped out by Native Americans, and later resettled by the British. Celts displaced from Britain filtered into the Appalachians, where they created a fiercely independent culture that persists today. Border disputes between Maryland, Delaware and Pennsylvania led to the creation of the Mason–Dixon line, which eventually separated the industrial North from the agrarian, slaveholding South.

The fighting part of the Revolutionary War finished here with the British surrender at Yorktown in 1781. Then, to diffuse regional tension, central, swampy Washington, District of Columbia (DC), was made the new nation's capital. But divisions of class, race and economy were strong, and this area in particular split along its seams during the Civil War: Virginia seceded from the Union while its impoverished western farmers, long resentful of genteel plantation owners, seceded from Virginia. Maryland stayed in the Union but her white slave-owners rioted against Northern troops, while thousands of black Marylanders joined the Union Army.

Local Culture

The North–South tension long defined this area, but the region has also jerked between the aristocratic pretensions of upper-class Virginia, miners and watermen, immigrant boroughs and the ever-changing rulers of Washington, DC. Since the Civil War, local economies have made the shift from agriculture and manufacturing to high technology and servicing and staffing the federal government.

Many blacks settled this border region, either as slaves or escapees running for Northern freedom. Today African Americans still form the visible underclass of major cities, but in the rough arena of the disadvantaged they compete with Latino immigrants, mainly from Central America. At the other end of the spectrum, ivory towers – in the form of world-class universities and research centers such as the National Institute of Health – attract intelligentsia from around the world. The local high schools are often packed with the children of scientists and consultants staffing some of the world's most prestigious think tanks.

All of this has spawned a culture that is, in turns, as sophisticated as a journalists' book club, as linked to the land as bluegrass festivals in Virginia and as hooked into the main vein of urban America as Tupac Shakur, go-go, Baltimore Club and DC Hardcore. And, of course, there's always politics, a subject continually simmering under the surface here.

WASHINGTON, DC

No stranger to the world's gaze, Washington, DC, is a proud and complicated city (politics makes it so) of grand boulevards, iconic monuments and idyllic vistas over the Potomac. Its museums and historic sites bear tribute to both the beauty and the horror of years past, and on even a short visit you can delve into the world of Americana – from moving artworks by Native American painters to memorable moonwalks from the likes of both Neil Armstrong and Michael Jackson.

Of course, DC is much more than mere museum piece or marble backdrop to nightly news reports. There are tree-lined neighborhoods and a vibrant theater scene, with ethnically diverse restaurants and a dynamism percolating just beneath the surface. The city has a growing number of markets, historic cobblestoned streets and a rich African American heritage that makes up nearly 50% of the population.

More than just a city of politicos, DC is home to folks who've passed homes through the family over generations, and new immigrants from El Salvador. Artists and creative types are drawn to Washington's undeniable intellectual energy, laboring alongside more

WASHINGTON, DC FACTS

» **Nicknames** DC, Chocolate City

» **Population** 602,000

» **Area** 68.3 sq miles

» **Capital city** Exactly!

» **Sales tax** 5.75%

» **Birthplace of** Duke Ellington (1899–1974), Marvin Gaye (1939–84), Dave Chappelle (b 1973)

» **Home of** The Redskins, cherry blossoms, all three branches of American government

» **Politics** Overwhelmingly democrat

» **Famous for** National symbols, crime, partying interns, struggle for Congressional recognition

» **Unofficial motto and license plate slogan** Taxation Without Representation

» **Driving distances** Washington, DC, to Baltimore 40 miles, Washington, DC, to Virginia Beach 210 miles

over-achieving and talented types than any city of this size deserves.

History

Like a lot of American history, the District of Columbia (DC) story is one of compromise. In this case, the balance was struck between Northern and Southern politicians who wanted to plant a federal city between their power bases. As potential capitals such as Boston, Philadelphia and Baltimore were rejected as too urban-industrial by Southern plantation owners, it was decided a new city would be carved at the 13 colonies' midway point, along the banks of the Potomac River. Maryland and Virginia donated the land (which Virginia took back in the 19th century).

DC was originally run by Congress, was torched by the British during the War of 1812, and lost the south-bank slave port of Alexandria to Virginia in 1846 (when abolition talk was buzzing in the capital). Over the years, DC evolved along diverging tracks; as a marbled temple to federal government and residential city for federal employees on the one hand, and an urban ghetto for northbound African Americans and overseas immigrants on the other.

The city finally got its own mayor in 1973 (Walter Washington, among the first African American mayors of a major American city). Ever under-funded, today DC residents are taxed like other American citizens, yet lack a voting seat in Congress. The educated upper class is leagues away from the neglected destitute; almost half the population has a university degree, yet a third are functionally illiterate.

With the election of Barack Obama in 2008, Washington, DC, has gained a bit of cool cachet – New Yorkers are coming here now, instead of the other way around! President Obama's habit of playing pickup basketball and patronizing local restaurants makes him the rarest of breeds: a president who doesn't just live in Washington, but is also a Washingtonian.

☉ Sights

The capital was designed by two planners to be perfectly navigable. Unfortunately, their urban visions have mashed up against each other. Pierre L'Enfant's diagonal state-named streets share space with Andrew Ellicott's grid (remember: letters go east–west, numbers north–south). On top of that the city is divided into four quadrants with identical addresses in different divisions – F and 14th NW puts you near the White House, while F and 14th NE puts you near Rosedale Playground.

The majority of sites lie in the Northwest (NW) quadrant, while the most run-down neighborhoods tend to be in the Southeast (SE). Keep your urban wits about you at night, and be prepared for crowds during events such as the Cherry Blossom Festival. The Potomac River is to your south and west; Maryland lies to the north and east; and the Beltway, the capital ring road, encircles the entire package.

NATIONAL MALL

Marble buildings that resemble Greek temples, Abe Lincoln and a reflecting pool, memorials commemorating tragic conflicts of the past – the Mall is all this and more. It is America's great public space, where citizens come to protest their government, go for scenic runs, visit museums and commune with America's most revered icons. The 1.9-mile-long lawn is anchored at one end by the Lincoln Memorial, at the other by Capitol Hill, intersected by the reflecting pool and WWII memorial, and centered by the Washington Monument.

Perhaps no other symbol has housed the national ideal of massed voice affecting radical change so much – from Martin Luther King's 1963 'I Have a Dream' speech to antiglobalization protests in the 1990s. But hundreds of other rallies occur here every year; the Mall, framed by great monuments and museums and shot through with tourists, dog-walkers and idealists, acts as loudspeaker for any cause.

Smithsonian Institution Museums

Massive in size and ambition, the 19 **Smithsonian museums** (☎202-633-1000; www.si.edu), galleries and zoo – all admission free – comprise the world's largest museum and research complex. You could spend weeks wandering endless corridors taking in the great treasures, artifacts and ephemera from America and beyond. Massive dinosaur skeletons, lunar modules and artworks from every corner of the globe are all part of the Smithsonian largesse. Thanks go to the curious Englishman James Smithson, who never visited the USA but willed the fledgling nation $500,000 to found an 'establishment for the increase and diffusion of knowledge' in 1826.

The Smithsonian's latest work in progress is the $500-million **National Museum of African American History and Culture** (www.nmaahc.si.edu; Constitution Ave & 14th St NW), scheduled to open in 2015. Until then, you can peruse its temporary galleries on the 2nd floor of the National Museum of American History.

All museums are open daily (except Christmas Day) 10am to 5:30pm unless noted. Some have extended hours in summer. Be prepared for lines and bag checks.

FREE National Air & Space Museum   MUSEUM
(cnr 6th St & Independence Ave SW) The Air & Space Museum is the most popular Smithsonian museum; everyone flocks to see the Wright brothers' flyer, Chuck Yeager's *Bell X-1*, Charles Lindbergh's *Spirit of St Louis* and the *Apollo 11* command module. An IMAX theater, planetarium and ride simulator are all here (adult/child $9/7.50 each). More avionic pieces reside in Virginia at the Steven F Udvar-Hazy Center (p286), an annex to hold this museum's leftovers.

FREE National Museum of Natural History   MUSEUM
(cnr 10th St & Constitution Ave SW) A favorite of the kids, the Museum of Natural History showcases dinosaur skeletons, an archaeology/anthropology collection, wonders from the ocean, and unusual gems and minerals, including the 45-carat Hope Diamond.

FREE National Museum of American History   MUSEUM
(cnr Constitution Ave & 14th St NW) The Museum of American History is accented with the daily bric-a-brac of the American experience – synagogue shawls, protest signs and cotton gins – plus an enormous display of the original Star-Spangled Banner and icons such as Dorothy's slippers and Kermit the Frog.

FREE National Museum of the
American Indian   MUSEUM
(cnr 4th St & Independence Ave SW) The Museum
of the American Indian provides a fine introduction to the indigenous people of the
Americas, with an array of costumes, video
and audio recordings, and cultural artifacts.
Don't miss the regionally specialized menu
of Native-inspired dishes at Café Mitsitam
on the ground floor.

FREE Hirshhorn Museum &
Sculpture Garden   MUSEUM
(cnr 7th St & Independence Ave SW; ⊙museum
10am-5:30pm, garden 7:30am-dusk) The dough-
nut-shaped Hirshhorn Museum & Sculpture
Garden houses a huge collection of modern sculpture, rotated regularly. It includes
works by Rodin, Henry Moore and Ron
Mueck, as well as paintings by O'Keeffe,
Warhol, Man Ray and de Kooning.

FREE National Museum of
African Art   MUSEUM
(950 Independence Ave SW) The National Museum of African Art showcases masks, textiles
and ceramics from the sub-Sahara, as well as
ancient and contemporary art from all over
the continent.

FREE Arthur M. Sackler Gallery   GALLERY
(1050 Independence Ave SW) Poring over ancient manuscripts and Japanese silk screens
is a peaceful way to spend an afternoon at
this quiet gallery and the adjoining Freer

Gallery of Art (cnr Jefferson Dr & 12th St SW).
Together they comprise the National Museum of Asian Art. The Freer, rather incongru-
ously, also houses more than 1300 works by
the American painter James Whistler.

Smithsonian Castle   VISITOR CENTER
(1000 Jefferson Dr SW; ⊙8:30am-5pm) The red-
turreted Smithsonian Castle is the visitor
center for all museums, but is not that interesting in and of itself.

Other Museums & Monuments

FREE National Gallery of Art   MUSEUM
(www.nga.gov; Constitution Ave NE, btwn 3rd & 4th
Sts NW; ⊙10am-5pm Mon-Sat, 11am-6pm Sun)
Set in two massive buildings, the National
Gallery of Art houses a staggering art collection (over 100,000 objects), spanning the
Middle Ages to the present. The neoclassical
west wing houses European art through the
1800s, with an excellent range of Italian Renaissance works (including the continent's
only da Vinci); the geometric east wing,
designed by IM Pei, showcases modern art,
with works by Picasso, Matisse, Pollock and
a massive Calder mobile over the entrance
lobby. An underground passage connects
the two buildings.

FREE US Holocaust
Memorial Museum   MUSEUM
(www.ushmm.org; 100 Raoul Wallenberg Pl;
⊙10am-5:20pm) For a deep understanding
of the Holocaust – its victims, perpetrators
and bystanders – this harrowing museum

THE CAPITAL REGION IN...

One Week

Follow a version of the two-day DC itinerary and spend a day exploring underrated **Balti-more** or historic **Annapolis** before heading to Maryland's gorgeous **Eastern Shore** and the **Delaware beaches**. Head south to cross over the Chesapeake Bay bridge-tunnel and time-warp through Virginia's history: visit the nation's birthplace at **Jamestown** and take a wander through the 18th century at **Williamsburg**, followed by the nation's post–Civil War reconciliation at **Appomattox Court House**. Swing north through **Richmond**, where students, Dixie aristocracy and African American neighborhoods combine to form a fascinating whole, before rolling back into DC.

Two Weeks

Head to **Charlottesville** to experience Virginia's aristocratic soul (and good dining and B&B scene), then drive down her mountainous backbone through **Staunton**, **Lexington** and **Roanoke**. Follow the **Crooked Road** on a weekend to hear some of the nation's best bluegrass. Truck through West Virginia, stopping to hike, mountain bike or ski in the **Monongahela National Forest**, then go rafting in **New River Gorge** before returning to Washington via the hallowed battlefields of **Antietam**.

Two Days

Start your DC adventure at the Mall's much-loved **Air & Space Museum** and **National Museum of Natural History**. Around lunchtime visit the **National Museum of the American Indian**, for aboriginal lore and a great meal. Wander down the **Mall** to the **Lincoln Memorial** and **Vietnam Veterans Memorial**. Before exhaustion creeps in, go to **U Street** for dining and drinks.

Next day, head to the **US Holocaust Memorial Museum**, **Arthur M Sackler Gallery** and **Freer Gallery of Art**. Catch the illuminated **White House** and the new **Martin Luther King Jr National Memorial** at night. For dinner, browse the restaurant-lined **Penn Quarter**.

Four Days

On day three, go to **Georgetown** for a morning stroll along the Potomac, followed by window-shopping and lunch at **Martin's Tavern**. Afterwards, visit the lovely **Dumbarton Oaks** gardens, then take a hike in **Rock Creek Park**. Head to **Dupont Circle** for dinner, followed by drinks at **Eighteenth Street Lounge**.

On the fourth day, visit the **Newseum**, **Capitol** and **Library of Congress**, then walk to **Eastern Market** for a meal. That evening, go to bohemian H Street NE; **Granville Moore's** is a good place to start off the night.

is a must-see. The main exhibit (not recommended for under-11s, who can go to a separate on-site exhibit that's also free) gives visitors the identity card of a single Holocaust victim, whom visitors can ponder while taking a winding route into a hellish past amid footage of ghettos, rail cars and death camps where so many were murdered. Only a limited number of visitors are admitted each day, so go early.

FREE **Washington Monument** MONUMENT (⊙9am-10pm Jun-Aug, to 5pm Sep-May) Just peaking at 555ft (and 5in), the Washington Monument is the tallest building in the district. It took two phases of construction to complete; note the different hues of the stone. Tickets are free but must be reserved from the kiosk (15th St, btwn Madison St & Jefferson Dr SW; ⊙8:30am-4:30pm), or you can order them in advance by calling the National Park Service (☎877-444-6777; www.recreation.gov; tickets $1.50).

FREE **Bureau of Engraving & Printing** LANDMARK (www.moneyfactory.gov; cnr 14th & C Sts SW; ⊙8:30am-3pm Mon-Fri) The Bureau of Engraving & Printing, aka the most glorified print shop in the world, is where all the US paper currency is designed. Some $32 million of it rolls off the presses daily. Get in line early at the ticket kiosk on Raoul Wallenberg Pl.

FREE **Lincoln Memorial** MONUMENT (⊙24hr) Anchoring the Mall's west end is the hallowed shrine to Abraham Lincoln, who gazes peacefully across the reflecting pool beneath his neoclassical Doric-columned abode. To the left of Lincoln you can read the words of the Gettysburg Address, and the hall below highlights other great Lincolnisms; on the steps, Martin Luther King Jr delivered his famed 'I Have a Dream' speech.

FREE **Vietnam Veterans Memorial** MONUMENT (Constitution Gardens; ⊙24hr) The opposite of DC's white, gleaming marble is this black, low-lying 'V,' an expression of the psychic scar wrought by the Vietnam War. The monument follows a descent deeper into the earth, with the names of the 58,267 dead soldiers – listed in the order in which they died – chiseled into the dark wall. It's a subtle, but profound monument – and all the more surprising as it was designed by 21-year-old undergraduate student Maya Lin in 1981.

FREE **Korean War Veterans Memorial** MONUMENT (Constitution Gardens; ⊙24hr) The elaborate memorial depicts a patrol of ghostly steel soldiers marching by a wall of etched faces from that conflict; seen from a distance, the images on the wall form the outline of the Korean mountains.

FREE **National WWII Memorial**   MONUMENT
(17th St, btwn Constitution & Independence Aves;
⏰24hr) Occupying one end of the reflecting
pool (and controversially, the center of the
Mall, the only war memorial to have that
distinction), the National WWII Memorial
honors the 400,000 Americans who died in
the war, along with the 16 million US soldiers who served during the conflict. Stirring
quotes are sprinkled about the monument.

Corcoran Gallery   MUSEUM
(www.corcoran.org; cnr 17th St & New York Ave NW;
adult/child $10/free; ⏰10am-5pm Wed-Sun, to
9pm Thu) DC's oldest art museum, the Corcoran Gallery, has had a tough time standing
up to the free, federal competition around
the block, but this hasn't stopped it from
maintaining one of the most eclectic exhibitions in the country.

Newseum   MUSEUM
(www.newseum.org; 555 Pennsylvania Ave NW;
adult/child $22/13) Although you'll have to
pay up, this massive, highly interactive news
museum is well worth the admission price.
You can delve inside the major events of recent years (the fall of the Berlin Wall, September 11, Hurricane Katrina), and spend
hours watching moving film footage, perusing Pulitzer Prize-winning photographs and
reading moving works by journalists killed
in the line of duty.

CAPITOL HILL
The Capitol, appropriately, sits atop Capitol
Hill (what L'Enfant called 'a pedestal waiting for a monument') across a plaza from
the almost-as-regal Supreme Court and
Library of Congress. Congressional office
buildings surround the plaza. A pleasant
residential district stretches from E Capitol
St to Lincoln Park. Union Station, Capitol
South and Eastern Market Metro stations
serve this area.

Capitol   LANDMARK
Since 1800, this is where the legislative
branch of American government – ie Congress – has met to write the country's laws.
The lower House of Representatives (435
members) and upper Senate (100) meet respectively in the south and north wings of
the building.

A **visitor center** (www.visitthecapitol.gov;
1st & E Capitol Sts NE; ⏰8:30am-4:30pm Mon-Sat)
showcases the exhaustive background of
a building that fairly sweats history. If you

book in advance (through http://tours.visit
thecapitol.gov) you can go on a free tour of
the building, which is as daunting as the
exterior, if a little cluttered with the busts,
statues and personal mementos of generations of Congress members.

To watch Congress in action, US citizens
can request visitor passes from their representatives or senators (☎202-224-3121);
foreign visitors show passports at the House
gallery. Congressional committee hearings
are actually more interesting (and substan-
tive) if you care about what's being debated;
check for a schedule, locations and to see if
they're open to the public (they often are) at
www.house.gov and www.senate.gov.

FREE **Library of Congress**   LANDMARK
(www.loc.gov; 1st St SE; ⏰8:30am-4:30pm Mon-
Sat) To prove to Europeans that America
was cultured, John Adams plunked the
world's largest library on Capitol Hill. The
LOC's motivation is simple: 'universality', the
idea that all knowledge is useful. Stunning
in scope and design, the building's baroque
interior and neoclassical flourishes are set
off by a Main Reading Room that looks like
an ant colony constantly harvesting 29 million books. The visitor center and tours of
the reading rooms are both located in the
Jefferson Building, just behind the Capitol
building.

FREE **Supreme Court**   LANDMARK
(www.supremecourt.gov; 11st St NE; ⏰9am-4:30pm
Mon-Fri) Even nonlaw students are impressed
by the highest court in America. Arrive early
to watch arguments (periodic Mondays
through Wednesdays October to April). You
can visit the permanent exhibits and the
building's seven-spiral staircase year-round.

FREE **Folger Shakespeare Library**   LIBRARY
(www.folger.edu; 201 E Capitol St SE; ⏰10am-5pm
Mon-Sat) Houses the world's largest collection of Shakespeare materials.

FREE **National Postal Museum**   MUSEUM
(www.postalmuseum.si.edu; 2 Massachusetts Ave
NE; ⏰10am-5:30pm) Has the planet's largest stamp collection, plus an antique mail
plane and touching war letters. A decent
microbrewery sits above the museum.

FREE **US Botanic Garden**   GARDENS
(www.usbg.gov; 100 Maryland Ave SW; ⏰10am-
5pm) Hot, sticky and green with over 4000
different plant species on display.

TIDAL BASIN

It's magnificent to stroll around this man-made inlet and watch the monument lights wink across the Potomac. The blooms are loveliest during the Cherry Blossom Festival (p253), the city's annual spring rejuvenation, when the basin bursts into a pink and white floral collage. The original trees were a gift from the city of Tokyo, and planted in 1912. Paddleboat rentals (1501 Maine Ave SW; 2-person boat per hr $12) are available at the boathouse.

FREE Jefferson Memorial   MONUMENT
(900 Ohio Dr SW; ⊙24hr) The domed memorial is etched with the Founding Father's most famous writings – although historians criticize some of the textual alterations (edited, allegedly, for space considerations).

FREE DR Memorial   MONUMENT
(Memorial Park; ⊙24hr) A 7.5-acre tribute to the longest-serving president in US history and the era he governed. In a thoughtful, well-laid-out path, visitors are taken through the Depression, the New Deal era and WWII. It's best visited at night, when the interplay of rock, fountains and the lights of the Mall are enchanting.

FREE Martin Luther
King Jr National Memorial   MONUMENT
(www.mlkmemorial.org) After 25 years of planning and fundraising, the Martin Luther King Jr National Memorial opened in August 2011, on the banks of the Tidal Basin. It is the Mall's first memorial dedicated to both a nonpresident and an African American, and pays moving tribute (through quotes taken from a dozen speeches) to one of the world's great peace advocates.

DOWNTOWN

Downtown Washington began in what is now called Federal Triangle, but has since spread north and east, encompassing the area east of the White House to Judiciary Sq at 4th St, and from the Mall north to roughly M St. Hours of operation for the attractions listed here are 10am to 5:30pm daily, unless otherwise noted.

FREE National Archives   LANDMARK
(www.archives.gov; 700 Constitution Ave NW; ⊙10am-7pm mid-Mar–early Sep, to 5:30pm Sep–mid-Mar) It's hard not to feel a little in awe of the big three documents in the National Archives. The Declaration of Independence, the Constitution and the Bill of Rights, plus one of four copies of the Magna Carta: taken together, it becomes clear just how radical the American experiment was for its time. The Public Vaults, a bare scratching of archival bric-a-brac, are a flashy rejoinder to the main exhibit.

FREE Reynolds Center for
American Art   MUSEUM
(cnr F & 8th Sts NW) Don't miss the Reynolds Center for American Art, which combines the National Portrait Gallery (www.npg.si.edu) with the American Art Museum (http://americanart.si.edu). From haunting depictions of the inner city and rural heartland to the self-taught visions of itinerant wanderers, the center has dedicated itself to capturing the optimism and critical self-appraisal of American art, and succeeds.

International Spy Museum   MUSEUM
(www.spymuseum.org; 800 F St NW; adult/child $18/15; ⊙10am-6pm Sep–mid-Apr, 9am-7pm mid-Apr–Aug) You like those bits in the Bond movies with Q? Then you'll like the immensely popular International Spy Museum. All the undercover tools of the trade on display make this place great for (secret) history buffs. Get there early.

National Building Museum   MUSEUM
(www.nbm.org; 401 F St NW; adult/child $8/5; ⊙10am-5pm Mon-Sat, from 11am Sun) Devoted to architecture and urban design, this under-appreciated museum is appropriately housed in a magnificent 19th-century edifice modeled after the Renaissance-era Palazzo Farnese in Rome. Four stories of ornamented balconies flank the dramatic 316ft-wide atrium, and the gold Corinthian columns rise 75ft high. Rotating exhibits on different aspects of the built environment are hidden in rooms off the atrium.

FREE Renwick Gallery   MUSEUM
(cnr 17th St & Pennsylvania Ave NW) Near the White House, the Renwick Gallery is set in a stately 1859 mansion and exhibits a superb collection of American crafts and decorative art pieces. Highlights include over-the-top works like Larry Fuente's extravagantly kitsch *Game Fish* and Beth Lipman's ethereal *Bancketje (Banquet)*.

FREE Old Post Office Pavilion   LOOKOUT
(www.oldpostofficedc.com; 1100 Pennsylvania Ave NW; ⊙10am-8pm Mon-Sat, noon-7pm Sun Apr-Aug,

10am-7pm Mon-Sat, noon-6pm Sun Sep-Mar) If you don't want to hassle with the lines at the Washington Monument, head to this little-visited 1899 Romanesque Revival building, where its 315ft observation tower gives great downtown panoramas. Down below, there's a floodlit atrium and international food court.

FREE **Ford's Theatre** HISTORIC SITE
(www.fordstheater.org; 511 10th St NW; ⊙9am-4pm) On April 14, 1865, John Wilkes Booth assassinated Abraham Lincoln in his box seat here. The theater still operates today; you can also take a tour of the theater, and learn about the events that transpired on that fateful April night. There's also a newly restored **Lincoln Museum** devoted to Lincoln's presidency that you can see as part of the tour. Arrive early to get a ticket, as limited numbers are admitted each day.

FREE **Peterson House** HISTORIC SITE
(www.fordstheater.org; 516 10th St NW; ⊙9am-5pm) Where Lincoln gave up the ghost the next morning. Closed indefinitely in 2010 for major renovations.

Marian Koshland Science Museum of the National Academy of Sciences MUSEUM
(www.koshland-science-museum.org; cnr 6th & E Sts NW; adult/child $5/3; ⊙10am-6pm Wed-Mon) A big, kid-friendly complex of hands-on, educational fun.

WHITE HOUSE & FOGGY BOTTOM

An expansive park called the Ellipse borders the Mall; on the east side is the powerbroker block of Pennsylvania Ave. Foggy Bottom was named for the mists that belched out of a local gasworks; now, as the home of the State Department and George Washington University, it's an upscale (if not terribly lively) neighborhood crawling with students and professionals.

White House LANDMARK
The White House has survived both fire (the Brits torched it in 1814 – only a thunderstorm saved its complete destruction) and insults (Jefferson groused that it was 'big enough for two emperors, one Pope and the grand Lama'). Although its facade has changed little since 1924, its interior has seen frequent renovations. Franklin Roosevelt added a pool; Truman gutted the whole place (and simply discarded many of its historical features – today's rooms are

thus historical replicas); Jacqueline Kennedy brought back antique furnishings and historic details; Nixon added a bowling alley; Carter installed solar roof panels, which Reagan then removed; Clinton added a jogging track; and George W Bush included a T-ball field. Cars can no longer pass the White House on Pennsylvania Ave, clearing the area for posing school groups and round-the-clock peace activists.

A self-guided **tour** (☎202-456-7041; ⊙7:30am-11am Tue-Sat) will lead you through the ground and 1st floors, but the 2nd and 3rd floors are off-limits. These tours must be arranged (up to six months) in advance. Americans must apply via one of their state's members of Congress, and non-Americans must apply through either the US consulate in their home country or their country's consulate in DC. If that sounds like too much work, pop into the **White House visitor center** (www.whitehouse.gov; cnr 15th & E Sts NW; ⊙7:30am-4pm); it's not the real deal, but hey, there's executive paraphernalia scattered about.

The riverfront **Watergate complex** (2650 Virginia Ave NW) encompasses apartments, boutiques and the office towers that made 'Watergate' a byword for political scandal after it broke that President Nixon's 'plumbers' had bugged the headquarters of the 1972 Democratic National Committee.

ADAMS MORGAN, SHAW & U STREET

If it's not party time in Adams Morgan, it's time to get a hangover-cure lunch from an Ethiopian or Central American diner. This multiethnic neighborhood (especially 18th St) becomes sin central on weekend nights. The area isn't easily Metro-accessible; try to catch bus 98, which runs between Adams Morgan and U St stations.

To the east, Shaw stretches from around Thomas Circle to Meridian Hill Park and from N Capitol St to 15th St NW.

Lincoln Theatre LANDMARK
(☎202-328-6000; 1215 U St NW) The historic Lincoln Theatre was an early cornerstone of the nation's African American renaissance when it was founded in 1922. Luminaries such as DC native Duke Ellington as well as Louis Armstrong, Ella Fitzgerald, Billie Holiday and Sarah Vaughn and many others have all lit up the stage here. Following the 1968 assassination of Dr Martin Luther King Jr, riots devastated the commercial district. This area has since undergone a second re-

naissance; there are lots of excellent restaurants and bars around.

DUPONT CIRCLE

A well-heeled splice of gay community and DC diplomatic scene, this is city life at its best. Great restaurants, bars, bookstores and cafes, captivating architecture and the electric energy of a lived-in, happening neighborhood make Dupont worth a linger. The historic mansions have largely been converted into embassies, and Embassy Row (on Massachusetts Ave) runs through DC's thumping gay heart.

Phillips Collection   MUSEUM
(www.phillipscollection.org; 1600 21st St NW; permanent collection admission free, special exhibitions adult/child $12/free; ⊘10am-5pm Tue-Sat, to 8:30pm Thu summer, 11am-6pm Sun) The first modern-art museum in the country (opened in 1921) houses a small but exquisite collection of European and American works – including pieces by Gauguin, van Gogh, Matisse, Picasso, O'Keefe, Hopper and many other greats. It's partially set in a beautifully restored Georgian Revival mansion.

Textile Museum   MUSEUM
(www.textilemuseum.org; 2320 S St NW; suggested donation $8; ⊘10am-5pm Tue-Sat, from 1pm Sun) Set in two historic mansions in the Kalorama neighborhood, the oft-overlooked Textile Museum showcases beautifully wrought creations from across the globe, including pre-Columbian weavings, American quilts and Ottoman embroidery.

FREE **National Geographic Society's Explorer Hall**   GALLERY
(1145 17 St NW; ⊘9am-5pm Mon-Sat, from 10am Sun) Rotating exhibits on worldwide expeditions are found here.

GEORGETOWN

Thousands of the bright and beautiful, from Georgetown students to ivory-tower academics and diplomats, call this leafy, aristocratic neighborhood home. At night, shop-a-block M St becomes congested with traffic, turning into a weird mix of high-school cruising and high-street boutique.

Get a historical overview from the **visitor center** (☏202-653-5190; 1057 Thomas Jefferson St NW; ⊘9am-4:30pm Wed-Sun), or join costumed guides on a history-intensive, hour-long, mule-driven barge trip along the **C&O Canal towpath** (adult/child $8/5; ⊘Apr–mid-Aug).

Dumbarton Oaks   GARDENS
(www.doaks.org; cnr R & 31st Sts NW) A free museum featuring exquisite Byzantine and pre-Columbian art is housed within this historic mansion. More impressive, are the 10 acres of beautifully designed formal **gardens** (adult/child $8/5 Apr-Oct, free Nov-Mar; ⊘2-6pm Tue-Sun), which are simply stunning during the springtime blooms. Visit on weekdays to beat the crowds.

Georgetown University   UNIVERSITY
(www.georgetown.edu; 37th & O Sts NW) Bill Clinton went to school here, which should give you an idea of the student body: smart, hard-working party people.

UPPER NORTHWEST DC

FREE **National Zoological Park**   ZOO
(http://nationalzoo.si.edu; 3000 Connecticut Ave NW; ⊘10am-6pm Apr-Oct, to 4:30pm Nov-Mar) Home to over 2000 individual animals (400 different species) in natural habitats, this 163-acre zoo is famed for its giant pandas Mei Xiang and Tian Tian. Other highlights include the African lion pride, Asian elephants and dangling orangutans swinging 50ft overhead from steel cables and interconnected towers (the 'O Line').

Washington National Cathedral   CHURCH
(☏202-537-6200; www.nationalcathedral.org; 3101 Wisconsin Ave NW; suggested donation $5; ⊘10am-5:30pm Mon-Fri, to 4:30pm Sat, 8am-5pm Sun) This Gothic cathedral, as dramatic as its European counterparts, blends both the spiritual and the profane in its architectural treasures. The stained-glass windows are stunning (check out the 'Space Window' with an imbedded lunar rock); you'll need binoculars to spy the Darth Vader gargoyle on the exterior. Specialized tours delve deeper into the esoteric; call or go online for the schedule.

ANACOSTIA

The drive from Georgetown to Anacostia takes about 30 minutes and the patience to endure a world of income disparity. The neighborhood's smack-, crack- and brick row houses sitting mere miles from the Mall form one of DC's great contradictory panoramas, yet strong communities persist. More tourists started arriving on the first day of the baseball season in 2008, when Nationals Stadium opened, bringing with it double-edged gentrification. The impact of renovation dollars can already be seen at some spruced-up intersections.

Frederick Douglass National Historic Site
LANDMARK

(www.nps.gov/frdo; 1411 W St SE; ⊙9am-4pm) Freedom fighter, author and statesman Frederick Douglass occupied this beautifully sited hilltop house from 1878 until his death in 1895. Original furnishings, books, photographs and other personal belongings paint a compelling portrait of both the private and public life of this great man. Visits into the home are by organized tour only; call ☏877-444-6777 for times and to reserve a space ($1.50 reservation fee per ticket).

FREE Anacostia Community Museum
MUSEUM

(☏202-633-4820; http://anacostia.si.edu; 1901 Fort Pl SE; ⊙10am-5pm) This Smithsonian museum is surrounded by the community that is the subject of its educational mission, and houses good rotating exhibits on the African American experience in the USA. Call ahead, as the museum closes for about a month between installations.

🏃 Activities

Under the auspices of the National Park Service (NPS), the 1754 acres of Rock Creek Park follow Rock Creek as it winds through the northwest of the city. There are miles of bicycling, hiking and horseback-riding trails, and even a few coyotes. The C&O Canal offers bicycling and hiking trails in canalside parks, and the lovely 11-mile Capital Crescent Trail (www.cctrail.org) connects Georgetown north to Silver Spring, MD, via some splendid Potomac River views. Fifteen miles north of DC, Great Falls National Park (www.nps.gov/grfa; per vehicle $5) is an outstanding slice of wilderness, great for rafting or rock climbing some of the beautiful cliffs that hang over the Potomac.

The Potomac Heritage National Scenic Trail (www.nps.gov/pohe) connects Chesapeake Bay to the Allegheny Highlands along an 830-mile network that includes the C&O Canal towpath, the 17-mile Mt Vernon Trail (Virginia) and the 75-mile Laurel Highlands Trail (Pennsylvania).

Thompson Boat Center
BOAT RENTAL

(☏202-333-9543; www.thompsonboatcenter.com; cnr Virginia Ave & Rock Creek Pkwy NW; ⊙8am-5pm) At the Potomac River end of Rock Creek Park, it rents canoes (per hour $12), kayaks (per hour single/double $10/17) and bikes (per hour/day $7/28).

Big Wheel Bikes
BICYCLE RENTAL

(☏202-337-0254; www.bigwheelbikes.com; 1034 33rd St NW; per hr/day $7/35; ⊙11am-7pm Tue-Fri, 10am-6pm Sat & Sun) A good bike-rental outfitter.

Capitol Bikeshare
BICYCLE RENTAL

(☏877-430-2453; www.capitolbikeshare.com) Modeled on bike-sharing schemes in Europe, Capitol Bikeshare has a network of 1000-plus bicycles scattered at 100-odd stations around DC. To check out a bike, select the membership (24 hours is $5, five days is $15), insert credit card, and off you go. The first 30 minutes are free; after that, rates rise exponentially ($1.50/3/6 per extra 30/60/90 minutes). Call or go online for complete details.

Washington, DC for Children

Top destination for families is undoubtedly the (free!) zoo (p251). Museums around the city will entertain and educate children of all ages. But if you – or they – tire of indoor attractions, there are plenty of enticing green spaces, such as the 328-acre East Potomac Park (Ohio Dr SW), with playground, outdoor swimming pool, mini-golf and picnic facilities; it runs southeast of the Tidal Basin.

The DC-area Our Kids (www.our-kids.com) website has loads of listings for kid-centric shows and events, family-friendly restaurants and loads of activity ideas.

Many hotels offer babysitting services, but you can also book through the reputable organization Mothers' Aides (☏703-250-0700; www.mothersaides.com), with rates from $15 to $20 per hour.

THE MALL

The wide-open spaces of the Mall are perfect for outdoor family fun, whether you want to throw a Frisbee, have a picnic, ride the old-fashioned carousel (tickets $2.50) or stroll through museums.

Kids like things that go squish and/or make other things go squish; they can find both in the dinosaurs and insects of the National Museum of Natural History (p245). The Kennedy Center (p260) puts on entertaining shows for tots, and the National Air & Space Museum (p245) has moon rocks, IMAX films and a wild simulation ride.

The National Theatre (p260) offers free Saturday-morning performances, from puppet shows to tap dancers (reservations required).

Discovery Theater
THEATER

(📞202-633-8700; www.discoverytheater.org; 1100 Jefferson Dr SW; adult/child $6/5) In the basement of the Ripley Center, stages entertaining shows for young audiences.

GREATER DC

National Children's Museum
MUSEUM

(📞301-686-0225; www.ncm.museum; 112 Waterfront St, National Harbor, MD) Will reopen its expanded doors in 2013 in the National Harbor Complex, 10 miles south of the Mall.

Six Flags America
AMUSEMENT PARK

(📞301-249-1500; www.sixflags.com/america; adult/child over 2yr $50/35; ☺May-Oct) Located about 15 miles east of downtown in Largo, MD; offers a full array of roller coasters and tamer kiddie rides.

👉 Tours

DC Metro Food Tours
WALKING

(📞800-979-3370; www.dcmetrofoodtours.com; per person $27-60) These walking tours take in the culinary riches of DC, exploring various neighborhoods and stopping for bites along the way. Offerings include Eastern Market, U Street, Little Ethiopia, Georgetown and Alexandria, VA.

DC by Foot
WALKING

(www.dcbyfoot.com) Guides for this free, tip-based walking tour dispense intriguing stories and historical details on different walks covering the National Mall, Arlington Cemetery and Lincoln's assassination.

Old Town Trolley Tours
BUS

(📞888-910-8687; www.trolleytours.com; adult/child $35/25) This open-sided bus offers hop-on, hop-off exploring of the major sights of DC. The outfit also offers a 'monuments by moonlight' tour and the DC Ducks tour, via amphibious vehicle that plunges into the Potomac.

Bike and Roll
BICYCLE

(📞202-842-2453; www.bikethesites.com; adult/child from $40/30; ☺Mar-Nov) Offers a handful of day and evening bike tours around the city (plus combo boat–bike trips to Mt Vernon).

City Segway Tours
SEGWAY

(📞202-626-0017; http://citysegwaytours.com/washington-dc) Extremely popular and relaxing way of seeing the major sites along the Mall and in Penn Quarter ($70).

✯ Festivals & Events

National Cherry Blossom Festival
CULTURAL

(www.nationalcherryblossomfestival.org) Held late March to early April. DC at her prettiest.

Smithsonian's Folklife Festival
CULTURAL

(www.festival.si.edu) This fun family event, held over two weekends in June and July, features distinctive regional folk art, crafts, food and music.

Independence Day
CULTURAL

Not surprisingly, a big deal here, celebrated on July 4 with a parade, an open-air concert and fireworks over the Mall.

🛏 Sleeping

For B&Bs and private apartments citywide, contact **Bed & Breakfast Accommodations** (📞877-893-3233; www.bedandbreakfastdc.com).

If you bring a car to DC, plan on $20 and up per day for in-and-out privileges (or stay in Arlington or Alexandria, where some hotels have free parking). Rates below don't include DC's hefty 14.5% hotel tax.

CAPITOL HILL

William Penn House
HOSTEL $

(📞202-543-5560; www.williampennhouse.org; 515 E Capitol St SE; dm incl breakfast from $40; ✳@) On a peaceful street five blocks east of the Capitol, this friendly Quaker-run guesthouse with garden offers clean, well-maintained dorms, but it could use more bathrooms. The curious and spiritually minded can rise for the 7:30am worship service.

DOWNTOWN & WHITE HOUSE AREA

Hay-Adams
LUXURY HOTEL $$$

(📞202-638-6600; www.hayadams-dc.com; 800 16th St NW; r from $379; P✳@🖥) One of the city's great heritage hotels, the Hay is a beautiful old building, where 'nothing is overlooked but the White House.' It's named for two mansions that once stood on the site (owned by secretary of state John Hay and historian Henry Adams) that were the nexus of Washington's political and intellectual elite. Today the hotel has a palazzo-style lobby and probably the best rooms of the old-school luxury genre in the city, all puffy mattresses like clouds shaded by four-poster canopies and gold braid tassels.

Morrison-Clark Inn
BOUTIQUE HOTEL $$$

(📞202-898-1200; www.morrisonclark.com; 1015 L St NW; r from $220; P✳@) Listed on the Register of Historic Places, this elegant inn comprises two 1864 residences filled with fine antiques, chandeliers, richly hued drapes and other features evocative of the antebellum South. Some rooms come with private balconies or decorative marble fireplaces. Doting staff and a super central location.

Chester Arthur House
B&B **$$**

(☎877-893-3233; www.chesterarthurhouse.com; 1339 14th St NW; r $175-250; ❄🖝) Run by a delightful couple with serious travel experience under their belts – they both have National Geographic credentials – this is a good option for those wanting to explore beneath Washington's surface. Accommodations are in one of three rooms in a beautiful Logan Circle row house that's filled with antiques and collected ephemera from the hosts' global expeditions.

HI-Washington, DC
HOSTEL **$**

(☎202-737-2333; 1009 11th St NW, at K St; dm incl breakfast from $35; ❄@🖝) Top of the budget picks, this large, friendly hostel attracts a laid-back international crowd and has loads of amenities – lounge rooms, pool table, free tours and movie nights, kitchen and laundry.

Hotel Harrington
HOTEL **$$**

(☎202-628-8140; www.hotel-harrington.com; 436 11th St NW; s/d from $125/145; ❄ 🖝) One of the most affordable options near the Mall, this aging, family-run hotel has small basic rooms that are clean but in definite need of an update. Helpful service and a great location make the Harrington a great value for travelers who don't mind roughing it a bit.

District Hotel
HOTEL **$$**

(☎202-232-7800; www.thedistricthotel.com; 1440 Rhode Island Ave NW; r $120-140; 🖝) Home to some of the smallest rooms in DC, the District Hotel has Spartan quarters that are comfy enough if you're low maintenance. It's in a decent location within walking distance to downtown and Dupont.

ADAMS MORGAN

American Guest House
B&B **$$**

(☎202-588-1180; www.americanguesthouse. com; 2005 Columbia Rd NW; r $160-220; ❄🖝) This 12-room B&B earns high marks for its warm, friendly service, good breakfasts and elegantly furnished rooms. Decor runs the gamut from Victorian vibe (room 203) to New England cottage (room 304) to colonial love nest (room 303). Some quarters are rather small.

Adam's Inn
B&B **$$**

(☎202-745-3600; www.adamsinn.com; 1746 Lanier Pl NW; r with shared/private bath from $109/139; P❄@) On a pretty, tree-lined street near Adams Morgan, this town house has small but nicely decorated rooms; thin walls mean you might hear your neighbor.

DUPONT CIRCLE

Carlyle Suites
HOTEL **$$$**

(☎202-234-3200; www.carlylesuites.com; 1731 New Hampshire Ave NW; r from $220; ❄@🖝) Inside this all-suites art-deco gem, you'll find sizable, handsomely furnished rooms with crisp white linens, luxury mattresses and full kitchens. The friendly staff is first-rate, and the added extras include free use of laptops and complimentary access to the Washington Sports Club.

Akwaaba
B&B **$$**

(☎877-893-3233; www.akwaaba.com; 1708 16th St NW; r $150-265; ❄) Part of a small chain of B&Bs that emphasize African American heritage in its properties, the well-located Dupont branch has uniquely furnished rooms set in a late-19th-century mansion. Expect a friendly welcome and excellent cooked breakfasts.

Dupont Collection
B&B **$$**

(☎202-467-6777; http://thedupontcollection.com; r $100-260; P ❄ 🖝) Brookland Inn (3742 12th St NE); Inn at Dupont Circle North (1620 T St NW); Inn at Dupont Circle South (1312 19th St NW) If you're craving a good range of B&B coziness in the heart of the capital, check out these three excellent heritage properties. Most centrally located are the inns at Dupont North and South; the former feels like the modern home of a wealthy friend, while the latter evokes much more of a chintz-and-lacy-linen sensibility. The Brookland is in the far northeast (but Metro accessible).

Tabard Inn
HOTEL **$$**

(☎202-785-1277; www.tabardinn.com; 1739 N St NW; r with shared/private bath from $120/165; P❄🖝) Set in a trio of 19th-century row houses, the Tabard Inn has attractive, antique-filled guest rooms sprinkled with unique flourishes – iron bedframes, wing-backed chairs, decorative fireplaces. There's an excellent restaurant here, with garden.

Hotel Helix
BOUTIQUE HOTEL **$$$**

(☎202-462-9001; www.hotelhelix.com; 1430 Rhode Island Ave NW; r from $240; P❄@🖝) Modish and highlighter bright, the Helix is playfully

Tryst CAFE $

(2459 18th St NW; ☺6:30am-late; 🛜) In Adams Morgan, stylish Tryst with its smattering of tables and sofas attracts the laptop crowd by day (free wi-fi) and a more garrulous gathering by night; there's live jazz Monday to Wednesday (from 8pm), an early happy hour (3pm to 5:30pm) and decent coffees, small plates and desserts.

Baked & Wired CAFE $

(1052 Thomas Jefferson St NW; mains $3; ☺7am-8pm Mon-Fri, from 8am Sat & Sun; 🛜) Baked & Wired is a cheery little Georgetown cafe that whips up beautifully made coffees and delectable desserts; it's a fine spot to join students in both real and virtual chatter (free wi-fi, of course).

Ching Ching Cha TEAHOUSE $$

(1063 Wisconsin Ave NW; teas $6-12; ☺11am-9pm) This airy, Zen-like teahouse feels a world away from the shopping mayhem of Georgetown's M Street. Stop in for a pot of rare tea (over 70 varieties). CCC also serves steamed dumplings, sweets and simple but flavorful three-course lunches ($14).

Pound CAFE $

(621 Pennsylvania Ave SE; mains $5-8; ☺7am-9:30pm Mon-Sat, 8am-8pm Sun; 🛜) In Capitol Hill, Pound serves high-quality coffees amid an elegant rustic interior (exposed brick and timber, original plaster ceilings, wood floors and nicely lit artwork). Breakfast quesadillas, panini and daily lunch specials are tops – as is the Nutella latte.

Filter CAFE $

(1726 20th St NW; ☺7am-7pm Mon-Fri, from 8am Sat & Sun; 🛜) On a quiet street in Dupont, Filter is a jewel-box-sized cafe with a tiny front patio, a hipsterish laptop-toting crowd and, most importantly, great coffee. Aussies and those who seek caffeinated perfection can get a decent flat white here.

cool – the perfect hotel for the bouncy international set that makes up the surrounding neighborhood of Dupont Circle.

GEORGETOWN

Hotel Monticello HOTEL $$$

(☎202-337-0900; www.monticellohotel.com; 1075 Thomas Jefferson St NW; r from $220; P❄🛜) In the heart of Georgetown, the Hotel Monticello has spacious rooms, with brass-and-crystal chandeliers, colonial-reproduction furniture, comfortable high-end mattresses and tasteful flower arrangements. Helpful staff.

✖ Eating

As you might expect of one of the world's most international cities, DC has an eclectic palate, with a superb array of restaurants serving Ethiopian, Indian, Southeast Asian, French, Italian and more, plus good old-fashioned Southern fare.

CAPITOL HILL

Sonoma INTERNATIONAL $$$

(☎202-544-8088; 223 Pennsylvania Ave SE; mains $12-38; ☺11:30am-2:30pm Mon-Fri, 5-10pm Mon-Sat, 5-9pm Sun) Warmly lit Sonoma is an elegant spot for enjoying high-end bistro fare with some great wines (more than 50 by the glass). In addition to seasonal fish, roast duck breast, pizzas and pastas, diners can linger over tasty small plates, charcuterie and rich cheese plates. True to name, California varietals predominate. Service receives mixed reviews.

Granville Moore's MODERN AMERICAN $$

(1238 H St NE; mains $12-16; ☺5pm-midnight Sun-Thu, to 3am Fri & Sat) One of the anchors of the bohemian Atlas District (which runs along H St NE), Granville Moore's bills itself as a gastropub with a Belgian fetish. Indeed you'll find more than 70 Belgian beers by the bottle and at least seven on tap. There's also good pub fare (and recommended mussels), a lively happy hour, and fun crowds most nights.

Eastern Market MARKET $

(225 7th St SE; ☺7am-7pm Tue-Fri, to 6pm Sat, 9am-5pm Sun) One of the icons of Capitol Hill, this covered arcade sprawls with delectable produce and good cheer on the weekends.

The crab cakes at the Market Lunch stall are divine.

Jimmy T's Place   DINER $

(501 E Capitol St SE; mains $6-10; ⊙7am-3pm Tue-Sun) Jimmy's is a neighborhood joint of the old school, where folks cram in to read the *Post,* have a burger or an omelet or some coffee and banter with staff behind the counter.

DOWNTOWN & WHITE HOUSE AREA

TOP CHOICE **Minibar at Café**

Atlantico   LATIN AMERICAN $$$

(☎202-393-0812; www.cafeatlantico.com; 405 8th St NW; tasting menu $150; ⊙6pm & 8:30pm, Tue-Sat) Atlantico's Minibar is foodie nirvana, where the lucky six (just six seats, folks) get wowed by animal bits spun into cotton candy and cocktails frothed into clouds. The tasting menu, entirely determined by the chef, is often delicious, and never dull. Reserve exactly one month in advance.

Maine Avenue Fish Market   SEAFOOD $

(1100 Maine Ave SW; ⊙8am-9pm) If you're a seafood-lover, this sprawling and bustling fish market should take high priority on your itinerary. Over a dozen vendors sell some of America's freshest, tastiest seafood – we're talking fresh-off-the-boat fresh. Big plump oysters ($7 for six), crab cakes, soft-shell crabs, steamed crabs and peel-and-eat shrimp are just the beginning...

Hill Country   BARBECUE $$

(www.hillcountrywdc.com; 410 7th St NW; mains $10-20; ⊙8am-9pm; ⊕) Straight from Texas by way of, uh, Manhattan, Hill Country made fast friends following its opening in 2011. The ribs, chicken and sausage are all respectable, but the brisket (order it 'moist') is phenomenal. The barn-sized space fills with noisy chatter most nights, and it's all very informal – order your sides and meat by the pound from the smokemasters in back. There's live music (downstairs) from Tuesday to Saturday.

Zaytinya   MEDITERRANEAN $$

(☎202-638-0800; 701 9th St NW; mezze $7-11; ⊙11:30am-11:30pm Tue-Sat, to 10pm Sun & Mon) One of the culinary crown jewels of chef José Andrés, ever-popular Zaytinya serves superb Greek, Turkish and Lebanese mezze (small plates) in a long narrow dining room with soaring ceilings and all-glass walls. Stop in for $4 happy hour specials (4:30pm to 6:30pm).

Ping Pong   ASIAN $$

(☎202-506-3740; 900 7th St NW; dim sum $5-7; ⊙11:30am-11pm Mon-Sat, 11am-10pm Sun) At Ping Pong you can enjoy delectable dim sum anytime, but the stylish and open dining room gathers the liveliest crowds at night. The pan-Asian menu features delicate steamed dumplings, honey-roasted pork buns, seafood clay pots and other hits, plus tasty libations like plum wine and elderflower saketini cocktails.

Matchbox Pizza   PIZZA $$

(☎202-289-4441; 713 H St NW; pizzas $14-21; ⊙11am-10:30pm Sun-Thu, to 1am Fri & Sat) One of the most popular pizzerias in DC serves celebrated thin-crust pies (like the spicy roasted pepper and smoked gouda 'fire & smoke'), plus much-lauded sliders (mini burgers; order them with gorgonzola). Prepare for big crowds on weekends.

Jaleo   SPANISH $$

(☎202-628-7949; 480 7th St NW; tapas $7-12, dinner mains $16; ⊙11:30am-11:30pm Tue-Sat, to 10pm Sun & Mon) Amid vintage murals and buzzing ambience, Jaleo serves some of DC's best tapas. Garlicky gambas al ajillo (garlic shrimps), beet salad with pistachios and house-made pork sausage with white beans are top choices. The bar has a great happy hour ($4 tapas and sangria).

Georgia Brown's   SOUTHERN $$

(☎202-393-4499; 950 15th St NW; mains $16-32; ⊙11:30am-10pm Mon-Thu, noon-11pm Fri & Sat, 10am-2:30pm & 5-10pm Sun) Georgia Brown's elevates the humble ingredients of the South (shrimp, cornmeal, catfish, grits and sausage) to high art in dishes like fried green tomatoes stuffed with herbed goat's cheese, and fried chicken marinated in sweet tea. The jazz brunch with a jaw-dropping buffet is probably DC's best.

ADAMS MORGAN, SHAW & U STREET

Busboys & Poets   INTERNATIONAL $$

(☎203-387-7638; www.busboysandpoets.com; 2021 14th St NW; mains $8-16; ⊙8am-midnight Mon-Fri, from 9am Sat & Sun; 🖘) A cultural icon, Busboys (named for a Langston Hughes poem) attracts an eclectic crowd who gather for coffee, bistro fare (pizzas, burgers, crab cakes) and a progressive line-up of events – book signings, poetry readings, film screenings.

Etete   ETHIOPIAN $$

(☎202-232-7600; 1942 9th St NW; mains $10-20; ⊙11:30am-11pm; ☂) In the small ethnic enclave sometimes called 'Little Ethiopia,' Etete serves authentic and high-quality food – fiery *yebeg wat* (spicy lamb stew), tender golden tibs (marinated short beef ribs), bountiful vegetarian platters and tangy *injera* (spongy flatbread) for soaking it all up. Culinary archrival Dukem (1114 U St NW) is up the street.

Cork   MODERN AMERICAN $$
(1720 14th St NW; small plates $7-15; ⊘5pm-1am) This dark 'n' cozy wine bar manages to come off as foodie magnet and friendly neighborhood hangout all at once. You'll find over 50 wines by the glass, which go nicely with the small plates and cheese selection.

Pasta Mia   ITALIAN $$
(1790 Columbia Rd NW; mains $10-15; ⊘6:30-10pm Mon-Sat) Even cold weather doesn't deter the faithful from lining up for their turn at affordable, monstrously portioned Italian on checkered tablecloths. No reservations, credit cards or line-jumping bribes accepted.

Diner   AMERICAN $$
(2453 18th St NW; mains $8-16; ⊘24hr; ⊕) The Diner is the ideal spot for late-night breakfast, (crowded) weekend bloody Mary brunches or anytime you want unfussy, well-prepared American fare (omelets, stuffed pancakes, mac 'n' cheese, grilled Portobello sandwiches, burgers and the like). It's a good spot for kids too (they'll even hang their Diner-made colorings on the wall).

Ben's Chili Bowl   FAST FOOD $
(1213 U St NW; mains $4-9; ⊘11am-2am Mon-Thu, to 4am Fri & Sat, to 11pm Sun) One of DC's landmarks, Ben's has been going strong for over 50 years, doling out burgers, fries and the well-loved chili-smothered half-smokes (pork and beef sausages) from its old-school U St storefront.

DUPONT CIRCLE

TOP CHOICE Bistro Du Coin   FRENCH $$
(✆202-234-6969; 1738 Connecticut Ave NW; mains $12-27; ⊘11:30am-11pm Sun-Wed, to 1am Thu-Sat) For a quick culinary journey across the Atlantic, the lively and much-loved Bistro Du Coin delivers the goods. You'll find consistently good onion soup, classic *steak-frites* (grilled steak and French fries), cassoulet, open-faced sandwiches and nine varieties of its famous *moules* (mussels). Try the *moules bretonnes* (with lobster) for pure decadence.

Malaysia Kopitiam   MALAYSIAN $$
(1827 M St NW; mains $10-15; ⊘noon-10pm) This hole-in-the-wall restaurant is a good spot to get your Malaysian fix. Standouts include the *laksas* (curry noodle soups), *roti canai* (flatbread served with chicken curry) and crispy squid salad. The big picture menu helps with ordering.

Afterwords   AMERICAN $$
(✆202-387-3825; 1517 Connecticut Ave NW; mains $12-20; ⊘7:30am-1am Sun-Thu, 24hr Fri & Sat; ⊛) Not your average bookstore cafe, this buzzing spot overflows with good cheer at its packed cafe tables and outdoor patio. The menu features tasty bistro fare and an ample beer selection, making it a prime spot for happy hour, brunch and at all hours on weekends.

Dolcezza   ICE CREAM $
(1704 Connecticut Ave NW; ice cream $4-7; ⊘8am-11pm Mon-Sat, to 8pm Sun; ⊛) DC's best gelateria spreads over a dozen unique, delectable flavors (like Thai coconut milk, wildflower honey and champagne mango). Good coffees, vintage-chic decor and free wi-fi. There's also a Georgetown branch.

GEORGETOWN

Citronelle   MODERN AMERICAN $$$
(✆202-625-2150; 3000 M St NW; tasting menu from $105; ⊘6-10pm Tue-Sat) Celebrated chef Michel Richard started this Georgetown dining destination, earning high marks for tender rack of lamb brushed with jalapeno-cumin sauce, wild salmon in lobster-saffron broth and other culinary gems. If you prefer not to shell out for the 10-course prix-fixe menu, you can dine à la carte in the more casual lounge.

Martin's Tavern   AMERICAN $$
(✆202-333-7370; 1264 Wisconsin Ave NW; lunch mains $12-15, dinner $13-30; ⊘from 11:30am) Martin's is a favorite with Georgetown students and US presidents, who all enjoy the tavern's old-fashioned dining room and unfussy classics like thick burgers, crab cakes and prime rib.

Dolcezza   ICE CREAM $
(1560 Wisconsin Ave NW; ice cream $4-7; ⊘noon-10pm Mon-Sat, to 9pm Sun) Serves amazingly good gelato from a menu that changes weekly. Recent hits include lime cilantro, Mexican coffee and lemon ricotta cardamom.

UPPER NORTHWEST DC

2 Amys   PIZZA $
(3715 Macomb St NW; mains $3-7.25; ⊘noon-2:30pm Tue-Sun, 5-11pm daily; ⊕) A bit out of

the way (but a stone's throw from Washington National Cathedral), 2 Amys serves some of DC's best thin-crust pizzas. Pies are sprinkled with market-fresh ingredients and baked to perfection in a wood-burning oven. Avoid the weekend crowds.

COLUMBIA HEIGHTS & AROUND
More and more restaurants and bars are opening in Columbia Heights and Petworth, north on the Green Line.

W Domku INTERNATIONAL $$
(☎202-722-7475; 821 Upshur St NW; mains $12-18; ☺6-11pm Tue-Thu, noon-midnight Fri, 10am-midnight Sat, 10am-10pm Sun) A gem in the midst of an uninspiring stretch of Petworth, W Domku spreads a broad mix of Polish, Russian and Scandinavian fare – from goulash, fish stew and gravlax to house-infused aquavit. Retro furnishings and an easy-going vibe add to the appeal.

Palena MODERN AMERICAN $$$
(☎202-537-9250; 3529 Connecticut Ave NW; fixed-price menu from $75; ☺11:30am-2pm & 5:30-10pm Tue-Sat, 10:30am-2pm Sun) Tucked away in Cleveland Park, northwest on the Red Line, Palena is one of DC's food-loving heavyweights. Red snapper with ramps (wild leeks) and oyster mushrooms, artichoke risotto and celery root soup with shrimp and almonds are recent favorites. Reserve ahead or eat in the more casual cafe (mains $14 to $26).

🍷 Drinking & Entertainment
See the weekly *Washington City Paper* (www.washingtoncitypaper.com) or *Washington Post* (www.washingtonpost.com) weekend section for comprehensive listings. Conveniently located at the Old Post Office Pavilion, Ticketplace (http://culturecapital.tix.com; 407 7th St NW; ☺11am-6pm Wed-Fri, 10am-5pm Sat) sells same-day concert and show tickets at half-price (no phone sales).

Bars & Nightclubs
CAPITOL HILL & DOWNTOWN
Hawk & Dove BAR
(329 Pennsylvania Ave SE; ☺from 10am) The quintessential Capitol Hill bar is a hot spot for political junkies, with intimate corner booths perfect for sipping pints and creating the next District scandal.

Red Palace LIVE MUSIC
(☎202-399-3201; http://redpalacedc.com; 1212 H St NE; ☺from 5pm) A pillar of the frenzied H St scene, Red Palace has three bars and

decent craft beer selections. The multiroom space books a mix of live bands and burlesque shows, with an abundance of indie rock and experimental sounds.

ADAMS MORGAN, SHAW & U STREET
Marvin LOUNGE
(2007 14th St NW; ☺5:30pm-2am) Stylish but unpretentious, Marvin has a low-lit lounge with vaulted ceilings where DJs spin soul and rare grooves to a mixed 14th St crowd. The upstairs roof deck is a draw both on summer nights and in winter, when folks huddle under roaring heat lamps sipping cocktails and Belgian beers. Good bistro fare too.

Cafe Saint-Ex BAR
(1847 14th St NW; ☺11am-1:30am) Amid framed drawings of *Le Petit Price* and wooden propellers (the place is named after French flyer and children's book author Antoine de Saint-Exupéry), this comfy classic serves up hearty bistro fare, a fine beer selection at the bar and DJs spinning fine grooves in the downstairs lounge, Gate 54. Head for the outdoor tables on warm nights.

Bar Pilar BAR
(1833 14th St NW; ☺from 5pm Mon-Fri, from 11am Sat & Sun) Friendly neighborhood favorite Bar Pilar serves seasonal organic tapas dishes and excellent cocktails in a small, nicely designed space. The mustard-colored walls and curious collections (hats, Hemingway regalia) give it an old-fashioned feel.

Chi-Cha Lounge LOUNGE
(1624 U St NW; ☺from 5pm) Slip through the double-sided mirror door, settle into a low settee and order up a hookah of fruit-flavored tobacco. Amid glowing candles and a backlit bar, the trendy clientele sip tropical cocktails and nosh on Andean-inspired tapas.

Madam's Organ LIVE MUSIC
(www.madamsorgan.com; 2461 18th St NW; cover $3-7; ☺5pm-2am Sun-Thu, to 3am Fri & Sat) The Organ is a well-loved standby, with lively crowds, cheap drinks, a rambling interior and roof deck, free pool and bands playing nightly.

Dan's Café BAR
(2315 18th St NW; ☺from 7:30pm Sun-Thu) Dan's dive is all the more grotty for its location: smack in the middle of the 18th St skimpy skirt parade. Inside this barely signed bar

One of Washington's gay bar scenes is concentrated around Dupont Circle.

Cobalt · BAR

(http://cobaltdc.com; 1639 R St NW; admission Sun-Thu free, Fri & Sat $5-8) Featuring lots of hair product and faux-tanned gym bodies, Cobalt tends to gather a better-dressed late-20s to 30-something crowd who come for fun (but loud!) dance parties throughout the week. Attractive bartenders, good DJs and daily drink specials add to the allure.

Nellie's Sports Bar · BAR

(www.nelliessportsbar.com; 900 U St NW) The vibe here is low-key, and Nellie's is a good place to hunker down among a friendly crowd for tasty bar bites, events' nights (including drag Bingo Tuesdays) or early drink specials. Twelve plasma screens show sporting events; there's also a roof deck and board games on hand.

Town Danceboutique · BAR

(www.towndc.com; 2009 8th St NW; admission Sun-Thu free, Fri & Sat $5-12) With a great sound system and fine DJs, Town is the go-to spot for dancing, with two floors, various rooms (including an outdoor smoking area) and hilarious drag shows on weekends.

JR's · BAR

(www.myjrsdc.com; 1519 17th St NW) This popular gay hangout is a great spot for happy hour, and is packed more often than not. Embarrassing show tunes karaoke is great fun on Monday nights.

is dim lighting, old locals, J Crew–looking types slumming it and cheap booze.

DUPONT CIRCLE

TOP CHOICE **Eighteenth Street Lounge** · LOUNGE
(www.eighteenthstreetlounge.com; 1212 18th St NW; cover $5-15; from 9:30pm Sat & Sun, from 5:30pm Tue-Fri) Chandeliers, velvet sofas, antique wallpaper and an attractive dance-loving crowd adorn this multifloored mansion. The DJs here – spinning funk, soul, Brazilian beats – are phenomenal, which is not surprising given Eric Hilton (of Thievery Corporation) is co-owner.

Russia House · LOUNGE
(1800 Connecticut Ave NW; from 5pm Mon-Fri, from 6pm Sat & Sun) Russophiles flock to this faded, elegant Dupont gem, with brassy chandeliers, candlelit chambers and stupefying vodka selection. A great spot for conversation and caviar – or heartier classics like pelmeni (dumplings), braised stuffed rabbit and shashlik (shish kabob).

Cafe Citron · LOUNGE
(1343 Connecticut Ave NW; from 4pm Mon-Sat) Citron is a festive, Latin-loving lounge with dance-happy crowds who come for salsa, world beats, and ever-flowing pitchers of *mojitos* and margaritas. With never a cover, there are free salsa lessons on Wednesdays and flamenco shows on Mondays.

Bier Baron · BAR
(1523 22nd St NW; from 11:30am Thu-Sun, from 4:30pm Mon-Wed) Since changing name and ownership, the former Brickskeller serves better food and has better service, with the same dark, pubby ambience and venerable selection of bottled and draft beer (over 500 brews!).

Current Sushi · LOUNGE
(1215 Connecticut Ave NW; cover $10-15; from 10pm Thu-Sat) Above a sleek, modern sushi restaurant, this ethereal, tent-like club becomes dance central on Thursday through Saturday night, with well-dressed crowds packing the dance floor.

Science Club · BAR
(www.scienceclubdc.com; 1136 19th St NW; from 5pm) In a warren of rooms scattered about a town house, the Science Club attracts a varied crowd of interns, transplants and young geeky types.

GEORGETOWN

Tombs · BAR
(1226 36 St, at P St NW; from 11:30am Mon-Sat, from 9:30am Sun) If it looks familiar, think back to the '80s; this was the setting for *St Elmo's Fire*. Today this cozy, windowless bar is a favorite with Georgetown students and teaching assistants boozing under crew regalia.

Mie N Yu Lounge
LOUNGE

(3125 M St NW; ⊙from 4pm) Mie N Yu (pronounced 'Me an you' – ugh) lays snob appeal and the Asian-fusion lounge thing on pretty thick, and the drink prices are equally excessive. But the wild decor – including themed rooms like the Tibetan Lounge, Turkish tent and Moroccan Bazaar – makes a colorful setting for a drink.

COLUMBIA HEIGHTS & AROUND

Red Derby
BAR

(3718 14th St NW; ⊙5pm-2am Mon-Thu, to 3am Fri, 11am-3am Sat & Sun) The unsigned Red Derby draws a fun eclectic crowd with its satisfying food and drinks menu (thick burgers, sweet-potato fries and dozens of exotic beers served in the can). There's an open-air deck up top (with heat lamps), films screening on the wall and riotous brunch crowds ($2 mimosas and bloody Marys keep things lively). Order the $5 shot-and-Schlitz combo to start the night off with a bang.

Wonderland
BAR

(1101 Kenyon St NW; ⊙5pm-2am Mon-Fri, from 11am Sat & Sun) In a residential stretch of Columbia Heights, Wonderland is friendly but divey with a spacious patio in front with outsize wooden benches just right on warm evenings. The upstairs dance floor sees a mix of DJs and bands, and gets packed on weekends.

Looking Glass Lounge
BAR

(3634 Georgia Ave NW; ⊙from 5pm) Petworth's best nightspot is an artfully designed neighborhood dive with a great jukebox, DJs on weekends and a fine outdoor patio.

Raven
BAR

(3125 Mt Pleasant Ave NW; ⊙from noon) The tattoo-loving Raven has cheap drinks, graffiti-stained bathrooms and more attitude than a pissed-off Ramone. Give it some respect and you may find this is DC's best spot for a $2 Schlitz.

Live Music

Black Cat
LIVE MUSIC

(www.blackcatdc.com; 1811 14th St NW; ⊙8pm-2am Sun-Thu, 7pm-3am Fri & Sat) A pillar of DC's music scene since the 1990s, the battered Black Cat has hosted all the greats of years past (White Stripes, the Strokes, Arcade Fire among others). If you don't want to pony up for $20-a-ticket bands on the upstairs main stage (or the smaller Backstage below), head to the Red Room for jukebox, pool and strong cocktails.

9:30 Club
LIVE MUSIC

(www.930.com; 815 V St NW) This spacious dive features two floors and a midsize stage (watch the action from the balcony or join the dancey mayhem below), with an excellent lineup of bands. Arrive early for a prime spot.

Blues Alley
LIVE MUSIC

(www.bluesalley.com; 1073 Wisconsin Ave NW; ⊙from 8pm) The classy Georgetown jazz supper club attracts some big-name players, as well as some forgettable proponents of smooth jazz. Enter through the alley just off M, south of Wisconsin.

Verizon Center
CONCERT VENUE

(☎202-628-3200; www.verizoncenter.com; 601 F St NW) DC's great big sports arena-cum-big-name-band venue.

Performing Arts

Kennedy Center
PERFORMING ARTS

(☎800-434-1324; www.kennedy-center.org; 2700 F St NW) Perched on 17 acres along the Potomac, the magnificent Kennedy Center hosts a staggering array of performances – more than 2000 each year among its multiple venues – including the Concert Hall (home to the National Symphony), the Opera House and Eisenhower Theater. The Millennium Stage puts on free performances at 6pm daily.

Wolf Trap Farm Park for the Performing Arts
PERFORMING ARTS

(☎703-255-1900; www.wolftrap.org; 1645 Trap Rd, Vienna, VA) This outdoor park some 40 minutes from downtown DC hosts summer performances by the National Symphony and other highly regarded musical and theatrical troupes.

National Theatre
THEATER

(☎202-628-6161; www.nationaltheatre.org; 1321 Pennsylvania Ave NW) Washington's oldest continuously operating theater.

Shakespeare Theatre
THEATER

(☎202-547-1122; www.shakespearedc.org; 450 7th St NW) The nation's foremost Shakespeare company presents masterfully staged pieces by the bard as well as works by George Bernard Shaw, Oscar Wilde, Ibsen, Eugene O'Neill and other greats.

Carter Barron Amphitheatre
PERFORMING ARTS

(☎202-426-0486; www.nps.gov/rocr; cnr 16th St & Colorado Ave NW) In a lovely wooded setting (inside Rock Creek Park), you can catch a mix of theater, dance and music (jazz, salsa, classical, reggae). Some events are free.

Sports

Washington Redskins   FOOTBALL
(📞301-276-6800; www.redskins.com) The city's football team plays at **FedEx Field** (1600 Fedex Way, Landover, MD; tickets $40-500), east of DC in Maryland. The season runs from September to February.

Washington Nationals   BASEBALL
(📞202-675-6287; http://washington.nationals. mlb.com) DC's baseball team plays at **Nationals Park** (1500 S Capitol St SE), along the Anacostia riverfront in southeast DC. The season runs from April through October.

DC United   SOCCER
(📞202-587-5000; www.dcunited.com) DC United play at **Robert F Kennedy (RFK) Memorial Stadium** (2400 E Capitol St SE). The season runs from March through October.

Washington Capitals   HOCKEY
(📞202-397-7328; http://capitals.nhl.com) DC's rough-and-tumble hockey team plays from October through April at the **Verizon Center** (601 F St NW).

Washington Wizards   BASKETBALL
(📞202-661-5050; www.nba.com/wizards) NBA season runs from October through April, with home games played at the **Verizon Center** (601 F St NW). DC's WNBA team, the **Washington Mystics** (📞877-324-6671; www.wnba.com/mystics), also play here May to September.

ⓘ Information

Internet Access
Kramerbooks (1517 Connecticut Ave NW, Dupont Circle; ⊘7:30am-1am Sun-Thu, 24hr Fri & Sat) One computer with free access in the bar.

Medical Services
CVS Pharmacy (📞202-785-1466; 6 Dupont Circle NW; ⊘24hr)

George Washington University Hospital (📞202-715-4000; 900 23rd St NW)

Post
Post office (2 Massachusetts Ave NE; ⊘9am-7pm Mon-Fri, to 5pm Sat & Sun)

Tourist Information
Destination DC (📞202-789-7000; www. washington.org; 901 7th St NW, 4th fl) Doles

out loads of information online, over the phone or in person at a handy downtown location.

Disability Guide (📞301-528-8664; www.disa bilityguide.org) Has useful info on museums, hotels and getting around; also publishes an annual accessibility guide ($5 available online).

International Visitors Information Desk (⊘9am-5pm Mon-Fri) At the Arrivals Terminal at Washington Dulles Airport, you'll find helpful multilingual staff at this post run by the Meridian International Center.

Websites
Online visitor information (www.washington. org, www.thedistrict.com)

Washington City Paper (www.washingtoncity paper.com) Free edgy weekly with entertainment and dining listings.

Washington Post (www.washingtonpost.com) Respected daily city (and national) paper. Its tabloid-format daily *Express* is free. Check online for events listings.

ⓘ Getting There & Away

Air
Washington Dulles International Airport (IAD; 📞703-572-2700), 26 miles west of the city center, and **Ronald Reagan Washington National Airport** (DCA; 📞703-417-8000), 4.5 miles south, are the main airports serving DC, although **Baltimore/Washington International Thurgood Marshall Airport** (BWI; 📞410-859-7111), 30 miles to the northeast, is also an option. All three airports, particularly Dulles and National, are major hubs for flights from around the world.

Bus
In addition to Greyhound, there are numerous cheap bus services to New York, Philadelphia and Richmond. Most charge around $20 for a one-way trip to NYC (it takes four to five hours). Pick-up locations are scattered around town, but are always Metro-accessible. Tickets usually need to be bought online, but can also be purchased on the bus itself if there is room.

Bolt Bus (📞877-265-8287; www.boltbus.com; 📶) The best of the budget options, Bolt Bus leaves from the upper level of Union Station.

DC2NY (📞202-332-2691; www.dc2ny.com; 20th St & Massachusetts Ave NW)

Greyhound (📞202-589-5141; www.greyhound. com; 1005 1st St NE) Provides nationwide service. The terminal is a few blocks north of Union Station; take a cab after dark.

Megabus (📞877-462-6342; www.us.megabus. com; 📶) Temporarily leaves from K & N Capitol Sts NW. Call to verify location.

New Century (📞202-789-8222; www.2001bus. com; 513 St NW)

Peter Pan Bus Lines (☎800-343-9999; www.peterpanbus.com) Travels to northeastern US; uses a terminal just opposite Greyhound's.

WashNY (☎866-287-6932; www.washny.com; 1333 19th St NW)

Train

Amtrak (☎800-872-7245; www.amtrak.com) Set inside the magnificent beaux-arts Union Station. Trains depart for nationwide destinations, including New York City (from $76, 3½ hours), Chicago (from $106, 18 hours), Miami (from $163, 24 hours) and Richmond, VA ($31, three hours).

MARC train (Maryland Rail Commuter; ☎866-743-3682; www.mtamaryland.com) This regional rail service for the Washington, DC–Baltimore metro area runs trains frequently to Baltimore ($7, 71 minutes) and other Maryland towns ($4 to $12); also goes to Harpers Ferry, WV ($15, 80 minutes).

ℹ Getting Around

To/From the Airport

If you're using Baltimore/Washington International Airport, you can travel between Union Station and the BWI terminal stop on either MARC train ($6, 40 minutes) or Amtrak ($14, 40 minutes).

Metrobus 5A (www.wmata.com) Runs from Dulles to Rosslyn Metro station (35 minutes) and central DC (L'Enfant Plaza, 48 minutes); it departs every 30 to 40 minutes. The combo bus/Metro fare is about $8.

Metrorail (www.wmata.com) National airport has its own Metro rail station, which is fast and cheap (around $2.50).

Supershuttle (☎800-258-3826; www.supershuttle.com) A door-to-door shuttle that connects downtown DC with Dulles ($29), National ($14) and BWI ($37).

Washington Flyer (www.washfly.com) Runs every 30 minutes from Dulles to West Falls Church Metro ($10).

Public Transportation

Metrorail (☎202-637-7000; www.wmata.com) One of the best transportation systems in the country will get you to most sights, hotel and business districts, and to the Maryland and Virginia suburbs. Trains start running at 5am Monday through Friday (from 7am on weekends); the last service is around midnight Sunday through Thursday and 3am on Fridays and Saturdays. Machines inside stations sell computerized fare cards; fares cost from $1.60 (children under five ride free). Unlimited travel passes are also available (one day/seven days from $9/33).

Circulator (www.dccirculator.com) Buses run along handy routes – including Union Station to/from Georgetown. One-way fare is $1.

Metrobus (www.wmata.com) Operates buses throughout the city and suburbs; have exact change handy (currently $1.70).

Taxi

For a cab, try **Capitol Cab** (☎202-636-1600), **Diamond** (☎202-387-6200) or **Yellow Cab** (☎202-544-1212).

MARYLAND

Maryland is often described as 'America in Miniature,' and for good reason. This small state has the best bits of the country, from the Appalachian Mountains in the west to sandy white beaches in the east. A blend of Northern streetwise and Southern down-home gives this most osmotic of border states an appealing identity crisis. Her main city, Baltimore, is a sharp, demanding port town; the Eastern Shore jumbles art-and-antique-minded city refugees and working fishermen; while the DC suburbs are packed with government and office workers seeking green space, and the poor seeking lower rents. Yet it all somehow works – scrumptious blue crabs, Natty Boh beer and

MARYLAND FACTS

Nickname The Old Line State, the Free State

» **Population** 5.8 million

» **Area** 12,407 sq miles

» **Capital city** Annapolis (population 36,600)

» **Sales tax** 6%

» **Birthplace of** Abolitionist Frederick Douglass (1818–95), baseball great Babe Ruth (1895–1948), actor David Hasselhoff (b 1952), author Tom Clancy (b 1947), swimmer Michael Phelps (b 1985)

» **Home of** 'The Star-Spangled Banner,' Baltimore Orioles, TV crime shows *The Wire* and *Homicide: Life on the Street*

» **Politics** Staunch democrats

» **Famous for** Blue crabs, lacrosse, Chesapeake Bay

» **State sport** jousting

» **Driving distances** Baltimore to Annapolis 29 miles, Baltimore to Ocean City 147 miles lovely Chesapeake country being the glue that binds all.

History

George Calvert established Maryland as a refuge for persecuted English Catholics in 1634 when he purchased St Mary's City from the local Piscataway, with whom he initially tried to coexist. Puritan refugees drove both Piscataway and Catholics from control and shifted power to Annapolis; their harassment of Catholics produced the Tolerance Act, a flawed but progressive law that allowed freedom of any (Christian) worship in Maryland – a North American first.

That commitment to diversity has always characterized this state, despite a mixed record on slavery. Although her loyalties were split during the Civil War, a Confederate invasion was halted here in 1862 at Antietam. Following the war, Maryland harnessed its black, white and immigrant work force, splitting the economy between Baltimore's industry and shipping, and the later need for services in Washington, DC. Today the answer to 'What makes a Marylander?' is 'all of the above': the state mixes rich, poor, the foreign-born, urban sophisticates and rural villages like few others.

Baltimore

Once one of the most important port towns in America, Baltimore – or 'Bawlmer' to locals – is a city of contradictions. On one hand she retains something of the ugly duckling – a defiant, working-class, somewhat gritty city still tied to her nautical past. But in recent years Baltimore has grown into a swan, filled with world-class museums, trendy shops, ethnic restaurants, boutique hotels, culture and sports. She does this all with a twinkle in the eye and a wisecrack on the lips. After all, this is a quirky city that spawned Billie Holiday and John Waters. Yet she remains intrinsically tied to the water, from the Disney-fied Inner Harbor and cobblestoned streets of portside Fells Point to the shores of Fort McHenry, birthplace of America's national anthem, 'The Star-Spangled Banner.' Baltimore lives up to her nickname, 'Charm City.'

⊙ Sights & Activities

HARBORPLACE & INNER HARBOR

This is where most tourists start and, unfortunately, end their Baltimore sightseeing.

The Inner Harbor is a big, gleaming waterfront renewal project of shiny glass, air-conditioned malls and flashy bars that manages to capture the maritime heart of this city, albeit in a safe-for-the-family kinda way. But it's also just the tip of Baltimore's iceberg.

TOP CHOICE National
Aquarium of Baltimore   AQUARIUM
(www.aqua.org; 501 E Pratt St; adult/child $25/20; ⊙9am-5pm Sun-Thu, to 8pm Fri, to 6pm Sat) Standing seven-stories high and capped by a glass pyramid, this is widely considered to be the best aquarium in America. It houses 16,500 specimens of 660 species, a rooftop rainforest, a central ray pool and multistory shark tank. There's also a reconstruction of the Umbrawarra Gorge in Australia's Northern Territory, complete with 35ft waterfall, rocky cliffs and free-roaming birds and lizards. Kids will love the dolphin show and new 4D Immersion Theater (together an additional $5). Go on weekdays to beat the crowds.

Baltimore Maritime Museum   MUSEUM
(www.baltomaritimemuseum.org; Piers 1, 3 & 5, off E Pratt St; 1/2/4 ships $11/14/18; ⊙10am-5:30pm) Ship-lovers can take a tour through four historic ships: a Coast Guard cutter, lightship, submarine and the USS Constellation, one of the last sail-powered warships built (in 1797) by the US Navy. Admission to the 1856 Seven Foot Knoll Lighthouse on Pier 5 is free.

Top of the World
Observation Deck   LOOKOUT
(www.viewbaltimore.org; 401 E Pratt St; adult/child $5/4; ⊙10am-6pm Wed-Thu, to 7pm Fri & Sat, 11am-6pm Sun) For a bird's-eye view of Baltimore, head to the observation deck at the World Trade Center.

DOWNTOWN & LITTLE ITALY
You can easily walk from downtown to Little Italy, but follow the delineated path as there's a rough housing project along the way.

National Great Blacks
in Wax Museum   MUSEUM
(www.greatblacksinwax.org; 1601 E North Ave; adult/child $12/10; ⊙9am-5pm Tue-Sat, noon-5pm Sun) In East Baltimore stands one of the country's best African American history museums, with exhibits on Frederick Douglass, Jackie Robinson, Martin Luther King Jr and Barack Obama, as well as lesser-known figures like explorer Matthew Henson. The

Baltimore

800 m
0.5 miles

N Washington St
N Wolfe St
Gay St
N Broadway
Johns Hopkins Hospital
Johns Hopkins
E Federal St
E Oliver St
E Bond St
N Caroline St
Ashland Ave
Orleans St
E Fairmont Ave
N Eden St
Madison Square
E Preston St
E Biddle St
E Chase St
E Eager St
E Madison St
E Monument St
Aisquith St
Aisquith St
E Fayette St
Ensor St
Ensor St
Greenmount Ave
Colvin St
Greenmount Cemetery
Johnston Square
DOWNTOWN
E Hoffman St
Greenmount Ave
Maryland State Penitentiary
The Fallsway
E Lanvale St
E Federal St
E Oliver St
The Fallsway
Jones Falls Expwy
Guilford Ave
Jones Falls Expwy
South St
Davis St
E Saratoga St
MT VERNON
Walters Art Gallery
N Calvert St
E Chase St
Saint Paul St
Penn Station
N Mount Royal Ave
Saint Paul St
N Charles St
E Read St
N Charles St
Maryland Ave
N Liberty St
W Madison St
W Centre St
W Mulberry St
Hillen St
University of Baltimore
Falls Rd
Cathedral St
W Mount Royal Ave
Maryland Historical Society
W Monument St
Park Ave
Tyson St
Lexington Market
N Howard St
Linden Ave
W Franklin St
W Lexington St
W Chase St
N Eutaw St
N Paca
SETON HILL
John St
Park Ave
Dolphin Ln
W Hoffman St
N Preston St
Lafayette Ave
Bolton St
Mason St
State Center
Eutaw Pl
Madison Ave
McCulloh St
MADISON PARK
Druid Hill Ave
N Martin Luther King Jr Blvd
St Mary's Park
St Mary's St
Pennsylvania Ave
Clay St
McMechen St
Wilson St
BOLTON HILL

S Chapel St
S Wolfe St
S Durham St
S Ann St
S Regester St
S Broadway
S Bethel St
S Bond St
S Caroline St
S Eden St
S Central Ave
Lloyd St
S Exeter St
High St
Albemarle St
President St

Gough St

E Baltimore St

Fell St
Thames St
Hull St

To Ale Mary's (0.2 miles);
Blue Hill Tavern (0.8 miles)

Market Square

Broadway Market

FELL'S POINT

Eastern Ave

Fleet St
Lancaster St
Aliceanna St
Philpot St

Patapsco River

E Pratt St

E Lombard St

LITTLE ITALY

Jewish Museum of Maryland

Star-Spangled Banner Flag House

E Falls Ave

Shot Tower
Market Pl

Water Taxi

Water Taxi

Baltimore Maritime Museum

National Aquarium of Baltimore

Market Pl
Water St
S Gay St
Commerce St

INNER HARBOR

Top of the World Observation Deck

E Pratt St

Inner Harbor

HARBORPLACE

E Cross St
Covington St
Henry St
Riverside Ave

Warren Ave

Federal Hill Park

Key Hwy

FEDERAL HILL

Grindall St
E West St
E Hamburg St

E Gittings St

S Calvert St

Light St

Charles Center

E Lexington St

Baltimore Area Visitor Center

OTTERBEIN

W Barre St
W Lee St

W Hughes St
W Montgomery St

S Charles St
E Henrietta St
E Hamburg St
S Hanover St

S Charles St
S Light St
E West St
E Gittings St
E Ostend St

W Conway St
S Sharp St

Convention Center

Hopkins Pl

Hopkins Plaza

Marion St
E Fayette St
W Baltimore St

S Howard St

To Bluegrass Tavern (0.2 miles)

University Square Park

University of Maryland at Baltimore

W Fayette St

W Lombard St
W Pratt St
W Camden St
N Greene St
Emory St
Penn St

N Paca St
W Baltimore St

RIDGELY'S DELIGHT

W Hamburg St
Russell St
Ridgely St
S Paca St
W Ostend St

Warner St

S Martin Luther King Jr Blvd

Washington Blvd

museum also covers slavery, the sickening Jim Crow era and African leaders – all told in surreal fashion through Madame Tussaud–style figures.

Star-Spangled Banner Flag House MUSEUM (www.flaghouse.org; 844 E Pratt St; adult/student $7/5; ⊙10am-4pm Tue-Sat) This historic home, built in 1793, is where Mary Pickersgill sewed the gigantic flag that inspired America's national anthem. Costumed interpreters and 19th-century artifacts transport visitors

back in time to dark days during the War of 1812; there's also a hands-on discovery gallery for kids.

Reginald F Lewis Museum of Maryland African American History & Culture MUSEUM (www.africanamericanculture.org; 830 E Pratt St; adult/student $8/6; ⊙10am-5pm Wed-Sat, noon-5pm Sun) Few states have been as defined by their African American population as Maryland, and the museum, across the street from a pre–Civil War slave market, effectively tells their complex tale.

Jewish Museum of Maryland
MUSEUM
(www.jewishmuseummd.org; 15 Lloyd St; adult/student/child $8/4/3; ☉noon-4pm Tue-Thu & Sun) Maryland has traditionally been home to one of the largest, most active Jewish communities in the country, and this is a fine place to explore the Jewish experience in America. It also houses two of the best-preserved historical synagogues in America.

Babe Ruth Birthplace & Museum
MUSEUM
(www.baberuthmuseum.com; 216 Emory St; adult/child $6/3; ☉10am-5pm, to 7pm during Orioles home games) Celebrates the Baltimore native son who happens to be the greatest baseball player in history. Four blocks east, **Sports Legends at Camden Yards** (Camden Station, cnr Camden & Sharp Sts; adult/child $8/4) honors more Maryland athletes. The museums share hours; combo tickets are $12/5.

B&O Railroad Museum
MUSEUM
(☑410-752-2490; www.borail.org; 901 W Pratt St; adult/child $14/8; ☉10am-4pm Mon-Sat, from 11am Sun) The Baltimore & Ohio railway was (arguably) the first passenger train in America, and the museum is a loving testament to both that line and American railroading in general. Train spotters will be in heaven among more than 150 different locomotives. Train rides cost an extra $3; call for the schedule.

Edgar Allan Poe House & Museum
MUSEUM
(☑410-396-7932; 203 N Amity St; adult/child $4/free; ☉noon-3:30pm Wed-Sat Apr-Nov) Home to Baltimore's most famous adopted son from 1832 to 1835, it was here that the macabre poet and writer first found fame after winning a $50 short-story contest. After moving around, Poe later returned to Baltimore in 1849, where he died in mysterious circumstances. His grave can be found in nearby **Westminster Cemetery** (cnr W Fayette & Greene Sts; admission free). The Poe House is located in a crime-ridden neighborhood, so it's best to drive or take a taxi; call to verify opening times before visiting.

National Museum of Dentistry
MUSEUM
(☑410-706-0600; www.dentalmuseum.org; 31 S Greene St; adult/student/child $7/5/3; ☉10am-4pm Wed-Sat, 1-4pm Sun) One of America's most unusual museums, this interactive museum traces the history of dental care from ancient Egypt to today. See George Washington's dentures (ivory, not wood) and old toothpaste, and check out Queen Victoria's 'toothbrush.'

Light Street Cycles
BICYCLE RENTAL
(☑410-685-2234; 1124 Light St; rental per day $25-50; ☉10am-8pm Mon-Fri, to 6pm Sat, 11am-3pm Sun) Rents out hybrids, mountain bikes and road bikes.

MT VERNON

FREE **Walters Art Gallery**
MUSEUM
(www.thewalters.org; 600 N Charles St; ☉10am-5pm Wed-Sun) Don't pass up this gallery, which spans over 55 centuries, from ancient to contemporary, with excellent displays of Asian treasures, rare and ornate manuscripts and books, and a comprehensive French paintings collection.

FREE **Contemporary Museum**
MUSEUM
(www.contemporary.org; 100 W Centre St; ☉noon-5pm Wed-Sun) So modern it's probably 'post,' this museum loves to ride the cutting edge of art. Auxiliary to the on-site exhibits is the museum's mission of bringing art to unexpected spots around the city.

Maryland Historical Society
MUSEUM
(www.mdhs.org; 201 W Monument St; adult/child $6/4; ☉10am-5pm Wed-Sat, noon-5pm Sun) With more than 5.4 million artifacts, this is one of the largest collections of Americana in the world, including Francis Scott Key's original manuscript of the 'Star-Spangled Banner.' There are often excellent temporary exhibits, as well as a fascinating permanent ones tracing Maryland's maritime history.

Washington Monument
MONUMENT
(699 Washington Pl; suggested donation $5; ☉10am-5pm Wed-Sun) For the best views of Baltimore, climb the 228 steps of the 178ft-tall Doric column dedicated to America's Founding Father, George Washington. It was designed by Robert Mills, who also created DC's Washington Monument. The ground floor contains a museum about Washington's life.

FEDERAL HILL & AROUND
On a bluff overlooking the harbor, **Federal Hill Park** lends its name to the comfortable neighborhood that's set around Cross St Market and comes alive after sundown.

TOP CHOICE **Fort McHenry National Monument & Historic Shrine**
HISTORIC SITE
(www.nps.gov/fomc; 2400 E Fort Ave; adult/child $7/free; ☉8am-4:45pm, to 7:45pm summer) On September 13 and 14, 1814, the star-shaped

fort successfully repelled a British navy attack during the Battle of Baltimore. After a long night of bombs bursting in the air, prisoner Francis Scott Key saw, 'by dawn's early light,' the tattered flag still waving, inspiring him to pen 'The Star-Spangled Banner' (set to the tune of a popular drinking song).

American Visionary Art Museum MUSEUM
(AVAM; www.avam.org; 800 Key Hwy; adult/child $16/10; ☺10am-6pm Tue-Sun) AVAM is a showcase for self-taught (or 'outsider' art), a celebration of unbridled creativity utterly free of arts-scene pretension. Some of the work comes from asylums, others are created by self-inspired visionaries, but it's all rather captivating and well worth a long afternoon.

FELL'S POINT & CANTON
Once the center of Baltimore's shipbuilding industry, the historic cobblestoned neighborhood is now a gentrified mix of 18th-century homes and restaurants, bars and shops. The neighborhood has been the setting for several films and TV series, most notably *Homicide: Life on the Street.* Further east, the slightly more sophisticated streets of Canton fan out, with its grassy square surrounded by great restaurants and bars. On weekends, both neighborhoods can get quite crowded with bar-hoppers.

NORTH BALTIMORE
The 'Hon' expression of affection, an oft-imitated, but never quite duplicated, 'Bawlmerese' peculiarity, was born from **Hampden**, an urban neighborhood at the pinnacle of hipness. Spend a lazy afternoon browsing kitsch, antiques and eclectic clothing along the Avenue (aka W 36th St).

To get to Hampden, take the I-83 N, merge onto Falls Rd (northbound) and take a right onto the Avenue. The prestigious **Johns Hopkins University** (3400 N Charles St) is nearby.

Baltimore Museum of Art MUSEUM
(www.artbma.org; 10 Art Museum Dr, at 31st & N Charles Sts; permanent collection free; ☺10am-5pm Wed-Fri, 11am-6pm Sat & Sun) With a massive collection (the early American, Asian and African galleries are particularly impressive) and a lovely sculpture garden, this museum easily competes with its Smithsonian cousins to the south.

Baltimore for Children

This city loves kids, and proves it with amazing museums, stroll-worthy water-front promenades and family-friendly restaurants. Most attractions are centered on the Inner Harbor, including the National Aquarium of Baltimore (p263), perfect for pint-sized visitors. Kids can run wild o'er the ramparts of historic Fort McHenry National Monument & Historic Shrine (p267) too.

Port Discovery
Children's Museum MUSEUM
(www.portdiscovery.org; Power Plant Live complex, 35 Market Pl; admission $13; ☺10am-5pm Mon-Sat, noon-5pm Sun) Swinging into a three-level jungle tree house, producing a TV show and solving riddles in the Mystery House are a few ways to spend a fun-filled afternoon at this sprawling kids' museum.

Maryland Zoo in Baltimore ZOO
(www.marylandzoo.org; Druid Hill Park; adult/child $16/11; ☺10am-4pm) Lily-pad hopping, adventures with Billy the Bog Turtle and grooming live animals are all in a day's play here. Prices are slightly cheaper on weekdays.

Maryland Science Center MUSEUM
(www.mdsci.org; 601 Light St; adult/child $15/12; ☺10am-5pm Mon-Fri, to 6pm Sat, 11am-5pm Sun) This awesome center features a three-story atrium, tons of interactive exhibits on dinosaurs, outer space and the human body, and the requisite IMAX theater ($4 extra). Hours change seasonally so it's best to check online or call ahead first.

☞ Tours

Baltimore Ghost Tours GHOST
(☏410-357-1186; www.baltimoreghosttours.com; adult/child $15/10; ☺7pm Fri & Sat Mar-Nov) Offers several walking tours exploring the spooky and bizarre side of Baltimore. The popular Fells Point ghost walk departs from Max's on Broadway, 731 S Broadway. There's also a Fell's Point Haunted pub crawl ($20, must be over 21) and a walk around Mt Vernon.

✸ Festivals & Events

Preakness HORSE RACING
(www.preakness.com) Held on the third Sunday of every May, the 'Freakness' is the second leg of the Triple Crown horse race.

Honfest CULTURAL
(www.honfest.net) Put on your best 'Bawlmerese' accent and head to Hampden for this June celebration of kitsch, beehive hairdos, rhinestone glasses and other Baltimore eccentricities.

Artscape CULTURAL
(www.artscape.org) America's largest free arts festival takes place in mid-July and features art displays, live music, theater and dance performances, international food vendors and more.

🛏 Sleeping

Stylish and affordable B&Bs are mostly found in the downtown burbs of Canton, Fell's Point and Federal Hill.

Inn at Henderson's Wharf HOTEL $$$
(☎410-522-7777; www.hendersonswharf.com; 1000 Fell St; r from $209; P❋⊛) A complimentary bottle of wine upon arrival sets the tone at this marvelously situated Fell's Point hotel, which began life as an 18th-century tobacco warehouse. Consistently rated one of the city's best lodges.

Inn at 2920 B&B $$
(☎410-342-4450, 877-774-2920; www.theinnat 2920.com; 2920 Elliott St; r incl breakfast $175-235; ❋@⊛) Housed in a former bordello, this boutique B&B has five individual rooms, high-thread-count sheets, sleek, avant-garde decor and the nightlife-charged neighborhood of Canton right outside your door. The Jacuzzi bathtubs and green sensibility of the owners are a nice touch.

Blue Door on Baltimore B&B $$
(☎410-732-0191; www.bluedoorbaltimore.com; 2023 E Baltimore St; r $140-180; ❋@⊛) In an early 1900s row house, this spotless inn has three elegantly furnished rooms, each with a king-sized bed, claw-foot bathtub (and separate shower) and thoughtful extras like an in-room fountain and fresh flowers. It lies just north of Fells Point.

Peabody Court HOTEL $$
(☎410-727-7101; www.peabodycourthotel.com; 612 Cathedral St; r from $120; P❋⊛) Right in the middle of Mt Vernon, this upscale 104-room hotel has large, handsomely appointed guest rooms with all-marble bathrooms and top-notch service. Often has great deals online.

Sleep Inn HOTEL $$
(☎410-779-6166; www.sleepinn.com; 301 Fallsway; d/ste from $130/150; P❋@⊛) Although it's part of a chain, this attractive, new (opened in 2011) hotel aims for a boutique feel with spacious rooms, high-end mattresses, big windows and artful details (like the B&W framed prints in the rooms, and a working vintage typewriter in the lobby). It's in a decent location, 10-minutes' walk to the Inner Harbor.

Mount Vernon Hotel HOTEL $$
(☎410-727-2000; www.mountvernonbaltimore. com; 24 W Franklin St; d $150; P❋⊛) The historic 1907 Mount Vernon Hotel is a good value for its comfortable, heritage-style rooms in a good location near the restaurant scene along Charles St. Hearty cooked breakfasts sweeten the deal.

HI-Baltimore Hostel HOSTEL $
(☎410-576-8880; www.hiusa.org/baltimore; 17 W Mulberry St; dm/d incl breakfast $25/65; ❋@⊛) Located in a beautifully restored 1857 mansion, the HI-Baltimore has four-, eight- and 12-bed dorms, plus a private double room. Helpful management, nice location and filigreed classical chic make this one of the region's best hostels.

🍴 Eating

Baltimore is an ethnically rich town that sits on top of the greatest seafood repository in the world, not to mention the fault line between the down-home South and cutting-edge innovation of the Northeast.

DOWNTOWN & LITTLE ITALY

Charleston SOUTHERN $$$
(☎410-332-7373; 1000 Lancaster St; 3-/6-courses $74/109; ⊙5:30-10pm Mon-Sat) One of Baltimore's most celebrated restaurants, Charleston serves beautifully prepared Southern-accented fare in a plush setting. Extensive wine list and superb desserts (always included).

Vaccaro's Pastry ITALIAN $
(222 Albemarle St; desserts $7; ⊙9am-10pm Sun-Thu, to midnight Fri & Sat) Vacarro's serves some of the best desserts and coffee in town. The cannoli are legendary, and the gelato and tiramisu are also quite good.

Isabella's PIZZA $$
(221 S High St; sandwiches $7-9, pizzas $13-15; ⊙11am-9pm Mon-Sat, to 5pm Sun) This casual neighborhood place has only a few tables, but it's worth crowding in to sample the excellent Italian pies and gourmet sandwiches, made from high-quality market-fresh ingredients.

Amicci's ITALIAN $$
(☎410-528-1096; 231 S High St; lunch mains $8-10, dinner $14-18; ⊙11am-10pm Sun-Thu, to midnight Fri & Sat; ☑) This local icon serves up traditional Italian comfort food at reasonable

prices. Seafood-lovers and vegetarians will be especially pleased.

MT VERNON

Helmand
AFGHAN $$
(☑410-752-0311; 806 N Charles St; mains $13-15; ⊙5-10pm Sun-Thu, to 11pm Fri & Sat) The Helmand is a longtime favorite for its *kaddo borawni* (pumpkin in yogurt-garlic sauce), vegetable platters and flavorful beef and lamb meatballs followed by cardamom ice cream. Good prices, but it's a dressy affair.

Cazbar
TURKISH $$
(☑410-528-1222; 316 N Charles St; lunch mains $8-10, dinner $16-20; ⊙11am-midnight Mon-Thu, to 2am Fri & Sat, 4pm-midnight Sun) Along a restaurant-sprinkled stretch of Charles St, Cazbar spreads tasty Turkish fare (including creamy hummus and char-grilled lamb and other meats) amid bold colors, multihued lamps and a belly dancer on weekends. Upstairs becomes a lounge on Friday and Saturday with DJs, hookahs and a small dance floor.

City Cafe
CAFE $$
(1001 Cathedral St; mains lunch $10-14, dinner $15-29; ⊙7:30am-10pm Mon-Fri, 10am-10pm Sat, 10am-8pm Sun; ⊛) Bright, inviting cafe with floor-to-ceiling windows, desserts and gourmet sandwiches; dining room in back serves high-end bistro fare.

Dukem
ETHIOPIAN $$
(☑410-385-0318; 1100 Maryland Ave; mains $12-16; ⊙11am-10:30pm) Delicious Ethiopian cooking, including spicy chicken, lamb and vegetarian dishes, all sopped up with spongy flatbread. There's live music some evenings.

Mekong
VIETNAMESE $
(105 W Saratoga St; mains $8-10; ⊙11am-9pm Tue-Sat) Much loved hole-on-the-wall place serving first-rate pho (beef and rice noodle soup).

Lexington Market
FAST FOOD $
(400 W Lexington St; ⊙9am-5pm Mon-Sat) Around since 1782, Lexington Market is famous but rather run-down. Don't miss the crab cakes at **Faidley's** (www.faidleyscrab cakes.com) seafood stall.

FEDERAL HILL & AROUND

Centro Tapas Bar
SPANISH $
(☑443-869-6871; 1444 Light St; small plates $4-10; ⊙6-10pm Tue-Sat) An elegant neighborhood favorite for tasty sharing plates (lobster croquettes, roasted pork belly, wild sautéed mushrooms) and good wines by the glass.

Warm nights offer dining on the backyard patio. Tuesday's $3 tapas menu is a draw.

Bluegrass Tavern
MODERN AMERICAN $$
(☑410-244-5101; 1500 S Hanover St; mains $12-28; ⊙5-10pm Tue-Wed, to 11pm Thu-Sat, 10am-10pm Sun) Warm woods and boutique bourbons set the scene at this welcoming bar and upscale eatery. You'll find house-made charcuterie, unique beers and cocktails, and market fresh fare with Southern accents. Superb Sunday brunches (fresh doughnuts).

Cross Street Market
MARKET $
(1065 Cross St, btwn Light & Charles Sts; ⊙7am-7pm Mon-Sat) This well-located food emporium has tempting stalls hawking oysters, crab cakes, sushi, fresh baked goodies, rotisserie chicken, and plenty of fruit, veg and picnic fare – plus beer (big ones) near the Charles St entrance.

FELL'S POINT & CANTON

TOP CHOICE Blue Hill Tavern
MODERN AMERICAN $$$
(☑443-388-9363; 938 S Conkling St; mains $25-31; ⊙11:30am-2:30pm & 5-10pm Mon-Thu, to 11pm Fri, 5-11pm Sat, 4-9pm Sun) The dining room has blue shimmery fabrics and dark wood furnishings, a subtle backdrop to the bold and flavorful dishes at this award-winning spot. Recent hits include grilled octopus on endive with cloves, and tender slow-cooked lamb loin. Good service (and wine recommendations) and an outdoor rooftop bar in summer.

Obrycki's
SEAFOOD $$$
(☑410-732-6399; 1727 E Pratt St; mains $19-30; ⊙11:30am-10pm Mon-Thu, to 11pm Fri & Sat, to 9:30pm Sun Mar-Nov) Despite its somewhat touristy reputation, Obrycki's is the go-to spot for crab-lovers, with crab soup, crab balls, crab cakes, steamed crabs and soft-shelled crabs.

HAMPDEN & NORTH BALITMORE

Cafe Hon
DINER $$
(1002 W 36th St; mains $7-17; ⊙7am-9pm Mon-Fri, 9am-9pm Sat & Sun) You don't have to be sporting rhinestone-studded glasses and a bouffant hairdo to eat here, but you'll earn serious brownie points. The American comfort food at this veggie-friendly diner is as hearty as the cafe's attitude. After dinner, slide over to adjacent Hon Bar.

PaperMoon Diner
DINER $$
(227 W 29th St; mains $7-16; ⊙7am-midnight Sun-Thu, to 2am Fri & Sat) Like a kaleidoscope

dream, this brightly colored, quintessential Baltimore diner is decorated with thousands of old toys, creepy mannequins and other quirky knickknacks. The real draw here is the anytime breakfast – fluffy French toast, crispy bacon and bagels with lox.

🍷 Drinking & Entertainment

On weekends, Fell's Point and Canton turn into temples of alcoholic excess that would make a Roman emperor blush. Mt Vernon and North Baltimore are a little more civilized, but any one of Baltimore's neighborhoods houses a cozy local pub. The Power Plant Live complex is filled with chain-brand clubs. In Federal Hill, Cross St is sprinkled with eat-and-drink spots. Unless otherwise noted, closing time is 2am.

Bars & Nightclubs
DOWNTOWN & LITTLE ITALY

Mick O'Shea's   PUB
(328 N Charles St; ⏰from 11:30am) Your standard paraphernalia-festooned Irish pub, with live Irish music Friday and Saturday.

Howl at the Moon   LIVE MUSIC
(22 Market Pl, Power Plant Live complex; cover Thu/Fri & Sat $5/7; ⏰from 7pm Wed-Sat) Howl stands out from the cookie-cutter clubs of Power Plant Live with its innovative theme: dueling pianos and a back-up band play audience requests, and everyone sings along.

MT VERNON

[TOP CHOICE] Brewer's Art   BAR
(1106 N Charles St; ⏰from 4pm Mon-Sat, from 5pm Sun) This subterranean cave mesmerizes the senses with an overwhelming selection of beers. Its upstairs embodiment serves respectable dinners in its classy dining room.

Club Charles   BAR
(1724 N Charles St; ⏰from 6pm) Hipsters adorned in the usual skinny jeans/vintage T-shirt uniform, as well as characters from other walks of life, flock to this 1940s art-deco cocktail lounge to enjoy good tunes and cheap drinks.

13th Floor   COCKTAIL BAR
(1 E Chase St; ⏰from 5pm Wed-Fri, from 6pm Sat) Atop the Gothic Belvedere Hotel, this iconic but dated spot has fantastic views over Baltimore. Also in the Belvedere, the **Owl Bar** is a nostalgic throwback to '50s Baltimore, with a long wooden bar that attracts a martini-sipping crowd.

Little Havana   BAR
(1325 Key Hwy; ⏰from 11:30am) A good after-work spot and a great place to sip *mojitos* on the waterfront deck, this converted brick warehouse is a major draw on warm, sunny days (especially around weekend brunch time).

8x10   LIVE MUSIC
(www.the8x10.com; 10 E Cross St; cover $10-20; ⏰from 7pm) Baltimore's premiere live music venue since 1983 mixes big-name acts with strong local talent in a funky concert hall that feels intimate and expansive all at once.

Pub Dog   PUB
(20 E Cross St; ⏰5pm-2am) Pictures of beloved canines adorn this cozy space (though their live compatriots are no longer allowed), which serves delicious brew (or two for $4), and tasty pizzas and bistro fare.

FELL'S POINT & CANTON

One-Eyed Mike's   PUB
(708 S Bond St; ⏰11am-2am) Handshakes and a hearty welcome will make you feel right at home at this popular pirate-themed spot. With tin ceilings and old-world details, it's also one of Baltimore's oldest taverns. There's gourmet grub and a handy outdoor patio/smoking space.

Ale Mary's   BAR
(1939 Fleet St; ⏰from 4pm Mon-Thu, from 11:30am Fri-Sun) Its name and decor pay homage to Maryland's Catholic roots, with crosses, rosaries and nun things scattered about. Aside from the kitsch factor, Ale Mary's brings in a fun festive crowd and serves satisfying food (crab cakes, tater tots, bread pudding).

Gay & Lesbian Venues

Baltimore has a remarkably vibrant, multiracial gay scene. Club admission ranges from $5 to $10.

Grand Central   GAY & LESBIAN
(www.centralstationpub.com; 1001 N Charles St; ⏰9pm-2am Wed-Sun) More of a complex than a club, Central spreads a fancy to suit all moods – dance floor, pub and Sappho's (free admission for the ladies). Probably boasts B's best dance floors.

Hippo   GAY
(www.clubhippo.com; 1 W Eager St; ⏰from 4pm) The Hippo has been around forever and is still one of the city's largest gay clubs

(though some nights the dance floor is dead), with themed nights (gay bingo, karaoke, hip-hop).

Performing Arts & Theater

The Baltimore Symphony Orchestra performs at the Meyerhoff Symphony Hall (410-783-8000; www.bsomusic.org; 1212 Cathedral St), while the Baltimore Opera performs at the Lyric Opera House (410-685-5086; www.lyricoperahouse.com; 140 W Mt Royal Ave).

Theater options include Center Stage (410-332-0033; www.centerstage.org; 700 N Calvert St), which stages Shakespeare, Wilde, Miller and contemporary works; and Charles Theatre (410-727-3456; www.thecharles.com; 1711 N Charles St), screening the best art-house films in the city.

Sports

Whether it's touchdowns, home runs, goals or monster-truck shows, Baltimoreans love their sports. The town plays hard and parties even harder, with tailgating parties in parking lots and games showing on numerous televisions.

Baltimore Orioles   BASEBALL
(888-848-2473; www.orioles.com) The Orioles play at Oriole Park at Camden Yards (333 W Camden St), arguably the best ballpark in America. Daily tours (admission $9) of the stadium are offered during regular season (April to October).

Baltimore Ravens   FOOTBALL
(410-261-7283; www.baltimoreravens.com) The Ravens play at M&T Bank Stadium (1101 Russell St) from September to January.

Homewood Field   LACROSSE
(410-516-7490; hopkinssports.cstv.com; Homewood Field on University Pkwy) Maryland is lacrosse heartland, and its residents are arguably the sport's most fanatic followers. The best place to watch 'lax' is at Johns Hopkins University's Homewood Field.

Baltimore Blast   INDOOR SOCCER
(410-732-5278; www.baltimoreblast.com) The National Indoor Soccer League team plays at the 1st Mariner Arena (410-347-2020; 201 W Baltimore St) from October to April.

Pimlico   HORSE RACING
(www.pimlico.com; 5201 Park Heights Ave) Horse racing is huge from April to late May, especially at Pimlico, which hosts the Preakness (p268). The track is roughly 7 miles north of downtown.

ℹ Information

Internet Access
Enoch Pratt Free Library (400 Cathedral St; 10am-8pm Mon-Wed, to 5pm Thu-Sat, 1-5pm Sun; 📶)

Media
Baltimore Sun (www.baltimoresun.com) Daily city newspaper.
City Paper (www.citypaper.com) Free alt-weekly.

Medical Services
University of Maryland Medical Center (410-328-8667; 22 S Greene St) Has a 24-hour emergency room.

Post
Post office (900 E Fayette St)

Tourist Information
Baltimore Area Visitor Center (877-225-8466; http://baltimore.org; 401 Light St; 9am-6pm Mon-Fri) Located on the Inner Harbor. Sells the Harbor Pass (adult/child $60/45), which gives admission to six major area attractions.

ℹ Getting There & Away

The **Baltimore/Washington International Thurgood Marshall Airport** (BWI; 410-859-7111, www.bwiairport.com) is 10 miles south of downtown via I-295.

Greyhound and **Peter Pan Bus Lines** (410-752-7682; 2110 Haines St) have numerous buses from Washington, DC (roughly every 45 minutes, one hour, $11 to $16); from New York they cost $14 to $35 (12 to 15 per day, 4½ hours). The **BoltBus** (877-265-8287; www.boltbus.com; 1610 St Paul St; 📶) has seven buses a day to/from NYC (3½ hours, $13 to $19).

Penn Station (1500 N Charles St) is in north Baltimore. MARC operates weekday commuter trains to/from Washington, DC ($7, 71 minutes). **Amtrak** (800-872-7245; www.amtrak.com) trains serve the East Coast and beyond.

ℹ Getting Around

Light Rail (tickets $1.60; 6am-11pm) runs from BWI airport to Lexington Market and Penn Station. Train frequency is every five to 10 minutes. MARC trains run hourly between Penn Station and BWI airport on weekdays for $4. **SuperShuttle** (800-258-3826; www.supershuttle.com) provides a BWI-van service to the Inner Harbor for $14. Check **Maryland Transit Administration** (MTA; www.mtamaryland.com) for all local transportation schedules and fares.

Baltimore Water Taxi (410-563-3901; www.baltimorewatertaxi.com; Inner Harbor; daily pass adult/child $10/5) docks at all harborside attractions and neighborhoods.

Annapolis

Annapolis is as charming as state capitals get. The Colonial architecture, cobblestones, flickering lamps and brick row houses are worthy of Dickens, but the effect isn't artificial; this city has preserved, rather than created, its heritage.

Perched on Chesapeake Bay, life in Annapolis (motto: 'Come Sail Away') revolves around the city's rich maritime traditions. It's home to the US Naval Academy, whose 'middies' (midshipmen students) stroll through town in their starched white uniforms. Sailing is not just a hobby, it's a way of life, and the city docks are crammed with vessels of all shapes and sizes. For landlubbers, the food is great, and a beer on the pier cooled by a salty headwind is even better.

There's a visitor center (www.visitannapolis. org; 26 West St; ⊗9am-5pm) and a seasonal information booth at City Dock. A Maryland Welcome Center (☑410-974-3400; 350 Rowe Blvd; ⊗9am-5pm) is inside the State House, and runs free tours of the building.

◉ Sights & Activities

Annapolis has more 18th-century buildings than any other city in America, including the homes of all four Marylanders who signed the Declaration of Independence.

Think of the State House as a wheel hub from which most attractions fan out, leading to the City Dock and historic waterfront.

US Naval Academy   UNIVERSITY
The undergraduate college of the US Navy is one of the most selective universities in America. The Armel-Leftwich visitor center (Gate 1, City Dock entrance; tours adult/child $9.50/7.50; ⊗9am-5pm) is the place to book tours and immerse yourself in all things Academy. Come for the formation weekdays at 12:05pm sharp, when the 4000 midshipmen and midshipwomen conduct a 20-minute military marching display in the yard. Photo ID is required for entry. If you've got a thing for American naval history, go on and revel in the Naval Academy Museum (118 Maryland Ave; admission free; ⊗9am-5pm Mon-Sat, from 11am Sun).

FREE Maryland State House   HISTORIC SITE
(25 State Circle; ⊗9am-5pm Mon-Fri, 10am-4pm Sat & Sun) The country's oldest state capitol in continuous legislative use, the stately 1772 State House also served as national capital from 1733 to 1734. The Maryland Senate is in action here from January to April. The upside-down giant acorn atop the dome stands for wisdom. Photo ID is required for entry.

Hammond-Harwood House   HISTORIC SITE
(www.hammondharwoodhouse.org; 19 Maryland Ave; adult/child $6/3; ⊗noon-5pm Tue-Sun Apr-Oct) Of the many historical homes in town, the 1774 HHH is the one to visit. It has a superb collection of decorative arts, including furniture, paintings and ephemera dating to the 18th century, and is one of the finest existing British Colonial homes in America.

St John's College   UNIVERSITY
(www.stjohnscollege.edu; cnr College Ave & King George St) Take a self-guided tour through the grounds. Originally founded in 1696 as the King William's preparatory school, it's one of the oldest institutions of higher learning in the country.

Kunta Kinte–Alex Haley Memorial   MONUMENT
At the City Dock, the Kunta Kinte–Alex Haley Memorial marks the spot where Kunta Kinte – ancestor of *Roots* author Alex Haley – was brought in chains from Africa. Haley received a 1977 special Pulitzer Prize Letters award for his epic.

William Paca House & Garden HISTORIC SITE
(annapolis.org; adult/child $8/5; ⊗10am-5pm Mon-Sat, noon-5pm Sun) An Annapolis highlight, founded in the 18th-century.

⌲ Tours

Four Centuries Walking Tour   WALKING
(www.watermarkcruises.com; adult/child $16/10) A costumed docent will lead you on this great introduction to all things Annapolis. The 10:30am tour leaves from the visitor center and the 1:30pm tour leaves from the information booth at the City Dock; there's a slight variation in sights visited by each, but both cover the country's largest concentration of 18th-century buildings, influential African Americans and colonial spirits who don't want to leave. The associated one-hour **Pirates of the Chesapeake Cruise** (adult/child $16/13; ⊗late May-early Sep) is good 'yar'-worthy fun, especially for the kids.

Watermark Cruises   CRUISE
(www.watermarkcruises.com; City Dock; 40min adult/child $13/5) The best way to explore the

city's maritime heritage is on the water. Watermark, which operates the Four Centuries Walking Tour, offers a variety of cruise options, with frequent departures.

Woodwind
CRUISE

(📞410-263-7837; www.schoonerwoodwind.com; 80 Compromise St; sunset cruise adult/child $39/25; 🕐May-Oct) This beautiful 74ft schooner offers two-hour day and sunset cruises. Or splurge for the Woodwind 'boat & breakfast' package (rooms $295, including breakfast), one of the more unique lodging options in town.

🛏 Sleeping

Historic Inns of Annapolis
INN $$

(📞410-263-2641; www.historicinnsofannapolis.com; 58 State Circle; r $100-170; ❊🔊) The Historic Inns comprise three different boutique guesthouses, each set in a heritage building in the heart of old Annapolis: the Maryland Inn, the Governor Calvert House and the Robert Johnson House. Common areas are packed with period details, and the best rooms boast antiques, a fireplace and attractive views (the cheapest are small and could use an update).

1908 William Page Inn
B&B $$$

(📞410-263-1506; www.1908-williampageinn.com; 8 Martin St; r incl breakfast $175-235; P❊🔊) For a romantic getaway, nothing beats this Victorian B&B. Beautifully decorated, comfortable rooms are capped with wonderful hospitality and delicious breakfast.

ScotLaur Inn
B&B $$

(📞410-268-5665; www.scotlaurinn.com; 165 Main St; r $95-140; P❊🔊) The folks from Chick & Ruth's Delly offer 10 simple pink-and-blue rooms with private bath at their B&B (bed and bagel) above the deli.

Country Inn & Suites
HOTEL $

(📞410-571-6700; www.countryinns.com; 2600 Housley Rd, at Hwy 450; r from $86; P❊🔊❄) As charming as chains get, plus it has free shuttles to the historic district.

🍴 Eating & Drinking

With the Chesapeake at its doorstep, Annapolis has superb seafood.

Middleton Tavern
SEAFOOD $$

(2 Market Space; mains $10-33; 🕐11:30am-1:30am Mon-Sat, from 10am Sun) One of the oldest continuously operating pubs in the country. As you'd expect from a waterside pub, the menu features some of the freshest seafood around. Live music most nights.

49 West
CAFE $$

(📞410-626-9796; 49 West St; mains lunch $8-10, dinner $15-23; 🕐8am-11pm) This art-filled hideaway in Annapolis serves eclectic cuisine – breakfast standards, gourmet sandwiches and salads for lunch, seafood and bistro fare by night (seared tuna with pesto, *mojito*-glazed chicken), and good wines and cocktails. Live music most nights.

Galway Bay
PUB $$

(📞410-263-8333; 63 Maryland Ave; mains $8-15; 🕐11am-midnight Mon-Sat, from 10:30am Sun) The epitome of a power-broker bar, this Irish-owned and -operated pub is the dark sort of hideaway where political deals go down over Jameson, stouts and mouth-watering seafood specials.

Chick & Ruth's Delly
DINER $

(165 Main St; mains $6-10; 🕐6:30am-10pm Sun-Thu, to 11:30pm Fri & Sat) A cornerstone of Annapolis, the Delly is bursting with affable quirkiness and a big menu, heavy on sandwiches and breakfast fare. Patriots can relive grade-school days reciting the Pledge of Allegiance, weekdays at 8:30am (9:30am on weekends).

Annapolis Ice Cream Company
ICE CREAM $

(196 Main St; ice cream $4-5; 🕐11am-10pm) Creamy ice cream made in-house from organic ingredients – good variety including seasonal flavors. Huge servings.

City Dock Cafe
CAFE $

(18 Market Space; 🕐6:30am-10pm; 🔊) A local favorite with excellent coffees and free wi-fi.

Rams Head Tavern
PUB $$$

(www.ramsheadtavern.com; 33 West St; mains $10-30; 🕐from 11am) Serves pub fare and refreshing microbrews in an attractive oak-paneled setting, with live bands (tickets $15 to $55) onstage.

❶ Getting There & Around

Greyhound runs buses to Washington, DC (once daily, $16). **Dillon's Bus** (www.dillonbus.com; tickets $5) has 26 weekday-only commuter buses between Annapolis and Washington, DC, connecting with various DC Metro lines. **Annapolis Transit** (📞410-263-7964) provides local transport.

Inexpensive **bikes** (per day $5; 🕐9am-8pm) are available for hire from the Harbormaster's office at the City Dock.

Eastern Shore

Just across the Chesapeake Bay Bridge, a short drive from the urban sprawl of the Baltimore–Washington corridor, Maryland's landscape makes a dramatic about-face. Nondescript suburbs and jammed highways give way to unbroken miles of bird-dotted wetlands, serene waterscapes, endless cornfields, sandy beaches and friendly little villages. The coastal flat plains are ideal for cycling. For the most part, the Eastern Shore retains its charm despite the growing influx of city-dwelling yuppies and day-trippers. This area revolves around the water: working waterfront communities still survive off Chesapeake Bay and its tributaries, and boating, fishing, crabbing and kayaking are a part of local life. This is America at its most genuine.

ST MICHAELS, TILGHMAN ISLAND & OXFORD

St Michaels, the prettiest little village on the Eastern Shore, lives up to its motto as 'the Heart & Soul of Chesapeake Bay.' It's a mix of old Victorian homes, quaint B&Bs, boutique shops and working docks, where escape artists from Washington mix with salty-dog crabbers. On weekends the village can get crowded with out-of-town boaters. During the War of 1812, inhabitants rigged up lanterns in a nearby forest and blacked out the town. British naval gunners shelled the trees, allowing St Michaels to escape de-struction. The building now known as the **Cannonball House** (Mulberry St) was the only structure to have been hit.

At the lighthouse, the **Chesapeake Bay Maritime Museum** (www.cbmm.org; 213 N Talbot St; adult/child $13/6; ⊙9am-6pm summer) delves into the deep ties between Shore folk and America's largest estuary. Narrated 60-minute cruises aboard the **Patriot** (☑410-745-3100; www.patriotcruises.com; Navy Point; adult/child $25/13) leave from the dock near the Crab Claw several times a day.

The Victorian red-brick **Parsonage Inn** (☑410-745-8383; www.parsonage-inn.com; 210 N Talbot St; r incl breakfast $150-210; P❖) offers floral decadence (curtains, duvets) and brass beds, plus a friendly welcome by its hospitable innkeepers.

Next door to the Maritime Museum the **Crab Claw** (☑410-745-2900; 304 Burns St; mains $15-30; ⊙11am-10pm) has a splendid open-air setting at the water's edge. Get messy eating delicious steamed crabs ($36 to $60 per dozen) at picnic tables, or head upstairs for more refined seafood feasting.

At the end of the road over the Hwy 33 drawbridge, tiny **Tilghman Island** still runs a working waterfront where local captains take visitors out on graceful oyster skipjacks; the historic **Rebecca T Ruark** (☑410-829-3976; www.skipjack.org; 2hr cruises adult/child $30/15), built in 1886, is the oldest certified vessel of its kind.

Oxford is a small village with a history dating back to the 1600s and a fine spread

WORTH A TRIP

SCENIC DRIVE: MARITIME MARYLAND

Maryland and Chesapeake Bay have always been inextricable, but there are some places where the old-fashioned way of life on the bay seems to have changed little over the passing centuries.

About 150 miles south of Baltimore, at the edge of the Eastern Shore, is **Crisfield**, the top working water town in Maryland. Get visiting details at the **visitor center** (☑410-968-2501; 3 9th St; ⊙10am-4pm Mon-Sat). Any seafood you eat here will be first-rate, but for a true Shore experience, **Watermen's Inn** (☑410-968-2119; 901 W Main St; mains $12-20; ⊙11am-9pm Wed-Fri, from 8am Sat & Sun) is legendary. In a simple, unpretentious setting, you can feast on local catch from an ever-changing menu.

From here you can leave your car and take a boat to **Smith Island** (www.visitsmithisland.com), the only offshore settlement in the state. Several small vessels make the journey, including the **Captain Jason II** (☑410-425-2771; www.smithislandcruises.com; adult/child round-trip $25/13; ⊙12:30pm mid-Jun–Sep); call for schedule off season. Settled by fisherfolk from the English West Country some 400 years ago, the island's tiny population still speak with what linguists reckon is the closest thing to a 17th-century Cornish accent. The island's website has information on island B&Bs, restaurants and activities. Ferries will take you back to the mainland and the present day at 3:45pm.

Eating at a crab shack, where the dress code stops at shorts and flip-flops, is the quint-essential Chesapeake Bay experience. Folks in these parts take their crabs seriously and can spend hours debating the intricacies of how to crack a crab, the proper way to prepare them and where to find the best crabs. There is one thing Marylanders can agree on: they must be blue crabs (scientific name: *Callinectes sapidus*), a critter indigenous to these parts and one of the bay's most important economic products.

Steamed crabs are prepared very simply, using beer and Old Bay seasoning. One of the best crab shacks in the state is **Jimmy Cantler's Riverside Inn** (458 Forest Beach Rd, Annapolis; ⏰11am-11pm Sun-Thu, to midnight Sun), where eating a steamed crab has been elevated to an art form – a hands-on, messy endeavor, normally accompanied by corn on the cob and ice-cold beer. Another fine spot is across the bay at the Crab Claw (p275).

Although the blue crab numbers are down from historical levels – due to overfishing and water pollution – recent studies are showing they may be on a comeback. In 2009, 223 million adult blue crabs were estimated to be living in the bay – a 70% increase over 2008 and the first time in nearly two decades that adult blue crab abundance exceeded the interim goal of 200 million crabs.

of leafy streets and waterfront homes. Al-though you can drive there via US-333, it's well worth taking the old-fashioned **ferry** (☎410-745-9023; www.oxfordbellevueferry.com; 1 way car/additional passenger/pedestrian $11/1/3; ⏰9am-sunset Apr-Nov) from Bellevue. Try to turn up around sunset for memorable views.

Once in Oxford, don't miss the chance to dine at the celebrated Robert Morris Inn (☎410-226-5111; www.robertmorrisinn.com; 314 N Morris St; mains $17-29; ⏰7:30am-10am, noon-2:30pm & 5:30-9:30pm) near the ferry dock. Award-winning crab cakes, grilled local rockfish and medallions of spring lamb are nicely matched by wines and best followed by pavlova with berries and other desserts. You can also overnight in one of the inn's heritage-style rooms (from $200).

BERLIN & SNOW HILL

Imagine 'small-town, main street Ameri-cana,' cute that vision up by a few points, and you've come close to these Eastern Shore villages. Most of the buildings here are preserved or renovated to look pre-served. Antiquity hunters will have to bud-get extra time to browse the antique shops littering this area.

In Berlin, the **Globe Theater** (☎410-641-0784; www.globetheater.com; 12 Broad St; lunch mains $6-12, dinner $11-25; ⏰11am-10pm; 🛜) is a lovingly restored main stage that serves as a restaurant, bar, art gallery and theater for nightly live music; the kitchen serves eclectic American fare with global accents

(seafood burritos, jerk chicken wraps). The nearby, still-functioning **Hair Shop** (17 N Main St) was used as a location in the 1999 film *Runaway Bride*.

There are B&Bs galore, but if you need an alternative try the **Atlantic Hotel** (☎410-641-3589; www.atlantichotel.com; 2 N Main St; r $115-245; P❄). This handsome, Gilded-era lodger gives guests the time-warp experience with all the modern amenities, and the attached Drummer's Cafe (lunch mains $9-14, dinner $17-34; ⏰11am-3pm & 5-10pm Mon-Sat, 10am-3pm Sun) serves up local favorites.

A few miles from Berlin, Snow Hill has a splendid location along the idyllic Po-comoke River. Get on the water with the **Pocomoke River Canoe Company** (☎410-632-3971; 312 N Washington St; canoe per hr/day $15/40). They'll even take you upriver so you can have a leisurely paddle downstream. Nearby **Furnace Town** (☎410-632-2032; www.furnacetown.com; Old Furnace Rd; adult/child $5/3; ⏰10am-5pm Apr-Oct), off Rte 12, is a living-history museum that marks the old location of a 19th-century iron-smelting town. In Snow Hill itself, while away an odd, reward-ing half-hour in the **Julia A Purnell Mu-seum** (☎410-632-0515; 208 W Market St; adult/child $2/50¢; ⏰10am-4pm Tue-Sat, from 1pm Sun Apr-Oct), a tiny structure that feels like an at-tic for the entire Eastern Shore.

Staying in town? Check out Snow Hill's **River House Inn** (☎410-632-2722; 201 E Mar-ket St; www.riverhouseinn.com; r $160-190, cottage $250-300; P❄🐾🏊), with a lush backyard that overlooks a scenic bend of the river.

Palette (☎410-632-0055; 104 W Market St; mains $18-2; ⏰11am-3pm Tue-Wed, to 9pm Thu-Sat, 10am-2pm Sun) serves a changing menu of contemporary American fare, using organic locally sourced ingredients.

Ocean City

'The OC' is where you'll experience the American seaside resort at its tackiest. Here you can take a spin on nausea-inducing thrill rides, buy a T-shirt with obscene slogans and drink to excess at cheesy theme bars. The center of action is the 2.5-mile-long boardwalk, which stretches from the inlet to 27th St. The beach is attractive, but you'll have to contend with packs of horny teenagers and noisy crowds; the beaches north of the boardwalk are much quieter.

The **visitor center** (☎800-626-2326; www.ococean.com; ⏰9am-5pm), in the convention center on Coastal Hwy at 40th St, can help you find lodging. In summer, the town's tiny year-round population of 7100 swells to over 150,000; traffic is jammed and parking scarce.

🛏 Sleeping

King Charles Hotel   GUESTHOUSE **$$**
(☎410-289-6141; www.kingcharleshotel.com; 1209 N Baltimore Ave, at 12th St; r $115-170; P❄🛜) This place could be a quaint summer cottage, except it happens to be a short stroll to the heart of the boardwalk action. It has aging but clean rooms with small porches attached, and it's quiet (owners discourage young partiers).

Spinnaker Motel   HOTEL **$$$**
(☎410-289-5444; http://ocmotels.com/spinnaker; cnr 18th St & Baltimore Ave; r $160-250; P❄🛜🏊)

Cheaper than most beachfront hotels, the Spinnaker has friendly staff, comfortable beds, and balconies with ocean views. It's in the thick of things, so it could get noisy.

🍴 Eating & Drinking

Surf 'n' turf and all-you-can-eat deals are the order of the day. Dance clubs cluster around the boardwalk's southern tip.

Liquid Assets   MODERN AMERICAN **$$**
TOP CHOICE
(☎410-524-7037; www.la94.com; 94th St & Coastal Hwy; mains $10-26; ⏰11:30am-11pm) Like a diamond in the rough, this bistro gem and wine shop complex is hidden in a strip mall in north OC. The menu is a refreshing mix of innovative seafood, grilled meats and regional classics (Carolina pork BBQ, 'ahi tuna burger).

Fager's Island   MODERN AMERICAN **$$$**
(☎410-524-5500; www.fagers.com; 60th St; mains $19-36; ⏰from 11am) The food is hit-and-miss, but it's a great place for a drink, with enviable views over Isle of Wight Bay. Live bands and DJs keep the bachelorettes rolling on weekends.

Seacrets   BAR
(www.seacrets.com; cnr W 49th St & the Bay; ⏰8am-2am) A water-laced, Jamaican-themed, rum-soaked bar straight out of MTV's *Spring Break*. You can drift around in an inner tube while sipping a drink and people-watching at OC's most famous meet-market.

ℹ Getting There & Around

Greyhound (☎410-289-9307; 12848 Ocean Gateway) buses run daily to and from Washington, DC ($62, four hours) and Baltimore ($55, 3½ hours).

WORTH A TRIP

ASSATEAGUE ISLAND

Just 8 miles south but a world away from Ocean City is Assateague Island seashore, a perfectly barren landscape of sand dunes and beautiful, secluded beaches. This undeveloped barrier island is populated by the only herd of wild horses on the East Coast, made famous in the book *Misty of Chincoteague*.

The island is divided into three sections. In Maryland there's **Assateague State Park** (☎410-641-2918; Rte 611; admission/campsites $4/31; ⏰campground open late Apr-Oct) and federally administered **Assateague Island National Seashore** (☎410-641-1441; www.nps.gov/asis; Rte 611; admission/vehicles/campsites $3/15/20; ⏰visitors center 9am-5pm). Chincoteague National Wildlife Refuge (see p298) is in Virginia.

As well as swimming and sunbathing, recreational activities include birding, kayaking, canoeing, crabbing and fishing. There are no services on the Maryland side of the island, so you must bring all your own food and drink. Don't forget insect repellent; the mosquitoes and biting horseflies can be ferocious!

Ocean City Coastal Highway Bus (day pass $3) runs up and down the length of the beach, from 6am to 3am.

Western Maryland

The western spine of Maryland is mountain country. The Appalachian peaks soar to 3000ft above sea level, and the surrounding valleys are packed with rugged scenery and Civil War battlefields. This is Maryland's outdoor playground, where hiking, skiing, rock climbing and white-water rafting are just a short drive from Baltimore.

FREDERICK

Halfway between the battlefields of Gettysburg, PA, and Antietam, Frederick is a popular stop along the Civil War trail. Its 50-square-block historic district is filled with 18th- and 19th-century buildings in various states of renovation. The visitor center (301-600-2888; 151 S East St), across from the MARC train station, is a 10-minute walk to the historic district.

The National Museum of Civil War Medicine (www.civilwarmed.org; 48 E Patrick St; adult/child $6.50/4.50; 10am-5pm Mon-Sat, from 11am Sun) gives a fascinating, sometimes gruesome look at the health conditions soldiers and doctors faced during the war, as well as important medical advances that resulted from the conflict.

Hollerstown Hill B&B (301-228-3630; www.hollerstownhill.com; 4 Clarke Pl; r $135-145; P✳️🛜) has four pattern-heavy rooms, an elegant billiards room and friendly, knowledgeable hosts.

On restaurant-lined Market St, Volt (301-696-3658; 228 N Market St; mains $29-40; noon-10pm) is one of Frederick's finest, with a seasonal, locally sourced menu, first-rate service and a loyal following who come from DC and beyond. It's set in a beautifully restored 19th-century mansion. Reserve months ahead for the Table 21 experience (21 courses for $121 served inside the kitchen). The three-course lunch for $25 is a great value.

Frederick is accessible via Greyhound (301-663-3311) and MARC trains (301-682-9716) located across from the visitor center at 100 S East St.

ANTIETAM NATIONAL BATTLEFIELD

The site of the bloodiest day in American history is, ironically, supremely peaceful, quiet and haunting, uncluttered save for plaques and statues. On September 17, 1862, General Robert E Lee's first invasion of the North was stalled here in a tactical stalemate that left over 23,000 dead, wounded or missing – more casualties than America had suffered in all her previous wars combined. Poignantly, many of the battlefield graves are inscribed with German and Irish names, a roll call of immigrants who died fighting for their new homeland.

The visitor center (301-432-5124; State Rd 65; 3-day individual/family pass $4/6; 8:30am-6pm, to 5pm low season) sells a range of books and materials, including self-guided driving and walking tours of the battlefield.

Ten miles southeast of Antietam, off I-67 in Burkittsville, is Gathland State Park (301-791-4767; admission free; 8am-sunset), with access to the Appalachian Trail. Burkittsville is also famous as the setting of *The Blair Witch Project*.

CUMBERLAND

At the Potomac River, the frontier outpost of Fort Cumberland (not to be confused with the Cumberland Gap between Virginia and Kentucky) was the pioneer gateway across the Alleghenies to Pittsburgh and the Ohio River. Today Cumberland has expanded into the outdoor recreation trade to guide visitors to the region's rivers, forests and mountains. The sights below are a short stroll from the pedestrian-friendly streets of downtown Cumberland.

👁 Sights & Activities

C&O Canal National Historic Park TRAIL
A marvel of engineering, the C&O Canal was designed to stretch alongside the Potomac River from Chesapeake Bay to the Ohio River. Construction on the canal began in 1828 but was halted here in 1850 by the Appalachian Mountains. The park's protected 185-mile corridor includes a 12ft-wide towpath/hiking and bicycling trail, which goes all the way from here to Georgetown in DC. The C&O Canal Museum (301-739-4200; 15 Canal Pl; 9am-5pm Mon-Fri) has displays chronicling the importance of river trade in eastern seaboard history.

Great Allegheny Passage TRAIL
(GAP; www.atatrail.org) Another great walking/cycling track is along this rail trail, which travels through valleys, along rivers and by small towns en route 135 miles northwest to Duquesne, PA. Still under construction, the GAP will eventually go all the way to Pittsburgh. The trail starts near Baltimore St and

the canal, and from here links with the C&O Canal path, 200m to the south.

Western Maryland Scenic Railroad TRAIN
(☎800-872-4650; www.wmsr.com; 13 Canal St; adult/child $30/16; ☺11:30am Fri-Sun May-Oct, Sat & Sun Nov-Dec) Outside the Allegheny County visitor center, near the start of the C&O Canal, passengers can catch steam-locomotive rides, traversing forests and steep ravines to Frostburg, a 3½-hour round-trip.

Cumberland Trail Connection CYCLING
(☎301-777-8724; www.ctcbikes.com; 14 Howard St, Canal Pl; half-day/day/week from $15/25/120; ☺10am-6pm) Conveniently located near the start of the C&O Canal, this outfit rents out bikes (cruisers, touring bikes and mountain bikes), and also arranges shuttle service anywhere from Pittsburgh to DC. Canoe rentals were in the works.

Allegany Expeditions ADVENTURE TOUR
(☎301-722-5170; www.alleganyexpeditions.com; 10310 Columbus Ave/Rte 2) Leads adventure tours, including rock-climbing, canoeing, cross-country skiing and fly-fishing.

✖ Eating

Queen City Creamery & Deli DINER $
(☎301-777-0011; 108 Harrison St; mains $6-8; ☺7am-9pm) This retro soda fountain is like a 1940s time warp, with creamy shakes and homemade frozen custard, thick sandwiches and belly-filling breakfasts.

DEEP CREEK LAKE
In the extreme west of the panhandle, Maryland's largest freshwater lake is an all-seasons playground. The crimson and copper glow of the Alleghenies attracts thousands during the annual **Autumn Glory Festival** (www.autumngloryfestival.com) in October, rivaling New England's leaf-turning backdrops. In McHenry, the **Garrett County visitor center** (☎301-387-4386; www.visitdeepcreek.com; 15 Visitor Center Dr), off US 219 on the north end, has information on all outdoor activities, including the nearby ski resort, **Wisp** (☎301-387-4911; www.wispresort.com).

DELAWARE

Diminutive, delectable Delaware, the nation's second-smallest state (96 miles long and less than 35 miles across at its widest point) is overshadowed by her neighbors and overlooked by visitors to the Capital Region. And that's too bad, because Delaware has a lot more on offer than just tax-free shopping and chicken farms.

You may be pleasantly surprised to learn that Delaware is home to long white sandy beaches, cute colonial villages, a cozy countryside and small-town charm. A whole state just waiting to be explored, Delaware still rides on her reputation as being the first state to ratify the US Constitution, hence her new slogan: 'It's Good Being First.'

History
In colonial days Delaware was the subject of an aggressive land feud between Dutch, Swedish and British settlers. The former imported classically northern European middle-class concepts, the latter a plantation-based aristocracy, which is partly why Delaware remains a typically mid-Atlantic cultural hybrid today.

The little state's big moment came on December 7, 1787, when Delaware became the first state to ratify the US Constitution and thus the first state in the Union. It remained in that union throughout the Civil War, despite supporting slavery. During this period, as throughout much of the state's history, the economy drew on its chemical industry. DuPont, the world's second-largest chemical company, was founded here in 1802 as

---

DELAWARE FACTS

» **Nickname** The First State

» **Population** 900,000

» **Area** 1982 sq miles

» **Capital city** Dover (population 36,000)

» **Sales tax** none

» **Birthplace of** Rock musician George Thorogood (b 1952), actress Valerie Bertinelli (b 1960), actor Ryan Phillippe (b 1974)

» **Home of** Vice President Joe Biden, the Du Pont family, DuPont chemicals, credit-card companies, lots of chickens

» **Politics** usually democrat

» **Famous for** tax-free shopping, beautiful beaches

» **State bird** blue hen chicken

» **Driving distances** Wilmington to Dover 52 miles, Dover to Rehoboth Beach 43 miles a gunpowder factory by French Immigrant Eleuthère Irénée du Pont. Low taxes drew other firms (particularly credit-card companies) in the 20th century, boosting the state's prosperity.

Delaware Beaches

Delaware's 28 miles of sandy Atlantic beaches are the best reason to linger. All businesses and services listed here are open year-round unless otherwise noted, and all prices are for the high season (June to August). Low-season bargains abound.

LEWES

In 1631 the Dutch gave this whaling settlement the pretty name of Zwaanendael, or valley of the swans, before promptly getting massacred by local Nanticoke. The name was changed to Lewes (pronounced LOO-iss) when William Penn gained control of the area. Today it's an attractive seaside gem with a mix of English and Dutch architecture.

The **visitor center** (www.leweschamber. com; 120 Kings Hwy; ⊙9am-5pm Mon-Fri) directs you to sights such as the **Zwaanendael Museum** (102 Kings Hwy; admission free; ⊙10am-4:30pm Tue-Sat, 1:30-4:30pm Sun), where the friendly staff explains the Dutch roots of this first state settlement.

At **Fisherman's Wharf** (☎302-645-8862; www.fishlewes.com; 7 Anglers Rd) you can book boat trips on the water for sunset cruises (adult/child $15/10), dolphin-watching (adult/child $35/20) and fishing trips (half-day/day $45/85).

For more aquatic action, you can rent kayaks from **Quest Fitness Kayak** (☎302-745-2925; www.questfitnesskayak.com; Savannah Rd; kayak per 2/8hr $25/50), which operates a rental stand next to the Beacon Motel. It also runs scenic paddle tours around the Cape (adult/child $65/35).

You'll find restaurant and hotel options in the small historic downtown, including **Hotel Rodney** (☎302-645-6466; www.hotel rodneydelaware.com; 142 2nd St; r $140-250; P❋@☎≋), a charming boutique hotel with exquisite bedding and antique furniture. On the other side of the canal, **Beacon Motel** (☎302-645-4888; www.beaconmotel.com; 514 Savannah Rd; r $95-190; P❋@☎≋) has large, quiet rooms within a 10-minute walk to the beach.

There are charming restaurants and cafes sprinkled along 2nd St. Located by the drawbridge over the canal, the clapboard **Striper**

BIKING THE JUNCTION & BREAKWATER TRAIL

For a fantastic ride between Rehoboth and Lewes, rent a bike and hit the 6-mile Junction and Breakwater Trail. Named after the former rail line, which operated here in the 1800s, this smooth, graded greenway travels through wooded and open terrain, over coastal marshes and past farmland. Pick up a map from the Rehoboth visitor center or from **Atlantic Cycles** (www.atlanticcycles.net; 18 Wilmington Ave) in Rehoboth, which offers inexpensive rentals (half-day/day from $12/18). In Lewes, try **Ocean Cycles** (www.oceancylces.com; 514 E Savannah Rd) at the Beacon Motel.

Bites Bistro (☎302-645-4657; 107 Savannah Rd; lunch mains $10-12, dinner $16-24; ⊙11:30am-late Mon-Sat) specializes in innovative seafood dishes like Lewes rockfish and fish tacos. Across the drawbridge, the **Wharf** (☎302-645-7846; 7 Anglers Rd; mains $10-24; ⊙7am-1am) has a relaxing waterfront location (facing the canal), and serves a big selection of seafood and pub grub. Live music throughout the week.

The **Cape May–Lewes Ferry** (☎800-643-3779; www.capemaylewesferry.com; 43 Cape Henlopen Dr; per vehicle $36-44, plus per adult/child passenger $10/5) runs daily 90-minute ferries across Delaware Bay to New Jersey from the terminal, 1 mile from downtown Lewes. For foot passengers, a seasonal shuttle bus ($4) operates between the ferry terminal and Lewes and Rehoboth Beach. Fares are lower Sunday through Thursday. Reservations are recommended.

CAPE HENLOPEN STATE PARK

One mile east of Lewes, more than 4000 acres of dune bluffs, pine forests and wetlands are preserved at this lovely **state park** (☎302-645-8983) that's popular with bird-watchers and beachgoers ($6 per out-of-state car). You can see clear to Cape May from the observation tower. **North Shores** beach draws many gay and lesbian couples. **Camping** (☎877-987-2757; campsites $30-32; ⊙Mar-Nov) includes oceanfront or wooded sites.

REHOBOTH BEACH & DEWEY BEACH

As the closest beach to Washington, DC (121 miles), Rehoboth is often dubbed 'the Nation's Summer Capital.' Founded in 1873 as a Christian seaside resort camp, Rehoboth is today a shining example of tolerance. It is both a family-friendly and gay-friendly destination, and has a particularly large lesbian community. There's even a gay beach – aka Poodle Beach – located, appropriately, at the end of Queen St.

Downtown Rehoboth is a mix of grand Victorian and gingerbread houses, tree-lined streets, boutique B&Bs and shops, posh restaurants, kiddie amusements and wide beaches fronted by a mile-long boardwalk. Rehoboth Ave, the main drag, is lined with restaurants and the usual tacky souvenir shops; it stretches from the visitor center (302-227-2233; www.beach-fun.com; 501 Rehoboth Ave; 9am-5pm Mon-Fri, to 1pm Sat & Sun) at the traffic circle to the boardwalk. Outside of town, Rte 1 is a busy highway crammed with chain restaurants, hotels and outlet malls, where bargain-hunters take advantage of Delaware's tax-free shopping.

Less than 2 miles south on Hwy 1 is the tiny hamlet of Dewey Beach. Unapologetically known as 'Do Me' beach for its hook-up scene (straight) and hedonistic nightlife, Dewey is a major party beach.

🛏 Sleeping

As elsewhere on the coast, prices sky rocket in high season (June to August). Cheaper lodging options are located on Rte 1.

TOP CHOICE Bellmoor Inn & Spa   BOUTIQUE HOTEL $$$
(800-425-2355; www.thebellmoor.com; 6 Christian St; r from $260; P❄@🐾🛜) If money were no object, we'd splurge for a room at Rehoboth's most luxurious inn. With its English country decor, fireplaces, quiet garden and secluded setting, this is not your usual seaside resort. A full-service day spa caps the amenities.

Hotel Rehoboth   BOUTIQUE HOTEL $$$
(302-227-4300; www.hotelrehoboth.com; 247 Rehoboth Ave; r $290-390; P❄@🐾🛜) Rehoboth's newest boutique hotel has gained a reputation for great service and luxurious amenities, including a free shuttle to the beach.

Crosswinds Motel   MOTEL $$$
(302-227-7997; www.crosswindsmotel.com; 312 Rehoboth Ave; r $150-250; P❄🛜) Located in the heart of Rehoboth Ave, this simple motel offers great value for your dollar, with welcome amenities (minifridge, coffeemaker, flat-screen TV). Walk to the beach in 12 minutes.

Walls Apartments   APARTMENT $
(302-227-2999; www.crosswindsmotel.com; cnr Christian St & Rehoboth Ave; r from $97; P) This aging complex of cabins and rustically furnished apartments sits in a great location a few blocks from the beach. The price is unbeatable, but the battered furniture and tattered carpets discourage most – plus some apartments have tubs but lack showers (there are outdoor showers, however). Cash only.

🍴 Eating & Drinking

Cheap eats are available on the boardwalk, with favorites like Thrasher's fries, Grotto's pizza and Dolle's saltwater taffy. For classier dining, browse the inviting restaurants sprinkled along Wilmington Ave.

TOP CHOICE Planet X   FUSION $$$
(302-226-1928; 35 Wilmington Ave; mains $16-33; from 5pm; 🌱) This stylish spot shows its Asian influence in menu and decor – red paper lanterns and Buddhas adorn the walls, while diners feast on red Thai curry with jumbo shrimp and crab cakes with spicy Asian sesame noodles. There's al fresco dining on the open-sided front porch.

Henlopen City Oyster House   SEAFOOD $$$
(50 Wilmington Ave; mains $21-26; from 3pm) Oyster- and seafood-lovers won't want to miss this elegant spot, where an enticing raw bar and beautifully prepared plates (soft-shell crabs, bouillabaisse, lobster mac 'n' cheese) draw crowds (arrive early; no reservations). Good microbrews, cocktails and wine selections make it an ideal early-evening drink–eat spot.

Cultured Pearl   JAPANESE $$$
(302-227-8493; 301 Rehoboth Ave; mains $16-33; 4:30pm-late) A longtime locals' favorite, this Asian restaurant has a Zen feel, with koi pond at the entrance and a pleasant rooftop deck. The sushi and appetizers are first-rate. Live music most nights.

Royal Treat   ICE CREAM $
(4 Wilmington Ave; ice cream $3.50; 8am-11:30pm) There's always a line outside this landmark ice-cream parlor, with giant servings of creamy rich concoctions. Breakfast is also popular.

Starboard   RESTAURANT, BAR $$
(2009 Hwy 1, Dewey Beach; mains $6-18; 9am-late Apr-Oct) A Dewey Beach tradition since 1960, the Starboard is the region's best bet

for brunch. Order the Eggs Del Marva – eggs Benedict topped with crab meat. At night, Starboard transforms into the area's biggest beach party with wall-to-wall drunks and live entertainment.

Dogfish Head　　　　MICROBREWERY **$$**
(www.dogfish.com; 320 Rehoboth Ave; mains $9-23; ☺noon-late) When a place mixes its own brewery with some of the best live music on the Eastern Shore, you know you've got a winning combination.

ⓘ **Getting There & Around**
The **Jolly Trolley** (one way $2.50; ☺8am-2am summer) connects Rehoboth and Dewey, and makes frequent stops along the way. Unfortunately, long-distance buses no longer serve Rehoboth.

BETHANY BEACH & FENWICK ISLAND

Want to get away from it all? The seaside towns of Bethany and Fenwick, about half-way between Rehoboth and Ocean City, are known as 'the Quiet Resorts.' They share a tranquil, almost boring, family-friendly scene.

There are only a few restaurants and even fewer hotels here; most visitors stay in rented apartments and beach houses. For a nice change of pace from the usual seafood fare, **Bethany Blues BBQ** (☏302-537-1500; www.bethanyblues.com; 6 N Pennsylvania Ave; mains $14-24; ☺4:30-9pm) has falling-off-the-bone ribs and pulled-pork sandwiches.

Northern & Central Delaware

The grit of Wilmington is balanced by the rolling hills and palatial residences of the Brandywine Valley, particularly the soaring estate of Winterthur. Dover is cute, friendly and gets a little lively after hours.

WILMINGTON

A unique cultural milieu (African Americans, Jews, Caribbean etc) and an energetic arts scene make this a town worth a visit. The central commercial district is along Market St, while Riverfront's old warehouses and other industrial sites have been transformed into shops, restaurants and museums. The **visitor center** (☏800-489-6664; www.visitwilmingtonde.com; 100 W 10th St; ☺9am-5pm Mon-Fri) is downtown.

The **Delaware Art Museum** (www.delart.org; 800 S Madison St; adult/child $12/6, Sun free;

☺10am-4pm Wed-Sat, from noon Sun) exhibits work of the local Brandywine School, including Edward Hopper, John Sloan and three generations of Wyeths. The **Delaware Center for the Contemporary Arts** (☏302-656-6466; www.thedcca.org; 200 S Madison St; admission free; ☺10am-5pm Tue & Thu-Sat, from noon Wed & Sun) is bringing some mind-expanding culture to the Riverfront district. Located in an art-deco Woolworth's building, the **Delaware History Museum** (www.hsd.org; 200 S Madison St; adult/child $6/4; ☺11am-4pm Sat) proves the First State has done loads more than earn its nickname.

The premier hotel in the state, the **Hotel du Pont** (☏302-594-3100; www.hoteldupont.com; cnr Market & 11th Sts, r $230-460; [P][✻][☎]) is luxurious and classy enough to satisfy its namesake (ie one of America's most successful industrialist families). On the riverfront, **Iron Hill Brewery** (☏302-472-2739; 710 South Madison St; mains $10-24; ☺11am-11pm) is a spacious and airy multilevel space set in a converted brick warehouse. Satisfying microbrews (try the seasonal Belgian ale) match nicely with hearty pub grub (pizzas, sandwiches, pan-roasted chicken, barbecued shrimp).

Wilmington is accessible by Greyhound or Peter Pan Bus Lines, which run to DC ($20, three hours) and New York ($30, 2½ hours). Both bus lines serve the **Wilmington Transportation Center** (101 N French St). **Amtrak trains** (100 S French St) connect Wilmington with DC ($45, 1½ hours), Baltimore ($37, 45 minutes) and New York ($56, 1¾ hours).

BRANDYWINE VALLEY

After making their fortune, the French-descended Du Ponts turned the Brandywine Valley into a sort of American Loire Valley, and it remains a nesting ground for the wealthy and ostentatious to this day. The **Brandywine Valley Tourist Information Center** (☏610-719-1730; www.brandywinevalley.com), outside Longwood Gardens in Kennett Square, PA, distributes information on the region's triple crown of chateaux and gardens: Winterthur, Longwood Gardens and Nemours.

◉ **Sights**

Winterthur　　　　　HISTORIC SITE
(☏302-888-4600; www.winterthur.org; Hwy 52; adult/child $18/5; ☺10am-5pm Tue-Sun) Six miles northwest of Wilmington is the 175-room country estate of industrialist Henry

Francis du Pont and his collection of antiques and American arts, one of the world's largest.

Hagley Museum   MUSEUM
(☑302-658-2400; www.hagley.org; Hwy 141; adult/child $11/4; ⊘9:30am-4:30pm) Another fascinating shrine to the Du Pont legacy, the sprawling outdoor museum includes the ruins of the original DuPont company mills, craftsmith demonstrations and exhibits on some of the DuPont company inventions such as nylon.

NEW CASTLE
New Castle is a web of cobblestoned streets and beautifully preserved 18th-century buildings, lying near the riverfront. The surrounding area, however, is a bit of an urban wasteland. Sights include the Old Court House (⊘closed Mon), the arsenal on the Green, churches and cemeteries dating back to the 17th century, and historic houses.

The five-room Terry House B&B (☑302-322-2505; www.terryhouse.com; 130 Delaware St; r $90-110; P 🛜) is idyllically set in the historic district. The owner will play the piano for you while you enjoy a full breakfast.

A few doors down, Jessop's Tavern (114 Delaware St; mains $12-22; ⊘11:30am-9pm) serves up Dutch pot roast, Pilgrim's feast (oven-roasted turkey with all the fixings) plus fish-and-chips and other pub grub in a colonial atmosphere – complete with costumed waitstaff, creaky wooden floors and antique decorations.

DOVER
Central Dover has stately brick buildings and shady, tree-lined boulevards that make for an intriguing half-day's exploration.

Walk beside the State House (25 The Green) to find the visitor center (☑302-739-4266; 406 Federal St; ⊘8:30am-4:30pm Mon-Sat, from 1:30pm Sun) and history exhibits at the foot of a long plaza. Ask here about free walking tours in the area led by costumed interpreters. Free tours of the State House are also given.

The Johnson Victrola Museum (cnr Bank & New Sts; admission free; ⊘9am-4:30pm Wed-Sat) honors 'talking machine' pioneer Eldridge Johnson, including an exhibit on the RCA Records trademark dog, Nipper. The Delaware Agriculture Museum and Village (☑302-734-1618; www.agriculturalmuseum.org; 866 N Dupont Hwy; adult/child $5/3; ⊘10am-3pm Tue-Sat) is a living-history museum featuring a re-creation of an 1890s farming community.

Southeast of town, Dover Air Force Base is the country's largest air base and the first stop for America's returning war dead. There are no public ceremonies to mark their homecoming, but you can visit the Air Mobility Command Museum (☑302-677-5938; www.amcmuseum.org; cnr Hwys 9 & 1; admission free; ⊘9am-4pm Tue-Sun), filled with vintage planes and other aviation artifacts.

NASCAR fans worldwide know of Dover International Speedway (☑302-883-6500; doverspeedway.com; 1131 N Dupont Hwy), considered one of the best tracks in the country. See its website for current race schedules and ticket information. At the same location is Dover's other major attraction, Dover Downs Casino (☑302-674-4600; doverdowns.com; ⊘8am-4am Mon-Sat, from noon Sun), an enormous entertainment complex with slot machines, horse racing, hotel, spa and concert venue.

The State Street Inn (☑302-734-2294; 228 N State St; r $110-135) is a well-located inn near the State House, with four bright rooms with wood floors and period furnishings.

A short stroll from the State House, Frazier's (☑302-674-8875; 9 E Lockerman St; mains $8-19; ⊘from 11am) is a wood-paneled eatery with outdoor tables facing the river, and decent burgers, sandwiches and seafood.

Neighborhood bar WT Smithers (☑302-674-8875; 140 S State St; mains $8-16; ⊘from 11am Mon-Sat) attracts a mix of students and State House staff sharing buffalo wings and excellent beer on tap.

VIRGINIA

Beautiful, passionate, lovely Virginia is a state steeped in history. It's the birthplace of America, where English settlers established the first permanent colony in the New World in 1607. From there, the Commonwealth of Virginia has played a lead role in nearly every major American drama, from the Revolutionary and Civil wars to the Civil Rights movement and September 11, 2001.

Virginia's natural beauty is as diverse as her history and people. Chesapeake Bay and the wide sandy beaches kiss the Atlantic Ocean. Pine forests, marshes and rolling green hills form the soft curves of the central Piedmont region, while the rugged Appalachian Mountains and stunning Shenandoah Valley line her back.

The nation's invisible line between North and South is drawn here, somewhere around Richmond; you'll know it as soon as you hear the sweet southern drawl offering plates of biscuits and Virginia ham. With something for everyone, it's easy to appreciate the state's motto: 'Virginia is for Lovers.'

History

Humans have occupied Virginia for at least 5000 years. Several thousand Native Americans were already here in May 1607 when Captain James Smith and his crew sailed up Chesapeake Bay and founded Jamestown, the first permanent English colony in the New World. Named for the 'Virgin Queen' Elizabeth I, the territory originally occupied most of America's eastern seaboard. By 1610 most of the colonists had died from starvation in their quest for gold, until colonist John Rolfe (husband of Pocahontas) discovered Virginia's real riches: tobacco.

A feudal aristocracy grew out of tobacco farming, and many gentry scions became Founding Fathers, including native son George Washington. In the 19th century the slave-based plantation system grew in size and incompatibility with the industrializing

VIRGINIA FACTS

» **Nickname** Old Dominion

» **Population** 8 million

» **Area** 42,774 sq miles

» **Capital city** Richmond (population 202,000)

» **Sales tax** 5%

» **Birthplace of** eight US presidents including George Washington (1732–99), Confederate General Robert E Lee (1807-70), tennis ace Arthur Ashe (1943–93), author Tom Wolfe (b 1931), actress Sandra Bullock (b 1964)

» **Home of** the Pentagon, the CIA, more technology workers than any other state

» **Politics** Republican

» **Famous for** American history, tobacco, apples, Shenandoah National Park

» **State beverage** milk

» **Driving distances** Arlington to Shenandoah 113 miles, Richmond to Virginia Beach 108 miles

North; Virginia seceded in 1861 and became the epicenter of the Civil War. Following its defeat the state walked a tense cultural tightrope, accruing a layered identity that included older aristocrats, a rural and urban working class, waves of immigrants and today, the burgeoning tech-heavy suburbs of DC. The state revels in its history, yet still wants to pioneer the American experiment; thus, while Virginia only reluctantly desegregated in the 1960s, today it houses one of the most ethnically diverse populations of the New South.

Northern Virginia

Hidden within its suburban sprawl exterior, 'NOVA' mixes small-town charm with metropolitan chic. Colonial villages and battlefields bump up against skyscrapers, shopping malls and world-class arts venues.

You'll discover unexpected green spaces like **Great Falls National Park** (☏703-285-2965; www.nps.gov/grfa; ⏰7am-sunset), a wilderness space that somehow survives despite being mere minutes from a major urban nexus. The park is a gorgeous, well-maintained forest cut through by the Potomac River, which surges over a series of white-water rapids. Kayaking (experienced paddlers only), rock climbing, hiking and fishing are all popular activities.

ARLINGTON

Just across the Potomac River from DC, Arlington County was once part of Washington until it was returned to Virginia in 1847. In recent years the gentrified neighborhoods of Arlington have spawned some tempting dining and nightlife options.

⊙ Sights & Activities

FREE **Arlington National Cemetery**   HISTORIC SITE (www.arlingtoncemetery.org; ⏰8am-7pm Apr-Sep, to 5pm Oct-Mar) The county's best-known attraction is the somber final resting place for more than 300,000 military personnel and their dependents, with veterans of every US war from the Revolution to Iraq. The cemetery is spread over 612 hilly acres. Departing from the visitor center, **Tourmobiles** (☏202-554-5100; www.tourmobile.com; adult/child $8.50/4.25) are a handy way to visit the cemetery's memorials.

Much of the cemetery was built on the grounds of **Arlington House**, the former

SCENIC DRIVE: VIRGINIA'S HORSE COUNTRY

About 40 miles west of Washington, DC, suburban sprawl gives way to endless green farms, vineyards, quaint villages and palatial estates and ponies. This is 'Horse Country,' where wealthy Washingtonians pursue their equestrian pastimes.

The following route is the most scenic drive to Shenandoah National Park. From DC, take Rte 50 West to **Middleburg**, a too-cute-for-words town of B&Bs, taverns, wine shops and boutiques. The **National Sporting Library** (☑540-687-6542; www.nsl.org; 102 The Plains Rd; ☺10am-4pm Tue-Fri, from 1pm Sat) is a museum and research center devoted to horse and field sports like foxhunting, dressage, steeplechase and polo.

Griffin Tavern (☑540-675-3227; 659 Zachary Taylor Hwy; mains $9-20; ☺11:30am-9pm) is a quintessential British pub with English and Irish food and beer; head southwest on Rte 522 and 211 to Flint Hill.

Six miles down Rte 211 is **Little Washington**, another cute town that's home to one of the finest B&B restaurants in America, the **Inn at Little Washington** (☑540-675-3800; www.theinnatlittlewashington.com; cnr Middle & Main Sts; r from $425). Further down the road at the foothills of the Blue Ridge Mountains is **Sperryville** and its many galleries and shops, a must-stop for antique-lovers. Continue 9 miles west to reach the Thornton Gap entrance of Skyline Dr in Shenandoah National Park (p301).

home of Robert E Lee and his wife Mary Anna Custis Lee, a descendant of Martha Washington. When Lee left to lead Virginia's army in the Civil War, Union troops confiscated the property to bury their dead. The **Tomb of the Unknowns** contains the remains of unidentified American servicemen from both World Wars and the Korean War; military guards retain a round-the-clock vigil and the changing of the guard (every half-hour March to September, every hour October to February) is one of Arlington's most moving sights. An eternal flame marks the **grave of John F Kennedy**, next to those of Jacqueline Kennedy Onassis and two of her infant children. The **Women in Military Service for America Memorial** (☑800-222-2294; www.womensmemorial.org) honors the two million women who have served in America's armed forces. Other points of interest include the **Pan Am Flight 103 cairn** and the **Space Shuttle Challenger memorial**.

Just north of the cemetery, the **Marine Corps Memorial** (N Meade & 14th Sts) depicts six soldiers raising the American flag on Iwo Jima. The Felix de Weldon–designed sculpture is based on an iconic photo by Associated Press photographer Joe Rosenthal.

Artisphere   ARTS CENTER
(www.artisphere.com; 1101 Wilson Blvd; ☎) For something completely different, check out the excellent exhibits at this sleek, modern, multistory arts complex, which opened in 2011. Its several theaters host live performances (many free) – world music, film, experimental theater – and there's a cafe, restaurant and bar. It's a short stroll from Rosslyn Metro station.

Pentagon   BUILDING
South of Arlington Cemetery is the Pentagon, the largest office building in the world. It's not open to the public, but outside you may visit the **Pentagon Memorial** (www.whs. mil/memorial; admission free; ☺24hr); 184 illuminated benches honor each person killed in the September 11, 2001, terrorist attack on the Pentagon. Nearby, the three soaring arcs of the **Air Force Memorial** (☑703-247-5805; www.airforcememorial.org) invoke the contrails of jets.

🛏 Sleeping & Eating

Dozens of hotels, chic restaurants and bars are located along Clarendon and Wilson Blvds, clustered near Rosslyn and Clarendon Metro stations.

Whitlow's on Wilson   AMERICAN $$
(☑703-276-9693; 2854 Clarendon Blvd; mains $8-21; ☺11am-2am Mon-Fri, from 9am Sat & Sun) The neighborhood's best Sunday-brunch menu, plus weekday happy hour specials and live bands on weekends.

Ray's Hell-Burger   BURGERS $
(1713 Wilson Blvd; burgers from $7; ☺noon-10pm Tue-Sun, from 5pm Mon) In a nondescript strip mall, amid wooden benches and minimal ambience, Ray's is famed for its 10-ounce burgers, served with an array of fixings.

WORTH A TRIP

STEVEN F UDVAR-HAZY CENTER

The Smithsonian National Air & Space Museum's **Steven F Udvar-Hazy Center** (☎703-572-4118; ⊙10am-5:30pm), located in Chantilly near Dulles airport, is a huge hangar filled with surplus planes and spacecraft that wouldn't fit at the museum's DC location. Highlights include the space shuttle *Enterprise*, the B-29 *Enola Gay*, SR-71 *Blackbird* and a Concorde supersonic airliner. While the museum is free, parking costs $15.

Order it with sweet potato fries. Obama took Russian pres Medvedev here (they apparently had cheddar cheese burgers).

Iota   LIVE MUSIC
(☎703-522-8340; www.iotaclubandcafe.com; 2832 Wilson Blvd; cover free-$15; ⊙7am-2am Mon-Fri, from 9am Sat & Sun; 🐾) Arlington's top spot to catch live local and national musicians nightly, with good food too; Norah Jones and John Mayer have performed here.

ALEXANDRIA

The charming colonial village of Alexandria is just 5 miles and 250 years away from Washington. Once a salty port town, Alexandria – known as 'Old Town' to locals – is today a posh collection of red-bricked colonial homes, cobblestoned streets, flickering gas lamps and a waterfront promenade. King St is packed with boutiques, outdoor cafes, and neighborhood bars and restaurants. The **visitor center** (☎703-838-5005; www.visitalexandriava.com; 221 King St; ⊙9am-5pm) issues parking permits and discount tickets to historic sites.

The 333ft-tall **George Washington Masonic National Memorial** (www.gwmemorial.org; 101 Callahan Dr & King St; admission free; ⊙9am-5pm) is an imposing tower modeled after Egypt's Lighthouse of Alexandria and dedicated to America's first president, who was a member of the shadowy Freemasons. **Gadsby's Tavern Museum** (www.gadsbystavernmuseum.us; 134 N Royal St; adult/child $5/3; ⊙10am-5pm Tue-Sat, from 1pm Sun & Mon) has exhibits on colonial life and is still a working pub and restaurant; past guests included George Washington and Thomas Jefferson.

Near the waterfront, the **Torpedo Factory Art Center** (www.torpedofactory.org; 105 N Union St; admission free; ⊙10am-6pm Fri-Wed, to 9pm Thu) is a former munitions factory that today houses dozens of galleries and studios.

A stylish new addition to Alexandria, the inviting and sunlit **Brabo Tasting Room** (1600 King St; mains around $15; ⊙11:30am-11pm Mon-Sat, to 10pm Sun) serves its signature mussels, tasty wood-fired tarts and gourmet sandwiches (like slow-roasted Angus beef with caramelized mushrooms), with a good beer and wine selection. Next door, high-end **Brabo** (☎703-894-3440; mains $28-38; ⊙from 5:30pm) serves superb seasonal fare.

One of Alexandria's best seafood spots is small, casual **Hank's Oyster Bar** (1026 King St; mains $6-28; ⊙5:30-9:30pm Tue-Thu, 11:30am-midnight Fri & Sat, 11am-9:30pm Sun), serving up daily fish specials, seared scallops, lobster rolls, crab cakes and its famous oysters. **Momo Sushi & Cafe** (☎703-299-9092; 212 Queen St; sushi $10-23; ⊙11:30am-2:30pm & 4-10pm Mon-Fri, noon-10pm Sat, 4pm-10pm Sun) has just 13 seats but serves excellent sushi.

The food is mediocre and beer selection weak, but the live bluegrass (from 8:30pm Friday and Saturday) hits the spot at the well-worn **Tiffany Tavern** (☎703-836-8844; 1116 King St; mains $10-20; ⊙5pm-midnight Mon-Thu, to 2am Fri & Sat).

Just north of Old Town by the Braddock Rd Metro station is one of America's premier music halls, the **Birchmere** (☎703-549-7500; www.birchmere.com; 3701 Mt Vernon Ave; tickets $25-70). The legendary venue stages an eclectic range of acts, from Shawn Colvin to Eric Benét, plus past legends like Doc Watson and America.

To get to Alexandria from downtown DC, get off at the King St Metro station. A free trolley makes the one-mile journey between the Metro station and the waterfront (every 20 minutes, 11:30am to 10pm).

MOUNT VERNON

One of the most visited historic shrines in the nation, **Mount Vernon** (☎703-780-2000; www.mountvernon.org; adult/child $15/7; ⊙9am-5pm, to 4pm Nov-Feb) was the beloved home of George and Martha Washington, who lived here from their marriage in 1759 until Washington's death in 1799. Now owned and operated by the Mount Vernon Ladies Association, the estate offers glimpses of 18th-century farm life and the first president's life as a country planter. Mount Vernon does not gloss over the Founding Father's slave ownership; visitors can tour the slave quarters and burial ground.

Other sights include Washington's **Distillery and Gristmill** (www.tourmobile.com; adult/child $4/2; incl Mount Vernon adult/child $30/15), 3 miles south of the estate. During warmer months, you can take a 40-minute **Sightseeing Cruise** (adult/child $9/5; ⊙Tue-Sun May-Aug, Sat & Sun Apr & Sep).

Mount Vernon is 16 miles south of DC off the Mount Vernon Memorial Hwy. By public transportation, take the Metro to Huntington, then switch to Fairfax Connector bus 101. **Tourmobile** (☑202-554-5100; www.tourmobile.com; adult/child incl admission $32/16; ⊙mid-Jun–Aug) offers one trip a day to Mount Vernon from Arlington National Cemetery. **Grayline** (☑202-289-1995; www.grayline.com; adult/child incl admission from $55/30) departs daily from DC's Union Station year-round.

Several companies offer seasonal boat trips from DC and Alexandria; the cheapest is **Potomac Riverboat Company** (☑703-684-0580; www.potomacriverboatco.com; adult/child incl admission $40/20). A healthy alternative is to take a lovely bike ride along the Potomac River from DC (18 miles from Roosevelt Island).

MANASSAS

On July 21, 1861, Union and Confederate soldiers clashed in the first major land battle of the Civil War. Expecting a quick victory, Union fans flocked here to picnic and watch the First Battle of Bull Run (known in the South as First Manassas). The surprise Southern victory erased any hopes of a quick end to the war. Union and Confederate soldiers again met on the same ground for the larger Second Battle of Manassas in August 1862; again the South was victorious. Today **Manassas National Battlefield Park** is a curving green hillscape, sectioned into fuzzy fields of tall grass and wildflowers by split-rail wood fences. Start your tour at the **Henry Hill Visitor Center** (☑703-361-1339; www.nps.gov/mana; adult/child $3/free; ⊙8:30am-5pm) to watch the orientation film and pick up park and trail maps.

Daily **Amtrak** (www.amtrak.com; one way $15-21) and **Virginia Railway Express** (VRE; www.vre.org; one way $9; ⊙Mon-Fri) trains make the 50-minute journey between DC's Union Station and the historic Old Town Manassas Railroad Station on 9431 West St; from there it's a 6-mile taxi ride to the park. There are several restaurants and bars around the Manassas train station, but the rest of the city is a mess of strip malls and suburban sprawl.

Fredericksburg

Fredericksburg is a pretty town with a historical district that is almost a cliché of small-town Americana. George Washington grew up here, and the Civil War exploded in the streets and surrounding fields. Today the main street is a pleasant amble of bookstores, gastropubs and cafes.

⊙ Sights

Fredericksburg & Spotsylvania National Military Park HISTORIC SITE
More than 13,000 Americans were killed during the Civil War in four battles fought in a 17-mile radius covered by this park and maintained by the NPS. Don't miss the burial site of Stonewall Jackson's amputated arm near the **Fredericksburg Battlefield visitor center** (1013 Lafayette Blvd; admission free, film $2; ⊙9am-5pm).

The **visitor center** (www.visitfred.com; 706 Caroline St; ⊙9am-5pm) offers a 'Timeless Fredericksburg' pass, which includes admission to nine local sights (adult/child $32/10).

James Monroe Museum & Memorial Library HISTORIC SITE
(908 Charles St; adult/child $5/1; ⊙10am-5pm Mon-Sat, from 1pm Sun) The museum's namesake was the nation's fifth president.

Mary Washington House HISTORIC SITE
(1200 Charles St; adult/child $5/2; ⊙11am-5pm Mon-Sat, noon-4pm Sun) The 18th-century home of George Washington's mother.

Rising Sun Tavern HISTORIC SITE
(1304 Caroline St; adult/child $5/2; ⊙10am-5pm Mon-Sat, noon-4pm Sun) A museum with tavern wenches.

🛏 Sleeping & Eating

You'll find dozens of restaurants and cafes along historic Caroline and William Sts.

Richard Johnston Inn B&B $$
(☑540-899-7606; www.therichardjohnstoninn.com; 711 Caroline St; r $115-225; [P][❄][@]) In an 18th-century brick mansion, this cozy B&B scores points for location, comfort and friendliness (especially from the two resident Scottie dogs). Guests get full breakfast on weekends.

Griffin Bookshop & Cafe CAFE $
(106 Hanover St; ⊙10am-6pm Mon-Sat, to 5pm Sun; [@]) The Griffin is a great spot for booklovers, with friendly staff, free wi-fi, good coffees and pastries, an outdoor patio and great reading selections.

Kybecca Wine Bar TAPAS $$
(☎540-373-3338; 400 William St; tapas $6-21; ⊙5-11pm Mon-Thu, 3pm-midnight Fri & Sat, 11am-8pm Sun) Kybecca adds verve to Fredericksburg's dining scene, with tasty sharing plates (sherry-braised short ribs, bison-and-blue-cheese sliders, seared tuna) and an excellent beer and wine selection. Sidewalk seating and live music (acoustic) on Thursday through Saturday nights.

❶ Getting There & Away

VRE ($11, 1½ hours) and **Amtrak** ($23 to $33, 1¼ hours) trains depart from the Fredericksburg train station (200 Lafayette Blvd) with service to DC. **Greyhound** has buses to/from DC ($15, five per day, 1½ hours) and Richmond ($18, three per day, one hour). The **Greyhound station** (☎540-373-2103; 1400 Jefferson Davis Hwy) is roughly 1.5 miles west of the historic district.

Richmond

Richmond has been the capital of the Commonwealth of Virginia since 1780. It was here during the American Revolution that patriot Patrick Henry gave his famous 'Give me Liberty, or give me Death!' speech. But Richmond is most notable for serving as the capital of the secessionist Confederate States of America during the Civil War from 1861 to 1865. Ironically, Richmond is now an ethnically diverse city, with a vibrant African American community. Of course, the attractive veneer of diversity cracks soon enough into ugly income disparities; most African American neighborhoods seem depressed compared with upmarket areas on the East and West ends of the center. This town also grapples with memorializing its controversial history. But in the end Richmond is a welcoming, warm traditional Southern city that is slowly being absorbed into the international milieu of the Northeast Corridor.

◉ Sights

The James River bisects Richmond, with most attractions to its north. Uptown residential neighborhoods include the Fan district, south of Monument Ave, and Carytown, in the west end. Downtown, Court End holds the capitol and several museums. On E Cary St between 12th and 15th Sts, converted warehouses in Shockoe Slip house shops and restaurants. Once you pass under the trestle-like freeway overpass, you're in Shockoe Bottom. Just north of Court End is

the historic African American neighborhood of Jackson Ward. Keep in mind that Cary St is more than 5 miles long; E Cary St is downtown, while W Cary St is in Carytown.

Monument Avenue, a tree-lined boulevard in northeast Richmond, holds **statues** of such revered Southern heroes as JEB Stuart, Robert E Lee, Matthew Fontaine Maury, Jefferson Davis, Stonewall Jackson and, controversially, African American tennis champion Arthur Ashe.

Jackson Ward, an African American neighborhood that was known as Little Africa in the late 19th century, is now a national historic landmark district. It comes off as a tough neighborhood (which it is), but there's a deep cultural legacy here as well.

The 1.25-mile waterfront **Canal Walk** between the James River and the Kanawha (ka-naw) and Haxall Canals is a lovely way of seeing a dozen highlights of Richmond history.

TOP CHOICE Museum & White House of the Confederacy HISTORIC SITE
(www.moc.org; cnr 12th & Clay Sts; adult/child $12/7; ⊙10am-5pm Mon-Sat, from noon Sun) Traces the history of the Confederate States of America with the country's largest collection of Confederate civilian and military artifacts. It's a must-see for any history and Civil War buff. The adjacent 1818 White House mansion was the home of CSA President Jefferson Davis.

American Civil War Center at Historic Tredegar MUSEUM
(www.tredegar.org; 500 Tredegar St; adult/child $8/2; ⊙9am-5pm) Located in an 1861 gun foundry, this fascinating site explores the causes and course of the Civil War from the perspectives of Union, Confederate and African American experiences. The center is one of 13 protected area sites that make up **Richmond National Battlefield Park** (www.nps.gov/rich).

FREE Virginia State Capitol BUILDING
(www.virginiacapitol.gov; cnr 9th & Grace Sts, Capitol Sq; ⊙9am-5pm Mon-Sat, 1-4pm Sun) Designed by Thomas Jefferson, the capitol building was completed in 1788 and houses the oldest legislative body in the Western Hemisphere, the Virginia General Assembly, established in 1619. Free tours.

Virginia Historical Society MUSEUM
(www.vahistorical.org; 428 N Blvd; adult/student $6/4; ⊙10am-5pm Tue-Sat, from 1pm Sat) Chang-

ing and permanent exhibits trace the history of the Commonwealth from prehistoric to present times.

St John's Episcopal Church CHURCH
(www.historicstjohnschurch.org; 2401 E Broad St; tours adult/child $7/5; ⊙10am-4pm, from 1pm Sun) It was here that firebrand Patrick Henry uttered his famous battle cry, 'Give me Liberty, or give me Death!' during the rebellious 1775 Second Virginia Convention. His speech is reenacted at 2pm on Sunday in summer.

FREE Virginia Holocaust Museum MUSEUM
(www.va-holocaust.com; 2000 E Cary St; ⊙9am-5pm Mon-Fri, from 11am Sat & Sun) The museum is structured like an attic/diorama of the Holocaust survivors who settled here after WWII. It's occasionally kitschy but still powerful, due to the personalized nature of the exhibits. Not recommended for children under 11.

Black History Museum & Cultural Center of Virginia MUSEUM
(www.blackhistorymuseum.org; 3 E Clay St; adult/child $5/3; ⊙10am-5pm Tue-Sat) Highlights the achievements of African American Virginians and displays collections of African arts, textiles and artifacts.

FREE Virginia Museum of Fine Arts MUSEUM
(VMFA; www.vmfa.state.va.us; 2800 Grove Ave; ⊙10am-5pm Sat-Wed, to 9pm Thu & Fri) Has a remarkable collection of European works, sacred Himalayan art and one of the largest Fabergé egg collections on display outside Russia. Also hosts excellent temporary exhibitions (admission free to $20).

Science Museum of Virginia MUSEUM
(www.smv.org; 2500 W Broad St; adult/child $11/10, incl IMAX adult/child $16/15; ⊙9:30am-5pm Mon-Sat, from 11:30am Sun) An interactive, educational, entertaining way to distract the kids.

Poe Museum MUSEUM
(www.poemuseum.org; 1914-16 E Main St; adult/student $6/5; ⊙10am-5pm Tue-Sat, from 11am Sun) Contains the world's largest collection of manuscripts and memorabilia of macabre poet Edgar Allan Poe, who lived and worked in Richmond.

FREE Hollywood Cemetery CEMETERY
(hollywoodcemetery.org; entrance cnr Albemarle & Cherry Sts; ⊙8am-5pm, to 6pm summer) This tranquil cemetery, perched above the James

River rapids, contains the gravesites of two US presidents (James Monroe and John Tyler), the only Confederate president (Jefferson Davis) and 18,000 Confederate soldiers. Free walking tours are given at 10am, Monday through Saturday.

🛏 Sleeping

TOP CHOICE Jefferson Hotel LUXURY HOTEL $$$
(☏804-788-8000; www.jeffersonhotel.com; 101 W Franklin St; r from $250; P❋❀☎⛱) The Jefferson is Richmond's grandest hotel and one of the finest in America. The vision of tobacco tycoon and Confederate Major Lewis Ginter, the beaux-arts-style hotel was completed in 1895. Today it offers luxurious rooms, topnotch service and one of Richmond's finest restaurants. According to rumor, the magnificent grand staircase in the lobby served as the model for the famed stairs in *Gone with the Wind*.

Linden Row Inn BOUTIQUE HOTEL $$
(☏804-783-7000; www.lindenrowinn.com; 100 E Franklin St; r incl breakfast $109-159, ste $239; P❋@☎) This antebellum gem has 70 attractive rooms (with period Victorian furnishings) spread among neighboring Greek Revival town houses in an excellent downtown location. Friendly southern hospitality and thoughtful extras (free passes to the YMCA, free around-town shuttle service) sweeten the deal.

Museum District B&B B&B $$
(☏804-359-2332; www.museumdistrictbb.com; 2811 Grove Ave; r $100-195; P❋☎) In a fine location near the dining and drinking of Carytown, this stately 1920s brick B&B has earned many admirers for its warm welcome. Rooms are comfortably set and guests can enjoy the wide front porch, cozy parlor with fireplace, and excellent cooked breakfasts – plus wine and cheese in the evenings.

Berkeley Hotel HOTEL $$
(☏804-780-1300; www.berkeleyhotel.com; 1200 E Cary St; d from $175; P❋☎) Located in Shockoe Slip, this European-style, four-star hotel has spacious rooms with cherry furnishings and gracious staff. Many rooms have fine views over downtown, and there's a good restaurant on-site.

Omni Hotel HOTEL $$$
(☏804-344-7000; www.omnihotels.com; 100 S 12th St; r from $250; P❋☎⛱) In a 19-story building overlooking the James River, this

high-end hotel has comfortable rooms and loads of amenities (including a heated indoor pool). It's in a great location in the heart of Shockoe Slip.

Holiday Inn Express   HOTEL $$

(📞804-788-1600; www.hiexpress.com; 201 E Cary St; r from $103; 🅿@🛜) The Holiday Inn is one of the cheapest options for staying in downtown Richmond, and earns decent marks for clean rooms and helpful staff.

✖ Eating

You'll find dozens of restaurants along the cobbled streets of Shockoe Slip and Shockoe Bottom. Further west in Carytown (W Cary St between S Blvd and N Thompson St), you'll find even more dining options.

TOP CHOICE Millie's Diner   MODERN AMERICAN $$$

(2603 E Main St; breakfast & lunch $7-10, dinner $20-32; ⏰11am-2:30pm & 5:30-10:30pm Tue-Fri, 10am-3pm & 5:30-10:30pm Sat & Sun) Breakfast, lunch or dinner, Millie's does it all, and does it well. But where this Richmond icon really shines is Sunday brunch: the Devil's Mess – an open-faced omelet with spicy sausage, curry, veg, cheese and avocado – is quite legendary.

Julep's   MODERN AMERICAN $$$

(📞804-377-3968; 1719 E Franklin St; mains $18-32; ⏰5:30-10pm Mon-Sat) One of Richmond's finest restaurants serves decadent New Southern cuisine in a classy old-fashioned dining room that's cinematically set inside a restored 1817 building. Start with a mint julep, fried green tomatoes or jumbo lump crab soup, followed by Julep's signature shrimp and grits with grilled andouille sausage.

Tarrants   MODERN AMERICAN $$$

(📞804-225-0035; 1 W Broad St; mains $9-24; ⏰11am-10pm Sun-Thu, to midnight Fri & Sat) With old-fashioned wooden booths, antique fixtures and a copper ceiling, Tarrants is a warm and inviting spot to linger over a meal. Top picks from the extensive menu include fish tacos, pizzas and crab cakes, plus nicely made cocktails.

Ipanema Café   AMERICAN $$

(917 W Grace St; mains $8-17; ⏰11am-11pm Mon-Fri, from 5:30pm Sat & Sun; 🍽) This underground den is much loved by the bohemian and art-student crowd, with a tempting selection of vegan and vegetarian fare (tempeh 'bacon' sandwich, curried vegetables, changing specials), plus *moules-frites,* tuna melts and a few other nonveg options. Vegan desserts are outstanding.

Edo's Squid   ITALIAN $$$

(📞804-864-5488; 411 N Harrison St; mains $12-30) Easily the best Italian restaurant in Richmond, Edo's serves up mouthwatering, authentic cuisine such as eggplant parmesan, spicy shrimp diavolo pasta, daily specials and, of course, squid. This place can get very crowded and noisy.

17th Street Farmers Market   MARKET $

(cnr 17th & E Main Sts; ⏰10am-7pm Thu, 5-9pm Fri, 10am-4pm Sat, 9am-4pm Sun) For cheap eats and fresh produce, check out the bustling market, which runs from early May through October. On Sundays, the market sells antiques.

🍷 Drinking & Entertainment

Lift   CAFE

(218 W Broad St; ⏰7am-7pm Mon-Fri, 8am-8pm Sat, 9am-7pm Sun; 🛜) Part coffeehouse, part art gallery, Lift serves stiff lattes and tasty sandwiches and salads. Sidewalk seating.

Tobacco Company Restaurant   BAR

(📞804-782-9555; www.thetobaccocompany.com; 1201 E Cary St; ⏰from 11:30am) An embodiment of the era when tobacco was king, the atmosphere of this three-story, brothel-like restaurant-bar is more of a draw than the food. Come instead for drinks and live music (from 9:30pm Wednesday through Saturday).

Capital Ale House   BAR

(623 E Main St; ⏰11am-1:30am) Popular with political wonks from the nearby state capitol, this downtown pub has a superb beer selection (over 50 on tap and 250 bottled) and decent pub grub. The frozen trough on the bar keeps your drink ice-cold.

Byrd Theater   CINEMA

(📞804-353-9911; www.byrdtheatre.com; 2908 W Cary St; tickets $2) You can't beat the price at this classic 1928 cinema, which shows second-run films. Wurlitzer-organ concerts precede the Saturday-night shows.

Richmond Centerstage   THEATER

(📞804-592-3400; www.richmondcenterstage.com; 600 E Grace St) In 2009 Richmond raised the curtain on the area's premier venue for concerts, dance and theater, including touring Broadway productions.

ⓘ Information

Media
Richmond-Times Dispatch (www2.timesdispatch.com) Daily newspaper.

Medical Services
Johnston-Willis Hospital (☏804-330-2000; 1401 Johnston-Willis Dr)
Richmond Community Hospital (☏804-225-1700; 1500 N 28th St)

Post
Post office (700 E Main St; ☺7:30am-5pm Mon-Fri)

Tourist Information
Richmond visitor center (☏804-783-7450; www.visitrichmondva.com; 405 N 3rd St; ☺9am-5pm)

ⓘ Getting There & Around

The cab fare from **Richmond International Airport** (RIC; ☏804-226-3000), 10 miles east of town, is about $26.

Amtrak (☏800-872-7245) Trains stop at the main station at 7519 Staples Mill Rd, 7 miles north of town (accessible to downtown on bus 27). More convenient but less frequent trains stop downtown at the Main Street Station (1500 E Main St).

Greater Richmond Transit Company (GRTC; ☏804-358-4782; www.ridegrtc.com) Runs local buses (base fare $1.50, exact change only).

Greyhound/Trailways bus station (☏804-254-5910; www.greyhound.com; 2910 N Blvd)

Petersburg

About 25 miles south of Richmond, the little town of Petersburg played a big role in the Civil War as a major railway junction, providing Confederate troops and supplies. Union troops laid a 10-month siege of Petersburg in 1864–65, the longest on American soil. The **Siege Museum** (☏804-733-2404; 15 W Bank St; adult/child $5/4, with Old Blandford Church $11/9; ☺10am-5pm) relates the plight of civilians during the siege. Several miles east of town, **Petersburg National Battlefield** (US 36; vehicle/pedestrian $5/3; ☺9am-5pm) is where Union soldiers planted explosives underneath a Confederate breastwork, leading to the Battle of the Crater (novelized and cinematized in *Cold Mountain*). West of downtown in Pamplin Historical Park, the excellent **National Museum of the Civil War Soldier** (☏804-861-2408; adult/child 6-12yr $10/5; ☺9am-5pm) illustrates the

hardships faced by soldiers on both sides of the conflict. South of town, **Old Blandford Church** (☏804-733-2396; 319 S Crater St; adult/child $5/4; ☺10am-5pm) has the largest collection of Tiffany glass windows in one place. Each exquisite pane is dedicated to one Confederate state and its war dead. More than 30,000 Confederate soldiers are buried on the church grounds.

Historic Triangle

This is America's birthplace. Nowhere else in the country has such a small area played such a pivotal role in the course of the nation's history. The nation's roots were planted in Jamestown, the first permanent English settlement in the New World. The flames of the American Revolution were fanned at the colonial capital of Williamsburg, and America finally won her independence from Britain at Yorktown.

You'll need at least two days to give the Triangle any justice. A daily free shuttle travels between the Williamsburg visitor center, Yorktown and Jamestown.

WILLIAMSBURG

If you visit only one historical town in Virginia, make it Williamsburg, home to Colonial Williamsburg, one of the most astounding and authentic living-history museums in the world. If any place is going to get kids into history, this is it, but it's plenty of fun for adults too.

The actual town of Williamsburg, Virginia's capital from 1699 to 1780, is a stately place. The prestigious campus of the College of William & Mary adds a decent dash of youth culture, with coffee shops, cheap pubs and fashion boutiques.

⦿ Sights & Activities

TOP CHOICE **Colonial Williamsburg** HISTORIC SITE (www.colonialwilliamsburg.org; adult/child $38/19; ☺9am-5pm) The restored capital of England's largest colony in the New World is a must-see attraction for visitors of all ages. This is not some cheesy, fenced-in theme park; Colonial Williamsburg is a living, breathing, working history museum that transports visitors back to the 1700s. The 301-acre historic area contains 88 original 18th-century buildings and several hundred faithful reproductions, including homes, taverns, shops and public buildings. The British Union Jack flutters everywhere. Costumed townsfolk and 'interpreters' in period dress go about their colonial jobs as blacksmiths, apothecaries, printers, barmaids, soldiers and patriots, breaking character only long enough to pose for a snapshot. Costumed patriots like Patrick Henry and Thomas Jefferson stand on their soapbox outside taverns, delivering impassioned speeches for freedom and democracy. Children will love the interactive, hands-on exhibits and activities, and hilarious skits such as witch trials, and tar and featherings.

Highlight buildings of Colonial Williamsburg include the reconstructed Capitol Building and Governor's Palace, the Bruton Parish Church and Raleigh Tavern. Walking around the historic district and patronizing the shops and taverns is free, but entry to building tours and most exhibits is restricted to ticket holders. Expect crowds, lines and petulant children, especially in summer.

To park and to purchase tickets, follow signs to the visitor center (☏757-229-1000; ☺8:45am-5pm), north of the historic district between Hwy 132 and Colonial Pkwy, where kids can hire out period costumes for $25 per day. Start off with a 30-minute film about Williamsburg, and peruse a copy of *Williamsburg This Week*, listing the day's programs and events. Most day activities are included with the admission price. Evening events (ghost walks, witch trials, chamber recitals) cost extra, typically $12.

Parking is free; shuttle buses run frequently to and from the historic district, or walk along the tree-lined footpath. You can also buy tickets at the Merchants Square information booth (☺9am-5pm) at the west end of Duke of Gloucester St.

Chartered in 1693, the College of William & Mary (www.wm.edu) is the second-oldest college in the country and retains the oldest academic building in continued use in the USA, the Sir Christopher Wren Building. The school's alumni include Thomas Jefferson, James Monroe and comedian Jon Stewart.

FREE Williamsburg Winery   WINERY
(☏757-229-0999; www.williamsburgwinery.com; 5800 Wessex Hundred; tasting tours $10; ☺11am-6pm) Four miles southwest of downtown, the largest winery in Virginia cranks out 60,000 cases a year and 25 varieties of the sweet nectar of the gods. Stay for lunch at the on-site Gabriel Archer Tavern, serving up tasty sand-

wich and wrap plates; or book a table at the high-end Cafe Provencal for dinner (lunch/dinner mains from $10/25, restaurants open 11am to 4pm and 6pm to 9pm).

🛏 Sleeping

The **Williamsburg Hotel & Motel Association** (☏800-446-9244; www.gowilliamsburg.com) at the visitor center will help find and book accommodations at no cost. If you stay in Colonial Williamsburg, guesthouses can provide discount admission tickets (adult/child $30/15).

Colonial Williamsburg
Historic Lodging   GUESTHOUSE $$$
(☏757-253-2277; www.history.org; r $150-270) For true 18th-century immersion, guests can stay in one of 26 original colonial houses inside the historic district. Accommodations range in size and style, though the best have period furnishings, canopy beds and wood-burning fireplaces.

Williamsburg White House   B&B $$
(☏757-229-8580; www.awilliamsburgwhitehouse.com; 718 Jamestown Rd; r $150-200; P❄) This romantic, beautifully furnished B&B decorated with red, white and blue bunting is located across the campus of William & Mary, just a few blocks' walk from Colonial Williamsburg.

Williamsburg Inn   INN $$$
(☏757-253-2277; www.colonialwilliamsburg.com; 136 E Francis St; r from $320; P❄✿🐾) Queen Elizabeth II has stayed here twice, so you know this place is palatial. Williamsburg's premier property is noted by its not-so-colonial price tag, but the pampering is nonstop at this prestigious resort.

Woodlands Hotel   HOTEL $$
(☏757-253-2277; www.colonialwilliamsburgresorts.com; 105 Visitor Center Dr; r $110-210; P❄✿🐾🚗) Next door to the visitor center, this huge complex has bright, well-equipped rooms and excellent facilities. With two pools, mini-golf and kid's play areas, it's a popular choice with families. It's a peaceful tree-lined stroll (a half-mile) to the colonial area.

Governor's Inn   HOTEL $
(☏757-253-2277; www.colonialwilliamsburgresorts.com; 506 N Henry St; r $60-110; P❄🐾) Williamsburg's official 'economy' choice is a big box by any other name, but rooms are clean, and guests can use the pool and facilities of the Woodlands Hotel. It's in a great location three blocks from the historic district.

Williamsburg & Colonial KOA Resorts
CAMPGROUND $

(☑800-562-1733; www.williamsburgkoa.com; 4000 Newman Rd, I-64 exit 234; campsites $22-37, cabins $52-70; ☎▣) With two campgrounds rolled into one, you'll find superb amenities such as a pool, games rooms, movies and laundry facilities.

✖ Eating

You will find many restaurants, cafes and pubs in Merchants Sq, adjacent to Colonial Williamsburg.

Fat Canary   MODERN AMERICAN $$$

(☑757-229-3333; 410 Duke of Gloucester St, Merchants Sq; mains $28-36; ⊙5-10pm) For a splurge, there's no better place in the historic triangle. Top-notch service, excellent wines and heavenly desserts are only slightly upstaged by the magnificent seasonal cuisine (recent favorites: pan-seared sea scallops with oyster mushrooms; crispy quail with goat's cheese tamales; and heritage breed pork chop with gruyere bread pudding, Swiss chard, apples and bacon). You can dine on the elegant outdoor patio, or in the subdued dining room.

Cheese Shop   DELI $

(410 Duke of Gloucester St, Merchants Sq; mains $6-7; ⊙10am-8pm Mon-Sat, 11am-6pm Sun) Adjoining Fat Canary, this gourmet deli showcases some flavorful sandwiches and antipasti, plus baguettes, pastries, wine, beer and wonderful cheeses.

King's Arms Tavern   MODERN AMERICAN $$

(☑757-229-2141; 416 E Duke of Gloucester St; lunch mains $13-15, dinner $31-37; ⊙11:30am-2:30pm & 5-9pm) Of the four restaurants located within Colonial Williamsburg, this is the most elegant, serving early American cuisine like game pie – venison, rabbit and duck braised in port wine sauce.

Aromas   CAFE $

(431 Prince George St; mains $5-15; ⊙7am-10pm Mon-Sat, 8am-8pm Sun; ☎) One block north of Merchants Sq, Aromas is an inviting coffeehouse serving a wide range of fare, plus wine and beer. Outdoor seating and occasional live music.

❶ Getting There & Around

Williamsburg Transportation Center (☑757-229-8750; cnr Boundary & Lafayette Sts) Amtrak trains run from here twice a day to Washington, DC ($40, four hours), Richmond ($20, 50 minutes) and New York ($84, eight

hours). Greyhound buses run to Richmond ($18, one hour) five times daily. Buses to other destinations require a transfer in Richmond.

TRIANGLE THEME PARKS

Three miles east of Williamsburg on Hwy 60, **Busch Gardens** (☑800-343-7946; www.buschgardens.com; adult/child $64/54; ⊙Apr-Oct) is a European-themed park with some of the best roller coasters on the East Coast. Just down the road, off Hwy 199 east of Williamsburg, **Water Country USA** (☑800-343-7946; www.watercountryusa.com; adult/child $47/40; ⊙May-Sep) is a kids' paradise, with twisty slides, raging rapids and wave pools. A three-day combo ticket for both parks is $75. Parking is $13 at both places.

JAMESTOWN

The first permanent English settlement in North America was a horrific struggle that for many ended in tragedy. On May 14, 1607, a group of 104 English men and boys settled on this swampy island with a charter from the Virginia Company of London to search for gold and other riches. Instead, they found starvation and disease. By January of 1608, only about 40 colonists were still alive. The colony survived the 'Starving Time' with the leadership of Captain James Smith and help from local Powhatan. In 1619 the elected House of Burgesses convened, forming the first democratic government in the Americas.

Historic Jamestowne (☑757-856-1200; www.historicjamestowne.org; adult/child $10/free; ⊙8:30am-4:30pm), run by the NPS, is the original Jamestown site. Start your visit at the on-site museum and check out the statues of John Smith and Pocahontas. The original Jamestown ruins were rediscovered in 1994; visitors can watch the ongoing archaeological work at the site.

More child-friendly, the state-run **Jamestown Settlement** (☑757-253-4838; www.historyisfun.org; adult/child $16/8, incl Yorktown Victory Center $20/10; ⊙9am-5pm) reconstructs the 1607 James Fort, a Native American village and full-scale replicas of the first ships that brought the settlers to Jamestown, along with multimedia exhibits and costumed interpreters portraying life in the 17th century.

YORKTOWN

On October 19, 1781, British General Cornwallis surrendered to George Washington here, effectively ending the American Revolution. Overpowered by massive American guns on land and cut off from the sea by the

French, the British were in a hopeless position. Although Washington anticipated a much longer siege, the devastating barrage quickly overwhelmed Cornwallis, who surrendered within days.

Yorktown Battlefield (☎757-898-3400; incl Historic Jamestowne adult/child $10/free; ⊙9am-5pm), run by the NPS, is the site of the last major battle of the American Revolution. Start your tour at the visitor center and check out the orientation film and the display of Washington's original tent. The 7-mile Battlefield Rd Tour takes you past the major highlights. Don't miss a walk through the last British defensive sites, Redoubts 9 and 10.

The state-run **Yorktown Victory Center** (☎757-253-4838; www.historyisfun.org; adult/child $10/5; ⊙9am-5pm) is an interactive, living-history museum that focuses on reconstruction, reenactment and the Revolution's impact on the people who lived through it. At the re-created encampment, costumed Continental soldiers fire cannons and discuss food preparation and field medicine of the day.

The actual town of Yorktown is a pleasant waterfront village overlooking the York River with a nice range of shops, restaurants and pubs. Set in an atmospheric 1720 house, the ⬚⬚⬚⬚⬚⬚⬚ (☎757-988-1999; 411 Main St; mains $10-16; ⊙11am-3:30pm daily, 5-8:30pm Thu-Sat) is a good, affordable spot serving playfully named dishes like Lord Nelson's BBQ and Battlefield beef stroganoff. Afterwards, grab a beer at the **Yorktown Pub** (112 Water St; mains $8-22; ⊙11am-midnight), which hosts live music on weekends. For a more upscale option, **Nick's Riverwalk Restaurant** (☎757-875-1522; 323 Water St; lunch mains $10-16, dinner $18-32; ⊙11:30am-2:30pm & 5-9pm) offers waterfront dining and modern American cuisine.

JAMES RIVER PLANTATIONS
The grand homes of Virginia's slaveholding aristocracy were a clear sign of the era's class divisions. A string of them line scenic Hwy 5 on the north side of the river, though only a few are open to the public. The ones listed here run from east to west.

Sherwood Forest (☎804-829-5377; sherwoodforest.org; 14501 John Tyler Memorial Hwy), the longest frame house in the country, was the home of 10th US president John Tyler. Tours are available by appointment for $35 per person. The grounds (and a touching pet

cemetery) are open to **self-guided tours** (adult/child $10/free; ⊙9am-5pm).

Berkeley (☎804-829-6018; www.berkeleyplantation.com; 12602 Harrison Landing Rd; adult/child $11/7.50; ⊙9:30am-4:30pm) was the site of the first official Thanksgiving in 1619. It was the birthplace and home of Benjamin Harrison V, a signer of the Declaration of Independence, and his son William Henry Harrison, ninth US president.

Shirley (☎800-232-1613; www.shirleyplantation.com; 501 Shirley Plantation Rd; adult/child $11/7.50; ⊙9am-5pm), situated picturesquely on the river, is Virginia's oldest plantation (1613) and perhaps the best example of how a British-model plantation actually appeared, with its tidy row of brick service and trade houses – tool barn, ice house, laundry etc – leading up to the big house.

Hampton Roads

The Hampton Roads (named not for asphalt, but the confluence of the James, Nansemond and Elizabeth Rivers and Chesapeake Bay) have always been prime real estate. The Powhatan Confederacy fished these waters and hunted the fingerlike protrusions of the Virginia coast for thousands of years before John Smith arrived in 1607. The pirate Blackbeard was killed here and had his head popped onto a pike, while navies from two continents littered the area with wreckage during the Revolutionary and Civil wars. Today Hampton Roads is known for its horribly congested roads as well as its cultural mishmash of history, the military and the arts.

NORFOLK

Home to the world's largest naval base, it's not surprising that Norfolk had a reputation as a rowdy port town filled with drunken sailors. In recent years, the city has worked hard to clean up its image through development, gentrification and focusing on its burgeoning arts scene. Norfolk is now the state's second-largest city, with a diverse population of 243,000. But at the end of the day, it still revolves around the US Navy, as evident by the frequent sights of mammoth warships offshore and sounds of screaming fighter jets above.

There are two visitor centers: **Interstate** (I-64 exit 273; ⊙9am-5pm; 🛈) and **Downtown** (www.visitnorfolktoday.com; 232 E Main St; ⊙9am-5pm Mon-Fri). The historic Ghent district, west of the city center, is where this town's refugee population of artsy types, foodies and cappuccino-lovers flocks.

⊙ Sights

Naval Station Norfolk   NAVY BASE
(☎757-444-7955; www.cnic.navy.mil/norfolksta; 9079 Hampton Blvd; adult/child $10/5) The world's largest navy base, and one of the busiest airfields in the country, this is a must-see. Depending on what ships are in port, you might see aircraft carriers, destroyers, frigates, amphibious assault ships and submarines. The 45-minute bus tours are conducted by naval personnel and must be booked in advance (hours vary). Photo ID is required for adults. Alternatively, view the docks from a narrated, two-hour cruise aboard the **Victory Rover** (☎757-627-7406; www.navalbasecruises.com; adult/child $18/10; ⊗Mar-Dec).

Nauticus   MUSEUM
(www.nauticus.org; 1 Waterside Dr; adult/child $12/10; ⊗10am-5pm May-Aug, 10am-5pm Tue-Sat, from noon Sun Sep-Apr) This massive interactive maritime-themed museum has exhibits on undersea exploration, aquatic life of the Chesapeake Bay and US Naval lore. The museum's highlight is clambering around the decks and inner corridors of the USS Wisconsin. Built in 1943, it was the largest (887ft long) and last battleship built by the US Navy.

FREE Chrysler Museum of Art   MUSEUM
(www.chrysler.org; 245 W Olney Rd; ⊗10am-9pm Wed, to 5pm Thu-Sat, noon-5pm Sun) A glorious setting for a spectacular and eclectic collection of artifacts from ancient Egypt to the present day, including works by Monet, Matisse, Renoir, Warhol and a world-class collection of Tiffany blown glass.

FREE MacArthur Memorial   MUSEUM
(www.macarthurmemorial.org; MacArthur Sq; ⊗10am-5pm Mon-Sat, from 11am Sun) Houses the final resting place of WWII hero General Douglas MacArthur and his wife, Jean. The complex includes a museum, theater and exhibits of the general's military and personal artifacts.

⏝ Sleeping

For waterfront digs, there are tons of budget to midrange options lining Ocean View Ave (which actually borders the bay).

Page House Inn   B&B $$$
(☎757-625-5033; www.pagehouseinn.com; 323 Fairfax Ave; r $150-230; P✳☎) Opposite the Chrysler Museum of Art, this luxurious B&B is a cornerstone of Norfolk elegance.

Residence Inn   HOTEL $$
(☎757-842-6216; 227 W Brambleton Ave; r $140-160; P✳☎≋) A short stroll to Granby St, this friendly chain hotel has a boutique feel, with stylish, spacious rooms with small kitchenettes and excellent amenities.

Tazewell Hotel   HOTEL $$
(☎757-623-6200; www.thetazewell.com; 245 Granby St; r $100-200; ✳☎) Set in a heritage 1906 building, the Tazewell overlooks the heart of the Granby St pub and restaurant district. Rooms are small and basic – some could use an update.

Best Western   MOTEL $$
(☎757-583-2621; 1330 E Ocean Ave; r from $120; P✳☎≋) Overlooking Chesapeake Bay, this place is a reliable and comfortable option.

✗ Eating

Two of the best dining strips are downtown's Granby St and Ghent's Colley Ave.

Luna Maya   LATIN AMERICAN $$
(☎757-622-6986; 2010 Colley Ave, Ghent; mains $13-19; ⊗4:30-10pm Tue-Sat; ✐) On Ghent's restaurant-lined Colley Ave, Luna Maya serves up delectable pan-Latin fare and ever-flowing *mojitos* in a stylish but somewhat rustic open dining room. It's run by two Bolivian sisters, and standouts include the *pastel de choclo con chorizo,* a Bolivian corn casserole with spicy chicken sausage.

Press 626 Cafe &
Wine Bar   MODERN AMERICAN $$$
(☎757-282-6234; 150 W Main St; mains $19-35; ⊗11am-11pm Mon-Fri, from 5pm Sat, 10:30am-2:30pm Sun; ✐) Embracing the slow food movement, Press 626 has a small high-end menu (pan-seared swordfish with sun-dried tomato polenta, for example), plus delectable cheeses and sharing plates. It's set in an elegant converted house, with tables scattered among warmly lit rooms and on the front porch. Great wine selection.

Todd Jurich's Bistro   MODERN AMERICAN $$$
(☎757-622-3210; Boush & W Main St; mains $19-35; ⊗11:30am-2:30pm Mon-Fri, 5:30-10pm Mon-Sat) This award-winning bistro serves innovative regional fare, like Virginia sea bass and

lump crab Norfolk with wilted greens and lemon confit.

Cutty Sark Marina
SEAFOOD $$

(☎757-362-2942; 4707 Pretty Lake Ave; mains $8-15; ⏱11:30am-2:30pm Mon-Fri, 5:30-10pm Mon-Sat) For an authentic slice of old-school Maryland, head to this waterside seafood shack serving steamed shrimp, homemade crab cakes and deep-fried seafood platters. It's set in a boatyard, with old salts hunkering over the bar and no-nonsense service. It's four blocks south of East Ocean View Ave near Shore Dr (US 60).

Doumar's
DINER $

(1919 Monticello Ave, at E 20th St, Ghent; mains $2-4; ⏱8am-11pm Mon-Sat) Since 1904 this slice of Americana has been the drive-up home of the world's original ice-cream-cone machine, plus great BBQ.

🍷 Drinking & Entertainment

Elliot's Fair Grounds
CAFE

(806 Baldwin Ave, Ghent; ⏱7am-10pm Mon-Sat, from 8am Sun; 🛜🌶) This tiny, funky coffeehouse attracts everyone from students to sailors. The menu also includes vegan and kosher items such as Boca burgers.

Taphouse Grill at Ghent
PUB

(931 W 21st St, Ghent) Good microbrews are served and good local bands jam at this warm little pub.

ℹ Getting There & Around

The region is served by **Norfolk International Airport** (NIA; ☎757-857-3351), 7 miles northeast of downtown Norfolk. **Greyhound** (☎757-625-7500; www.greyhound.com; 701 Monticello Ave) runs buses to Virginia Beach ($14, 35 minutes), Richmond ($28, 2¾ hours) and Washington, DC ($45, 6½ hours).

Hampton Roads Transit (☎757-222-6100; www.hrtransit.org) serves the entire Hampton Roads region. Buses ($1.50) run from downtown throughout the city and to Newport News and Virginia Beach. **Norfolk Electronic Transit** (NET; ⏱6:30am-11pm Mon-Fri, noon-midnight Sat, noon-8pm Sun) is a free bus service that connects Norfolk's major downtown sites, including Nauticus and the Chrysler Museum.

NEWPORT NEWS & HAMPTON

The city of Newport News comes off as a giant example of suburban sprawl, but there are several attractions here, notably the amazing **Mariners' Museum** (☎757-596-2222; www.marinersmuseum.org; 100 Museum Dr; adult/child $12/7; ⏱10am-5pm Wed-Sat, from noon Sun), one of the biggest, most comprehensive maritime museums in the world. The on-site **USS Monitor Center** houses the dredged carcass of the Civil War–era *Monitor,* one of the world's first ironclad warships, as well as a life-size replica of the real deal.

The **Virginia Living Museum** (☎757-595-1900; thevlm.org; 524 J Clyde Morris Blvd; adult/child $17/13; ⏱9am-5pm) is a fine introduction to Virginia's terrestrial and aquatic life set in naturalistic ecosystems. The complex comprises open-air animal enclosures, an aviary, gardens and a planetarium.

In nearby Hampton, the **Virginia Air & Space Center** (☎757-727-0900; www.vasc. org; 600 Settlers Landing Rd; adult/child $12/10; ⏱10am-5pm Mon-Wed, to 7pm Thu-Sun) will fascinate budding aeronautic geeks with exhibits like the *Apollo 11* command module and a DC-9 passenger plane. IMAX films cost extra.

Virginia Beach

With 35 miles of sandy beaches, a 3-mile concrete oceanfront boardwalk and nearby outdoor activities, it's no surprise that Virginia Beach is the largest city in the state (population 438,000) and a prime tourist destination. In recent years the city has worked hard to shed its unfortunate reputation as a rowdy 'Redneck Riviera.' With a $300 million facelift, the beach is wider and cleaner than ever, with dolphins frolicking offshore, and a heightened police presence (and antiprofanity signs!) aimed at keeping loutish drunken crowds in check. The town's appeal, however, is limited: uninspiring high-rise hotels dominate the horizon, while the crowded beachfront and traffic-choked streets leave much to be desired.

The I-264 runs straight to the **visitor center** (☎800-822-3224; www.visitvirginiabeach. com; 2100 Parks Ave; ⏱9am-5pm) and the beach. Surfing is permitted at the beach's southern end near Rudee Inlet and alongside the 14th St pier.

◉ Sights

Virginia Aquarium & Marine Science Center
AQUARIUM

(www.virginiaaquarium.com; 717 General Booth Blvd; adult/child $21/15; ⏱9am-6pm) If you want to see an aquarium done right, this is one of the country's best. Get up close and personal with marine life on one of the aquarium's dolphin- (adult/child $21/15, April to October) or whale-watching (adult/child $28/24, January to March) boat trips.

FREE **Mt Trashmore** PARK
(310 Edwin Dr; ☉7:30am-dusk) Off I-64 exit 17B, Virginia Beach's only verticality was the creative solution to a landfill problem. Today the 165-acre park serves as a prime picnicking and kite-flying venue, with two lakes, playgrounds, a skate park and other recreational areas.

Fort Story HISTORIC SITE
(cnr 89th St & Pacific Ave) This active army base at Cape Henry is home to the 1791 **Old Cape Henry Lighthouse** (adult/child $5/3), offering spectacular views of the surrounding area from its observation deck. On summer Saturdays, the fort stages a re-created Native American village and 17th-century colonial outpost at the **Historic Villages at Cape Henry** (www.firstlandingfoundation.com; adult/child $8/5; ☉2-6pm Jun-Aug). All adults must have a photo ID to enter the base.

First Landing State Park NATURE RESERVE
(☎800-933-7275; 2500 Shore Dr; admission per vehicle $4-5) Virginia's most-visited state park is a vast 2888-acre woodland with 20 miles of hiking trails, plus camping, biking, fishing, kayaking and swimming.

FREE **Edgar Cayce Association for Research & Enlightenment** SPIRITUAL
(☎800-333-4499; www.edgarcayce.org; 215 67th St; ☉10am-8pm Mon-Sat, noon-6pm Sun) Founded by the self-proclaimed psychic of the early 20th century, the center has an extensive library and bookstore (with shelving categories like 'Life after Life' and 'Intuitive Arts'), a full schedule of drop-in lectures, and therapies such as massages, acupuncture, meditation and colonics.

Contemporary Arts Center of Virginia MUSEUM
(www.cacv.org; 2200 Parks Ave; adult/child $7/5; ☉10am-5pm Tue-Fri, to 4pm Sat, noon-4pm Sun) Has excellent rotating exhibitions housed in a fresh, ultramodern building that lovingly focuses natural light onto an outstanding collection of local and international artwork.

Back Bay National Wildlife Refuge NATURE RESERVE
(www.fws.gov/backbay; per vehicle/pedestrian $5/2 Apr-Oct, free Nov-Mar; ☉sunrise-sunset) This 9250-acre wildlife and migratory bird marshland habitat is most stunning during the December migration season.

FREE **Great Dismal Swamp National Wildlife Refuge** NATURE RESERVE
(☉sunrise-sunset) Some 30 miles southwest of Virginia Beach, this 112,000-acre refuge, which straddles the North Carolina border, is rich in flora and fauna, including black bears, bobcats and more than 200 species of bird.

🛏 Sleeping

Angie's Guest Cottage & Hostel GUESTHOUSE $
(☎757-491-1830; www.angiescottage.com; 302 24th St; dm $23-31, s/d $52/64, cottages per week from $650; P❄) Located just one block from the beach, Angie's HI-USA-affiliated hostel offers five dormitories, two private rooms and a communal kitchen.

First Landing State Park CAMPGROUND $
(☎800-933-7275; dcr.virginia.gov; Cape Henry; campsites $24-30, cabins from $75) You couldn't ask for a prettier campground than the one at this bayfront state park, though cabins have no water view.

Cutty Sark Motel MOTEL $$
(☎757-428-2116; www.cuttysarkvb.com; 3614 Atlantic Ave; r $140-160, apt per week from $1000; P❄) Rooms at Cutty Sark have private balconies and kitchenettes, but check that the view you're promised doesn't look out onto a parking lot.

🍴 Eating & Drinking

There is no shortage of restaurants along the boardwalk and Atlantic Ave, most geared toward local seafood. A bevy of interchangeable clubs and bars sit between 17th and 23rd Sts around Pacific and Atlantic Aves.

Catch 31 SEAFOOD $$$
(☎757-213-3474; 3001 Atlantic Ave; mains $18-35; ☉7am-11pm) One of the top seafood restaurants on the boardwalk has a sleek interior and a popular deck that's great for people-watching and catching a bit of an ocean breeze. Find it in the Hilton.

Mahi Mah's SEAFOOD $$$
(☎757-437-8030; www.mahimahs.com; 615 Atlantic Ave; mains $18-30; ☉5pm-late Mon-Fri, from 7am Sat & Sun) Located in the Ramada Inn, this oceanfront local has some fantastic sushi, which makes up for the snail-paced service. After

SCENIC DRIVE: VIRGINIA'S EASTERN SHORE

Across the 17-mile Chesapeake Bay bridge-tunnel (fee $12), Virginia's isolated Eastern Shore has the feel of a remote, maritime escape, dotted with fishing villages and serene, low-lying natural refuges. A drive up or down the peninsula takes a little over an hour.

Tucked behind windswept Assateague Island (p277), the town of **Chincoteague** (shink-o-teeg), on the island of the same name, is Virginia's principal Eastern Shore destination. Chincoteague is famous for its oysters and late-July wild pony swim, when the small horses that inhabit Assateague are led across the channel for annual herd-thinning foal auctions.

The **chamber of commerce** (☎757-336-6161; www.chincoteaguechamber.com; 6733 Maddox Blvd; ☺9am-4:30pm Mon-Sat) has maps of hiking and bicycling trails up to and into the incredibly relaxing **Chincoteague National Wildlife Refuge** (per vehicle $8; ☺6am-8pm), a lovely wetland repose for migratory waterfowl. Five miles west of Chincoteague, stop by **NASA Wallops Flight Facility** (☎757-824-1344; admission free; ☺10am-4pm Thu-Mon), where you can watch occasional rocket launches and enjoy exhibits of the facility's work.

dark, this is one of the most popular nightspots on the beach.

Mary's Restaurant
DINER **$**
(616 Virginia Beach Blvd; mains $4-9; ☺6am-3pm) A local institution for more than 40 years, Mary's is a great place to start the day with a tasty, filling, cheap breakfast. Fluffy, gooey, chocolate chip waffles have earned many fans.

❶ Getting There & Around

Greyhound (☎757-422-2998; www.greyhound.com; 971 Virginia Beach Blvd) has several buses a day to Richmond ($33, 3½ hours), which also stop in Norfolk and Newport News; transfer in Richmond for services to Washington, DC, Wilmington, NYC and beyond. Buses depart from Circle D Food Mart, 1 mile west of the boardwalk.
Hampton Roads Transit runs the Virginia Beach Wave trolley (tickets $1), which plies Atlantic Ave in summer.

The Piedmont

Central Virginia's rolling green landscape separates the coastal lowlands from the mountainous frontier. The fertile valley gives way to dozens of wineries, country villages and grand colonial estates.

CHARLOTTESVILLE

Set in the shadow of the Blue Ridge Mountains, Charlottesville is regularly ranked as one of the country's best places to live. This culturally rich town of 45,000 is home to the University of Virginia, which attracts Southern aristocracy and artsy lefties in equal proportion. With the UVA grounds and pedestrian downtown area overflowing with students, couples, professors and the occasional celebrity under a blanket of blue skies, 'C-ville' is practically perfect.

Charlottesville Visitor Center (☎877-386-1103; www.visitcharlottesville.org; 610 E Main St; ☺9am-5pm) is a helpful office in the heart of downtown.

MONTICELLO & AROUND

Monticello (☎434-984-9822; www.monticello.org; adult/child $22/8; ☺9am-6pm Mar-Oct, 10am-5pm Nov-Feb) is an architectural masterpiece designed and inhabited by Thomas Jefferson, Founding Father and third US president. 'I am as happy nowhere else and in no other society, and all my wishes end, where I hope my days will end, at Monticello,' wrote Jefferson, who spent 40 years building his dream home, finally completed in 1809. Today it is the only home in America designated a UN World Heritage site. Built in Roman neoclassical style, the house was the centerpiece of a 5000-acre plantation tended by 150 slaves. Monticello today does not gloss over Jefferson's role as a slave owner nor the likelihood that he fathered children with slave Sally Hemings, the complicated past of the man who declared that 'all men are created equal' in the Declaration of Independence. Jefferson and his family are buried in a small wooded plot near the home.

Visits to the house are conducted by guided tours only; you can take self-guided tours of the plantation grounds, gardens and cemetery. A high-tech exhibition center that opened in 2009 delves deeper into Jefferson's world – including exhibits on architecture, enlightenment through education and the complicated idea of liberty. The Griffin Discovery Room allows kids to put their hands on models of clever Jeffersonian inventions – like the duplicating polygraph machine. Frequent shuttles run from the visitor center to the hilltop house, or you can take the wooded footpath. *(path)*

Tours are also offered of the nearby 1784 Michie Tavern (☑434-977-1234; www.michie tavern.com; 683 Thomas Jefferson Pkwy; adult/child $9/7; ☺9am-4:20pm) and James Monroe's estate, Ash Lawn-Highland (☑434-293-8000; www.ashlawnhighland.org; adult/child $12/6; ☺9am-6pm Apr-Oct, 11am-5pm Nov-Mar), 2.5 miles east of Monticello. A combo ticket for all three is $36. Visit the Michie Tavern during lunchtime, when its dining room, the Ordinary (meals $17; ☺11:15am-3:30pm), serves lunch buffets of Southern delights like fried chicken with biscuits.

UNIVERSITY OF VIRGINIA

One of the most beautiful college campuses in America, Thomas Jefferson's University of Virginia is a must-see. The classically designed buildings and grounds embody the spirit of communal living and learning that Jefferson envisioned. The centerpiece is the Jefferson-designed Rotunda (☑434-924-7969), a scale replica of Rome's Pantheon. Free, student-led tours of the Rotunda meet inside the main entrance daily at 10am, 11am, 2pm, 3pm and 4pm. The UVA Art Museum (155 Rugby Rd; admission free; ☺noon-5pm Tue-Sun) has an eclectic and interesting collection of American, European and Asian arts.

🛏 Sleeping

There's a good selection of budget and mid-range chain motels lining Emmet St/US 29 north of town. If you're after a reservation service, try Guesthouses (☑434-979-7264; www.va-guesthouses.com; r from $150), which provides cottages and B&B rooms in private homes. Two-night minimum stays are common on weekends.

Inn at Monticello   B&B $$$
(☑434-979-3593; www.innatmonticello.com; 1188 Scottsville Rd; r $215; P❀☎) Located across from Monticello, this Victorian B&B is set off against the Piedmont's rolling hillscape. Every one of the lodge's five rooms are cozy little testaments to colonial grandeur. Excellent cooked breakfasts.

South Street Inn   B&B $$$
(☑434-979-0200; www.southstreetinn.com; 200 South St; r incl breakfast $160-255; P❀) In the heart of downtown, this elegant 1856 building went through previous incarnations as a girl's finishing school, boarding house and brothel. Now, it houses heritage-style rooms, some with antiques and working fireplaces. There's wine and cheese in the evenings.

Alexander House   GUESTHOUSE $
(☑434-327-6447; www.alexanderhouse.us; 1205 Monticello Rd; dm/r $30/75; P@☎) This friendly, laid-back guesthouse has three comfortable rooms as well as a separate six-bed bunkhouse for budget travelers. Those staying in the house share a bathroom but have free rein of the kitchen, living room and common areas. It's located in peaceful Belmont, home to an up-and-coming dining and cafe scene, a 15-minute walk to the downtown mall.

VIRGINIA VINEYARDS

Now the fifth-biggest wine producer in the USA, Virginia has 192 vineyards around the state, many located in the pretty hills around Charlottesville. Particularly notable is the Virginia Viognier. For more information on Virginia wine, visit www.virginiawine.org.

Jefferson Vineyards   WINERY
(☑434-977-3042; www.jeffersonvineyards.com; 1353 Thomas Jefferson Pkwy, Charlottesville) Known for consistent quality vintage, this winery harvests from its namesake's original 1774 vineyard site.

Keswick Vineyards   WINERY
(☑434-244-3341; www.keswickvineyards.com; 1575 Keswick Winery Dr, Keswick) Keswick won a wave of awards for its first vintage and has since been distilling a big range of grapes. It's off Rte 231.

Kluge Estate   WINERY
(☑434-977-3895; www.klugeestateonline.com; 100 Grand Cru Dr, Charlottesville) Oenophiles regularly rate Kluge wine as the best in the state.

English Inn
HOTEL $$

(☎434-971-9900; www.englishinncharlottesville.com; 2000 Morton Dr; r incl breakfast $100-160; P🖥🖨) British hospitality and furnishings and a Tudor facade accent this unique hotel. It's 1.5 miles north of UVA. Cheaper rates on weekdays.

🌿 White Pig
B&B $$

(☎434-831-1416; www.thewhitepig.com; 5120 Irish Rd, Schuyler; r $160-185; P🖨🐾) Vegans and vegetarians should make a pilgrimage to the White Pig, about 22 miles southwest of Monticello. Located on the 170-acre Briar Creek Farm, this B&B/animal sanctuary has one of the most innovative vegan menus in the state. Rooms have pleasant meadow and garden views, and there's a hot tub for guests.

✗ Eating & Drinking

The Downtown Mall, a pedestrian zone lined with dozens of shops and restaurants, is great for people-watching and outdoor dining on warm days. At night the bars along University Ave attract students and 20-somethings.

Local
MODERN AMERICAN $$

(☎434-984-9749; 824 Hinton Ave; mains $11-25; ⏱5:30-10pm Sun-Thu, to 11pm Fri & Sat) Amid Belmont's growing restaurant scene, the Local has earned many fans for its locavore-loving menu (black truffle mac 'n' cheese, roast duck with blood orange gastrique) and the elegant, warmly lit interior (exposed brick trimmed with colorful oil paintings). There's sidewalk and rooftop dining in warmer months, plus great cocktails.

Blue Moon Diner
AMERICAN $$

(512 W Main St; mains $10-20; ⏱8am-10pm Mon-Fri, from 9am Sat, 9am-3pm Sun) One of Charlottesville's best breakfast and weekend brunch spots is a festive retro-style diner that serves up delicious fare using locally sourced ingredients. You'll also find Virginia beers on tap, old-school rock on the radio, and the occasional live band.

Continental Divide
MEXICAN $$

(811 W Main St; mains $10-15; ⏱5:30-10pm) This fun, easy-going spot has no sign (look for the neon 'Get in Here' in the window) but is well worth seeking out for its Mexican fusion fare – tacos with slow-cooked pork, tuna tostadas, nachos with bison chili – and C-ville's best margaritas.

Zocalo
FUSION $$$

(☎434-977-4944; 201 E Main St; mains $19-26; ⏱5:30pm-2am Tue-Sun) This sleek and stylish restaurant-bar serves nicely turned-out Latin-inspired dishes (spicy tuna tartar, chili-dusted sea scallops, achiote-rubbed grilled pork). There's an outdoor patio for warm nights and a crackling fireplace in winter.

Mudhouse
CAFE $

(213 W Main St; ⏱7am-10pm Mon-Thu, to 11pm Fri & Sat, to 7pm Sun; 🖨) Do as the cool kids do and come here for bracing espresso, wi-fi and daily artsy happenings.

Splendora's Gelato Cafe
ICE CREAM $

(317 E Main St; ⏱9am-10pm Mon-Sat, from noon Sun; 🖨) Splendora's prepares creamy rich gelato, including flavors like pistachio, hazelnut, dulce de leche and gianduia.

Christian's Pizza
PIZZA $$

(118 W Main St; slices $2-4, pies $10-16; ⏱11am-9pm) A C-ville institution in the Downtown Mall, Christian's serves up tasty slices with a thin, crispy crust.

South Street Brewery
SOUTHERN $$

(106 W South St; mains $9-18; ⏱from 5pm Mon-Sat) In a restored 1800s brick warehouse, you'll find tasty craft brews, good Southern bistro fare (barbecue pulled pork, crawfish-and-mushroom-stuffed trout) and occasional live bands (currently Wednesday nights from 10pm). It's a short stroll from the downtown mall.

Backyard
BAR

(20 Elliewood Ave; ⏱11am-2am Mon-Sat) The Backyard is a lively collegiate bar with a spacious outdoor space that gets packed on weekends. It's on a narrow lane sprinkled with restaurants and cafes, just off University Ave.

❶ Getting There & Around

Amtrak (www.amtrak.com; 810 W Main St) Two daily trains to Washington, DC ($30, three hours).

Charlottesville Albemarle Airport (CHO; ☎434-973-8342; www.gocho.com) Ten miles north of downtown; offers regional flights.

Greyhound/Trailways terminal (☎434-295-5131; 310 W Main St) Runs three daily buses to both Richmond ($20, 1¼ hours) and Washington, DC ($23, three hours).

Trolley (⏱6:40am-11:30pm Mon-Sat, 8am-5pm Sun) A free trolley connects W Main St with UVA.

APPOMATTOX COURT HOUSE & AROUND

At the McLean House in the town of Appomattox Court House, General Robert E Lee surrendered the Army of Northern Virginia to General Ulysses S Grant, in effect ending the Civil War. Instead of coming straight here, follow **Lee's retreat** (☏800-673-8732; www.varetreat.com) on a winding 25-stop tour that starts in Petersburg at Southside Railroad Station (River St and Cockade Alley) and cuts through some of the most attractive countryside in Virginia. Best take a detailed road map, as the trail is not always clearly marked. You'll finish at the 1700-acre **Appomattox Court House National Historic Park** (☏434-352-8987; www.nps.gov/apco; summer $4, Sep-May $3; ⊘8:30am-5pm). Most of the 27 restored buildings are open to visitors.

Shenandoah Valley Maybe

Local lore says Shenandoah was named for a Native American word meaning 'Daughter of the Stars.' True or not, there's no question that this is God's country, one of the most beautiful places in America. The 200-mile-long valley and its Blue Ridge Mountains hold amazing wonders at every turn, from small towns and wineries to battlefields and caverns. This was once the western border of colonial America, settled by Scotch–Irish frontiersmen who were Highland Clearance refugees. The area offers an array of outdoor activities including hiking, camping, fishing, horseback riding and canoeing.

SHENANDOAH NATIONAL PARK

One of the most spectacular national parks in the country, **Shenandoah** (☏540-999-3500; www.nps.gov/shen; week pass per car Mar-Nov $15, Dec-Feb $10) is like a new smile from nature: in spring and summer the wildflowers explode, in fall the leaves burn bright red and orange, and in winter a cold, starkly beautiful hibernation period sets in. White-tailed deer are a common sight and, if you're lucky, you might spot a black bear, bobcat or wild turkey. The park lies just 75 miles west of Washington, DC. Whatever your agenda, don't miss a visit to this amazing wonderland.

◉ Sights & Activities

There are two visitor centers in the park, **Dickey Ridge** (Mile 4.6; ⊘8:30am-5pm mid-Apr–Oct) in the north and **Harry F Byrd** (Mile

51; ⊘8:30am-5pm Mar 31-Oct 27) in the south. Both have maps, backcountry permits and information on horseback riding, hang gliding, cycling (only on public roads) and other wholesome goodness. Shenandoah has more than 500 miles of hiking trails, including 101 miles of the Appalachian Trail. The trails described in this section are listed from north to south.

TOP CHOICE Skyline Drive   SCENIC ROUTE

A 105-mile-long road running down the spine of the Blue Ridge Mountains, the Skyline Drive redefines the definition of 'Scenic Route.' You're constantly treated to an impressive view, but keep in mind the road is bendy, slow-going (35mph limit) and (in peak season) congested.

Old Rag Mountain   HIKING

This is a tough, 8-mile circuit trail that culminates in a rocky scramble only suitable for the physically fit. Your reward is the summit of Old Rag Mountain and, along the way, some of the best views in Virginia.

Skyland   HIKING

There are four easy trails here, none exceeding 1.6 miles, with a few steep sections throughout. Stony Man Trail gives great views for not-too-strenuous trekking.

Big Meadows   HIKING

A very popular area with four easy-to-mid-level difficulty hikes. The Lewis Falls and Rose River trails run by the park's most spectacular waterfalls, and the former accesses the Appalachian Trail.

Bearfence Mountain   HIKING

A short trail leads to a spectacular 360-degree viewpoint. The circuit hike is only 1.2 miles, but it involves a strenuous scramble over rocks.

Riprap   HIKING

Three trails of varying difficulty. Blackrock Trail is an easy 1-mile loop that yields fantastic views. You can either hike the moderate 3.4-mile Riprap Trail to Chimney Rock, or detour and make a fairly strenuous 9.8-mile circuit that connects with the Appalachian Trail.

🛏 Sleeping & Eating

Camping is at four **NPS campgrounds** (☏877-444-6777; www.recreation.gov): **Mathews Arm** (Mile 22.1; campsites $15), **Big Meadows** (Mile 51.3; campsites $20), **Lewis Mountain** (Mile 57.5; campsites $15; no reservations)

and **Loft Mountain** (Mile 79.5; campsites $15). Most are open mid-May to October. Camping elsewhere requires a free back-country permit, available from any visitor center.

For not-so-rough lodging, stay at **Sky-land Lodge** (Mile 41.7; r $87-200), **Big Meadows** (Mile 51.2; r $99-159) or **Lewis Mountain** (Mile 57.5; cabins from $76), all open from early March to mid-November. Reservations can be made by calling ☎800-999-4714 or booking online at www.visitshenandoah.com.

Skyland and Big Meadows both have restaurants and taverns with nightly live music. Big Meadows is the prettiest and largest resort in the park and offers the most services, including gas, laundry and camp store. It's best to bring your own food into the park if you're going camping or on extended hikes.

❶ Getting There & Around
Amtrak trains run to Staunton, in the Shenandoah Valley, once a day from Washington, DC ($66, four hours). You'll really need your own wheels to explore the length and breadth of the park, which can be easily accessed from several exits off I-81.

FRONT ROYAL & AROUND
The northernmost tip of Skyline Dr initially comes off as a drab strip of gas stations, but there's a friendly enough main street and some cool caverns nearby. Stop in at the **visitor center** (☎800-338-2576; 414 E Main St; ☯9am-5pm) and the **Shenandoah Valley Travel Association** (☎800-847-4878; www.visitshenandoah.org; US 211 W, I-81 exit 264; ☯9am-5pm) before heading 'up' (a reference to altitude, not direction) the valley.

Front Royal's claim to fame is **Skyline Caverns** (☎540-635-4545; www.skylinecaverns.com; US 340; adult/child $16/8; ☯9am-5pm Mon-Fri, to 6pm Sat, Sun & summer), which boast rare white-spiked anthodites – delicate mineral formations that resemble sea urchins. Kids may enjoy mini train rides ($3) and the mirror maze ($5).

Woodward House on Manor Grade (☎540-635-7010; www.acountryhome.com; 413 S Royal Ave/US 320; r $110-155, cottage $225; ℗🛜) is a cluttered B&B with seven cheerful rooms and two separate cottages (with wood-burning fireplaces). Sip your coffee from the deck and don't let the busy street below distract from the Blue Ridge Mountain vista.

Element (☎540-636-9293; jsgourmet.com; 206 S Royal Ave; mains $12-18; ☯11am-3pm & 5-10pm Tue-Sat) is a foodie favorite for its quality bistro fare. The small dinner menu features changing specials like horseradish-crusted red snapper; for lunch, come for gourmet sandwiches ($8 to $10), soups and salads.

Upstairs from Element, **Apartment 2G** (☎540-636-9293; jsgourmet.com; 206 S Royal Ave; 5 courses $50; ☯from 6:30pm Sat) serves decadent five-course dinners on Saturday evening in a cozy space (like dining at a friend's place). Reservations essential. Check the website for other culinary happenings.

Soul Mountain Cafe (☎540-636-0070; 1303 117 E Main St; mains $12-24; ☯noon-9pm Mon-Sat, to 4pm Sun) serves tasty eclectic fare (pan-seared tuna, barbecue pulled pork) beneath a large portrait of Bob Marley.

Some 25 miles north, in the town of Winchester, is the **Museum of the Shenandoah Valley** (☎888-556-5799; www.shenandoahmuseum.org; 901 Amherst St; adult/student $12/10; ☯10am-4pm Tue-Sun), which comprises an 18th-century period-filled house museum, 6-acre garden and a multimedia museum that delves into the valley's history. There's also a cafe.

If you can only fit one cavern into your itinerary, head 25 miles south from Front Royal to the world-class **Luray Caverns** (☎540-743-6551; www.luraycaverns.com; I-81 exit 264; adult/child $23/11; ☯9am-6pm, to 7pm summer, to 4pm winter) and hear the 'Stalacpipe Organ,' hyped as the largest musical instrument on earth.

GEORGE WASHINGTON & JEFFERSON NATIONAL FORESTS
Stretching along the entire western edge of Virginia, these two mammoth **forests** (www.fs.fed.us/r8/gwj; campsites around $12, primitive camping free) comprise more than 1562 sq miles of mountainous terrain bordering the Shenandoah Valley. They contain challenging to easy trail networks, which include 330 miles of the **Appalachian Trail** (www.appalachiantrail.org) and mountain-biking routes. Hundreds of developed campgrounds are scattered throughout (most open mid-May to mid-September). **USDA Forest Service headquarters** (☎540-265-5100; 5162 Valleypointe Pkwy; ☯8am-4:30pm Mon-Fri), off the Blue Ridge Pkwy in Roanoke, oversees a dozen ranger stations along the ranges.

STAUNTON & AROUND
This pretty little town jumps out of the mountains with its cozy college (Mary Bald-

win), old time-y avenues and, oddly enough, one of America's premier Shakespeare companies. The **visitor center** (www.visitstaunton.com; 35 S New St; ⊘9am-6pm) is in the small historic downtown.

The excellent **Frontier Culture Museum** (☑540-332-7850; overlooking I-81 exit 222; adult/student/child $10/9/6; ⊘9am-5pm mid-Mar–Nov, 10am-4pm Dec–mid-Mar) has authentic historic buildings from Germany, Ireland and England, plus re-created West African dwellings and a separate area of American frontier dwellings on the site's 100-plus acres. Costumed interpreters (aided by bleating livestock) do an excellent job showing what life was like for the disparate ancestors of today's Virginians.

Woodrow Wilson Presidential Library (www.woodrowwilson.org; 18-24 N Coalter St; adult/student/child $14/7/5; ⊘9am-5pm Mon-Sat, from noon Sun) is a scholarly peek into the life of the 28th president and founder of the League of Nations, as well as the pre- and post-WWI era he emerged from.

Don't leave without catching a show at the 300-seat **Blackfriars Playhouse** (☑540-851-1733; www.americanshakespearecenter.com; 10 S Market St; tickets $20-42), where the American Shakespeare Center company performs in a stunning re-creation of Shakespeare's original indoor theater.

To stay right downtown, the thoroughly mauve and immensely welcoming **Frederick House** (☑540-885-4220; www.frederickhouse.com; 28 N New St; r incl breakfast $130-240; P❄🕙) consists of five historical residences with 25 varied rooms and suites, all with private bathrooms and some with antique furnishings and decks.

Nearby, the **Miller House** (☑540-886-3186; www.millerhousebandb.com; 210 N New St; r incl breakfast $155-175; P❄) offers beautiful guestrooms with chandeliers, four-poster beds and decorative fireplaces in a beautifully restored Victorian.

Howard Johnson Express (☑540-886-5330; www.hojo.com; 268 N Central Ave; r $58; P❄🕙🏊) is a clean, good-value cheapie, a short stroll to the historic district.

West Beverley St is sprinkled with restaurants and cafes. Leading Staunton's culinary renaissance, **Zynodoa** (☑540-885-7775; 115 E Beverley St; mains $21-28; ⊘5-11:30pm Wed-Sat, noon-8pm Sun) serves delectable seasonal fare, sustainably sourced. Recent hits: Ayrshire roasted pork with spicy black beans and Southern fried soft-shell crabs.

Another farm-to-table favorite, the **Staunton Grocery** (☑540-886-6880; 105 W Beverley St; lunch/dinner mains from $9/18; ⊘11am-2pm Wed-Sat, 5:30-9pm Tue-Sat) serves innovative fare with Southern accents (like roasted catfish with beluga lentils and bacon vinaigrette).

Split Banana (7 W Beverley St; ice cream from $3.15; ⊘11am-11pm; ⊛) is an inviting, retro-style ice-cream parlor with 18 or so gelato-style flavors, all made on-site.

A valley tradition since 1947, **Mrs Rowe's** (☑540-886-1833; I-81 exit 222; mains $5-16; ⊘7am-8pm Mon-Sat, to 7pm Sun) offers home-cooked Southern fare and hospitality.

LEXINGTON & AROUND

This is the place to see Southern gentry at their stately best, as cadets from the Virginia Military Institute jog past the prestigious academics of Washington & Lee University. The **visitor center** (☑540-463-3777; 106 E Washington St; ⊘9am-5pm) has free parking.

You can learn about one of Lexington's favorite former residents at the **Stonewall Jackson House** (8 E Washington St; adult/child $8/6; ⊘9am-5pm Mon-Sat, from 1pm Sun). The future Confederate general lived (and did the polka) in the house from 1851 to 1861 before going off to war and into history.

You'll either feel admiration or pity for the disciplined cadets at **Virginia Military Institute** (VMI; Letcher Ave; ⊘9am-5pm when campus & museums open), the only university to have sent its entire graduating class into combat (plaques to student war dead are touching and ubiquitous). A full-dress parade takes place most Fridays at 4:30pm during the school year. The school's **George C Marshall Museum** (☑540-463-7103; adult/student $5/2; ⊘9am-5pm Tue-Sat, from 1pm Sun) honors the creator of the Marshall Plan for post-WWII European reconstruction. The **VMI Cadet Museum** (☑540-464-7334; admission free; ⊘9am-5pm) houses the stuffed carcass of Stonewall Jackson's horse, a homemade American flag made by an alumnus prisoner of war in Vietnam, and a tribute to VMI students killed in the War on Terror. Contact the museum for a free guided tour of the campus offered at noon.

Founded in 1749, colonnaded Washington & Lee University is one of the top small colleges in America. The **Lee Chapel & Museum** (☑540-458-8768; ⊘9am-4pm, from 1pm Sun) inters Robert E Lee, while his horse Traveller is buried outside. One of the four Confederate banners surrounding Lee's tomb is set in an original flagpole, a branch a rebel soldier turned into a makeshift standard.

Historic Country Inns (☎877-283-9680; 11 N Main St; r $110-145, ste $170-190; P❄) operates two inns downtown and one outside town. All of the buildings have some historical significance to Lexington, and most of the rooms are individually decorated with period antiques. The charming, eco-minded **Applewood Inn & Llama Trekking** (☎800-463-1902; www.applewoodbb.com; 242 Tarn Beck Lane; r $155-165; P❄) offers a slew of outdoorsy activities on a farm 12-minutes' drive southeast of Lexington.

Reserve well ahead for a memorable meal at **Red Hen** (☎540-464-4401; 11 E Washington St; mains $17-25; ⊙5:30-9pm Tue-Sat), with a creative menu that showcases the fine local produce (roasted pork loin with savory beer bread pudding and oyster mushrooms).

Bistro on Main (8 N Main St; mains $9-24; ⊙11:30am-2:30pm & 5-9pm Tue-Sat) is a bright, welcoming spot with big windows onto the main street, tasty bistro fare and a bar.

For old-fashioned amusement, catch a movie at **Hull's Drive-in** (☎540-463-2621; http://hullsdrivein.com; 2367 N Lee Hwy/US 11; per person $6; ⊙7pm Thu-Sun May-Oct), 5.5 miles north of town.

NATURAL BRIDGE & FOAMHENGE

Yes, it's a kitschy tourist trap, and yes, vocal creationists who insist it was made by the hand of God are dominating the site, but the 215ft-high **Natural Bridge** (www.naturalbridgeva.com; bridge adult/child $18/10, bridge & caverns $24/14; ⊙9am-dusk), 15 miles from Lexington, is still pretty cool. It was surveyed by 16-year-old George Washington, who supposedly carved his initials into the wall, and was once owned by Thomas Jefferson. You can also take a tour of some exceptionally deep caverns here.

Just up the road, check out **Foamhenge** (Hwy 11; admission free), a marvelous full-size replica of Stonehenge made entirely of Styrofoam. There are fine views – and even an onsite wizard. It's a mile north of Natural Bridge.

Blue Ridge Highlands & Southwest Virginia

The southwestern tip of Virginia is the most rugged part of the state. Turn onto the Blue Ridge Pkwy or any side road and you'll immediately plunge into dark strands of dogwood and fir, fast streams and white water-

falls. You're bound to see Confederate flags in the small towns, but there's a proud hospitality behind the fierce veneer of independence.

BLUE RIDGE PARKWAY

Where Skyline Dr ends, the **Blue Ridge Parkway** (www.blueridgeparkway.org, www.nps.gov/blri) picks up. The road is just as pretty and runs from the southern Appalachian ridge in Shenandoah National Park at Mile 0 to North Carolina's Great Smoky Mountains National Park at Mile 469. Wildflowers bloom in spring, and fall colors are spectacular, but watch out for foggy days; no guardrails can make for hairy driving. There are a dozen visitor centers scattered over the Pkwy, and any of them make a good kick-off point to start your trip. For more details, see p327.

☉ Sights & Activities

There are all kinds of sights running along the Pkwy; these are a handful, listed from north to south:

Humpback Rocks   HIKING
(Mile 5.8) Tour 19th-century farm buildings or take the steep trail to Humpback Rocks, offering spectacular 360-degree views.

Sherando Lake Recreation Area   SWIMMING
(Off Mile 16; ☎540-291-2188) In George Washington National Forest (p302), you'll find two pretty lakes (one for swimming, one for fishing), with hiking trails and campsites. To get there, take Rte 664 W.

James River & Kanawha Canal   HISTORIC SITE
(Mile 64) A footpath here leads to the 19th-century canal locks and, if you have time, a pleasant amble over river bluffs.

Peaks of Otter   HIKING
(Mile 86) There are trails to the tops of these mountains: Sharp Top, Flat Top and Harkening Hill. Shuttles run to the top of Sharp Top or you can try a fairly challenging hike (3 miles return) to the summit.

Mabry Mill   HISTORIC SITE
(Mile 176) One of the most photographed buildings in the state, the mill nests in such a fuzzy green vale you'll think you've entered the opening chapter of a Tolkien novel.

🛏 Sleeping

There are nine local **campgrounds** (☎877-444-6777; www.recreation.gov; campsites $16; ⊙May-Oct), four in Virginia. Every year the staggered opening date of facilities changes, but sites are generally accessible from April to November. Two NPS-approved indoor facilities are on the Pkwy in Virginia.

Peaks of Otter
LODGE $$
(540-586-1081; www.peaksofotter.com; Mile 86, 85554 Blue Ridge Pkwy; r $110-140; 🅿) A pretty, split-rail-surrounded lodge on a small lake that's nestled between two of its namesake mountains. There's a restaurant, but no public phones and no cellphone reception.

Rocky Knob Cabins
CABINS $
(540-593-3503; Mile 174, 256 Mabry Mill Rd; cabin with shared bath $65; ⊘May-Oct) Rustic cabins set in a secluded stretch of forest. Bring food, as eating options are limited along the Pkwy.

ROANOKE & AROUND
Illuminated by the giant star atop Mill Mountain, Roanoke is the largest city in the valley and is the self-proclaimed 'Capital of the Blue Ridge.' It has a compact set of attractions based around the bustling indoor-outdoor Historic City Market (213 Market St; ⊘7:30am-4:30pm Mon-Sat), a sumptuous farmers market loaded with temptations. For local information, check out the Roanoke Valley Visitor Information Center (540-342-6025; www.visitroanokeva.com; 101 Shenandoah Ave NE; ⊘9am-5pm) in the old Norfolk & Western train station.

The striking Taubman Museum of Art (www.taubmanmuseum.org; 110 Salem Ave SE; adult/child $7/4; ⊘10am-5pm Tue-Sat, to 8pm Fri, noon-5pm Sun), opened in 2008, is set in a sculptural steel-and-glass edifice that's reminiscent of the Guggenheim Bilbao (it's no coincidence, as architect Randall Stout was a one-time associate of Frank Gehry). Inside, you'll find a superb collection of artworks spanning 3500 years (particularly strong in 19th- and 20th-century American works).

Currently undergoing a massive $27 million renewal project, Center in the Square (540-342-5700; www.centerinthesquare.org; 1 Market Sq; ⊘10am-5pm Tue-Sat, from 1pm Sun) is the city's cultural heartbeat, with a science museum and planetarium (adult/child $8/6), local history museum (adult/child $3/2) and theater. The site of the Harrison Museum of African American Culture (admission free) was the first public high school for African Americans in America. It showcases local African American culture, and traditional and contemporary African art.

About 30 miles east of Roanoke, the tiny town of Bedford suffered the most casualties per capita during WWII, and hence was chosen to host the moving National D-Day Memorial (540-586-3329; US 460 & Hwy 122; adult/child $7/5; ⊘10am-5pm). Among its towering arch and flower garden is a cast of bronze figures re-enacting the storming of the beach, complete with bursts of water symbolizing the hail of bullets the soldiers faced. Walking tours ($3) leave hourly between 10:30am and 3:30pm.

Rose Hill (540-400-7785; www.bandbrose hill.com; 521 Washington Ave; r $100-125) is a charming and welcoming three-room B&B in Roanoke's historic district.

Market St is dotted with eateries, including much-loved, family-owned Thelma's Chicken & Waffles (315 Market St; mains $4-10; ⊘7am-10pm Tue-Sat, 10am-9pm Sun & Mon), serving tasty Southern classics like baby-back ribs, mac 'n' cheese, meatloaf and, of course, fried chicken and waffles.

MT ROGERS NATIONAL RECREATION AREA
This seriously beautiful district is well worth a visit from outdoor enthusiasts. Hike, fish or cross-country ski among ancient hardwood trees and the state's tallest peak. The park headquarters (276-783-5196; Hwy 16, Marion) offers maps and recreation directories. The NPS operates five campgrounds in the area; contact park headquarters for details.

ABINGDON
One of the most photogenic towns in Virginia, Abingdon retains fine Federal and Victorian architecture in its historic district, and hosts the bluegrass Virginia Highlands Festival over the first half of August. The visitor center (800-435-3440; 335 Cummings St; ⊘9am-5pm) has exhibits on local history.

Fields-Penn 1860 House Museum (208 W Main St; adult/child $3/2; ⊘11am-4pm Wed, from 1pm Thu-Sat) has exhibits on 19th-century life in southwest Virginia. Founded during the Depression, Barter Theatre (276-628-3991; www.bartertheatre.com; 133 W Main St; performances from $20) earned its name from audiences trading food for performances. Actors Gregory Peck and Ernest Borgnine (and uh, Wayne Knight, *Seinfeld*'s 'Newman') cut their teeth on Barter's stage.

The Virginia Creeper Trail (www.vacreeper trail.org), named for the railroad that once ran this route, travels 33 miles between Whitetop Station near the North Carolina border and downtown Abingdon. Several outfitters rent bikes, organize outings and run shuttles, including **Virginia Creeper Trail Bike Shop** (☏276-676-2552; www.vacreepertrailbikeshop.com; 201 Pecan St; per 2hr/day $10/20; ⏱9am-6pm Sun-Fri, from 8am Sat) near the trailhead.

Martha Washington Inn (☏276-628-3161; www.marthawashingtoninn.com; 150 W Main St; r from $225; P❄@🛜🏊), opposite the Barter, is the region's premier historic hotel, a Victorian sprawl of elegant rooms and excellent amenities (wood-paneled library, outdoor Jacuzzi, saltwater pool, tennis courts).

Step back in time at **Pop Ellis Soda Shoppe** (217 W Main St; mains $8-11; ⏱11am-4pm Mon, to 9pm Tue-Sat) with a beautifully restored interior reminiscent of 1920s-era soda fountains. Thick burgers, wraps and nachos are a fine accompaniment to hand-jerked sodas and milkshakes.

Equal parts cafe and bookstore, **Zazzy'z** (380 E Main St; mains around $5; ⏱8am-6pm Mon-Sat, 9am-3pm Sun) serves inexpensive quiches, lasagnas and panini, plus decent coffee.

THE CROOKED ROAD

When Scotch–Irish fiddle-and-reel married African American banjo-and-percussion, American mountain or 'old-time' music was born, with such genres as country and bluegrass. The latter genre still dominates the Blue Ridge, and Virginia's Heritage Music Trail, the 250-mile-long **Crooked Road** (www.thecrookedroad.org), takes you through nine sites associated with that history, along with some eye-stretching mountain scenery. It's well worth taking a detour and joining the music-loving fans of all ages who kick up their heels (many arrive with tap shoes) at these festive jamborees. During a live show you'll witness elders connecting to deep cultural roots and a new generation of musicians keeping that heritage alive and evolving.

FLOYD

Tiny, cute-as-a-postcard Floyd is nothing more than an intersection between Hwy 8 and 221, but life explodes on Friday nights at the **Floyd Country Store** (☏540-745-4563; www.floydcountrystore.com; 206 S Locust St; ⏱10am-11pm Fri, to 5:30pm Sat). Every Friday starting at 6:30pm, $5 gets you four bluegrass bands in four hours and the chance to watch happy crowds jam along to regional heritage. No smokin', no drinkin', but there's plenty of dancin' (of the jig-and-tap style)

and good cheer. On weekends, there's lots of live music happening nearby.

Built in 2007 with ecofriendly materials and furnishings, **Hotel Floyd** (☏540-745-6080; www.hotelfloyd.com; 120 Wilson St; r $100-160; P❄🛜) is one of the most 'green' hotels in Virginia, and is a model of sustainability. Each of the 14 unique rooms were decorated by local artisans. Eight miles west of Floyd, **Miracle Farm B&B** (☏540-789-2214; www.miraclefarmbnb.com; 179 Ida Rose Lane; r $125-155; P❄🛜) has lovely ecofriendly cabins amid lush scenery.

When you're all jigged out, head for **Oddfella's** (110 N Locust St; lunch mains $7-14, dinner $8-21; ⏱11am-2:30pm Wed-Sat, 5-9pm Thu-Sun, 10am-3pm Sun), which has a woodsy, organic mostly Tex-Mex menu – and satisfying locally produced microbrews from the Shooting Creek Brewery.

Above the Harvest Moon health-food store, **Natasha's Market Cafe** (☏540-745-2450; 227 N Locust St; lunch/dinner mains from $8/16; ⏱11am-3pm Tue-Sat, 5:30-9pm Thu-Sat) is a bright and cheery spot serving organic local produce.

GALAX

Galax claims to be the world capital of mountain music, although it feels like anywhere-else-ville outside of the immediate downtown area, which is on the National Register of Historic Places. The main attraction is the **Rex Theater** (☏276-236-0329; www.rextheatergalax.com; 113 E Grayson St), a musty, red-curtained belle of yore. Frequent bluegrass acts cross its stage, but the easiest one to catch is the free Friday-night live WBRF 98.1 show, which pulls in crowds from across the mountains.

For a touch of the great outdoors, go for a hike or bike ride along the **New River Trail**, a 57-mile-long greenway along an abandoned railroad track north to Pulaski. It parallels the New River for 39 miles.

Tom Barr of **Barr's Fiddle Shop** (105 S Main St) is the Stradivarius of the mountains, a master craftsman sought out by fiddle and mandolin aficionados from across the world. The **Old Fiddler's Convention** (www.oldfiddlersconvention.com) is held on the second weekend in August in Galax; it's one of the premier mountain music festivals in the world.

Doctor's Inn (☏276-238-9998; thedoctorsinnvirginia.com; 406 W Stuart Dr; r $140-150; P❄🛜) is a welcoming guesthouse with antique-filled chambers and excellent breakfasts.

The **Galax Smokehouse** (101 N Main St; mains $5-14; ⊙11am-9pm Mon-Sat, to 3pm Sun) serves platters of sweetly sauced Memphis-style BBQ.

CARTER FAMILY FOLD

In a tiny hamlet of SW Virginia, formerly known as Maces Spring (today part of Hiltons), you'll find one of the hallowed birthplaces of mountain music. The **Carter Family Fold** (☑276-386-6054; www.carterfamilyfold.org; AP Carter Hwy/Rte 614; adult/child $7/1; ⊙7:30pm Sat) continues the musical legacy begun by the talented Carter family back in 1927. Every Saturday night, the 900-person arena hosts first-rate bluegrass and gospel bands; there's also a museum with family memorabilia and the original mid-1800s log cabin where AP Carter was born. With no nearby lodging, your best bet is to stay in Abingdon (30 miles east), Kingsport, TN (12 miles southwest) or Bristol (25 miles southeast).

WEST VIRGINIA

Wild and wonderful West Virginia is often overlooked by American and foreign travelers. It doesn't help that the state can't seem to shake its negative stereotypes. That's too bad, because West Virginia is one of the prettiest states in the Union. With its line of unbroken green mountains, raging whitewater rivers and snowcapped ski resorts, this is an outdoor-lovers' paradise.

Created by secessionists from secession, the people here still think of themselves as hardscrabble sons of miners, and that perception isn't entirely off. But the Mountain State is also gentrifying and, occasionally, that's a good thing: the arts are flourishing in the valleys, where some towns offer a welcome break from the state's constantly evolving outdoor activities.

History

Virginia was once the biggest state in America, divided between the plantation aristocracy of the Tidewater and the mountains of what is now West Virginia. The latter were settled by tough farmers who staked out independent freeholds across the Appalachians. Always resentful of their Eastern brethren and their reliance on cheap (ie slave) labor, the mountaineers of West Virginia declared their independence from Virginia when the latter tried to break off from America during the Civil War.

» **Nickname** Mountain State

» **Population** 1.9 million

» **Area** 24,230 sq miles

» **Capital city** Charleston (population 52,000)

» **Sales tax** 6%

» **Birthplace of** Olympic gymnast Mary Lou Retton (b 1968), writer Pearl S Buck (1892–1973), pioneer aviator Chuck Yeager (b 1923), actor Don Knotts (1924–2006)

» **Home of** The National Radio Astronomy Observatory, much of the American coal industry

» **Politics** Republican

» **Famous for** mountains, John Denver's 'Take Me Home, Country Roads,' the Hatfield–McCoy feud

» **State slogan** 'Wild and Wonderful'

» **Driving distances** Harpers Ferry to Fayetteville 280 miles, Fayetteville to Morgantown 148 miles

Yet the scrappy, independent-at-all-costs stereotype was challenged in the late 19th and early 20th centuries, when miners here formed into cooperative unions and fought employers in some of the bloodiest battles in American labor history. That mix of chip-on-the-shoulder resentment toward authority and look-out-for-your-neighbor community values continues to characterize West Virginia today, although the creeping blandness of suburbia threatens this regional culture.

❶ **Information**

West Virginia Division of Tourism (☑800-225-5982; www.wvtourism.com) operates welcome centers at interstate borders and in **Harpers Ferry** (☑304-535-2482). Check www.adventuresinwv.com for info on the state's myriad adventure tourism opportunities.

Many hotels and motels tack on a $1 'safe' fee, refundable upon request at checkout. So if you didn't use that room safe, get your dollar back.

Eastern Panhandle

The most accessible part of the state has always been a mountain getaway for DC types.

HARPERS FERRY

History lives on in this attractive town, set with steep cobblestoned streets framed by the Shenandoah Mountains and the confluence of the rushing Potomac and Shenandoah Rivers. The lower town functions as an open-air museum, with over a dozen buildings that you can wander through to get a taste of 19th-century life in the small town. Exhibits narrate the town's role at the forefront of westward expansion, American industry, and most famously, the slavery debate. In 1859 old John Brown tried to spark a slave uprising here and was hanged for his efforts; the incident rubbed friction between North and South into the fires of Civil War.

Pick up a pass to visit the historic buildings at the **Harpers Ferry National Historic Park Visitor Center** (☎304-535-6029; www.nps.gov/hafe; 171 Shoreline Dr; vehicle/pedestrian $6/4; ⏱8am-5pm) off Hwy 340. You can also park and take a free shuttle from here. Parking is extremely limited in Harpers Ferry proper.

◉ Sights & Activities

There are great hikes in the area, from three-hour scrambles to the scenic overlook from the Maryland Heights Trail, past Civil War fortifications on the Loudoun Heights Trail or along the Appalachian Trail. You can also bike or walk along the C&O Canal towpath.

Master Armorer's House   BUILDING
Among the free sites in the historic district, this 1858 house explains how rifle technology developed here revolutionized the firearms industry.

Appalachian Trail Conservancy   HIKING
(☎304-535-6331; www.appalachiantrail.org; cnr Washington & Jackson Sts; ⏱9am-5pm Mon-Fri Apr-Oct) The 2160-mile Appalachian Trail is headquartered at this tremendous resource for hikers.

Storer College building   MUSEUM
Long ago a teachers' college for freed slaves, it now traces the town's African American history.

John Brown Museum   MUSEUM
(http://johnbrownwaxmuseum.com; 168 High St; adult/child $7/5; ⏱9am-4:30pm) This laughably tacky museum tells the story of Brown's life through music, voice recordings and life-size wax figures.

River Riders   ADVENTURE SPORTS
(☎800-326-7238; www.riverriders.com; 408 Alstadts Hill Rd) The go-to place for rafting, canoeing, tubing, kayaking and multiday biking trips, plus bike rental (four hours $20).

O Be Joyfull   WALKING TOURS
(☎732-801-0381; www.obejoyfull.com; 175 High St; adult/child from $8/5) Offers a variety of historical walking tours around Harpers Ferry, including a spooky 90-minute evening tour.

🛏 Sleeping & Eating

Jackson Rose   B&B $$
(☎304-535-1528; www.thejacksonrose.com; 1167 W Washington St; r weekday/weekend $135/150; ❄🐾) This marvelous brick 18th-century residence with stately gardens has three attractive guestrooms, including a room where Stonewall Jackson briefly lodged during the Civil War. Antique furnishings and vintage curios are sprinkled about the house, and the cooked breakfast is excellent. It's a 600m walk downhill to the historic district. No children under 12.

Town's Inn   B&B $$
(☎304-702-1872, 877-489-2447; www.thetownsinn.com; 175 & 179 High St; r $70-140; ❄) Spread between two neighboring pre–Civil War residences, the Town's Inn has rooms ranging from small and minimalist to charming heritage-style quarters. It's set in the middle of the historic district with an indoor-outdoor restaurant as well.

HI-Harpers Ferry Hostel   HOSTEL $
(☎301-834-7652; www.hiusa.org; 19123 Sandy Hook Rd, Knoxville, MD; dm $20; ⏱mid-Apr–mid-Oct; 🅿❄@🐾) Located 2 miles from downtown on the Maryland side of the Potomac River, this friendly hostel has plenty of amenities including a kitchen, laundry and lounge area with games and books.

Canal House   AMERICAN $$
(1226 Washington St; mains $7-14; ⏱11am-3pm Wed-Sat, 5:30-8:30pm Thu-Sat, noon-6pm Sun; 🚲) Roughly 1 mile west (and uphill) from the historic district, Canal House is a perennial favorite for delicious sandwiches and friendly service in a flower-trimmed stone house. Outdoor seating.

Anvil   AMERICAN $$
(☎304-535-2582; 1270 Washington St; lunch mains $8-12, dinner $15-24; ⏱11am-9pm Wed-Sun) Local trout melting in honey-pecan butter and an elegant Federal dining room equals excellence at Anvil, in next-door Bolivar.

Beans in the Belfry TOP CHOICE AMERICAN $$

(☑301-834-7178; 122 W Potomac St, Brunswick, MD; ☺9am-9pm Mon-Sat, to 7pm Sun; @🛜🚗) Across the river in Brunswick (roughly 10 miles east), you'll find this converted red-brick church, sheltering mismatched couches and kitsch-laden walls, light fare (chili, sandwiches, quiche) and a tiny stage where live folk, blues and bluegrass bands strike up most nights. Sunday jazz brunch ($16) is a hit.

❶ Getting There & Around

Amtrak (www.amtrak.com) trains run to Washington's Union Station (one daily, 71 minutes, $14). **MARC trains** (mta.maryland.gov) run three times daily, Monday to Friday ($11).

BERKELEY SPRINGS

America's first spa town (George Washington relaxed here) is an odd jumble of spiritualism, artistic expression and pampering spa centers. Farmers in pickups sporting Confederate flags and acupuncturists in tie-dye smocks regard each other with bemusement on the roads of Bath (still the official name).

The Berkeley Springs State Park's **Roman Baths** (☑304-258-2711; 2 S Washington St; bath $22; ☺10am-6pm) are uninspiring (soaks are in dimly lit individual tile-lined rooms), but it's the cheapest spa deal in town. (Fill your water bottle with some of the magic stuff at the fountain outside the door.) For a more indulgent experience, book a treatment (massages, facials, aromatherapy) across the green at the **Bath House** (☑800-431-4698; www.bathhouse.com; 21 Fairfax St; 1hr massage $75; ☺10am-5pm).

Inn & Spa at Berkeley Springs (☑304-258-2210; thecountryinnatberkeleysprings.com; r from $110; 🅿🛜), right next to the park, has a wide range of accommodations, from bright, comfortable rooms with wood floors to more elegant suites. There's a good spa on-site.

Cacapon State Park (☑304-258-1022; 818 Cacapon Lodge Dr; lodge/cabins from $85/91) has simple lodge accommodations plus modern and rustic cabins (with fireplaces) in a peaceful wooded setting, 9 miles south of Berkeley Springs (off US 522). There's hiking, lake swimming and a golf course.

Tari's (33 N Washington St; lunch $8-10, dinner $15-2; ☺11am-9pm) is a casual spot serving gourmet sandwiches and salads by day, and heartier fare (seafood, ribs, thyme-crusted lamb) by night. Reserve ahead for high-end cuisine at the elegant, award-winning **Lot**

12 Public House (☑304-258-6264; 117 Warren St; mains $23-30; ☺from 5pm Thu-Sun), halfway up the hill.

Monongahela National Forest

Almost the entire eastern half of West Virginia is marked green parkland on the map, and all that goodness falls under the auspices of this stunning national forest. Within its 1400 sq miles are wild rivers, caves and the highest peak in the state (Spruce Knob). More than 850 miles of trails include the 124-mile **Allegheny Trail**, for hiking and backpacking, and the 75-mile rails-to-trails **Greenbrier River Trail**, popular with bicyclists.

Elkins, at the forest's western boundary, is a good base of operations. The **National Forest Service Headquarters** (☑304-636-1800; 200 Sycamore St; campsites $5-30, primitive camping free) distributes recreation directories for hiking, bicycling and camping. Stock up on trail mix, energy bars and hippie auras at **Good Energy Foods** (214 3rd St; ☺9am-5:30pm Mon-Sat).

In the southern end of the forest, **Cranberry Mountain Nature Center** (☑304-653-4826; cnr Hwys 150 & 39/55; ☺9am-4:30pm Thu-Mon May-Oct) has scientific information on the forest.

The surreal landscapes at **Seneca Rocks**, 35 miles southeast of Elkins, attract rock climbers up the 900ft-tall sandstone strata. **Seneca Shadows Campground** (☑877-444-6777; campsites $11-30; ☺Apr-Oct) is 1 mile east.

An 8-mile portion of the Allegheny Trail links two full-service state parks 30 miles northeast of Elkins: **Canaan Valley Resort** (☑304-866-4121; www.canaanresort.com), a downhill ski resort, and **Blackwater Falls State Park** (☑304-259-5216; www.blackwaterfalls.com), with backcountry ski touring. Further south, **Snowshoe Mountain** (☑877-441-4386; www.snowshoemtn.com; lift tickets adult/student/child $79/76/66) is the state's largest downhill ski and snowboard resort, with a beautiful alpine-inspired, pedestrian village. Snowshoe is a popular mountain-biking center from spring to fall.

Nearby, the **Cass Scenic Railroad State Park** (☑304-456-4300; www.cassrailroad.com; train rides from $18) runs steam trains, from an old logging town to mountaintop overlooks, daily in summer and for peak fall foliage. Accommodations include cottages ($103 to $122) and cabooses ($85 to $119).

ROADSIDE MYSTERIES

See gravity and the known limits of tackiness defied at the **Mystery Hole** (☑304-658-9101; 16724 Midland Trail, Ansted, WV; adult/child $6/5; ☺10:30am-6pm), one of the great attractions of roadside America. Everything inside this madhouse *tilts at an angle!* It's located 1 mile west of Hawks Nest State Park. Call ahead to check open days.

The **National Radio Astronomy Observatory** (☑304-456-2150; www.gb.nrao.edu; Green Bank; admission & tour free; ☺9am-6pm summer, from 10am Thu-Mon rest of year) is home to the 328ft Green Bank Telescope, the largest movable radio dish in the world. The center lies within the country's only federal radio-free zone, which is why your car won't pick up any stations within 25 miles of the center.

Southern West Virginia

This part of the state has carved out a viable stake as adventure-sports capital of the eastern seaboard.

NEW RIVER GORGE NATIONAL RIVER

The New River is actually one of the oldest in the world, and the primeval forest gorge it runs through is one of the most breathtaking in the Appalachians. The NPS protects a stretch of the New River that falls 750ft over 50 miles, with a compact set of rapids up to Class V concentrated at the northernmost end.

Canyon Rim visitor center (☑304-574-2115; ☺9am-5pm), just north of the impressive gorge bridge, is only one of five NPS visitor centers along the river, with information on scenic drives, river outfitters, gorge climbing, hiking and mountain biking, as well as white-water rafting to the north on the Gauley River. Rim and gorge trails offer beautiful views. There are several free basic camping areas.

Nearby **Hawks Nest State Park** offers views from its rim-top **lodge** (☑304-658-5212; www.hawksnestsp.com; r $77-84; ✱☎); from June through October it operates an aerial tram (closed Wednesday) to the river, where you can catch a cruising boat ride.

Babcock State Park (☑304-438-3004; www.babcocksp.com; cabins $77-88, campsites $20-23) has hiking, canoeing, horseback riding, camping and cabin accommodations. The park's highlight is its photogenic Glade Creek Grist Mill.

FAYETTEVILLE & AROUND

Dubbed one of the coolest small towns in America, pint-sized Fayetteville acts as the jumping-off point for New River thrill-seekers. On the third Saturday in October, hundreds of base jumpers parachute from the 876ft-high New River Gorge Bridge for the **Bridge Day Festival**.

Among the many state-licensed rafting outfitters in the area, **Cantrell Ultimate Rafting** (☑800-470-7238; www.ultimaterafting.com; packages from $60) stands out for its white-water rafting trips. For rock climbers, **Hard Rock** (☑304-574-0735; www.hardrockclimbing.com; 131 South Court St; half-day/day from $75/140) offers trips and training courses.

The **Beckley Exhibition Coal Mine** (☑304-256-1747; www.beckleymine.org; adult/child $20/12; ☺10am-6pm Apr-Oct) in nearby Beckley is a museum on the region's coal heritage. Visitors can descend 1500ft to a former coal mine. Bring a jacket, as it's cold underground!

River Rock Retreat Hostel (☑304-574-0394; www.riverrockretreatandhostel.com; Lansing-Edmond Rd; dm $23; ℗✱) located less than 1 mile north of the New River Gorge Bridge, has basic, clean rooms and plenty of common space. Owner Joy Marr is a wealth of local information. Two miles south of the bridge, **Rifrafters Campground** (☑304-574-1065; www.rifrafters.com; Laurel Creek Rd; campsites per person $12, cabins d/q $40/80) has primitive campsites, comfy cabins and hot-shower and bathroom facilities.

TOP CHOICE **Pies & Pints** (219 W Maple Ave; pizza small/large $13/22; ☺11:30am-9pm; ✈) has delicious and innovative pizzas (like Cuban pork pie or eggplant and roasted red peppers), plus a huge beer selection (try the local Bridge Brew Works lager on draft).

Start the day with breakfast and coffee under stained-glass windows at **Cathedral Café & Bookstore** (134 S Court St; mains $5-8; ☺8am-4pm; @☎).

GREENBRIER VALLEY

Tucked between the Allegheny Mountains, the eclectic Greenbrier Valley is home to breathtaking natural beauty and hot-spring spa towns, all anchored by the sophisticated artsy town of Lewisburg. The valley's star attraction is **Greenbrier** (☎800-453-4858; www.greenbrier.com; 300 W Main St, White Sulphur Springs; r from $279; P❄@🛜🏊), an unparalleled, luxurious hotel and spa resort. Dubbed the Queen of the Southern Spas, it was originally built in 1778 to pamper wealthy Southerners. In the 20th century, the Greenbrier housed a more covert amenity: a **nuclear**

bunker. In the 1950s during the height of the Cold War, the government built this massive bunker under Greenbrier to house Congress in the event of a nuclear holocaust. It remained a secret until 1992, when *The Washington Post* spilled the beans; the bunker shut down three years later. Today visitors can take a guided **bunker tour** (adult/child $30/15, closed Jan-Mar) of this unique and fascinating bit of American lore.

The South

Includes »

Best Places to Stay

» Ansonborough Inn (p334)

» Music City Hostel (p356)

» 21c (p364)

» Kate Shepard House (p393)

» Shack Up Inn (p396)

Best Places to Eat

» Husk (p335)

» Prince's Hot Chicken (p356)

» Cochon (p414)

» Doe's Eat Place (p312)

» Commander's Palace (p415)

Why Go?

More than any other part of the country, the South has an identity all its own – a musical way of speaking, a complicated political history and a pride in a shared culture that cuts across state lines.

Nurtured by deep roots yet shaped by hardship, the South has produced some of America's most important culture, from novelists like William Faulkner and Flannery O'Connor, to foodstuffs like barbecue, bourbon and Coca-Cola, to music like blues and rock and roll. The cities of the South are some of the country's most fascinating, from antebellum beauties like New Orleans and Savannah to New South powerhouses like Atlanta and Charlotte.

But it's the legendary Southern hospitality that makes travel in the region such a pleasure. People round here *love* to talk. Stay long enough and you'll no doubt be invited for dinner.

When to Go
New Orleans

Nov–Feb Winter is generally mild here, and Christmas is a capital-E Event.

Apr–Jun Springs are lush and warm, abloom with fragrant jasmine, gardenia and tuberose.

Jul–Sep Summer is steamy, often unpleasantly so, and locals hit the beaches.

Understanding Southern Culture

Southerners have long been the butt of their fellow countrymen's jokes. They're slow-moving, hard-drinking, funny-talking and spend all their time fixing their pickup trucks and marrying their cousins. Or so the line goes. Well, while Southerners do tend to be relatively friendly and laid-back, the drawling country bumpkin is more the exception than the norm. Today's Southerner is just as likely to be a Mumbai-born motel owner in rural Arkansas, a fast-talking Atlanta investment banker with a glitzy high-rise condo, or a 20-something gay hipster in trendy Midtown Memphis.

Southerners do love sports, especially football, college basketball and NASCAR, while fine arts thrive in historic cities like Charleston and Savannah, and college towns like Chapel Hill, Knoxville and Athens are famed for their indie-music scenes. Religion is hugely important here – the so-called Bible belt runs smack through the South, with about half of all Southerners identifying as Evangelical Christians.

THE SOUTH FOR MUSIC LOVERS

The history of American music is the history of Southern music: the blues, bluegrass, jazz, gospel, country and rock and roll were all born here. Music hot spots include: Nashville, the birthplace of country music and home to more boot-stompin' honky-tonks than anywhere in the world; Memphis, where bluesmen still groove in the clubs of Beale St; and New Orleans, where you can hear world-class jazz, blues and zydeco every night of the week. Asheville, NC, is an emerging center of Appalachian revival music, while Kentucky claims bluegrass as its own.

Must-Eat Southern Foods

» Barbecue (region-wide, especially in North Carolina and Tennessee)

» Fried chicken (region-wide)

» Cornbread (region-wide)

» Shrimp and grits (South Carolina and Georgia coasts)

» Boudin (Cajun pork and rice sausage; Southern Louisiana)

» Gumbo/jambalaya/étouffée (rice and seafood or meat stew or mixture; Southern Louisiana)

» Po'boy (sandwich, traditionally with fried seafood or meat; Southern Louisiana)

» Hot tamales (cornmeal stuffed with spiced beef or pork; Mississippi Delta)

» Collards (a leafy green, often cooked with ham; region-wide)

» Pecan pie, coconut cake, red velvet cake, sweet-potato pie (region-wide)

» Bourbon (Kentucky)

DID YOU KNOW?

The South is America's fastest-growing region, with 14.3% of the country's population.

Fast Facts

» Nickname: Dixie

» Top three biggest cities: Atlanta, Charlotte, Memphis

» Time zones: Eastern, Central

Best Scenic Drives

» Blue Ridge Parkway – North Carolina to Virginia (www.blueridgeparkway. org)

» Natchez Trace – Tennessee to Mississippi (www. nps.gov/natr)

» Hwy 12 – North Carolina's Outer Banks

» Country Music Hwy/US 23 – Kentucky (countrymusichighway.com)

» Cherokee Foothills Scenic Hwy/SC 11 – South Carolina (www.discoversouthcarolina.com)

» Great River Road – Louisiana to Minnesota, including parts of Mississippi, Tennessee, Arkansas and Kentucky (www.experiencemississippiriver.com)

Resources

» www.visitsouth.com

» www.discoversouthcarolina.com

» www.visitnc.com

» www.tnvacation.com

» www.louisianatravel.com

The South Highlights

① Stomping your boots at **Tootsie's Orchid Lounge** (p358) on Nashville's honky-tonk-lined Lower Broadway

② Hiking and camping in the magnificent **Great Smoky**

Mountains National Park (p330)

③ Driving windswept Hwy 12 the length of North Carolina's **Outer Banks** (p317) and riding the ferry to Ocracoke Island

④ Touring the grand antebellum homes and cotton plantations of **Charleston** (p332)

⑤ Putting yourself into a Cajun-Creole food-induced

coma in **New Orleans** (p413), one of America's most treasured foodie havens.

⑥ Immersing yourself in the soul, rhythm, history and perseverance of the **Delta** **blues** (p396) in Clarksdale, MS

⑦ Exploring the caverns, mountains, rivers and forests of Arkansas' **Ozark Mountains** (p429), where folk music reigns

⑧ Falling for the hauntings, murderous tales and Southern hospitality in Georgia's living romance novel, the architecturally pristine **Savannah** (p383)

NORTH CAROLINA

It's trailer parks next to McMansions in North Carolina, where the Old South stands shoulder-to-shoulder with the New South. From the ancient mountains in the west to the sandy barrier islands of the Atlantic you'll find a variety of cultures and communities not easy to stereotype.

The fast-growing state is a patchwork of the progressive and the Stone Age: Asheville was named the 'New Freak Capital of the US' by *Rolling Stone,* while cohabitation of unmarried couples was technically illegal until 2006. The Raleigh area has the highest concentration of PhDs in the country, yet North Carolina routinely ranks 48th in education. Important industries range from tobacco and hogs to finance and nanotechnology.

Though the bulk of North Carolinians live in the business-oriented urban centers of the central Piedmont region, most travelers tend to stick to the scenic routes along the coast and through the Appalachian Mountains.

So come on down, ya'll, grab a plate of 'cue and watch the Duke Blue Devils and the Carolina Tar Heels battle it out on the basketball court – college hoops rival Jesus for Carolinians' souls.

History

Native Americans have inhabited North Carolina for more than 10,000 years. Major tribes included the Cherokee, in the mountains, the Catawba in the Piedmont and the Waccamaw in the Coastal Plain.

North Carolina was the second territory to be colonized by the British, named in memory of King Charles I (Carolus in Latin), but the first colony to vote for independence from the Crown. Several important Revolutionary War battles were fought here.

The state was a sleepy agricultural backwater through the 1800s, earning it the nickname the 'Rip Van Winkle State.' Divided on slavery (most residents were too poor to own slaves), North Carolina was the last state to secede during the Civil War, but went on to provide more Confederate soldiers than any other state.

North Carolina was a civil rights hotbed in the mid-20th century, with highly publicized lunch-counter sit-ins in Greensboro and the formation of the influential Student Nonviolent Coordinating Committee (SNCC) in Raleigh. The later part of the century brought finance to Charlotte, and technology and medicine to the Raleigh-Durham area, driving a huge population boom and widening cultural diversity.

ℹ Information

North Carolina Division of Tourism (☏919-733-8372; www.visitnc.com; 301 N Wilmington St, Raleigh) Sends out good maps and information, including its annual *Official Travel Guide.*

North Carolina State Parks (☏919-733-4181; www.ncparks.gov) Offers info on North Carolina's 40 state parks, some of which have camping (prices range from free to more than $20 a night).

THE SOUTH IN...

One Week

Fly into **New Orleans** and stretch your legs with a walking tour in the legendary French Quarter before devoting your remaining time to celebrating jazz history and partying the night away on **Bourbon St**. Then wind your way upward through the languid Delta, stopping in **Clarksdale** for a sultry evening of blues at the juke joints before alighting in **Memphis** to walk in the footsteps of the King at **Graceland**. From here, head on down the Music Hwy to **Nashville** to see Elvis' gold Cadillac at the **Country Music Hall of Fame** and practice your line dancing at the honky-tonks (country-music clubs) of the **District**.

Two to Three Weeks

Head east to hike amid the craggy peaks and waterfalls of **Great Smoky Mountains National Park** before a revitalizing overnight in the arty mountain town of **Asheville** and a tour of the scandalously opulent **Biltmore Estate**, America's largest private home. Plow straight through to the coast to loll on the sandy barrier islands of the isolated **Outer Banks**, then head down the coast to finish up in **Charleston**, with decadent food and postcard-pretty architecture.

North Carolina Coast

Which one of the following does not belong? A) windswept barrier islands; B) dignified Colonial villages once frequented by pirates; C) laid-back beach towns full of locally owned ice-cream shops and mom 'n' pop motels; D) flashy resort areas with megamalls and beach-themed chain restaurants. If you answered 'D,' buy yourself a celebratory shrimp sandwich. The North Carolina coast is relatively undeveloped, so even the most touristy beaches still have a small-town vibe. If it's solitude you seek, head to the isolated Outer Banks (OBX), where fishermen still make their living hauling in shrimp and the older locals speak in an archaic British-tinged brogue. Further south, Wilmington is known as a center of film and TV production and its surrounding beaches are popular with local spring breakers and tourists.

OUTER BANKS

These fragile ribbons of sand trace the coastline for 100 miles, cut off from the mainland by various sounds and waterways. From north to south, the barrier islands of Bodie (pronounced 'Body'), Roanoke, Hatteras and Ocracoke, essentially large sandbars, are linked by bridges and ferries. The far-northern communities of Corolla (pronounced kur-*all*-ah, not like the car), Duck and Southern Shores are former duck-hunting grounds for the northeastern rich, and are quiet and upscale. The nearly contiguous Bodie Island towns of Kitty Hawk, Kill Devil Hills and Nags Head are heavily developed and more populist in nature, with fried-fish joints, outdoor bars, motels and dozens of sandals 'n' sunblock shops. Roanoke Island, west of Bodie Island, is home to tons of Colonial history and the quaint waterfront town of Manteo. Further south, Hatteras Island is a protected national seashore with a few teeny villages and a wild, windswept beauty. At the tail end of the banks, wild ponies run free and salty old Bankers shuck oysters and weave hammocks on Ocracoke Island, accessible only by ferry.

A meandering drive down Hwy 12, which connects much of the Outer Banks, is one of the truly great American road trips, whether you come during the stunningly desolate winter months or the sunny summer.

◉ Sights

The following places are listed from north to south.

NORTH CAROLINA FACTS

» **Nickname** Tar Heel State

» **Population** 9.4 million

» **Area** 48,711 sq miles

» **Capital city** Raleigh (population 400,000)

» **Other cities** Charlotte (population 730,000)

» **Sales tax** 7%, plus an additional hotel-occupancy tax of up to 6%

» **Birthplace of** President James K Polk (1795–1849), jazzman John Coltrane (1926–67), NASCAR driver Richard Petty (b 1937), singer-songwriter Tori Amos (b 1963)

» **Home of** America's first state university, the Biltmore House, Krispy Kreme doughnuts

» **Politics** conservative in rural areas, increasingly liberal in urban ones

» **Famous for** The Andy Griffith Show, first airplane flight, college basketball

» **Pet name** natives are called 'tar heels,' a nickname of uncertain origin but said to be related to their pine tar production and their legendary stubbornness

» **Driving distances** Asheville to Raleigh 247 miles, Raleigh to Wilmington 131 miles

Currituck Heritage Park   HISTORIC BUILDINGS

The sunflower-yellow, art-nouveau-style Whalehead Club (www.whaleheadclub.org; Corolla; tours $9; ☺sunrise-sunset), built in the 1920s as a hunting 'cottage' for a Philadelphia industrialist, is the centerpiece of this manicured park in the village of Corolla. You can also climb the Currituck Beach Lighthouse (www.currituckbeachlight.com; adult/child $7/free) and visit the Victorian lighthouse-keeper's home, or check out the modern Outer Banks Center for Wildlife Education (admission free; ☺9am-5pm) for an interesting film on area history, info on local hiking trails and duck-decoy carving classes.

Wright Brothers National Memorial   PARK, MUSEUM

(www.nps.gov/wrbr; Kitty Hawk; admission $4; ☺9am-5pm, to 6pm summer) This historic site is located among the same windswept Kitty Hawk dunes where self-taught engineers Wilbur and Orville Wright launched the world's first successful airplane flight on December 17, 1903 (it lasted 12 seconds). A boulder now marks the take-off spot. Climb a nearby hill where the brothers conducted earlier glider experiments for fantastic views of sea and sound. The on-site **Wright Brothers Visitor Center** has a reproduction of the 1903 flyer and offers exhibits and lectures on aviation history.

Fort Raleigh National Historic Site
HISTORIC BUILDINGS

In the late 1580s, three decades before the Pilgrims landed at Plymouth Rock, a group of 116 British colonists disappeared without a trace from their Roanoke Island settlement. Were they killed off by drought? Did they run away with a Native American tribe? Did they try to sail home and capsize? The fate of the 'Lost Colony' remains one of America's greatest mysteries, and the **visitor center** (www.nps.gov/fora; 1401 National Park Dr, Manteo; ⊗9am-5pm, to 6pm summer) has exhibits, artifacts, maps and a free film to fuel the imagination.

Attractions at the site include the **Lost Colony Outdoor Drama** (www.thelostcolony.org; adult/child $20/10; ⊗8pm Mon-Sat Jun-Aug). This beloved long-running musical from Pulitzer Prize–winning North Carolina playwright Paul Green dramatizes the fate of the colonists. It plays at the Waterside Theater throughout summer.

The 16th-century-style **Elizabethan Gardens** (www.elizabethangardens.org; adult/child $8/5; ⊗9am-8pm daily summer, shorter hr fall-spring) include a Shakespearian herb garden and rows of beautifully manicured flower beds.

North Carolina Aquarium
AQUARIUM

(www.ncaquariums.com/roanoke-island; 374 Airport Rd, Roanoke Island; adult/child $8/6; ⊗9am-5pm; ⁂) Watch tiger sharks glide through the gloomy depths, chill by the gator pond or stroke the slimy bellies of (de-barbed) stingrays in the touch tank. Great for kids.

Cape Hatteras National Seashore
ISLANDS

Extending some 70 miles from south of Nags Head to the south end of Okracoke Island, this fragile necklace of islands remains blissfully free of overdevelopment. Natural attractions include local and migratory water birds, marshes, woodlands, dunes and miles of empty beaches. Don't miss the 156ft striped **Bodie Island Lighthouse**, south of Nags Head. You can't climb it, but it's darn photogenic. The following other attractions are listed north to south.

Pea Island National Wildlife Refuge
(www.fws.gov/peaisland; ⊗9am-4pm, to 5pm summer) At the northern end of Hatteras Island, this 5834-acre preserve is a birdwatcher's heaven, with nature trails and 13 miles of unspoiled beach.

Chicamacomico Lifesaving Station
(www.chicamacomico.net; Rodanthe village; admission $6; ⊗10am-5pm Mon-Fri Apr-Oct) Built in 1874, this was the first lifesaving station in the state, now a museum filled with pre–Coast Guard artifacts.

Cape Hatteras Lighthouse
(www.nps.gov/caha; climbing tours adult/child $7/3.50; ⊗9am-4:30pm, to 5:30pm Apr-Oct) At 208ft, this striking black-and-white-striped edifice is the tallest brick lighthouse in the US and is one of North Carolina's most iconic images. Climb the 248 steps and check out the visitor center (open year-round).

Graveyard of the Atlantic Museum
(www.graveyardoftheatlantic.com; Hatteras; admission by donation; ⊗10am-4pm) This museum is all about preserving the Outer Banks' maritime history, with exhibits about shipwrecks, piracy and salvaged cargo.

Ocracoke Island
ISLAND

Accessed via the free Hatteras–Ocracoke ferry, **Ocracoke Village** (www.ocracokevillage.com) sits at the south end of 14-mile-long Ocracoke Island. It's a funky little village that's crowded in summer and desolate in winter, where the older residents still speak in the 17th-century British dialect known as 'Hoi Toide' (their pronunciation of 'high tide') and refer to nonislanders as 'dingbatters.' Edward Teach, aka Blackbeard the pirate, used to hide out in the area and was killed here in 1718. You can camp by the beach where the wild ponies run, have a fish sandwich in a local pub, ride a rented scooter or bike around the village's narrow streets or visit the 1823 **Ocracoke Lighthouse**, the oldest one still operating in North Carolina.

The island makes a terrific day trip from Hatteras Island, or you can stay the night. The island has a handful of B&Bs, an NPS (National Parks Service) campground and tons of rental cottages. Or try the **Island Inn** (☑252-928-4351, 877-456-3466; www.ocracokeislandinn.com; 25 Lighthouse Rd, Ocracoke; r from $99, villas from $199; ᴘ❋☏☲), a grand

OUTER BANKS ORIENTATION

Hwy 12, also called Virginia Dare Trail or 'the coast road,' runs close to the Atlantic for the length of the Outer Banks. US 158, usually called 'the Bypass,' begins just north of Kitty Hawk and merges with US 64 as it crosses onto Roanoke Island. Locations are usually given in terms of 'mile posts' (Mile or MP), beginning with Mile 0 at the foot of the Wright Memorial Bridge at Kitty Hawk.

old turn-of-the-century clapboard inn built entirely from shipwrecked wood. Shabby-chic inn rooms come with mismatched bedspreads, spooky oil portraits and pedestal sinks, while two-story modern 'villas' across the street are bright and beachy.

For eats, grab a slice of the island's famous fig cake at the **Fig Tree Bakery** (Ocracoke Village; mains $2-6; ☺8am-9pm summer, off-season hr vary), or head to **Howard's Pub** (Ocracoke Village; mains $6-16; ☺11am-10pm Mon-Thu, to midnight Fri & Sat), a big old wooden pub that's been an island tradition for beer and fried seafood since the 1850s.

🏃 Activities

The same strong wind that helped the Wright brothers launch their biplane today propels windsurfers, sailors and hang gliders. Other popular activities include kayaking, fishing, cycling, horse tours and scuba diving – all well catered for in the northern resort areas. The usually calm coastal waters kick up between August and October, creating perfect conditions for bodysurfing.

TOP CHOICE **Kitty Hawk Kites** ADVENTURE SPORTS
(☎252-441-4124, 877-359-2447; www.kittyhawk.com; 3933 Croatan Hwy, Nags Head; bike/kayak rental per day $25/39) Has locations all over the Banks offering beginners' kiteboarding lessons (three hours $200) and hang-gliding lessons at Jockey's Ridge State Park (from $89). It also rents kayaks, sailboats, bikes and in-line skates and has a variety of tours and courses.

Wild Horse Adventure Tours DRIVING TOURS
(☎252-489-2020; wildhorsetour.com; 2hr tour adult/child $44/29) Offers guided 4WD tours over the dunes and through the maritime forest to see the unique wild mustang ponies that roam the Outer Banks.

Outer Banks Dive Center DIVING
(☎252-449-8349; www.obxdive.com; 3917 S Croatan Hwy, Nags Head; wreck dives $120) Has NAUI-certified instructors who run everything from basic classes to guided dives of the shipwrecks of the Graveyard of the Atlantic.

🛏 Sleeping

Crowds swarm the Outer Banks in summer, so reserve in advance. The area has few massive chain hotels, but hundreds of small motels, efficiencies and B&Bs; the visitor centers offer referrals. Also check www.outer-banks.com.

TOP CHOICE **Roanoke Island Inn** B&B $$$
(☎252-473-5511; www.roanokeislandinn.com; 305 Fernando St, Manteo; r from $198; P✳🛜; ☺Apr-Nov) One of historic downtown Manteo's sweetest inns, this sprawling white cottage wraps around a hidden garden and koi pond. Guests are welcome to lounge on the many porches, or borrow bikes to ride around the island. When evenings grow cool, retreat to your rustic-chic, warmly lit guest room and snuggle under the handmade quilt.

Sanderling Resort & Spa RESORT $$$
(☎252-261-4111, 877-650-4812; www.thesanderling.com; 1461 Duck Rd, Duck; r $349-459; P✳🛜≋) The poshest digs in the Outer Banks has impeccably tasteful neutral-toned rooms with decks and flat-screen TVs, several restaurants and bars, and a spa offering luxe oceanside massage.

Buccaneer Motel MOTEL $$
(☎252-261-2030, 800-442-4412; www.buccaneermotelouterbanks.com; Mile 5 Kitty Hawk; r from $99; P✳🛜≋) One of many deliciously retro motor motels lining the Coast Rd, the Buccaneer has clean, tile-floor rooms with wooden pirate swords on the doors, at bargain-basement rates.

Campgrounds CAMPGROUND $
(☎800-365-2267; www.nps.gov/caha/planyourvisit/campgrounds.htm; tent sites $20-23) The National Park Service runs four summer-only campgrounds on the islands, which feature cold-water showers and flush toilets. They are located at Oregon Inlet, near Bodie Island Lighthouse, Cape Point and Frisco near Cape Hatteras Lighthouse and **Ocracoke** (☎800-365-2267; www.recreation.gov) at Oregon Inlet (near Bodie Island Lighthouse), Cape Point and Frisco (both near Cape Hatteras Lighthouse), and Ocracoke Island. Only sites

THE SOUTH NORTH CAROLINA COAST

at Ocracoke can be reserved; the others are first-come, first-served.

✗ Eating & Drinking

The main tourist strip on Bodie Island has the most restaurants and nightlife, but many are only open Memorial Day through early fall.

Awful Arthur's Oyster Bar   SEAFOOD $$$

(www.awfularthursobx.com; Mile 6; mains $6-23; ⏰11am-10:30pm) Oysters go down easy at this friendly restaurant and raw bar (emphasis on the 'bar'), as do the excellent soft-shell crab sandwiches and sky-high, homemade key lime pie. Don't be shy about ordering a beer before noon; the locals aren't.

John's Drive-In   SEAFOOD, AMERICAN $$

(3716 Virginia Dare Trail, Kitty Hawk; mains $5-13; ⏰11am-6pm summer, shorter hr spring & fall, closed winter) A Kitty Hawk institution for perfectly fried baskets of 'dolphin' (mahimahi) and rockfish, to be eaten at outdoor picnic tables and washed down with one of hundreds of possible milkshake varieties.

Jolly Roger   ITALIAN, AMERICAN $$$

(www.jollyrogerobx.com; Mile 6.5, Kill Devil Hills; mains $10-24; ⏰6am-late) The atmosphere in this OBX institution could be described as 'pirate bordello,' with Christmas lights, mermaid murals and evening karaoke contests. Come for huuuuge Southern breakfasts, groaning platters of shrimp fettuccine, or late-night burgers at the bar.

Rundown Cafe   CARIBBEAN, INTERNATIONAL $

(MP1, Kitty Hawk; mains $6-11; ⏰11:30am-9pm, shorter hr fall-spring) Kiteboarders and surfers slurp up rundown (a Jamaican stew) and nibble on conch fritters, nachos, wontons and other global munchies at this big blue beach shack.

ℹ Information

The best sources of information are at the main visitor centers. Many smaller centers are open seasonally. Also useful is www.outerbanks.org. The entire Manteo waterfront has free wi-fi.

Corolla public library (1123 Ocean Trail/Hwy 12) Free internet access.

Visitor centers (⏰9am-5pm) Hatteras (☎252-441-5711; ⏰Apr-Oct); Kitty Hawk (☎252-261-4644); Manteo (☎252-473-2138, 877-629-4386); Ocracoke (☎252-928-4531)

ℹ Getting There & Away

No public transportation exists to or on the Outer Banks. However, the **North Carolina Ferry**

System (☎800-293-3779; www.outer-banks.com/ferry) operates several routes, including the free 40-minute Hatteras–Ocracoke car ferry, which runs at least hourly from 5am to 10pm; reservations aren't necessary. North Carolina ferries also run between Ocracoke and Cedar Island (one way $15, 2¼ hours) and Ocracoke and Swan Quarter on the mainland ($15, 2½ hours) every two hours or so; reservations are recommended in summer.

CRYSTAL COAST

The southern Outer Banks are collectively called the 'Crystal Coast,' at least for tourist offices' promotional purposes. Less rugged than the northern beaches, they include several historic coastal towns, a number of sparsely populated islands, and some vacation-friendly beaches.

A rather unappealing industrial and commercial stretch of US 70 goes through More-head City, with plenty of chain hotels and restaurants. Stop here for shrimp burgers at El's Drive-In (3706 Arendell St; mains $3-6; ⏰10:30am-10pm), a legendary seafood spot where your food is brought to you by carhop.

Down the road, postcard-pretty Beaufort (bow-fort), the third-oldest town in the state, has a charming boardwalk and mountains of B&Bs. The pirate Blackbeard was a frequent visitor to the area in the early 1700s – in 1996 the wreckage of his flagship, the Queen Anne's Revenge, was discovered at the bottom of Beaufort Inlet. See artifacts from the ship and meet modern shipbuilders at the North Carolina Maritime Museum (www.ncmaritimemuseum.org; 315 Front St; admission free; ⏰9am-5pm Mon-Sat, from 1-5pm Sun). Blackbeard himself is said to have lived in the Hammock House off Front St. You can't go inside, but some claim you can still hear the screams of the pirate's murdered wife at night.

Small ferries leave regularly from the Beaufort boardwalk for the isolated islands of the Cape Lookout National Seashore (www.nps.gov/calo; ferries $14-25). Highlights include Shackleford Banks, an uninhabited sandbar with spectacular seashells and herds of wild ponies, and the diamond-patterned Cape Lookout Lighthouse. Primitive camping is allowed in some areas – the coolest place to sleep is on Portsmouth Island, where you can wander an abandoned 18th-century settlement and sleep on the beach. Hire a private ferry from Beaufort or Ocracoke and bring plenty of bug spray – the mosquitoes are absolutely notorious. There are also rustic multiroom cabins (South Core 252-241-6783, North Core 252-732-4424; www.nps.gov/calo; from $73) popular with fishermen.

The **Bogue Banks**, across the Sound from Morehead City via the Atlantic Beach Causeway, have several well-trafficked beach communities – try Atlantic Beach if you like the smell of coconut suntan oil and doughnuts. Pine Knoll Shores is home to the **North Carolina Aquarium** (www.ncaquariums.com; 1 Roosevelt Blvd; adult/child $8/6; ⊙9am-5pm; 🐾), with an ultracool exhibit re-creating local shipwrecks. In Atlantic Beach, **Fort Macon State Park** (www.ncparks.gov; admission free; ⊙8am-9pm in summer, shorter hr in winter) draws crowds to its reconstructed Civil War fort.

WILMINGTON

Wilmington may not have the name recognition of other antebellum tourist destinations like Charleston and Savannah, but eastern North Carolina's largest city has historic neighborhoods, azalea-choked gardens and cute cafes aplenty. All that plus reasonable hotel prices and a lack of crowds make Wilmington a hidden gem, in our book. At night the historic riverfront downtown becomes the playground for local college students, tourists and the occasional Hollywood type – there are so many movie studios here the town has earned the nickname 'Wilmywood'.

⊙ Sights

Wilmington sits at the mouth of the Cape Fear River, about 8 miles from the beach. The historic **riverfront** is perhaps the city's most important sight, abounding with boutiques and boardwalks.

A **free trolley** runs through the historic district from morning through evening.

TOP CHOICE **Cape Fear Serpentarium** SNAKE ZOO
(www.capefearserpentarium.com; 20 Orange St; admission $8; ⊙11am-5pm Mon-Fri, to 6pm Sat & Sun) The place to go if you don't mind keeping reptilian company. You can gawk at yellow eyelash vipers, read about how it feels to die from the bite of the deadly bushmaster, and, at 3pm on Saturday and Sunday, watch gonzo herpetologist/ringmaster Dean Ripa hand-feed mice to his 100-plus species of beasties.

Battleship North Carolina HISTORIC SHIP
(www.battleshipnc.com; adult/child $12/6; ⊙8am-5pm, to 8pm summer) Take a river taxi ($5 round-trip) or cross the Cape Fear Bridge to get here. Self-guided tours take you through the decks of this 45,000-ton megaship, which earned 15 battle stars in the Pacific theater in WWII before being decommissioned in 1947.

Screen Gems Studios MOVIE STUDIO
(☎910-343-3433; www.screengemsstudios.com; 1223 N 23rd St; adult/child $12/5; ⊙noon & 2pm Sat & Sun summer) Offers a fun, one-hour, behind-the-scenes tour of the working studio where shows such as *Dawson's Creek* and *One Tree Hill* were filmed.

Airlie Gardens GARDEN
(www.airliegardens.org; 300 Airlie Rd; adult/child $5/3; ⊙9am-5pm, closed Sun winter) Wander

---

WILMINGTON-AREA BEACHES

While riverfront Wilmington doesn't have its own beach, there are plenty of sandy stretches just a few minutes away. These are listed from north to south.

» Surf City: a low-key beach town with good waves.

» Topsail Beach: a clean, white-sand beach, home to a sea-turtle rehab center.

» Wrightsville Beach: the closest to Wilmington, with plenty of fried-fish joints, sunglass shops and summer crowds.

» Carolina Beach: warm water and boardwalk equal row upon row of beach umbrellas.

» Kure Beach: a popular fishing beach and home to the North Carolina Aquarium at Fort Fisher.

» Southport: not a swimming beach, but a quaint town with tons of antique stores.

» Bald Head Island: accessible by ferry from Southport. This secluded sea-turtle sanctuary forbids cars, making travel difficult for those for who don't rent a golf cart.

» Caswell Beach: a quiet beach with nearby golf course.

» Oak Island: the largest beach community in North Carolina, with three piers.

beneath the wisteria, with 67 acres of bewitching formal flower beds, lakes and trails.

Sleeping & Eating

There are numerous budget hotels on Market St, just north of downtown. Restaurants directly on the waterfront can be crowded and mediocre; head a block or two inland for the best eats and nightlife.

Graystone Inn B&B $$$
(☏910-763-2000; www.graystoneinn.com; 100 S 3rd St; r incl breakfast $169-379; P⊛) Built as the home of a turn-of-the-century railroad magnate, this imposing Renaissance-style mansion has nine splendiferous guest rooms with period furnishings such as clawfoot tubs, all walking distance from the downtown action.

Clarendon Inn HOTEL $$
(☏910-343-1990; www.clarendoninn.com; 117 S Second St; r from $99; P⊛⊛) Hovering in the gray zone between hotel and B&B, the friendly 11-room Clarendon offers an excellent location, comfy beds and a plethora of angel statutes on every surface. Good value.

Crow Hill MODERN AMERICAN $$
(☏910-228-5332; www.crowhillnc.com; 9 Front St; mains $13-20; ⊙5-10pm Tue-Sun, late night to 1am Fri & Sat; brunch 10am-2pm Sun) The city's current foodie darling for its local, seasonal approach to Southern fare – NC soft-shell crabs with sweet-pea custard, local pork cheeks with fried green tomatoes. Decor is very 'haute farm' – reclaimed wood tables, vintage hoes on the wall. Great brunch.

Front Street Brewery PUB $
(www.frontstreetbrewery.com; 9 N Front St; mains $7-14; ⊙11:30am-10pm Sun-Wed, to 2am Thu-Sat)

THE BARBECUE TRAIL

North Carolina pulled-pork BBQ is practically a religion in these parts, and the rivalry between Eastern Style (with a thin vinegar sauce) and Western Style (with a sweeter, tomato-based sauce) occasionally comes to blows. The North Carolina Barbecue Society has an interactive Barbecue Trail map (www.ncbbqsociety.com), directing 'cue pilgrims to the best spots. So try both styles, then take sides (hint: Eastern style is better. Just kidding! Sort of).

This two-story downtown pub is madly popular for simple grub, like drippy burgers and crab cakes, and for its microbrews. There are free beer tastings and brewery tours daily from 3pm to 5pm.

ⓘ Information

The **visitor center** (☏910-341-4030, 800-222-4757; 505 Nutt St; ⊙8:30am-5pm Mon-Fri, 9am-4pm Sat, from 1-4pm Sun), an 1800s freight warehouse, has a walking-tour map.

The Triangle

In the central North Carolina region known as the Piedmont, the cities of Raleigh, Durham and Chapel Hill form a rough triangle. Three top research universities – Duke, University of North Carolina and North Carolina State – are located here, as is the 7000-acre computer and biotech-office campus known as Research Triangle Park. Swarming with egghead computer programmers, bearded peace activists and hip young families, each town has its own unique personality, despite being only a few miles apart. Come here in March to see everyone – we mean *everyone* – go crazy for college basketball.

ⓘ Getting There & Around

Raleigh-Durham International Airport (RDU; ☏919-840-2123; www.rdu.com), a significant hub, is a 25-minute (15 mile) drive northwest of downtown Raleigh. **Carolina Trailways/Greyhound** Raleigh (☏919-834-8275; 314 W Jones St); Durham (☏919-687-4800; 820 W Morgan St) serve Raleigh and Durham. The **Triangle Transit Authority** (☏919-549-9999; www.triangletransit.org; adult $2) operates buses linking Raleigh, Durham and Chapel Hill to each other and the airport.

RALEIGH

Founded in 1792 specifically to serve as the state capital, Raleigh remains a rather staid government town with some major sprawl issues. Still, the handsome downtown has some neat (and free!) museums and galleries, and the food and music scene is on the upswing.

⊙ Sights

Check out the handsome 1840 **state capitol** on Edenton St, one of the best examples of Greek Revival architecture. It's open for tours.

TOP
CHOICE **North Carolina Museum of Art** MUSEUM
(www.ncartmuseum.org; 2110 Blue Ridge Rd; admission free; ⊙9am-5pm Tue-Thu & Sat, 9am-9pm

Fri, 10am-5pm Sun) Worth the trip for the building alone – the light-filled glass-and-anodized-steel West Building won praise from architecture critics nationwide when it opened in 2010. The fine and wide-ranging collection, with everything from ancient Roman sculpture to Raphael to graffiti artists, is worthy as well, of course, as is the winding outdoor sculpture trail. A few miles west of downtown.

FREE **North Carolina**
Museum of Natural Sciences   MUSEUM
(www.naturalsciences.org; 11 W Jones St; ⊙9am-5pm Mon-Sat, noon-5pm Sun) See Willo, the world's only dinosaur with a heart (it's fossilized), at this modern, airy museum. There's also a unique and scary Acrocanthosaurus skeleton, five habitat dioramas and lots of well-done taxidermy.

FREE **North Carolina**
Museum of History   MUSEUM
(www.ncmuseumofhistory.org; 5 E Edenton St; ⊙9am-5pm Mon-Sat, noon-5pm Sun) Has all kinds of artifacts, such as Civil War photos, Cherokee crafts, 19th-century costumes and a special exhibit on stock-car racing.

🛌 Sleeping & Eating

Downtown is pretty quiet on nights and weekends, except for the City Market area at E Martin and S Person Sts. Just to the northwest, the Glenwood South neighborhood hops with cafes, bars and clubs. You'll find plenty of moderately priced chain hotels around Exit 10 off I-440 and off I-40 near the airport.

Umstead Hotel & Spa   HOTEL $$$
(☑919-447-4000; www.theumstead.com; 100 Woodland Pond, Cary; r from $279; P❋@🛜♨) Computer chips embedded in the silver room-service trays alert bellhops to whisk away leftovers post haste at this lavish new boutique hotel. How's that for taking care of details? In a wooded suburban office park, the Umstead caters to visiting biotech CEOs with simple, sumptuous rooms and a Zen-like spa.

Poole's Downtown Diner MODERN AMERICAN $$
(www.poolesdowntowndiner.com; 426 S McDowell St; mains $9-15; ⊙6pm-midnight Wed-Sat, brunch 10:30am-3pm Sat) Chef Ashley Christensen sautés burgers in duck fat and bakes the world's most exquisitely creamy mac 'n' cheese at this Southern diner-meets-Parisian bistro, the toast of the local food scene. Don't miss the haute takes on classic American pies like banana cream.

Raleigh Times   PUB $
(www.raleightimesbar.com; 14 E Hargett St; mains $8-11; ⊙11:30am-2am) Chase plates of BBQ nachos with pints of North Carolina craft brews at this popular downtown pub.

❶ Information

The **Raleigh Convention & Visitors Bureau** (☑866-724-8687; www.visitraleigh.com; 220 Fayetteville St; ⊙10am-5pm Mon-Sat) hands out maps and other info.

DURHAM & CHAPEL HILL

Ten miles apart, these two university towns are twinned by their rival basketball teams and left-leaning cultures. Most similarities end here, though. Chapel Hill is a postcard-pretty Southern college town whose culture revolves around the 30,000 students at the prestigious University of North Carolina, founded in 1789 as the nation's first state university. A funky, forward-thinking place, Chapel Hill is renowned for its indie rock scene and loud 'n' proud hippie culture. Down the road, Durham is a once-gritty tobacco-and-railroad town whose fortunes collapsed in the 1960s and have only recently begun to revive. Though still fundamentally a working-class Southern city, the presence of top-ranking Duke University has long drawn progressive types to the area and Durham is now making its name as hot spot for foodies, artists and gays and lesbians.

The hip former mill town of Carrboro is to the west. Here, the big lawn at **Weaver Street Market** (www.weaverstreetmarket.com) grocery co-op serves as an informal town square, with live music and free wi-fi.

In Durham, activity centers around the renovated brick tobacco warehouses of the handsome downtown: check out Brightleaf Sq and the American Tobacco Campus for shopping and outdoor dining.

◉ Sights

TOP CHOICE **Duke Lemur Center**   ZOO
(☑919-489-3364; www.lemur.duke.edu; ♿) Perhaps the coolest, least-known sight in Durham, the Lemur Center has the largest collection of endangered prosimian primates outside their native Madagascar. Only a robot could fail to melt at the sight of these big-eyed fuzzy-wuzzies. Call well in advance for tours, held Monday to Saturday by appointment only.

Duke University
UNIVERSITY, GALLERY

(www.duke.edu) Endowed by the Duke family's cigarette fortune, the university has a Georgian-style East Campus and a neo-Gothic West Campus notable for its towering 1930s chapel. The **Nasher Museum of Art** (2001 Campus Dr; admission $5) is also worth a gander, as is the heavenly 55-acre **Sarah P Duke Gardens** (426 Anderson St; admission free).

University of North Carolina
UNIVERSITY

(www.unc.edu) America's oldest public university has a classic quad lined with flowering pear trees and gracious antebellum buildings. Don't miss the Old Well, said to give good luck to students who drink from it.

Durham Bulls Athletic Park
SPECTATOR SPORT

(www.dbulls.com; 409 Blackwell St; tickets $7-9; 🚻) Have a quintessentially American afternoon of beer and baseball watching the minorleague Durham Bulls (of 1988 Kevin Costner film *Bull Durham* fame), who play from April to September.

🛏 Sleeping

There are plenty of cheap chain motels off I-85 in north Durham.

⌂ TOP CHOICE Inn at Celebrity Dairy
B&B $$

(✆919-742-5176; www.celebritydairy.com; 144 Celebrity Dairy Way; r incl breakfast $90-150; ⓟ❄🛜) Thirty miles west of Chapel Hill in rural Chatham County, this working goat dairy offers B&B accommodations in a Greek Revival farmhouse. Savor goat's-cheese omelets for breakfast then head out to the barn to pet the goat who provided the milk.

🏠 King's Daughters Inn
INN $$

(✆919-354-7000; thekingsdaughtersinn.com; 204 N Buchanan Blvd; r incl breakfast from $165; ⓟ❄🛜) Once a charity home for elderly women, this 1926 Colonial Revival has been newly renovated into an ecofriendly inn with 11 elegant guest rooms and a yummy sun porch. On the edge of Duke campus, it's a fave with visiting professors.

Duke Tower
HOTEL $

(✆919-687-4444, 866-385-3869; www.duketower.com; 807 W Trinity Ave; ste $85; ⓟ❄🛜♿) For less than most local hotel rooms you can have a contemporary condo with hardwood floors, full kitchen and flat-screen TV, in Durham's historic downtown tobacco-mill district.

✗ Eating

Durham and Chapel Hill were recently named 'America's Foodiest Small Town' by *Bon Appétit*, and with good reason: the area abounds with top-notch restaurants of all stripes. Downtown Durham has scads of great restaurants, coffee shops and bars. Most of Chapel Hill's better restaurants are found along Franklin St.

⌂ TOP CHOICE Scratch
BAKERY $

(www.piefantasy.com; 111 Orange St, Durham; mains $5-10; ⓣ7:30am-4pm Tue-Fri, 9am-3pm Sat & Sun) Baker Phoebe Lawless shoots sunshine and rainbows out of her fingertips at this nationally praised nook of a bakery, famed for its hyper-seasonal pies (fresh lavender in spring, local muscadine grape in fall) and delectable sandwiches and salads (try the pickled-egg salad).

Allen & Son's Barbecue
BARBECUE $

(6203 Millhouse Rd, Chapel Hill; mains $7-10; ⓣ10am-5pm Tue-Wed, to 8pm Thu-Sat) Owner Keith Allen splits his own hickory wood behind this cinder-block cabin to smoke what many consider the best pork BBQ in the state. Try it topped with slaw on a soft bun with a side of hush puppies (balls of fried cornmeal) and a slice of frozen peanut butter pie.

Watts Grocery
NEW SOUTHERN $$$

(✆919-416-5040; 1116 Broad St, Durham; mains $16-23; ⓣ11am-2:30pm & 5:30-10pm) Durham's hippest 'farm-to-table' joint serves upscale takes on local bounty (think bourbon-glazed pork belly, hand-cut buttermilk onion rings) in an airy renovated storefront. Sausage- and avocado-laden bowls of grits might just well be the best weekend brunch in town.

Lantern
ASIAN $$$

(✆919-969-8846; www.lanternrestaurant.com; 243 W Franklin St, Chapel Hill; mains $17-26; ⓣ5:30-10pm Mon-Sat) Tea-smoked chicken and roll-your-own bento boxes have earned this modern Asian spot a shower of James Beard Awards.

Sunrise Biscuit Kitchen
BREAKFAST, SOUTHERN $

(1305 E Franklin St, Chapel Hill; mains $2-4; ⓣ6am-2pm) Fried chicken biscuits washed down with sweet tea are one of America's truly great breakfasts, and the reason this venerable drive-thru is always jam-packed at 7am.

Drinking & Entertainment

Chapel Hill has an excellent music scene, with shows nearly every night of the week. For entertainment listings, pick up the free weekly *Independent* (www.indyweek.com).

Fullsteam Brewery BREWPUB
(www.fullsteam.ag; 726 Rigsbee Ave, Durham) Calling itself a 'plow-to-pint' brewery, Fullsteam has gained national attention for pushing the boundaries of beer with wild, super-Southern concoctions like sweet-potato lager and persimmon ale. Mixed-age crowds.

Top of the Hill PUB
(100 E Franklin St, Chapel Hill) The 2nd-story patio of this downtown restaurant and microbrewery is *the* place for the Chapel Hill preppy set to see and be seen after football games.

Cat's Cradle MUSIC
(www.catscradle.com; 300 E Main St, Carrboro) Everyone from Nirvana to Arcade Fire has played the Cradle, hosting the cream of the indie-music world for three decades. Most shows all-ages.

Information

Visitor center Durham (919-687-0288, 800-446-8604; www.durham-nc.com; 101 E Morgan St; 8:30am-5pm Mon-Fri, 10am-2pm Sat); Chapel Hill (501 W Franklin St; www.visitchapelhill.org) For information and maps.

Charlotte

The largest city in North Carolina and the biggest US banking center after New York, Charlotte has the sprawling, sometimes faceless look of many New South suburban megalopolises. But although the Queen City, as it's known, is primarily a business town, it's got a few good museums, stately old neighborhoods and lots of fine food.

Busy Tryon St cuts through skyscraper-filled 'uptown' Charlotte, home to banks, hotels, museums and restaurants. The renovated textile mills of the NoDa neighborhood (named for its location on N Davidson St) and the funky mix of boutiques and restaurants in the Plaza–Midwood area, just northeast of uptown, have a hipper vibe.

Sights & Activities

FREE **Billy Graham Library** RELIGIOUS
(www.billygrahamlibrary.org; 4330 Westmont Dr; 9:30am-5pm Mon-Sat) Those interested in

the phenomenon of Christian evangelism in America will be fascinated (or annoyed) by this multimedia 'library,' a tribute to the life of superstar evangelist and 'pastor to the presidents' Billy Graham, a Charlotte native. The 90-minute tour starts with a gospel-preaching animatronic cow and ends with a paper questionnaire asking whether or not you've been moved to accept Christ today.

Mint Museum of Art MUSEUM
(www.mintmuseum.org; 2730 Randolph Rd; adult/child $10/5; 10am-9pm Tue, 10am-5pm Wed-Sat, noon-5pm Sun) Housed in the imposing 19th-century US mint building. The hushed halls display historic maps, American paintings and an impressive number of gruesome Spanish Colonial bleeding-saint statues.

Levine Museum of the New South MUSEUM
(www.museumofthenewsouth.org; 200 E 7th St; adult/child $6/5; 10am-5pm Mon-Sat, noon-5pm Sun) This slick museum has an informative permanent exhibit on post–Civil War Southern history and culture, from sharecropping to sit-ins.

US National Whitewater Center ADVENTURE SPORTS
(www.usnwc.org; 500 Whitewater Center Pkwy; all-sport day pass adult/child $49/39, individual activities $15-25, 3hr canopy tour $89; 10am-6pm, later in summer) A beyond-awesome hybrid of nature center and waterpark, this 400-acre facility is home to the largest manmade white-water river in the world, whose rapids serve as training grounds for Olympic canoe and kayak teams. Paddle it yourself as part of a guided rafting trip, or try one of the center's other high-octane activities: zip-lines, an outdoor rock climbing wall, multiple ropes courses, paddleboarding, aerial canopy tours of the surrounding forest, miles of wooded hiking and mountain-biking trails.

Charlotte Motor Speedway SPEEDWAY
(www.charlottemotorspeedway.com; tours $9; tours 9:30am-3:30pm Mon-Sat, 1:30-3:30pm Sun) NASCAR races, a homegrown Southeastern obsession, are held at the visible-from-outer-space speedway, 12 miles northeast of town. For the ultimate thrill/near-death experience, ride shotgun at up to 165 miles per hour in a real stock car with the **Richard Petty Driving Experience** (800-237-3889; www.1800bepetty.com; rides from $149).

🛏 Sleeping & Eating

Because so many uptown hotels cater to the business traveler, rates are often lower on weekends. Cheaper chains cluster off I-85 and I-77. Uptown eating and drinking options cater to the preppy young banker set; you'll see more tattoos at the laid-back pubs and bistros of NoDa.

Duke Mansion B&B **$$**
(☎704-714-4400; www.dukemansion.com; 400 Hermitage Rd; r from $179; P❄@🖙) Tucked away in an oak-shaded residential neighborhood, this stately white-columned inn was the residence of 19th-century tobacco millionaire James B Duke and still retains the quiet, discreet feel of a posh private home. Most rooms have high ceilings and their own screened-in sleeping porches.

Hotel Sierra HOTEL **$$**
(☎704-373-9700; www.hotel-sierra.com; 435 E Trade St; r from $148; P❄@🖙) With a space-agey lime-and-charcoal color scheme and a gleaming lobby full of business travelers typing frantically into their BlackBerrys, the brand-new Sierra is *very* Charlotte.

TOP
CHOICE **Price's Chicken Coop** SOUTHERN **$**
(1614 Camden Rd; mains $5-10; ⊙10am-6pm Tue-Sat) A Charlotte institution, scruffy Price's regularly makes 'Best Fried Chicken in America' lists. Line up to order your 'dark quarter' or 'white half' from the army of white-jacketed cooks, then take your bounty outside – there's no seating.

Bar-B-Q King BARBECUE **$**
(2900 Wilkinson Blvd; mains $4-9; ⊙10:30am-10:30pm Tue-Thu, 10am-11:30pm Fri & Sat) A venerable retro drive-in, where carhops deliver minced-pork platters and perfectly fried trout sandwiches to your driver's side window.

Rí Rá PUB **$$**
(www.rira.com; 208 N Tryon St; mains $11-19; ⊙11am-2am) A friendly mixed-age crowd downs Guinness and nibbles fish-and-chips at this Victorian-style uptown Irish pub.

ℹ Information

The downtown **visitor center** (☎704-331-2700, 800-231-4636; www.charlottesgotalot.com; 330 S Tryon St; ⊙8:30am-5pm Mon-Fri, 9am-3pm Sat) publishes maps and a visitor's guide. The **public library** (College St) has 90 terminals with free internet. Check out the alt-weekly Creative *Loafing* (charlotte.creativeloafing.com) for entertainment listings.

ℹ Getting There & Around

Charlotte Douglas International Airport (CLT; ☎704-359-4027; www.charmeck.org/departments/airport; 5501 Josh Birmingham Pkwy) is a US Airways hub with direct flights from Europe and the UK. Both the **Greyhound station** (601 W Trade St) and **Amtrak** (1914 N Tryon St) are handy to Uptown. **Charlotte Area Transit** (www.charmeck.org) runs local bus and light-rail services; its main station is at 310 E Trade St.

North Carolina Mountains

Seekers of all sorts have been drawn to these ancient mountains for hundreds of years. The Cherokee came to hunt, Scots-Irish immigrants came in the 1700s looking for a better life, fugitives hid from the law in the deep forests, the ill came to take in the fresh air, and naturalists came to hike the craggy trails.

The Appalachians in the western part of the state include the Great Smoky, Blue Ridge, Pisgah and Black Mountain subranges. Carpeted in blue-green hemlock, pine and oak trees, these cool hills are home to cougars, deer, black bears, wild turkeys and great horned owls. Hiking, camping, climbing and rafting adventures abound, and there's another jaw-dropping photo opportunity around every bend.

HIGH COUNTRY

The northwestern corner of the state is known as 'High Country.' Its main towns are Boone, Blowing Rock and Banner Elk, all short drives from the Blue Ridge Pkwy. **Boone** is a lively college town, home to Appalachian State University (ASU). **Blowing Rock** and **Banner Elk** are quaint tourist centers near the winter ski areas.

◉ Sights & Activities

Hwy 321 from Blowing Rock to Boone is studded with gem-panning mines and other tourist traps.

Tweetsie Railroad AMUSEMENT PARK
(www.tweetsie.com; adult/child $34/22; 🚗) A much-loved Wild West–themed amusement park. Opening hours vary by season.

Grandfather Mountain HIKING
(www.grandfather.com; Blue Ridge Pkwy Mile 305; adult/child $15/7; ⊙8am-6pm) This place rakes in car tourists who tiptoe across its vertigo-

Commissioned by President Franklin D Roosevelt as a Depression-era public-works project, the glorious Blue Ridge Pkwy traverses the southern Appalachians from Virginia's Shenandoah National Park at Mile 0 to the Great Smoky Mountains National Park at Mile 469. North Carolina's piece of the parkway twists and turns for 262 miles of killer alpine vistas. The National Park Service **campgrounds and visitor centers** (☏877-444-6777; www.blueridgeparkway.org; tent sites $16) are open May to October. Parkway entrance is free; be aware that restrooms and gas stations are few and far between.

Parkway highlights and campgrounds include the following:

Cumberland Knob (Mile 217.5) NPS visitor center, easy walk to the knob.

Doughton Park (Mile 241.1) Gas, food, trails and camping.

Blowing Rock (Mile 291.8) Small tourist town, named for a craggy, commercialized cliff that offers great views, occasional updrafts and a Native American love story.

Moses H Cone Memorial Park (Mile 294.1) A lovely old estate with pleasant walks and a craft shop.

Julian Price Memorial Park (Mile 296.9) Camping.

Grandfather Mountain (Mile 305.1) Hugely popular for its mile-high pedestrian 'swinging bridge.'

Linville Falls (Mile 316.4) Short hiking trails to the falls, campsites.

Linville Caverns (Mile 317) Limestone cave with neat formations and underground streams; tours $7.

Little Switzerland (Mile 334) Old-style mountain resort.

Crabtree Meadows (Mile 339.5) Camping.

Mt Mitchell State Park (Mile 355.5) Highest peak east of the Mississippi (6684ft); hiking and camping.

Craggy Gardens (Mile 364) Hiking trails explode with rhododendron blossoms in summer.

Folk Art Center (Mile 382) Local crafts for sale.

Mount Pisgah (Mile 408.8) Hiking and camping.

inducing mile-high suspension bridge. Lose the crowds on one of 11 hiking trails, the most difficult of which include steep hands-and-knees scrambles.

River and Earth Adventures OUTDOORS
(☏828-963-5491; www.raftcavehike.com; 1655 Hwy 105, Boone; half-/full-day rafting from $65/100) Offers everything from family-friendly caving trips to rafting Class V rapids at Watauga Gorge. Ecoconscious guides even pack organic lunches. Bike and kayak rentals.

🛏 Sleeping & Eating

Chain motels abound in Boone. You'll find private campgrounds and B&Bs scattered throughout the hills.

Mast Farm Inn B&B **$$**
(☏828-963-5857, 888-963-5857; www.mastfarm inn.com; 2543 Broadstone Rd, Blowing Rock; r/

cottages from $99/149; P❀🤶) In the achingly beautiful hamlet of Valle Crucis, this restored farmhouse defines rustic chic with worn hardwood floors, claw-foot tubs and handmade toffees on your bedside table. The upscale mountain cuisine at the inn's restaurant, Simplicity, is worth a trip in itself.

Hob Nob Farm Cafe CAFE **$$**
(www.hobnobfarmcafe.com; 506 West King St, Boone; mains $7-14; ⊙10am-10pm Wed-Sun) Inside a wildly painted cottage, mountain town hippie types gobble up avocado-tempeh melts, Thai curry bowls and sloppy burgers made from local beef. Brunch is served until 5pm.

Knights on Main SOUTHERN **$$**
(www.knightsonmainrestaurant.com; 870 Main St, Blowing Rock; mains $7-17; ⊙7am-8:30pm, to 2:30pm Sun) This wood-paneled family diner

is *the* place to try livermush, a mountain specialty consisting of...well, you can guess.

❶ Information

The High Country **visitor center** (📞828-264-1299, 800-438-7500; www.highcountryhost.com; 1700 Blowing Rock Rd, Boone; ⏰9am-5pm) has info on accommodations and outdoors outfitters.

ASHEVILLE

This Jazz Age gem of a city appears like a mirage out of the mists of the Blue Ridge Mountains. Long a vacation destination for moneyed East Coasters (F Scott Fitzgerald was a fan), the city now has a huge artist population and a highly visible contingent of hard-core hippies. The art-deco buildings of downtown remain much the same as they were in 1930, though the area is now hopping with decidedly modern boutiques, restaurants, vintage stores and record shops. Visit Asheville once and you'll likely find yourself perusing local real-estate listings on the sly once you've returned home.

◉ Sights

Downtown is compact and easy to negotiate on foot. The shopping's fantastic, with everything from hippie-dippy candle shops to vintage shops to high-end local art. West Asheville is an up-and-coming area, still gritty but very cool.

TOP CHOICE Biltmore Estate   HOUSE, GARDENS

(www.biltmore.com; adult/child under 17 $59/5; ⏰9am-4:30pm) With 43 bathrooms, 65 fireplaces and a private bowling alley, the Gilded Age estate is a veritable American Versailles. The country's largest private home and Asheville's number-one tourist attraction, it was built in 1895 for shipping and railroad heir George Washington Vanderbilt II, who modeled it after the grand chateaux he'd seen on his various European jaunts. Viewing the estate and its 250 acres of gorgeously manicured grounds and gardens takes several hours. There are numerous cafes, a gift shop the size of a small supermarket, a hoity-toity hotel, and an award-winning winery that offers free tastings.

Chimney Rock Park   PARK

(www.chimneyrockpark.com; adult/child $14/6; ⏰8:30am-4:30pm) A 20-mile drive southeast of Asheville, the American flag flaps in the breeze atop this popular park's namesake 315ft granite monolith. An elevator takes visitors up to the chimney, but the real draw is the exciting hike around the cliffs to a 404ft waterfall.

Thomas Wolfe Memorial   HOUSE

(www.wolfememorial.com; 52 N Market St; admission $1; ⏰9am-5pm Tue-Sat, 1-5pm Sun) Downtown, this is *Look Homeward Angel* author Thomas Wolfe's childhood home, displaying artifacts from his brief life.

🛏 Sleeping

The **Asheville Bed & Breakfast Association** (📞877-262-6867; www.ashevillebba.com) handles bookings for numerous area B&Bs, from gingerbread cottages to alpine cabins.

Sweet Peas   HOSTEL $

(📞828-285-8488; www.sweetpeashostel.com; 23 Rankin Ave; dm/pod/r $28/35/60; 🅿❄@🛜) Asheville's newest hostel looks as if it tumbled out of the IKEA catalog, with shipshape steel bunk beds and blond wood sleeping 'pods' with retractable curtains and reading lamps. The loftlike space is very open and can be noisy (a downstairs pub adds to the ruckus) – what you lose in privacy and quiet, you gain in style, cleanliness, sociability and an unbeatable downtown location.

Grove Park Inn Resort & Spa   RESORT $$

(📞828-252-2711; www.groveparkinn.com; 290 Macon Ave; r from $135; 🅿❄🛜≋) Built in 1913, this titanic arts-and-crafts-style stone lodge clings to the side of the mountain like the castle of a goblin king. Inside is a mini-village of 510 richly appointed rooms, four restaurants, numerous shops and an underground grotto of a spa, complete with stone pools and an indoor waterfall.

Campfire Lodgings   CAMPGROUND $$

(📞828-658-8012; www.campfirelodgings.com; 116 Appalachian Village Rd; tent sites $38, yurts from $115; 🅿❄🛜) All yurts should have flat-screen TVs, don't you think? Sleep like the world's most stylish Mongolian nomad in one of these furnished multiroom tents, on the side of a hill with stunning valley views. Cabins and tent sites are also available.

Lion and the Rose   B&B $$$

(📞828-546-6988; www.lion-rose.com; 276 Montford Ave; r $135-225; 🅿❄🛜) The recipe for a perfect B&B: a grand Queen Anne in a historic neighborhood, with a gorgeous English garden, grand but unfussy decor, friendly owners and an even friendlier little fox terrier.

Bon Paul & Sharky's Hostel HOSTEL **$**
(☎828-350-9929; www.bonpaulandsharkys.com; 816 Haywood Rd; tent sites per person $15, dm/r $24/65; P❋@🛜) In the hip West Asheville residential neighborhood, this cottage has a friendly college-dorm vibe and sweet amenities including foosball, communal bikes and backyard tent space.

✖ Eating

Asheville is a great foodie town – many visitors come here just to eat!

TOP CHOICE Admiral MODERN AMERICAN **$$$**
(☎828-252-2541; www.theadmiralnc.com; 400 Haywood Rd; mains $17-26; ⊙5pm-11pm Mon-Sat) Walking by, you might guess this little concrete bunker was a dive bar. That's what they want you to think. This purposefully inconspicuous West Asheville spot is one of the state's – perhaps the country's – finest New American restaurants, serving wildly creative and irreverent dishes like duck breast with pimento cheese, steak tartare with Sriracha (hot chili sauce) aioli, and banana-Nutella-marshmallow cake with tempura apples. Phone a week ahead for reservations and *maybe* you'll get lucky and score a table.

French Broad Chocolate Lounge BAKERY, DESSERTS **$**
(frenchbroadchocolates.com; 10 S Lexington; snacks $2-6; ⊙11am-11pm, to midnight Fri & Sat) Small-batch organic chocolates in flavors like masala chai and orange-fennel, fat slices of maple cake with smoked salt, shot glasses full of 'liquid truffles,' pints of local stout served á la mode with vanilla ice cream... hey, where'd you go?

Salsa's CARIBBEAN **$$**
(www.salsas-asheville.com; 6 Patton Ave; mains $9-17; ⊙11:30am-2:30pm & 5:30-9pm) This tiny, brightly painted joint serves amazing, mutant Latin-fusion cuisine – think lamb empanadas with goat's cheese and banana salsa or crab-jalapeño-saffron-fennel egg rolls.

Rosetta's Kitchen VEGETARIAN **$**
(rosettaskitchen.com; 116 N Lexington Ave; mains $7-10; ⊙11am-11pm Mon-Thu, to 3am Fri & Sat, to 9pm Sun; ✍) An institution among Asheville's dreadlocked set, where you can belly up to the counter for a bowl of peanut-butter tofu (looks awful, tastes heavenly) at 2am.

Tupelo Honey NEW SOUTHERN **$$**
(☎828-255-4863; www.tupelohoney.com; 12 College St; mains $9-22; ⊙9am-10pm) A longtime favorite for New Southern fare like pork chops with peach salsa. We especially like this cozy bistro for breakfast – try the sweet-potato pancakes.

Grove Arcade SELF-CATERING
(Page Ave) Try this massive Gothic-style building for fancy groceries and produce.

🍷 Drinking & Entertainment

Downtown Asheville has all types of bars and cafes, from frat-boy beer halls to hookah-n-sprout hippie holes-in-the-wall. West Asheville has a more laid-back townie vibe.

TOP CHOICE Southern BAR
(www.southernkitchenandbar.com; 41 N Lexington Ave) Fantastic new spot with upscale Southern pub grub (truffled deviled eggs, chicken 'n' waffles), a breezy patio and a long bar slinging fancy retro cocktails and local brews.

Jack of the Wood PUB
(jackofthewood.com; 95 Patton Ave) This Celtic pub is a good place to bond with local 20- and 30-somethings over a bottle of organic ale.

Asheville Pizza & Brewing Company BREWERY, CINEMA
(www.ashevillebrewing.com; 675 Merrimon Ave; movies $3; ⊙movies 1pm, 4pm, 7pm & 10pm) Catch a flick at the small theater inside this one-of-a-kind spot.

Orange Peel LIVE MUSIC
(www.theorangepeel.net; 101 Biltmore Ave; tickets $10-25) For live music, try this warehouse-sized place for big-name indie and punk.

Grey Eagle LIVE MUSIC
(www.thegreyeagle.com; 185 Clingman Ave; tickets $8-15) For bluegrass and jazz.

ℹ Information

The shiny new **visitor center** (☎828-258-6129; www.exploreasheville.com; 36 Montford Ave; ⊙9am-5pm) is at I-240 exit 4C.

The **public library** (67 Haywood Ave) has computers with free internet.

ℹ Getting There & Around

Asheville Transit (www.ashevilletransit.com; tickets $1) has 24 local bus routes running from 6am to 11:30pm Monday to Saturday. Twenty minutes south of town, **Asheville Regional Airport** (AVL; ☎828-684-2226; www.flyavl.com) has a handful of direct flights, including to/from

Atlanta, Charlotte and New York. **Greyhound** (2 Tunnel Rd) is just northeast of downtown.

GREAT SMOKY MOUNTAINS NATIONAL PARK

More than 10 million visitors a year come through this majestic park, one of the world's most biodiverse areas. Landscapes range from deep, dim spruce forest to sunny meadows carpeted with daisies and Queen Anne's lace to wide, coffee-brown rivers. There's ample hiking and camping, and opportunities for horseback riding, bike rental and fly-fishing. The North Carolina side has less traffic than the Tennessee side, so even at the height of summer tourist season you'll still have room to roam. For more information about the Tennessee section of this park, see p361.

Newfound Gap Rd/Hwy 441 is the only thoroughfare that crosses Great Smoky Mountains National Park, winding through the mountains from Gatlinburg, TN, to the town of Cherokee and the busy **Oconaluftee Visitor Center** (☑865-436-1200; Hwy 441), in the southeast. Pick up your backcountry camping permits here. The Oconaluftee River Trail, one of only two in the park that allows leashed pets, leaves from the visitor center and follows the river for 1.5 miles.

Nearby attractions include the 1886 **Mingus Mill** (self-guided tours free; ⊙9am-5pm 15 Mar-1 Dec), 2 miles west of Cherokee, a turbine-powered mill that still grinds wheat and corn much as it always has. The on-

site **Mountain Farm Museum** is a restored 19th-century farmstead, complete with barn, blacksmith shop and smokehouse (with real pig heads!), assembled from original buildings from different parts of the park. A few miles away the **Smokemont Campground** (www.nps.gov/grsm; tent & RV sites $20) is the only North Carolina campground open year-round.

To the east, remote **Cataloochee Valley** has several historic buildings to wander through and is a prime location for elk and black bears.

SOUTHWESTERN NORTH CAROLINA

The state's westernmost tip is blanketed in parkland and sprinkled with tiny mountain towns. The area has a rich but sad Native American history – many of the original Cherokee inhabitants were forced off their lands during the 1830s and marched to Oklahoma on the Trail of Tears. Descendants of those who escaped are known as the Eastern Band of the Cherokee, about 12,000 of whom now occupy the 56,000-acre Qualla Boundary territory at the edge of Great Smoky Mountains National Park.

The unlovely town of **Cherokee** anchors the Qualla Boundary with ersatz Native American souvenir shops, fast-food joints and **Harrah's Cherokee Casino** (www.harrahs.com). The best sight is the modern **Museum of the Cherokee Indian** (www.cherokeemuseum.org; cnr Hwy 441 & Drama Rd; adult/child $10/6; ⊙9am-5pm), with an informative exhibit on the Trail of Tears and eerily realistic dioramas.

South of Cherokee, the contiguous **Pisgah** and **Nantahala National Forests** have more than a million acres of dense hardwood trees, windswept mountain balds and some of the country's best white water. Both contain portions of the Appalachian Trail. Pisgah highlights include the bubbling baths in the village of **Hot Springs** (www.hotspringsnc.org), the natural waterslide at **Sliding Rock**, and the 30-mile **Art Loeb Trail**, which skirts Cold Mountain of book and movie fame. Nantahala has several recreational lakes and dozens of roaring waterfalls, several of which can be easily accessed via the **Mountain Waters Scenic Byway**.

For plush accommodations try **Brevard**, a cute mountain town with tons of B&Bs on the east edge of Pisgah. Or head just north of Nantahala to quaint **Bryson City**, an ideal jumping-off point for outdoor adventures. It's home to the huge and highly

---

SMOKY MOUNTAIN DAY HIKES

These are a few of our favorite short hikes in the North Carolina side of the park:

Big Creek Trail Hike an easy 2 miles to Mouse Creek Falls or go another 3 miles to backcountry campground; the trailhead's near I-40 on the park's northeastern edge.

Boogerman Trail Moderate 7-mile loop passing old farmsteads; access via Cove Creek Rd.

Chasteen Creek Falls From Smokemont campground, this 4-mile round-trip passes a small waterfall.

Shustack Tower Starting at massive Fontana Dam, climb 3.5 miles for killer views from an old fire tower.

recommended **Nantahala Outdoor Center** (☎828-488-2176, 828-586-8811; www.noc.com; 13077 Hwy 19/74; guided rafting trips $37-177), which specializes in wet and wild rafting trips down the Nantahala, French Broad, Pigeon and Ocoee Rivers, and rents out bikes, kayaks and more. It even has its own lodge and restaurant. From the Bryson City depot, the **Great Smoky Mountain Railroad** (☎800-872-4681; www.gsmr.com; Nantahala Gorge trip adult/child $53/31) runs scenic train excursions through the dramatic river valley.

SOUTH CAROLINA

Cross the border of South Carolina and plunge back in time. For a traveler heading down the eastern seaboard, venturing into South Carolina marks the beginning of the Deep South, where the air is hotter, the accents are thicker and traditions are clung to with even more fervor.

Starting at the silvery sands of the Atlantic Coast, the state climbs westward from the Coastal Plain and up through the Piedmont and into the Blue Ridge Mountains. Most travelers stick to the coast, with its splendid antebellum cities and palm-tree-studded beaches. But the interior has a wealth of sleepy old towns, wild and undeveloped state parks and spooky black-water swamps just waiting to be explored by canoe. Along the sea islands you hear the sweet songs of the Gullah, a culture and language created by former slaves who held onto many West African traditions through the ravages of time.

Whether you're looking for a romantic weekend in genteel, gardenia-scented Charleston or a week of riotous fun at bright, tacky Myrtle Beach, South Carolina is a lovely, affordable destination.

History

More than 28 separate tribes of Native Americans have lived in what is now South Carolina, many of them Cherokee who were later forcibly removed during the Trail of Tears era.

The English founded the Carolina colony in 1670, with settlers pouring in from the royal outpost of Barbados, giving the port city known as Charles Towne a Caribbean flavor. West African slaves were brought over to turn the thick coastal swamps into rice paddies and by the mid-1700s the area was deeply divided between the slave-

SOUTH CAROLINA FACTS

» **Nickname** Palmetto State

» **Population** 4.5 million

» **Area** 30,109 sq miles

» **Capital city** Columbia (population 130,000)

» **Other cities** Charleston (120,000)

» **Sales tax** 5%, plus up to 10% extra tax on accommodations

» **Birthplace of** jazzman Dizzy Gillespie (1917–93), political activist Jesse Jackson (b 1941), boxer Joe Frazier (b 1944), Wheel of Fortune hostess Vanna White (b 1957)

» **Home of** first US public library (1698), museum (1773) and steam railroad (1833)

» **Politics** one of America's top 10 most conservative states

» **Famous for** firing the first shot of the Civil War, from Charleston's Fort Sumter

» **Smelliest festival** Chitlin' Strut festival in Salley, a celebration of the odiferous stuffed pig's intestine dish chitterlings, or chitlins, a dubious Southern delicacy

» **Driving distances** Columbia to Charleston 115 miles, Charleston to Myrtle Beach 97 miles

owning aristocrats of the Lowcountry and the poor Scots-Irish and German farmers of the rural backcountry.

South Carolina was the first state to secede from the Union, and the first battle of the Civil War occurred at Fort Sumter in Charleston Harbor. The end of the war left much of the state in ruins.

South Carolina traded in cotton and textiles for most of the 20th century. It remains a relatively poor agricultural state, though with a thriving coastal tourism business.

❶ Information

South Carolina Department of Parks, Recreation & Tourism (☎803-734-1700 www.discoversouthcarolina.com; 1205 Pendleton St, Room 505, Columbia) Sends out *South Carolina Smiles,* the state's official vacation guide.

South Carolina State Parks (☎888-887-2757; www.southcarolinaparks.com) This helpful website lists activities, hiking trails and allows online reservations for campsites (prices vary).

Charleston

Put on your twinset and pearls or your seersucker suit, have a fortifying sip of sherry, and prepare to be thoroughly drenched in Southern charm. Charleston is a city for strolling, for admiring antebellum architecture, stopping to smell the blooming jasmine and long dinners on the verandah. A tooth-achingly romantic place, everywhere you turn another blushing bride is standing on the steps of yet another charming church.

Named the 'Best-Mannered City in America' 11 years in a row, Charleston is one of the most popular tourist destinations in the Southeast. In the high season the scent of gardenia and honeysuckle mixes with the tang of horse from the innumerable carriage tours that clip-clop down the cobblestones day and night. In winter the weather is milder and the crowds thinner, making Charleston a great bet for off-season travel.

History

Well before the Revolutionary War, Charles Towne (named for Charles II) was one of the busiest ports on the eastern seaboard, the center of a prosperous rice-growing and trading colony. With influences from the West Indies and Africa, France and other European countries, it became a cosmopolitan city, often compared to New Orleans.

The first shots of the Civil War rang out at Fort Sumter, in Charleston's harbor. After the war, as the labor-intensive rice plantations became uneconomical without slave labor, the city's importance declined. But much of the town's historic fabric remains, to the delight of four million tourists every year.

DON'T MISS

CHARLESTON'S SPECIAL CHARMS

» Eating fried shrimp in an old bait warehouse at the **Wreck of the Richard & Charlene** (p336)

» Ogling the oh-so-photogenic painted town houses of **Rainbow Row** (p333)

» Strolling past ancient churchyards abloom with flowers on the **Gateway Walk** (p332)

» Peeking into the lives of the 19th-century Southern aristocracy at **Middleton Place** (p338)

» Watching the sun set in a blaze of orange over the river at the **Rooftop at Vendue Inn** (p337)

◉ Sights & Activities

HISTORIC DISTRICT

The quarter south of Beaufain and Hasell Sts has the bulk of the antebellum mansions, shops, bars and cafes. At the southernmost tip of the peninsula are the antebellum mansions of the Battery.

Gateway Walk   CHURCHES
Long a culturally diverse city, Charleston gave refuge to persecuted French Protestants, Baptists and Jews over the years and earned the nickname the 'Holy City' for its abundance of houses of worship. The Gateway Walk, a little-known garden path between Archdale St and Philadelphia Alley, connects four of the city's most beautiful historic churches: the white-columned **St John's Lutheran Church**; the Gothic Revival **Unitarian Church**; the striking Romanesque **Circular Congregational Church**, originally founded in 1681; and **St Philip's Church**, with its picturesque steeple and 17th-century graveyard, parts of which were once reserved for 'strangers and transient white persons.'

Gibbes Museum of Art   GALLERY
(www.gibbesmuseum.org; 135 Meeting St; adult/child $9/7; ☉10am-5pm Tue-Sat, 1-5pm Sun) Houses a decent collection of American and Southern works; the most interesting way to visit is in conjunction with a two-hour **walking tour** (www.oldcharlestontours.com; tours $20) that combines the museum with various artistically significant city sights.

Old Slave Mart Museum   MUSEUM
(www.nps.gov/nr/travel/charleston/osm.htm; 6 Chalmers St; adult/child $7/5; ☉9am-5pm Mon-Sat) African men, women and children were once auctioned off here, now a museum of South Carolina's shameful past. Text-heavy exhibits illuminate the slave experience; the few artifacts, such as leg shackles, are especially chilling.

**Old Exchange &
Provost Dungeon**   HISTORIC BUILDING
(www.oldexchange.com; 122 E Bay St; adult/child $8/4; ☉9am-5pm; ⊕) Kids love this dungeon, built in 1771 as a customs house and later used as a prison for pirates. Costumed guides lead tours.

Kahal Kadosh Beth Elohim SYNAGOGUE

(www.kkbe.org; 90 Hasell St; tours 10am-noon & 1:30-3:30pm Mon-Thu, 10am-noon Fri) The oldest continuously used synagogue in the country. There are free tours by appointment.

City Market MARKET

(Market St) The historic market is the crowded center of the district, with vendors hawking junky souvenirs from open-air stalls.

White Point Park GARDEN

Take a seat in this shady park and ponder whether 'filthy-rich merchant seaman' is still a viable career.

Rainbow Row NEIGHBORHOOD

Around the corner from White Point Park, a stretch of lower E Bay St known as Rainbow Row is one of the most photographed areas of town for its candy-colored houses.

HISTORIC HOMES

About half a dozen majestic historic homes are open to visitors. Discounted combination tickets may tempt you to see more, but one or two will be enough for most people. Most houses are open from 10am to 5pm Monday to Saturday, 1pm to 5pm Sunday and run guided tours every half-hour. Admission is $10.

Heyward-Washington House HISTORIC BUILDING

(www.charlestonmuseum.org; 87 Church St), Built in 1772, this house belonged to Thomas Heyward Jr, a signer of the Declaration of Independence, and contains some lovely examples of Charleston-made mahogany furniture and the city's only preserved historic kitchen.

Nathaniel Russell House HISTORIC BUILDING

(www.historiccharleston.org; 51 Meeting St) Built by a Rhode Islander, known in Charleston as 'the king of the Yankees,' the 1808 Federal-style house is noted especially for its spectacular, self-supporting spiral staircase and lush English garden.

Joseph Manigault House HISTORIC BUILDING

(www.charlestonmuseum.org; 350 Meeting St) The three-story house was once the showpiece of a French Huguenot rice planter. Don't miss the tiny neoclassical temple in the garden.

Aiken-Rhett House HISTORIC BUILDING

(www.historiccharleston.org; 48 Elizabeth St) The only surviving urban plantation; it gives a fascinating look into antebellum life, including the role of slaves.

Lowcountry Oyster Festival In January oyster-lovers in Mt Pleasant feast on 65,000lb of the salty bivalves.

Charleston Food & Wine Festival This newish March event draws celebrity chefs and well-heeled foodies.

Spoleto USA This 17-day performing arts festival in May is Charleston's biggest event, with operas, dramas and musicals staged across the city, and artisans and food vendors lining the streets.

Charleston Harbor Fest In June antique tall ships sail into town; visitors can take tours and sailing lessons.

MOJA Arts Festival Spirited poetry jams and gospel concerts mark this two-week September celebration of African American culture.

MARION SQUARE

Formerly home to the state weapons arsenal, this 10-acre park is Charleston's living room, with various monuments and an excellent Saturday farmers market.

Charleston Museum MUSEUM

(www.charlestonmuseum.org; 360 Meeting St; adult/child $10/5; ⊙9am-5pm Mon-Sat, from 1pm Sun) Founded in 1773, this claims to be the country's oldest museum, with exhibits from various periods of Charleston's long and storied history, from prehistoric whale skeletons to slave tags and Civil War weapons.

Children's Museum of the Lowcountry MUSEUM

(www.explorecml.org; 25 Ann St; admission $7; ⊙10am-5pm Tue-Sat, 1-5pm Sun; ⊞) Has eight interactive exhibit areas, including a 30ft replica shrimp boat where kids can play captain.

AQUARIUM WHARF

Aquarium Wharf surrounds pretty Liberty Sq and is a great place to stroll around and watch the tugboats guiding ships into the seventh-largest container port in the US. The wharf is the embarkation point for tours to Fort Sumter.

Fort Sumter
HISTORIC SITE

The first shots of the Civil War rang out at Fort Sumter, on a pentagon-shaped island in the harbor. A Confederate stronghold, the fort was shelled to bits by Union forces from 1863 to 1865. A few original guns and fortifications give a feel for the momentous history. The only way to get here is by boat tour (☑843-883-3123; www.nps.gov/fosu; adult/child $17/10; ⊙tours 9:30am, noon & 2:30pm summer, fewer winter), which also depart from Patriot's Point in Mt Pleasant, across the river.

South Carolina Aquarium
AQUARIUM

(www.scaquarium.org; 100 Aquarium Wharf; adult/child $20/13; ⊙9am-5pm; ☕) The massive, excellent aquarium showcases the state's diverse aquatic life, from the otters of the Blue Ridge Mountains to the loggerhead turtles of the Atlantic. The highlight is the 42ft Great Ocean Tank, which teems with sharks and alien-looking puffer fish.

Arthur Ravenel Jr Bridge
BRIDGE

Stretching across the Cooper River like some massive stringed instrument, the 3-mile-long Arthur Ravenel Jr Bridge is a triumph of contemporary engineering. Cycling or jogging across the protected no-car lane is one of active Charlestonians' go-to weekend activities. Rent a cruiser at Charleston (☏843-407-0482; www.charlestonbicyclecompany.com; 334 M E Bay St; bikes per day $27).

Tours

Listing all of Charleston's walking, horse-carriage, bus and boat tours could take up this entire book. Ask at the visitor center for the gamut.

Culinary Tours of Charleston
CULINARY TOUR

(☑800-918-0701; www.culinarytoursofcharleston.com; 2½hr tour $42) Sample grits, pralines, BBQ and more on this walking tour of Charleston's restaurants and markets.

Adventure Harbor Tours
BOAT TOUR

(☑843-442-9455; www.adventureharbortours.com; Morris Island tour adult/child $55/25, off-the-beaten path tour adult/child $75/40) Runs fun trips to uninhabited Morris Island, great for shelling, and a quirky 'off-the-beaten-path' history tour of the harbor.

Charleston Footprints
WALKING TOUR

(☑843-478-4718; www.charlestonfootprintss.com; 2hr tour $20) A highly rated walking tour of historical Charleston sights.

Olde Towne Carriage Company
CARRIAGE TOUR

(☑843-722-1315; www.oldetownecarriage.com; 20 Anson St; 45min tour adult/child $20/12) Guides on this popular horse-drawn-carriage tour offer colorful commentary as you clip-clop around town.

Sleeping

Staying in the historic downtown is the most attractive option, but it's the most expensive, especially on weekends and in high season. The rates below are for high season (spring and early summer). The chain hotels on the highways offer significantly lower rates. Hotel parking in central downtown is usually between $15 and $20 a night; accommodations on the fringes of downtown often have free parking.

The city is bursting with charming B&Bs serving up Southern breakfasts and Southern hospitality. They fill up fast, so try using an agency such as Historic Charleston B&B (☑843-722-6606; www.historiccharlestonbedandbreakfast.com; 57 Broad St).

★ Ansonborough Inn
HOTEL $$$

(☑800-522-2073; www.ansonboroughinn.com; 1 Maiden Ln; r $149-290; ☀☏) A central atrium done up with burnished pine, exposed beams and nautical-themed oil paintings makes this intimate Historic District hotel feel like being inside an antique sailing ship. Droll neo-Victorian touches like the Persian-carpeted glass elevator and the closet-sized British pub add a sense of fun. Huge guest rooms mix old and new, with worn leather couches, high ceilings and flat-screen TVs.

Battery Carriage House Inn
B&B $$$

(☑843-727-3100; www.batterycarriagehouse.com; 20 S Battery; r from $219; P☀☏) Step through the iron gates and into this secluded 11-room treasure, where an interior garden filled with roses and whimsically trimmed topiary hedges begs you to sit down for a cup of tea. A 'gentleman ghost' is said to wander the Victorian-style rooms at night.

Restoration on King
HOTEL $$$

(☑843-518-5100; www.restorationonking.com; 75 Wentworth St; r $299-499; ☀☏) Charleston's newest sleeping spot is an antidote to the city's traditional antiques-and-pineapples hotel decor. The 16 ultramodern luxury suites are more like private apartments, with exposed brick, sleek stainless steel and gorgeous spa-style bathrooms. Splash out for one with a balcony.

Vendue Inn
INN $$$

(☎843-577-7970; www.vendueinn.com; 19 Vendue Range; r incl breakfast $145-255; ✳☎) This teeny boutique hotel, in the part of downtown known as the French Quarter, is decked out in a trendy mix of exposed brick and eccentric antiques. Rooms have cool amenities like deep soaking tubs and gas fireplaces. Even cooler is the aptly named Rooftop bar.

NotSo Hostel
HOSTEL $

(☎843-722-8383; www.notsohostel.com; 156 Spring St; dm/r $23/60; P✳@☎) On the north edge of downtown, three tottering old houses have been carved into dorms and private rooms, the verandahs decked with hammocks. Get local tips from friendly staff members during the shared morning breakfast. A new nearby annex offers queen beds and a quieter vibe, good for couples.

Mills House Hotel
HOTEL $$

(☎843-577-2400; www.millshouse.com; 115 Meeting St; r from $189; ✳☎☎) This grand old dame (150 years young, *merci*) has had an $11-million facelift, and is now one of the most opulent choices in the area. Gilded elevators lead from an enormous marble lobby to 214 lushly upholstered rooms. The sun has still not set on the British Empire inside the clubby, wood-paneled Barbados Room restaurant.

1837 Bed & Breakfast
B&B $$

(☎843-723-7166, 877-723-1837; www.1837bb.com; 126 Wentworth St; r incl breakfast $109-195; P✳☎) Like staying at the home of your eccentric, antique-loving aunt, 1837 has nine charmingly overdecorated rooms, including three in the old brick carriage house.

Palmer Pinckney Inn
INN $$$

(☎843-722-1733; www.pinckneyinn.com; 19 Pinckney St; r $150-300; P✳☎) This bubblegum-pink 'single house' (a narrow building style characteristic of Charleston) has five twee guest rooms tucked away on a Historic District side street.

James Island County Park
CAMPGROUND $

(☎843-795-7275; www.ccprc.com; 871 Riverland Dr; tent sites from $25, 8-person cottages $159) Southwest of town, this park offers shuttle services downtown. Reservations are highly recommended.

Anchorage Inn
INN $$

(☎843-723-8300; www.anchoragecharleston.com; 26 Vendue Range; r from $99; ✳☎) One of the best-value of Charleston's intimate Historic District inns, its rooms have the dark and small feel of ship's quarters but they're plenty plush.

✖ Eating

Charleston is one of America's finest eating cities, and there are enough fabulous restaurants here for a town three times its size. The 'classic' Charleston establishments stick to fancy seafood with a French flair, while many of the trendy up-and-comers are reinventing Southern cuisine with a focus on the area's copious local bounty, from oysters to heirloom rice to heritage pork. On Saturday, stop by the terrific **farmers market** (Marion Sq; ⊙8am-1pm Sat Apr-Oct).

TOP CHOICE Husk
NEW SOUTHERN $$$

(☎843-577-2500; www.huskrestaurant.com; 76 Queen St; mains $22-26; ⊙11:30am-2:30pm Mon-Sat, 5:30-10pm daily, brunch 10am-2:30pm Sun) The brain child of chef Sean Brock, the current toast of the foodie world, Husk was the South's most buzzed-about restaurant when it burst onto the scene in late 2010, and for damn good reason. Everything – *everything* – on the menu is grown or raised in the South, from the jalapeño marmalade-topped

---

LOWCOUNTRY CUISINE

The traditional cooking style of the South Carolina and Georgia coasts, Lowcountry cuisine is seafood-centric Southern fare with a heavy dash of West African influence. Dishes to look for:

» She-crab soup: cream-based crab soup fortified with sherry

» Lowcountry boil/Frogmore stew: crabs, shrimp, oysters and other local seafood boiled in a pot with corn and potatoes, generally eaten at picnics

» Country Captain: curried chicken stew, brought to the city via India by British sea captains

» Perlau: a rice-and-meat dish, cousin to rice pilaf

» Shrimp and grits: a classic Charleston fisherman's breakfast, now a ubiquitous main course

» Hoppin' John: a rice and bean dish, sometimes spicy

» Benne wafers: sesame-seed cookies

Georgia corn soup to the yuzu-scented Cooper River oysters, to the local lard featured in the 'pork butter' brought out with the restaurant's addictive sesame-seed rolls. The setting, in a two-story mansion, is elegant but unfussy, and the adjacent speakeasy-style bar (see Drinking) is straight-up terrific.

Wreck of the Richard & Charlene
SEAFOOD $$$

(www.wreckrc.com; 106 Haddrell St; mains $12-25; ⏰5:30-8:30pm Sun-Thu, to 9:30pm Fri & Sat) It's practically impossible to find, but don't give up! This unmarked warehouse, down a dirt road overlooking Shem Creek in suburban Mt Pleasant, has what many consider the best fried seafood in the state. Kick back in a plastic chair with a free bowl of boiled peanuts while you wait; finish with the key lime bread pudding. No credit cards.

O-Ku
JAPANESE $$$

(☎843-737-0112; www.o-kusushi.com; 463 King St; mains $16-29; ⏰11:30am-2pm Mon-Fri, 5-10:30pm Sun-Thu, to midnight Fri & Sat) Scenesters dine on irreverent sushi (try the fried potato-wrapped roll), Japanese street food (try Kurobuta pork sliders with grapefruit puree) and lavish seafood dishes at this new rock star of a restaurant, a big high-ceilinged space with a glammy black paint-and-mirrors decor. The lunchtime bento box ($10) is a steal.

FIG
NEW SOUTHERN $$$

(☎843-805-5900; www.eatatfig.com; 232 Meeting St; mains $28-32; ⏰5:30-10:30pm Mon-Thu, to 11pm Fri-Sun) Foodies swoon over inspired nouvelle-Southern fare like crispy pig's trotters (that means 'feet' – local and hormone-free, of course) with celery-root remoulade in this rustic-chic dining room.

Glass Onion
NEW SOUTHERN $$

(☎843-225-1717; www.ilovetheglassonion.com; 1219 Savannah Hwy; mains $12-19; ⏰11am-9pm Mon-Sat) In-the-know foodies flock across the bridge to West Ashley for Tuesday-night fried-chicken suppers at this funky art-filled diner, Charleston's newest spot for creative takes on Southern classics. The perfect stop for lunch on the way to visit the Ashley River plantations.

S.N.O.B.
NEW SOUTHERN $$$

(☎843-723-3424; www.mavericksouthernkitchens.com; 192 E Bay St; mains $18-34; ⏰11:30am-3pm Mon-Fri, 5:30pm-late nightly) The cheeky name (it stands for 'slightly north of Broad,' as in Broad St) reflects the anything-goes spirit of this upscale-casual spot, which draws raves for its eclectic menu, filled with treats such as house-smoked salmon or sautéed squab breast over cheese grits.

Gullah Cuisine
SOUTHERN $

(1717 Hwy 17 N. Mt Pleasant; mains $7-11; ⏰9am-3pm & 5-9:30pm) It's not much to look at,

---

CHARLESTON'S BEST BAKERIES

Ever the European-style city, Charleston has some of the finest bakeries outside the Continent.

Wildflour Pastry
BAKERY $

(73 Spring St; pastries $1-3; ⏰6:30am-4pm Tue-Fri, 8am-3pm Sat, 8am-1pm Sun) On rapidly gentrifying Spring St, this sweet slip of a bakery turns out glorious Nutella-raspberry turnovers, jam scones and coffee cake muffins.

Sugar Bakeshop
BAKERY $

(59 Cannon St; pastries $1-3; ⏰11am-6pm Mon-Fri, noon-5pm Sat) Pop into this teensy space on Thursdays for the Lady Baltimore cupcake, a retro Southern specialty with dried fruit and white frosting.

Baked
BAKERY $

(160 E Bay St; pastries $1-5; ⏰7:30am-7pm; 🖧) Salty caramel cake, red velvet whoopie pies and homemade marshmallows (and lots of table space with free wi-fi) make this Historic District spot a winner.

Macaroon Boutique
BAKERY $

(45 John St; bags of macarons $7; ⏰8:30am-6pm Tue-Sat, to 4pm Sun) With perfect golden croissants and baggies of crisp, chewy macaroons, you might as well be in Paris. No seating.

but this dowdy suburban cafe is the best place to taste South Carolina's West African-influenced Gullah cooking. Go for the lunch buffet, groaning with red rice, okra gumbo (roux-based stew), oxtail stew and fried fish, and skip the dinner.

Hominy Grill   NEW SOUTHERN **$$**
(www.hominygrill.com; 207 Rutledge Ave; mains $7-18; ☺7:30am-9pm Mon-Fri, 9am-3pm Sat & Sun) Slightly off the beaten path, this neighborhood cafe serves modern, vegetarian-friendly Lowcountry cuisine in an old barbershop. The shady patio is tops for brunch.

Gaulart & Maliclet   FRENCH **$$**
(www.fastandfrench.org; 98 Broad St; mains $8-15; ☺8am-4pm Mon, 8am-10pm Tue-Thu, to 10:30pm Fri-Sun) Locals crowd around the shared tables at this tiny spot, known as 'Fast & French,' to nibble on Gallic cheeses and sausages or nightly specials ($15) that include bread, soup, a main dish and wine.

Drinking

Balmy Charleston evenings are perfect for lifting a cool cocktail or dancing to live blues. Check out the weekly *Charleston City Paper* and the 'Preview' section of Friday's *Post & Courier*.

TOP CHOICE / Husk Bar   BAR
(462 King St) Adjacent to the excellent new Husk restaurant (see Eating), this intimate brick-and-worn-wood spot recalls a speakeasy, with historic cocktails such as the Monkey Gland (gin, OJ, raspberry syrup). Very cool.

Rooftop at Vendue Inn   BAR
(23 Vendue Range) This two-level rooftop bar has the best views of downtown, and the crowds to prove it. Enjoy afternoon nachos or late-night live blues.

Belmont   BAR
(511 King St) Young hipsters mellow out with small-batch bourbon at this low-key new lounge, in a narrow 1930s-style King St storefront.

Blind Tiger   PUB
(36-38 Broad St) A cozy and atmospheric dive, with stamped tin ceilings, a worn wood bar and good pub grub.

Closed for Business   PUB
(535 King St) Charleston's best beer selection and a raucous neighborhood pub vibe.

Shopping

The historic district is clogged with over-priced souvenir shops and junk markets. Heading to King St is a better bet: hit lower King for antiques, middle King for scads of cool boutiques, and upper King for trendy design and gift shops. The main stretch of Broad St is known as 'Gallery Row' for its many art galleries.

Shops of Historic
Charleston Foundation   GIFTS
(108 Meeting St) This place showcases jewelry, home furnishings and furniture inspired by the city's historic homes, like earrings based on the cast-iron railings at the Aiken-Rhett House. Pick up a 'Charleston' candle, scented with hyacinth, white jasmine and tuberose.

Carolina Antique Maps & Prints   MAPS, ART
(91 Church St) Buy a vintage map of Charleston or a magnolia-blossom botanical print at this crowded little shop, tucked away on a residential street.

Charleston Crafts Cooperative   CRAFT
(161 Church St) A pricey, well-edited selection of contemporary South Carolina-made crafts such as sweetgrass baskets, hand-dyed silks and wood carvings.

Blue Bicycle Books   BOOKS
(420 King St) Excellent local bookshop with a great selection of Southern history and culture.

Information

The City of Charleston maintains free public internet (wi-fi) access throughout the downtown area.
Charleston City Paper (www.charlestoncity paper.com) Published each Wednesday, this alt-weekly has good entertainment and restaurant listings.
Main police station (☎843-577-7434; 180 Lockwood Blvd)
Post & Courier (www.charleston.net) Charleston's daily newspaper.
Post office (83 Broad St)
Public library (68 Calhoun St) Free internet access.
University Hospital (MUSC; ☎843-792-2300; 171 Ashley Ave; ☺24hr) Emergency room.
Visitor center (☎843-853-8000; www. charlestoncvb.com; 375 Meeting St; ☺8:30am-5pm) Find help with accommodations and tours or watch a half-hour video on Charleston history in this spacious renovated warehouse.

ⓘ Getting There & Around

Charleston International Airport (CHS; ☏843-767-7009; www.chs-airport.com; 5500 International Blvd) is 12 miles outside of town in North Charleston, with 124 daily flights to 17 destinations.

The **Greyhound station** (3610 Dorchester Rd) and the **Amtrak train station** (4565 Gaynor Ave) are both in North Charleston.

CARTA (www.ridecarta.com; fare $1.75) runs city-wide buses; the free DASH streetcars do four loop routes from the visitor center.

Around Charleston

MT PLEASANT

Across the Cooper River is the residential and vacation community of Mt Pleasant, originally a summer retreat for early Charlestonians, along with the slim barrier resort islands of Isle of Palms and Sullivan's Island. Though increasingly glutted with traffic and strip malls, the area still has some charm, especially in the historic downtown, called the Old Village. Some good seafood restaurants sit overlooking the water at Shem Creek, where it's fun to dine creekside at sunset and watch the incoming fishing-boat crews unload their catch. This is also a good place to rent kayaks to tour the estuary.

Patriot's Point Naval & Maritime Museum (www.patriotspoint.org; 40 Patriots Point Rd; adult/child $18/11; ☺9am-6:30pm) is home to the USS *Yorktown,* a giant aircraft carrier used extensively in WWII. You can tour the ship's flight deck, bridge and ready rooms and get a glimpse of what life was like for its sailors. Also on site are a small museum, submarine, naval destroyer, Coast Guard cutter and a re-created 'fire base' from Vietnam. You can also catch the Fort Sumter boat tour from here.

Just 7 miles from Charleston on Hwy 17 N, Boone Hall Plantation (www.boonehall plantation.com; 1235 Long Point Rd; adult/child $19.50/9.50; ☺9am-5pm Mon-Sat, noon-5pm Sun) claims to be America's most photographed plantation. It's famous for its magical Avenue of Oaks, planted by Thomas Boone in 1743. Boone Hall is still a working plantation, though strawberries, tomatoes and Christmas trees long ago replaced cotton as the primary crop.

Near Boone Hall, the Charles Pinckney National Historic Site (1254 Long Point Rd; admission free; ☺9am-5pm) sits on the remaining 28 acres of Snee Farm, once the expansive plantation of statesman Charles Pinckney. There are archaeological and historical exhibits in the 1820s cottage turned museum, and several walking trails meandering through the magnolias.

ASHLEY RIVER PLANTATIONS

Only 20 minutes' drive from Charleston, three spectacular plantations are worthy of a detour. You'll be hard-pressed for time to visit all three in one outing, but you could squeeze in two (allow at least a couple of hours for each). Ashley River Rd is also known as SC 61, which can be reached from downtown Charleston via Hwy 17.

TOP CHOICE Middleton Place   PLANTATION
(www.middletonplace.org; 4300 Ashley River Rd; gardens adult/child $22/10, house tour add $12; ☺9am-5pm) Designed in 1741, this plantation's vast gardens are the oldest in the US. One hundred slaves spent a decade terracing the land and digging the precise geometric canals for the owner, wealthy South Carolina politician Henry Middleton. The grounds are truly bewitching, a mix of classic formal French gardens and romantic woodland settings, bounded by real flooded rice paddies and fields full of rare breed farm animals (horse-drawn carriage tours are $15). In contrast to the antebellum plantation house, the very cool on-site inn (r incl plantation admission from $209) is a series of ecofriendly modernist glass boxes overlooking the Ashley River. Even if you don't stay the night, don't miss a traditional Lowcountry plantation lunch of she-crab soup and pole beans at the highly regarded cafe (lunch $11-13, dinner $23-32; ☺11am-3pm daily & 6-8pm Tue-Sun).

Magnolia Plantation   HOUSE, GARDENS
(www.magnoliaplantation.com; 3550 Ashley River Rd; adult/child $15/10, house tour add $8; ☺8am-5:30pm) Sitting on 500 acres owned by the Drayton family since 1676, Magnolia Plantation is enjoyable even for those who disdain 'boring historical stuff.' It's a veritable plantation theme park, complete with a tram tour of the flora and fauna, boat tours, a swamp walk, a petting zoo, and an outdoor cafe full of wandering peacocks, in addition to the guided house tour. Don't miss the reconstructed cabins of the slaves who once tended the indigo, cotton, corn and sugarcane.

Drayton Hall   HISTORIC BUILDING
(www.draytonhall.org; 3380 Ashley River Rd; adult/child $18/8; ☺9am-4:30pm, shorter hr in winter)

This 1738 Palladian brick mansion was the only structure on the Ashley River to survive the Revolutionary and Civil Wars and the great earthquake of 1886. Guided tours through the empty house will appeal to history and architecture buffs.

Lowcountry

From just north of Charleston, the southern half of the South Carolina coast is a tangle of islands cut off from the mainland by inlets and tidal marshes. Here, descendants of West African slaves known as the Gullah maintain small communities in the face of resort and golf-course development. The landscape ranges from tidy stretches of shimmery, oyster-gray sand, to wild, moss-shrouded maritime forests.

CHARLESTON COUNTY SEA ISLANDS

The following islands are all within an hour's drive from Charleston.

About 8 miles south of Charleston, Folly Beach is good for a day of sun and sand. Folly Beach County Park (cars/pedestrians $7/free; ☉10am-6pm), on the west side, has public changing areas and beach-chair rentals. The other end of the island is popular with surfers.

Upscale rental homes and golf courses abound on Kiawah Island, just southeast of Charleston, while nearby Edisto Island (ed-is-tow) is a homespun family vacation spot without a single traffic light. At its southern tip, Edisto Beach State Park (admission $5; tent sites from $17, furnished cabins from $70) has a gorgeous, uncrowded beach and oak-shaded hiking trails and campgrounds.

Between Kiawah and Edisto, agricultural Wadmalaw Island is home to Charleston Tea Plantation (www.charlestonteaplantation.com; 6617 Maybank Hwy; trolley tours/factory tours $10/free; ☉10am-4pm, noon-4pm Sun), America's only working tea farm. Ride a trolley through the fields, or buy prettily packaged Plantation Peach and Island Green teas in the gift shop.

BEAUFORT & HILTON HEAD

The southernmost stretch of South Carolina's coast is popular with a mostly upscale set of golfers and B&B aficionados, but the area's got quirky charms aplenty for everyone.

On Port Royal Island, the darling colonial town of Beaufort (byoo-furt) is often used as a set for Hollywood films about the South. The streets of the historic district are

BOWEN'S ISLAND RESTAURANT

Down a long dirt road through Low-country marshland near Folly Beach, this unpainted wooden shack is one of the South's most venerable seafood dives – grab an oyster knife and start shucking! Cool beer and friendly locals give the place its soul. You'll find the restaurant at 1870 Bowen's Island Rd, open Tuesday to Saturday, 5pm to 10pm.

lined with antebellum homes and magnolias dripping with Spanish moss, and the riverfront downtown has gobs of linger-worthy cafes and galleries. The most romantic of the city's handful of B&Bs is the Cuthbert House (☑843-521-1315; www.cuthberthouseinn.com; 1203 Bay St; r from $169; ☏), a sumptuously grand white-columned mansion straight out of Gone With the Wind II. Bay St has the bulk of the cute bistros, but for some hardcore local flavor head inland to Sgt White's (1908 Boundary St; mains $6-12; ☉11am-3pm Mon-Fri), where a retired Marine sergeant serves up juicy BBQ ribs, collards and cornbread.

South of Beaufort, some 20,000 young men and women go through boot camp each year at the Marine Corps Recruit Depot on Parris Island, made notorious by Stanley Kubrick's Full Metal Jacket. The fascinating base museum (admission free; ☉10am-4:30pm) has antique uniforms and weaponry. Come for Friday graduations to see newly minted marines parade proudly in front of weeping family and friends.

East of Beaufort, the Sea Island Pkwy/Hwy 21 connects a series of marshy, rural islands, including St Helena Island, considered the heart of Gullah country. Once one of the nation's first schools for freed slaves, the Penn Center (www.penncenter.com; adult/child $5/2; ☉11am-4pm Mon-Sat) has a small museum of Gullah culture and is a good place to get info for further exploration. Further down the road, Hunting Island State Park (☑843-838-2011; www.huntingisland.com; adult/child $5/3; tent sites/cabins from $17/107) has acres of spooky maritime forest, tidal lagoons, and empty, bone-white beach. The Vietnam War scenes from Forrest Gump were filmed in the marsh, a nature-lover's dream. Campgrounds fill up quickly in summer.

GULLAH CULTURE

Many parts of the US resemble the European cities from which the founding settlers emigrated, but only on remote islands along the Georgia and South Carolina coast can the same claim be given to Africa. From the region known as the Rice Coast (Sierra Leone, Senegal, the Gambia and Angola), African slaves were transported across the Atlantic to a landscape that was shockingly similar – swampy coastlines, tropical vegetation and hot, humid summers.

These new African Americans were able to retain many of their homeland traditions, even after the fall of slavery and well into the 20th century. The resulting Gullah (also known as Geechee) culture has its own language, an English-based Creole with many African words and sentence structures, and many traditions, including fantastic storytelling, art, music and crafts. The Gullah culture is celebrated annually with the energetic **Gullah Festival** (www.gullahfestival.org) in Beaufort. As many as 70,000 people gather on the last weekend in May to enjoy music, dance and crafts, including the famous Gullah sweetgrass baskets, and to eat traditional foods such as fried whiting, candied yams and okra gumbo.

Across Port Royal Sound, tony **Hilton Head Island** is South Carolina's largest barrier island and one of America's top golf spots. There are literally dozens of courses, many enclosed in posh private residential communities called 'plantations.' Though summer traffic and miles of stoplights make it hard to see the forest (or a tree) along Hwy 278, there are some lush nature preserves and wide white beaches hard enough to ride a bike on. At the entrance to the island is the visitor center (9:30am-5pm), with a small museum and info on accommodations and, well, golf.

North Coast

The coastline from the North Carolina border to the city of Georgetown is known as the Grand Strand, with some 60 miles of fast-food joints, beach resorts and three-story souvenir shops. What was once a laid-back summer destination for working-class people from across the Southeast has become some of the most overdeveloped real estate in the country. Whether you're ensconced in a behemoth resort or sleeping in a tent at a state park, all you need to enjoy your stay is a pair of flip-flops, a margarita and some quarters for the pinball machine.

MYRTLE BEACH

Love it or hate it, Myrtle Beach means summer vacation, American-style.

Bikers take advantage of the lack of helmet laws to let their graying ponytails fly in the wind, bikini-clad teenagers play Pac-Man and eat hot dogs in smoky arcades, and

whole families roast like chickens on the white sand.

North Myrtle Beach, actually a separate town, is slightly lower-key, with a thriving culture based on the 'shag' (no, not that kind of shag) – a jitterbug-like dance invented here in the 1940s.

It ain't for nature-lovers, but with enormous outlet malls and innumerable mini-golf courses, water parks, daiquiri bars and T-shirt shops, it's a rowdy good time.

◉ Sights & Activities

The beach itself is pleasant enough – wide, hot and crowded with umbrellas. Beach-front Ocean Blvd has the bulk of the hamburger stands and seedy gift shops. Hwy 17 is utterly choked with **mini-golf** courses, boasting everything from animatronic dinosaurs to faux volcanoes spewing lurid-pink water.

Several amusement park–shopping mall hybrids teem with people at all hours.

Brookgreen Gardens GARDENS
(www.brookgreen.org; adult/child $12/6; 9:30am-5pm) These magical gardens, 16 miles south of town on Hwy 17 S, are home to the largest collection of American sculpture in the country, set amid 9000 acres of rice plantation turned subtropical garden paradise.

Wonderworks MUSEUM
(www.wonderworksonline.com; tickets adult/child from $23/15; 10am-10pm;) In a fake upside-down building, this new interactive museum/amusement zone perfectly encapsulates Myrtle Beach's fun-but-migraine-inducing spirit, with ropes courses,

laser tag and various beeping, flashing 'science exhibits' such as an 'anti-gravity chamber.'

Broadway at the Beach MALL, LANDMARK
(www.broadwayatthebeach.com; 1325 Celebrity Circle) With shops, restaurants, nightclubs, rides and an IMAX theater, this is Myrtle Beach's nerve center.

Family Kingdom AMUSEMENT PARK
(www.family-kingdom.com; combo pass $35; 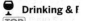) An old-fashioned amusement-and-water-park combo overlooking the ocean. Hours vary by season; it's closed in winter.

🛏 Sleeping

Hundreds of hotels, ranging from retro family-run motor inns to vast resort complexes, have prices that vary widely by season; a room might cost $30 in January and more than $150 in July. The following are high-season rates.

Serendipity Inn INN $$
(☎800-762-3229; www.serendipityinn.com; 407 71st Ave N; r incl breakfast $89-109; P❋🛜🏊) The closest thing to a B&B in resort-crazed Myrtle Beach, this intimate Spanish-style inn hides from the city's buzz on a quiet side street. Rooms, done up with florals and knickknacks, are comfy but not fancy.

Myrtle Beach State Park CAMPGROUND $$
(☎843-238-5325; www.southcarolinaparks.com; tent & RV sites $21-25, cabins & apts $65-176; P🛜🏊👪) Most campgrounds are veritable parking lots catering to families with RVs, but the best camping is found in the shady sites of this state park, 3 miles south of central Myrtle Beach.

Breakers RESORT $$
(☎800-952-4507; www.breakers.com; 2006 N Ocean Blvd; r $112-195; P❋🛜🏊👪) This long-standing megaresort has three towers of crisp, summery-yellow suites, with only-in-Myrtle-Beach amenities like a pirate-ship swimming pool and a pirate-themed bar.

🍴 Eating

The thousands of restaurants high-volume and middlebrow fets longer than bowling alleys doughnut shops. Ironically, go hard to come by; locals go to th ing village of **Murrells Inlet**.

Prosser's BBQ
(3750 Business Hwy 17; b $7.50/13; ☺6am-8:30pm; on Murrells Inlet's 'resta Prosser's has a gut-bust fish and chicken, swee cheese, and vinegary vary by season. Wort'

Duffy Street Seafo $
(www.duffyst.com; 202 h; mains $8-20; ☺4pm-l di-vey, peanut-shells- nce and a raw bar 'hap imp.

🍷 Drinking & [

TOP CHOICE Fat Harol DANCE
(www.fatharolds.c h Myrtle Beach) It's a ga g beach bums groove -time rock and roll at institution, which calls Shag.' The dance, that are offered at 7pm eve

Carolina (MUSICAL THEATER
(☎843-913 pry.com; 8901a Business 1 s glittery musicals an ets from $35.

ℹ Inf[

Chapin 00 14th Ave N)
Interne'

Visito -7444, 800-496-8250 fo.com; 1200 N Oak St; ☺8:3ua... ri, 10am-2pm Sat) Has loads of maps and brochures.

ℹ Getting There & Around

The traffic coming and going on Hwy 17 Business/Kings Hwy can be infuriating. To avoid 'the

---

MEXICAN HAT DANCE

Yes, that's a giant sombrero rising above I-95 on the North Carolina–South Carolina state line. *Bienvenidos* to **South of the Border**, a Mexican-flavored monument to American kitsch. Begun in the 1950s as a fireworks stand – pyrotechnics are illegal in North Carolina – it's since morphed into a combo rest stop, souvenir mall, motel and (mostly defunct) amusement park, promoted on hundreds of billboards by a wildly stereotypical Mexican cartoon character named Pedro. Stop for a photo, some taffy, and a key chain that pees when you squeeze it.

Strand' altogether, stay on the Hwy 17 bypass, or take Hwy 31/Carolina Bays Pkwy, which parallels Hwy 17 between Hwy 501 and Hwy 9.

Myrtle Beach International Airport (MYR; ☑843-448-1589; 1100 Jetport Rd) is located within the city limits, as is the **Greyhound** (511 7th Ave N) station.

AROUND MYRTLE BEACH

Fifteen minutes down I-17 is Pawleys Island, a narrow strip of pastel sea cottages that's worlds away from the neon of Myrtle Beach. There's not much to do here but kayak and fish, but that's just fine. Another 15 minutes will bring you to mellow Georgetown, South Carolina's third-oldest city. Have lunch on Front St, with photogenic 19th-century storefronts overlooking the water, or use it as a quiet jumping-off point for exploring the Francis Marion National Forest.

Columbia

South Carolina's state capital is a quiet place, with wide, shady streets and the kind of old-fashioned downtown where pillbox hats are still on display in the windows of family-run department stores. The University of South Carolina adds a youthful vibe, and college students whoop it up over basketball wins in campus-side bars. Though Columbia is a pleasant stop, most visitors, like General Sherman's troops, charge on through to the coast.

The grand, Corinthian-columned State House (www.scstatehouse.gov; 1100 Gervais St; admission free; ◷9am-5pm Mon-Fri, 10am-5pm Sat)

has bronze stars on its west side to mark the impacts from Northern troops' cannonballs.

The South Carolina State Museum (www.museum.state.sc.us; 301 Gervais St; adult/child $7/3; ◷10am-5pm Tue-Sat, 1-5pm Sun) is housed in an 1894 textile factory building, one of the world's first electrically powered mills. Exhibits on science, technology and the state's cultural and natural history make a nice activity for a rainy day.

For eating and entertainment, head down Gervais St to the Vista, a hip renovated warehouse district popular with young professionals. For coffee and cheap ethnic food, mingle with USC students in Five Points, where Harden, Greene and Devine Sts meet Saluda Ave. Stop at popular new Pawley's Front Porch (www.pawleys5pts.com; 827 Harden St; mains $7-10; ◷11:30am-10pm) to try a pimento cheeseburger (a burger topped with a cheese, mayonnaise and red pepper mixture), Columbia's answer to New York's pizza slice or Chicago's hot dog.

There are plenty of chain hotels off I-26. In Five Points, the 28-room Inn at Claussen's (☑803-765-0440; www.theinnatclaussens.com; 2003 Greene St; r $112-154; 🖥) gamely attempts a boutique art-deco look, with modest success.

TENNESSEE

Most states have one official state song. Tennessee has seven. And that's not just a random fact – Tennessee has music deep within its soul. Here, the folk music of the Scots-Irish in the eastern mountains com-

---

EXPLORING SOUTH CAROLINA SWAMPS

Inky-black water, dyed with tannic acid leached from decaying plant matter. Bone-white cypress stumps like the femurs of long-dead giants. Spanish moss as dry and gray as witches' hair. There's nothing like hiking or canoeing through one of South Carolina's unearthly swamps to make you feel like a character in a Southern Gothic novel.

About 45 minutes from Charleston, Beidler Forest (www.beidlerforest.com; 336 Sanctuary Rd, Harleyville; ◷9am-5pm Tue-Sun; adult/child $8/4) is a spooky 1800 acres of cypress swamp managed by the Audubon Society, who lead springtime weekend canoe trips (adult/child $30/15).

Near Columbia, the 22,000-acre Congaree National Park (www.nps.gov/cong; 100 National Park Rd, Hopkins; ◷8:30am-5pm), America's largest contiguous, old-growth flood-plain forest, has camping and free ranger-led canoe trips (reserve in advance; ☑803-776-4396). Casual day-trippers can wander the 2.4-mile elevated boardwalk.

Between Charleston and Myrtle Beach, Francis Marion National Forest (5821 Hwy 17 N, Awendaw) has 259,000 acres of black-water creeks, camping, and hiking trails, including the 42-mile Palmetto Trail, which runs along old logging routes. Charleston-based Nature Adventures Outfitters (☑843-568-3222; www.natureadventuresoutfitters.com; adult/child half-day $55/39) leads kayak and canoe trips.

bined with the bluesy rhythms of the African Americans in the western Delta to give birth to the modern country music that makes Nashville famous.

These three geographic regions, represented by the three stars on the Tennessee flag, have their own unique beauty: the heather-colored peaks of the Great Smoky Mountains descend into lush green valleys in the central plateau around Nashville and then onto the hot, sultry lowlands near Memphis.

In Tennessee you can hike shady mountain trails in the morning, and by evening whoop it up in a Nashville honky-tonk or walk the streets of Memphis with Elvis' ghost.

From country churches where snake handlers still speak in tongues, to modern cities where record execs wear their sunglasses even at night, Tennesseans are a zesty lot.

History

Spanish settlers first explored Tennessee in 1539 and French traders were plying the rivers by the 17th century. Virginian pioneers soon established their own settlement and fought the British in the American Revolution. Tennessee joined the United States as the 16th state in 1796, taking its named from the Cherokee town of Tanasi.

The Cherokee themselves were brutally booted from their homes, along with many other Tennessee tribes, in the mid-1800s and marched west along the Trail of Tears.

Tennessee was the second-to-last Southern state to secede during the Civil War, and many important battles were fought here. Immediately following the war, six Confederate veterans from the town of Pulaski formed the infamous Ku Klux Klan to disenfranchise and terrorize the newly free blacks.

Major industries today are textiles, tobacco, cattle and chemicals, with tourism, especially in Nashville and Memphis, raking in hundreds of millions of dollars a year.

🛈 Information

Department of Environment & Conservation (☎888-867-2757; www.state.tn.us/environ ment/parks) Check out this well-organized website for camping (prices range from free to $27 or more), hiking and fishing info for Tennessee's more than 50 state parks.

Department of Tourist Development (☎615-741-2159, 800-462-8366; www.tnvacation.com; 312 8th Ave N, Nashville) Has welcome centers at the state borders.

TENNESSEE FACTS

» **Nickname** Volunteer State

» **Population** 6.3 million

» **Area** 41,217 sq miles

» **Capital city** Nashville (population 630,000)

» **Other cities** Memphis (population 650,000)

» **Sales tax** 7%, plus local taxes of up to about 15%

» **Birthplace of** frontiersman Davy Crockett (1786–1836), soul diva Aretha Franklin (b 1942), singer Dolly Parton (b 1946)

» **Home of** Graceland, Grand Ole Opry, Jack Daniel's distillery

» **Politics** pretty darn conservative, with liberal hot spots in urban areas

» **Famous for** 'Tennessee Waltz,' country music, Tennessee walking horses

» **Odd law** in Tennessee, it's illegal to fire a gun at any wild game, other than whales, from a moving vehicle

» **Driving distances** Memphis to Nashville 213 miles, Nashville to Great Smoky Mountains National Park 223 miles

Memphis

Memphis doesn't just attract tourists. It draws pilgrims. Music-lovers come to lose themselves amid the throb of blues guitar on Beale St. Barbecue connoisseurs come to stuff themselves sick on smoky pulled pork and dry-rubbed ribs. Elvis fanatics fly in from London and Reykjavik and Osaka to worship at the altar of the King at Graceland. You could spend days hopping from one museum or historic site to another, stopping only for a spot o' barbecue, and leave happy.

But once you get away from the lights and the tourist buses, Memphis is a different place entirely. Named after the capital of ancient Egypt, it has a certain baroquely ruined quality that's both sad and beguiling. Poverty is rampant – Victorian mansions sit beside tumbledown shotgun shacks (a narrow style of house popular in the South), college campuses lie in the shadow of eerie abandoned factories, and whole neighborhoods seem to have been almost reclaimed by kudzu and honeysuckle vines.

But Memphis' wild river-town spirit reveals itself to visitors willing to look. Keep your eyes open and you'll find some of the country's strangest museums, most deliciously oddball restaurants (barbecued spaghetti, anyone?), spookiest cemeteries and craziest dive bars.

History

Union troops occupied Memphis during the Civil War, but the postwar collapse of the port city's cotton trade was far more devastating. After a yellow fever outbreak caused most whites to flee the city, Memphis was forced to declare bankruptcy. The African American community revived the town, led by Robert Church, a former slave. By the early 1900s Beale St was the hub of black social and civic activity, becoming an early center for what was to be known as blues music. In the '50s and '60s, local recording companies cut tracks for blues, soul, R & B and rockabilly artists such as Al Green, Johnny Cash and Elvis, cementing Memphis' place in the American music firmament.

Memphis

Sights & Activities

DOWNTOWN

TOP CHOICE | National Civil Rights Museum
MUSEUM

(www.civilrightsmuseum.org; 450 Mulberry St; adult/child $13/9.50; ⊙9am-5pm Mon & Wed-Sat, 1-5pm Sun Sep-May, to 6pm Jun-Aug) Housed in the Lorraine Motel, where the Reverend Dr Martin Luther King Jr was fatally shot on April 4, 1968, is the gut-wrenching National Civil Rights Museum. Five blocks south of Beale St, this museum's extensive exhibits, detailed timeline and accompanying audio-guide chronicle the ongoing struggles for African American freedom and equality in the US. Both Dr King's cultural contribution and his assassination serve as prisms for looking at the Civil Rights movement, its precursors and its indelible and continuing impact on American life. The turquoise exterior of the 1950s motel and two preserved interior rooms remain much as they were at the time of King's death, and serve as pilgrimage points in their own right.

FREE | Peabody Ducks
MARCHING DUCKS

(www.peabodymemphis.com; 11am & 5pm daily; ⊕) Every day at 11am sharp, five ducks file from the Peabody Hotel's gilded elevator, waddle across the red-carpeted lobby, and decamp in the marble lobby fountain for a day of happy splashing. The ducks make the reverse march at 5pm, when they retire to their penthouse accompanied by their red-coated Duckmaster. The march of the ducks, which dates back to a 1930s-era drunken prank, is a quintessential Memphis tradition. It always draws major crowds – get here early to secure your spot (the mezzanine has the best views).

Mud Island
PARK, MUSEUM

(www.mudisland.com; park free; 125 N Front St; ⊙10am-5pm Tue-Sun Apr-Oct, later Jun-Aug; ⊕) A small peninsula jutting into the Mississippi, Mud Island is downtown Memphis' best-loved green space. The top part of the peninsula is a residential subdivision, while the bottom is home to the delightful **Mud Island River Park**. Hop the monorail ($4, or free with museum admission) or walk across the bridge to the park, where you can jog, rent bikes, or wade through a super-cool scale model of the Mississippi, which empties into a 1.3-million-gallon 'Gulf of Mexico' where visitors tool around in pedal boats. The park's **Mississippi River Museum** (adult/child $8/5; ⊙10am-5pm Apr-May & Sep-Oct, to 6pm Jun-Aug, closed Mon) has a cool full-size replica of a packet boat and other historical displays.

FREE | Center for Southern Folklore
ARTS CENTER

(☎901-525-3655; www.southernfolklore.com; 119 S Main St; ⊙11am-6pm Mon-Sat, to 5pm winter) A well-tended community space with a cafe, craft gallery and frequent (free!) local music performances and film screenings.

BEALE STREET

The pedestrian-only stretch of Beale St is a 24-hour carnival zone, where you'll find deep-fried funnel cakes, to-go beer counters, and music, music, music. Although locals don't hang out here much, visitors tend to get a kick out of the ribald, party-happy atmosphere.

Memphis

Memphis Rock 'n' Soul Museum MUSEUM
(www.memphisrocknsoul.org; cnr Lt George W Lee Ave & 3rd St; adult/child $11/8; ☉10am-7pm) The Smithsonian's museum, next to FedEx Forum, examines how African American and white music mingled in the Mississippi Delta to create modern sound. The audio tour has more than 100 songs.

Gibson Beale Street Showcase FACTORY TOUR
(www.gibson.com; 145 Lt George W Lee Ave; admission $10, no children under 5; ☉tours 11am-4pm Mon-Sat, noon-4pm Sun) Take the fascinating 45-minute tour of this enormous place to see master craftspeople transform solid blocks of wood into legendary Gibson guitars. Tours leave on the hour.

Orpheum Theatre THEATER
(www.orpheum-memphis.com; 203 S Main St) Originally built for vaudeville, the Orpheum has been restored to its glittering 1928 glory. Today you can catch big comedy and Broadway shows; but beware – the ghost of a pig-tailed little girl named Mary is said to giggle eerily between acts. Tours available – call ahead (☎901-525-7800).

A Schwab's HISTORIC STORE
(163 Beale St; ☎9am-5pm Mon-Sat) The original dry-goods store has three floors of voodoo powders, $1 neckties and Elvis shot glasses.

EAST OF DOWNTOWN

TOP CHOICE Sun Studio STUDIO TOUR
(www.sunstudio.com; 706 Union Ave; adult/child $12/free; ☉10am-6pm) It doesn't look like much from outside, but this dusty storefront is ground zero for American rock and roll music. Starting in the early 1950s, Sun's Sam Phillips recorded blues artists such as Howlin' Wolf, BB King and Ike Turner, followed by the rockabilly dynasty of Jerry Lee Lewis, Johnny Cash, Roy Orbison and, of course, the King himself (who started here in 1953). Today packed 40-minute guided tours through the tiny studio offer a chance to hear original tapes of historic recording sessions. Guides are witty and full of anecdotes; many are musicians themselves. Pose for photos in the old recording studio on the 'X' where Elvis once stood, or buy a CD of the 'Million Dollar Quartet,' Sun's spontaneous 1956 jam session between Elvis, Johnny Cash, Carl Perkins and Jerry Lee Lewis.

From here, you can hop on the studio's free shuttle (hourly, starting at 11:15am), which does a loop between Sun Studio, Beale St and Graceland.

Pink Palace Museum & Planetarium MUSEUM, PLANETARIUM
(www.memphismuseums.org; 3050 Central Ave; adult/child $9.75/6.25, ☉9am-5pm Mon-Sat, noon-5pm Sun) The 1923 building was built as a residence for Piggly Wiggly founder Clarence Saunders and opened in 1996 as a natural- and cultural-history museum. It mixes fossils, Civil War exhibits and a replica of the original 1916 Piggly Wiggly, the world's first self-service grocery store.

Children's Museum of Memphis MUSEUM
(www.cmom.com; 2525 Central Ave; admission $10; ☉9am-5pm; ⓜ) Gives the kids a chance to let loose and play in, on and with exhibits such as an airplane cockpit, tornado generator and waterwheel.

OVERTON PARK
Off Poplar Ave in Midtown, stately homes surround Overton Park, a 342-acre rolling green oasis in the middle of this often gritty city. If Beale St is Memphis' heart, then Overton Park is its lungs.

Memphis Zoo ZOO
(www.memphiszoo.org; 2000 Prentiss Pl; adult/child $15/10; ☉9am-4pm Mar-Oct, to 4pm Nov-Feb; ⓜ) At the park's northwestern corner, this world-class zoo hosts two giant panda stars, Ya Ya and Le Le, in a $16-million exhibit on native Chinese wildlife and habitat. Other residents include the full gamut of monkeys, polar bears, penguins, eagles, sea lions and so on. Imagine an animal, the zoo probably has it.

Brooks Museum of Art GALLERY
(www.brooksmuseum.org; 1934 Poplar Ave; adult/child $7/3; ☉10am-4pm Wed-Sat, to 8pm Thu, 11am-5pm Sun) At the park's western fringe, this well-regarded art museum has an excellent permanent collection encompassing everything from Renaissance sculpture to Impressionists (eg Renoir) to abstract expressionists (eg Robert Motherwell).

Levitt Shell AMPHITHEATER
(www.levittshell.org) This historic band shell was the site of Elvis' first concert, in 1954. Today the mod-looking white shell hosts free concerts all summer.

SOUTH OF DOWNTOWN

TOP CHOICE Graceland ELVIS' HOUSE
(☎901-332-3322, 800-238-2000; www.elvis.com; Elvis Presley Blvd/US 51; tours adult/child house-

only \$31/14, full \$35/17; ☺9am-5pm Mon-Sat, to 4pm Sun, shorter hr & closed Tue winter) If you only make one stop in Memphis, it ought to be here: the sublimely kitschy, gloriously bizarre home of the King of Rock and Roll.

Though born in Mississippi, Elvis Presley was a true son of Memphis, raised in the Lauderdale Courts public housing projects, inspired by the blues in the Beale St clubs, and discovered at Sun Studio on Union Ave. In the spring of 1957, the already-famous 22-year-old spent \$100,000 on a Colonial-style mansion, named Graceland by its previous owners. Priscilla Presley (who divorced Elvis in 1973) opened Graceland to tours in 1982, and now millions come here to pay homage to the King and gawk at the infamous decor. The King himself had the place redecorated in 1974; with a 15ft couch, fake waterfall, yellow vinyl walls and green shag-carpet ceiling – it's a virtual textbook of ostentatious '70s style. Elvis died here (in the upstairs bathroom) from heart failure in 1977. Throngs of fans still weep at his grave, next to the swimming pool out back.

You begin your tour at the high-tech visitor plaza on the other side of seedy Elvis Presley Blvd. Book ahead in the busy season to ensure a prompt tour time. The basic self-guided mansion tour comes with a headset audio narration with the voices of Elvis, Priscilla and Lisa Marie. Buy a package to see the entire estate, or pay extra for additional attractions: several clothing museums, the car museum, and two custom airplanes (check out the blue-and-gold private bathroom on the *Lisa Marie,* a Convair 880 Jet). Parking costs \$10.

Graceland is 9 miles south of downtown on US 51, also called 'Elvis Presley Blvd.' Nondrivers can take bus 43 from downtown, or hop on the free Sun Studio shuttle.

Stax Museum of American Soul Music   MUSEUM

(www.staxmuseum.com; 926 E McLemore Ave; adult/child \$12/9; ☺10am-5pm Mon-Sat, 1-5pm Sun Mar-Oct, closed Mon Nov-Mar) Wanna get funky? Head directly to Soulsville USA, where this 17,000-sq-ft museum sits on the site of the old Stax recording studio. This venerable spot was soul music's epicenter in the 1960s, when Otis Redding, Booker T and the MGs and Wilson Pickett recorded here. Dive into soul-music history with photos, displays of '60s and '70s peacock clothing and, above all, Isaac Hayes' 1972 Superfly

Cadillac outfitted with shag-fur carpeting and 24-carat-gold exterior trim.

Full Gospel Tabernacle Church   CHURCH

(www.algreenmusic.com; 787 Hale Rd; ☺services 11:30am & 4pm Sun) If you're in town on a Sunday, put on your least-wrinkled pants and head to services at South Memphis, where soul music legend turned reverend Al Green presides over a powerful choir. Visitors are welcome, and usually take up about half the pews. Join in the whooping 'hallelujahs,' but don't forget the tithe (about \$1 is fine). Green is not around every single weekend, but the services are a fascinating cultural experience nonetheless.

☞ Tours

TOP CHOICE American Dream Safari   DRIVING TOUR

(☎901-527-8870; www.americandreamsafari.com; walking tour per person \$15, driving tours per vehicle from \$125) Southern culture junkie Tad Pierson shows you the quirky, personal side of Memphis – juke joints, gospel churches, eerie decaying buildings – on foot or by car (in his pink Cadillac). Ask about day trips to the Delta and special photography tours.

Memphis Rock Tours   DRIVING TOUR

(☎901-359-3102; www.shangrilaprojects.com; 2-person tour \$75) Quirky custom tours of music sites and local restaurants.

Blues City Tours   BUS TOUR

(☎901-522-9229; www.bluescitytours.com; adult/child from \$24/16) A variety of bus tours, including an Elvis tour.

Memphis Riverboats   BOAT TOUR

(☎901-527-5694, 800-221-6197; www.memphisriverboats.net; adult/child from \$20/10) Sightseeing and dinner cruises on the Mississippi.

✯✯ Festivals & Events

International Blues Challenge   MUSIC

(www.blues.org) Sponsored by the Blues Foundation, each January/February blues acts do battle in front of a panel of judges.

Memphis in May   CULTURAL

(www.memphisinmay.org) Every Friday, Saturday and Sunday in May something's cookin', whether it's the Beale St Music Festival, the barbecue contest or the grand finale sunset symphony.

Mid-South Fair   FAIR

(www.midsouthfair.org) Since 1856, folks come out each September to this combo amusement park and agricultural fair.

🛏 Sleeping

Cheap and ultracheap chain motels lie off I-40, exit 279, across the river in West Memphis, AR. Prices jump during the Memphis in May festival.

DOWNTOWN

TOP CHOICE **Talbot Heirs**   GUESTHOUSE **$$**
(☎901-527-9772, 800-955-3956; www.talbothouse.com; 99 S 2nd St; ste from $130; ✳🕾) Inconspicuously located on the 2nd floor of a busy downtown street, this cheerful guesthouse is one of Memphis' best kept and most unique secrets. Suites are more like studio apartments than hotel rooms, with Oriental rugs and funky local artwork, and kitchens stocked with snacks. Innkeepers Tom and Sandy know all the best local restaurants and bars – just ask. Parking costs $10.

Peabody Hotel   HOTEL **$$$**
(☎901-529-4000; www.peabodymemphis.com; 149 Union Ave; r from $209; ✳🕾≋) The Mississippi Delta's most storied hotel, the Peabody has been catering to a Who's Who of Southern gentry since the 1860s. The hotel's current incarnation, a 13-story Italian Renaissance Revival-style building, dates to the 1920s. The Peabody continues to be a social center, with a spa, shops, various restaurants and a fabulously atmospheric marble-and-gold lobby bar. The daily march of the lobby fountain's resident mallard ducks (p345) is a legendary Memphis tradition.

Inn at Hunt Phelan   B&B **$$**
(☎901-525-8225; www.huntphelan.com; 533 Beale St; r from $155; 🅿✳🕾) Outside the gates are dystopian warehouses and vacant lots. But inside the gates it's still 1828, the year this aristocratic mansion was built. Sip complimentary evening cocktails by the courtyard fountain and wander the 4.5-acre gardens before retiring to your four-poster bed (or heading to the Beale St bars, just down the road).

Sleep Inn at Court Square   HOTEL **$$**
(☎901-522-9700; www.sleepinn.com; 400 N Front St; r from $110; ✳🕾) Our pick of the cheaper downtown digs, this stubby stucco box has pleasant, airy rooms with flat screen TVs. Parking is $12.

MIDTOWN

TOP CHOICE **Pilgrim House Hostel**   HOSTEL **$**
(☎901-273-8341; 1000 S Cooper St; dm/r $15/30; 🅿✳@🕾) Yes, it's in a church. No, no one will try to convert you but the chatty young live-in staff may well invite you for a beer down the street, in Midtown's trendy Cooper-Young neighborhood. An international crowd plays cards and chats (no alcohol) in a sunny, open common area resembling an IKEA catalog. Dorms and private rooms are clean and spare. All guests must do a brief daily chore, like taking out the trash.

GRACELAND AREA

Heartbreak Hotel   HOTEL **$$**
(☎901-332-1000, 877-777-0606; www.elvis.com/epheartbreakhotel/; 3677 Elvis Presley Blvd; d from $112; 🅿✳@🕾≋) At the end of Lonely St (seriously) across from Graceland, this basic hotel is tarted up with all things Elvis. Ramp up the kitsch with one of the themed suites, such as the red-velvet monstrosity that is the Burnin' Love room.

Memphis Graceland RV Park & Campground   CAMPGROUND **$**
(☎901-396-7125; www.elvis.com; 3691 Elvis Presley Blvd; tent sites/cabins from $23/42; 🅿✳≋) Next to Graceland and owned by Elvis Presley Enterprises. Keep Lisa Marie in business when you camp out or sleep in the no-frills log cabins (with shared bathrooms).

Days Inn Graceland   MOTEL **$**
(☎901-346-5500; www.daysinn.com; 3839 Elvis Presley Blvd; r from $85; 🅿✳🕾) With a guitar-shaped pool, 24-hour Elvis channel, and neon Cadillacs on the roof, the Days Inn manages to out-Elvis the neighboring Heartbreak Hotel. Guest rooms themselves are clean but nothing special.

🍴 Eating

Locals come to blows over which of the city's chopped-pork sandwiches or dry-rubbed ribs are the best. Barbecue joints are scattered across the city; the ugliest exteriors often yield the tastiest goods. Beale St is lined with corporate barbecue and soul-food joints; few are worth the crowds or the price. Hip young locals head to the South Main Arts District or Midtown's Cooper-Young neighborhood for dinner and drinks.

DOWNTOWN

TOP CHOICE **Gus's World Famous Fried Chicken**   CHICKEN **$**
(☎901-527-4877; 310 S Front St; mains $5-9; ⊙11am-9pm Sun-Thu, to 10pm Fri & Sat) Fried-chicken connoisseurs across the globe twitch in their sleep at night, dreaming about the gossamer-light fried chicken at this down-

town concrete bunker. On busy nights, waits can top an hour. So worth it.

Alcenia's
SOUTHERN $

(alcenias.com; 317 N Main St; mains $6-9; ⊙11am-5pm Tue-Fri, 9am-3pm Sat) The only thing sweeter than Alcenia's famous 'ghetto juice' (a diabetes-inducing fruit drink) is owner Betty-Joyce 'BJ' Chester-Tamayo – don't be surprised to receive a kiss on the top of the head as soon as you sit down. The lunch menu at this funky little gold- and purple-painted cafe rotates daily – look for killer fried chicken and catfish, melt-in-your-mouth spiced cabbage and an exquisite eggy custard pie.

Charlie Vergos' Rendezvous
BARBECUE $$

(☎901-523-2746; www.hogsfly.com; 52 S 2nd St; mains $7-18; ⊙4:30-10:30pm Tue-Thu, 11am-11pm Fri & Sat) Tucked in an alleyway off Union Ave, this subterranean institution sells an astonishing 5 tons of its exquisite dry-rubbed ribs weekly. Friendly service and walls plastered with historic memorabilia make eating here an event. Expect a wait.

Arcade
DINER $

(www.arcaderestaurant.com; 540 S Main St; mains $6-8; ⊙7am-3pm, plus dinner Fri) Elvis used to eat at this ultra-retro diner, Memphis' oldest. Crowds still pack in for sweet-potato pancakes and cheeseburgers.

Dyer's
FAST FOOD $

(www.dyersonbeale.com; 205 Beale St; mains $6-8; ⊙11am-1am Sun-Thu, to 5am Fri & Sat) Dyer's legendary deep-fried burgers, fried using the same (continuously filtered) cooking grease since 1912, will sound far less disgusting when it's 3am and you've been sucking back beers on Beale St all night.

EAST OF DOWNTOWN

TOP CHOICE Cozy Corner
BARBECUE $$

(www.cozycornerbbq.com; 745 N Pkwy; mains $5-16; ⊙10:30am-5pm Tue-Sat, later in summer) Slouch in a torn vinyl booth and devour an entire barbecued Cornish game hen, the house specialty at this pug-ugly cult favorite. Ribs and wings are spectacular too, and the fluffy, silken sweet-potato pie is an A-plus specimen of the classic Southern dessert.

Restaurant Iris
NEW SOUTHERN $$$

(☎901-590-2828; www.restaurantiris.com; 2146 Monroe Ave; mains $23-34; ⊙5-10pm Mon-Sat, Sun brunch 3rd Sun each month) Chef Kelly English richly deserved his recent James Beard Award nomination, one of a pile of accolades he's accumulated since opening Iris in 2008. His avant-garde Creole menu sends foodies into paroxysms of delight, with playful dishes like a 'knuckle sandwich' of tarragon-flecked lobster, or an oyster-stuffed steak 'surf 'n' turf.' The setting, in a turreted cottage on a residential Midtown block, is so low-profile it feels like a speakeasy.

Sweet Grass
SOUTHERN $$

(☎901-278-0273; www.sweetgrassmemphis.com; 937 S Cooper St; mains $16-23; ⊙5:30pm-late Tue-Sun, 11am-2pm Sun) Contemporary Low County cuisine (the seafood-heavy cooking of the South Carolina and Georgia coasts) wins raves at this sleek new Midtown bistro. Shrimp and grits, a classic fisherman's breakfast, is a crowd-pleaser.

Bar-B-Q Shop
BARBECUE $$

(www.dancingpigs.com; 1782 Madison Ave; mains $9-16; ⊙11am-8:45pm) Chopped pork on grilled Texas toast and barbecued spaghetti (just try it) are house favorites at this friendly neighborhood spot, whose spacious wooden booths are popular with families.

Payne's Bar-B-Q
BARBECUE $

(1762 Lamar Ave; mains $4-6; ⊙11am-6:30pm Tue-Sat) We'd say this converted gas station has the best chopped-pork sandwich in town, but we don't want to have to fight anyone. Decide for yourself.

🍷 Drinking & Entertainment

Many Memphis restaurants and bars mix food, drinks and music, so it's easy to turn a meal into a party. Beale St is the obvious spot for live blues, country, rock and jazz. Cover for most clubs is free or only a few bucks. Beale St warms up early, and its bars are open all day, while neighborhood clubs tend to start filling up around 10pm. Last call for alcohol is 3am, but bars sometimes close earlier on quiet nights. Hip locals head to the Cooper-Young neighborhood for everything from margarita bars to Irish pubs. To find out what's up tonight, check the Memphis Flyer's online calendar (www.memphisflyer.com).

Bars

TOP CHOICE Earnestine & Hazel's
BAR

(531 S Main St) One of the great dive bars has a 2nd floor full of rusty bedsprings and claw-foot tubs, remnants of its brothel past. Climb the creaky stairs to shoot the breeze with Nate, a courtly gentleman who regales you with tales of Memphis past as he pours you a Miller Lite – he works the upstairs bar

on weekends. The Soul Burger, the bar's only food, is the stuff of legend. Watch out for ghosts. Things heat up after midnight.

Cove
BAR

(www.thecovememphis.com; 2559 Broad Ave) Far from the Beale St crowds, this hipster-ish new dive rocks a nautical theme while serving retro cocktails (sidecars, Singapore Slings) and upscale bar snacks (oysters on the half shell, chips with fresh anchovies). A good place to meet locals.

Silky O'Sullivan's
BAR

(silkyosullivans.com; 183 Beale St) Party-happy youth swill 'divers' out of yellow plastic buckets while goats graze in the courtyard of this massive bizarro Beale St tavern.

Live Music

Wild Bill's
BLUES

(1580 Vollentine Ave; ⊙10pm-late Fri & Sat) Don't even think of showing up at this gritty, hole-in-the-wall juke joint before midnight. Order a 40oz beer and a basket of wings then sit back to watch some of the greatest blues acts in Memphis. Expect some stares from the locals; it's worth it for the kickass, ultra-authentic jams.

TOP CHOICE Hi-Tone Cafe
LIVE MUSIC

(www.hitonememphis.com; 1913 Poplar Ave) Near Overton Park, this unassuming little dive is one of the city's best places to hear live local bands and touring indie acts.

Young Avenue Deli
LIVE MUSIC

(www.youngavenuedeli.com; 2119 Young Ave) This Midtown favorite has food, pool, live music and a hip, laid-back young crowd.

Rum Boogie
BLUES

(www.rumboogie.com; 182 Beale St) Huge, popular and noisy, this Cajun-themed Beale club hops every night to the tunes of the house blues band.

Minglewood Hall
CONCERT VENUE

(www.minglewoodhall.com; 1555 Madison) In a former bread factory, this new space is part concert venue, part tattoo studio, part cafe.

🛍 Shopping

Beale St abounds with cheesy souvenir shops, while Cooper-Young is the place for boutiques and bookshops.

Lanksy Brothers
CLOTHING

(149 Union Ave) The 'Clothier to the King,' this mid-century men's shop once outfitted Elvis with his two-tone shirts. Today it has a retro line of menswear, plus gifts and women's clothes. In the Peabody Hotel.

Burke's Book Store
BOOKS

(936 S Cooper St) A delightfully disorganized 122-year-old bookshop, with an emphasis on Southern literature.

Memphis Flea Market
MARKET

(777 Walnut Grove Rd, at The Agricenter) Nicknamed 'The Big One,' this 1000-plus vendor junque and antiques extravaganza is held on the third Saturday and Sunday of each month.

ℹ Information

Almost all hotels, and many restaurants, have free wi-fi.

Commercial Appeal (www.commercialappeal.com) Daily newspaper.

Main post office (555 S 3rd St)

Memphis Flyer (www.memphisflyer.com) Free weekly distributed on Thursday; has entertainment listings.

Police station (☏901-545-2677; 545 S Main St)

Public library (33 S Front St; ⊙10am-5pm Mon-Fri) Computers with free internet access.

Regional Medical Center (☏901-545-7100; 877 Jefferson Ave) Has the only level-one trauma center in the region.

Tennessee State Visitor Center (☏901-543-5333, 888-633-9099; www.memphistravel.com; 119 N Riverside Dr; ⊙9am-5pm Nov-Mar, to 6pm Apr-Oct) Brochures for the whole state.

ℹ Getting There & Around

Memphis International Airport (MEM; ☏901-922-8000; www.memphisairport.org; 2491 Winchester Rd) is 12 miles southeast of downtown via I-55; taxis to downtown cost about $30.

Memphis Area Transit Authority (www.mata transit.com; 444 N Main St; fares $1.50) operates local buses; 2A and 32A go to the airport.

MATA's vintage **trolleys** ($1, every 12 minutes) ply Main St and Front St downtown. **Greyhound** (www.greyhound.com; 203 Union Ave) is right downtown, as is **Central Station** (www.amtrak.com; 545 S Main St), the Amtrak terminal.

Shiloh National Military Park

'No soldier who took part in the two days' engagement at Shiloh ever spoiled for a fight again,' said one veteran of the bloody 1862 battle, which took place among these lovely fields and forests. During the fight 3400 soldiers died, and the Confederate forces were eventually repelled by the Union.

The **Shiloh National Military Park** (www.nps.gov/shil; per vehicle $5; ⊙park dawn-dusk, visitor center 8am-5pm) is located just north of the Mississippi border near the town of Crump, TN. The visitor center gives out maps and shows a video about the battle, and sells an audio tour.

The vast park can only be seen by car. Sights along the route include the Shiloh National Cemetery, an overlook of the Cumberland River where Union reinforcement troops arrived by ship, and various markers and monuments.

Nashville

Imagine you're an aspiring country singer arriving in downtown Nashville after days of hitchhiking, with nothing but your battered guitar on your back. Gaze up at the neon lights of Lower Broadway, take a deep breath of smoky, beer-perfumed air, feel the boot-stompin' rumble from deep inside the crowded honky-tonks, and say to yourself 'I've made it.'

For country-music fans and wannabe songwriters all over the world, a trip to Nashville is the ultimate pilgrimage. Think of any song involving a pickup truck, a bottle of booze, a no-good woman or a late, lamented hound dog, and chances are it came from Nashville. Since the 1920s the city has been attracting musicians who have taken the country genre from the 'hillbilly music' of the early 20th century to the slick 'Nashville sound' of the 1960s to the punk-tinged alt-country of the 1990s.

Nashville has many attractions to keep you busy, from the Country Music Hall of Fame and the revered Grand Ole Opry House to rough blues bars, historic buildings and big-name sports. It also has friendly people, a lively university community, excellent fried chicken and an unrivaled assortment of tacky souvenirs.

History

In 1925, this river port became known for its live-music radio program *Barn Dance*, later nicknamed the *Grand Ole Opry*. Its popularity soared, the city proclaimed itself the 'country-music capital of the world' and recording studios sprang up in Music Row.

Today Nashville is the second most populous city in Tennessee, with more than a doz-

NASHVILLE'S TOP EXPERIENCES

» Watching the singin', stompin', fiddlin' extravaganza at the venerable **Grand Ole Opry** (p354)

» Feasting on diabolically spicy fried chicken at 3am at **Prince's Hot Chicken** (p356)

» Whooping it up at **Tootsie's Orchid Lounge** (p358), the grandmama of all honky-tonks

» Shopping for vintage cowboy boots at **Katy K's Ranch Dressing** (p355)

» Admiring Elvis' gold Caddy and other treasures at the vast **Country Music Hall of Fame** (p351)

en colleges and universities and an economy based on music, tourism, health care and publishing.

⊙ Sights & Activities

Nashville sits on a rise beside the Cumberland River, with the state capitol situated at the highest point.

DOWNTOWN

The historic 2nd Ave N business area was the center of the cotton trade in the 1870s and 1880s, when most of the Victorian warehouses were built; note the cast-iron and masonry facades. Today it's the heart of the **District**, with shops, restaurants, underground saloons and nightclubs. Two blocks west, **Printers Alley** is a narrow cobblestoned lane known for its nightlife since the 1940s. Along the Cumberland River, Riverfront Park is a landscaped promenade featuring **Fort Nashborough**, a 1930s replica of the city's original outpost.

TOP CHOICE **Country Music Hall of Fame & Museum**   MUSEUM
(www.countrymusichalloffame.com; 222 5th Ave S; adult/child $22/15; ⊙9am-5pm) 'Honor Thy Music' is the catchphrase of this monumental museum, reflecting the near-biblical importance of country music to Nashville's soul. See case upon case of artifacts including Patsy Cline's cocktail gown, Johnny Cash's guitar, Elvis' gold Cadillac and Conway Twitty's yearbook picture (back when he was Harold Jenkins). There are written

THE SOUTH TENNESSEE

exhibits tracing country's roots, computer touch screens to allow access to recordings and photos from the Country Music Foundation's enormous archives and walk-in listening booths. The fact- and music-filled **audio tour** (additional $5) is narrated by contemporary country musicians. From here you can also take the **Studio B Tour** (1hr tour adult/child $13/11), which shuttles you to Radio Corporation of America's (RCA's) famed Music Row studio, where Elvis recorded 'Are You Lonesome Tonight?' and Dolly Parton cut 'I Will Always Love You.'

Ryman Auditorium   HISTORIC BUILDING
(www.ryman.com; 116 5th Ave N; self-guided tour adult/child $13/6.50, backstage tour $17/10.50; ☺9am-4pm) The so-called 'Mother Church of Country Music' has hosted a laundry list of 20th-century performers, from Martha Graham to Elvis to Katherine Hepburn to Bob Dylan. The soaring brick tabernacle was built in 1890 by wealthy riverboat captain Thomas Ryman to house religious revivals, and watching a show from one of its 2000 seats can still be described as a spiritual experience. The *Grand Ole Opry* took place here for 31 years, until it moved out to the Opryland complex in Music Valley in 1974. Today the *Opry* returns to the Ryman during winter.

Tennessee State Capitol   HISTORIC BUILDING
(Charlotte Ave; tours free; ☺tours 9am-4pm Mon-Fri) At the northeast edge of downtown, this 1845 Greek Revival building was built from local limestone and marble by slaves and prison inmates working alongside European artisans. Around back, steep stairs lead down to the **Tennessee Bicentennial Mall**, whose outdoor walls are covered with historical facts about Tennessee's history, and the wonderful daily **Farmers Market**.

FREE Tennessee State Museum   MUSEUM
(www.tnmuseum.org; 5th Ave, btwn Union & Deaderick Sts; ☺10am-5pm Tue-Sat, 1-5pm Sun) For history buffs, this engaging but not flashy museum offers a worthy look at the state's past, with Native American handicrafts, a life-size log cabin and quirky historical artifacts such as President Andrew Jackson's inaugural hat.

Frist Center for the Visual Arts   GALLERY
(www.fristcenter.org; 919 Broadway; adult/child $10/free; ☺10am-5:30pm Mon, Tue, Wed & Sat, to 9pm Thu & Fri, 1-5pm Sun) Hosts traveling exhibitions of everything from American folk

THE SOUTH NASHVILLE

art to Picasso in the grand, refurbished post office building.

MIDTOWN

Along West End Ave, starting at 21st Ave, sits prestigious **Vanderbilt University**, founded in 1883 by railway magnate Cornelius Vanderbilt. The 330-acre campus buzzes with some 12,000 students, and student culture influences much of Midtown's vibe.

Parthenon   PARK, GALLERY
(www.parthenon.org; 2600 West End Ave; adult/child $6/4; ⊘9am-4:30pm Tue-Sat, plus Sun in summer) Yes, that is indeed a reproduction Athenian parthenon sitting in **Centennial Park**. Originally built in 1897 for Tennessee's Centennial Exposition and rebuilt in 1930 due to popular demand, the full-scale plaster copy of the 438-BC original now houses an art museum with a collection of American paintings and a 42ft statue of the Greek goddess Athena.

Music Row   NEIGHBORHOOD
Just west of downtown, a stretch of 16th and 17th Aves are home to the production companies, agents, managers and promoters who run Nashville's country-music industry. There's not much to see, but you can pay to cut your own record at some of the smaller studios (about $25 to $100 an hour). 'World's Greatest Love Songs on the Kazoo,' anyone?

MUSIC VALLEY

This suburban tourist zone is about 10 miles northeast of downtown at Hwy 155/Briley Pkwy exits 11 and 12B, and reachable by bus.

Grand Ole Opry House   TOUR, MUSEUM
(☑615-871-6779; www.opry.com; 2802 Opryland Dr; tours adult/child $17.50/12.50) This unassuming modern brick building seats 4400 for the *Grand Ole Opry* on Friday and Saturday from March to November. Guided backstage tours are offered daily by reservation – book online up to two weeks ahead. Across the plaza, a small, free museum (⊘10:30am-6pm Mar-Dec) tells the story of the Opry with wax characters, colorful costumes and dioramas.

Gibson Bluegrass Showcase   GUITAR FACTORY
(www.gibson.com; 161 Opry Mills Dr; ⊘10am-9:30pm Mon-Sat, to 7pm Sun) Through the glass you can see banjos, mandolins and resonator guitars being made.

PLANTATIONS

Hermitage   MUSEUM, GARDENS
(www.thehermitage.com; 4580 Rachel's Lane; adult/child $18/12; ⊘8:30am-5pm Apr-Oct, 9am-4:30pm Oct-Mar) The former home of seventh president Andrew Jackson lies 15 miles east of downtown. The 1000-acre plantation is a peek into what life was like for a Mid-South gentleman farmer in the 19th century. Tour the Federal-style brick mansion, now a furnished house museum with costumed interpreters, and see Jackson's original 1804 log cabin and the old slave quarters (Jackson was a lifelong supporter of slavery, at times owning up to 150 slaves; a special exhibit tells their stories). The arcadian gardens and grounds are lovely to wander, though somewhat marred by the highway passing nearby.

Belle Meade Plantation
HISTORIC BUILDING

(www.bellemeadeplantation.com; 5025 Harding Pike; adult/child $16/8; ⏰9am-5pm Mon-Sat, 11am-5pm Sun) The Harding-Jackson family began raising thoroughbreds here (6 miles west of Nashville) in the early 1800s. Every horse entered in the Kentucky Derby in the past five years is a descendant of Belle Meade's studly sire, Bonnie Scotland, who died in 1880. The 1853 mansion is open to visitors, as are various interesting outbuildings, including a model slave cabin.

👉 Tours

Ask at the visitor center for a list of the many theme tours available in Nashville.

🏆 TOP CHOICE NashTrash
BUS TOUR

(☎615-226-7300; www.nashtrash.com; 900 8th Ave N; 1½hr tours $32) The big-haired 'Jugg Sisters' lead a campy frolic through the risqué side of Nashville history while guests sip BYO booze. Buy in advance: tours can sell out *months* in advance.

Tommy's Tours
BUS TOUR

(☎615-335-2863; www.tommystours.com; tours from $40) Joke-cracking local Tommy Garmon leads highly entertaining three-hour tours of country music sights.

General Jackson Showboat
BOAT TOUR

(☎615-458-3900; www.generaljackson.com; tours from $46) Paddleboat sightseeing cruises of varying length on the Cumberland River, some with music and food.

🎆 Festivals & Events

CMA Music Festival
MUSIC

(www.cmafest.com) Draws tens of thousands of country-music fans to town each June.

Tennessee State Fair
FAIR

(www.tennesseestatefair.org) Nine days of racing pigs, mule-pulls and cake bake-offs every September.

🛌 Sleeping

Bargain-bin chain motels cluster on all sides of downtown, along I-40 and I-65. Music Valley has a glut of family-friendly midprice chains.

DOWNTOWN

🏆 TOP CHOICE Union Station Hotel
HOTEL $$$

(☎615-726-1001; www.unionstationhotelnashville. com; 1001 Broadway; r from $209; P❄🐾) This soaring Romanesque stone castle was Nashville's train station back in the days when travel was a grand affair; today's it's downtown's most iconic hotel. The vaulted lobby is dressed in peach and gold with inlaid marble floors and a stained-glass ceiling. Rooms are tastefully modern, with flat-screen TVs and deep soaking tubs. Parking costs $20.

Hermitage Hotel
HOTEL $$$

(☎615-244-3121, 888-888-9414; www.thehermitagehotel.com; 231 6th Ave N; r from $259; P❄🐾) Nashville's first million-dollar hotel was a hit with the socialites when it opened in 1910.

VIVA NASHVEGAS!

Brash, glittery Nashville is proud to have earned the nickname NashVegas. So put on your rhinestone cowboy boots and explore the weird and wild side of town.

'Outlaw Country' star Willie Nelson sold all his worldly goods to pay off $16.7 million in unpaid taxes in the early 1990s. You can see them at the **Willie Nelson Museum** (www.willienelsongeneralstore; McGavock Pike, Music Valley; admission $10; ⏰8:30am-9pm), which might as well be called the Everything-But-Willie-Nelson's-Used-Toothbrush Museum. Up the street is the **Music City Wax Museum** (2515 McGavock Pike; admission $3; ⏰8am-10pm), with eerie, corpse-like statues of country stars dead and alive.

The Tuesday-night **Doyle and Debbie** show at the Station Inn (p358) is a cult-hit parody of a washed-up country-music duo.

Printer's Alley, once the epicenter of NashVegas vice, has cleaned up but still has at least one bar advertising **nude karaoke**. That's all we have to say about that.

Also downtown, the **Charlie Daniels Museum** (110 2nd Ave N; admission free; ⏰9am-late) is less museum and more gift shop, hawking everything from bacon-scented air fresheners to T-shirts bearing the likeness of 'Devil Went Down to Georgia' singer Daniels, who looks like a chicken-fried Santa Claus.

In the quirky 12th Ave S neighborhood, a former stylist to New York City's drag queens stocks bouffant wigs, vintage cowboy boots and handmade bolo ties at **Katy K's Ranch Dressing** (2407 12th Ave S).

JACK DANIEL'S DISTILLERY

The irony of the Jack Daniel's Distillery (www.jackdaniels.com; Rte 1, Lynchburg; tours free; ⊙9am-4:30pm) being in a 'dry county' is lost on no one – local liquor laws dictate that no hard stuff can be sold within county lines, thus the distillery cannot give out samples of its famous whiskey. But it can give hour-long free tours, where visitors are encouraged to take long sniffs of the golden brew. It's the oldest registered distillery in the US: the folks at Jack Daniels have been dripping whiskey through layers of charcoal then aging it in oak barrels since 1866. The distillery is located off Hwy 55 in the diminutive town of Lynchburg, which freely admits that all visitors are either here to see the distillery or they are lost.

The lobby feels like a Czar's palace, every surface covered in rich tapestries and ornate carvings. Rooms are generic upscale, with plush beds and mahogany furniture. Parking costs $20.

Indigo Nashville Downtown HOTEL $$
(☑877-846-3446; www.ichotelsgroup.com; 301 Union St; r from $139; P⚹☎) Most of downtown's midprice hotels are corporate behemoths catering to conventioneers. Not so the newly opened Indigo, with its mod high-ceiling lobby, space age violet-and-lime color schemes, and arty floor-to-ceiling photomurals of Nashville landmarks. Parking is $20.

WEST END

Music City Hostel HOSTEL $
(☑615-692-1277; www.musiccityhostel.com; 1809 Patterson St; dm/r $25/70; P⚹@☎) These squat brick bungalows are less than scenic, but Nashville's only hostel is lively and welcoming, with bike rental, common kitchen, a computer and free wi-fi. The crowd is young, international and fun – you can almost guarantee an evening jam session in the courtyard. Many kickin' West End bars are within walking distance.

Hutton Hotel HOTEL $$$
(☑615-340-9333; www.huttonhotel.com; 1808 West End Ave; r from $189; P⚹@☎) Nashville's newest hotel is also its slickest, riffing on mid-Century Modern design with bamboo-paneled walls and grown-up beanbags in the lobby. Rust- and chocolate-colored rooms have miniature cactus gardens and a number of ecofriendly touches.

1501 Linden Manor B&B $$
(☑615-298-2701; www.nashville-bed-breakfast. com; 1501 Linden Ave; r from $125; P⚹☎☒) The husband-and-wife owners have filled this yellow Victorian cottage with antiques collected through their world travels – Persian rugs, Asian carvings, old Victrolas. Have homemade egg soufflés for breakfast in the sunny dining room, or dip your hand into the 'bottomless cookie jar' anytime.

MUSIC VALLEY

Gaylord Opryland Hotel RESORT $$$
(☑615-889-1000, 866-972-6779; www.gaylord hotels.com; 2800 Opryland Dr; r from $199; P⚹@☎☒) This whopping 2881-room hotel is a universe unto itself. Why set foot outdoors when you could ride a paddleboat along an artificial river, eat sushi beneath a faux waterfall in an indoor garden, shop for bolo ties in a model 19th-century town, or sip Scotch in an antebellum-style mansion, all *inside* the hotel's three massive glass atriums.

Nashville KOA Kampground CAMPGROUND $
(☑615-889-0282, 800-562-7789; www.koa.com; 2626 Music Valley Dr; campsites $39, cabins from $60, lodges $129; P☎☒) Popular with RVers, this well-manicured, wholesome campground also has tent sites, cabins, and lodges with kitchenettes, all set back from the road. Amenities include a pool, game room, and snack bar.

✗ Eating

The classic Nashville meal is the 'meat-and-three' – a heaping portion of fried chicken, meatloaf etc with your choice of three home-style sides. Many of the restaurants in the District are high-volume tourist traps and are best avoided.

Prince's Hot Chicken CHICKEN $
(123 Ewing Dr; mains $4-8; ⊙noon-10pm Tue-Thu, noon-4am Fri & Sat) Cayenne-rubbed 'hot chicken,' fried to succulent perfection and served on a piece of white bread with a side

of pickles, is Nashville's unique contribution to the culinary universe. Tiny, faded Prince's, in a northside strip mall, is a local legend that's gotten shout-outs everywhere from the *New York Times* to *Bon Appétit*. In mild, medium, hot and death-defying extra hot, its chicken will burn a hole in your stomach and you'll come back begging for more.

City House NEW SOUTHERN **$$$**
(☎615-736-5838; cityhousenashville.com; 1222 4th Ave N; mains $9-24; ⊙5pm-10pm Wed-Mon) This signless brick building in Nashville's gentrifying Germantown neighborhood hides one of the South's best new restaurants. The food, cooked in an open kitchen in the warehouselike space, is a crackling bang-up of Italy-meets-New South – local chicken livers with red-onion jam, pizza with house-cured pork belly, root-beer layer cake with buttermilk buttercream. Cocktails are a high art here: try a Kubric (Tennessee whiskey, artisan pear brandy, ginger ale).

Arnold's SOUTHERN **$**
(605 8th Ave S; mains $5-8; ⊙6am-2:30pm Mon-Fri) Grab a tray and line up with college students, garbage collectors and country-music stars at Arnold's, king of the meat-and-three. Slabs of drippy roast beef are the house specialty, along with fried green tomatoes, cornbread two ways, and big gooey wedges of chocolate cream pie. This is Southern food at its finest.

Family Wash PUB **$$**
(www.familywash.com; 2038 Greenwood Ave; mains $9-15; ⊙6pm-midnight Tue-Sat) This East Nashville neighborhood gastropub is the kind of place where you can eat a sublime roast garlic shepherd's pie and nurse a microbrew while watching the bartender shoot the breeze with the regulars and kids play with toy cars on the floor. Live music gets rolling on the small stage around 9pm most nights.

WORTH A TRIP

FRANKLIN

About 20 miles south of Nashville off I-65, the historic town of **Franklin** (www.historicfranklin.com) has a charming downtown and beautiful B&Bs. Stop off at **Puckett's Grocery** (www.puckettsgrocery.com; 120 4th Ave S; mains $10-20; ⊙6am-6pm Sun-Thu, to late Fri & Sat) for a fried-catfish sandwich and some bluegrass.

Monell's SOUTHERN **$$**
(www.monellstn.com; 1235 6th Ave N; all-you-can-eat $16; ⊙10:30am-2pm Mon, 10:30am-2pm & 5-8:30pm Tue-Fri, 8:30am-1pm & 5-8:30pm Sat, 8:30am-4pm Sun) In an old brick house just north of the District, Monell's is beloved for down-home Southern food served communally, meaning you sit with strangers and pass the food around the table yourselves. This being Nashville, you'll all be friends before you're done with your fried catfish.

Marché Artisan Foods BISTRO **$$**
(www.marcheartisanfoods.com; 1000 Main St; mains $9-16; ⊙8am-9pm Tue-Sat, to 4pm Sun) In rapidly gentrifying East Nashville, this airy bistro has a veggie-friendly menu of light French- and Italian-inflected fare, made with seasonal local ingredients. Drop in for a cinnamon brioche at breakfast, or a plate of homemade gnocchi with sweet corn for dinner.

Pancake Pantry BREAKFAST **$**
(www.pancakepantry.com; 1796 21st Ave S; mains $5-9; ⊙6am-3pm) For 50-plus years, crowds have been lining up for tall stacks of pancakes every-which-way at this iconic breakfast joint. Try the sweet-potato kind.

Elliston Place Soda Shop DINER **$**
(2111 Elliston Pl; mains $3-6; ⊙7am-7pm Mon-Sat) This venerable eatery has served fountain Cokes and meat-and-threes to Vandy students since the 1930s, and the decor hasn't changed much since.

🍷 Drinking & Entertainment

Nashville has the nightlife of a city three times its size, and you'll be hard-pressed to find a place that *doesn't* have live music. College students, bachelor-party-goers, Danish backpackers and conventioneers all rock out downtown, where neon-lit Broadway looks like a country-fried Las Vegas. Bars and venues west and south of downtown tend to attract more locals, with many places clustered near Vanderbilt University. Last call is at 3am, so many bars stay open until then when it's busy.

Bars & Nightclubs

Cafe Coco CAFE, BAR
(www.cafecoco.com; 210 Louise Ave; ⊙24hr) In a ramshackle old cottage just off Elliston Pl, Cafe Coco is like an especially groovy frat house, with a 24-hour whirl of action. Twenty-somethings snack on sandwiches and cake in the front parlor, smoke on the

BEST POPSICLES EVER

Locals know just where to head on steamy Tennessee afternoons: **Las Paletas Gourmet Popsicles** (2907 12th Ave S; ⊙Tue-Sat noon-7pm, to 5pm Sun), a groovy little popsicle shop selling icy treats in wild flavors such as chocolate-wasabi, hibiscus and olive oil.

large patio, drink at the bar and tap away on laptops in the old bedrooms (there's free wi-fi).

Whiskey Kitchen   PUB
(www.whiskeykitchen.com; 118 12th Ave S) In the Gulch, an up-and-coming patch of rehabbed warehouses adjacent to downtown, this neo-Southern gastropub with a mile-long whiskey menu is one of Nashville's trendiest spots. Expect crowds.

Rumours Wine and Art Bar   BAR
(www.rumourswinebar.com; 2404 12th Ave S) In the hip but low-key 12th Ave S neighborhood, this arty hangout is good for a chilling with a glass of Malbec.

Tribe   BAR
(www.tribenashville.com; 1517 Church St) Ultra-friendly Tribe caters to a largely gay male crowd, though everyone is welcome to sip martinis, watch music videos and dance the night away.

Live Music
Nashville's opportunities for hearing live music are unparalleled. As well as the big venues, many talented country, folk, bluegrass, Southern-rock and blues performers play smoky honky-tonks, college bars, coffee shops and organic cafes for tips. Many places are free Monday to Friday or if you arrive early enough.

[TOP CHOICE] Tootsie's Orchid Lounge   HONKY-TONK
(☎615-726-7937; www.tootsies.net; 422 Broadway) The most venerated of the downtown honky-tonks, Tootsie's vibrates with boot-stompin' every night of the week. In the 1960s club owner and den mother 'Tootsie' Bess nurtured the likes of Willie Nelson, Kris Kristofferson and Waylon Jennings. Now up-and-coming country musicians play the two tiny stages and it's not unusual for big stars to stop by for an impromptu jam session.

Grand Ole Opry   MUSICAL THEATER
(☎615-871-6779; www.opry.com; 2802 Opryland Dr, Music Valley; adult $28-88, child $18-53) Though you'll find a variety of country shows throughout the week, the performance to see is the *Grand Ole Opry,* a lavish tribute to classic Nashville country music, every Tuesday, Friday and Saturday night. Shows return to the Ryman from November to February.

Bluebird Cafe   CLUB
(☎615-383-1461; www.bluebirdcafe.com; 4104 Hillsboro Rd; cover free-$15; ⊙shows 6pm & 9:30pm) It's in a strip mall in suburban South Nashville, but don't let that fool you: some of the best original singer-songwriters in country music have graced this tiny stage. Steve Earle, Emmylou Harris and the Cowboy Junkies have all played the Bluebird, which was the setting for the 1993 Sandra Bullock and River Phoenix movie *The Thing Called Love.* Try your luck at Monday open mike nights.

Robert's Western World   HONKY-TONK
(www.robertswesternworld.com; 416 Broadway) Buy a pair of boots, a beer or a burger at Robert's, a longtime favorite on the strip. Music starts at 11am and goes all night; Brazilbilly, the house band, rocks it after 10pm on weekends.

Station Inn   CLUB
(☎615-255-3307; www.stationinn.com; 402 12th Ave S) South of downtown, this unassuming stone building is the best place in town for serious bluegrass. Don't miss the Tuesday-night Doyle and Debbie show (see p355).

Ryman Auditorium   CONCERT VENUE
(☎tickets 615-458-8700, info 615-889-3060; www.ryman.com; 116 5th Ave) The Ryman's excellent acoustics, historic charm and large seating capacity have kept it the premier venue in town. The *Opry* returns for winter runs.

Bourbon Street Blues & Boogie Bar   BLUES
(www.bourbonstreetblues.com; 220 Printer's Alley) A Printer's Alley standby, with low ceilings, sweet blues and Mardi Gras beads everywhere.

Tired of country?

Basement   CLUB
(www.thebasementnashville.com; 1604 8th Ave S) Beneath Grimey's Records, has intimate alt-rock and folk shows.

Mercy Lounge   CLUB
(www.mercylounge.com; 1 Cannery Row) Up the street, with arty rock-and-roll shows in an old brick cannery.

Exit/In
CLUB

(www.exitin.com; 2208 Elliston Pl) On Elliston Pl, opened in 1971, does indie rock, hip-hop and more.

Shopping

Lower Broadway has tons of record shops, boot stores and souvenir stalls, but you can generally get better prices elsewhere. The 12th Ave South neighborhood is the spot for ultra-trendy boutiques and vintage stores. Don't miss the iconic Katy K's Ranch Dressing (p355).

TOP CHOICE Hatch Show Print
ART, SOUVENIRS

(316 Broadway) One of the oldest letterpress print shops in the US, Hatch has been using old-school cut blocks to print its bright, iconic posters since the early days of Vaudeville. The company has produced graphic ads and posters for almost every country star since.

Ernest Tubb
MUSIC

(417 Broadway) Marked by a giant neon guitar sign, this is the best place to shop for country and bluegrass records. Open late.

Third Man Records
MUSIC

(623 7th Ave S) Music geeks freak out over this tiny new record shop and recording studio, owned by White Stripes frontman Jack White.

Elder's Bookstore
BOOKS

(2115 Elliston Pl) This excellent used-book shop has been around since the 1930s.

Gruhn Guitars
MUSIC

(400 Broadway) This renowned vintage instrument store has expert staff.

Opry Mills Mall
MALL

(☉10am-9:30pm Mon-Sat, to 7pm Sun) Next door to the Opry, this sprawling outlet mall houses an IMAX theater, theme restaurants and dozens of big name retailers.

THREE-FOR-ONE COWBOY BOOTS

Embroidered leather cowboy boots, the unofficial Nashville uniform, are the city's quintessential souvenir and dozens of shops along Lower Broadway hawk overpriced pairs to tourists. But in-the-know shoppers will head to Boot Country (304 Broadway) for their legendary 'buy one, get two free' deal on everything from flashy alligator to rough 'n' ready riding boots.

ⓘ Information

Downtown Nashville and Centennial Park have free wi-fi, as do nearly all hotels and many restaurants and coffee shops.

InsideOut (www.insideoutnashville.com) A weekly covering the local gay and lesbian scene.

Main police station (☎615-862-8600; 310 1st Ave S)

Nashville Scene (www.nashvillescene.com) Free alternative weekly with entertainment listings.

Nashville Visitors Information Center (☎615-259-4747; www.visitmusiccity.com; 501 Broadway, Sommet Center; ☉8:30am-5:30pm) Pick up free city maps here at the glass tower. Great online resource.

Post office (1718 Church St)

Public library (www.library.nashville.org; 615 Church St) Free internet access.

Tennessean (www.tennessean.com) Nashville's daily newspaper.

Vanderbilt University Medical Center (☎615-322-5000; 1211 22nd Ave S)

ⓘ Getting There & Around

Nashville International Airport (BNS; ☎615-275-1675; www.nashintl.com), 8 miles east of town, is not a major air hub. MTA bus 18 links the airport and downtown; the **Gray Line Airport Express** (www.graylinenashville.com; one way/return $12/20; ☉5am-11pm) serves major downtown and West End hotels. Taxis charge a flat rate of $25 to downtown or Opryland.

Greyhound (1030 Charlotte Ave) is downtown. The **Metropolitan Transit Authority** (www.nashvillemta.org; fares $1.60) operates city bus services based downtown at **Music City Central** (400 Charlotte Ave). Express buses go to Music Valley.

Eastern Tennessee

Dolly Parton, Eastern Tennessee's most famous native, loves her home region so much she has made a successful career out of singing about girls who leave the honeysuckle-scented embrace of the Smoky Mountains for the false glitter of the city. They're always sorry.

Largely a rural region of small towns, rolling hills and river valleys, the eastern third of the state has friendly folks, hearty country food and pastoral charm to make most anyone feel at home.

The lush, heather-tinted Great Smoky Mountains are great for hiking, camping and rafting, while the region's two main

SCENIC DRIVE: NATCHEZ TRACE PARKWAY

About 25 miles southwest of Nashville off Hwy 100, drivers pick up the Natchez Trace Pkwy, which leads 444 miles southwest to Natchez, MS. This northern section is one of the most attractive stretches of the entire route, with broad-leafed trees leaning together to form an arch over the winding road. There are three primitive campsites along the way, free and available on a first-come, first-served basis. Near the parkway entrance, stop at the landmark Loveless Cafe, a 1950s roadhouse famous for its biscuits and homemade preserves, country ham and ample portions of Southern fried chicken.

urban areas, Knoxville and Chattanooga, are easygoing riverside cities with lively college populations and kicking music scenes.

CHATTANOOGA

Named 'the dirtiest city in America' in the 1960s, Chattanooga was shamed into cleaning up rampant industrial pollution and focusing on downtown revitalization. Today the city is recognized as being one of the country's greenest, with miles of well-used waterfront trails, free electric buses and pedestrian bridges crossing the Tennessee River. With world-class rock-climbing, hiking, biking and water-sports opportunities, it's one of the South's best cities for outdoorsy types.

The city was once a major railway hub throughout the 19th and 20th centuries, hence the 'Chattanooga Choo-Choo,' which was originally a reference to the Cincinnati Southern Railroad's passenger service from Cincinnati to Chattanooga and later the title of a 1941 Glen Miller song.

The Bluff View Art District at High and E 2nd Sts has upscale shops and restaurants overlooking the river.

👁 Sights & Activities

On the North Shore, Coolidge Park is a good place to start a riverfront stroll. There's a carousel, well-used playing fields and a 50ft climbing wall attached to one of the columns supporting the Walnut Street Bridge.

Lookout Mountain OUTDOORS
(www.lookoutmtnattractions.com; 827 East Brow Rd; adult/child $46/24; 🔊) Some of Chattanooga's oldest and best-loved attractions are 6 miles outside the city. Admission price includes: the Incline Railway, which chugs up a steep incline to the top of the mountain; the world's longest underground waterfall, Ruby Falls; and Rock City, a garden with a dramatic cliff-top overlook. Opening hours vary by season. The mountain is also a popular hang-gliding location. The folks at Lookout Mountain Flight Park (☎800-688-5637; www.hanglide.com; 7201 Scenic Hwy, Rising Fawn, GA; intro tandem flight $199) give lessons.

Tennessee Aquarium AQUARIUM
(www.tnaqua.org; 1 Broad St; adult/child $25/15; ⏰10am-6pm; 🔊) That glass pyramid looming over the riverside bluffs is the world's largest freshwater aquarium. Climb aboard the aquarium's high-speed catamaran for two-hour excursions through the Tennessee River Gorge (adult/child $29/22). While here, check out a show at the attached IMAX theater (adult/child $8.50/7).

Outdoor Chattanooga OUTDOORS
(☎423-643-6888; www.outdoorchattanooga.com) Hop on the pedestrian-only bridge to cross into downtown. Below you'll notice the grass-covered 'living roof' of this city-run agency promoting active recreation. It leads hiking, kayaking and biking trips – call or check the website for schedules. It's also a good resource for outdoor info and trail suggestions.

Hunter Museum of American Art GALLERY
(www.huntermuseum.org; 10 Bluff View; adult/child $10/5; ⏰10am-5pm Mon, Tue & Thu-Sat, noon-5pm Wed & Sun) East of the aquarium is the equally striking glass lobby of this museum, which has a fantastic 19th- and 20th-century collection. Check out the vertigo-inducing glass pedestrian bridge.

🛏 Sleeping & Eating

You can find plenty of budget motels around I-24 and I-75.

Chattanooga Choo-Choo Holiday Inn HOTEL $$
(☎423-266-5000; www.choochoo.com; 1400 Market St; r/railcars from $145/179; 🅿️✳️@🍴🏊) The city's grand old railway terminal has been transformed into a bustling hotel, complete with 48 authentic Victorian railcar rooms, a retro Gilded Age bar and numerous shops.

Standard rooms and suites, in separate buildings, are clean but ordinary.

Stone Fort Inn
B&B $$

(☑423-267-7866; www.stonefortinn.com; 120 E 10th St; r from $120; P✻☎) Exposed brick and a stylish mix of antiques, vintage Coke art and kitschy-cool mounted deer heads make this downtown boutique hotel the hippest digs in town.

Raccoon Mountain Campground
CAMPGROUND $

(☑423-821-9403; www.raccoonmountain.com; 319 W Hills Dr; tent sites from $18) The closest campsite to downtown has shady tent sites and well-maintained facilities, at the base of the nifty tour-able caverns of the same name.

TOP CHOICE Zarzour's
SOUTHERN $

(1627 Rossville Ave; mains $5-8; ☺11am-3:30pm Mon-Fri) 'We treat you like family here,' says the waitress at this tiny wood-paneled slip of a diner, Chattanooga's oldest restaurant. 'We just don't like our family very much!' She's kidding (we think), but that kind of salty banter is what makes Zarzour's such an experience: that, and the just-like-grammy-used-to-make hamburger steak, baked spaghetti and lemon ice box pie (a true classic of the genre).

Big River Grille & Brewing Works
PUB $$

(222 Broad St; mains $9-20; ☺11am-midnight Sun-Thu, to 2am Fri & Sat) A lively crowd drinks beer and chows down on crowd-pleasing upmarket pub grub – burgers, calamari, barbecue chicken pizza – in a warehouse-y downtown space with a big front patio.

ⓘ Information
The **visitor center** (☑423-756-8687, 800-322-3344; www.chattanoogafun.com; 215 Broad St; ☺8:30am-5:30pm) is huge and modern, with friendly staff.

ⓘ Getting There & Around
Chattanooga's modest **airport** (CHA; ☑423-855-2202; www.chattairport.com; 1001 Airport Rd) is just east of the city. The **Greyhound station** (960 Airport Rd) is just down the road.

For access to most downtown sites, ride the free electric **shuttle buses** that ply the center. The visitor center has a route map.

KNOXVILLE
Once known as the 'underwear capital of the world' for its numerous textile mills, Knoxville is now home to the University of Tennessee and a vibrant arts and music scene. Downtown's Market Square is full of ornate, slightly crumbling 19th-century buildings and lovely outdoor cafes shaded by pear trees, while Old Town, an arty, renovated warehouse district centered on Gay St, is a food and nightlife hot spot.

The **visitor center** (☑865-523-7263, 800-727-8045; www.knoxville.org; 301 S Gay St; ☺9am-5pm Mon-Sat, 1-5pm Sun) is downtown. If you're here at lunchtime, don't miss the hallowed Blue Plate Special (www.wdvx.com; admission free; ☺noon Mon-Sat), a daily live concert put on at the visitor center by WDVX, Knoxville's venerable country and roots music radio station.

The city's visual centerpiece is the Sunsphere, a gold orb atop a tower that's the main remnant of the 1982 World Fair. You can take the elevator up to the (usually deserted) viewing deck to see the skyline and a dated exhibit on Knoxville's civic virtues.

You can't miss the massive orange basketball that marks the Women's Basketball Hall of Fame (www.wbhof.com; 700 Hall of Fame Dr; adult/child $8/6; ☺10am-5pm Mon-Sat summer, 11am-5pm Tue-Sat winter), a nifty look at the sport from the time when women were forced to play in full-length dresses.

GREAT SMOKY MOUNTAINS NATIONAL PARK
The Cherokee called this territory Shaconage (shah-*cone*-ah-jey), meaning roughly 'land of the blue smoke,' for the heather-colored mist that hangs over the ancient peaks. The Southern Appalachians are the world's oldest mountain range, with mile upon mile of cool, humid deciduous forest.

The 815-sq-mile park is the country's most visited and, while the main arteries and attractions can get crowded, studies have shown that 95% of visitors never venture further than 100yd from their cars, so it's easy to leave the teeming masses behind.

Unlike most other national parks, Great Smoky charges no admission fee, nor will it ever; this proviso was written into the park's original charter as a stipulation for a $5-million Rockefeller family grant. Stop by a visitor center to pick up a park map and the free park newspaper, *Smokies Guide*. For more information about the North Carolina section of this park, see p330.

The remains of the 19th-century settlement at Cades Cove are some of the park's most popular sights, as evidenced by the teeth-grinding summer traffic jams on the loop road.

Mt LeConte has some of the park's best hikes, as well as the only non-camping accommodations, LeConte Lodge (☏865-429-5704; www.leconte-lodge.com; cabins per person $79). Though the only way to get to the lodge's rustic, electricity-free cabins is via an 8-mile uphill hike, it's so popular you need to reserve up to a year in advance. Dinner and breakfast are available for $37. You can drive right up to the dizzying heights of Clingmans Dome, the third-highest mountain east of the Mississippi, with a futuristic observation tower.

With 10 developed campgrounds offering about 1000 campsites, you'd think finding a place to pitch would be easy. Not so in the busy summer season: your best bet is to plan ahead. You can make reservations (☏800-365-2267; www.nps.gov/grsm) for some sites; others are first-come, first-served. Camping fees are $14 to $23 per night. Of the park's 10 campgrounds, only Cades Cove and Smokemont are open year-round; others are open March to October.

Backcountry camping (☏reservations 865-436-1231) is an excellent option. A (free) permit is required; you can make reservations and get permits at the ranger stations or visitor centers.

ⓘ Information

The park's three interior visitor centers are Sugarlands Visitor Center (☏865-436-1291; ⊙8am-4:30pm, to later spring & summer), at the park's northern entrance near Gatlinburg; Cades Cove Visitor Center (☏877-444-6777; ⊙9am-4:30pm, to later spring & summer), halfway up Cades Cove Loop Rd, off Hwy 441 near the Gatlinburg entrance; and Oconaluftee Visitor Center (p330), at the park's southern entrance near Cherokee, NC.

GATLINBURG

Wildly kitschy Gatlinburg hunkers at the entrance of the Great Smoky Mountains National Park, waiting to stun hikers with the scent of fudge and cotton candy. Tourists flock here to ride the ski lifts, shop for Confederate-flag undershorts, get married at the many wedding chapels and play hillbilly-themed mini-golf. Love it or hate it, the entire village is a gin-u-wine American roadside attraction.

Amuse yourself Gatlinburg-style at the city's various Ripley's franchise attractions (a 'Believe it or Not!' museum of oddities, a mirror maze, a haunted house, a massive aquarium), at the one-of-a-kind Salt and Pepper Shaker Museum (www.thesaltand peppershakermuseum.com; Winery Sq; adult/child

DOLLYWOOD

Dollywood (www.dollywood.com; 1020 Dollywood Lane; adult/child $57/46; ⊙Apr-Dec) is a self-created ode to the patron saint of East Tennessee, the big-haired, bigger-bosomed country singer Dolly Parton. The park features Appalachian-themed rides and attractions, from the Mystery Mine roller coaster to the bald-eagle sanctuary, to the faux one-room chapel named after the doctor who delivered Dolly.

$3/free; ⊙10am-4pm), or by riding the scenic 2-mile aerial tramway (adult/child $11/8.50) to the Bavarian-themed Ober Gatlinburg ski resort. Afterwards, suck down free samples of white lightnin' at the Ole Smoky Moonshine Distillery (www.olesmokymoonshine. com; 903 Parkway; ⊙10am-10pm), the country's first licensed moonshine maker (sounds like an oxymoron to us!). Cap your day off with a frolic inside a giant hamster ball (yes, seriously) at Zorb (www.zorb.com; 203 Sugar Hollow Rd, Pigeon Forge; rides $37). It's all in day's fun in Gatlinburg.

Pigeon Forge (www.mypigeonforge.com), 10 miles north of Gatlinburg, is a tacky complex of motels, outlet malls and country-music theaters and restaurants, all of which have grown up in the shadow of Dollywood.

KENTUCKY

With an economy based on bourbon, horse racing and tobacco, you might think Kentucky would rival Las Vegas as Sin Central. Well, yes and no. For every whiskey-soaked Louisville bar there's a dry county where you can't get anything stronger than ginger ale. For every racetrack there's a Catholic monastery or a Southern Baptist church.

Kentucky's full of strange juxtapositions like that. A geographic and cultural crossroads, the state combines the friendliness of the South, the rural frontier history of the West, the industry of the North and the aristocratic charm of the East.

Every corner of the state is easy on the eye. In spring the pastures of central Kentucky bloom with tiny azure buds, earning it the moniker 'Bluegrass State.' There are few sights more heartbreakingly beautiful than the rolling limestone hills of horse country, where thoroughbred breeding is a multimillion-dollar industry. Even the mountains, often maligned as 'hillbilly country,' blaze with color and culture.

History

British and French forces battled for control of Kentucky in the mid-1700s, recognizing the value of the fertile land that was once used by Native Americans as a hunting ground.

Legendary frontiersman Daniel Boone blazed a trail through the Cumberland Gap and the British began pouring over the Appalachians in 1775. The state became a battleground during the Revolutionary War, with local Shawnee allying with the crown.

Though a slave state, Kentucky was bitterly divided during the Civil War, with 30,000 fighting for the Confederacy and 64,000 for the Union. Both the Union president Abraham Lincoln and Confederacy president Jefferson Davis were Kentucky-born.

After the war, Kentucky built up its economy on railways, tobacco and coal-mining. Today its motto, 'Unbridled Spirit,' reflects the dominance of scenic horse country.

KENTUCKY FACTS

» **Nickname** Bluegrass State

» **Population** 4.3 million

» **Area** 39,728 sq miles

» **Capital city** Frankfort (pop 28,000)

» **Other cities** Louisville (pop 600,000), Lexington (pop 300,000)

» **Sales tax** 6%

» **Birthplace of** 16th US president Abraham Lincoln (1809–65), 'gonzo' journalist Hunter S Thompson (1937–2005), boxer Muhammad Ali (b 1942), actress Ashley Judd (b 1968)

» **Home of** Kentucky Derby, Louisville Slugger, bourbon

» **Politics** generally conservative; extremely conservative in rural areas

» **Famous for** horses, bluegrass music, fried chicken, caves

» **Interesting place names** Monkeys Eyebrow, Chicken Bristle, Shoulderblade, Hippo, Petroleum

» **Driving distances** Louisville to Lexington 77 miles, Lexington to Mammoth Cave National Park 135 miles

---

❶ Information

The boundary between Eastern and Central time goes through the middle of Kentucky.

Kentucky State Parks (☑800-255-7275; www.parks.ky.gov) Offers info on hiking, caving, fishing, camping and more in Kentucky's 52 state parks. So-called 'Resort Parks' have more upscale options, like lodges, while 'Recreation Parks' are all about roughin' it.

Kentucky Travel (☑502-564-4930, 800-225-8747; www.kentuckytourism.com) Sends out a detailed booklet on the state's attractions.

Louisville

Best known as the home of the Kentucky Derby, Louisville (or Louahvul, as the locals say) is a handsome, underrated city. A major Ohio River shipping center during the days of westward expansion, Kentucky's largest city now has a lively working-class vibe, with corner pool halls, punk-rock bars and drive-through chili restaurants. It's a fun place to spend a day or two, checking out the museums, wandering the old neighborhoods, drinking a little bourbon.

⊙ Sights

The Victorian-era Old Louisville neighborhood, just south of downtown, is well worth a drive or stroll. Don't miss St James Court, just off Magnolia Ave, with its utterly charming gas lamp-lit park. There are several wonderful historic homes (www.historichomes.org) in the area open for tours, including Thomas Edison's old shotgun cottage.

TOP CHOICE Churchill Downs   RACETRACK

(www.churchilldowns.com; 700 Central Ave) On the first Saturday in May, a who's who of upper-crust America puts on their pinstripe suits and most flamboyant hats and descends for the 'greatest two minutes in sports,' the Kentucky Derby. After the race, the crowd sings 'My Old Kentucky Home' and watches as the winning horse is covered in a blanket of roses. Then they party.

To be honest, they've been partying for a while. The Kentucky Derby Festival (www.kdf.org), which includes a balloon race and the largest fireworks display in North America, starts two weeks before the big event.

Most seats at the derby are by invitation only or they've been reserved years in advance. On Derby Day, $40 gets you into the paddock party scene (no seat) if you arrive early, but it's so crowded you won't see much of the race. Don't fret, though. From April through to November, you can get a $3 seat at the Downs for many exciting races, often warm-ups for the big events.

Kentucky Derby Museum
(www.derbymuseum.org; Gate 1, Central Ave; adult/child $13/5; ◷8am-5pm Mon-Sat, 11am-5pm Sun) On the grounds, the museum has exhibits on derby history, including a peek into the life of jockeys and a roundup of the most illustrious horses. There is a 360-degree audiovisual about the race, and a behind-the-scenes track tour ($10) that leads you through the jockey's quarters and posh VIP seating areas.

Louisville Slugger Museum   MUSEUM
(www.sluggermuseum.org; 800 W Main St; adult/child $10/5; ◷9am-5pm Mon-Sat, noon-5pm Sun;) Look for the 120ft baseball bat leaning against the museum – ya can't miss it. Hillerich & Bradsby Co have been making the famous Louisville Slugger here since 1884. The admission fee includes a plant tour, a hall of baseball memorabilia such as Babe Ruth's bat, a batting cage and a free mini slugger. Customized bats are sold in the lobby. Note: bat production halts on Sunday, as well as on Saturday in the winter.

CULTURAL CENTER
(www.alicenter.org; 144 N 6th St; adult/child $9/4; ◷9:30am-5pm Mon-Sat, noon-5pm Sun) A love offering to the city from its most famous native. Self-guided tours include a stirring film on Ali's life and video projections of his most famous fights, as well as exhibits about the racial segregation and humanitarian issues that so vexed the outspoken man once known as the 'Louisville Lip.'

Frazier International History Museum   MUSEUM
(www.fraziermuseum.org; 829 W Main St; adult/child $12/9; ◷9am-5pm Mon-Sat, noon-5pm Sun) Surprisingly ambitious for a midsized city, this state-of-the-art museum covers 1000 years of history with grisly battle dioramas and costumed interpreters demonstrating swordplay and staging mock debates.

Speed Art Museum   MUSEUM
(www.speedmuseum.org; 2035 S 3rd St; adult/child $10/5; ◷10am-5pm Tue, Wed & Fri, to 9pm Thu, noon-5pm Sun) A handsome Greek Revival-style building with more than 12,000 pieces of art, from classical sculptures to Kentucky mint julep cups.

🛏 Sleeping

Chain hotels cluster near the airport off I-264. Check out www.louisvillebedandbreakfast.org for the lowdown on the city's many reasonably priced, historic B&Bs.

CHOICE 21c   HOTEL $$$
(☎502-217-6300; www.21chotel.com; 700 W Main St; r from $240; P❀❁) This contemporary art-museum–hotel would be edgy anywhere; in laid-back Louisville, it's practically in a different dimension. Video screens project your distorted image on the wall as you wait for the elevator. Chandeliers made from scissors dangle weirdly in the hallways. Sexually suggestive sculptures in the lobby make even normally unflappable guidebook authors blush. Urban-loftlike rooms have iPod docks and mint julep kits in the minifridge. The hotel restaurant, Proof on Main, is one of the city's hippest New Southern bistros. Parking is $18.

Central Park B&B   B&B $$
(☎502-638-1505, www.centralparkbandb.com; 1353 S 4th St; r incl breakfast $135-195; P❀❁) Sleep in Gilded Age style at this 1884 stone mansion, overlooking Old Louisville's Central Park. The decor is very 'Victorian maximalist' – chandeliers, stained glass everywhere and huge flower arrangements on every surface.

INTERNATIONAL BLUEGRASS MUSIC MUSEUM

Kentuckian Bill Monroe is considered the founding father of bluegrass music; his band, the Blue Grass Boys, gave the genre its name. Bluegrass has its roots in the old-time mountain music, mixed with the fast tempo of African songs and spiced with lashings of jazz. Any banjo picker or fiddle fan will appreciate the historic exhibits at the International Bluegrass Music Museum (www.bluegrass-museum.org; 107 Daviess St; admission $5; ◷10am-5pm Tue-Sat, 1-4pm Sun) in Owensboro. The pretty Ohio River town, about 100 miles west of Louisville, also hosts the ROMP Bluegrass Festival (www.bluegrass-museum.org/riverofmusic) in June.

THE HAUNTED HOSPITAL

Towering over Louisville like a mad king's castle, the abandoned Waverly Hills Sanatorium once housed victims of an early 20th-century tuberculosis epidemic. When patients died, workers dumped their bodies down a chute into the basement. No wonder the place is said to be one of America's most haunted buildings. Search for spooks with a nighttime ghost-hunting tour (502-933-2142; www.therealwaverly hills.com; 2hr tours/2hr ghost hunts/ overnights $22/50/100; Mar-Aug); the genuinely fearless can even spend the night! Many claim it's the scariest place they've ever been.

Brown Hotel
HOTEL $$$
(502-583-1234; www.brownhotel.com; 335 West Broadway; r from $250; P✱☺☎) Opera stars, queens and prime ministers have trod the marble floors of this storied downtown hotel, now restored to all its 1920s gilded glamour with 293 comfy rooms and a swank bar. Parking is $18.

✖ Eating

The Highlands area around Bardstown and Baxter Rds is the spot for locally owned cafes and bars. Downtown's 'Fourth Street Live' is a rather contrived 'entertainment district' of casual shopping and dining; there are better pickings in the area, so don't be afraid to wander.

610 Magnolia
NEW SOUTHERN $$$
(502-636-0783; www.610magnolia.com; 610 W Magnolia Ave; 3-/4-course prix fixe menu $50/60; 6pm-10pm Thu-Sat) Only open three evenings a week, this sleek Scandinavia-meets-Kentucky bistro is Louisville's hottest-ticket restaurant (and the hardest to find – there's no sign, just look for the numbers '610' on the front). Local seasonal ingredients get a global treatment – chili-rubbed crispy pork belly, sashimi with bourbon-soy sauce, sweet-potato bread pudding – to jaw-dropping effect.

Lynn's Paradise Cafe
DINER $$
(www.lynnsparadisecafe.com; 984 Barret Ave; mains $7-15; 7am-10pm Mon-Fri, 8am-10pm Sat & Sun; 🚼) It's breakfast anytime at this psychedelic diner, marked by the 10ft-tall teapot outside. Don't miss the homemade biscuits with sor-

ghum butter, or the Hot Brown sandwich, a Louisville classic invented in the 1920s at the Brown Hotel.

Doc Crow's Southern Smokehouse & Raw Bar
SOUTHERN, BARBECUE $$
(doccrows.com; 127 W Main St; mains $7-18; 11am-10pm Mon-Thu, to 11pm Fri & Sat) In an 1880s-era distillery trendily rehabbed with exposed brick and reclaimed wood, Louisville hipsters sip bourbon, slurp oysters and munch on house-smoked BBQ ribs.

♟ Drinking & Entertainment

The free weekly *Leo* (www.leoweekly.com) lists gigs and entertainment. You'll have no problem finding a watering hole in the Highlands area.

Old Seelbach Bar
BAR
(www.seelbachhilton.com; 500 4th St) In the Gilded Era Seelbach Hilton, this is the city's top spot for elegant bourbon-sipping.

Holy Grale
PUB
(www.holygralelouisville.com; 1034 Bardstown Rd) One of Bardstown's newest and most interesting bars is housed in an old church, with a menu of funked-up pub grub (Scotch quail eggs, kimchee hot dogs) and a dozen rare German, Belgian and Japanese brews on tap.

Rudyard Kipling
BAR, MUSIC
(www.therudyardkipling.com; 422 W Oak St) In Old Louisville, this place is loved by arty locals for its intimate indie-bluegrass shows and Kentucky bar food (try the 'snappy cheese').

Actors Theatre of Louisville
THEATER
(www.actorstheatre.org; 504 W Main St) This highly regarded theater performs everything from Shakespeare to contemporary musicals and has premiered several Pulitzer Prize–winning plays.

❶ Information

Public library (301 York St) Surf the web free, downtown.

Visitor center (502-582-3732, 888-568-4784; www.gotolouisville.com; 301 S 4th St; 10am-6pm Mon-Sat, noon-5pm Sun) Has a free exhibit about that great Kentucky icon, KFC founder Colonel Sanders.

❶ Getting There & Around

Louisville's International Airport (SDF; 502-367-4636; www.flylouisville.com) is 5 miles south of town on I-65. Get there by cab (around

$18) or local bus 2. The **Greyhound station** (720 W Muhammad Ali Blvd) is just west of downtown. **TARC** (www.ridetarc.org; 1000 W Broadway) runs local buses ($1.50) from the Union Station depot.

Bluegrass Country

Drive through northeast Kentucky's Bluegrass Country on a sunny day and you'll get an idea of what the ancient Greeks were imagining when they wrote about the Elysian fields of paradise. Horses graze in the brilliant-green hills dotted with ponds, poplar trees and handsome estate houses. These once-wild woodlands and meadows have been a center of horse breeding for almost 250 years – the region's natural limestone deposits are said to produce especially nutritious grass. The area's principal city, Lexington, is known as the 'Horse Capital of the World.'

LEXINGTON

Even the prison looks like a country club in Lexington, home of million-dollar houses and multimillion-dollar horses. Once the wealthiest and most cultured city west of the Allegheny Mountains, it was called 'the Athens of the West' and today is home to the University of Kentucky and the heart of the thoroughbred-racehorse industry. The small downtown has some pretty Victorian

---

WORTH A TRIP

NATIONAL CORVETTE MUSEUM

All hail America's favorite sports car, the made-in-Kentucky Chevrolet Corvette! Auto fans should not miss the pilgrimage to Bowling Green's space-agey **National Corvette Museum** (www.corvettemuseum.com; I-65, exit 28, Bowling Green; adult/child $10/5; ⊙8am-5pm), home to 80 Corvette models and walk-through dioramas filled with memorabilia (check out the 'Main Street,' a mockup of Corvette-loving 1950s America). The nearby **Bowling Green Assembly Plant** (www.bowling greenassemblyplant.com; ⊙tours 8:30am, 11:30am, 12:45pm & 2pm Mon-Thu) gives guided factory tours – book online at least nine days in advance, or show up 45 minutes early and hope for a walk-in spot.

---

neighborhoods, but most of the attractions are in the countryside outside the metro area.

◉ Sights & Activities

Most of Lexington's sights are horse-related, or involve the city's many historic homes and estates.

TOP CHOICE **Headley-Whitney Museum**   MUSEUM
(www.headley-whitney.org; 4435 Old Frankfort Pike; adult/child $10/7; ⊙10am-5pm Tue-Fri, noon-5pm Sat & Sun) This marvelously old place holds the private collection of the late George Headley, a jewelry designer whose gemstone trinkets and handmade dollhouses are on display, along with a truly bizarre garage turned 'seashell grotto.'

Kentucky Horse Park   MUSEUM, PARK
(www.kyhorsepark.com; 4089 Iron Works Pkwy; adult/child $16/8; ⊙9am-5pm daily mid-Mar–Oct, Wed-Sun Nov–mid-Mar; ⊕) An educational theme park and equestrian sports center sits on 1200 acres just north of Lexington. Horses representing 50 different breeds live in the park and participate in special live shows. Also included, the international **Museum of the Horse** has neat dioramas of the horse through history, from the tiny prehistoric 'eohippus' to the pony express mail carriers. Seasonal **horseback riding** costs $22. The adjacent American Saddlebred Museum focuses on America's first registered horse breed – for hard-core enthusiasts only.

Keeneland Race Course   RACETRACK
(www.keeneland.com; 4201 Versailles Rd; tickets $5) Watch 'em run, with races in April and October and horse sales throughout the year. From March to November you can watch the champions train from sunrise to 10am.

Red Mile   RACETRACK
(www.theredmile.com; 1200 Red Mile Rd) Head here to see harness racing, where jockeys are pulled behind horses in special two-wheeled carts. Live races are in the fall, but you can watch and wager on simulcasts of races from around the world year-round.

Thoroughbred Center   TOUR
(www.thethoroughbredcenter.com; 3380 Paris Pike; adult/child $15/8; ⊙tours 9am Mon-Sat Apr-Oct, Mon-Fri Nov-Mar) Most farms are closed to the public, but you can see working racehorses up close here, with tours of the stables, practice tracks and paddocks.

BELIEVE IT OR NOT

Fact: nearly half of Americans don't believe in evolution. Hence the popularity of Petersburg, Kentucky's new multimillion-dollar **Creation Museum** (www.creationmuseum.org; 2800 Bullittsburg Church Rd; adult/child $25/15; ⊙10am-6pm Mon-Sat, noon-6pm Sun), an interactive tour through a biblical interpretation of history. The scientific-minded will fume at what may be seen as an antirational message. But that doesn't mean they won't enjoy the walk-through Noah's Ark, animatronic dinosaurs (creationists believe they coexisted with humans) and the zonkeys (zebra-donkey hybrids) in the petting zoo.

Mary Todd-Lincoln House HISTORIC BUILDING
(www.mtlhouse.org; 578 W Main St; adult/child $9/4; ⊙10am-3pm Mon-Sat) The 1806 house has articles from the first lady's childhood and her years as Abe's wife.

Waveland HISTORIC BUILDING
(http://parks.ky.gov/findparks/histparks/wl; 225 Waveland Museum Lane; ⊙9am-4pm) A 19th-century plantation.

Ashland HISTORIC BUILDING
(www.henryclay.org; 120 Sycamore Rd; adult/child $9/4; ⊙10am-4pm Tue-Sat, 1-4pm Sun) Just 1.5 miles east of downtown, it was the Italianate estate of statesman Henry Clay (1777–1852).

Whispering Woods HORSEBACK RIDING
(☑502-570-9663; www.whisperingwoodstrails. com; 265 Wright Lane; trail rides per hr $25; ⊙Mar-Nov) Call to arrange guided trail rides; in bucolic Georgetown.

🛏 Sleeping & Eating

There are several downtown cafes and bars with outdoor seating around Main and Limestone Sts. S Limestone, across from the UK campus, has student-friendly nightlife.

Kentucky Horse Park CAMPGROUND $
(☑859-259-4257, 800-370-6416; www.kyhorsepark. com; 4089 Iron Works Pkwy; electric/primitive campsites from $29/19; ☒) The 260 paved sites are open year-round. There are showers, laundry, a grocery, playgrounds and more. Primitive camping is also available.

Gratz Park Inn HOTEL $$
(☑859-231-1777; www.gratzparkinn.com; 120 W 2nd St; r from $179; P☀☎) On a quiet downtown street, this 40-room hotel feels like a genteel hunt club, with mahogany furnishings and Old World oil paintings in heavy frames. The attached restaurant, Jonathan's, serves fine regional cuisine.

TOP CHOICE **Holly Hill Inn** NEW SOUTHERN $$$
(☑859-846-4732; www.hollyhillinn.com; 426 N Winter St, Midway; 3-/5-course dinner menu $35-55; ⊙5:30-10pm Thu-Sat, 11am-2pm Sun year-round, plus 11am-2pm Fri & Sat spring & summer) Guests dine in the converted bedrooms and parlors of an elegant old farmhouse, just west of Lexington in the town of Midway. The husband-and-wife owners serve local bounty with a deft touch – lamb with scallion ravioli, farmstead egg custard with fiddlehead ferns – earning scads of foodie praise.

Horse & Barrel PUB $$
(101 N Broadway; mains $10-15; ⊙from 5pm) Part of DeSha's restaurant, this is a local favorite for bourbon sipping – there are more than 70 varieties on offer.

❶ Information

Pick up maps and area information from the **visitor center** (☑859-233-7299, 800-845-3959; www.visitlex.com; 301 E Vine St; ⊙8:30am-5pm Mon-Fri, 10am-4pm Sat). The **public library** (140 E Main St; ⊙10am-5pm Tue-Fri, noon-5pm Sat & Sun; ☎) has free internet access and free wi-fi for those with laptops.

❶ Getting There & Around

Blue Grass Airport (LEX; ☑859-425-3114; www.bluegrassairport.com; 4000 Terminal Dr) is west of town, with about a dozen domestic nonstops. **Greyhound** (477 W New Circle Rd) is 2 miles from downtown. **Lex-Tran** (www.lextra nonthemove.org) runs local buses (bus 6 goes to the Greyhound station).

FRANKFORT

A pretty little postcard of a town, all red brick and gingerbread trim, Kentucky's diminutive capital lies 26 miles west of Lexington on the banks of the Kentucky River. There are some notable historic buildings, including the **old state capitol** (admission free; ⊙10am-5pm Tue-Sat), which functioned from 1827 to 1910. Nearby is the handsome **Kentucky History Center** (www.history. ky.gov; 100 W Broadway St; admission free; ⊙8am-4pm Tue-Sat), for those truly interested in state history. Daniel Boone is buried in the **Frankfort Cemetery** (E Main St).

Central Kentucky

The Bluegrass Pkwy runs from I-65 in the west to Rte 60 in the east, passing through some of the most luscious pasturelands in Kentucky.

About 40 miles south of Louisville is Bardstown, the 'Bourbon Capital of the World'. The historic downtown comes alive in September for the Kentucky Bourbon Festival (www.kybourbonfestival.com). Have a meal, some bourbon and a good night's sleep in the dim limestone environs of Old

Talbott Tavern (☎502-348-3494; www.talbotts. com; 107 W Stephen Foster Ave; r from $59; [P]✿), which has been welcoming likes of Abraham Lincoln and Daniel Boone since the late 1700s.

Follow Hwy 31 southwest and turn left at Monks Rd to visit the ascetically beautiful Abbey of Gethsemani, a Trappist monastery once home to famed Catholic thinker Thomas Merton. You can buy monk-made fudge at the gift shop (⊘9am-5pm Mon-Fri). Continue on Hwy 31 to Hodgenville and the Abraham Lincoln Birthplace (www.nps.

THE BOURBON TRAIL

Silky, caramel-colored bourbon whiskey was likely first distilled in Bourbon County, north of Lexington, around 1789. Today 90% of all bourbon is produced here in Kentucky (no other state is allowed to put its own name on the bottle). Good bourbon must contain at least 51% corn, and must also be stored in charred oak barrels for a minimum of two years. While most connoisseurs drink it straight or with water, you must try a mint julep, the archetypal Southern drink made with bourbon, sugar syrup and crushed mint.

The Oscar Getz Museum of Whiskey History (www.whiskeymuseum.com; 114 N 5th St; donations appreciated; ⊘10am-4pm Mon-Sat, noon-4pm Sun), in Bardstown, tells the bourbon story with old moonshine stills and other artifacts.

Most of Kentucky's distilleries, which are centered on Bardstown and Frankfort, offer free tours. Check out Kentucky's official Bourbon Trail website (wwwkybourbontrail. com) – though note that it doesn't include every distillery.

Distilleries near Bardstown:

Heaven Hill (www.bourbonheritagecenter.com; 1311 Gilkey Run Rd, Bardstown) Not a distillery tour, but an interactive Bourbon Heritage Center, with a tasting room inside a giant barrel.

Jim Beam (www.jimbean.com; 149 Happy Hollow Rd, Clermont) Watch a film about the Beam family and sample small-batch bourbons at the country's largest bourbon distillery.

Maker's Mark (www.makersmark.com; 3350 Burks Spring Rd, Loretto) This restored Victorian distillery is like a bourbon theme park, with an old gristmill and a gift shop where you can seal your own bottle in red wax.

Tom Moore (www.1792bourbon.com; 300 Barton Rd, Bardstown) Connoisseur-quality 1792 Ridgemont Reserve is produced at this small distillery, the only one within Bards-town city limits.

Distilleries near Frankfort/Lawrenceburg:

Buffalo Trace (www.buffalotrace.com; 1001 Wilkinson Blvd, Frankfort) The nation's oldest continuously operating distillery has highly regarded tours and free tastings.

Four Roses (www.fourroses.us; 1224 Bonds Mills Rd, Lawrenceburg) One of the most scenic distilleries, in a riverside Spanish Mission-style building. Free tastings.

Wild Turkey (www.wildturkey.com; Hwy 62 E, Lawrenceburg) Master distiller Jimmy Russell has been making this extra-dark bourbon since 1954. The factory is more industrial than scenic.

Woodford Reserve (www.woodfordreserve.com; 7855 McCracken Pike, Versailles) The historic site along a creek is restored to its 1800s glory; the distillery still uses old-fashioned copper pots.

OTHER 'CAVE COUNTRY' CAVES

By the early-20th century Mammoth Cave had become such a popular attraction that owners of smaller local caves began diverting travelers heading to Mammoth by claiming it was flooded or quarantined. The inevitable conflicts became known as the 'Cave Wars.' Today you'll still see plenty of billboards beseeching you to visit other caves around Mammoth. Here are a few that are actually worth the drive:

Cub Run Cave (www.cubruncave.net; admission $14; ⊙9:30am-4:30pm, shorter hr winter) One of the 'newest' caves, discovered in 1950, with tons of colorful formations.

Diamond Caverns (1hr guided tours adult/child $16/8) Has guided tours of its vast cathedrals dripping stalactites and draped in pearly flowstone.

Hidden River Cave (www.cavern.org; admission $15; ⊙9am-5pm) A cave museum and a one-hour tour that takes you by the ruins of a turn-of-the-20th-century hydroelectric system. Special off-trail adventure tours can be arranged in advance during summer.

Lost River Cave (www.lostrivercave.com; admission $15; ⊙9am-6pm, shorter hr winter) Offers a family-friendly 25-minute boat ride through an underground river. There are 2 miles of hiking trails on-site.

gov/abli; admission free; ⊙8am-4:45pm, to 6:45pm summer), a faux-Greek temple constructed around an old log cabin. Ten minutes away is Honest Abe's boyhood home at Knob Creek, with hiking trails.

About 25 miles (30 minutes) southwest of Lexington is **Shaker Village at Pleasant Hill** (www.shakervillageky.org; 3501 Lexington Rd, Harrodsburg; adult/child $15/5; ⊙10am-5pm), home to a community of the Shaker religious sect until the early 1900s. Tour 14 impeccably restored buildings, set amid buttercup meadows and winding stone paths. There's an inn and restaurant, and a gift shop selling the Shakers' famous handicrafts.

Forty miles south of Lexington is **Berea**, famed for its folk art. The **Kentucky Artisan Center** (www.kentuckyartisancenter.ky.gov; Exit 77, off Hwy 75; ⊙8am-8pm) has a large variety of handcrafts and food.

DANIEL BOONE NATIONAL FOREST

These 707,000 acres of rugged ravines and gravity-defying sandstone arches cover much of the Appalachian foothills of eastern Kentucky. The forest has numerous state-and federal-run areas; the main **ranger station** (☎859-745-3100; www.fs.fed.us/r8/boone) is in Winchester.

An hour southeast of Lexington is **Red River Gorge** area, whose cliffs and natural arches make for some of the best rock climbing in the country. **Red River Outdoors** (☎859-230-3567; www.redriveroutdoors. com; 415 Natural Bridge Rd, Slade; full-day guided climb from $115) offers guided climbing trips.

Climbers can also pay $2 to camp out behind **Miguel's Pizza** (1890 Natural Bridge Rd, Slade; mains $10-14; ⊙7am-10pm Mon-Thu, to 11pm Fri & Sat) in the hamlet of Slade. Bordering Red River Gorge is the **Natural Bridge State Resort Park** (☎606-663-2214; www.parks. ky.gov; 2135 Natural Bridge Rd, Slade), notable for its gravity-defying 78ft-high sandstone arch. It's a family-friendly park, with camping, a variety of short hiking trails, and a lake with an island known as 'hoedown island' for its occasional clogging performances.

Further south, the **Cumberland Falls State Resort Park** (☎606-528-4121; admission free; tent sites $22, lodge r from $69) is one of the few places in the world to see a moonbow, a rainbow that sometimes forms in the fall's mist at night. The park has a rustic lodge and campgrounds. While you're there, head over to the adjacent **Natural Arch Scenic Area** to see the 90ft sandstone arch and hike the half-dozen trails. The nearby town of **Corbin** has the original Kentucky Fried Chicken restaurant, with a rather disturbing life-size statue of the Colonel.

MAMMOTH CAVE NATIONAL PARK

With the longest cave system on earth, **Mammoth Cave National Park** (www.nps. gov/maca; Exit 53, off I-65; ⊙8:45am-5:15pm) has some 300 miles of surveyed passageways. Mammoth is at least three times bigger than any other known cave, with vast interior cathedrals, bottomless pits and strange, undulating rock formations. The caves have been used for prehistoric mineral-gathering, as a source of saltpeter for gunpowder and as a tuberculosis hospital. Tourists started visiting around 1810 and guided tours have been offered since the 1830s. The area became a national park in 1926 and now brings nearly two million visitors each year.

The only way to see the caves is on the excellent ranger-guided tours (☏800-967-2283; adult $5-48) and it's wise to book ahead, especially in summer. Tours range from subterranean strolls to strenuous, day-long spelunking adventures. The history tour is especially interesting.

In addition to the caves, the park contains 70 miles of trails for hiking, horseback riding and mountain biking. There are also three campsites with restrooms, but no electricity or water hookups ($12 to $30), 12 free backcountry campsites, and the Mammoth Cave Hotel (☏270-758-2225; www.mammothcavehotel.com; r $89, cottages from $79; P❋), next to the visitor center, which has standard hotel rooms and, in spring and summer, rustic cottages. There is a gas station and convenience store near the visitor center. But to be honest, we prefer to drive down to shabby Cave City to sleep in the giant concrete tipis at the Wigwam Village Inn (☏270-773-3381; www.wigwamvillage.com; 601 N Dixie Hwy, Cave City; wigwams $40-70; P❋), a 1937 chunk of pure American kitsch.

GEORGIA

Vastly different at each of its edges, Georgia – the largest state east of the Mississippi River – is in many ways the perfect distillation of everything the South has to offer. It's a state of wild geographic and cultural extremes: right-leaning Republican politics rub against liberal idealism, small towns merge with gaping cities, northern mountains rise to the clouds and produce roaring rivers, while coastal marshlands teem with fiddler crabs and swaying cordgrass.

Atlanta is the state capital and the region's transportation hub, a sprawling metropolis with friendly neighborhoods alongside multinational corporations such as UPS and Coca-Cola. So start your trip in the city known as 'the ATL' then road-trip across the state to fall under the spell of Savannah's live oaks, seafood, antebellum homes and humid nights. From here you're close to the coastal barrier islands – bring your tuxedo to Jekyll Island and your hiking boots to Cumberland Island.

GEORGIA FACTS

» **Nickname** Peach State

» **Population** 9.7 million

» **Area** 59,425 sq miles

» **Capital city** Atlanta (population metro area 5.2 million)

» **Other cities** Savannah (population 136,286)

» **Sales tax** 7%

» **Birthplace of** baseball legend Ty Cobb (1886–1961), president Jimmy Carter (b 1924), civil rights leader Martin Luther King Jr (1929–68), singer Ray Charles (1930–2004)

» **Home of** Coca-Cola, the world's busiest airport, the world's biggest aquarium

» **Politics** socially conservative as a whole; Atlanta has been known to swing both ways

» **Famous for** peaches

» **Odd Law** donkeys may not be kept in bathtubs. Seriously, don't do it.

» **Driving distances** Atlanta to St Marys 343 miles, Atlanta to Dahlonega 75 miles

History

Permanent English settlement dates from 1733, when James Edward Oglethorpe founded Savannah. By the time of the Revolutionary War almost half the population was made up of slaves. Georgia held two crucial battlefronts in the latter part of the Civil War: Chickamauga, where Union troops were defeated, and Atlanta, which they conquered and burned.

In the 20th century the state vaulted to national prominence on the back of an eclectic group of events: the wildly popular novel and film *Gone With the Wind;* Reverend Martin Luther King Jr and civil rights protests; 39th US President Jimmy Carter; and Atlanta's rise as a global media and business center, culminating in the 1996 Summer Olympics.

❶ Information

For statewide tourism information, contact the **Georgia Department of Economic Development** (☏800-847-4842; www.exploregeorgia.org). For information on state parks, contact the **Georgia Department of Natural Resources**

(📱800-864-7275; www.gastateparks.org), where you can find information on camping and activities in parks statewide. Forty-one parks offer tent-only and RV-site camping for around $25 to $28 per night. Most parks have laundry facilities.

Cars are the most convenient way to move around Georgia. (Atlanta has a citywide train system called MARTA, but service is limited. Some cyclists brave the city streets.) I-75 bisects the state running north-south; I-20 runs east-west.

You can expect to pay an additional 6% tax on hotel accommodations in Georgia.

Atlanta

With five million residents in the metro and outlying areas, the so-called capital of the South continues to experience explosive growth thanks to southbound Yankees and international immigrants alike. It's also booming as a tourist destination thanks to two glitzy 21st-century attractions – the Georgia Aquarium and the World of Coca-Cola – plus giant panda exhibits at Zoo Atlanta. Beyond the attractions you'll find a constellation of superlative restaurants, ample Civil War lore, miles of walking trails and a plethora of African American history.

Without natural boundaries to control development, Atlanta keeps growing – sometimes up, but mostly out. Suburban sprawl has turned Atlanta into an almost endless city. Increased car dependence creates horrendous traffic and pollution.

For all this suburbanization, Atlanta is a pretty city covered with trees and elegant homes. Distinct neighborhoods are like friendly small towns. Racial tensions are minimal in 'the city too busy to hate,' which prides itself as hometown to the civil rights titan Martin Luther King Jr.

History

Born as a railroad junction in 1837, Atlanta became a major Confederate transportation and munitions center for General William T Sherman, whose Union forces blazed through Georgia in 1864, leaving more than 90% of Atlanta's buildings in ruins.

After the war, Atlanta became the epitome of the 'New South,' a concept that entailed reconciliation with the North, the promotion of industrialized agriculture and a progressive business outlook. Segregation ended relatively painlessly here compared with other Southern cities, and President John F Kennedy lauded this transition as a model for other communities facing integration.

For the 1996 Summer Olympic Games the city put on her prettiest debutante gown and CNN beamed her picture worldwide. People took notice, the moving trucks came rolling down the freeways and, like summer weeds, condos sprouted everywhere. Since then, the city has focused its development energy on the downtown and midtown neighborhoods, both of which have flourished in recent years. Georgia's capital has also become known as the 'Motown of the South' thanks to its sizzling hip-hop and R & B scene.

⊙ Sights & Activities

DOWNTOWN

In recent years developers and politicians have been focusing on making the urban core more vibrant and livable. Big attractions in the city have contributed to the success.

TOP CHOICE **Georgia Aquarium** AQUARIUM
(www.georgiaaquarium.com; 225 Baker St; adult/child $25/19, with Dolphin combo $38/26; ⊙10am-5pm Sun-Fri, 9am-6pm Sat; ▣) The world's largest aquarium is Atlanta's showstopper. It's crowded, like Venice, but it's awesomeness is hard to deny: whale sharks, beluga whales and the new $110 million AT&T Dolphin Tales gallery, theater and show ($13.50 add-on), where human actors/trainers and majestic bottlenose dolphins perform together in a Vegas-meets-Broadway production of spectacle and cheese (think more *Pirates of the Caribbean* than underwater Cirque du Soleil).

World of Coca-Cola MUSEUM
(www.woccatlanta.com; 121 Baker St; adult/child $15/10; ⊙10am-6:30pm Sun-Thu, 9am-6:30pm Fri & Sat) Next door to the Georgia Aquarium, this self-congratulatory museum might prove entertaining to fans of the fizzy beverage and rash commercialization. The climactic moment comes when guests sample Coke products from around the world – a taste-bud-twisting good time! But there are also Andy Warhol pieces to view, a 4-D film to catch, company history to learn, and what seems like 20 billion promotional materials to behold.

CNN Center TV LOCATION
(📱404-827-2300; www.cnn.com/tour/atlanta; 1 CNN Center; 50min tour adult/child $15/10; ⊙9am-5pm) The headquarters of the cable-TV news

THE SOUTH ATLANTA

Atlanta

N
0 .... 1 km
0 .... 0.5 miles

To Virginia Highlands
Bars & Restaurants (0.5mi)

Ponce de Leon Pl

To St Charles
Inn (0.5mi)

To Fernbank Museum of
Natural History (2mi);
Decatur Bars &
Restaurants (4mi);
Stone Mountain (17mi)

To Manuel's Tavern (1mi);
Highland Inn (1mi)

City
Hall
East

Monroe Dr

Virginia Ave

Ponce de Leon Pl

Seal Pl

Greenwood

Ave

Glen Iris Dr

Dallas St

Rankin St

Winton Tce

Morgan St

Boulevard Pl

Parkway Dr

Charles Allen Dr

Monroe Dr

North Ave

Ponce de Leon Ave

Durant Pl

Glendale

Argonne Ave

9th St

8th St

6th St

5th St

3rd St

Penn Ave

Myrtle St

Piedmont Ave

Linden Ave

Pine St

Renaissance
Park

Renaissance Pkwy

Piedmont
Park

To Atlanta Botanical
Garden (0.7mi);
Fat Matt's &
Woodfire Grill (1.5mi)

To High Museum of Art (0.3mi);
Amtrak Station (1.3mi);
Piedmont Hospital (1.9mi)

10th St

12th St

13

20

8th St

Juniper St

6th St

5th St

4th St

3rd St

Pine St

nd St

To Hotel
Artmore
(0.3mi)

Crescent Ave

Peachtree Pl

7th St

Biltmore Pl

Cypress St

Peachtree St NE

N4 Midtown

W Peachtree St

Spring St

22

Linden Ave

Prescott St

MIDTOWN

8

16

To Center for Puppetry
Arts (0.6mi)

11th St

Old 10th St

Spring St NW

Williams St

Techwood Dr

75

85

401

Downtown Connector

18

Spring St

Crescent Ave

10th St

8th St

6th St

Fowler St

5th St

Georgia
Institute of
Technology

4th St

Bobby
Dodd
Stadium

Techwood Dr

North Ave

Bobby Dodd Way

Luckie St

Merritts Ave

Pine St

Tech Pkwy NW

To West Side (1mi);
Octane Cafe (1mi)

THE SOUTH ATLANTA

service. You might be tempted to take the CNN tour, a behind-the-scenes glance at the 24-hour news organization, but don't be heartbroken if you miss it. Visitors don't get close enough to the action to feel connected. They do, however, get to ride on an enormous escalator that climbs above a food court and into the CNN facility.

Georgia State Capitol   HISTORIC BUILDING
(☎404-463-4536; www.sos.ga.gov/archives/state _capitol; 214 State Capitol; ◎8am-5pm Mon-Fri, tours 11:30am) The gold-domed capitol is Atlanta's political hub. The free tours include a film about the legislative process and a glance at the government's communications facility.

MIDTOWN
Midtown is like a hipper, second downtown, with plenty of great bars, restaurants and cultural venues.

TOP CHOICE **High Museum of Art**   GALLERY
(www.high.org; 1280 Peachtree St NE; adult/child $18/11; ◎10am-5pm Tue-Wed, Fri & Sat, 10am-8pm Thu, noon-5pm Sun) Atlanta's modern High Museum was the first museum in the world to ever exhibit art lent from Paris' Louvre and is a destination as much for its architecture as its world-class exhibits. The striking whitewashed multi-level building houses a permanent collection of eye-catching late-19th-century furniture and countless European and American collections, contemporary pieces and Georgian folk art.

Atlanta Botanical Garden   GARDENS
(☎404-876-5859; www.atlantabotanicalgarden.org; 1345 Piedmont Ave NE; adult/child $18.95/12.95; ◎9am-5pm Tue-Sun, to 7pm Apr-Oct) In the northwest corner of Piedmont Park, the stunning 30-acre botanical garden has a Japanese garden, winding paths and the amazing Fuqua Orchid Center.

Margaret Mitchell
House & Museum   HISTORIC BUILDING
(www.margaretmitchellhouse.com; 990 Peachtree St, at 10th St; adult/child $13/10; ◎10am-5:30pm Mon-Sat, noon-5:30pm Sun) A shrine to the author of *Gone With the Wind*. Mitchell wrote her epic in a small apartment in the basement of this historic house, though nothing inside it actually belonged to her.

Piedmont Park   PARK
(www.piedmontpark.org) In the middle of midtown, a glorious, rambling urban park and the setting of many cultural and music festivals. The park has fantastic bike paths, a Saturday Green Market, a well-loved dog area and pleasant green spaces.

Skate Escape CYCLING
(📞404-892-1292; www.skateescape.com; 1086 Piedmont Ave NE) Rents out bicycles (from $6 per hour) and in-line skates ($6 per hour). It also has tandems ($12 per hour) and mountain bikes ($25 for three hours).

SWEET AUBURN

Auburn Ave was the thumping commercial and cultural heart of African American culture in the 1900s. Today a collection of sights is associated with Sweet Auburn's most famous son, Martin Luther King Jr, who was born and preached here and whose grave now looks onto the street.

All of the King sites are a few blocks' walk from the MARTA (Metropolitan Atlanta Rapid Transit Authority) King Memorial station.

Martin Luther King Jr
National Historic Site HISTORIC SITE
The historic site commemorates the life, work and legacy of the civil rights lodestar. The center takes up several blocks. A stop by the excellent bustling visitor center (www. nps.gov/malu; 450 Auburn Ave NE; admission free; ⊙9am-5pm, to 6pm in summer) will help you get oriented with a map and brochure of area sites and exhibits.

King Center for Non-Violent
Social Change MUSEUM
(www.thekingcenter.org; 449 Auburn Ave NE; ⊙9am-5pm, to 6pm summer) Across from the visitor center, it has more information on King's life and work and a few of his personal effects, including his Nobel Peace Prize. His gravesite, between the church and center, is surrounded by a long reflecting pool and can be viewed any time. From here, sign up for 30-minute first-come, first-served guided tours for the Martin Luther King Jr Birthplace (501 Auburn Ave; admission free).

FREE Ebenezer Baptist Church CHURCH
(www.historicebenezer.org; 407 Auburn Ave NE; ⊙tours 9am-6pm Mon-Sat, 1:30-6pm Sun) The preaching ground for King Jr, his father and grandfather, who were all pastors here, is also where King Jr's mother was murdered in 1974. A multimillion-dollar restoration of the church's balcony, hardwood flooring, pews, pulpit, altar furniture, stained-glass windows and baptismal pool to the 1960–68 period when King Jr served as co-pastor with his father, was completed in 2011. Tours are self-guided. Sunday services are now held at a new Ebenezer across the street.

GRANT PARK
Grant Park PARK
(www.grantpark.org) A large oasis of green situated on the edge of the city center, the park is home to Zoo Atlanta (www.zooatlanta.org; adult/child $20/16; ⊙9:30am-5:30pm Mon-Fri, to 6:30pm Sat & Sun; 🚼), which features flamingos, elephants, kangaroos and the odd tiger. But the zoo's pride and joy are the giant pandas. They tend to have cubs that slaughter you with cuteness. Be prepared to wait to see the cubs.

For history buffs, on the south side of Grant Park is the Cyclorama building that houses the gigantic mural *Battle of Atlanta,* which visually recounts the history of the fight.

THE SHORT LIFE OF A CIVIL RIGHTS GIANT

Martin Luther King Jr, the quintessential figure of the American Civil Rights movement, was born in 1929, the son of an Atlanta preacher. His lineage was significant not only because he followed his father to the pulpit of Ebenezer Baptist Church, but also because his political speeches rang out with a preacher's inflections.

In 1955 King led the 'bus boycott' in Montgomery, AL. After a year of boycotting, the US Supreme Court removed laws that enforced segregated buses. From this successful beginning King emerged as an inspiring moral voice in civil rights.

His nonviolent approach to racial equality and peace makes his death all the more ironic: he was assassinated on a Memphis hotel balcony in 1968, four years after receiving the Nobel Peace Prize and five years after giving his legendary 'I Have a Dream' speech in Washington, DC.

King remains one of the most recognized and respected figures of the 20th century. Over 10 years he led a movement that essentially ended a system of statutory discrimination in existence since the country's founding. The Martin Luther King Jr National Historic Site and the King Center for Non-Violent Social Change in Atlanta are testaments to his moral vision, his ability to inspire others and his lasting impact on the fundamental fabric of American society.

GAY & LESBIAN ATLANTA

Atlanta – or 'Hotlanta' as some might call it – is one of the few places in Georgia, perhaps in the South, with a noticeable and active gay and lesbian population. Midtown is the center of gay life; the epicenter is around Piedmont Park and the intersection of 10th St and Piedmont Ave. The town of Decatur, east of downtown Atlanta, has a significant lesbian community. For news and information, grab a copy of the *Southern Voice* newspaper (www.sovo.com); also check out www.gayatlanta.com.

Atlanta Pride Festival (www.atlantapride.org) is a massive annual celebration of the city's gay and lesbian community. Held at the end of June in and around Piedmont Park, it attracts people from all over the country.

LITTLE FIVE POINTS & EAST ATLANTA

These two bohemian neighborhoods are close to one another, but miles away from mainstream Atlanta's genteel sensibilities. They're young, hipster neighborhoods with a definite alternative edge. Both are dominated by a main drag – in L5P and Flat Shoals Ave in East Atlanta – and both are anchored by popular music venues, Variety Playhouse and the EARL, respectively. These neighborhoods offer Atlanta's most dense concentration of funky local boutiques; the stretch of Moreland Ave separating the two 'hoods is equally dense with big chain stores. Both neighborhoods can be explored well on foot, and both are jammed with restaurants.

VIRGINIA-HIGHLAND

Atlanta's preppiest neighborhood is populated by adorable homes (with big price tags) and beautiful boutiques (with big price tags). Highland Ave, running through the heart of the neighborhood, makes for a pleasant stroll.

POINTS EAST & DECATUR

Carter Presidential Library & Museum LIBRARY, MUSEUM
(404-865-7100; www.jimmycarterlibrary.org; 441 Freedom Pkwy; adult/child $8/free; 9am-4:45pm Mon-Sat, noon-4:45pm Sun) Located on a hilltop overlooking downtown, it features exhibits highlighting Jimmy Carter's 1977–81 presidency, including a replica of the Oval Office. Carter's Nobel Prize is also on display. Don't miss the tranquil Japanese garden out back.

Festivals & Events

Atlanta Jazz Festival MUSIC
(www.atlantafestivals.com) A city-sponsored month-long event culminating in live concerts in Piedmont Park on Memorial Day weekend in late May.

Atlanta Pride Festival CULTURAL
(www.atlantapride.org) End of June.

National Black Arts Festival CULTURAL
(404-730-7315; www.nbaf.org) Artists from across the country converge on Atlanta for this festival celebrating African American music, theater, literature and film. Held in July at various locations.

Sleeping

Rates at downtown hotels tend to fluctuate wildly depending on whether there is a large convention in town. At weekends rates often go down away from downtown and rise in the city. A cheap option is to stay in one of the many chain hotels along the MARTA line outside downtown and take the train into the city for sightseeing.

St Charles Inn B&B $$
(404-875-1001; www.thesaintcharlesinn.com; 1001 St Charles Ave NE; r incl breakfast $115-215; P@) Ideally located steps from the shops and restaurants of Highland Ave and 15 minutes from everything else, this homey B&B – the friendliest we encountered – does all things right and cozy. There are seven fireplaces and some rooms have Jacuzzi tubs. The friendly innkeepers are a young hipster couple that can point you down the gastro/libation path of choice.

Hotel Artmore BOUTIQUE HOTEL $$
(404-876-6100; www.artmorehotel.com; 1302 W Peachtree St; r $99-209; @) This funky art-deco gem wins all sorts of accolades: Excellent service, a wonderful, wine-inviting courtyard with fire pit and a superb location across the street from Arts Center MARTA station. The 1924 Spanish-Mediterranean architectural landmark was completely revamped in 2009 resulting in an artistic boutique hotel that's become an urban sanctuary for those who appreciate their trendiness with a dollop of discretion. Parking is $18.

Stonehurst Place B&B **$$$**
(☑404-881-0722; www.stonehurstplace.com; 923 Piedmont Ave NE; r $159-399; P❈@🛜) Built in 1896 by the Hinman family, this elegant, almost Parisian B&B has all the modern amenities one could ask for and is fully updated with ecofriendly water treatment and heating systems. Smack in the middle of midtown, this is truly an exceptional place to stay in Atlanta if you have the budget.

Highland Inn INN **$$**
(☑404-874-5756; www.thehighlandinn.com; 644 N Highland Ave; s/d/ste incl breakfast $100/121/130; P❈🛜) This aged European-style inn has a great location in the middle of Virginia-Highland. Appealing to touring musicians over the years and with its own casual music venue, the Ballroom Lounge, on the bottom floor, this ragged but clean hotel has lyrical personality.

Loews Atlanta BUSINESS HOTEL **$$**
(☑404-745-5000; ww.loewshotels.com; 1065 Peachtree St; r from $189; ❈@🛜) Smart and modern, Atlanta's newest boutique business hotel is part of the Loews chain and offers luxury with all the fixings smack-dab in the heart of the arts in Midtown, walking distance from the Woodruff Arts Center and Fox Theatre. The attached Exhale Spa will soothe your weary heart after the board meetings and contemporary art – studio soundboard paintings, etc – add a bit of hi-tech artistic flair.

✗ Eating

After New Orleans, Atlanta is the best city in the South to eat and food culture here is nothing short of obsessive. At time of writing, the gourmet burger, craft beer and mixology cultures are approaching fetish levels and the farm-to-table trend was a near given. Some of the most iconic eats of the USA were also born here: Krispy Kreme and Waffle House among them.

DOWNTOWN, MIDTOWN & NORTH

🍴 **Woodfire Grill** MODERN AMERICAN **$$$**
(☑404-347-9055; www.woodfiregrill.com; 1782 Cheshire Bridge Rd; mains $28-36; ☺5:30-10pm Tue-Thu, till 11pm Fri & Sat) Fiercely bearded *Top Chef* Season 6 finalist Kevin Gillespie is at the helm at this superb choice, offering one of the city's most memorable foodie bangs for the buck and sublime service. À la carte is limited, but five-course ($65) and

---

ATLANTA FOR CHILDREN

Atlanta has plenty of activities to keep children entertained, delighted and – perhaps against their will – educated.

Fernbank Museum of Natural History MUSEUM
(☑404-929-6300; www.fernbankmuseum.org; 767 Clifton Rd NE; adult/child $17.50/15.50; ☺10am-5pm Mon-Sat, noon-5pm Sun; ⛹) There are better natural history museums, but Fernbank is especially kid-friendly with its new Naturequest exhibit. The museum covers the natural world from seashells to giant lizards, and it has an **IMAX theater** (adult/child $13/12).

Center for Puppetry Arts MUSEUM
(www.puppet.org; 1404 Spring St NW; museum $8.25; ☺9am-3pm Tue-Fri, 9am-5pm Sat, 11am-5pm Sun; ⛹) A wonderland for visitors of all ages and, hands-down, one of Atlanta's most unique attractions, the museum houses a treasury of puppets, some of which you get to operate yourself. Separate tickets are required for the performances.

Stone Summit ROCK CLIMBING
(www.ssclimbing.com; 3701 Presidential Pkwy; adult/child $12/10; ☺6am-10pm Mon & Wed, 11am-10pm Tue & Thu-Fri, 10am-8pm Sat, noon-6pm Sun; ⛹) The nation's largest climbing gym is especially welcoming for beginners and kids, so grab the whole family and get up those walls!

Imagine It! Children's Museum of Atlanta MUSEUM
(www.childrensmuseumatlanta.org; 275 Olympic Centennial Park Dr NW; admission $12.50; ☺10am-4pm Mon-Fri, to 5pm Sat & Sun; ⛹) A hands-on museum geared toward kids aged eight and under. Adults aren't allowed in without a youngster in tow.

seven-course ($85) tasting menus are given the attention of a *Top Chef* challenge with a Slow Food mentality: a stunning fried green tomato with bacon-hot sauce aioli, chili-rubbed Angus strip-loin in cumin-orange vinaigrette, wood-grilled honey-lacquered local quail – everything sourced, prepared and served according to all the sustainable buzz words.

Ecco
EUROPEAN $$$

(404-347-9555; www.ecco-atlanta.com; 40 7th St NE; mains $19-25; 5:30-10pm Sun-Thu, till 11pm Fri & Sat) The vehemently sustainable Ecco was named America's best new restaurant in 2006 by *Esquire* magazine, and you can certainly have a blowout meal here. But you can also go the tapas/small bite route ($4 to $14) and leave floored with some change in your pocket. The fried goat's cheese with honey and black pepper and the chili-braised pork with garlic and homemade pappardelle are both extraordinary.

Fat Matt's Rib Shack
BARBECUE $$

(www.fatmattsribshack.com; 1811 Piedmont Ave NE; sandwiches from $3.95; 11:30am-11:30pm Mon-Fri, to 12:30am Sat, 1-11:30pm Sun) A classic shrine to two great Southern traditions: barbecue and the blues. Take special note of the Brunswick stew, a delicious side dish best described as barbecue soup.

Varsity
FAST FOOD $

(www.thevarsity.com; 61 North Ave, at Spring St; dogs from $1.35; 10am-11:30pm Mon-Thu, to 12:30am Fri & Sat) This drive-in restaurant on steroids (it's the world's largest) has been an Atlanta institution since 1928. It's little more than a glorified fast-food joint, but it's always packed.

WEST SIDE

Miller Union
NEW SOUTHERN $$$

(404-685-3191; www.millerunion.com; 999 Brady Ave; mains $19-26; 11:30am-2:30pm Tue-Sat & 5-10pm Mon-Thu, 5-11pm Fri & Sat) Former stockyards have been transformed into Atlanta's most exciting newcomer, a lesson in restrained subtlety disguised as sustainable New Southern gastro-science in a city obsessed with both. Chef Steven Satterfield has wooed everyone from us to Martha Stewart with his appetizer egg cooked in celery cream.

Bocado
AMERICAN $$

(www.bocadoatlanta.com; 887 Howell Mill Rd; lunch mains $8-11; 11am-2pm Mon-Fri, 5-10pm Mon-Sat) The name loosely translates as mouthful/morsel/bite from Spanish/Portuguese/Italian, but there's nothing little about the flavor packed into the viciously creative sandwiches and salads on offer at this West Side farm-to-table newcomer. Hello roasted poblano (a type of chili) and pimento cheese sandwich with bacon and fried green tomatoes, it's a pleasure to meet you.

SWEET AUBURN

Sweet Auburn Curb Market
MARKET $

(www.sweetauburncurbmarket.com; 209 Edgewood Ave SE; mains $5-9; 8am-6pm Mon-Sat) This small market allows foodies to browse countless stalls for cooking ingredients or hot meals served on the premises, from organic coffee to Italian deli fare. Bell Street Burritos is particularly worthy of a trip here, serving up the sort of fresh, fat burritos that evoke San Francisco's Mission District.

LITTLE FIVE POINTS

Vortex Bar & Grill
BURGERS $

(www.thevortexbarandgrill.com; 438 Moreland Ave; burgers from $6.45; 11am-midnight Sun-Thu, to 3am Fri & Sat) A scrappy joint where alterna-hipsters mingle alongside Texas tourists and Morehouse College steppers. The snarky menu boasts loads of gourmet burgers, but don't discount the sublime black bean veggie melt. There's also a branch in Midtown (878 Peachtree St). No kids.

VIRGINIA-HIGHLAND & INMAN PARK

Goin' Coastal
TOP CHOICE
SEAFOOD $$$

(www.goincoastalseafood.com; 1021 Virginia Ave NE; mains $18-26; 5-10pm Mon-Thu, 10am-10pm Fri, 11:30am-11pm Sat & Sun) Atlanta needs another holy ethics-toting restaurant like it needs more traffic; but great seafood is still pretty off the radar here. That changes with this casual neighborhood seafood place in the heart of the Highlands run by a bunch of good ol' fishing buddies. Fresh blackboard catches of the day supplement stunning staples such as lobster tacos ($18), coastal trout ($24) and a heap of delicious sides (creamy grits, jalapeño corn-bread pudding). It only serves eco-acceptable fish and uses hydroponic greens grown with reclaimed water from high-tech urban farms inside reused shipping containers. Futuristic, fun and fabulous.

Fritti
PIZZERIA $$

(www.frittirestaurant.com; 309 N Highland Ave NE; pizza $10-15; 11:30-3pm & 5:30-11pm, till midnight Fri & Sat, 12:30-10pm Sun) Staunchly traditional pizza Napoletana emerges from an $18,000, 13,000lb, 1100°F (593°C) Uno Forno brick oven, hand-built brick-by-brick by *the* Stefano Ferrara – Naples' pizza God – with 100% Italian materials including volcanic ash from Mount Vesuvius. Fritti is not messing around. Cooking time: 45 seconds.

DECATUR
Independent Decatur, 6 miles east of downtown, has grown into a bohemian enclave of counterculture over the years and is now a bonafide foodie destination.

TOP CHOICE Leon's Full Service
FUSION $$

(www.leonsfullservice.com; 131 E Ponce de Leon Ave; mains $11-19; ⊙5pm-1am Mon, 11:30am-1am Tue-Thu & Sun, till 2am Fri & Sat) If your indie rock friends got together and dreamed up a holier-than-thou menu and beer list, this is it. Everyone here thinks they are cooler than you, but the food excels: slow-roasted beef brisket in black peppercorn gravy, killer pub frites with specialty sauces, etc. It's all the rage in Decatur rightfully so.

Farm Burger
BURGERS $

(www.farmburger.net; 410b W Ponce de Leon Ave; burgers from $6; ⊙11:30am-10pm Sun-Thu, 11:30am-10pm Fri & Sat) Southeastern sweetgrass-fed, locally farm-raised beef is the calling at this gourmet farm-to-table burger joint, the current trailblazer in an ongoing Atlanta burger war. Build your own from $6 from an unorthodox list that includes oxtail marmalade, roasted bone marrow and pimento and cheese (a Southern staple); or go for the daily-changing chalkboard special.

Taqueria del Sol
MEXICAN $

(359 W. Ponce de Leon Ave; tacos $2.39; ⊙11am-2pm Mon-Fri & 5:30-9pm Tue-Thu, 12-3pm Sat & 5:30-10pm Fri & Sat) Smoked pork or fried chicken tacos and to-die-for shrimp corn chowder are highlights of this Mexican–Southern marriage, a great value in a city that can overwhelm with both sides of that culinary coin otherwise.

🍺 Drinking

Brick Store Pub
BAR

(www.brickstorepub.com; 125 E Court Sq) Beer hounds geek out on Atlanta's best beer selection, with some 17 meticulously chosen draughts (so underground, they're striking oil) and a separate Belgian beer bar upstairs.

In total, nearly 200 by the bottle and a cool quotient approaching exhausting.

Park Tavern
BAR

(www.parktavern.com; 500 10th Street NE) This microbrewery/restaurant may not be on the modster It List, but its outdoor patio on the edge of Piedmont Park is one of the most beautiful spots in Atlanta to sit back and drink away a weekend afternoon.

Euclid Avenue Yacht Club
BAR

(1136 Euclid Ave) A divey bar ideal for grabbing a drink before a show at the nearby Variety Playhouse.

Octane
CAFE

(www.octanecoffee.com; 1009-B Marietta St; sandwiches $4-6; ⊙7am-11pm Mon-Thu, to midnight Fri, 8am-11pm Sat & Sun; 🛜) This industrial-hip coffeehouse near Georgia Tech's campus brews the joe of choice for severe caffeine junkies, following a 'direct trade' philosophy.

Manuel's Tavern
BAR

(www.manuelstavern.com; 602 N Highland Ave) A longtime political hangout that draws a good, conversational beer-drinking crowd.

Blake's
GAY & LESBIAN

(www.blakesontheparkatlanta.com; 227 10th St NE) Right on Piedmont Park, Blake's bills itself as 'Atlanta's favorite gay bar since 1987.'

☆ Entertainment

Atlanta has big-city nightlife with lots of live music and cultural events. Check out **Atlanta Coalition of Performing Arts** (www.atlantaperforms.com), which has info and links about the city's music, film, dance and theater scene. The **Atlanta Music Guide** (www.atlantamusicguide.com) maintains a live-music schedule, plus a directory of local venues and links to online ticketing.

Theater

Woodruff Arts Center
ARTS CENTER

(www.woodruffcenter.org; 1280 Peachtree St NE, at 15th St) An arts campus hosting the High Museum, the Atlanta Symphony Orchestra and the Alliance Theatre.

Fox Theatre
THEATER

(www.foxtheatre.org; 660 Peachtree St NE) A spectacular 1929 movie palace with fanciful Moorish and Egyptian designs. It hosts Broadway shows, and concerts in an auditorium holding more than 4500 people.

Live Music & Nightclubs

Cover charges at the following vary nightly. Check their respective websites for music calendars and ticket prices.

EARL
LIVE MUSIC

(www.badearl.com; 488 Flat Shoals Ave) The indie rocker's pub of choice – a smoky restaurant with surprisingly good food; it's also a bar and a busy live-music venue.

Eddie's Attic
LIVE MUSIC

(www.eddiesattic.com; 515b N McDonough St, Decatur) One of the city's best venues to hear live folk and acoustic music, renowned for breaking local artists, in a nonsmoking atmosphere seven nights a week.

MJQ Concourse
CLUB

(☑404-870-0575; 736 Ponce de Leon Place NE) This club inside a former underground parking garage is now all the young indie scenester rage – you enter through a small retractable garage door in what looks like an indiscreet tool shed behind a Chipotle – I mean, where else?

Variety Playhouse
LIVE MUSIC

(www.variety-playhouse.com; 1099 Euclid Ave NE) A smartly booked and well-run concert venue for a variety of touring artists.

Sports

Order tickets to sporting events through Ticketmaster (☑404-249-6400; www.ticketmaster.com).

Atlanta Braves
BASEBALL

(☑404-522-7630; www.atlantabraves.com; tickets $8-90) The Major League Baseball (MLB) team plays at Turner Field. The MARTA/Braves shuttles to the games leave from **Underground Atlanta** (www.underground-atlanta.com; cnr Peachtree & Alabama Sts; ⊙10am-9pm Mon-Sat, 11am-6pm Sun) at Steve Polk Plaza beginning 90 minutes before the first pitch.

ⓘ Information

Emergency & Medical Services

Atlanta Medical Center (www.atlantamedcenter.com; 303 Pkwy Dr NE)

Atlanta Police Department (☑404-614-6544; www.atlantapd.org)

Emory University Hospital (www.emoryhealthcare.org; 1364 Clifton Rd NE)

Piedmont Hospital (www.piedmonthospital.org; 1968 Peachtree Rd NW)

Internet Access

Central Library (www.afpls.org; 1 Margaret Mitchell Sq; ⊙9am-9pm Mon-Sat, 2-6pm Sun)

Many branches of the public library offer two free 15-minute internet sessions daily, including this main branch.

Internet Resources

Access Atlanta (www.accessatlanta.com) A great place to find out about Atlanta news and upcoming events.

Atlanta Travel Guide (www.atlanta.net) Official site of the Atlanta Convention & Visitors Bureau with excellent links to shops, restaurants, hotels and upcoming events.

Media

Atlanta (www.atlantamagazine.com) A monthly general-interest magazine covering local issues, arts and dining.

Atlanta Daily World (www.atlantadailyworld.com) The nation's oldest continuously running African American newspaper (since 1928).

Atlanta Journal-Constitution (www.ajc.com) Atlanta's major daily newspaper, with a good travel section on Sunday.

Creative Loafing (www.clatl.com) For hip tips on music, arts and theater, this free alternative weekly comes out every Wednesday.

Post

For general postal information call ☑800-275-8777.

Post office CNN Center (190 Marietta St NW); Little Five Points (455 Moreland Ave NE); North Highland (1190 N Highland Ave NE); Phoenix Station (41 Marietta St NW)

Tourist Information

Atlanta Convention & Visitors Bureau (☑404-521-6600; www.atlanta.net; 233 Peachtree St; ⊙9am-5pm Mon-Fri) Has an online neighborhood guide, a restaurant guide and a link to info for gay and lesbian travelers – in six languages. Its website also lets you buy a CityPass, a tremendous money saver that bundles admission to five attractions for the discounted price of $69.

ⓘ Getting There & Away

Atlanta's huge **Hartsfield-Jackson International Airport** (ATL; www.atlanta-airport.com), 12 miles south of downtown, is a major regional hub and an international gateway. It's the busiest airport in the world in overall passenger traffic.

The **Greyhound terminal** (232 Forsyth St) is next to the MARTA Garnett station. Some destinations include Nashville, TN (five hours), New Orleans, LA (10½ hours), New York (20 hours), Miami, FL (16 hours) and Savannah, GA (4¾ hours).

The **Amtrak station** (1688 Peachtree St NW, at Deering Rd) is just north of downtown.

Getting Around

The **Metropolitan Atlanta Rapid Transit Authority** (MARTA; www.itsmarta.com; fares $2.50) rail line travels to/from the airport to downtown, along with a few less-useful routes used mostly by commuters. Individual tokens are no longer sold – every customer must purchase a Breeze card ($1), which can be loaded and reloaded as necessary.

The shuttle and car-rental agencies have desks in the airport situated at the baggage-claim level.

Driving in Atlanta can be infuriating. You'll often find yourself sitting in traffic jams, and it's easy to get disoriented – a road map is invaluable.

North Georgia

The southern end of the great Appalachian Range extends some 40 miles into Georgia's far north, providing some superb mountain scenery and wild white-water rivers. The landscape is unlike anywhere else in Georgia. The fall colors emerge late here, peaking in October.

A few days are warranted to see sites like the 1200ft-deep **Tallulah Gorge** (www.gastateparks.org/TallulahGorge), the mountain scenery and hiking trails at **Vogel State Park** (www.gastateparks.org/Vogel) and **Unicoi State Park** (www.gastateparks.org/Unicoi), and the interesting collection of Appalachian folk arts at the **Foxfire Museum** (www.foxfire.org; adult/child $6/3; ☺8:30am-4:30pm Mon-Sat) in Mountain City.

DAHLONEGA

In 1828 Dahlonega was the site of the first gold rush in the USA. The boom these days, though, is in tourism. It's an easy day excursion from Atlanta and is a fantastic destination if you want to get away to the mountains.

Walking around the historic main square is an event in itself. Many offbeat shops compete for tourist dollars. The **visitor center** (☎706-864-3513; www.dahlonega.org; 13 S Park St; ☺9am-5:30pm Mon-Fri, 10am-5pm Sat) has plenty of information on area sites and activities (including hiking, canoeing, kayaking, rafting and mountain biking).

Amicalola Falls State Park (☎706-265-4703; www.amicalolafalls.com), 18 miles west of Dahlonega on Hwy 52, features the 729ft **Amicalola Falls**, the highest waterfall in Georgia. The park offers spectacular scenery, a lodge, and excellent hiking and mountain-biking trails.

The **cycling** (www.cyclenorthgeorgia.com) was fantastic enough for Lance Armstrong to train here. **Dalhonega Wheelworks** (www.wheelworksga.com; 24 Alicia Lane; ☺11am-6pm Mon, Tue, Thu, Fri, 1:30-6pm Wed, 9am-5pm Sat) is a nice bike shop in town with mountain and road bike rentals, bike guides and daily rides offered at the shop. The 35-mile **Three Gap** cycling loop is spectacular, but bring your climbing legs.

A number of wineries near Dahlonega actually produce some tasty products, but it's especially worth going to hang out at the gorgeous vineyards. **Frogtown Cellars** (www.frogtownwine.com; 700 Ridge Point Dr; ☺noon-5pm Sun-Fri, to 6pm Sat, 12:30-5pm Sun) is a beautiful winery with a killer deck on which to sip libations and enjoy a panini lunch. It's one of the East Coast's most award-winning producers.

Crimson Moon Café (24 N Park St; mains $8-15; ☺11am-3pm Mon, till 9pm Wed, till 10pm Thu-Fri, 8am-1pm Sat, 8am-8pm Sun) is an organic coffeehouse offering great Southern comfort food and an intimate live music venue.

Hiker Hostel (☎770-312-7342; www.hikerhostel.com; 7693 Hwy 19N; dm/r $17/40; P✻@☎), on Hwy 19N near the Three Gap Loop, is owned by an avid couple of cycling and outdoors enthusiasts. The hostel is newish, wonderfully kept with extra-cool dorm-bed drapes for privacy, and provides hearty breakfasts. The only downside is the blurred lines between staff and guest regarding bed maintenance in private rooms.

Central Georgia

Central Georgia is a kind of catch-all for everything that's not metro Atlanta, mountainous north Georgia or swampy Savannah-centric south Georgia. The remaining area feels rustic and Southern.

ATHENS

A beery, artsy and laid-back college town roughly 70 miles east of Atlanta, Athens has an extremely popular football team (the University of Georgia Bulldogs), a world-famous music scene (which has launched artists including the B-52s, R.E.M. and Widespread Panic) and a burgeoning restaurant culture. The university drives the culture of Athens and ensures an ever-replenishing supply of young bar-hoppers and concertgoers. The pleasant, walkable downtown offers a plethora of funky choices for eating, drinking and shopping.

For a more detailed music sites tour, pick up a copy of Lonely Planet's *The Carolinas, Georgia & the South Trips*.

◉ Sights & Activities

State Botanical Garden of Georgia
GARDENS

(www.uga.edu/~botgarden; 2450 S Milledge Ave; suggested donation $2; ⊗8am-6pm, to 8pm summer) Truly gorgeous, with winding outdoor paths and a socio-historical edge to boot, Athens' gardens rivals Atlanta's. Signs provide smart context for its amazing collection of plants, which runs the gamut from rare and threatened species to nearly 5 miles of top-notch woodland walking trails.

Georgia Museum of Art
MUSEUM

(www.georgiamuseum.org; 90 Carlton St; suggested donation $3; ⊗10am-5pm Tue-Wed, Fri & Sat, to 9pm Thu, 1-5pm Sun) Fresh off a $20 million expansion, the state's modern, excellent art museum now boasts 16,000 sq ft of new galleries and an outdoor sculpture garden.

🛏 Sleeping & Eating

Athens does not have an awesome variety of places to stay. There are standard chains just out of town on W Broad St.

Hotel Indigo
BOUTIQUE HOTEL $$
TOP CHOICE

(☎706-546-0430; www.indigoathens.com; 500 College Ave; r weekend/weekday from $159/139; P✳@🛜🏊) Athens' first – and desperately needed – boutique hotel is part of the Indigo chain, but here is a LEED Gold-certified sustainable standout (the first of InterContinental's 4500 hotels worldwide). Green elements throughout (regenerative elevators, priority parking for hybrid vehicles, 30% of the building constructed from recycled content) means it's environmentally sound,

---

BUCK MANOR

For a glimpse of a classic Athens musical legend, do a drive-by of 748 Cobb St, a Second Empire Victorian home painted 12 different colors and known as Buck Manor. R.E.M. guitarist Peter Buck lived here until his divorce from his wife, Barrie; and R.E.M. filmed the *Nightswimming* video here as well as a prerelease promotional video for *Out of Time*. Nirvana spent the night here when they played the 40 Watt Club in 1991.

---

and the 130-room eco-chic hotel is steeped in local color (Jittery Joe's coffee instead of Starbucks, reclaimed barn-wood-framed posters of R.E.M. and the like).

Foundry Park Inn & Spa
INN $$

(☎706-549-7020; www.foundryparkinn.com; 295 E Dougherty St; r $130-150; P✳@🛜🏊) An upscale, non-corporate choice on pleasant grounds, including the restored Confederate iron foundry. In addition to its on-site spa the hotel campus includes a restaurant and the Melting Point, a cozy music venue.

Five & Ten
AMERICAN $$$
TOP CHOICE

(☎706-546-7300; www.fiveandten.com; 1653 S Lumpkin St; mains $18-29; ⊗5:30-10pm Sun-Thu, to 11pm Fri & Sat, 10:30am-2:30pm Sun) Driven by sustainable ingredients, Five & Ten ranks among the South's best restaurants. Its menu is earthy and slightly gamey: sweatbreads, hand-cut pasta and Frogmore stew (stewed corn, sausage and potato). Reservations mandatory.

Farm 255
AMERICAN $$

(www.farm255.com; 255 W Washington St; mains $12-21; ⊗5:30-10pm Tue-Thu, to 10:30pm Fri & Sat, 11am-2pm & 5:30-9:30pm Sun) This stylish, light-filled bistro gets much of its meat and vegetables from its own 5-acre, organic/biodynamic Blue Moon Farms outside of Athens. The operative word here is *fresh*.

Grit
VEGETARIAN $

(www.thegrit.com; 199 Prince Ave; mains $5-8; ⊗11am-10pm Mon-Fri 10am-3pm & 5-10pm Sat & Sun; 🍴🛜) Get your tofu Reuben (grilled rye sandwich) or black-eyed pea burger on at this pioneering vegetarian spot whose landlord is R.E.M.'s Michael Stipe.

Grill
DINER $

(www.thegrit.com; 171 College Ave; mains $5-8; ⊗24hr) Downtown diner that's an Athens institution for curing late-night, drunken munches. It's all about the fries dipped in feta cheese.

🍷 Drinking & Entertainment

Nearly 100 bars and restaurants dot Athens' compact downtown area, so it's not hard to find a good time. Pick up a free *Flagpole* (www.flagpole.com) weekly to find out what's on.

Trappeze Pub
PUB

(www.trappezepub.com; 269 W Washington St; draft beers $4-8; ⊗11am-2am Mon-Sat, to midnight Sun) Those 'beer weirdos,' as one local put it, flock here to enjoy a choice of 35 beers on tap and 260 by the bottle, with bartenders who wax poetic about suds like sommeliers talk Château d'Yquem. The above-average pub menu takes full advantage of the stock – pulled pork marinated in Unibroue Ephemere? Don't mind if I do.

40 Watt Club   LIVE MUSIC
(www.40watt.com; 285 W Washington St) It has lounges, a tiki bar, $2 PBR beers, and indie rock on stage. It's where the big hitters in town play. No wonder it's legendary.

Manhattan Cafe   BAR
(337 N Hull St) The antithesis of most downtown Athens bars, this dive is the spot to tie one on if you don't have an 8am Psych class to concern you. It's all funky lighting, mismatched reclaimed furniture and townie attitude.

❶ Information
The **Athens Welcome Center** (☎706-353-1820; www.athenswelcomecenter.com; 280 E Dougherty St; ◷10am-5pm Mon-Sat, noon-5pm Sun), in a historic antebellum house at the corner of Thomas St, provides maps and information on local tours – these include a Civil War tour and the 'Walking Tour of Athens Music History.'

Savannah

Like a Southern belle who wears hot pants under her skirt, this grand historic town revolves around formal antebellum architecture and the revelry of local students from Savannah College of Art & Design. It sits alongside the Savannah River, about 18 miles from the coast, amid Lowcountry swamps and mammoth live oak trees dripping with Spanish moss. With its gorgeous mansions, cotton warehouses, wonderfully beautiful squares and Colonial public buildings, Savannah preserves its past with pride and grace. However, unlike its sister city of Charleston, SC, which retains its reputation as a dignified and refined cultural center, Savannah isn't clean-cut – the town has been described as 'a beautiful lady with a dirty face.'

◉ Sights & Activities
The Central Park of Savannah is a sprawling rectangular green space called **Forsyth Park**. The park's beautiful fountain is a quintessential photo op.

Owens-Thomas House   HISTORIC BUILDING
(www.telfair.org; 124 Abercorn St; adult/child $15/5; ◷noon-5pm Mon, 10am-5pm Tue-Sat, 1-5pm Sun) Completed in 1819 by British architect William Jay, this gorgeous villa exemplifies English Regency-style architecture, which is known for its symmetry. The guided tour is fussy, but it delivers interesting trivia about the spooky 'haint blue' ceiling paint in the slave's quarters (made from crushed indigo, buttermilk and crushed oyster shells) and the number of years by which this mansion preceded the White House in getting running water (nearly 20).

Jepson Center for the Arts   GALLERY
(JCA; www.telfair.org; 207 W York St; multivenue ticket adult/child $20/5; ◷10am-5pm Mon, Wed, Fri & Sat, 10am-8pm Thu, noon-5pm Sun; ⊞) Now over five years old but still looking pretty darn space-age by Savannah's standards, the JCA focuses on 20th- and 21st-century art. Its contents are modest in size but intriguing. There's also a neat interactive area for kids. The $20 multivenue ticket allows discounted admission to two affiliated museums, the Telfair and the Owens-Thomas House.

Mercer-Williams House   HISTORIC BUILDING
(www.mercerhouse.com; 429 Bull St; adult/child $12.50/8) Although Jim Williams, the Savannah art dealer portrayed by Kevin Spacey in the film version of *Midnight in the Garden of Good and Evil,* died back in 1990, his infamous mansion didn't become a museum until 2004. You're not allowed to see the upstairs, where Williams' family still lives, but the downstairs is an interior decorator's fantasy.

Telfair Museum of Art   MUSEUM
(www.telfair.org; 121 Barnard St; multi-venue ticket adult/child $20/5; ◷noon-5pm Mon, 10am-5pm Tue-Sat, 1-5pm Sun) Along with silver from the 1800s and a colossal oil painting depicting a scene from the Hundred Years War, Sylvia Shaw's famous 1936 *Bird Girl* sculpture – the one on the cover of *Midnight in the Garden of Good and Evil* – stands inside this museum.

Cathedral of St John the Baptist   CHURCH
Completed in 1896 but destroyed by fire two years later, this impressive cathedral, reopened in 1912, features stunning stained-glass transept windows from Austria depicting Christ's ascension into heaven as well as

THE SOUTH GEORGIA

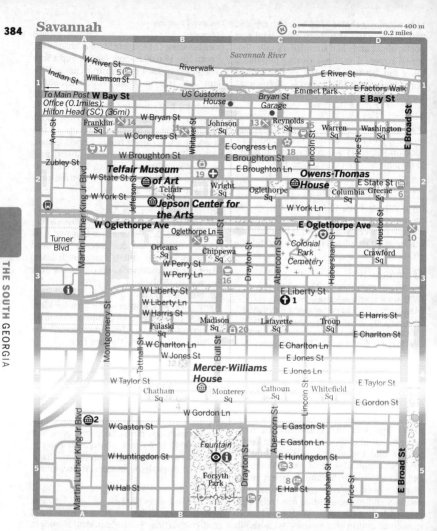

ornate Station of the Cross woodcarvings from Bavaria.

Ralph Mark Gilbert
Civil Rights Museum   MUSEUM
(460 Martin Luther King Jr Blvd; adult/child $8/4; ☉9am-5pm Tue-Sat) Focuses on the local history of segregated schools, hotels, hospitals, jobs and lunch counters. Push the buttons at the Levy's lunch counter – a dramatization, but no less stinging.

🛏 Sleeping

Luckily for travelers, it's become stylish for Savannah hotels and B&Bs to serve hors d'oeuvres and wine to guests in the evening. Accommodations by the river have lots of hype and make your wallet quiver.

Bohemian Hotel   BOUTIQUE HOTEL **$$$**
(☎912-721-3800; www.bohemianhotelsavannah .com; 102 West Bay St; r weekend/weekday $319/229; P✳@🅰) Though it was meant to evoke a maritime theme (how awful?), thankfully it didn't take – stunning hot Gothic hallways and dark, dungeon-chic art are better adjectives to describe Savannah's new waterfront hotel. Staying here feels almost medieval, which is really kind of sinister and

Savannah

THE SOUTH SAVANNAH

great save the low-lit guest rooms – the one outright flaw. Small touches like driftwood and oyster chandeliers are fabulous and personalized service makes it feel far more intimate than its 75 rooms indicate. The views, especially from the Rocks rooftop bar, are exemplary. Parking is $21.

Thunderbird Inn   MOTEL $
(☎912-232-2661; www.thethunderbirdinn.com; 611 W Oglethorpe Ave; r $99; P❋☎) A little dab of Palm Springs, a little dip of Vegas best describes this renovated vintage-chic 1964 motel that wins its own popularity contest – a 'Hippest hotel in Savannah' proclamation greets guests in his '60s-soundtracked lobby. But in a land of stuffy B&Bs this groovy place is an oasis, made all the better by a fresh coat of soothing paints and local SCAD (Savannah College of Art and Design) student art. The hotel is just outside the tourist area, across from the Greyhound station. Krispy Kreme donuts for breakfast!

Mansion on Forsyth Park   HOTEL $$$
(☎912-238-5158; www.mansiononforsythpark.com; 700 Drayton St; r weekday/weekend $249/199; ❋@☎☒) A choice location and chic design highlight the luxe accommodations on offer at the 18,000-sq-ft Mansion – the sexy bathrooms alone are practically worth the money. The best part of the hotel-spa is the amazing local and international art that crowds its walls and hallways, over 400 original pieces in all. Parking costs $20 per day.

Green Palm Inn   B&B $$
(☎912-447-8901; www.greenpalminn.com; 548 E President St; r from $149-189; P❋☎) With the capacity to host up to nine people, this cute B&B off Green Sq provides an intimate B&B experience. The rooms are meticulously cared for and staff is helpful and friendly.

Bed & Breakfast Inn   B&B $$
(☎912-238-0518; www.savannahbnb.com; 117 W Gordon St; r weekday/weekend from $159/179; P❋☎) Spittin' distance from Savannah's most architecturally diverse square (Monterrey), this is a well-loved, well-worn establishment, but the rooms are crisp, unique and tidy. Easy to walk right by on a uniform street of 1850 row houses, the rooms are scattered about six buildings along the street.

Savannah Pensione   GUESTHOUSE $
(☎912-236-7744; www.savannahpensione.com; 304 E Hall St; dm $23, r $45-60; ❋☎) It was run as a hostel for some 15 years but the owner of this basic neighborhood crash-pad got tired of backpackers traipsing up and down the historic steps in his 1894 Italianate mansion. Fair enough. Now a bare-bones pensione, it still has a vaguely hostel-like vibe and fills a definite niche in the market: dorms bed can be had for $23, but only for groups of three or more who know each other.

Azalea Inn   B&B $$$
(☎912-236-2707; www.azaleainn.com; 217 E Huntingdon St; r from $200; P❋☎☒) Located on

a quiet street, the Azalea has lovely rooms and a little pool in the back. The mural in the dining room, created by art students, is a highlight.

✗ Eating

TOP CHOICE Mrs Wilkes' SOUTHERN $$

(www.mrswilkes.com; 107 W Jones St; lunch $16; 11am-2pm Mon-Fri) The line outside can begin as early as 8am at this first-come, first served, Southern comfort food institution. Once the lunch bell rings and you are seated family-style, the kitchen unloads on you: fried chicken, beef stew, meatloaf, cheese potatoes, collard greens, black-eyed peas, mac 'n' cheese, rutabaga, candied yams, squash casserole, creamed corn *and* biscuits. It's like Thanksgiving and the Last Supper rolled into one massive feast chased with sweet tea.

Olde Pink House NEW SOUTHERN $$$

(☏912-232-4286; 23 Abercorn St; mains $25-31; ⏰5-10:30pm Sun-Mon,11am-10:30pm Tue-Thu, 11am-11pm Fri & Sat) There are fancier and trendier restaurants in Savannah but this 1771 National Landmark on Reynolds Sq is rarely trumped for food or experience. The whole place epitomizes antebellum romance and you'll fall in love with the signature crispy scored flounder (though the menu is chock-full of irresistible Southern-bent delights). The service is casually flawless; the dark and cozy downstairs bar is also worthy of a cocktail pop-in. Damn near perfect.

Angel's BBQ BARBECUE $

(www.angels-bbq.com; 21 West Oglethorpe Lane; pulled-pork sandwich $6; ⏰11:30am-3pm Tue, till 6pm Wed-Sat) Utterly low-brow and hidden down a uneventful lane, Angel's pulled-pork sandwich and sea-salted fries will leave you humbled and thoroughly satisfied – and that's before you tear through the impressive list of housemade sauces, one made with scary-hot ghost and Chiltepin chilies.

🖊 Cha Bella AMERICAN $$$

(102 E Broad St; brunch $15.95, dinner mains $17-32; ⏰5:30-9pm Tue-Thu, till 10pm Fri & Sat, 5:30-9pm Sun) With a commitment to organic, local and well-presented vittles, this welcoming restaurant leaves pretension behind: swings hang on the lovely patio. The Georgia white-shrimp risotto or fish-market special will not leave you unpleased.

Lady & Sons SOUTHERN $$

(☏912-233-2600; www.ladyandsons.com; 102 W Congress St; buffets $14-18; ⏰11am-9pm Mon-Thu, to 10pm Sat & Sun) Savannah's irrepressible culinary doyenne Paula Deen has created a monster – and, some say, lost the magic in the process. Her country cookin' is indeed delicious, but showing up at 9:30am for lunch or 3:30pm for dinner to put your name on the list means the whole thing has gotten a bit out of hand. Perhaps Deen might consider putting the soul back into her South?

Vinnie Van GoGo's PIZZERIA $

(www.vinnievangogo.com; 317 W Bryan St; pizza slices from $2.50; ⏰4-11pm Mon-Thu, noon-midnight Fri & Sat, noon-11:30pm Sun) This locally owned pizzeria draws legions of locals for its Neapolitan brick-oven pizza.

🍷 Drinking

Rocks on the Roof BAR

(102 West Bay St; ⏰from 11am) The expansive rooftop bar at the new Bohemian Hotel is just what Savannah needed: a breezy, lipstick-red wrap-around rooftop set to an indie-cred soundtrack with lovely river views – best seen from seats on the northwest corner. There's live music Thursday to Saturday – prepare to rub elbows with the velvet rope.

Lulu's Chocolate Bar CAFE

(www.luluschocolatebar.net; 42 Martin Luther King Jr Blvd) More a place to sink yourself into a sugar coma than catch a buzz, Lulu's is an adorable yet chic neighborhood martini and dessert bar. The heavenly signature Lulutini here is pure chocolate decadence.

Gallery Espresso CAFE

(www.galleryespresso.com; 234 Bull St; ⏰7:30am-10pm Mon-Fri, 8am-11pm Sat & Sun) Savannah's best coffee shop; this and the Sentient are two of the South's best as well. Gallery is cozier, more conveniently located and is near-fiendish regarding its teas. There's also light fare and scrumptious desserts.

🖊 Sentient Bean CAFE

(www.sentientbean.com; 13 E Park Ave; ⏰7am-10pm; 📶🖊) This green coffeehouse cares about coffee and community. It has vegan treats, organic cafe fare and live music or performance art on its stage.

Abe's on Lincoln BAR

(17 Lincoln St) Ditch the tourists – drink with the locals.

⭐ Entertainment

Wormhole LIVE MUSIC
(www.wormholebar.com; 2307 Bull St; 📶) Embracing a broad scope of the alternative-music scene, this dive bar and venue is in the seedier part of town but will let you experience how alternative Savannah kicks it.

Lucas Theatre for the Arts THEATER
(📞912-525-5040; www.scad.edu/venues/lucas; 32 Abercorn St) Hosting concerts (guitarist Jonny Lang), plays *(Guys and Dolls)* and films *(The Day the Earth Stood Still)* in a historic building dating from 1921.

🛍 Shopping

TOP CHOICE **Savannah Bee Company** FOOD
(www.savannahbee.com; 104 W Broughton St) This internationally renowned honey dreamland is one of Savannah's must-stops: artisanal honey of infinitesimal varieties (free tastings) dots the wonderful store, as well as soaps, honey coffee and unique art and homewares.

ShopSCAD ARTS & CRAFTS
(www.shopscadonline.com; 340 Bull St; ⊙9-5:30pm Mon-Wed, till 8pm Thu-Fri, 10am-8pm Sat, noon-5pm Sun) All the wares at this funky, kitschy boutique were designed by students, faculty and alumni of Savannah's prestigious art college.

E Shaver, Bookseller BOOKSHOP
(326 Bull St; ⊙9:30am-5pm Mon-Sat) Shelves are stocked with tomes on local and regional history.

ℹ Information

Candler Hospital (www.sjchs.org; 5353 Reynolds St)

CVS Pharmacy (cnr Bull & W Broughton Sts)

Main Library (www.liveoakpl.org; 2002 Bull St; ⊙9am-8pm Mon-Tue, to 6pm Wed-Fri, 2-6pm Sun; 📶) Offers free internet and wi-fi access.

Post office Historic District (118 Barnard Street; ⊙8am-5pm Mon-Fri); Main (1 E Bay St; ⊙8am-5:30pm Mon-Fri, 9am-1pm Sat)

Savannah Chatham Metropolitan Police (📞912 651-6675; www.scmpd.org; cnr E Oglethorpe Ave & Habersham St)

Visitor center (📞912-944-0455; www.savannahvisit.com; 301 Martin Luther King Jr Blvd; ⊙8:30am-5pm Mon-Fri, 9am-5pm Sat & Sun) Excellent resources and services are available in this center, based in a restored 1860s train station. Many privately operated city tours start here and there's tons of information about various city tours, from carriage to bus. There is also a small interactive tourist info kiosk in the new Visitor Center at Forsyth Park.

ℹ Getting There & Around

The **Savannah/Hilton Head International Airport** (SAV; www.savannahairport.com) is about 5 miles west of downtown off I-16. The visitor center runs shuttles from the airport to Historic District hotels for $25 round-trip.

Greyhound (610 W Oglethorpe Ave) has connections to Atlanta (about five hours), Charleston, SC (about two hours) and Jacksonville, FL (2½ hours).

The **Amtrak station** (2611 Seaboard Coastline Dr) is just a few miles west of the Historic District.

You won't need a car. It's best to park it and walk or take tours. Another Earth-friendly and entertaining way to get around is by bike taxi with **Savannah Pedicab** (📞912-232-7900; www.savannahpedicab.com; 30/60min $25/45, full day $150).

Chatham Area Transit (CAT; www.catchacat.org) operates local hybrid buses that run on used cooking oil, including a free shuttle that makes its way around the Historic District and stops within a couple of blocks of nearly every major site.

Brunswick & the Golden Isles

Georgia has a coast? Oh yes, a righteously beautiful one, blessed with a string of picturesque islands. The islands have very different characters and provide experiences ranging from the rustic to the spoiled rotten.

With its large shrimp-boat fleet and downtown historic district shaded beneath lush live oaks, **Brunswick** dates from 1733 and has charms you might miss when sailing by on I-95 or the Golden Isle Pkwy (US Hwy 17). During WWII Brunswick shipyards constructed 99 Liberty transport ships for the navy. Today a new 23ft scale model at **Mary Ross Waterfront Park** (Bay St) stands as a memorial to those ships and their builders.

Forest Hostel (📞912-264-9738; www.foresthostel.com; Hwy 82; per person $25; 🅿), an International Youth Hostel, is worth checking out if you're up for staying in little nature-loving tree houses (sans air or heat) on an ecofriendly, sustainable campus. It's 10 miles outside Brunswick; phone reservations only.

Brunswick-Golden Isles Visitors Bureau (☎912-265-0620; www.bgivb.com; Hwy 17, St Simons Causeway; ⊘8:30am-5pm Mon-Fri) has loads of practical information about all the Golden Isles.

ST SIMONS ISLAND

Famous for its golf courses, resorts and majestic live oaks, St Simons Island is the largest and most developed of the Golden Isles. It lies 75 miles south of Savannah and just 5 miles from Brunswick. While the southern half of the island is a thickly settled residential and resort area, the northern half and adjacent Sea Island (www.explorestsimonsisland.com) and Little St Simons offer tracts of coastal wilderness amid a tidewater estuary.

JEKYLL ISLAND

An exclusive refuge for millionaires in the late 19th and early 20th centuries, Jekyll Island is a 4000-year-old barrier island with 10 miles of beaches. Today it's an unusual clash of wilderness, historically preserved buildings, modern hotels and a massive campground (complete with wi-fi). It's an easily navigable place – you can get around by car, horse or bicycle, but there's a $5 parking fee per day. The posh Jekyll Island Club Hotel (☎800-535-9547; www.jekyllclub.com; 371 Riverview Dr; d/ste from $209/319; P✳@⊕≋) looms large on this island. It's a great place for a drink after a sunset seafood dinner at nearby waterfront restaurant Latitude 31 (www.latitude31andrahbar.com; mains $14-23; ⊘from 11:30am Tue-Sun), located right on the wharf. An endearing attraction is the Georgia Sea Turtle Center (www.georgiaseaturtlecenter.org; Hopkins Rd; adult/child $6/4; ⊘9am-5pm Sun-Tue, 10am-2pm Mon; ♿), a conservation center and turtle hospital where patients are on view for the public.

CUMBERLAND ISLAND & ST MARYS

An unspoiled paradise, a backpacker's fantasy, a site for day trips or extended stays – it's clear why the Carnegie family used Cumberland as a retreat long ago. Most of this southernmost barrier island is now occupied by the Cumberland Island National Seashore (www.nps.gov/cuis; admission $4). Almost half of its 36,415 acres consists of marsh, mudflats and tidal creeks. On the ocean side are 16 miles of wide, sandy beach that you might have all to yourself. The island's interior is characterized by a maritime forest. Ruins from the Carnegie estate

Dungeness are astounding, as are the wild turkeys, tiny fiddler crabs and beautiful butterflies. Feral horses roam the island and are a common sight.

The only public access to the island is via boat to/from the quirky, lazy town of St Marys (www.stmaryswelcome.com). A convenient and pleasant ferry (☎912-882-4335; adult/child $20/14; ⊘departures 9am & 11:45am) leaves from the mainland at the St Marys dock. Reservations are staunchly recommended well before you arrive, and visitors are required to check in at the Visitor's Center (☎912-882-4336; ⊘8am-4:30pm) at the dock at least 30 minutes prior to departure. December through February, the ferry does not operate on Tuesday or Wednesday.

St Marys caters to tourists visiting Cumberland. This tiny, lush one-horse town has a number of comfortable B&Bs, including the lovely Emma's Bed and Breakfast (☎912-822-4199; www.emmasbedandbreakfast.com; 300 W Conyers St; r from $129; P✳☎⊕), which is right off the main street on a quiet road. The decorations are thankfully not of the common Southern frilly variety and the staff is helpful. Ask for a midweek special. For something cheap and in the 'action' by the dock, the tattered Riverview Hotel (☎912-882-3242; www.riverviewhotelstmarys.com; 105 Osborne St; r from $79; P✳☎) might be worth braving to save a dime.

On Cumberland Island, the only private accommodations are at the Greyfield Inn (☎904261-6408; www.greyfieldinn.com; r incl meals $395-595), a mansion built in 1900, with a two-night minimum stay. Camping is available at Sea Camp Beach (☎912-882-4335; tent sites per person $4), a campground set among magnificent live oaks.

Note: there are no stores or waste bins on the island. Eat before arriving or bring lunch, and keep your trash with you.

OKEFENOKEE NATIONAL WILDLIFE REFUGE

Established in 1937, the Okefenokee National Wildlife Refuge (www.fws.gov/okefenokee) is a national gem, encompassing 396,000 acres of bog in a giant saucer-shaped depression that was once part of the ocean floor. The swamp is home to an estimated 9000 to 15,000 alligators, 234 bird species, 49 types of mammal and 60 amphibian species. The Okefenokee Swamp Park (www.okeswamp.com; US 1 South, Waycross; adult/child $12/11; ⊘9am-5:30pm) maintains around 3000 acres of the refuge and captive bears and gators on-site, or you can explore the swamp in a canoe or on a boat tour. The ultimate experience is a multiday canoe trip on the swamp's 120 miles of waterways. Call the US Fish & Wildlife Service's **Okefenokee National Wildlife Refuge Wilderness Canoe Guide** (☏912-496-7836; www.fws.gov /okefenokee) if you're considering a trip. Guided boat trips are also available if the water levels are high enough.

ALABAMA

Obsessed with football and race – two things Southerners never stop discussing – Alabama has been home to one of gridiron's most legendary coaches, Paul 'Bear' Bryant, and Jefferson Davis, the first president of the Confederacy in 1861 (the year the Civil War began).

In the 1950s and '60s, Alabama led the way for civil rights triumphs throughout the country and it continues to deal with its reputation and legacy of rebels, segregation, discrimination and wayward politicians – in the face of both progress and setbacks. Exploring Alabama provides a powerful insight into the racial dynamic and history in the USA.

Geographically, Alabama has a surprising diversity of landscapes, from foothills in the north and a gritty city in the middle to the subtropical Gulf Coast down south. Visitors come to see the heritage of antebellum architecture, to celebrate the country's oldest Mardi Gras, in Mobile, and to learn about the civil rights struggle. Every fall the University of Alabama Crimson Tide and the Auburn University Tigers continue one of college football's greatest rivalries.

History

Alabama was among the first states to secede in the Civil War. Montgomery was the first Confederate capital. Alabama lost around 25,000 soldiers in the war, and reconstruction came slowly and painfully.

Racial segregation and Jim Crow laws survived into the mid-20th century, when the Civil Rights movement campaigned for desegregation of everything from public buses to private universities, a notion that Governor George Wallace opposed. In perhaps the most famous moment in civil rights history, an African American woman named Rosa Parks refused to give up her bus seat to a white passenger and was arrested; the ensuing uproar began to turn the tide in favor of racial equality. Alabama saw brutal repression and hostility, but federal civil rights and voting laws eventually prevailed. At a political level, reform has seen the election of dozens of African American mayors and representatives.

❶ Information

Alabama Bureau of Tourism & Travel (☏334-242-4169, 800-252-2262; www.alabama.travel) Sends out a vacation guide and has a website with extensive tourism options. Foodies will definitely want to pick up a copy of *100 Dishes To Eat in Alabama Before You Die*.

Alabama State Parks (☏888-252-7272; www.alapark.com) There are 23 parks statewide with camping facilities ranging from primitive ($12) to RV hookups ($26). Advanced reservations are suggested for weekends and holidays.

ALABAMA FACTS

» **Nickname** The Heart of Dixie

» **Population** 4.7 million

» **Area** 52,419 sq miles

» **Capital city** Montgomery (population 224,119)

» **Other cities** Birmingham (population 212,237)

» **Sales tax** 4%, but up to 11% with local taxes

» **Birthplace of** Author Helen Keller (1880–1968), civil rights activist Rosa Parks (1913–2005), musician Hank Williams (1923–53)

» **Home of** US Space & Rocket Center

» **Politics** GOP stronghold – Alabama hasn't voted democratic since 1976

» **Famous for** Rosa Parks and the Civil Rights movement

» **Bitterest rivalry** University of Alabama vs Auburn University

» **Driving distances** Montgomery to Birmingham 91 miles, Mobile to Dauphin Island 38 miles

---

Birmingham

No one can ignore Birmingham's checkered past – civil rights violence earned it the nickname 'Bombingham.' Even though that was decades ago, invisible racial boundaries are still evident and smack of the city's history. Yet this midsize, blue-collar city has made progress, can show you a good time, has a surprising amount of culture to offer and has integrated its civil rights struggle into the tourist experience.

⊙ Sights & Activities

Art-deco buildings in trendy **Five Points South** house shops, restaurants and nightspots. Equally noteworthy is the **Homewood** community's quaint commercial drag on 18th St S.

TOP CHOICE Birmingham Civil Rights Institute
MUSEUM
(www.bcri.org; 520 16th St N; adult/child $12/3, Sun free; ⊙10am-5pm Tue-Sat, 1-5pm Sun) A maze of moving audio, video and photography exhibits tell the story of racial segregation in the USA, from WWI and the Civil Rights movement to racial and human-rights issues around the world today, and it reveals the complicated and shocking layers of Birmingham's history. A new $2.5-million renovation has spruced up displays and added an extensive exhibit on the 16th Street Baptist Church bombing in 1963.

16th Street Baptist Church
CHURCH
(www.16thstreetbaptist.org; cnr 16th St & 6th Ave N; donation $5; ⊙ministry tours 10am-4pm Tue-Fri, 10am-1pm Sat) This became a gathering place for meetings and protests in the 1950s and '60s. When Ku Klux Klan members bombed the church in 1963, killing four girls, the city was flung into a whirlwind of social change. Today the rebuilt church is a memorial and a house of worship (services 10:45am Sunday).

Vulcan Park
PARK
(www.visitvulcan.com; 1701 Valley View Dr; ⊙7am-10pm) Visible from all over the city thanks to the world's largest cast-iron statue, the park offers fantastic views for free, and an **observation tower** (adult/child $6/4; ⊙from 10am Mon-Sat, from 1pm Sun).

FREE Birmingham Museum of Art
GALLERY
(www.artsbma.org; 2000 Rev Abraham Woods Jr Blvd; ⊙10am-5pm Tue-Sat, noon-5pm Sun) Collects work from Asia, Africa, Europe and the Americas. Don't miss the work of Rodin, Botero and Dalí in the sculpture garden.

🛏 Sleeping

Redmont Hotel
HISTORIC HOTEL $$
(☏205-324-2101; www.theredmont.com; 2101 5th Ave N; r from $129; ❋@�⌁) It's a toss up be-

tween here and Tutwiler for Birmingham's best, but the Redmont, born in the roaring '20s, wins since it's not a Hampton Inn. The hotel's piano and chandelier in the lobby lend a certain historical, old-world feel throughout and all deluxe rooms were just renovated giving it modern edge. The spacious rooftop bar doesn't hurt, either.

Hotel Highland
HOTEL $$
(☏205-271-5800; www.thehotelhighland.com; 1023 20th St S; r from $119; P❋@�⌁) Nuzzled right up next to the lively Five Points district, this colorful, slightly trippy, modern hotel manages to be very comfortable and a good deal. The rooms are a bit less bright and funky than the lobby, eliminating the need for sunglasses at night. Rates include a continental breakfast.

Cobb Lane Bed and Breakfast
B&B $
(☏205-918-9090; www.cobblanebandb.com; 1309 19th St S; r from $89; P❋�⌁) Aims for the traditional debutante-esque of Southern B&Bs, but ends up with a giant stuffed peacock in the fireplace, numerous porcelain dolls and the gaudy frilliness of an underage Southern beauty pageant.

🍴 Eating & Drinking

For such a small Southern city, student-tilted Birmingham has a wide variety of eateries and cafes, from ethnic to local, for all budgets.

TOP CHOICE Hot & Hot Fish Club
SEAFOOD $$$
(www.hotandhotfishclub.com; 2180 11th Court South; mains $29-36; ⊙5:30-10:30pm Tue-Sat) This crazy-awesome Southside Birmingham restaurant – one of the South's best – will bring you to your knees hollerin' Gastro-Hallelujah's! Chef Chris Hastings was a James Beard Best Chef in the South finalist three years in a row – his daily-changing seasonal menu (including cocktails) is a knockout (the vanilla bean-infused lemonade with sweet tea vodka might be the best cocktail ever). Best seat in the house? The lengthy chef's counter, where Hastings chats up the guests while his unbelievably diverse and chill sous chefs work his creations into culinary genius.

Rib-It-Up
BARBECUE $
(830 1st Ave North; mains $4-11; ⊙10:30am-9pm Mon-Thu, till midnight Fri & Sat) Barbecue rib *sandwich* – an absolute hot mess. What else do you need to know? OK, the neighborhood isn't the best, but there is no such thing as authentic barbecue next door to a Pottery Barn!

Garage Café   CAFE $

(www.garagecafe.us; 2304 10th Ter S; sandwiches $7; ⊗3pm-midnight Sun-Mon, 11-2am Tue-Sat) By day it's a great soup and create-your-own-sandwich spot; by night eclectic crowds knock back myriad beer choices while tapping their toes to live music in a courtyard full of junk, antiques, ceramic statues *and* the kitchen sink.

J Clyde   BEER HALL $$

(www.jclyde.com; 1312 Cobb Lane S; mains $8 to $18; ⊗3pm-midnight Mon, to 2am Tue-Thu & Sun, to 4am Fri) Over 40 beers on draft, hundreds in bottles and an additional one to three cask-conditioned ales with traditional British Beer Engines – the only Alabama bar to boast such devotion to suds. It sits on charming Cobb Lane in Five Points and there's plenty of good late-night pub grub to wash down the beer.

Lucy's Coffee and Tea   CAFE

(www.lucyscoffeeandtea.com; 2007 University Blvd; mains $6-10; ⊗7am-5pm Mon-Fri) Next door to the University of Alabama-Birmingham not far from Five Points, this artsy coffee shop is good for an espresso fix and solid paninis for lunch.

☆ Entertainment

TOP CHOICE Gip's Place   LIVE MUSIC

(www.myspace.com/gipsjukejoint; 3101 Ave C, Bessemer) You'll need to ask a local for directions to this tin-roof makeshift backyard shack in a dicey neighborhood in Bessemer, one of the only truly authentic juke joints left outside Mississippi. Gip, a gravedigger by day, opens the doors on Saturday only, when the place is shoulder-to-shoulder with blues fans come one come all. It's BYOB but there's no need – *free* moonshine is passed around in Mason jars, permitted by a legal loophole in Alabama that says it must be given away, not sold.

❶ Information

Greater Birmingham Convention & Visitors Bureau (✆205-458-8000, 800-458-8085; www.sweetbirmingham.com; 2200 9th Ave N; ⊗8:30am-5pm Mon-Fri) Tourist information.

❶ Getting There & Around

The **Birmingham International Airport** (BHM; www.flybirmingham.com) is about 5 miles northeast of downtown.

Greyhound (✆205-253-7190; 618 19th St N), north of downtown, serves cities including

Huntsville, Montgomery, Atlanta, GA, Jackson, MS, and New Orleans, LA (10 hours). **Amtrak** (✆205-324-3033; 1819 Morris Ave), downtown, has trains daily to New York and New Orleans.

Birmingham Transit Authority (www.bjcta. org; adult $1.25) runs local buses.

Around Birmingham

North of Birmingham, the aerospace community of Huntsville hosts the US space program that took off and attracted international aerospace-related companies.

US Space & Rocket Center (www.space camp.com/museum; I-565, exit 15; adult/child museum $20/15, with IMAX $28/22; ⊗9am-5pm; ♿) is a combination science museum and theme park. It's a great place to take a kid, or to become one again. The center has IMAX films, exhibits, rides and video presentations.

East of Huntsville, in Scottsboro, you'll find the infamous **Unclaimed Baggage Center** (✆256-259-1525; www.unclaimedbag gage.com; 509 W Willow St; ⊗9am-6pm Mon-Fri, 8am-6pm Sat), which draws pilgrims from far and wide who peruse the now-for-sale belongings of unfortunate air travelers who have lost their baggage irrevocably down the dark annals of fate. Finders keepers.

The area receives some acclaim for music history, and the cheesy-cool **Alabama Music Hall of Fame** (www.alamhof.org; 617 Hwy 72 W, Tuscumbia; adult/child $8/5; ⊗9am-5pm Mon-Sat, 1-5pm Sun summer) immortalizes both Hank Williams and Lionel Richie.

THE SOUTH AROUND BIRMINGHAM

WORTH A TRIP

AVE MARIA GROTTO

Located 50 miles north of Birmingham on the grounds of the only Benedictine monastery in Alabama, the amazing **Ave Maria Grotto** (www.avemaria-grotto.com; 1600 St. Bernard Dr, Cullman; adult/child $7/4.50; ⊗9am-6pm) is more or less the work of one man, Brother Joseph Zoettl, who spent the better part of 35 years hand-sculpting stone and cement miniatures of the world's most prominent religious buildings. The attention to detail and level of skill in the 125 pieces is amazing, regardless of your personal views on religion. From an art perspective, it's even more miraculous yet – after all, this was just Brother Joseph's hobby.

Montgomery

In 1955 Rosa Parks refused to give up her seat to a white man on a Montgomery bus, launching a bus boycott and galvanizing the Civil Rights movement nationwide. The city has commemorated that incident with a museum, which (along with an excellent Shakespeare program) is the main reason to visit.

Although it's Alabama's capital city, Montgomery feels more like a sleepy little city with a dead downtown. To its credit, it covers both fine and folk arts well, with a terrific Shakespeare festival and a museum devoted to country-music legend Hank Williams.

◉ Sights & Activities

Civil Rights Memorial Center   MEMORIAL
(www.civilrightsmemorialcenter.org; 400 Washington Ave; adult/child $2/free; ◷9am-4:30pm Mon-Fri, 10am-4pm Sat) With its circular design crafted by Maya Lin, this haunting memorial focuses on 40 martyrs of the Civil Rights movement, all murdered for countless senseless reasons, many of which have never been solved. MLK Jr was the most famous, but there were many 'faceless' deaths along the way, white and African American alike, that here provide some of the most somber moments in American history.

Rosa Parks Museum   MUSEUM
(http://montgomery.troy.edu/rosaparks/museum; 251 Montgomery St; adult/child $6/4; ◷9am-5pm Mon-Fri, 9am-3pm Sat; ⊕) A tribute to Mrs Parks (who died in October 2005), the mu-seum features a sophisticated and wacky video re-creation of Montgomery's history of racial conflict and also the bus-seat protest.

Scott & Zelda Fitzgerald Museum   MUSEUM
(919 Felder Ave; donation adult/child $5/2; ◷10am-2pm Wed-Fri, 1-5pm Sat & Sun) The writers' home from 1931 to '32 now houses first editions, translations and original artwork including a mysterious self-portrait of Zelda in pencil.

Hank Williams Museum   MUSEUM
(www.thehankwilliamsmuseum.com; 118 Commerce St; adult/child $8/3; ◷9am-4:30pm Mon-Fri, 10am-4pm Sat, 1-4pm Sun) Pays homage to the country-music giant and Alabama native, a pioneer who effortlessly fused hillbilly music with African American blues.

🍴 Sleeping & Eating

Montgomery may not be known for its restaurants and accommodations but there are a couple of finds. The opening of the Alley, a new dining and entertainment district, shows great promise for revitalizing downtown.

Lattice Inn   B&B $
(☎334-262-3388; www.thelatticeinn.com; 1414 S Hull St; r from $90; P❋@☞❄) Most definitely this cute little B&B in the Garden District is a lovely alternative to chain hotels in Montgomery's downtown and outskirts. It's not fancy-pants, but well executed and homey with a consummate host.

Butterfly Inn   B&B $$
(☎334-230-9708; www.butterflyinn.net; 135 Mildred St; r $96-126; P❋) Montgomery's first African American-owned B&B is cool and comfortable, but Isaiah's restaurant on site is the real coup, famous for its lemon pepper catfish ($8.75), peach cobbler and other soul food favorites.

Dreamland BBQ   BARBECUE $
(www.dreamlandbbq.com; 101 Tallapoosa St; mains $8-11; ◷11am-9pm Sun-Thu, till 10pm Sat) It's a chain but, before you poo-poo it, it's an Alabama chain and the ribs, chopped pork sandwich and traditional banana pudding are all extraordinary. It's the culinary cradle of the Alley, the focal point of Montgomery's downtown makeover.

Farmer's Market Cafe   SOUTHERN $
(315 N McDonough St; meals without/with tea from $7.50/6.75; ◷5:30am-2pm Mon-Fri) This oversized downtown cafeteria serves up God-fearing Southern home cooking at recession-friendly prices according to the meat/veggie combo of your choice. Don't skip the grits casserole.

Chris' Hot Dog   FAST FOOD $
(www.chrishotdogs.com; 138 Dexter Ave; hot dogs $2.15; ◷10am-7pm Mon-Thu & Sat, till 8pm Fri) This funky hot-dog dive has been a Montgomery institution since 1917 and was a favorite drinking den of Hank Williams.

❶ Information

Montgomery Area Visitor Center (☎334-262-0013; www.visitingmontgomery.com; 300 Water St; ◷8:30am-5pm Mon-Sat) Has tourist information and a helpful website.

❶ Getting There & Around

Montgomery Regional Airport (MGM; www.montgomeryairport.org; 4445 Selma Hwy) is about 15 miles from downtown and is served by daily flights from Atlanta, Charlotte, Cincinnati, Houston and Memphis. **Greyhound** (📞334-286-0658; 950 W South Blvd) also serves the city. The **Montgomery Area Transit System** (www.montgomerytransit.com; tickets $1) operates the city buses.

Selma

On Bloody Sunday, March 7, 1965, the media captured state troopers and deputies beating and gassing African Americans and white sympathizers near the Edmund Pettus Bridge. Led by Martin Luther King Jr, the crowd was marching to the state capital (Montgomery) to demonstrate for voting rights. This was the culmination of two years of violence, which ended when President Johnson signed the *Voting Rights Act* of 1965. Today Selma is a quiet town and though its attractions are few they do provide an excellent insight into the voting rights protests that were at the crux of the Civil Rights movement.

Selma's key attraction, the **National Voting Rights Museum** (www.nvrm.org; 1012 Water Ave; adult/senior & student $6/4; ⊙9am-5pm Mon-Fri, 10am-3pm Sat), near the Edmund Pettus Bridge, is an important stop as it honors the movement's 'foot soldiers' – the unsung heroes who marched for freedom.

Mobile

Wedged between Mississippi and Florida, the only real Alabama coastal town is Mobile (mo-*beel*), a seaport with green spaces, shady boulevards and four historic districts. It's ablaze with azaleas in early spring, and festivities are held throughout February for **Mardi Gras** (www.mobilemardigras.com), which has been celebrated here for nearly 200 years. Mobile can be fun like New Orleans, only the volume and brightness are turned way down. The Dauphin St historic district is where you'll find many bars and restaurants, and it's where much of the Mardi Gras action takes place.

Government St, near downtown, makes for a lovely drive thanks to its mansions and tree canopy. The **Leinkauf Historic District** has more great homes.

USS Alabama (www.ussalabama.com; 2703 Battleship Pkwy; adult/child $12/6; ⊙8am-6pm Apr-Sep, 8am-4pm Oct-Mar) is a 690ft behemoth famous for escaping nine major WWII battles unscathed. It's a worthwhile self-guided tour for its awesome size and might. While there, you can also tour a submarine and get up close and personal with military aircraft. Parking's $2.

Kate Shepard House (📞251-479-7048; www.kateshepardhouse.com; 1552 Monterrey Pl; r $160; P❀🛜) is an adorable, meticulously restored 1897 Queen Anne–style B&B run by gracious host Wendy James. Everything in this charmer is perfect, personified most memorably in the pecan praline French toast. Foodgasm!

Home to Mobile's best burgers and consistently voted one of America's best bars, the ramshackle **Callaghan's Irish Social Club** (www.callaghansirishsocialclub.com; 916 Charleston St; burgers $7-9; ⊙11am-9pm Mon, 11am-10pm Tue & Wed, 11am-11pm Thu-Sat) in a 1920s-era building that used to house a meat market in the Oakleigh District, is unmissable.

WORTH A TRIP

DAUPHIN ISLAND

Alabama has an island? Yes, but many write it off because oil rigs grace its horizon. However unsung it may be, it's a worthwhile destination. The whole 14-mile-long, 1¾-mile-wide island is a designated bird sanctuary, with 6 miles for public use and 8 miles of private property. Though it has its fair share of traditional beach-vacation kitsch and the water is not sparkly turquoise, it's still pretty nice. The white-blonde beaches are stellar and prices reasonable. The island is accessed from the north by Hwy 193 and from the east by **ferry** (📞251-861-3000; www.mobilebayferry.com) shuttling from Fort Morgan.

For helpful maps and information, contact the **Dauphin Island Chamber of Commerce** (📞251-861-5524; www.dauphinislandcoc.com).

The biggest highlight is the **Dauphin Island Bird Sanctuary** (📞251-861-2120; www.coastalbirding.org), where you'll find what many people consider to be some of the best birding in the southeast. In addition, you'll encounter uncrowded beaches accessed only by hiking paths, placards explaining the flora and fauna, and several miles of winding trails.

MISSISSIPPI

One of the USA's most misunderstood (and yet most mythologized) states, Mississippi is home to gorgeous country roads, shabby juke joints, crispy catfish, hallowed authors and acres of cotton. Most people feel content to malign Mississippi, long scorned for its lamentable civil rights history and its low ranking on the list of nearly every national marker of economy and education, without ever experiencing it firsthand. But unpack your bags for a moment and you'll glimpse the real South. It lies somewhere amid the Confederate defeat at Vicksburg, the literary legacy of William Faulkner in bookish Oxford, the birthplace of the blues in the Mississippi Delta and the humble origins of Elvis Presley in Tupelo.

History

Stay in Mississippi long enough and you'll hear folks refer to a time 'when cotton was king.' That time dates back at least to 1860, when Mississippi was the country's leading cotton producer and one of the 10 wealthiest states. The Civil War wrecked Mississippi's economy, and reconstruction was traumatic.

And the state's racist history – from slavery through the civil rights era – has left deep scars. (One of the most famous incidents came in 1962, when violence erupted as student James Meredith became the first African American to attend the University of Mississippi.)

Today, though Mississippi is still a poor state, people have come to realize that the blues of the Delta – one of America's richest and most distinctive art forms – is worth celebrating. And that Mississippi has been disproportionately blessed with literary luminaries. Therefore, the state has developed a tourist industry revolving around its proud cultural history, as well as its waterfront casinos.

❶ Information

Mississippi Division of Tourism Development (☑601-359-3297; www.visitmississippi.org) Has a directory of visitor bureaus.

Mississippi Wildlife, Fisheries, & Parks (☑1-800-467-2757; www.mississippistateparks. reserveamerica.com) Camping costs $11 to $22, depending on the facilities, and some parks have cabins for rent.

Tupelo

Unless you have an unhealthy Elvis obsession or want to pick up the Natchez Trace Pkwy, you probably shouldn't plan to spend a long time in Tupelo. But an afternoon pop-in is rewarding indeed if you are a fan of the King.

Elvis Presley's Birthplace (www.elvispresleybirthplace.com; 306 Elvis Presley Blvd; adult/child $12/6; ☺9am-5:30pm Mon-Sat, 1-5pm Sun) is east of downtown off Hwy 78. The 15-acre park complex contains the two-room shack Elvis lived in as a boy, a museum displaying personal items, a modest chapel and a massive gift shop.

Oxford

A refreshingly sophisticated little town that's bustling and prosperous, Oxford was named after the English city by colonists who hoped it would open a school as revered as its namesake. The University of Mississippi (Ole Miss) opened in 1848 and provides Oxford's heartbeat. (You know a town has an intellectual bent when its favorite native son is a literary lion like William Faulkner. But former Ole Miss quarterback Archie Manning runs a close second; the speed limit

---

MISSISSIPPI FACTS

» **Nickname** The Magnolia State

» **Population** 2.9 million

» **Area** 48,430 sq miles

» **Capital city** Jackson (population 173,514)

» **Other cities** Biloxi 45,670

» **Sales tax** 7%

» **Birthplace of** Author Eudora Welty (1909–2001), musicians Robert Johnson (1911–38) and Elvis Presley (1935–77), puppeteer Jim Henson (1936–90)

» **Home of** the blues

» **Politics** traditionally conservative, but has voted for third-party candidates more than any other state since WWII.

» **Famous for** cotton fields

» **Kitschiest souvenir** Elvis lunchbox in Tupelo

» **Driving distances** Jackson to Clarksdale 187 miles, Jackson to Ocean Springs 176 miles here on campus is 18mph, in deference to his old uniform number.)

Social life in Oxford revolves around 'the Square' (Courthouse Sq), a series of downtown blocks dotted with shops and eateries.

◉ Sights & Activities

Rowan Oak   HISTORIC BUILDING
(off Old Taylor Rd; www.rowanoak.com; adult/child $5/ free; ⊙10am-4pm Tue-Sat, 1-4pm Sun) Literary pilgrims head directly here, to the graceful 1840s home of William Faulkner, who authored so many brilliant and dense novels set in Mississippi, and whose work is celebrated in Oxford with an annual conference in July. Tours of Rowan Oak – where Faulkner lived from 1930 until he died in 1962 – are self-guided. The staff can also provide directions to **Faulkner's grave**, which is located in St Peter's Cemetery, northeast of the Square.

Square Books   CULTURAL BUILDING
(www.squarebooks.com; 160 Courthouse Sq; ⊙9am-9pm Mon-Thu, to 10pm Fri & Sat, 9am-6pm Sun) One of America's great independent bookstores is the epicenter of Oxford's lively literary scene and a frequent stop for traveling authors. There's a cafe and balcony upstairs, along with an immense section devoted to Faulkner.

FREE **University of Mississippi Museum**   MUSEUM
(University Ave, at 5th St; www.museum.olemiss. edu; ⊙10am-6 Tue-Sat) This museum has fine arts, folk arts, a Confederate uniform and a plethora of science-related marvels, including a microscope and electromagnet from the 19th century.

⌂ Sleeping & Eating

The cheapest accommodations are on the outskirts of town at chain hotels. But there are some other choices with more personality. A number of high-quality restaurants dot the Square.

Inn at Ravine   B&B $$
(☑662-234-4555; www.oxfordravine.com; 53 County Rd 321; r from $100; P✳☎) For those wanting a peaceful stay on Oxford's green fringes, there are two B&B-style guest rooms above the lovely restaurant Ravine, as well as a cabin.

(5) Twelve   B&B $$
(☑662-234-8043; www.the512oxford.com; 512 Van Buren Ave; r from $115; P✳☎) Formerly the

Oliver Britt House (now under new management), this six-room B&B has an antebellum-style exterior, modern interior and Southern breakfasts to order. It's an easy walk from shops and restaurants at the Square.

TOP CHOICE **Ravine**   AMERICAN $$$
(☑662-234-4555; www.oxfordravine.com; 53 County Rd 321; mains $16-32; ⊙Wed-Thu 6-9pm, Fri & Sat til 10pm, 10:30am-2pm & 6-9pm Sun; ☎) About 3 miles outside the city, this unpretentious, cozily elegant restaurant nuzzles up to the forest. Chef Joel Miller picks and pulls much of the produce and herbs from his garden outside and buys locally and organically when he can. The result is simply wonderful food and a delicious experience.

Taylor Grocery   SEAFOOD $$
(www.taylorgrocery.com; 4 County Rd 338 A, Taylor; dishes $9-15; ⊙5-10pm Thu-Sat, till 9pm Sun) Be prepared to wait – and to tailgate in the parking lot – at this splendidly rusticated catfish haunt. Get your cat fried or grilled, and bring a marker to sign your name on the wall. The joint is about 7 miles from downtown Oxford, south on Old Taylor Rd.

Bottletree Bakery   BAKERY $
(923 Van Buren; cinnamon rolls $3.75; ⊙7am-4pm Tue-Fri, 9am-4pm Sat, 9am-2pm Sun; ☎) Saucer-sized, sweet, sticky cinnamon rolls are the source of this bakery's acclaim. But it also has sandwiches, espresso drinks and 'humble pie.'

☆ Entertainment

Proud Larry's   LIVE MUSIC
(www.proudlarrys.com; 211 S Lamar Blvd) On the Square, this iconic music venue hosts some of the bigger names passing through town.

Rooster's Blues House   BLUES
(www.roostersblueshouse.com; 114 Courthouse Sq) Also on the Square, this is where you'll find that soulful crooning on the weekends.

Mississippi Delta

One of the most mythical places in the USA, the Delta is a panoramic agricultural expanse that thrums with historic significance. Its vernacular food culture ranks as one of America's great folk arts, but even the grub is trumped by the Delta's other great cultural export: blues music. David L Cohn, Greenville native and author of *God Shakes Creation*, devised a geo-cultural definition of the region. He wrote that 'the Delta begins in the lobby of the Peabody Hotel in Memphis and ends on Catfish Row in Vicksburg.'

CLARKSDALE

If you come here for anything, come for the love of music. Clarksdale is the real deal. It hosts a healthy blues-lovin' tourist industry and also caters to moneyed patrons, but what keeps Clarksdale genuine is its residents: they adore music. It's no surprise that big-name blues bands still honor Clarksdale on the weekends and that music museums sprinkle the area. Over the twists and turns of its intriguing past, this little juke-jointed Delta town continues to navigate contradictions: wealth, poverty, white culture, black culture and blues culture.

◉ Sights & Activities

Delta Blues Museum MUSEUM
(www.deltabluesmuseum.org; 1 Blues Alley; adult/child $7/5; ◔9am-5pm Mon-Sat) A small but exciting and well-presented collection of memorabilia is on display, including Charlie Musselwhite's harmonica and BB King's guitar, Lucille. The shrine to Delta legend Muddy Waters is being expanded into a new 7000-sq-ft annex by 2012; local art exhibits and a gift shop round out the revelry.

Rock N' Roll & Blues Heritage Museum MUSEUM
(☎901-605-8662; www.blues2rock.com; 113 E Second St; admission $5; ◔11am-5pm Fri-Sun) Theo, a jovial Dutch transplant and blues fanatic,

has on display an impressive personal collection of records, memorabilia, and artifacts that traces the roots of rock and roll from blues through the '70s. His collection features all sorts of rare and interesting items (check out one of Muddy Waters' riders) and if he's not too busy, he's all too enthusiastic to compliment the display with loads of fascinating historical rhetoric. Open by appointment outside posted hours.

✯✯ Festivals & Events

Clarksdale has two bluesy throw-downs.

Juke Joint Festival MUSIC
(www.jukejointfestival.com) Held in April, it's more about the venues than the headliners.

Sunflower River Blues & Gospel Festival MUSIC
(www.sunflowerfest.org) In August. Draws bigger names than Juke.

🛏 Sleeping & Eating

TOP CHOICE Shack Up Inn INN $$
(☎662-624-8329; www.shackupinn.com; r $65-165; P☀❄☎) At the cheeky Hopson Plantation, this self-titled 'bed and beer' 2 miles south on the west side of Hwy 49 evokes the blues like no other. Guests stay in refurbished sharecropper cabins or the creatively renovated cotton gin. The cabins have covered porches and are filled with old furniture and musical instruments. The old commissary, the Juke Joint Chapel (equipped with pews), is an atmospheric venue inside the cotton gin for live-music performances. The whole place reeks of down home dirty blues and

A WHOLE LOTTA JUKIN' GOING ON

It's believed that 'juke' is a West African word that survived in the Gullah language, the Creole–English hybrid spoken by isolated African Americans in the US. The Gullah 'juke' means 'wicked and disorderly.' Little wonder, then, that the term was applied to the roadside sweatboxes of the Mississippi Delta, where secular music, suggestive dancing, drinking and, in some cases, prostitution were the norm. The term 'jukebox' came into vogue when recorded music, spun on automated record-changing machines, began to supplant live musicians in such places, as well as in cafes and bars.

Most bona-fide juke joints are African American neighborhood clubs, and outside visitors can be a rarity. Many are mostly male hangouts. There are very few places that local women, even in groups, would turn up without a male chaperone. Otherwise, women can expect a lot of persistent, suggestive attention.

For a taste of the juke-joint scene, we recommend **Ground Zero** (www.groundzero-bluesclub.com; 0 Blues Alley, Clarksdale; ◔11am-2pm Mon-Tue, to 11pm Wed & Thu, to 2am Fri & Sat), a huge and friendly (read: somewhat sugar-coated) hall graffitied to death and owned by Morgan Freeman. By contrast, **Red's** (☎662-627-3166; 395 Sunflower Ave, Clarksdale), which is usually open on Friday and Saturday nights, looks a little scary to first-timers, but it is one of Clarksdale's best jukes. If the pit's smoking, order whatever's cooking.

Deep South character – possibly the coolest place you'll ever stay.

Riverside Hotel
HISTORIC HOTEL $

(☑662-624-9163; ratfrankblues@yahoo.com; 615 Sunflower Ave; r with/without bath $70/65; ✷) Don't let a well-worn exterior put you off: this hotel, soaked in blues history – Bessie Smith died here when it was a hospital, everyone else has stayed here – offers clean and tidy rooms wrought with the spirits of the blues. It's family-run since 1944, when it was 'the black hotel' in town. The original proprietor's son, Rat, will charm your socks off with history, hospitality and prices.

Rust
SOUTHERN $$

(218 Delta Ave; mains $12-26; ☺6-9pm Wed-Thu, till 10pm Fri & Sat) A beacon of culinary cool in an otherwise downtrodden downtown, the souped-up Southern comfort food served here (blackened rib eye with red chili mustard, fried green tomatoes with citrus cream sauce) amid junkyard chic decor is hopefully the shape of things to come.

Madidi
SOUTHERN $$$

(☑662-627-7770; www.madidires.com; 164 Delta Ave; mains $24-36; ☺6-9pm Tue-Sat) Handsome and refined, just like cofounder Morgan Freeman, this upscale eatery has a menu including buttermilk fried quail, braised beef short ribs and wild-mushroom risotto. Reservations requested.

Hick's
FAST FOOD $

(305 S State St; mains $2-8.50; ☺11am-6pm Mon-Thu, to 10pm Fri & Sat) A don't-miss dive that's been here forever on the outskirts of town. It has the best Delta hot tamales in town (half a dozen for $5), as well as the best pulled pork.

🔒 Shopping

Cat Head Delta Blues & Folk Art
ARTS & CRAFTS

(252 Delta Ave; ☺10am-5pm Mon-Sat) Friendly St Louis carpetbagger Roger Stolle runs a colorful, all-purpose, blues emporium. The shelves are jammed with books, face jugs, local art and blues records. Stolle seems to know everyone in the Delta; skip the Chamber of Commerce and stop here for the lowdown.

AROUND CLARKSDALE

For such a poor, flat part of the country, the Delta has a surprisingly deep list of funky little towns with food, gambling and history to offer.

DOE'S EAT PLACE

James Beard Award–winning **Doe's Eat Place** (☑662-334-3315; www.does eatplace.com; 502 Nelson St, Greenville; steaks $35-55; ☺5:30-9pm Mon-Sat) is the priciest dive you're likely to ever come across, but the world-class steaks served here, in the middle of a poor neighborhood, are unforgettable, as is the experience in general, with the open kitchen smack-dab in the middle of the old-school family restaurant. It used to be you paid a kid a dollar to 'watch your car,' ie not break into it. Now there's a security guard outside. The family's third generation runs the show, one that began in 1941 with an African American–only honky-tonk (bar) in the front of the house and a restaurant serving steaks for whites in the back. Come early or make a reservation – this is the American dream on a plate.

The Delta's largest city, **Greenville** is roughly midway between Clarksdale and Vicksburg. It was here that the levee broke during the catastrophic Great Flood of 1927. Today it has some riverboat gambling and not much else. But in September, Greenville hosts the **Mississippi Delta Blues & Heritage Festival** (www.deltablues.org) near the intersection of Hwys 454 and 1.

East of Greenville, Hwy 82 heads out of the Delta. The **Highway 61 Blues Museum** (www.highway61blues.com; 307 N Broad St; ☺10am-4pm Tue-Sat Nov-Feb, 10am-5pm Mon-Sat Mar-Oct), packs a mighty wallop in a condensed, six-room space venerating local bluesman from the Delta. The best part of a visit here is the presence, music and impromptu cat sketches of Pat Thomas, son of legendary local bluesman James 'Son Ford' Thomas, a real character you won't soon forget. **Leland** (www.lelandms.org) hosts the **Highway 61 Blues Festival** in June as well as the **Crawfish Festival** (crayfish) at the beginning of May.

Stopping in the tiny Delta town of **Indianola** is well worthwhile, to visit the incredible, modern **BB King Museum and Delta Interpretive Center** (www.bbkingmuseum.org; 400 Second St; adult/student/child $10/5/free; ☺10am-5pm Tue-Sat, noon-5pm Sun-Mon, closed

Mon Nov-Mar). Situated in between Greenville and Greenwood on Hwy 82, this center, filled with interactive displays, video exhibits and an amazing array of blues and BB King artifacts, effectively communicates the history and legacy of the blues while shedding light on the soul of the Delta.

Greenwood is a poor Delta town furnished with one block of opulence due to Viking Range Corporation's investment (its headquarters is here). Visitors are usually wealthy patrons or splurging travelers who want to take advantage of the tourist beacon of Greenwood, the **Alluvian** (☎662-453-2114; www.thealluvian.com; 318 Howard St; r incl breakfast $195-340; P❄@☎), owned by Viking. This shockingly luxurious boutique hotel is equipped with a high-class spa, gourmet restaurant, Giardina's (locally pronounced 'Gardinia's'), and an unbelievably outfitted cooking school. If you feel like splurging, this might be the place, though some find the oasis of wealth a disturbing contrast to the poverty of the surrounding town.

As an alternative to the Alluvian, 3 miles north of Greenwood **Tallahatchie Flats** (☎662-453-1854; www.tallahatchieflats.com; 58458 County Rd 518; shacks $65-85; P❄) is a compound of shacks simulating rural homes called 'tenant houses' that once dotted the area. They're now outfitted for guests. Each sleeps two to four.

VICKSBURG

Vicksburg is famous for its strategic location in the Civil War, thanks to its position on a high bluff overlooking the Mississippi River, and history buffs dig it. General Ulysses S Grant besieged the city for 47 days, until its surrender on July 4, 1863, at which point the North gained dominance over North America's greatest river.

◉ Sights & Activities

The major sights are readily accessible from I-20 exit 4B (Clay St). The old, slow downtown stretches along several cobblestoned blocks of Washington St, and **historic-house museums** cluster in the Garden District. Vicksburg's stretch of the **Mississippi River** has casinos. Down by the water is a block of murals depicting the history of the area, and a **Children's Art Park**.

National Military Park (www.nps.gov/vick; Clay St; per car/individual $8/4; ⊙8am-5pm Oct-Mar, til 7pm Apr-Sep), north of I-20 is a massive battlefield, Vicksburg's main attraction for Civil War buffs. A 16-mile driving tour passes

historic markers explaining battle scenarios and key events. You can buy an audiotape tour on cassette or CD in the visitor center gift shop, or drive through on your own using the free map distributed on-site (but plan for at least two hours to do it justice). If you have your bike, cycling is a fantastic way to tour the place. Locals use the scenic park for walking and running, too. The cemetery contains some 17,000 Union graves, and a museum houses the ironclad gunboat USS *Cairo*. **Civil War reenactments** are held in May and July.

🛏 Sleeping & Eating

Corners Mansion   B&B **$$**
(☎601-636-7421; www.thecorners.com; 601 Klein St; r incl breakfast $125-170; P❄❄) The best part of this Old South 1873 B&B could be looking over the Yazoo and Mississippi Rivers from your porch-swing vantage point. The gardens and Southern breakfast don't hurt either.

Battlefield Inn   HOTEL **$**
(☎601-638-5811; www.battlefieldinn.org; 4137 N I-20 Frontage Rd; r incl breakfast from $85; P❄☎❄❄) Shouting distance from the National Military Park and next door to the Battlefield Museum, there's a karaoke bar inside the hotel, a wet bar by the swimming pool and cannons on the property, but other than the vague 'Robert E Lee meets *Gone with the Wind*' theme, there is little reason to stay here over the surrounding chain hotels.

Walnut Hills   SOUTHERN **$$**
(www.walnuthillsms.net; 1214 Adams St; mains $8-25; ⊙11am-9pm Mon-Sat, 11am-2pm Sun) For a dining experience that brings you back in time, head to this eatery where you can enjoy the utterly delectable, down-home Southern food elbow-to-elbow, family-style at a round table from 11am to 2pm. Try the blue-plate special ($9).

🌿 Highway 61 Coffeehouse   CAFE **$**
(www.61coffee.blogspot.com; 1101 Washington St; ⊙7am-5pm Mon-Fri, 9am-5pm Sat; ☎) This surprisingly awesome coffee shop has occasional live music on Saturday afternoons, serves Fair Trade coffee and is a minuscule epicenter of artsy-ness.

❶ Information

Visitor center (☎601-636-9421; www.visit vicksburg.com; 3300 Clay St; ⊙8am-5pm Mon-Sat & 10am-5pm Sun Mar-Oct, till 7pm

Mon-Sat & 10am-5pm Sun Nov-Feb) Hands out indispensable free maps that mark color-coded scenic driving paths into and out of the city.

Jackson

Mississippi's capital and largest city is victim to the common car-culture phenomenon of a latent (though stately and gentrifying) downtown surrounded by plush suburbs – sitting on top of an extinct volcano (most locals don't know that). However, interesting areas like the funky Fondren District, along with a cluster of well-done museums, historic sites and bars and restaurants, give insight into the culture of Mississippi and are elevating Jackson to a definite good time.

◉ Sights

FREE **Mississippi Museum of Art**   GALLERY
(www.msmuseumart.org; 380 South Lamar St; ☺10am-5pm Tue-Sat, noon-5pm Sun) This is the one fantastic attraction in Jackson. The collection of Mississippi art – a permanent exhibit dubbed 'The Mississippi Story' – is nothing less than superb. A new downtown green space called the Art Garden, with a symphony stage and live music, was underway at the time of writing.

FREE **Old Capitol Museum**   MUSEUM
(http://mdah.state.ms.us/museum; 100 State St; ☺9am-5pm Tue-Sati, 1-5pm Sun) The state's Greek Revival capitol building from 1839 to 1903 received a stellar renovation in 2009. It now houses an extremely well-done museum that covers Mississippi's history from prehistoric to modern times.

Eudora Welty House   HISTORIC BUILDING
(☑601-353-7762;   www.mdah.state.ms.us/welty; 1119 Pinehurst St; ☺tours 9am, 11am, 1pm & 3pm Tue-Fri) Southern-literature buffs should make a reservation to tour the Welty. The Pulitzer Prize–winning author lived in this Tudor Revival house for more than 75 years. It's now a true historical preservation down to the most minute details.

Smith Robertson Museum   MUSEUM
(www.jacksonms.gov/visitors/museums/smithrobertson; 528 Bloom St; adult/child $4.50/1.50; ☺9am-5pm Mon-Fri, 10am-1pm Sat, 2-5pm Sun) Housed in Mississippi's first public school for African American kids, is the alma mater of author Richard Wright. It offers insight and explanation into the pain and perseverance of the African American legacy in Mississippi.

Mississippi Children's Museum   MUSEUM
(www.mississippichildrensmuseum.com;   2148 Riverside Dr; admission $8; ☺9am-5pm Tue-Sat, 1-6pm Sun; ▣) Jackson's brand new children's museum, opened in December 2010, was quickly recognized as one of the country's best. Many of the exhibits have a sustainable or Mississippi slant, and all are aimed educating the youngsters – the digestive-tract jungle gym that ends in a toilet might have gone too far, though.

🛏 Sleeping & Eating

Fondren District is the budding artsy, boho area of town, ie fun restaurants, art galleries and cafes dot a strip of traffic-heavy road. Farish St, a dilapidated downtown street thoroughly soaked in blues history, was being gutted and revitalized at the time of writing, with a BB King blues club on the way.

Old Capitol Inn   BOUTIQUE HOTEL $$
(☑601-359-9000;   www.oldcapitolinn.com; 226 N State St; r incl breakfast from $99; ▣※@🛜🏊) A heck of a deal, this 24-room boutique hotel, near museums and restaurants, has up-to-date rooms that are comfortably and uniquely furnished. The rooftop deck, complete with hot tub, overlooks a courtyard and pool. A full Southern breakfast (and early-evening wine and cheese) are included and the thoughtful service is exemplified by details such as handwritten weather reports brought to your room.

Fairview Inn   INN $$
(☑601-948-3429;   www.fairviewinn.com;   734 Fairview St; s/d incl breakfast from $139/154; ▣※@🛜) For a colonial estate experience, the 18-room Fairview Inn will not let you down when it comes to Southern formality and traditions, including a grits-and-bacon kind of breakfast. It also has a full spa.

Two Sisters Kitchen   SOUTHERN $$
(707 N Congress St; buffet weekends/weekdays $14.80/12.50; ☺11am-2pm Sun-Fri) Some serious Southern business is happening at this down-home buffet in a historical 1903 home: fried okra, cheese grits and legendary *skinless* fried chicken among the highlights. The line stretches out the door pretty much always and the all-you-can-eat price includes salad and dessert as well.

Walker's Drive-In SOUTHERN $$$
(www.walkersdrivein.com; 3016 N State St; dinner mains $28-32; ⏲11am-2pm Mon-Fri & from 5:30pm Tue-Sat) This truly outstanding restaurant calls itself a drive-in, but it's really a gussied-up diner that serves lusciously tweaked Southern staples. And it serves things like heavenly barbecued oysters dolloped with brie, and incredible fish dishes. There's an excellent wine list and service is impeccable.

🌱 **High Noon Cafe** VEGETARIAN
(2807 Old Canton Rd; mains $9-11; ⏲11:30am-2pm; 🖉) Tired of fried green pulled-pork-covered catfish? This organic vegetarian grill, inside the Rainbow Co-op grocery store in the Fondren District (which also has a free internet cafe, incidentally), does beet burgers, portabello Reubens and other healthy delights. Stock up on healthy groceries, too.

☆ Entertainment

📍 **F Jones Corner** BLUES
(www.fjonescorner.com; 303 N Farish St; ⏲Tue-Fri 11am-2pm, Thu-Sat 10am-late) The real deal. All shapes and sizes descend on this down-home club when everywhere else closes; a race, color and creed potpourri on Farish St that hosts some seriously authentic Delta musicians who have been known to play until sunrise. Don't show up before 1am.

119 Underground BLUES
(www.underground119.com; 119 S President St; ⏲4pm-midnight Wed-Thu, 4pm-2am Fri, Sat 6pm-2am Sat) A funky, supremely cool supper club throwback serving up blues, jazz and bluegrass alongside excellent eats (the chef's Southern fusion comes from his extended travels and backyard urban garden) and juiced up creative cocktails (try the Robert Johnson – sweet tea vodka with fresh lemon juice).

ℹ Information

Convention & visitors bureau (📞601-960-1891; www.visitjackson.com; 111 E Capitol St, Suite 102; ⏲8am-5pm Mon-Fri) Free information.

ℹ Getting There & Away

At the junction of I-20 and I-55, it's easy to get in and out of Jackson. Its international **airport** (JAN; www.jmaa.com) is 10 miles east of downtown. **Greyhound** (📞601-353-6342; 300 W Capitol St) buses serve Birmingham, AL, Memphis, TN, and New Orleans, LA. Amtrak's *City of New Orleans* stops at the station.

Natchez

A tiny dollop of cosmopolitan in Mississippi, adorable Natchez stews together a wide variety of folks, from gay log-cabin republicans to intellectual liberals, to down-home folks. Perched on a bluff overlooking the Mississippi, it's the oldest town on the river and attracts tourists in search of antebellum history and architecture – 668 antebellum homes pepper the oldest civilized settlement on the Mississippi River (beating New Orleans by two years). It's also the end (or the beginning!) of the scenic 444-mile Natchez Trace Pkwy (p360), the state's cycling and recreational jewel.

The **visitor and welcome center** (📞601-446-6345; www.visitnatchez.org; 640 S Canal St; tours adult/child $12/8; ⏲8:30am-5pm Mon-Sat, 9am-4pm Sun) is a large, well-organized tourist resource with little exhibits of area history and a ton of information on local sites. Tours of the historic downtown and antebellum mansions leave here. During the 'pilgrimage' seasons in spring and fall, local mansions are opened to visitors.

Ever wish you could sleep in one of those historic homes with every room roped off? At the **Historic Oak Hill Inn** (📞601-446-2500; www.historicoakhill.com; 409 S Rankin St; r incl breakfast from $125; 🅿✳🛜), you can sleep in an original 1835 bed and dine on pre–Civil War Old Paris porcelain under 1850 Waterford crystal gasoliers – it's all about purist antebellum aristocratic living at this classic Natchez B&B. A high-strung staff makes for an immaculate experience and it's gay-friendly. The **Sunset View Guest Cottages** (📞601-870-2662; www.asunsetview.com; 26 Cemetery Rd; cottages $165-195; 🅿✳🛜) are warmly decorated cottages with private, stunning views of the Mississippi River. You can skip rocks into the Mississippi from the **Mark Twain Guesthouse** (📞601-446-8023; www.underthehillsaloon.com; 33 Silver St; r without bath $65-85; ✳🛜) where three rooms (two with views) sit on top of a good local watering hole, the **Under the Hill Saloon**.

Economy options are limited here, but there is camping at **Natchez State Park** (www.mississippistateparks.reserveamerica.com; 230 Wickcliff Rd B; tent sites $13-24, RV sites $18, cabins $77-87). It's 1 mile east of the parkway on Hwy 61, 10 miles north of Natchez. Within the park is Emerald Mound, the second-largest Native American ceremonial mound of its type in the United States.

To get your fill of Southern eats, follow your nose to the **Pig Out Inn** (www.pigoutinnb bq.com; 116 S Canal St; pulled-pork sandwich $4.75; ☺11am-9pm Mon-Sat, to 3pm Sun), where some people say you'll find the best ribs in town. **Natchez Coffee Co.** (509 Franklin St; mains $5-8; ☺7am-6pm Mon-Fri, 8am-5pm Sat & Sun; ☎) is the spot for a latte or nicely done light bites.

Gulf Coast

In the backyard of New Orleans, the Gulf Coast's economy, traditionally based on the seafood industry, got a shot of adrenaline in the 1990s when big Vegas-style casinos muscled in alongside the sleepy fishing villages. And then a double whammy of disasters: just when the casinos in Biloxi had been rebuilt following Hurricane Katrina in 2005, the Deepwater Horizon oil spill in the Gulf in 2010 dealt the coast another unexpected blow. However, Mississippi's barrier islands help divert much of the oil problems toward New Orleans and Alabama, so Biloxi and Gulfport were largely spared and tourism had returned to 75% pre-spill levels at time of writing. The appeal? The manmade beaches are pleasant, and if you're a gambler you can jostle at the blackjack tables alongside Southern-speaking Vietnamese, Irish fishermen and bigwigs and environmentalists who have jetted in from big cities – all collaborating to rebuild a hard-luck area.

Keep track of what's open for business through the **Mississippi Gulf Coast Convention & Visitors Bureau** (☎228-896-6699; www.gulfcoast.org; 2350 Beach Blvd, Biloxi), which has a website that lists openings and reopenings.

Ocean Springs is one of the coolest, non-destroyed places on the Mississippi coast. Its **visitor center** (☎228-875-4424; www. oceanspringschamber.com; 1000 Washington St; ☺9am-4pm Mon-Fri) is at the head of Washington St, where you'll find a slew of cute shops, restaurants and coffeehouses.

Walter Anderson Museum (www.walter andersonmuseum.org; 510 Washington St; adult/child $10/5; ☺9:30am-4:30pm Mon-Sat, 12:30-4:30pm Sun) is a highlight of the city (and probably the state). A consummate artist and lover of Gulf Coast nature, Anderson had his fair share of turmoil and love that spurred his talent to great heights. After he died, the beachside shack where he lived

was found to be completely covered in mind-blowing murals, which are now transplanted to the museum.

Hotels line the highway, or stay at **Oak Shade B&B** (☎888-875-4711; www.oakshade. net; 1017 La Fontaine Ave; r $95-140; ✺❊☎). A visit here is very similar to just being a guest in a friend's home: comfy and relaxed. There's a lovely courtyard too. Marian, the owner, is laid-back and loves to help you do whatever you want to do in the area. Nice camping (and a visitor center) can be found at **Gulf Islands National Seashore Park** (www.nps.gov/guis; camping $16-20), which is a little bit out of town.

LOUISIANA

In the words of William Faulkner: 'The past is never dead. It's not even past.' Nowhere is that as true in the US as it is in Louisiana. Nostalgia for times long gone and recognition of hardships endured are found at every turn. This leads to a dynamic sense of place – natives are rooted here, and embrace what makes them unique. This is a state where African American cowboys strap washboards to their chests and strum the distinctive clicking sound of zydeco, and where gators lurk in swamps and are hunted by French-speaking Cajuns. Different cultures coexist – after all, don't we all just want to eat well and dance?

In the rolling hills and pine forests of northern Louisiana, the mostly Protestant population shares similar traits with other Southern states. But the world becomes a different place amid the swamps of southern Louisiana and the debauched streets of New Orleans – where jazz and Afro-Caribbean sounds are thick in the sultry air and make you unable to resist the urge to let loose.

History

The lower Mississippi River area was dominated by the Mississippian mound-building culture until around 1592 when Europeans arrived and decimated the Native Americans with the usual combination of disease, unfavorable treaties and outright hostility.

The land was then passed back and forth between France, Spain and England. After the American Revolution the whole area passed to the USA in the 1803 Louisiana Purchase, and Louisiana became a state in 1812.

LOUISIANA FACTS

» **Nicknames** Bayou State, Pelican State, Sportsman's Paradise

» **Population** 4.5 million

» **Area** 51,843 sq miles

» **Capital city** Baton Rouge (population 229,553)

» **Other cities** New Orleans (population 343,829)

» **Sales tax** 4%, plus local city and county taxes

» **Birthplace of** jazz, naturalist John James Audubon (1785–1851), trumpeter Louis 'Satchmo' Armstrong (1901–71), author Truman Capote (1924–84), musician Antoine 'Fats' Domino (b 1928), pop star Britney Spears (b 1981)

» **Home of** Tabasco sauce, chef Emeril Lagasse

» **Politics** normally a Republican stronghold but isn't afraid to veer left on occasion

» **Famous for** drive-thru margaritas

» **Official state reptile** alligator

» **Driving distances** New Orleans to Lafayette 137 miles, New Orleans to St Francisville 112 miles

Steamboats opened a vital trade network across the continent. New Orleans became a major port, and Louisiana's slave-based plantation economy kept up a flowing export of rice, tobacco, indigo, sugarcane and especially cotton. After the Civil War, Louisiana was readmitted to the Union in 1868, and the next 30 years saw political wrangling, economic stagnation and renewed discrimination against African Americans.

In the 1920s, industry and tourism developed, but the tradition of unorthodox and sometimes ruthless politics continues today. Race and economics are ongoing sources of struggle: witness the post-Katrina rebuilding process (p403). The 2005 hurricane and the flooding in its aftermath have reshaped southern Louisiana. Locals have negotiated the tricky path through redevelopment, the return of displaced peoples, wetland restoration and outsider involvement. Though revitalization has been more successful in some places, progress has been painfully slow in others, especially the poorer areas.

ⓘ Information

Sixteen welcome centers dot freeways throughout the state, or contact the **Louisiana Office of Tourism** (☑225-342-8119; www.louisianatravel.com).

Louisiana State Parks (☑877-226-7652; www.crt.state.la.us/parks; primitive/premium sites $1/18) Louisiana has 22 state parks that offer camping. Some parks offer lodge accommodations and cabins. Reservations can be made on the **internet** (www.reserveamerica.com), by phone, or on a drop-in basis if there's availability.

New Orleans

New Orleans gets called the 'Big Easy' in all its promotional material, and this city does take it easy, to some degree. It's rare in America to see folks hold up traffic for the sake of pulling over and calling out, 'Yo Dante, wassup,' and rarer still for the people behind them to accept this nonchalantly and find another way around.

But when it comes to having a good time, New Orleanians are kind of like Manhattanites on a deadline. Just one more beer? Nah son, have a shot with that. You want a burger? How's about we put peanut butter and bacon on top? And throw in a huge baked potato with sour cream on the side. And hell, some crawfish (crayfish).

At the mouth of the Mississippi, remember the three 'I's. The first two, indulgence and immersion, are easy to pick up on. It's brown sugar on bacon instead of oatmeal for breakfast; a double served neat instead of light beer; sex in the morning instead of being early for work ('My streetcar was down'). But the biggest 'I' here is *intermixing*. Tolerating everything and learning from it is the soul of this city. Social tensions and divisions of race and income keep New Orleans jittery, but when its citizens aspire to that great Creole ideal – a mix of all influences into something better – we get: jazz; Nouveau Louisiana cuisine; storytellers from African *griots* (West African storyteller) to Seventh Ward rappers to Tennessee Williams; French town houses a few blocks from Foghorn Leghorn mansions groaning under sweet myrtle and bougainvillea; Mardi Gras celebrations that mix pagan mysticism with Catholic pageantry. Just don't forget the indulgence and immersion, because that Creole-ization gets watered down when folks don't live life to its intellectual and epicurean hilt.

New Orleans may take it easy, but it takes it. The whole hog.

History

The town of Nouvelle Orléans was founded as a French outpost in 1718 by Jean-Baptiste Le Moyne de Bienville. Early settlers arrived from France, Canada and Germany, and the French imported thousands of African slaves. The city became a central port in the slave trade; due to local laws some slaves were allowed to earn their freedom and assume an established place in the Creole community as *les gens de couleur libres* (free people of color).

The Spanish were largely responsible for building the French Quarter as it still looks today because fires in 1788 and 1794 decimated the earlier French architecture. The influx of Anglo-Americans after the Louisiana Purchase led to an expansion of the city into the Central Business District (CBD), Garden District and Uptown. By 1840 New Orleans was the nation's fourth-largest city, with more than 100,000 people.

New Orleans survived the Civil War intact after an early surrender to Union forces, but the economy languished with the end of the slavery-based plantations. In the early 1900s, New Orleans was the birthplace of jazz music. Many of the speakeasies and homes of the jazz originators have been destroyed through neglect, but the cultural claim was canonized in 1994 when the NPS established the New Orleans Jazz National Historical Park to celebrate the origins and evolution of America's most widely recognized indigenous musical art form. Oil and petrochemical industries developed in the 1950s, and today tourism is the other lifeblood of the local economy.

In 2005 Katrina, a relatively weak Category 3 hurricane, overwhelmed New Orleans' federal flood protection system in over 50 places. Some 80% of the city was flooded, over 1800 people lost their lives and the entire city was evacuated. Today the population stands at 70% of pre-Katrina levels. Although much has rebuilt and tourists are back with a bead-throwing vengeance, the city has irrevocably changed.

⊙ Sights & Activities

FRENCH QUARTER

Elegant, Caribbean-colonial architecture, lush gardens and wrought-iron accents are the visual norm in the French Quarter. But this is also the heart of New Orleans' tourism scene. Bourbon St generates a loutish membrane that sometimes makes the rest of the Quarter difficult to appreciate. Look past this. The 'Vieux Carré' (Old Quarter, first laid out in 1722) is the focal point of much of this

---

RENEWED ORLEANS

New Orleans is back. The 'Katrina Tattoo,' the line on thousands of buildings that marked the top elevation of 2005's Hurricane Katrina floodwaters, has faded, and talk of 'The Storm' is slowly but surely fading into the history books. The city has survived floods, fires, epidemics, oil spills and the Indianapolis Colts, so it's no surprise that Katrina would be any different. Sure, there are still buildings left scarred with international rescue codes and plenty of rebuilding to do, but it's business as usual in the 'Who Dat' Nation, especially on the 'sliver by the River' extending from the blocks of Riverbend down in a curve along Uptown and Magazine St, up into the CBD, French Quarter and Faubourg Marigny.

There are new hot spots as well, from art gallery row on St Claude Ave, recently made-over Oak St in Riverbend and the Tremé neighborhood of HBO fame. Thanks to the thousands of new arrivals, affectionately nicknamed YURPs – Young, Urban Rebuilding Professionals (they've even got a website: www.nolayurp.com) – who came to carve the city back to life from the sludge and muck, as well as returnees. There are also signs of renewed life in the embattled Ninth Ward, Gentilly, Lakeview and Broadmoor neighborhoods, where Idealistic 20- and 30-somethings are buying property and starting new businesses.

New Orleans has always been a beacon for the misfits of America. Now add entrepreneurs, techies and actors to that list. The newly coined 'Silicon Bayou' and 'Hollywood South' – at least four flicks are being shot on location here at any given time lately – are also becoming a litmus test for new frontiers of urban planning. Brad Pitt's Make It Right campaign (p408) has turned much of the Lower Ninth Ward into a model sustainable neighborhood with a retro futuristic vibe so cool that it's worth a visit just to gawk at the homes.

New Orleans

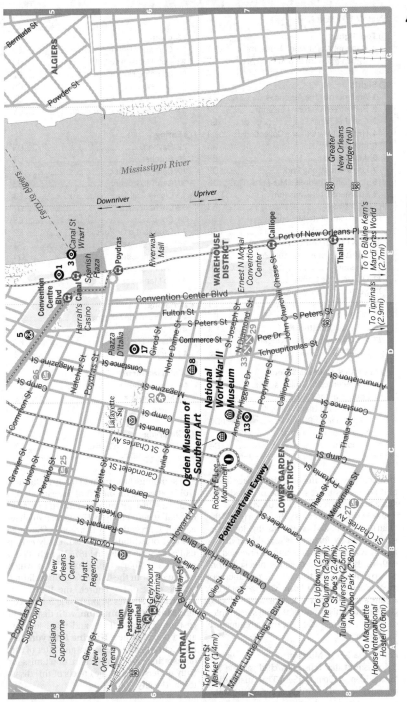

ALGIERS

Bermuda St

Powder St

Mississippi River

Downriver

Upriver

Ferry to Algiers

1

3 Canal St Wharf

Spanish Plaza

Poydras

Riverwalk Mall

WAREHOUSE DISTRICT

Ernest N Morial Convention Center

Calliope

Port of New Orleans Pl

Thalia

Greater New Orleans Bridge (toll)

To Blaine Kern's Mardi Gras World (2.7mi)

Convention Centre Blvd

Harrah's Casino

Convention Center Blvd

Fulton St

S Peters St

S Joseph St

S Peters St

To Tipitina's (2.9mi)

5

Piazza D'Italia

Girod St

Notre Dame St

Commerce St

N Diamond St

29

Poe Dr

John Churchill Chase St

Tchoupitoulas St

17

Constance St

Magazine St

Poydras St

Natchez St

National World War II Museum

8

33

Andrew Higgins Dr

Poeyfarre St

Calliope St

Annunciation St

Magazine St

20

Camp St

Church St

Julia St

13

Ogden Museum of Southern Art

St Charles Av

Carondelet St

Baronne St

Robert E Lee Monument

Erato St

Thalia St

Constance St

Camp St

Camp St

Magazine St

Lafayette St

9

Common St

Gravier St

Union St

Perdido St

O'Keefe St

S Rampart St

Lafayette St

25

Howard Av

Pontchartrain Expwy

LOWER GARDEN DISTRICT

Carondelet St

Baronne St

Thalia St

Prytania St

Melpomene St

St Charles Av

27

New Orleans Centre

Hyatt Regency

Loyola Av

Julia St

Bolivar St

Ophelia Castle-Haley Blvd

Thalia St

Erato St

Ophelia Castle-Haley Blvd

To Uptown (2mi);
The Columns (2.3mi);
St Joe's (2.4mi);
Tulane University (2.5mi);
Audubon Park (2.8mi)

Poydras Av

Sugarbowl Dr

Louisiana Superdome

Union Passenger Terminal

Greyhound Terminal

Girod St

New Orleans Arena

Simon Bolivar St

Oretha Castle-Haley Blvd

Erato St

CENTRAL CITY

To Freret St Market (1.4mi)

Martin Luther King Jr Blvd

To Marquette House International Hostel (0.6mi)

New Orleans

city's culture and in the quieter back lanes and alleyways there's a sense of faded time shaken and stirred with joie de vivre.

Jackson Square is the heart of the Quarter. Sprinkled with lazing loungers, surrounded by fortune-tellers, sketch artists and traveling showmen and overlooked by cathedrals, offices and shops plucked from a Parisian fantasy, this is one of America's great green spaces. **St Louis Cathedral** is the square's masterpiece. Designed by Gilberto Guillemard, this is one of the finest examples of French ecumenical (church) architecture in America.

Louisiana State Museum   MUSEUM
(http://lsm.crt.state.la.us; adult/child per bldg $6/free; ⊙10am-4:30pm Tue-Sun) This institution operates several institutions across the state.

The standouts here include the 1911 **Cabildo** (701 Chartres St), on the left of the cathedral, a Louisiana history museum located in the old city hall where Plessy vs Ferguson (which legalized segregation) was argued. The huge amount of exhibits inside can easily eat up half a day (don't miss the 1875 Upright Piano on the 3rd floor), the remainder of which can be spent in the Cabildo's sister building, on the right of the church, the 1813 **Presbytère** (751 Chartres St; ⓘ). Inside is an excellent **Mardi Gras museum**, with displays of costumes, parade floats and royal jewelry; and a poignant new **Katrina & Beyond** exhibit, chronicling the before and after of this devastating storm – a surefire don't miss for truly understanding the effects of this disaster on the city.

Historic New Orleans Collection   MUSEUM
(www.hnoc.org; 533 Royal St; admission free, tours $5; ☺9:30am-4:30pm Tue-Sat, 10:30am-4:30pm Sun) In several exquisitely restored buildings are thoughtfully curated exhibits with an emphasis on archival materials, such as the original transfer documents of the Louisiana Purchase. Separate home, architecture/courtyard and history tours also run at 10am, 11am, 2pm and 3pm, the home being the most interesting.

Old Ursuline Convent   HISTORIC BUILDING
(1112 Chartres St; adult/child $5/3; ☺tours 10am-4pm Mon-Sat) In 1727, 12 Ursuline nuns arrived in New Orleans to care for the French garrison's 'miserable little hospital' and to educate the young girls of the colony. Between 1745 and 1752 the French colonial army built what is now the oldest structure in the Mississippi River Valley and the only remaining French building in the Quarter. The self-guided tour takes in various rotating exhibits and the beautiful St Mary's chapel.

THE TREMÉ
The oldest African American neighborhood in the city is obviously steeped in a lot of history.

Louis Armstrong Park (☺9am-10pm) encompasses Congo Square, an American cultural landmark. Now a brick open space, it was the one place where enslaved people were allowed to congregate and play the music they had carried over the seas – a practice outlawed in most other slaveholding societies. The preservation of this musical heritage helped lay the groundwork for rhythms that would eventually become jazz. It was cordoned off and under a controversial facelift on our visit.

Backstreet Cultural Museum   MUSEUM
(www.backstreetmuseum.org; 1116 St Claude Ave; admission $8; ☺10am-5pm Tue-Sat) This is the place to see one facet of this town's distinctive customs – its African American side – and how they're expressed in daily life. The term 'backstreet' refers to New Orleans' 'back o' town,' or the poor African American neighborhoods. If you have any interest in Mardi Gras Indian suits (African Americans who dress up in Carnival-esque Native American costume), second lines and the activities of social aid and pleasure clubs (the local African American community version of civic associations), you need to stop by.

Le Musée de FPC   MUSEUM
(Free People of Color Museum; www.lemuseed efpc.com; 2336 Esplanade Ave; adult/child $10/5; ☺11am-4pm Wed-Sat or by appt) Inside a lovely 1859 Greek Revival mansion in the Upper Tremé, this newcomer showcases a 30-year collection of artifacts, documents, furniture and art telling the story of a forgotten subculture: the 'free people of color' before the Civil War. The small but fascinating collection includes original documentation of slaves who became free, either by *coartación* (buying their own freedom) or as a reward for particularly good service.

St Louis Cemetery No 1   CEMETERY
(Basin St; ☺9am-3pm Mon-Sat, til noon Sun; ⊕) This cemetery received the remains of most early Creoles. The shallow water table necessitated aboveground burials, with bodies placed in the family tombs you see to this day. The supposed grave of voodoo queen Marie Laveau is here, scratched with 'XXX's from spellbound devotees – this is graffiti you shouldn't add to, per the request of the family that owns the tomb.

New Orleans African American Museum of Art, Culture & History   MUSEUM
(www.thenoaam.org; 1418 Governor Nicholls St; adult/student/child $7/5/3; ☺11am-4pm Wed-Sat) Well-presented museum exhibiting rotating displays of local artists and more semipermanent installations on slavery and African American history in a series of tidy Creole homes.

St Augustine's Church   CHURCH
(☏504-525-5934; www.staugustinecatholic church-neworleans.org; 1210 Governor Nicholls St) The 1824 church is the second-oldest African American Catholic church in the US; many jazz funeral processions originate here. It has Sunday services but you'll need to call ahead for a tour – it's still understaffed post-Katrina and usually closed.

FAUBOURG MARIGNY, THE BYWATER & THE NINTH WARD
North of the French Quarter are the Creole suburbs ('faubourgs,' which more accurately means 'neighborhoods') of the Marigny and the Bywater. The Marigny is the heart of the local gay scene. Frenchman St, which runs through the center of the 'hood, is a fantastic strip of live-music goodness – what Bourbon St used to be before the strip clubs and daiquiri factories took over. The Bywater is

an edgier area, where a good mix of white, African American working class and artists are straddling the edge of urban cool. A lot of new New Orleanians have moved into this area, bringing a bit of gentrification along with some decent funkiness to the pretty rows of shotgun shacks.

Make It Right   NEIGHBORHOOD
(www.makeitrightnola.org; N Clairborne at Tennessee St) Brad Pitt's futuristic green building project in the Lower Ninth Ward, Make It Right, dots the former devastated landscape like *Jetsons*-style living quarters. Some 75 sustainable, storm-resistant homes had been built at time of writing (45 of which are LEED-certified platinum), giving the neighborhood a beautiful kaleidoscopic aura that is in striking contrast to the despairing images beamed around the world during Katrina. The US Green Building Council has named the neighborhood the 'largest, greenest neighborhood of single family homes in America.'

Musicians' Village   NEIGHBORHOOD
(www.nolamusiciansvillage.com; btwn North Roman, Alvar & North Johnson Sts) An 8-acre tract of some 81 houses, built primarily for musicians, a vital component of the city's cultural and economic landscape. If you visit, please bear in mind this is a living neighborhood; folks can get understandably tetchy if you take pictures of them or their property without asking permission or even getting out of your car. The brightly painted houses brighten up the surrounding neighborhood.

CBD & WAREHOUSE DISTRICT
The CBD and Warehouse District comprise the commercial section established after the Louisiana Purchase. Several outstanding museums anchor the Warehouse District and local art galleries cluster along Julia St, holding openings on the first Saturday evening of each month.

TOP CHOICE **National World War II Museum**   MUSEUM
(www.nationalww2museum.org; 945 Magazine St; adult/student/child $18/9/free, with film $23/12/5; ⊙9am-5pm) The extensive, heart-wrenching museum should satisfy the historical curiosity of anyone with even a passing interest in WWII. The museum presents an admirably nuanced and thorough analysis of the biggest war of the 20th century. Of particular note is the **D-Day exhibition**, arguably the most in-depth of its type in the country. The new 4-D *Beyond All Boundaries* film, narrated by Tom Hanks and shown on a 120ft-wide immersive screen in the new **Solomon Victory Theater**, is a loud, proud and awesome extravaganza well worth the extra $5. Chef John Besh's casual American diner, the **American Sector** (mains $9.50-18) has also been added here – make it a day.

Ogden Museum of Southern Art   MUSEUM
(www.ogdenmuseum.org; 925 Camp St; adult/student/child $10/8/5; ⊙10am-5pm Wed-Mon, 6-8pm Thu) One of our favorite museums in the city manages to be beautiful, educating and unpretentious all at once. New Orleans entrepreneur Roger Houston Ogden has assembled one of the finest collections of Southern art anywhere – far too large to keep to himself – which includes huge galleries ranging from Impressionist landscapes to outsider folk-art quirkiness, to contemporary installation work. There's live music from 6pm to 8pm Thursday for $10.

Blaine Kern's Mardi Gras World   MUSEUM
(www.mardigrasworld.com; 1380 Port of New Orleans Pl; adult/child $19.95/12.95; ⊙tours 9:30am-4:30pm; 🚗) This garish and good-fun place houses (and constructs) many of the greatest floats used in Mardi Gras parades. You can see them being built or on display any time of the year by popping by the facilities. After an outdated film on Mardi Gras history and a sample of King Cake, the tour takes you through the giant workshops where artists create elaborate floats for New Orleans krewes (marching clubs), Universal Studios and Disney World.

Aquarium of the Americas   AQUARIUM
(www.audoninstitute.org; 1 Canal St; adult/child $19.95/12.95; ⊙10am-5pm; 🚗) Simulates an eclectic selection of watery habitats – look for the rare white alligator. You can buy combination tickets to the IMAX theater next door or the Audubon Zoo in Uptown.

Insectarium   MUSEUM, GARDEN
(www.audoninstitute.org; 423 Canal St; adult/child $15.95/10.95; ⊙10am-5pm; 🚗) A supremely kid-friendly learning center that's a joy for budding entomologists. The Japanese garden dotted with whispering butterflies is particularly beautiful.

Canal Street Ferry   RIVER
(pedestrian & cyclist/car free/$1; ⊙6:15am-12:15am) Departing from the foot of Canal St is a fast and fabulous ride across the

Mississippi to Algiers, an attractive historic neighborhood just across the river, and back.

GARDEN DISTRICT & UPTOWN

The main architectural division in New Orleans is between the elegant town houses of the Creole and French northeast and the magnificent mansions of the American district, settled after the Louisiana Purchase. These huge structures, plantationesque in their appearance, are most commonly found in the Garden District and Uptown. Magnificent oak trees arch over St Charles Ave, which cuts through the heart of this sector and where the supremely picturesque St Charles Avenue streetcar (per ride $1.25; 🔊) runs. The boutiques and galleries of Magazine St form the best shopping strip in the city.

Further west, Tulane and Loyola universities occupy adjacent campuses alongside expansive Audubon Park. Tulane was founded in 1834 as a medical college in an attempt to control repeated cholera and yellow fever epidemics. Today the verdant campuses offer a welcome respite from city streets, while the universities host plenty of concerts and lectures.

Audubon Zoological Gardens   ZOO
(www.auduboninstitute.org; 6500 Magazine St; adult/child $15/10; ⊙10am-5pm Tue-Sun) Among the country's best zoos. It contains the ultra-cool **Louisiana Swamp** exhibit, full of alligators, bobcats, foxes, bears and snapping turtles.

CITY PARK & MID-CITY

New Orleans Museum of Art   MUSEUM
(www.noma.org; 1 Collins Diboll Circle; adult/child $10/6; ⊙10am-5pm Tue-Thu, Sat & Sun, to 9pm Fri) Inside the park, the elegant museum

was opened in 1911 and is well worth a visit both for its special exhibitions and top-floor galleries of African, Asian (don't miss the outstanding Qing dynasty snuff-bottle collection), Native American and Oceanic art. Its sculpture garden (admission free; ⊙10am-4:30pm Sat-Thu, til 8:45pm Fri) contains a cutting-edge collection in lush, meticulously planned grounds.

City Park   PARK
(www.neworleanscitypark.com) The Canal streetcar makes the run from the CBD to City Park. Three miles long, 1 mile wide, stroked by weeping willows and Spanish moss and dotted with museums, gardens, waterways, bridges, birds and the occasional alligator, City Park is the nation's fifth-largest urban park (bigger than Central Park in NYC) and New Orleans' prettiest green lung.

Fair Grounds   PARK
(1751 Gentilly Blvd, btwn Gentilly Blvd & Fortin St) Besides hosting the regular horse-racing season, the fair grounds are also home to the huge springtime New Orleans Jazz & Heritage Festival.

🔊 Courses

New Orleans School of Cooking   COOKING
(☎504-525-2665; www.neworleansschoolof cooking.com; 524 St Louis St; $23-27) A food demonstration – not a hands-on class. Menus rotate daily, but rest assured you'll be snacking on creations such as gumbo, jambalaya and pralines at the end of class, all the while learning about the history of the city as told by the charismatic chefs.

Wine Institute of New Orleans (WINO)   COOKING
(☎504-324-8000; www.winoschool.com; 610 Tchoupitoulas St; classes from $35) The 'institute'

NEW ORLEANS FOR CHILDREN

Many of New Orleans' daytime attractions are well suited for kids: the Audubon Zoological Gardens, Aquarium of the Americas (p408) and Mardi Gras World (p408), for example.

Carousel Gardens   AMUSEMENT PARK
(www.neworleanscitypark.com; admission $3; ⊙11am-6pm spring & fall, 10am-4pm Thu, 10am-10pm Fri, 11am-10pm Sat, 11am-6pm summer; 🔊) The 1906 carousel is a gem of vintage carny-ride happiness inside City Park.

Louisiana Children's Museum   MUSEUM
(www.lcm.org; 420 Julia St; admission $8; ⊙9:30am-4:30pm Tue-Sat, noon-4:30pm Sun, 9:30-4:30pm Mon in summer; 🔊) Great hands-on exploratory exhibits and toddler area. Children under 16 must be accompanied by an adult.

runs classes on wine tasting, food pairing and the like, aimed at both amateur enthusiasts and folks looking to get professionally employed in the wine and spirit industry. It's also a wine bar and shop with 120 wines on tap for tasting.

New Orleans GlassWorks & Printmaking Studio ART
(504-529-7279; www.neworleansglassworks. com; 727 Magazine St; classes $75-125) Try your hand at glassblowing (really!) or printmaking or both: you can design your own wine glasses and labels in the two-hour Wine and Design combo. Prices fluctuate with natural gas prices.

Tours

Tours, tours everywhere! Check the *New Orleans Official Visitors Guide* for a full selection of the myriad offerings. Some companies now give post-Katrina devastation/rebuilding tours. The Jean Lafitte National Historic Park and Preserve Visitor Center (p417) leads free walking tours of the French Quarter at 9:30am (get tickets at 9am).

Confederacy of Cruisers CYCLING
(504-400-5468; www.confederacyofcruisers. com; tour $45) Get yourself out of the Quarter and on two wheels – this super informative, laid-back bike tour takes you through Nola's non-Disneyland neighborhoods – Faubourg Marigny, Esplanade Ridge, the Tremé – often with a bar stop and the occasional jazz funeral pop-in along the way.

Friends of the Cabildo WALKING
(504-523-3939; 1850 House Museum Store, 523 St Ann St; adult/student/child $15/10/free; tours 10am & 1:30pm Tue-Sun) Volunteers lead the best available walking tours of the Quarter.

Festivals & Events

New Orleans never needs an excuse to party – whether in commemoration of shrimp and petroleum or the mighty mirliton (a kind of squash), there's almost always some celebration in town. Just a few listings follow; check www.neworleanscvb.com for more.

Mardi Gras CULTURAL
In February or early March, Fat Tuesday marks the orgasmic finale of the Carnival season.

St Patrick's Day CULTURAL
March 17 and its closest weekend see parades of cabbage-wielding Irishfolk.

St Joseph's Day – Super Sunday CULTURAL
March 19 and its nearest Sunday bring 'gangs' of Mardi Gras Indians out into the streets in all their feathered, drumming glory. The Super Sunday parade usually begins around noon at Bayou St John and Orleans Ave, but follows no fixed route.

Tennessee Williams Literary Festival LITERARY
(www.tennesseewilliams.net) In March, five days of literary panels, plays and parties celebrate the author's work.

French Quarter Festival MUSIC
(www.fqfi.org) The second weekend of April; free music on multiple stages.

Jazz Fest MUSIC
The last weekend of April and the first weekend of May; a world-renowned extravaganza of music, food, crafts and good living.

Southern Decadence GAY & LESBIAN
(www.southerndecadence.net) A huge gay, lesbian and transgender festival, including a leather block party, on Labor Day weekend (first weekend in September).

Sleeping

Rates peak during Mardi Gras and Jazz Fest, and fall in the hot summer months. Book early and call or check the internet for special deals. Hotel sales tax is 13%, plus $1 to $3 per person per night. Parking in the Quarter costs $15 to $25 per day.

TOP CHOICE Columns HISTORIC HOTEL $$
(504-899-9308; www.thecolumns.com; 3811 St Charles Ave; r incl breakfast weekend/weekday from $160/120;) A steal in low season (from $99), still a deal in high, this stately 1883 Italianate mansion in the Garden District is both elegant and relaxed, boasting all sorts of extraordinary original features: a stained-glass-topped staircase, elaborate marble fireplaces, richly carved woodwork throughout etc. To top it off, there's a lovely 2nd-floor porch overlooking oak-draped St Charles Ave and a damn inviting bar. It's everything that's wonderful about Nola.

Loft 523 BOUTIQUE HOTEL $$$
(504-200-6523; www.loft523.com; 523 Gravier St; r low/high season $79/299;) The hip industrial-minimalist style of Loft 523's 16 lodgings is a jarring change of pace for New Orleans (that's a compliment). Those are $5000 Fortuny lamps, for Godsakes.

Walking Tour
French Quarter

❯ Begin your walk at the ❶ **Presbytère** on Jackson Sq and head down Chartres St to the corner of Ursulines Ave and the ❷ **Old Ursuline Convent**.

Directly across Chartres St, at No 1113, the 1826 ❸ **Beauregard-Keyes House** combines Creole and American-style design. Walk along Ursulines Ave to Royal St – the soda fountain at the ❹ **Royal Pharmacy** is a preserved relic from halcyon malt-shop days.

Continue up Ursulines Ave and then turn left onto Bourbon St. The ramshackle one-story structure on the corner of St Philip St is a salty little tavern and National Historic Landmark called ❺ **Lafitte's Blacksmith Shop**. Head down St Philip back to Royal St and take a right.

When it comes to quintessential New Orleans postcard images, Royal St takes the prize. Cast-iron galleries grace the buildings and a profusion of flowers garland the facades.

At No 915 the ❻ **Cornstalk Hotel** stands behind one of the most frequently photographed fences anywhere. At Orleans Ave, stately magnolia trees and lush tropical plants fill ❼ **St Anthony's Garden**, behind ❽ **St Louis Cathedral**.

Alongside the garden, take the inviting Pirate's Alley and turn right down Cabildo Alley and then right up St Peter St toward Royal St. Tennessee Williams shacked up at No 632 St Peter, the ❾ **Avart-Peretti House** in 1946–47 while he wrote *A Streetcar Named Desire*.

Turn left on Royal St. At the corner of Royal and Toulouse Sts stands a pair of houses built by Jean François Merieult in the 1790s. The ❿ **Court of Two Lions**, at 541 Royal St, opens onto Toulouse St and next door is the ⓫ **Historic New Orleans Collection**.

On the next block, the massive 1909 ⓬ **State Supreme Court Building** was the setting for many scenes in director Oliver Stone's movie *JFK*.

Head down St Louis St to Chartres St and turn left. As Jackson Sq comes into view, you'll reach the Presbytère's near-identical twin, the ⓭ **Cabildo**.

ART FOR EVERY WEEKEND

You can discover local art and meet local artists every weekend in New Orleans.

New Orleans Arts District Art Walk (www.neworleansartsdistrict.com; Julia St) The first Saturday of each month beginning at 6pm until close (whenever, really), the fine art galleries in New Orleans Art District celebrate the opening night of month-long feature artist exhibitions.

Freret Street Market (www.freretmarket.org; cnr Freret St & Napoleon Ave) A combination farmers, flea and art show, this market offers a great mix of local culture. Held the first Saturday of the month (except for July and August) from noon to 5pm.

Saint Claude Arts District Gallery Openings (www.scadnola.com) New Orleans' newest arts district, this growing collective of art exhibition spaces spans Faubourg Marigny and the Bywater, home to some of New Orleans' more eclectic artists. Ask locals for weekend recommendations and you may be rewarded with a fire-eating display or impromptu collective installations at a secret, hidden art space.

Art Market of New Orleans (www.artscouncilofneworleans.org; Palmer Park, cnr Carrolton & Claiborne Aves) Last Saturday of every month. Featuring hundreds of the area's most creative local artists, this monthly market is juried for quality and always features local food, music and kids' activities. Perfect on warm-weather days.

With thanks to Lindsay Glatz, Arts Council of New Orleans.

Whirligig-shaped fans circle over low-lying Mondo beds and polished concrete floors and that half-egg-shaped tub is about as inviting as the Pearly Gates themselves. The sustainable angle – keys made from corn, partially-used toiletries being shipped off to countries in need – are mere bonuses. In summer, the $79 rate is downright theft.

Prytania Park Hotel HOTEL $
(☎504-524-0427; www.prytaniaparkhotel.com; 1525 Prytania St; r from $49-69; P※🐾📶) This great-value complex of three separate hotels offers friendly, well-located bang-for-the-buck. The Prytania Park's offers clean-cut, smallish rooms with flat-screen TVs for budget travelers. The **Prytania Oaks** (r $79-109) is sleeker and the **Queen Anne** (rooms $99-119) is an exquisite boutique hotel, newly renovated and bedecked with antiques. It's a perfect spot for folks of all budgets bouncing between the Quarter and the Garden District and/or Uptown. Parking is free and so is access to St Charles Ave Atheltic Club.

Lamothe House HISTORIC B&B $$$
(☎504-947-1161; www.lamothehouse.com; 621 Esplanade Ave; r incl breakfast $109-189, ste incl breakfast $209-399; ※📶🐾) Splashes of blue or green have lightened up the grand rooms in this 1839 mansion complete with gilt accents, rococo carvings and delicate oil paintings. Starker rooms in the outbuildings

adjoin easily for families, and the spacious courtyard lets you all spread out.

Degas House HISTORIC HOTEL $$
(☎504-821-5009; www.degashouse.com; 2306 Esplanade Ave; r incl breakfast from $199; P※🐾📶) Edgar Degas, the famed French Impressionist, lived in this 1852 Italianate house when visiting his mother's family in the early 1870s. Arty rooms recall the painter's stay with reproductions of his work and period furnishings. The suites have balconies and fireplaces, while the less-expensive garret rooms are the cramped top-floor quarters that once offered resident artist's some much-need respite.

Cornstalk Hotel B&B $$$
(☎504-523-1515; www.cornstalkhotel.com; 915 Royal St; r $115-250; ※🐾📶) Pass through the famous cast-iron fence and into a plush, antiqued B&B where the serenity sweeps away the whirl of the busy streets outside. Gemlike rooms are all luxurious and clean – carpets are given the once-over monthly! Limited parking.

Hotel Maison de Ville HISTORIC HOTEL $$$
(☎504-561-5858; www.hotelmaisondeville.com; 727 Toulouse St; ※🐾📶) New owners were redoing the courtyard, renovating the slave quarter suites, the facade, balconies etc at time of writing. The one- and two-bedroom Audubon Cottage suites (where artist John J Audubon

stayed and painted while in town) surround a lushly landscaped courtyard; the pool is rumored to be the oldest in the Quarter (from the late 1700s). It's all scheduled to reopen in the fall of 2011 so if genteel Southern comfort and polished charm are what you're after, it's worth looking into when it does.

Le Pavillon HISTORIC HOTEL **$$$**
(☎504-581-3111; www.lepavillon.com; 833 Poydras Ave; r $129-299, ste $199-499; ❄️🖥️🏊) Built in 1907, this elegant European-style hotel's opulent marble lobby, plush, classic rooms and rooftop pool are a steal. Decadent suites might prevent you from ever leaving the building. If booking a queen room, request a bay window. Parking costs $25.

India House Hostel HOSTEL **$**
(☎504-821-1904; www.indiahousehostel.com; 124 S Lopez St; dm/d $20/55; @🖥️🏊) In Mid-City, this place has a free-spirited party atmosphere. A large aboveground swimming pool and cabana-like patio add ambience to the three well-used old houses that serve as sparse but nice dorms. As for staff, Dutch trainees and Dutch management are lovely and helpful, others are is a bit off-putting. Many of the private rooms are little more than private dorms, so ask ahead if you want an actual double bed.

Marquette House International Hostel HOSTEL **$**
(☎504-523-3014; www.neworleansinternational hostel.com; 2249 Carondelet St; dm $17-25, s/d from $53/66; ☺office 7am-noon & 5-10pm; P❄️) A sprawling compound of both dorms and private rooms (with refrigerators and microwaves) near the Garden District. Serviceable, but certainly not luxurious, the rooms are upstaged by the lush garden area, perfect for hanging out and meeting fellow travelers.

✖️ Eating

Louisiana may have the greatest native culinary tradition in the USA – not necessarily by dint of the quality of food (although quality is very high) but from the long history that lies behind dishes that are older than most American states; and, while the rest of us eat to live, New Orleanians live to eat – despite the post-Katrina drop in population, there are 15% more restaurants now!

FRENCH QUARTER
GW Fins SEAFOOD, CAJUN **$$$**
(☎504-581-3467; www.gwfins.com; 808 Bienville St; mains $26-36; ☺5-10pm Sun-Thu, to 10:30pm

Fri & Sat) Fins focuses almost entirely on fish: fresh caught and prepped so the flavor of the sea is always accented and never overwhelmed. And it's not your average dishes, either: wood-grilled mangrove snapper, parmesan-crusted sheep's head, and hell, why not go for the bourbon-and-vanilla mashed potatoes to round it all out? For New Orleans this is light, almost delicate dining – a refreshing breath of salty air if you're getting jambalaya-ed out.

Bayona MODERN AMERICAN **$$$**
(☎504-525-4455; www.bayona.com; 430 Dauphine St; mains $27-32; ☺11:30am-2pm Mon-Fri & 6-10pm Mon-Thu, 6-11pm Fri & Sat) Bayona is a great splurge in the Quarter. It's rich but not overwhelming, classy but unpretentious, innovative without being precocious. Expect fish, fowl and game on the daily-changing menu divided between long-time classics and daily specials (about four of each), all done up in a way that makes you raise an eyebrow, then smile like you've discovered comfort food gone classy.

Green Goddess FUSION **$$**
(www.greengoddessnola.com; 307 Exchange Pl; mains $7-17; ☺11:30am-3:30pm Mon & Wed, 11am-3:30pm & 6pm-late Thu-Sun) Down a quiet alley off the Quarter, the Green Goddess is not only part of Nola's current mixologist craze (blueberry, basil, black pepper and jalapeño martini, anyone?) but is a global fusion godsend when you just can't bear another plate of red beans and rice. Not that an Irish porter cheddar grilled cheese melted with pear butter is any healthier, but it sure does send your taste buds on a welcomed journey elsewhere.

Coop's CAJUN, CREOLE **$$**
(1109 Decatur St; mains $8-17.50; ☺11am-3am) For a cheap but thoroughly satisfying meal in the Quarter, this Cajun country shack disguised as a divey bar is as good as it gets: try the rabbit and sausage jambalaya or the red beans and rice for a taste of Cajun heaven. You can get out of here stuffed to a Creole stupor for under $15.

Central Grocery ITALIAN **$$**
(923 Decatur St; half/full muffuletta $7.50/14.50; ☺9am-5pm Mon-Sat) Here, in 1906, a Sicilian immigrant invented the world-famous *muffuletta* sandwich – a round, seeded loaf of bread stuffed with ham, salami, provolone and marinated olive salad that's roughly the size of a manhole cover. This is still the best place in town to get one.

THE SOUTH LOUISIANA

Yo Mama's
BURGERS $

(www.yomamasbarandgrill.com; 727 St Peters St; burgers $6.50-10.50; ☺11am-3am) Let us lay it on the line: peanut butter and bacon burger. That's right: looks like a cheeseburger, but that ain't melted cheddar on top. Honestly, it's great: somehow the stickiness of the peanut butter compliments the char-grilled edge of the meat. New Orleans: peanut butter and bacon burger.

Croissant D'Or Patisserie
CAFE $

(617 Ursulines Ave; items $1.50-5.75; ☺6:30am-3pm Mon & Wed-Sun) This ancient and spotlessly clean pastry shop is where many Quarter locals start their day. Bring a paper, order coffee and a croissant and bliss out. On your way in, check out the tiled sign on the threshold that says 'ladies entrance' – a holdover from pre-feminist days that is no longer enforced.

Clover Grill
DINER $

(900 Bourbon St; mains $3-8; ☺24hr) Gay greasy spoon? Yup. It's all slightly surreal, given this place otherwise totally resembles a '50s diner, but nothing adds to the Americana like a prima-donna-style argument between an out-of-makeup drag queen and a drunk club kid, all likely set to blaring disco music.

[unreadable]
CAFE $

(800 Decatur St; beignets $2.14; ☺24hr; 🚼) Du Monde is overrated, but you're probably gonna go there, so here goes: the coffee is decent and the beignets (square, sugar-coated fritters) are inconsistent. The atmosphere is off-putting: you're a number forced through the wringer, trying to shout over Bob and Fran while they mispronounce 'jambalaya' and a street musician badly mangles John Lennon's 'Imagine.' At least it's open 24 hours.

THE TREMÉ

Willie Mae's Scotch House
SOUTHERN $$

(2401 St Ann St; fried chicken $10; ☺11am-7pm Mon-Sat) The fried chicken at Willie Mae's is good. Very good. But it's not the best in the world, despite being named an 'American Classic' by the James Beard foundation in 2005.

Dooky Chase
SOUTHERN $$

(2301 Orleans Ave; buffet $17.95; ☺11am-3pm Tue-Fri) Ray Charles wrote 'Early in the Morning' about Dooky's, local civil rights leaders used the spot as an informal headquarters in the 1960s and Bush and Barack have tucked into the refined soul food at this overpriced Tremé backbone.

FAUBOURG MARIGNY & THE BYWATER

Bacchanal
CAFE $$

(www.bacchanalwine.com; 600 Poland Ave; mains $8-14, cheese per piece from $5; ☺11am-midnight) Grab a bottle of wine, let the folks behind the counter prep your *fromage* into a work of art, then kick back in a backyard of overgrown garden green scattered with rusted-out lawn chairs and tatty foldouts set to whoever showed up to play live that day. Or order from the limited but inventive full menu. It's a sort of high-end hillbilly wine and cheese hangout – and it's great.

Elizabeth's
CAJUN, CREOLE $$$

(www.elizabeths-restaurant.com; 601 Gallier St; mains $16-26; ☺8am-2:30pm & 6-10pm Tue-Sat, 8am-2:30pm Sun) Elizabeth's is deceptively divey, way too dark and probably too laid-back. The food is overly simplistic at times, startlingly out-of-the-box at others. But it tastes as good as the best haute New Orleans chefs can offer. Be sure to order some praline bacon, no matter the time of day: fried up in brown sugar and, as far as we can tell, God's own cooking oil.

CBD & WAREHOUSE DISTRICT

TOP CHOICE / Cochon
CONTEMPORARY CAJUN $$$

(☎504-588-2123; www.cochonrestaurant.com; 930 Tchoupitoulas St; mains $19-25; ☺11am-10pm Mon-Fri, 5:30-10pm Sat) James Beard Award–winning chef Donald Link's fabulous brasserie serves up gourmet Southern comfort food in such curious and intriguing ways, you won't know what to do with yourself. The housemade Louisiana *cochon* – moist, pulled-pork heaven on the inside, crusty, pan-seared perfection on the outside – is probably the best swine you will ever have, unless you eat here twice. The mac 'n' cheese? It's laced with bacon fat – end of story. Link's fearless willingness to pair the simply succulent with the exceptionally extravagant catapult this cultishly loved spot into the echelons of truly unique cuisine – and there's moonshine to wash it all down. Reservations essential.

Butcher
CAJUN, SOUTHERN $$

(www.cochonbutcher.com; 930 Tchoupitoulas St; sandwiches $9-12; ☺10am-10pm Mon-Thu, til 11pm Fri & Sat, til 4pm Sun) Around the corner from Cochon, Chef Donald Link makes his in-house cured meat philosophy accessible to all budgets at this don't-miss butcher shop–deli and bar. Sandwich highlights here include milk-fed pork Cubans, Carolina-style pulled pork, the Cochon muffaletta and the Buckboard bacon melt. Pair it with pancetta mac 'n' cheese and bacon pralines. This is an empire in the making.

GARDEN DISTRICT & UPTOWN

TOP CHOICE Commander's
Palace   CONTEMPORARY CREOLE **$$$**
(☑504-899-8221; www.commanderspalace.com; 1403 Washington Ave; dinner mains $28-45; ⊘11:30am-2pm Mon-Fri, to 1pm Sat, 10:30am-1:30pm Sun & 6:30-10pm Mon-Sat) It's no small coincidence that some of the most famous Nola chefs – check that, US chefs – got their start in this kitchen (Paul Prudhomme, Emeril Lagasse); this New Orleans grand dame is outstanding across the board. Chef Tory McPhail's (remember that name!) shrimp-and-tasso appetizer swimming in Louisiana hot sauce and the hickory-grilled pork are two of the most explosively satisfying dishes you will ever encounter. It's an impeccable mainstay of Creole cooking and knowledgeable, friendly service, in the heart of the gorgeous Garden District. Pop in for the lunchtime 25¢ martinis and a cup of the signature turtle soup ($8), or a *prix fixe* extravaganza. No shorts allowed.

Boucherie   NEW SOUTHERN **$$**
(☑504-862-5514; www.boucherie-nola.com; 8115 Jeannette St; large plates $12-15; ⊘11am-3pm & 5:30-9pm Tue-Sat) Just when you thought a Krispy Kreme doughnut was already perfection personified, Boucherie comes along and turns it into a bread pudding. When married to a honey-glazed, drowning in syrup, that heavy bread pudding becomes airy yet drool-tastically unforgettable! For dinner, blackened shrimp-and-grits cakes are darkly sweet and savory, garlic parmesan fries are gloriously stinky and gooey and the smoked Wagyu beef brisket just melts in your mouth. And it's all so reasonably priced.

Mat and Naddie's   CONTEMPORARY CREOLE **$$$**
(☑504-861-9600; www.matandnaddies.com; 937 Leonidas St; mains $22-29; ⊘11am-2pm Mon-Fri, 5:30-9:30pm Thu-Sat & Mon) Set in a beautiful riverfront shotgun house with a Christmas-light-bedecked patio in the back, M&N's is rich, innovative, even outlandish: artichoke, sun-dried tomato and roasted garlic cheese-cake (oh yes!), sherry-marinated grilled quail with waffles, pecan sweet-potato pie – all crazy delicious. It's high quality topped with quirkiness and a great indicator of

what chefs can do when they think outside the gastro box around here.

🖊 **Cowbell**   AMERICAN **$$**
(www.cowbell-nola.com; 8801 Oak St; mains $10-14; ⊘11:30am-3pm Tue-Sat & 5-10pm Tue-Thu, till 11pm Fri & Sat) This hipster farm-to-table hangout in a former gas station dishes out simple, sustainable comfort food free of horrible stuff like hormones, pesticides and other crap that makes food taste like cardboard – so says the owner. The natural, grass-fed burger is indeed great and the limited menu features Gulf fish tacos, adult-style grilled cheese and organic lime chicken, which is gobbled down by Riverbend's cooler-than-thou set in an aluminum-sided, silo-chic gourmet shack.

Domilise's Po-Boys   CREOLE **$$**
(5240 Annunciation St; po'boys $9-13; ⊘10am-7pm Mon-Wed & Fri, 10:30am-7pm Sat) A dilapidated white shack by the river serving Dixie beer (brewed in Wisconsin!), staffed by folks who've worked here for decades and dressing one of the most legendary po' boys (traditional Louisiana submarine sandwich) in the city. It's cash only and prepare to hurry up and wait on weekends.

🍷 **Drinking**

New Orleans is a drinking town. Heads up: Bourbon St sucks. Get into the neighborhoods and experience some of the best bars in America. The kinder, gentler strip runs along Frenchmen St in Faubourg Marigny.

Most bars open every day, often by noon, get hopping around 10pm, and can stay open all night. There's no cover charge unless there's live music. It's illegal to have open glass liquor containers in the street, so all bars dispense plastic 'go cups' when you're ready to wander.

Spotted Cat   LIVE MUSIC
(www.spottedcatmusicclub.com; 623 Frenchmen St) A throwback retro cool permeates through this excellent Frenchman staple you might recognize from numerous episodes of *Tremé*. Hipster jazz is on nightly and there's never a cover unless a special event is on.

Mimi's in the Marigny   BAR
(2601 Royal St; ⊘til 5am) Great bi-level bar (pool downstairs, music upstairs) serving up excellent Spanish tapas ($5 to $8), casual neighborhood jazz (most nights) and DJs on

the weekend (Swamp Pop every other Friday, Retro Soul otherwise).

Tonique
BAR

(www.bartonique.com; 820 Rampart St) If you're going to drink in the Quarter (on the edge of it, anyway), this serious cocktail bar is the place, where cool folks who appreciate an excellent concoction gather over the best Sazerac we had in town. And we had many.

St Joe's
BAR

(5535 Magazine St) Good-time Uptown pious-themed bar with great blueberry mojitos (praise the Lord!), a cool back courtyard and friendly ambience.

R Bar
BAR

(1431 Royal St) Somewhere between a dive and a neighborhood joint; a beer and a shot runs you $5.

☆ Entertainment

What's New Orleans without live local music? Almost any weekend night you can find something for every taste: jazz, blues, brass band, country, Dixieland, zydeco, rock or Cajun. Free shows in the daytime abound. Check *Gambit* (www.bestofneworleans. com), *Offbeat* (www.offbeat.com) or www. nolafunguide.com for schedules.

Three Muses
JAZZ

(www.thethreemuses.com; 536 Frenchman St; ⊙4-10pm Wed-Thu & Sun-Mon, til 2am Fri & Sat) This newcomer was an instant hit with both musicians and foodies – they've managed to happily marry an excellent soundtrack with gourmet cuisine in a more intimate room than most on Frenchman. There's loads of great local art to peruse between acts and courses. Start here.

Preservation Hall
JAZZ

(www.preservationhall.com; 726 St Peter St; ⊙8-11pm) A veritable museum of traditional and Dixieland jazz, Preservation Hall is a pilgrimage. But like many religious obligations, it ain't necessarily easy, with no air-conditioning, limited seating and no refreshments (you can bring your own water, that's it).

Snug Harbor
JAZZ

(www.snugjazz.com; 626 Frenchmen St) In the Marigny, the city's best contemporary jazz venue is all about world-class music and a good variety of acts. If you can't spring for the show (cover $15 to $25), sit downstairs at the bar and watch on close-circuit.

Maple Leaf Bar
LIVE MUSIC

(☎504-866-9359; 8316 Oak St) Riverbend's pride and joy, its pressed-tin ceiling and close atmosphere get especially heated late. Big nights are Papa Grows Funk on Mondays and Rebirth Brass Band on Tuesdays.

Tipitina's
LIVE MUSIC

(www.tipitinas.com; 501 Napoleon Ave) Always drawing a lively crowd, this legendary Uptown club rocks out like the musical mecca it is: local jazz, blues, soul and funk stop in, as well as national touring bands.

Vaughan's
LIVE MUSIC

(800 Lesseps St) A great Bywater neighborhood bar that hosts local favorite and awesome trumpeter Kermit Ruffins on Thursday nights.

🛍 Shopping

Faulkner House Books
BOOKSHOP

(www.faulknerhousebooks.net; 624 Pirate's Alley; ⊙10am-5:30pm) The erudite owner of this former residence of author William Faulkner sells rare first editions and new titles.

Maple Street Book Shop
BOOKSHOP

(www.maplestreetbookshop.com; 7523 Maple St; ⊙9am-7pm Mon-Sat, 11am-5pm Sun) A mainstay independent bookstore in Uptown, with a used bookstore affiliate next door.

ⓘ Information

Dangers & Annoyances

New Orleans has a high violent-crime rate, and neighborhoods go from good to ghetto very quickly. Be careful walking too far north of Faubourg Marigny and the Bywater (St Claude Ave is a good place to stop), south of Magazine St (things get dodgier past Laurel St) and too far north of Rampart St (Lakeside) from the French Quarter into Tremé without a specific destination in mind. Stick to places that are well peopled, particularly at night, and spring for a cab to avoid dark walks. In the Quarter, street hustlers frequently approach tourists – just walk away. With all that said, don't be paranoid. Crime here, as in most of America, tends to be between people who already know each other.

Emergency & Medical Services

Medical Center of Louisiana (www.mclno.org; 2021 Perdido St; ⊙24hr) Has an emergency room.

Internet Access

There's pretty good wi-fi coverage in the CBD, French Quarter, Garden and Lower Garden Districts and Uptown. Almost every coffee shop in the city has wi-fi coverage. Libraries have free internet access for cardholders.

Zotz (8210 Oak St; per 30min $4; ⊙7m-1am; 🖧) Appropriately funky coffee shop in Riverbend neighborhood, popular with Tulane types. Coffee is here is organic/Fair Trade.

Internet Resources & Media

Gambit Weekly (www.bestofneworleans.com) Free weekly hot sheet of music, culture, politics and classifieds.

NOLA Fun Guide (www.nolafunguide.com) Great website for up-to-date info on gigs, gallery openings and the like.

Offbeat Magazine (www.offbeat.com) Free monthly specializing in music.

Times-Picayune (www.nola.com) New Orleans' daily newspaper has an entertainment calendar, and 'Lagniappe,' a more extensive guide, is included every Friday.

WWOZ 90.7 FM (www.wwoz.org) Tune in here for Louisiana music and more.

Post

Post office Lafayette Sq (610 S Maestri Pl; ⊙8:30am-4:30pm Mon-Fri); Main branch (701 Loyola Ave; ⊙7am-7pm Mon-Fri, 8am-4pm Sat) Mail sent General Delivery, New Orleans, LA 70112, goes to the main branch. Postboxes in outlying areas are not necessarily reliable since Katrina.

Tourist Information

The city's official visitor website is www.neworleansonline.com.

Jean Lafitte National Historic Park and Preserve Visitor Center (☑504-589-2636; www.nps.gov/jela; 419 Decatur St; ⊙9am-5pm) Operated by the NPS, with exhibits on local history, guided walks and daily live music. There's not much in the park office itself, but educational musical programs are held on most days of the week. Many of the park rangers are musicians and knowledgeable lecturers, and their presentations discuss musical developments, cultural changes, regional styles, myths, legends and musical techniques in relation to the broad subject of jazz.

Basin St Visitor's Center (☑504-293-2600; www.neworleanscvb.com; 501 Bason St; ⊙9am-5pm) Affiliated with the New Orleans CVB, this interactive tourist info center inside the former freight administration building of the Southern Railway has loads of helpful info and maps as well as an historical overview film and a small rail museum component. It's next door to St Louis Cemetery No 1.

Louisiana Visitor's Center (☑504-566-5661; www.louisianatravel.com; 529 St Ann St; ⊙8:30am-5pm) Provides lots of free information and maps for Nola and the state.

ℹ Getting There & Away

Louis Armstrong New Orleans International Airport (MSY; www.flymsy.com; 900 Airline Hwy), 11 miles west of the city, handles primarily domestic flights.

The **Union Passenger Terminal** (☑504-299-1880; 1001 Loyola Ave) is home to **Greyhound** (☑504-525-6075; ⊙5:15am-1pm & 2:30-6pm), which has regular buses to Baton Rouge ($18 to $23, two hours), Memphis, TN ($63 to $79, 11 hours) and Atlanta, GA ($84 to $106, 12 hours). **Amtrak** (☑504-528-1610; ⊙ticketing 5:45am-10pm) trains also operate from the Union Passenger Terminal, running to Jackson, MS; Memphis, TN; Chicago, IL. Birmingham, AL; Atlanta, GA; Washington, DC; New York City; Los Angeles, CA; and Miami, FL.

ℹ Getting Around

To/From the Airport

There's an information booth at the airport's A&B concourse. The **Airport Shuttle** (☑866-596-2699; www.airportshuttleneworleans.com; one way per person $20) runs to downtown hotels. The **Jefferson Transit** (☑504-364-3450; www.jeffersontransit.org; adult $2) airport route E2 picks up outside entrance 7 on the airport's upper level; it stops along Airline Hwy (Hwy 61) on its way into town (final stop Tulane and Loyola Aves). After 7pm it only goes to Tulane and Carrollton Aves in Mid-City; a solid 5 miles through a dreary neighborhood to get to the CBD, from here you must transfer to a Regional Transit Authority (RTA) bus – a haphazard transfer at best, especially with luggage.

Taxis downtown cost $33 for one or two people, $14 more for each additional passenger.

Car & Motorcycle

Bringing a car is a useful way of exploring beyond the Quarter; just be aware that parking in the Quarter is a hassle. Garages charge about $13 for the first three hours and $30 to $35 for 24 hours.

> ℹ **BIG EASY PARKING**
>
> It's not a hard and fast rule, but New Orleans lost numerous bus lines post-Katrina, especially in the French Quarter, where buses no longer go. Locals in the know often park in now-unused bus lanes regardless of the outdated signage banning parking there. It's still a risk if a particular parking enforcement officer is having a bad day, but locals report that you will almost always be OK.

Public Transportation

The **Regional Transit Authority** (RTA; www. norta.com) runs the local bus service. Bus and streetcar fares are $1.25, plus 25¢ for transfers; express buses cost $1.50. Exact change is required. RTA Visitor Passes for one/three days cost $5/12.

The RTA also operates three **streetcar** lines. The historic St Charles streetcar is running only a short loop in the CBD due to hurricane damage to the Uptown tracks. The Canal streetcar makes a long journey up Canal St to City Park, with a spur on Carrollton Ave. The Riverfront line runs 2 miles along the levee from the Old US Mint, past Canal St, to the upriver convention center and back.

For a taxi, call **United Cabs** (☑504-522-9771; www.unitedcabs.com) or **White Fleet Cabs** (☑504-822-3800).

Rent bicycles at **Bicycle Michael's** (☑504-945-9505; www.bicyclemichaels.com; 622 Frenchmen St; rentals per day $35; ◷10am-7pm Mon, Tue & Thu-Sat, to 5pm Sun), in Faubourg Marigny.

Around New Orleans

Leaving gritty, colorful New Orleans quickly catapults you into a world of swamps, bayous, antebellum plantation homes and laid-back small communities. A foray into these lesser-known environs makes for an off-the-beaten-path adventure.

THE NORTH SHORE

Bedroom communities sprawl along Lake Ponchartrain's north shore, but head north of Mandeville and you'll reach the bucolic village of Abita Springs, which was popular in the late 1800s for its curative waters. Today the spring water still flows from a fountain in the center of the village, but the primary liquid attraction here is the Abita Brew Pub (www.abitabrewpub.com; 7201 Holly St; tours free; ◷11am-9pm Tue-Fri, to 10pm Sat), where you can choose from 10 Abita beers on tap that are made a mile west of town at Abita Brewery (www.abita.com; 166 Barbee Rd; tours free; ◷tours 2pm Wed-Fri, 11am, noon, 1pm & 2pm Sat).

Other local libations can be found on Hwy 1082, where you'll encounter Louisiana's finest wines at Ponchartrain Vineyards (www.pontchartrainvineyards.com; 81250 Old Military Rd; ◷tasting room noon-5pm Wed-Sun). It's a pleasant surprise that tends to diverge from the syrupy sweet wines usually produced down South. To the south, Covington has a worthwhile downtown with funky antique shops.

The 31-mile **Tammany Trace trail** (www.tammanytrace.org) connects north shore towns, beginning in Covington, passing through Abita Springs and Fontainebleau State Park, on the lakeshore near Mandeville, and terminating in Slidell. This converted railroad makes for a lovely bike ride that drops you into each town's center. In Mandeville you can rent bikes at the Old Mandeville Café and Kickstand Bike Rental (www.kickstand.bz; 690 Lafitte St; ◷8am-4pm Mon-Sat, 10am-4pm Sun).

BARATARIA PRESERVE

This section of the Jean Lafitte National Historical Park & Preserve, south of New Orleans near the town of Marrero, provides the easiest access to the dense swamplands that ring New Orleans. The 8 miles of platform trails are a stunning way to tread lightly through the fecund, thriving swamp where you can check out gators and other fascinating plant life and creatures. The preserve is home to alligators, nutrias, tree frogs and hundreds of species of birds. It is well worth taking a ranger-led walk to learn about the many ecosystems that make up what are often lumped together as 'wetlands.'

Start at the NPS Visitors Center (☑504-589-2330; www.nps.gov/jela; Hwy 3134; admission free; ◷9am-5pm; 🖢), 1 mile west of Hwy 45 off the Barataria Blvd exit, where you can pick up a map or join a guided walk or canoe trip (most Saturday mornings and monthly on full-moon nights; call to reserve a spot). The center has informational exhibits and a 25-minute documentary on swampland habitats. To rent canoes or kayaks for a tour or an independent paddle, go to **Bayou Barn** (☑504-689-2663; www.bayoubarn.net; canoes per person $20, 1-person kayak per day $25; ⊙10am-6pm Thu-Sun) on the Bayou de Familles just outside the park entrance.

RIVER ROAD

Elaborate plantation homes dot the east and west banks of the Mississippi River between New Orleans and Baton Rouge. First indigo, then cotton and sugarcane, brought great wealth to these plantations, many of which are open to the public. Most tours focus on the lives of the plantation owners, the restored architecture and the ornate gardens of antebellum Louisiana, and they skip over the story of plantation slaves who made up the majority of the plantations' population. It's easy to explore the area by car or organized tour.

Laura Plantation (www.lauraplantation.com; 2247 Hwy 18; adult/child $18/5; ⊙10am-4pm), in Vacherie on the west bank, offers the most dynamic and informative tour. This ever-evolving and popular tour teases out the distinctions between Creole, Anglo and African American antebellum life via meticulous research and the written records of the Creole women who ran the place for generations.

Also in Vacherie, the most impressive aspect of **Oak Alley Plantation** (www.oakalleyplantation.com; 3645 Hwy 18; adult/child $18/4.50; ⊙9am-4:40pm) is its canopy of 28 majestic live oaks lining the entry to the grandiose Greek Revival-style house – even better with a fresh mint julep ($6). The tour is relatively staid, but there are guest cottages ($130 to $170) and a restaurant on-site.

Be sure to flesh out any plantation tour with a visit to the **River Road African American Museum** (www.africanamericanmuseum.org; 406 Charles St; museum $4; ⊙10am-5pm Wed-Sat, 1-5pm Sun), 25 miles further along in Donaldsonville. This excellent museum preserves the important history of African Americans in the rural communities along the Mississippi.

BATON ROUGE

In 1699 French explorers named this area *baton rouge* (red stick) when they came upon a reddened cypress pole that Bayagoulas and Houma Native Americans had staked in the ground to mark the boundaries of their respective hunting territories.

An industrial town with a bustling port and the state capital, formerly lethargic Baton Rouge has swollen in size as relocated New Orleanians settle post-Katrina. Visitors are mostly drawn to Baton Rouge for Louisiana State University (LSU) and Southern University (the largest historically African American university in the country).

◉ Sights & Activities

FREE **Louisiana State Capitol** HISTORIC BUILDING
(⊙9am-4pm Tue-Sat) The art-deco skyscraper looming over town is a must-visit. Built at the height of the Great Depression to the tune of $5 million, it's populist governor 'Kingfish' Huey Long's most visible legacy. The 27th-floor **observation deck** offers stunning views and the ornate lobby is equally impressive. There are hourly free tours.

Louisiana Arts & Science Museum MUSEUM
(www.lasm.org; 100 S River Rd; adult/child $7/6, with planetarium show $9/8; ⊙10am-3pm Tue-Fri, 10am-5pm Sat, 1-4pm Sun; 🚸) Interesting arts and natural-history installations, and planetarium shows. If you just want a good stretch of the legs, there's a pleasant **pedestrian/bike path** along the Mississippi River, stretching 2.5 miles from the downtown promenade to LSU.

FREE **Old State Capitol** HISTORIC BUILDING
(www.crt.state.la.us/tourism/capitol; 100 North Blvd; ⊙9am-4pm Tue-Sat) The Gothic Revival, pink fairytale-castlelike building makes you think Governor Bobby Jindal is going to 'throw down his long hair' to Louisianans. It houses exhibits about the state's colorful political history.

LSU Museum of Art MUSEUM
(www.lsumoa.com; 100 Lafayette St; adult/child $5/free; ⊙10am-5pm Tue-Sat, to 8pm Thu, 1-5pm Sun) Across the street it holds a small exhibit, the highlight being about Louisiana 'Old and New.'

Dixie Landin & Blue Bayou AMUSEMENT PARK
(www.bluebayou.com; adult/child $35/28; 🚸) Just east of town at I-10 and Highland Rd. Kids will love the respective amusement and water park; check the online calendar for opening hours.

🛏 Sleeping & Eating

Stockade Bed & Breakfast B&B $$$
(☑225-769-7358; www.thestockade.com; 8860 Highland Rd; r incl breakfast $135-215; P🅿❄️)

DON'T MISS

PO'BOY PERFECTION

Louisiana's best po'boy ain't in N'Awlins, you'll find it under an I-10 overpass in Baton Rouge. How legit is *that?* Georges (www.georgesbr.com; 2943 Perkins Rd; meals $5-12; ◷11am-10:30pm Sun-Thu, till 11pm Fri & Sat) is a divey bar with dollar bills stapled to the ceiling and a chalkboard menu that is cause for genuflecting. The menu, among other things, boasts 13 po'boys, from exotic choices like spicy BBQ pork to the classic shrimp – a perfectly seasoned, crispy, batter-fried pile of heavenly goodness on Louisiana French bread. Can't decide between that and the equally killer cheeseburgers? Go for the cheeseburger po'boy. Done deal.

Chain hotels line the sides of I-10, but for a more intimate stay, try this wonderful B&B with five spacious, comfortable and elegant rooms just 3½ miles southeast of LSU and within earshot of several standout neighborhood restaurants. Book ahead on weekends, especially during football season.

BAR, PIZZERIA **$$**
(www.schlittz.com; 301 3rd St; pizzas $10-22; ◷11am-midnight Mon-Thu, to 3am Fri-Sun; ◈) The food stands up to the awesomely named downtown late-night bar and pizzeria. Bubbly coeds serve up thin-as-black-ice pizza slices ($3 to $3.50) and fabulous paninis to a student crowd, while a gaggle of old-timer locals tend to belly up at the bar.

Buzz Café CAFE **$**
(www.thebuzzcafe.org; 340 Florida St; meals $7-9; ◷7:30am-2pm Mon-Fri; ◈) For an awesome cup of joe and a plethora of creative wraps and sandwiches at a funky coffee shop in a historic building, try the Buzz.

☆ Entertainment

Varsity Theatre LIVE MUSIC
(www.varsitytheatre.com; 3353 Highland Rd; ◷8pm-2am) At the gates of LSU, you'll find live music here, often on weeknights. The attached restaurant boasts an extensive beer selection and a raucous college crowd.

Boudreaux and Thiboudeux LIVE MUSIC
(www.bandtlive.com; 214 3rd St) Try this place downtown for live music Thursday to Saturday and a great upstairs balcony bar.

❶ Information

Visitor center (☎800-527-6843; www.visit batonrouge.com; 358 3rd St; ◷8am-5pm) The downtown city branch has maps, brochures of local attractions, and festival schedules.

Capital Park Visitor Center (☎225-219-1200; www.louisianatravel.com; 702 River Rd N; ◷8am-4:30pm) Near the visitor center, it's even more extensive.

❶ Getting There & Around

Baton Rouge lies 80 miles west of New Orleans on I-10. **Baton Rouge Metropolitan Airport** (BTR; www.flybtr.com) is north of town off I-110. **Greyhound** (☎225-383-3811; 1253 Florida Blvd, at N 12th St) has regular buses to New Orleans, Lafayette and Atlanta, GA. **Capitol Area Transit System** (CATS; www.brcats.com) operates buses around town.

ST FRANCISVILLE

North of Baton Rouge, the lush town of St Francisville and its neighboring plantations have historically been, and continue to be, a lovely respite from the heat of the Delta. During the antebellum decade it was home to plantation millionaires, and much of their architecture is still intact. Its lazy tree-lined streets and plethora of historic homes and churches, as well as galleries and antique shops, are well worth a visit.

◉ Sights & Activities

In town, stroll down historic Royal St to catch a glimpse of antebellum homes and buildings-turned-homes. The visitor center has pamphlets that lead you on self-guided tours.

Myrtles Plantation HISTORIC BUILDING
(☎225-635-6277, 800-809-0565; www.myrtles plantation.com; 7747 US Hwy 61 N; ◷9am-4:30pm, tours 6pm, 7pm & 8pm Fri & Sat) An especially notable B&B because supposedly it's haunted, and it has night mystery tours (by reservation) on the weekend. We heard secondhand corroboration of the supernatural presence, so it might be fun to stay overnight (rooms from $115) to commune with the other world.

⌷ Sleeping & Eating

TOP CHOICE **3-V Tourist Court** HISTORIC INN **$$**
(☎225-721-7003; 5689 Commerce St; 1-/2-bed cabins $80/130; ▣❄◈) One of the oldest motor inns in the United States (started in the 1930s and on the National Register of Historic Places), these five units bring you back to simpler times. Rooms have period decorations and fixtures, though a recent

renovation upgraded the beds, hardwood floors and flat-screen TVs into borderline trendy territory.

Shadetree Inn Bed and Breakfast B&B $$
(225-635-6116; www.shadetreeinn.com; cnr Royal St & Ferdinand St; r from $175; P✱🤖) Sidled up against the historic district and a bird sanctuary, this super cozy B&B has a gorgeous flower-strewn, hammock-hung courtyard and spacious, upscale rustic rooms. A deluxe continental breakfast can be served in your room and is included along with a bottle of wine or champagne.

Magnolia Café CAFE $$
(www.themagnoliacafe.com; 5687 Commerce St; mains $7-12; 10am-4pm Sun-Wed, to 9pm Thu-Sat) The nucleus of what's happening in St Francisville, the Magnolia Café used to be a health-food store/VW bus repair shop. Now it's where people go to eat, socialize and dance to live music on Friday night. Try the cheesy shrimp po'boy.

Birdman Coffee and Books CAFE $
(Commerce St; mains $5-6.50; 7-5pm Mon-Fri, 8am-5pm Sat & Sun; 🤖) Right in front of the Magnolia Café lies the Birdman, *the* spot for a local breakfast (old-fashioned yellow grits, sweet-potato pancakes etc) and local art.

ℹ️ Information
Tourist information (225-635-4224; www.stfrancisville.us; 11757 Ferdinand St) Provides helpful information about the numerous plantations open for view in the area, many of which offer B&B services.

Cajun Country

One of the truly unique parts of the US, Acadiana is named for French settlers exiled from L'Acadie (now Nova Scotia, Canada) by the British in 1755. As they lived alongside Native Americans and Creoles, 'Acadian' eventually morphed into 'Cajun.' The harrowing journey to Louisiana and the fight for survival in its swamplands are points of cultural pride for modern-day Cajuns, and do a lot to explain their combination of toughness and absolute ease.

Cajuns are the largest French-speaking minority in the US – prepare to hear it on radios and in the sing-song lilt of their English. While Lafayette is the nexus of Acadiana, getting out and around the waterways, villages and ramshackle roadside taverns really drops you straight into Cajun living. It's hard to

find a bad meal here; jambalaya (rice-based dish with tomatoes, sausage and shrimp) and crawfish étouffée (a thick Cajun stew) are prepared slowly with pride (and cayenne!), and if folks aren't fishing, then they are probably dancing. Don't expect to sit on the sidelines...*allons danson* (let's dance).

LAFAYETTE
At its edges Lafayette looks like Anytown USA, but venture into its nucleus and you'll find an unsung jewel, especially if you like to shake your moneymaker. Surprisingly, its incredibly vibrant music scene remains relatively under the radar. Around the university town, bands are rocking most any night, and you'll drink a beer next to genuine, life-lovin', laid-back folks looking for a dance or to kick back and appreciate the show. Between venues, there are some of the best restaurants and bars in Louisiana outside New Orleans, all nicely organized for your eating and drinking pleasure in the compact and cool historic downtown, and a fascinating hipster retro bike culture.

👁️ Sights & Activities
Acadiana Center for the Arts GALLERY
(337-233-7060; www.acadianacenterforthearts.org; 101 W Vermilion St; adult/child/student $5/2/3; 10am-5pm Tue-Fri, to 6pm Sat) This arts center in the heart of downtown maintains three chic galleries and hosts dynamic theater, lectures and special events.

University Art Museum MUSEUM
(museum.louisiana.edu; 710 E St Mary Blvd; adult/youth $5/3; 9am-5pm Tue-Thu, 9am-noon Fri, 10am-5pm Sat) Just south of Girard Park, the sleek museum hosts beautifully curated exhibits, often leaning toward an educational slant.

Vermilionville CULTURAL BUILDING
(www.vermilionville.org; 300 Fisher Rd; adult/student $8/5; 10am-4pm Tue-Sun; ♿) A tranquil restored/re-created 19th-century Cajun village wends along the bayou near the airport. Friendly costumed docents explain Cajun, Creole and Native American history; local bands perform on Sundays. They also offer guided **boat tours** (337-233-4077; adult/students $12/8; 10:30am Tue-Sat Mar-May & Sep-Nov) of Bayou Vermilion.

FREE **Acadian Cultural Center** MUSEUM
(www.nps.gov/jela; 501 Fisher Rd; 8am-5pm) The best NPS museum in Cajun Country, next door to Vermilionville.

✤✤ Festivals & Events

At the fabulous, free **Festival International de Louisiane** (www.festivalinternational.com), hundreds of local and international artists rock out for five days in April – the largest *free* music festival of its caliber in the US.

🛏 Sleeping & Eating

Chains clump near exits 101 and 103, off I-10 (doubles from $65). Head to Jefferson St mid downtown to take your choice of bars and restaurants, from sushi to Mexican.

TOP CHOICE Blue Moon Guest House   GUESTHOUSE $

(☎337-234-2422, 877-766-2583; www.bluemoon guesthouse.com; 215 E Convent St; dm $18, r $73-94; P✸@♠) This tidy old home is one of Louisiana's travel gems, an upscale hostel-like hangout, walking distance from downtown. Snag a bed and you'll be on the guest list for Lafayette's most popular down-home music venue, located in the backyard. The friendly owners, full kitchen, and camaraderie among guests create a unique music-meets-migration environment catering to backpackers, flashpackers and those in transition (flashbackpackers?). Prices skyrocket during festival time.

Buchanan Lofts   BOUTIQUE APARTMENTS $$

(☎337-534-4922; www.buchananlofts.com; 403 S Buchanan; r per night/week from $100/600; P✸@♠)These tragically hip lofts could be in New York City if they weren't so big: Doused in contemporary cool art and design – all fruits of the friendly owner's globetrotting – the extra spacious units all come with kitchenettes and are awash in exposed brick and hardwoods, with small knickknacks such as steel drums livening up the industrial motif.

TOP CHOICE Johnson's Boucanière   CAJUN $

(1111 St John St; mains $5-8; ☺10am-5pm Thu-Fri, 7am-3pm Sat) This resurrected 70-year-old family prairie smoker business turns out detour-worthy *boudin* (Cajun-style pork and rice sausage) and an unstoppable smoked pork-brisket sandwich topped with smoked sausage. You can smell it from a block away and can't miss the chic aluminum-sided shack with wraparound porch.

French Press   BREAKFAST $$

(www.thefrenchpresslafayette.com; 214 E Vermillion; breakfast $6-$10.50; ☺7am-2pm Tue-Thu, 7am-2pm & 5:30-9pm Fri, 9am-2pm & 5:30-9pm Sat, 9am-2pm Sun; ♠) This new French-Cajun hybrid is a breakfast pleaser, with an outstanding breakfast sandwich, cheddar grits (that will kill you dead), organic granola (offset the grits) and black bean and crab cake eggs benedict, served in a modern cafe atmosphere with excellent French press coffee.

Pamplona Tapas Bar   TAPAS $$

(www.pamplonatapas.com; 631 Jefferson St; tapas from $4; ☺11am-2pm & 5-20pm Tue-Thu, to 11pm Fri, 5-11pm Sat; ♠) A bit more upscale, this place does a robust trade in excellent Spanish tapas (eg bacon-wrapped dates on a bed of blue cheese; chorizo-stuffed mushrooms) and a fabulous Spanish wine selection (by the glass $6 to $11).

Old Tyme Grocery   CAJUN $

(218 W St Mary St; po'boys $6-10; ☺9am-10pm Mon-Fri, 9am-7pm Sat) Famous po'boys.

☆ Entertainment

To find out what's playing around town, pick up the free weekly *Times* (www.thetimeso facadiana.com) or *Independent* (www.the ind.com).

Blue Moon Saloon   LIVE MUSIC

(www.bluemoonpresents.com; 215 E Convent St; cover $5-8) This intimate venue on the back porch of the accompanying guesthouse is what Louisiana is all about: good music, good people and good beer. What's not to love?

Lafayette specializes in big ol' dance halls that offer one-stop entertainment, dancing and local cuisine. Some standout Cajun music and dance joints:

Mulate's   DANCE

(325 Mills Ave, Breaux Bridge) On the way to Breaux Bridge.

Randol's   DANCE

(www.randols.com; 2320 Kaliste Saloom Rd, Lafayette; ☺5-10pm Sun-Thu, to 11pm Fri & Sat) South of town.

Prejean's   DANCE

(www.prejeans.com; 3480 NE Evangeline Thruway/I-49, North Lafayette) Two miles north of town.

❶ Information

Visitor center (☎337-232-3737, 800-346-1958; www.lafayettetravel.com; 1400 NW Evangeline Thruway; ☺8:30am-5pm Mon-Fri, 9am-5pm Sat & Sun)

❶ Getting There & Away

From I-10, exit 103A, the Evangeline Thruway (Hwy 167) goes to the center of town. **Grey-**

hound (☎337-235-1541; 315 Lee Ave) operates from a hub beside the central commercial district, making several runs daily to New Orleans (3½ hours) and Baton Rouge (one hour).
Amtrak's (133 E Grant St) *Sunset Limited* goes to New Orleans three times a week.

CAJUN WETLANDS

In 1755, *le Grande Dérangement,* the British expulsion of the rural French settlers from Acadiana, created a homeless population of Acadians who searched for decades for a place to settle. In 1785, seven boatloads of exiles arrived in New Orleans. By the early 19th century, 3000 to 4000 Acadians oc-cupied the swamplands southwest of New Orleans. Native American tribes such as the Attakapas helped them learn to eke out a living based upon fishing and trapping, and the aquatic way of life is still the backdrop to modern living.

East and south of Lafayette, the **Atchafa-laya Basin** is the preternatural heart of the Cajun wetlands. Stop in to the **Atchafalaya Welcome Center** (☎337-228-1094; Butte La Rose; ⊙8:30am-5pm), at Exit 121 from I-10, to learn how to penetrate the dense jungle protecting these swamps, lakes and bayous from the casual visitor. They'll fill you in on camping in **Indian Bayou** and exploring the **Sherburne Wildlife Management Area**, as well as the exquisitely situated **Lake Fausse Pointe State Park**.

Eleven miles east of Lafayette in the sleepy, crawfish-lovin' town of **Breaux Bridge**, you'll find sophisticated **Café des Amis** (www.cafedesamis.com; 140 E Bridge St; mains $14-24; ⊙11am-2pm Tue, to 9pm Wed & Thu, 7:30am-9:30pm Fri & Sat, 8am-2pm Sun), where you can relax amid funky local art as wait-ers trot out sumptuous weekend breakfasts, sometimes set to a zydeco jam. If you just want good coffee, friendly folks and wi-fi, **Fly's Coffee House** (109 N Main St; ⊙7am-6pm Sun-Thu, to 7pm Fri & Sat; 🛜) is your place.

Check out the friendly **Tourist Center** (☎337-332-8500; www.breauxbridgelive.com; 318 E Bridge St; ⊙8am-4pm Mon-Fri, to noon Sat), who can hook you up with one of numerous B&Bs in town, like tidy **Maison des Amis** (☎337-507-3399; www.maisondesamis.com; 111 Washington St; r $100-125; 🅿✳🛜) right along Bayou Teche. If you're in town the first week of May, don't miss the gluttony of music, dancing and Cajun food at the **Crawfish Festival** (www.bbcrawfest.com).

Tiny **St Martinville** (www.stmartinville. org), 15 miles southeast of Lafayette, packs

SPICE ISLAND

Drive southwest of New Iberia along Hwy 329 through cane fields to lush and lovely **Avery Island** (admission per vehicle $1), home of **McIlhenny Tabasco** (☎337-365-8173; tours free; ⊙9am-4pm) and its excellent **wildlife sanctuary** (adult/child $8/5; ⊙9am-5:30pm). The beautiful, manicured paths around the island actually cover a salt dome that extends 8 miles below the surface. Even though the air smells lightly of Tabasco, alligators and egrets bask in the protected sunshine – bring a lunch and mosquito repellent.

At the Tabasco store, you can sample Tabasco-laced grub, including sweet and spicy ice cream and jalapeño soda.

a mighty punch. Within one block of the bayou in the town center, visit the **African American Museum & Acadian Memorial** (www.acadianmemorial.org; adult/child $3/free; ⊙10am-4pm) to learn about the diasporas of both Cajuns and African Americans.

One mile north of the town center, **Longfellow-Evangeline State Historic Site** (www.lastateparks.com; 1200 N Main St; adult/child $4/free; ⊙9am-5pm) explains the nuances of Creole and Acadian history, and gives tours of its restored Raised Creole Cot-tage and replica Acadian farmstead.

CAJUN PRAIRIE

Think: dancing cowboys! Cajun and African American settlers to the higher, drier terrain north of Lafayette developed a culture based around animal husbandry and farming, and the ten-gallon hat still rules. It's also the hot-bed of Cajun and zydeco music (and thus ac-cordions) and crawfish farming.

Opelousas squats sleepily alongside Hwy 49, and its historic downtown is home to the esoteric **Museum & Interpretive Center** (315 N Main St; admission free; ⊙9am-5pm Mon-Sat); check out the doll collection.

The top zydeco joints in Acadiana, **Slim's Y-Ki-Ki** (www.slimsykiki.com; Hwy 182 N), a few miles north on Main St, across from the Pig-gly Wiggly, and the **Zydeco Hall of Fame** (11154 Hwy 190), 4 miles west in Lawtell, strike it up most weekends. Wear your dancing shoes and don't be afraid to sweat!

Plaisance, northwest of Opelousas, hosts the grassroots, fun-for-the-family **Southwest**

Louisiana Zydeco Festival (www.zydeco.org) in August.

In **Eunice** (www.eunice-la.com) there's the Saturday-night 'Rendez-Vous des Cajuns' at the **Liberty Theater** (200 Park Ave; admission $5), which is broadcast on local radio. In fact, visitors are welcome all day at **KBON** (www.kbon.com; 109 S 2nd St), 101.1FM. Browse the capacious Wall of Fame, signed by visiting musicians. Two blocks away, the **Cajun Music Hall of Fame & Museum** (www.cajunfrenchmusic.org; 230 S CC Duson Dr; admission free; ☺9am-5pm Tue-Sat) caters to the die-hard music buff, and the NPS runs the **Prairie Acadian Cultural Center** (cnr 3rd St & Park Ave; admission free; ☺8am-5pm Tue-Fri, to 6pm Sat) with interesting exhibits on swamp life and Cajun culture, and showing a variety of documentaries explaining the history of the area.

If all this leaves you in need of a respite, try centrally located **Potier's Cajun Inn** (☎337-457-0440; 110 W Park Ave; r from $55; P❋) for spacious, down-home-Cajun-style cozy apartments with kitchenettes. **Ruby's Café** (221 W Walnut Ave; meals $7; ☺6am-2pm Mon-Fri) does popular plate lunches in a 1950s diner setting and **Café Mosaic** (202 S 2nd St; meals $3-4.50; ☎) is a smart coffeehouse with waffles and grilled sandwiches.

Though ▮▮▮▮▮▮ has a great name, the main thing the town's got going for it is **Fred's Lounge** (420 6th St; ☺8am-1:30pm Sat), with its Saturday-morning live Cajun band and charming country waltzes.

Cane River Country

The central part of the state is a crossroads of Louisiana's distinct cultures, politics and religions, with bilingual French Catholic and Franco African people along the Cane River, and monolingual, chiefly Protestant residents to the north. Hwy 119 meanders alongside the Cane River. You'll pass locals dipping fishing poles into the lazy water or whiling away the day on front-porch rockers.

Melrose Plantation (☎318-379-0055; I-49, exit 119; adult/child $10/4; ☺noon-4pm Tue-Sun) is a complex of interesting buildings built by a family of 'free people of color' headed by Marie Therese Coincoin. The early-20th-century owner, Cammie Henry, housed artists and writers such as William Faulkner and Sherwood Anderson in the 1796 Yucca House. Congo-style Africa House contains a vivid 50ft mural depicting plantation life by Clementine Hunter, the renowned folk artist. Hunter had been a field-hand and cook at Melrose before picking up a paintbrush at age 50. The nearby **Kate Chopin House** (243 Hwy 495, Cloutierville) was the author's residence while she wrote *The Awakening*.

NATCHITOCHES

A bit further north you'll find French architecture in historic Natchitoches (mysteriously pronounced *nak*-id-esh), which is split scenically by the Cane River and is the oldest permanent settlement in the Louisiana Purchase. It gained significant notoriety after Hollywood filmmakers arrived in 1988 to film the blockbuster movie *Steel Magnolias*. Head to the **Visitor Bureau** (☎800-259-1714; www.natchitoches.net; 781 Front St; ☺9am-5pm) for information about the tours of Creole plantation estates and the numerous B&Bs in town.

Not to be missed is the Natchitoches meat pie famously served by **Lasyone's** (www.lasyones.com; 622 Second St; meat pies $4; ☺7am-3pm Mon-Sat). The meat pie's heritage dates back to the 1800s when African American youngsters sold them from street corners. Today this crispy fried savory remains ever-popular, with Lasyone's at the epicenter.

If you don't want to stay in a B&B, the 20-room **Church Street Inn** (☎318-238-8890; www.churchstinn.com; 120 Church St; r incl breakfast from $99; P❋☎) is a solid option. From here, you can stroll to downtown eateries and shops then cozy up in your room or do yoga on the communal balcony.

Right in the thick of this densely forested and sparsely populated part of Louisiana, just a short drive from Natchitoches, is the gorgeous **Kisatchie National Forest** (☎318-473-7160; www.fs.fed.us/r8/kisatchie), 937 sq miles of hilly Southern yellow pine and hardwood. Trails aren't incredibly well maintained, as they are mostly used by hunters in the hunting season, but there are opportunities to mountain bike, hike, swim and go on scenic drives. It's especially splendid during the shoulder seasons. Bring repellent in summer.

Northern Louisiana

Make no mistake: the rural, oil-industry towns along the Baptist Bible belt make northern Louisiana as far removed from New Orleans as Paris, TX, is from Paris, France. Even in the commercial center of

Shreveport, in the far northwest corner of Louisiana, this is a region battling to find self-definition after decades of decline.

Captain Henry Shreve cleared a 165-mile logjam on the Red River and founded the river-port town of Shreveport, in 1839. The city boomed with oil discoveries in the early 1900s, but declined after WWII. Some revitalization came in the form of huge Vegas-sized casinos and a riverfront entertainment complex. The visitor center (☑318-222-9391, 800-458-4748; www.shreveport-bossier.org; 629 Spring St; ☺8am-5pm Mon-Fri, 10am-2pm Sat) is downtown. If you're a rose-lover, it would be a shame to miss the Gardens of the American Rose Center (www.ars.org; 8877 Jefferson Paige Rd; adult/child $5.50/4.50; ☺9am-5pm Mon-Sat, 1-5pm Sun), which contains more than 65 individual gardens designed to show how roses can be grown in a home garden – take Exit 5 off the I-20. Columbia Cafe (www.columbiacafe.com; 3030 Creswell St; mains $8-17; ☺7am-10pm Tue-Fri, 10am-10pm Sat, 10am-2pm Sun) might entice you to stop and grab a bite. Eat outside on the patio or inside among local art. The New American fusion is uncomplicated and surprisingly progressive, as in buffalo burgers instead of beef. Tasty!

About 50 miles northeast of Monroe on Hwy 557 near the town of Epps, the Poverty Point State Historic Site (www.crt.state.la.us; 6859 Hwy 577, Pioneer; adult/child $4/free; ☺9am-5pm) has a remarkable series of earthworks and mounds along what was once the Mississippi River. A two-story observation tower gives a view of the site's six concentric ridges. Around 1000 BC this was the hub of a civilization comprising hundreds of communities, with trading links as far north as the Great Lakes.

ARKANSAS

Tucked smack in the center of the US, hiding out between the Midwest and the Deep South, Arkansas is America's overlooked treasure. The natural areas are off the charts: the worn slopes of the Ozarks and the Ouachita (wash-ee-tah) mountains; clean, gushing rivers; and lakes bridged by crenelated granite and limestone outcroppings. The entire state is dotted with exceptionally well-presented state parks and tiny, empty roads crisscrossing dense forests that let out onto surprising, sweeping vistas and gentle pastures dotted with grazing horses. The rural towns of Mountain View and Eureka Springs hold quirky charm. Don't be fooled by talk of Wal-Mart or backwoods culture. As one local put it, 'Say what you want about Arkansas, but it's a outdoor paradise.'

History

Caddo, Osage and Quapaw Native Americans had permanent settlements here when Spaniard Hernando de Soto visited in the mid-1500s. Frenchman Henri de Tonti founded the first white settlement in 1686. After the 1803 Louisiana Purchase, Arkansas became a US territory, and slave-holding planters moved into the Delta to grow cotton. Poorer immigrants from Appalachia settled in the Ozark and Ouachita plateaus.

On the edge of the frontier, lawlessness persisted until the Civil War. Reconstruction was difficult, and development only came after 1870 with the expansion of railroads. Racial tension peaked in 1957, with the incident at Central High School in Little Rock.

The state has one of the lowest per-capita incomes in the US, with many poor African Americans in the Delta and poor whites in the Ozarks.

ARKANSAS FACTS

» **Nickname** Natural State

» **Population** 2.9 million

» **Area** 52,068 sq miles

» **Capital city** Little Rock (population 193,524)

» **Other cities** Fayetteville (population 77,143)

» **Sales tax** 6%, plus 2% visitors tax and local taxes

» **Birthplace of** General Douglas MacArthur (1880–1964), musician Johnny Cash (1932–2003), former President Bill Clinton (b 1946), author John Grisham (b 1955), actor Billy Bob Thornton (b 1955)

» **Home of** Wal-Mart

» **Politics** like most Southern states, opposition to Civil Rights turned the state Republican in the '60's

» **Famous for** football fans 'calling the Hogs'

» **Official state instrument** fiddle

» **Driving distances** Little Rock to Eureka Springs 182 miles, Eureka Springs to Mountain View 123 miles

❶ Information

Arkansas State Parks (☏888-287-2757; www.arkansasstateparks.com) Arkansas' well-reputed park system has 52 state parks, 30 offering camping (tent and RV sites $13 to $30, depending on amenities). A number of the parks offer lodge and cabin accommodations. Due to popularity, reservations on weekends and holidays often require multiday stays.

Department of Parks & Tourism (☏501-682-7777; www.arkansas.com; 1 Capitol Mall, Little Rock) Sends out a vacation planning kit; ask for the excellent annual *State Parks Guide* and *Adventure Guide*.

Little Rock

Downtown Little Rock, strangled in the last several decades by parking lots and bad city planning, is now perking up a bit with the burgeoning River Market district. Across the river, North Little Rock, with a growing enclave of shops and restaurants, stretches alongside the extensive riverfront park. This conservative city definitely has some worthwhile things going on, but you just have to know where to look or it all might blur in strip-mall whiplash.

◉ Sights

The best stroll is in the River Market district (www.rivermarket.info), an area of shops, galleries, restaurants and pubs on W Markham St and President Clinton Ave along the riverbank. **Ottenheimer Market Hall** (btwn S Commerce & S Rock Sts; ⊙7am-6pm Mon-Sat) houses an eclectic collection of food stalls and shops.

The **Hillcrest Neighborhood** toward west Little Rock is a tiny epicenter of cafes and funky shops and is a communing ground for minority strains of counterculture in the city.

FREE **Little Rock Central High School** HISTORIC SITE
(www.nps.gov/chsc; 2125 Daisy Bates Dr; ⊙9:30am-4:30pm, tours 9am & 1:15pm Mon-Fri mid-Aug–early Jun) Little Rock's most riveting attraction is the site of the 1957 desegregation crisis that changed the country forever. It was here that a group of African American students known as the Little Rock Nine were first denied entry inside the then all-white high school (despite a 1954 Supreme Court ruling forcing the integration of public schools) then escorted by the 1200-man 101st Airborne Battle Group, a pivotal moment in the American Civil Rights Movement. Today it's both a National Historic Site and a working high school – the most beautiful one you will ever see. There's a spiffy new visitor center airing all the dirty laundry and putting the crisis into perspective alongside the greater Civil Rights Movement. The guides are fantastic, including Spirit Trickey, the daughter of one of the nine.

William J Clinton Presidential Center LIBRARY
(www.clintonlibrary.gov; 1200 President Clinton Ave; adult/child $7/3, with audio $10/6; ⊙9am-5pm Mon-Sat, 1-5pm Sun) Houses the largest archival collection in presidential history, including 80 million pages of documents and two million photographs. Peruse the full-scale replica of the Oval Office, the exhibits on all stages of Clinton's life or the gifts from visiting dignitaries (such as Lance Armstrong's yellow jersey). The entire complex is built to environmentally friendly 'green' standards.

FREE **Old State House Museum** MUSEUM
(www.oldstatehouse.com; 300 W Markham St; ⊙9am-5pm Mon-Sat, 1-5pm Sun) The state capitol from 1836 to 1911 now holds impressively restored legislative chambers and displays on Arkansas history and culture.

Riverfront Park PARK
Just northwest of downtown, Riverfront Park rolls pleasantly along the Arkansas River and both pedestrians and cyclists take advantage of this fantastic city park daily. You can't miss the **Big Dam Bridge** (www.bigdambridge.com; ♿), which is the largest bridge built specifically for pedestrians and cyclists in the United States; it connects 17 miles of multiuse trails in Little Rock and North Little Rock that form a complete loop thanks to the renovation of the Rock Island railroad bridge – now renamed the Clinton Presidential Park Bridge – by the Clinton Foundation. For a proper perusal of Riverfront Park rent a bike (or tandem) from **River Trail Rentals** (☏501-374-5505; www.rivertrailrentals.com; 200 S Olive St; per 4-hr/day from $16/30; ⊙by appt Mon-Tue, 10-7pm Wed-Fri, 7am-7pm Sat, 11-6pm Sun) – outside opening hours you can call for a reservation. Otherwise **Chainwheel** (☏501-224-7651; www.chainwheel.com; 10300 Rodney Parham Rd; ⊙10am-6pm Mon-Fri, to 5pm Sat) is the best bike shop in town and can rent higher-end road or mountain bikes, depending on availability.

Sleeping & Eating

Because of government and convention-center traffic, it's difficult to find inexpensive hotels in downtown, and rates fluctuate wildly. Budget motels lie off the interstates.

Capital Hotel BOUTIQUE HOTEL **$$**
(☑501-374-7474, 888-293-4121; www.capitalhotel.com; 111 W Markham St; r from $160; P✳@☎) Renovated into the stately Capital Hotel, this 1872 former bank building with a cast-iron facade – a near-extinct architectural feature – is top digs in Little Rock. There is a wonderful outdoor mezzanine for cocktails (and, unfortunately, smokers) and massive elevators, the largest hydraulic lifts in Arkansas, to whisk you away all of four floors. The chef at Ashley's, one of two restaurants on the premises, won *Food & Wine*'s People's Choice Best New Chef for the Midwest in 2011 (except this ain't the Midwest, though it's no fault of the food).

Rosemont HISTORIC B&B **$$**
(☑501-374-7456; www.rosemontoflittlerock.com; 515 W 15th St; r incl breakfast from $99; P✳☎) In an 1880s restored farmhouse near the Governor's mansion, this place oozes cozy Southern charms. The proprietors have also opened some historic cottages a block away (from $160).

House PUB **$$**
(www.facebook.com/TheHouseInHillcrest; 722 N Palm St; mains $9-14; ☺7am-6pm Mon-Sat; ☺11am-2pm Mon-Fri; ☎) Arkansas' first gastropub is run by Hillcrest hipsters who know their way around an eclectic menu that traverses from burgers and BBQ to Thai and Greek (and maybe the best sweet-potato fries – ever).

Homer's DINER **$**
(www.homersrestaurant.com; 2001 East Roosevelt; mains $2-7; ☺7am-2pm Mon-Fri) It's a schlep out by the airport in the industrial district, but businessmen smoking stogies rubbing elbows with hunters in overalls and Air Force officers on break and high-ranking politicos hatching plans make a visit to this country-cooking classic worth it for local theater alone.

Acadia SOUTHERN **$$$**
(www.acadiahillcrest.com; 3000 Kavanaugh Blvd; dinner mains from $18-24; ☺11am-2pm Mon-Fri & 5:30-10pm Mon-Sat; ☎) Another Hillcrest standout, Acadia's multilevel patio with twinkling lights is a fabulous place to enjoy fancy-shmancy Southern dishes like smoked Gouda mac 'n' cheese. Lunch is a steal here (mains $9 to $12).

Flying Fish SEAFOOD **$$**
(511 President Clinton Ave; meals $5.50-17; ☺11am-10pm) The idea was hatched out of East Texas, but the catfish at this down-home seafood place walkable from Clinton library is classic: you *can* get it grilled, but you know deep down fried is the only way to go, served with (fried) fries and (fried) hush puppies. When in Rome, folks, when in Rome...

River City CAFE **$**
(www.rivercityteacoffeeandcream.com; 2715 Kavanaugh Blvd; ☺5:30-10pm Mon-Sat) Killer Hillcrest tea and coffeehouse. Espresso: 75¢!

❶ Information

Visitor center (☑501-371-0076, 877-220-2568; www.littlerock.com; 615 E Capitol Ave; ☺9am-5pm Mon-Sat, 1-5pm Sun) Housed in 1842 Curran Hall.

❶ Getting There & Around

Little Rock National Airport (LIT; ☑501-372-3439; www.lrn-airport.com) lies just east of downtown. The **Greyhound station** (☑501-372-3007; 118 E Washington St), in North Little Rock, serves Hot Springs (one to two hours), Memphis, TN (2½ hours), and New Orleans, LA (18 hours). Amtrak occupies **Union Station** (☑501-372-6841; 1400 W Markham St). **Central Arkansas Transit** (CAT; ☑501-375-6717; www.cat.org) runs local buses; a trolley makes a loop on W Markham St and President Clinton Ave (adult/child $1.35/60¢).

Hot Springs

It's a wonder that the little city of Hot Springs, with its strip malls, mini-golf suburbs and gasping downtown, hosted the vacationing elite of New York City's organized crime. At full throttle in the 1930s, the city was a hotbed of gambling, bootlegging, prostitution, opulence and dangerous thugs. Yet it was also a spot of truce between warring gangs, a place where it was decreed that all criminals could be gluttonous hedonists in peace. When gambling was squelched, so was the city's economy.

Though it still hasn't recovered from that blow, the healing waters have always drawn people, everyone from the Native American populations to present-day pilgrims. Elaborate restored bathhouses, where you can still get old-school spa treatments, line

Bathhouse Row behind shady magnolias on the east side of Central Ave.

◉ Sights & Activities

A promenade runs through the park around the hillside behind Bathhouse Row, where some springs survive intact, and a network of trails covers Hot Springs' mountains. Unfortunately, only two of the historic Bathhouse Row bathhouses are in operation, but bids were being evaluated by the NPS at time of writing to rechristen the others, including one as a microbrewery.

Gangster Museum of America   MUSEUM
(www.tgmoa.com; 510 Central Ave; adult/child $10/4; ⊙10am-6pm Sun-Thu, to 7pm Fri & Sat) See the intriguing underbelly of Hot Springs' history, which explains the sin-filled glory days of Hot Springs when this small town in the middle of nowhere turned into a pinpoint of lavish wealth. Highlights include original slots – that still spew money! – and other gambling tables and equipment.

Que Paw Baths   SPA
(www.quapawbaths.com; 413 Central Ave; thermal bath $18, with 25min massage $50; ⊙10am-6pm Mon & Wed, 10am-7pm Thu-Sat,10am-3pm Sun) If the traditional 'wham, bam, thank you, ma'am' approach at the Buckstaff Bathhouse isn't your thing, the newly remodeled Qua Paw offers a more 21st-century approach, with lovely restored thermal baths, green treatments and a sustainable-minded outlook throughout.

FREE NPS Visitor Center   MUSEUM
(☎501-620-6715; 369 Central Ave; ⊙9am-5pm) On Bathhouse Row in the 1915 Fordyce bathhouse, the NPS visitor center and museum have exhibits about the park's history first as a Native American free-trade zone, and later as a turn-of-the-19th-century European spa.

Hot Springs Mountain Tower   OUTDOORS
(adult/child $7/4; ⊙9am-5pm Nov-Feb, til 6pm Mar-May 15 & Labor Day-Oct, til 9pm May 16-Labor Day) On the top of Hot Springs Mountain, the 216ft tower has spectacular views of the surrounding mountains covered with dogwood, hickory, oak and pine – lovely in the spring and fall.

🛏 Sleeping & Eating

Chain motels line highways around town; the visitor center has a list of lakeside rental properties and area B&Bs. Some restaurants congregate along the Central Ave tourist strip and offer ho-hum food.

Alpine Inn   INN $
(☎501-624-9164; www.alpine-inn-hot-springs.com; 741 Park Ave/Hwy 7 N; r $55-90; P❄🐾📶≋) The friendly Scottish owners of this inn, less than a mile from Bathhouse Row, have spent a few years upgrading this old motor court hotel. The tidily maintained row of somewhat-themed, impeccable rooms include new flat-screen TVs and scrumptious beds; and some offer kitchenettes. The Mackintosh room, a nod to Scotland's architectural son, is our favorite.

**Arlington Resort
Hotel & Spa**   HISTORIC HOTEL $
(☎501-623-7771; www.arlingtonhotel.com; 239 Central Ave; s/d from $79/89, with mineral baths $139; P❄🐾📶≋) This imposing historic hotel tops Bathhouse Row and constantly references its glory days. The grand lobby tries to set the tone for the antique in-house spa and aging rooms and there's a half-hearted Starbucks if you're looking for decent coffee. Catch a foxtrot on the weekend when there might be a live band.

Cajun Boilers   CAJUN, SEAFOOD $$
(www.cajunboilers.com; 2806 Albert Pike Rd; mains $8-20; ⊙11am-10pm Mon-Sat to 9pm Sun; 👪) A loud and boisterous seafood spot right on Lake Hamilton, a few miles from Bathhouse Row. The outdoor patio is a fabulous setting to tear into the famous crawfish boil, catfish fried or blackened, or shrimp étouffée. You can boat up or drive up.

McClard's   BARBECUE $$
(www.mcclards.com; 505 Albert Pike; mains $4-15; ⊙11am-8pm Tue-Sat) Southwest of the center, it may be Bill Clinton's favorite boyhood BBQ but reviews are seriously mixed about whether the ribs, slow-cooked beans and creamy slaw here are truly up to snuff.

ⓘ Information

Visitor center (☎501-321-2277, 800-772-2489; www.hotsprings.org; 629 Central Ave; ⊙9am-5pm, until 7pm Jun-Aug) For city information or to pick up a map of Clinton-related sites.

ⓘ Getting There & Away

Greyhound (☎501-623-5574; 1001 Central Ave) has buses heading to Little Rock (1½ hours, three daily).

Around Hot Springs

The wild, pretty **Ouachita National Forest** (☎501-321-5202; welcome center 100 Reserve St, Hot Springs; ☺8am-4:30pm) is studded with lakes and draws hunters, fisherfolk, mountain bikers and boaters. The small roads through the mountains unfailingly bring hidden nooks and wonderful views. The Ouachita boasts two designated National Forest Scenic Byways: Arkansas Scenic Hwy 7 and Talimena Scenic Byway, navigating mountain ranges from Arkansas into Oklahoma. If you stop in the welcome center, leave your camera behind – it's a federal building.

Hot Springs National Park (www.nps. gov/hosp), a tiny preserve nearby, has thermal waters in and around town from which spew a collected 700,000 gallons of 143°F (62°C) water daily from 47 natural springs, and attract modern-day pilgrims who bathe in or sip its waters.

Clinton buffs might stop at **Hope**, where the ex-pres spent his first seven years, but there's not much to see other than the spiffy **Hope Visitor Center & Museum** (www.hope arkansas.net; 100 E Division St; ☺8:30am-5pm Mon-Fri, from 9am Sat, 1-4pm Sun), in the old depot, and the **President Bill Clinton First Home Museum** (www.clintonchildhoodhome museum.com; 117. S. Hervey St; admission free; ☺8:30am-4:30pm), now part of the National Park Service.

If you want to test your luck and diamond-spotting skills, head to **Crater of Diamonds State Park** (www.craterofdiamondsstatepark. com; 209 State Park Rd; ☺8am-5pm), where you can scour the **diamond field** (adult/child $7/4) in which three- to 40-carat diamonds have been found, and where valuable diamonds continue to be found today.

Arkansas River Valley

The Arkansas River cuts a swath across the state from Oklahoma to Mississippi. Folks come to fish, canoe and camp along its banks and tributaries.

The excellently maintained trails of **Petit Jean State Park** (☎501-727-5441; www.peti tjeanstatepark.com; ☝), west of Morrilton, wind past a lush 95ft waterfall, romantic grottoes, expansive vistas, and dense forests. There's a rustic stone lodge, reasonable **cabins** (per night $100-175) and campgrounds. Another stellar state park is **Mount Magazine** (☎479-963-8502; www.mountmagazinestatepark.

com; 16878 Hwy 309 S, Paris), which maintains 14 miles of trails around Arkansas' highest point. Outdoor enthusiasts enjoy great hang gliding and rock climbing here as well as hiking.

The spectacular **Highway 23/Pig Trail Byway**, lined with wild echinacea and lilies, climbs up through **Ozark National Forest** and into the mountains; an excellent way to reach Eureka Springs in the Ozark Mountains.

The **Arkansas and Missouri Railway** (www.arkansasmissouri-rr.com; adult/child from $35/18; ☺Fri & Sat Apr-Sep) offers a 70-mile trip through the Boston Mountain Range from **Van Buren** to **Winslow** and back.

Ozark Mountains

Stretching from northwest and central Arkansas into Missouri, the **Ozark Mountains** (☎870-404-2741; www.ozarkmountainregion.com) are an ancient range, once surrounded by sea and now well worn by time. Verdant rolling mountains give way to misty fields, and dramatic karst formations line sparkling lakes, meandering rivers and scenic back roads. Though some of the towns bank on kitschy hillbilly culture, scratch below the surface to find the unique cultural traditions, such as acoustic folk music and home-cooked hush puppies and catfish.

MOUNTAIN VIEW

Detour east of US 65 or along Hwy 5 to this wacky Ozark town, known for its tradition of informal music-making at Courtsquare. Creeping commercialism is taking its toll, as the **Visitor Information Center** (☎870-269-8068; www.yourplaceinthemountains.com; 107 N Peabody Ave; ☺9am-4:30pm Mon-Sat) promotes the place as the 'Folk Music Capital of the World,' but loads of live folk-music and bizarre festivals keep it real, including the **Championship Outhouse Races**, where crowds cheer on their favorite 'people-powered potty' racing to the finish line – it usually takes place around the last week in October. Cutesy sandstone architecture downtown, one of Arkansas' last standing drive-in movie theaters, and the pickin' parks and impromptu hill music, gospel and bluegrass hootenannies (jam sessions and folk music parties) in the **Courtsquare** by the Stone County Courthouse (especially on Saturday night) – and on porches all around town anytime – make a visit here quirky and fun.

A LOVELY LOOP

Downtown Eureka Springs is beautiful in and of itself, but the town's real coup is its easily overlooked Historic Loop, a 3.5-mile ring of history through downtown and around neighboring residential neighborhoods that will blow your mind. The route is dotted with over 300 Victorian homes, all built before 1910, each and every one of them a jaw-dropper and on par with any preserved historic district in the USA.

There are several ways to enjoy the route if you don't have your own wheels. Pick up a *Six Scenic Walking Tours* brochure from the visitor center in Eureka Springs; rent a bike from Adventure Mountain Outfitters (☑479-253-0900; www.adventuremountainoutfitters.com; 151 Spring St, Eureka Springs; half day $50; ☺9am-5pm Wed-Sat); or catch the Red Line of the Eureka Trolley (www.eurekatrolley.org; adult/child $5/1; ☺9am-5pm Jan-Apr & Nov-Dec, til 8pm Sun May-Oct).

Ozark Folk Center State Park (www.ozarkfolkcenter.com; auditorium adult/child $10/6; ☺10am-5pm Wed-Sat), just north of town, hosts ongoing craft demonstrations and a traditional herb garden, as well as nightly live music from 7pm that brings in an avid, older crowd.

The spectacular Blanchard Springs Caverns (☑888-757-2246; off Hwy 14; adult/child $10.50/5.50, wild cave tour $75; ☺9am-6pm Apr-Sep; ♿), located 15 miles northwest of Mountain View, were carved by an underground river and rival those at Carlsbad Caverns National Park, Southeastern New Mexico. It's another little-known, mind-blowing spot in Arkansas. Three Forest Service guided tours range from disabled-accessible to adventurous three- to four-hour spelunking sessions. The welcoming and historic 1918 Wildflower B&B (☑870-269-4383; www.wildflowerbb.com; 100 Washington; r incl breakfast from $89; P❄❂) is right on the Courtsquare with a rocking chair-equipped wraparound porch, cozy down-home trappings and a $20 midweek discount. Breakfast connoisseurs will be particularly pleased, especially if they get the guava puff pastry or baked hash browns. Tommy's Famous Pizza and BBQ (cnr Carpenter & W Main Sts; pizza $5.50-24, mains $6.40-13.20; ☺from 3pm) is run by the friendliest bunch of backwoods hippies you could ask for. The pulled-pork BBQ pizza marries Tommy's specialties indulgently.

EUREKA SPRINGS

Artsy, quirky and drop-dead gorgeous, Eureka Springs, near Arkansas' Northwestern corner, perches in a steep valley and is one of the coolest towns in the South. Victorian buildings line crooked streets and a crunchy local population welcomes all – it's one of the most explicitly gay-friendly towns in the Ozarks and an island of Democratic blue in an absolute sea of Republican red. On the surface, art galleries and kitschy shops compete with commercialized country music and the 70ft Christ of the Ozarks statue for your attention. But bend a local's ear and find out who's playing at the nearest pub or the location of their favorite swimming hole and this idiosyncratic village will take on new dimensions. Furthermore, hiking, biking, and horseback-riding opportunities abound. Adding to its appeal, there are no red lights or perpendicular cross streets, so zipping around its historical beauty is a breeze.

The visitor center (☑479-253-8737; www.eurekaspringschamber.com; 516 Village Circle, Hwy 62 E; ☺9am-5pm) has information about lodging, activities, tours and local attractions, such as the rockin' Blues Festival (www.eurekaspringsblues.com) at the end of May. The old ES & NA Railway (www.esnarailway.com; 299 N Main St; adult/child $13.50/6.75; ☺Tue-Sat Apr-Oct) puffs through the Ozark hills on an hour-long tour three times a day (four times on Saturday).

Thorncrown Chapel (☑479-253-7401; www.thorncrown.com; 12968 Hwy 62 West; donation suggested; ☺9am-5pm Apr-Nov, 11am-4pm Mar & Dec) is a magnificent sanctuary made of glass, with its 48ft-tall wooden skeleton holding 425 windows. There's not much between your prayers and God's green earth here. It's just outside of town in the woods. The exquisite Queen Anne Mansion (www.thequeenannemansion.com; 115 W Van Buren; tours adult/child $15/9, guided $25/15), originally built in Carthage, Missouri in 1891, debuted in 2010 after a five-year, multimillion-dollar restoration. Original period pieces dot the gorgeously furnished home, a non-negotiable stop for architecture and antique buffs.

If your budget can stand it, bypass the cheap motels on the rim of the canyon and splurge on lodging in the town center. Right in the historic downtown is the super-comfortable and historic **New Orleans Hotel and Suchness Spa** (☑479-253-8630; www.neworleanshotelandspa.com; 63 Spring St; r $84-204; P❄️📶), which sends you reeling back in time, except that it houses a spa with a menu fully loaded for your body and chakra needs. **Treehouse Cottages** (☑479-253-8667; www.treehousecottages.com; 165 W Van Buren St; from $145; P❄️📶) offers gorgeous sunlit, Jacuzzi-equipped tree houses (that are more like cottages on stilts) in the woods.

Right across the street is **Bubba's BBQ** (www.bubbasbarbecueeurekasprings.com; 166 W Van Buren St; mains $5.50-13; ☺11am-9pm Mon-Sat), which is a genuine Southern meat joint in a town that has its fair share of tourist contrivance. At **Mud Street Café** (www.mudstreetcafe.com; 22 G S Main St; mains $9-13; ☺8am-3pm Thu-Tue) in downtown, the coffee drinks and breakfasts are renowned. The cheese plate menu reads like a work of art at the sophisticated wine and cheese bar, the **Stone House** (www.eurekastonehouse.com; 89 S Main St; cheese plates $25-47; ☺1-10pm Wed-Sat), which serves captivating European and artisan Stateside cheese paired with some 30 wines by the glass ($8 to $15).

BUFFALO NATIONAL RIVER

Yet another under-acknowledged Arkansas gem, this 135-mile river flows beneath dramatic bluffs through unspoiled Ozark forest. The upriver section tends to have most of the white water, while the lower reaches ease lazily along – perfect for a float. The **Buffalo National River** (☑870-741-5443; www.nps.gov/buff) has 10 **campgrounds** (☑877-444-6777; www.recreation.gov; tent/RV sites $10/20) and three designated wilderness areas; the most accessible is through the **Tyler Bend visitor center** (☑870-439-2502; ☺8:30am-4:30pm), 11 miles north of Marshall on Hwy 65, where you call also pick up a list of approved outfitters for self-guided rafting or canoe trips, the best way to tour the park and see the gargantuan limestone bluffs.

Evidence of human occupation here dates back some 10,000 years, but this wild and naturally bountiful area kept even modern Ozark settlers isolated and self-sufficient. They developed a distinct dialect, along with unique craftsmanship and musical traits. Thanks to its National River designation in 1972, the Buffalo is one of the few remaining unpolluted, free-flowing rivers in the country.

Arkansas Delta

Roughly 120 miles east of Little Rock, the Great River Rd follows the west bank of the Mississippi River through the Arkansas Delta. Blues town of yesteryear, **Helena** is now a depressed little Arkansas town. However, it explodes for its annual **Arkansas Blues & Heritage Festival** (www.bluesandheritagefest.com; admission free) when blues musicians and 100,000 fans take over downtown for three days in early October. Food stalls sell home-cooked soul food and BBQ.

Year-round, blues fans and history buffs should visit the **Delta Cultural Center** (☑870-338-4350; www.deltaculturalcenter.com; 141 Cherry St; admission free; ☺9am-5pm Tue-Sat), which is in two buildings: the Train Depot and the Visitor Center. The museum displays all manner of blues memorabilia such as Albert King's and Sister Rosetta Tharpe's guitars, and John Lee Hooker's signed handkerchief.

The world's longest-running blues radio program, *King Biscuit Time,* is broadcast here (12:15pm Monday to Friday), and *Delta Sounds* (1pm Monday to Friday) often has live musicians. Other than that, music in Helena is not to be found.

Florida

Best Places to Eat

» Senora Martinez (p448)

» Sustain (p449)

» Café Solé (p465)

» Floridian (p471)

» Refinery (p475)

Best Places to Stay

» Pelican Hotel (p447)

» Biltmore Hotel (p447)

» Dickens House (p477)

» Pillars (p452)

» Everglades International Hostel (p457)

Why Go?

Blessed with almost year-round sunshine, Florida is a hot-house orchid – a bold, sexy, semitropical peninsula edged with bone-white beaches, caressed by teal waters and clad in lurid neon sunsets. Surreal, garish, wacky and perpetually self-amused, Florida is a fantasy-filled swampy wonderland of giddy delights, from alligators, mermaids and Mickey Mouse to Miami's hedonistic, art-fueled, celebrity playground.

Florida's gorgeous beaches are its calling card, and you could visit one every day of the year and still not see them all. But the state offers much more: the prehistoric Everglades, Orlando's phantasmagorical theme parks, the pastel-colored eye candy of South Beach, Key West's nightly carnival, Key Largo's coral reefs. In ways natural and unnatural, Florida's perpetual promise is of escape, both from mundane life and the reasoned constraints of polite society.

When to Go

Miami

Feb-Apr During the last of the winter dry period, the south Florida high season coincides with spring break.

Jun-Aug The hot, humid wet months are peak season for northern Florida beaches and theme parks.

Sep-Oct The ideal shoulder season with fewer crowds, cooler temperatures and warm waters.

Spring Training

Every March, 13 major league baseball teams hold their spring training in stadiums across central and south Florida. That's around 240 exhibition games in 30 days, and it's a pilgrimage for many fans, since the intimate stadiums put you within spitting and signing distance of big leaguers and future hall of famers. For information, visit www.floridagrapefruitleague.com.

AMERICA'S BEST STATE PARKS

Encountering Florida's bizarre, beautiful terrain and its wealth of ancient critters, migratory seabirds and imposing wildlife is unquestionably a highlight. Thankfully, Florida makes it easy for travelers with one of the nation's best state park systems. It is the first and only state to be a two-time recipient of the National Gold Medal Award for Excellence (in 1999 and 2005), and was a finalist once again in 2011.

The state's 160 state parks span an overwhelming array of environments, home to epic coral reefs (John Pennekamp), thousands of alligators (Myakka River), otherworldly limestone karst terrain (Paynes Prairie) and crystal springs (Wakulla Springs). Of course, Florida is also legendary for the quality of its beaches, including such top beach parks as Grayton Beach, Fort DeSoto, Honeymoon Island and St Joseph Peninsula.

For the full list, visit **Florida State Parks** (www.floridastateparks.org). For advice on wildlife watching (what, when and how), visit the **Florida Fish & Wildlife Commission** (http://myfwc.com), which also facilitates boating, hunting and fishing.

Green Florida

Until recently, Florida wasn't known for conservation and ecotourism, but that's changing fast. Here are some resources for local issues and sustainable travel.

» Department of Environmental Protection (**DEP; www.dep.state.fl.us**) State-run agency tackles ecological and sustainability issues.

» Green Lodging Program (**www.dep.state.fl.us/greenlodging**) DEP-run program recognizes lodgings committed to conservation and sustainability.

» Florida Sierra Club (**http://florida.sierraclub.org**) Venerable outdoors and advocacy group.

» Florida Surfrider (**http://florida.surfrider.org**) Grassroots surfer-run nonprofit dedicated to protecting America's beaches; 11 Florida chapters.

» Greenopia (**www.greenopia.com**) Rates ecofriendly businesses in six major Florida cities.

HIAASEN'S FLORIDA

Writer Carl Hiaasen's unique, black-comic vision of Florida is a hilarious gumbo of misfits and murderous developers. Try *Skinny Dip* (for adults), *Hoot* (for kids) and *Paradise Screwed* (for his selected columns).

Fast Facts

» Population: Miami 399,460, Miami-Dade County 2.5 million

» Distances from Miami: Key West (160 miles), Orlando (235 miles)

» Time zones: Eastern (eastern Florida), Central Time Zone (western Panhandle)

Kid Stuff

Need to rent baby gear? Want formula and diapers shipped ahead to your hotel? Need a babysitter?

» Baby's Away (www.babysawayrentals.com)

» Babies Travel Lite (www.babiestravellite.com)

» Kids' Nite Out (www.kidsniteout.com)

Resources

» Visit Florida (www.visitflorida.com) is the official state tourism website.

» My Florida (www.myflorida.com) is the official government portal.

» Florida Smart (www.floridasmart.com) provides comprehensive Florida links.

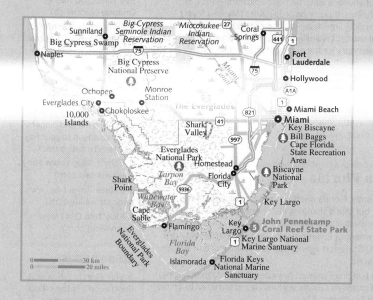

Florida Highlights

1 Marvel at the bright-painted works of art in **Miami's museums and galleries** (p437)

2 Paddle among the alligators and saw grass of the **Everglades** (p455)

3 Be swept up in the nostalgia and thrill rides of **Walt Disney World** (p485)

4 Join Mallory Square's sunset bacchanal in **Key West** (p462)

5 Snorkel and dive the USA's most extensive coral reef at **John Pennekamp** (p459)

ATLANTIC
OCEAN

See Everglades Enlargement

⑥ Relax on the sugar sand
beaches of Sarasota's **Siesta
Key** (p478)

⑦ Ponder the symbolism of
the Hallucinogenic Toreador at

St Petersburg's **Salvador Dalí
Museum** (p477)

⑧ Growl like a pirate among
the historic Spanish buildings
of **St Augustine** (p470)

⑨ Road-trip through the fun-
loving beach towns and quiet
silken sands of the **Panhandle**
(p489)

History

Florida has the oldest recorded history of any US state, and also the most notorious and bizarre. The modern tale begins with Ponce de León, who arrived in 1513 and claimed La Florida (for the Easter 'Feast of Flowers') for Spain. Supposedly, he was hunting for the mythical fountain of youth (the peninsula's crystal springs), while later Spanish explorers like Hernando de Soto sought gold. All came up empty handed.

Within two centuries, Florida's original native inhabitants – who formed small tribes across a peninsula they'd occupied for over 11,000 years – were largely decimated by Spanish-introduced diseases. Today's Seminoles are the descendents of native groups who moved into the territory and intermingled in the 1700s.

Through the 18th century, Spain and England played hot potato with Florida as they struggled to dominate the New World, finally tossing the state to America, who admitted it to the Union in 1845. Sixteen years later, Florida joined the Confederacy and seceded from the US at the onset of the 1861–65 Civil War. Afterward, Florida society was cleaved by social and institutional racism that by the 1950s and '60s would make it a battleground for civil rights.

Meanwhile, developers and speculators were working hard to turn the swampy peninsula into a vacation and agricultural paradise. By the turn of the 20th century, railroad tycoons like Henry Flagler had unlocked Florida's coastlines, while a frenzy of canal-building drained the wetlands. The rush was on, and in the 1920s the South Florida land boom transformed Miami from sandbar to metropolis in 10 years.

Things went bust with the Great Depression, which set the pattern: Florida has ever since swung between intoxicating highs and brutal lows, riding the vicissitudes of immigration, tourism, hurricanes and real estate speculation (not to mention a thriving black market).

Following Castro's Cuban revolution in the 1960s, Cuban exiles flooded Miami, and each successive decade has seen the ranks of Latin immigrants grow and diversify. As for tourism, it was never the same after 1971, when Walt Disney built his Magic Kingdom, embodying the vision of eternal youth and perfected fantasy that Florida has packaged and sold since the beginning.

Local Culture

Florida is one of the USA's most diverse states. Broadly speaking, northern Florida reflects the culture of America's South, while southern Florida has welcomed so many Cuban, Caribbean, and Central and South American immigrants, it's been dubbed 'the Capital of Latin America.' As such, there is no 'typical Floridian,' and about the only thing that unifies state residents is that the great majority are transplants from someplace else. While this has led to its share of conflicts, tolerance is more often the rule. Most Floridians are left to carve their own self-defined communities, be they gays, retirees, Cubans, Haitians, bikers, evangelicals, Nascar-loving good old boys or globetrotting art-world sophisticates.

ℹ Getting There & Around

Miami International Airport (MIA; www.miami-airport.com) is an international gateway, as are Orlando, Tampa and Fort Lauderdale. The Fort Lauderdale and Miami airports are about 30 minutes apart; it's almost always cheaper to fly into Fort Lauderdale. Miami is also home to the world's busiest cruise port.

FLORIDA FACTS

» **Nickname** Sunshine State

» **Population** 18.8 million

» **Area** 53,927 sq miles

» **Capital city** Tallahassee (population 168,979)

» **Other cities** Jacksonville (821,780), Tampa (335,700)

» **Sales tax** 6% (some towns add 9.5% to 11.5% to accommodations and meals)

» **Birthplace of** Author Zora Neale Hurston (1891–1960), actor Faye Dunaway (b 1941), musician Tom Petty (b 1950), author Carl Hiaasen (b 1953)

» **Home of** Cuban Americans, manatees, Mickey Mouse, retirees, key lime pie

» **Politics** sharply divided between Republicans and Democrats

» **Famous for** theme parks, beaches, alligators, art deco

» **Notable local invention** frozen concentrated orange juice (1946)

» **Driving distances** Miami to Key West 160 miles, Miami to Orlando 235 miles

One Week

Start in **Miami** and plan on spending three full days exploring the museums and galleries, the art-deco district, Little Havana and the South Beach scene. Take a day to hike and kayak the **Everglades**, and don't miss **Coral Castle**. Then spend three days in the Keys: snorkel at **John Pennekamp Coral Reef State Park**, go tarpon fishing in **Islamorada** and let yourself get loose in **Key West**.

Two Weeks

Spend one or two days at the theme parks of **Orlando**, then scoot over to **Tampa** for fine cuisine and Ybor City nightlife. Get surreal in **St Petersburg** at the Salvador Dalí Museum, and visit a few **Tampa Bay Area beaches**. Finally, save a couple of days for **Sarasota**, with its jaw-dropping Ringling Museum Complex and the dreamy sands of **Siesta Key**.

Greyhound (www.greyhound.com) has widespread service throughout the state. **Amtrak** (www.amtrak.com) *Silver Meteor* and *Silver Star* trains run daily between New York and Miami.

Car-rental rates in Florida tend to fluctuate, but expect to pay at least $300 to $350 a week for a typical economy car.

SOUTH FLORIDA

Exemplifying the state's diversity, South Florida is a vivid pastiche of all that makes Florida wicked and wild. First is the multicultural entrepôt of Miami, and the sophisticated, rich beach communities stretching north from Fort Lauderdale to Palm Beach. In striking contrast, the beaches are bordered by the subtropical wilderness of the Everglades, while the tip of the state peters out in an ellipsis of fun-loving islands, culminating in anything-goes Key West.

Miami

Miami moves to a different rhythm from anywhere else in the USA. Pastel-hued, subtropical beauty and Latin sexiness are everywhere: from the cigar-filled dance halls where Havana expats dance to *son* and boleros to the exclusive nightclubs where stiletto-heeled Brazilian models shake to Latin hip-hop. Whether you're meeting avant-garde gallery hipsters or passing the buffed, perfect bodies recumbent along South Beach, everyone can seem oh-so-artfully posed. Meanwhile, street vendors and restaurants dish out flavors of the Caribbean, Cuba, Argentina and Haiti. For travelers, the city can be as intoxicating as a sweaty-glassed *mojito*.

Miami is its own world, an international city whose tempos, concerns and inspirations often arrive from distant shores. Over half the population is Latino and over 60% speak predominantly Spanish. In fact, many northern Floridians don't consider immigrant-rich Miami to be part of the state, and many Miamians, particularly Cubans, feel the same way.

⊙ Sights

Greater Miami is a sprawling metropolis that includes suburbs such as Coral Gables and Coconut Grove, and neighborhoods such as Little Havana and Little Haiti. Miami is on the mainland, while Miami Beach lies 4 miles east across Biscayne Bay.

Downtown Miami operates on a fairly normal grid system, with Flagler St as the main east–west drag, and 2nd Ave as the main north–south conduit. North of downtown (along NE 2nd Ave from about 17th St to 41st St), Wynwood and the Design District are focal points for art, food and nightlife. Just north again is Little Haiti.

To reach Little Havana, head west on SW 8th St, or Calle Ocho, which pierces the heart of the neighborhood (and becomes the Tamiami Trail/Hwy 41). Just south of Little Havana are Coconut Grove and Coral Gables.

South Beach is actually the southern part of Miami Beach, extending from 5th St north to 21st St. Washington Ave is the main commercial artery.

For more on South Florida, pick up a copy of Lonely Planet's guide to *Miami & the Keys*.

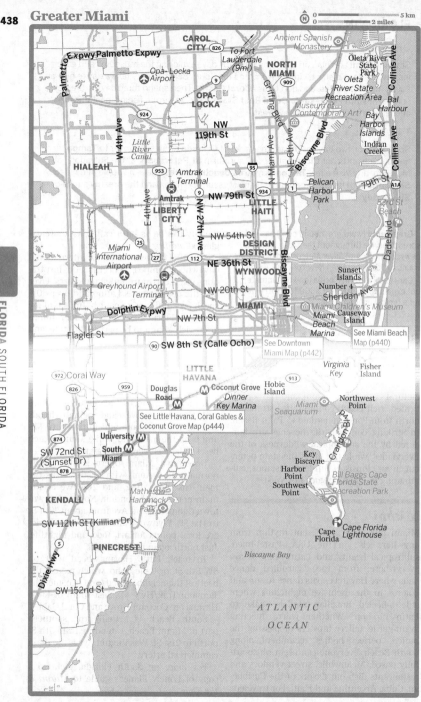

MIAMI BEACH

Miami Beach has some of the best beaches in the country, with white sand and warm aquamarine water that rivals the Bahamas. That movie in your head of art-deco hotels, in-line-skating models, preening young studs and cruising cars? That's **Ocean Drive** (from 1st to 11th Sts), with the beach merely a backdrop for strutting peacocks. This confluence of waves, sunshine and exhibitionist beauty is what made South Beach (or 'SoBe') world-famous.

In the evening, stroll down **Española Way**, a *trés* European strip lined with restaurants and cafes. Just a few blocks north, **Lincoln Road** (between Alton Rd and Washington Ave) becomes a pedestrian mall, or outdoor fashion runway, so all may admire SoBe's fabulously gorgeous creatures.

TOP CHOICE ▸ Art Deco Historic District   NEIGHBORHOOD

The well-preserved, pastel-hued Art Deco Historic District verily screams 'Miami.' It's the largest concentration of deco anywhere in the world, with approximately 1200 buildings lining the streets around Ocean Dr and Collins Ave. For tours and info, make your first stop the **Art Deco Welcome Center** (Map p440; ☏305-531-3484; www.mdpl.org; 1200 Ocean Dr; ⊙9:30am-7pm).

Wolfsonian-FIU   MUSEUM

(Map p440; www.wolfsonian.org; 1001 Washington Ave; adult/child $5/3.50; ⊙11am-9pm Thu, to 6pm Fri & Sat, noon-5pm Sun) A fascinating collection that spans transportation, urbanism, industrial design, advertising and political propaganda from the late 19th to mid-20th century.

Bass Museum of Art   MUSEUM

(off Map p440; www.bassmuseum.org; 2121 Park Ave; adult/child $8/6; ⊙noon-5pm Wed-Sun) The best art museum in Miami Beach has a playfully futurist facade, and the collection isn't shabby either, ranging from 16th-century European religious works to Renaissance paintings.

World Erotic Art Museum   MUSEUM

(Map p440; www.weam.com; 1205 Washington Ave; adult over 18yr $15; ⊙11am-10pm, to midnight Fri & Sat) Unfazed by SoBe's bare flesh? Something will get your attention here, with an amazingly extensive collection of naughty and erotic art, and even furniture depicting all sorts of parts and acts.

DOWNTOWN MIAMI

Downtown isn't a tourist magnet, outside of the Arsht performing arts center and sports arena. Still the **Metro-Dade Cultural Center Plaza** (Map p442; 101 W Flagler St) is home to two worthwhile museums; a $10 combo ticket is good for both.

History Miami   MUSEUM

(Map p442; www.historymiami.org; adult/child $8/5; ⊙10am-5pm Tue-Fri, from noon Sat & Sun) South Florida's complex, excitable history of Seminole warriors, rumrunners, pirates, land grabbers, tourists and Latin American immigrants is succinctly and vividly told.

MIAMI IN...

Two Days

Focus your first day on South Beach. Bookend an afternoon of sunning and swimming with a walking tour through the **Art Deco Historic District** and a visit to **Wolfsonian-FIU**, which explains it all. That evening, sample some Haitian cuisine at **Tap Tap**, while away the evening with swanky cocktails at **Skybar** or, for a low-key brew, head to **Room**. For a late jolt, stop by the **World Erotic Art Museum**, open to midnight on weekends. Next morning, shop for Cuban music along Calle Ocho in **Little Havana**, followed by classic Cuban cuisine at **Versailles**. Go for a stroll at **Vizcaya Museum & Gardens**, cool off with a dip at the **Venetian Pool**, then end the day with dinner and cocktails at **Senora Martinez**.

Four Days

Follow the two-day itinerary, then head to the **Everglades** on day three and jump in a kayak. For your last day, immerse yourself in art and design in **Wynwood** and the **Design District**, followed by a visit to the **Miami Art Museum** or **Museum of Contemporary Art**. In the evening, party with the hipsters at the **Electric Pickle** or check out some live music: enjoy rock at **Tobacco Road** or Latin grooves at **La Covacha**.

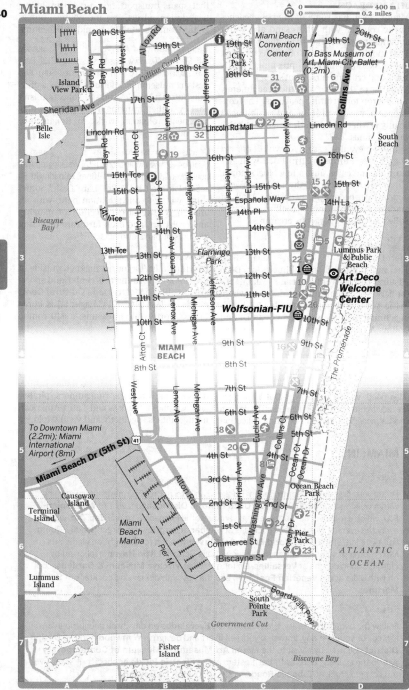

Miami Art Museum
MUSEUM

(MAM; Map p442; www.miamiartmuseum.org; adult/child $8/free, 2nd Sat free; ☉10am-5pm Tue-Fri, from noon Sat & Sun) Philip Johnson–designed building features rotating exhibits on post-WWII international art. It is scheduled to move to Bicentennial Park in 2013.

LITTLE HAVANA

As SW 8th St heads away from downtown, it becomes Calle Ocho (pronounced *kah*-yeh *oh*-cho, Spanish for 'Eighth Street'). That's when you know you've arrived in Little Havana, the most prominent community of Cuban Americans in the US. Despite the cultural monuments, this is no Cuban theme park. The district remains a living, breathing immigrant enclave, though one whose residents have become, admittedly, more broadly Central American. One of the best times to come is the last Friday of the month during Viernes Culturales (www.viernesculturales.com; ☉6-11pm), or 'Cultural Fridays,' a street fair showcasing Latino artists and musicians.

TOP CHOICE Máximo Gómez Park
PARK

(Map p444; cnr Calle Ocho & SW 15th Ave) Get a sensory-filled taste of old Cuba. It's also known as 'Domino Park,' and you'll un-derstand why when you see the old-timers throwing bones.

Cuba Ocho
GALLERY

(Map p444; ☎305-285-5880; cubaocho.com; 1465 SW 8th St; ☉9am-6pm) The jewel of the Little Havana Art District, Cuba Ocho functions as a Cuban community center, art gallery and research outpost. Check for events and performances.

El Crédito Cigars
CIGARS

(Map p444; ☎305-858-4162; 1106 SW 8th St) One of Miami's most popular cigar stores; watch *tabaqueros* hand-roll them.

FREE Bay of Pigs
Museum & Library
LIBRARY

(Map p444; www.bayofpigsmuseum.org; 1821 SW 9th St; ☉9am-4pm Mon-Sat) History buffs can stop by to learn more about the ill-fated Cuban invasion and pay tribute to the 2506 Brigade.

DESIGN DISTRICT, WYNWOOD & LITTLE HAITI

Proving that SoBe doesn't hold the lease on hip, these two trendy areas north of downtown – all but deserted 25 years ago – have

FLORIDA MIAMI

Miami Beach

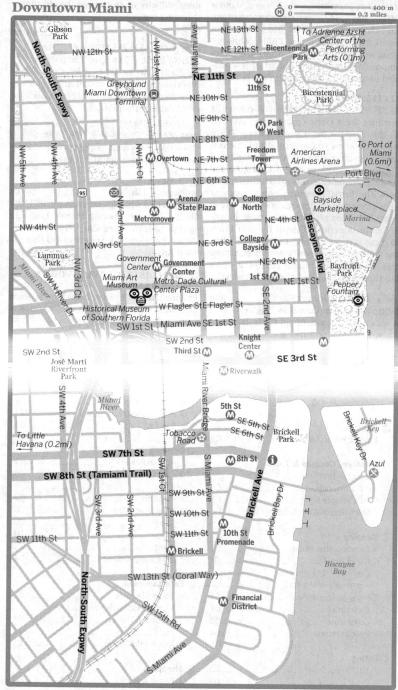

ensconced themselves as bastions of art and design. The **Design District** (Map p438; www.miamidesigndistrict.net) is a mecca for interior designers, home to dozens of galleries and contemporary furniture, fixture and design showrooms. Just south of the Design District, **Wynwood** is a notable arts district, with myriad galleries and art studios housed in abandoned factories and warehouses.

The home of Miami's Haitian refugees, **Little Haiti** is defined by brightly painted homes, markets and *botanicas* (voodoo shops).

Little Haiti Cultural Center   GALLERY
([phone icon]305-960-2969; www.miamigov.com/LHCultur alcenter; 212 NE 59th Tce; [clock icon]9am-5pm) Miami has the largest community of *Ayisens* (Haitians) in the world outside Haiti, and this cultural center is the place to learn about their story. Time your visit for **Big Night in Little Haiti** (www.bignightlittlehaiti.com), a monthly street celebration on the third Friday from 6pm to 10pm.

CORAL GABLES & COCONUT GROVE
For a slower pace and a more European feel, head inland. Designed as a 'model suburb' by George Merrick in the early 1920s, Coral Gables is a Mediterranean-style village that's centered around the shops and restaurants of the **Miracle Mile** (Map p444), a four-block section of Coral Way between Douglas and LeJeune Rds.

[TOP CHOICE] **Vizcaya Museum & Gardens**   HISTORIC BUILDING
(Map p444; www.vizcayamuseum.org; 3251 S Miami Ave; adult/child $12/5; [clock icon]9:30am-4:30pm Wed-

Mon) In Coconut Grove, this Italian Renaissance-style villa, the housing equivalent of a Fabergé egg, is Miami's most fairy-tale residence. The 70 rooms are stuffed with centuries-old furnishings and art, and the 30-acre grounds contain splendid formal gardens and Florentine gazebos.

Biltmore Hotel   HISTORIC BUILDING
(Map p444; www.biltmorehotel.com; 1200 Anastasia Ave) Architecturally speaking, the crown jewel of Coral Gables is this magnificent edifice that once housed a speakeasy run by Al Capone. Even if you don't stay, drop by for afternoon tea or a drink at the bar and gawk at the pool.

Venetian Pool   SWIMMING POOL
(Map p444; www.coralgablesvenetianpool.com; 2701 DeSoto Blvd; adult/child $11/7.35; [clock icon]10am-4:30pm) 'Swimming pool' doesn't even begin to describe this spring-fed goblet, made by filling in the limestone quarry used to build Coral Gables. With waterfalls, grottos and an Italianate feel, it looks like a vacation home for rich mermaids. Don't settle for a peek through wrought-iron fences – best to dive right in.

Lowe Art Museum   MUSEUM
(Map p444; www.lowemuseum.org, 1301 Stanford Dr; adult/student $10/5; [clock icon]10am-4pm Tue-Sat, from noon Sun) The Lowe's tremendous collection satisfies a wide range of tastes, but it's particularly strong in Asian, African and South Pacific art and archaeology, and its pre-Columbian and Mesoamerican collection is stunning.

WYNWOOD GALLERIES

In Wynwood, Miami's hip proving ground for avant-garde art, 'Wypsters' (Wynwood hipsters) stock dozens of galleries with 'guerrilla' installations, new murals, graffiti and other inscrutableness. The neighborhood is roughly bound by NW 20th and NW 37th streets on the south and north, and N Miami Ave and NW 3rd Ave east and west.

The best way to experience the scene is to attend the **Wynwood and Design District Arts Walks** (www.artcircuits.com), with music, food and wine on the second Saturday of the month from 7pm to 10pm.

» **PanAmerican Art Projects** (www.panamericanart.com; 2450 NW 2nd Ave; [clock icon]9:30am-5:30pm Tue-Fri, from noon Sat) Showcases work from European and Chinese artists as well as those from the Americas.

» **Art Modern Gallery** (www.artmoderngallery.com; 175 NW 23rd St; [clock icon]noon-4:30pm Mon-Sat) Surprise! Focuses on modern, contemporary and pop art.

» **Curator's Voice Art Projects** (www.curatorsvoiceartprojects.com; 2509 NW 2nd Ave; [clock icon]9:30am-5:30pm Mon-Fri, from noon Sat) A large and elegant showplace for the avant-garde.

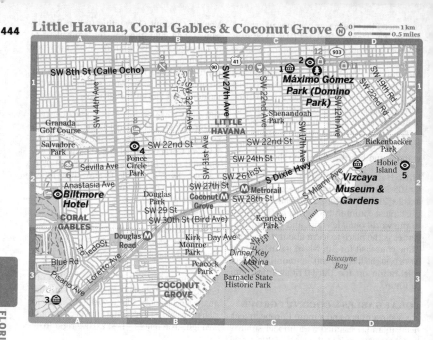

GREATER MIAMI

Museum of Contemporary Art MUSEUM
(MoCA; Map p438; www.mocanomi.org; 770 NE
125th St; adult/student $5/3; ⏲11am-5pm Tue &
Thu-Sat, 1-9pm Wed, noon-5pm Sun) North of
downtown, MoCA has frequently changing
exhibitions focusing on international, national and emerging artists.

Ancient Spanish Monastery CHURCH
(Map p438; ☎305-945-1461; www.spanishmon
astery.com; 16711 W Dixie Hwy; adult/child $8/4;
⏲10am-4pm Mon-Sat, from 11am Sun) Said to
be the oldest building in the Western Hemisphere, this monastery was built in Segovia,
Spain, in 1141 and shipped here by William
Randolph Hearst. Call to confirm hours.

KEY BISCAYNE

**Bill Baggs Cape Florida
State Recreation Park** PARK
(Map p438; www.floridastateparks.org/capeflorida;
1200 S Crandon Blvd; car/bicycle $8/2; ⏲8am-
dusk) Serene beaches and stunning sunsets
are just across the Rickenbacker Causeway
(toll $1) at Key Biscayne, where you'll find
the boardwalks and bike trails of this beachfront park. From the park's southern shore
you can catch a glimpse of Stiltsville, seven
colorful houses hovering on pilings in the
shallow waters of Biscayne Bay.

🏃 Activities

Cycling & In-Line Skating

Skating or cycling the strip along Ocean Dr in South Beach is pure Miami; also try the Rickenbacker Causeway to Key Biscayne.

Fritz's Skate Shop   CYCLING
(Map p440; ☑305-532-1954; www.fritzmiami beach.com; 1620 Washington Ave; ☺10am-10pm) Rentals and free in-line skate lessons (10:30am Sunday).

Miami Beach Bicycle Center   CYCLING
(Map p440; www.bikemiamibeach.com; 601 5th St; per hr/day $8/24; ☺10am-7pm Mon-Sat, to 5pm Sun) Convenient bike rentals in the heart of SoBe.

Water Sports

**Boucher Brothers
Watersports**   WATER SPORTS
(Map p440; www.boucherbrothers.com; 161 Ocean Dr; ☺10:30am-4:30pm) Rentals and lessons for all sorts of water-related activities: kayaking, waterskiing, windsurfing, parasailing, waverunners and boats.

Sailboards Miami   WATER SPORTS
(Map p444; www.sailboardsmiami.com; 1 Rickenbacker Causeway; ☺10am-6pm Fri-Tue) The waters off Key Biscayne are perfect for windsurfing, kayaking and kiteboarding; get your gear and lessons here.

Miami for Children

The best beaches for kids are in Miami Beach north of 21st St, especially at 53rd St, which has a playground and public toilets, and the dune-packed beach around 73rd St. Also head south to Matheson Hammock Park (Map p438), which has calm artificial lagoons.

Miami Seaquarium   AQUARIUM
(Map p438; ☑305-361-5705; www.miamiseaquari um.com; 4400 Rickenbacker Causeway; adult/child $38.95/29.95; ☺9:30am-6pm, last entry 4:30pm) On Key Biscayne, this 38-acre marine-life park is more extensive than the usual aquarium; it also rehabilitates dolphins, manatees and sea turtles, and presents great animal shows. You can also swim with the dolphins.

Miami Children's Museum   MUSEUM
(www.miamichildrensmuseum.org; 980 MacArthur Causeway; admission $15; ☺10am-6pm) On Watson Island, between downtown Miami and Miami Beach, this hands-on museum has fun music and art studios, as well as some branded 'work' experiences that make it feel a tad corporate.

Jungle Island   ZOO
(www.jungleisland.com; 1111 Parrot Jungle Trail, off MacArthur Causeway; adult/child $33/25; ☺10am-5pm) Also on Watson Island, Jungle Island is packed with tropical birds, alligators, orangutans, chimps and (wait for it, *Napoleon Dynamite* fans) a liger, a cross between a lion and a tiger.

Miami Metrozoo   ZOO
(www.miamimetrozoo.com; 12400 SW 152nd St; adult/child $16/12; ☺9:30am-5:30pm, last entry 4pm) A huge zoo in far south Miami with all the exotic Asian and African species.

Monkey Jungle   ZOO
(www.monkeyjungle.com; 14805 SW 216th St; adult/child $30/24; ☺9:30am-5pm, last entry 4pm) The tagline – 'Where humans are caged and monkeys run free' – tells you all you need to know. Unforgettable fun, also in south Miami.

👉 Tours

**Miami Design Preservation
League**   WALKING
(☑305-531-3484; guided tours adult/child $20/free; ☺10:30am Fri-Wed, 6:30pm Thu) Learn about art deco and its icons on a 90-minute walking tour departing from the Art Deco Welcome Center (Map p440) at 1200 Ocean Dr, Miami Beach.

Dr Paul George   WALKING, CYCLING
(☑305-375-1621; www.hmsf.org/programs-adult. htm; tours $25-42) Historian extraordinaire Dr Paul George leads fascinating bike, boat, coach and walking tours, including those that focus on Stiltsville. Get the full menu online.

South Beach Bike Tours   CYCLING
(☑305-673-2002; www.southbeachbiketours.com; half-day tour per person $59) Three-hour, two-wheel tours of South Beach.

🎊 Festivals & Events

Calle Ocho Festival   CULTURAL
(www.carnavalmiami.com) This massive street party in March is the culmination of Carnaval Miami, a 10-day celebration of Latin culture.

Winter Music Conference   MUSIC
(www.wmcon.com) The SXSW of dance music and electronica takes place every March.

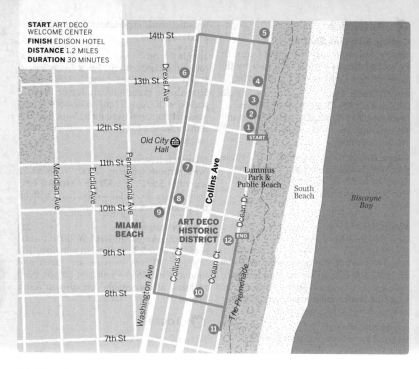

START ART DECO WELCOME CENTER
FINISH EDISON HOTEL
DISTANCE 1.2 MILES
DURATION 30 MINUTES

14th St

13th St

Drexel Ave

12th St

Old City Hall

11th St

Pennsylvania Ave

Euclid Ave

Meridian Ave

10th St

9th St

MIAMI BEACH

8th St

Washington Ave

7th St

Collins Ave

Collins Ct

ART DECO HISTORIC DISTRICT

Ocean Ct

Ocean Dr

The Promenade

START

END

Lummus Park & Public Beach

South Beach

Biscayne Bay

Walking Tour

> There are excellent walking tours available for the Art Deco Historic District – both guided and self-guided – but if you just want to hit the highlights, follow this quick and easy path.

Start at the ❶ **Art Deco Welcome Center** at the corner of Ocean Dr and 12th St, and head inside for a taste of deco style. Next, go north on Ocean Dr. Between 12th and 14th Sts, you'll see three classic examples of deco hotels: the ❷ **Leslie**, with classic 'eyebrows' and a typically boxy shape; the ❸ **Carlyle**, which was featured in the film *The Birdcage;* and the graceful ❹ **Cardozo Hotel**, with sleek, rounded edges. At 14th St, peek inside the ❺ **Winter Haven Hotel** to see its fabulous terrazzo floors.

Turn left and head along 14th St to Washington Ave, and turn left again to find the ❻ **US Post Office** at 13th St. Step inside to admire the domed ceiling and marble stamp tables, and try whispering into the domed ceiling. Two blocks down on your left is the ❼ **11th St Diner**, a gleaming aluminum

deco-style Pullman car where you can also stop for lunch. At 10th St, you'll find the ❽ **Wolfsonian-FIU**, an excellent museum with many deco-era treasures, and across the street is the beautifully restored ❾ **Hotel Astor**.

Turn left on 8th St and head east to Collins Ave. On the corner, you'll see ❿ **Hotel** – originally the Tiffany Hotel and still topped by a deco-style neon spire bearing that name. Continue to Ocean Dr and turn right to see the ⓫ **Colony Hotel** and its famous neon sign, then double back to find the 1935 ⓬ **Edison Hotel**, another creation of deco legend Henry Hohauser, half a block past 9th St.

Goombay Festival CULTURE
(www.goombayfestivalcoconutgrove.com) This massive fest, held in Coconut Grove on the first week of June, celebrates Bahamian culture.

White Party MUSIC
(www.whiteparty.net) This weeklong extravaganza in November draws more than 15,000 gay men and women for nonstop partying all over town.

Art Basel Miami Beach ART
(www.artbaselmiamibeach.com) An internationally important art show held each December – a sister event to Art Basel Switzerland.

🛏 Sleeping

Miami Beach is the well-hyped mecca for stylish boutique hotels in renovated art-deco buildings. To find them and other chic options, check out www.miamiboutiquehotels. com. Rates vary widely by season and all bets are off during spring break, when rates can quintuple; the summer months are slowest. For hotel parking, expect to pay $20 to $35 a night.

SOUTH BEACH

TOP CHOICE Pelican Hotel BOUTIQUE HOTEL $$$
(Map p440; 305-673-3373; www.pelicanhotel. com; 826 Ocean Dr; r $225-345; ❄🛜) The name and deco facade don't hint at anything unusual, but the decorators went wild inside with great themes such as 'Best Whorehouse,' 'Executive Zebra' and 'Me Tarzan, You Vain.'

TOP CHOICE Hotel St Augustine BOUTIQUE HOTEL $$$
(Map p440; 305-532-0570; www.hotelstaugus tine.com; 347 Washington Ave; r $180-280; P❄🛜) Wood that's blonder than Barbie and a crisp-and-clean deco theme combine to create one of South Beach's most elegant yet stunningly modern sleeps. A hip-and-homey standout.

Lords Hotel BOUTIQUE HOTEL $$
(Map p440; 877-448-4754; www.lordsouthbeach. com; 1120 Collins Ave; r $120-240, ste $330-540; P❄🛜) The epicenter of South Beach's gay scene is this cream puff of a hotel, with rooms decked out in lemony yellow and offset by pop art. Lords is hip, yet doesn't affect an attitude.

Kent Hotel BOUTIQUE HOTEL $$
(Map p440; 305-604-5068; www.thekenthotel. com; 1131 Collins Ave; r $79-220; P❄🛜) The lobby is a kick, filled with fuchsia and electric-orange geometric furniture plus bright Lucite toy blocks. Rooms continue the playfulness. One of South Beach's better deals.

Cadet Hotel BOUTIQUE HOTEL $$$
(Map p440; 305-672-6688; www.cadethotel.com; 1701 James Ave; r $170-280; ❄🛜📶) This unassuming little boutique hotel has the perfect deco aesthetic, with creative embellishments everywhere and a shaded verandah that's an oasis of calm.

Miami Beach International Hostel HOSTEL $
(Map p440; 305-534-2988; www.clayhotel.com; 1438 Washington Ave; dm $25-29, r $60-120; ❄📶@🛜) Nestled off Española Way and just blocks from the beach, this century-old Spanish-style building has an illustrious history and clean, affordable rooms.

Beachcomber Hotel HOTEL $$
(Map p440; 305-531-3755; www.beachcomber miami.com; 1340 Collins Ave; r $89-189; P❄@) Inside the green-banana-colored exterior, the Beachcomber has 29 cozy rooms.

NORTHERN MIAMI BEACH

TOP CHOICE Circa 39 BOUTIQUE HOTEL $$
(305-538-3900; www.circa39.com; 3900 Collins Ave; r $90-150; P❄@📶) If you love South Beach style but loathe South Beach attitude, Circa has got your back. Combines one of the funkiest lobbies in Miami, hip icy-blue-and-white rooms and a welcoming attitude. Web rates are phenomenal.

CORAL GABLES

TOP CHOICE Biltmore Hotel HOTEL $$$
(Map p444; 305-913-3158; www.biltmorehotel. com; 1200 Anastasia Ave; r $240-400; P❄🛜📶📶) This 1926 hotel is a National Historic Landmark and an icon of luxury. Standard rooms may be small, but public spaces are palatial; its fabulous pool is the largest hotel pool in the country.

Hotel St Michel HOTEL $$
(Map p444; 305-444-1666; www.hotelstmichel. com; 162 Alcazar Ave; r $125-220; P❄🛜📶) You could conceivably think you're in Europe in this vaulted place at Coral Gables, with inlaid floors, old-world charm and just 28 rooms.

🍴 Eating

Florida's most international city has an international-level food scene.

SOUTH BEACH

TOP CHOICE Tap Tap
HAITIAN $$

(Map p440; ☎305-672-2898; www.taptaprestaurant.com; 819 5th St; mains $9-20; ☺noon-11pm Mon-Thu, to midnight Fri & Sat) In this tropi-psychedelic Haitian eatery, you dine under bright murals of Papa Legba, enjoying cuisine that's a happy marriage of West Africa, France and the Caribbean: try spicy pumpkin soup, curried goat and *mayi moulen*, a signature side of cornmeal.

TOP CHOICE Osteria del Teatro
ITALIAN $$

(Map p440; ☎305-538-7850; http://osteriadelteatromiami.com; 1443 Washington Ave; mains $16-31; ☺6-11pm Mon-Thu, to 1am Fri-Sun) Stick to the specials of one of Miami's oldest and best Italian restaurants, and you can't go wrong. Better yet, let the gracious Italian waiters coddle and order for you. They never pick wrong.

Puerto Sagua
CUBAN $

(Map p440; ☎305-673-1115; 700 Collins Ave; mains $6-17; ☺7:30am-2am) Pull up to the counter for authentic, tasty and inexpensive *ropa vieja* (shredded beef), black beans and *arroz con pollo* (rice with chicken) – plus some of the best Cuban coffee in town – at this beloved Cuban diner.

11th St Diner
DINER $

(Map p440; www.eleventhstreetdiner.com; 1065 Washington Ave; mains $8-16; ☺24hr) This deco diner housed inside a gleaming Pullman train car sees round-the-clock activity and is especially popular with people staggering home from clubs.

Pizza Rustica
PIZZERIA $

(Map p440; www.pizza-rustica.com; 863 Washington Ave; slices $3-5; ☺11am-6pm) Big square slices that are a meal in themselves – when you're wandering around hungry, there's nothing better. Also at 1447 Washington Ave and 667 Lincoln Rd.

Jerry's Famous Deli
DELI $$

(Map p440; www.jerrysfamousdeli.com; 1450 Collins Ave; mains $9-18; ☺24hr) Jerry's does it all – from pastrami melts to Chinese chicken salad to fettuccine Alfredo – and does it all day long. It also does it big, with huge portions served in a large, open, deco space.

Front Porch Cafe
AMERICAN $$

(Map p440; ☎305-531-8300; 1418 Ocean Dr; mains $10-18; ☺7am-11pm) Pull up a chair on the front porch of the Penguin Hotel for great breakfasts, huge portions and reasonable prices, all overlooking the ocean.

DOWNTOWN MIAMI

Azul
FUSION $$$

(Map p442; ☎305-913-8288; 500 Brickell Key Dr; mains $30-72; ☺7-11pm Mon-Sat) Be pampered at this terrific restaurant on Brickell Key with a stellar Asian fusion menu. In addition to a massive wine list and waterfront views of downtown, Azul offers some of the best service in Miami.

LITTLE HAVANA

Versailles
CUBAN $

(Map p444; ☎305-444-0240; 3555 SW 8th St; mains $5-20; ☺8am-2am) *The* Cuban restaurant in town is not to be missed. It finds room for everybody in the large, cafeteria-style dining rooms.

DESIGN DISTRICT & WYNWOOD

TOP CHOICE Senora Martinez
FUSION $$$

(☎305-573-5474; www.sramartinez.com; 4000 NE 2nd Ave; mains $13-30; ☺noon-3pm Tue-Sun, 6-11pm

---

EATING MIAMI: LATIN AMERICAN SPICE

Thanks to its immigrant heritage, Miami is legendary for its authentic Cuban, Haitian, Brazilian and other Latin American cuisines. Cuban food is a mix of Caribbean, African and Latin American influences, and the fertile cross-pollination of these traditions has given rise to endlessly creative, tasty gourmet fusions, sometimes dubbed 'nuevo Latino,' 'nouvelle Floridian' or 'Floribbean' cuisine.

For a good introduction to Cuban food, sidle up to a Cuban *loncheria* (snack bar) and order a *pan cubano*: a buttered, grilled baguette stuffed with ham, roast pork, cheese, mustard and pickles. For dinner, order the classic *ropa vieja*: shredded flank steak cooked in tomatoes and peppers, and accompanied by fried plantains, black beans and yellow rice.

Other treats to look for include Haitian *griots* (marinated fried pork), Jamaican jerk chicken, Brazilian BBQ, Central American *gallo pinto* (red beans and rice) and *batidos*, a milky, refreshing Latin American fruit smoothie.

Tue-Thu, to midnight Fri-Sat, to 10pm Sun; 🍴) One of Miami's most exciting top-end restaurants, Senora Martinez pushes the boundaries of experimentation and plain good food. The menu is eclectic – exemplifying Miami itself.

🌱 **Sustain** AMERICAN $$$
(☎305-424-9079; www.sustainmiami.com; 3252 NE 1st Ave; mains $13-30; ⊙11:30am-3pm & 5-10:30pm; 🍴) Sustain is one of Miami's leading – and more affordable – purveyors of locally sourced, organically grown food. The lovely dining room and fantastic cuisine make a meal both carnivores and vegetarians adore.

🍷 Drinking & Entertainment

Miami truly comes alive at night. There is always something going on, and usually till the wee hours, with many bars staying open till 3am or 5am. For events calendars and gallery, bar and club reviews, check out www.cooljunkie.com, www.miaminights.com and www.beachedmiami.com.

Bars

There are tons of bars along Ocean Dr; a happy-hour meander unearths half-price drinks.

TOP CHOICE **Room** BAR
(Map p440; www.theotheroom.com; 100 Collins Ave) This dark, atmospheric, boutique beer bar is a gem: hip and sexy as hell but with a low-key attitude. Per the name, it's small and gets crowded.

Abraxas BAR
(Map p440; 407 Meridian Ave) In a classic deco building, Abraxas couldn't be friendlier. Uncrowded and serving fantastic beer from around the world, it's tucked away in a residential part of South Beach.

Zeke's Roadhouse BAR
(Map p440; 625 Lincoln Rd) Great beer selection, and lots of it, cheaply priced; the outdoor seating on Lincoln Rd doesn't hurt either.

Electric Pickle BAR
(www.electricpicklemiami.com; 2826 N Miami Ave) Wynwood's arty hipsters become glamorous club kids in this two-story hepcat hot spot. The Pickle is sexy, gorgeous and literate.

Abbey Brewery BAR
(Map p440; www.abbeybrewinginc.com; 1115 16th St) The only brewpub in South Beach is packed with friendly folks listening to the

Grateful Dead and slinging back the excellent homebrew.

B Bar BAR
(Map p440; Betsy Hotel, 1440 Ocean Ave) This basement bar, under the Betsy Hotel, draws the usual crowd of beautiful, in-the-know, SoBe-tastic types and has some unusual entertainment: an odd, low-hanging reflective ceiling that ripples when touched.

Nightclubs

To increase your chances of getting into the major nightclubs, call ahead to get on the guest list. Having gorgeous, well-dressed females in your group doesn't hurt either (unless you're going to a gay bar). In South Beach clubs and live music venues, covers range from $20 to $25, and half that elsewhere.

Bardot CLUB
(☎305-576-5570; www.bardotmiami.com; 3456 N Miami Ave) In Wynwood, Bardot is a saucy vision of decadent excess, yet the glam local scene is more laid-back than SoBe.

Skybar CLUB
(Map p440; ☎305-695-3900; Shore Club, 1901 Collins Ave) Sip chic cocktails on the alfresco terrace – they're too expensive to guzzle. Or, if you're 'somebody,' head for the indoor A-list Red Room. Both have a luxurious Moroccan theme and beautiful people-watching.

Twist CLUB
(Map p440; ☎305-538-9478; www.twistsobe.com; 1057 Washington Ave) This (free) gay hangout has serious staying power and a little bit of something for everyone, including dancing, drag shows and go-go dancers.

Nikki Beach Club CLUB
(Map p440; ☎305-538-1111; www.nikkibeach.com; 1 Ocean Dr; cover from $25) Lounge on beds or inside your own tipi in this beach-chic outdoor space that's right on the sand.

Mansion CLUB
(Map p440; ☎305-532-1525; www.mansionmiami. com; 1235 Washington Ave; cover from $20; ⊙Thu-Sun) *Was that Lindsay Lohan?* Prepare for some quality time with the velvet rope and wear fly duds to enter this grandiose, exclusive megaclub, which lives up to its name.

Live Music

La Covacha LIVE MUSIC
(☎305-594-3717; www.lacovacha.com; 10730 NW 25th St, Doral) Well-loved, tourist-free, very

hip Latin club for up-and-coming bands and DJs. A long drive.

Tobacco Road   BAR
(Map p442; ☎305-374-1198; www.tobacco-road. com; 626 S Miami Ave) Old-school roadhouse around since 1912; blues, jazz and occasional impromptu jams by well-known rockers.

Hoy Como Ayer   LIVE MUSIC
(Map p444; ☎305-541-2631; www.hoycomoayer. us; 2212 SW 8th St) Authentic Cuban music.

Jazid   LOUNGE
(Map p440; ☎305-673-9372; www.jazid.net; 1342 Washington Ave) Jazz in a candlelit lounge; upstairs, DJ-fueled soul and hip-hop.

Churchill's   BAR
(☎305-757-1807; www.churchillspub.com; 5501 NE 2nd Ave) The best of indie/punk music – as well as UK football broadcasts.

Theater & Culture

Adrienne Arsht Center for the
Performing Arts   PERFORMING ARTS
(off Map p442; ☎305-949-6722; www.arshtcenter. org; 1300 Biscayne Blvd) Showcases jazz from around the world, as well as theater, dance, music, comedy and more.

New World Center   CLASSICAL MUSIC
(Map p440; ☎305-673-3330; www.nws.edu; 500 17th St) The new home of the acclaimed New World Symphony is one of the most beautiful buildings in Miami.

Colony Theater   PERFORMING ARTS
(Map p440; ☎305-674-1040; www.mbculture.com; 1040 Lincoln Rd) Everything – from off-Broadway productions to ballet and movies – plays in this renovated 1934 art-deco showpiece.

Miami City Ballet   DANCE
(off Map p440; ☎305-929-7000; www.miamicity ballet.org; 2200 Liberty Ave) One of the USA's premier Ballanchine companies.

Fillmore Miami Beach at
Jackie Gleason Theater   PERFORMING ARTS
(Map p440; ☎305-673-7300; www.gleasontheater. com; 1700 Washington Ave) Miami Beach's premier showcase for Broadway shows, headliners and the Miami City Ballet.

Sports

Miami hosts pro teams in all four major US team sports.

Miami Dolphins   FOOTBALL
(www.miamidolphins.com; Sun Life Stadium, 2269 Dan Marino Blvd; tickets from $35) NFL football season runs from August to December.

Florida Marlins   BASEBALL
(www.marlins.mlb.com; Sun Life Stadium, 2269 Dan Marino Blvd; tickets from $15) MLB baseball season is May to September.

Miami Heat   BASKETBALL
(Map p442; www.nba.com/heat; American Airlines Arena, 601 Biscayne Blvd; tickets from $20) NBA basketball season is November to April.

Florida Panthers   HOCKEY
(☎954-835-7000; http://panthers.nhl.com; Bank Atlantic Center, 1 Panther Pkwy, Sunrise; tickets from $15) NHL hockey season runs mid-October to mid-April.

🔒 Shopping

Browse for one-of-a-kind and designer items at the South Beach boutiques around Collins Ave between 6th and 9th Sts and along Lincoln Rd mall. For unique items, try Little Havana and the Design District.

Bal Harbour Shops   MALL
(www.balharbourshops.com; 9700 Collins Ave) Miami's most elegant mall.

Bayside Marketplace   MALL
(Map p442; www.baysidemarketplace.com; 401 Biscayne Blvd) Near the marina, a buzzy if touristy shopping and entertainment hub.

Little-Havana-to-Go   CUBAN
(Map p444; www.littlehavanatogo.com; 1442 SW 8th St/Calle Ocho) Stocks authentic Cuban goods and clothing.

Books & Books   BOOKS
(www.booksandbooks.com; 927 Lincoln Rd) Best indie bookstore in South Florida; the original location is at 265 Aragon Ave and there's another in Bal Harbour Shops.

ℹ Information

Dangers & Annoyances

Miami has a few areas considered dangerous at night: Little Haiti, stretches of the Miami riverfront and Biscayne Blvd, and areas below 5th St in South Beach. Downtown, use caution near the Greyhound station and shantytowns around causeways, bridges and overpasses.

Emergency
Beach Patrol (☎305-673-7714)

Internet Access

Most hotels offer wi-fi access (as do Starbucks), and libraries also have free internet terminals.

Internet Resources
Art Circuits (www.artcircuits.com) Insider info on art events; neighborhood-by-neighborhood gallery maps.

Mango & Lime (www.mangoandlime.net) The best local food blog.

Miami Beach 411 (www.miamibeach411.com) A great general guide for Miami Beach visitors.

Media

El Nuevo Herald (www.elnuevoherald.com) Spanish-language daily published by the *Miami Herald*.

Miami Herald (www.miamiherald.com) The city's major English-language daily.

Miami New Times (www.miaminewtimes.com) Edgy, alternative weekly.

Medical Services

Mount Sinai Medical Center (☑305-674-2121, 24hr visitors medical line 305-674-2222; 4300 Alton Rd) The area's best emergency room.

Money

Bank of America has branch offices all over Miami and Miami Beach. To get currency exchanged, go to **Amex** (www.amex.com; 100 N Biscayne Blvd; ⊘9am-5pm Mon-Fri) in downtown Miami.

Tourist Information

Greater Miami & the Beaches Convention & Visitors Bureau (☑305-539-3000; www.miamiandbeaches.com; 701 Brickell Ave, 27th fl; ⊘8:30am-5pm Mon-Fri)

Miami Beach Chamber of Commerce (☑305-672-1300; www.miamibeachchamber.com; 1920 Meridian Ave; ⊘9am-5pm Mon-Fri)

ⓘ Getting There & Away

Miami International Airport (MIA; www.miami-airport.com) is about 6 miles west of downtown and is accessible by **SuperShuttle** (☑305-871-8210; www.supershuttle.com), which costs about $26 to South Beach.

Greyhound goes to all major cities in Florida. Main terminals are the **Airport terminal** (☑305-871-1810; 4111 NW 27th St) and **Miami Downtown terminal** (☑305-374-6160; 1012 NW 1st Ave).

Amtrak (☑305-835-1222; 8303 NW 37th Ave) has a main Miami terminal. The **Tri-Rail** (☑800-874-7245; www.tri-rail.com) commuter system serves Miami (with a free transfer to Miami's transit system) and MIA, Fort Lauderdale and its airport, and West Palm Beach and its airport ($11.55 round-trip).

ⓘ Getting Around

Metro-Dade Transit (☑305-891-3131; www.miami dade.gov/transit) runs the local Metrobus and Metrorail ($2), as well as the free **Metro-mover** monorail serving downtown.

Fort Lauderdale

Fort Lauderdale was once known as spring break party central, but like the drunken teens who once littered the beach, the town has grown up and moved on. It's now a stylish, sophisticated city known more for museums, Venice-style waterways, yachting and open-air cafes than wet T-shirt contests and beer bongs. It's also a very popular gay and lesbian destination, along with most of South Florida. Of course, the beach is as lovely as always.

For local information, head to the **visitor bureau** (☑954-765-4466; www.sunny.org; 100 E Broward Blvd, Suite 200).

◉ Sights & Activities

Fort Lauderdale
Beach & Promenade   BEACH

Fort Lauderdale's promenade – a wide, brick, palm-tree-dotted pathway swooping along the beach and A1A – is a magnet for runners, in-line skaters, walkers and cyclists. The white-sand beach, meanwhile, is one of the nation's cleanest and best, stretching 7 miles to Lauderdale-by-the-Sea, with dedicated family-, gay- and dog-friendly sections. Boating, diving, snorkeling and fishing are all extremely popular.

Museum of Art   MUSEUM

(www.moaflnsu.org; 1 E Las Olas Blvd; adult/child $10/7; ⊘11am-6pm, to 8pm Wed, noon-5pm Sun) A curvaceous Florida standout with an impressive collection of modern masters (Picasso, Matisse, Warhol), plus Cuban, African and South American art.

Museum of Discovery & Science   MUSEUM

(www.mods.org; 401 SW 2nd St; adult/child $11/9; ⊘10am-5pm Mon-Sat, noon-6pm Sun) A 52ft kinetic-energy sculpture greets you, and fun exhibits include Gizmo City and Runways to Rockets – where it actually *is* rocket science. Plus there's an Everglades exhibit and IMAX theater.

Fort Lauderdale Antique Car Museum   MUSEUM

(www.antiquecarmuseum.org; 1527 Packard Ave; adult/child $8/5; ⊘9am-3pm Mon-Fri) Nostalgic car-lovers should motor here; it features 22 vintage Packards and auto memorabilia.

Bonnet House   HISTORIC HOME

(www.bonnethouse.org; 900 N Birch Rd; adult/child $20/16, grounds only $10; ⊘10am-4pm Tue-Sat,

Sure, Miami's South Beach is a mecca for gay travelers, but Fort Lauderdale has long been nipping at the high heels of its southern neighbor. Plus, compared to South Beach, Lauderdale's scene is less exclusive and more rainbow-flag oriented.

Fort Lauderdale is home to several dozen gay bars and clubs, as many gay guesthouses, and a couple of way-gay residential hubs, including **Victoria Park**, the established gay ghetto, and **Wilton Manors**, more recently gay-gentrified and boasting endless nightlife options.

Two places catering exclusively to gay male clients, and that just happen to be clothing optional, are the stylish **Schubert Resort** (✆954-763-7434; www.schubertresort.com; 855 NE 20th Ave; ste $99-309; P❄@🐾🛜🏊) and **Pineapple Point** (✆888-844-7295; www.pineapplepoint.com; 315 NE 16th Tce; r $199-279, ste $299-399; P@🛜🏊), an intimate guesthouse tucked away in a quiet residential neighborhood.

For more information on local gay life, visit www.gayftlauderdale.com. Other resources that cover South Florida include the glossy weekly *Hot Spots* (www.hotspotsmagazine.com), the insanely comprehensive www.jumponmarkslist.com, and www.sunny.org/glbt.

from 11am Sun) Wandering the 35 acres of lush, subtropical gardens, you might just spot the resident Brazilian squirrel monkeys. The art-filled house is open to guided tours only.

Gondola Man   GONDOLA RIDE
(✆877-926-2467; www.gondolaman.com; ride $125) Explore the 'Venice of America' with a romantic ride that takes you up and down the canals of the rich and famous.

WATER TAXI
(www.watertaxi.com; all-day pass adult/child $20/12) For the best unofficial tour of the city, hop on the water taxi, whose drivers offer a lively narration as they ply Fort Lauderdale's canals and waterways. Check online for locations.

🛏 Sleeping

The area from Rio Mar St in the south to Vistamar St in the north, and from Hwy A1A in the east to Bayshore Dr in the west, offers the highest concentration of accommodations in all price ranges. Check out **Superior Small Lodgings** (www.sunny.org/ssl).

TOP CHOICE Pillars   B&B $$$
(✆954-467-9639; www.pillarshotel.com; 111 N Birch Rd; r $179-520; P❄🛜🏊) From the harp in the sitting area to the private balconies and the intimate prearranged dinners for two, this tiny boutique B&B radiates hushed good taste. A block from the beach, facing one of the best sunsets in town.

Riverside Hotel   HOTEL $$
(✆954-467-0671; www.riversidehotel.com; 620 E Las Olas Blvd; r $143-200; P❄🛜🏊) This Fort Lauderdale landmark – fabulously located downtown on Las Olas – has three room types: more modern rooms in the newer tower, restored rooms in the original property and the more old-fashioned 'classic' rooms.

Shell Motel   MOTEL $
(✆954-463-1723; www.sableresorts.com; 330 Bayshore Dr; r/ste from $85/150; P🛜🏊) One of six modest motels owned by the same company, this sweet Old Florida–style spot has bright, clean rooms surrounding a small pool. Splash out for a roomy suite.

🍴 Eating

TOP CHOICE Gran Forno   ITALIAN $
(www.granforno.com; 1235 E Las Olas Blvd; mains $6-12; ⏱7:30am-7pm Tue-Sun) The best lunch spot in downtown Fort Lauderdale is this delightfully old-school Milanese-style bakery and cafe: warm crusty pastries, bubbling pizzas, and fat golden loaves of ciabatta, sliced and stuffed with ham, roast peppers, pesto and other delicacies.

Rustic Inn   SEAFOOD $$$
(✆954-584-1637; www.rusticinn.com; 4331 Ravenswood Rd; mains $14-45; ⏱10:30am-10:45pm, to 9pm Sun) Hungry locals at this messy, noisy crab house use wooden mallets at long, newspaper-covered tables to get at the Dungeness, blue and golden crabs drenched in garlic.

Casablanca Cafe   MEDITERRANEAN $$$
(✆954-764-3500; 3049 Alhambra St; mains $10-38; ⏱11:30am-1am Sun-Tue, to 2am Wed-Sat) Try

to score a seat on the upstairs balcony of this Moroccan-style home where Mediterranean-inspired food and Florida-style ocean views are served. Live music Wednesdays through Sundays.

11th Street Annex
AMERICAN $

(http://twouglysisters.com; 14 SW 11th St; lunch $9; ⊙11:30am-2pm Mon-Fri) In this off-the-beaten-path peach cottage, the 'two ugly sisters' serve whatever strikes their fancy: perhaps brie mac 'n' cheese, chicken confit and sour cream chocolate cake. Most of the vegetables are grown from the cottage's garden.

Cafe Sharaku
ASIAN FUSION $$$

(☑954-563-2888; www.cafesharaku.com; 2736 N Federal Hwy; mains $25-32; ⊙11:30am-3pm Tue-Fri, 5:30-10pm Tue-Sun) Local foodies whisper to one another about this exquisite 18-seat bistro, but the cat's out of the bag: Sharaku is a fabulous temple of gemlike fish and seafood creations.

🍷 Drinking & Entertainment

Bars generally stay open until 4am on weekends and 2am during the week. Meander the **Riverwalk** (www.goriverwalk.com) along the New River, where you'll find the alfresco mall **Las Olas Riverfront** (SW 1st Ave at Las Olas Blvd), with stores, restaurants, a movie theater and entertainment.

Elbo Room
BAR

(www.elboroom.com; 241 S Fort Lauderdale Beach Blvd) Featured in the movie *Where the Boys Are,* Elbo Room hangs onto its somewhat seedy reputation as one of the oldest and diviest bars around.

Lulu's Bait Shack
BAR

(www.lulusbaitshack.com; 17 S Fort Lauderdale Beach Blvd) Lures 'em in with buckets of beer, bowls of mussels and fishbowl drinks at the ocean's edge.

Voodoo Lounge
NIGHTCLUB

(www.voodooloungeflorida.com; 111 SW 2nd Ave; ⊙10pm-4am Wed-Sun) A massive nightclub – look for Sunday drag nights, Latin nights and other themed events.

❶ Getting There & Around

The **Fort Lauderdale-Hollywood International Airport** (FLL; www.fll.net) is served by more than 35 airlines, some with nonstop flights from Europe. A taxi from the airport to downtown costs around $20.

The **Greyhound station** (☑954-764-6551; 515 NE 3rd St at Federal Hwy) is four blocks from Broward Central Terminal, with multiple daily services. The **train station** (200 SW 21st Tce) serves **Amtrak** (☑800-872-7245; www.amtrak. com), and the **Tri-Rail** (www.tri-rail.com) has services to Miami and Palm Beach.

Hail a **Sun Trolley** (www.suntrolley.com; per ride 50¢) for rides between downtown, the beach, Las Olas and the Riverfront.

Palm Beach & Around

Palm Beach isn't all yachts and mansions – but just about. This area, 45 miles north of Fort Lauderdale, is where railroad baron Henry Flagler built his winter retreat, and it's also home to Donald Trump's **Mar-a-Lago** (cnr Southern & S Ocean Blvds). In other words, if you're looking for middle-class tourism or Florida kitsch, keep driving. Contact the Palm Beach County **Convention & Visitor Bureau** (☑800-544-2756; www.palmbeachfl.com; 1555 Palm Beach Lakes Blvd) in West Palm Beach for area information and maps.

BOCA RATON

Halfway between Fort Lauderdale and Palm Beach is this largely residential stretch of picturesque coast that's been preserved from major development. For a great taste, hike the elevated boardwalks of the **Gumbo Limbo Nature Center** (www.gumbolimbo.

FLORIDA'S SEMINOLES

If you want to learn about Florida's Seminole people, the best place is the **Ah-Tah-Thi-Ki Museum** (☑877-902-1113; www.ahtahthiki.com; Big Cypress Seminole Indian Reservation, Clewiston; adult/child & senior $9/6; ⊙9am-5pm), 17 miles north of I-75, west of Fort Lauderdale. The museum is set within a cypress dome cut through with an interpretive boardwalk, so from the start it strikes a balance between environmentalism and education. Permanent exhibits include dioramas depicting scenes of traditional Seminole life, an old school 'living village' and re-created ceremonial grounds. Temporary exhibits have even more academic polish, and overall the museum does an excellent job of presenting Seminole history and tribal life today.

org; 1801 N Ocean Blvd; admission by donation; ☉9am-4pm Mon-Sat, from noon Sun), a beautiful wetlands preserve; also visit its sea turtle rehabilitation center. Another good reason to stop is the outstanding **Boca Raton Museum of Art** (www.bocamuseum.org; 501 Plaza Real, Mizner Park; adult/child $8/4; ☉10am-5pm Tue-Fri, from noon Sat & Sun), with a permanent collection of contemporary works by Picasso, Matisse, Warhol and more. The museum is in **Mizner Park** (www.miznerpark.org; cnr US 1 & Mizner Blvd), a ritzy outdoor mall with stores, restaurants and regular free concerts.

PALM BEACH

About 30 miles north of Boca Raton are Palm Beach and West Palm Beach. The two towns have flip-flopped the traditional coastal hierarchy: Palm Beach, the beach town, is more upscale, while West Palm Beach on the mainland is younger and livelier. Because Palm Beach is an enclave of the ultrawealthy, especially during its winter 'social season,' most travelers just window-shop the oceanfront mansions and boutiques lining the aptly named **Worth Avenue** (www.worth-avenue.com).

One of the country's most fascinating museums is the resplendent **Flagler Museum** (www.flagler.org; 1 Whitehall Way; adult/child $18/10; ☉10am-5pm Tue-Sat, from noon Sun), housed in the railroad magnate's 1902 winter estate, Whitehall Mansion. The elaborate 55-room palace is an evocative immersion in Gilded Age opulence.

Modeled after Rome's Villa Medici, Flagler's opulent oceanfront 1896 hotel, the **Breakers** (☎561-655-6611; www.thebreakers.com; 1 S County Rd; r $270-1250; P✳@☎☀), is a super-luxurious world unto itself, encompassing two golf courses, 10 tennis courts, a three-pool Mediterranean beach club and a trove of restaurants.

In the trendy Omphoy Hotel, **Michelle Bernstein's** (☎561-540-6440; www.omphoy.com; 2842 S Ocean Blvd; mains $29-38; ☉5:30-10pm) is the latest outpost for this Miami celebrity chef. Come for gourmet riffs on Nouvelle Floridian cuisine, emphasizing South Florida produce. Or, kick it Formica-style with an egg cream and a low-cal platter at the lunch counter in **Green's Pharmacy** (151 N County Rd; mains $4-13; ☉7am-3pm Mon-Sat, to 2pm Sun).

WEST PALM BEACH

Henry Flagler initially developed West Palm Beach as a working-class community to support Palm Beach, and indeed, West Palm today works harder, plays harder and is simply cooler and more relaxed. It's a groovy place to explore.

Florida's largest museum, the **Norton Museum of Art** (www.norton.org; 1451 S Olive Ave; adult/child $12/5; ☉10am-5pm Tue-Sat, to 9pm Thu, from 11am Sun) houses an enormous collection of American and European modern masters and Impressionists, along with a large Buddha head presiding over an impressive Asian art collection. If you like that, you'll love the outdoor **Ann Norton Sculpture Garden** (www.ansg.org; 253 Barcelona Rd; admission $7; ☉10am-4pm Wed-Sun). This serene collection of sculptures sprinkled among verdant gardens is a real West Palm gem.

If you have children, take them to **Lion Country Safari** (www.lioncountrysafari.com; 2003 Lion Country Safari Rd; adult/child $26.50/19.50; ☉9:30am-5:30pm), the country's first cageless drive-through safari, where around 900 creatures roam freely around 500 acres.

The coolest lodging in town is **Hotel Biba** (☎561-832-0094; www.hotelbiba.com; 320 Belvedere Rd; r summer/winter $79/129; P✳☎☀). The retro-funky exterior looks like a cute, 1950s motel in honeydew-melon green, but the rooms have a modern boutique style that would be right at home in Miami's SoBe.

Much of the action centers around **City-Place** (www.cityplace.com; 700 S Rosemary Ave), a European village-style outdoor mall with splashing fountains and a slew of dining and entertainment options. Clematis St also has several worthy bars, live-music clubs and restaurants, and every Thursday **Clematis by Night** (www.clematisbynight.net; ☉6-9:30pm Thu) hosts friendly outdoor concerts. If you're hungry, try **Rocco's Tacos & Tequila Bar** (www.roccostacos.com; 224 Clematis St; mains $12-19; ☉11:30am-11pm, to midnight Tue-Wed, to 1am Thu-Sat), a saucy *nuevo* Mexican restaurant with funky decor, tableside guacamole and 175 different kinds of tequila – no wonder it's so loud in here!

Admirably servicing its migration of snowbirds is **Palm Beach International Airport** (PBI; www.pbia.org), 2.5 miles west of downtown West Palm Beach. The downtown **Tri-Rail station** (☎800-875-7245; 201 S Tamarind Ave) also serves as the **Amtrak station** (☎561-832-6169).

The Everglades

Contrary to what you may have heard, the Everglades is not a swamp. Or at least, it's not *only* a swamp. Its complex taxonomy of environments is most accurately characterized as a wet prairie – grasslands that happen to be flooded most of the year. Nor is it stagnant. In the wet season, a horizon-wide river creeps ever-so-slowly beneath the rustling saw grass and around the subtly raised cypress and hardwood hammocks toward the ocean. The Everglades are indeed filled with alligators – and perhaps a few dead bodies, as *CSI: Miami* would have it. Yet its beauty is not measured in fear or geological drama, but in the timeless, slow Jurassic flap of a great blue heron as it glides over its vast and shockingly gentle domain.

Which is one reason that exploring the Everglades by foot, bicycle, canoe and kayak (or camping) is so much more satisfying than by noisy, vibrating airboat. There is an incredible variety of wonderful creatures to see within this unique, subtropical wilderness: all those alligators, bottlenose dolphins, manatees, snowy egrets, herons, anhingas, bald eagles and ospreys. And there are accessible entrances that, at the cost of a few hours, get you easily into the Everglades' soft heart.

The Everglades has two seasons: the summer wet season and the winter dry season.

Winter – from December to April – is the prime time to visit: the weather is mild and pleasant, and the wildlife is out in abundance. In summer – May through October – it's stiflingly hot, humid and buggy, with frequently afternoon thunderstorms. In addition, as water sources spread out, the animals disperse.

EVERGLADES NATIONAL PARK

While the Everglades have a history dating back to prehistoric times, the park wasn't founded until 1947. It's considered the most endangered national park in the USA, but the Comprehensive Everglades Restoration Plan has been enacted to undo some of the damage done by draining and development.

The park has three main entrances and areas: in the south along Rte 9336 through Homestead and Florida City to Ernest Coe Visitor Center and, at road's end, Flamingo; along the Tamiami Trail/Hwy 41 in the north to Shark Valley; and on the Gulf Coast near Everglades City.

The main park entry points have visitor centers where you can get maps, camping permits and ranger information. You only need to pay the entrance fee (per car/pedestrian $10/5 for seven days) once to access all points.

Even in winter it's almost impossible to avoid mosquitoes, but they're ferocious in summer: bring *strong* repellent. Alligators are also prevalent. As obvious as it sounds,

FLORIDA THE EVERGLADES

SAVING THE EVERGLADES

For most of human history, the Everglades were an utter and almost entirely uninhabited wilderness. But by 1900 the desire to settle South Florida led Florida governor Napoleon Bonaparte Broward to envision an 'Empire of the Everglades.' Broward set in motion 70 years of canal building that drained about half the swamp and effectively cut off what had been a vibrant 100-mile-long river from its source, Lake Okeechobee.

South Florida's burgeoning cities, suburbs and agriculture then did two things: thirstily sucked up the fresh water while dumping pollutants into what is, essentially, the peninsula's kidney – vital wetlands that help cleanse the Florida Aquifer. If allowed to continue unabated, this process would eventually kill the Everglades and leave South Florida uninhabitable.

Marjory Stoneman Douglas, who famously dubbed the Everglades a 'river of grass,' almost single-handedly raised the alarm in the 1940s, and in 1947 the Everglades were protected as a national park, the first for reasons of conservation, not natural beauty. This, however, was only a first step.

Fast forward to today: in 2000 the Comprehensive Everglades Restoration Plan (CERP; www.evergladesplan.org) was approved, a 30-year proposal to fill in canals, remove levees and restore the water flow. Yet political battles and the high estimated price tag ($15 billion and counting) have slowed progress. And as funding has fallen to a fraction of what's needed, some wonder about the future viability of one of the USA's biggest, most ambitious environmental projects.

For an overview of Everglades history, visit www.theevergladesstory.org.

never, ever feed them: it's illegal and is a sure way to provoke attacks. Four types of poisonous snakes call the Everglades home; avoid all snakes, just in case, and wear long, thick socks and lace-up boots.

Sights & Activities

Shark Valley Visitor Center   PARK
(305-221-8776; Tamiami Trail; 8:30am-6pm) For a quick peek from Miami, come here. On the excellent two-hour tram tour (305-221-8455; www.sharkvalleytramtours.com; adult/child $18.25/11.50) along the 15-mile asphalt road, you'll see copious numbers of alligators and lots of migratory herons and ibis in winter. The narration by park rangers is both knowledgeable and witty, providing an ideal overview of the Everglades and its inhabitants. Halfway along the trail is the 50ft-high observation tower, an ugly concrete structure that offers a dramatic panorama of the 'river of grass.' The pancake-flat road is also perfect for cycling (rental per hr $7.50); stop and gawk as long and often as you wish. Bring water.

Ernest Coe Visitor Center   PARK
(305-242-7700; www.nps.gov/ever; Hwy 9336; 8am-5pm) Those with a day to give the Glades could start with this visitor center in the south. It has excellent, museum-quality exhibits and tons of activity info: the road accesses numerous short trails and lots of top-drawer canoeing opportunities. Call for a schedule of fun ranger-led programs, such as the two-hour 'slough slog.' Most programs start at the nearby Royal Palm Visitor Center (305-242-7700; Hwy 9336; 8am-4:15pm), where you can catch two short trails. The Anhinga Trail is great for wildlife spotting, especially alligators in winter, and the Gumbo-Limbo showcases plants and trees.

Flamingo Visitor Center   PARK
(239-695-2945; 8am-4:15pm) From Royal Palm, Hwy 9336 cuts through the belly of the park for 38 miles until it reaches the isolated Flamingo Visitor Center, which has maps of canoeing and hiking trails. Call ahead about the status of facilities: the former Flamingo Lodge was wiped out by hurricanes in 2005, and at the time of research Flamingo Marina (239-695-3101) was closed for renovations. It should reopen again and offer backcountry boat tours and kayak/canoe rentals for self-guided trips along the coast.

Gulf Coast Visitor Center   PARK
(239-695-3311; 815 Oyster Bar Lane, off Hwy 29, Everglades City; 9am-4:30pm) Those with more time should also consider visiting the northwestern edge of the Everglades, where the mangroves and waterways of the 10,000 Islands offer incredible canoeing and kayaking opportunities, and great boat tours with a chance to spot dolphins. The visitor center is next to the marina, with rentals (from $13 per hour) and various guided boat trips (from $25). Everglades City also has other private tour operators who can get you camping in the 10,000 Islands.

Sleeping

Everglades National Park has two developed campgrounds (877-444-6777; www.recreation.gov; campsites Nov-Apr $16, low season free). The best are the first-come, first-served sites at Long Pine Key (305-242-7873); reserve ahead for campsites at Flamingo. They both have water, toilets and grills; Flamingo adds cold-water showers and electricity. Camping is free in summer because it's brutally hot and wet.

Backcountry camping (permit $10, plus per person per night $2) is throughout the park and includes beach sites, ground sites and chickees (covered wooden platforms above the water). A permit from the visitor center is required.

Around the Everglades

Coming from Miami, the gateway town of Homestead on the east side of the park can make a good base, especially if you're headed for the Keys.

BISCAYNE NATIONAL PARK

Just south of Miami (and east of Homestead), this national park is only 5% land. The 95% that's water is Biscayne National Underwater Park (305-230-1100; www.nps.gov/bisc, www.biscayneunderwater.com), containing a portion of the world's third-largest coral reef, where manatees, dolphins and sea turtles highlight a vibrant, diverse ecosystem. Get general park information from Dante Fascell Visitor Center (305-230-7275; 9700 SW 328th St, Homestead; 8:30am-5pm). The park offers canoe/kayak rentals, snorkel and dive trips, and popular three-hour glass-bottom boat tours; all require reservations.

HOMESTEAD & FLORIDA CITY

Homestead and Florida City don't look like much, but they have some true Everglades highlights. Without question the most heart-warming is the **Everglades Outpost** (☎305-247-8000; www.evergladesoutpost.org; 35601 SW 192nd Ave, Homestead; admission $20; ◷10am-4pm Sat & Sun, by appointment Mon-Fri), which cares for neglected and abused wild animals; residents include gibbons, wolves, cobras and a pair of majestic tigers.

Much more than a farmer's stand, **Robert Is Here** (☎305-246-1592; www.robertishere.com; 19200 SW 344th St, Homestead; ◷8am-7pm Nov-Aug) is a kitschy Old Florida institution with a petting zoo, live music and crazy-good milk shakes.

The Homestead–Florida City area has no shortage of chain motels; try Rt 1 Krome Ave. If you don't mind hostel living, seriously consider the **Everglades International Hostel** (☎305-248-1122; www.evergladeshostel. com; 20 SW 2nd Ave, Florida City; camping/dm/r $18/28/75; P❄@☎). Rooms are good value, the vibe is very friendly, but the back gardens – wow. It's a fantasia of natural delights, and the hostel conducts some of the best Everglades tours around. For a more pampered, personal touch than the chain hotels, book a room at the historic **Redland Hotel** (☎305-246-1904; www.redlandhotel.com; 5 S Flagler Ave, Homestead; r $83-150; P☎). Homestead's modestly quaint main street, along Krome Ave, is the central restaurant and shopping district.

TAMIAMI TRAIL
The Tamiami Trail/Hwy 41 starts in Miami and beelines to Naples along the north edge of Everglades National Park.

The first sign you've left the city behind is **Pit BBQ** (16400 SW 8th St; mains $4-9; ◷11am-

11:30pm), between Shark Valley and Miami. A bastion of country music and Confederate flags, it's as cheesy as a dairy.

At the entrance to the Everglades' Shark Valley is **Miccosukee Village** (☎305-552-8365; www.miccosukee.com; village/airboat ride $8/10; ◷9am-5pm), an informative, entertaining open-air museum showcasing Miccosukee culture. Tour traditional homes, attend performances (from dance to gator wrestling), take an airboat ride and peruse handmade crafts in the gift store.

About 20 miles west of Shark Valley, you reach the **Oasis Visitor Center** (☎239-695-1201; ◷9am-4:30pm) for 1139-sq-mile **Big Cypress National Preserve** (www.nps.gov/bicy). Good exhibits and short trails bring the region's ecology to life, though the adventurous might consider tackling a portion of the **Florida National Scenic Trail** (www.florida trail.org); 31 miles cut through Big Cypress.

Half a mile east of the visitor center, drop into the **Big Cypress Gallery** (☎941-695-2428; www.clydebutcher.com; 52388 Tamiami Trail; ◷10am-5pm Wed-Mon), displaying Clyde Butcher's work; his large-scale B&W landscape photographs spotlight the region's unusual beauty.

The tiny town of **Ochopee** is home to the country's smallest post office. If that's not enough to make you pull over, then stop into the eccentric **Skunk Ape Research Headquarters** (☎239-695-2275; www.skunkape.info; 40904 Tamiami Trail E; ◷7am-7pm), dedicated to tracking Bigfoot's legendary, if stinky, Everglades kin. They're goofy but sincere. Based out of Skunk Ape HQ, **Everglades Adventure Tours** (☎800-504-6554; www.ever gladesadventuretours.com; tours from $69) offers knowledgeable swamp hikes, 'safaris,' airboats, and best of all, trips being poled around in a canoe or skiff.

Finally, just east of Ochopee, is the quintessential 1950s-style swamp shack, **Joanie's Blue Crab Cafe** (☎239-695-2682; 39395 Tamiami Trail; mains $9-15; ◷10am-5pm Wed-Mon), with open rafters, colorful, shellacked picnic tables and a swamp dinner of gator nuggets and fritters.

EVERGLADES CITY
This small town at the edge of the park makes a good base for exploring the 10,000 Islands region. With large renovated rooms, **Everglades City Motel** (☎239-695-4244; www.evergladescitymotel.com; 310 Collier Ave; r from $80; ❄☎) is an exceptionally good value, and the fantastically friendly staff can hook

A KINDER, GENTLER WILDERNESS ENCOUNTER

As you explore Florida's outdoors and encounter its wildlife, keep in mind the following guidelines.

» **Airboats and swamp buggies** For exploring wetlands, airboats are better than big-wheeled buggies, but nonmotorized (and silent) canoes and kayaks are least-damaging and disruptive.

» **Wild dolphins** Captive dolphins are typically rescued animals already acclimated to humans. However, federal law makes it illegal to feed, pursue or touch wild dolphins in the ocean.

» **Manatee swims** When swimming near manatees, a federally protected endangered species, look but don't touch. 'Passive observation' is the standard.

» **Feeding wild animals** In a word, don't. Acclimating wild animals to humans usually leads to the animal's death, whether because of accidents or aggression.

» **Sea-turtle nesting sites** It's a federal crime to approach nesting sea turtles or hatchling runs. Observe beach warning signs. If you encounter nesting turtles, keep your distance and no flash photos.

» **Coral-reef etiquette** Never touch the coral reef. It's that simple. Coral polyps are living organisms. Touching or breaking coral creates openings for infection and disease.

you up with any kind of tour. The same can be said for the Ivey House Bed & Breakfast (☎239-695-3299; www.iveyhouse.com; 107 Camellia St; lodge $74-120, inn $99-209; ❄️🛜). Choose between basic lodge accommodations or somewhat sprucer inn rooms, then book some of the region's best nature trips with the on-site Everglades Adventure Tours (☎941-695-3299/4666; www.evergladesadventures.com; tours $25-65; ☀️Nov–mid-Apr). Ask about room/tour packages.

A mile or so south, JT's Island Grill & Gallery (☎239-695-3633; 238 Mamie St, Chokoloskee; mains $5-16; ☀️11am-3pm late Oct-May) serves up delicious lunches in a restored 1890 general store with retro kitsch and charm to spare.

For dinner, try the Seafood Depot (☎239-695-0075; 102 Collier Ave; mains $14-33; ☀️10:30am-9pm), a haven of fried seafood and a great place to sample gator and frog's legs; just douse with Tabasco and devour.

Florida Keys

Before Henry Flagler completed his railroad in 1912, which connected the Keys to the mainland, this 126-mile string of islands was just a series of untethered bumps of land accessible only by boat. (Little surprise, then, that their early economies were built on piracy, smuggling, ship salvaging and fishing.) Flagler's railroad was destroyed by a hurricane in 1935, but what remained of its bridges allowed the Overseas Hwy to be completed in 1938. Now, streams of travelers swarm down from the mainland to indulge in the alluring jade-green waters, laid-back island lifestyle, great fishing, and idyllic snorkeling and diving.

The islands are typically divided into the Upper Keys (Key Largo to Islamorada), Middle Keys and Lower Keys (from Little Duck Key). Yet far from petering out, they crescendo at highway's end, reaching their grand finale in Key West – the Keys' gloriously unkempt, bawdy, freak-loving exclamation point.

Many addresses in the Keys are noted by their proximity to mile markers (indicated as MM), which start at MM126 in Florida City and count down to MM0 in Key West. They also might indicate whether they're 'oceanside' (the south side of the highway) or 'bayside' (which is north).

The Florida Keys & Key West Visitors Bureau (☎800-352-5397; www.fla-keys.com) has information; also check www.keysnews.com.

KEY LARGO

Stretching from Key Largo to Islamorada, the Upper Keys are cluttered with touristy shops and motels. At first you can't even see the water from the highway, then – bam – you're in Islamorada and water is everywhere.

Key Largo has long been romanticized in movies and song, so it can be a shock to arrive and find...no Bogart, no Bacall, no lovesick Sade. Yes, Key Largo is underwhelming, a sleepy island and town with middling views. That is, if all you do is stick to the highway and keep your head above water. Root down side roads for those legendary island idiosyncracies, and dive underwater for the most amazing coral reef in the continental US.

For maps and brochures, visit the **chamber of commerce** (☑305-451-4747; www.key largo.org; MM 106 bayside; ⊙9am-6pm).

◉ Sights & Activities

John Pennekamp Coral Reef State Park PARK
(☑305-451-6300; www.pennekamppark.com; MM 102.5 oceanside; car/pedestrian or bicycle $8/2; ⊙8am-sunset) This park has boardwalk trails through mangroves and a cute aquarium, but as the USA's first underwater park, it's true jewel box is beneath the sea, a vast living coral reef that's home to a panoply of sea life (and the oft-photographed statue *Christ of the Deep*).

Your options for seeing the reef are many: take a 2½-hour **glass-bottom boat tour** (adult/child $24/17; ⊙9:15am, 12:15pm & 3pm) on a thoroughly modern 38ft catamaran. Dive in with a **snorkeling trip** (adult/child $30/25) or two-tank **diving trip** (☑305-451-6322; $60); half-day trips leave twice daily, usually around 9am and 1pm. Or go DIY and rent a **canoe or kayak** (per hr single/double $12/17) and journey through a 3-mile network of water trails. Call the park for boat-rental information.

Florida Bay Outfitters KAYAKING
(☑305-451-3018; www.kayakfloridakeys.com; MM 104 bayside; kayak rental per half-day $40) All sorts of guided kayak trips and rentals.

Horizon Divers DIVING
(☑305-453-3535; www.horizondivers.com; 100 Ocean Dr, off MM 100 oceanside; snorkel/scuba trips $50/80) Friendly crew; offers rentals, dive trips and scuba instruction.

⌸ Sleeping

In addition to luxe resorts, Key Largo has loads of bright, cheery motels and camping.

Largo Lodge HOTEL $$
(☑305-451-0424; www.largolodge.com; MM 102 bayside; cottages $125-195; ℗) These six charming, sunny cottages with their own private beach – family owned since the '50s – are surrounded by palm trees, tropical flowers and lots of roaming birds, for a taste of Florida in the good old days.

Key Largo House Boatel HOUSEBOAT $$
(☑305-766-0871; www.keylargohouseboatel.com; Shoreland Dr, MM 103.5 oceanside; houseboats from $75-150) These five houseboats are a steal. The largest is incredibly spacious, sleeping six people comfortably. The boats are right on the docks, so no possibility of being isolated from land (or booze). Call for directions.

Kona Kai Resort & Gallery HOTEL $$$
(☑305-852-7200; www.konakairesort.com; MM 97.8 bayside; r $199-369; ℗❋◈☎◲) This intimate hideaway features 11 airy rooms and suites (with full kitchens). They're all bright and comfortable, but some feel a little too old-fashioned. Tons of activities, plus its own beach.

John Pennekamp Coral Reef State Park CAMPGROUND $
(☑800-326-3521; www.pennekamppark.com; camp-sites $32) Sleep near the fishes at one of the 47 coral-reef-adjacent sites here. Camping's popular; reserve well in advance.

✕ Eating & Drinking

TOP CHOICE **Key Largo Conch House** FUSION $$
(☑305-453-4844; www.keylargocoffeehouse.com; MM 100.2 oceanside; mains $8-25; ⊙7am-10pm) Now *this* feels like the islands: conch architecture, tropical foliage, a parrot, and crab and conch dishes that ease you off the mainland.

Mrs Mac's Kitchen AMERICAN $$
(MM 99.4 bayside; mains $7-18; ⊙7am-9:30pm Mon-Sat) This cute roadside diner bedecked with rusty license plates serves classic highway food such as burgers and fish baskets.

Fish House SEAFOOD $$
(☑305-451-4665; www.fishhouse.com; MM 102.4 oceanside; mains $12-28; ⊙11:30am-10pm) Delivers on its name, serving fish, fish and more fish that's as fresh as it gets. Your main decision: fried, broiled, jerked, blackened or grilled?

Alabama Jack's BAR
(http://alabamajacks.com; 58000 Card Sound Rd; mains $5-25; ⊙11am-7pm) On the back road between Key Largo and Florida City, this funky open-air joint draws an eclectic booze-hungry crowd of genuine Keys characters. Try the rave-worthy conch fritters.

ISLAMORADA

Things finally get pretty around Islamorada, which is actually a long string of several islands (from MM90 to MM74); the epicenter is Upper Matecumbe Key. Several little nooks of beach are easily accessible, providing scenic rest stops. Housed in an old red caboose, the **chamber of commerce** (☑305-664-4503; www.islamoradachamber.com; MM 83.2 bayside; ⊙9am-5pm Mon-Fri, 10am-3pm Sat & Sun) has area information.

◉ Sights & Activities

Billed as 'the Sportfishing Capital of the World,' Islamorada is an angler's paradise. Indeed, most of its highlights involve getting on or in the sea.

TOP
CHOICE **Robbie's Marina** MARINA
(☑305-664-9814; www.robbies.com; MM 77.5 bayside; ⊙8am-6pm) This marina/roadside attraction offers the buffet of boating options: fishing charters, jet skiing, party boats, ecotours, snorkeling trips, kayak rentals and more (come here to visit the area's island parks). At a minimum, stop to feed the freakishly large tarpon from the dock ($3 per bucket, $1 to watch), and sift the flea market/tourist shop for tacky seaside trinkets.

Indian Key Historic State Park ISLAND
(☑305-664-2540; www.floridastateparks.org/indiankey; ⊙8am-sunset) A few hundred yards offshore, this peaceful little island contains the derelict, crumbling foundations of a 19th-century settlement that was wiped out by Native Americans during the Second Seminole War. It's a moody ramble, accessible only by kayak or boat.

Lignumvitae Key State Botanical Park ISLAND
(☑305-664-2540; www.floridastateparks.org/lignumvitaekey; ⊙9am-5pm Thu-Mon) It'll feel like just you and about a jillion mosquitoes on this bayside island park, with virgin tropical forests and the 1919 Matheson House. Come for the shipwrecked isolation. Robbie's Marina offers boat rentals and tours.

Florida Keys History of Diving Museum MUSEUM
(www.divingmuseum.org; MM 83; adult/child $12/6; ⊙10am-5pm, to 7pm Wed) Don't miss this collection of diving paraphernalia from around the world, including diving 'suits' and technology from the 19th century. This charmingly eccentric museum embodies the quirky Keys.

Theater of the Sea DOLPHIN ENCOUNTER
(☑305-664-2431; www.theaterofthesea.com; MM 84.5 bayside; adult/child $27/19.45; ⊙9:30am-4pm) Dolphins and sea lions perform in an intimate, close-up setting, and for an extra fee you can meet or swim with them.

Windley Key Fossil Reef Geological State Site PARK
(☑305-664-2540; www.floridastateparks.org/windleykey; MM 85.5 oceanside) Check out layer after layer of geological history in the quarry, with 8ft walls of fossilized coral.

FREE **Anne's Beach** BEACH
(MM 73.5 oceanside) The area's best public beach; shaded picnic tables and a bright ribbon of sand.

⌂ Sleeping & Eating

Casa Morada BOUTIQUE HOTEL **$$$**
(☑305-664-0044; www.casamorada.com; 136 Madeira Rd, off MM 82.2; ste summer $239-459, winter $299-659; P❋◉❦) Come for a welcome dash of South Beach sophistication mixed with laid-back Keys style. The slick bar is a great oceanside sunset perch.

Ragged Edge Resort RESORT **$$**
(☑305-852-5389; www.ragged-edge.com; 243 Treasure Harbor Rd; apt $69-259; P❋❦) Swim off the docks at this happily unpretentious oceanfront complex off MM 86.5. It has 10 spotless and popular efficiencies and apartments, and a happily comatose vibe.

Long Key State Recreation Area CAMPGROUND **$**
(☑305-664-4815, 305-326-3521; www.floridastateparks.org/longkey; MM 67.5; campsites $38.50) Book as far ahead as possible for the 60 coveted oceanfront campsites in this shady, 965-acre park.

Midway Cafe CAFE **$**
(80499 Overseas Hwy; mains under $5; ⊙7am-3pm Thu-Tue, to 2pm Sun) The lovely folks who run this art-filled cafe roast their own beans and make destination-worthy baked goods. Celebrate your Keys adventure with a friendly cup of joe.

Morada Bay AMERICAN **$$$**
(☑305-664-0604; www.moradabay-restaurant.com; MM 81.6 bayside; lunch $10-15, dinner $21-29; ⊙11:30am-10pm) Grab a table under a palm tree on the white-sand beach and sip a rum drink with your fresh seafood for a lovely, easygoing Caribbean experience. Don't miss the monthly full-moon party.

Hog Heaven BAR **$$**
(☑305-664-9669; MM 83 oceanside; mains $10-18; ⊙11am-3:30am) From sandwiches and salads

to seafood nachos and T-bone steaks, the diverse menu rocks. Come during happy hour (4pm to 8pm) and bring a designated driver; the drinks are practically free.

GRASSY KEY

To reach Grassy Key in the Middle Keys, you enjoy a vivid sensation of island-hopping, ending with the biggest hop, the Seven Mile Bridge, one of the world's longest causeways.

Sedate Grassy Key was once the village-like heart of the Keys. Today, the main reason for travelers to pause is the Dolphin Research Center (305-289-1121; www.dolphins.org; MM 59 bayside; adult/child $20/15, swim program $180-650; 9am-4pm). Of all the dolphin swimming spots in the Keys, this is preferred simply because the dolphins are free to leave the grounds and a lot of marine-biology research goes on behind the scenes.

MARATHON

Halfway between Key Largo and Key West, Marathon is the most sizable town between them; it's a good base and a hub for commercial fishing and lobster boats. Get local information at the visitor center (305-743-5417; www.floridakeysmarathon.com; MM 53.5 bayside; 9am-5pm).

⊙ Sights & Activities

Crane Point Museum   MUSEUM
(www.cranepoint.net; MM 50.5 bayside; adult/child $12.50/8.50; 9am-5pm Mon-Sat, from noon Sun) Escape all the development at this 63-acre reserve, where you'll find a vast system of nature trails and mangroves, a raised boardwalk and a rare early-20th-century Bahamian-style house. Kids will enjoy pirate and wreck exhibits, a walk-through coral reef tunnel and the bird hospital.

Turtle Hospital   ANIMAL SANCTUARY
(305-743-2552; www.theturtlehospital.org; 2396 Overseas Hwy; adult/child $15/7.50; 9am-6pm) Call ahead to make sure hospital staff are around. This labor of love is a heart-warming encounter with injured and diseased sea turtles, who are sweetly cared for.

**Pigeon Key National
Historic District**   ISLAND
(305-743-5999; www.pigeonkey.net; adult/child $12/9; tours 10am, 11:30am, 1pm & 2:30pm) On the Marathon side of Seven Mile Bridge, this tiny key served as a camp for the workers who toiled to build the Overseas Hwy in the 1930s. You can tour the historic structures or just sun and snorkel on the beach. Reach it by ferry, included in admission. Also here, the Old Seven Mile Bridge is closed to traffic and serves as the 'World's Longest Fishing Bridge.'

Sombrero Beach   BEACH
(Sombrero Beach Rd, off MM 50 oceanside) One of the few white-sand, mangrove-free beaches in the Keys; good swimming.

Marathon Kayak   KAYAKING
(305-395-0355; www.marathonkayak.com; 6363 Overseas Hwy/MM 50 oceanside) Kayak instruction and three-hour guided eco-tours (from $45 per person).

🍴 Sleeping & Eating

Seascape   MOTEL $$
(305-743-6212; 1275 76th St, btwn MM 51 & 52; r from $125; P✳︎🛜🏊♿) The classy, understated luxury in this B&B manifests in the nine rooms, which all have a different feel, from old-fashioned cottage to sleek boutique. Seascape also has a waterfront pool, kayaks for guest use and includes breakfast.

Siesta Motel   MOTEL $
(305-743-5671; www.siestamotel.net; MM 51 oceanside; r $75-105; P✳︎🛜) Head here for one of the cheapest, cleanest flops in the Keys, located in a friendly cluster of cute Marathon homes – with great service, to boot.

Keys Fisheries   SEAFOOD $
(305-743-4353; 35th St, off MM 49 bayside; mains $7-16; 11:30am-9pm) Shoo the seagulls from your picnic table on the deck and dig in to fresh seafood in a down-and-dirty dockside atmosphere. The lobster reuben is the stuff of legend.

Hurricane   AMERICAN $$
(www.hurricaneblues.com; MM 49.5 bayside; mains $12-19; 11am-midnight) As well as being a favorite Marathon bar, the Hurricane also serves an excellent menu of creative South Florida–inspired goodness, like snapper stuffed with crabmeat and conch sliders jerked in Caribbean seasoning.

Wooden Spoon   AMERICAN $
(MM 51 oceanside; mains $3-9; 7am-3pm) It's the best breakfast around, served by sweet Southern women who know their way around a diner. The biscuits are fluffy, the sausage gravy is delicious, and the grits buttery and creamy.

LOWER KEYS

The Lower Keys (MM 46 to MM 0) are fierce bastions of conch culture in all its variety. The **chamber of commerce** (☑305-872-2411; www.lowerkeyschamber.com; MM 31 oceanside; ⊙9am-5pm Mon-Fri, to 3pm Sat) is on Big Pine Key.

One of Florida's most acclaimed beaches – and certainly the best in the Keys for its shallow, warm water – is at **Bahia Honda State Park** (www.bahiahondapark.com; MM 36.8 oceanside; per car/bicycle $5/2; ⊙8am-sunset), a 524-acre park with nature trails, ranger-led programs and water-sports rentals. Snorkel some of the best coral reefs outside Key Largo.

Drive slowly: along the highway in Big Pine Key is the 84,000-acre **National Key Deer Refuge**. Stop by or contact the **visitor center** (☑305-872-2239; www.fws.gov/nation alkeydeer; MM30.5 bayside; ⊙8am-5pm Mon-Fri) at Big Pine Shopping Center to learn more about these endangered, miniature deer and the trails where you can view them; Key Deer are easiest to spot at dusk and dawn.

Looe Key (floridakeys.noaa.gov) is actually an offshore marine sanctuary teeming with colorful tropical fish and coral; try **Looe Key Dive Center** (☑305-872-2215; www.diveflakeys. com; MM 27.5 oceanside; snorkel/dive $44/84) on Ramrod Key for snorkeling and diving day trips; the sanctuary contains wreck dives as well.

To spend the night, camping at **Bahia Honda State Park** (☑800-326-3521; campsites/cabins $36/160) is sublime; it'd be perfect except for the sandflies. There are also six popular waterfront cabins. Reserve far ahead for all. For a completely different experience, book one of the four cozily scrumptious rooms at **Deer Run Bed & Breakfast** (☑305-872-2015; www.deerunflori dabb.com; 1997 Long Beach Dr, Big Pine Key, off MM 33 oceanside; r $235-355; ❄☀). This state-certified green lodge and vegetarian B&B is a garden of quirky delights, and the owners are extremely helpful and decidedly not self-righteous.

It's hard to miss the jumbo shrimp statue that marks your arrival at the **Good Food Conspiracy** (☑305-872-3945; MM 30 oceanside; mains $7-10; ⊙9:30am-7pm Mon-Sat, 11am-5pm Sun), where you'll find healthy hippie food along with your classic Keys photo op.

The proprietors at the **No Name Pub** (☑305-872-9115; N Watson Blvd, off MM 30.5 bayside; mains $8-20; ⊙11am-11pm), 1.5 miles north of US 1 on Big Pine Key, know where their retirement is coming from: the approximately $60,000 in $1 bills stapled to the walls by customers; stop by for pizza, beer and kooky ambience.

KEY WEST

While parts of Big Pine Key would fit easily in Florida's rural Panhandle, crazy, cultured, gay-friendly Key West would fit nowhere else. It's an eccentric frontier town that fosters and promotes its own brand of funky insanity. Perhaps this is a quirk of geography: Key West is the literal end of the road on the map of the continental US, closer to Cuba than the rest of America and a welcoming port for all sorts of global wayfarers. Or perhaps, as a local saying goes, 'They shook the United States and all the nuts fell to the bottom.'

Artists, renegades, homosexuals and free spirits have long made Key West their own. It's impossible to tease apart high and low culture: on one side are expensive art galleries, literary festivals, Caribbean villas and Hemingway's legacy. On the other are S&M fetish parades, frat boys toppling black-out drunk and 30-something women tossing their bras to the rafters.

Originally called 'Cayo Hueso' – Spanish for 'Bone Island' – Key West was named for all the skeletons that early explorers found littering the beach. These days, people flock to Key West to soak up the sun, the mellow atmosphere, more than a little booze, and to reset their internal clocks to 'island time.'

◎ Sights

Key West has more than its fair share of historic homes, buildings and districts (like the colorful Bahama Village); it's a walkable town that rewards exploring. Naturally, you'll snap a pic at the USA's much ballyhooed **Southernmost Point Marker**; just know that the red-and-black buoy isn't even the proper southernmost point on Key West.

TOP CHOICE ⬥ Mallory Square   SQUARE

Sunset at Mallory Sq, at the end of Duval St, is a bizzaro attraction of the highest order. It takes all those energies, subcultures and oddities of Keys life – the hippies, the rednecks, the foreigners and the tourists – and focuses them into one torchlit, playfully edgy (but family-friendly) street party. Come for the jugglers, fire-eaters, sassy acrobats and tightrope-walking dogs, and stay for the after-dark madness.

Duval Street
STREET

Key West locals have a love–hate relationship with their island's most famous road. Duval, Old Town Key West's main drag, is a miracle mile of booze, tacky everything and awful behavior that still manages, somehow, to be fun. At the end of the night, the 'Duval Crawl' is one of the best pub crawls in the country.

Hemingway House
HOUSE

(☏305-294-1136; www.hemingwayhome.com; 907 Whitehead St; adult/child $12.50/6; ◷9am-5pm) Ernest Hemingway lived in this Spanish-Colonial house from 1931 to 1940 – to write, drink and fish, if not always in that order. Tours run every half-hour, and as you listen to docent-spun yarns of Papa, you'll see his studio, his unusual pool, and the descendents of his six-toed cats languishing in the sun, on furniture and pretty much wherever they feel like.

FREE Florida Keys Eco-Discovery Center
MUSEUM

(☏305-809-4750; http://eco-discovery.com/ecokw. html; 35 East Quay Rd; ◷9am-4pm Tue-Sat) This excellent nature center pulls together all the plants, animals and habitats that make up the Keys' unique ecosystem and presents them in fresh, accessible ways. A great place for kids and the big picture.

Key West Cemetery
CEMETERY

(cnr Margaret & Angela Sts) This dark, alluring Gothic labyrinth is in the center of town. Livening up the mausoleums are famous epitaphs like 'I told you I was sick.'

Key West Butterfly & Nature Conservatory
ANIMAL SANCTUARY

(☏305-296-2988; www.keywestbutterfly.com; 1316 Duval St; adult/child $12/8.50; ◷9am-5pm) Even if you have only the faintest interest in butterflies, you'll find yourself entranced by the sheer quantity flittering around you here.

Museum of Art & History at the Custom House
MUSEUM

(☏305-295-6616; www.kwahs.com/customhouse; 281 Front St; adult/child $7/5; ◷9:30am-4:30pm) Offering a more low-key, less swashbuckling version of Key West history, this is an interesting collection of folklore, international art and historical exhibits housed in the impressive former Customs House.

Fort East Martello Museum & Gardens
MUSEUM

(☏305-296-3913; www.kwahs.com/martello.htm; 3501 S Roosevelt Blvd; adult/child $7/5; ◷9:30am-4:30pm) This fortress preserves interesting historical artifacts and some fabulous folk art by Mario Sanchez and 'junk' sculptures by Stanley Papio. Yet Martello's most famous resident – Robert the Doll – is a genuinely creepy, supposedly haunted, 19th-century doll that's kept in a glass case to keep him from making mischief.

FLORIDA FLORIDA KEYS

WORTH A TRIP

DRY TORTUGAS

Seventy miles west of the Keys in the middle of the Gulf, **Dry Tortugas National Park** (☏305-242-7700; www.nps.gov/drto) is America's most inaccessible national park. Reachable only by boat or plane, it rewards your efforts to get there with amazing snorkeling, diving, bird-watching and stargazing.

Ponce de León christened the area *Las Tortugas* (the Turtles) after the abundant sea turtles; a lack of fresh water led sailors to add 'dry.' But this is more than just a pretty cluster of islands with no drinking water. The never-completed Civil War–era **Fort Jefferson** provides a striking hexagonal centerpiece of red brick rising up from the emerald waters on **Garden Key** – which has a visitor center and 13 first-come, first-served **campsites** (per person per night $3). Reserve far ahead, and bring everything you need, including water, though you might be able to barter with the Cuban-American fishing boats for lobster.

To get there, the **Yankee Freedom II** (☏305-294-7009; www.yankeefreedom.com) operates a fast ferry between Garden Key and the Historic Seaport (north end of Margaret St). Round-trip fares cost $165/120 per adult/child. Reserve ahead; includes breakfast, a picnic lunch, snorkeling gear and tour of the fort.

Key West Seaplanes (☏305-294-0709; www.seaplanesofkeywest.com) can take up to 10 passengers. A four-hour trip costs $250/190 per adult/child; an eight-hour trip costs $515/365. Reserve a week ahead.

⚓ Activities

Fort Zachary Taylor BEACH
(www.floridastateparks.org/forttaylor; per car/pedestrian $6/2; ⊙8am-sunset) Key West has three city beaches, but they aren't special; most head to Bahia Honda. That said, Fort Zachary Taylor has the best beach on Key West, with white sand, decent swimming and some near-shore snorkeling; it's great for sunsets and picnics.

Dive Key West DIVING
(☎305-296-3823; www.divekeywest.com) Key West generally doesn't have great reefs for snorkeling, but it has some wreck diving, such as a massive WWII ship sunk purposefully in 2009. Dive Key West arranges trips.

Subtropic Dive Center DIVING
(☎305-296-9914; www.subtropic.com) Arranges wreck-diving trips.

Charter Boat Key West FISHING
(www.charterboatkeywest.com) Fishing and cruising charters.

Reelax Charters KAYAKING
(☎305-304-1392; www.keyskayaking.com; MM 17 Sugarloaf Key Marina; kayak trips $200) Runs guided kayaks from nearby Sugarloaf Key.

Jolly II Rover CRUISE
(☎305-304-2235; www.schoonerjollyrover.com; cnr Greene & Elizabeth Sts. Schooner Wharf; cruise $39) Book a sunset cruise on a pirate ship.

☞ Tours

Both the **Conch Tour Train** (☎305-294-5161; adult/child $29/26; ⊙9am-4:30pm) and **Old Town Trolley** (☎305-296-6688; adult/child $29/26; ⊙9am-4:30pm) offer tours leaving from Mallory Sq. The train offers a 90-minute narrated tour in a breezy, open car, while the hop-on/hop-off trolley makes 12 stops around town.

Original Ghost Tours GHOST
(☎305-294-9255; www.hauntedtours.com; 423 Fleming St; adult/child $15/10; ⊙8pm & 9pm) Is your guesthouse haunted? Probably. Why should you fear Robert the Doll in East Martello? Don't ask.

✹✹ Festivals & Events

Key West hosts a party every sunset, but residents don't need an excuse to go crazy.

Conch Republic
Independence Celebration CULTURE
(www.conchrepublic.com) A 10-day tribute to Conch Independence, held every April; vie for (made-up) public offices and watch a drag queens footrace.

Hemingway Days Festival CULTURE
(www.hemingwaydays.net) Includes a bull run, marlin tournament and look-alike contest, as well as literary events, in late July.

Fantasy Fest CULTURE
(www.fantasyfest.net) Room rates get hiked to the hilt for this raucous, 10-day Halloween-meets-Carnivale event in late October.

🛏 Sleeping

Key West lodging is generally pretty expensive – especially in the wintertime and even *more* especially during special events, when room rates can triple. Book ahead, or you may well end up joining the long traffic jam headed back to the mainland.

You can find chain motels in New Town, but you've got to stay in Old Town to truly experience Key West. Visit the **Key West Innkeepers Association** (www.keywestinns. com) for more guesthouses; pretty much all are gay-friendly.

Curry Mansion Inn HOTEL $$$
(☎305-294-5349; http://currymansion.com; 511 Caroline St; r winter $240-365, summer $195-285; P❄✳🔊❄) In a city full of stately 19th-century homes, the Curry Mansion is especially handsome. It's a pleasing mix of aristocratic American elements, but especially the bright Floridian rooms with canopied beds. Enjoy bougainvillea and breezes on the verandah.

Mermaid & the Alligator GUESTHOUSE $$$
(☎305-294-1894; www.kwmermaid.com; 729 Truman Ave; r winter $218-298, summer $148-198; P❄✳@🔊❄) Book way ahead: with only nine rooms, this place's charm exceeds its capacity. It's chock-a-block with treasures collected from the owners' travels, giving it a worldly flair that's simultaneously European and Zen.

L'Habitation GUESTHOUSE $$
(☎305-293-9203; www.lhabitation.com; 408 Eaton St; r $109-179; ✳🔊) At this beautiful classic Keys cottage, the friendly, bilingual owners welcome guests in English or French. The cute rooms come kitted out in light tropical shades, with lamps that look like contemporary art pieces and skittles-bright quilts.

Big Ruby's Guesthouse HOTEL $$$
(☎305-296-2323; www.bigrubys.com; 409 Appelrouth Lane; r $195-305; P❄🔊❄) Catering exclusively to a gay clientele, the hotel's exterior is all refined Conch mansion, while

inside, the rooms are sleekly contemporary. The capper is the clothing-optional lagoon pool. Breakfast is included.

Caribbean House
GUESTHOUSE $

(☑305-296-0999; www.geocities.com/caribbean housekw; 226 Petronia St; r from $85; P✲@) In the heart of Bahama Village, rooms are tiny, but they're clean, cozy and cheery. Add free breakfast and welcoming hosts and you get a rare find in Key West: a bargain.

Key Lime Inn
HOTEL $$

(☑800-559-4430; www.historickeywestinns.com; 725 Truman Ave; r $99-229; P🅿🛜🏊) These cozy cottages are scattered around a tropical hardwood backdrop. Inside, the blissfully cool rooms are greener than a jade mine, with wicker furniture and tiny flat-screens to keep you from ever leaving.

✕ Eating

You aren't technically allowed to leave the island without sampling the conch fritters – like hushpuppies, but made with conch – or the key lime pie, made with key limes, sweetened condensed milk, eggs and sugar on a Graham-cracker crust.

TOP CHOICE Café Solé
FRENCH $$$

(☑305-294-0230; www.cafesole.com; 1029 Southard St; lunch $5-11, dinner $25-32; ⏰5:30-10pm) Conch carpaccio with capers? Yellowtail fillet and foie gras? Oh yes. This locally and critically acclaimed venue is known for its cozy back-porch ambience and innovative menus, the result of a French-trained chef exploring island ingredients.

Mo's Restaurant
CARIBBEAN $$

(http://salsalocakeywest.com; 1116 White St; mains $11-16; ⏰11am-10pm Mon-Sat) If the phrase 'Caribbean home cooking' causes drool to form in the corners of your mouth, don't hesitate. The dishes are mainly Haitian, and they're delicious.

Blue Heaven
AMERICAN $$$

(☑305-296-8666; http://blueheavenkw.homestead.com; 729 Thomas St; dinner $19-38; ⏰8am-3pm & 5-10pm) One of the island's quirkiest venues (and it's a high bar), where you dine in an outdoor courtyard with a flock of chickens. Customers gladly wait, bemusedly, for Blue Heaven's well-executed, Southern-fried interpretation of Keys cuisine.

Camille's
FUSION $$

(☑305-296-4811; 1202 Simonton St; lunch $4-13, dinner $14-25; ⏰8am-10pm; ♪) This healthy and tasty neighborhood joint is where local families go for a casual meal. Still, homey Camille's keeps its knives sharp, and the inventive menu ranges from French toast with Godiva liqueur to tasty chicken salad.

El Siboney
CUBAN $$

(900 Catherine St; mains $10-16; ⏰11am-9:30pm) Key West is only 90 miles from Cuba, so this awesome rough-and-ready corner establishment is quite literally the closest you can get to real Cuban food in the US. Cash only.

Conch Town Café
SEAFOOD $

(801 Thomas St; mains $5-18; ⏰11:30am-7:30pm) Many bypass this walk-up/carry-out, with its plastic patio furniture and scruffy island vibe. It's a shame, as it serves deliciously 'cracked' (deep-fried) conch with a lip-puckeringly sour-lime marinade.

🍷 Drinking

Another way to think of Key West is as a floating bar. You can crawl your way along Duval St till about 3am, when most bars close.

TOP CHOICE Green Parrot
BAR

(www.greenparrot.com; 601 Whitehead St) This rogue's cantina has the longest tenure of any bar on the island (since 1890). It's a fabulous dive drawing a lively mix of locals and out-of-towners, with a century's worth of strange decor. Men, don't miss the urinal.

La Te Da
CABARET

(www.lateda.com; 1125 Duval St) Look for drag queens to mark your arrival at this complex that has three bars and a cabaret space famous for its drag shows.

Porch
BAR

(429 Caroline St) Escape the Duval St frat boy bars at the Porch, where knowledgeable bartenders dispense artisan beers. It sounds civilized, and almost is, by Key West standards.

Garden of Eden
BAR

(224 Duval St) You can make like Adam and Eve at this clothing-optional rooftop bar; the fig leaf is also optional.

Captain Tony's Saloon
BAR

(www.capttonyssaloon.com; 428 Greene St) This former icehouse, morgue and Hemingway haunt is built around the town's old hanging tree. The eclectic decor includes emancipated bras and signed dollar bills.

Virgilio's   JAZZ
(www.virgilioskeywest.com; 524 Duval St) Thank
God for a little variety. This town needs a
dark, candlelit martini lounge where you
can chill to jazz and salsa. Enter on Appelrouth Lane.

801 Bourbon Bar   GAY
(www.801bourbon.com; 801 Duval St) Boys will
be boys.

Aqua   GAY & LESBIAN
(www.aquakeywest.com; 711 Duval St) All
genders.

Pearl's Rainbow   LESBIAN
(www.pearlsrainbow.com; 525 United St) Lesbian
pool bar.

ⓘ Information

A great trip-planning resource is www.fla-keys.
com/keywest. In town, get maps and brochures
at **Key West Chamber of Commerce** (☑305-
294-2587; www.keywestchamber.org; 510 Greene
St; ⊘8am-6:30pm Mon-Sat, to 6pm Sun).

Gay and lesbian visitors can get information
at the **Gay & Lesbian Community Center**
(☑305-292-3223; http://lgbtcenter.com; 513
Truman Ave).

ⓘ Getting There & Around

The easiest way to travel around Key West and
the Keys is by car, though traffic along the one
major route, US 1, can be maddening during the
winter high season. **Greyhound** (☑305-296-
9072; www.greyhound.com; 3535 S Roosevelt
Blvd) serves the Keys along US Hwy 1 from
downtown Miami.

You can fly into **Key West International Airport** (EYW; www.keywestinternationalairport.
com) with frequent flights from major cities,
most going through Miami. Or, take a fast cata-
maran from Fort Myers or Miami; call the **Key
West Express** (☑888-539-2628; www.seakey
westexpress.com) for schedules and fares.

Within Key West, bicycles are the preferred
mode of travel (rentals along Duval St run $10
a day). **City Transit System** (www.kwtransit.
com; tickets $2) runs color-coded buses through
downtown and the Lower Keys.

ATLANTIC COAST

Florida's East Coast is a study in contrasts:
there are the astronaut training and (now-
ended) space shuttle launches of Kennedy
Space Center, and the cobblestone streets of
the nation's oldest city, St Augustine. There
are Daytona's screaming, oval Nascar racetrack and the undeveloped beaches and in-
tercoastal waterways of Canaveral National

Seashore. There's rocking out in Jacksonville, skimming stones on Amelia Island,
and catching waves on Cocoa Beach.

Space Coast

They call the Titusville–Cocoa Beach–Melbourne area the Space Coast because it's
home to NASA, but it could just as easily be
referring to the miles of undeveloped beaches and protected national parkland, where
space is plentiful. Once the setting for the
iconic 1960s TV series *I Dream of Jeannie,*
the Space Coast is the real-life home to the
Kennedy Space Center, with its massive visitor complex. Cocoa Beach is also a magnet
for surfers, with Florida's best waves. Visitor
information is available through **Florida's
Space Coast Office of Tourism** (☑321-
433-4470; www.space-coast.com; 430 Brevard Ave,
Cocoa Village; ⊘8am-5pm Mon-Sat).

◉ Sights & Activities

**Kennedy Space Center
Visitor Complex**   MUSEUM
(☑321-449-4444; www.kennedyspacecenter.com;
adult/child $41/31; ⊘9am-5:30pm) Houston, we
have an attraction. It was perhaps inevitable
that, considering its proximity to Orlando,
the space center would develop a ride, and
thus Shuttle Launch Experience officially
achieved lift-off. Reaching a top 'speed' of
17,500mph – vertically – this realistic simulator ride was designed by astronauts to feel
just like a space-shuttle takeoff, but without
the teary goodbyes.

Your ticket to the complex includes a two-
hour bus tour, a 45-minute IMAX film, live-
action stage shows, exhibits on subjects such
as early space exploration and encounters
with astronauts. It also includes the **Astronaut Hall of Fame**, where you'll experience
the G-Force Trainer and other simulator
rides.

Add-on options abound, depending on
how serious you are about your astronaut
experience (they're popular – book in advance). **Discover KSC** (adult/child $21/15)
includes a visit to the massive Vehicle Assembly Building, while **Cape Canaveral:
Then & Now** (adult/child $21/15) is an extend-
ed guided tour that includes the Air Force
Space & Missile Museum. Hungry space
enthusiasts can have **Lunch with an Astronaut** (adult/child $44/33), and the action-
oriented **Astronaut Training Experience**

(ticket $145) prepares you for spaceflight, should the opportunity arise.

As of 2011, NASA ended its space shuttle program indefinitely, which means an end to watching shuttle launches at Kennedy. However, because of this you can expect changes, both with exhibits and visitor facilities as well as with Kennedy's role in the next phase of the US space program.

FREE **Merritt Island**

National Wildlife Refuge WILDLIFE RESERVE
(www.merrittisland.com; SR 402, Titusville; ☉visitor center 8am-4:30pm Mon-Fri, 9am-5pm Sat & Sun, closed Sun Apr-Oct) This unspoiled 140,000-acre refuge is one of the country's best birding spots, especially from October to May (early morning and after 4pm). More endangered and threatened species of wildlife inhabit the swamps, marshes and hardwood hammocks here than at any other site in the continental US. The best viewing is on Black Point Wildlife Dr.

Canaveral National Seashore PARK
(☑386-428-3384; www.nps.gov/cana; adult/child $3/free; ☉6am-6pm Oct-Mar, to 8pm Apr-Sep) The 24 miles of pristine, windswept beaches comprise the longest stretch of undeveloped beach on Florida's east coast. They include family-friendly **Apollo Beach** on the north end with its gentle surf, untrammeled **Klondike Beach** in the middle – a favorite of campers and nature lovers – and **Playalinda Beach** at the south end, which is surfer central.

Mosquito Lagoon, with islands and mangroves teeming with wildlife, hugs the west side of the barrier island. Rent kayaks in Cocoa Beach. Rangers offer **pontoon boat tours** (per person $20) from the visitor information center on most Sundays. From June through August, rangers lead groups on nightly **sea turtle nesting tours** (adult/child 8-16yr $14/free; ☉7am-11:30pm); reservations required.

Water Sports

In addition to surfing the region's beaches, the Banana River, Indian River Lagoon and Mosquito Lagoon lure folks into all kinds of watercraft.

Island Watercraft Rental BOATING
(☑321-454-7661; www.islandwatercraftrentals.com; 1872 E 520 Causeway, Cocoa Beach) Offers pontoons (half-day $250), fishing boats (two hours $90) and motorboats (half-day $225), as well as inner-tubes and skis.

SURF'S UP ON THE SPACE COAST

For surfers, the 70 miles of Space Coast beaches from New Smyrna to Sebastian Inlet get the state's best waves. Ten-time world champion surfer Kelly Slater was born in Cocoa Beach, which remains the epicenter of the surf community. For the local scene and surf reports, visit **Florida Surfing** (www.floridasurfing.com) and **Surf Guru** (www.surfguru.com).

In Cocoa Beach, the long-running **Ron Jon Surf School** (☑321-868-1980; www.cocoabeachsurfingschool.com; 3901 N Atlantic Ave; per hr $50-65) offers lessons for all ages and levels, and sponsors the Ron Jon Easter Surf Festival, Florida's largest.

Ron Jon's Surf Shop SURFING, BOATING
(☑321-799-8888; www.ronjons.com; 4151 N Atlantic Ave, Cocoa Beach) Local icon rents just about anything water-related, from fat-tired beach bikes ($15 daily) to surfboards ($30 daily); also a huge store.

🛌 Sleeping

Charming Cocoa Beach has the most options, as well as the most chains. For a quieter stay, Vero Beach is also attractive.

Beach Place Guesthouses APARTMENT $$$
(☑321-783-4045; www.beachplaceguesthouses.com; 1445 S Atlantic Ave, Cocoa Beach; ste $195-350; ☮♿) A slice of heavenly relaxation in Cocoa Beach's partying beach scene, this laid-back two-story guesthouse in a residential neighborhood has roomy suites with hammocks and a lovely deck, all just steps from the dunes and beach.

Fawlty Towers MOTEL $
(☑321-784-3870; www.fawltytowersresort.com; 100 E Cocoa Beach Causeway, Cocoa Beach; r $90-114; ⓟ❄☮♨) Beneath this motel's gloriously garish and extremely pink exterior lie fairly straightforward rooms with an unbeatable beachside location; quiet pool and tiki bar.

South Beach Place MOTEL $$
(☑772-231-5366; www.southbeachplacevero.com; 1705 S Ocean Dr, Vero Beach; ste per day $125-175, per week $700-1050; ☮♨♿) Old Florida with a facelift, this tasteful and bright two-story motel in Vero Beach sits in a particularly

FLORIDA SPACE COAST

quiet stretch across from the beach. One-bedroom suites have a full kitchen.

Eating

Fat Snook
SEAFOOD $$$
(☑321-784-1190; http://thefatsnook.com; 2464 S Atlantic Ave, Cocoa Beach; mains $21-34; ☺5-10pm) Hidden inside an uninspired building, yet sporting cool, minimalist decor, tiny Fat Snook stands out as an oasis of fine cooking. Yes, there's a distinct air of food snobbery here, but it's so tasty, no one seems to mind.

Slow and Low Barbecue
BARBECUE $$
(306 N Orlando Ave, Cocoa Beach; mains $8-20; ☺11am-midnight) After a day on the beach, nothing satisfies better than a plate over-flowing with barbecue ribs, fried okra, turnip greens and sweet fried potatoes. There's a daily happy hour and live music Thursday through Sunday.

Simply Delicious
CAFE $
(125 N Orlando Ave, Cocoa Beach; mains $6-12; ☺8am-3pm Tue-Sat, to 2pm Sun) You can't miss this little yellow house on the southbound stretch of A1A. It's a homey Americana place – nothing fancy, nothing trendy, just simply delicious.

Maison Martinique
FRENCH $$$
(☑772-231-5366; Caribbean Court Boutique Hotel, 1601 S Ocean Dr, Vero Beach; mains $18-35; ☺5-10pm) In Vero Beach, outstanding French cuisine with first-rate service and intimate surrounds. On warm evenings, eat by the little pool; for something more casual, head to the piano bar upstairs.

❶ Getting There & Away

From Orlando take Hwy 528 east, which connects with Hwy A1A. **Greyhound** (www.greyhound.com) has services from West Palm Beach and Orlando to Titusville. **Vero Beach Shuttle** (☑772-267-0550; www.verobeachshuttle.com) provides airport shuttle service.

Daytona Beach

With typical Floridian hype, Daytona bills itself as 'the World's Most Famous Beach.' Well, not really, and anyway, its fame is less about quality than the size of the parties this expansive beach has witnessed. To wit: spring break and Nascar.

Daytona has long been, and remains, a family destination, and it preserves some retro '50s carnival attractions. Until recently,

it also hosted the quintessential *Girls Gone Wild* spring break madness. However, the town has cracked down on drunken loutish-ness and wardrobe malfunctions, and spring break here isn't what it used to be, though it still draws crowds.

What hasn't slowed down (pun intended) is Nascar, which was born here in 1947. As early as 1902, pioneers in the auto industry would drag race down the beach's hard-packed sands to test their inventions. That gave way to stock-car racing, which was eventually formalized and moved to the Daytona International Speedway.

Today the population quintuples during February's **Speed Weeks**, and half a million bikers roar into town for motorcycle events in spring and fall. Be aware that traffic police, cognizant of the local need for speed, are vigilant.

The **Daytona Beach Convention & Visitors Bureau** (☑386-255-0415; www.daytonabeach.com; 126 E Orange Ave; ☺9am-5pm Mon-Fri) has great lodging listings. Gay and lesbian travelers can visit www.gaydaytona.com.

◉ Sights & Activities

Daytona Beach
BEACH
(per car $5) This perfectly planar stretch of sand was once the city's raceway. You can still drive sections at a strictly enforced top speed of 10mph. Or rent an ATV, fat-tired cruiser or recumbent trike. Water sports rentals are ubiquitous.

Daytona International Speedway
RACETRACK
(☑800-748-7467; www.daytonaintlspeedway.com; 1801 W International Speedway Blvd; tickets from $20) The Holy Grail of raceways has a diverse race schedule. Ticket prices accelerate rapidly for the big races, headlined by the **Daytona 500** in February, but you can wander the massive stands for free on nonrace days. Two first-come, first-served **tram tours** (tickets $15-22) take in the track, pits and behind-the-scenes areas. Real fanatics can indulge in the **Richard Petty Driving Experience** (☑800-237-3889; www.drivepetty.com), where you can either ride shotgun ($135) around the track or take a day to become the driver ($2200); check schedule online.

Museum of Arts & Sciences
MUSEUM
(www.moas.org; 1040 Museum Blvd; adult/student $13/7; ☺9am-5pm Tue-Sat, from 11am Sun) A wonderful mishmash of everything from

Cuban art to Coca-Cola relics to a 13ft giant sloth skeleton.

a full-service spa and sophisticated color palette.

Marine Science Center   AQUARIUM
(www.marinesciencecenter.com; 100 Lighthouse Dr; adult/child $5/2; ⊙10am-4pm Tue-Sat, from noon Sun) Sea turtles nest on Daytona's beaches, and this rehab center cares for the sick and injured. Lots of seabirds too.

Ponce de León Inlet Lighthouse   LIGHTHOUSE
(www.ponceinlet.org; 4931 S Peninsula Dr; adult/child $5/1.50; ⊙10am-6pm winter, to 9pm summer) About 6 miles south of Daytona Beach, it's 203 steps up to the top of Florida's tallest lighthouse.

Daytona Beach Drive-In Church   CHURCH
(www.driveinchurch.net; 3140 S Atlantic Ave; ⊙services 8:30am & 10am Sun) In auto-obsessed Daytona, cars are a religion, and in this former drive-in movie theater you can get religion in your car.

🛏 Sleeping

Daytona lodging is plentiful and spans all budgets and styles. Prices soar during events; book well ahead.

[TOP CHOICE] August Seven Inn   B&B $$
(⌨386-248-8420; www.jpaugust.net; 1209 S Peninsula Dr; r $99-155; [P✱🕸🌀]) The friendly innkeepers of this gorgeous B&B have stocked it with period antiques and stylish deco, creating a soothing haven from Daytona's typical Nascar-and-spring-break carnival.

Tropical Manor   RESORT $$
(⌨386-252-4920; www.tropicalmanor.com; 2237 S Atlantic Ave; r $88-315; [P✱🕸🌀]) This immaculate beachfront property is like a playful pastel vision of Candy Land. Every room type is available, from motel rooms to efficiencies, large suites to cottages.

Sun Viking Lodge   RESORT $$
(⌨386-252-6252; www.sunviking.com; 2411 S Atlantic Ave; r $80-285; [P✱🕸🌀🛶]) Most rooms have kitchenettes, but they could stand a reno – oh never mind. For families, it's ideal: two pools, a 60ft waterslide, beach access, shuffleboard, endless activities and a Viking theme!

Shores   RESORT $$$
(⌨386-767-7350; www.shoresresort.com; 2637 N Atlantic Ave; r $120-320; [P✱🕸🌀]) One of Daytona's most elegant offerings, this chic, beachfront boutique has hand-striped walls,

✗ Eating & Drinking

Dancing Avocado Kitchen   MEXICAN $
(110 S Beach St; mains $6-11; ⊙8am-4pm Mon-Sat; 🍴) Fresh, healthful, yummy Mexican dishes like extreme burritos and quesadillas dominate the menu at this vegetarian-oriented cafe, but the signature dancing avocado melt is tops.

Rose Villa   CONTINENTAL $$$
(⌨386-615-7673; www.rosevillaormond.com; 43 West Granada Blvd, Ormond Beach; mains $18-32; ⊙5-10pm Tue-Thu, to 11pm Fri & Sat) This lovely new under-the-radar bistro is in a renovated Victorian house a few miles north of Daytona. The menu is charmingly old-fashioned 'Continental' – veal chop in cream sauce, Scottish salmon with caper butter – and the vintage setting enchanting.

Pasha Middle East Cafe   MIDDLE EASTERN $
(www.pashacafedaytona.com; 919 W International Speedway Blvd; mains $5-14; ⊙10am-7pm Mon-Sat, noon-6pm Sun) Chow on falafel, kabob, hummus, tabbouleh – and of course baklava – in a casual, family-run cafe and deli.

Aunt Catfish's on the River   SOUTHERN $$
(⌨386-767-4768; www.auntcatfishontheriver.com; 4009 Halifax Dr, Port Orange; mains $8-25; ⊙11:30am-9pm) Southern-style seafood lolling in butter and Cajun-spice catfish make this place insanely popular.

☆ Entertainment

Daytona's entertainment scene skews to rocking biker bars (mostly along Main St) and high-octane dance clubs (on or near Seabreeze Blvd).

Razzles   CLUB
(www.razzlesnightclub.com; 611 Seabreeze Blvd) The reigning dance club, permanently thumping.

Froggy's Saloon   BAR
(www.froggyssaloon.com; 800 Main St) It's bike week all year long; check your liver at the door.

ⓘ Getting There & Around

Daytona Beach International Airport (DAB; www.flydaytonafirst.com) is just east of the Speedway, and the **Greyhound bus station** (www.greyhound.com; 138 S Ridgewood Ave) is the starting point for services around Florida.

Daytona is close to the intersection of two of Florida's major interstates: I-95 is the quickest way to Jacksonville (about 90 miles) and Miami (260 miles), and I-4 leads to Orlando in an hour.

Votran (www.votran.com; adult/child $1.25/ free) runs buses and trolleys throughout the city.

St Augustine

The first this, the oldest that...St Augustine was founded by the Spanish in 1565, which means it's chock-full of age-related superlatives. Tourists flock here to stroll the ancient streets, and horse-drawn carriages clip-clop past townsfolk dressed in period costume around the National Historic Landmark District, aka the oldest permanent settlement in the US.

At times St Augustine screams, 'Hey, everyone, look how quaint we are!' but it stops just short of theme park plastic-ness because, well, the buildings and monuments are real, and the narrow, cafe-strewn lanes are genuinely charming. Walk the cobblestoned streets or stand where Juan Ponce de León landed in 1513, and the historical distance occasionally collapses into present-moment chills.

The main visitor center (☏904-825-1000; www.floridashistoriccoast.com; 10 Castillo Dr; ☉8:30am-5:30pm) screens a 45-minute film on the town's history. Also visit the city website, www.ci.st-augustine.fl.us.

◉ Sights & Activities

The town's two Henry Flagler buildings shouldn't be missed.

Lightner Museum   MUSEUM
(☏904-824-2874; www.lightnermuseum.org; 75 King St; adult/child $10/5; ☉9am-5pm) Flagler's former Hotel Alcazar is now home to this wonderful museum, with a little bit of everything from ornate Gilded Age furnishings to collections of marbles and cigar-box labels.

Hotel Ponce de León   HISTORIC BUILDING
(74 King St; tours adult/child $7/1; ☉tours hourly 10am-3pm) Across the street is this gorgeous former hotel, which was built in the 1880s and is now the world's most gorgeous dormitory, belonging to Flagler College. Take a guided tour (summer only) – or at least step inside to gawk at the lobby for free.

Spanish Quarter Museum   HISTORIC BUILDINGS
(☏904-825-6830; 53 St George St; adult/child $7/4; ☉9am-4:45pm) See how they did things

back in the 18th century at this re-creation of Spanish-colonial St Augustine, complete with craftspeople demonstrating blacksmithing, leather working and other trades.

Pirate & Treasure Museum   MUSEUM
(www.thepiratemuseum.com; 12 S Castillo Dr; adult/ child $12/7; ☉9am-8pm) A mash-up of theme park and museum, this celebration of all things pirate has real historical treasure (and genuine gold) as well as animatronic pirates, blasting cannons and a kid-friendly treasure hunt.

Castillo de San Marcos National Monument   FORT
(www.nps.gov/casa; btwn San Marcos Ave & Matanzas River; adult/child $6/free; ☉8:45am-5:15pm) This incredibly photogenic fort is another atmospheric monument to longevity: it's the country's oldest masonry fort, completed by the Spanish in 1695. Park rangers lead programs hourly and shoot off cannons most weekends.

Oldest Houses   HISTORIC BUILDINGS
The **González-Alvarez House** (www.oldesthouse.com; 14 St Francis St; adult/student $8/4; ☉9am-5pm) is the oldest house in the US, on a site occupied since the 1600s. The **Oldest Wooden School House** (www.oldestwoodenschoolhouse.com; 14 St George St; adult/child $3/2; ☉10am-4:30pm Mon-Sat, from 11am Sun) is peopled by animatronic teachers and pupils, and includes a dungeon!

Fountain of Youth   HISTORIC SITE
(www.fountainofyouthflorida.com; 11 Magnolia Ave; adult/child $10/6; ☉9am-5pm) Insert tongue firmly in cheek and step right up for an acrid cup of eternal youth at this 'archaeological park.' As the story goes, Spanish explorer Juan Ponce de León came ashore here in 1513, and he considered this freshwater stream the possible legendary Fountain of Youth.

Anastasia State Recreation Area   PARK
(☏904-461-2033; 1340 Hwy A1A; car $8) Locals escape the tourist hordes here, with a terrific beach, a campground (campsites $28) and rentals for all kinds of water sports.

☞ Tours

TOP CHOICE **St Augustine City Walks**   WALKING
(☏904-540-3476; www.staugustinecitywalks.com; tours $14-45) Extremely fun walking tours of all kinds, from silly to serious.

Old Town Trolley Tours
TROLLEY

(☎904-829-3800; www.trolleytours.com; 167 San Marco Ave; adult/child $23/10) Hop-on/hop-off narrated trolley tours.

St Augustine Sightseeing Trains
TRAIN

(☎904-829-6545; www.redtrains.com; 170 San Marco Ave; adult/child $22/9) Hop-on/hop-off narrated train tours.

🛏 Sleeping

St Augustine is a popular weekend escape; expect room rates to rise about 30% on Friday and Saturday. Inexpensive motels and chain hotels line San Marco Ave, near where it meets US Hwy 1. More than two dozen atmospheric B&Bs can be found at www.staugustineinns.com.

TOP CHOICE At Journey's End
B&B $$

(☎904-829-0076; www.atjourneysend.com; 89 Cedar St; r $129-219; P❄🐾🛜) Free from the granny-ish decor that haunts many St Augustine B&Bs, this pet-friendly, kid-friendly and gay-friendly spot is outfitted in a chic mix of antiques and modern furniture, and run by some affable hosts. Breakfast is included.

🏨 Casa Monica
HOTEL $$$

(☎904-827-1888; www.casamonica.com; 95 Cordova St; r $179-779; P❄🛜🏊) Built in 1888, this is *the* luxe hotel in town, with turrets and fountains adding to the Spanish-Moorish castle atmosphere. Rooms are also richly appointed, with wrought-iron beds and every amenity.

Casa de Solana
B&B $$

(☎877-824-3555; www.casadesolana.com; 21 Aviles St; r $129-249; P🛜) Just off pedestrian-only Aviles St in the oldest part of town, this utterly charming little inn remains faithful to its early-1800s period decor. Rooms are a bit small, but price and location make it a great deal.

Pirate Haus Inn
HOSTEL $

(☎904-808-1999; www.piratehaus.com; 32 Treasury St; dm $20, r $50-95; P❄🛜) It's not fancy, but this family-friendly European-style guesthouse-hostel has an unbeatable location. Includes 'pirate pancake' breakfast.

🍴 Eating & Drinking

St Augustine has a notable dining scene, though it's also rife with overpriced tourist traps.

TOP CHOICE Floridian
NEW AMERICAN $$

(☎904-829-0655; www.thefloridianstaug.com; 39 Cordova St; mains $12-20; ⏰11am-3pm & 5-9pm Wed-Mon, to 10pm Fri & Sat) Though it oozes with hipster-locavore earnestness, this new farm-to-table restaurant is so friggin' fabulous you won't mind. The chef-owners serve whimsical neo-Southern creations in an oh-so-cool dining room.

Spanish Bakery
BAKERY $

(www.thespanishbakery.com; 42½ St George St; mains $3-5.50; ⏰9:30am-3pm) Through an arched gate in a table-filled courtyard, this diminutive stucco bakeshop serves empanadas, sausage rolls and other conquistador-era favorites. Don't hesitate; they sell out quick.

Casa Maya
MEXICAN $$

(17 Hypolita St; mains $6-18; ⏰10am-3:30pm daily, 5:30-9pm Wed-Sun; 🥗) Snappy jazz wafts through the jasmine-shaded patio of this tasty vegetarian-friendly Mayan (or Northern Central American) restaurant. Don't miss the hibiscus sangria!

Collage
INTERNATIONAL $$$

(☎904-829-0055; www.collagestaug.com; 60 Hypolita St; mains $26-36; ⏰from 5:30pm) This upscale spot feels a world away from the bustling touristy downtown. The seafood-heavy menu wins raves for its subtle touch with global flavors.

Scarlett O'Hara's
PUB $

(www.scarlettoharas.net; 70 Hypolita St; mains $5-14; ⏰11am-1am) Leave your hoop skirt at home. This rowdy place is a fine spot for beer and pub grub.

Taberna del Gallo
BAR

(53 St George St; ⏰2-9:30pm Thu-Sat, noon-7pm Sun) Flickering candles provide the only light at this 1736 stone tavern. Sing sea shanties on weekends.

AIA Ale Works
PUB

(www.a1aaleworks.com; 1 King St; ⏰11am-11:30pm Sun-Thu, to midnight Fri & Sat) Who needs historical ambience with fine-crafted beer like this?

ℹ Getting There & Around

The **Greyhound bus station** (☎904-829-6401; 1711 Dobbs Rd) is a few miles from the heart of things. Once you're in Old Town, you can get almost everywhere on foot.

Jacksonville

Are we there yet? Have we left yet? It's hard to tell, because Jacksonville sprawls out over a whopping 840 sq miles, making it the largest city by area in the continental US (eclipsed only by Anchorage, AK). Jacksonville Beach, known locally as 'Jax Beach,' is about 17 miles east of the city center and is where you'll find white sand and most of the action. For information, peruse www.visit jacksonville.com.

Sights & Activities

TOP CHOICE Cummer Museum of Art & Gardens MUSEUM
(www.cummer.org; 829 Riverside Ave; adult/student $10/6; ⊙10am-9pm Tue, to 5pm Wed-Sat, noon-5pm Sun) This handsome museum, Jacksonville's premier cultural space, has a genuinely excellent collection of American and European paintings, Asian decorative art and antiquities.

Museum of Science & History MUSEUM
(www.themosh.org; 1025 Museum Circle; adult/child $10/8; ⊙10am-5pm Mon-Fri, to 6pm Sat, 1-6pm Sun) Packing kids? This museum offers dinosaurs, a planetarium and educational exhibits on Jacksonville's cultural and natural history.

FREE Anheuser-Busch Brewery BREWERY TOUR
(www.budweisertours.com; 111 Busch Dr; ⊙10am-4pm Mon-Sat) Enjoy a free tour (and free beer if you're over 21).

Jacksonville Museum of Modern Art MUSEUM
(www.mocajacksonville.org; 333 N Laura St; adult/child $8/5; ⊙10am-4pm Tue-Sat, to 9pm Thu, from noon Sun) The focus of this ultramodern space extends beyond painting: get lost among contemporary sculpture, prints, photography and film.

Sleeping & Eating

The cheapest rooms are along I-95 and I-10, where the lower-priced chains congregate. Beach lodging rates often rise in summer.

Inn at Oak Street B&B $$
(☎904-379-5525; www.innatoakstreet.com; 2114 Oak St; r $120-165; P❀❀) This gabled three-story 1902 house, with views of the St Johns River, is a peaceful B&B with loads of upscale touches. Handsome, unfussy and includes gourmet breakfast.

Riverdale Inn B&B $$
(☎904-354-5080; www.riverdaleinn.com; 1521 Riverside Ave; r $120-220; P❀❀) In the early 1900s this was one of 50 or so mansions lining Riverside. Now there are only two left, and you're invited to enjoy its lovely rooms with full breakfast.

TOP CHOICE Clark's Fish Camp SOUTHERN $$
(www.clarksfishcamp.com; 12903 Hood Landing Rd; mains $13-22; ⊙5:30-9:30pm Mon-Fri, from 11:30am Sat & Sun) Sample Florida's Southern 'Cracker' cuisine of gator, snake, catfish and frog's legs while surrounded by the surreal animal menagerie of 'America's largest private taxidermy collection.' This swamp shack is unforgettable. It's far south of downtown Jacksonville.

Aix MEDITERRANEAN $$$
(☎904-398-1949; www.bistrox.com; 1440 San Marco Blvd; mains $14-28; ⊙11am-10pm Mon-Thu, to 11pm Fri, 5-11pm Sat, 5-9pm Sun) Dine with the fashionable food mavens on fusion-y Mediterranean dishes at Aix, whose menu bursts with global flavors. Reservations recommended.

River City Brewing Company SEAFOOD $$$
(☎904-398-2299; www.rivercitybrew.com; 835 Museum Circle; mains $18-30; ⊙10am-3pm & 5-10pm Mon-Sat, 10:30am-2:30pm Sun) The perfect place to quaff a microbrew and enjoy some upscale seafood overlooking the water.

☆ Entertainment

Jacksonville Landing MALL
(www.jacksonvillelanding.com; 2 Independent Dr) Downtown, has restaurants, shops, bars and free outdoor entertainment.

Freebird Live LIVE MUSIC
(☎904-246-2473; www.freebirdlive.com; 200 N 1st St; ⊙8pm-2am) At the beach, a rocking music venue and home of the band Lynyrd Skynyrd.

❶ Getting There & Around

North of the city, **Jacksonville International Airport** (JAX; www.jia.aero) has rental cars. **Greyhound** (www.greyhound.com; 10 N Pearl St) serves numerous cities, and **Amtrak** (☎904-766-5110; www.amtrak.com; 3570 Clifford Lane) has trains from the north and south. The **Jacksonville Transportation Authority** (www.jtafla.com) runs a monorail and **city buses** (fare $1).

Amelia Island & Around

Residents are quick to tell you: Amelia Island is just as old as that braggart St Augustine – they just can't prove it. Unfortunately, no Ponce de León, no plaque, so they have to content themselves with being a pretty little island of moss-draped Southern charm and home to **Fernandina Beach**, a shrimping village with 40 blocks of historic buildings and romantic B&Bs. Pick up walking-tour maps and information at the **visitor center** (☏904-261-3248; www.ameliaisland.org; 102 Centre St; ◷11am-4pm Mon-Sat, from noon Sun).

To learn about Amelia Island's intricate history, which has seen it ruled under eight different flags starting with the French in 1562, check out the **Amelia Island Museum of History** (www.ameliamuseum.org; 233 S 3rd St; adult/student $7/4; ◷10am-4pm Mon-Sat, from 1pm Sun). Admission includes tours at 11am and 2pm.

Take a half-hour horse-drawn carriage tour with the **Old Towne Carriage Co** (☏904-556-2662; www.ameliacarriagetours.com; adult/child $15/7.50) or **Amelia Island Carriages** (☏904-556-2662; adult/child $15/7). If you'd rather a carriage didn't come between you and your horse, **Kelly's Seahorse Ranch** (☏904-491-5166; www.kellyranchinc.com; ride per hr $60) offers beachfront trail rides for riders aged 13 and over.

Capping the north end of the island, the Spanish moss–draped **Fort Clinch State Park** (☏904-277-7274; 2601 Atlantic Ave; pedestrian/car $2/6; ◷8am-dusk) has beaches, camping ($26), bike trails and a commanding Civil War–era **fort** (◷9am-5pm), with reenactments taking place the first full weekend of every month.

Amelia Island is part of the **Talbot Islands State Parks** (☏904-251-2320; ◷8am-dusk), which includes the pristine shoreline at **Little Talbot Island** (car $5) and the 'boneyard beach' at **Big Talbot Island State Park** (car $3), where silvered tree skeletons create a dramatic landscape. Both are south of Amelia Island down the First Coast Hwy.

From fall through spring, surfable beach breaks can be common, especially at Main Beach. **Pipeline Surf Shop** (☏904-277-3717; 2022 1st Ave) rents boards and wetsuits, and gives lessons.

At Fernandina Beach, **Elizabeth Pointe Lodge** (☏904-277-4851; www.elizabethpointelodge.com; 98 S Fletcher Ave; r $215-460; P✳🛜) looks like an old Nantucket-style sea captain's house with wraparound porches, gracious service and beautifully appointed rooms. Also at the beach is the Victorian Gothic **Fairbanks House** (☏904-277-0500; www.fairbankshouse.com; 227 S 7th St; r $175-265; P✳🛜), an atmospheric mansion where Indiana Jones might retire, as well as **Hoyt House** (☏904-277-4300; www.hoythouse.com; 804 Atlantic Ave; r $185-240; P✳🛜≋), another lovely inn with lavish breakfasts and a pool (a rarity among Amelia B&Bs).

Downtown Fernandina Beach is the place to eat. Small plates and mains link arms happily at the tiny, stylish **29 South** (☏904-277-7919; www.29southrestaurant.com; 29 S 3rd St; mains $18-28; ◷11:30am-2:30pm Tue-Sat, 5:30-9:30pm Mon-Sat, 10am-2pm Sun), a neo-Southern gourmet bistro. Another foodie destination is **Merge** (☏904-277-8797; 510 S 8th St; meals $20-26; ◷from 5pm), featuring exquisite seafood dishes using local ingredients. For something more low-key and funky, try **Café Karibo & Karibrew** (www.cafekaribo.com; 27 N 3rd St; mains $8-24; ◷11am-9pm Tue-Sun, to 3pm Mon), with a two-story cafe on one side and a down-home brewpub on the other.

Fernandina does beat out St Augustine in one 'oldest' category: Florida's oldest bar, the **Palace Saloon** (www.thepalacesaloon.com; 113 Centre St), with swinging doors, draped velvet and a deadly Pirate's Punch.

WEST COAST

Every evening along the seemingly endless powdery white-sand beaches of the Gulf Coast, the tangerine sun kisses the silver-mantled indigo waters before slipping off to bed. The west coast's barrier islands are a Florida promoter's dream – not only are they less commercially cluttered than their Atlantic counterparts, they remain equally rich in cultural sophistication, gourmet cuisine and natural beauty. Searching for mermaids and flamenco dancers, manatees and open-mouthed alligators, the circus and Salvador Dalí? Look no further.

Tampa

From the outside, Florida's third-largest city seems all business, even generically so. But Tampa surprises: its revitalized riverfront is a sparkling green swathe dotted with intriguing cultural institutions, and its historic Ybor City district preserves the city's Cuban cigar-industry past while, at night, transforming into the Gulf Coast's hottest bar and nightclub scene. South Tampa, meanwhile, has a cutting-edge dining scene that's drawing food mavens from Orlando and Miami.

⊙ Sights

DOWNTOWN TAMPA

Aside from the zoo, downtown's sights are in or along Tampa's attractive green space, Riverwalk (www.thetampariverwalk.com).

TOP CHOICE Florida Aquarium   AQUARIUM
(☎813-273-4000; www.flaquarium.org; 701 Channelside Dr; adult/child $20/15; ◷9:30am-5pm) Tampa's excellent aquarium is among the state's best. Cleverly designed, the re-created swamp lets you walk among herons and ibis as they prowl the mangroves. Programs let you swim with the fishes (and the sharks) or take a catamaran ecotour in Tampa Bay.

Lowry Park Zoo   ZOO
(www.lowryparkzoo.com; 1101 W Sligh Ave; adult/child $24/19; ◷9:30am-5pm) North of downtown, Tampa's zoo gets you as close to the animals as possible, with several free-flight aviaries, a camel ride, giraffe feeding, wallaby enclosure and rhino 'encounter.'

Tampa Museum of Art   MUSEUM
(www.tampamuseum.org; 120 W Gasparilla Plaza; adult/child $10/5; ◷11am-7pm Mon-Thu, to 8pm Fri, to 5pm Sat & Sun) In 2010 the museum christened its dramatically cantilevered new home. Six galleries balance Greek and Roman antiquities, contemporary photography and new media with major traveling exhibitions.

Tampa Bay History Center   MUSEUM
(www.tampabayhistorycenter.org; 801 Old Water St; adult/child $12/7; ◷10am-5pm) This first-rate history museum presents the region's Seminole people, Cracker pioneers and Tampa's Cuban community and cigar industry. The cartography collection dazzles.

Henry B Plant Museum   MUSEUM
(www.plantmuseum.org; 401 W Kennedy Blvd; admission $10; ◷10am-5pm Tue-Sat, from noon Sun) The silver minarets of Henry B Plant's 1891 Tampa Bay Hotel glint majestically. Now part of the University of Tampa, one section re-creates the original hotel's luxurious, gilded late-Victorian world.

Glazer Children's Museum   CHILDREN'S MUSEUM
(www.glazermuseum.org; 110 W Gasparilla Plaza; adult/child 1-12yr $15/9.50; ◷10am-5pm Mon-Fri, to 6pm Sat, 1-6pm Sun) Creative play spaces for kids don't get any better than this crayon-bright, inventive museum. Eager staff and tons of coolio fun; adjacent Curtis Hixon Park is picnic-and-playground friendly.

YBOR CITY

Like the illicit love child of Key West and Miami's Little Havana, Ybor City's cobblestoned 19th-century historic district is a redolent mix of wrought-iron balconies, globe streetlamps, immigrant history, ethnic cuisine, cigars and hip, happening nightlife. Diverse and youthful, Ybor (ee-bore) City oozes rakish, scruffy charm.

The **visitor center** (www.ybor.org; 1600 E 8th Ave; ◷9am-5pm Mon-Sat, from noon Sun) is itself an excellent small museum. The main drag – along 7th Ave (La Septima) between 14th

---

MANATEES & MERMAIDS

Apparently, Florida's Spanish discoverers confused manatees with mermaids, but it's not hard to tell them apart. Mermaids are those beautiful long-haired women with the spangly tails swimming in the underwater theater at Weeki Wachee Springs (www.weekiwachee.com; 6131 Commercial Way, Weeki Wachee; adult/child $25/17; ◷10am-4pm). Their graceful adagios and The Little Mermaid show (three times daily) are Florida's most delightfully kitschy entertainment (just 45 minutes north of Tampa).

Lovable, ponderous, 1000lb manatees are the ones nibbling lettuce in the crystal bathtub of Homosassa Springs Wildlife State Park (www.floridastateparks.org/homosassasprings; adult/child $13/5; ◷9am-5:30pm, last entry 4pm), with its own underwater observatory (20 minutes north of Weeki Wachee).

Sadly, you can't swim with the mermaids, but you can with the manatees. Head a few miles north to King's Bay, within the Crystal River National Wildlife Refuge (www.fws.gov/crystalriver; 1502 SE Kings Bay Dr; ◷visitor center 8am-4pm Mon-Fri), where the visitor center can guide you to nearly 40 commercial operators that, had they existed, would have spared the Spaniards lots of heartache.

and 21st Sts – is packed with eats, drinks, shops and cigar stores.

Ybor City Museum State Park MUSEUM
(www.ybormuseum.org; 1818 E 9th Ave; admission $4; ☉9am-5pm) This dusty, old-school history museum preserves a bygone era, with cigar-worker houses and wonderful photos. Best is the museum store; get expert cigar advice and join its **walking tour** (☏813-428-0854; tour $8; ☉10:30am Sat), run by a cigar-maker with a PhD.

BUSCH GARDENS & ADVENTURE ISLAND
No, it's not as thematically immersive as Orlando's Disney World or Universal, but Tampa's big theme park, **Busch Gardens** (www.buschgardens.com; 10000 McKinley Dr; adult/child $80/70), will satisfy your adrenaline craving with epic roller coasters and flume rides that weave through an African-theme wildlife park. Music, performances and interactive 4D movies round out a full day. Check the website for opening hours, which vary seasonally.

Adjacent **Adventure Island** (www.adventureisland.com; 10001 McKinley Dr; adult/child $43/39; ☉daily mid-Mar–Aug, weekends only Sep-Oct) is a massive water park with slides and rides galore. Discounts and combination tickets are available online.

🛏 Sleeping
Chains abound along Fowler Ave and Busch Blvd (Hwy 580), near Busch Gardens.

TOP CHOICE Gram's Place HOSTEL $
(☏813-221-0596; www.grams-inn-tampa.com; 3109 N Ola Ave; dm $23, r $25-70; ❋@) As charismatic as an aging rock star, Gram's is a tiny, welcoming hostel for international travelers who prefer personality over perfect linens. Dig the in-ground hot tub and Saturday night jams.

Tahitian Inn HOTEL $$
(☏813-877-6721; www.tahitianinn.com; 601 S Dale Mabry Hwy; r $100-170; P❋@🛜♨♿) This family-owned, full-service hotel offers fresh, boutique stylings at midrange prices. Nice pool, and airport transportation.

Don Vicente de Ybor Historic Inn HISTORIC HOTEL $$
(☏813-241-4545; www.donvicenteinn.com; 1915 Republica de Cuba; r $130-200; P❋🛜) Slightly faded, the 1895 Don Vicente recalls Ybor City's glory days. Unfortunately, rooms

are less warmly dramatic than the atmospheric Old World public spaces. Breakfast included.

✖ Eating
At mealtime, focus on Ybor City, South Tampa's SoHo area (South Howard Ave) and up-and-coming Seminole Heights.

TOP CHOICE Columbia Restaurant SPANISH $$$
(☏813-248-4961; www.columbiarestaurant.com; 2117 E 7th Ave; mains $17-28; ☉11am-10pm Mon-Thu, to 11pm Fri & Sat, noon-10pm Sun) Definitely reserve ahead for the exuberant, twice-nightly flamenco shows, and enjoy robust, classic Spanish cuisine and heady *mojitos* and sangria. It's an Old World Iberian time warp.

🍴 Refinery FUSION $$
(☏813-237-2000; www.thetamparefinery.com; 5137 N Florida Ave; mains $12-18; ☉5-10pm Tue-Thu, to 11pm Fri & Sat, 11am-3pm Sun; 🍴) This blue-collar gourmet joint promises chipped plates and no pretensions, just playful, delicious hyperlocal cuisine that cleverly mixes a sustainability ethic with a punk attitude.

La Teresita SPANISH $
(www.lateresitarestaurant.com; 3246 W Columbus Dr; mains $5-7; ☉5am-midnight Mon-Wed, 24hr Thu-Sat, to 10pm Sun) Experience 'real' Tampa at the horseshoe-shaped counters of this Cuban cafeteria (skip the restaurant): order Spanish comfort food of grilled steak, plantains, neon-yellow rice and black beans.

Bern's Steak House STEAKHOUSE $$$
(☏813-251-2421; www.bernssteakhouse.com; 1208 S Howard Ave; mains $25-60; ☉from 5pm) This legendary, nationally renowned steakhouse is an event as much as a meal. Dress up, order caviar and on-premises dry-aged beef, ask to tour the wine cellar and kitchens, and *don't* skip dessert.

🍴 Sidebern's FUSION $$$
(☏813-258-2233; www.sideberns.com; 2208 W Morrison Ave; mains $29-40; ☉5-10pm Mon-Thu, to 11pm Fri & Sat; 🍴) Don't feel like steak? This trendy alternative to Bern's offers inventive, big-city gourmet cuisine, locally sourced. Impeccable service.

🍴 Restaurant BT FUSION $$$
(☏813-258-1916; www.restaurantbt.com; 2507 S MacDill Ave; lunch $10-13, dinner $23-34; ☉11:30am-2:30pm & 5:30-10pm Mon-Sat, to 11pm Fri & Sat) Chef Trina Nguyen-Batley has

The barrier islands of the Tampa Bay Area are graced with some of Florida's best beaches, whether you define 'best' as 'gorgeous untrammeled solitude' or 'family fun and thumping beach parties.' For more information, visit www.tampabaybeaches.com and www.visitstpeteclearwater.com. North to south, some highlights:

» **Honeymoon & Caladesi Islands** Two of Florida's most beautiful beaches; unspoiled, lightly visited Caladesi Island is only reachable by ferry.

» **Clearwater Beach** Idyllic soft white sand hosts raucous spring-break-style parties; huge resorts cater to the masses.

» **St Pete Beach** Double-wide strand is epicenter of activities and all-ages fun; packed with hotels, bars and restaurants.

» **Pass-a-Grille Beach** Most popular with city-based day-trippers; extremely long and backed by houses (not resorts); cute-as-a-button village for eats.

» **Fort DeSoto Park** North Beach is one of Florida's finest white-sand beaches; ideal for families. Extensive park includes bike and kayak rentals, fishing piers and a cafe.

combined her high-fashion background and Vietnamese upbringing to create this ultrachic temple to sustainable, locavore gastronomy.

🍷 Drinking & Entertainment

For nightlife, Ybor City is party central, though SoHo and Seminole Heights are also hip and happening. Tampa Bay's alternative weekly, Creative Loafing (www.cltampa.com), lists events and bars. Ybor City is also the center of Tampa's GLBT life; check out the GaYbor District Coalition (www.gaybor.com) and Gay Tampa (www.gaytampa.com).

TOP CHOICE **Skipper's Smokehouse** LIVE MUSIC (www.skipperssmokehouse.com; cnr Skipper Rd & Nebraska Ave; cover $5-25; ⏲11am-midnight Tue-Sun) Feeling like it blew in from the Keys, Skipper's is a beloved, unpretentious open-air venue for blues, folk, reggae and gator-swamp rockabilly. Get directions online.

Straz Center for the Performing Arts PERFORMING ARTS (☑813-229-7827; www.strazcenter.org; 1010 MacInnes Pl) This enormous, multivenue complex draws the gamut of fine arts performances: touring Broadway shows, pop concerts, opera, ballet, drama and more.

ℹ Information

Media

The Tampa Bay area has two major daily newspapers.

St Petersburg Times (www.tampabay.com)
Tampa Tribune (www.tampatrib.com)

Tourist Information

Tampa Bay Convention & Visitors Bureau (☑813-223-1111; www.visittampabay.com; 615 Channelside Dr; ⏲9:30am-5:30pm Mon-Sat, 11am-5pm Sun) The visitor center has good free maps and lots of information. Book hotels directly through the website.

ℹ Getting There & Around

Tampa International Airport (TPA; www.tampaairport.com; 5503 W Spruce St) has car-rental agencies. **Greyhound** (www.greyhound.com; 610 E Polk St) has numerous services. Trains run south to Miami and north through Jacksonville from the **Amtrak station** (www.amtrak.com; 601 Nebraska Ave). **Hillsborough Area Regional Transit** (HART; www.gohart.org; single/day pass $1.75/3.75) connects downtown and Ybor City with buses, trolleys and old-style streetcars.

St Petersburg

In the bay area, St Petersburg is the more arty, youthful sibling. It also has a more compact and walkable tourist district along its attractive harbor. For a cultural city base within easy striking distance of the region's excellent beaches, St Pete is a great choice.

For maps and info, visit the **chamber of commerce** (☑727-821-4069; http://pleasure.stpete.com; 100 2nd Ave N; ⏲9am-5pm Mon-Fri).

◉ Sights

Most of the action is around and along Central Ave, from 8th Ave to Bayshore Dr, which fronts the harbor and tourist pier.

St Petersburg Museum of Fine Arts
MUSEUM
(www.fine-arts.org; 255 Beach Dr NE; adult/child $17/10; ⊙10am-5pm Mon-Sat, from noon Sun) The Museum of Fine Arts collection is as broad as the Dalí's is deep, traversing the world's antiquities and following art's progression through nearly every era.

Florida Holocaust Museum
MUSEUM
(www.flholocaustmuseum.org; 55 5th St S; adult/child $14/8; ⊙10am-5pm, to 8pm Thu) The understated exhibits of this Holocaust museum, one of the country's largest, present these mid-20th-century events with moving directness.

Chihuly Collection
GALLERY
(www.chihulycollectionstpete.com; 400 Beach Dr; adult/child $15/12; ⊙10am-6pm Mon-Sat, from noon Sun) A paean to Chihuly's glass artistry, with galleries designed to hold the dramatic installations.

🛏 Sleeping

TOP CHOICE Dickens House
B&B $$
(☏727-822-8622; www.dickenshouse.com; 335 8th Ave NE; r $130-230; P✳@🛜) Five lushly designed rooms await in this passionately restored arts-and-crafts-style home. The gregarious, gay-friendly owner whips up a gourmet breakfast.

Ponce de Leon
BOUTIQUE HOTEL $$
(☏727-550-9300; www.poncedeleonhotel.com; 95 Central Ave; r $110-150; P✳@🛜) A boutique hotel with Spanish flair in the heart of downtown. Splashy murals, designer-cool decor, and the hot restaurant and bar are highlights; off-site parking is not.

Renaissance Vinoy Resort
LUXURY HOTEL $$$
(☏727-894-1000; www.vinoyrenaissanceresort.com; 501 5th Ave NE; r $250-310; P✳@🛜🏊) St Pete's coral pink grande dame, the newly renovated 1925 Vinoy is a sumptuous concoction with take-notice off-season and online deals. It's worth it just for the gorgeous pool.

🍴 Eating & Drinking
At night, focus on Central Ave between 2nd and 3rd Sts, and along the harborfront. Many restaurants have lively, late bar scenes.

TOP CHOICE Ceviche
TAPAS $$
(☏727-209-2302; www.ceviche.com/1828; 95 Central Ave; tapas $5-13, mains $15-23; ⊙5-10pm Sun & Mon, to midnight Tue-Sat) Panache counts and Ceviche has it in spades, with an upbeat Spanish atmosphere and flavorful, creative, generously portioned tapas. End the evening in the sexy, cavernlike Flamenco Room below, with live flamenco Thursday and Saturday nights.

Bella Brava
ITALIAN $$
(☏727-895-5515; www.bellabrava.com; 204 Beach Dr NE; lunch $7-10, dinner $14-20; ⊙11:30am-10pm, to 11pm Fri & Sat, 3-9pm Sun) Anchoring the prime waterfront intersection, Bella Brava specializes in contemporary northern Italian cooking and breezy, sidewalk dining.

DON'T MISS

SALVADOR DALÍ MUSEUM

Unveiled in 2011, the theatrical exterior of the new Dalí Museum (☏727-823-3767; www.thedali.org; 1 Dali Blvd; adult/child 6-12yr $21/7, after 5pm Thu $10; ⊙10am-5pm Mon-Wed, to 8pm Thu, to 5:30pm Fri & Sat, noon-5:30pm Sun) augurs great things: out of a wound in the towering white shoebox oozes the 75ft geodesic atrium Glass Enigma. Even better, what unfolds inside is a blueprint of what a modern art museum should be, or at least one that's devoted to understanding the life, art and impact of a revolutionary artist.

The new Dalí Museum is designed specifically to display all 96 oil paintings in the collection, along with 'key works from every moment and in every medium': drawings, prints, sculptures, photos, manuscripts, even movies, everything arranged chronologically and explained in context. Free docent tours and audioguides help unlock the rich symbolism of Dalí's monumental works, and the museum is so popular it's been known to draw 3000 people in a day.

Even if you dismiss his dripping clocks and curlicue mustache, this stunning museum – a crown jewel among Florida cultural institutions – makes a convincing case for Salvador Dalí's passionate, daring intellectualism and his visionary, even prescient 'surrealism.'

Garden
MEDITERRANEAN **$$**

(☎727-896-3800; www.thegardendtsp.com; 217
Central Ave; lunch $7-10, dinner $14-20; ☺11am-
10pm Mon-Sat, to 2am Fri & Sat, 10am-2pm Sun)
In a pretty hidden courtyard, Garden em-
phasizes Mediterranean-influenced salads
and pastas. There's live jazz and DJs on
weekends.

AnnaStella Cajun Bistro
CAJUN **$**

(☎727-498-8978; www.annastellacajunbistro.com;
300 Beach Dr N; dishes $6-15; ☺8am-10pm Sun-
Thu, to 11pm Fri & Sat; 🛜) Enjoy a Cajun-spiced
breakfast or lunch and harbor views; great
gumbo and fresh beignets.

☆ Entertainment

Jannus Live
CONCERT VENUE

(www.jannuslive.com; 16 2nd St N; tickets $15-30)
Well-loved outdoor concert venue inside
an intimate courtyard; national and local
bands reverberate downtown.

ⓘ Getting There & Around

**St Petersburg-Clearwater International Air-
port** (PIE; www.fly2pie.com) is served by several
major carriers. **Greyhound** (☎727-898-1496;
www.greyhound.com; 180 9th St N) services
include Tampa.

Pinellas Suncoast Transit Authority (PSTA;
www.psta.net; fare $2) operates buses citywide
and the Suncoast Beach Trolley that links the
beaches from Clearwater to Pass-a-Grille. The
Looper trolley (www.loopertrolley.com; fare
25¢) links downtown sights on a 30-minute
narrated loop.

Sarasota

Sarasota is a welcoming, well-to-do bastion
of the arts, with a performer's weakness for
the theater's sodium lights. John Ringling
set it on this course in 1911, when he made
the town the winter home of his famous cir-
cus. Today the Ringling Museum Complex
is a regional highlight, and Sarasota spills
over with opera, theater and art. Stop by the
Visitor Information Center (☎941-957-1877;
www.sarasotafl.org; 701 N Tamiami Trail; ☺10am-
5pm Mon-Sat) for info and maps.

Yet Sarasota wouldn't be half as popular
if it didn't have such luscious white-sand
beaches. **Lido Beach** is closest and has free
parking, but 5 miles away **Siesta Key** (www.
siestakeychamber.com) has sand like confec-
tioner's sugar and is one of Florida's best
and most popular strands; Siesta Village is
also a lively, family-friendly beach town.

Mote Aquarium (☎941-388-4441; www.mote.
org; 1600 Ken Thompson Pkwy; adult/child $17/12;
☺10am-5pm) is a leading shark research
center providing intimate encounters with
sharks, manatees, sea turtles, rays and more,
plus marine biologist-led sea-life cruises.

Boasting the world's largest scientific col-
lection of orchids and bromeliads, **Marie
Selby Botanical Gardens** (www.selby.org; 811
S Palm Ave; adult/child $17/6; ☺10am-5pm) is a
relaxing yet fascinating botanical encounter.

About a half-hour from downtown, visit
Myakka River State Park (www.myakkariver.
org; per car $6; ☺8am-sunset) to kayak or air-

RINGLING'S LEGACY: ART, ARCHITECTURE & THE CIRCUS

Circus impresario John Ringling was an avid fine art collector with upper-class aspira-
tions who died flat broke. Rather than sell his art and estate, however, he willed both to
the state of Florida.

Today the 66-acre **Ringling Museum Complex** (☎941-359-5700; www.ringling.org;
5401 Bayshore Rd; adult/child $25/10; ☺10am-5:30pm, to 8pm Thu) is one of the Gulf Coast's
premier attractions; it's worth a day and more. A good introduction is the 30-minute
film in the historic 18th-century **Asolo Theater**, then tour Ringling's Venetian Gothic
mansion, **Ca d'Zan**. Theatrically over-the-top Renaissance and Baroque decor includes
masterful painted ceilings; guided tours grant access to the extravagant 2nd-floor living
quarters.

Even more impressive, the **John & Mabel Ringling Museum of Art** is packed with
imposing, passionate religious and mythological works from the 14th to 18th centuries.
One wing presents contemporary exhibits and, in 2012, a new James Turrell–designed
'Sky Space.'

Finally, there's the one-of-a-kind **Circus Museum**. Really several museums, it dis-
plays ephemera from Ringling's traveling show, a history of the circus from sideshow to
Cirque du Soleil, and in the center ring, a truly epic scale re-creation of the entire Ringling
Bros circus in action. It's as thrilling as the circus itself.

boat among hundreds of alligators, and for the area's best hiking and camping; get directions and tour times online.

For arts and performance information, check out the **Arts and Cultural Alliance** (www.sarasotaarts.org). The all-encompassing **Van Wezel Performing Arts Hall** (☑941-953-3368; www.vanwezel.org; 777 N Tamiami Trail) showcases all types of performances, while the **Asolo Repertory Theatre** (☑941-351-8000; www.asolorep.org; 5555 N Tamiami Trail) is a lauded regional theater company.

🛏 Sleeping & Eating

In addition to downtown Sarasota and Siesta Village, **St Armands Circle** on Lido Key is an evening social hub, with a proliferation of stylish shops and restaurants.

TOP CHOICE Hotel Ranola   BOUTIQUE HOTEL **$$**
(☑941-951-0111; www.hotelranola.com; 118 Indian Pl; r $180-190; P ❄ @) The nine rooms feel like a designer's brownstone apartment: free-spirited and effortlessly artful, but with real working kitchens. It's urban funk, walkable to downtown Sarasota.

Sunsets on the Key   APARTMENT **$$$**
(☑941-312-9797; www.sunsetsonthekey.com; 5203 Avenida Navarre; apt $230-340; P ❄ 🌊 🐾) In Siesta Village, eight well-kept, rigorously clean condo apartments are run like a hotel.

Owen's Fish Camp   SOUTHERN **$$**
(☑941-951-6936; www.owensfishcamp.com; 516 Burns Lane; mains $9-20; ⏱4-10pm, to 11pm Fri & Sat) This ironically hip swamp shack downtown serves upscale versions of Florida-style Southern cuisine. The emphasis is on seafood, and the energy is high.

Broken Egg   BREAKFAST **$**
(www.thebrokenegg.com; 140 Avenida Messina; mains $7-14; ⏱7:30am-2:30pm) This diner-style breakfast institution on Siesta Key, known for huge pancakes and cheddary home fries, is a social hub each morning.

Fort Myers

Workaday, sprawling Fort Myers is overshadowed by the region's pretty beaches and upscale, sophisticated towns. However, a recent facelift has spruced up the historic riverfront district (along 1st St between Broadway and Lee St) into an attractive, brick-lined collection of restaurants and bars. Visit www.fortmyers.org for information.

Fort Myers' main claim to fame is the **Edison & Ford Winter Estates** (www.edisonfordwinterestates.org; 2350 McGregor Blvd; adult/child $20/11; ⏱9am-5:30pm). Famous inventor Thomas Edison built a winter home and lab here in 1885, and automaker Henry Ford became his neighbor in 1916. The excellent museum focuses mainly on the overwhelming scope of Edison's genius, and their homes are genteel, landscaped delights.

From November through March, one of the easiest ways to encounter wintering manatees is at **Lee County Manatee Park** (www.leeparks.org; 10901 State Rd 80; parking per hr/day $1/5; ⏱park 8am-sunset year-round, visitorscenter 9am-4pm Nov-Mar), a warm-water power-plant discharge canal that's now a protected sanctuary. The park is signed off Hwy 80, about 6.5 miles from downtown.

For an easily accessible taste of South Florida wetlands, meander the 1.2-mile boardwalk trail of the **Six Mile Cypress Slough Preserve** (www.leeparks.org/sixmile; 7791 Penzance Blvd; parking per hr/day $1/5; ⏱dawn-dusk).

Fort Myers Beach

Fifteen miles south of Fort Myers, Fort Myers Beach is 7 miles of talcum powder-fine sand along Estero Island, presided over by one of Florida's quintessential activity-and-party-fueled beach towns. Families often prefer Fort Myers Beach because it's more affordable than neighboring coastal towns, and coeds like it because its bars are louder and more raucous. For town information, visit www.fortmyersbeachchamber.org.

The only draw, and it's a good one, is the beachy fun, but nearby **Lovers Key State Park** (www.floridastateparks.org/loverskey; car/bike $8/2; ⏱sunrise-sunset) adds great shelling as well as hiking and kayaking among quiet islands and canals (frequented by manatees).

Impeccably clean and well maintained, **Edison Beach House** (☑239-463-1530; www.edisonbeachhouse.com; 830 Estero Blvd; r $200-335; ❄ 🌊 🐾) is perfectly situated near action central (the so-called Times Sq area), yet soothingly comfortable, with full kitchens. For funky charm in a more low-key beach section, nab one of the six rooms at **Mango Street Inn** (☑239-233-8542; www.mangostreetinn.com; 126 Mango St; r $145-165; ❄), an idiosyncratic B&B serving delectable breakfasts by a Cajun-trained chef.

Sanibel & Captiva Islands

Shaped like a fish hook trying to lure Fort Myers, these two slivers of barrier island lie across a 2-mile causeway (toll $6). Upscale but unpretentious, with a carefully managed shoreline that feels remarkably lush and undeveloped, the islands are idyllic, cushy getaways, where bikes are the preferred mode of travel, the shelling is legendary and romantic meals are a reservation away. The **Sanibel & Captiva Islands Chamber of Commerce** (☏239-472-1080; www.sanibel-captiva.org; 1159 Causeway Rd, Sanibel; ☉9am-5pm; ☎) is one of the most helpful VCs around and can help with accommodations.

In addition to its fabulous beaches, Sanibel's 6300-acre **JN 'Ding' Darling National Wildlife Refuge** (www.fws.gov/dingdarling; MM2 Sanibel-Captiva Rd, Sanibel; car/bike $5/1; ☉visitor center 9am-5pm, refuge 7am-7pm Sat-Thu) is a splendid refuge that's home to an abundance of seabirds and wildlife. It has an excellent nature center, a 5-mile Wildlife Drive, narrated tram tours and easy kayaking in Tarpon Bay. For tours and boat rentals, contact **Tarpon Bay Explorers** (☏239-472-8900; www.tarponbayexplorers.com; 900 Tarpon Bay Rd, Sanibel).

Like a mermaid's jewel box, the **Bailey-Matthews Shell Museum** (www.shellmuseum.org; 3075 Sanibel-Captiva Rd, Sanibel; adult/child $7/4; ☉10am-5pm) is a natural history of the sea, with covetous displays of shells worldwide. To rent bikes or any other wheeled contrivance, visit **Billy's Rentals** (☏239-472-5248; www.billysrentals.com; 1470 Periwinkle Way, Sanibel; bikes per 2hr/day from $5/15; ☉8:30am-5pm).

On Captiva, the **'Tween Waters Inn** (☏239-472-5161; www.tween-waters.com; 15951 Captiva Dr, Captiva; r $160-215, ste $220-405; P❄@☎❄⛵) is a full-service yet low-key resort with a variety of good-value lodging choices; ask for a renovated room. In addition to a big pool, tennis courts and spa, its marina offers various kayak rentals, guided trips and boat cruises.

For a more personal experience, stay in the five-room **Tarpon Tale Inn** (☏239-472-0939; www.tarpontale.com; 367 Periwinkle Way, Sanibel; r $150-260; ❄@☎❄), which does a nice imitation of a charming, hammock-strung B&B, but without breakfast.

Instead, start your day at the **Over Easy Cafe** (www.overeasycafesanibel.com; 630 Tarpon Rd, Sanibel; mains $8-13; ☉7am-2:30pm), which is where everyone goes for a top-quality,

diner-style breakfast. For romantic gourmet, one excellent choice is **Sweet Melissa's Cafe** (☏239-472-1956; www.sweetmelissascafe.net; 1625 Periwinkle Way, Sanibel; tapas $11-14, mains $26-34; ☉11:30am-2:30pm Mon-Fri, from 5pm nightly), which offers creative, relaxed refinement.

If you have kids, prepare yourself for the spectacularly kitschy **Bubble Room** (www.bubbleroomrestaurant.com; 15001 Captiva Dr, Captiva; lunch $10-15, dinner $20-30; ☉11:30am-3pm & 4:30-9pm), a riotous pastiche of retro cartoons, superheroes, Christmas and Golden Era movie stars.

Naples

The Gulf Coast's answer to Palm Beach, Naples is a perfectly manicured, rich town with an adult sense of self and one of the most pristine, relaxed city beaches in the state. While it is certainly family friendly, it appeals most to romance-minded travelers seeking fine art and fine dining, trendy cocktails, fashion-conscious shopping and luscious sunsets. Visit www.napleschamber.org for city information.

For contemporary art, the sophisticated **Naples Museum of Art** (www.thephil.org; 5833 Pelican Bay Blvd; adult/child $8/4; ☉10am-4pm Tue-Sat, from noon Sun Oct-Jun) is a rewarding collection with cleverly designed exhibits. Meanwhile, one of the state's best nature conservancies and rehabilitation centers is **Naples Nature Center** (www.conservancy.org; 14th Ave N & Goodlette-Frank Rd; adult/child $10/5; ☉9am-4:30pm Mon-Sat), recently renovated into a LEED-certified campus with fantastic exhibits.

For well-polished, Mediterranean-style luxury in the heart of downtown's 5th Ave corridor, stay at the historic **Inn on 5th** (☏239-403-8777; www.innonfifth.com; 699 5th Ave S; r $320-500; ❄@☎❄). For a well-located, good-value midrange motel, the **Lemon Tree Inn** (☏239-262-1414; www.lemontreeinn.com; 250 9th St S, at 3rd Ave S; r $130-200; ❄@☎❄⛵) is a pretty, bright choice.

Good eats are abundant. Top choices for a special meal include **Cafe Lurcat** (☏239-213-3357; www.cafelurcat.com; 494 5th Ave; lunch $14-18, dinner $25-40; ☉5-9:30pm Sun-Thu, to 10pm Fri & Sat), a sexy, multilevel restaurant and lively bar (open to 11pm or midnight nightly), and the off-the-beaten-path **IM Tapas** (☏239-403-8272; http://imtapas.com; 965 4th Ave N; tapas $9-21; ☉from 5:30pm), where a mother-and-daughter team serves Madrid-worthy Spanish tapas.

CENTRAL FLORIDA

For a century, tourists came to Florida for, in essence, two things: its white-sand beaches and teal waters (and the resorts serving them), and to peek inside the alligator-infested Everglades. Walt Disney changed all that when he opened the Magic Kingdom in 1971. Today Orlando is the theme park capital of the world, and Walt Disney World is Florida's number one attraction.

Orlando

Like Las Vegas, Orlando is almost entirely given over to fantasy. It's a place to come when you want to imagine you're somewhere else: Hogwarts, perhaps, or Cinderella's Castle, or ancient Jerusalem, or Dr Seuss' world, or an African safari. And like Vegas' casinos, Orlando's theme parks work hard to be constantly entertaining thrill rides where the only concern is your pleasure. Even outside the theme parks, Orlando can exhibit a hyper atmosphere of fiberglass-modeled, cartoon-costumed pop culture amusement.

Yet there is, in fact, a real city to explore, one with tree-shaded parks of the natural variety, art museums, orchestras, and dinners that don't involve high-fiving Goofy. And just outside the city, Florida's wilderness and wildlife, particularly its crystal springs, can be as memorably bizarre as anything Ripley ever dreamed up.

◉ Sights & Activities

DOWNTOWN & LOCH HAVEN PARK
Fashionable Thornton Park has several good restaurants and bars, while Loch Haven Park is home to a cluster of cultural institutions.

Orlando Museum of Art   MUSEUM
(☑407-896-4231; www.omart.org; 2416 N Mills Ave; adult/child $8/5; ◷10am-4pm Tue-Fri, from noon Sat & Sun) Spotlighting American and African art as well as unique traveling exhibits.

Mennello Museum of American Art   MUSEUM
(☑407-246-4278; www.mennellomuseum. org; 900 E Princeton St; adult/child $4/free; ◷10:30am-4:30pm Tue-Sat, from noon Sun)

Features the bright folk art of Earl Cunningham, plus traveling exhibitions.

Orlando Science Center   MUSEUM
(☑407-514-2000; www.osc.org; 777 E Princeton St; adult/child $15/10; ◷10am-5pm Thu-Tue) Candy-coated hands-on science for the whole family.

Harry P Leu Gardens   PARK
(www.leugardens.org; 1920 N Forest Ave; adult/child $7/2; ◷9am-5pm) One mile east of Loch Haven Park is this 50-acre tranquil escape from all the gloss.

INTERNATIONAL DRIVE
Like a theme park itself, International Dr (I-Dr) is shoulder to shoulder with high-energy amusements: sprinkled among the major theme, wildlife and water parks, smaller attractions shout for attention: Ripley's Believe It or Not, the upside-down Wonder-Works and an indoor skydiving experience. Chain restaurants and hotels also crowd the thoroughfare.

Universal Orlando Resort   THEME PARK
(☑407-363-8000;www.universalorlando.com;1000 Universal Studios Plaza; 1-day ticket 1/2 parks $82/112, 4 days $140/150; ◷from 9am) Smaller, easier to navigate and more pedestrian-friendly than Walt Disney World, Universal Orlando is everything you wish Disney could be. Universal features two theme parks, a water park, three hotels and an entertainment district. The megaplex is as absorbingly themed as Disney, but it replaces Snow White and the Seven Dwarves with Spider-Man, the Simpsons and – to widespread acclaim in 2010 – Harry Potter.

For good ol' scream-it-from-the-rooftops, no-holds-barred, laugh-out-loud fun, explore the multiple worlds within Islands of Adventure, which is packed with adrenaline rides. Marvel Super Hero Island is a sensory overload of comic book characters; there's dino-happy Jurassic Park; the ersatz-mystical Lost Continent; and the kid-friendly Toon Lagoon and Seuss Landing. But most famously of all, there is now the Wizarding World of Harry Potter, which brings to life Hogwarts and Hogsmeade in exquisite, rib-tickling detail.

At Universal Studios, the central question is: would you like to live the movies? Do battle with the Terminator? Go *Back to the Future?* Escape Jaws, Beetlejuice, the Mummy, *Men in Black* aliens and a *Twister* tornado? Do Lucille Ball, Curious George,

Shrek and the Simpsons amuse you? With a Hollywood backlot feel, Universal Studios' simulation-heavy rides are dedicated to silver screen and TV icons.

Review multiple ticket options online, which can include add-ons like Express Plus line skipping and a dining plan; resort hotel guests also get nice park perks.

SeaWorld AMUSEMENT PARK
(☏407-351-3600; www.seaworld.com; 7007 Sea-World Dr; 2-day ticket $72; ☺from 9am) A peculiarly Floridian blend of marine animal shows and thrill rides, SeaWorld is home to both Shamu the killer whale and Kraken the

floorless roller coaster. While the rides provide jolts of adrenaline, the real draws are the up-close sea life encounters (with manta rays, sharks, penguins, beluga whales) and the excellent dolphin, sea lion and killer whale shows. Make sure to check show and feeding times online before visiting, and plan your day accordingly.

Check online for combo tickets with Discovery Cove and Aquatica.

Discovery Cove WATER PARK
(☏407-370-1280; www.discoverycove.com; 6000 Discovery Cove Way; admission $129-169, incl dolphin swim $199-319; ☺8:30am-5:30pm) Attendance is

limited, ensuring Discovery Cove retains the feel of an exclusive tropical resort, complete with beaches, a fish-filled reef and an aviary. No high-speed thrills or frantic screaming, just blessed relaxation and the chance to swim with dolphins. The price is steep, but everything is included: buffet lunch, beer, towels, parking, even a day pass to SeaWorld.

Aquatica WATER PARK
(☑407-351-3600; www.aquaticabyseaworld.com; admission $42) Orlando's latest water park is newer, cleaner and prettier than the others, but in the end, it's the same combination of lazy rivers, splash zones, wave pools and slippery slides that everyone looks for.

Holy Land Experience THEME PARK
(☑407-872-2272; www.holylandexperience.com; 4655 Vineland Rd; adult/child 6-12yr $35/20; ☉10am-6pm Mon-Sat) Just north of I-Dr, this is an earnest re-creation of ancient Jerusalem and biblical times, which makes it a theme park, but without roller coasters and pop culture sarcasm.

WINTER PARK

On the northern edge of Orlando, Winter Park is a friendly college town with some outstanding museums and a relaxing downtown.

**Charles Hosmer Morse
Museum of American Art** MUSEUM
(www.morsemuseum.org; 445 N Park Ave; adult/child $5/free; ☉9:30am-4pm Tue-Sat, from 1pm Sun) Internationally famous, with the world's most comprehensive collection of Tiffany glass; stunning centerpiece is a chapel interior.

FREE **Zora Neale Hurston National
Museum of Fine Arts** MUSEUM
(www.zoranealehurstonmuseum.com; 227 E Kennedy Blvd, Eatonville; ☉9am-4pm Mon-Fri, 11am-1pm

Sat) In neighboring Eatonville (get directions online), this museum is dedicated to Florida novelist Zora Neale Hurston; changing exhibits of African American artists.

GREATER ORLANDO

Gatorland AMUSEMENT PARK
(www.gatorland.com; 14501 S Orange Blossom Trail/ Hwy 17; adult/child $23/15; ☉9am-5pm) This Old Florida throwback is small, silly and kitschy. It's all about alligators, with gator wrestling, gators jumping, feeding gators hot dogs and other great squeal-worthy moments.

Legoland THEME PARK
(http://florida.legoland.com; 1 Legoland Way, Winter Haven; adult/child $65/55; ☉10am-5pm) In Winter Haven, Florida's newest theme park was not yet open at the time of research. Like its California cousin, Legoland rebuilds the world brick by brick, but to scale, with rides and build-your-own fun that are heaven for the 12-and-under set.

🛏 Sleeping

In addition to the Walt Disney World resorts, Orlando has countless lodging options. Most are clustered around I-Dr, US 192 in Kissimmee and I-4. **Reserve Orlando** (www.reserveorlando.com) is a central booking agency. **Universal Orlando Resort** (☑407-363-8000; r & ste from $270) has three recommended hotels.

EO Inn & Spa BOUTIQUE HOTEL **$$**
(☑407-481-8485; www.eoinn.com; 227 N Eola Dr; r $139-229; P✳☎☙) Sleek and understated, this downtown boutique inn overlooks Lake Eola near Thornton Park, with neutral-toned rooms that are elegant in their simplicity.

Courtyard at Lake Lucerne B&B **$$**
(☑407-648-5188; www.orlandohistoricinn.com; 211 N Lucerne Circle E; r $99-225; P✳☎☙) This lovely

historic inn, with enchanting gardens and genteel breakfast, has roomy art-deco suites and handsome antiques throughout. Unfortunately, it sits directly under two highway overpasses.

Veranda Bed & Breakfast   B&B $$
(☑407-849-0321; www.theverandabandb.com; 115 N Summerlin Ave; r $110-270; P❄️🛜🏊) Ideal for wandering Thornton Park and Lake Eola, this European-style B&B has big antique beds and is a lovely retreat from all the bustle.

Barefoot'n in the Keys   MOTEL $$
(☑407-397-1144; www.barefootn.com; 2750 Florida Plaza Blvd; ste $80-300; @🛜🏊) Clean, bright and spacious suites in a yellow six-story building. Low-key, friendly and close to Disney, this makes an excellent alternative to generic chains.

✖ Eating

On and around I-Dr you'll find an explosion of chains; a half-mile stretch of Sand Lake Rd has been dubbed 'restaurant row' for its upscale dining.

Dessert Lady Café   CAFE $
(☑407-999-5696; 120 W Church St; mains $5-10; ⏱11:30am-11pm Tue-Thu, to midnight Fri, 4pm-midnight Sat) There's a bordello atmosphere and a bistro menu of pulled-pork sliders, chicken salad, soups and quiches to go with the sinful desserts, from fruit cobbler to bourbon pecan pie.

Graffiti Junktion American Burger Bar   BURGERS $$
(900 E Washington St, Thornton Park; mains $12-25; ⏱11pm-1am, to midnight Sun) This neon graffiti-covered happenin' hangout is all about massive burgers with attitude. Top yours with a fried egg, artichoke hearts, chili, avocado and more.

Ravenous Pig   AMERICAN $$$
(☑407-628-2333; 1234 Orange Ave, Winter Park; mains $14-29; ⏱11:30am-2pm & 5:30-9:30pm Tue-Thu, to 10:30pm Fri & Sat) One of Orlando's most talked-about foodie destinations, this bustling hot spot serves designer cocktails and creative, delicious versions of shrimp and grits, and lobster tacos. Reservations recommended.

Yellow Dog Eats   BARBECUE $$
(☑407-296-0609; www.yellowdogeats.com; 1236 Hempel Ave, Windermere; mains $10-20; ⏱11am-9pm) Housed in an old, tin-roof general store,

and quirky to the extreme, it's not your typical barbecue. Try the excellent Cuban-style black beans and the Florida Cracker (pulled pork with gouda, bacon and fried onions). It's a drive; get directions online.

🌱 Dandelion Communitea Café   VEGETARIAN $
(☑407-362-1864; http://dandelioncommunitea.com; 618 N Thornton Ave; mains $5-10; ⏱11am-10pm Mon-Sat, to 5pm Sun; 🍴) Unabashedly crunchy and definitively organic, this pillar of creative, sustainable, locavore vegetarianism is genuinely delicious, with tons of community spirit. Look for events.

🍷 Drinking & Entertainment

Orlando Weekly (www.orlandoweekly.com) is the best source for entertainment listings. There's plenty to do downtown, where there's a happening bar district around Orange Ave between Church St and Jefferson St.

Universal Studio's **CityWalk** (www.citywalkorlando.com) has a concentration of cinemas, restaurants, clubs and big-name shows.

Social   LIVE MUSIC
(www.thesocial.org; 54 N Orange Ave) Check out great live music.

Latitudes   BAR
(www.churchstreetbars.com; 33 W Church St) Island-inspired rooftop bar, with two more bars below.

Wall St Plaza   BAR
(www.wallstplaza.net; 25 Wall St Plaza) Eight theme bars, with live music, all in one plaza.

Parliament House   GAY
(www.parliamenthouse.com; 410 N Orange Blossom Trail) Legendary gay resort and drag shows; six bars.

ℹ Information

For city information, good multilingual guides and maps, visit Orlando's **Official Visitor Center** (☑407-363-5872; www.visitorlando.com; 8723 International Dr; ⏱8:30am-6:30pm). Gay travelers can peruse www.orlandogaycities.com. For theme park advice, visit www.themeparkinsider.com.

ℹ Getting There & Around

Orlando International Airport (MCO; www.orlandoairports.net) has buses and taxis to major tourist areas. **Mears Transportation** (☑407-423-5566; www.mearstransportation.com) provides shuttles for $20 to $30 per person.

Greyhound (www.greyhound.com; 555 N John Young Pkwy) serves numerous cities. **Amtrak** (www.amtrak.com; 1400 Sligh Blvd) has daily trains south to Miami and north to New York City.

Orlando's bus network is operated by **Lynx** (www.golynx.com; ride/day pass $2/4.50). **I-Ride Trolley** (www.iridetrolley.com; adult/child $1/free; ⊙8am-10:30pm) buses run along I-Dr.

When driving, note that I-4 is the main north–south connector, though it's confusingly labeled east–west. To go north, take I-4 east (toward Daytona); to go south, get on I-4 west (toward Tampa). The main east–west roads are Hwy 50 and Hwy 528 (the Bee Line Expwy), which accesses Orlando International Airport.

Walt Disney World Resort

Covering 40 sq miles, Walt Disney World (WDW; http://disneyworld.disney.go.com) is the largest theme park resort in the world. It includes four separate theme parks, two water parks, a sports complex, five golf courses, two dozen hotels, 100 restaurants and two shopping and nightlife districts – proving that it's not such a small world, after all. At times it feels ridiculously crowded and corporate, but with or without kids, you won't be able to inoculate yourself against Disney's highly infectious enthusiasm and warm-hearted nostalgia. Naturally, expectations run high, and even the self-proclaimed 'happiest place on earth' doesn't always live up to its billing. Still, it always happens: Cinderella curtsies to your little Belle, your own Jedi knight vanquishes Darth Maul, or you tear up on that corny ride about our tiny planet, and you're swept up in the magic.

◉ Sights & Activities

Anytime schools are out – during summer and holidays – WDW will be the most crowded. The least crowded times are January to February, mid-September through October and early December. Late fall tends to have the best weather; frequent downpours accompany the hot, humid summer months.

Magic Kingdom   THEME PARK

When people think of WDW, they picture the Magic Kingdom, from the iconic Cinderella's Castle to Space Mountain, the Haunted Mansion and Pirates of the Caribbean (now including Johnny Depp's Jack Sparrow). This is where the fireworks and nighttime light parade illuminate Main Street, USA. For Disney mythology, it doesn't get better,

and rides and shows aim squarely at young kids and their parents and grandparents.

Disney Hollywood Studios   THEME PARK

Formerly Disney-MGM Studios, this is the least-charming of Disney's parks. However, it does have two of WDW's most exciting rides: the unpredictable elevator in the Twilight Zone Tower of Terror and the Aerosmith-themed Rock 'n' Roller Coaster. Wannabe singers can audition for the American Idol Experience, kids can join the Jedi Training Academy, and various programs present Walt Disney himself and how Disney's movies are made.

Epcot   THEME PARK

An acronym for 'Experimental Prototype Community of Tomorrow,' Epcot was Disney's vision of a high-tech city when it opened in 1982. It's divided into two halves: Future World, with rides and corporate-sponsored interactive exhibits, and World Showcase, providing an interesting toe-dip into the cultures of 11 countries. Epcot is much more soothingly low-key than other parks, and it has some of the best food and shopping. Plus, a few rides are WDW highlights, like Soarin' and Mission: Space. The interactive Turtle Talk with Crush is delightful.

Animal Kingdom   THEME PARK

This sometimes surreal blend of African safari, zoo, rides, costumed characters, shows and dinosaurs establishes its own distinct tone. It's best at animal encounters and shows, with the 110-acre Kilimanjaro Safaris as its centerpiece. The iconic Tree of Life houses the fun It's Tough to Be a Bug! show, and Expedition Everest and Kali River Rapids are the top thrill rides.

Tickets

The simple logic behind ticket options is the longer you stay, the less you pay (per day). Tickets allow entrance to one park per day, and can range from one to 10 days: adults from $82 to $262, and children aged three to nine from $74 to $239. By day six, the per day cost is 50% the single-day ticket, and so on. Buy in advance to avoid lines at the gate.

Options you can add (for extra cost) are discount passes to other Disney areas, a no-expiration option (for unused days) and, the most recommended, Park Hopper ($56), allowing entrance to all four WDW parks in a day. Check online for packages.

For discounts, check out www.mousesavers.com and www.undercovertourist.com.

🛏 Sleeping

WDW has 24 family-friendly sleeping options, from camping to deluxe resorts, and Disney guests receive great perks (extended park hours, discount dining plans, free transportation, airport shuttles). Rates vary by season, and there are 20 seasons! Disney's thorough website outlines rates and amenities for every property. Approximate rates given below are for peak season.

For the most amenities, choose a roomy **Deluxe Villa** (villas $540-1600), the only properties with full kitchen and in-room washer/dryer. At the other end of the scale, the **campground** (campsites $70-100, cabins $360) is meticulously maintained, with lots of activities. **Value Resorts** (r $120-150) are the least-expensive option (besides camping); quality is equivalent to basic chain hotels, and (fair warning) they are favored by school groups.

When evaluating properties, the main thing to consider is their location to the parks you want to visit; room quality is uniformly average except at the handful of top deluxe properties. Many visitors prefer the Deluxe Resort hotels in Epcot (Boardwalk Inn, Beach Club and Yacht Club, Swan and Dolphin); these are walkable to Epcot, Hollywood Studios and Disney's Boardwalk.

🍴 Eating

Theme park food ranges from OK to awful; the most interesting is served in Epcot's World Showcase. Sit-down meals are best, but *always* make reservations; seats can be impossible to get without one. For any dining, you can call **central reservations** (☎407-939-3463) up to 180 days in advance.

Disney has three dinner shows (a luau, country-style BBQ and vaudeville show) and about 15 character meals, and these are insanely popular (see website for details). Book them the minute your 180-day window opens. The most sought-after meal is **Cinderella's Royal Table** (adult $33-45, child $24-28) inside the Magic Kingdom's castle, where you dine with Disney princesses.

Sci-Fi Dine-In Theater   AMERICAN
(Hollywood Studios; mains $11-21) Dine in Cadillacs and watch classic sci-fi flicks.

California Grill   AMERICAN
(Contemporary Resort; mains $15-38) Coveted seats with great views of the Magic Kingdom fireworks.

O'Hana   HAWAIIAN
(Polynesian Resort; mains $15-30) Great South Pacific decor and interactive Polynesian-themed luau shenanigans.

Boma   BUFFET
(Animal Kingdom Lodge; adult/child breakfast $17/10, dinner $27/13) African-inspired eatery with pleasant surroundings and a buffet several notches above the rest.

Victoria and Albert   AMERICAN
(Grand Floridian; prix fixe $125-200) A true jacket-and-tie, crystal goblet romantic gourmet restaurant – no kidding, and no kids (under 10).

⭐ Entertainment

In addition to theme park events like Magic Kingdom parades and fireworks and Epcot's Illuminations, Disney has two entertainment districts – Downtown Disney and Disney's Boardwalk – with eats, bars, music, movies, shops and shows.

Cirque du Soleil   CIRCUS
(☎407-939-7600; www.cirquedusoleil.com; adult $76-132, child $61-105; ☺6pm & 9pm Tue-Sat) The best live show in Disney World; exquisite theatrical acrobatics.

House of Blues   LIVE MUSIC
(☎407-934-2583; www.houseofblues.com) Top acts visit this national chain; Sunday's Gospel Brunch truly rocks.

DisneyQuest   ARCADE
(1 day $36-42; ☺11:30am-10pm Sun-Thu, to 11pm Fri & Sat) Five floors of virtual reality and arcade games.

ESPN's Wide World of Sports Complex   SPECTATOR SPORT
(www.espnwwos.disney.go.com) This 220-acre sports facility hosts hundreds of amateur and professional sporting events.

ℹ Getting There & Around

Most hotels in Kissimmee and Orlando – and all Disney properties – offer free transportation to WDW. Disney-owned resorts also offer free transportation from the airport. Drivers can reach all four parks via I-4 and park for $14. The Magic Kingdom lot is huge; trams get you to the entrance.

Within WDW, a complex network of monorails, boats and buses get you between the parks, resorts and entertainment districts. Pick up a transportation map at your resort or at Guest Relations; Disney's official **phone apps** (http://m.disneyworld.go.com) can also be helpful.

Around Orlando

Just north of Orlando await some of Florida's best outdoor adventures, particularly swimming, snorkeling and kayaking in its crystal-clear, 72°F (22°C) natural springs. Closest is **Wekiwa Springs State Park** (407-884-2008; www.floridastateparks.org/wekiwasprings; car/campsites $6/24), with 13 miles of hiking trails, a spring-fed swimming hole, nice campground and the tranquil 'Wild and Scenic' Wekiva River; rent kayaks from **Nature Adventures** (407-884-4311; www.canoewekiva.com; kayak rental $15-20).

Blue Spring State Park (386-775-3663; www.floridastateparks.org/bluespring; car/campsites $6/24) is a favorite of wintering manatees, and two-hour cruises ply the St John's River. Just north of Deland, **De Leon Springs State Park** (386-985-4212; www.floridastateparks.org/deleonsprings; car $6; 8am-dusk) has a huge swimming area, more kayaking and tours of the Ponce de León's alleged fountain of youth.

Connoisseurs of Old Florida shouldn't miss **Silver Springs** (www.silversprings.com; adult/child under 10yr $30/25; 10am-5pm), near Ocala, which invented the glass-bottom boat and remains a delightfully old-fashioned nature theme park.

To really escape into raw wilderness, head for the **Ocala National Forest** (http://fs.usda.gov/ocala), which has dozens of campgrounds, hundreds of miles of trails and 600 lakes. The hiking, biking, canoeing and camping are some of the state's best. See the website for visitor centers and descriptions.

FLORIDA PANHANDLE

Take all the things that are great about the Deep South – friendly people, molasses-slow pace, oak-lined country roads, fried food galore – and then add several hundred miles of sugar-white beaches, dozens of gin-clear natural springs and all the fresh oysters you can suck down, and there you have it: the fantastic, highly underrated Florida Panhandle.

Tallahassee

Florida's capital, cradled between gently rising hills and beneath tree-canopied roadways, is a calm and gracious city. Geographically and culturally, it's closer to Atlanta than it is to Miami, and far more Southern than the majority of the state it administrates. Despite the city's two major universities (Florida State and Florida Agricultural and Mechanical University) and its status as a government center, there's not much to detain a visitor for more than a day or two.

Get information from the **visitor center** (850-413-9200; www.visittallahassee.com; 106 E Jefferson St; 8am-5pm Mon-Fri).

◉ Sights & Activities

Mary Brogan Museum of Art & Science   MUSEUM
(www.thebrogan.org; 350 S Duval St; adult/child $7.50/5; 10am-5pm Mon-Sat, from 1pm Sun) Affiliated with the Smithsonian, this museum mixes a kid-friendly, hands-on science center with the Tallahassee art museum to good effect.

FREE **Museum of Florida History**   MUSEUM
(www.museumoffloridahistory.com; 500 S Bronough St; 9am-4:30pm Mon-Fri, from 10am Sat, from noon Sun) Here it is, Florida's history splayed out in fun, crisp exhibits: from mastodon skeletons to Florida's Paleo-Indians and Spanish shipwrecks, the Civil War to 'tin-can tourism.'

Mission San Luis   HISTORIC SITE
(www.missionsanluis.org; 2020 W Mission Rd; adult/child $5/2; 10am-4pm Tue-Sun) The 60-acre site of a 17th-century Spanish and Apalachee mission that's been wonderfully reconstructed, especially the soaring Council House. Good tours included with admission provide a fascinating taste of 300 years ago.

FREE **Florida Capitol Buildings**   HISTORIC BUILDING
Old and new, side by side. The current **Florida State Capitol** (cnr Pensacola & Duval Sts; 8am-5pm Mon-Fri), is, in a word, ugly, but its observation deck is worth seeing. Next door, the **Historic Capitol** (www.flhistoriccapitol.gov; 400 S Monroe St; 9am-4:30pm Mon-Fri, from 10am Sat, from noon Sun) is the more charming 1902 predecessor. Inside, the **Florida Legislative Research Center and Museum** (www.flrcm.com) has intriguing government and cultural exhibits, including one on the infamous 2000 US presidential election.

🛏 Sleeping & Eating

Chains are clumped at exits along I-10 and along Monroe St between I-10 and downtown.

Hotel Duval　　　　　　　　HOTEL **$$**
(☎850-224-6000; www.hotelduval.com; 415 N Monroe St; r from $119; P❋☀☎) Tallahassee's slickest digs. This new 117-room hotel goes in for a neo-mod look. A rooftop bar and lounge is open until 2am most nights, and Shula's, a fancy chain steakhouse, is off the lobby.

Governor's Inn　　　　　　　HOTEL **$$**
(☎850-681-6855; www.thegovinn.com; 209 S Adams St; r $129-149; P❋☎) In a stellar downtown location, this warm, inviting inn has everything from single rooms to two-level loft suites, plus a daily cocktail hour.

Catfish Pad　　　　　　　　SEAFOOD **$**
(www.catfishpad.com; 4229 W Pensacola St; mains $4-11; ⏰11am-3pm & 5-9pm Mon-Sat) There's no doubt you're in the South at this home-style seafood joint. Go for a plate of cornmeal-battered catfish with a side of grits, chased down with a cup of sweet tea. Yum.

Reangthai　　　　　　　　　THAI **$$**
(☎850-386-7898; reangthai.com; 2740 Capital Circle NE; mains $13-20; ⏰11am-2pm Tue-Fri, 5-10pm Mon-Sat) The real deal, and elegant despite its strip mall setting, Reangthai serves the kind of spicy, fish sauce-y, explode-in-your-mouth cuisine so many American Thai restaurants shy away from.

Andrew's Downtown　　　　ITALIAN **$$**
(☎850-222-3444; www.andrewsdowntown.com; 228 S Adams St; mains $9-36; ⏰11:30am-10pm) Downtown's see-and-be-seen political hot spot. At this split-level place, the downstairs grill serves casual burgers and beer, while upstairs serves upscale neo-Tuscan dishes.

☆ Entertainment

Bradfordville Blues Club　　LIVE MUSIC
(☎850-906-0766;　www.bradfordvilleblues.com; 7152 Moses Lane, off Bradfordville Rd; tickets $15-20; ⏰8pm-2am Fri & Sat) Down the end of a dirt road lit by tiki torches, you'll find a bonfire raging under the live oaks at this hidden-away juke joint that hosts excellent national blues acts.

❶ Getting There & Around

The **Tallahassee Regional Airport** (TLH; www.talgov.com/airport) is about 5 miles southwest of downtown, off Hwy 263. The **Greyhound station** (www.greyhound.com; 112 W Tennessee St, at Duval St) is right downtown. **Star Metro** (www.talgov.com/starmetro; fare $1.25) provides local bus service.

Apalachicola & Around

Slow, mellow and perfectly preserved, Apalachicola is one of the Panhandle's most irresistible, romantic villages. Perched on the edge of a broad bay famous for its oysters, the oak-shaded town is a hugely popular getaway, with a new wave of bistros, art galleries, eclectic boutiques and historic B&Bs.

For town information, visit www.apalachicolabay.org. For nature, the pristine **St Vincent Island** (www.fws.gov/saintvincent) holds pearly dunes, pine forests and wetlands teeming with wildlife. Neighboring **St George Island State Park** (www.floridastateparks.org/stgeorgeisland; car $6) offers 9 miles of glorious, undeveloped beaches. In town, seek out fishing charters and wildlife cruises.

Ensure romance with a night's stay at **Coombs House Inn** (☎850-653-9199; www.coombshouseinn.com; 80 6th St; r $129-269; P❋☎), a stunning Victorian home transformed into a luscious, luxury B&B. Sample the town's famous bivalve, freshly shucked, baked or fried, at **Papa Joe's Oyster Bar & Grill** (www.papajoesoysterbar.com; 301b Market St; mains $8-18; ⏰11:30am-10pm).

Panama City Beach

There's no mistaking Panama City Beach for anything other than it is: a quintessentially Floridian, carnival-esqe beach town. Spring breakers and summer vacationers flock here for the beautiful white-sand beaches and the hurdy-gurdy of amusements, while mile after mile of high-rise condos insist on disrupting the view. Stop by the **visitor bureau** (☎850-233-5070; www.visitpanamacitybeach.com, www.pcbeach.org; 17001 Panama City Beach Pkwy; ⏰8am-5pm) for information.

A renowned wreck-diving site, the area around Panama City Beach has dozens of natural, historic and artificial reefs. **Dive Locker** (☎850-230-8006; www.divelocker.net; 106 Thomas Dr; ⏰8am-6pm Mon-Sat) has dives from $90, gear included. Get inspiration at the **Museum of Man in the Sea** (www.manthesea.org; 17314 Panama City Beach Pkwy; adult/child $5/free; ⏰10am-4pm Tue-Sun), showcasing the history of diving.

St Andrews State Park (www.floridastateparks.org/standrews; car $8) is a peaceful escape with nature trails, swimming beaches and wildlife. Just offshore, **Shell Island** has fantastic snorkeling, and **shuttles** (www.

Along the Panhandle coast between Panama City Beach and Destin, skip the main highway (Hwy 98) in favor of one of the most enchanting drives in Florida: Scenic Hwy 30A. This 18-mile stretch of road hugs what's referred to as the Emerald Coast for its almost fluorescent, gem-colored waters lapping brilliant white beaches of ground-quartz crystal.

Leading off Scenic Hwy 30A are pristine, wild parklands like **Grayton Beach State Park** (www.floridastateparks.org/graytonbeach; 357 Main Park Rd, Santa Rosa Beach; car $5), considered one of Florida's prettiest, most pristine strands. About 15 quaint communities hug the coast, some arty and funky, and some master-planned resorts with matchy-matchy architectural perfection. Of these, the most intriguing and surreal is the little village of **Seaside** (www.seasidefl.com), a Necco Wafer–colored town that was hailed as a model of New Urbanism in the 1980s.

Seaside is such an idealized vision that, unaltered, it formed the setting for the 1998 film *The Truman Show*, about a man whose 'perfect life' is nothing but a TV show. Other variations on this theme are WaterColor, Alys Beach and Rosemary Beach.

Good online resources are www.30a.com and www.visitsouthwalton.com.

---

shellislandshuttle.com; trip plus gear $22) depart every 30 minutes in summer.

🛏 Sleeping

Summer is the high season for Panhandle beaches. Panama City doesn't lack for choice; to avoid spring breakers, look for the code phrase 'family-friendly.'

Wisteria Inn MOTEL **$$**
(📞850-234-0557; www.wisteria-inn.com; 20404 Front Beach Rd; r from $109; 🅿❄🐾) This sweet little 15-room motel has a bright, Caribbean theme, poolside mimosa hours and an 'adults only' policy that discourages spring breakers.

Beachbreak by the Sea MOTEL **$**
(📞850-234-3870; www.beachbreakbythesea.com; 15405 Front Beach Rd; d $79-169; 🅿❄🐾) A refreshing four-story spot in a sea of high-rises, this place offers basic motel-style rooms, a central beachfront location and continental breakfast.

✖ Eating & Drinking

Pineapple Willy's CARIBBEAN **$$**
(www.pwillys.com; 9875 S Thomas Dr; mains $15-22; ⊙11am-late) Ask for a table on the restaurant pier for breezy beachside dining. Famed for its signature drinks and its house special: Jack Daniels BBQ ribs.

Firefly NOUVELLE CUISINE **$$$**
(📞850-249-3359; www.fireflypcb.com; 535 Beckrich Rd; mains $22-36; ⊙5-10pm) This uber atmospheric, fine dining establishment beckons with clever seafood dishes and its cool

Library Lounge. It's good enough for the US president – Obama ate here in 2010.

Tootsie's Orchid Lounge HONKY TONK
(www.tootsies.net; Pier Park; ⊙10am-late) Lacks the dusty character of the Nashville original, but the nonstop live country music is still plenty boot stompin'.

❶ Getting There & Around

The **Panama City International Airport** (PFN; www.iflybeaches.com) is served by a few major airlines. The **Greyhound Station** (www.greyhound.com; 917 Harrison Ave) is in Panama City, and the limited **Bay Town Trolley** (www.baytowntrolley.org; fare $1.50) runs only weekdays from 6am to 8pm.

Pensacola & Pensacola Beach

Neighbors with Alabama, Pensacola and its adjacent beach town welcome visitors driving in from the west. Its gorgeous snow-white beaches and tolerance of the annual spring break bacchanal ensure Pensacola's popularity. There is also a thrumming military culture and a sultry, Spanish-style downtown. The **visitor bureau** (📞850-434-1234; www.visitpensacola.com, www.visitpensacolabeach.com; 1401 E Gregory St; ⊙8am-5pm; @) has maps.

The region has taken its licks in recent years. In 2004 Hurricane Ivan did its best to smash the place, and in 2010 the Deepwater Horizon oil spill in the Gulf of Mexico tainted beaches with tar balls. However, today, all Panhandle beaches are clean of oil, Pensacola's buildings and roads are repaired, and the region is eager to welcome travelers back.

⊙ Sights & Activities

In 2007 a 910ft-long aircraft carrier was intentionally sunk off the coast of Pensacola to make the world's largest artificial reef. Now dubbed 'the Great Carrier Reef,' the USS Oriskany sits in the sand 210ft below the surface. One of many outfitters, MBT Divers (☑850-455-7702; www.mbtdivers.com; 3920 Barrancas Ave) offers two-tank Oriskany dives for $150, plus various other charters.

Historic Pensacola Village   HISTORIC BUILDINGS
(www.historicpensacola.org; Zaragoza St, btwn Tarragona & Adams Sts; adult/child $6/3; ⊙10am-4pm Tue-Sat, tours 11am, 1pm & 2:30pm) Pensacola says 'take that, St Augustine!' with this village, a self-contained enclave of historic homes and museums. Admission is good for one week and includes a guided tour and entrance to each building.

FREE **National Museum of Naval Aviation**   MUSEUM
(www.navalaviationmuseum.org; 1750 Radford Blvd; ⊙9am-5pm) The Pensacola Naval Air Station (NAS) is home to both the museum – a don't-miss collection of jaw-dropping military aircraft – and the elite Blue Angels (www.blueangels.navy.mil) squadron. You can watch the Blue Angels practice their death-defying air show at 8:30am most Tuesdays and Wednesdays between March and November.

Pensacola Museum of Art   ART MUSEUM
(www.pensacolamuseumofart.org; 407 S Jefferson St; adult/child $5/free; ⊙10am-5pm Tue-Fri, from noon Sat) In the city's old jail (1908), this lovely art museum features an impressive, growing collection of major 20th- and 21st-century artists, spanning cubism, realism, pop art and folk art.

Gulf Islands National Seashore   PARK
(www.nps.gov/guis; 7-day pedestrian & cyclist/car $3/8; ⊙sunrise-sunset) To enjoy the area's lovely white sands, head to the easy-access Pensacola Beach or the neighboring Gulf Islands National Seashore, part of a 150-mile stretch of undeveloped beach. Aim for the Naval Live Oaks section for a calm, family-friendly beach, and drive out to Fort Pickens to poke around this crumbling wreck of a 19th-century fort.

WHAT THE...?

Every April, locals gather along the Florida–Alabama state line on Perdido Key for a time-honored tradition: the Interstate Mullet Toss. The idea – apart from a great excuse for a party – is to see who can throw their (dead) mullet the furthest into Alabama (we're talking fish, not the unfortunate '80s hairstyle). The event is organized by the Flora-Bama Lounge, Package and Oyster Bar (www.florabama.com; 17395 Perdido Key Dr; ⊙10am-10pm Mon-Thu, to late Fri-Sun), a legendary roadhouse that's worth visiting even when the fish aren't flying.

⊨ Sleeping

Pensacola Victorian B&B   B&B $$
(☑850-434-2818; www.pensacolavictorian.com; 203 W Gregory St; r $85-125; P❋⊛) This stately 1892 Queen Anne building offers four lovingly maintained guest rooms – we especially like Suzanne's Room, with its hardwood floors, blue toile prints and clawfoot tub. It's about a mile north of downtown Pensacola.

New World Inn   HOTEL $$
(☑850-432-4111; www.newworldlanding.com; 600 S Palafox St; r from $109; P❋⊛) Peek under the lid of this former box factory and you'll find surprisingly lovely rooms with luxe bedding and real carpeting (a beach-town luxury).

Paradise Inn   MOTEL $$
(☑850-932-2319; www.paradiseinn-pb.com; 21 Via de Luna Dr; r $100-200; P❋⊛☒) Across from the beach, this sherbet-colored motel is a lively, cheery place thanks to its popular bar and grill (for quiet, ask for rooms on the parking lot's far side). Rooms are small and clean, with tiled floors and brightly painted walls.

✕ Eating & Drinking

TOP CHOICE **Joe Patti's**   SEAFOOD $
(www.joepattis.com; 534 South B St, at Main St; ⊙7am-6pm Mon-Thu & Sat, to 7pm Fri) At this beloved seafood emporium, get dock-fresh fish and seafood, prepared picnic food and sushi.

Dharma Blue   INTERNATIONAL $$
(☑850-433-1275; www.dharmablue.com; 300 S Alcaniz St; mains $9-21; ⊙11am-4pm & 5-9:30pm Mon-Sat) Many locals consider this the area's

best restaurant. The eclectic menu goes from fried green tomatoes to luscious sushi rolls.

Jerry's Drive-In AMERICAN $
(2815 E Cervantes St; mains $7-12; ☺10am-10pm Mon-Fri, from 7am Sat) No longer a drive-in or owned by Jerry, but this greasy spoon is always packed – possibly because you can hardly eat for less. Cash only.

Peg Leg Pete's SEAFOOD $$
(☏850-932-4139; 1010 Fort Pickens Rd; mains $8-20; ☺11am-10pm) Raw? Rockefeller? Casino? Get your oysters any way you like 'em at this popular beach hangout with live music and pirate decor.

McGuire's Irish Pub IRISH $$
(www.mcguiresirishpub.com; 600 E Gregory St; mains $11-30; ☺11am-late) Promising 'feasting, imbibery and debauchery,' this barnlike spot delivers all three. Stick to steaks and burgers, and don't mind the animal heads or dollar-bill-adorned walls. Stay late, and be prepared to sing along.

TOP CHOICE **Seville Quarter** CLUB
(www.sevillequarter.com; 130 E Government St; ☺11am-late) Taking up an entire city block, this massive entertainment complex contains seven separate eating, drinking and music venues, along with an HG Wells-ian 1890s decor.

ⓘ Getting There & Around

Five miles northeast of downtown, **Pensacola Regional Airport** (PNS; www.flypensacola.com) is served by major airlines. The **Greyhound station** (www.greyhound.com; 505 W Burgess Rd) is 9 miles north of downtown.

FLORIDA PENSACOLA & PENSACOLA BEACH

Great Lakes

Best Places to Eat

» Zingerman's Roadhouse (p555)

» Terry's Turf Club (p545)

» Slows Bar BQ (p552)

» Next (p518)

» Bryant-Lake Bowl (p579)

Best Places to Stay

» Inn on Ferry Street (p551)

» Hotel Burnham (p514)

» Arbor House (p569)

» Lighthouse B&B (p587)

» Inn Serendipity (p571)

Why Go?

Don't be fooled by all the corn. Behind it lurks surfing beaches and Tibetan temples, car-free islands and the green-draped night-lights of the aurora borealis. The Midwest takes its knocks for being middle-of-nowhere boring. So consider the moose-filled national parks, urban five-ways and Hemingway, Dylan and Vonnegut sites its little secret.

Roll call for the Midwest's cities starts with Chicago, which unfurls what is arguably the country's mightiest skyline. Milwaukee keeps the beer-and-Harley flame burning, while Minneapolis shines a hipster beacon out over the fields. Detroit rocks, plain and simple.

The Great Lakes themselves are huge, like inland seas, offering beaches, dunes, resort towns and lots of lighthouse-dotted scenery. Dairy farms and fruit orchards blanket the region, meaning that fresh pie and ice cream awaits road trippers. And when the Midwest does flatten out? There's always a goofball roadside attraction, like the meaty Spam museum or world's biggest ball of twine, to revive imaginations.

When to Go

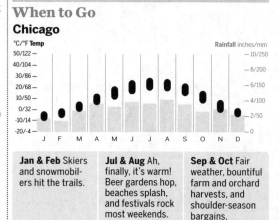

Jan & Feb Skiers and snowmobilers hit the trails.

Jul & Aug Ah, finally, it's warm! Beer gardens hop, beaches splash, and festivals rock most weekends.

Sep & Oct Fair weather, bountiful farm and orchard harvests, and shoulder-season bargains.

Getting There & Around

Chicago's O'Hare International Airport (ORD) is the main air hub for the region. Detroit (DTW), Cleveland (CLE) and Minneapolis (MSP) also have busy airports.

A car is the easiest way to get around, especially if you want to head down Route 66 or dawdle on scenic backroads. Small change is useful for tollways such as the I-80 and I-90 through northern Illinois, Indiana and Ohio.

Greyhound (www.greyhound.com) connects many local cities and towns. Upstart **Megabus** (www.megabus.com/us) provides an efficient alternative between major Great Lakes cities. Note that Megabus has no terminals (drop-off and pickup are at various street corners), and all purchases must be made in advance online (you cannot buy a ticket from the driver).

Amtrak's national rail network centers on Chicago. Trains depart at least once daily for San Francisco *(California Zephyr)*, Seattle *(Empire Builder)*, New York City *(Lake Shore Limited)*, New Orleans *(City of New Orleans)* and San Antonio *(Texas Eagle)*. Regional trains chug to Milwaukee (seven daily) and Detroit (three daily).

Two car/passenger ferries sail across Lake Michigan, providing a shortcut between Wisconsin and Michigan. The **Lake Express** (www.lake-express.com) crosses between Milwaukee and Muskegon. The older **SS Badger** (www.ssbadger.com) crosses between Manitowoc and Ludington.

TOP FIVE ACTIVITY HOT SPOTS

» Boundary Waters (p588) Canoe where wolves and moose roam

» Wisconsin's Rails to Trails (p565) Pedal through cow-dotted farmland

» Apostle Islands (p573) Kayak through sea caves

» New Buffalo (p557) Learn to surf in Harbor Country

» Isle Royale (p563) Hike and camp in pristine backcountry

Pre-Planning

A couple of things to know before you go: pre-booking accommodation during summer is a good idea, especially in resort-orientated places such as Mackinac Island in Michigan, and the North Shore in Minnesota. It's also advised for festival-packed cities such as Milwaukee and Chicago.

Chowhounds who crave dinner at top-end restaurants such as Chicago's Alinea, Next or Frontera Grill/Topolobampo should make reservations six to eight weeks in advance.

Eyeing a nice beachfront campsite at one of the state parks? Better nab it early on; most parks take online reservations for a small fee.

Bring insect repellent, especially if you're heading to the Northwoods. The blackflies in spring and mosquitoes in summer can be brutal.

DON'T MISS

Only in the Midwest can you fork into proper cheese curds (Wisconsin), deep-dish pizza (Chicago) and sugar cream pie (Indiana).

Fast Facts

» Hub cities: Chicago (population 2.8 million), Minneapolis (population 372,800)

» Chicago to Minneapolis: 400 miles

» Chicago to Detroit: 285 miles

» Time zone: Eastern (IN, OH, MI), Central (IL, WI, MN)

» States covered in this chapter: Illinois, Indiana, Ohio, Michigan, Wisconsin, Minnesota

Did You Know?

The Great Lakes possess about 20% of the earth's and 95% of America's fresh water.

Resources

» Midwest Microbrews (www.midwestmicrobrews.com) The sudsy lowdown

» Great Lakes Information Network (www.great-lakes.net) Environmental news

» Changing Gears (www.changinggears.info) Rust Belt reinvention stories

Great Lakes Highlights

1 Absorbing the skyscrapers, museums, festivals and foodie bounty of **Chicago** (p497)

2 Beach lounging, berry eating and surfing on Michigan's **Gold Coast** (p557)

3 Slowing down for clip-clopping horses and buggies in **Amish Country** (p534 and p540)

4 Polka dancing at a Friday-night fish fry in **Milwaukee** (p564)

5 Paddling the **Boundary Waters** (p588) and sleeping under a blanket of stars

6 Cycling along the river against the urban backdrop of **Detroit** (p547)

7 Taking the slowpoke, pie-filled route through Illinois on **Route 66** (p526)

History

The region's first residents included the Hopewell (around 200 BC) and Mississippi River mound builders (around AD 700). Both left behind mysterious piles of earth that were tombs for their leaders and possibly tributes to their deities. You can see remnants at Cahokia in southern Illinois, and Mound City in southeastern Ohio.

The mound-building cultures began to decline around AD 1000, and over the next centuries the Miami, Shawnee and Winnebago moved in.

French voyageurs (fur traders) arrived in the early 17th century and established missions and forts. The British turned up soon after that, with the rivalry spilling over into the French and Indian Wars (Seven Years' War, 1754–61), after which Britain took control of all of the land east of the Mississippi. Following the Revolutionary War, the Great Lakes area became the new USA's Northwest Territory, which soon was divided into states and locked to the region after it developed its impressive canal and railroad network. But conflicts soon erupted between the newcomers and the Native Americans, including the 1811 Battle of Tippecanoe in Indiana; the bloody 1832 Black Hawk War in Wisconsin, Illinois and around, which forced indigenous people to move west of the Mississippi; and the 1862 Sioux uprising in Minnesota.

Throughout the late 19th and early 20th centuries, industries sprang up and grew quickly, fueled by resources of coal and iron, and cheap transport on the lakes. The work available brought huge influxes of immigrants from Ireland, Germany, Scandinavia and southern and eastern Europe. For decades after the Civil War, a great number of African Americans also migrated to the region's urban centers from the South.

The area prospered during WWII and throughout the 1950s, but was followed by 20 years of social turmoil and economic stagnation. Manufacturing industries declined, which walloped Rust Belt cities such as Detroit and Cleveland with high unemployment and 'white flight' (ie white middle-class families who fled to the suburbs).

The 1980s and '90s brought urban revitalization. The region's population increased, notably with newcomers from Asia and Mexico. Growth in the service and high-tech sectors resulted in economic balance, although manufacturing industries such as car making and steel still played a big role, meaning that when the economic crisis hit in 2008, Great Lakes towns felt the pinch first and foremost.

Local Culture

The Great Lakes region – aka the Midwest – is the USA's solid, sensible heartland. Folks here shrug at the brash glitz of the East Coast and flaky sex appeal of the West Coast, happy instead to be in the plain-speaking middle. It's no surprise that novelist Ernest Hemingway hailed from this part of the country, where words are seldom wasted.

If the Midwest had a mantra, it might be to work hard, go to church, and stick to the straight and narrow...unless there's a sports game happening, and then it's OK to slather on the body paint and dye your hair purple (or whatever team colors dictate). Baseball, football, basketball and ice hockey are all hugely popular, with the big cities sponsoring pro teams for each sport.

Music has always been a big part of local culture. Muddy Waters and Chess Re-

---

GREAT LAKES IN...

Five Days

Spend the first two days in **Chicago**. On your third day, make the 1½-hour trip to Milwaukee for culture, both high- and lowbrow. Take the ferry over to Michigan and spend your fourth day beaching in **Saugatuck**. Circle back via **Indiana Dunes** or **Indiana's Amish Country**.

10 Days

After two days in **Chicago**, on day three make for **Madison** and its surrounding quirky sights. Spend your fourth and fifth days at the **Apostle Islands**, and then head into the Upper Peninsula to visit **Marquette** and **Pictured Rocks** for a few days, followed by **Sleeping Bear Dunes** and the wineries around **Traverse City**. Return via the galleries, pies and beaches of **Saugatuck**.

cords spawned the electric blues in Chicago. Motown Records started the soul sound in Detroit. Alt rock shakes both cities (think Wilco in Chicago, White Stripes in Detroit), and has come out of Minneapolis (the Replacements, Hüsker Dü), and Dayton, Ohio (Guided By Voices, the Breeders), as well.

The region is more diverse than outsiders might expect. Immigrants from Mexico, Africa, the Middle East and Asia have established communities throughout the Midwest, mostly in the cities, where they are making welcomed contributions, especially to local dining scenes.

ILLINOIS

Chicago dominates the state with its sky-high architecture and superlative museums, restaurants and music clubs. But venturing further afield reveals Hemingway's hometown of 'wide lawns and narrow minds,' scattered shrines to local hero Abe Lincoln, and a trail of corn dogs, pies and drive-in movie theaters down Route 66. A cypress swamp and a prehistoric World Heritage site make appearances in Illinois too.

ⓘ Information

Illinois Bureau of Tourism (www.enjoyillin ois.com)

Illinois Highway Conditions (www.getting aroundillinois.com)

Illinois State Park Information (www.dnr. illinois.gov) State parks are free to visit. Campsites cost $6 to $35; some accept reservations (www.reserveamerica.com; $5).

Chicago

Loving Chicago is 'like loving a woman with a broken nose: you may well find lovelier lovelies, but never a lovely so real.' Writer Nelson Algren summed it up well in *Chicago: City on the Make*. There's something about this cloud-scraping city that bewitches. Well, maybe not during the six-month winter, when the 'Windy City' gets slapped by snowy blasts; however, come May, when the weather warms and everyone dashes for the outdoor festivals, ballparks, lakefront beaches and beer gardens – ahh, nowhere tops Chicago. Literally: the Willis Tower is here, the USA's tallest building.

Beyond its mighty architecture, Chicago is a city of Mexican, Polish, Vietnamese and other ethnic neighborhoods in which to wan-

ILLINOIS FACTS

» **Nicknames** Prairie State, Land of Lincoln

» **Population** 12.9 million

» **Area** 57,900 sq miles

» **Capital city** Springfield (population 116,500)

» **Other cities** Chicago (population 2.8 million)

» **Sales tax** 6.25%

» **Birthplace of** author Ernest Hemingway (1899–1961), animator Walt Disney (1901–66), jazz musician Miles Davis (1926–91), actor Bill Murray (b 1950)

» **Home of** cornfields, Route 66 starting point

» **Politics** Democratic in Chicago, Republican downstate

» **Famous for** skyscrapers, corn dogs, Abe Lincoln sights

» **Official snack food** popcorn

» **Driving distances** Chicago to Milwaukee 92 miles, Chicago to Springfield 200 miles

der. It's a city of blues, jazz and rock clubs any night of the week. And it's a chowhound's town, where the queues for hot dogs equal those of North America's top restaurant.

Forgive us, but it has to be said: the Windy City will blow you away with its low-key, cultured awesomeness.

History

In the late 17th century, the Potawatomi gave the name Checagou – meaning wild onions – to the once-swampy environs. The new city's pivotal moment happened on October 8, 1871, when (so the story goes) Mrs O'Leary's cow kicked over the lantern that started the Great Chicago Fire. It torched the entire inner city and left 90,000 people homeless.

'Damn,' said the city planners. 'Guess we shouldn't have built everything from wood. It's flammable.' So they rebuilt with steel and created space for bold new structures, such as the world's first skyscraper, which popped up in 1885.

Al Capone's gang more or less ran things during the 1920s and corrupted the city's political system. Local government has had issues ever since, with 30 city council members going to jail since 1970.

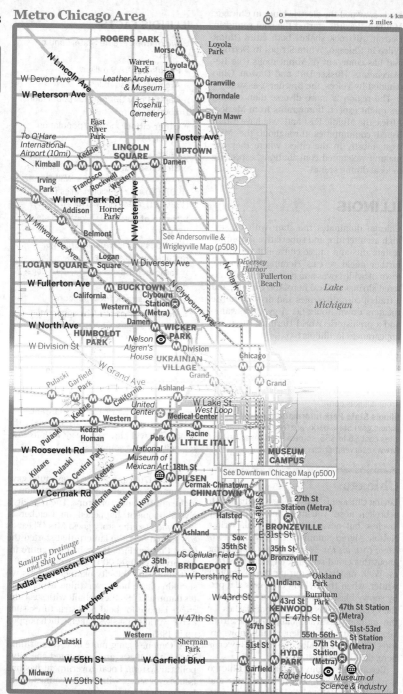

For the last half-century, the biggest name in Chicago has been Daley: Richard J Daley, mayor from 1955 to 1976; and son Richard M Daley, who governed from 1989 to 2011.

◉ Sights

Chicago's main attractions are found mostly in or near the city center, though visits to distant neighborhoods, like Pilsen and Hyde Park, can also be rewarding.

The city's streets are laid out on a grid and numbered. Madison and State Sts in the Loop are the grid's center. As you go north, south, east or west from here, each increase of 800 in street numbers corresponds to 1 mile. For instance, Chicago Ave (800 N) is followed by North Ave (1600 N) and Fullerton Ave (2400 N), at which point you're 3 miles north of downtown.

For more in-depth city explorations, pick up Lonely Planet's *Chicago* guide or *Chicago Encounter* guide.

THE LOOP

The city center and financial district is named for the elevated train tracks that lasso its streets. It's busy all day, though not much happens at night other than in Millennium Park and the Theater District, near the intersection of N State and W Randolph Sts.

FREE **Millennium Park** PARK
(Map p500; www.millenniumpark.org; Welcome Center, 201 E Randolph St; ☉6am-11pm; ⊛) Rising boldly by the lakefront, Millennium Park is a treasure trove of free and arty sights. Frank Gehry's 120ft-high swooping silver band shell anchors what is, in essence, an outdoor modern design gallery. It includes Jaume Plensa's 50ft-high **Crown Fountain**, which projects video images of locals spitting water, gargoyle style; the Gehry-designed **BP Bridge** that spans Columbus Dr and offers great skyline views; and the **McCormick Tribune Ice Rink** that fills with skaters in winter (and alfresco diners in summer). The newest installment is the **Nichols Bridgeway** that arches from the park up to the Art Institute's 3rd-floor contemporary sculpture garden (free to view).

However, the thing that has become the park's biggest draw is 'the Bean' – officially titled **Cloud Gate** – Anish Kapoor's ridiculously smooth, 110-ton, silver-drop sculpture. Locals and visitors alike find it hard to resist such playful art, as you'll see from all the folks splashing around in Crown Fountain and touching the sculpture.

In summer, Millennium's acoustically awesome band shell – **Pritzker Pavilion** – hosts free concerts at lunchtime and at 6:30pm. For the latter, bring a picnic and bottle of wine and tune in to new music on Mondays, jazz and world music on Thursdays, and classical music on most other days. Each Saturday free exercise classes (yoga at 8am, Pilates at 9am and dance at 10am) take place on the Great Lawn. And

---

CHICAGO IN...

Two Days

On your first day, take an **architectural tour** and gaze up at the city's skyscrapers. Look down from the **John Hancock Center**, one of the world's tallest buildings. See 'the Bean' reflect the skyline, and splash with Crown Fountain's human gargoyles at **Millennium Park**. Hungry after all that walking? Chow down on a deep-dish pizza at **Giordano's**.

Make the second day a cultural one: explore the **Art Institute of Chicago** or **Field Museum of Natural History**. Browse boutiques and grab a stylish dinner in **Wicker Park**. Then head north to Al Capone's gin joint, the **Green Mill**, for an evening of jazz.

Four Days

Follow the two-day itinerary and, on your third day, rent a bicycle, dip your toes in Lake Michigan at **North Avenue Beach** and cruise through **Lincoln Park**, making stops at the zoo and conservatory. If it's baseball season, head to **Wrigley Field** for a Cubs game. A smoky blues club, such as **Buddy Guy's Legends**, is a fine way to finish the day (or start the morning).

Pick a neighborhood on your fourth day, and eat, shop and soak up the culture: murals and mole sauce in **Pilsen**, pagodas and Vietnamese sandwiches in **Uptown**, or Obama and the Nuclear Energy sculpture in **Hyde Park**. Then see a play at one of Chicago's 200 theaters, or a comedy at **Second City**.

0 — 1 km
0 — 0.5 miles

Lake Shore Park
E Chicago Ave

Lakefront Path

N Lake Shore Dr

Water Filtration Plant

Olive Park

E Ontario St
STREETERVILLE

Ohio St Beach

Navy Pier

E Grand Ave
E Illinois St

4
55
62
23

32

30
22

E North Water St
River Esplanade

E Wacker Dr

E Randolph St

Millennium Park

N Lake Shore Dr

Lake Michigan

Butler Field

8
2

Lakefront Path

Hutchinson Field

S Lake Shore Dr

Shedd Aquarium

Adler Planetarium & Astronomy Museum

MUSEUM CAMPUS

Field Museum of Natural History

Solidarity Dr

Burnham Park

Burnham Harbor

S Lynn White Dr

1

18

72

Downtown Chicago

the Family Fun Tent provides free kids' activities daily between 10am and 3pm. Free walking tours (Welcome Center; ⊙11:30am and 1pm) take place daily, or do it yourself with a downloadable tour from the website.

Technically, Millennium is part of the northwest corner of Grant Park (see p503).

Art Institute of Chicago MUSEUM

(Map p500; ☑312-443-3600; www.artic.edu/aic; 111 S Michigan Ave; adult/child $18/free; ⊙10:30am-5pm, to 8pm Thu; ☑) The second-largest art museum in the country, the Art Institute houses treasures and masterpieces from around the globe, including a fabulous selection of both impressionist and post-impressionist paintings. The Modern Wing dazzles with natural light, and hangs Picassos and Mirós on its 3rd floor.

Allow two hours to browse the museum's highlights; art buffs should allocate much longer. Ask at the front desk about free talks and tours once you're inside. Note that the 3rd-floor contemporary sculpture garden is always free. It has great city views and connects to Millennium Park via the mod, pedestrian-only Nichols Bridgeway.

Willis Tower TOWER

(Map p500; ☑312-875-9696; www.the-skydeck.com; 233 S Wacker Dr; adult/child $17/11; ⊙9am-10pm Apr-Sep, 10am-8pm Oct-Mar) Yes, you're at the right place. Willis Tower was the Sears Tower until mid-2009, when insurance broker Willis Group Holdings bought the naming rights. No matter what you call it, it's still the USA's tallest building (1454ft), and its 103rd-floor Skydeck puts visitors way up in the clouds.

Enter via Jackson Blvd, then take the elevator down to the waiting area, where you go through security and pay admission.

Queues can be up to an hour on busy days (peak times are in summer, between 11am to 4pm Friday through Sunday). There's a factoid-filled film to watch, and then the ear-popping, 70-second ride to the top. Step onto the glass-floored Ledge for a feeling of mid-air suspension and knee-buckling view straight down. For those who prefer a drink with their vista, the Gold Coast's John Hancock Center (p505) is a better choice.

FREE Chicago Cultural Center CULTURAL BUILDING

(Map p500; ☑312-744-6630; www.chicagoculturalcenter.org; 78 E Washington St; ⊙8am-7pm Mon-Thu, 8am-6pm Fri, 9am-6pm Sat, 10am-6pm Sun; ☜) The block-long, beaux arts building houses art exhibitions, foreign films, and jazz and world music concerts at 12:15pm on weekdays. It also contains the world's largest Tiffany stained-glass dome, Chicago's main visitor center and a local authors' gallery, in which you can browse Nelson Algren and Studs Terkel books.

Grant Park PARK

(Map p500; Michigan Ave btwn 12th & Randolph Sts; ⊙6am-11pm) Grant Park hosts the city's mega-events, such as Taste of Chicago, Blues Fest and Lollapalooza. **Buckingham Fountain** (cnr Congress Pkwy & Columbus Dr) is Grant's centerpiece. The fountain is one of the world's largest, with a 1.5-million-gallon capacity. It lets loose on the hour every hour between 10am and 11pm mid-April to mid-October, accompanied at night by multicolored lights and music.

Public Artworks MONUMENTS

(Map p500) Chicago has commissioned several head-scratching public sculptures

---

ⓘ ONLINE TICKETS & DISCOUNT CARDS

Most major sights, including the Art Institute, Shedd Aquarium and Willis Tower, allow you to buy tickets online. The advantage is that you're assured entry and you get to skip the regular ticket lines. The disadvantage is that you have to pay a service fee of $1.50 to $4 per ticket (sometimes it's just per order), and at times the prepay line is almost as long as the regular one. Our suggestion: consider buying online in summer and for big exhibits; otherwise, there's no need.

Chicago offers a couple of discount cards that also let you skip the regular queues:

» **Go Chicago Card** (www.gochicagocard.com) Allows you to visit an unlimited number of attractions for a flat fee; good for one, two, three, five or seven consecutive days.

» **CityPass** (www.citypass.com) Gives access to five of the city's top draws, including Shedd Aquarium and Willis Tower, over nine days; a better option if you prefer a more leisurely sightseeing pace.

FAMOUS LOOP ARCHITECTURE

Ever since it presented the world with the first skyscraper, Chicago has thought big with its architecture and pushed the envelope of modern design. The Loop is a fantastic place to roam and gawk at these ambitious structures.

The **Chicago Architecture Foundation** (Map p500; www.architecture.org) runs tours that explain the following buildings and more:

» **Chicago Board of Trade** (Map p500; 141 W Jackson Blvd) A 1930 art deco gem. Inside, manic traders swap futures and options. Outside, check out the giant statue of Ceres, the goddess of agriculture, that tops the building.

» **Rookery** (Map p500; 209 S LaSalle St) The 1888 Rookery looks fortresslike outside, but the inside of this office building is light and airy thanks to Frank Lloyd Wright's atrium overhaul. Pigeons used to roost here, hence the name.

» **Monadnock Building** (Map p500; 53 W Jackson Blvd) Architectural pilgrims get weak-kneed when they see the Monadnock Building, which is two buildings in one. The north is the older, traditional design from 1891, while the south is the newer, mod half from 1893. See the difference? The Monadnock remains true to its original purpose as an office building.

throughout the decades. The Loop's triumvirate of puzzlement includes:

Untitled (50 W Washington St) Pablo Picasso's work, which everyone just calls 'the Picasso.'

Sun, the Moon and One Star (69 W Washington St) Joan Miro's work, which everyone just calls 'Miró's Chicago.'

Monument with Standing Beast (100 W Randolph St) Jean Dubuffet's creation, which everyone calls 'Snoopy in a Blender.'

Route 66 Sign (Adams St btwn Michigan & Wabash Aves) Attention Route 66 buffs: the Mother Road's starting point is here. Look for the marker on Adams St's north side as you head west toward Wabash Ave.

SOUTH LOOP

The South Loop, which includes the lower ends of downtown and Grant Park, has soared recently, from dereliction to development central. The Museum Campus is the lakefront area south of Grant Park, where three top attractions huddle.

Field Museum of Natural History MUSEUM
(Map p500; ☎312-922-9410; www.fieldmuseum.org; 1400 S Lake Shore Dr; adult/child $15/10; ☉9am-5pm; ⓐ) The mammoth Field Museum houses everything but the kitchen sink – beetles, mummies, gemstones, Bushman the stuffed ape. The collection's rockstar is Sue, the largest *Tyrannosaurus rex* yet discovered. She even gets her own gift shop. Special exhibits, like the 3D movie, cost extra.

Shedd Aquarium AQUARIUM
(Map p500; ☎312-939-2438; www.sheddaquarium.org; 1200 S Lake Shore Dr; adult/child $29/20; ☉9am-6pm Jun-Aug, to 5pm Sep-May; ⓐ) Top draws at the kiddie-mobbed Shedd Aquarium include the Oceanarium, with its beluga whales and frolicking white-sided dolphins, and the shark exhibit, where there's just 5in of Plexiglas between you and two dozen fierce-looking swimmers. The 4D theater and the odd aquatic show cost extra (around $4 each).

Adler Planetarium & Astronomy Museum MUSEUM
(Map p500; ☎312-922-7827; www.adlerplanetarium.org; 1300 S Lake Shore Dr; adult/child $12/8; ☉9:30am-6pm Jun-Aug, 10am-4pm Sep-May; ⓐ) Space enthusiasts will get a big bang (pun!) out of the Adler. There are public telescopes from which to view the stars, 3D lectures where you can learn about supernovas, and the Planet Explorers exhibit where kids can 'launch' a rocket. The Adler's front steps offer Chicago's primo skyline view (and are a renowned spot for the adults to smooch). Other sights around the Museum Campus:

12th Street Beach BEACH
(Map p500) A path runs south from the planetarium to this handsome, secluded crescent of sand.

Northerly Island PARK
(Map p500; 1400 S Lynn White Dr) Hosts big-name summer concerts (which you can hear from 12th St Beach), trails and bird-watching.

FREE Museum of
Contemporary Photography   MUSEUM
(Map p500; ☎312-663-5554; www.mocp.org; Columbia College, 600 S Michigan Ave; ⊙10am-5pm Mon-Sat, to 8pm Thu, noon-5pm Sun) A small museum worth exploring.

NEAR NORTH
The Loop may be where Chicago fortunes are made, but the Near North is where those fortunes are spent. Shops, restaurants and amusements abound.

FREE Navy Pier   WATERFRONT
(Map p500; ☎312-595-7437; www.navypier.com; 600 E Grand Ave; ⊙10am-10pm, to midnight Fri & Sat; 🖘) Half-mile-long Navy Pier is Chicago's most-visited attraction, sporting a 150ft Ferris wheel (per ride $6), an IMAX theater, a beer garden and gimmicky chain restaurants. Locals groan over its commercialization, but its lakefront view and cool breezes can't be beat. The fireworks displays on summer Wednesdays (9:30pm) and Saturdays (10:15pm) are a treat too.

The Chicago Children's Museum (p512) and gorgeous Smith Museum of Stained Glass Windows (Map p500; ☎312-595-5024; Festival Hall; admission free; ⊙10am-10pm, to midnight Fri & Sat) are also on the pier, as are several boat-cruise operators. Try the Shoreline water taxi (Map p500; www.shorelinesightseeing.com; ⊙10am-7pm late May–early Sep) for a fun ride to the Museum Campus (adult/child $7/4).

Magnificent Mile   STREET
(Map p500; www.themagnificentmile.com; N Michigan Ave) Spanning Michigan Ave between the river and Oak St, the Mag Mile is the much-touted upscale shopping strip, where Bloomingdales, Neiman's and Saks will lighten your wallet.

Tribune Tower   TOWER
(Map p500; 435 N Michigan Ave) Take a close look when passing by the gothic tower to see chunks of the Taj Mahal, Parthenon and other famous structures embedded in the lower walls.

Trump Tower   TOWER
(Map p500; 401 N Wabash Ave) The Donald's 1360ft tower is now Chicago's second-tallest building, though architecture critics have mocked its 'toothpick' look.

Wrigley Building   TOWER
(Map p500; 400 N Wabash Ave) Built by the chewing-gum maker, the white terra-cotta exterior glows as white as the Doublemint Twins' teeth.

GOLD COAST
The Gold Coast has been the address of Chicago's wealthiest residents for more than 125 years.

John Hancock Center   TOWER
(off Map p500; ☎888-875-8439; www.hancockobservatory.com; 875 N Michigan Ave; adult/child $15/10; ⊙9am-11pm) Get high in Chicago's third-tallest skyscraper. In many ways the

---

CAPONE'S CHICAGO

The city would rather not discuss its gangster past; consequently there are no brochures or exhibits about infamous sites. So you'll need to use your imagination when visiting the following as most are not designated as notorious.

Two murders took place near Holy Name Cathedral (Map p500; 735 N State St). In 1924 North Side boss Dion O'Banion was gunned down in his florist shop (738 N State St) after he crossed Al Capone. O'Banion's replacement, Hymie Weiss, fared no better. In 1926 he was killed on his way to church by bullets flying from a window at 740 N State St.

The St Valentine's Day Massacre Site (2122 N Clark St, Lincoln Park) is where Capone's goons, dressed as cops, lined up seven members of Bugs Moran's gang against the garage wall that used to be here and sprayed them with bullets. The garage was torn down in 1967.

In 1934, the 'lady in red' betrayed John Dillinger at the Biograph Theater (2433 N Lincoln Ave, Lincoln Park). Dillinger was shot by the FBI outside it.

The speakeasy in the basement of the glamorous jazz bar Green Mill (p520) was a Capone favorite.

Capone's Chicago Home (7244 S Prairie Ave) is deep on the South Side in a sketchy area, so use caution. The residence was used mostly by Capone's wife, Mae, his mom and other relatives.

view here surpasses the one at Willis Tower, as the Hancock is closer to the lake and a little further north. Those needing a city history lesson should ascend to the 94th-floor observatory, and listen to the archaic audio tour that comes with admission. Those secure in their knowledge should shoot up to the 96th-floor Signature Lounge, where the view is free if you buy a drink ($6 to $14).

Museum of Contemporary Art   MUSEUM
(Map p500; 📞312-280-2660; www.mcachicago. org; 220 E Chicago Ave; adult/student $12/7; 🕙10am-8pm Tue, 10am-5pm Wed-Sun) Consider it the Art Institute's brash, rebellious sibling, with especially strong minimalist, surrealist and book arts collections, and permanent works by Franz Kline, Rene Magritté, Cindy Sherman and Andy Warhol.

Original Playboy Mansion   BUILDING
(1340 N State St) Hugh Hefner began wearing his all-day jammies here, when the rigors of magazine production and heavy partying prevented him from getting dressed. The building contains condos now, but a visit still allows you to boast, 'I've been to the Playboy Mansion.' Head east a block to Astor St and ogle more manors between the 1300 and 1500 blocks.

Water Tower   LANDMARK
(Map p500; cnr Chicago & Michigan Aves) The 154ft-tall, turreted tower is a defining city landmark: it was the sole downtown survivor of the 1871 Great Fire.

Oak Street Beach   BEACH
(off Map p500; 1000 N Lake Shore Dr) Packs in bodies beautiful at the edge of downtown.

LINCOLN PARK & OLD TOWN

Lincoln Park (off Map p500) is Chicago's largest green space, an urban oasis spanning 1200 leafy acres along the lakefront. 'Lincoln Park' is also the name for the abutting neighborhood. Both are alive day and night with people jogging, walking dogs, pushing strollers and driving in circles looking for a place to park.

Old Town rests at the southwest foot of Lincoln Park. The intersection of North Ave and Wells St is the epicenter, with saucy restaurants, bars and the Second City improv club fanning out from here.

FREE **Lincoln Park Zoo**   ZOO
(📞312-742-2000; www.lpzoo.org; 2200 N Cannon Dr; 🕙10am-4:30pm Nov-Mar, to 5pm Apr-Oct, to 6:30pm Sat & Sun Jun-Aug; 👶) It's a local family favorite, filled with gorillas, lions, tigers and other exotic creatures in the shadow of downtown. Check out the Regenstein African Journey, Primate House and Nature Boardwalk for the cream of the crop.

FREE **Lincoln Park Conservatory**   GARDENS
(📞312-742-7736; 2391 N Stockton Dr; 🕙9am-5pm) Near the zoo's north entrance, the magnificent 1891 hothouse coaxes palms, ferns and orchids to flourish. In winter, it becomes a soothing, 75-degree escape from the icy winds raging outside.

North Avenue Beach   BEACH
(1600 N Lake Shore Dr; 👶) Chicago's most popular and amenity-laden stretch of sand wafts a southern California vibe. You can rent bikes, kayaks, volleyballs and lounge chairs, as well as eat and drink at the party-orientated beach house. It's 2 miles north of the Loop.

Chicago History Museum   MUSEUM
(off Map p500; 📞312-642-4600; www.chicago history.org; 1601 N Clark St; adult/child $14/free; 🕙9:30am-4:30pm Mon-Sat, noon-5pm Sun) Multimedia displays cover it all, from the Great Fire to the 1968 Democratic Convention. President Lincoln's deathbed is here; so is the chance to 'become' a Chicago hot dog covered in condiments (in the kids' area, but adults are welcome for the photo op).

LAKE VIEW & WRIGLEYVILLE

North of Lincoln Park, these neighborhoods can be enjoyed by ambling along Halsted St, Clark St, Belmont Ave or Southport Ave, which are well supplied with restaurants, bars and shops. Ivy-covered **Wrigley Field** (Map p508; 1060 W Addison St) is named after the chewing-gum guy and is home to the much-loved but perpetually losing Chicago Cubs. If they're playing a game, you can peep through the 'knothole,' a garage door-sized opening on Sheffield Ave, to watch the action for free. For ticket information, see p521.

ANDERSONVILLE & UPTOWN

These northern neighborhoods (Map p508) are good for a delicious browse. Andersonville is an old Swedish enclave centered on Clark St, where timeworn, European-tinged businesses mix with new foodie restaurants, funky boutiques, vintage shops and gay and lesbian bars. Take the CTA Red Line to the Berwyn stop, and walk west for about a mile.

Around the corner to the south, Uptown is a whole different scene. Take the Red Line to the Argyle stop, and you're in the heart of 'Little Saigon' and its pho-serving storefronts.

WICKER PARK, BUCKTOWN & UKRAINIAN VILLAGE

West of Lincoln Park, these three neighborhoods (Map p498) – once havens for working-class, central European immigrants and bohemian writers – are hot property. Heaps of fashion boutiques, hipster record stores, thrift shops and cocktail lounges have shot up, especially near the Milwaukee-North-Damen Aves intersection. Division St is also prime wandering territory. It used to be called 'Polish Broadway' for all the polka bars that lined it, but now the requisite cafes and crafty businesses have taken over. There aren't many actual sights here, aside from **Nelson Algren's House** (Map p498; 1958 W Evergreen Ave), where he wrote several gritty, Chicago-based novels. Alas, it's a private residence, so you can only admire it from the sidewalk. Take the CTA Blue Line to Damen (for Algren) or Division.

LOGAN SQUARE & HUMBOLDT PARK

When artists and hipsters got priced out of Wicker Park, they moved west to the Latino communities of Logan Square and Humboldt Park (Map p498). For visitors, these are places for small, cool-cat eateries, brewpubs and music clubs. Take the CTA Blue Line to Logan Square or California.

From 1957 to 1967, the humble building at 2120 S Michigan Ave was Chess Records, the seminal electric blues label. Muddy Waters, Howlin' Wolf and Bo Diddley cut tracks here, and paved the way for rock 'n' roll with their sick licks and amped-up sound. Chuck Berry and the Rolling Stones arrived soon after. The studio is now called **Willie Dixon's Blues Heaven** (312-808-1286; www.bluesheaven.com; 2120 S Michigan Ave; tours $10; 11am-4pm Mon-Fri, noon-2pm Sat), named for the bassist who wrote most of Chess' hits. Staff give tours that take in the reception area (Minnie Ripperton worked the desk) and main studio. Free blues concerts rock the side garden on summer Thursdays at 6pm. The building is near Chinatown, and about a mile south of the Museum Campus.

NEAR WEST SIDE & PILSEN

Just west of the Loop is, well, the **West Loop** (Map p500). It's akin to New York City's Meatpacking District, with chic restaurants, clubs and galleries poking out between meat-processing plants. W Randolph St and W Fulton Market are the main veins. Nearby **Greektown** (off Map p500) runs along S Halsted St near W Jackson Blvd. The areas are about 1.25 miles west of the Loop and most easily reached by taxi.

Southwest lies the enclave of **Pilsen** (Map p498), a festive mix of art galleries, Mexican bakeries, hipster cafes and murals on the buildings. The CTA Pink Line to 18th St drops you in the midst.

FREE **National Museum of Mexican Art**   MUSEUM

(Map p498; 312-738-1503; www.nationalmuseum ofmexicanart.org; 1852 W 19th St; 10am-5pm Tue-Sun) The largest Latino arts institution in the US, this museum's vivid permanent collection includes classical paintings, shining gold altars, skeleton-rich folk art and colorful beadwork.

Pilsen Mural Tours   WALKING TOUR

(773-342-4191; per group 1½hr tour $100) Local artist Jose Guerrero leads the highly recommended tours, during which you can learn more about this traditional art form; call to arrange an excursion.

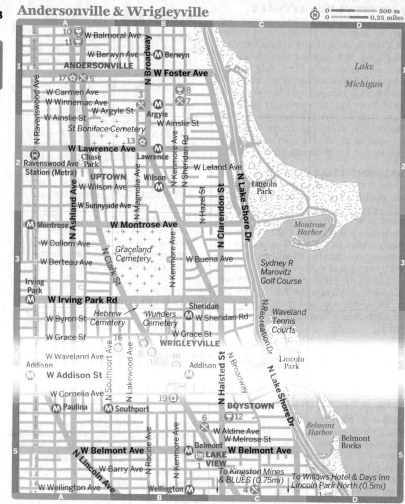

CHINATOWN

Chinatown's (off Map p500) charm is best enjoyed by going bakery to bakery, nibbling chestnut cakes and almond cookies, and shopping for Hello Kitty items. Wentworth Ave, south of Cermak Rd, is the retail heart of old Chinatown; Chinatown Sq, along Archer Ave north of Cermak, is the newer commerce district. It's an easy 10-minute train ride from the Loop. Take the CTA Red Line to the Cermak-Chinatown stop.

HYDE PARK & SOUTH SIDE

The South Side is the generic term applied to Chicago's myriad neighborhoods, including some of its most impoverished, that lie south of 25th St. Hyde Park and abutting Kenwood are the South Side's stars, catapulted into the spotlight by local boy Barack Obama. Unless stated otherwise, sights are reached via Metra Electric Line trains from Millennium Station downtown to the 55th-56th-57th St stop.

InstaGreeter (www.chicagogreeter.com/insta greeter) offers free one-hour walking tours from the **Hyde Park Art Center** (5020 S Cornell Ave; ☺10am-3pm Sat Jun-early Oct). Several bicycle tours (p509) also cruise by all the highlights.

Obama Sights
BUILDINGS

Hefty security means you can't get close to **Obama's house** (5046 S Greenwood Ave), but you can stand across the street on Hyde Park Blvd and try to glimpse the red-brick Georgian-style manor. Better yet, visit his barber Zariff and the bulletproof glass-encased presidential barber chair at the **Hyde Park Hair Salon** (5234 S Blackstone Ave). Take the Metra Electric Line to 51st-53rd St.

University of Chicago
UNIVERSITY

(5801 S Ellis Ave) Faculty and students have racked up more than 80 Nobel prizes within U of C's hallowed halls. The economics and physics departments lay claim to most. It's also where the nuclear age began: Enrico Fermi and his Manhattan Project cronies built a reactor and carried out the world's first controlled atomic reaction on December 2, 1942. The **Nuclear Energy sculpture** (S Ellis Ave btwn E 56th & E 57th Sts), by Henry Moore, marks the spot where it blew its stack.

Museum of Science & Industry
MUSEUM

(Map p498; ☎773-684-1414; www.msichicago.org; 5700 S Lake Shore Dr; adult/child $15/10; ☺9:30am-5:30pm Jun-Aug, reduced Sep-May) This colossal play-palace will overstimulate the serenest of souls with its flashy exhibits. Highlights include a WWII German U-boat nestled in an underground display ($8 extra to tour it) and the 'Science Storms' exhibit with a mock tornado.

Robie House
ARCHITECTURE

(Map p498; ☎708-848-1976; www.gowright.org; 5757 S Woodlawn Ave; adult/child $15/12; ☺11am-4pm Thu-Mon) Of the numerous buildings that Frank Lloyd Wright designed around Chicago, none is more famous or influential than Robie House. The resemblance of its horizontal lines to the flat landscape of the Midwestern prairie became known as the Prairie style. Inside are 174 stained-glass windows and doors, which you'll see on the hour-long tours (frequency varies by season).

🏃 Activities

Tucked away among Chicago's 552 parks are public golf courses, ice rinks, swimming pools and more. Activities are free or low cost, and the necessary equipment is usually available for rent. The **Chicago Park District** (www.chicagoparkdistrict.com) runs the show; **golf information** (☎312-245-0909; www.cpdgolf.com) is separate.

Cycling

Riding along the 18.5-mile lakefront path is a fantastic way to see the city. Two companies rent wheels. The cost is roughly $10 per hour, or $35 per day (helmet and lock included). Both companies also offer two-to four-hour tours ($35 to $60, including bikes) that cover themes like the lakefront, beer and pizza munching, or Obama sights (highly recommended!). The **Active Transportation Alliance** (www.activetrans.org) lists bike events around town.

Bike Chicago
CYCLING

(Map p500; ☎888-245-3929; www.bikechicago.com; 239 E Randolph St; ☺6:30am-8pm Mon-Fri, from 8am Sat & Sun, closed Sat & Sun Nov-Mar) This one's quite corporate, and has multiple locations. The main one is at Millennium Park; there's another at Navy Pier.

Bobby's Bike Hike
CYCLING

(Map p500; ☑312-915-0995; www.bobbysbikehike. com; 465 N McClurg Ct; ☺8:30am-7pm Jun-Aug, closed Dec-Feb) The eager upstart; located at the River East Docks' Ogden Slip.

Water Sports

Take a dip, build a sand castle or laze in the sun at any of Chicago's 30-plus beaches. Lifeguards patrol the shores in summer; check with the **Chicago Park District** (www. chicagoparkdistrict.com) for water-quality advisories before embarking. **North Avenue Beach** (p506) and **Oak Street Beach** (off Map p500), both close to downtown, are particularly body-filled. Brace yourself as the water remains butt-numbing well into July.

Ice Skating

Millennium Park's **McCormick Tribune Ice Rink** (Map p500; ☑312-742-5222; www.millenniumpark.org; 55 N Michigan Ave; skate rental $10; ☺late Nov-Feb) heats up when the temperature plummets.

Offbeat Chicago

Sure, your friends will listen politely as you describe your trip to the Willis Tower's tip, but you'll stop them mid-yawn when you unleash stories of how you boozed with roller babes and honed your cornhole strategy (see p510). Chicago has a fine collection of unusual sights and activities to supplement its standard attractions.

Cornhole
GAME

(www.chicagoleaguesports.com) Get your mind out of the gutter; we're not talking dirty here. We mean an activity in which small corn-filled bags (aka beanbags) are tossed into a sloped box with a hole in it. Cornhole is a game! Several bars have leagues and tournaments.

International Museum of Surgical Science
MUSEUM

(☑312-642-6502; www.imss.org; 1524 N Lake Shore Dr; adult/child $15/7, admission free Tue; ☺10am-5pm Tue-Sat, noon-5pm Sun) A blood-letting exhibit and fine collection of 'stones' (as in kidney stones and gallstones) are among the offerings at this museum, and the hemorrhoid surgery toolkit serves as a reminder to eat lots of fiber. It's in the Gold Coast, about a mile north of the Water Tower area.

Windy City Rollers
SPECTATOR SPORT

(www.windycityrollers.com; UIC Pavilion, 525 S Racine Ave; tickets $20-40) The bang-'em-up sport of roller derby was born in Chicago in 1935, and the battlin' babes here will show you how it's played, bruises and all. Matches take place monthly at UIC Pavilion, west of the Loop (take the Blue Line to Racine).

Leather Archives & Museum
MUSEUM

(Map p498; ☑773-761-9200; www.leatherarchives. org; 6418 N Greenview Ave; admission $10; ☺11am-7pm Thu & Fri, to 5pm Sat & Sun) Who knew Ben Franklin liked to be flogged and Egypt's Queen Hatshepsut had a foot fetish? This museum reveals these facts and more in its displays of leather, fetish and S&M subcultures. It's 8 miles north of the Loop, and 1.5 miles north of Andersonville.

Weird Chicago Tours
BUS TOUR

(www.weirdchicago.com) Drives by kinky and spooky spots.

Chic-A-Go-Go
TV SHOW

(www.roctober.com/chicagogo) The cable-access show's live dance audience isn't just kids: adults, too, can shake it on the dancefloor with Miss Mia and Ratso.

☞ Tours

Tours get you out on the water and into further-flung neighborhoods, and many companies offer discounts if you book online. Outdoor-oriented tours operate from April to November only, unless specified otherwise. For cycling jaunts, see p509.

If guided tours aren't your thing, you can always do it yourself with free downloadable audio tours, such as the Buddy Guy–narrated **Chicago Blues Tour** (www.downloadchicago tours.com/bluesmedia), or the **Chicago Movie Tour** (www.onscreenillinois.com), providing a peek at sites from *The Untouchables* and other famous flicks.

FREE Chicago Greeter
WALKING TOUR

(Map p500; ☑312-744-8000; www.chicagogreeter. com; ☺year-round) This outfit pairs you with a local city dweller who will take you on a personal two- to four-hour tour customized by theme (architecture, history, gay and lesbian and more) or neighborhood. Travel is by foot and/or public transportation; reserve seven business days in advance.

FREE InstaGreeter
WALKING TOUR

(Map p500; www.chicagogreeter.com/instagreeter; 77 E Randolph St; ☺10am-4pm Fri-Sun year-round) The quicker version of Chicago Greeter, offering on-the-spot one-hour tours from the

START CHICAGO BOARD OF TRADE
FINISH BILLY GOAT TAVERN
DISTANCE 3 MILES
DURATION ABOUT 2 HOURS

Walking Tour
The Loop

❯ This tour swoops through the Loop, highlighting Chicago's revered art and architecture, with a visit to Al Capone's dentist thrown in for good measure.

Start at the ① **Chicago Board of Trade**, where guys in Technicolor coats swap corn (or something like that) inside a cool art deco building. Step into the nearby ② **Rookery** to see Frank Lloyd Wright's handiwork in the atrium.

Head east on Adams St to the ③ **Art Institute**, one of the city's most-visited attractions. The lion statues out front make a classic keepsake photo. Walk a few blocks north to avant-garde ④ **Millennium Park**, and saunter in to explore 'the Bean' sculpture, human-gargoyle fountains and other contemporary designs.

Leave Millennium Park and head west on Washington St to ⑤ **Hotel Burnham**. It's housed in the Reliance Building, which was the precursor to modern skyscraper design; Capone's dentist drilled teeth in what's now room 809. Just west, Picasso's ⑥ **Untitled**,

created by Mr Abstract himself, is ensconced in Daley Plaza. Bird, dog, woman? You decide. Then go north on Clark St to ⑦ **Monument with Standing Beast**, another head-scratching sculpture.

Walk east on Randolph St through the theater district. Pop into the ⑧ **Cultural Center** to get a soda in the cafe and maybe catch a free concert. Refreshed? Now go north on Michigan Ave and cross the Chicago River. Just north of the bridge you'll pass the ⑨ **Wrigley Building**, shining bright and white, and the nearby Gothic, eye-popping ⑩ **Tribune Tower**.

To finish your tour, visit ⑪ **Billy Goat Tavern**, a vintage Chicago dive that spawned the Curse of the Cubs. Just look around at the walls and you'll get the details, but in short: the tavern's owner, Billy Sianis, once tried to enter Wrigley Field with his pet goat. The smelly creature was denied entry, so Sianis called down a mighty curse on the baseball team in retaliation. They've stunk ever since.

CHICAGO FOR CHILDREN

Chicago is a kid's kind of town. **Time Out Chicago Kids** (www.timeoutchicagokids.com) and **Chicago Parent** (www.chicagoparent.com) are indispensible resources. Top choices for toddlin' times include:

» **Chicago Children's Museum** (Map p500; ☑312-527-1000; www.chicagochildrens museum.org; 700 E Grand Ave; admission $12, free Thu evening; ⊙10am-5pm, to 8pm Thu) Climb, dig and splash in this educational playland on Navy Pier; follow with an expedition down the carnival-like wharf itself, including spins on the Ferris wheel and carousel.

» **Chicago Children's Theatre** (☑773-227-0180; www.chicagochildrenstheatre.org) See a show by one the best kids' theater troupes in the country. Performances take place at venues around town.

» **American Girl Place** (Map p500; www.americangirl.com; 835 N Michigan Ave; ⓓ) Young ladies sip tea and get new hair-dos with their dolls at this multistory, girl-power palace.

» **Chic-A-Go-Go** (www.roctober.com/chicagogo) Groove at a taping of this cable-access TV show that's like a kiddie version of *Soul Train*. Check the website for dates and locations.

Other kid-friendly activities:

» **North Avenue Beach** (p506)
» **Field Museum of Natural History** (p504)
» **Shedd Aquarium** (p504)
» **Lincoln Park Zoo** (p506)
» **Art Institute of Chicago** (p503)
» **Museum of Science & Industry** (p509)

Chicago Cultural Center visitor center. InstaGreeter also has outlets open on summer Saturdays at Second City and the Hyde Park Art Center (p508).

🔝 **Chicago Architecture Foundation**   BOAT TOUR, WALKING TOUR
(Map p500; ☑312-922-3432; www.architecture. org; 224 S Michigan Ave; tours $5-40) The gold-standard boat tours ($35) sail from Michigan Ave's river dock, while the popular Rise of the Skyscraper walking tours ($16) leave from the downtown Michigan Ave address. Weekday lunchtime tours ($5) explore individual landmark buildings.

Wateriders   KAYAKING
(☑312-953-9287; www.wateriders.com; 950 N Kingsbury St; 2½hr tours $50-60) Slither through a canyon of glass and steel while kayaking the Chicago River. The daily 'Ghost and Gangster' trips glide by notorious downtown venues. The launch site is west of downtown, near where Chicago Ave meets the river.

Chicago History Museum   BOAT TOUR, WALKING TOUR
(off Map p500; ☑312-642-4600; www.chicagohistory.org; tours $15-45) It counts pub crawls, kayak jaunts and cemetery walks among its tour arsenal. Departure points and times vary.

Weird Chicago Tours   BUS TOUR
(Map p500; ☑888-446-7859; www.weirdchicago. com; cnr Clark & Ontario Sts; 3hr tours $30; ⊙7pm Thu-Sat, 3pm Sat & Sun) Drives by ghost, gangster and red-light sites. Departs from outside the Hard Rock Cafe.

Chicago Food Planet Tours   WALKING TOUR
(☑212-209-3370; www.chicagofoodplanet.com; 3hr tours $45) Graze through Wicker Park, Near North or Chinatown. Departure points and times vary.

Chicago Rocks Tour   BUS TOUR
(www.chicagorockstour.com; 3½hr tours $28) For the music fans in the crowd: sites, sounds and stories of the Smashing Pumpkins, Wilco and other Chicago bands from the 1980s onward. Departure points and times vary.

🎉 **Festivals & Events**

Chicago has a full events calendar all year, but the biggies take place in the summer. The following events are held downtown on a weekend, unless noted otherwise. Explore

Chicago (www.explorechicago.org/specialevents) has exact dates and other details.

FREE St Patrick's Day Parade   CULTURAL
(www.chicagostpatsparade.com; ☉mid-Mar) The local plumbers union dyes the Chicago River shamrock green; a big parade follows.

FREE Blues Festival   MUSIC
(www.chicagobluesfestival.us; ☉early Jun) It's the biggest free blues fest in the world, with three days of the music that made Chicago famous.

FREE Taste of Chicago   FOOD
(www.tasteofchicago.us; ☉late Jun–early Jul) The 10-day bash in Grant Park includes bands and lots of food on a stick.

FREE SummerDance   MUSIC
(www.chicagosummerdance.org; 601 S Michigan Ave; ☉6pm Thu-Sat, 4pm Sun early Jul–mid-Sep) Bands play rumba, samba and other world music preceded by fun dance lessons; held

at the Spirit of Music Garden in Grant Park.

Pitchfork Music Festival   MUSIC
(www.pitchforkmusicfestival.com; day pass $45; ☉mid-Jul) Indie bands strum for three days in Union Park.

Lollapalooza   MUSIC
(www.lollapalooza.com; day pass around $100; ☉early Aug) Up to 130 bands spill off eight stages at Grant Park's three-day mega-gig.

FREE Jazz Festival   MUSIC
(www.chicagojazzfestival.us; ☉early Sep) Top names on the national jazz scene play over Labor Day weekend.

🛏 Sleeping

Chicago lodging doesn't come cheap. The best way to cut costs is to use a bidding site like Priceline or Hotwire (look for 'River North' or 'Mag Mile' locations). On weekends and when the frequent big conventions

---

GAY & LESBIAN CHICAGO

Chicago has a flourishing gay and lesbian scene. **Gay Chicago** (www.gaychicagonews.com), the **Windy City Times** (www.windycitymediagroup.com) and **Pink magazine** (www.pinkmag.com) provide the local lowdown.

The **Chicago Area Gay & Lesbian Chamber of Commerce** (www.glchamber.org) has an online tourism directory. Chicago Greeter (see p510) offers personalized sight-seeing trips.

The biggest concentration of bars and clubs is in Wrigleyville on N Halsted St between Belmont Ave and Grace St, an area known as Boystown. Andersonville, aka Girls' Town, is another area with many choices. Top picks:

Big Chicks   BAR
(Map p508; www.bigchicks.com; 5024 N Sheridan Rd; 🕿) Despite the name, both men and women frequent Big Chicks, with its weekend DJs, art displays and next-door organic restaurant **Tweet** (www.tweet.biz; 5020 N Sheridan Ave; ☉9am-3pm Wed-Mon; 🕿), where weekend brunch packs 'em in.

Sidetrack   CLUB
(Map p508; www.sidetrackchicago.com; 3349 N Halsted St) Massive Sidetrack thumps dance music and show tunes and is prime for people watching.

Hamburger Mary's   BAR
(Map p508; www.hamburgermarys.com/chicago; 5400 N Clark St) Cabaret, karaoke, burgers and a booze-soaked outdoor patio make for good times at this hot spot.

Chance's Dances   DANCE
(www.chancesdances.org) Organizes queer dance parties at clubs around town.

Pride Parade   FESTIVAL
(www.chicagopridecalendar.org; ☉late Jun) Pride winds through Boystown and attracts more than 450,000 revelers.

North Halsted Street Market Days   FESTIVAL
(www.northhalsted.com; ☉early Aug) Another raucous event on the Boystown calendar, featuring a street fair and wild costumes.

trample through town, your options become much slimmer, so plan ahead to avoid unpleasant surprises. The prices we've listed are normal midweek rates in summer, the high season. Taxes add 15.4%.

B&Bs give a nice bang for the midrange buck. Contact the **Chicago Bed & Breakfast Association** (www.chicago-bed-breakfast.com; r $125-250), which represents 18 guesthouses. Many properties have two- to three-night minimum stays. Vacation rentals in local apartments are also a good deal here. Try **Vacation Rental By Owner** (www.vrbo.com) or **Craigslist** (www.chicago.craigslist.org).

Hotels in the Loop are convenient to Grant Park, the museums and business district, but the area is pretty dead come nightfall. Accommodations in the Near North and Gold Coast are most popular, given their proximity to eating, shopping and entertainment venues. Rooms in Lincoln Park, Lake View and Wicker Park entice because they're often cheaper than rooms downtown; they are also near swingin' nightlife.

Wi-fi is free unless noted otherwise. You pay dearly for parking in Chicago, around $45 per night downtown, and $22 in outlying neighborhoods.

LOOP & NEAR NORTH

TOP

HOTEL $$$

(Map p500; ☎312-782-1111; www.burnhamhotel.com; 1 W Washington St; r from $189; P✆❄@⚡) The proprietors brag that the Burnham has the highest guest return rates in Chicago; it's easy to see why. Housed in the Loop's landmark 1890s Reliance Building (precedent for the modern skyscraper), its super-slick decor woos architecture buffs. The bright, butter-colored rooms are furnished with mahogany writing desks and chaise lounges. The hotel also hosts a complimentary wine happy hour each evening.

Hotel Felix HOTEL $$
(Map p500; ☎312-447-3440; www.hotelfelixchicago.com; 111 W Huron St; r $139-189; P✆❄@⚡) Opened in 2009 in the Near North, the 225-room, 12-story Felix is downtown's first hotel to earn ecofriendly LEED certification (Silver status, to be exact). The earth-toned, mod-furnished rooms are small but efficiently and comfortably designed. Parking is free if you drive a hybrid.

HI-Chicago HOSTEL $
(Map p500; ☎312-360-0300; www.hichicago.org; 24 E Congress Pkwy; dm incl breakfast $29-38;

P✆❄@⚡) Chicago's best hostel is immaculate, conveniently placed in the Loop, and offers bonuses like a staffed information desk, free volunteer-led tours and discount passes to museums and shows. The simple dorm rooms have six to 12 beds, and most have attached baths.

Best Western River North HOTEL $$
(Map p500; ☎312-467-0800; www.rivernorthhotel.com; 125 W Ohio St; r $159-219; P✆❄⚡❄✆) Well-maintained rooms with maple veneer beds and desks, together with free parking (!), an indoor pool and sundeck overlooking the city, make this Near North value.

Wit HOTEL $$$
(Map p500; ☎312-467-0200; www.thewithotel.com; 201 N State St; r from $229; P✆❄@⚡) Viewtastic rooms, a rooftop bar and an onsite movie theater draw holidaying hipsters and business travelers to the design-savvy, green-glass Wit. Wi-fi costs $10 per day (though it's free in the lobby).

Central Loop Hotel HOTEL $$
(Map p500; ☎312-601-3525; www.centralloophotel.com; 111 W Adams St; r $119-179; P✆@⚡) This small business hotel has good prices if you're stuck paying rack rates. The owners have a similar property called Club Quarters at 75 E Wacker Dr.

LAKEVIEW & WICKER PARK/BUCKTOWN

Willows Hotel HOTEL $$
(off Map p508; ☎773-528-8400; www.willowshotelchicago.com; 555 W Surf St; r incl breakfast $169-229; P✆❄⚡) Small and stylish, the Willows wins an architectural gold star. The chic little lobby provides a swell refuge of overstuffed chairs by the fireplace, while the 55 rooms, done up in shades of peach, cream and soft green, evoke a 19th-century French countryside feel. It's a block north of the commercial hub where Broadway, Clark and Diversey streets intersect.

Wicker Park Inn B&B $$
(☎773-486-2743; www.wickerparkinn.com; 1329 N Wicker Park Ave; r incl breakfast $149-199; ✆❄⚡) This brick row house is steps away from Chicago's most rockin' bar-restaurant scene. The sunny rooms aren't huge, but have hardwood floors, pastel colors and small desk spaces. Across the street, two apartments with kitchens provide a self-contained experience. The inn is about a half-mile southeast of the CTA Blue Line stop at Damen.

Days Inn Lincoln Park North   HOTEL **$$**

(off Map p508; ☑773-525-7010; www.lpndaysinn. com; 644 W Diversey Pkwy; r incl breakfast $120–180; ⓟ☺✳@⑦) This well-maintained chain hotel in Lincoln Park is a favorite of both families and touring indie bands, providing good service and perks like free health club access. It's an easy amble to the lakefront's parks and beaches, and a 15-minute bus ride to downtown. It's right at the hustle-bustle intersection of Broadway, Clark and Diversey streets.

Longman & Eagle   INN **$$**

(☑773-276-7110; www.longmanandeagle.com; 2657 N Kedzie Ave; r $75-200; ☺✳⑦) Check in at the Michelin-starred gastropub downstairs, then head to your wood-floored, vintage-stylish accommodation on the floor above. The six rooms aren't particularly sound-proofed, but after using your whiskey tokens in the bar, you probably won't care. Take the Blue Line to Logan Sq and walk a block north on Kedzie Ave.

The owners of the Willows Hotel have two other similarly styled and priced properties in the Lake View neighborhood:

City Suites Hotel   HOTEL **$$**

(Map p508; ☑773-404-3400; www.chicagocity suites.com; 933 W Belmont Ave) Located near the CTA Red/Brown Line Belmont station, City Suites is a bit noisier than its counterparts.

Majestic Hotel   HOTEL **$$**

(Map p508; ☑773-404-3499; www.majestic -chicago.com; 528 W Brompton Ave) The Majestic lies east toward the lake and is more remote than its counterparts.

✗ Eating

For years epicures wrote off Chicago as a meaty backwater. Then a funny thing happened: the city won a heap of James Beard awards, and foodie magazines like *Saveur* ranked it as the nation's top restaurant scene. The beauty here is even the buzziest restaurants are accessible: they're visionary yet traditional, pubby at the core and decently priced. You can also fork into a superb range of ethnic eats, especially if you break out of downtown and head for neighborhoods such as Pilsen or Uptown.

Need help deciding where to eat? Check these local resources: LTH Forum (www.lthfo rum.com) and Chicago Gluttons (www.chica gogluttons.com).

THE LOOP & SOUTH LOOP

Most Loop eateries are geared to lunch crowds of office workers.

Cafecito   CUBAN **$**

(Map p500; www.cafecitochicago.com; 26 E Congress Pkwy; sandwiches $4-6; ⊙6am-9pm Mon-Fri, 10am-6pm Sat & Sun; ⑦) Attached to the hostel and perfect for the hungry, thrifty traveler,

---

EATING CHICAGO: THE HOLY TRINITY

Chicago cooks up three beloved specialties. Foremost is deep-dish pizza, a hulking mass of crust that rises two or three inches above the plate and cradles a molten pile of toppings. One gooey piece is practically a meal. A large pizza averages $20 at the following places (all open from 11am to 10pm or so daily):

» **Pizzeria Uno** (Map p500; www.unos.com; 29 E Ohio St) The deep-dish concept originated here in 1943; sister outlet Due is one block north.

» **Gino's East** (Map p500; www.ginoseast.com; 162 E Superior St) Write on the walls while you wait for your pie.

» **Lou Malnati's** (Map p500; www.loumalnatis.com; 439 N Wells St) Famous for its butter crust.

» **Giordano's** (Map p500; www.giordanos.com; 730 N Rush St) Perfectly tangy tomato sauce.

» **Pizano's** (Map p500; www.pizanoschicago.com; 864 N State St) Oprah's favorite.

No less iconic is the Chicago hot dog – a wiener that's been 'dragged through the garden' (ie topped with onions, tomatoes, shredded lettuce, bell peppers, pepperoncini and sweet relish, or variations thereof, but *never* ketchup), and then cushioned on a poppy-seed bun. Hot Doug's (p518) does it right.

The city is also revered for its spicy, drippy, only-in-Chicago Italian beef sandwiches. Mr Beef (p516) serves the gold standard.

FARM TO FORK FARE

These entities provide unique ways to eat local, sustainable foods:

» The outdoor **Green City Market** (www.chicagogreencitymarket.org; 1790 N Clark St; ⏰7am-1pm Wed & Sat mid-May–late Oct) offers heirloom veggies, homemade pies, chef demos and much more at Lincoln Park's south end.

» **Chicago's Downtown Farmstand** (Map p500; www.chicagofarmstand.com; 66 E Randolph St; ⏰11am-7pm Tue-Fri, to 4pm Sat) sells locally made honey, pastries and produce. Farmers come in to share stories on Fridays at noon.

» **Clandestino** (www.clandestinodining.com; multicourse meals $65-100) is an underground, 'community dining project,' where chef Efrain Cuevas serves sustainable meals in changing locations, such as galleries or lofts. Sign up for the online mailing list, and grab a spot when he sends out event invitations.

Cafecito serves killer Cuban sandwiches layered with citrus-garlic-marinated roasted pork and ham. Strong coffee and hearty egg sandwiches make a fine breakfast.

Gage
PUB $$$

(Map p500; ☎312-372-4243; www.thegagechicago.com; 24 S Michigan Ave; mains $16-32; ⏰11am-11pm, to midnight Fri) This gastropub dishes up Irish-tinged grub with a fanciful twist, such as Guinness-battered fish and chips, and fries smothered in curry gravy. The booze rocks, too, including a solid whiskey list and small-batch beers that pair with the food.

BREAKFAST $

(www.loumitchellsrestaurant.com; 565 W Jackson Blvd; mains $6-11; ⏰5:30am-3pm Mon-Sat, 7am-3pm Sun) A relic of Route 66, Lou's old-school waitresses deliver double-yoked eggs and thick-cut French toast just west of the Loop by Union Station. There's usually a queue, but free doughnut holes and Milk Duds help ease the wait.

NEAR NORTH

This is where you'll find Chicago's mother lode of restaurants.

Frontera Grill
MEXICAN $$$

(Map p500; ☎312-661-1434; www.rickbayless.com; 445 N Clark St; ⏰lunch Tue-Fri, dinner Tue-Sat, brunch Sat) Perhaps you've seen chef Rick Bayless on TV, stirring up pepper sauces and other jump-off-the-tongue Mexican creations. His isn't your typical taco menu: Bayless uses seasonal, sustainable ingredients for flavor-packed fare. No wonder it's a fave of President Obama. Sister restaurant **Topolobampo**, in an adjoining room, is sleeker and pricier, with similar hours.

Xoco
MEXICAN $$

(Map p500; www.rickbayless.com; 449 N Clark St; mains $8-13; ⏰8am-9pm Tue-Thu, 8am-10pm Fri & Sat) Next door to Frontera Grill, crunch into warm *churros* (spiraled dough fritters) for breakfast, meaty *tortas* (sandwiches) for lunch and rich *caldos* (soups) for dinner at Rick Bayless' Mexican street-food joint.

Billy Goat Tavern
BURGERS $

(Map p500; www.billygoattavern.com; lower level, 430 N Michigan Ave; burgers $4-6; ⏰6am-2am Mon-Fri, 10am-2am Sat & Sun) *Tribune* and *Sun-Times* reporters have guzzled in the subterranean Billy Goat for decades. Order a 'cheezborger' and Schlitz, then look around at the newspapered walls to get the scoop on infamous local stories, such as the Cubs Curse.

Purple Pig
MEDITERRANEAN $

(Map p500; ☎312-464-1744; www.thepurplepigchicago.com; 500 N Michigan Ave; small plates $7-9; ⏰11:30am-midnight Sun-Thu, to 1am Fri & Sat; 🖉) The Pig's Magnificent Mile location, wide-ranging meat and veggie menu, long list of affordable vinos, and late-night serving hours make it a crowd pleaser. Milk-braised pork shoulder is the hamtastic specialty.

Mr Beef
SANDWICHES $

(666 N Orleans St; sandwiches $4-7; ⏰8am-7pm Mon-Thu, to 5am Fri, 10:30am-3:30pm & 10:30pm-5am Sat) A Chicago specialty, the Italian beef sandwich stacks up like this: thin-sliced, slow-cooked roast beef that's sopped in natural gravy and *giardiniera* (spicy, pickled vegetables), and then heaped on a hoagie roll. Mr Beef serves the best at its picnic-style tables. It's about four blocks west of Hotel Felix.

LINCOLN PARK & OLD TOWN

Halsted, Lincoln and Clark Sts are the main veins teeming with restaurants and bars. Parking is frightful, but the CTA Red Line to North or Fullerton will put you in their midst.

Alinea   NEW AMERICAN $$$
(✍312-867-0110; www.alinea-restaurant.com; 1723 N Halsted St; multicourse tastings $150-225; ⏰5:30-9:30pm Wed-Sun) Superstar chef Grant Achatz is the guy behind Alinea's 'molecular gastronomy.' If you secure a coveted reservation, prepare for roughly 12 to 24 courses of mind-bending, space-age cuisine. Dishes may emanate from a centrifuge or be pressed into a capsule. *Restaurant Magazine* has named it North America's number-one restaurant; reserve as far ahead as possible.

Wiener's Circle   AMERICAN $
(✍773-477-7444; 2622 N Clark St; items $3-6; ⏰10:30am-4am Sun-Thu, to 5am Fri & Sat) As famous for its unruly, foul-mouthed ambience as its char-dogs and cheddar fries, the Wiener Circle is *the* place for late-night munchies. It helps to be shnockered before entering.

LAKE VIEW & WRIGLEYVILLE

Clark, Halsted, Belmont and Southport are fertile streets. Parking stinks, so take the CTA Red Line to Addison (for Wrigleyville) or the Brown Line to the Belmont or Southport stops.

Crisp   ASIAN $
(Map p508; www.crisponline.com; 2940 N Broadway; mains $7-12; ⏰11:30am-9pm Tue-Thu & Sun, to 10:30pm Fri & Sat) Music pours from the stereo, and cheap, delicious Korean fusions

arrive from the kitchen at this cheerful cafe. The 'Bad Boy Buddha' bowl, a variation on *bi bim bop* (mixed vegetables with rice), is one of the best cheap lunches in town.

Mia Francesca   ITALIAN $$
(Map p508; ✍773-281-3310; www.miafrancesca.com; 3311 N Clark St; mains $13-27; ⏰5-10pm Sun-Thu, to 11pm Fri & Sat) Local chain Mia's buzzes with regulars who come for the trattoria's Italian standards, such as seafood linguine, spinach ravioli and mushroom-sauced veal medallions, all prepared with simple flair.

ANDERSONVILLE & UPTOWN

For 'Little Saigon' take the CTA Red Line to Argyle. For the European cafes in Andersonville, go one stop further to Berwyn.

Hopleaf   EUROPEAN $$
(Map p508; ✍773-334-9851; www.hopleaf.com; 5148 N Clark St; mains $10-17; ⏰5-11pm Mon-Thu, to midnight Fri & Sat, 4-10pm Sun) A cozy, European-style tavern, Hopleaf draws crowds for its Montréal-style smoked brisket, cashew-butter-and-fig-jam sandwich and the house-specialty – *frites* and ale-soaked mussels. It also pours 200 types of brew. Prepare to queue.

Ba Le Bakery   VIETNAMESE $
(Map p508; ✍773-561-4424; 5016 N Broadway; sandwiches $3-5; ⏰7:30am-8pm) Ba Le serves Saigon-style *banh mi* sandwiches, with steamed pork, shrimp cakes or meatballs on fresh baguettes made right here.

WICKER PARK, BUCKTOWN & UKRAINIAN VILLAGE

Trendy restaurants open almost every day in these 'hoods. Take the CTA Blue Line to Damen.

Handlebar Bar & Grill   INTERNATIONAL $$
(✍773-384-9546; www.handlebarchicago.com; 2311 W North Ave; mains $9-14; ⏰10am-midnight Mon-Thu, to 2am Fri & Sat, to 11pm Sun; ✍) Local cyclists congregate around the eclectic, vegetarian-friendly menu (ie West African groundnut stew) and summertime patio to quaff from the well-curated beer list.

Big Star Taqueria   MEXICAN $
(www.bigstarchicago.com; 1531 N Damen Ave; tacos $3-4; ⏰11:30am-2am) This honky-tonk gets packed, but damn, the tacos are worth the wait – pork belly in tomato-*guajillo* (chili) sauce and lamb shoulder with *queso fresco* (white cheese) accompany the specialty whiskey list. Cash only.

ROLLING WITH FOOD TRUCKS

Chicago is finally getting in on the food truck action. Perhaps you'd like tortilla soup ladled by gentlemen in Mexican wrestling masks? The Tamale Spaceship can deliver. Other popular purveyors include the Gaztro-Wagon (Indian-style 'naan-wiches') and Meatyballs Mobile ('globes of goodness'). Most trucks tweet their location; the **Tribune's food blog** (www.twitter.com/@tribstew/chicago-food-trucks) amalgamates them.

DIY: HOW TO FIND A REAL CHICAGO BAR

Unfortunately, we can't list every watering hole in town, but we can give you the tools to go out and discover classic, character-filled bars on your own. Look for the following:

» an 'Old Style' beer sign swinging out front

» a well-worn dart board and/or pool table inside

» patrons wearing Cubs-, White Sox- or Bears-logoed ballcaps

» bottles of brew served in buckets of ice

» sports on TV (with the latter being a 1974 Zenith, not some fancy flat-screen thing).

LOGAN SQUARE & HUMBOLDT PARK

Eats and drinks ring the intersection of Milwaukee, Logan and Kedzie Blvds. Get the CTA Blue Line to Logan Square or California.

TOP CHOICE Hot Doug's   AMERICAN $
(773-279-9550; www.hotdougs.com; 3324 N California Ave; mains $3-8; 10:30am-4pm Mon-Sat) Doug's the man to fulfill all your hot-dog fantasies. He serves multiple dog styles (Polish, bratwursts, Chicago) cooked multiple dog ways (char-grilled, deep-fried, steamed). Confused? He'll explain it all. Doug also makes gourmet 'haute dogs,' such as blue-cheese pork with cherry cream sauce. It's sublime, but a heck of a haul unless you're traveling by car. Cash only.

Bonsoiree   NEW AMERICAN $$$
(773-486-7511; www.bonsoireechicago.com; 2728 W Armitage Ave; multicourse meal $60-90; 5-10pm Tue-Sat, to 9pm Sun) It started as an underground supper club, and Saturdays are still an invitation-only event (go to the website to get on the mailing list). Otherwise, dinner at Bonsoiree is a leisurely, multicourse affair where the chefs whip up inspired comfort foods (often with a Japanese bent). It's unusually casual for such fine dining, right up to being BYOB.

NEAR WEST SIDE & PILSEN

Greektown extends along S Halsted St (take the Blue Line to UIC-Halsted), and the Mexican Pilsen enclave centers around W 18th St (take the Pink Line to 18th). The West Loop holds several stylish eateries along Randolph and Fulton Market Sts (taxi from downtown $10).

Next   ECLECTIC $$$
(312-226-0858; www.nextrestaurant.com; 953 W Fulton Market; multicourse meal $100; 5:30-9:30pm Wed-Sun) Grant Achatz's West Loop restaurant, which opened in 2011, is the hottest ticket in town. And we mean it literally – you need a ticket to dine at Next, which operates like a time machine. It started by serving an eight-course French meal from 1906 Paris, but every three months the whole thing changes: new era, new menu, new decor. Sign up for tickets at the website as early as possible. Prices vary by date, time and menu (early weekdays cost less than prime-time weekends), and you pay when you book. Check the Twitter feed (@nextres taraunt) for possible last-minute seats.

Don Pedro Carnitas   MEXICAN $
(1113 W 18th St; tacos $1.50-2; 6am-6pm Mon-Fri, 5am-5pm Sat, to 3pm Sun) At this no-frills Pilsen meat hive, a man with a machete salutes you at the front counter. He awaits your command to hack off pork pieces, and then wraps the thick chunks with onion and cilantro in a fresh tortilla. Cash only.

Publican   AMERICAN $$$
(312-733-9555; www.thepublicanrestaurant.com; 837 W Fulton Market; mains $16-30; 3:30-10:30pm Mon-Thu, to 11:30pm Fri & Sat, 10am-2pm & 5-10pm Sun) Set up like a swanky beer hall, Publican specializes in oysters, hams and fine suds – all from small family farms and microbrewers.

🍷 Drinking

During the long winters, Chicagoans count on bars for warmth. The usual closing time is 2am, but some places stay open until 4am or 5am. In summer many bars boast beer gardens.

THE LOOP & NEAR NORTH

Restaurants such as the Gage, Billy Goat Tavern and Purple Pig (see Eating) make fine drinking destinations, too.

Signature Lounge   LOUNGE
(Map p500; www.signatureroom.com; John Hancock Center, 875 N Michigan Ave; from 11am) Have the Hancock Observatory view without the Hancock Observatory admission price. Grab the elevator up to the 96th floor and order

a beverage while looking out over the city. Ladies: don't miss the bathroom view.

Clark Street Ale House   BAR
(Map p500; 742 N Clark St; ⊗from 4pm) Do as the retro sign advises and 'Stop & Drink Liquor.' Midwestern microbrews are the main draw; order a three-beer sampler for $5.

Intelligentsia Coffee   CAFE
(Map p500; www.intelligentsia.com; 53 E Randolph St; ⊗from 6am Mon-Fri, 7am Sat & Sun) The local chain roasts its own beans and percolates strong stuff. Staff recently won the US Barista Championship.

Harry Caray's Tavern   BAR
(Map p500; www.harrycaraystavern.com; 700 E Grand Ave; ⊗from 11am) Relieves thirst on Navy Pier; it has decent brews and a small sports memorabilia 'museum.'

OLD TOWN & WRIGLEYVILLE

TOP CHOICE Old Town Ale House   BAR
(www.oldtownalehouse.net; 219 W North Ave; ⊗from 8am Mon-Sat, from noon Sun) This unpretentious favorite lets you mingle with beautiful people and grizzled regulars, seated pint by pint under the nude-politician paintings. It's across the street from Second City.

Gingerman Tavern   BAR
(Map p508; 3740 N Clark St; ⊗from 3pm Mon-Fri, from noon Sat & Sun) The pool tables, good beer selection and pierced-and-tattooed patrons make Gingerman wonderfully different from the surrounding Wrigleyville sports bars.

WICKER PARK, BUCKTOWN & UKRAINIAN VILLAGE

Map Room   PUB
(www.maproom.com; 1949 N Hoyne Ave; ⊗from 6:30am Mon-Fri, 7:30am Sat, 11am Sun; 🕏) At this map-and-globe-filled 'travelers' tavern' artsy types sip coffee by day and suds from the 200-strong beer list by night. There's free ethnic food on Tuesdays at 7pm.

Danny's   BAR
(1951 W Dickens Ave) Danny's comfortably dim and dog-eared ambience is perfect for conversations over a pint. A poetry-reading series and occasional DJs add to the scruffy artiness.

Matchbox   BAR
(770 N Milwaukee Ave; ⊗from 4pm) Lawyers, artists and bums all squeeze in for retro cocktails. It's small as – you got it – a match-

box, with about 10 barstools; everyone else stands against the back wall. Matchbox sits by its lonesome northwest of downtown, near the Blue Line stop at Chicago.

WEST LOOP

Aviary   COCKTAIL BAR
(www.twitter.com/@aviarycocktails; 955 W Fulton Market; ⊗from 6pm Wed-Sun) Grant Achatz's bar beside Next (see p518) is more in spirit (pun!) with his other restaurant, Alinea. The lounge shakes and stirs one-of-a-kind drinks such as Buttered Popcorn, which tastes as advertised. The selection changes frequently, as do the 19 different types of ice. Drinks cost around $16 each.

☆ Entertainment

Check the **Reader** (www.chicagoreader.com) and **Time Out Chicago** (www.timeoutchicago.com) for listings.

Live Music
Blues and jazz have deep roots in Chicago, and indie rock clubs slouch on almost every corner. Cover charges range from $5 to $20.

BLUES

Buddy Guy's Legends   BLUES
(Map p500; www.buddyguys.com; 700 S Wabash Ave) Top local and national acts wail on the stage of local icon Buddy Guy. The man himself usually plugs in his axe in January.

Kingston Mines   BLUES
(www.kingstonmines.com; 2548 N Halsted St) Two stages, seven nights a week, ensure somebody's always on. It's noisy, hot, sweaty, crowded and conveniently located in Lincoln Park.

ⓘ DISCOUNT TICKETS

National ticket broker **Goldstar** (www.goldstar.com) sells half-price tickets to all sorts of Chicago entertainment, including theater performances, sports events and concerts. You'll fare best if you sign up at least three weeks ahead of time, as Goldstar typically releases its seats well in advance of shows.

For same-day theater seats at half-price, try **Hot Tix** (www.hottix.org). You can buy them online, or in person at booths in the **Chicago Tourism Center** (Map p500; 72 E Randolph St) and **Water Works Visitor Center** (Map p500; 163 E Pearson St).

BLUES
BLUES
(www.chicagobluesbar.com; 2519 N Halsted St)
Across the street from Kingston Mines, this
veteran club draws a slightly older crowd
that soaks up every crackling, electrified
moment.

Rosa's
BLUES
(www.rosaslounge.com; 3420 W Armitage Ave;
⊙closed Sun, Mon & Wed) Rosa's is a real-deal
venue that brings in local talent and dedicated fans to a somewhat dodgy Logan Sq block.

Lee's Unleaded Blues
BLUES
(www.leesunleadedblues.com; 7401 S South Chicago Ave; ⊙closed Mon-Thu) Buried deep on the
South Side, Lee's is a genuine juke joint. The
crowd dresses in their finest threads, and everyone jams until dawn.

JAZZ
Green Mill
JAZZ
(Map p508; www.greenmilljazz.com; 4802 N Broadway) The timeless Green Mill earned its notoriety as Al Capone's favorite speakeasy (the
tunnels where he hid the booze are still underneath the bar), and you can feel his ghost
urging you on to another martini. Local and
national artists perform six nights per week;
Sundays are for the nationally acclaimed poetry slam.

JAZZ
(Map p500; www.jazzshowcase.com; 806 S Plymouth Court) The gorgeous room is the top spot
for national acts to blow their horns.

Andy's
JAZZ
(Map p500; www.andysjazzclub.com; 11 E Hubbard
St) Andy's is affordable and mixed, from its
multiage clientele to its fusion of swing, bop
and Afro-pop.

ROCK & FOLK
Hideout
LIVE MUSIC
(www.hideoutchicago.com; 1354 W Wabansia Ave)
Hidden behind a factory at the edge of
Bucktown, this two-room lodge of indie rock
and alt-country is well worth seeking out.
The owners have nursed an outsider, underground vibe, and the place feels like the
downstairs of your grandma's rumpus room.
Music and other events (bingo, literary readings etc) take place nightly.

Metro
LIVE MUSIC
(Map p508; www.metrochicago.com; 3730 N Clark
St) The Metro is legendary for loud rock. Local bands on the verge of stardom and national names looking for an 'intimate' venue
turn up the volume.

Empty Bottle
LIVE MUSIC
(www.emptybottle.com; 1035 N Western Ave) The
scruffy, go-to club for edgy indie rock and
jazz; Monday's show is always free (and
there's $1.50 Pabst).

Double Door
LIVE MUSIC
(www.doubledoor.com; 1572 N Milwaukee Ave) Alternative rock that is *just* under the radar
finds a home a this former liquor store.

Theater
Chicago's reputation for stage drama is
well deserved. Many productions export to
Broadway. The city's top troupes:

Steppenwolf Theatre
THEATER
(☑312-335-1650; www.steppenwolf.org; 1650 N
Halsted St) Drama club of Malkovich, Sinise
and other Hollywood stars; 2 miles north of
the Loop in Lincoln Park.

Goodman Theatre
THEATER
(Map p500; ☑312-443-3800; www.goodmanthe
atre.org; 170 N Dearborn St) Known for new and
classic American works.

Other first-rate companies:

Chicago Shakespeare Theater
THEATER
(Map p500; ☑312-595-5600; www.chicagoshakes.
com; 800 E Grand Ave) Will's comedies and
tragedies at Navy Pier.

THEATER
(Map p500; ☑312-337-0665; www.lookingglass
theatre.org; 821 N Michigan Ave) Improv-based
works, often incorporating acrobatics.

Neo-Futurists
THEATER
(Map p508; ☑773-275-5255; www.neofuturists.org;
5153 N Ashland Ave) Original works that make
you ponder and laugh simultaneously.

Dreamboat old theaters that host touring
shows cluster at State and Randolph Sts.
Broadway in Chicago (☑800-775-2000; www.
broadwayinchicago.com) handles tickets for
most:

Auditorium Theater
THEATER
(Map p500; 50 E Congress Pkwy)

Bank of America Theatre
THEATER
(Map p500; 18 W Monroe St)

Cadillac Palace Theater
THEATER
(Map p500; 151 W Randolph St)

Chicago Theater
THEATER
(Map p500; 175 N State St)

Ford Center/Oriental Theatre
THEATER
(Map p500; 24 W Randolph St)

Comedy

Improv comedy began in Chicago, and the city still nurtures the best in the business.

Second City   COMEDY

(off Map p500; ☑312-337-3992; www.secondcity.com; 1616 N Wells St) It's the cream of the crop, where Bill Murray, Stephen Colbert, Tina Fey and many more honed their sharp, biting wit. Bargain: turn up after the evening's last show (Friday excluded), and watch the comics improv a performance for free.

iO Improv   COMEDY

(Map p508; ☑773-880-0199; www.ioimprov.com; 3541 N Clark St) Chicago's other major improv house.

Sports

Chicago Cubs   BASEBALL

(www.cubs.com) The Cubs last won the World Series in 1908, but their fans still pack baseball's most charming stadium, **Wrigley Field** (Map p508; 1060 W Addison St), which dates from 1914 and is known for its ivy-walled field and classic neon entrance sign. For tickets, check the website for deals, or try the box office two to three hours before game time. Take the CTA Red Line to Addison; it's 4.5 miles north of the Loop.

Chicago White Sox   BASEBALL

(www.whitesox.com) The Sox are the Cubs' South Side rivals and play in the more modern 'Cell,' aka **US Cellular Field** (Map p498; 333 W 35th St). Tickets are usually cheaper and easier to get than at Wrigley; Monday is half-price night. Take the CTA Red Line to the Sox-35th St station; it's 4.5 miles south of the Loop.

Chicago Bulls   BASKETBALL

(www.nba.com/bulls) Is Derrick Rose the new Michael Jordan? Find out at the **United Center** (Map p498; 1901 W Madison St), where the Bulls shoot hoops. It's about 2 miles west of the Loop. CTA runs special buses (No 19) on game days; it's best not to walk here.

Chicago Blackhawks   HOCKEY

(www.chicagoblackhawks.com) The 2010 Stanley Cup winners skate in front of big crowds. They share the United Center with the Bulls.

Chicago Bears   FOOTBALL

(www.chicagobears.com) Da Bears, Chicago's NFL team, tackle at **Soldier Field** (Map p500; 425 E McFetridge Dr), recognizable by its classical-meets-flying-saucer architecture. Expect beery tailgate parties, sleet and snow.

Clubs

Clubs in the Near North and West Loop tend to be cavernous and luxurious (with dress codes). Clubs in Wicker Park-Ukrainian Village are usually more casual.

Late Bar   CLUB

(www.latebarchicago.com; 3534 W Belmont Ave; ⊙Tue-Sat) Owned by a couple of DJs, Late Bar's weird, new wave vibe draws fans of all stripes. It's off the beaten path in a forlorn stretch of Logan Sq, though easily reachable via the Blue Line train to Belmont.

Smart Bar   CLUB

(Map p508; www.smartbarchicago.com; ⊙Wed-Sat) Long-standing, unpretentious favorite for dancing, attached to the Metro rock club.

Darkroom   CLUB

(www.darkroombar.com; 2210 W Chicago Ave) Welcomes everyone from goths to reggae-heads with its eclectic spins in Ukrainian Village.

Performing Arts

FREE Grant Park Orchestra   CLASSICAL MUSIC

(Map p500; ☑312-742-7638; www.grantparkmusicfestival.com) The beloved group puts on free classical concerts in Millennium Park throughout the summer.

Symphony Center   CLASSICAL MUSIC

(Map p500; ☑312-294-3000; www.cso.org; 220 S Michigan Ave) The Chicago Symphony Orchestra plays in the Daniel Burnham–designed hall.

Civic Opera House   OPERA

(☑312-332-2244; www.lyricopera.org; 20 N Wacker Dr) The renowned Lyric Opera of Chicago high C's in this chandeliered venue. It's a few blocks west of the Loop.

Hubbard Street Dance Chicago   DANCE

(☑312-850-9744; www.hubbardstreetdance.com) Chicago's preeminent dance company performs at the **Harris Theater for Music and Dance** (Map p500; www.harristheaterchicago.org; 205 E Randolph St).

🔒 Shopping

The shoppers' siren song emanates from N Michigan Ave, along the Magnificent Mile. **Water Tower Place** (Map p500; 835 N Michigan Ave) is among the large vertical malls here. Moving onward, boutiques fill Wicker Park/Bucktown (indie and vintage), Lincoln Park (posh), Lake View (countercultural) and Andersonville (all of the above).

FREEBIES

The city's official portal, **Explore Chicago** (www.explorechicago.org), provides a Twitter feed (twitter.com/explorechicago) of free events each day, as well as excellent free neighborhood maps and guides.

Chicago Architecture Foundation Shop
SOUVENIRS

(Map p500; www.architecture.org/shop; 224 S Michigan Ave) Skyline posters, Frank Lloyd Wright note cards, skyscraper models and more for those with an edifice complex.

Strange Cargo
CLOTHING

(Map p508; www.strangecargo.com; 3448 N Clark St) The retro store stocks kitschy iron-on T-shirts featuring Ditka, Obama and other renowned Chicagoans.

Jazz Record Mart
MUSIC

(Map p500; www.jazzmart.com; 27 E Illinois St) One-stop shop for Chicago jazz and blues CDs and vinyl.

Quimby's
BOOKS

(www.quimbys.com; 1854 W North Ave) Ground Zero for comics, zines and underground culture; in Wicker Park.

ⓘ Information

Emergency & Medical Services

Northwestern Memorial Hospital (☎312-926-5188; 251 E Erie St) Well-respected hospital downtown.

Stroger Cook County Hospital (☎312-864-1300; 1969 W Ogden Ave) Public hospital serving low-income patients; 2.5 miles west of the Loop.

Walgreens (☎312-664-8686; 757 N Michigan Ave; ⊙24hr) On the Mag Mile.

Internet Access

Many bars and restaurants have free wi-fi, as does the Chicago Cultural Center. Or try:

Harold Washington Library Center (www.chipublib.org; 400 S State St; ⊙9am-9pm Mon-Thu, to 5pm Fri & Sat, 1-5pm Sun) A grand, art-filled building with free wi-fi throughout and 3rd-floor internet terminals (get a day pass at the counter).

Media

Chicago Reader (www.chicagoreader.com) Free alternative newspaper with comprehensive arts and entertainment listings.

Chicago Sun-Times (www.suntimes.com) The *Tribune's* daily, tabloidesque competitor.

Chicago Tribune (www.chicagotribune.com) The city's stalwart daily newspaper; its younger, trimmed-down, freebie version is *RedEye*.

Time Out Chicago (www.timeoutchicago.com) Weekly magazine with all-encompassing listings.

Money

ATMs are plentiful downtown, with many near Chicago and Michigan Aves. To change money, try Terminal 5 at O'Hare International or the following places in the Loop:

Travelex (☎312-807-4941; 19 S LaSalle St; ⊙Mon-Fri)

World's Money Exchange (☎312-641-2151; 203 N LaSalle St; ⊙Mon-Fri)

Post

Post office Fort Dearborn (540 N Dearborn St); Main (433 W Harrison St; ⊙7:30am-midnight)

Tourist Information

The **Chicago Office of Tourism** (☎312-744-2400; www.explorechicago.org) operates two well-stocked visitor centers, each with a staffed information desk, ticket outlet, cafe and free wi-fi:

Chicago Cultural Center Visitors Center (77 E Randolph St; ⊙8am-7pm Mon-Thu, 8am-6pm Fri, 9am-6pm Sat, 10am-6pm Sun)

Water Works Visitors Center (163 E Pearson St; ⊙8am-7pm Mon-Thu, 8am-6pm Fri, 10am-6pm Sat, 10am-4pm Sun)

Websites

Chicagoist (www.chicagoist.com) Quirky take on news, food, arts and events.

Gaper's Block (www.gapersblock.com) News and events site with Chicago attitude.

Huffington Post Chicago (www.huffingtonpost.com/chicago) Amalgamates news from major local sources.

ⓘ Getting There & Away

Air

Chicago Midway Airport (MDW; off Map p498; www.flychicago.com) The smaller airport used mostly by domestic carriers, such as Southwest; often has cheaper flights than from O'Hare.

O'Hare International Airport (ORD; off Map p498; www.flychicago.com) Chicago's larger airport, and among the world's busiest. Headquarters for United Airlines and a hub for American. Most non-US airlines and international flights use Terminal 5 (except Lufthansa and flights from Canada).

Bus

Greyhound (☎312-408-5800; www.grey hound.com; 630 W Harrison St) Main station is two blocks southwest from the CTA Blue Line Clinton stop. Buses run frequently to Cleveland (7½ hours), Detroit (seven hours) and Minneapolis (nine hours), as well as to small towns throughout the USA.

Megabus (Map p500; www.megabus.com/us; southeast cnr Canal St & Jackson Blvd) Travels only to major Midwestern cities. Prices are often less, and quality and efficiency are better than Greyhound on these routes. The bus stop is adjacent to Union Station.

Train

Chicago's classic **Union Station** (Map p500; 225 S Canal St) is the hub for **Amtrak's** (☎800-872-7245; www.amtrak.com) national and regional service. Routes include:

DETROIT (5½ hours, three trains daily)

MILWAUKEE (1½ hours, seven trains daily)

MINNEAPOLIS/ST PAUL (eight hours, one train daily)

NEW YORK (20½ hours, one train daily)

SAN FRANCISCO (EMERYVILLE) (53 hours, one train daily)

ST LOUIS (5½ hours, five trains daily)

❶ Getting Around

To/From the Airport

CHICAGO MIDWAY AIRPORT 11 miles southwest of the Loop, connected via the CTA Orange Line ($2.25). Other options include shuttles (per person $24) and cabs ($30 to $40).

O'HARE INTERNATIONAL AIRPORT 17 miles northwest of the Loop. The cheapest, and often the quickest, way to/from O'Hare is by the CTA Blue Line ($2.25), but the station is a long walk from the flight terminals. Airport Express shuttles run between the airport and downtown hotels (per person $29). Cabs to/from downtown cost about $45.

Bicycle

Chicago has 120 miles of bike lanes. Get free maps from the city's **transportation department** (www.chicagobikes.org). Bike racks are plentiful; the biggest, with showers, is at the **McDonalds Cycle Center** (www.chicagobike station.com; 239 E Randolph St) in Millennium Park. Lock it or lose it. For bike-rental information, see p509.

Car & Motorcycle

Be warned: street and garage/lot parking is expensive. If you must, try **East Monroe Garage** (www.millenniumgarages.com; Columbus Dr btwn Randolph & Monroe Sts; per day $24). Chicago's rush-hour traffic is abysmal.

Public Transportation

The **Chicago Transit Authority** (CTA; www. transitchicago.com) operates the city's buses and the elevated/subway train system (aka the El). CTA buses go everywhere from early morning until late evening. Two of the eight color-coded train lines – the Red Line, and the Blue Line to O'Hare International Airport – operate 24 hours a day. The other lines run from about 5am to midnight daily. During the day, you shouldn't have to wait more than 15 minutes for a train. Get free maps at any station.

The standard fare per train is $2.25; per bus, it is $2. Transfers cost 25¢. On buses, you can use a fare card (called a Transit Card) or pay with exact change (in which case the price goes up to $2.25). On the train, you must use a Transit Card, which is sold from vending machines at train stations. Day passes (one-/three-day pass $5.75/14) provide excellent savings, but they can be purchased only at airports and various drug stores and currency exchanges.

Metra commuter trains (www.metrarail.com) have 12 routes serving the suburbs from four terminals ringing the Loop: LaSalle St Station, Millennium Station, Union Station and Richard B Ogilvie Transportation Center (a few blocks north of Union Station). Some lines run daily, while others operate only during weekday rush hours. Metra fares cost $2.25 to $8.50. An all-weekend pass costs $7.

PACE (www.pacebus.com) runs the suburban bus system that connects with city transport.

Taxi

Cabs are plentiful in the Loop, north to Andersonville and northwest to Wicker Park/Bucktown. Flagfall is $2.25, plus $1.80 per mile and $1 per extra passenger; a 15% tip is expected. Venture outside city limits and you'll pay one and a half times the fare. Recommended companies:

Flash Cab (☎773-561-1444)

Yellow Cab (☎312-829-4222)

Around Chicago

OAK PARK

Located 10 miles west of the Loop and easily reached via CTA train, Oak Park has spawned two famous sons: novelist Ernest Hemingway was born here, and architect Frank Lloyd Wright lived and worked here from 1889 to 1909.

During Wright's 20 years in Oak Park, he designed many houses. Stop at the **visitor center** (☎888-625-7275; www.visitoakpark.com; 158 N Forest Ave; ⊙10am-5pm) and buy an architectural site map ($4), which gives their locations. To actually get inside a Wright-designed dwelling, you'll need to visit the

Frank Lloyd Wright Home & Studio ([📞]708-848-1976; www.gowright.org; 951 Chicago Ave; adult/child $15/12; [⏰]11am-4pm). Tour frequency varies, from every 20 minutes on summer weekends to every hour in winter. The Studio also offers guided neighborhood walking tours, as well as a self-guided audio version.

Despite Hemingway calling Oak Park a 'village of wide lawns and narrow minds,' the town still pays homage to him at the **Ernest Hemingway Museum** ([📞]708-848-2222; www.ehfop.org; 200 N Oak Park Ave; adult/child $10/8; [⏰]1-5pm Sun-Fri, 10am-5pm Sat). Admission also includes access to **Hemingway's Birthplace** (339 N Oak Park Ave) across the street.

From downtown Chicago, take the CTA Green Line to its terminus at the Harlem stop, which lands you about four blocks from the visitor center. The train traverses some bleak neighborhoods before emerging into Oak Park's wide-lawn splendor.

EVANSTON & NORTH SHORE

Evanston, 14 miles north of the Loop and reached via the CTA Purple Line, combines sprawling old houses with a compact downtown. It's home to Northwestern University.

Beyond are Chicago's northern lakeshore suburbs, which became popular with the wealthy in the late 19th century. A classic 30-mile drive follows Sheridan Rd through various well-off towns to the socioeconomic apex of Lake Forest. Attractions include the **Baha'i House of Worship** (www.bahai.us/bahai-temple; 100 Linden Ave, Wilmette; admission free; [⏰]6am-10pm), a glistening white architectural marvel, and the **Chicago Botanic Garden** ([📞]847-835-5440; www.chicagobotanic.org; 1000 Lake Cook Rd, Glencoe; admission free; [⏰]8am-sunset), with hiking trails, 255 bird species and weekend cooking demos by well-known chefs. Parking costs $20.

Inland lies the **Illinois Holocaust Museum** ([📞]847-967-4800; www.ilholocaustmuseum.org; 9603 Woods Dr, Skokie; adult/child $12/6; [⏰]10am-5pm Mon-Fri, to 8pm Thu, 11am-4pm Sat & Sun). Besides its excellent videos of survivors' stories from WWII, the museum contains thought-provoking art about genocides in Armenia, Rwanda, Cambodia and others.

Galena & Northern Illinois

The highlight is the hilly northwest, where cottonwood trees, grazing horses and twisty roads over old stagecoach trails fill the pocket around Galena.

En route is Union, where the **Illinois Railway Museum** ([📞]815-923-4000; www.irm.org; US 20 to Union Rd; adult $8-12, child $4-8 depending upon season; [⏰]hours vary Apr-Oct) sends trainspotters into fits of ecstasy with 200 acres of locomotives.

GALENA

Galena, spread across wooded hillsides near the Mississippi River, amid rolling, barn-dotted farmland, draws hordes of Chicagoans to its perfectly preserved, Civil War–era streets. While it sometimes gets chided as a place for the 'newly wed and nearly dead,' thanks to all the tourist-oriented B&Bs, fudge and antique shops, there's no denying the little town's beauty. Red-brick mansions in Greek Revival, Gothic Revival and Queen Anne styles fill the streets, left over from Galena's heyday in the mid-1800s, when local lead mines made it rich. Throw in cool kayak trips, foodie farm tours and winding backroad drives, and you've got a lovely, slowpoke getaway.

The **visitor center** ([📞]877-464-2536; www.galena.org; 101 Bouthillier St; [⏰]9am-5pm), in the 1857 train depot as you enter from the east, is a good place to start. Get a map, leave your car in the lot ($5 per day) and explore on foot.

Elegant old Main St curves around the hillside and the historic heart of town. Among numerous sights is the **Ulysses S Grant Home** ([📞]815-777-3310; www.granthome.com; 500 Bouthillier St; adult/child $4/2; [⏰]9am-4:45pm Wed-Sun, reduced hrs Nov-Mar), which was a gift from local Republicans to the victorious general at the Civil War's end. Grant lived here until he became the country's 18th president. The elaborate Italianate **Belvedere Mansion** ([📞]815-777-0747; www.belvederemansionandgardens.com; 1008 Park Ave; adult/child $13/free; [⏰]11am-4pm Sun-Fri, to 5pm Sat, closed mid-Nov–mid-May) hangs the green drapes from *Gone With the Wind*.

Outdoors enthusiasts should head to **Fever River Outfitters** ([📞]815-776-9425; www.feverriveroutfitters.com; 525 S Main St; [⏰]10am-5pm, closed Tue-Thu early Sep-late May), which rents canoes, kayaks, stand up paddleboards, bicycles and snowshoes. It also offers guided tours, such as two-hour kayak trips ($45 per person, equipment included) on the Mississippi River's backwaters. Or visit local bison ranches, artisan cheesemakers and herb farms on a culinary tour with **Learn Great Foods** ([📞]866-240-1650; www.learngreatfoods.com; tours $50-125).

Excursions vary; check online for the schedule and locations.

Galena brims with quilt-laden B&Bs. Most cost $100 to $200 nightly and fill up during weekends. The visitor center website provides contact information. Presidential types can be like Grant and Lincoln and stay in the well-furnished rooms at DeSoto House Hotel (☑815-777-0090; www.desoto house.com; 230 S Main St; r $128-200; ☺✲☎), which dates from 1855. Grant Hills Motel (☑877-421-0924; www.granthills.com; 9372 US 20; r $70-90; ☺✲☎☎) is a no-frills option 1.5 miles east of town, with countryside views and a horseshoe pitch.

111 Main (☑815-777-8030; www.oneeleven main.com; 111 N Main St; mains $16-24; ☺11am-10pm) makes meatloaf, pork-and-mashed-potatoes and other Midwestern favorites using ingredients sourced from local farms. Victory Cafe (www.victorycafes.com; 200 N Main St; mains $5-11; ☺6am-3pm) is ideal for biscuit-and-gravy breakfasts or lunchtime sandwiches. The VFW Hall (100 S Main St) provides a sublime opportunity to sip cheap beers and watch TV alongside veterans of long-ago wars. Don't be shy: as the sign out front says, the public is welcome.

QUAD CITIES

South of Galena along a pretty stretch of the Great River Road (www.greatriverroad-illinois. org) is scenic Mississippi Palisades State Park (☑815-273-2731), a popular rock-climbing, hiking and camping area; pick up trail maps at the north entrance park office.

Further downstream, the Quad Cities (www.visitquadcities.com) – Moline and Rock Island in Illinois, and Davenport and Bettendorf across the river in Iowa – make a surprisingly good stop. Rock Island has an appealing downtown (based at 2nd Ave and 18th St), with a couple of cafes and a lively pub and music scene. On the edge of town, Black Hawk State Historic Site (www.black hawkpark.org; 1510 46th Ave; ☺sunrise-10pm) is a huge park with trails by the Rock River. Its Hauberg Indian Museum (☑309-788-9536; Watch Tower Lodge; admission free; ☺9am-noon & 1-5pm Wed-Sun) outlines the story of Sauk leader Black Hawk and his people.

Out in the Mississippi River, the actual island of Rock Island once held a Civil War–era arsenal and POW camp. It now maintains an impressive arms museum (☺Tue-Sun), Civil War cemetery, national cemetery and visitor center for barge viewing. All are

free, but bring photo ID as the island is still an active army facility.

Moline is the home of John Deere, the international farm machinery manufacturer. Downtown holds the John Deere Pavilion (www.johndeerepavilion.com; admission free; 1400 River Dr; ☺9am-5pm Mon-Fri, 10am-5pm Sat, noon-4pm Sun; ♿), a museum/showroom loved by kiddies.

Springfield & Central Illinois

Abraham Lincoln and Route 66 sights are sprinkled liberally throughout central Illinois, which is otherwise farmland plain. East of Decatur, Arthur and Arcola are Amish centers.

SPRINGFIELD

The small state capital has a serious obsession with Abraham Lincoln, who practiced law here from 1837 to 1861. Many of the attractions are walkable downtown and cost little or nothing.

⊙ Sights & Activities

FREE Lincoln Home & Visitor Center HISTORIC SITE
(☑217-492-4150; www.nps.gov/liho; 426 S 7th St; ☺8:30am-5pm) Start at the National Park Service visitor center, where you must pick up a ticket to enter Lincoln's 12-room abode, located directly across the street. You can then walk through the house where Abe and Mary Lincoln lived from 1844 until they moved to the White House in 1861; rangers are stationed throughout to provide background information and answer questions.

Lincoln Presidential Library & Museum MUSEUM
(☑217-558-8844; www.presidentlincoln.org; 212 N 6th St; adult/child $12/6; ☺9am-5pm; ♿) It contains the most complete Lincoln collection in the world. Real-deal artifacts like Abe's shaving mirror and briefcase join whiz-bang exhibits and Disneyesque holograms that keep the kids agog.

FREE Lincoln's Tomb CEMETERY
(1441 Monument Ave; ☺9am-5pm, closed Sun & Mon Sep-May) After his assassination, Lincoln's body was returned to Springfield, where it lies in an impressive tomb in Oak Ridge Cemetery, 1.5 miles north of downtown. The gleam on the nose of Lincoln's

ROUTE 66: GET YOUR KICKS IN ILLINOIS

America's 'Mother Road' kicks off in Chicago on Adams St, just west of Michigan Ave. Before embarking, fuel up at Lou Mitchell's (p516) diner near Union Station. After all, it's 300 miles from here to the Missouri state line.

Sadly, most of the original Route 66 has been superseded by I-55 in Illinois, though the old road still exists in scattered sections often paralleling the interstate. Keep an eye out for brown 'Historic Route 66' signs, which pop up at crucial junctions to mark the way.

Our first stop rises from the cornfields 60 miles south in Wilmington. Here the Gemini Giant – a 28ft fiberglass spaceman – stands guard outside the **Launching Pad Drive In** (810 E Baltimore St; burgers $2-6; ☺11am-7:30pm). To reach it, exit I-55 at Joliet Rd, and follow it south as it becomes Hwy 53 into town.

Motor 45 miles onward to Pontiac and the tchotchke-and-photo-filled **Route 66 Hall of Fame** (☎815-844-4566; 110 W Howard St; admission free; ☺9am-5pm Mon-Fri, 10am-4pm Sat). Cruise another 50 miles to Shirley and **Funk's Grove** (☎309-874-3360; www.funks maplesirup.com; ☺call for seasonal hrs), a pretty 19th-century maple syrup farm and nature preserve (exit 154 off I-55).

Ten miles later you'll reach the throwback hamlet of Atlanta. Pull up a chair at the **Palms Grill Cafe** (☎217-648-2233; 110 SW Arch St; mains $4-9; ☺8am-5pm Sun-Thu, to 8pm Fri & Sat), where thick slabs of gooseberry, sour cream raisin and other retro pies tempt from the glass case. Then walk across the street to snap a photo with **Tall Paul**, a sky-high statue of Paul Bunyan clutching a hot dog.

The state capital of Springfield, 50 miles further on, harbors a trio of sights: **Shea's Gas Station Museum** (p526), the **Cozy Dog Drive In** (p527) and **Route 66 Drive In** (p526).

Further south, a good section of old Route 66 parallels I-55 through Litchfield, where you can fork into chicken fried steak while chatting up locals at the 1924 **Ariston Cafe** (www.ariston-cafe.com; S Old Rte 66; mains $7-15; ☺11am-9pm Tue-Fri, 4-10pm Sat, 11am-8pm Sun). Finally, before driving into Missouri, detour off I-270 at exit 3. Follow Hwy 203 south, turn right at the first stoplight and drive west to the 1929 (☺9am-sunset). Only open to pedestrians and cyclists these days, the mile-long span over the Mississippi River has a 22-degree angled bend (cause of many a crash, hence the ban on cars).

For more information, visit the **Route 66 Association of Illinois** (www.il66assoc.org) or **Illinois Route 66 Scenic Byway** (www.illinoisroute66.org). Detailed driving directions are at www.historic66.com/illinois.

---

bust, created by visitors' light touches, indicates the numbers of those who pay their respects here.

FREE Old State Capitol HISTORIC SITE
(☎217-785-9363; www.oldstatecapitol.org; cnr 5th & Adams Sts; ☺9am-5pm, closed Sun & Mon Sep-May) Chatterbox docents will take you through the building and regale you with more Lincoln stories, such as how he gave his famous 'House Divided' speech here in 1858. Suggested donation is $4.

Springfield's Lincoln-free attractions are:

Shea's Gas Station Museum MUSEUM
(☎217-522-0475; 2075 Peoria Rd; admission $2; ☺8am-4pm Tue-Fri, to noon Sat) Octogenarian Bill Shea shares his famed collection of Route 66 pumps and signs.

Route 66 Drive In CINEMA
(☎217-698-0066; www.route66-drivein.com; 1700 Recreation Dr; adult/child $7/4; ☺nightly Jun-Aug, weekends mid-Apr–May & Sep) It screens first-run flicks under the stars.

🍴 Sleeping & Eating

Statehouse Inn HOTEL **$$**
(☎217-528-5100; www.thestatehouseinn.com; 101 E Adams St; r incl breakfast $95-155; P❉@☎) It looks concrete-drab outside, but inside, the Statehouse shows its style. Comfy beds and large baths fill the rooms; a retro bar fills the lobby.

Inn at 835 B&B **$$**
(☎217-523-4466; www.innat835.com; 835 S 2nd St; r incl breakfast $130-200; P❉☎) The historic, arts and crafts–style manor offers 10

rooms of the four-post bed, claw-foot bathtub variety.

Cozy Dog Drive In
DINER $

(www.cozydogdrivein.com; 2935 S 6th St; mains $2-4; ⊙8am-8pm Mon-Sat) It's a Route 66 legend – the reputed birthplace of the corn dog! – with memorabilia and souvenirs in addition to the deeply fried main course on a stick.

D'Arcy's Pint
PUB $

(www.darcyspintonline.com; 661 W Stanford Ave; mains $6-12; ⊙11am-10pm Mon-Thu, to 11pm Fri & Sat) D'Arcy's piles up Springfield's best 'horseshoe,' a local sandwich of fried meat on toasted bread, mounded with french fries and smothered in melted cheese. It's 4 miles south of downtown.

❶ Information

Springfield Convention & Visitors Bureau (www.visitspringfieldillinois.com) Produces a useful visitors' guide.

❶ Getting There & Around

The downtown **Amtrak station** (☑217-753-2013; cnr 3rd & Washington Sts) has five trains daily to/from St Louis (two hours) and Chicago (3½ hours).

PETERSBURG

When Lincoln first arrived in Illinois in 1831, he worked variously as a clerk, storekeeper and postmaster in the frontier village of New Salem before studying law and moving to Springfield. In Petersburg, 20 miles northwest of Springfield, **Lincoln's New Salem State Historic Site** (☑217-632-4000; www.lincolnsnewsalem.com; Hwy 97; suggested donation adult/child $4/2; ⊙9am-5pm, closed Mon & Tue mid-Sep–mid-Apr) reconstructs the village with building replicas, historical displays and costumed performances – a pretty informative and entertaining package.

Southern Illinois

A surprise awaits near Collinsville, 8 miles east of East St Louis: classified as a Unesco World Heritage site with the likes of Stonehenge, the Acropolis and the Egyptian pyramids is **Cahokia Mounds State Historic Site** (☑618-346-5160; www.cahokiamounds.org; Collinsville Rd; suggested donation adult/child $4/2; ⊙visitor center 9am-5pm, grounds 8am-dusk). Cahokia protects the remnants of North America's largest prehistoric city (20,000 people, with suburbs), dating from AD 1200. While the 65 earthen mounds, including the enormous Monk's Mound and the 'Woodhenge' sun calendar, are not overwhelmingly impressive in themselves, the whole site is worth seeing. If you're approaching from the north, take exit 24 off I-255 S; if approaching from St Louis, take exit 6 off I-55/70.

A short distance north of St Louis, Hwy 100 between **Grafton** and **Alton** is perhaps the most scenic 15 miles of the entire Great River Road. As you slip under wind-hewn bluffs, keep an eye out for the turnoff to itty-bitty **Elsah** (www.elsah.org), a hidden hamlet of 19th-century stone cottages, wood buggy shops and farmhouses.

An exception to the state's flat farmland is the green southernmost section, punctuated by rolling **Shawnee National Forest** (☑618-253-7114; www.fs.usda.gov/shawnee) and its rocky outcroppings. The area has numerous state parks and recreation areas good for hiking, climbing, swimming, fishing and canoeing, particularly around **Little Grassy Lake** and **Devil's Kitchen**. And who would think that Florida-like swampland, complete with bald cypress trees and croaking bullfrogs, would be here? But it is, at **Cypress Creek National Wildlife Refuge** (☑618-634-2231; www.fws.gov/midwest/cypresscreek).

Union County, near the state's southern tip, has wineries and orchards. Sample the wares on the 35-mile **Shawnee Hills Wine Trail** (www.shawneewinetrail.com), which connects 12 vineyards.

INDIANA

The state revs up around the Indy 500 race, but otherwise it's about slow-paced pleasures in corn-stubbled Indiana: pie-eating in Amish Country, meditating in Bloomington's Tibetan temples and admiring the big architecture in small Columbus. For the record, folks have called Indianans 'Hoosiers' since the 1830s, but the word's origin is unknown. One theory is that early settlers knocking on a door were met with 'Who's here?' which soon became 'Hoosier.' It's certainly something to discuss with locals, perhaps over a traditional pork tenderloin sandwich.

❶ Information

Indiana Highway Conditions (☑800-261-7623; www.trafficwise.in.gov)

Indiana State Park Information (☑800-622-4931; www.in.gov/dnr/parklake) Park entry costs $2 per day by foot or bicycle, $5 to $10 by vehicle. Campsites cost $6 to $39;

reservations accepted (☎866-622-6746; www.
camp.in.gov).

Indiana Tourism (☎888-365-6946; www.
visitindiana.com)

Indianapolis

Clean-cut Indy is the state capital and a perfectly pleasant place to ogle racecars and take a spin around the renowned speedway. The art museum and White River State Park have their merits, as do the Mass Ave and Broad Ripple 'hoods for eating and drinking. And Kurt Vonnegut fans are in for a treat.

Many early carmakers opened shop in the city, but were eclipsed by the Detroit giants. They did leave a lasting legacy – a 2.5-mile test track, which became the site for the first Indianapolis 500 race in 1911 (won at an average speed of 75mph).

◉ Sights & Activities

Downtown's bulls-eye is Monument Circle. White River State Park and its many attractions lie about three-quarters of a mile west. The Broad Ripple neighborhood is 7 miles north at College Ave and 62nd St.

Indianapolis Motor Speedway   MUSEUM
(☎317-492-6784; www.indianapolismotorspeedway
.com; 4790 W 16th St) The Speedway, home of the Indianapolis 500 motor race, is Indy's supersight. The **Hall of Fame Museum** (adult/child $5/3; ☉9am-5pm) features 75 racing cars (including former winners), a 500lb Tiffany trophy and a track tour ($5 extra). OK, so you're on a bus for the latter and not even beginning to burn rubber at 37mph, but it's still fun to pretend.

The big race itself is held on Memorial Day weekend (last weekend of May) and attended by 450,000 crazed fans. **Tickets** (☎317-484-6700, 800-822-4639; www.imstix.com; $30-150) can be hard to come by. Try the prerace trials and practices for easier access and cheaper prices.

Other races at the Speedway are the NASCAR **Brickyard 400** in late July and the **Motorcycle Grand Prix** in late August. The track is about 6 miles northwest of downtown.

White River State Park   PARK
(http://inwhiteriver.wrsp.in.gov) The expansive park, located at the edge of downtown, contains several worthwhile sights. The adobe **Eiteljorg Museum of American Indians &** **Western Art** (☎317-636-9378; www.eiteljorg.org; 500 W Washington St; adult/child $8/5; ☉10am-5pm Mon-Sat, noon-5pm Sun) features Native American basketry, pots and masks, as well as a realistic/romantic Western painting collection with works from Frederic Remington and Georgia O'Keeffe.

The **NCAA Hall of Champions** (☎800-735-6222; www.ncaahallofchampions.org; 700 W Washington St; adult/child $5/3; ☉10am-5pm Tue-Sat, noon-5pm Sun) reveals the country's fascination with college sports. The interactive exhibits let you shoot free throws or climb onto a swimming platform à la Michael Phelps. You'll probably find most Hoosiers hovering around the basketball exhibits, as locals are renowned hoop-ball fanatics.

Other park highlights include an atmospheric **minor-league baseball stadium**, a **zoo**, a **canal walk**, **gardens**, a **science museum** and a military **Medal of Honor Memorial**.

FREE **Indianapolis Museum of Art**   MUSEUM
(☎317-920-2660; www.imamuseum.org; 4000 Michigan Rd; ☉11am-5pm Tue-Sat, to 9pm Thu & Fri, noon-5pm Sun; ☎) The museum has a terrific collection of European art (especially Turner and some post-Impressionists), African tribal art, South Pacific art and Chinese

INDIANA FACTS

» **Nickname** Hoosier State

» **Population** 6.4 million

» **Area** 36,420 sq miles

» **Capital city** Indianapolis (population 785,600)

» **Sales tax** 7%

» **Birthplace of** Author Kurt Vonnegut (1922–2007), actor James Dean (1931–55), TV host David Letterman (b 1947), rocker John Mellencamp (b 1951), King of Pop Michael Jackson (1958–2009)

» **Home of** farmers, corn

» **Politics** typically Republican

» **Famous for** Indy 500 motor race, basketball fanaticism, pork tenderloin sandwich

» **Official pie** sugar cream

» **Driving distances** Indianapolis to Chicago 185 miles, Indianapolis to Bloomington 53 miles works. The venue is linked to Oldfields – Lilly House & Gardens (⊙11am-5pm Tue-Sat, noon-5pm Sun), the 26-acre estate of the Lilly pharmaceutical family, and Fairbanks Art & Nature Park (⊙sunrise-sunset), which features sculptures and audio installations amid 100 acres of woodlands.

FREE Kurt Vonnegut Memorial Library   MUSEUM
(www.vonnegutlibrary.org; 340 N Senate Ave; ⊙noon-5pm Thu-Tue) Author Kurt Vonnegut was born and raised in Indy, and this humble museum pays homage with displays including his typewriter, Pall Mall cigarettes and Purple Heart medal from WWII. Don't miss the painting of the Tralfamadorians (from *Slaughterhouse-Five*) and his raft of rejection letters from publishers. Vonnegut's children donated most of the artifacts.

Monument Circle   MONUMENT, MUSEUM
(1 Monument Circle) At Monument Circle, the city center is marked by the jaw-dropping 284ft Soldiers & Sailors Monument. For a bizarre (and cramped) experience, take the elevator ($2) to the top. Beneath is the Civil War Museum (admission free; ⊙10:30am-5:30pm Wed-Sun), which neatly outlines the conflict and Indiana's abolition position. A few blocks north, the World War Memorial (cnr Vermont & Meridian Sts) is another impressively beefy monument.

Indiana Medical History Museum   MUSEUM
(☎317-635-7329; www.imhm.org; 3045 W Vermont St; adult/child $5/1; ⊙10am-4pm Thu-Sat) A guide leads you through century-old pathology labs. The highlight, especially for zombies, is the room full of brains in jars. There's also a healing herb garden to walk through. It's a few miles west of White River park.

FREE Indianapolis Hiking Club   HIKING
(www.indyhike.org) Who knew you could hike in Indy? Join free, 5- to 8-mile jaunts around downtown, Broad Ripple, rugged Eagle Creek Park and elsewhere. Check the website for times and departure points.

★ Festivals

The city celebrates the Indy 500 throughout May with the 500 Festival (www.500festival.com; tickets from $7). Events include a racecar drivers' parade and a community shindig at the racetrack.

🛏 Sleeping

Hotels cost more and are usually full during race weeks in May, July and August. Add 17% tax to the prices listed here. Look for low-cost motels off I-465, the freeway that circles Indianapolis.

Indy Hostel   HOSTEL $
(☎317-727-1696; www.indyhostel.us; 4903 Winthrop Ave; weekday/weekend dm $26/29, r $58/64; P🅿✳@🛜) This small, friendly hostel has four dorm rooms in configurations from four to six beds. One room is for females only, while the others are mixed. There are also a couple of private rooms. The Monon Trail hiking/cycling path runs beside the property. It's located by Broad Ripple, so a bit of a haul from downtown (though on bus 17).

Conrad Indianapolis   HOTEL $$$
(☎317-713-5000; www.conradindianapolis.com; 50 W Washington St; r from $250; P✳@🛜🏊) The Conrad is Indy's top address: a 241-room beauty near the sports venues. Spa services, 42-inch plasma screen TVs and bath telephones are part of the package. Wi-fi costs $14, and parking is $33.

Stone Soup   B&B $$
(☎866-639-9550; www.stonesoupinn.com; 1304 N Central Ave; r incl breakfast $85-145; P➰✳🛜) The nine rooms sprawl throughout a rambling house filled with antiques and stained glass. The less-expensive rooms share a bath.

Hampton Inn   HOTEL $$
(☎317-261-1200; www.hamptondt.com; 105 S Meridian St; r incl breakfast $139-169; P✳@🛜) Handsome-looking public areas, plush beds and the prime downtown location make this a fine chain hotel choice. Parking is $15.

✗ Eating

Massachusetts Ave (www.discovermassave.com), by downtown, is bounteous when the stomach growls. Broad Ripple (www.discoverbroadripple.com), 7 miles north, has pubs, cafes and ethnic eateries.

Mug 'N' Bun   AMERICAN $
(www.mug-n-bun.com; 5211 W 10th St; mains $3-5; ⊙10am-9pm Sun-Thu, to 10pm Fri & Sat) The mugs are frosted and filled with a wonderful home-brewed root beer. The buns contain burgers, chili dogs and juicy pork tenderloins. And don't forget the fried macaroni-and-cheese wedges. At this vintage drive-in near the Speedway, you are served – where else? – in your car.

ℹ INDIANA FOODWAYS

Which restaurants serve the best pork tenderloin and sugar cream pie? Where are the local farmers markets and rib fests? What's the recipe for corn pudding? The Indiana Foodways Alliance (www.indianafoodways.com) is your one-stop shop for Hoosier cuisine information.

Shapiro's Deli   DELI **$$**
(☎317-631-4041; www.shapiros.com; 808 S Meridian St; mains $8-15; ☺6:45am-8pm; ☎) Chomp into a towering corned beef or peppery pastrami sandwich on homemade bread, and then chase it with fat slices of chocolate cake or fruit pie.

Bazbeaux   PIZZERIA **$$$**
(www.bazbeaux.com; 329 Massachusetts Ave; large pizza $19-23; ☺11am-10pm Sun-Thu, to 11pm Fri & Sat) A local favorite, Bazbeaux offers an eclectic pizza selection, like the 'Tchoupitoulas,' topped with Cajun shrimp and andouille sausage. Muffaletta sandwiches, stromboli and Belgian beer are some of the other unusual offerings.

MARKET **$**
(www.indycm.com; 222 E Market St; ☺6am-3pm Mon-Fri, 10am-4pm Sat) Ethnic food stalls and local produce vendors fill the city's old marketplace, which dates from 1886. It's ideal for lunchtime grazing.

🍷 Drinking & Entertainment

Downtown and Mass Ave have some good watering holes; Broad Ripple has several.

Bars & Nightclubs

Slippery Noodle Inn   BAR
(www.slipperynoodle.com; 372 S Meridian St) Downtown's Noodle is the oldest bar in the state, and has seen action as a whorehouse, slaughterhouse, gangster hangout and Underground Railroad station; currently, it's one of the best blues clubs in the country. There's live music nightly, and it's cheap.

Rathskeller   BEER HALL
(www.rathskeller.com; 401 E Michigan St) Quaff German brews at the outdoor beer garden's picnic tables in summer, or at the deer-headlined indoor beer hall once winter strikes. The six-beer sampler gets you acquainted

with the wares. It is located in the historic Athenaeum building near Mass Ave.

Plump's Last Shot   BAR
(6416 Cornell Ave) Bobby Plump inspired the iconic movie *Hoosiers*. He's the kid who swished in the last-second shot, so his tiny school beat the 'big city' school in the 1950s state basketball championship. There's sports memorabilia everywhere, and sometimes Bobby himself is on-site. It's located in a big house in Broad Ripple – great for people-watching and sipping a cold one on the dog-friendly patio.

Sports

The motor races aren't the only coveted spectator events. The NFL's Colts win football games under a huge retractable roof at Lucas Oil Stadium (☎317-262-3389; www. colts.com; 500 S Capitol Ave). The NBA's Pacers shoot hoops at Conseco Fieldhouse (☎317-917-2500; www.pacers.com; 125 S Pennsylvania St).

🔒 Shopping

You could buy a speedway flag or Colts jersey as your Indy souvenir. Or you could purchase a bottle of mead made by a couple of enthusiastic former beekeepers at New Day Meadery (www.newdaymeadery.com; 1102 E Prospect St; ☺2-9pm Tue-Fri, noon-9pm Sat, noon-4pm Sun). Sip the honeyed wares in the tasting room (eight samples for $5) before making your selection.

ℹ Information

Emergency & Medical Services

Indiana University Medical Center (☎317-274-4705; 550 N University Blvd)

Media

Gay Indy (www.gayindy.org) Gay and lesbian news and entertainment listings.

Indianapolis Star (www.indystar.com) The city's daily newspaper.

Nuvo (www.nuvo.net) Free, weekly alternative paper with the arts and music low-down.

Tourist Information

Indianapolis Convention & Visitors Bureau (☎800-323-4639; www.visitindy.com) Download a free city app and print out coupons from the website.

ℹ Getting There & Around

The fancy **Indianapolis International Airport** (IND; www.indianapolisairport.com; 7800 Col H Weir Cook Memorial Dr) is 16 miles southwest of town. The Washington bus (8) runs between the airport and downtown ($1.75, 50 minutes); the Green Line bus does it quicker ($7, 20 minutes). A cab to downtown costs about $35.

Greyhound (☏317-267-3076; www.grey hound.com) shares **Union Station** (350 S Illinois St) with Amtrak. Buses go frequently to Cincinnati (two hours) and Chicago (3½ hours). **Megabus** (www.megabus.com/us) stops at 200 E Washington St, and is often cheaper. Amtrak travels these routes but takes almost twice as long and (nonsensically) costs more.

IndyGo (www.indygo.net; fare $1.75) runs the local buses. Bus 17 goes to Broad Ripple. Service is minimal during weekends.

For a taxi, call **Yellow Cab** (☏317-487-7777).

Bloomington & Central Indiana

Bluegrass music, architectural hot spots, Tibetan temples and James Dean all furrow into the farmland around here.

FAIRMOUNT

This small town, north on Hwy 9, is the birthplace of James Dean, one of the original icons of cool. Fans should head directly to the **Historical Museum** (☏765-948-4555; www.jamesdeanartifacts.com; 203 E Washington St; admission free; ⊙10am-5pm Mon-Sat, noon-5pm Sun Mar-Nov) to see Dean's bongo drums, among other artifacts. This is also the place to pick up a free map that will guide you to sites like the farmhouse where Jimmy grew up and his red-lipstick-kissed grave site. The museum sells Dean posters, zippo lighters and other memorabilia, and sponsors the annual **James Dean Festival** (admission free; ⊙late Sep), when as many as 50,000 fans pour in for four days of music and revelry. The privately owned **James Dean Gallery** (☏765-948-3326; www.jamesdeangallery.com; 425 N Main St; admission free; ⊙9am-6pm) has more memorabilia a few blocks away.

COLUMBUS

When you think of the USA's great architectural cities – Chicago, New York, Washington, DC – Columbus, Indiana, doesn't quite leap to mind, but it should. Located 40 miles south of Indianapolis on I-65, Columbus is a remarkable gallery of physical design. Since the 1940s the city and its leading corporations have commissioned some of the world's best architects, including Eero Saarinen, Richard Meier and IM Pei, to create both public and private buildings. Stop at the **visitor center** (☏812-378-2622;

www.columbus.in.us; 506 5th St; ⊙9am-5pm Mon-Sat, noon-5pm Sun Mar-Nov, closed Sun Dec-Feb) to pick up a self-guided tour map ($3) or join a two-hour bus tour (adult/child $20/10); they depart at 10am Monday to Friday, 10am and 2pm Saturday, and 3pm Sunday. Over 70 notable buildings and pieces of public art are spread over a wide area (car required), but about 15 diverse works can be seen on foot downtown.

Hotel Indigo (☏812-375-9100; www.hotelin digo.com; 400 Brown St; r from $135-180; ❋☏☰), also downtown, offers the chain's trademark mod, cheery rooms, plus a fluffy white dog who works as the lobby ambassador (he even has his own email address). A few blocks away you can grab a counter stool, chat up Wilma and her fellow servers, and let the sugar buzz begin at retro **Zaharakos** (www.zaharakos.com; 329 Washington St; ⊙8am-8pm Mon-Fri, 9am-8pm Sat & Sun), a 1909 soda fountain.

NASHVILLE

Gentrified and antique-filled, this 19th-century town west of Columbus on Hwy 46 is now a bustling tourist center, at its busiest in fall when leaf-peepers pour in. The **visitor center** (☏800-753-3255; www.browncounty. com; 10 N Van Buren St; ⊙10am-5pm Mon-Thu, to 6pm Fri & Sat, 10:30am-4pm Sun; ☏) provides maps and online coupons.

Beyond gallery browsing, Nashville is the jump-off point to **Brown County State Park** (☏812-988-6406; www.browncountystate park.us; tent & RV sites $13-26, cabins from $72), a 15,700-acre stand of oak, hickory and birch trees, where trails give hikers, mountain bikers and horseback riders access to the area's green hill country.

Among several B&Bs, central **Artists Colony Inn** (☏812-988-0600; www.artistscolo nyinn.com; 105 S Van Buren St; r incl breakfast $112-170; ❃☏) stands out for its spiffy, Shaker-style rooms. The **dining room** (mains $9-17; ⊙7:30am-8pm Sun-Thu, to 9pm Fri & Sat) offers traditional Hoosier fare, such as catfish and pork tenderloins.

As with Nashville, Tennessee, Nashville, Indiana enjoys country music, and bands play regularly at several venues. To shake a leg, mosey into **Mike's Music & Dance Barn** (☏812-988-8636; www.thedancebarn.com; 2277 Hwy 46; ⊙Thu-Mon). The **Bill Monroe Museum** (☏812-988-6422; 5163 Rte 135 N, Bean Blossom; adult/child $4/free; ⊙9am-5pm, closed Tue & Wed Nov-Apr), 5 miles north of town, hails the bluegrass hero.

BLOOMINGTON

Lively and lovely Bloomington, 53 miles south of Indianapolis via Hwy 37, is the home of Indiana University. The town centers on Courthouse Sq, surrounded by restaurants, bars, bookshops and the historic facade of Fountain Sq Mall. Nearly everything is walkable. The Bloomington CVB (www.visitbloomington.com) has a downloadable guide.

On the expansive campus, the Art Museum (✆812-855-5445; www.indiana.edu/~iuam; 1133 E 7th St; admission free; ⏰10am-5pm Tue-Sat, noon-5pm Sun, reduced hr summer), designed by IM Pei, contains an excellent collection of African art, as well as European and US paintings.

The colorful, prayer flag-covered Tibetan Mongolian Buddhist Cultural Center (✆812-336-6807.tibetancc.com; 3655 Snoddy Rd; admission free; ⏰sunrise-sunset) and stupa, as well as the Dagom Gaden Tensung Ling Monastery (✆812-339-0857; www.dgtlmonastery.org; 102 Clubhouse Dr; admission free; ⏰9am-6pm), indicate Bloomington's significant Tibetan presence. Both offer free teachings and meditation sessions; check the websites for weekly schedules.

If you arrive in mid-April and wonder why an extra 20,000 people are hanging out in town, it's for the Little 500 (www.iusf.indiana.edu; tickets $25). Lance Armstrong called the bike race, where amateurs ride one-speed Schwinns for 200 laps around a quarter-mile track, 'the coolest event I ever attended.'

Look for cheap lodgings along N Walnut St near Hwy 46. Grant Street Inn (✆800-328-4350; www.grantstinn.com; 310 N Grant St; r incl breakfast $149-229; @🛜) fluffs up 24 rooms in a Victorian house and annex near campus.

For a town of its size, Bloomington offers a mind-blowing array of ethnic restaurants – everything from Burmese to Eritrean to Mexican. Browse Kirkwood Ave and E 4th St. Anyetsang's Little Tibet (✆812-331-0122; www.anyetsangs.com; 415 E 4th St; mains $9-13; ⏰11am-9:30pm Wed-Mon) offers specialties from the Himalayan homeland. Pubs on Kirkwood Ave, close to the university, cater to the student crowd. Nick's English Hut (www.nicksenglishhut.com; 423 E Kirkwood Ave) pours not only for students and professors, but has filled the cups of Kurt Vonnegut, Dylan Thomas and Barack Obama, as well.

Southern Indiana

The pretty hills, caves, rivers and utopian history of southern Indiana mark it as a completely different region from the flat and industrialized north.

OHIO RIVER

The Indiana segment of the 981-mile Ohio River marks the state's southern border. From tiny Aurora, in the southeastern corner of the state, Hwys 56, 156, 62 and 66, known collectively as the Ohio River Scenic Route, wind through a varied landscape.

Coming from the east, a perfect place to stop is little Madison, a well-preserved river settlement from the mid-19th century where architectural beauties beckon genteelly from the streets. At the visitor center (✆812-265-2956; www.visitmadison.org; 601 W First St; ⏰9am-5pm Mon-Fri, 10am-3pm Sat, 11am-5pm Sun), pick up a walking tour brochure, which will lead you by notable landmarks.

Madison has motels around its edges, as well as several B&Bs. Main St lines up numerous places for a bite, interspersed with antique stores. Large, wooded Clifty Falls State Park (✆812-273-8885; tent & RV sites $10-26), off Hwy 56 and a couple of miles west of town, has camping, hiking trails, views and waterfalls.

In Clarksville, Falls of the Ohio State Park (✆812-280-9970; www.fallsoftheohio.org; 201 W Riverside Dr) has only rapids, no falls, but is of interest for its 386-million-year-old fossil beds. The interpretive center (adult/child $5/2; ⏰9am-5pm Mon-Sat, 1-5pm Sun) explains it all. Quench your thirst in adjacent New Albany, home to New Albanian Brewing Company Public House & Pizzeria (www.newalbanian.com; 3312 Plaza Dr; ⏰11am-midnight Mon-Sat). Or cross the bridge to Louisville, Kentucky, where the tonsil-singeing native bourbon awaits....

Scenic Hwy 62 heads west and leads to the Lincoln Hills and southern Indiana's limestone caves. A plunge into Marengo Cave (✆812-365-2705; www.marengocave.com; ⏰9am-6pm, to 5pm Sep-May), north on Hwy 66, is highly recommended. It offers a 40-minute tour (adult/child $13.50/7), 70-minute tour ($15/7.50) or combination tour ($21/11) walking past stalagmites and other ancient formations. The same group operates Cave Country Canoes (www.cavecountrycanoes.com; ⏰May-Oct) in nearby Milltown, with half-day ($23), full-day ($26) or longer trips on the scenic Blue River; keep an eye out for river otters and rare hellbender salamanders.

Four miles south of Dale, off I-64, is the **Lincoln Boyhood National Memorial** (812-937-4541; www.nps.gov/libo; adult/child $3/free; 8am-5pm), where young Abe lived from age seven to 21. This isolated site also includes admission to a working **pioneer farm** (8am-5pm mid-Apr–Sep).

NEW HARMONY

In southwest Indiana, the Wabash River forms the border with Illinois. Beside it, south of I-64, captivating **New Harmony** is the site of two early communal-living experiments and is worth a visit. In the early 19th century a German Christian sect, the Harmonists, developed a sophisticated town here while awaiting the Second Coming. Later, the British utopian Robert Owen acquired the town. Learn more and pick up a walking-tour map at the angular **Atheneum Visitors Center** (812-682-4474; www.usi. edu/hnh; 401 N Arthur St; 9:30am-5pm).

Today New Harmony retains an air of contemplation, if not otherworldliness, which you can experience at its newer attractions, such as the templelike Roofless Church and the Labyrinth, a maze symbolizing the spirit's quest. The town has a couple of guesthouses and camping at **Harmonie State Park** (812-682-4821; campsites $11-27). Pop into **Main Cafe** (508 Main St; mains $4-7; 5:30am-1pm Mon-Fri) for a ham-bean-and-cornbread lunch, but save room for the coconut cream pie.

Northern Indiana

The truck-laden I-80/I-90 tollways cut across Indiana's northern section. Parallel US 20 is slower and cheaper, but not much more attractive.

INDIANA DUNES

Hugely popular on summer days with sunbathers from Chicago and South Bend, **Indiana Dunes National Lakeshore** (219-926-7561; www.nps.gov/indu; admission free, tent & RV sites $15) stretches along 21 miles of Lake Michigan shoreline. In addition to its beaches, the area is noted for its plant variety: everything from cacti to pine trees sprouts here. Hiking trails crisscross the dunes and woodlands, winding by a peat bog, a still-operating 1870s farm and a blue heron rookery, among other payoffs. Mt Baldy is the top

dune to climb. Oddly, all this natural bounty lies smack-dab next to smoke-belching factories, which you'll also see at various vantage points. Stop at the **Dorothy Buell Visitor Center** (219-926-7561; Hwy 49; 8:30am-6:30pm Jun-Aug, to 4:30pm Sep-May) for beach details, a schedule of ranger-guided walks and activities, and to pick up hiking, biking and birding maps. Or get guides in advance via the **Porter County Convention & Visitors Bureau** (www.indianadunes.com).

Indiana Dunes State Park (219-926-1952; www.dnr.in.gov/parklake; per car $10, tent & RV sites $17-28) is a 2100-acre, shoreside pocket within the national lakeshore; it's located at the end of Hwy 49, near Chesterton. It has more amenities, but also more regulation and more crowds (plus the vehicle entry fee). Wintertime brings out the cross-country skiers; summertime brings out the hikers. Seven trails zigzag over the landscape; No 4 up Mt Tom rewards with Chicago skyline views.

Other than a couple of beachfront snack bars, you won't find much to eat in the parks, so stop at homey, Italian **Lucrezia** (219-926-5829; www.lucreziacafe.com; 428 S Calumet Rd; mains $17-27; 11am-10pm Sun-Thu, to 11pm Fri & Sat) in Chesterton.

The Dunes are an easy day trip from Chicago. Driving takes one hour. The **South Shore Metra train** (www.nictd.com) makes the journey from Millennium Station downtown, and it's about 1¼ hours to the Dune Park or Beverly Shores stops (note both stations are a 1½-mile walk from the beach). Those who want to make a night of it can camp (national lakeshore campsites $15, state park tent and RV sites $17 to $28).

Near Illinois, the steel cities of **Gary** and **East Chicago** present some of the bleakest urban landscapes anywhere. Taking the train (Amtrak or South Shore line) through here will get you up close and personal with the industrial underbelly.

SOUTH BEND

South Bend is home to the **University of Notre Dame**. You know how people in certain towns say, 'football is a religion here'? They mean it at Notre Dame, where *Touchdown Jesus* lords over the 80,000-capacity stadium (it's a mural of the resurrected Christ with arms raised, though the pose bears a striking resemblance to a referee signaling a touchdown). Tours of the pretty campus, including the Lourdes Grotto replica, start at the **visitor center** (www.nd.edu/

visitors; 111 Eck Center). Less visited but worth a stop is the **Studebaker National Museum** (☎574-235-9714; www.studebakermuseum. org; 201 S Chapin St; adult/child $8/5; ☺10am-5pm Mon-Sat, noon-5pm Sun) near downtown, where you can gaze at a gorgeous 1956 Packard and other classic beauties.

AMISH COUNTRY

East of South Bend, around **Shipshewana** and **Middlebury**, is the USA's third-largest Amish community. Horses and buggies clip-clop by, and long-bearded men hand-plow the tidy fields. Get situated with maps from the **Elkhart County CVB** (☎800-517-9739; www.amishcountry.org). Better yet, pick a backroad between the two towns and head down it. Often you'll see families selling beeswax candles, quilts and fresh produce on their porch, which beats the often-touristy shops and restaurants on the main roads. Note most places close on Sunday.

Village Inn (☎574-825-2043; 105 S Main St; mains $3-7; ☺5am-8pm Mon-Fri, to 2pm Sat), in Middlebury, sells real-deal pies; bonneted women in pastel dresses come in at 4:30am to bake the flaky wares. Arrive before noon, or you'll be looking at crumbs.

AUBURN

Just before reaching the Ohio border, classic car connoisseurs should dip south on I-69 to the town of Auburn, where the Cord Company produced the USA's favorite cars in the 1920s and '30s. The **Auburn Cord Duesenberg Museum** (☎260-925-1444; www.automobilemuseum.org; 1600 S Wayne St; adult/child $10/6; ☺9am-5pm, to 8pm Thu) has a wonderful display of early roadsters in a beautiful art deco setting. Next door are the vintage rigs of the **National Automotive and Truck Museum** (☎260-925-9100; www. natmus.org; 1000 Gordon Buehrig Pl; adult/child $7/4; ☺9am-5pm).

OHIO

All right, time for your Ohio quiz. In the Buckeye State you can 1) watch butter churn on an Amish farm; 2) party your ass off at an island resort; 3) lose your stomach on one of the world's fastest roller coasters; 4) suck down a dreamy creamy milk shake fresh from a working dairy; or 5) examine a mon-do, mysterious snake sculpture built into the earth. And the answer is...all of these. It hurts locals' feelings when visitors think the

---

OHIO FACTS

» **Nickname** Buckeye State

» **Population** 11.5 million

» **Area** 44,825 sq miles

» **Capital city** Columbus (population 733,200)

» **Other cities** Cleveland (population 444,300), Cincinnati (population 332,250)

» **Sales tax** 5.5%

» **Birthplace of** inventor Thomas Edison (1847–1931), author Toni Morrison (b 1931), entrepreneur Ted Turner (b 1938), filmmaker Steven Spielberg (b 1947)

» **Home of** sows, roller coasters, aviation pioneers Wright Brothers

» **Politics** swing state

» **Famous for** first airplane, first pro baseball team, birthplace of seven US presidents

» **State rock song** 'Hang On Sloopy'

» **Driving distances** Cleveland to Columbus 142 miles, Columbus to Cincinnati 108 miles

---

only thing to do here is tip over cows. C'mon, give Ohio a chance. Besides these activities, you can partake in a five-way in Cincinnati (see p545) and rock out in Cleveland.

ℹ Information

Ohio Division of Travel and Tourism (☎800-282-5393; www.discoverohio.com)

Ohio Highway Conditions (www.buckeyetraf fic.org)

Ohio State Park Information (☎614-265-6561; www.ohiodnr.com/parks) State parks are free to visit; some have free wi-fi. Tent and RV sites cost $10 to $36; reservations accepted (☎866-644-6727; www.ohio.reserveworld. com; fee $8.25).

Cleveland

Does it or does it not rock? That is the question. Drawing from its roots as a working man's town, Cleveland has toiled hard in recent years to prove it does. Step one was to control the urban decay/river-on-fire thing – the Cuyahoga River was once so polluted that it actually burned. Check. Step two was to bring a worthy attraction to town, say the Rock and Roll Hall of Fame. Check. Step three was to get grub beyond steak-and-potatoes. Check. So can Cleveland finally wipe the sweat from its brow? More or less. Much of the downtown area remains bleak, though there are definite pockets of freshness.

◉ Sights & Activities

Cleveland's center is Public Sq, dominated by the conspicuous Terminal Tower. Most attractions are downtown on the lakefront or at University Circle (the area around Case Western Reserve University, Cleveland Clinic and other institutions).

DOWNTOWN

Keep an eye out for the **Greater Cleveland Aquarium** (www.greaterclevelandaquarium.com), slated to open by 2012 in the Flats.

Rock and Roll Hall of Fame & Museum   MUSEUM
(📞216-781-7625; www.rockhall.com; 1 Key Plaza; adult/child $22/13; ⊙10am-5:30pm, to 9pm Wed year-round, to 9pm Sat Jun-Aug) Cleveland's top attraction is more than a collection of memorabilia, though it does have Jimi Hendrix's Stratocaster, Keith Moon's platform shoes and Ray Charles' sunglasses. Interactive multimedia exhibits trace the history and social context of rock music and the performers who created it. Why is the museum in Cleveland? Because this is the hometown of Alan Freed, the disk jockey who popularized the term 'rock 'n' roll' in the early 1950s, and because the city lobbied hard and paid big. Be prepared for crowds (especially thick until 1pm or so). In summer, Johnny Cash's tour bus parks outside; climb aboard to see how the Man in Black lived.

Great Lakes Science Center   MUSEUM
(📞216-694-2000; www.glsc.org; 601 Erieside Ave; adult/child $11/9; ⊙10am-5pm; 🖽) One of 10 museums in the country with a NASA affiliation, Great Lakes goes deep in space with rockets and moon stones, as well as exhibits on the lakes' environmental problems. The wind turbine and solar panels out front provide 6% of the museum's energy.

William G Mather   MUSEUM
(📞216-574-6262; http://wgmather.nhlink.net; 305 Mather Way; adult/child $7/5; ⊙11am-5pm daily Jun-Aug, Fri-Sun only May, Sep & Oct, closed Nov-Apr) Take a self-guided walk-about on this humungous freighter incarnated as a steam-

ship museum. It's docked beside the Science Center, which manages it.

USS Cod   MUSEUM
(📞216-566-8770; www.usscod.org; 1089 E 9th St; adult/child $7/4; ⊙10am-5pm May-Sep) The storied submarine *USS Cod* saw action in WWII. You're free to climb through it, tight spaces, ladders and all, while listening to audio stories about life on board.

OHIO CITY & TREMONT

West Side Market   MARKET
(www.westsidemarket.org; cnr W 25th St & Lorain Ave; ⊙7am-4pm Mon & Wed, to 6pm Fri & Sat) The European-style market overflows with greengrocers and their fruit and vegetable pyramids, as well as purveyors of Hungarian sausage, Mexican flat breads and Polish pierogi.

Christmas Story House & Museum   FILM LOCATION
(📞216-298-4919; www.achristmasstoryhouse.com; 3159 W 11th St; adult/child $8/6; ⊙10am-5pm Thu-Sat, noon-5pm Sun) Remember the beloved 1983 film *A Christmas Story*, in which Ralphie yearns for a Red Ryder BB gun? The original house sits in Tremont, complete with leg lamp. This attraction's for true fans only.

UNIVERSITY CIRCLE

Several museums and attractions are within walking distance of each other at University Circle, 5 miles east of downtown. Carless? Take the HealthLine bus to Adelbert.

FREE Cleveland Museum of Art   MUSEUM
(📞216-421-7340; www.clevelandart.org; 11150 East Blvd; ⊙10am-5pm Tue-Sun, to 9pm Wed & Fri) The gem of the group, the art museum houses an excellent collection of European paintings, as well as African, Asian and American art. It's undergoing a whopping expansion, to be completed in 2013. Head to the 2nd floor for rock star works from Impressionists, Picasso and surrealists.

Cleveland Botanical Garden   GARDENS
(📞216-721-1600; www.cbgarden.org; 11030 East Blvd; adult/child $8.50/3; ⊙10am-5pm Tue-Sat, noon-5pm Sun, to 9pm Wed Jun-Aug) Has a Costa Rican cloud forest and Madagascan desert exhibits. An ice-skating rink opens nearby in winter; skate rentals cost $3. Parking costs $5 to $10 per day and gives access to all the museums here.

Lakeview Cemetery   GARDENS
(☎216-421-2665;   www.lakeviewcemetery.com;
12316 Euclid Ave; ⊙7:30am-7:30pm) Beyond the
circle further east, don't forget this eclectic
'outdoor museum' where President Garfield
and John Rockefeller rest, or more intrigu-
ingly, local comic book hero Harvey Pekar
and crimefighter Eliot Ness.

🛏 Sleeping

Prices listed are for summer, which is high
season, and do not include the 16.25% tax.
Modest motels are southwest of Cleveland's
center, near the airport. The W 150th exit
off I-71 (exit 240) has several options for less
than $100.

Brownstone Inn   B&B $$
(☎216-426-1753;   www.brownstoneinndowntown.
com; 3649 Prospect Ave; r incl breakfast $89-
139; P❄@🛜) This Victorian townhouse
B&B has a whole lotta personality. All five
rooms have a private bath, and each comes
equipped with robes to lounge in and an
invitation for evening aperitifs. It's between
downtown and University Circle, though in
a bit of a no-man's-land for walkable enter-
tainment.

University Circle B&B   B&B $$
(☎866-735-5960; www.ucbnb.com; 1575 E 108th
St; r incl breakfast $110-145; P❄🛜) Located in
the heart of University Circle and within
walking distance of its museums, this four-
room B&B gets lots of academic visitors. Two
rooms share a bath.

Hilton Garden Inn   HOTEL $$
(☎216-658-6400; www.hiltongardeninn.com; 1100
Carnegie Ave; r $110-169; P❄@🛜🛏) While
nothing fancy, the Hilton's rooms are good
value with comfy beds, wi-fi-rigged worksta-
tions and mini refrigerators. It's right by the
baseball park. Parking costs $16.

Holiday Inn Express   HOTEL $$
(☎216-443-1000; www.hiexpress.com; 629 Euclid
Ave; r incl breakfast $115-180; P❄@🛜) Another
OK chain option, in an old bank building
that's conveniently located near the E 4th St
entertainment strip. Parking costs $14.

✖ Eating

There's more range than you might expect
in a Rust Belt town. TV food dudes from
Anthony Bourdain to Guy Fieri have filmed
shows here and raved over the offerings.

DOWNTOWN

The Warehouse District, between W 6th and
W 9th Sts, jumps with trendy restaurants.
Off the beaten path and east of the city center, Asiatown (bounded by Payne and St
Clair Aves, and E 30th and 40ths Sts) has
several Chinese, Vietnamese and Korean
eateries.

Lola   AMERICAN $$$
(☎216-621-5652; www.lolabistro.com; 2058 E 4th
St; mains $22-31; ⊙11:30am-2:30pm Mon-Fri,
5-10pm Mon-Thu, to 11pm Fri & Sat) Famous for
his piercings, Food Channel TV appearances
and multiple national awards, local boy Mi-
chael Symon has put Cleveland on the food-
ie map with Lola. The lower-priced lunch
dishes are the most fun; say, coconut-and-
lime-tinged scallop ceviche, or the show-
stopper – an egg-and-cheese-topped fried
bologna sandwich.

OHIO CITY & TREMONT

Ohio City and Tremont, which straddle I-90
south of downtown, are areas that have lots
of new establishments popping up. Buzz-
worthy, sustainably focused **Crop Bistro**
(www.cropbistro.com) should open by the West
Side Market by the time you're reading this.

West Side Market Cafe   CAFE $
(☎216-579-6800; 1995 W 25th St; mains $6-9;
⊙7am-4pm Mon-Thu, to 6pm Fri & Sat, 9am-3pm
Sun) This is a smart stop if you're craving
well-made breakfast and lunch fare, and
cheap fish and chicken mains. The cafe is
inside West Side Market itself, which over-
flows with prepared foods that are handy for
picnicking or road-tripping.

**Sokolowski's
University Inn**   EASTERN EUROPEAN $$
(☎216-771-9236;   www.sokolowskis.com;   1201
University Rd; mains $7-15; ⊙11am-3pm Mon-Fri,
5-9pm Fri, 4-9pm Sat) The portions are huge,
enough to fuel the hungriest steelworker. It's
cafeteria style, so grab a tray and fill it with
plump pierogi, cabbage rolls and other rib-
sticking Polish fare.

Lolita   AMERICAN $$
(☎216-771-5652; www.lolitarestaurant.com; 900
Literary Rd; mains $9-17; ⊙5-11pm Tue-Thu, to 1am
Fri & Sat, 4-9pm Sun) It's the lighter-fare sister
of Lola (downtown). Munch on Iowa pro-
sciutto, mussels and Neapolitan-style pizzas
with cold local beer. Five-dollar food specials
rock happy hour (5pm to 6:30pm, and after
9:30pm or so).

South Side
AMERICAN $$

(216-937-2288; 2207 W 11 St; sandwiches $9-11, mains $14-19; 11am-2am;) Local athletes, blue-collar electricians and everyone in between pile into this sleek Tremont establishment to drink at the winding granite bar. They come for the late-night food too, like the grouper sandwich, veggie Reuben and Kobe burger.

LITTLE ITALY & COVENTRY

These two neighborhoods make prime stops for refueling after hanging out in University Circle. Little Italy is closest: it's along Mayfield Rd, near Lake View Cemetery (look out for the Rte 322 sign). Alternatively, relaxed Coventry Village is a bit further east off Mayfield Rd.

Presti's Bakery
BAKERY $

(www.prestisbakery.com; 12101 Mayfield Rd; items $2-6; 6am-9pm Mon-Thu, to 10pm Fri & Sat, to 6pm Sun) Try Presti's for its popular sandwiches, stromboli and divine pastries.

Tommy's
INTERNATIONAL $

(216-321-7757; www.tommyscoventry.com; 1823 Coventry Rd; mains $6-10; 9am-9pm Sun-Thu, to 10pm Fri, 7:30am-10pm Sat;) Tofu, seitan and other old-school veggie dishes emerge from the kitchen, though carnivores have multiple options, too.

Drinking

The downtown action centers on the young, testosterone-fueled Warehouse District (around W 6th St), and around E 4th St's entertainment venues. Tremont is also chockablock with chic bars. Most places stay open until 2am.

Great Lakes Brewing Company
BREWERY

(www.greatlakesbrewing.com; 2516 Market Ave; Mon-Sat) Great Lakes wins numerous prizes for its brewed-on-the-premises beers. Added historical bonus: Eliot Ness got into a shootout with criminals here; ask the bartender to show you the bullet holes.

Major Hoopples
BAR

(1930 Columbus Rd; Mon-Sat) Look over the bar for Cleveland's best skyline view from this friendly, eclectic watering hole. They project films and sports games on the bridge abutment out back.

Johnny's Little Bar
BAR

(www.johnnyscleveland.com; 614 Frankfort Ave) One of the Warehouse District's more ca-

sual, compact offerings. The hard-to-find entrance is on Frankfort Ave, a side street.

☆ Entertainment

Gordon Square Arts District (www.gordonsquare.org) has a fun pocket of theaters, live music venues and cafes along Detroit Ave between W 56th and W 69th Sts, a few miles west of downtown.

Live Music

Check *Scene* (www.clevescene.com) and Friday's *Plain Dealer* (www.cleveland.com) for listings.

TOP CHOICE Happy Dog
LIVE MUSIC

(www.happydogcleveland.com; 5801 Detroit Ave) Listen to scrappy bands while munching on a wienie, for which you can choose from among 50 toppings, from gourmet (black truffle) to, er, less gourmet (peanut butter and jelly); in the Gordon Sq district.

Grog Shop
LIVE MUSIC

(216-321-5588; www.grogshop.gs; 2785 Euclid Hts Blvd) Up-and-coming rockers thrash at Coventry's long-established music house.

Beachland Ballroom
LIVE MUSIC

(www.beachlandballroom.com; 15711 Waterloo Rd) Hip young bands play at this venue east of downtown.

Sports

Cleveland is a serious jock town with three modern downtown venues. Whatever you do, don't mention the name 'LeBron' (the basketball player who famously defected to Miami).

Progressive Field
BASEBALL

(www.indians.com; 2401 Ontario St) The Indians (aka 'the Tribe') hit here; great sightlines make it a good park to see a game.

Quicken Loans Arena
BASKETBALL

(www.nba.com/cavaliers; 1 Center Ct) The Cavaliers play basketball at 'the Q,' which doubles as an entertainment venue.

Cleveland Browns Stadium
FOOTBALL

(www.clevelandbrowns.com; 1085 W 3rd St) The NFL's Browns pass the football and score touchdowns on the lakefront.

Performing Arts

Severance Hall
CLASSICAL MUSIC

(216-231-1111; www.clevelandorchestra.com; 11001 Euclid Ave) The acclaimed Cleveland Symphony Orchestra holds its season (August to May) at Severance Hall, located by the University Circle museums. The orchestra's summer home is Blossom Music Center in Cuyahoga Valley National Park, about 22 miles south.

Playhouse Square Center THEATER
(☎216-771-4444; www.playhousesquare.com; 1501 Euclid Ave) This elegant center hosts theater, opera and ballet. Check the website for $10 'Smart Seats.'

❶ Information

Emergency & Medical Services
MetroHealth Medical Center (☎216-778-7800; 2500 MetroHealth Dr)

Internet Access
Many of Cleveland's public places have free wi-fi, such as Tower City and University Circle.

Media
Gay People's Chronicle (www.gaypeoples chronicle.com) Free weekly publication with entertainment listings.
Plain Dealer (www.cleveland.com) The city's daily newspaper.
Scene (www.clevescene.com) A weekly entertainment paper.

Tourist Information
Cleveland Convention & Visitors Bureau (www.positivelycleveland.com) Official website; the Twitter feed lists daily deals.
Visitor center (☎216-875-6680; 100 Public Sq, Suite 100; ⊙9am-5pm Mon-Fri, plus 10am-3pm Sat Jun-Aug) Staffed desk, coupons and computers to make reservations; in the Higbee Building.

Websites
Cool Cleveland (www.coolcleveland.com) Hip arts and cultural happenings.
Ohio City (www.ohiocity.org) Eats and drinks in the neighborhood.
Tremont (www.restoretremont.com) Eats, drinks and gallery hops in the neighborhood.

❶ Getting There & Around
Eleven miles southwest of downtown, **Cleveland Hopkins International Airport** (CLE; www.clevelandairport.com; 5300 Riverside Dr) is linked by the Red Line train ($2.25). A cab to downtown costs about $30.

From downtown, **Greyhound** (☎216-781-0520; 1465 Chester Ave) offers frequent departures to Chicago (7½ hours) and New York City (13 hours). **Megabus** (www.megabus.com/us) also goes to Chicago, often for lower fares; check the website for the departure point.

ICE WINE VINEYARDS

Canada may grab all the glory for its ice wines, but Ohio has some chilled grapes up its sleeve, too. Tour and try sips at **Debonne Vineyards** (☎440-466-3485; www.debonne.com; 7743 Doty Rd; 8-sample tasting $6; ⊙noon-6pm Mon & Tue, to 11pm Wed & Fri, to 8pm Thu & Sat, 1-6pm Sun) in Madison, 40 miles northeast of Cleveland, which reaps praise for its sweet concoctions with hints of melon and apricot. Several other ice wine makers are also in the area, thanks to the local climate of long autumns, followed by winters cold enough to freeze grapes but not so cold that the vines die. Check the **Wine Growers of the Grand River Valley** (www.wggrv.com) for thirst-quenching locations.

Amtrak (☎216-696-5115; 200 Cleveland Memorial Shoreway) runs once daily to Chicago (seven hours) and New York City (13 hours).

The **Regional Transit Authority** (RTA; www.riderta.com; fare $2.25) operates the Red Line train that goes to both the airport and Ohio City. It also runs the HealthLine bus that motors along Euclid Ave from downtown to University Circle's museums. Day passes are $5.

For cab service, try phoning **Americab** (☎216-429-1111).

Around Cleveland

Sixty miles south of Cleveland, **Canton** is the birthplace of the NFL and home to the **Pro Football Hall of Fame** (☎330-456-8207; www.profootballhof.com; 2121 George Halas Dr; adult/child $21/15; ⊙9am-8pm, to 5pm Sep-May), a shrine for the gridiron-obsessed. Look for the football-shaped tower off I-77.

West of Cleveland, attractive **Oberlin** is an old-fashioned college town, with noteworthy architecture by Cass Gilbert, Frank Lloyd Wright and Robert Venturi. Further west, just south of I-90, the tiny town of **Milan** is the birthplace of Thomas Edison. His home, restored to its 1847 likeness, is now a small **museum** (☎419-499-2135; www.tomedison.org; 9 Edison Dr; adult/child $7/4; ⊙10am-5pm Tue-Sat, 1-5pm Sun, reduced hrs winter, closed Jan) outlining his inventions, like the light bulb and phonograph.

Still further west, on US 20 and surrounded by farmland, is Clyde, which bills itself as the USA's most famous small town. It got that way when native son Sherwood Anderson published *Winesburg, Ohio* in 1919. It didn't take long for the unimpressed residents to figure out where the fictitious town really was. Stop at the Clyde Museum (☏419-547-7946; www.clydeheritageleague.org; 124 W Buckeye St; admission free; ☺1-4pm Thu Apr-Sep & by appointment) in the old church for Anderson tidbits or at the library, a few doors down.

Erie Lakeshore & Islands

In summer this good-time resort area is one of the busiest – and most expensive – places in Ohio. The season lasts from mid-May to mid-September, and then just about everything shuts down. Make sure you prebook your accommodations.

Sandusky, long a port, now serves as the jump-off point to the Erie Islands and a mighty group of roller coasters (see boxed text, p539). The visitor center (☏419-625-2984; www.shoresandislands.com; 4424 Milan Rd; ☺8am-8pm Mon-Fri, 9am-6pm Sat, 9am-3pm Sun) provides lodging and ferry information. Loads of chain motels line the highways heading into town.

BASS ISLANDS

In the war of 1812's Battle of Lake Erie, Admiral Perry met the enemy English fleet near South Bass Island. His victory ensured that all the lands south of the Great Lakes became US, not Canadian, territory. But history is all but forgotten on a summer weekend in packed Put In Bay, the island's main town and a party place full of boaters, restaurants and shops. Move beyond it, and

you'll find a winery and opportunities for camping, fishing, kayaking and swimming.

A singular attraction is the 352ft Doric column known as Perry's Victory and International Peace Memorial (www.nps.gov/pevi; admission $3; ☺10am-7pm). Climb to the observation deck for views of the battle site and, on a good day, Canada.

The Chamber of Commerce (☏419-285-2832; www.visitputinbay.com; 148 Delaware Ave; ☺10am-4pm Mon-Fri, to 5pm Sat & Sun) has information on activities and lodging. Ashley's Island House (☏419-285-2844; www.ashleysislandhouse.com; 557 Catawba Ave; r with shared/private bath from $70/100; ✳☏) is a 13-room B&B, where naval officers stayed in the late 1800s. The Beer Barrel Saloon (www.beerbarrelpib.com; Delaware Ave; ☺11am-1am) has plenty of space for imbibing – its bar is 406ft long.

Cabs and tour buses serve the island, though cycling is a fine way to get around. Two ferry companies make the 20-minute trip regularly from the mainland. Jet Express (☏800-245-1538; www.jet-express.com) runs passenger-only boats direct to Put In Bay from Port Clinton (one way adult/child $14/2) almost hourly. It also departs from Sandusky ($18/5), stopping at Kelleys Island en route. Leave your car in the lot (per day $10) at either dock. Miller Boatline (☏800-500-2421; www.millerferry.com) operates a vehicle ferry that is the cheapest option, departing from further-flung Catawba (one way adult/child $6.50/1.50, car $15) every 30 minutes. It also cruises to Middle Bass Island, a good day trip from South Bass, offering nature and quiet.

KELLEYS ISLAND

Peaceful and green, Kelleys Island is a popular weekend escape, especially for families. It has pretty 19th-century buildings, Native

DON'T MISS

CEDAR POINT'S RAGING ROLLER COASTERS

Cedar Point Amusement Park (☏419-627-2350; www.cedarpoint.com; adult/child $47/21; ☺10am-10pm, closed Nov–mid-May) regularly wins the 'world's best amusement park' award, chosen each year by the public, which goes wild for the venue's 17 adrenaline-pumping roller coasters. Stomach droppers include the Top Thrill Dragster, one of the globe's tallest and fastest rides. It climbs 420ft into the air before plunging and whipping around at 120mph. Meanwhile, the Maverick drops at a 95-degree angle (that's steeper than straight down) and blasts over eight hills. If those and the 15 other coasters aren't enough to keep you occupied, the surrounding area has a nice beach, a water park and a slew of old-fashioned, cotton-candy-fueled attractions. It's about 6 miles from Sandusky. Parking costs $10.

American pictographs, a good beach and glacial grooves raked through its landscape. Even its old limestone quarries are scenic.

The **Chamber of Commerce** (☏419-746-2360; www.kelleysislandchamber.com; Seaway Marina Bldg; ☉9:30am-4pm), by the ferry dock, has information on accommodations and activities – hiking, camping, kayaking and fishing are popular. The Village, the island's small commercial center, has places to eat, drink, shop and rent bicycles – the recommended way to sightsee.

Kelleys Island Ferry (☏419-798-9763; www.kelleysislandferry.com) departs from the wee village of Marblehead (one way adult/child $9.50/6, car $15). The crossing takes about 20 minutes and leaves hourly (more frequently in summer). **Jet Express** (☏800-245-1538; www.jet-express.com) departs from Sandusky (one way adult/child $14/4, no cars) and also goes onward to Put In Bay on South Bass Island (island-hopping one way $20/6, no cars).

PELEE ISLAND

Pelee, the largest Erie island, is a ridiculously green, quiet wine-producing and bird-watching destination that belongs to Canada. **Pelee Island Transportation** (☏800-661-2220; www.ontarioferries.com) runs a ferry (one way adult/child $13.75/6.75, car $30) from Sandusky to Pelee and onward to Ontario's mainland. Check www.pelee.org for lodging and trip planning information.

Amish Country

Rural Wayne and Holmes counties are home to the USA's largest Amish community. They're only 80 miles south of Cleveland, but visiting here is like entering a pre-industrial time warp.

Descendants of conservative Dutch-Swiss religious factions who migrated to the USA during the 18th century, the Amish continue to follow the *ordnung* (way of life), in varying degrees. Many adhere to rules prohibiting the use of electricity, telephones and motorized vehicles. They wear traditional clothing, farm the land with plow and mule, and go to church in horse-drawn buggies. Others are not so strict.

Unfortunately, what would surely be a peaceful country scene is often disturbed by behemoth tour buses. Many Amish are happy to profit from this influx of outside dollars, but don't equate this with free photographic access – the Amish typically view photographs as taboo. Drive carefully as roads are narrow and curvy, and there's always the chance of pulling up on a slow-moving buggy just around the bend. Many places are closed Sunday.

◉ Sights & Activities

Kidron, on Rte 52, makes a good starting point. A short distance south, **Berlin** is the area's tchotchke-shop-filled core, while **Millersburg** is the region's largest town, more antique-y than Amish; US 62 connects these two 'busy' spots.

To get further off the beaten path, take Rte 557 or County Rd 70, both of which twist through the countryside to wee **Charm**, about 5 miles south of Berlin.

Lehman's   DEPARTMENT STORE
(www.lehmans.com; 4779 Kidron Rd, Kidron; ☉8am-6pm Mon-Sat) Lehman's is an absolute must-see. It is the Amish community's main purveyor of modern-looking products that use no electricity, housed in a 32,000-sq-ft barn. Stroll through to ogle wind-up flashlights, wood-burning stoves and hand-cranked meat grinders.

FREE **Kidron Auction**   MARKET
(www.kidronauction.com; 4885 Kidron Rd, Kidron; ☉ from 10am Thu) If it's Thursday, follow the buggy line-up down the road from Lehman's to the livestock barn. Hay gets auctioned at 10am, cows at 11am and pigs at 1pm. A flea market rings the barn for folks seeking nonmooing merchandise. Similar auctions take place in Sugarcreek (Monday and Friday), Farmerstown (Tuesday) and Mt Hope (Wednesday).

FREE **Heini's Cheese Chalet**   CHEESEMAKING FACTORY
(☏800-253-6636; www.heinis.com; 6005 Hwy 77, Berlin; tours free; ☉8:30am-5pm Mon-Sat) Heini's whips up more than 70 cheeses. Learn how Amish farmers hand-milk their cows and spring-cool (versus machine-refrigerate) the output before delivering it each day. Then grab abundant samples and peruse the kitschy 'History of Cheesemaking' mural. To see the curd-cutting in action, come before 11am weekdays (except on Wednesdays).

Hershberger's Farm & Bakery   FARM
(☏330-674-6096; 5452 Hwy 557, Millersburg; ☉bakery 8am-5pm Mon-Sat year-round, farm from 10am mid-Apr–Oct; ⊕) Gorge on 25 kinds of

pie, homemade ice cream cones and seasonal produce from the market inside. Pet the farmyard animals (free) and take pony rides ($3) outside.

Yoder's Amish Home   FARM

(☑330-893-2541; www.yodersamishhome.com; 6050 Rte 515, Walnut Creek; tours adult/child $11/7; ☺10am-5pm Mon-Sat mid-Apr–late Oct; 🚼) Peek into a local home and one-room schoolhouse, and take a buggy ride through a field at this Amish farm that's open to visitors.

🛏 Sleeping & Eating

Hotel Millersburg   HISTORIC HOTEL $$

(☑330-674-1457; www.hotelmillersburg.com; 35 W Jackson St, Millersburg; r $79-149; ❄️🐕) Built in 1847 as a stagecoach inn, the property still provides lodging in its 26 casual rooms, which sit above a modern dining room and tavern (one of the few places to get a beer in Amish Country).

Guggisberg Swiss Inn   HOTEL $$

(☑330-893-3600; www.guggisbergswissinn.com; 5025 Rte 557, Charm; r incl breakfast $100-150; ❄️🐕🚼) The 24 tidy, compact rooms are bright with quilts and light-wood furnishings. A cheesemaking facility and horseback riding stable are on the grounds, too.

Boyd & Wurthmann Restaurant   AMERICAN $

(☑330-893-3287; Main St, Berlin; mains $5-10; ☺5:30am-8pm Mon-Sat) Hubcap-sized pancakes, 23 pie flavors, fat sandwiches and Amish specialties such as country-fried steak draw locals and tourists alike. Cash only.

ℹ Information

Holmes County Chamber of Commerce
(www.visitamishcountry.com)

Columbus

Ohio's capital city is like the blind date your mom arranges – average looking, restrained personality, but solid and affable. Better yet, she's easy on the wallet, an influence from Ohio State University's 55,000 students (the uni is the nation's second largest). A substantial gay population has taken up residence in Columbus in recent years.

👁 Sights & Activities

German Village   NEIGHBORHOOD

(www.germanvillage.com) The remarkably large, all-brick German Village, a half mile south of downtown, is a restored 19th-century neighborhood with beer halls, cobbled streets and Italianate and Queen Anne architecture.

Short North   NEIGHBORHOOD

(www.shortnorth.org) Just north of downtown, the browse-worthy Short North is a redeveloped strip of High St that holds contemporary art galleries, restaurants and jazz bars.

Wexner Center for the Arts   ARTS CENTER

(☑614-292-3535; www.wexarts.org; cnr 15th & N High Sts; admission $5; ☺11am-6pm Tue, Wed & Sun, to 8pm Thu-Sat) The campus' arts center offers cutting-edge art exhibits, films and performances.

🛏 Sleeping & Eating

German Village and the Short North provide fertile grazing and guzzling grounds. The **Arena District** (www.arenadistrict.com) bursts with midrange chains and brewpubs. Around the university and along N High St from 15th Ave onward, you'll find everything from Mexican to Ethiopian to sushi.

Short North B&B   B&B $$

(☑614-299-5050; www.columbus-bed-breakfast. com; 50 E Lincoln St; r incl breakfast $129-149; 🅿❄️🐕) The seven well-maintained rooms are steps away from the eponymous neighborhood's scene.

Red Roof Inn   HOTEL $$

(☑614-224-6539; www.redroof.com; 111 E Nationwide Blvd; r incl breakfast $85-139; 🅿🐾❄️🐕) Located in the Arena District, it's not bad as far as the chain goes. Parking is $10.

Schmidt's   GERMAN $$

(☑614-444-6808; www.schmidthaus.com; 240 E Kossuth St; mains $8-15; ☺11am 9pm Sun & Mon, to 10pm Tue-Thu, to 11pm Fri & Sat) In German Village, shovel in Old Country staples like sausage and schnitzel, but save room for the whopping half-pound cream puffs. Oompah bands play Wednesday to Saturday.

🍳 Skillet   AMERICAN $$

(☑614-443-2266; www.skilletruf.com; 410 E Whittier St) A teeny restaurant in German Village serving rustic, locally sourced fare.

North Market   MARKET $

(www.northmarket.com; 59 Spruce St; ☺9am-5pm Mon, to 7pm Tue-Fri, 8am-5pm Sat, noon-5pm Sun) Local farmers' produce and prepared foods; renowned ice cream by Jeni.

☆ Entertainment

Spectator sports rule the city.

Ohio Stadium FOOTBALL
(☎800-462-8257; www.ohiostatebuckeyes.com;
411 Woody Hayes Dr) The Ohio State Buckeyes
pack a rabid crowd into legendary, horse-
shoe-shaped Ohio Stadium for their games,
held on Saturdays in the fall. Expect 102,000
extra partiers in town.

Nationwide Arena HOCKEY
(☎614-246-2000; www.bluejackets.com; 200 W
Nationwide Blvd) The pro Columbus Blue Jackets slap the puck at downtown's big arena.

Crew Stadium SOCCER
(☎614-447-2739; www.thecrew.com) The popular Columbus Crew pro soccer team kicks
north off I-71 and 17th Ave, from March to
October.

❶ Information

Media
Alive (www.columbusalive.com) Free weekly
entertainment newspaper.
Columbus Dispatch (www.dispatch.com) The
daily newspaper.
Outlook (www.outlookmedia.com) Monthly gay
and lesbian publication.

Tourist Information

Columbus Convention & Visitors Bureau
(☎866-397-2657; www.experiencecolum
bus.com)

❶ Getting There & Away

The **Port Columbus Airport** (CMH; www.port
-columbus.com) is 10 miles east of town. A cab
to downtown costs about $25.

Greyhound (☎614-221-4642; www.grey
hound.com; 111 E Town St) buses run at least six
times daily to Cincinnati (two hours) and Cleveland (2½ hours). Often cheaper, **Megabus** (www.
megabus.com/us) runs a couple times daily to
Cincinnati and Chicago. Check the website for
locations.

Athens & Southeastern Ohio

Ohio's southeastern corner cradles most of
its forested areas, as well as the rolling foothills of the Appalachian Mountains and scattered farms.

Around Lancaster, southeast of Columbus, the hills lead gently into Hocking
County, a region of streams and waterfalls,
sandstone cliffs and cavelike formations.
It's splendid to explore in any season, with
miles of trails for hiking and rivers for canoeing, as well as abundant campgrounds
and cabins at **Hocking Hills State Park**
(☎740-385-6165; www.hockinghills.com; 20160
Hwy 664; campsites/cottages from $24/130). **Old
Man's Cave** is a scenic winner for hiking.
Hocking Valley Canoe Livery (☎740-385-
8685; www.hockinghillscanoeing.com; 31251 Chieftain Dr; 2hr tours $42; �rApr-Oct) lets you paddle
by moonlight and tiki torch from nearby
Logan. **Earth-Water-Rock: Outdoor Adventures** (☎740-664-5220; www.ewroutdoors.
com; half-day tour $85-110) provides thrills with
guided rock climbing and rappelling trips;
beginners are welcome.

Athens (www.athensohio.com) makes a
lovely base for seeing the region. Situated
where US 50 crosses US 33, it's set among
wooded hills and built around the Ohio University campus (which comprises half the
town). Student cafes and pubs line Court St,
Athens' main road. The **Village Bakery &
Cafe** (www.dellazona.com; 268 E State St; mains
$4-8; �8:7:30am-8pm Tue-Sat, 9am-2pm Sun)
uses organic veggies, grass-fed meat and
farmstead cheeses in its pizzas, soups and
sandwiches.

The area south of Columbus was a center
for the fascinating ancient Hopewell people,
who left behind huge geometric earthworks
and burial mounds from around 200 BC to
AD 600. For a fine introduction visit the
**Hopewell Culture National Historical
Park** (☎740-774-1126; www.nps.gov/hocu; Hwy
104 north of I-35; admission free; �8:30am-6pm
Jun-Aug, to 4:30pm Sep-May), 3 miles north of
Chillicothe. Stop in the visitor center, and
then wander about the variously shaped
ceremonial mounds spread over 13-acre
Mound City, a mysterious town of the dead.
Serpent Mound (☎937-587-2796; www.ohiohis
tory.org; 3850 Hwy 73; per vehicle $7; �10am-5pm
Fri-Sun Jun-Aug), southwest of Chillicothe and
4 miles northwest of Locust Grove, is perhaps the most captivating site of all. The giant, uncoiling snake stretches over a quarter
of a mile and is the largest effigy mound in
the USA.

Dayton & Yellow Springs

Dayton has the aviation sights, but little Yellow Springs (18 miles northeast on US 68)
has much more to offer in terms of accommodations and places to eat.

❍ Sights & Activities

FREE **National Museum of the US Air Force** MUSEUM
(☑937-255-3286; www.nationalmuseum.af.mil; 1100 Spaatz St; ⊘9am-5pm) Located at the Wright-Patterson Air Force Base, 6 miles northeast of Dayton, the museum has everything from a Wright Brothers exhibit and Sopwith Camel (WWI biplane) to a Stealth bomber. Don't miss the annex with its collection of presidential planes; a free shuttle bus takes you over to the hangar (which you'll need a passport or driver's license to enter). Expect your visit to take three or more hours.

Carillon Historical Park HISTORIC SITE
(☑937-293-2841; www.daytonhistory.org; 1000 Carillon Blvd; adult/child $8/5; ⊘9:30am-5pm Mon-Sat, noon-5pm Sun) The many heritage attractions include the 1905 Wright Flyer III biplane and a replica of the Wright workshop.

FREE **Dayton Aviation Heritage National Historical Park** HISTORIC SITE
(☑937-225-7705; www.nps.gov/daav; 16 S Williams St; ⊘8:30am-5pm) Includes the Wright Cycle Company Complex, where the brothers developed bikes and aviation ideas.

🛏 Sleeping & Eating

The following listings are located in Yellow Springs, a top-notch place to experience down-home Ohio.

Morgan House B&B $$
(☑937-767-1761; www.arthurmorganhouse.com; 120 W Limestone St; r incl breakfast $90-125; ⊖❄🐾) The six comfy rooms have super-soft linens and private baths. Breakfasts are organic, with free-trade African coffee.

TOP CHOICE **Young's Jersey Dairy** AMERICAN $$
(☑937-325-0629; www.youngsdairy.com; 6880 Springfield-Xenia Rd) Young's is a working dairy farm with two restaurants: the **Golden Jersey Inn** (mains $9-15; ⊘lunch & dinner Mon-Fri, plus breakfast Sat & Sun), serving dishes like buttermilk chicken; and the **Dairy Store** (sandwiches $3.50-6.50; ⊘7am-11pm Sun-Thu, to midnight Fri & Sat), serving sandwiches, dreamy ice cream and Ohio's best milk shakes. There's also minigolf, batting cages and opportunities to watch the cows get milked.

Winds Cafe AMERICAN $$$
(☑937-767-1144; www.windscafe.com; 215 Xenia Ave; mains $18-25; ⊘11:30am-2pm & 5-10pm Tue-Sat, 10am-3pm Sun) A hippie co-op 30 years ago, the Winds has grown up to become a sophisticated foodie favorite plating seasonal dishes like fig-sauced asparagus crepes and rhubarb halibut.

Cincinnati

Cincinnati splashes up the Ohio River's banks. Its prettiness surprises, as do its haunted music-club mansions, its twisting streets to hilltop Mt Adams, and the locals' unashamed ardor for a five-way (see boxed text, p545). Amid all that action, don't forget to catch a baseball game, stroll the riverfront and gape at some serious neon.

❍ Sights & Activities

Many attractions are closed on Monday.

DOWNTOWN

National Underground Railroad Freedom Center MUSEUM
(☑513-333-7500; www.freedomcenter.org; 50 E Freedom Way; adult/child $12/8; ⊘11am-5pm Tue-Sat) Cincinnati was a prominent stop on the Underground Railroad and a center for abolitionist activities led by residents, such as Harriet Beecher Stowe. The Freedom Center tells their stories. Exhibits show how slaves escaped to the north, and the ways in which slavery still exists today. Download the free iPhone app for extra insight while touring.

Findlay Market MARKET
(www.findlaymarket.org; 1801 Race St; ⊘9am-6pm Tue-Fri, 8am-6pm Sat, 10am-4pm Sun) Indoor-outdoor Findlay Market greens the somewhat blighted area at downtown's northern edge. It's a good stop for fresh produce, meats, cheeses and baked goods. The Belgian waffle guy will wow your taste buds.

Rosenthal Center for Contemporary Arts MUSEUM
(☑513-721-0390; www.contemporaryartscenter. org; 44 E 6th St; adult/child $7.50/4.50, admission free Mon evening; ⊘10am-9pm Mon, 10am-6pm Wed-Fri, 11am-6pm Sat & Sun) This center displays modern art in an avant-garde building designed by Iraqi architect Zaha Hadid. The structure and its artworks are a pretty big deal for traditionalist Cincy.

AMERICAN SIGN MUSEUM

The American Sign Museum (☏513-258-4020; www.signmuseum.net; 2515 Essex Pl; adult/child $10/free; ☺10am-4pm Sat or by appointment) is a bit out of the way and challenging to find, but the cache of flashing, lightbulb-studded beacons offers a mighty reward. Passionate proprietor Tod Swormstedt likely will show you around the warehouse, where you'll burn your retinas staring at vintage neon drive-in signs, hulking genies and the Frisch's Big Boy, among many other nostalgic novelties. It's a one-of-a-kind horde for people who treasure the past. Located in the Essex building of artists' studios, 3 miles north of downtown, just west of I-71.

Fountain Square   PLAZA
(www.myfountainsquare.com; cnr 5th & Vine Sts; ☎) Fountain Square is the city's centerpiece, a public space with a seasonal ice rink, chess tables, concerts, a Reds ticket kiosk and the fancy old 'Spirit of the Waters' fountain.

An amble along the riverfront is well worthwhile, taking you past several parks and bridges:

Roebling Suspension Bridge   BRIDGE
(www.roeblingbridge.org) The elegant 1876 spanner was a forerunner of John Roebling's famous Brooklyn Bridge in New York. It's cool to walk across while passing cars make it 'sing' around you. It links to Covington, Kentucky (see p544).

Purple People Bridge   BRIDGE
(www.purplepeoplebridge.com) This pedestrian-only bridge provides a unique crossing from Sawyer Point (a nifty park dotted by whimsical monuments and flying pigs) to Newport, Kentucky (see p544).

COVINGTON & NEWPORT

Covington and Newport, Kentucky, are sort of suburbs of Cincinnati, just over the river from downtown. Newport is to the east and known for its massive Newport on the Levee (www.newportonthelevee.com) restaurant and shopping complex. Covington lies to the west and has the MainStrasse (www.mainstrasse.org) quarter, filled with funky restaurants and bars in the neighborhood's 19th-century brick row houses. Antebellum mansions fringe Riverside Dr, and old paddle-wheel boats tie up along the water's edge.

Newport Aquarium   AQUARIUM
(☏859-491-3467; www.newportaquarium.com; One Aquarium Way; adult/child $22/15; ☺9am-7pm Jun-Aug, 10am-6pm Sep-May) Meet parading penguins, Sweet Pea the shark ray and lots of other razor-toothed fish at Newport's large, well-regarded facility.

MT ADAMS

It might be a bit of a stretch to compare Mt Adams, immediately east of downtown, to Paris' Montmartre, but this hilly 19th-century enclave of narrow, twisting streets, Victorian town houses, galleries, bars and restaurants is certainly a pleasurable surprise. Most visitors ascend for a quick look around and a drink.

To get here, follow 7th St east of downtown to Gilbert Ave, bear northwest to Elsinore Ave, and head up the hill to reach the lakes, paths and cultural offerings in Eden Park. The yard at nearby Immacula Church (30 Guido St) is worth a stop for its killer views over the city.

FREE Cincinnati Art Museum   MUSEUM
(☏513-721-5204; www.cincinnatiartmuseum.org; 953 Eden Park Dr; ☺11am-5pm Tue-Sun) The collection spans 6000 years, with an emphasis on ancient Middle Eastern art and European old masters, plus a wing devoted to local works. Parking costs $4.

FREE Krohn Conservatory   GARDENS
(☏513-421-4086; www.cincinnatiparks.com/krohn-conservatory; 1501 Eden Park Dr; ☺10am-5pm Tue-Sun) The vast greenhouse sprouts a rainforest, desert flora and glorious seasonal flower shows (separate admission $3 to $6).

WEST END

Cincinnati Museum Center   MUSEUM
(☏513-287-7000; www.cincymuseum.org; 1301 Western Ave; adult/child $12.50/8.50; ☺10am-5pm Mon-Sat, 11am-6pm Sun; ☺) Two miles northwest of downtown, this museum complex occupies the 1933 Union Terminal, an art deco jewel still used by Amtrak. The interior has fantastic murals made of Rookwood tiles. The Museum of Natural History & Science is mostly geared to kids, but it does have a limestone cave with real bats inside. A history museum, children's museum and Omnimax theater round out the offerings; the admission fee provides entry to all. Parking costs $6.

⛬ Tours

Architreks WALKING
(📞513-421-4469; www.cincinnati-walks.org; tours adult/child $15/5; ☺May-Oct) Guided walking tours of various neighborhoods, including downtown, Mt Adams and Northside. Departure points and days/times vary.

🎊 Festivals & Events

Oktoberfest FOOD
(www.oktoberfestzinncinnati.com; ☺mid-Sep) German beer, brats and mania.

Midpoint Music Festival MUSIC
(www.mpmf.com; ☺late Sep) Indie bands flood various venues; three-day passes cost $49.

🛏 Sleeping

Hotel tax is cheaper on the Kentucky side at 11.3%, versus the 17% charged in Cincinnati. Tax is not included in the following prices.

Several midrange chain options line up on the Kentucky riverfront. You'll save money (less tax, free parking), but be prepared either to walk a few miles or take a short bus ride to reach downtown Cincy.

The **Greater Cincinnati B&B Network** (www.cincinnatibb.com) has links to Kentucky-side properties.

Cincinnatian Hotel HOTEL $$$
(📞513-381-3000; www.cincinnatianhotel.com; 601 Vine St; r $160-260; 🅿☺✳🛜) The Cincinnatian is in a magnificent 1882 Victorian building; the spacious rooms have fluffy towels, silk-soft sheets and huge round bathtubs. Rates drop to the lower end of the price range during weekends. Parking costs $28.

Best Western Mariemont Inn HOTEL $$
(📞513-271-2100; www.mariemontinn.com; 6880 Wooster Pike; r $150-209; 🅿☺✳🛜) If you're looking for something unusual and out of the rat race, try this Tudor-style lodge with massive beamed ceilings and a fireplace in every room. It sits on the town square in a quiet neighborhood 10 miles northeast of downtown.

Residence Inn
Cincinnati Downtown HOTEL $$$
(📞513-651-1234; www.marriott.com; 506 E 4th St; r incl breakfast $199-299; 🅿☺✳@🛜) Welcome to Cincy's first new downtown hotel in 30 years. The glistening rooms are suites with full kitchens. Parking costs $20.

Holiday Inn Express HOTEL $$
(📞859-957-2320; www.hiexpress.com; 109 Landmark Dr; r incl breakfast $125-180; 🅿✳@🛜) It's a good pick among the riverfront chains; located about three-quarters of a mile east of Newport on the Levee.

🍴 Eating

In addition to downtown, dining options concentrate along the Kentucky riverfront and in the Northside neighborhood (north of where I-74 and I-75 intersect, 5 miles north of downtown).

TOP CHOICE Terry's Turf Club BURGERS $$
(📞513-533-4222; 4618 Eastern Ave; mains $8-15; ☺4pm-midnight Mon-Wed, from 11am Thu, 11am-2:30am Fri & Sat, noon-10pm Sun) Burger aficionados practically pee in their pants waiting for Terry's fat patties. The wine-with-wild-mushroom sauce is the epic topper, though other concoctions (rosemary garlic, wasabi red curry ginger) will blow your mind, too. And fear not, vegetarians: the mushroom burger gets plaudits. Terry's eccentricity reflects in his decor, with enough neon and cra-zee signs to light up Vegas. Located 7 miles east of downtown via Columbia Pkwy.

Hathaway's DINER $
(📞513-621-1332; Carew Tower, 441 Vine St; $5-8; ☺6:30am-4pm Mon-Fri, 8am-3pm Sat) Hathaway's hasn't changed its retro dinette

> **DON'T MISS**
>
> ## CHILI FIVE-WAY
>
> Don't worry – you can keep your clothes on for this experience, though you may want to loosen your belt. A 'five-way' in Cincinnati has to do with chili, which is a local specialty. It comprises meat sauce (spiced with chocolate and cinnamon) ladled over spaghetti and beans, then garnished with cheese and onions. Although you can get it three-way (minus onions and beans) or four-way (minus onions *or* beans), you should go the whole way – after all, life's an adventure. **Skyline Chili** (www.skylinechili.com; 643 Vine St; items $3.50-7.50; ☺10:30am-8pm Mon-Fri, 11am-4pm Sat) has a cultlike following devoted to its version. There are outlets throughout town; this one is downtown near Fountain Sq.

tables, or apron-wearing waitresses, since it started feeding hungry businesspeople 30-plus years ago. Try the goetta (pork, oats, onions and herbs) for breakfast – it's a Cincy specialty. The milk shakes will please sweet tooths.

Honey AMERICAN **$$**
(☎513-541-4300; www.honeynorthside.com; 4034 Hamilton Ave; mains $15-23; ⏰5-9pm Tue-Thu, to 10pm Fri & Sat, 11am-2pm Sun; 🌿) Seasonal comfort food – maybe Creole meatloaf or sweet pea ravioli – fills the plates on Honey's low-lit, sturdy wood tables. Brunch is a fan favorite, offering a special gift to herbivores: vegan goetta.

Otto's CAFE **$$$**
(☎859-491-6678; www.ottosonmain.com; 521 Main St; sandwiches $8-11, mains $19-23; ⏰11am-3pm Mon, to 10pm Tue-Sat, 10am-9pm Sun) Fork into 'hot brown' (a local meat-and-cheese specialty) and thick-cut sandwiches for lunch, or shrimp and grits with wine for dinner at this Covington bistro.

Graeter's Ice Cream ICE CREAM **$**
(www.graeters.com; 511 Walnut St; scoops $2.50-5; ⏰6:30am-9pm Mon-Fri, 7am-9pm Sat, 11am-7pm Sun) It's a local delicacy, with scoop shops around the city. The flavors that mix in the gargantuan, chunky chocolate chips top the list.

🍷 Drinking

Both Mt Adams and Northside are busy nightspots.

Blind Lemon BAR
(www.theblindlemon.com; 936 Hatch St) Head down the passageway to enter this atmospheric old speakeasy in Mt Adams. It has an outdoor courtyard in summer, with a fire pit added in winter, and there's live music nightly.

Motr Pub BAR
(www.motrpub.com; 1345 Main St) Located in the on again, off again – currently on again – gritty Over-the-Rhine neighborhood on downtown's northern edge, Motr lets arty types congregate around their Hudepohls (local beer) and rockumentary movie nights.

Comet BAR
(www.cometbar.com; 4579 Hamilton Ave; 🖥) The casual Comet, in Northside, has the city's best jukebox and bar food; try the burrito.

City View Tavern BAR
(www.cityviewtavern.com; 403 Oregon St) From atop Mt Adams, the city sparkles out in front of you at this unassuming boozer.

☆ Entertainment

Scope for free publications like *CityBeat* for current listings.

Sports

Great American Ballpark BASEBALL
(☎513-765-7000; www.cincinnatireds.com; 100 Main St) Home to the Reds – pro baseball's first team – Cincy is a great place to catch a game thanks to its bells-and-whistles riverside ballpark.

Paul Brown Stadium FOOTBALL
(☎513-621-3550; www.bengals.com; 1 Paul Brown Stadium) The Bengals pro football team scrimmages a few blocks west of the ballpark.

Live Music

Southgate House LIVE MUSIC
(☎859-431-2201; www.southgatehouse.com; 24 E 3rd St) Big and small, touring and local bands alike play in this 1814 haunted mansion in Newport, which also happens to be the birthplace of the tommy gun.

Northside Tavern LIVE MUSIC
(☎513-542-3603; www.northside-tavern.com; 4163 Hamilton Ave) Local bands plug in their amps here, and it's always free.

Performing Arts

Music Hall CLASSICAL MUSIC
(☎513-721-8222; www.cincinnatiarts.org; 1241 Elm St) The acoustically pristine Music Hall is where the symphony orchestra, pops orchestra, opera and ballet hold their seasons. This is not the best neighborhood, so be cautious and park nearby.

Aronoff Center THEATER
(☎513-621-2787; www.cincinnatiarts.org; 650 Walnut St) The mod Aronoff hosts touring shows.

① Information

Media

Cincinnati Enquirer (www.cincinnati.com) Daily newspaper.

CityBeat (www.citybeat.com) Free alternative weekly paper with good entertainment listings.

Rainbow Cincinnati (www.gaycincinnati.com) GLBT news and business listings.

Tourist Information
Cincinnati USA Regional Tourism Network
(☑800-344-3445; www.cincinnatiusa.com)
Call or go online for a visitor's guide.

❶ Getting There & Around

The **Cincinnati/Northern Kentucky International Airport** (CVG; www.cvgairport.com)
is actually in Kentucky, 13 miles south. To get
downtown, take the TANK bus ($1.75) from near
Terminal 3; a cab costs about $30.

Greyhound (☑513-352-6012; www.greyhound.com; 1005 Gilbert Ave) buses travel daily
to Indianapolis (2½ hours) and Columbus (two
hours). Often cheaper and quicker, **Megabus**
(www.megabus.com/us) travels the same
routes, and goes to Chicago (six hours). It departs from downtown Cincy at 4th and Race Sts.

Amtrak (☑513-651-3337; www.amtrak.com)
choo-choos into **Union Terminal** (1301 Western
Ave) thrice weekly en route to Chicago (9½
hours) and Washington, DC (14½ hours), departing in the middle of the night.

Metro (www.go-metro.com; fare $1.75) runs
the local buses and links with the **Transit Authority of Northern Kentucky** (TANK; www.
tankbus.org; fare $1-1.75).

MICHIGAN

More, more, more – Michigan is the Midwest
state that cranks it up. It sports more beaches than the Atlantic seaboard. More than
half the state is covered by forests. And more
cherries and berries get shoveled into pies
here than anywhere else in the USA. Plus
its gritty city Detroit is the Midwest's rawest
of all – and we mean that in a good way. Of
course, there's more unemployment in Michigan than any other state, but we digress...

Michigan occupies prime real estate, surrounded by four of the five Great Lakes – Superior, Michigan, Huron and Erie. Islands
freckle its coast – Mackinac, Beaver and Isle
Royale – and make top touring destinations.
Surfing beaches, colored sandstone cliffs
and trekkable sand dunes also woo visitors.

The state consists of two parts split by water: the larger Lower Peninsula, shaped like
a mitten; and the smaller, lightly populated
Upper Peninsula, shaped like a slipper. They
are linked by the gasp-worthy Mackinac
Bridge, which spans the Straits of Mackinac
(pronounced *mac*-in-aw).

❶ Information

Michigan Highway Conditions (☑800-381-
8477; www.michigan.gov/mdot)

MICHIGAN FACTS

» **Nicknames** Great Lakes State,
Wolverine State

» **Population** 10 million

» **Area** 96,720 sq miles

» **Capital city** Lansing (population
114,300)

» **Other cities** Detroit (population
871,100)

» **Sales tax** 6%

» **Birthplace of** industrialist Henry
Ford (1863–1947), filmmaker Francis
Ford Coppola (b 1939), musician Stevie Wonder (b 1950), singer Madonna
(b 1958), Google co-founder Larry
Page (b 1973)

» **Home of** auto assembly plants,
freshwater beaches

» **Politics** leans Democratic

» **Famous for** cars, Cornflakes, tart
cherries, Motown music

» **State reptile** painted turtle

» **Driving distances** Detroit to
Traverse City 255 miles, Detroit to
Cleveland 168 miles

Michigan State Park Information (☑800-
447-2757; www.michigan.gov/stateparks) Park
entry requires a vehicle permit (per day/year
$8/29). Campsites cost $16 to $33; reservations accepted (www.midnrreservations.com;
fee $8). Some parks have wi-fi.
Travel Michigan (☑800-644-2489; www.
michigan.org)

Detroit

Tell any American that you're planning to
visit Detroit, and then watch their eyebrows
shoot up quizzically. They'll ask 'Why?' and
warn you about the off-the-chart homicide
rates, boarded-up buildings with trash
swirling at their bases, and whopping high
foreclosure rates where homes sell for $1.
'Detroit's a crap-hole. You'll get killed there.'

While the aforementioned attributes are
true, and although the city does waft a sort
of bombed-out, apocalyptic vibe, it's these
same qualities that fuel a raw urban energy
you won't find anywhere else. Artists, entrepreneurs and young people are moving in,
and a DIY spirit pervades. They're converting

vacant lots into urban farms and abandoned buildings into hostels and museums. Plus, they shred a mean guitar in 'the D.' Very mean.

History

French explorer Antoine de La Mothe Cadillac founded Detroit in 1701. Sweet fortune arrived in the 1920s, when Henry Ford began churning out cars. He didn't invent the automobile, as so many mistakenly believe, but he did perfect assembly-line manufacturing and mass-production techniques. The result was the Model T, the first car the USA's middle class could afford to own.

Detroit quickly became the motor capital of the world. General Motors (GM), Chrysler and Ford were all headquartered in or near Detroit (and still are). The 1950s were the city's heyday, when the population exceeded two million and Motown music hit the airwaves. But racial tensions in 1967 and Japanese car competitors in the 1970s shook the city and its industry. Detroit entered an era of deep decline, losing about two-thirds of its population.

The D resurged somewhat in the mid-2000s, only to see the global economic crisis of 2008–09 crush the auto industry. GM and Chrysler filed for bankruptcy, and thousands of blue- and white-collar workers lost their jobs. The city continues to 'restructure.'

⊙ Sights & Activities

Downtown revolves around the riverfront Renaissance Center and nearby Hart Plaza. Woodward Ave, the city's main boulevard, heads north from here to Midtown (containing the Cultural Center and its museums, plus Wayne State University) and on to architecturally rich New Center (a mile beyond). Bar-filled Corktown sits west of downtown. The Mile Roads are Detroit's major east-west arteries; 8 Mile forms the city-suburbs boundary. Across the Detroit River lies Windsor, Canada.

Sights are commonly closed on Monday and Tuesday.

MIDTOWN & CULTURAL CENTER

Detroit Institute of Arts MUSEUM
(☑313-833-7900; www.dia.org; 5200 Woodward Ave; adult/child $8/4; ◷10am-4pm Wed & Thu, 10am-10pm Fri, 10am-5pm Sat & Sun) It's the cream of the local museum crop, lauded

for its American collection. The centerpiece is Diego Rivera's mural *Detroit Industry*, which fills an entire room and reflects the city's blue-collar labor history.

FREE Museum of
Contemporary Art Detroit   MUSEUM
(☏313-832-6622; www.mocadetroit.org; 4454 Woodward Ave; ⊙11am-5pm Wed-Sun, to 8pm Thu & Fri) MOCAD opened in 2006 in an abandoned, graffiti-slathered auto dealership. Heat lamps hang from the ceiling over peculiar exhibits that change every few months.

Wright Museum of
African American History   MUSEUM
(☏313-494-5800; www.maah-detroit.org; 315 E Warren Ave; adult/child $8/5; ⊙9am-5pm Tue-Sat, 1-5pm Sun) It holds less than it appears to from the impressive exterior, though it's worth a look inside. The full-scale model of slaves chained up on a dark, creaking slave ship will leave you chilled.

NEW CENTER
Motown Historical Museum   MUSEUM
(☏313-875-2264; www.motownmuseum.com; 2648 W Grand Blvd; adult/child $10/8; ⊙10am-6pm Tue-Sat, plus Mon Jul & Aug) In this row of modest houses Berry Gordy launched Motown Records – and the careers of Stevie Wonder, Diana Ross, Marvin Gaye and Michael Jackson – with an $800 loan in 1959. Gordy and Motown split for Los Angeles in 1972, but you can still step into humble Studio A and see where the famed names recorded their first hits. A tour takes about 1½ hours, and consists mostly of looking at old photos and listening to guides' stories. The museum is 2 miles northwest of Midtown.

Model T Automotive
Heritage Complex   MUSEUM
(☏313-872-8759; www.tplex.org; 461 Piquette Ave; adult/child $10/free; ⊙10am-4pm Wed-Fri, 9am-4pm Sat, noon-4pm Sun Apr-Nov) Henry Ford cranked out the first Model T in this landmark factory. Admission includes a tour into the workshop and 'experimental room,' plus loads of classic cars to view. It's about 1 mile northeast of the Detroit Institute of Arts.

DOWNTOWN & AROUND
Busy Greektown (centered on Monroe St) has restaurants, bakeries and a casino.

Riverwalk & Dequindre Cut   WALKING, CYCLING
(www.detroitriverfront.org) The city's swell riverfront path runs for 3 miles along the churning Detroit River west from Hart Plaza east to Mt Elliott St, passing several parks, outdoor theaters, riverboats and fishing spots en route. Eventually it will extend all the way to beachy Belle Isle (detour onto Jefferson Ave to get there now). About halfway along the Riverwalk, near Orleans St, the 1.5-mile Dequindre Cut Greenway path juts north, offering a convenient passageway to Eastern Market.

Wheelhouse Bikes   BICYCLE RENTAL
(☏313-656-2453; www.wheelhousedetroit.com; 1340 E Atwater St; per 2hr $15; ⊙11am-8pm Mon-Sat, to 5pm Sun) Cycling is a great way to explore the city. Wheelhouse rents sturdy two-wheelers (helmet and lock included) on the Riverwalk at Rivard Plaza. Tours ($35 including bike rental) on weekends roll by various neighborhoods and architectural sites.

Eastern Market   MARKET
(www.detroiteasternmarket.com; Gratiot Ave & Russell St) Produce, cheese, spice and flower vendors fill the large halls on Saturday, but you also can turn up Monday through Friday to browse the specialty shops (props to the peanut roaster), cafes and ethnic eats that flank the market on Russell and Market Sts.

Renaissance Center   BUILDING
(RenCen; www.gmrencen.com; 330 E Jefferson Ave; ☏) GM's glossy, cloud-poking headquarters is a fine place to grab a bite (in the Wintergarden), take a free hour-long tour (Monday through Friday at noon and 2pm) or embark on the riverfront walkway.

Hart Plaza   PLAZA
(cnr Jefferson & Woodward Aves) This is the site of many free, summer weekend festivals and concerts. While there, check out the sculpture of Joe Louis' mighty fist.

Campus Martius   PLAZA
(www.campusmartiuspark.org; 800 Woodward Ave) It's another communal hot spot downtown, with an outdoor ice rink in winter, and eating areas, concerts and films in summer.

People Mover   MONORAIL
(www.thepeoplemover.com; fare $0.50) As mass transit, the monorail's 3-mile loop on elevated tracks around downtown won't get you very far. As a tourist attraction, it's a sweet ride providing great views of the city and riverfront.

FREE Heidelberg Project   ART INSTALLATION
(www.heidelberg.org; 3600 Heidelberg St; ⊙sunrise-sunset) Polka-dotted streets, houses

covered in Technicolor paint blobs, strange sculptures in yards – this is no acid trip, but rather an art installation that covers an entire neighborhood. It's the brainchild of street artist Tyree Guyton, who wanted to beautify his run-down community (which has the dubious distinction of being the USA's most economically depressed 'hood). Get here by taking Gratiot Ave northwest to Heidelberg St; the project spans from Ellery to Mt Elliott Sts.

☞ Tours

Preservation Wayne
WALKING

(☎313-577-7674; www.preservationwayne.org; 2.5hr tours $10-15; ☺5:30pm Tue & 10am Sat May-Sep) offers architectural walking tours through downtown, Midtown and other neighborhoods; departure points vary.

✦ Festivals & Events

North American International Auto Show
CARS

(www.naias.com; tickets $12; ☺mid-Jan) It's autos galore for two weeks in mid-January at the Cobo Center.

Movement Electronic Music Festival
MUSIC

(www.movement.us; day pass $40; ☺late May) The world's largest electronic music festival congregates in Hart Plaza over Memorial Day weekend.

🛏 Sleeping

Add 9% to 15% tax (it varies by lodging size and location) to the rates listed here, unless stated otherwise.

Affordable motels abound in Detroit's suburbs. If you're arriving from Metro Airport, follow the signs for Merriman Rd when leaving the airport and take your pick.

TOP CHOICE Inn on Ferry Street
INN $$

(☎313-871-6000; www.innonferrystreet.com; 84 E Ferry St; r incl breakfast from $149; P☺✳@�) Forty guest rooms fill a row of Victorian mansions right by the art museum. The lower-cost rooms are small but have deliciously soft bedding; the larger rooms feature plenty of antique wood furnishings. The healthy hot breakfast and shuttle to downtown are nice touches.

Detroit Hostel
HOSTEL $

(☎248-807-2131; www.hosteldetroit.com; 2700 Vermont St; dm $18-27, r $40-45; P☺@late) Vol-

unteers rehabbed this old building, gathered up recycled materials and donations for the patchwork furnishings, and opened it to the public in 2011. There's a 10-bed dorm, two two-bed dorms and five private rooms; everyone shares the four bathrooms, three kitchens and backyard herb garden. Bookings are taken online only (and must be done at least 24 hours in advance). Parking costs $10 per day, as do bicycle rentals. The hostel is located in Corktown on a desolate street, but near several good bars and restaurants.

Ft Shelby Doubletree Hotel
HOTEL $$

(☎313-963-5600, 800-222-8733; http://doubletree1.hilton.com; 525 W Lafayette Blvd; ste $126-169; P☺✳@late) This new hotel fills a historic beaux arts building downtown. All rooms are suites, with both the sitting area and bedroom equipped with HDTV and free wi-fi. Parking costs $20, and there's free shuttle service around downtown.

Westin Book Cadillac
HOTEL $$$

(☎313-442-1600; www.bookcadillacwestin.com; 1114 Washington Blvd; r weekend/weekday from $179/299; P☺✳@late) Opened in 2008, 'the Book' swooped into a 1924 landmark building and took over as the top address in town. It has all the amenities you'd expect at a swanky, 453-room hotel. In-room wi-fi costs $8 per day; parking costs $25.

✕ Eating

Two nearby suburbs also have caches of hip restaurants and bars: walkable, gay-oriented Ferndale at 9 Mile Rd and Woodward Ave, and Royal Oak just north of Ferndale between 12 and 13 Mile Rds.

MIDTOWN & CULTURAL CENTER

Good Girls Go to Paris Crepes
CREPERIE $

(☎877-727-4727; www.goodgirlsgotopariscrepes.com; 15 E Kirby St; mains $5-8; ☺9am-4pm Mon-Wed, to 8pm Thu, to 10pm Fri & Sat, to 5pm Sun) This red-walled, French-style cafe transports diners across the pond via its sweet (Heath Bar and ricotta) and savory (goat cheese and fig) pancakes.

Cass Cafe
CAFE $$

(☎313-831-1400; www.casscafe.com; 4620 Cass Ave; mains $8-15; ☺11am-11pm Mon-Thu, 11am-1am Fri & Sat, 5-10pm Sun; ☺late) The Cass is a bohemian art gallery fused with a bar and restaurant that serves soups, sandwiches and veggie beauties, like the lentil-walnut burger. Service can be fickle.

Avalon International Breads
BAKERY $

(☎313-832-0008; www.avalonbreads.net; 422 W Willis St; mains $5-9; ⊙6am-6pm Tue-Sat, 8am-4pm Sun) Detroit's earthy types huddle round the hearth at Avalon, where its fresh-baked bread (like scallion dill or country Italian) makes an excellent base for the sandwiches it serves.

DOWNTOWN

Foran's Grand Trunk Pub
PUB $$

(☎313-961-3043; www.grandtrunkpub.com; 612 Woodward Ave; mains $7-12; ⊙11am-2am) If the high vaulted ceiling and long narrow space make you feel like you're in an old railroad ticket station, that's because you are. The food is pub grub – sandwiches, burgers and shepherd's pie – but made with local ingredients such as Avalon bread and Eastern Market produce. The taps pour 18 Michigan craft brews.

Lafayette Coney Island
AMERICAN $

(☎313-964-8198; 118 Lafayette Blvd; items $2.50-4; ⊙7:30am-4am Mon-Thu, to 5am Fri & Sat, 9:30am-4am Sun) The 'coney' – a hot dog smothered with chili and onions – is a Detroit specialty. When the craving strikes (and it will), take care of business at Lafayette. The minimalist menu consists of burgers, fries and beer, in addition to the signature item. Cash only.

Laikon Cafe
GREEK $$

(☎313-963-7058; 569 Monroe St; mains $9-14; ⊙11am-10pm Sun-Thu, to midnight Fri & Sat, closed Tue) Chef-owner Kostas has cooked staples like lamb and flaming cheese in his homey, old-school Greek restaurant for decades.

CORKTOWN & MEXICANTOWN

Mexicantown, along Bagley St 3 miles west of downtown, offers several inexpensive Mexican restaurants.

Slows Bar BQ
TOP CHOICE
BARBECUE $$

(☎313-962-9828; www.slowsbarbq.com; 2138 Michigan Ave; mains $10-18, half-rack ribs $19; ⊙11am-10pm Sun & Mon, to 11pm Tue-Thu, to midnight Fri & Sat; 🛜) Mmm, slow-cooked southern-style barbecue in Corktown. Carnivores can carve into the three-meat combo plate (brisket, pulled pork and chicken). Vegetarians have options from okra fritters to a faux-meat chicken sandwich. The taps yield 21 quality beers.

🍷 Drinking

Bronx
TOP CHOICE
BAR

(4476 2nd Ave; 🛜) There's not much inside Detroit's best boozer besides a pool table, dim lighting and a couple of jukeboxes filled with ballsy rock and soul. But that's the way the hipsters, slackers and rockers (the White Stripes used to hang here) like their dive bars. They're also fond of the beefy burgers served late at night and the cheap beer selection.

Honest John's
BAR

(www.honestjohnsdetroit.com; 488 Selden St; ⊙7am-2am; 🛜) There really is a John and he's a Detroit classic, as is his unassuming bar where cops, nurses and other local workers toss back a cold one postshift.

D'Mongo's
BAR

(www.cafedmongos.com; 1439 Griswold St; ⊙6pm-2am Fri) With its retro ambience, ribs cookin' on the outdoor smoker, and jazz or country bands croonin', it's a pity this secret hideaway is open on Fridays only.

☆ Entertainment

Live Music

Cover charges hover between $5 and $15.

FROM MOTOWN TO ROCK CITY

Motown Records and soul music put Detroit on the map in the 1960s, while the thrashing punk rock of the Stooges and MC5 was the 1970s response to that smooth sound. By 1976, Detroit was dubbed 'Rock City' by a Kiss song (though – just Detroit's luck – the tune was eclipsed by its B-side, 'Beth'). In recent years it has been hard-edged rock – aka whiplash rock 'n' roll – that has pushed the city to the music scene forefront. Homegrown stars include the White Stripes, Von Bondies and Dirtbombs. Rap (thank you, Eminem) and techno are Detroit's other renowned genres. Many music aficionados say the city's blight is what produces such a beautifully angry explosion of sound, and who's to argue? Scope free publications like the *Metro Times* and *Real Detroit Weekly*, or blogs like 'Motor City Rocks' (www.motorcityrocks.com), for current show and club listings.

Magic Stick & Majestic Theater LIVE MUSIC

(www.majesticdetroit.com; 4120-4140 Woodward Ave) The White Stripes and Von Bondies are rockers who've risen from the beer-splattered ranks at the Magic Stick. The Majestic Theater next door hosts larger shows. There's bowling, billiards, a pizza joint and cafe. Something cool rocks here nightly.

PJ's Lager House LIVE MUSIC

(www.pjslagerhouse.com; 1254 Michigan Ave) This Corktown punk-underground club is dingy in an atmospheric way, with scrappy bands or DJs playing most nights.

Cliff Bell's Jazz Club LIVE MUSIC

(www.cliffbells.com; 2030 Park Ave; ⊙Tue-Sun) With its dark wood, candlelight and art deco decor, Bell's evokes 1930s elegance. Local jazz bands and poetry readings attract a diverse young audience nightly.

Baker's Keyboard Lounge LIVE MUSIC

(www.bakerskeyboardlounge.com; 20510 Livernois Ave; ⊙Tue-Sun) Everyone from Miles Davis to Thelonious Monk to Nina Simone has let loose at the self-proclaimed 'world's oldest jazz club' on Detroit's far northwest side.

St Andrew's Hall LIVE MUSIC

(www.facebook.com/standrewshall; 431 E Congress St) St Andrew's is a well-known alternative band venue in an old church. Downstairs is Shelter, a smaller music/dance club.

Performing Arts

Puppet ART/Detroit

Puppet Theater THEATER

(☑313-961-7777; www.puppetart.org; 25 E Grand River Ave; adult/child $10/5; 🚼) Soviet-trained puppeteers perform beautiful shows in this 70-person theater; a small museum displays puppets from different cultures. Shows are typically held on Saturday afternoons.

Detroit Opera House OPERA

(☑313-237-7464; www.motopera.com; 1526 Broadway) Gorgeous interior, top-tier company and nurturer of many renowned African American performers.

Fox Theatre THEATER

(☑313-983-6611; 2211 Woodward Ave) This is a gloriously restored 1928 venue that large touring shows occupy.

Sports

Comerica Park BASEBALL

(www.detroittigers.com; 2100 Woodward Ave; 🚼) The Detroit Tigers play pro baseball at Comerica, one of the league's most decked-out stadiums. The park is particularly kid friendly, with a small Ferris wheel and carousel inside (per ride $2 each).

Joe Louis Arena HOCKEY

(www.detroitredwings.com; 600 Civic Center Dr) The much-loved Red Wings play pro ice hockey at this arena where, if you can wrangle tickets, you might witness the strange octopus-throwing custom.

Ford Field FOOTBALL

(www.detroitlions.com; 2000 Brush St) The struggling Lions toss the pigskin at this indoor stadium next to Comerica Park.

Palace of Auburn Hills BASKETBALL

(www.nba.com/pistons; 5 Championship Dr) The Palace hosts the Pistons pro basketball team. It's about 30 miles northwest of downtown; take I-75 to exit 81.

🛍 Shopping

Pure Detroit SOUVENIRS

(www.puredetroit.com; 500 Griswold St; ⊙10:30am-5:30pm Mon-Sat) Local artists create stylish products for Pure Detroit that celebrate the city's fast-cars-and-rock-music culture. Pick up handbags made from recycled seatbelts, groovy hoodies and local Pewabic pottery. Located in the landmark, mosaic-strewn Guardian Building (worth a peek in its own right).

People's Records MUSIC

(3161 Woodward Ave; ⊙10am-6pm Mon-Sat) Calling all crate-diggers: DJ-owned People's Records is your vinyl Valhalla. Used 45s are the specialty, with more than 80,000 jazz, soul and R & B titles filling bins.

John King Books BOOKS

(www.rarebooklink.com; 901 W Lafayette Blvd; ⊙9:30am-5:30pm Mon-Sat) Set aside some time to browse this insanely massive, musty warren of secondhand books.

ℹ Information

The area between the sports arenas north to around Willis Rd is pretty deserted and best avoided on foot come nighttime.

Emergency & Medical Services

Detroit Receiving Hospital (☑313-745-3000; 4201 St Antoine St)

Internet Access

You'll find free wi-fi in many cafes and bars, as well as the Renaissance Center lobby.

Media

Between the Lines (www.pridesource.com) Free, weekly gay and lesbian paper.

Detroit Free Press (www.freep.com) Daily.

Detroit News (www.detnews.com) Daily.

Metro Times (www.metrotimes.com) Free alternative weekly that is the best guide to the entertainment scene.

Real Detroit Weekly (www.realdetroitweekly. com) Another free weekly for entertainment listings.

Tourist Information

Detroit Convention & Visitors Bureau (☎800-338-7648; www.visitdetroit.com)

Websites

DetroitYES (www.detroityes.com) Images organized as 'tours' reveal the city's soul.

Forgotten Detroit (www.forgottendetroit.com) A website devoted to Detroit's 'ruins' (ie decaying buildings).

Model D (www.modelmedia.com) Weekly e-zine about local developments and food/ entertainment options, broken down by neighborhood.

❶ Getting There & Around

Detroit Metro Airport (DTW; www.metroair port.com), a Delta Airlines hub, is about 20 miles southwest of Detroit. Transport options from the airport to the city are few: you can take a cab for about $45; or you can take the 125 SMART bus ($2), but it takes one to 1½ hours to get downtown.

Greyhound (☎313-961-8005; 1001 Howard St) runs to various cities in Michigan and beyond. **Megabus** (www.megabus.com/us) runs to/from Chicago (5½ hours) daily; departures are from downtown (corner of Cass and Michigan) and Wayne State University (corner off Cass and Warren Aves).

Amtrak (☎313-873-3442; 11 W Baltimore Ave) trains go thrice daily to Chicago (5½ hours). You can also head east – to New York (16½ hours) or destinations en route – but you'll first be bused to Toledo.

Transit Windsor (☎519-944-4111; www.city windsor.ca/001209.asp) operates the Tunnel Bus to Windsor, Canada. It costs $3.75 (American or Canadian) and departs by Mariner's Church (corner of Randolph St and Jefferson Ave) near the Detroit-Windsor Tunnel entrance, as well as other spots downtown. Bring your passport.

For information on the People Mover city-rail line, see p550.

For taxi service, call **Checker Cab** (☎313-963-7000).

Around Detroit

Stunning Americana and good eatin' lie just down the road from Detroit.

DEARBORN

Dearborn is 10 miles west of downtown Detroit and home to two of the USA's finest museums. The indoor **Henry Ford Museum** (☎313-982-6001; www.thehenryford.org; 20900 Oakwood Blvd; adult/child $15/11; ☉9:30am-5pm) contains a fascinating wealth of American culture, such as the chair Lincoln was sitting in when he was assassinated, the presidential limo in which Kennedy was killed, the hot-dog-shaped Oscar Mayer Wienermobile (photo op!) and the bus on which Rosa Parks refused to give up her seat. Don't worry: you'll get your vintage car fix here too. Parking is $5. The adjacent, outdoor **Greenfield Village** (adult/child $22/16; ☉9:30am-5pm daily mid-Apr–Oct, 9:30am-5pm Fri-Sun Nov & Dec) features historic buildings shipped in from all over the country, reconstructed and restored, such as Thomas Edison's laboratory from Menlo Park and the Wright Brothers' airplane workshop. Plus you can add on the **Rouge Factory Tour** (adult/child $15/11; ☉9:30am-3pm Mon-Sat) and see F-150 trucks roll off the assembly line where Ford first perfected his self-sufficient, mass-production techniques.

The three attractions are separate, but you can get a **combination ticket** (adult/child $32/24) for Henry Ford and Greenfield Village. Plan on at least one very full day at the complex.

Dearborn has the nation's greatest concentration of people of Arab descent, so it's no surprise that the **Arab American National Museum** (☎313-582-2266; www. arabamericanmuseum.org; 13624 Michigan Ave; adult/child $6/3; ☉10am-6pm Wed-Sat, noon-5pm Sun) popped up here. It's a noble concept, located in a pretty, bright-tiled building, but it's not terribly exciting unless actor Jamie Farr's *M*A*S*H* TV-show script wows you. The thousand-and-one Arabian eateries lining Michigan Ave provide a more engaging feel for the culture. Cavernous **La Pita** (www. lapitadearborn.com; 22681 Newman St; sandwiches $4-5, mains $10-19; ☉10am-11pm Mon-Sat, 11am-10pm Sun) is a classic; it's a block south of Michigan Ave, tucked into one of the many strip malls along the road.

ANN ARBOR

Forty-odd miles west of Detroit, liberal and bookish Ann Arbor is home to the Univer-

More than sand dunes, beaches and Mackinac Island fudge, Michigan is synonymous with cars. While the connection hasn't been so positive in recent years, the state commemorates its glory days via several auto museums. The following fleets are within a few hours' drive from the Motor City.

Henry Ford Museum (p554) This Dearborn museum is loaded with vintage cars, including the first one Henry Ford ever built. In adjacent Greenfield Village you can ride in a Model T that rolled off the assembly line in 1923.

Automotive Hall of Fame (☏313-240-4000; www.automotivehalloffame.org; 21400 Oakwood Blvd, Dearborn; adult/child $8/4; ☺9am-5pm Wed-Sun) Next door to the Henry Ford Museum, the interactive Auto Hall focuses on the people behind famed cars, such as Mr Ferdinand Porsche and Mr Soichiro Honda.

Walter P Chrysler Museum (☏248-944-0001; www.chryslerheritage.com; 1 Chrysler Dr, Auburn Hills; adult/child $8/4; ☺10am-5pm Tue-Sat, noon-5pm Sun) This museum at Chrysler's headquarters (take exit 78 off I-75) has 70 beauties on display, including rare Dodge, DeSoto, Nash and Hudson models.

Gilmore Car Museum (☏269-671-5089; www.gilmorecarmuseum.org; 6865 Hickory Rd, Hickory Corners; adult/child $10/8; ☺9am-5pm Mon-Fri, to 6pm Sat & Sun, closed Nov-Apr) North of Kalamazoo along Hwy 43, this museum complex offers 22 barns filled with 120 vintage autos, including 15 Rolls Royces dating back to a 1910 Silver Ghost.

RE Olds Transportation Museum (☏517-372-0529; www.reoldsmuseum.org; 240 Museum Dr, Lansing; adult/child $5/3; ☺10am-5pm Tue-Sat year-round, noon-5pm Sun Apr-Oct) Twenty vintage cars sit in the old Lansing City Bus Garage, including the first Oldsmobile, which was built in 1897.

sity of Michigan. The walkable downtown, which abuts the campus, is loaded with free-trade coffee shops, bookstores, brewpubs and independent record stores. It's also a mecca for chowhounds; follow the drool trail toward anything named 'Zingerman's.'

◉ Sights & Activities

FREE **University of Michigan Museum of Art**   MUSEUM
(☏734-764-0395; www.umma.umich.edu; 525 S State St; ☺10am-5pm Tue-Sat, noon-5pm Sun) The campus' big, bold, massively expanded art museum impresses with its collections of Asian ceramics, Tiffany glass and German expressionist works.

Ann Arbor Farmers Market   MARKET
(www.a2gov.org/market; 315 Detroit St; ☺7am-3pm Wed & Sat May-Dec, Sat only Jan-Apr) Given the surrounding bounty of orchards and farms, it's no surprise this place is stuffed to the rafters with everything from spicy pickles to cider to mushroom-growing kits; located downtown near Zingerman's Deli.

Zingerman's Bakehouse   COOKING COURSE
(www.bakewithzing.com; 3723 Plaza Dr) Part of Zingerman's epicurean empire, the Bakehouse offers popular 'bake-cations,' from two-hour cookie-making classes to week-long pastry courses.

✖ Eating & Drinking

TOP CHOICE **Zingerman's Roadhouse** AMERICAN **$$**
(☏734-663-3663; www.zingermansroadhouse.com; 2501 Jackson Ave; burgers $12-15, mains $17-27; ☺7am-10pm Mon-Thu, to 11pm Fri, 9am-11pm Sat, 9am-9pm Sun) Two words: doughnut sundae. The bourbon-caramel-sauced dessert is pure genius, as are the traditional American dishes like Carolina grits, Iowa pork chops and Massachusetts oysters using sustainably produced ingredients. It's 2 miles west of downtown.

Zingerman's Delicatessen   DELI **$$**
(☏734-663-3354; www.zingermansdeli.com; 422 Detroit St; sandwiches $10-16; ☺7am-10pm) The shop that launched the foodie frenzy, Z's deli piles local, organic and specialty ingredients onto towering sandwiches in a downtown location.

Arbor Brewing Company   BREWERY
(www.arborbrewing.com; 114 E Washington St) Swig handcrafted beer, like the crisp Sacred Cow IPA.

☆ Entertainment

If you happen to arrive on a fall weekend and wonder why 110,000 people – the size of Ann Arbor's entire population, more or less – are crowding into the school's stadium, the answer is football. Tickets are nearly impossible to purchase, especially when nemesis Ohio State is in town. You can try by contacting the **U of M Ticket Office** (☎734-764-0247; www.mgoblue.com/ticketoffice).

Blind Pig   LIVE MUSIC
(www.blindpigmusic.com; 208 S 1st St) Everyone from John Lennon to Nirvana to the Circle Jerks has rocked the storied stage.

Ark   LIVE MUSIC
(www.a2ark.org; 316 S Main St) The Ark hosts acoustic and folk-oriented tunesmiths.

❶ Information

There are several B&Bs within walking distance of downtown. Hotels tend to be about 5 miles out, with several clustered south on State St. The CVB website has contact details.

Ann Arbor Convention & Visitors Bureau (www.annarbor.org)

Lansing & Central Michigan

Michigan's heartland, plunked in the center of the Lower Peninsula, alternates between fertile farms and highway-crossed urban areas.

LANSING

Smallish Lansing is the state capital; a few miles east lies East Lansing, home of Michigan State University. The **Greater Lansing CVB** (www.lansing.org) has information on both.

Between Lansing's downtown and the university is the **River Trail** (www.lansingrivertrail.org), which extends 8-plus miles along the shores of Michigan's longest river, the Grand. The paved path is popular with cyclists, joggers and inline skaters, and links a number of attractions, including a children's museum, zoo and fish ladder.

Downtown, the **Michigan Historical Museum** (☎517-373-3559; www.michigan.gov/museum; 702 W Kalamazoo St; admission free; ⊙9am-4:30pm Mon-Fri, 10am-4pm Sat, 1-5pm Sun) features 26 permanent galleries, including a replica UP copper mine you can walk through. The **RE Olds Transportation Museum** (see the boxed text, p555) will please car buffs.

Lansing's downtown hotels feed off politicians and lobbyists, so they're fairly expensive. It's best to head to East Lansing's **Wild Goose Inn** (☎517-333-3334; www.wildgooseinn.com; 512 Albert St; r incl breakfast $139-159; ❄🛜), a six-room B&B one block from Michigan State's campus. All rooms have fireplaces and most have Jacuzzis.

Kewpee's (www.kewpees.com; 118 S Washington Sq; mains $3-7; ⊙8am-6pm Mon-Fri, 11am-2pm Sat) has been feeding folks olive burgers and crisp onion rings by the capitol for more than 85 years. For breakfast, **Golden Harvest** (☎517-485-3663; 1625 Turner St; mains $7-9; ⊙7am-2:30pm Mon-Fri, from 8am Sat & Sun) is a loud, punk-rock-meets-hippie diner serving the sausage-and-French-toast Bubba Sandwich and hearty omelets; cash only. Abundant restaurants, pubs and nightclubs also fill Michigan State's northern campus area.

GRAND RAPIDS

The second-largest city in Michigan, Grand Rapids is known for office-furniture manufacturing, a conservative Dutch Reform attitude and the fact that it's only 30 miles from Lake Michigan's Gold Coast. The **Grand Rapids CVB** (www.visitgrandrapids.org) provides maps, coupons and any other information you'll need.

The downtown Gerald R Ford Museum (☎616-254-0400; www.fordlibrarymuseum.gov; 303 Pearl St NW; adult/child $7/3; ⊙9am-5pm) is dedicated to the only Michigander president (he was born with a different name in Nebraska). Ford stepped into the Oval Office after Richard Nixon and his vice president, Spiro Agnew, resigned in disgrace. It's an intriguing period in US history, and the museum does an excellent job of covering it, down to displaying the burglary tools used in the Watergate break-in. Ford died in 2006 and is buried on the museum's grounds.

The 118-acre **Frederik Meijer Gardens** (☎616-957-1580; www.meijergardens.org; 1000 E Beltline NE; adult/child $12/6; ⊙9am-5pm Mon-Sat, to 9pm Tue, 11am-5pm Sun) features impressive blooms and sculptures by Auguste Rodin, Henry Moore and others. It is 5 miles east of downtown via I-196.

If you're whizzing through Grand Rapids with time for only one stop, make it **Founders Brewing Company** (www.foundersbrewing.com; 235 Grandville Ave SW; sandwiches $6-8; ⊙11am-2am Mon-Sat, 3pm-2am Sun; 🅿). The ruby-tinged Dirty Bastard Ale is good swillin', and there's meaty (or vegetable-y, for vegetarians) deli sandwiches to soak it up.

Lake Michigan Shore

They don't call it the Gold Coast for nothing. Michigan's 300-mile western shoreline features seemingly endless stretches of beaches, dunes, wineries, orchards and B&B-filled towns that boom during the summer – and shiver during the snow-packed winter. Note all state parks listed here take campsite reservations (☎800-447-2757; www.midnrreservations.com; fee $8) and require a vehicle permit (day/year $8/29), unless specified otherwise.

HARBOR COUNTRY

Harbor Country refers to a group of eight small, lake-hugging towns just over the Michigan border (an easy day trip from Chicago). Yep, they've got your requisite beaches, wineries and antique shops; they've got a couple of big surprises too. The Harbor Country Chamber of Commerce (www.harborcountry.org) has the basics.

First up, surfing. Believe it, people: you can surf Lake Michigan, and the VW-bus-driving dudes at Third Coast Surf Shop (☎269-932-4575; www.thirdcoastsurfshop.com; 22 S Smith St; ☉10am-6pm mid-May–mid-Sep) will show you how. They provide wetsuits and boards for surfing, skim boarding and paddle boarding (rentals per day $20 to $35). For novices, they offer 1½-hour lessons (incl equipment $55-75) right on the public beach June through mid-September. The surf shop is in New Buffalo, Harbor Country's biggest town.

Three Oaks is the only Harbor community that's inland (6 miles in, via US 12). Here Green Acres meets Greenwich Village in a funky farm-and-arts blend. By day, rent bikes at Dewey Cannon Trading Company (☎269-756-3361; www.applecidercentury.com; 3 Dewey Cannon Ave; bike per day $15; ☉10am-4pm Sun-Fri, to 9pm Sat) and cycle lightly used rural roads past orchards and wineries. By eve, catch a provocative play or art-house flick at Three Oaks' theaters.

Hungry? Get a wax paper-wrapped cheeseburger, spicy curly fries and cold beer at Redamak's (www.redamaks.com; 616 E Buffalo St; burgers $5-10; ☉noon-10:30pm Mar-Oct) in New Buffalo.

SAUGATUCK & DOUGLAS

Saugatuck is one of the Gold Coast's most popular resort areas, known for its strong arts community, numerous B&Bs and gay-

A dozen wineries cluster between New Buffalo and Saugatuck. The Lake Michigan Shore Wine Trail (www.lakemichiganshorewinetrail.com) provides a downloadable map of vineyards and tasting rooms. Most are signposted off the highway.

friendly vibe. Douglas is its twin city a mile or so south, and they've pretty much sprawled into one. The Saugatuck/Douglas CVB (www.saugatuck.com) provides maps and more.

The best thing to do in Saugatuck is also the most affordable. Jump aboard the clackety Saugatuck Chain Ferry (foot of Mary St; one way $1; ☉9am-9pm late May-early Sep) and the operator will pull you across the Kalamazoo River. On the other side, walk to the dock's left and soon you'll come to Mt Baldhead, a 200ft-high sand dune. Huff up the stairs to see the grand view, and then race down the north side to beautiful Oval Beach.

Galleries and shops proliferate downtown on Water and Butler Sts. Antiquing prevails on the Blue Star Hwy running south for 20 miles. Blueberry U-pick farms share this stretch of road and make a juicy stop, too.

Several frilly B&Bs are tucked into the Saugatuck's century-old Victorian homes, with most ranging from $125 to $300 per night. Try the Bayside Inn (☎269-857-4321; www.baysideinn.net; 618 Water St; r incl breakfast $150-280; ☏), a 10-room former boathouse on Saugatuck's waterfront, or the retro-cool Pines Motorlodge (☎269-857-5211; www.thepinesmotorlodge.com; 56 Blue Star Hwy; r incl breakfast $129-189; ☏), with rooms amid the firs in Douglas.

For eats, Wicks Park Bar & Grill (☎269-857-2888; www.wickspark.com; 449 Water St; mains $11-25; ☉11:30am-10pm), by the chain ferry, gets props for its lake perch and live music. Locals like to hang out and sip the house-made suds at Saugatuck Brewing Company (www.saugatuckbrewing.com; 2948 Blue Star Hwy; ☉11am-11pm Sun-Thu, to midnight Fri & Sat). For dessert, buy a bulging slice at Crane's Pie Pantry (☎269-561-2297; www.cranespiepantry.com; 6054 124th Ave; ☉9am-8pm Mon-Sat, 11am-8pm Sun May-Oct, reduced hr Nov-Apr), or pick apples and peaches in the surrounding orchards. Crane's is in Fennville, 3 miles south on the Blue Star Hwy, then 4 miles inland on Hwy 89.

HOLLAND

Holland (www.holland.org) lies 11 miles north of Saugatuck via US 31. Yes, there's plenty of kitschy tulips, windmills and clogs. But there's also an excellent brewery and eco-hotel hiding in town. They sit a block apart, making it way too easy to raise another Dragon's Milk ale at the New Holland Brewing Company Pub (www.newhollandbrew.com; 66 E 8th St; ⊙from 11am) before stumbling into your bamboo sheets at the Gold-LEED-certified City Flats Hotel (☏616-796-2100; www.cityflatshotel.com; 61 E 7th St; r $119-219; 🛜).

MUSKEGON & LUDINGTON

These towns are jump-off points for the two ferries that sail across the lake, providing a shortcut between Michigan and Wisconsin. The Lake Express (☏866-914-1010; www.lake-express.com; ⊙May-Oct) crosses between Muskegon and Milwaukee (one way adult/child/car $95/28/101, 2½ hours). The older SS Badger (☏888-337-7948; www.ssbadger.com; ⊙mid-May–mid-Oct) crosses from Ludington to Manitowoc (one way adult/child/car $70/24/59, four hours).

The towns themselves aren't much, but the Muskegon Luge & Sports Complex (☏231-744-9629; www.msports.org; 442 Scenic Dr) kicks butt with its full-on luge track (usable during summer, too) and cross-country ski trails. And lakeside Ludington State Park (☏231-843-8671; tent & RV sites $16-29, cabins $45; ⊙year-round), beyond the city limits on M-116, is one of Michigan's largest and most popular playlots. It has a top-notch trail system, a renovated lighthouse to visit (or live in, as a volunteer lighthouse keeper) and miles of beach.

ℹ **HIKING TRAIL MAPS**

Plot out your walk in the woods with Michigan Trail Maps (www.michigan trailmaps.com), a free resource with more than 100 trail guides. Search by county, trail length or activity (ie birding), then download and print the high-quality maps as pdfs. So far the trails covered are on the Lower Peninsula, but Upper Peninsula treks are reportedly in the works.

SLEEPING BEAR DUNES NATIONAL LAKESHORE

This national park stretches from north of Frankfort to just before Leland, on the Leelanau Peninsula. Stop at the park's visitor center (☏231-326-5134; www.nps.gov/slbe; 9922 Front St; ⊙8:30am-6pm Jun-Aug, to 4pm Sep-May) in Empire for information, trail maps and vehicle entry permits (week/annual $10/20).

Attractions include the famous dune climb along Hwy 109, where you trudge up the 200ft-high dune and then run or roll down. Gluttons for leg-muscle punishment can keep slogging all the way to Lake Michigan, a strenuous 1½-hour trek one way; bring water. There are also plenty of easier hikes; ask at the visitor center. Short on time or stamina? Take the 7-mile, one-lane, picnic-grove-studded Pierce Stocking Scenic Drive, perhaps the best way to absorb the stunning lake vistas.

After you leave the park, swing into little Leland (www.lelandmi.com). Grab a bite at a waterfront restaurant downtown, and poke around atmospheric Fishtown with its weather-beaten shacks-cum-shops. Boats depart from here for the Manitou Islands (see the boxed text, p559).

TRAVERSE CITY

Michigan's 'cherry capital' is the largest city in the northern half of the Lower Peninsula. It's got a bit of urban sprawl, but it's still a happenin' base from which to see the Sleeping Bear Dunes, Mission Peninsula wineries, U-pick orchards and other area attractions.

Stop at the downtown visitor center (☏231-947-1120; www.traversecity.com; 101 W Grandview Pkwy; ⊙9am-5pm Mon-Fri, 9am-3pm Sat) for maps and the do-it-yourself foodie tour brochure (also available online; click 'Things to Do' on the website). Or see what Learn Great Foods (☏866-240-1650; www.learngreatfoods.com; tours $50-125) has on its guided tour schedule; there's usually a weekly jaunt to farms and fisheries on the Leelanau Peninsula, including alfresco dinner among the greens.

Road tripping out to the wineries is a must. Head north from Traverse City on Hwy 37 for 20 miles to the end of the grape- and cherry-planted Old Mission Peninsula. You'll be spoiled for choice: Chateau Grand Traverse (www.cgtwines.com; ⊙10am-7pm Mon-Sat, to 6pm Sun) and Chateau Chantal (www.chateauchantal.com; ⊙11am-8pm Mon-Sat, to 5pm Sun) pour crowd-pleasing Chardonnay and Pinot Noir. Peninsula Cellars (www.peninsulacellars.com; ⊙10am-6pm), in an old schoolhouse, makes fine whites and is often less crowded. Whatever bottle you buy, take it out to Lighthouse Park beach, at the peninsula's tip, and enjoy it with the waves chilling your toes. The wineries stay open year-round, though they reduce their hours in winter.

The town goes all Hollywood during the **Traverse City Film Festival** (www.traversecityfilmfest.org; ⊙late Jul), when founder (and native Michigander) Michael Moore comes in and unspools a six-day slate of documentaries, international flicks and 'just great movies.'

Dozens of beaches, resorts, motels and water sports operators line US 31 around Traverse City. Lodgings are often full – and more expensive – during weekends; the visitor center website has contact details. Most resorts overlooking the bay cost $150 to $250 per night. The aforementioned Chantal and Grand Traverse wineries also double as B&Bs and fit into this price range.

Guests can rent jet skis and enjoy nightly bonfires at **Park Shore Resort** (☎877-349-8898; www.parkshoreresort.com; 1401 US 31 N; r incl breakfast weekday/weekend from $150/190; ❄☎☼). Motels on the other side of US 31 (away from the water) are more moderately priced, such as **Mitchell Creek Inn** (☎231-947-9330; www.mitchellcreek.com; 894 Munson Ave; r/cottages from $60/125; ☎), near the state park beach.

After a day of fun in the sun, refresh with sandwiches at gastronome favorite **Folgarelli's** (☎231-941-7651; www.folgarellis.net; 424 W Front St; sandwiches $6-9; ⊙9:30am-6:30pm Mon-Fri, to 5:30pm Sat, 11am-4pm Sun) and Belgian and Michigan craft beers at **7 Monks Taproom** (www.7monkstap.com; 128 S Union St).

CHARLEVOIX & PETOSKEY

These two towns hold several Hemingway sights. They're also where Michigan's upper-crusters maintain summer homes. The downtown areas of both places have gourmet restaurants and high-class shops, and the marinas are filled with yachts.

In Petoskey, **Stafford's Perry Hotel** (☎231-347-4000; www.staffords.com; Bay at Lewis St; r $129-259; ❄@☎) is a grand historic place in which to stay. **Petoskey State Park** (☎231-347-2311; 2475 Hwy 119; tent & RV sites $27-29; ⊙year-round) is north along Hwy 119 and has a beautiful beach. Look for indigenous Petoskey stones, which are honeycomb-patterned fragments of ancient coral. From

MANITOU ISLANDS

If you're looking for a wilderness adventure, the Manitou Islands – part of Sleeping Bear Dunes National Lakeshore – deliver. **Manitou Island Transit** (☎231-256-9061; www.manitoutransit.com) can help plan overnight camping trips on North Manitou, or day trips to South Manitou. Kayaking and hiking are popular activities, especially the 7-mile trek to the Valley of the Giants, a mystical stand of cedar trees on South Manitou. **Ferries** (round-trip adult/child $32/18, 1½hr) sail from Leland two to seven times per week from May to mid-October.

here, Hwy 119 – aka the **Tunnel of Trees scenic route** – dips and curves through thick forest as it rolls north along a sublime bluff, en route to the Straits of Mackinac.

Straits of Mackinac

This region, between the Upper and Lower Peninsulas, features a long history of forts and fudge shops. Car-free Mackinac Island is Michigan's premier tourist draw.

One of the most spectacular sights in the area is the 5-mile-long **Mackinac Bridge** (known locally as 'Big Mac'), which spans the Straits of Mackinac. The $3.50 toll is worth every penny as the views from the bridge, which include two Great Lakes, two peninsulas and hundreds of islands, are second to none in Michigan.

And remember: despite the spelling, it's pronounced *mac*-in-aw.

MACKINAW CITY

At the south end of Mackinac Bridge, bordering I-75, is touristy Mackinaw City. It serves mainly as a jump-off point to Mackinac Island, but it does have a couple of interesting sights.

Next to the bridge (its visitor center is actually beneath the bridge) is **Colonial Michilimackinac** (☎231-436-5564; www.mackinacparks.com; adult/child $10.50/6.50; ⊙9:30am-7pm Jun-Aug, to 5pm May & Sep–mid-Oct), a National Historic Landmark that features a reconstructed stockade first built in 1715 by the French. Some 3 miles southeast of the city on US 23 is **Historic Mill Creek** (☎231-436-4226; www.mackinacparks.com; adult/child

HEMINGWAY'S HAUNTS

A number of writers have ties to northwest Michigan, but none are as famous as Ernest Hemingway, who spent the summers of his youth at his family's cottage on Walloon Lake. Hemingway buffs often tour the area to view the places that made their way into his writing.

First up: Horton Bay. As you head north on US 31, past yacht-filled Charlevoix, look for Boyne City Rd veering off to the east. It skirts Lake Charlevoix and eventually arrives at the **Horton Bay General Store** (231-582-7827; www.hortonbaygeneralstore.com; 05115 Boyne City Rd; late May–early Sep). Hemingway fans will recognize the building, with its 'high false front,' from his short story 'Up in Michigan.' For the mother lode of Hemingway books and souvenirs, pop into the **Red Fox Inn Bookstore** (05156 Boyne City Rd; late May–early Sep) next door.

Further up Hwy 31 in Petoskey, you can see the Hemingway collection at the **Little Traverse History Museum** (231-347-2620; www.petoskeymuseum.org; 100 Depot Ct; adult/child $2/1; 10am-4pm Mon-Fri, 1-4pm Sat Jun–mid-Oct), including rare first-edition books that the author autographed for a friend when he visited in 1947. Afterward, toss back a drink at **City Park Grill** (231-347-0101; www.cityparkgrill.com; 432 E Lake St; 11:30am-11pm Mon-Fri, to midnight Sat & Sun), where Hemingway was a regular.

The **Michigan Hemingway Society** (www.michiganhemingwaysociety.org) provides further information for self-guided tours. It also hosts the weekend-long **Hemingway festival** (mid-Oct).

$8/4.75; 9am-5:30pm Jun-Aug, to 4:30pm May & Sep–mid-Oct), which has an 18th-century sawmill, historic displays and nature trails. A combination ticket for both sights, along with Fort Mackinac (p561), is available at a discount.

If you can't find lodging on Mackinac Island – which should be your first choice – motels line I-75 and US 23 in Mackinaw City. Most cost $100-plus per night. Try **Days Inn** (231-436-8961; www.daysinnbridgeview.com; 206 N Nicolet St; r incl breakfast $115-170;).

ST IGNACE

At the north end of Mackinac Bridge is St Ignace, the other departure point for Mackinac Island and the second-oldest settlement in Michigan – Père Jacques Marquette founded a mission here in 1671. As soon as you've paid your bridge toll, you'll pass a huge **visitor center** (906-643-6979; I-75N; 8am-6pm summer, 9am-5pm rest of year) which has racks of statewide information.

MACKINAC ISLAND

From either Mackinaw City or St Ignace you can catch a ferry to Mackinac Island, Michigan's top crowd-puller. The island's location in the straits between Lake Michigan and Lake Huron made it a prized port in the North American fur trade, and a site the British and Americans battled over many times.

The most important date on this 3.8-sq-mile island was 1898 – the year cars were banned in order to encourage tourism. Today all travel is by horse or bicycle; even the police use bikes to patrol the town. The crowds of tourists – called Fudgies by the islanders – can be crushing at times, particularly during summer weekends. But when the last ferry leaves in the evening and clears out the day-trippers, Mackinac's real charm emerges and you drift back into another, slower era.

The **visitor center** (800-454-5227; www.mackinacisland.org; Main St; 9am-5pm), by the Arnold Line ferry dock, has maps for hiking and cycling. Eighty percent of the island is state parkland. Not much stays open between November and April.

Sights & Activities

Edging the island's shoreline is Hwy 185, the only Michigan highway that doesn't permit cars. The best way to view the incredible scenery along this 8-mile road is by bicycle; bring your own or rent one in town for $8 per hour at one of the many businesses. You can loop around the flat road in about an hour.

The two best attractions – **Arch Rock** (a huge limestone arch that sits 150ft above Lake Huron) and **Fort Holmes** (the island's other fort) – are both free. You can also ride past the **Grand Hotel**, which boasts a porch stretching halfway to Detroit. Unfortunately, if you're not staying at the Grand (minimum $235 per night per person), it costs $10 to stroll its long porch. Best to admire from afar.

Fort Mackinac   HISTORIC SITE

(☎906-847-3328; www.mackinacparks.com; adult/child $10.50/6.50; ⏰9:30am-6pm Jun-Aug, 9:30am-4:30pm May & Sep-mid-Oct; ♿) Fort Mackinac sits atop limestone cliffs near downtown. Built by the British in 1780, it's one of the best-preserved military forts in the country. Costumed interpreters and cannon and rifle firings (every half-hour) entertain the kids. Stop into the tearoom for a bite and million-dollar view of downtown and the Straits of Mackinac from the outdoor tables.

The fort admission price also allows you entry to five other museums in town along Market St, including the Dr Beaumont Museum (where the doctor performed his famous digestive tract experiments) and Benjamin Blacksmith Shop. The **Mackinac Art Museum** (adult/child $5/3.50), housing Native American and other arts by the fort, is the newest member of the fold.

🛏 Sleeping

Rooms are booked far in advance during summer weekends; July to mid-August is peak season. The visitor center website has lodging contacts. Camping is not permitted anywhere on the island.

Most hotels and B&Bs charge at least $180 for two people. Exceptions (all are walkable from downtown) include:

Bogan Lane Inn   B&B $$

(☎906-847-3439; www.boganlaneinn.com; Bogan Lane; r incl breakfast $85-125; ⏰year-round; 🐾) Four rooms, shared bath.

Cloghaun B&B   B&B $$

(☎906-847-3885; www.cloghaun.com; Market St; r incl breakfast $110-195; ⏰mid-May-late Oct; 🐾🛜) Eleven rooms, some with shared bath.

Hart's B&B   B&B $$

(☎906-847-3854; www.hartsmackinac.com; Market St; r incl breakfast $150-180; ⏰mid-May-late Oct; ❄🐾) Eight rooms, all with private bath.

✖ Eating & Drinking

Fudge shops are the island's best-known eateries; resistance is futile when they use fans to blow the aroma out onto Huron St. Hamburger and sandwich shops abound downtown.

JL Beanery Coffeehouse   CAFE $

(☎906-847-6533; Huron St; mains $6-13; ⏰7am-7pm; 🛜) Read the newspaper, sip a steaming cup of joe and gaze at the lake at this waterside cafe. It serves dandy breakfasts, sandwiches and soups.

Horn's Bar   BURGERS, MEXICAN $$

(☎906-847-6154; www.hornsbar.com; Main St; mains $10-19; ⏰11am-2am) Horn's saloon serves American burgers and south-of-the-border fare, and there's live entertainment nightly.

Village Inn   AMERICAN $$$

(☎906-847-3542; www.viofmackinac.com; Hoban St; mains $18-23; ⏰8am-10pm) Planked whitefish, pan-fried perch and other fresh-from-the-lake fish, meat and pasta dishes stuff diners at this year-round local hangout with a bar and outdoor seating.

❶ Getting There & Around

Three ferry companies – **Arnold Line** (☎800-542-8528; www.arnoldline.com), **Shepler's** (☎800-828-6157; www.sheplersferry.com) and **Star Line** (☎800-638-9892; www.mackinacferry.com) – operate out of Mackinaw City and St Ignace, and charge the same rates: round-trip adult/child/bicycle $22/11/8. Book online and you'll save a few bucks. The ferries run several times daily from May to October; Arnold Line runs longer, weather permitting. The trip takes about 15 minutes, and once on the island, horse-drawn cabs will take you anywhere, or rent a bicycle.

Upper Peninsula

Rugged and isolated, with hardwood forests blanketing 90% of its land, the Upper Peninsula (UP) is a Midwest highlight. Only 45 miles of interstate highway slice through the trees, punctuated by a handful of cities, of which Marquette (population 20,000) is the largest. Between the small towns lie miles of undeveloped shoreline on Lakes Huron, Michigan and Superior; scenic two-lane roads; and pasties, the local meat-and-vegetable pot pies brought over by Cornish miners 150 years ago.

You'll find it's a different world up north. Residents of the UP, aka 'Yoopers,' consider themselves distinct from the rest of the state – they've even threatened to secede in the past.

SAULT STE MARIE & TAHQUAMENON FALLS

Founded in 1668, Sault Ste Marie (Sault is pronounced 'soo') is Michigan's oldest city and the third oldest in the USA. The town is best known for its locks that raise and lower 1000ft-long freighters between the different lake levels. **Soo Locks Park & Visitors Center** (admission free; ⊙9am-9pm mid-May–mid-Oct) is on Portage Ave downtown (take exit 394 off I-75 and go left). It features displays, videos and observation decks from which you can watch the boats leap 21ft from Lake Superior to Lake Huron. Pubs and cafes line Portage Ave. The **Sault CVB** (www.saultstemarie.com) has all the lowdown.

An hour's drive west of Sault Ste Marie, via Hwy 28 and Hwy 123, is eastern UP's top attraction: lovely **Tahquamenon Falls**, with tea-colored waters tinted so by upstream hemlock leaves. The Upper Falls in **Tahquamenon Falls State Park** (☏906-492-3415; per vehicle $8), 200ft across with a 50ft drop, wow onlookers – including Henry Wadsworth Longfellow, who mentioned them in his *Song of Hiawatha*. The Lower Falls are a series of small cascades that swirl around an island; many visitors rent a rowboat and paddle out to it. The large state park also has camping (tent & RV sites $16 to $23), great hiking and – bonus – a brewpub near the park entrance.

North of the park, beyond the little town of Paradise, is the fascinating Great Lakes Shipwreck Museum (☏888-492-3747; www.shipwreckmuseum.com; 18335 N Whitefish Point Rd; adult/child $13/9; ⊙10am-6pm May-Oct), whose intriguing displays include items trawled up from sunken ships. Dozens of vessels – including the *Edmund Fitzgerald* that Gordon Lightfoot crooned about – have sunk in the area's congested sea lanes and storm-tossed weather, earning it such nicknames as the 'Shipwreck Coast' and 'Graveyard of the Great Lakes.' The grounds also include a lighthouse President Lincoln commissioned and a bird observatory that 300 species fly by. To have the foggy place to yourself, spend the night at **Whitefish Point Light Station B&B** (☏888-492-3747; r $150; ⊙Apr–mid-Nov), which offers five rooms in the old Coast Guard crew quarters on-site.

PICTURED ROCKS NATIONAL LAKESHORE

Stretching along prime Lake Superior real estate, **Pictured Rocks National Lakeshore** (www.nps.gov/piro) is a series of wild cliffs and caves where blue and green minerals have streaked the red and yellow sandstone into a kaleidoscope of color. Rte 58 (Alger County Rd) spans the park for 52 slow miles from Grand Marais in the east to Munising in the west. Top sights (from east to west) include **Au Sable Point Lighthouse** (reached via a 3-mile round-trip walk beside shipwreck skeletons), agate-strewn **Twelvemile Beach**, hike-rich **Chapel Falls** and view-worthy **Miners Castle Overlook**.

Several boat tours launch from Munising. **Pictured Rock Cruises** (☏906-387-2379; www.picturedrocks.com; 100 W City Park Dr; 2½hr tours adult/child $35/10) departs from the city pier downtown and glides along the shore to Miners Castle. **Shipwreck Tours** (☏906-387-4477; www.shipwrecktours.com; 1204 Commercial St; 2hr tours adult/child $30/12) sails in glass-bottom boats to see sunken schooners.

Grand Island (www.grandislandmi.com), part of Hiawatha National Forest, is also a quick jaunt from Munising. Hop aboard the **Grand Island Ferry** (☏906-387-3503; round-trip adult/child $15/10; ⊙late May–mid-Oct) to get there and rent a mountain bike (per day $25) to zip around. There's also a ferry/bus tour package ($22). The ferry dock is on Hwy 28, which is about 4 miles west of Munising.

Munising has lots of motels, such as tidy **Alger Falls Motel** (☏906-387-3536; www.algerfallsmotel.com; E9427 Hwy 28; r $50-70; ❄️ 🛜). Falling Rock Cafe & Bookstore (☏906-387-3008; www.fallingrockcafe.com; 104 E Munising Ave; mains $5-9; ⊙9am-8pm Sun-Fri, to 10pm Sat; 🛜) provides sandwiches and live music.

Staying in wee Grand Marais, on the park's east side, is also recommended. Turn in at **Hilltop Cabins and Motel** (☏906-494-2331; www.hilltopcabins.net; N14176 Ellen St; r & cabins $75-150; 🛜) after a meal of whitefish sandwiches and brewskis at rustic **Lake Superior Brewing Company** (☏906-494-2337; N14283 Lake Ave; mains $7-13; ⊙noon-11pm).

MARQUETTE

From Munising, Hwy 28 heads west and hugs Lake Superior. This beautiful stretch of highway has lots of beaches, roadside parks and rest areas where you can pull over and enjoy the scenery. Within 45 miles you'll reach outdoorsy, oft-snowy Marquette.

Stop at the log-lodge **visitor center** (☏906-249-9066; www.marquettecountry.org; 2201 US 41; ⊙9am-5pm) as you enter the city for brochures on local hiking trails and waterfalls.

The easy **Sugarloaf Mountain Trail** and the harder, wildernesslike **Hogsback Mountain Trail** offer panoramic views. Both are reached from County Rd 550, just north

WHAT THE...?

Behold Big Gus, the world's largest chainsaw. And Big Ernie, the world's largest rifle. Kitsch runs rampant at **Da Yoopers Tourist Trap and Museum** (☑800-628-9978; www.dayoopers.com; admission free; ☉9am-7pm Mon-Sat, 11am-6pm Sun, with seasonal variations), 15 miles west of Marquette on Hwy 28/41, past Ishpeming. Browse the store for only-in-the-UP gifts, say, a polyester moose tie or beer-can wind chimes.

of Marquette. In the city, the high bluffs of **Presque Isle Park** make a great place to catch the sunset. The **Noquemanon Trail Network** (www.noquetrails.org) is highly recommended for mountain biking and cross-country skiing.

Marquette is the perfect place to stay put for a few days to explore the central UP. Budgeteers can bunk at **Value Host Motor Inn** (☑906-225-5000; www.valuehostmotorinn.com; 1101 US 41 W; r incl breakfast $55-65; ✷🛜) a few miles west of town. Downtown's **Landmark Inn** (☑906-228-2580; www.thelandmarkinn.com; 230 N Front St; r $139-229; ✷🛜) fills a historic lakefront building and has a couple of resident ghosts.

Sample the local meat-veggie pie specialty at **Jean Kay's Pasties & Subs** (www.jeankayspasties.com; 1635 Presque Isle Ave; items $4-6; ☉11am-9pm Mon-Fri, to 8pm Sat & Sun). In a quonset hut at Main St's foot, **Thill's Fish House** (☑906-226-9851; 250 E Main St; items $4-9; ☉8am-5:30pm Mon-Fri, to 4pm Sat) is Marquette's last commercial fishing operation, and it hauls in fat catches daily; try the smoked whitefish sausage. **UpFront and Company** (www.upfrontandcompany.com; 102 E Main St; mains $13-19; ☉11am-10pm Mon-Fri, 2-10pm Sat, closed Mon in winter) fires up the wood oven for pizzas, the taps for hearty beers and the amps for live music.

ISLE ROYALE NATIONAL PARK

Totally free of vehicles and roads, **Isle Royale National Park** (www.nps.gov/isro; fee per day $4; ☉mid-May-Oct), a 210-sq-mile island in Lake Superior, is certainly the place to go for peace and quiet. It gets fewer visitors in a year than Yellowstone National Park gets in a day, which means the packs of wolves and moose creeping through the forest are all yours.

The island is laced with 165 miles of hiking trails that connect dozens of campgrounds along Superior and inland lakes. You must be totally prepared for this wilderness adventure, with a tent, camping stove, sleeping bags, food and water filter. Otherwise, be a softie and bunk at the **Rock Harbor Lodge** (☑906-337-4993; www.isleroyaleresort.com; cottages $229-254; ☉late May-early Sep).

From the dock outside the **park headquarters** (800 E Lakeshore Dr) in Houghton, the **Ranger III** (☑906-482-0984) departs at 9am on Tuesday and Friday for the six-hour boat trip (round trip adult/child $120/40) to Rock Harbor, at the east end of the island. **Royale Air Service** (☑877-359-4753; www.royaleairservice.com) offers a quicker trip, flying from Houghton County Airport to Rock Harbor in 30 minutes (round trip $290). Or head 50 miles up the Keweenaw Peninsula to Copper Harbor (a beautiful drive) and jump on the **Isle Royale Queen** (☑906-289-4437; www.isleroyale.com) for the 8am three-hour crossing (round-trip adult/child $130/65). It usually runs daily during peak season from late July to mid-August. Bringing a kayak or canoe on the ferries costs an additional $40 to $50 round-trip, and ensure you make reservations well in advance. You can also access Isle Royale from Grand Portage, Minnesota (p587).

PORCUPINE MOUNTAINS WILDERNESS STATE PARK

Michigan's largest state park, with 90 miles of trails, is another UP winner, and it's a heck of a lot easier to reach than Isle Royale. 'The Porkies,' as they're called, are so rugged that loggers bypassed most of the range in the early 19th century, leaving the park with the largest tract of virgin forest between the Rocky Mountains and Adirondacks.

From Silver City, head west on Hwy 107 to reach the **Porcupine Mountains visitors center** (☑906-885-5275; www.porcupinemountains.com; 412 S Boundary Rd; ☉10am-6pm mid-May–mid-Oct), where you buy vehicle entry permits (per day/year $8/29) and backcountry permits (one to four people per night $14). Continue to the end of Hwy 107 and climb 300ft for the stunning view of **Lake of the Clouds**.

Winter is also a busy time at the Porkies, with downhill skiing (a 787ft vertical drop) and 26 miles of cross-country trails on offer; check with the **ski area** (☑906-289-4105; www.skitheporkies.com) for conditions and costs.

The park rents **rustic cabins** (☎906-885-5275; www.mi.gov/porkies; cabins $60) perfect for wilderness adventurers, as you have to hike in 1 to 4 miles, boil your own water and use a privy. **Sunshine Motel & Cabins** (☎906-884-2187; www.ontonagon.net/sun shinemotel; 24077 Hwy 64; r $60, cabins $66-104), 3 miles west of Ontonagon, provides another good base.

WISCONSIN

Wisconsin is cheesy and proud of it. The state pumps out 2.4 billion pounds of cheddar, Gouda and other smelly goodness – a quarter of America's hunks – from its cow-speckled farmland per year. Local license plates read 'The Dairy State' with udder dignity. Folks here even refer to themselves as 'cheeseheads' and emphasize it by wearing novelty foam rubber cheese-wedge hats for special occasions (most notably during Green Bay Packers football games).

So embrace the cheese thing, because there's a good chance you'll be here for a while. Wisconsin has heaps to offer: exploring the craggy cliffs and lighthouses of Door County, kayaking through sea caves at Apostle Islands National Lakeshore, cow chip throwing along US 12 and soaking up beer, art and festivals in Milwaukee and Madison.

❶ Information

Travel Green Wisconsin (www.travelgreenwis consin.com) Certifies businesses as ecofriendly by grading them on waste reduction, energy efficiency and seven other categories.

Wisconsin B&B Association (www.wbba.org)

Wisconsin Department of Tourism (☎800-432-8747; www.travelwisconsin.com) Produces loads of free guides on subjects like bird-watching, biking, golf and rustic roads; also a free app.

Wisconsin Highway Conditions (☎511; www.511wi.gov)

Wisconsin Milk Marketing Board (www.eatwisconsincheese.com) Provides a free statewide map of cheesemakers titled *A Traveler's Guide to America's Dairyland*.

Wisconsin State Park Information (☎608-266-2181; www.wiparks.net) Park entry requires a vehicle permit (per day/year $10/35). Campsites cost from $12 to $25; **reservations** (☎888-947-2757; www.wisconsinstateparks. reserveamerica.com; fee $10) accepted.

WISCONSIN FACTS

» **Nicknames** Badger State, America's Dairyland

» **Population** 5.7 million

» **Area** 65,500 sq miles

» **Capital city** Madison (population 223,400)

» **Other cities** Milwaukee (population 573,360)

» **Sales tax** 5%

» **Birthplace of** author Laura Ingalls Wilder (1867–1957), architect Frank Lloyd Wright (1867–1959), painter Georgia O'Keeffe (1887–1986), actor Orson Welles (1915–85), guitar maker Les Paul (1915–2009)

» **Home of** 'Cheesehead' Packer fans, dairy farms, water parks

» **Politics** leans Democratic

» **Famous for** breweries, artisanal cheese, first state to legislate gay rights

» **Official dance** polka

» **Driving distances** Milwaukee to Minneapolis 336 miles, Milwaukee to Madison 80 miles

Milwaukee

Here's the thing about Milwaukee: it's cool, but for some reason everyone refuses to admit it. Yes, the reputation lingers as a working man's town of brewskis, bowling alleys and polka halls. But attractions like the Calatrava-designed art museum, badass Harley-Davidson Museum and stylish eating and shopping 'hoods have turned Wisconsin's largest city into a surprisingly groovy place. In summertime, festivals let loose with revelry by the lake almost every weekend. And where else on the planet will you see racing sausages?

History

Milwaukee was first settled by Germans in the 1840s. Many started small breweries, but a few decades later the introduction of bulk brewing technology turned beer production into a major industry here. Milwaukee earned its 'Brew City' and 'Nation's Watering Hole' nicknames in the 1880s when Pabst, Schlitz, Blatz, Miller and 80 other breweries made suds here. Today, only Miller and a few microbreweries remain.

TWO-WHEELING WISCONSIN

Wisconsin has converted an impressive number of abandoned railroad lines into paved, bike-only paths. They go up hills, through old tunnels, over bridges and alongside pastures. Wherever you are in the state, there's likely a sweet ride nearby; check the **Department of Tourism's Bike Path Directory** (www.travelwisconsin.com/bike_path_and_touring_directory.aspx). The **400 State Trail** (www.400statetrail.org) and **Elroy-Sparta Trail** (www.elroy-sparta-trail.com) top the list.

Bike rentals are available in gateway towns, and you can buy trail passes (per day/year $4/20) at area businesses or trailhead drop-boxes.

⊙ Sights & Activities

Lake Michigan sits to the east of the city, and is rimmed by parkland. The Riverwalk path runs along both sides of the Milwaukee River downtown.

Harley-Davidson Museum & Plant   MUSEUM, TOUR

(☑877-436-8738; www.h-dmuseum.com; 400 W Canal St; adult/child $16/10; ⊙9am-6pm, to 8pm Thu May-Oct, reduced rest of year) In 1903 local schoolmates William Harley and Arthur Davidson built and sold their first Harley-Davidson motorcycle. A century later the big bikes are a symbol of American manufacturing pride. The Harley-Davidson Museum pays homage in a sprawling industrial building just south of downtown. Hundreds of bikes show the styles through the decades, including the flashy rides of Elvis and Evel Knievel. Plus you get to sit in the saddle of various bikes (on the bottom floor, behind the Design Lab), as well as get a minilesson on how to ride (by the front entrance). Even nonbikers will enjoy the place.

Hog-heads can get another fix at the **Harley-Davidson plant** (☑877-883-1450; www.harley-davidson.com; W156 N9000 Pilgrim Rd; 30min tours free; ⊙9am-2pm Mon), in the suburb of Menomonee Falls, a 25-minute drive northwest of downtown. This is where the engines are built. Longer tours also take place on Wednesday and Friday, but only as part of a package deal you buy from the museum (per person $38, including tour, museum admission, and a bus ride between the two venues). No open shoes are permitted.

Milwaukee Art Museum   MUSEUM

(☑414-224-3200; www.mam.org; 700 N Art Museum Dr; adult/child $14/12; ⊙10am-5pm, to 8pm Thu, closed Mon Sep-May; ⓦ) Even those who aren't usually museum-goers will be struck by this lakeside museum, which features a stunning winglike addition by Santiago Calatrava. It soars open and closed every day at 10am, noon and at closing time, which is wild to see. There are fabulous folk and outsider art galleries, and a sizeable collection of Georgia O'Keeffe paintings.

FREE Miller Brewing Company   TOUR

(☑414-931-2337; www.millercoors.com; 4251 W State St; ⊙10:30am-3:30pm Mon-Sat, to 4:30pm in summer) Pabst and Schlitz have moved on, but Miller preserves Milwaukee's beer legacy. Join the legions of drinkers lined up for the free tours. Though the mass-produced beer may not be your favorite, the factory impresses with its sheer scale: you'll visit the packaging plant where 2000 cans are filled each minute, and the warehouse where a half-million cases await shipment. And then there's the generous tasting session at the tour's end, where you can down three full-size samples. Don't forget your ID.

Lakefront Brewery   TOUR

(☑414-372-8800; www.lakefrontbrewery.com; 1872 N Commerce St; 1hr tours $7; ⊙Mon-Sun) Well-loved Lakefront Brewery, across the river from Brady St, has afternoon tours, but the swellest time to visit is on Friday nights when there's a fish fry, 16 beers to try and a polka band letting loose. Tour times vary throughout the week, but there's usually at least a 2pm and 3pm walk-through.

Sprecher Brewing Company   TOUR

(☑414-964-2739; www.sprecherbrewery.com; 701 W Glendale Ave; tours $4; ⊙4pm Mon-Fri, noon-2pm Sat & Sun) The small microbrewery's tour includes a museum of memorabilia from long-gone Milwaukee suds-makers and a beer garden replete with oompah music. It's 6 miles north of downtown; reservations are required.

Discovery World at Pier Wisconsin   MUSEUM

(☑414-765-9966; www.discoveryworld.org; 500 N Harbor Dr; adult/child $17/13; ⊙9am-5pm Tue-Fri, 10am-5pm Sat & Sun; ⓦ) The city's lakefront science and technology museum is primarily a kid-pleaser, with freshwater and saltwater

GREAT LAKES WISCONSIN

WHAT THE...?

Rumor has it the **Bronze Fonz** (east side of the Riverwalk, just south of Wells St downtown) is the most photographed sight in Milwaukee. Fonz, aka Arthur Fonzarelli, was a character from the 1970s TV show *Happy Days*, which was set in the city. What do you think – do the blue pants get an 'Aaay' or 'Whoa!'?

aquariums (where you can touch sharks and sturgeon) and a dockside, triple-masted Great Lakes schooner to climb aboard ($5 extra). Adults will appreciate the Les Paul exhibit, showcasing the Wisconsin native's pioneering guitars and sound equipment.

Lakefront Park   PARK
The parkland edging Lake Michigan is prime for walking, cycling and in-line skating. Also here is Bradford Beach, which is good for swimming and lounging.

✫✫ Festivals & Events

Summerfest   MUSIC
(www.summerfest.com; day pass $15; ☉late Jun-early Jul) It's dubbed 'the world's largest music festival,' and indeed hundreds of rock, blues, jazz, country and alternative bands swarm its 10 stages over 11 days. The scene totally rocks; it is held at downtown's lakefront festival grounds.

Other popular parties, held downtown during various summer weekends:

PrideFest   CULTURAL
(www.pridefest.com; ☉mid-Jun)

Polish Fest   CULTURAL
(www.polishfest.org; ☉late Jun)

German Fest   CULTURAL
(www.germanfest.com; ☉late Jul)

Irish Fest   CULTURAL
(www.irishfest.com; ☉mid-Aug)

🛏 Sleeping

Rates in this section are for summer, the peak season, when you should book in advance. Tax (15.1%) is not included. For cheap chain lodging, try Howell Ave, south near the airport.

Comfort Inn & Suites Downtown Lakeshore   HOTEL $$
(☎414-276-8800; www.choicehotels.com; 916 E State St; r incl breakfast $110-170; P☻✳🖥)

Check in here and you'll be laying low in the same digs as touring indie bands who come to town. The breakfast buffet, location near the lakefront and shuttle bus to local sights supplement the contemporary rooms. Parking costs $10.

County Clare Irish Inn   INN $$
(☎414-272-5273; www.countyclare-inn.com; 1234 N Astor St; r incl breakfast $129-179; P☻✳🖥) It's another winner near the lakefront. Rooms have that snug Irish-cottage feel, with four-post beds, white wainscot walls and whirlpool baths. There's free parking and an on-site Guinness-pouring pub, of course.

Iron Horse Hotel   HOTEL $$$
(☎888-543-4766; www.theironhorsehotel.com; 500 W Florida St; r from $189-259; P✳🖥) This boutique hotel near the Harley Museum is geared toward motorcycle enthusiasts, with covered parking for bikes. Most of the loft-style rooms retain the post-and-beam, exposed-brick interior of what was once a bedding factory. Parking costs $25.

Aloft   HOTEL $$
(☎414-226-0122; www.aloftmilwaukeedowntown.com; 1230 Old World Third St; r $129-179; P☻✳🖥) The chain's Milwaukee property has the usual compact, industrial-looking tone. It's inland and not as convenient for festival-goers, though it is near sausagey Old World Third St and Water St's bar action (thus a bit noisy). Parking costs $23.

🍴 Eating

Good places to scope for eats include Germanic N Old World 3rd St downtown; the fashionable East Side by the University of Wisconsin-Milwaukee; hip, Italian-based Brady St by its intersection with N Farwell Ave; and the gastropub-filled Third Ward, anchored along N Milwaukee St south of I-94.

The Friday night fish fry is a highly social tradition observed throughout Wisconsin and all over Milwaukee. Try it at Lakefront Brewery (see p565), which complements its fish with microbrews and a polka band.

Another Milwaukee specialty is frozen custard, which is like ice cream only smoother and richer. **Leon's** (www.leonsfrozencustard.us; 3131 S 27th St; ☉11am-midnight) and **Kopp's** (www.kopps.com; 5373 N Port Washington Rd, Glendale; ☉10:30am-11:30pm) are popular purveyors.

Roots Restaurant and Cellar   AMERICAN $$$
(☎414-374-8480; www.rootsmilwaukee.com; 1818 N Hubbard St; small plates $8-15, mains $19-36;

5-9pm Mon-Thu, to 10pm Fri & Sat, 10am-2pm & 5-9pm Sun; ☑) The Slow Food chefs host two options for dining. Upstairs is the sleek, pricier main room with mains like soy-grilled tilapia. The funky downstairs offers small plates, like the seafood sausage corn dog. The outdoor patio with views is prime for cocktails. It is located across the river from Brady St.

Distil
AMERICAN $$

(☑414-220-9411; www.distilmilwaukee.com; 722 N Milwaukee St; mains $10-20; ☺from 5pm Mon-Sat) It's all about artisanal fare at dark, coppery Distil. The menu focuses on cheese and charcuterie (burgers, too). Heck, the beef comes from the owner's cow. Mixologists stir up Corpse Revivers and Sidecars to accompany the food.

Milwaukee Public Market
MARKET $

(www.milwaukeepublicmarket.org; 400 N Water St; ☺10am-8pm Mon-Fri, 8am-7pm Sat, 10am-6pm Sun; ☜) This Third Ward market stocks mostly prepared foods – cheese, chocolate, beer, frozen custard. Take them upstairs where there are tables, free wi-fi and $1 used books.

☕ Drinking & Entertainment

Bars

Several bars tap kegs around N Water and E State Sts downtown, in the Third Ward and along Brady St between Astor and Farwell Sts. Drinkeries stay open to 2am.

[TOP CHOICE] Palm Tavern
BAR

(2989 S Kinnickinnic Ave; ☺from 5pm Mon-Sat, from 7pm Sun) Located in the fresh south-side neighborhood of Bay View, this warm, jazzy little bar has a mammoth selection of beer (heavy on the Belgians) and single-malt Scotches.

Von Trier
BAR

(www.vontriers.com; 2235 N Farwell Ave) The German Von Trier is a long-standing, real-deal favorite, with plenty of good stuff on tap, a *biergarten* and the famed free popcorn.

Kochanski's Concertina Beer Hall
BAR

(www.beer-hall.com; 1920 S 37th St; ☺Wed-Sun; ☜) Live polka music rules at kitschy Kochanski's, with beers from Schlitz to Polish drafts to Wisconsin craft labels. It's 5 miles southwest of downtown.

Sports

Miller Park
BASEBALL

(www.milwaukeebrewers.com; 1 Brewers Way) The Brewers play baseball at fab Miller Park, which has a retractable roof, real grass and racing sausages (see the boxed text, p563). It's located near S 46th St.

Bradley Center
BASKETBALL

(www.nba.com/bucks; 1001 N 4th St) The NBA's Milwaukee Bucks dunk here.

❶ Information

Emergency & Medical Services
Froedtert Hospital (☑414-805-3000; 9200 W Wisconsin Ave)

Internet Access
The East Side neighborhood near the University of Wisconsin-Milwaukee has several coffee shops with free wi-fi.

Media
Milwaukee Journal Sentinel (www.jsonline. com) The city's daily newspaper.

Quest (www.quest-online.com) GLBT entertainment magazine.

Shepherd Express (www.expressmilwaukee. com) Free alternative weekly paper.

Tourist Information
Milwaukee Convention & Visitors Bureau (☑800-554-1448; www.visitmilwaukee.org)

Websites
On Milwaukee (www.onmilwaukee.com) Site for traffic and weather updates, plus restaurant and entertainment reviews.

❶ Getting There & Around

General Mitchell International Airport (MKE; www.mitchellairport.com) is 8 miles south of downtown. Take public bus 80 ($2.25) or a cab ($30).

AMERICA'S BOWLING CAPITAL

You're in Milwaukee, so you probably should just do it: bowl. The city once had more than 200 bowling alleys, and many retro lanes still hide in timeworn dives. To get your game on try **Landmark Lanes** (www.landmarklanes.com; 2220 N Farwell Ave; per game $2.50-3.50; ☺5pm-1:30am Mon-Thu, noon-1:30am Fri-Sun; ☜), offering 16 beat-up alleys in the historic 1927 Oriental Theater. An arcade, three bars and butt-cheap beer round out the atmosphere.

WHAT THE...?

It's common to see strange things after too many stadium beers. But a group of giant sausages sprinting around Miller Park's perimeter – is that for *real*? It is if it's the middle of the 6th inning. That's when the famous 'Racing Sausages' (actually five people in costumes) waddle onto the field to give the fans a thrill. If you don't know your encased meats, that's Brat, Polish, Italian, Hot Dog and Chorizo vying for supremacy.

The **Lake Express ferry** (☎866-914-1010; www.lake-express.com) sails from downtown (the terminal is located a few miles south of the city center) to Muskegon, Michigan, providing easy access to Michigan's beach-lined Gold Coast. See p558 for details.

Greyhound (☎414-272-2156; 433 W St Paul Ave) runs frequent buses to Chicago (two hours) and Minneapolis (seven hours). **Badger Bus** (☎414-276-7490; www.badgerbus.com; 635 N James Lovell St) goes to Madison ($19, two hours). **Megabus** (www.megabus.com/us) runs express to Chicago (two hours) and Minneapolis (six hours), often for lower fares than Greyhound.

Amtrak (☎414-271-0840; 433 W St Paul Ave) runs the *Hiawatha* train seven times a day to/from Chicago ($22, 1½ hours); catch it downtown (it shares the station with Greyhound) or at the airport.

The **Milwaukee County Transit System** (www.ridemcts.com; fare $2.25) provides the local bus service. Bus 31 goes to Miller Brewery; bus 90 goes to Miller Park.

For taxi service, try phoning **Yellow Cab** (☎414-271-1800).

Madison

Madison reaps a lot of kudos – most walkable city, best road-biking city, most vegetarian friendly, gay friendly, environmentally friendly and just plain all-round friendliest city in the USA. Ensconced on a narrow isthmus between Mendota and Monona Lakes, it's a pretty combination of small, grassy state capital and liberal, bookish college town. An impressive foodie/locavore scene has been cooking here for years.

◎ Sights & Activities

State St runs from the capitol west to the University of Wisconsin. The lengthy avenue is lined with free-trade coffee shops, parked bicycles and incense-wafting stores selling hacky sacks and flowy Indian skirts.

⟦🌿⟧ Dane County Farmers Market   MARKET
(www.dcfm.org; Capitol Sq; ⊙6am-2pm Sat, late Apr-early Nov) On Saturdays, a food bazaar takes over Capitol Sq. It's one of the nation's most expansive markets, famed for its artisanal cheeses. All the cheese, veggies, flowers and breads are made by the folks behind the 150 vendor tables.

FREE State Capitol   BUILDING
(☎608-266-0382; ⊙8am-6pm Mon-Fri, to 4pm Sat & Sun) The X-shaped capitol is the largest outside Washington, DC, and marks the heart of downtown. Tours are available on the hour most days, or you can go up to the observation deck on your own for a view. Recently the capitol has been the site of big-time protests pitting state Democrats against Republicans.

FREE Museum of Contemporary Art   MUSEUM
(☎608-257-0158; www.mmoca.org; 227 State St; ⊙noon-5pm Tue-Thu, to 8pm Fri, 10am-8pm Sat, noon-5pm Sun) The glassy museum holds works by Diego Rivera, Claes Oldenburg, Cindy Sherman and others. Exhibits change several times a year, so you never know what you'll see. There's also a rooftop garden and martini lounge. The museum connects to the **Overture Center for the Arts** (www.overturecenter.com; 201 State St), home to jazz, opera, dance and other performing arts.

Machinery Row   CYCLING
(☎608-442-5974; www.machineryrowbicycles.com; 601 Williamson St; rental per day $20; ⊙9am-9pm Mon-Fri, to 7pm Sat, 10am-7pm Sun) It'd be a shame to leave town without taking advantage of the city's 120 miles of bike trails. Get wheels and maps at this shop, located near the hostel and by various trailheads.

Rutabaga Paddlesports   WATER SPORTS
(☎608-223-9300; www.rutabaga.com; 220 W Broadway; rental per half-/full day $25/40; ⊙10am-8pm Mon-Fri, to 6pm Sat, 11am-5pm Sun) Rent a canoe or kayak to paddle the lakes; it's 5 miles southeast of Capitol Sq and right on the water.

FREE Arboretum   GARDENS
(☎608-263-7888; http://uwarboretum.org; 1207 Seminole Hwy; ⊙7am-10pm) The campus' 1260-acre arboretum is dense with lilac.

⚜ Festivals & Events

FREE **World's Largest Brat Fest** FOOD
(www.bratfest.com; ☺late May) At this Memorial Day weekend festival, 208,000 bratwursts go down the hatch, accompanied by rides and bands.

**Great Taste of the Midwest
Beer Festival** FOOD
(www.mhtg.org; tickets $50; ☺early Aug) Tickets sell out fast for this festival where 120 craft brewers pour their elixirs.

🛏 Sleeping

Moderately priced motels can be found off I-90/I-94 (about 6 miles from the town center), off Hwy 12/18 and also along Washington Ave.

TOP
CHOICE **Arbor House** B&B $$
(✆608-238-2981; www.arbor-house.com; 3402 Monroe St; r incl breakfast weekday $110-175, weekend $150-230; 🐾) Arbor House was an old tavern back in the mid-1800s. Now it's a wind-powered, energy-efficient-appliance-using, vegetarian-breakfast-serving B&B. It's located about 3 miles southwest of the State Capitol but accessible to public transportation. The owners will lend you mountain bikes, too.

HI Madison Hostel HOSTEL $
(✆608-441-0144; www.hiusa.org/madison; 141 S Butler St; dm $22-27, r $57; ⓟ@🐾) The brightly painted, 33-bed brick house is located on a quiet street a short walk from the State Capitol. Dorms are gender segregated; linens are free. A Costa Rican restaurant cooks below the hostel, which is handy for dinner. Parking is $7.

University Inn HOTEL $$
(✆608-285-8040, 800-279-4881; www.universityinn.org; 441 N Frances St; r $89-129; ⓟ❄@🐾) The rooms are fine, though nothing special; the inn's greatest asset is its handy location right by State St and university action. Rates are highest at weekends.

🍴 Eating & Drinking

A global smorgasbord of restaurants peppers State St amid the pizza, sandwich and cheap-beer joints; many places have inviting patios. Cruising Williamson ('Willy') St turns up cafes, dumpling bars and Lao and Thai joints. Bars stay open to 2am. Isthmus (www.

thedailypage.com) is the free entertainment paper.

569

TOP
CHOICE **The Old Fashioned** AMERICAN $$
(✆608-310-4545; www.theoldfashioned.com; 23 N Pinckney St; mains $8-16; ☺7:30am-10:30pm Mon & Tue, 7:30am-2am Wed-Fri, 9am-2am Sat, 9am-10pm Sun) With its dark, woodsy decor, the Old Fashioned evokes a supper club, a type of time-warped eatery common in the upper Midwest. The menu is all Wisconsin specialties, including walleye, cheese soup and sausages. There's even a relish tray, for those who know their supper club staples. It's hard to choose among the 150 types of state-brewed suds in bottles, so opt for a sampler (four or eight little glasses) from the 30 Wisconsin tap beers.

🍴 **Graze & L'Etoile** AMERICAN $$$
(✆608-251-0500; www.letoile-restaurant.com; 1 S Pinckney St; pub mains $16-22, restaurant mains $29-42; ☺pub breakfast, lunch & dinner Mon-Sat, brunch Sun, restaurant dinner Mon-Sat) Slow Food pioneer Odessa Piper offered farm-to-table dinners at L'Etoile for 30 years. These days, chef Tory Miller does the cooking with seasonal ingredients sourced at the farmers market. He also helms Graze, the gastropub next door, that dishes up sustainable comfort foods such as fried chicken and waffles, mussels and *frites,* and burgers.

Food Trucks ECLECTIC $
(mains $1-8; 🐾) Madison's fleet impresses. The more traditional ones, serving barbecue, burritos, southwestern-style fare and Chinese food, ring the Capitol. The corner of King St is well endowed. Trucks ladling out more adventurous dishes – ie East African, Jamaican, Indonesian, vegan – huddle at the foot of State St by campus.

Himal Chuli ASIAN $$
(✆608-251-9225; 318 State St; mains $8-15; ☺11am-9pm Mon-Thu, to 10pm Fri & Sat, noon-8pm Sun; 🐾) Cheerful and cozy Himal Chuli serves up homemade Nepali fare, including lots of vegetarian dishes.

Ian's Pizza PIZZERIA $
(✆608-257-9248; www.ianspizza.com; 115 State St; slices $3.50; ☺11am-2am) Crazy slices topped by macaroni and cheese (most popular), guacamole taco, barbecue chicken and about 20 other items are in high demand, especially late at night.

WORTH A TRIP: ODDBALL US 12

Unusual sights huddle around US 12, all easy to experience on a northerly day trip from Madison.

Heading west out of town (take University Ave), stop first at the **National Mustard Museum** (☑800-438-6878; www.mustardmuseum.com; 7477 Hubbard Ave; admission free; ⊙10am-5pm) in suburban Middleton. Born of one man's ridiculously intense passion, the building houses 5200 mustards and kooky condiment memorabilia. Tongue-in-cheek humor abounds, especially if CMO (chief mustard officer) Barry Levenson is there to give you the shtick.

About 20 miles further on US 12 is the town of Prairie du Sac. It hosts the annual **Cow Chip Throw** (www.wiscowchip.com; admission free; ⊙1st weekend Sep), where 800 competitors fling dried manure patties as far as the eye can see; the record is 248ft.

Seven miles onward is **Dr Evermor's Sculpture Park** (www.worldofevermor.com; admission free; ⊙9am-5pm Mon & Thu-Sat, noon-5pm Sun). The doc welds old pipes, carburetors and other salvaged metal into a hallucinatory world of futuristic birds, dragons and other bizarre structures. The crowning glory is the giant, egg-domed Forevertron, once cited by *Guinness World Records* as the globe's largest scrap metal sculpture. Finding the park entrance is tricky. Look for the Badger Army Ammunition Plant, and then a small sign leading you into a driveway across the street.

Baraboo, about 45 miles northwest of Madison, was once the winter home of the Ringling Brothers Circus. **Circus World Museum** (☑608-356-8341; www.wisconsinhistory. org/circusworld; 550 Water St; adult/child summer $15/8, winter $7/3.50; ⊙9am-6pm summer, reduced hr winter; ▣) preserves a nostalgic collection of wagons, posters and equipment from the touring big-top heyday. In summer, admission includes clowns, animals and acrobats doing the three-ring thing.

Continue north another 12 miles to the **Wisconsin Dells** (☑800-223-3557; www.wis dells.com; ▣), a megacenter of kitschy diversions, including 21 water parks, water-skiing thrill shows and super-minigolf courses. It's a jolting contrast to the natural appeal of the area, with its scenic limestone formations carved by the Wisconsin River. To appreciate the original attraction, take a boat tour or walk the trails at Mirror Lake or Devil's Lake state parks.

Memorial Union AMERICAN
(www.union.wisc.edu/venue-muterrace.htm; 800 Langdon St) The campus Union is Madison's gathering spot. The festive lakeside terrace pours microbrews and hosts free live music and free Monday night films, while the indoor ice cream shop scoops hulking cones from the university dairy.

🛍 Shopping

🧀 **Fromagination** (☑608-255-2430; www. fromagination.com; 12 S Carroll St; ⊙9:30am-6pm Mon-Fri, 9am-4pm Sat) specializes in small-batch and hard-to-find local cheese. If you miss the Saturday farmers market, you can find many of the same cheeses here. Be sure to pick up some cheese curds to experience their squeaky bite.

ℹ Information

Madison Convention & Visitors Bureau (www. visitmadison.com)

ℹ Getting There & Around

Badger Bus (www.badgerbus.com) uses Memorial Union as its pick-up/drop-off point for trips to Milwaukee ($19, two hours), as does **Megabus** (www.megabus.com/us) for trips to Chicago (four hours) and Minneapolis (4½ hours).

Taliesin & Southern Wisconsin

This part of Wisconsin has some of the prettiest landscapes in the state, particularly the hilly southwest. Architecture fans can be unleashed at Taliesin, the Frank Lloyd Wright ubersight, and Racine, where two of his other works stand. Dairies around here cut a lot of cheese.

RACINE

Racine is an unremarkable industrial town 30 miles south of Milwaukee, but it has two key Frank Lloyd Wright sights, both of which offer 45-minute tours that must be prebooked. The first, the **Johnson Wax Company Administration Building** (262-260-2154; 1525 Howe St; admission free; tours 11:45am & 12:45pm Fri, noon Sat), dates from 1939 and is a magnificent space with tall, flared columns. The second is the lakeside **Wingspread** (262-681-3353; www.johnsonfdn.org; 33 E Four Mile Rd; admission free; 9:30am-2:30pm Tue-Fri), the last and largest of Wright's Prairie houses.

GREEN COUNTY

This pastoral area holds the nation's greatest concentration of cheesemakers, and **Green County Tourism** (www.greencounty.org) will introduce you to them. Monroe is a fine place to start sniffing. Follow your nose to **Roth Käse** (657 Second St; 9am-6pm Mon-Fri, 10am-5pm Sat & Sun), a store and factory where you can watch cheesemakers in action from the observation deck (weekday mornings only) and delve into the 'bargain bin' for hunks. Bite into a fresh limburger-and-raw-onion sandwich at **Baumgartner's** (www.baumgartnercheese.com; 1023 Sixteenth Ave; sandwiches $4-7; 8am-11pm), an old Swiss tavern on the town square. At night, catch a flick at the local drive-in movie theater, and then climb into bed at **Inn Serendipity** (608-329-7056; www.innserendipity.com; 7843 County Rd P; r incl breakfast $110-125), a two-room, wind-and-solar-powered B&B on a 5-acre organic farm in Browntown, about 10 miles west of Monroe.

For more on local dairy producers and plant tours, pick up **A Traveler's Guide to America's Dairyland** (www.eatwisconsincheese.com) map.

SPRING GREEN

Forty miles west of Madison and 3 miles south of the small town of Spring Green, **Taliesin** was the home of Frank Lloyd Wright for most of his life and is the site of his architectural school. It's now a major pilgrimage destination for fans and followers. The house was built in 1903, the Hillside Home School in 1932, and the **visitor center** (608-588-7900; www.taliesinpreservation.org; Hwy 23; 9am-5:30pm May-Oct) in 1953. A wide range of guided tours ($16 to $80) cover various parts of the complex; reserve in advance for the lengthier ones. The one-hour Hillside Tour ($16) provides a nice introduction to Wright's work.

A few miles south of Taliesin is the **House on the Rock** (608-935-3639; www.thehouseontherock.com; 5754 Hwy 23; adult/child $12.50/7.50; 9am-6pm May-Aug, to 5pm rest of year, closed Tue-Thu Nov-Apr), one of Wisconsin's busiest attractions. Alex Jordan built the structure atop a rock column in 1959 (some say as an 'up yours' to neighbor Frank Lloyd Wright). He then stuffed the house to mind-blowing proportions with wonderments, including the world's largest carousel, whirring music machines, freaky dolls and crazed folk art. The house is broken into three parts, each with its own tour. Visitors with stamina (and about four hours to kill) can experience the whole shebang for adult/child $28.50/15.50.

Spring Green has a B&B in town and six motels strung along Hwy 14, north of town. Small **Usonian Inn** (877-876-6426; www.usonianinn.com; E 5116 Hwy 14; r $85-135;) was designed by a Wright student. Check www.springgreen.com for more options.

Chomp sandwiches or inventive specials like sweet potato stew at **Spring Green General Store** (www.springgreengeneralstore.com; 137 S Albany St; mains $5-7; 9am-6pm Mon-Fri, 8am-6pm Sat, 8am-4pm Sun).

The **American Players Theatre** (608-588-2361; www.playinthewoods.org) stages classical productions at an outdoor amphitheater by the Wisconsin River.

Along the Mississippi River

The Mississippi River forms most of Wisconsin's western border, and alongside it run some of the most scenic sections of the **Great River Road** (www.wigreatriverroad.org) – the designated route that follows Old Man River from Minnesota to the Gulf of Mexico.

From Madison, head west on US 18. You'll hit the River Road (aka Hwy 35) at **Prairie du Chien**. North of town, the hilly riverside wends through the scene of the final battle in the bloody Black Hawk War. Historic markers tell part of the story, which finished at the Battle of Bad Ax when Native American men, women and children were massacred trying to flee across the Mississippi.

At Genoa, Hwy 56 leads inland for 20 miles to the trout-fishing mecca of **Viroqua** (www.viroquatourism.com), a pretty little town surrounded by organic farms and distinctive round barns. Pop into **Viroqua Food Cooperative** (www.viroquafood.coop; 609 Main St; 7am-9pm Mon-Sat, 9am-8pm Sun) to meet farmers and munch their wares.

Back riverside and 18 miles upstream, La Crosse (www.explorelacrosse.com) has a historic center nestling restaurants and pubs. Grandad Bluff offers grand views of the river. It's east of town along Main St (which becomes Bliss Rd); follow Bliss Rd up the hill and then turn right on Grandad Bluff Rd. The World's Largest Six-Pack (3rd St S) is also in town. The 'cans' are actually storage tanks for City Brewery and hold enough beer to provide one person with a six-pack a day for 3351 years (or so the sign says).

For destinations on up the road, see Southern Minnesota (p584).

Door County & Eastern Wisconsin

Rocky, lighthouse-dotted Door County draws crowds in summer, while Green Bay draws crazed football fans in the freakin' freezing winter.

GREEN BAY

Green Bay (www.greenbay.com) is a modest industrial town best known as the fabled 'frozen tundra' where the Green Bay Packers win Super Bowls. The franchise is unique as the only community-owned nonprofit team in the NFL; perhaps pride in ownership is what makes the fans so die-hard (and wear foam-rubber cheese wedges on their head).

While tickets are nearly impossible to obtain, you can always get into the spirit by joining a pregame tailgate party. The generous flow of alcohol has led to Green Bay's reputation as a 'drinking town with a football problem.' On nongame days, visit the Green Bay Packer Hall of Fame (920-569-7512; www.lambeaufield.com; adult/child $10/5; 9am-6pm Mon-Sat, 10am-5pm Sun) at Lambeau Field, which is indeed packed with memorabilia and movies that'll intrigue any pigskin fan.

The National Railroad Museum (920-437-7623; www.nationalrrmuseum.org; 2285 S Broadway; adult/child $9/6.50 May-Sep; 9am-5pm Mon-Sat, 11am-5pm Sun, closed Mon Jan-Apr) features some of the biggest locomotives ever to haul freight into Green Bay's vast yards; train rides ($2) are offered in summer.

Bare-bones Bay Motel (920-494-3441; www.baymotelgreenbay.com; 1301 S Military Ave; r $52-75;) is a mile from Lambeau Field. Hinterland (920-438-8050; www.hinterland beer.com; 313 Dousman St) gastropub brings a touch of rustic swankiness to beer drinkers.

DOOR COUNTY

With its rocky coastline, picturesque lighthouses, cherry orchards and small 19th-century villages, you have to admit Door County is pretty damn lovely. The area spreads across a narrow peninsula jutting 75 miles into Lake Michigan, and visitors usually loop around on the county's two highways. Hwy 57 runs beside Lake Michigan and goes through Jacksonport and Baileys Harbor; this is known as the more scenic 'quiet side.' Hwy 42 borders Green Bay and passes through (from south to north) Egg Harbor, Fish Creek, Ephraim and Sister Bay; this side is more action oriented. Only about half the businesses stay open from November to April.

Sights & Activities

Parkland blankets the county. Bayside Peninsula State Park is the largest, with bluffside hiking and biking trails and a beach for kayaking and sailing. In winter, cross-country skiers and snowshoers take over the trails. On the lake side, secluded Newport State Park offers trails, backcountry camping and solitude. Whitefish Dunes State Park has sandscapes and a wide beach (beware of riptides). Adjacent Cave Point Park is known for its sea caves and kayaking. Multiactivity outfitters include:

(920-854-9220; www.kayakdoorcounty.com; Sister Bay)

Nor Door Sport & Cyclery (920-868-2275; www.nordoorsports.com; Fish Creek)

Sleeping & Eating

The bay side has the most lodging. Prices listed are for July and August, the peak season; many places have minimum-stay requirements. Local restaurants often host a 'fish boil,' a regional specialty started by

---

i TALK LIKE A LOCAL

Admit it: you're puzzled by how to pronounce town names like Prairie du Chien and Lac du Flambeau. Lucky for you, Miss Pronouncer (www.miss pronouncer.com) provides recordings of how to say it in Wisconsinese. She covers 190 cities, 1260 towns and heaps of famous locals' names. Soon you'll be chattering on about your visit to Rio (rye-o) or Chequamegon (sheh wom again) with confidence.

Scandinavian lumberjacks, in which white-fish, potatoes and onions are cooked in a fiery cauldron. Finish with Door's famous cherry pie.

Egg Harbor Lodge INN $$
(✆920-868-3115; www.eggharborlodge.com; Egg Harbor; r $159-199; ⊝❄🤶🏊) All rooms have a water view and free bike use.

Julie's Park Cafe and Motel MOTEL $
(✆920-868-2999; www.juliesmotel.com; Fish Creek; r $82-106; ⊝❄🤶) It's tidy and relatively low cost; located beside Peninsula State Park.

Peninsula State Park CAMPGROUND $
(✆920-868-3258; tent & RV sites $17-25; Fish Creek) Peninsula holds nearly 500 amenity-laden campsites.

JJ's PUB $$
(✆920-854-4513; jjslapuerta.com; Sister Bay; mains $9-16; ⊙11am-2am, closed Sun-Tue in winter) Hang with the young boater types at this good-time pub attached to a Mexican restaurant.

Village Cafe AMERICAN $
(✆920-868-3342; www.villagecafe-doorcounty. com; Egg Harbor; sandwiches $6.50-8.50, mains $14-16; ⊙7am-8pm) Delicious breakfast, lunch and dinner platters.

ⓘ Information
Door County Visitors Bureau (✆800-527-3529; www.doorcounty.com) Special-interest brochures on art galleries, biking and lighthouses.

Apostle Islands & Northern Wisconsin

The north is a thinly populated region of forests and lakes, where folks paddle and fish in summer, and ski and snowmobile in winter. The cliffy, windswept Apostle Islands steal the show.

NORTHWOODS & LAKELANDS

Nicolet National Forest is a vast, wooded district ideal for outdoor activities. The simple crossroads of **Langlade** is a center for white-river river adventures. **Wolf River Guides** (✆715-882-3002; www.wolfriverguides. com) provides half-day kayak-paddling classes followed by a half-day trip on the water (per person $110), while **Wolf River Lodge** (✆715-882-2182; www.wolfriverlodge.com; r incl breakfast $100; ❄) provides accommodation where you can dry off, get warm and cele-

SCENIC DRIVE: HIGHWAY 13 **573**

After departing Bayfield, Hwy 13 takes a fine route around the Lake Superior shore, past the Ojibwa community of **Red Cliff** and the Apostle Islands' mainland segment, which has a beach. Tiny **Cornucopia**, looking every bit like a seaside village, has great sunsets. The road runs on through a timeless countryside of forest and farm reaching US 2 for the final miles back to civilization at Superior.

brate your accomplishments in the on-site bar.

North on Hwy 13, folk artist and retired lumberjack Fred Smith's **Concrete Park** (www.friendsoffredsmith.org; admission free; ⊙sunrise-sunset) in Phillips is extraordinary, with 200-plus whimsical, life-size sculptures.

West on Hwy 70, **Chequamegon National Forest** offers exceptional mountain biking with 300 miles of off-road trails. The **Chequamegon Area Mountain Bike Association** (www.cambatrails.org) has trail maps and bike rental information. The season culminates in mid-September with the **Chequamegon Fat Tire Festival** (www.cheqfattire. com), when 1700 strong-legged men and women peddle 40 grueling miles through the woods. The town of **Hayward** (www.haywardareachamber.com) makes a good base.

APOSTLE ISLANDS

The 21 rugged Apostle Islands, floating in Lake Superior and freckling Wisconsin's northern tip, are a state highlight. Jump off from **Bayfield** (www.bayfield.org), a humming resort town with hilly streets, Victorian-era buildings, apple orchards and nary a fast-food restaurant in sight.

The **Apostle Islands National Lakeshore visitors center** (✆715-779-3397; www. nps.gov/apis; 410 Washington Ave; ⊙8am-4:30pm Jun-Sep, closed Sat & Sun Oct-May) has camping permits (per night $10) and paddling and hiking information. The forested islands have no facilities, and walking is the only way to get around.

Various companies offer seasonal boat trips around the islands, and kayaking is very popular. Try **Living Adventure** (✆715-779-9503; www.livingadventure.com; Hwy 13; half-/full-day tour $59/99; ⊙Jun-Sep) for a guided paddle through arches and sea caves; beginners are welcome. If you prefer a motor to power your explorations, climb aboard the Apostle Islands Cruise Service (☎715-779-3925; www.apostleisland.com; ☺mid-May–mid-Oct) boat. It departs at 10am from Bayfield's City Dock for a three-hour narrated trip past sea caves and lighthouses (adult/child $40/24).

Inhabited Madeline Island (www.madeline island.com), a fine day trip, is reached by a 20-minute ferry (☎715-747-2051; www.mad-ferry.com) from Bayfield (round-trip adult/child/bicycle/car $12/6/6/24). Its walkable village of La Pointe has some mid-priced places to stay, and restaurants. Bus tours are available, and you can rent bikes and mopeds – everything is near the ferry dock. Big Bay State Park (☎715-747-6425; tent & RV sites $15-17, vehicle $10) has a beach and trails.

Back in Bayfield, there are loads of B&Bs and inns, but reserve ahead in summer; see www.bayfield.org for options. Most rooms at no-frills Seagull Bay Motel (☎715-779-5558; www.seagullbay.com; 325 S 7th St; r $75-105; ☺☎) have decks; ask for a lake view. Going upscale: Pinehurst Inn (☎877-499-7651; www.pinehurstinn.com; 83645 Hwy 13; r incl breakfast $119-199; ☺☎) is a carbon-neutral, solar-heated, eight-room B&B.

Ecoconscious Big Water Cafe (www.big watercoffee.com; 117 Rittenhouse Ave; mains $5-10; ☺7am-8pm summer, to 4pm winter) serves sandwiches, local farmstead cheeses and area microbrews. Kitschy, flamingo-themed Maggie's (☎715-779-5641; www.maggies-bayfield.com; 257 Manypenny Ave; mains $7-16; ☺11:30am-9pm Sun-Thu, to 10pm Fri & Sat) is the place to sample local lake trout and whitefish; there are pizza and burgers too.

The Big Top Chautauqua (☎888-244-8368; www.bigtop.org) is a major regional summer event with big-name concerts and musical theater; call for schedule and prices.

MINNESOTA

Is Minnesota really the land of 10,000 lakes, as so often advertised? You betcha. Actually, in typically modest style, the state has undermarketed itself – there are 11,842 lakes. Which is great news for travelers. Intrepid outdoorsfolk can wet their paddles in the Boundary Waters, where nighttime brings a blanket of stars and the lullaby of wolf howls. Those wanting to get further off the beaten path can journey to Voyageurs National Park, where there's more water than roadway. If that all seems too far-flung, stick

MINNESOTA FACTS

» **Nicknames** North Star State, Gopher State

» **Population** 5.3 million

» **Area** 86,940 sq miles

» **Capital city** St Paul (population 273,500)

» **Other cities** Minneapolis (population 372,800)

» **Sales tax** 6.88%

» **Birthplace of** author F Scott Fitzgerald (1896–1940), songwriter Bob Dylan (b 1941), filmmakers Joel Coen (b 1954) and Ethan Coen (b 1957)

» **Home of** lumberjack legend Paul Bunyan, Spam, walleye fish, Hmong and Somali immigrants

» **Politics** leans Democratic

» **Famous for** niceness, funny accents, snowy weather, 10,000 lakes

» **Official muffin** blueberry

» **Driving distances** Minneapolis to Duluth 153 miles, Minneapolis to Boundary Waters 245 miles

to the Twin Cities of Minneapolis and St Paul, where you can't swing a moose without hitting something cool or cultural. And for those looking for middle ground – a cross between the big city and big woods – the dramatic, freighter-filled port of Duluth beckons.

ⓘ **Information**
Minnesota Highway Conditions (☎511; www.511mn.org)
Minnesota Office of Tourism (☎888-868-7476; www.exploreminnesota.com)
Minnesota State Park Information (☎888-646-6367; www.mnstateparks.info) Park entry requires a vehicle permit (per day/year $5/25). Campsites cost $12 to $25; **reservations** (☎866-857-2757; www.stayatmnparks.com; fee $8.50) accepted.

Minneapolis

Minneapolis is the biggest and artiest town on the prairie, with all the trimmings of progressive prosperity – swank art museums, rowdy rock clubs, organic and ethnic eateries, and enough theaters to be nicknamed Mini-Apple (second only to the

Big Apple). It's always happenin', even in winter. But there's no attitude to go along with the abundance. It's the kind of place where homeless people are treated kindly at the coffee shops, where the buses are kept immaculately clean, and where the public workers tell everyone to 'Have a nice day,' rain or shine (or snow). The city is 'Minnesota Nice' in action.

History

Timber was the city's first boom industry, and water-powered sawmills rose along the Mississippi River in the mid-1800s. Wheat from the prairies also needed to be processed, so flour mills churned into the next big business. The population boomed in the late 19th century with mass immigration, especially from Scandinavia and Germany. Today Minneapolis' Nordic heritage is evident, whereas twin city St Paul is more German and Irish-Catholic.

⊙ Sights & Activities

The Mississippi River flows northeast of downtown. Despite the name, Uptown is actually southwest of downtown, with Hennepin Ave as its main axis. Minneapolis' twin city, St Paul, is 10 miles east.

Most attractions are closed Monday; many stay open late Thursday.

DOWNTOWN & LORING PARK

Nicollet Mall   STREET

Nicollet Mall is the pedestrian-friendly portion of Nicollet Ave in the heart of downtown, dense with stores, bars and restaurants. It's perhaps most famous as the spot where Mary Tyler Moore (of '70s TV fame) threw her hat into the air during the show's opening sequence. A cheesy MTM statue (8th St S & Nicollet Mall) depicts our girl doing just that. A farmers market (www.mplsfarmersmarket.com; ⊙6am-6pm) takes over the mall on Thursdays from May to November.

FREE Minneapolis
Sculpture Garden   GARDENS

(726 Vineland Pl; ⊙6am-midnight) The 11-acre garden, studded with contemporary works such as the oft-photographed *Spoonbridge & Cherry* by Claes Oldenburg, sits beside the Walker Art Center. The Cowles Conservatory, abloom with exotic hothouse flowers, is also on the grounds. The garden connects to attractive Loring Park by a sculptural pedestrian bridge over I-94.

Walker Art Center   MUSEUM

(☑612-375-7622; www.walkerart.org; 725 Vineland Pl; adult/child $10/free, admission free Thu evening; ⊙11am-5pm Tue-Sun, to 9pm Thu) The first-class center has a strong permanent collection of 20th-century art and photography, including big-name US painters and great US pop art.

RIVERFRONT DISTRICT

At the north edge of downtown at the foot of Portland Ave is the St Anthony Falls Heritage Trail, a recommended 2-mile path that provides both interesting history (placards dot the route) and the city's best access to the banks of the Mississippi River. View the cascading St Anthony Falls from the car-free Stone Arch Bridge. On the north side of the river, Main St SE has a stretch of redeveloped buildings housing restaurants and bars. From here you can walk down to Water Power Park and feel the river's frothy spray. Pick up a free trail map at the Mill City Museum.

Definitely head next door to the cobalt-blue Guthrie Theater (see p580) and make your way up to its 'Endless Bridge,' a cantilevered walkway overlooking the river. You don't need a theater ticket – it's intended as a public space – though see a show if you can as the Guthrie is one of the Midwest's finest companies. Gold Medal Park spirals next door.

Mill City Museum   MUSEUM

(☑612-341-7555; www.millcitymuseum.org; 704 2nd St S; adult/child $10/5; ⊙10am-5pm Tue-Sat, noon-5pm Sun, open Mon Jul & Aug) The building is indeed a former mill, and highlights include a ride inside an eight-story grain elevator ('the Flour Tower'), Betty Crocker exhibits and a baking lab. It's not terribly exciting unless you're really into milling history. The Mill City Farmer's Market (www.millcityfarmersmarket.org; ⊙8am-1pm Sat mid-May–mid-Oct) takes place in the museum's attached train shed; cooking demos fire up at 10am.

NORTHEAST

Once a working-class Eastern European neighborhood, Northeast (so named because of its position to the river) is where urbanites and artists now work and play. They appreciate the dive bars pouring microbrews along with Pabst, and boutiques selling ecogifts next to companies grinding sausage. Hundreds of craftsfolk and galleries fill historic industrial buildings. They fling open their doors the first Thursday of each month when

GREAT LAKES MINNESOTA

the **Northeast Minneapolis Arts Association** (www.nemaa.org) sponsors a gallery walk. Heady streets include 4th St NE and 13th Ave NE.

UNIVERSITY AREA

The **University of Minnesota**, by the river southeast of Minneapolis' center, is one of the USA's largest campuses, with over 50,000 students. Most of the campus is in the **East Bank** neighborhood.

Dinkytown, based at 14th Ave SE and 4th St SE, is dense with student cafes and bookshops. A small part of the university is on the **West Bank** of the Mississippi River, near the intersection of 4th St S and Riverside Ave. This area has a few restaurants, some student hangouts and a big Somali community.

FREE **Weisman Art Museum**   MUSEUM
(☎612-625-9494; www.weisman.umn.edu; 333 E River Rd; ☺10am-5pm Tue-Fri, to 8pm Thu, 11am-

5pm Sat & Sun) The Weisman, which occupies a swooping silver structure by architect Frank Gehry, is a uni (and city) highlight. It was in expansion mode at the time of writing, set to reopen with double the space and five new galleries for American art, ceramics and works on paper.

UPTOWN, LYN-LAKE & WHITTIER

These three neighborhoods are south of downtown.

Uptown, based around the intersection of Hennepin Ave S and Lake St, is a punk-yuppie collision of shops and restaurants that stays lively until late. **Lyn-Lake** abuts Uptown to the east and sports a similar urban-cool vibe; it's centered on Lyndale and Lake Sts. (Get the name?)

Uptown is a convenient jump-off point to the 'Chain of Lakes' – Lake Calhoun, Lake of the Isles, Lake Harriet, Cedar Lake and Brownie Lake. It seems all of Minneapolis is out frolicking by the water – not surprising, really, since this is known as the 'city of lakes.' Paved cycling paths (which double as cross-country ski trails in winter) meander around the five lakes, where you can go boating in summer or ice skating in winter.

Lake Calhoun sits at the foot of Lake St, where there are amenities galore. Further around Lake Calhoun, Thomas Beach is popular for swimming. Cedar Lake's freewheeling Hidden Beach (aka East Cedar Beach) used to bring out the nudists, though it's mostly clothed folks lolling about these days.

FREE **Minneapolis Institute of Arts**   MUSEUM
(612-870-3131; www.artsmia.org; 2400 3rd Ave S; 10am-5pm Tue-Sat, to 9pm Thu, 11am-5pm Sun) This museum is a huge treasure trove housing a veritable history of art. The modern and contemporary collections astonish, while the Prairie School and Asian galleries are also highlights. Brochures at the front desk can help you winnow it down to the

must-sees if you're short on time. The museum is 1 mile due south of the convention center via 3rd Ave S.

Calhoun Rental   CYCLING
(612-827-8231; www.calhounbikerental.com; 1622 W Lake St; per half-/full day $25/35; 10am-7pm Mon-Fri, 9am-8pm Sat, 10am-8pm Sun Apr-Oct) In Uptown, a couple blocks west of Lake Calhoun, this shop rents bikes (helmet, lock and bike map included); credit card and driver's license are required. It also offers two- to four-hour cycling tours ($39 to $49) around the water Friday through Sunday; reserve in advance.

Lake Calhoun Kiosk   WATER SPORTS
(612-823-5765; base of Lake St; per hr $11-17; 10am-8pm late May-Aug, weekends only Sep & Oct) The kiosk, at the foot of Lake St, rents canoes, kayaks and paddleboats. It's a busy spot as there's also a patio restaurant and sailing school here.

Minneapolis

★★ Festivals & Events

Art-A-Whirl　　　　　　　　　　MUSIC
(www.nemaa.org; ⊙mid-May) The Northeast's weekend-long, rock-and-roll gallery crawl heralds the arrival of spring.

Minneapolis Aquatennial　　　CULTURAL
(www.aquatennial.org; ⊙mid-Jul) Ten days celebrating the ubiquitous lakes via parades, beach bashes and fireworks.

Holidazzle　　　　　　　　　　CULTURAL
(www.holidazzle.com; ⊙Dec) Parades, lights and lots of good cheer downtown throughout December.

🛏 Sleeping

B&Bs offer the best value – they've got budget prices but are solidly midrange in quality. Tax adds 13.4% to prices.

Wales House　　　　　　　　　　B&B $
(☎612-331-3931; www.waleshouse.com; 1115 5th St SE; r without/with shared bath, incl breakfast from $65/75; P⊖❋🛜) This cheery 10-bedroom B&B often houses scholars from the nearby University of Minnesota. Curl up with a book on the porch, or lounge by the fireplace. A two-night minimum stay is required.

Le Meridien Chambers Hotel　　HOTEL $$$
(☎612-767-6900; www.lemeridienchambers.com; 901 Hennepin Ave S; r $189-289; P⊖❋🛜) It's

an art gallery – no, it's a hotel. Actually, it's both, with 200 artworks (including Damien Hirst's floating bull's head at the front desk) spread throughout, and 60 minimalist rooms with luxury touches, like heated bathroom floors. Parking costs $28, wi-fi costs $13 per day.

Aloft　　　　　　　　　　　　　HOTEL $$
(☎612-455-8400; www.alofthotels.com/minneapolis; 900 Washington Ave S; r $109-149; P⊖❋@🛜🏊) Aloft's compact, efficiently designed, industrial-toned rooms draw a younger clientele. The clubby lobby has board games, a cocktail lounge and 24-hour snacks. There's a tiny pool and decent fitness room. Parking costs $15.

Evelo's B&B　　　　　　　　　　B&B $
(☎612-374-9656; 2301 Bryant Ave S; r with shared bath, incl breakfast $75-95; ⊖🛜) Evelo's three rooms creak and charm in this polished-wood-filled Victorian home. They're close quartered, but the B&B's strategic location between the Walker Art Center and Uptown compensates.

Minneapolis International Hostel　HOSTEL $
(☎612-522-5000; www.minneapolishostel.com; 2400 Stevens Ave S; dm $28-34, r without/with bath $60/81; ⊖❋@🛜) This homey hostel beside the Minneapolis Institute of Arts has antique furniture, wood floors and fluffy quilts

on the beds. The 48 beds come in a variety of configurations, from a 15-bed male dorm to private rooms with en suite bath. It's easy to miss, as there's no sign on the front (due to the building's historic designation). Reservations are recommended.

✖ Eating

Minneapolis has ripened into a rich dining scene known for its many restaurants that use local, sustainable ingredients.

DOWNTOWN & NORTHEAST
Nicollet Mall is loaded with eateries.

Bar La Grassa ITALIAN $$$
(☎612-333-3837; www.barlagrassa.com; 800 Washington Ave N; pastas $12-24, mains $16-45; ⏲5pm-midnight Mon-Thu, to 1am Fri & Sat, to 10pm Sun) Chef Isaac Becker won the 2011 James Beard award for 'best in the midwest,' so expect great things from the small plates menu of fresh pastas, bruschetta and secondi. It is located about a mile northwest of downtown's core.

Hell's Kitchen AMERICAN $$
(☎612-332-4700; www.hellskitcheninc.com; 80 9th St S; mains $10-20; ⏲6:30am-9pm Mon-Wed, to 2am Thu & Fri, 7:30am-2am Sat, 7:30am-9pm Sun; ☻) Descend the stairs to Hell's devilish lair, where spirited waitstaff bring you uniquely Minnesotan foods, like the walleye bacon-lettuce-tomato sandwich, bison burger and lemon-ricotta hotcakes. Happy hour (3pm to 6pm) at the bar is a dandy deal. It morphs into a club with DJs late on weekend nights.

Red Stag Supper Club AMERICAN $$$
(☎612-767-7766; www.redstagsupperclub.com; 509 1st Ave NE; bar menu $8-13, mains $18-27; ⏲11am-2am Mon-Fri, 9am-2am Sat & Sun) The exposed-beam Northwoods lodge look belies Red Stag's LEED-certified architecture. The locally sourced arugula-and-pine-nut flatbread sandwiches, smelt fries, smoked trout and cassoulet soothe the stomach. There are good deals for Tuesday dinner.

UNIVERSITY AREA
Low-priced eateries cluster in the campus area by Washington Ave and Oak St.

Al's Breakfast BREAKFAST $
(☎612-331-9991; 413 14th Ave SE; mains $4-8; ⏲6am-1pm Mon-Sat, 9am-1pm Sun) It's the ultimate hole-in-the-wall: 14 stools at a tiny counter. Whenever a customer comes in, everyone picks up their plates and scoots down to make room for the newcomer. Fruit-full pancakes are the big crowd-pleaser. Cash only.

UPTOWN, LYN-LAKE & WHITTIER
Vietnamese, Greek, African and other ethnic restaurants line Nicollet Ave S between Franklin Ave (near the Minneapolis Institute of Arts) and 28th St – the stretch is known as 'Eat Street.' Lake St in Uptown is a rich vein for stylish bars and cafes.

TOP CHOICE Bryant-Lake Bowl AMERICAN $$
(☎612-825-3737; www.bryantlakebowl.com; 810 W Lake St; sandwiches $7-9, mains $11-16; ⏲8am-12:30am; ☻) A workingman's bowling alley meets epicurean food at the BLB. Artisanal cheese plates, mock duck rolls, cornmeal-crusted walleye strips and organic oatmeal melt in the mouth. A long list of local beers washes it all down. The on-site theater always has something intriguing and odd going on too.

MINNEAPOLIS FOR CHILDREN

Note that many of the top sights for wee ones are in St Paul, at the Mall of America and at Fort Snelling. Others include:

» **Minnesota Zoo** (☎952-431-9500; www.mnzoo.org; 13000 Zoo Blvd; adult/child $18/12; ⏲9am-6pm summer, 9am-4pm winter; ☻) You'll have to travel a way to get to the respected zoo in suburban Apple Valley, which is 20 miles south of town. It has naturalistic habitats for its 400-plus species, with an emphasis on cold-climate creatures. Parking is $5.

» **Valleyfair** (☎952-445-7600; www.valleyfair.com; 1 Valleyfair Dr; adult/child $42/10; ⏲from 10am mid-May–Aug, weekends only Sep & Oct, closing times vary; ☻) If the rides at the Mall of America aren't enough, drive out to this full-scale amusement park 25 miles southwest in Shakopee. Parking costs $10.

» **Children's Theatre Company** (☎612-874-0400; www.childrenstheatre.org; 2400 3rd Ave S; ☻) So good it won a Tony award for 'outstanding regional theater.'

Peninsula ASIAN $$

(612-871-8282; www.peninsulamalaysiancuis ine.com; 2608 Nicollet Ave S; mains $9-15; 11am-10pm Sun-Thu, to 11pm Fri & Sat;) Malaysian dishes – including *achat* (tangy vegetable salad in peanut dressing), red curry hot pot, spicy crab and fish in banana leaves – rock the palate in this contemporary restaurant.

Uptown Cafeteria &
Support Group AMERICAN $$

(612-877-7263; www.uptowncafeteria.com; 3001 Hennepin Ave; mains $13-22; 11:30am-late Mon-Fri, 9am-late Sat & Sun;) One of Uptown's concept-y hot spots, the Cafeteria features a great roof deck and pretty darn good comfort food along the lines of chicken pot pie and meatloaf.

🍷 Drinking

Bars stay open until 2am. Happy hour typically lasts from 3pm to 6pm.

Brit's Pub PUB

(www.britspub.com; 1110 Nicollet Mall) A lawn bowling green on the roof, plus Brit's sweeping selection of Scotch, port and beer, is sure to unleash skills you never knew you had.

Grumpy's BAR

(www.grumpys-bar.com/nordeast; 2200 4th St NE) Grumpy's is the Northeast's classic dive, with cheap (but good) beer and an outdoor patio. Sample the specialty 'hot dish' on Tuesdays for $1.

☆ Entertainment

With its large student population and thriving performing-arts scene, Minneapolis has an active nightlife. Check *Vita.MN* (www. vita.mn) and *City Pages* (www.citypages. com) for current goings on.

Live Music

Minneapolis rocks; everyone's in a band, it seems. Acts such as Prince and post-punkers Hüsker Dü and the Replacements cut their teeth here.

First Avenue & 7th St Entry LIVE MUSIC

(www.first-avenue.com; 701 1st Ave N) This is the bedrock of Minneapolis' music scene, and it still pulls in top bands and big crowds. Check out the exterior stars; they're all bands that have graced the stage.

Nye's Polonaise Room LIVE MUSIC

(www.nyespolonaise.com; 112 E Hennepin Ave) The World's Most Dangerous Polka Band lets loose Friday and Saturday. It's smashing fun, and enhanced if you find yourself an old-timer to twirl you around the room.

Triple Rock Social Club LIVE MUSIC

(www.triplerocksocialclub.com; 629 Cedar Ave) Triple Rock is a popular punk-alternative club.

Lee's Liquor Lounge LIVE MUSIC

(www.leesliquorlounge.com; 101 Glenwood Ave) Rockabilly and country-tinged alt bands twang here.

Dakota Jazz Club LIVE MUSIC

(www.dakotacooks.com; 1010 Nicollet Mall) The Dakota is a classy venue that gets big-name jazz acts.

Theater & Performing Arts

They don't call it Mini-Apple for nothing, with 100-plus theater groups here. The Guthrie and other venues put unsold tickets on sale 15 minutes before showtime for $15 to $30.

Guthrie Theater THEATER

(612-377-2224; www.guthrietheater.org; 818 2nd St S) This is Minneapolis' top-gun theater troupe, with the jumbo facility to prove it.

GAY & LESBIAN MINNEAPOLIS

Minneapolis has one of the country's highest percentages of gay, lesbian, bisexual and transgender (GLBT) residents, and the city enjoys strong GLBT rights. The Minneapolis Convention & Visitors Association (www.glbtminneapolis.org) has a comprehensive website for events, nightlife, news and attractions. Or pick up the free, biweekly magazine *Lavender* (www.lavendermagazine.com) at coffee shops around town.

For nightlife, Gay Nineties (www.gay90s.com; 408 Hennepin Ave S) has dancing, dining and drag shows that attract both gay and straight clientele. Wilde Roast Cafe (www. wilderoastcafe.com; 65 Main St SE) features amazing baked goods, riverfront digs and a Victorian ambience worthy of its namesake, Oscar Wilde; it was ranked 'best cafe' by *Lavender*.

The Pride Festival (www.tcpride.com; late Jun), one of the USA's largest, draws about 400,000 revelers.

Historic Pantages, State & Orpheum Theatres
THEATER

(☑612-339-7007; www.hennepintheatretrust.org) These classy palaces are main venues for Broadway shows and touring acts, all in a row on Hennepin Ave S at street Nos 710, 805 and 910, respectively.

Brave New Workshop Theatre
THEATER

(☑612-332-6620; www.bravenewworkshop.com; 2605 Hennepin Ave S) An established venue for musical comedy, revue and satire; in Uptown.

Orchestra Hall
CLASSICAL

(☑612-371-5656; www.minnesotaorchestra.org; 1111 Nicollet Mall) Superb acoustics for concerts by the acclaimed Minnesota Symphony Orchestra.

Sports

Minnesotans love their sports teams. Note that ice hockey happens in St Paul (see p583).

Target Field
BASEBALL

(www.minnesotatwins.com; 3rd Ave N btwn 5th & 7th Sts N) The new stadium for the Twins pro baseball team is notable for its beyond-the-norm, locally focused food and drink.

Hubert H Humphrey Metrodome
FOOTBALL

(www.vikings.com; 900 5th St S) The Vikings pro football team passes in the marshmallow-like 'Dome (notable for its roof crashing in 2010 under the weight of too much snow).

Target Center
BASKETBALL

(www.nba.com/timberwolves; 600 1st Ave N) This is where the Timberwolves pro basketball team plays.

ℹ Information

Emergency & Medical Services
Fairview/University of Minnesota Medical Center (☑612-273-6402; 2450 Riverside Ave)

Internet Access
Minneapolis Public Library (www.hclib.org; 300 Nicollet Mall; ☺10am-8pm Tue & Thu, to 6pm Wed, Fri & Sat, noon-5pm Sun) Mod facility with free internet and wi-fi.

Media
City Pages (www.citypages.com) Weekly entertainment freebie.

Pioneer Press (www.twincities.com) St Paul's daily.

Star Tribune (www.startribune.com) Minneapolis' daily.

Vita.MN (www.vita.mn) The *Star Tribune*'s weekly entertainment freebie.

Tourist Information
Minneapolis Convention & Visitors Association (☑612-767-8000; www.minneapolis.org) Coupons, maps, guides and bike-route info online.

Websites
Ask the Minneapolitan (www.asktheminneapolitan.wordpress.com) Scenesters' guide to art shows, concerts and festivals.

Minneapolis Bicycle Program (www.ci.minneapolis.mn.us/bicycles) Trail maps and anything else you want to know about local cycling.

ℹ Getting There & Around

Air
The **Minneapolis-St Paul International Airport** (MSP; www.mspairport.com) is between the two cities to the south. It's the home of Delta Airlines, which operates several direct flights to/from Europe.

The Hiawatha light-rail line (regular/rush-hour fare $1.75/2.25, 25 minutes) is the cheapest way into Minneapolis. Bus 54 (regular/rush-hour fare $1.75/2.25, 25 minutes) goes to St Paul. Taxis cost around $45.

Bicycle
Minneapolis hovers near the top of rankings for 'best bike city' in the US. It has 84 miles of off-street paths, plus a large bicycle-share program, à la Paris. **Nice Ride** (www.niceridemn.com; ☺Apr-Oct) has 1000 bikes in 80 self-serve kiosks around the city. Users pay a subscription fee (per day/month $5/30) online or at the kiosk, plus a small fee per half-hour of use (with the first half-hour free). Bikes can be returned to any kiosk. For traditional rentals (which work better if you're riding for recreation versus transportation purposes), see p577.

Bus
Greyhound (☑612-371-3325; 950 Hawthorne Ave) Runs frequent buses to Milwaukee (seven hours), Chicago (nine hours) and Duluth (three hours).

Megabus (www.megabus.com/us) Runs express to Milwaukee (six hours) and Chicago (eight hours), often for lower fares than Greyhound. It departs from both downtown and the university; check the website for exact locations.

Public Transportation
Metro Transit (www.metrotransit.org; regular/rush-hr fare $1.75/2.25) runs frequent buses throughout the area, as well as the excellent Hiawatha light-rail line between downtown and

the Mall of America. Express bus 94 (regular/rush-hour fare $2.25/3) connects Minneapolis to St Paul; it departs from 6th St N's south side, just west of Hennepin Ave. A day pass ($6) is available from any rail station or bus driver.

Taxi

Call **Yellow Cab** (☑612-824-4444).

Train

The **Amtrak station** (☑651-644-6012; 730 Transfer Rd), off University Ave SE, is between Minneapolis and St Paul. Trains go daily to Chicago (eight hours) and Seattle (37 hours). The ride east to La Crosse (three hours), Wisconsin, is beautiful, skirting the Mississippi River and offering multiple eagle sightings.

St Paul

Smaller and quieter than its twin city Minneapolis, St Paul has retained more of a historic character. Walk through F Scott Fitzgerald's old stomping grounds, trek the trails along the mighty Mississippi River, or slurp some Lao soup.

◉ Sights & Activities

Downtown and Cathedral Hill hold most of the action. The latter features eccentric shops, Gilded Age Victorian mansions and, of course, the hulking church that gives the area its name. Downtown has the museums. An insider's tip: there's a shortcut between the two areas, a footpath that starts on the Hill House's west side and drops into downtown.

Revitalized **Harriet Island**, running south off Wabasha St downtown, is a lovely place to meander; it has a park, river walk, concert stages and fishing dock.

F Scott Fitzgerald Sights &
Summit Avenue   STREET

Great Gatsby author F Scott Fitzgerald is St Paul's most celebrated literary son. The Pullman-style apartment at **481 Laurel Avenue** is his birthplace. Four blocks away, Fitzgerald lived in the brownstone at **599 Summit Avenue** when he published *This Side of Paradise*. Both are private residences. From here stroll along Summit Ave toward the cathedral and gape at the Victorian homes rising from the street. Literature buffs should grab the *Fitzgerald Homes and Haunts* map at the visitor center to see other footprints.

FREE **Landmark Center**   MUSEUM
(www.landmarkcenter.org; 75 W 5th St; ☺8am-5pm Mon-Fri, to 8pm Thu, 10am-5pm Sat, noon-5pm Sun)

Downtown's turreted 1902 Landmark Center used to be the federal courthouse, where gangsters such as Alvin 'Creepy' Karpis were tried; plaques by the various rooms show who was brought to justice here. In addition to the city's visitor center, the building also contains a couple of small museums. On the 2nd floor the **Schubert Club Museum** (☑651-292-3267; www.schubert.org; ☺noon-4pm Sun-Fri) has a brilliant collection of old pianos and harpsichords – some tickled by Mozart, Beethoven and the like – as well as old manuscripts and letters from famous composers. The club plays free chamber music concerts Thursdays at noon from October to April. A free wood-turning museum (it's a decorative form of woodworking) is also on the 2nd floor.

FREE **Mississippi River**
Visitors Center   INTERPRETIVE CENTER
(☑651-293-0200; www.nps.gov/miss; ☺9:30am-5pm Sun-Thu, to 9pm Fri & Sat) The National Park Service visitor center occupies an alcove in the science museum's lobby. Definitely stop by to pick up trail maps and see what sort of free ranger-guided walks and bike rides are going on. Most take place at 10am on Wednesday, Thursday and Saturday in summer. In winter, the center hosts ice-fishing and snowshoeing jaunts.

MUSEUM
(☑651-221-9444; www.smm.org; 120 W Kellogg Blvd; adult/child $11/8.50; ☺9:30am-9:30pm, reduced hr in winter) Has the usual hands-on kids' exhibits and Omnimax theater ($5 extra). Adults will be entertained by the wacky quackery of the 4th floor's 'questionable medical devices.'

St Paul Curling Club   SNOW SPORTS
(www.stpaulcurlingclub.org; 470 Selby Ave; ☺from 11am Oct-May) For those uninitiated in northern ways, curling is a winter sport that involves sliding a hubcap-sized 'puck' down the ice toward a bull's-eye. The friendly folks here don't mind if you stop in to watch the action. Heck, they might invite you to share a Labatt's from the upstairs bar.

Cathedral of St Paul   CHURCH
(www.cathedralsaintpaul.org; 239 Selby Ave; ☺7am-7pm Sun-Fri, to 9pm Sat) Modeled on St Peter's Basilica in Rome, the cathedral presides over the city from its hilltop perch.

James J Hill House   HISTORIC BUILDING
(☑651-297-2555; www.mnhs.org/hillhouse; 240 Summit Ave; adult/child $8/5; ☺10am-3:30pm

ST PAUL FOR CHILDREN

Add the Science Museum of Minnesota (see p582) to the list below. Kids love its laser show and Omnimax.

» **Minnesota Children's Museum** (☑651-225-6000; www.mcm.org; 10 W 7th St; admission $9; ☺9am-4pm Mon-Thu, to 8pm Fri & Sat, to 5pm Sun; 🚼) Has the usual gamut of hands-on activities, as well as a giant anthill to burrow through, and the 'One World' intercultural community where kids can shop and vote.

» **Minnesota History Center** (☑651-259-3000; www.minnesotahistorycenter. org; 345 W Kellogg Blvd; adult/child $10/5, admission free Tue evening; ☺10am-8pm Tue, 10am-5pm Wed-Sat, noon-5pm Sun; 🚼) Educates with its 'A to Z' treasure hunt and climbable boxcar.

Wed-Sat, 1-3:30pm Sun) Tour the palatial stone mansion of railroad magnate Hill. It's a Gilded Age beauty, with five floors and 22 fireplaces.

☞ Tours

Down In History Tours   WALKING
(☑651-292-1220; www.wabashastreetcaves.com; 215 S Wabasha St; 45min tours $6; ☺5pm Thu, 11am Sat & Sun) Explore St Paul's underground caves, which gangsters once used as a speakeasy. The fun ratchets up on Thursday nights, when a swing band plays in the caverns (admission $7).

✴ Festivals & Events

St Paul Winter Carnival   CULTURAL
(www.winter-carnival.com; ☺late Jan) Ten days of ice sculptures, ice skating and ice fishing.

🛏 Sleeping

You'll find a bigger selection of accommodations in Minneapolis.

Covington Inn   B&B $$
(☑651-292-1411; www.covingtoninn.com; 100 Harriet Island Rd; r incl breakfast $150-235; P☻❄) This four-room, Harriet Island B&B is on a tugboat floating in the Mississippi River; watch the river traffic glide by while sipping your morning coffee.

Holiday Inn   HOTEL $$
(☑651-225-1515; www.holiday-inn.com/stpaulmn; 175 W 7th St; r $99-169; P☻❄🛜🏊) The rooms

are the usual decent quality you expect from the Holiday Inn chain; the perks are the location adjacent to the RiverCentre (convention center), a small pool and an on-site Irish pub. Parking is $15.

✕ Eating & Drinking

Grand Ave between Dale and Victoria Sts is a worthy browse, with cafes, foodie shops and ethnic eats in close proximity. Selby Ave by the intersection of Western Ave N also holds a quirky line-up.

Mickey's Dining Car   DINER $
(www.mickeysdiningcar.com; 36 W 7th St; mains $4-9; ☺24hr) Mickey's is a downtown classic, the kind of place where the friendly waitress calls you 'honey' and satisfied regulars line the bar with their coffee cups and newspapers. The food has timeless appeal, too: burgers, malts and apple pie.

WA Frost & Company   AMERICAN $$
(☑651-224-5715; www.wafrost.com; 374 Selby Ave; small plates $9-16, mains $18-34; ☺11am-1:30pm Mon-Fri, 10:30am-2pm Sat & Sun, 5-10pm daily) Frost's tree-shaded, ivy-covered, twinkling-light patio is right out of a Fitzgerald novel, perfect for a glass of wine, beer or gin. The restaurant locally sources many ingredients for dishes like the artisanal cheese plate, glazed tofu steak and cardamom-glazed duck.

Hmongtown Marketplace   ASIAN $
(www.hmongtownmarketplace.com; 217 Como Ave; mains $5-8; ☺8am-8pm) The nation's largest enclave of Hmong immigrants lives in the Twin Cities, and this market delivers their favorite Vietnamese, Lao and Thai dishes at its humble food court. Find the West Building and head to the back where vendors ladle hot-spiced papaya salad, beef ribs, sticky rice and curry noodle soup. Then stroll the market, where you can fix your dentures or buy a cockatoo or brass gong.

Happy Gnome   PUB
(www.thehappygnome.com; 498 Selby Ave; ☺from 11:30am; 🛜) Seventy craft beers flow from the taps, best sipped on the fireplace-warmed outdoor patio. The pub sits across the parking lot from the St Paul Curling Club.

★ Entertainment

Fitzgerald Theater   THEATER
(☑651-290-1221; www.fitzgeraldtheater.org; 10 E Exchange St) Where Garrison Keillor tapes his *Prairie Home Companion* radio show.

Ordway Center for
Performing Arts   CLASSICAL MUSIC
(☎651-224-4222; www.ordway.org; 345 Washington
St) Chamber music and the Minnesota Opera fill the hall here.

Xcel Energy Center   HOCKEY
(www.wild.com; 199 Kellogg Blvd) The Wild pro
hockey team skates at Xcel.

🔒 Shopping

Common Good Books   BOOKS
(www.commongoodbooks.com; 165 Western Ave
N; ⊙10am-10pm, to 8pm Sun) Garrison Keillor
owns this skylit, basement bookstore, tucked
under a coffee shop. It stacks shelves of fiction and nature books by Midwest authors –
many of whom may be in the upstairs cafe
tapping away at their laptops (the list by the
front door shows all the novels written by
patrons at the tables).

ⓘ Information

Visitor center (☎651-292-3225; www.visitst
paul.com; 75 W 5th St; ⊙10am-4pm Mon-Sat,
noon-4pm Sun) In the Landmark Center; makes
a good first stop for maps and DIY walking tour
info.

ⓘ Getting There & Around

St Paul is served by the same transit systems
as Minneapolis; see p581 for details. Greyhound
bus routes serving Minneapolis usually stop at
the **St Paul station** (☎651-222-0507; 166 W
University Ave) too.

Around Minneapolis-St Paul

Mall of America   MALL, AMUSEMENT PARK
(www.mallofamerica.com; off I-494 at 24th Ave;
⊙10am-9:30pm Mon-Sat, 11am-7pm Sun; 🚼)
The Mall of America, located in suburban
Bloomington near the airport, is the USA's
largest shopping center. Yes, it's just a mall,
filled with the usual stores, movie theaters
and eateries. But there's also a wedding chapel inside. And an 18-hole minigolf course
(☎952-883-8777; 3rd fl; admission $8). And an
amusement park, aka Nickelodeon Universe (☎952-883-8600; www.nickelodeonuni
verse.com), with 24 rides, including a couple
of scream-inducing roller coasters. To walk
through will cost you nothing; a one-day,
unlimited-ride wristband is $30; or you can
pay for rides individually ($3 to $6). What's
more, the state's largest aquarium, Minne-

WHAT THE...?

Behold the World's Largest Ball of
Twine (☎320-693-7544; www.darwin
twineball.com; 1st St; admission free;
⊙24hr) in Darwin, 62 miles west of Minneapolis on US 12. To be specific, it's
the 'Largest Built by One Person' –
Francis A Johnson wrapped the
17,400lb whopper on his farm over the
course of 29 years. Gawk at it in the
town gazebo. Better yet, visit the museum (⊙1-4pm Apr-Sep, by appointment
Oct-Mar) beside it and buy your own
twine ball starter kit in the gift shop.

sota Sea Life (☎952-883-0202; www.sealifeus.
com; adult/child $20/16) – where children can
touch sharks and stingrays – is in the mall
too. Combination passes are available to
save dough. The Hiawatha light-rail runs to/
from downtown.

Fort Snelling   HISTORIC SITE
(☎612-726-1171; www.historicfortsnelling.org; cnr
Hwys 5 & 55; adult/child $10/5; ⊙10am-5pm Tue-
Sat, noon-5pm Sun Jun-Aug, Sat only Sep & Oct;
🚼) East of the mall, Fort Snelling is the
state's oldest structure, established in 1820
as a frontier outpost in the remote Northwest Territory. Guides in period dress show
restored buildings and reenact pioneer life.

Southern Minnesota

Some of the scenic southeast can be seen on
short drives from the Twin Cities. Better is
a loop of a few days' duration, following the
rivers and stopping in some of the historic
towns and state parks.

Due east of St Paul, on Hwy 36, touristy
Stillwater (www.ilovestillwater.com), on the
lower St Croix River, is an old logging town
with restored 19th-century buildings, river
cruises and antique stores. It's also an official 'booktown,' an honor bestowed upon a
few small towns worldwide that possess an
extraordinary number of antiquarian bookshops. What's more, the town is filled with
classy historic B&Bs.

Larger Red Wing, to the south on US
61, is a similar but less-interesting restored
town, though it does offer its famous Red
Wing Shoes – actually more like sturdy
boots – and salt glaze pottery.

The prettiest part of the **Mississippi Valley** area begins south of here. To drive it and see the best bits, you'll need to flip-flop back and forth between Minnesota and Wisconsin on the Great River Road.

From Red Wing, cross the river on US 63. Before heading south along the water though, let's make a cheesy detour. Go north on US 63 in Wisconsin for 12 miles until you hit US 10. Turn right, and within a few miles, you're in Ellsworth, the 'Cheese Curd Capital.' Pull into **Ellsworth Cooperative Creamery** (☑715-273-4311; www.ellsworthcheesecurds. com; 232 N Wallace St; ⊗8am-5pm Mon-Fri, 8am-2pm Sat) – curd-maker for A&W and Dairy Queen – and savor squeaky goodness hot off the press (11am is prime time).

Back along the river on Wisconsin Hwy 35, a great stretch of road edges the bluffs beside **Maiden Rock**, **Stockholm** and **Pepin**. Follow your nose to local bakeries and cafes in the area.

Continuing south, cross back over the river to **Wabasha** in Minnesota, which has a historic downtown and large population of bald eagles that congregate in winter. To learn more, visit the **National Eagle Center** (☑651-565-4989; www.nationaleaglecenter.org; 50 Pembroke Ave; adult/child $8/5; ⊗10am-5pm Sun-Thu, 9am-6pm Fri & Sat).

Inland and south, the Bluff Country is dotted with limestone bluffs, southeast Minnesota's main geological feature. **Lanesboro** is a gem for rails-to-trails cycling and canoeing. Seven miles westward on County Rd 8 (call for directions) is **Old Barn Resort** (☑507-467-2512; www.barnresort.com; dm/r $25/50, camp/RV site $28/36; ⊗Apr–mid-Nov; ⊛), a pastoral hostel-cum-campground-restaurant-outfitter. **Harmony**, south of Lanesboro, is the center of an Amish community and another welcoming town.

Duluth & Northern Minnesota

Northern Minnesota is where you come to 'do some fishing, do some drinking,' as one resident summed it up.

DULUTH

At the Great Lakes' westernmost end, Duluth (with its neighbor, Superior, Wisconsin) is one of the busiest ports in the country. The town's dramatic location spliced into a cliff makes it a fab place to see changeable Lake Superior in action. The water, along with the area's trails and natural splendor, has earned Duluth a reputation as a hot spot for outdoors junkies.

◎ Sights & Activities

The waterfront area is distinctive. Mosey along the Lakewalk trail and around Canal Park, where most of the sights cluster. Look for the Aerial Lift Bridge, which rises to let ships into the port; about 1000 ships a year pass through here.

Maritime Visitors Center   MUSEUM
(☑218-720-5260; www.lsmma.com; 600 Lake Ave S; admission free; ⊗10am-9pm Jun-Aug, reduced hours Sep-May) Check the computer screens inside to learn what time the big ships will be sailing through port. The first-rate center also has exhibits on Great Lakes shipping and shipwrecks.

William A Irvin   MUSEUM
(☑218-722-7876; www.williamairvin.com; 350 Harbor Dr; adult/child $10/8; ⊗9am-6pm Jun-Aug, 10am-4pm May, Sep & Oct) To continue the nautical theme, tour this mighty 610ft Great Lakes freighter.

Great Lakes Aquarium   AQUARIUM
(☑218-740-3474; www.glaquarium.org; 353 Harbor Dr; adult/child $14.50/8.50; ⊗10am-6pm; ⊛) One of the country's few freshwater aquariums, the highlights here include the daily stingray feedings at 2pm, and the otter tanks.

Vista Fleet   BOAT TOUR
(☑218-722-6218; www.vistafleet.com; 323 Harbor Dr; adult/child $16/8; ⊗mid-May–Oct) Ah, everyone loves a boat ride. Vista's two-hour harbor cruise is a favorite, departing from the dock beside the *William A Irvin* in Canal Park.

SPAM MUSEUM

Sitting by its lonesome in Austin, near where I-35 and I-90 intersect in southern Minnesota, lies the **Spam Museum** (☑800-588-7726; www.spam. com; 1101 N Main St; admission free; ⊗10am-5pm Mon-Sat, noon-5pm Sun; ⊛), an entire institution devoted to the peculiar meat. It educates on how the blue tins have fed armies, become a Hawaiian food staple and inspired legions of haiku writers. What's more, you can chat up the staff (aka 'spambassadors'), indulge in free samples, and try your hand at canning the sweet pork magic.

DYLAN IN DULUTH

While Hibbing and the Iron Range are most often associated with Bob Dylan, he was born in Duluth. You'll see brown-and-white signs on Superior and London streets for **Bob Dylan Way** (www.bobdylanway.com), pointing out places associated with the legend (like the armory where he saw Buddy Holly in concert, and decided to become a musician). But you're on your own to find **Dylan's birthplace** (519 3rd Ave E), up a hill a few blocks northeast of downtown. Dylan lived on the top floor until age six, when his family moved inland to Hibbing. It's a private residence (and unmarked), so all you can do is stare from the street.

Leif Erikson Park   PARK

(cnr London Rd & 14th Ave E) This is a lakefront sweet spot with a rose garden, replica of Leif's Viking ship and free outdoor movies each Friday night in summer. Take the Lakewalk from Canal Park (about 1½ miles) and you can say you hiked the Superior Trail (p588), which traverses this stretch.

Outdoor Program   OUTDOORS

(☎218-726-6134, 218-726-7128; www.umdrsop.org; 154 Sports & Health Center; rental per day $20-40) Rent kayaks, camping gear and other equipment from the university. It also offers rock climbing, paddleboarding and snow-kiting programs; beginners are welcome for all activities.

Spirit Mountain   SKIING

(☎218-628-2891; www.spiritmt.com; 9500 Spirit Mountain Pl; per day adult/child $47/37; ⊙9am-8pm Sun-Thu, to 9pm Fri & Sat mid-Nov–Mar) Skiing and snowboarding are big pastimes come winter; a new zip line is in the works for summer. The mountain is 10 miles south of Duluth.

Enger Park   PARK

(Skyline Pkwy) For a spectacular view of the city and harbor, climb the rock tower in Enger Park, located a couple miles southwest by the golf course.

🛏 Sleeping

Duluth has several B&Bs; rooms cost at least $125 in the summer. Check **Duluth Historic Inns** (www.duluthbandb.com) for listings. The town's accommodations fill up fast in summer, which may mean you'll have to try your luck across the border in Superior, Wisconsin (where it's cheaper too).

Fitger's Inn   HOTEL $$

(☎218-722-8826; www.fitgers.com; 600 E Superior St; r incl breakfast $99-209; ❸@🛜) Fitger's carved its 62 large rooms, each with slightly varied decor, from an old brewery. Located on the Lakewalk, the pricier rooms have great water views. The free shuttle to local sights is handy.

Willard Munger Inn   INN $$

(☎218-624-4814, 800-982-2453; www.mungerinn.com; 7408 Grand Ave; r incl breakfast $70-136; ❸@🛜) Family-owned Munger Inn offers a fine variety of rooms (budget to Jacuzzi suites), along with perks for outdoor enthusiasts, such as hiking and biking trails right outside the door, free use of bikes and canoes and a fire pit. It's near Spirit Mountain.

🍴 Eating & Drinking

Most restaurants and bars reduce their hours in winter. The Canal Park waterfront area has eateries in all price ranges.

DeWitt-Seitz Marketplace   ECLECTIC $$

(www.dewittseitz.com; 394 Lake Ave S) This building in Canal Park holds several eateries, including vegetarian-friendly (⊙11am-8:30pm Sun-Thu, to 9:30pm Fri & Sat; 🍴), hippyish cafe **Amazing Grace** (⊙7am-10pm) and **Northern Waters Smokehaus** (⊙10am-9pm Mon-Sat, 11am-5pm Sun), with sustainably harvested salmon and whitefish (primo for picnics).

Chester Creek Cafe   CAFE $$

(☎218-723-8569; www.astccc.net; 1902 E 8th St; mains $7-14; ⊙7am-9pm Mon-Sat, 7:30am-8pm Sun; 🍴) Earthy and pinewood-boothed, Chester Creek plates omelets, tempeh Reubens, Thai tofu curry, and fish and meat dishes. It's in the university area, about 2 miles from downtown.

🌿 Pizza Luce   PIZZERIA $$

(☎218-727-7400; www.pizzaluce.com; 11 E Superior St; large pizza $20-22; ⊙8am-1:30am Sun-Thu, to 2:30am Fri & Sat; 🍴) It cooks locally sourced breakfasts and gourmet pizzas. It's also plugged into the local music scene and hosts bands. Fully licensed.

Fitger's Brewhouse   BREWERY

(www.fitgersbrewhouse.net; 600 E Superior St; ⊙from 11am) In the hotel complex, the Brewhouse rocks with live music and fresh brews. Try them via the seven-beer sampler (3oz glasses $7).

TOP CHOICE **Thirsty Pagan** BREWERY
(www.thirstypaganbrewing.com; 1623 Broadway St; ⊙from 4pm) This one's a bit of a trek, over the bridge in Superior, Wisconsin (a 10-minute drive), but worth it for the aggressive, spicy beers to wash down hand-tossed pizzas.

🛍 Shopping

Electric Fetus MUSIC
(☑218-722-9970; www.electricfetus.com; 12 E Superior St; ⊙9am-9pm Mon-Fri, 9am-8pm Sat, 11am-6pm Sun) Sells a whopping selection of CDs, vinyl and local arts and crafts, including Dylan tunes and T-shirts. It sits across the street from Pizza Luce.

ℹ Information

Duluth Visitors Center (☑800-438-5884; www.visitduluth.com; Harbor Dr; ⊙9:30am-7:30pm summer) Seasonal center, opposite the Vista dock.

ℹ Getting There & Around

Greyhound (☑218-722-5591; 4426 Grand Ave) has a couple of buses daily to Minneapolis ($20 to $36, three hours).

NORTH SHORE

Hwy 61 (see p587) is the main vein through the North Shore. It edges Lake Superior and passes numerous state parks, waterfalls, hiking trails and mom-and-pop towns en route to Canada. Lots of weekend, summer and fall traffic makes reservations essential.

Two Harbors (www.twoharborschamber.com) has a museum, lighthouse and B&B. Actually, the latter two are one and the same, with the Lighthouse B&B (☑218-834-4814; www.lighthousebb.org; r incl breakfast $135-155) being a unique place to spend the night if you can snag one of its four rooms. Nearby, Betty's Pies (www.bettyspies.com; 1633 Hwy 61; sandwiches $5-9; ⊙7am-9pm, reduced Oct-May) wafts a five-layer chocolate tinful among its rackful of wares.

Route highlights north of Two Harbors are Gooseberry Falls, Split Rock Lighthouse and Palisade Head. About 110 miles from Duluth, artsy little Grand Marais (www.grandmarais.com) makes an excellent base for exploring the Boundary Waters and environs. For Boundary permits and information, visit the Gunflint Ranger Station (☑218-387-1750; ⊙7am-5pm May-Sep), just south of town.

Do-it-yourself enthusiasts can learn to build boats, tie flies or brew beer at the North House Folk School (☑218-387-9762; www.northhousefolkschool.com; 500 Hwy 61). The course list is phenomenal – as is the school's two-hour sailing trip aboard the Viking schooner *Hjordis* (adult/child $45/35). Reserve in advance.

Grand Marais' lodging options include camping, resorts and motels, like the Harbor Inn (☑218-387-1191; www.bytheharbor.com; 207 Wisconsin St; r $115-135; 🛜) in town or rustic, trail-encircled Naniboujou Lodge (☑218-387-2688; www.naniboujou.com; 20 Naniboujou; r $95-115), which is 14 miles north of town. Sven and Ole's (☑218-387-1713; www.svenandoles.com; 9 Wisconsin St; sandwiches $6-8; ⊙11am-8pm, to 9pm Thu-Sat) is a classic for sandwiches and pizza; beer flows from the attached Pickled Herring Pub. Ecofriendly Angry Trout Cafe (☑218-387-1265; www.angrytroutcafe.com; 416 Hwy 61; mains $19-25; ⊙11am-8:30pm May–mid-Oct) grills fresh-plucked lake fish in a converted fishing shanty.

Hwy 61 continues to Grand Portage National Monument (☑218-475-0123; www.nps.gov/grpo; admission free; ⊙hrs vary, mid-May–mid-Oct), beside Canada, where the early

SCENIC DRIVE: HIGHWAY 61

Hwy 61 conjures a headful of images. Local boy Bob Dylan mythologized it in his angry 1965 album *Highway 61 Revisited*. It's the fabled 'Blues Highway' clasping the Mississippi River en route to New Orleans (see p36). And in northern Minnesota, it evokes red-tinged cliffs and forested beaches as it follows Lake Superior's shoreline.

But let's back up and get a few things straight. The Blues Highway is actually US 61, and it starts just north of the Twin Cities. Hwy 61 is a state scenic road, and it starts in Duluth. To confuse matters more, there are two 61s between Duluth and Two Harbors: a four-lane expressway and a two-lane 'Old Hwy 61' (also called North Shore Scenic Drive, which morphs from London Rd in Duluth). Whatever the name, take it. After Two Harbors, it's one wondrous strip of pavement all the way to the Canadian border. For more information, check the North Shore Scenic Drive at www.superiorbyways.com.

voyageurs had to carry their canoes around the Pigeon River rapids. This was the center of a far-flung trading empire, and the reconstructed 1788 trading post and Ojibwe village is well worth seeing. **Isle Royale National Park** in Lake Superior is reached by daily **ferries** (☎218-475-0024; www.isleroyale boats.com; day trip adult/child $53/30) from May to October. (The park is also accessible from Michigan; see p563.)

BOUNDARY WATERS

From Two Harbors, Hwy 2 runs inland to the legendary **Boundary Waters Canoe Area Wilderness (BWCAW)**. This pristine region has more than 1000 lakes and streams in which to dip a paddle. It's possible to go just for the day, but most people opt for at least one night of camping. If you're willing to dig in and canoe for a while, you'll lose the crowds. Camping then becomes a wonderfully remote experience where it will be you, the howling wolves, the moose who's nuzzling the tent and the aurora borealis' greenish light filling the night sky. Beginners are welcome, and everyone can get set up with gear from local lodges and outfitters. **Permits** (☎877-550-6777; www.recreation.gov; adult/child $16/8, plus $6 reservation fee) are required for overnight stays. Day permits, though free, are also required; get them at BWCAW entry point kiosks or ranger stations. Call **Superior National Forest** (☎218-626-4300; www.fs.fed.us/r9/forests/superior/bwcaw) for details; the website has a useful trip planning guide. Try to plan ahead, as permits are quota restricted and sometimes run out.

Many argue the best BWCAW access is via the engaging town of **Ely** (www.ely.org), northeast of the Iron Range area, which has accommodations, restaurants and scores of outfitters. The **International Wolf Center** (☎218-365-4695; www.wolf.org; 1369 Hwy 169; adult/child $8.50/4.50; ⊙10am-5pm, closed Sun-Thu mid-Oct–mid-May) offers intriguing exhibits and wolf-viewing trips. Across the highway from the center, **Kawishiwi Ranger Station** (☎218-365-7600; 1393 Hwy 169; ⊙7am-4:30pm May-Sep) provides expert BWCAW camping and canoeing details, trip suggestions and required permits.

In winter, Ely gets mushy – it's a renowned dogsledding town. Outfitters such as **Wintergreen Dogsled Lodge** (☎218-365-6022; www.dogsledding.com; 4hr tour $125) offer numerous packages.

IRON RANGE DISTRICT

An area of red-tinged scrubby hills rather than mountains, Minnesota's Iron Range District consists of the Mesabi and Vermilion Ranges, running north and south of Hwy 169 from roughly Grand Rapids northeast to Ely. Iron was discovered here in the 1850s, and at one time more than three-quarters of the nation's iron ore was extracted from these vast open-pit mines. Visitors can see working mines and the terrain's raw, sparse beauty all along Hwy 169.

In **Calumet**, a perfect introduction is the **Hill Annex Mine State Park** (☎218-247-7215; www.mnstateparks.info; 880 Gary St; tours adult/child $10/6; ⊙9am-5pm Wed-Sat), with its open-pit tours and exhibit center. Tours are held in summertime only, from Wednesday to Saturday at 12:30pm and 3pm; there's also a fossil tour at 10am.

An even bigger pit sprawls in **Hibbing**, where a must-see **viewpoint** (admission free; ⊙9am-5pm mid-May–mid-Sep) north of town overlooks the 3-mile Hull-Rust Mahoning Mine. Bob Dylan lived at 2425 E 7th Ave as a boy and teenager; the **Hibbing Public Library** (☎218-362-5959; www.hibbing.lib.mn.us; 2020 E 5th Ave; ⊙9am-8pm Mon-Thu, to 5pm Fri) has well-done Dylan displays and a free walking tour map (available online, too) that takes you past various sites, like the place

---

SUPERIOR HIKING TRAIL

The 205-mile **Superior Hiking Trail** (www.shta.org) follows the lake-hugging ridgeline between Two Harbors and the Canadian border. Along the way it passes dramatic red-rock overlooks and the occasional moose and black bear. Trailheads with parking lots pop up every 5 to 10 miles, making it ideal for day hikes. The **Superior Shuttle** (☎218-834-5511; www.superiorhikingshuttle.com; from $17; ⊙Fri-Sun mid-May–mid-Oct) makes life even easier, picking up trekkers from 17 stops along the route. Overnight hikers will find 81 backcountry campsites and several lodges to cushion the body come nightfall; the trail website has details. The whole footpath is free, with no reservations or permits required. Duluth also sports 39 miles of the trail, which should be connected to Two Harbors by 2012.

where Bobby had his bar mitzvah. **Zimmy's** (www.zimmys.com; 531 E Howard St; mains $14-20; 11am-1am) has more memorabilia, plus drinks and pub grub. For a bed, try **Hibbing Park Hotel** (218-262-3481; www.hibbingpark hotel.com; 1402 E Howard St; r $60-95;).

Soudan sports the area's only **underground mine** (218-753-2245; www.soudan. umn.edu; 1379 Stuntz Bay Rd; tours adult/child $10/6; 10am-4pm late May–early Sep); wear warm clothes. A fire halted tours in 2011, but they should be operating again by 2012.

VOYAGEURS NATIONAL PARK

In the 17th century, French-Canadian fur traders, or voyageurs, began exploring the Great Lakes and northern rivers by canoe. **Voyageurs National Park** (www.nps.gov/voya) covers part of their customary waterway, which became the border between the USA and Canada.

It's all about water up here. Most of the park is accessible only by hiking or motorboat – the waters are mostly too wide and too rough for canoeing, though kayaks are becoming popular. A few access roads lead to campgrounds and lodges on or near Lake Superior, but these are mostly used by people putting in their own boats.

The visitor centers are car accessible and good places to begin your visit. Twelve miles east of International Falls on Hwy 11 is **Rainy Lake Visitors Center** (218-286-5258; 9am-5pm late May–Sep, closed Mon & Tue rest of year), the main park office. Ranger-guided walks and boat tours are available here. Seasonal visitor centers are at **Ash River** (218-374-3221; 9am-5pm late May–Sep) and **Kabetogama Lake** (218-875-2111; 9am-5pm late May–Sep). These areas have outfitters, rentals and services, plus some smaller bays for canoeing.

Houseboating is the region's rage. Outfitters such as **Ebel's** (888-883-2357; www. ebels.com; 10326 Ash River Trail, Orr) and **Voyagaire Houseboats** (800-882-6287; www. voyagaire.com; 7576 Gold Coast Rd, Crane Lake) can set you up. Rentals range from $275 to $700 per day, depending on boat size. Novice boaters are welcome and receive instruction on how to operate the vessels.

Otherwise, for sleeping, your choices are pretty much camping or resorts. The 12-room, shared-bath **Kettle Falls Hotel** (218-240-1724; www.kettlefallshotel.com; r/cottage incl breakfast $80/160; May–mid-Oct) is an exception, located in the park's midst and accessible only by boat; make arrangements

ⓘ GREEN & NATIVE-OWNED BUSINESSES

Green Routes (www.greenroutes.org) lists sustainable, community-oriented eateries, accommodations, shops and activity providers, including many that are Native American–owned. Most listings are in Minnesota, though there are a few from surrounding states such as Wisconsin and South Dakota, too.

with the owners for pick-up (per person round-trip $45). **Nelson's Resort** (800-433-0743; www.nelsonsresort.com; 7632 Nelson Rd; cabins from $180) at Crane Lake is a winner for hiking, fishing and relaxing under blue skies.

While this is certainly a remote and wild area, those seeking wildlife, canoeing and forest camping in all their glory are best off in the Boundary Waters.

BEMIDJI & CHIPPEWA NATIONAL FOREST

This area is synonymous with outdoor activities and summer fun. Campsites and cottages abound, and almost everybody is fishing-crazy.

Itasca State Park (218-266-2100; www. mnstateparks.info; off Hwy 71 N; per vehicle $5, tent & RV sites $16-25) is an area highlight. You can walk across the tiny headwaters of the mighty Mississippi River, rent canoes or bikes, hike the trails and camp. The log **HI Mississippi Headwaters Hostel** (218-266-3415; www.mississippiheadwatershostel.org; dm $24-27, r $80-130;) is in the park; winter hours vary, so call ahead. Or if you want a little rustic luxury, try the venerable **Douglas Lodge** (866-857-2757; r $75-130;), run by the park, which also has cabins and two good dining rooms.

On the western edge of the forest, about 30 miles from Itasca, tidy **Bemidji** is an old lumber town with a well-preserved downtown and a giant statue of logger Paul Bunyan and his faithful blue ox, Babe. The **visitor center** (800-458-2223; www.visitbe midji.com; 300 Bemidji Ave N; 8am-5pm Mon-Fri, 10am-4pm Sat, 11am-2pm Sun Jun-Aug, closed Sat & Sun Sep-May) displays Paul's toothbrush. Stay by the lake and fish at **Taber's Log Cabins** (218-751-5781; www.taberslogcabins. com; 2404 Bemidji Ave N; cabins $69-79; May-Oct;).

Understand
Eastern USA

population per sq mile

AUSTRALIA   USA   CANADA

= 11 people

Eastern USA Today

Economic Woes

» Household income New Hampshire (2008-2010): $66,300

» Household income Mississippi (2008-2010): $36,850

» Population density New York City: 27,530 per sq mi

» Population density Maine: 43 per sq mi

» Cheese produced annually Wisconsin: 2.4 billion pounds

» Number of vacant homes in Florida (2010): 1.5 million

The East, along with the rest of the country, has experienced a tumultuous economy in recent years. What started as a collapse of the US real estate market in 2007 spread to the banking sector, and some financial institutions subsequently failed. Thus began the nation's largest fiscal crisis since the Great Depression. In 2009, Congress passed an ambitious $800 billion stimulus package, but it didn't bear much fruit in the eyes of many locals – even though economists estimated the stimulus did soften the blow of the recession.

While the faltering economy has affected the entire country, some states in the East have been especially hard hit. In Florida, home foreclosures flooded the market, so that by 2010, 18% of houses were vacant. Meanwhile, Michigan can't shake one of the nation's highest unemployment rates (more than 11%), which has plagued it since the recession's start, and is due to its economic reliance on the beleaguered car-making industry. Many other Midwestern Rust Belt economies – in northern Ohio, Indiana and Illinois – have also felt the manufacturing pinch, and states there join Florida at the top of the foreclosure rolls.

Political Fraction

With lost jobs, overvalued mortgages and little relief in sight, the conditions were ripe for the Tea Party. Named after the infamous 1773 event in Boston, during which patriots dumped British tea to protest the government's tax on it, today's Tea Party is a populist movement of politically conservative republicans who decry high taxes and federal spending. Government bailouts (the banking and auto industries) and President Obama's healthcare reform (derisively named Obamacare) particularly capture their ire.

Classic Reads

To Kill a Mockingbird (1960) Harper Lee's Pulitzer winner about racism in Depression-era Alabama.
A Walk in the Woods (1998) Humorist Bill Bryson attempts to hike the Appalachian Trail.

A Confederacy of Dunces (1980) John Kennedy Toole's tale of a misfit questing for a job.
Walden (1854) Thoreau's tale of living simply near a pond.
The Orchid Thief (1998) Yankee Journalist Susan Orlean loses her head in the swamp.

Rock Playlist

Highway 61 Revisited Bob Dylan
My City was Gone Pretenders
Atlantic City Bruce Springsteen
Sweet Home Alabama Lynyrd Skynard
No Sleep till Brooklyn Beastie Boys

USA belief systems
(% of population)

52 Protestant

24 Roman Catholic

2 Mormon

2 Jewish

20 Other

if USA were 100 people

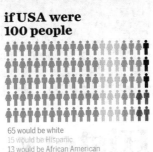

65 would be white
15 would be Hispanic
13 would be African American
4 would be Asian American
3 would be other

The Tea Party and fellow republicans have made inroads into traditionally liberal regions of the East. The most dramatic example is the Massachusetts Senate seat they won in 2010. Held by Ted Kennedy for almost a half-century until his death, the seat was considered a shoo-in for Democrats – until Tea Party support helped carry pickup-truck-driving Republican Scott Brown into office.

In essence, the region is becoming more and more divided. Wisconsin took center stage in 2011, as battles raged between Republican Governor Scott Walker (with Tea Party supporters) and pro-union government workers fighting over wages and collective bargaining rights. Despite huge protests Walker got his way, but the resulting acrimony led to recall elections (permitted in Wisconsin) for many lawmakers. Walker himself is eligible for a recall vote in 2012. The presidential election also takes place in 2012.

Getting Back on Track

Hurricane Katrina and its aftermath have reshaped much of the Gulf Coast. Locals have negotiated the tricky path through redevelopment, the return of displaced peoples, wetlands restoration and outsider involvement. Though revitalization has been successful in some areas – including parts of New Orleans, which has become a spawning ground for new frontiers of urban planning – progress has been painfully slow in other areas, especially the poorer ones.

In April 2010 the Gulf Coast suffered another major blow: the Deepwater Horizon oil spill in the Gulf of Mexico. Roughly five million barrels of crude oil gushed into the water before British Petroleum plugged the leak. The extent of damage to local wildlife and the fisheries is still being assessed, but the region is hanging tough, as always.

Classic Films

Gone with the Wind (1939) Civil War–era saga of the South.
Mr Smith Goes to Washington (1939) Jimmy Stewart gets a crash course in politics and corruption.
The Untouchables (1987) Eliot Ness takes down Al Capone in gangster-era Chicago.
Key Largo (1948) Bogart, Bacall and Florida gangsters.
Do the Right Thing (1989) NYC's racial melting pot boils over on a Brooklyn block.

Blues Playlist

Take the A Train Ella Fitzgerald
Georgia on My Mind Ray Charles
Cross Road Blues Robert Johnson
Potato Head Blues Louis Armstrong

History

The startling New World for Europeans was ancient homeland for thousands of indigenous tribes. Sadly, introduced diseases would decimate their numbers, followed by centuries of warfare to push them off the land.

The earliest colonies struggled to survive. By the 17th century, however, British colonials in present-day Virginia and Massachusetts had put down permanent roots. From there, the American colony flourished, helped along by slaves and a plantation economy.

By 1776, the colonists had developed an independent streak, and waged war for their autonomy. Washington, Adams, Jefferson, Franklin and others laid the foundations for an ingenious new type of government by the people.

In the 19th century the survival of the fledgling nation was at stake when the slave-owning south seceded from the union. Seeing no other way to keep the nation intact, Abraham Lincoln led the nation into a bloody, four-year-long Civil War.

The republic survived, and more importantly slavery was abolished. The north helped rebuild the south, but bitterness lived on. Freed blacks soon found themselves disenfranchised, and 'separate but equal' became a justification for overt discrimination. America became deeply segregated.

World war soon overshadowed racial strife, followed by the 'roaring twenties'. The good times didn't last, and the Great Depression erupted in 1929, destroying banks, farms and businesses and leaving millions unemployed. Roosevelt's New Deal helped pull the nation back together. But then fascist and totalitarian regimes in Europe and the Pacific stoked world war once again, which drew in the US and 16 million Americans who served in the military.

The 1950s were boom days once again, with suburban homes and fancy highways all the rage. However, the threat of nuclear annihilation seemed ever-present as the Cold War kicked into high gear, with proxy wars against communism waged in Korea and Vietnam.

Colonial Sights

» Williamsburg, Virginia

» Jamestown, Virginia

» Plymouth, Massachusetts

North End, Boston

Philadelphia

Annapolis, Maryland

» Charleston, South Carolina

TIMELINE	7000 BC–AD 100	1492	1620
	'Archaic period' marked by nomadic hunter-gatherer lifestyle. By the end of this period, corn, beans and squash (the agricultural 'three sisters') and permanent settlements are well established.	Italian explorer Christopher Columbus 'discovers' America. He names the indigenous inhabitants 'Indians,' mistakenly thinking he had reached the Indies.	The *Mayflower* lands at Plymouth with 102 English Pilgrims, who have come to the New World to escape religious persecution. The Wampanoag tribe saves them from starvation.

Assassinations (John F Kennedy, Martin Luther King Jr, Robert F Kennedy), riots, a devastating and unpopular war, political corruption (Watergate) and sexual liberation ensured the tumultuous 1960s and 70s never had a dull moment. It was also a time of momentous change as African Americans achieved hard-won victories in the realm of civil rights.

The 1980s saw decaying cities and a stratified society as whites took flight to the suburbs. The 1990s brought good times again, with peace, prosperity, budget surpluses and a growing high-tech sector. The 21st century began ominously with the terrorist attacks on New York and Washington, followed by two costly, ongoing wars in Iraq and Afghanistan and a real bummer of an economy.

First Inhabitants

Among North America's most significant prehistoric cultures were the Mound Builders, who inhabited the Ohio and Mississippi River valleys from around 3000 BC to AD 1200. In Illinois, Cahokia (p527) was once a metropolis of 20,000 people, the largest in pre-Columbian North America. Similar mounds rise up throughout the Eastern USA, including several along the Natchez Trace (p39) in Mississippi.

By the time the first Europeans arrived, several different groups of Native Americans occupied the land, such as the Wampanoag in New England, the Calusa in southern Florida and the Shawnee in the Midwest. Two centuries later, they were all but gone. European explorers left diseases in their wake to which indigenous peoples had no immunity. More than any other factor – war, slavery or famine – disease epidemics devastated Native American populations by anywhere from 50% to 90%.

European claims

In 1492, Italian explorer Christopher Columbus, backed by Spain, voyaged west looking for the East Indies. He found the Bahamas. With visions of gold, Spanish explorers quickly followed: Cortés conquered much of today's Mexico; Pizarro conquered Peru; and Ponce de León wandered through Florida looking for the fountain of youth. Not to be left out, the French explored Canada and the Midwest, while the Dutch and English cruised North America's eastern seaboard.

With all the ensuing action in the north, it's easy to forget the USA's first city was St Augustine, Florida, where the Spanish set up shop in 1565. Up the coast in 1607, a group of English noblemen established that country's first permanent North American settlement at Jamestown (p293). Earlier English settlements had ended badly, and Jamestown almost did too: the noblemen chose a swamp, planted their crops late and died from disease and starvation. Local tribes provided the settlement with enough aid to survive.

Before Jamestown or Plymouth Rock, a group of 116 British men and women set up a colony at Roanoke, North Carolina in the late 1580s. When a supply ship returned three years later, the settlers had disappeared without a trace. The fate of the 'Lost Colony' remains one of America's greatest mysteries.

1675	1773	1775	1776
For decades, the Pilgrims and local tribes live fairly cooperatively, but deadly conflict erupts in 1675. King Philip's War lasts 14 months and kills over 5000 people (mostly Native Americans).	To protest a British tax on tea, Bostonians dress as Mohawks, board East India Company ships and toss their tea overboard during what would be named the Boston Tea Party.	Paul Revere rides from Boston to warn colonial 'Minutemen' that the British are coming. The next day, 'the shot heard round the world' is fired at Lexington, starting the Revolutionary War.	On July 4, colonies sign the Declaration of Independence. Creators of the document include John Hancock, Samuel Adams, John Adams, Benjamin Franklin and Thomas Jefferson.

For Jamestown and America, 1619 proved a pivotal year: the colony established the House of Burgesses, a representative assembly of citizens to decide local laws, and it received its first boatload of 20 African slaves.

The next year was equally momentous, as a group of radically religious Puritans pulled ashore at what would become Plymouth, Massachusetts (p177). The Pilgrims were escaping religious persecution under the 'corrupt' Church of England, and in the New World they saw a divine opportunity to create a new society that would be a religious and moral beacon. The Pilgrims signed a 'Mayflower Compact,' one of the seminal texts of American democracy, to govern themselves by consensus.

Capitalism & Colonialism

For the next two centuries, European powers competed for position and territory in the New World, extending European politics into the Americas. As Britain's Royal Navy came to rule Atlantic seas, England increasingly profited from its colonies and eagerly consumed the fruits of their labors – sweet tobacco from Virginia, sugar and coffee from the Caribbean.

Over the 17th and 18th centuries, slavery in America was slowly legalized into a formal institution to support this plantation economy. By 1800, one out of every five persons was a slave.

Meanwhile, Britain mostly left the American colonists to govern themselves. Town meetings and representative assemblies, in which local citizens (that is, white men with property) debated community problems and voted on laws and taxes, became common.

However, by the end of the Seven Years' War in 1763, Britain was feeling the strains of running an empire: it had been fighting France for a century and had colonies scattered all over the world. It was time to clean up bureaucracies and share financial burdens.

The colonies, however, resented English taxes and policies. Frustrations came to a head with the Boston Tea Party in 1773, after which Britain clamped down hard, shutting Boston's harbor and increasing its military presence. In 1774 representatives from 12 colonies convened the First Continental Congress in Philadelphia's Independence Hall (p127) to air complaints and prepare for the inevitable war ahead.

Revolution & The Republic

In April 1775, British troops skirmished with armed colonists in Massachusetts (who were prepared for the fight, thanks to Paul Revere's famous warning), and the Revolutionary War began. George Washington, a wealthy Virginia farmer, was chosen to lead the American army. Trouble was, Washington lacked gunpowder and money (the colonists resisted taxes even for their own military), and his troops were a motley

The whaling industry thrived in New England in the 18th century, especially around Massachusetts. Buzzards Bay, Nantucket Island and New Bedford were all prominent centers. New Bedford eventually hosted a whaling fleet of over 300 ships, employing 10,000 people directly and indirectly, and earning over $12 million in profits.

According to legend, George Washington was so honest that after chopping down his father's cherry tree when he was just a child, he admitted, 'I cannot tell a lie. I did it with my little hatchet.'

1787	1791	1803–06	1812
The Constitutional Convention in Philadelphia draws up the US Constitution. Federal power is balanced between the presidency, Congress and the judiciary.	Bill of Rights is adopted as 10 constitutional amendments articulating citizens' rights, including freedom of speech, a free press and the right to bear arms.	President Thomas Jefferson sends Meriwether Lewis and William Clark west. Guided by the Shoshone tribeswoman Sacajawea, they trailblaze from St Louis, Missouri, to the Pacific Ocean and back.	The War of 1812 begins with battles against the British and Native Americans in the Great Lakes region. Even after the 1815 Treaty of Ghent, fighting continues along the Gulf Coast.

collection of poorly armed farmers, hunters and merchants, who regularly quit and returned to their farms due to lack of pay. On the other side, the British 'Redcoats' represented the world's most powerful military. The inexperienced General Washington had to improvise constantly, sometimes wisely retreating, sometimes engaging in 'ungentlemanly' sneak attacks. During the winter of 1777–78, the American army nearly starved at Valley Forge, Pennsylvania (p142).

Meanwhile, the Second Continental Congress tried to articulate what exactly they were fighting for. In January 1776, Thomas Paine published the wildly popular *Common Sense,* which passionately argued for independence from England. Soon, independence seemed not just logical, but noble and necessary, and on July 4, 1776, the Declaration of Independence was finalized and signed. Largely written by Thomas Jefferson, it elevated the 13 colonies' particular gripes against the monarchy into a universal declaration of individual rights and republican government.

However, to succeed on the battlefield, General Washington needed help, not just patriotic sentiment. In 1778, Benjamin Franklin persuaded France (always eager to trouble England) to ally with the revolutionaries, and they provided the troops, material and sea power that helped win the war. The British surrendered at Yorktown, Virginia, in 1781, and two years later the Treaty of Paris formally recognized the 'United States of America.'

At first, the nation's loose confederation of fractious, squabbling states were hardly 'united.' So the founders gathered again in Philadelphia, and in 1787 drafted a new-and-improved Constitution: the US government was given a stronger federal center, with checks and balances between its three major branches; and to guard against the abuse of centralized power, a citizen's Bill of Rights was approved in 1791.

As radical as it was, though, the Constitution also preserved the economic and social status quos. Rich landholders kept their property, which included their slaves; Native Americans were excluded from the nation; and women were excluded from politics. These blatant discrepancies and injustices, which were widely noted, were the result of pragmatic compromise (eg to get slave-dependent Southern states to agree) and also widespread beliefs in the essential rightness of things as they were.

Louisiana Purchase & the Move West

As the 19th century dawned on the young nation, optimism was the mood of the day. Agriculture was industrialized, and US commerce surged. In 1803, Thomas Jefferson bought land from Frenchman Napoleon Bonaparte. The Louisiana Purchase included New Orleans and about 15 present-day states west of the Mississippi River. Expansion began in earnest.

Great History Museums

» Henry Ford Museum/Greenfield Village, Detroit

» National Civil Rights Museum, Memphis

» New Bedford Whaling Museum, Massachusetts

» National Museum of the American Indian, Washington, DC

1861–65
American Civil War erupts between North and South (delineated by the Mason–Dixon line). The war's end on April 9, 1865, is marred by President Lincoln's assassination five days later.

1870
Freed black men are given the vote, but the South's segregationist 'Jim Crow' laws (which remain until the 1960s) effectively disenfranchise blacks from every meaningful sphere of daily life.

RICHARD CUMMINS/LONELY PLANET IMAGES ©

» Lincoln Memorial (p247), Washington, DC

Relations between the US and Britain – despite lively trade – remained tense, and in 1812, the US declared war on England again. The two-year conflict ended without much gain by either side, although the British abandoned their forts, and the US vowed to avoid Europe's 'entangling alliances.'

In the 1830s and 1840s, with growing nationalist fervor and dreams of continental expansion, many Americans came to believe it was 'Manifest Destiny' that all the land should be theirs. The 1830 Indian Removal Act aimed to clear one obstacle. It designated land west of the Mississippi as 'Indian territory.' Native Americans were meant to relocate themselves there, thus clearing fertile valleys in eastern states like Georgia, and Alabama for settlement and capitalism. Many tribes resisted removal, including the Seminole in Florida, but the US government cajoled, threatened and bribed Native Americans to sign treaties and cooperate; when that failed, the government used guns.

Meanwhile, newly built railroads cleared another hurdle, linking midwestern and western lands with East Coast markets. As new states joined the USA, a troubling question loomed: would they be slave states or free states? The nation's future depended on the answer

The Civil War

The US Constitution hadn't ended slavery, but it had given Congress the power to approve (or not) slavery in new states. Public debates raged constantly over the expansion of slavery, particularly since this shaped the balance of power between the industrial North and the agrarian South.

Since the founding, Southern politicians had dominated government and defended slavery as 'natural and normal,' which an 1856 *New York Times* editorial called 'insanity.' The Southern proslavery lobby enraged northern abolitionists. But even many Northern politicians feared that ending slavery with a pen-stroke would be ruinous. Limit slavery, they reasoned, and in the competition with industry and free labor, slavery would wither without inciting a violent slave revolt – a constantly feared possibility. Indeed, in 1859, radical abolitionist John Brown tried unsuccessfully to spark such an uprising at Harpers Ferry (p308).

The economics of slavery were undeniable. In 1860, there were over four million slaves in the US, most held by Southern planters – who grew 75% of the world's cotton, accounting for over half of US exports. Thus, the Southern economy supported the nation's economy, and it required slaves. The 1860 presidential election became a referendum on this issue, and the election was won by a young politician from Illinois who favored limiting slavery: Abraham Lincoln.

Civil War Onscreen

» *Civil War* (documentary), Ken Burns

» *Glory*, Edward Zwick

» *Gods & General*, Ronald Maxwell

» *Gettysburg*, Ronald Maxwell

» *Gone With the Wind*, Victor Fleming

1880–1920	1896	1908	1917
Millions of immigrants flood in from Europe and Asia, fueling the age of cities. New York, Chicago and Philadelphia swell in size, becoming global centers of industry and commerce.	In *Plessy v. Ferguson*, the US Supreme Court rules that 'separate but equal' public facilities for blacks and whites are legal, arguing that the Constitution addresses only political, not social, equality.	The first Model T (aka 'Tin Lizzie') car is built in Detroit, MI; assembly-line innovator Henry Ford is soon selling one million automobiles annually.	President Woodrow Wilson enters US into WWI. The US mobilizes 4.7 million troops, and suffers around 110,000 of the war's 9 million military deaths.

THE AFRICAN AMERICAN EXPERIENCE: THE STRUGGLE FOR EQUALITY

It's impossible to grasp American history without taking into account the great struggles and hard-won victories of African Americans from all spheres of life.

Slavery

From the early 1600s until the 1800s, an estimated 600,000 slaves were brought from Africa to America. Those who survived the horrific transport on crowded ships (which sometimes had 50% mortality rates) were sold in slave markets (African males cost $27 in 1638). The majority of slaves ended up in southern plantations where conditions were usually brutal – whipping and branding were commonplace.

All (White) Men are Created Equal

Many of the founding fathers – George Washington, Thomas Jefferson and Benjamin Franklin – owned slaves, though privately expressed condemnation for the abominable practice. The abolition movement, however, wouldn't appear until the 1830s, long after the appearance on the Declaration of Independence of the rousing but ultimately hollow words 'all men are created equal'.

Free at Last

While some revisionist historians describe the Civil War as being about states rights, most scholars agree that the war was really about slavery. Following the Union victory at Antietam, Lincoln drafted the Emancipation Proclamation, which freed all blacks in occupied territories. African Americans joined the Union effort, with more than 180,000 serving by war's end.

Jim Crow Laws

During Reconstruction (1865–77) federal laws provided civil rights protection for newly freed blacks. Southern bitterness, however, coupled with centuries of prejudice fueled a backlash. By the 1890s, the Jim Crow laws (named after a derogatory character in a minstrel show) appeared. African Americans were effectively disenfranchised, and America became a deeply segregated society.

The Civil Rights Movement

Beginning in the 1950s, a movement was underway in African American communities to fight for equality. Rosa Parks, who refused to give up her seat to a white passenger, inspired the Montgomery bus boycott. There were sit-ins at lunch counters where blacks were excluded; massive demonstrations led by Martin Luther King Jr in Washington, DC; and harrowing journeys by 'freedom riders' aiming to end bus segregation. The work of millions paid off: in 1964, President Johnson signed the Civil Rights Act, which banned discrimination and racial segregation.

1919	1920s	1933–38	1941–45
The temperance movement champions the 18th amendment, which bans alcohol. Prohibition is unsuccessful, leading to bootlegging and organized crime. The amendment is repealed in 1933.	Spurred by massive African American migration to northern cities, the Harlem Renaissance inspires an intellectual flowering of literature, art and music.	Roosevelt's New Deal establishes federal programs and legislation including Social Security, the Fair Labor Standards Act and the Civilian Conservation Corps to provide unemployment relief.	WWII: America deploys 16 million troops and suffers 400,000 deaths. Overall, civilian deaths outpace military deaths two to one, and total 50 to 70 million people from over 50 countries.

The Perilous Fight: America's World War II in Color (2003) is a groundbreaking documentary featuring previously lost footage of US military battles abroad, focusing on the Pacific theater and war efforts on the home front.

In the South, even the threat of federal limits was too onerous to abide, and as President Lincoln took office, 11 states seceded from the union and formed the Confederate States of America. Lincoln faced the nation's greatest moment of crisis. He had two choices: let the southern states secede and dissolve the union, or wage war to keep the union intact. He chose the latter, and war soon erupted.

It began in April 1861, when the Confederacy attacked Fort Sumter in Charleston, South Carolina, and raged on for the next four years – in the most gruesome combat the world had ever known until that time. By the end, over 600,000 soldiers, nearly an entire generation of young men, were dead. Southern plantations and cities (most notably Atlanta) lay sacked and burned. The North's industrial might provided an advantage, but its victory was not preordained; it unfolded battle by bloody battle.

As fighting progressed, Lincoln recognized that if the war didn't end slavery outright, victory would be pointless. In 1863, his Emancipation Proclamation expanded the war's aims and freed all slaves. In April 1865, Confederate General Robert E Lee surrendered to Union General Ulysses S Grant in Appomattox, Virginia. The Union had been preserved, but at a staggering cost.

Great Depression, the New Deal & World War II

In October 1929, investors, worried over a gloomy global economy, started selling stocks, and seeing the selling, everyone panicked until they'd sold everything. The stock market crashed, and the US economy collapsed like a house of cards.

Thus began the Great Depression. Frightened banks called in their dodgy loans, people couldn't pay, and the banks folded. Millions lost their homes, farms, businesses and savings, and as much as 33% of the American workforce became unemployed. Bread lines and shanty towns sprang up in cities; New York's Central Park held one of the biggest camps.

In 1932, Democrat Franklin D Roosevelt was elected president on the promise of a 'New Deal' to rescue the US from its crisis, which he did with resounding success. When war once again broke out in Europe in 1939, the isolationist mood in America was as strong as ever. However, the extremely popular President Roosevelt, elected to an unprecedented third term in 1940, understood that the US couldn't sit by and allow victory for fascist, totalitarian regimes. Roosevelt sent aid to Britain and persuaded a skittish Congress to go along with it.

Then, on December 7, 1941, Japan launched a surprise attack on Hawaii's Pearl Harbor, killing over 2000 Americans and sinking several battleships. US isolationism transformed overnight into outrage, and

1948–51	1954	1963	1965–75
The US-led Marshall Plan funnels $12 billion in material and financial aid to help Europe recover from WWII. The plan also aims to contain Soviet influence and reignite America's economy.	The Supreme Court rules that segregation in public schools is 'inherently unequal' and orders desegregation 'with all deliberate speed.' The fight to integrate schools spurs the civil rights movement.	On November 22, President John F Kennedy is publicly assassinated by Lee Harvey Oswald while riding in a motorcade through Dealey Plaza in Dallas, Texas.	US involvement in the Vietnam War tears the nation apart as 58,000 Americans die, along with four million Vietnamese and 1.5 million Laotians and Cambodians.

America reached its lowest point in history during the Great Depression. By 1932, nearly one third of all American workers were unemployed. National output fell by 50%, hundreds of banks shuttered, and great swaths of the country seemed to disappear beneath enormous dust storms.

Franklin Roosevelt easily won the 1932 election, and rather casually promised to give Americans a new deal. So began one of America's most progressive eras in history, under the rule of one of its most popular presidents.

Roosevelt wasted no time getting down to work. During his first 100 days, he completed the rescue of the ailing banking system with the creation of deposit insurance. He sent $500 million to states for direct relief and saved a fifth of all homeowners from foreclosure.

He also sent people back to work on a grand scale. He created the Civilian Conservation Corps, which gave jobs to 250,000 young men to work in the parks and forests; they would go on to plant two billion trees. He also created the Works Progress Administration (WPA), which put another 600,000 to work on major projects across the country – building bridges, tunnels, dams, power plants, waterworks, highways, schools and town halls.

The New Deal wasn't just about infrastructure. Some 5000 artists (including famed Mexican painter Diego Rivera) were employed painting murals and creating sculptures in public buildings – many still in existence today. Over 6000 writers were put to work crisscrossing the country, recording oral histories and folktales and compiling ethnographic studies.

Roosevelt suddenly had the support he needed. Germany also declared war on the US, and America joined the Allied fight against Hitler and the Axis powers. From that moment, the US put almost its entire will and industrial prowess into the war effort.

Fighting went on for over two years in both the Pacific and in Europe. The US finally dealt the fatal blow to Germany with its massive D-Day invasion of France on June 6, 1944: Germany surrendered in May 1945.

Nevertheless, Japan continued fighting. Newly elected President Harry Truman – ostensibly worried that a US invasion of Japan would lead to unprecedented carnage – chose to drop experimental atomic bombs on Hiroshima and Nagasaki in August 1945. Created by the government's top-secret Manhattan Project, the bombs devastated both cities, killing over 200,000 people. Japan surrendered days later. The nuclear age was born.

Red Scare, Civil Rights & Vietnam War

The US enjoyed unprecedented prosperity in the decades after WWII but little peace.

1969	1973	1980s	1989
American astronauts land on the moon, fulfilling President Kennedy's unlikely 1961 promise to accomplish this feat within a decade and culminating the 'space race' between the US and USSR.	In *Roe v. Wade*, the Supreme Court legalizes abortion. Still today, this decision remains controversial and socially divisive, pitting 'right to choose' advocates against the 'right to life' anti-abortion lobby.	New Deal-era financial institutions, deregulated under President Reagan, gamble with their customers' savings and loans, and ultimately fail, leaving the government with the bill.	The 1960s-era Berlin Wall is torn down, marking the end of the Cold War between the US and the USSR (now Russia). The USA becomes the world's last remaining superpower.

Though the town of Woodstock, NY, lent its name to the mythic music fest of 1969, the event actually took place in the nearby hamlet of Bethel, where dairy farmer Max Yasgur rented his alfalfa field to organizers. Ticket price for the bash: $18 for a three-day pass ($24 at the gate).

Formerly wartime allies, the communist Soviet Union and the capitalist USA soon engaged in a running competition to dominate the globe. The superpowers engaged in proxy wars – notably the Korean War (1950–53) and Vietnam War (1959–75) – with only the mutual threat of nuclear annihilation preventing direct war.

Meanwhile, with its continent unscarred and its industry bulked up by WWII, the American homeland entered an era of growing affluence. In the 1950s, a mass migration left the inner cities for the suburbs, where affordable single-family homes sprang up. Americans drove cheap cars using cheap gas over brand-new interstate highways. They relaxed with the comforts of modern technology, swooned over TV, and got busy, giving birth to a 'baby boom.'

Middle-class whites did, anyway. African Americans remained segregated, poor and generally unwelcome at the party. Echoing 19th-century abolitionist Frederick Douglass, the Southern Christian Leadership Coalition (SCLC), led by African American preacher Martin Luther King Jr (p375), aimed to end segregation and 'save America's soul': to realize color-blind justice, racial equality and fairness of economic opportunity for all.

Beginning in the 1950s, King preached and organized nonviolent resistance in the form of bus boycotts, marches and sit-ins, mainly in the South. White authorities often met these protests with water hoses and batons, and demonstrations sometimes dissolved into riots, but with the 1964 Civil Rights Act, African Americans spurred a wave of legislation that swept away racist laws and laid the groundwork for a more just and equal society.

Civil Rights on Film

King, Sidney Lumet

Mississippi Burning, Alan Parker

» *Ghosts of Mississippi,* Rob Reiner

» *Black Like Me,* Carl Lerner

» *Long Walk Home,* Richard Pearce

Meanwhile, the 1960s saw further social upheavals: rock 'n' roll spawned a youth rebellion, and drugs sent Technicolor visions spinning in their heads. President John F Kennedy was assassinated in Dallas in 1963, followed by the assassinations in 1968 of his brother, Senator Robert Kennedy, and of Martin Luther King (in Memphis). Americans' faith in their leaders and government was further shocked by the bombings and brutalities of the Vietnam War, as seen on TV, which led to widespread student protests.

Yet President Richard Nixon, elected in 1968 partly for promising an 'honorable end to the war,' instead escalated US involvement and secretly bombed Laos and Cambodia. Then, in 1972, the Watergate scandal broke: a burglary at Democratic Party offices in Washington was, through dogged journalism, tied to 'Tricky Dick,' who, in 1974, became the first US president to resign from office.

The tumultuous 1960s and '70s also witnessed the sexual revolution, women's liberation and other events challenging the status quo. Milestones include the 1969 Stonewall riots in Greenwich Village, NYC, which

1990s	2001	2003
The world-wide-web debuts in 1991. Silicon Valley, CA, leads a high-tech internet revolution, remaking communications and media, and overvalued tech stocks drive the massive boom (and subsequent bust).	On September 11, Al-Qaeda terrorists hijack four commercial airplanes, flying two into NYC's twin towers, and one into the Pentagon (the fourth crashes in Pennsylvania); nearly 3000 people are killed.	After citing evidence that Iraq possesses weapons of mass destruction, President George W Bush launches a preemptive war that will cost over 4000 American lives and some $3 trillion.

STEVEN GREAVES/LONELY PLANET IMAGES ©

» September 11th tribute

galvanized the gay rights movement when patrons of a gay bar – the Stonewall Inn – fought back after a police raid, demanding equal rights and an end to persecution. A few months later, the Woodstock Festival defined the Vietnam era with its peace-love-and-flowers hippies swaying in the fields to rock music.

Pax Americana & the War On Terror

In 1980, Republican California governor and former actor Ronald Reagan campaigned for president by promising to make Americans feel good about America again. The affable Reagan won easily, and his election marked a pronounced shift to the right in US politics.

Military spending and tax cuts created enormous federal deficits, which hampered the presidency of Reagan's successor, George HW Bush. Despite winning the Gulf War – liberating Kuwait in 1991 after an Iraqi invasion – Bush was soundly defeated in the 1992 presidential election by Southern Democrat Bill Clinton. Clinton had the good fortune to catch the 1990s high-tech internet boom, which seemed to augur a 'new economy' based on white-collar telecommunications. The US economy erased its deficits and ran a surplus, and Clinton presided over one of America's longest economic booms.

In 2000, George W Bush, the eldest son of George HW Bush, won the presidential election – barely. Florida was the tie-breaking state that put him there, but its results unraveled into a fiasco of 'irregularities,' including defective ballots, wrongly purged voter rolls and mysterious election-day roadblocks – all under the watch of Jeb Bush, Florida's governor and George W's brother. 'Dubya' won the presidency again in 2004. Tax cuts and elevated federal deficits marked his tenure, along with a moral, religious and cultural campaign of 'family values.'

The catastrophic terrorist attacks on September 11, 2001 united Americans behind their president as he vowed revenge and declared a 'war on terror.' Bush soon attacked Afghanistan in an unsuccessful hunt for Al-Qaeda terrorist cells, then he attacked Iraq in 2003 and toppled its anti-US dictator, Saddam Hussein. Meanwhile, Iraq descended into civil war.

Following scandals and failures – torture photos from Abu Ghraib prison in Baghdad, the inadequate federal response in the aftermath of Hurricane Katrina and the inability to bring the Iraq War to a close – Bush's approval ratings reached historic lows in the second half of his presidency. Hungry for change, Americans responded by electing political newcomer, Barack Obama, who became America's first African American president in 2008.

Ronald Reagan broke 'Tecumseh's Curse'. Tecumseh was a Shawnee warrior from Ohio whom William Henry Harrison defeated at the Battle of Tippecanoe in 1811. As revenge, Tecumseh supposedly invoked a hex: Harrison would become president in 1840 but would die in office, and the same fate would befall presidents elected in 1860, 1880 and every 20 years thereafter. Sure enough, Harrison died. Lincoln and Kennedy were also among the cursed.

2005	2008–09	2010	2011
On August 29, Hurricane Katrina hits the Mississippi and Louisiana coasts, rupturing poorly maintained levees and flooding New Orleans. More than 1800 people die, and cost estimates exceed $110 billion.	The stock market crashes due to mismanagement by American financial institutions. The crisis spreads worldwide as the US struggles with its worst economic recession since the Great Depression.	America's worst natural disaster occurs when a deep-water oil rig off the Louisiana coast explodes, killing 11 workers and releasing an estimated five million barrels of oil into the Gulf.	As unemployment remains high and household income drops, activists launch Occupy Wall Street in NYC to protest economic and social inequality. The movement spreads to cities worldwide.

The Way of Life

The Eastern USA is a compelling mix of accents and rhythms, of big-city financiers and small-town farmers, of university students and sun-seeking retirees, of Yankees and Southerners.

Multiculturalism

From the get-go, the cities in the East were 'melting pots,' with a long and proud heritage of welcoming newcomers from all over the world. So it's no surprise the region's diversity is vast.

In the Northeast, Irish and Italian communities have been well established in the urban areas since the 19th century. In Chicago, Latinos (mostly from Mexico) comprise roughly one-quarter of the population. The upper Great Lakes states are home to the nation's biggest enclaves of Somali and Hmong immigrants, a result of the area's long tradition of resettling refugees. In Florida, Cubans lead the multicultural pack. They began arriving in Miami in the 1960s following Castro's revolution and created a politically powerful community. Nicaraguans followed in the 1980s, fleeing war in their country, and now number over 100,000. The city's Little Haiti adds 70,000 Haitians to the mix. The South, more than any other region, is a culture unto itself; over half of all black Americans live here. These examples are just a fraction of the complex whole.

The East, like the rest of the country, can never quite decide if the continual influx of newcomers is its saving grace or what will eventually strain society to the breaking point. 'Immigration reform' has been a Washington buzzword for over a decade. Some people believe the nation's current system deals with illegal immigrants (there are 11 million of them, compared to 470,000 legal immigrants) too leniently – that we should deport immigrants who are here unlawfully and fine employers who hire them. Other Americans think those rules are too harsh – that immigrants who have been here for years working, contributing to society and abiding by the law deserve amnesty. Despite several attempts, Congress has not been able to pass a comprehensive package addressing illegal immigration.

Religion

Separation of church and state has been the law of the land ever since the Pilgrims came ashore in Massachusetts in the early 1600s. Their religion – Protestantism – continues to be the main one in the East.

Protestantism covers a wide swath of denominations. They fall under two main headings: evangelical Protestantism, of which Baptists form the biggest contingent; and mainline Protestantism, which includes groups such as Lutherans, Methodists and Presbyterians. Evangelicals have the greater number of worshippers, and that number has grown in recent years. Baptists are their powerhouse, accounting for one-third of all Protestants and close to one-fifth of the USA's total adult population. Their numbers stack up in the South. In contrast, Lutherans (who are concentrated in Minnesota and Wisconsin, as well as the Dakotas) and the other mainline denominations have experienced declining figures.

Catholicism is the East's second-most-practiced religion. In fact, New England is the country's most Catholic zone, and the numbers trickle down to the Mid-Atlantic states. Rhode Island is the most Catholic state, with 64% of residents worshipping in the tradition. Baltimore is the country's oldest archdiocese, established in 1789. States with large Latino populations, such as Florida and Illinois, also support big concentrations of Catholics.

Judaism has a significant presence in the Eastern USA. Jews make up roughly 12% of the population in both south Florida and the New York metro area. The latter is a major center of Orthodox Judaism and home to more Jews than anywhere outside Tel Aviv.

Also in the East: Muslim-Americans cluster in the New York, Chicago and Detroit metro areas. Hindu Americans bunch in New York and New Jersey, as well as big cities like Chicago, Washington DC and Atlanta.

Lifestyle

In general, the Eastern USA has one of the world's highest standards of living, though there are some shocking variances by region. At the top end sits New Hampshire, with a median household income of $66,300 (based on a three-year average from 2009 through 2011). Mississippi dwells at the opposite end of the scale at $36,850. These amounts are the high/low not just for the region, but for the nation. They uphold the pattern whereby households in the Northeast earn the most, followed by the Midwest and the South. Wages also vary by ethnicity, with African Americans and Latinos earning less than whites and Asians ($34,000 and $38,000 respectively, versus $52,000 and $66,000, according to census data).

Nearly 87% of Americans are high-school graduates, while some 30% go on to graduate from college with a four-year bachelor's degree. The university life (ie cafes, bookshops and progressive mindsets) is especially prevalent in the Northeast, where the eight Ivy League schools amass, along with the 'Little Ivies' (a self-anointed collection of a dozen elite liberal-arts colleges) and the 'Seven Sisters' (top-tier women's colleges, founded in the days when the Ivy League was still a boys-only club). More than 50 institutions of higher learning throng around Boston alone.

If you peeked in a house, you'd typically find a married couple with two kids occupying it. Both parents usually work, and 28% work more than 40 hours per week. Divorce is common – 40% of first marriages go kaput – but both divorce and marriage rates have declined over the last three decades. Single parents head 9% of households.

Four million Americans tune in every week to Midwestern raconteur Garrison Keillor's old-timey radio show, *A Prairie Home Companion*; listen to the live music, sketches and storytelling online at http://prairiehome.publicradio.org.

STATES & TRAITS

Regional US stereotypes now have solid data behind them, thanks to a 2008 study titled 'The Geography of Personality.' Researchers processed more than a half-million personality assessments collected from individual US citizens, then looked at where certain traits stacked up on the map. Turns out 'Minnesota nice' is for real – the most 'agreeable' states cluster in the Midwest, Great Plains and South. These places rank highest for friendliness and cooperation. The most neurotic states? They line up in the Northeast. But New York didn't place number one, as you might expect; that honor goes to West Virginia. Many of the most 'open' states lie out West. California, Nevada, Oregon and Washington all rate high for being receptive to new ideas – although they lag behind Washington DC and New York.

The Super Bowl costs America $800 million dollars in lost workplace productivity as employees gossip about the game, make bets and shop for new TVs online.

While many Americans hit the gym or walk, bike or jog regularly, over 50% don't exercise at all during their free time, according to the Centers for Disease Control (CDC). Health researchers speculate this lack of exercise and Americans' fondness for sugary and fatty foods have led to rising obesity and diabetes rates. The South fares the worst. Mississippi, Alabama, West Virginia, Tennessee and Louisiana lead the obesity rankings, with the condition affecting one-third of residents.

About 26% of Americans volunteer their time to help others or help a cause. This is truer in the Midwest, followed by the West, South and Northeast, according to the Corporation for National and Community Service. Eco-consciousness has entered the mainstream: over 75% of Americans recycle at home, and most big chain grocery stores – including Wal-Mart – now sell organic foods.

Sports

What really draws folks together, sometimes slathered in blue body paint or with foam-rubber cheese wedges on their heads, is sports. In spring and summer there's baseball nearly every day. In fall and winter there's football, and through the long days and nights of winter there's plenty of basketball to keep the adrenaline going. Those are the big three sports. Car racing has revved up interest, especially in the South. Major League Soccer (MLS) is attracting an ever-increasing following. And ice hockey, once favored only in northern climes, has fans throughout the area.

Baseball

Despite high salaries and its biggest stars being dogged by steroid rumors, baseball remains America's favourite pastime. It may not command the same TV viewership (and subsequent advertising dollars) as football, but baseball has 162 games over a season versus 16 for football.

Besides, baseball isn't about seeing it on TV – it's all about the live version: being at the ballpark on a sunny day, sitting in the bleachers with a beer and hot dog, and indulging in the seventh-inning stretch, when the entire park erupts in a communal sing-along of 'Take Me Out to the Ballgame.' The play-offs, held every October, still deliver excitement and unexpected champions. The New York Yankees, Boston Red Sox and Chicago Cubs continue to be America's favorite teams, even when they're abysmal (the Cubs haven't won a World Series in over 100 years).

Key Sports Sites

» Baseball: www.mlb.com

» Basketball: www.nba.com

» Football: www.nfl.com

» Hockey: www.nhl.com

Nascar: www.nascar.com

Soccer: www.mlssoccer.com

ICONIC SPORTING VENUES

» **Yankee Stadium, NYC** The Bronx's fabled baseball field, steeped in history and the ghost of Babe Ruth.

» **Lambeau Field, Green Bay** Stadium of the NFL's Packers; nicknamed The Frozen Tundra for its insanely cold weather.

» **Fenway Park, Boston** Baseball's oldest park, from 1912; home of the 'Green Monster' (aka the tall, left field wall).

» **Wrigley Field, Chicago** Another throwback ballpark (from 1914), with ivy walls, a classic neon sign and good-time neighborhood bars all around.

» **Madison Square Garden, NYC** Not only do the Knicks dribble at the 'Mecca of Basketball,' but Ali boxed here and Elvis rocked here.

» **Joe Louis Arena, Detroit** The badass rink of pro hockey's Red Wings; witness the strange octopus-throwing custom.

» **Churchill Downs, Louisville** Fine hats, mint juleps and the 'greatest two minutes in sports' sum up the Kentucky Derby's grounds.

» **Indianapolis Motor Speedway, Indianapolis** Racecars scream by at 170 miles per hour at the hard-partying Indy 500.

Tickets are relatively inexpensive – seats average about $25 at most stadiums – and are easy to get for most games. Minor-league baseball games cost half as much, and can be even more fun, with lots of audience participation, stray chickens and dogs running across the field and wild throws from the pitcher's mound. For information, click to www. minorleaguebaseball.com.

Football

Football is big, physical, and rolling in dough. With the shortest season and least number of games of any of the major sports, every match takes on the emotion of an epic battle, where the results matter and an unfortunate injury can deal a lethal blow to a team's play-off chances.

Football's also the toughest because it's played in fall and winter in all manner of rain, sleet and snow. Some of history's most memorable matches have occurred at below-freezing temperatures. Green Bay Packers fans are in a class by themselves when it comes to severe weather. Their stadium in Wisconsin (Lambeau Field) was the site of the infamous Ice Bowl, a 1967 championship game against the Dallas Cowboys where the temperature plummeted to 13°F below zero – mind you, that was with a wind-chill factor of -48°F.

The rabidly popular Super Bowl is pro football's championship match, held in late January or early February. The bowl games (such as the Sugar Bowl in New Orleans and Orange Bowl in Miami) are college football's title matches, held on and around New Year's Day.

Basketball

The teams bringing in the most fans these days include the Chicago Bulls (thanks to the lingering Michael Jordan effect), Detroit Pistons (a rowdy crowd where riots have broken out), Miami Heat (home of Lebron James, the league's most loved – and hated – player) and New York Knicks (where Woody Allen and other famous people sit courtside).

College level basketball also draws millions of fans, especially every spring when March Madness rolls around. This series of college play-off games culminates in the Final Four, when the remaining quartet of teams competes for a spot in the championship game. The Cinderella stories and unexpected outcomes rival the pro league for excitement. The games are widely televised – and bet upon. This is when Las Vegas bookies earn their keep.

Even college and high-school football games enjoy an intense amount of pomp and circumstance, with cheerleaders, marching bands, mascots, songs and mandatory pre- and post-game rituals, especially the tailgate – a full-blown beer-and-barbecue feast that takes place over portable grills in parking lots where games are played.

THE WAY OF LIFE SPORTS

TAILGATE

Food & Drink

The East's cuisine mixes myriad cultures, and each region has evolved its own unique flavor. Tipplers will find the East to be the country's most spirited side.

Local Flavors

NYC: Foodie Heaven

The weak US dollar has made the occasional foray into a posh restaurant here far less expensive than in cities like London, Paris and Tokyo. Always call to make a reservation, ask if there is a dress code, and be prepared to accept a very early or quite late table at popular star-chefs' restaurants.

They say that you could eat at a different restaurant every night of your life in New York City and not exhaust the possibilities. It's likely true, since according to the Zagat Guide (www.zagat.com), there are over 23,000 restaurants in the five boroughs (go ahead, do the math). Owing to its huge immigrant population and an influx of 49 million tourists annually, New York captures the title of America's greatest restaurant city. Its diverse neighborhoods serve up authentic Italian food and thin crust-style pizza, all manner of Asian food, French *haute cuisine* and classic Jewish deli food, from bagels to piled-high pastrami on rye. More exotic cuisines are found here as well, from Ethiopian to Slavic.

Don't let NYC's image as expensive get to you: the *Zagat Guide* says the average cost of a meal – including drink, tax and tip – is $42. There may be no free lunch in New York, but compared to other world cities, eating here can be a bargain.

New England: Clambakes and Lobster Boils

New England claims to have the nation's best seafood, and who's to argue? The North Atlantic Ocean offers up clams, mussels, oysters and huge lobsters, along with shad, bluefish and cod. The bounty stirs into a mighty fine chowder (soup), for which every seafoood shack up the coast has its own secret recipe and puts to the test during summertime chowder fests and cook-offs. The clambake is another tradition, where shellfish are buried in a pit fire with foil-wrapped corn, chicken and sausages. Fried clam fritters and lobster rolls (lobster meat with mayonnaise served in a bread bun) are served throughout the region. Vermont makes excellent cheeses, Massachusetts harvests cranberries (a Thanksgiving staple), and New England's forests drip sweet maple syrup. Still hungry? Lobster shacks line Maine's coast; Boston specializes in baked beans and brown bread; and Rhode Islanders pour coffee syrup into milk and embrace traditional cornmeal johnnycakes.

Weird Regional Foods

» Scrapple (rural Pennsylvania)

» Lutefisk (Minnesota)

» Deep fried cheese curds (Wisconsin)

» Beef on Weck (Western New York)

» Horseshoe Sandwich (Illinois)

» Spiedie (Binghamton, NY)

Mid-Atlantic: Cheesesteaks, Crabcakes and Scrapple

From New York down through Virginia, the Mid-Atlantic states share a long coastline and a cornucopia of apple, pear and berry farms. New Jersey wins prizes for tomatoes and New York's Long Island for potatoes. Chesapeake Bay's blue crabs make diners swoon, as do Pennsylvania-Dutch country's heaped plates of chicken pot pie, noodles and meatloaf-like scrapple. In Philadelphia, you can gorge on 'Philly' cheesesteaks, made with thin, sautéed beef and onions and melted cheese on a bun. Virginia serves its salt-cured 'country-style' ham with biscuits. New York's Finger Lakes, Hudson Valley and Long Island uncork highly regarded wines to accompany the region's well-set table.

The South: BBQ, Biscuits and Gumbo

No region is prouder of its food culture than the South, which has a long history of mingling Anglo, French, African, Spanish and Native American foods. Slow-cooked barbecue is one of the top stokers of regional pride; there are as many meaty and saucy variations as there are towns in the South. Southern fried chicken and catfish pop out of the pan crisp outside and moist inside. Fluffy hot biscuits, corn bread, sweet potatoes, collard greens, and – most passionately – grits (ground corn cooked to a cereal-like consistency) accompany Southern plates, all butter smothered. Treasured dessert recipes tend to produce big layer cakes or pies made with pecans, bananas and citrus. Sweet iced-tea (non alcoholic) or a cool mint julep cocktail (with bourbon) help wash it down.

For the region's crème de la crème, pull up a chair at Louisiana's tables. The state stands out for its two main cuisines – Cajun food is found in the bayou country and marries native spices like sassafras and chili peppers to provincial French cooking. Creole food is more urban and centered in New Orleans, where zippy dishes like shrimp remoulade, crabmeat ravigote and gumbo (soupy stew of chicken, shellfish and/or sausage, and okra) have eaters dabbing their brow.

Midwest: Burgers, Bacon and Beer

Midwesterners eat big and with gusto. Portions are huge – this is farm country, after all, where people need sustenance to get their work done. The region is tops for serving American classics like pot roast, meatloaf, steak and pork chops; add walleye, perch and other freshwater fish to menus in towns near the Great Lakes. Count on a nice cold beer to complement the wares. Chicago stands tall as the region's best place to pile a plate, with hole-in-the-wall ethnic eateries cooking alongside many of the country's most-acclaimed restaurants. Another great place to sample Midwestern foods is at a county fair, which offers everything from bratwurst to fried dough to grilled corn on the cob. Elsewhere at diners and family restaurants, you'll taste the varied influences of Eastern European, Scandinavian, Latino and Asian immigrants, especially in the cities.

Habits & Customs

For breakfast Americans love their eggs and bacon, waffles and hash browns, and big glasses of orange juice. Most of all, they love a steaming cup of coffee. After a midmorning snack break, most American workers' lunch hour affords time enough for just a sandwich, quick burger or hearty salad. While you may spot (rarely) diners drinking a glass of wine or beer with their noontime meal, the days of the 'three martini lunch' are long gone. Early in the evening, people settle in to a more substantial weeknight dinner, which, given the workload of so many two-career families, might be takeout or prepackaged dishes.

Americans tend to eat dinner early, usually between 6pm and 8pm. In smaller towns, it may be hard to find anywhere to eat after 8:30pm or so. Dinner parties usually begin around 6:30pm or 7pm with cocktails followed by a meal. If invited to dinner, it's polite to be prompt: ideally, you should plan to arrive within 15 minutes of the designated time. Americans are notoriously informal in their dining manners, although they will usually wait until everyone is served before eating.

FOOD & DRINK HABITS & CUSTOMS

Lip-Smacking Festivals

» Maine Lobster Festival, Rockland, ME

» Kentucky Bourbon Festival, Bardstown, KY

» National Buffalo Wing Festival, Buffalo, NY

» Crawfish Festival, Breaux Bridge, LA

Thanksgiving may be the only holiday (held the last Thursday in November) where most Americans would agree on the menu – roast turkey, stuffing, mashed potatoes, cranberry sauce and pumpkin pie – but even then appetizers, side dishes and desserts might freestyle into Latino, African or Hawaiian flavors.

Vegetarian and vegan restaurants abound in major cities, though not always in small towns and rural areas away from the coasts. Throughout this book we've noted eateries that focus heavily on vegetarian or vegan dishes using the ✐icon. To find more, browse the online directory at www.happycow.net. Here are a few of our go-to faves for when the veggie craving hits.

» **Green Elephant**, Portland, ME (p227)
» **Veggie Planet**, Cambridge, MA (p172)
» **Counter**, NYC (p91)
» **Blossom**, NYC (p93)
» **Moosewood Restaurant**, Ithaca, NY (p113)
» **Mama's Vegetarian**, Philadelphia (p138)
» **Café Zenith**, Pittsburgh (p151)
» **Grit**, Athens, Georgia (p382)

Cooking Courses

Cooking schools that offer courses for enthusiastic amateur chefs include the following (though this list is by no means exhaustive):

Kitchen Window (www.centralmarket.com) Minneapolis cooking school hosts market tours and restaurant crawls, plus classes on baking, outdoor grilling, and world cuisine.

Chopping Block Cooking School (www.thechoppingblock.net) Master knife skills and meet the 'Wine Goddess' in Chicago.

Cookin' Cajun Cooking School (www.cookincajun.com) Feast on Cajun and Creole delicacies in New Orleans.

Heat and Spice Cooking School (http://heatandspice.com) Vegetarian, grilling, New Orleans-style, Floribbean and world cuisine classes in Chicago.

International Culinary Center (www.internationalculinarycenter.com) Hosts the French Culinary Institute and Italian Culinary Academy in New York City.

Natural Gourmet Cookery School (www.naturalgourmetschool.com) Focuses on vegetarian and healthy 'flexitarian' cooking in NYC.

Drinks

Beer

After founding the American beer industry in Milwaukee, 19th-century German immigrants developed ways to make beer in vast quantities and to deliver it all over America. Today about 80% of domestic beer still comes from the Midwest.

Despite their ubiquity, popular brands of American beer have long been the subject of ridicule abroad due to their low alcohol content and 'light' taste. The antithesis to strong European beers, American lager – far and away the most popular type – has a relatively low alcohol content between 3% and 5%. Regardless of what critics say, sales indicate it is more popular than ever, far surpassing wine and spirits.

Thanks to the meteoric rise of microbreweries and craft beer production, the suds market is in the midst of reinventing (and many would say upgrading) itself. The nation's 1500-plus craft breweries accounted for 11% of domestic sales in 2010. It has become possible to 'drink local' all over the region as microbreweries pop up in urban centers and unexpected small towns. Some restaurants now have beer 'sommeliers,' while others host beer dinners, where you can experience how small-batch brews pair with different foods. And so you know: Vermont boasts the most microbreweries per capita.

Wine

About 20% of Americans drink wine on a regular basis. The West Coast states, predominately California, produce the majority of domestic vino. In the East, New York yields the most – enough to rank fourth nationwide when gauged by number of producers. The Finger Lakes region is the hot spot, awash in Riesling grapes and prime for sipping a good Chardonnay, Gewürztraminer or ice wine. Virginia is the fifth-biggest wine-producing state, with 192 vineyards within its borders, many located in the pretty hills around Charlottesville. Particularly notable is the Virginia Viognier (an exotic white grape). Michigan's west coast offers another vine-striped landscape; its winemakers are known for everything from lush Cabernet Franc to high-end sparkling wines. All of these bucolic regions have spawned entire industries of sip-tripping and bed-and-breakfast tourism.

In general, wine isn't cheap in the US, as it's considered a luxury rather than a staple (in contrast to some European countries). But it's possible to procure a perfectly drinkable bottle of American wine at a liquor or wine shop for around $10 to $12.

Spirits

The East is the cradle of the good stuff. Jack Daniels remains the most well-known brand of American whiskey around the world, and is also the oldest continually operating US distillery, going strong in Lynchburg, Tennessee, since 1870. Bourbon, made from corn, is the nation's only native spirit. Kentucky produces 95% of the world supply, most of which flows from seven distilleries in the state's central zone. The 225-mile loop between the booze-makers here is known as the Bourbon Trail, and road tripping to visit the distilleries and sample their wares has become an offbeat version of California's Napa Valley.

Cocktails were invented in New Orleans, appropriately enough, before the Civil War. The first cocktail was the Sazerac – a mix of rye whiskey or brandy, simple syrup, bitters and a dash of absinthe. American cocktails created at bars in the late 19th and early 20th centuries include such long-standing classics as the martini, the Manhattan, and the Old-Fashioned.

The Vintage Cocktail Craze

Across US cities, it has become decidedly cool to party like it's 1929 by drinking retro cocktails from the days – less than a century ago – when alcohol was illegal. Good old Prohibition: instead of spawning a nation of teetotalers, it arguably only solidified a culture for which the forbidden became appealing – it felt good to be bad, and so-called respectable citizens congregated in secret 'speakeasies' to drink homemade moonshine and dance to hot jazz.

Fast forward to the 21st century. While Prohibition isn't in any danger of being reinstated, you'll find plenty of bars in the region where the spirit of the Roaring '20s and illicit 1930s lives on. Inspired by vintage recipes calling for natural and homemade elixirs, these cocktails – blending ingredients such as small-batch liqueurs, whipped egg whites, hand-chipped ice and fresh fruits – are lovingly concocted by nattily dressed bartenders who regard their profession as something between art and a science.

In many parts of the South, a 'coke' means any kind of soda, so you may have to specify which kind you mean (ie if you say 'I'll have a Coke,' the waiter might ask, 'Which kind?'). In the Midwest, soda is called 'pop.' On the East Coast, it's called 'soda.' Go figure...

FOOD & DRINK DRINKS

Throwback Cocktail Bars

» The Aviary, Chicago

» Tonique, New Orleans

» Franklin Mortgage & Investment Co, Philadelphia

» Weather Up, NYC

» Mulberry Project, NYC

» On the Rocks, NYC

» Alibi, Boston

Arts & Architecture

Music

Blues

Willie Dixon said it best: 'the blues is the roots, and everything else is the fruits.' He meant that all US music starts with the blues. And the blues started in the South. That's where the genre developed out of the work songs, or 'shouts,' of black slaves and out of black spiritual songs and their 'call-and-response' pattern, both of which were adaptations of African music.

By the 1920s, Delta blues typified the sound. Musicians from Memphis to Mississippi sung passionate, plaintive melodies accompanied by a lonely slide guitar. Traveling blues musicians, and particularly female blues singers, gained fame and employment across the South. Early pioneers included Robert Johnson, WC Handy, Ma Rainey, Huddie Ledbetter (aka Lead Belly) and Bessie Smith, who some consider the best blues singer who ever lived.

After WWII many musicians headed north to Chicago, which had become a hub for African American culture. And here the genre took a turn – it went electric. A new generation of players such as Muddy Waters, Buddy Guy, BB King and John Lee Hooker plugged in to amps, and their screaming guitars laid the groundwork for rock and roll.

Shrines for Music Fans

Sun Studio, Memphis

Rock and Roll Hall of Fame, Cleveland

» Preservation Hall, New Orleans

» BB King Museum, Indianola, MS

Jazz

Down in New Orleans, Congo Sq, where slaves gathered to sing and dance from the late 18th century onward, is considered the birthplace of jazz. There ex-slaves adapted the reed, horn and string instruments used by the city's multiracial Creoles – who themselves preferred formal European music – to play their own African-influenced music. This fertile cross-pollination produced a steady stream of innovative sound.

The first variation was ragtime, so-called because of its 'ragged,' syncopated African rhythms. Next came Dixieland jazz, centered on New Orleans' infamous Storyville red-light district. In 1917 Storyville shut down, and the musicians dispersed. Key player Louis Armstrong moved to Chicago to blow his trumpet, and set the tone for decades to come.

The 1920s and '30s are known as the Jazz Age, and New York City's Harlem was its hot spot, where Duke Ellington and Count Basie led their swingin' big bands. In the 1950s and '60s, Miles Davis, John Coltrane and others deconstructed the sound and made up a new one that was cool, free and avant-garde. NYC, New Orleans and Chicago remain the core of the scene today.

Country

Early Scottish, Irish and English immigrants brought their own instruments and folk music to America, and what emerged over time in the secluded Appalachian Mountains was fiddle-and-banjo hillbilly, or 'country,' music. In the Southwest, steel guitars and larger bands distinguished 'western' music. In the 1920s, these styles merged into 'country-and-western' music and Nashville became its center, especially once the *Grand Ole Opry* began its radio broadcasts in 1925.

Something about the 'cry a tear in your beer' twanging resonated with listeners, because country music is now big business. Singer-songwriters such as Shania Twain, Tim McGraw and Taylor Swift have sold millions of albums. Subsequent riffs on the genre include bluegrass, rockabilly and alt country. The South remains the genre's boot-wearin' stronghold.

Rock

Most say rock and roll was born in 1954 the day Elvis Presley walked into Sam Philips' Sun Studios and recorded 'That's All Right.' Initially, radio stations weren't sure why a white country boy was singing black music, or whether they should play him. It wasn't until 1956 that Presley scored his first big breakthrough with 'Heartbreak Hotel,' and in some ways, America never recovered from the rock and roll aftermath.

Musically, rock was a hybrid of guitar-driven blues, black rhythm and blues (R&B), and white country-and-western music. R&B evolved in the 1940s out of swing and the blues, and was then known as 'race music.' With rock and roll, white musicians (and some African American musicians) transformed 'race music' into something that white youths could embrace freely – and boy, did they.

Rock morphed into the psychedelic sounds of the Grateful Dead and Jefferson Airplane, and the electric wails of Janis Joplin, Jimi Hendrix, Bob Dylan and Patti Smith. Since then, rock has been about music and lifestyle, alternately torn between hedonism and seriousness, commercialism and authenticity. Woodstock exemplified the scene in 1969, transforming a little patch of upstate New York into a legend.

Punk arrived in the late 1970s, led by the Ramones and the Dead Kennedys, as did the working-class rock of Bruce Springsteen (the pride of New Jersey). But it wasn't long before a new sound on the block took over the 'outlaw' mantle: rap. In the east, New York and Detroit became spawning grounds. Jay Z and Eminem are its current frontmen.

Literature

The 'Great American Novel' has stirred the imagination for more than 150 years. Edgar Allan Poe told spooky short stories in the 1840s, and is credited with inventing the detective story, horror story and science fiction. Four decades later Samuel Clemens, aka Mark Twain, also made a literary splash. Twain wrote in the vernacular, loved 'tall tales' and reveled in absurdity, which endeared him to everyday readers. His novel *Huckleberry Finn* (1884) became the quintessential American narrative: compelled by a primal moment of rebellion against his father, Huck embarks on a search for authenticity through which he discovers himself. The Mississippi River provides the backdrop.

The Lost Generation brought American literature into its own in the early 20th century. These writers lived as expatriates in Europe post-WWI and described a growing sense of alienation. Plain-speaking Midwesterner Ernest Hemingway exemplified the era with his spare, stylized realism. Minnesotan F Scott Fitzgerald eviscerated East Coast society life with his fiction. Back on home turf, William Faulkner examined the South's social rifts in dense, caustic prose, and African Americans such

Best Music Festivals

» Winter Music Conference, Miami, March

» New Orleans Jazz Festival, April

» Bonnaroo, Manchester, TN, June

» Lollapalooza, Chicago, August

Great American Novels

» *The Sun Also Rises,* Ernest Hemingway

» *The Great Gatsby,* F Scott Fitzgerald

» *The Sound and the Fury,* William Faulkner

» *Beloved,* Toni Morrison

ARTS & ARCHITECTURE FILM & TELEVISION

THE GOLDEN AGE OF AMERICAN TELEVISION

By the 21st century, cable TV was targeting all manner of niche audiences and producing sophisticated, complex dramas that surpassed most risk-averse Hollywood fare. The result? Some might say that the 2000s, not the mid-20th century, have proved to be the 'golden age' of American TV. Shows that give an Eastern USA perspective include:

» *The Sopranos:* Mafia, murder, and marriage in New Jersey, plus a lot of trips to the psychologist's office.

» *The Wire:* Politicians versus police versus drug dealers on the mean streets of Baltimore.

» *Dexter:* Can a serial killer have morals? A Miami police detective with a big secret proves that the answer just may be 'yes.'

» *Tremé:* New Orleans gets its close-up in this drama of the city's historic African American neighborhood trying to rebuild post-Katrina.

» *30 Rock:* OK, this one's not on cable, but airs on regular ol' network TV. It's comedy queen Tina Fey's brainchild, inspired by her years writing for *Saturday Night Live*.

as poet Langston Hughes and novelist Zora Neale Hurston undermined racist stereotypes during New York's Harlem Renaissance.

After WWII, American writers began depicting regional and ethnic divides, experimented with style and often bashed middle-class society's values. The 1950s Beat Generation, with Jack Kerouac, Allen Ginsberg and William S Burroughs at the center, was particularly hard-core.

Today's literature reflects an ever-more-diverse panoply of voices. Toni Morrison, Amy Tan, Ana Castillo and Sherman Alexie have all written best sellers and given voice to, respectively, African American, Asian American, Mexican American and Native American issues, among many others.

Film & Television

The studio system actually began in Manhattan, where Thomas Edison – inventor of the industry's earliest moving picture technology – tried to create a monopoly with his patents. This drove many independents to move to a suburb of Los Angeles, where they could easily flee to Mexico in case of legal trouble – and *ta-da,* Hollywood was born.

While most of the movie magic still happens on the west coast, New York retains its fair share of film and TV studios. ABC, CBS, NBC, CNN, MTV and HBO are among the Big Apple's big shots, and many visitors come expressly to see David Letterman, Dr Oz or their other favorite talk show taping. Many filmmakers and actors prefer New York to the west coast – Robert DeNiro, Spike Lee and Woody Allen most famously – so keep an eye out on local streets. Other film-friendly cities include Miami and Chicago, and one you normally wouldn't think of: Wilmington, North Carolina, which hosts enough studios to earn the nickname 'Wilmywood'.

As YouTube, Blip.tv and their ilk have entered the industry, the networks have responded by creating more edgy, long-narrative serial dramas, as well as cheap-to-produce, 'unscripted' reality TV: what *Survivor* started in 2000, the contestants and 'actors' of *American Idol, Project Runway* and *The Jersey Shore* keep alive today, for better or for worse.

Theater

Eugene O'Neill put American drama on the map with his trilogy *Mourning Becomes Electra* (1931), which sets a tragic Greek myth in post-Civil War New England. O'Neill was the first major US playwright, and is still widely considered to be the best.

After WWII two playwrights dominated the stage: Arthur Miller, who famously married Marilyn Monroe and wrote about everything from middle-class male disillusionment (*Death of a Salesman,* 1949) to the mob mentality of the Salem Witch Trials (*The Crucible,* 1953); and Tennessee Williams, whose explosive works *The Glass Menagerie* (1945), *A Streetcar Named Desire* (1947) and *Cat on a Hot Tin Roof* (1955) dig deep into the Southern psyche.

Edward Albee gave the 1960s a healthy dose of absurdism, and David Mamet and Sam Shepard filled the '70s and '80s with rough and tough guys. These days Pulitzer Prize winner Tracy Letts writes family dramas that are often compared to O'Neill, bringing the scene full circle.

Broadway is where shows get star treatment. During the 2010/2011 season, the famed NYC district sold over a billion dollars in tickets – a new record even as costly productions like 'Spiderman: Turn Off the Dark' closed and reopened amid bad reviews and artistic feuds. But it's away from Broadway's bright lights, in regional theaters such as Chicago's Steppenwolf, Minneapolis' Guthrie and hundreds more, where new plays and playwrights emerge that keep the art vital.

Painting

In the wake of WWII, the USA developed its first truly original school of art: abstract expressionism. New York painters Jackson Pollock, Franz Kline, Mark Rothko and others explored freely created, non-representational forms. Pollock, for example, made drip paintings by pouring and splattering pigments over large canvases.

Pop art followed, where artists drew inspiration from bright, cartoony consumer images. Andy Warhol was the king (or Pope of Pop, as he's sometimes called). Minimalism came next, and by the 1980s and 90s, the canvas was wide open – any and all styles could take their place at the arts table. New York remains the red-hot center of the art world, and its make-or-break influence shapes tastes across the nation and around the globe.

Architecture

In 1885, a group of designers in Chicago shot up the pioneering skyscraper. It didn't exactly poke the clouds, but its use of steel framing launched modern architecture.

Around the same time, another Chicago architect was doing radical things closer to the ground. Frank Lloyd Wright created a building style that abandoned historical elements and references, which had long been the tradition, and instead he went organic. He designed buildings in relation to the landscape, which in the Midwest were the low-slung, horizontal lines of the surrounding prairie. An entire movement grew up around Wright's Prairie Style.

European architects absorbed Wright's ideas, and that influence bounced back when the Bauhaus school left Nazi Germany and set up in the USA. Here it became known as the International Style, an early form of modernism. Ludwig Mies van der Rohe was the main man with the plan, and his boxy, metal-and-glass-type behemoths rose high on urban horizons, especially in Chicago and New York City. Postmodernism followed, reintroducing color and the decorative elements of art deco, beaux arts and other earlier styles to the region's sky-high designs.

Today architects are being challenged to 'go green,' and the creativity unleashed is riveting, transforming skylines and changing the way Americans think about their built environments.

Best Modern Art Museums

» Museum of Modern Art, NYC

» Whitney Museum of American Art, NYC

» Salvador Dalí Museum, St Petersburg, FL

» Andy Warhol Museum, Pittsburgh

Chicago's Willis Tower (nee Sears) has been the tallest since 1972, though the new One World Trade Center in New York City is set to eclipse it in 2014.

The Land & Wildlife

Whether you've come to glimpse alligators, whales, manatees or moose, the Eastern USA delivers. Its coasts, mountains, swamps and forests have heaps of habitat for wildlife spotting.

The Landscape

The Eastern USA is a land of temperate, deciduous forests and contains the ancient Appalachian Mountains, a low range that parallels the Atlantic Ocean. Between the mountains and the coast lies the country's most populated, urbanized region, particularly in the corridor between Washington, DC, and Boston, MA.

Geologists believe that roughly 460 million years ago the Appalachian Mountains were the highest mountains on earth – higher even than the Himalayas are today.

To the north are the Great Lakes, which the USA shares with Canada. These five lakes, part of the Canadian Shield, are the greatest expanse of fresh water on the planet, constituting nearly 20% of the world's supply.

Going south along the East Coast, things get wetter and warmer till you reach the swamps of southern Florida and make the turn into the Gulf of Mexico, which provides the USA with a southern coastline.

West of the Appalachians are the vast interior plains, which lie flat all the way to the Rocky Mountains. The eastern plains are the nation's breadbasket, roughly divided into the northern 'corn belt' and the southern 'cotton belt.' The plains, an ancient sea bottom, are drained by the mighty Mississippi River, which together with the Missouri River forms the world's fourth-longest river system, surpassed only by the Nile, Amazon and Yangtze rivers.

Beyond the East, the Rocky Mountains and southwestern deserts eventually give way to the Pacific Ocean.

Land Mammals

Moose

Moose nibble shrubs throughout the northern part of the region, specifically Maine, New Hampshire, Vermont, upstate New York and the Michigan-Minnesota-Wisconsin north woods. They're part of the deer family, but far more humungous, with skinny, ballerina-like legs that support a hulking body. Males weigh up to 1200lb, all put on by a vegetarian diet of twigs and leaves. Despite their odd shape, moose can move it: they run up to 35 miles per hour, and in water, they can swim as fast as two men paddling a canoe.

Males grow a spectacular rack of antlers every summer, only to discard it in November. You'll spot moose foraging near lakes and streams.

INFAMOUS NATURAL DISASTERS

Earthquakes, wildfires, tornadoes, hurricanes and blizzards – the US certainly has its share of natural disasters. A few of the more infamous events that have shaped the national conscience:

Hurricane Katrina August 29, 2005, is not a day easily forgotten in New Orleans. A massive hurricane swept across the Gulf of Mexico and slammed into Louisiana. As levees failed, floods inundated over 80% of the city. The death toll reached 1836, with over $100 billion in estimated damages – making it America's costliest natural disaster. Heartbreaking images of the destroyed city and anger over the government's bungled response still linger.

Tornado Alley In April 2011, the US experienced its largest tornado outbreak in recorded history. More than 300 confirmed tornadoes raged across 21 states over three harrowing days. Amazingly, this occurred just weeks after the second-largest tornado outbreak in US history. The storms left more than 300 dead and $10 billion in damages.

Hurricane Irene On August 27 and 28, 2011, a mammoth storm blew over the Eastern Seaboard, battering 15 states from Florida through to New England and as far inland as Pennsylvania. New York City evacuated many residents and took the unprecedented step of shutting down all public transit. More than 7.4 million homes lost electrical power, rivers ran wild, and at least 45 people died. The damage has been estimated to be $7 billion.

East Coast Earthquake On August 23, 2011, a rare earthquake rattled the Eastern USA. The 5.8 magnitude tremor had its epicenter located in Mineral, Virginia, but was felt from Maine right through to South Carolina. It was the strongest quake since 1897. There was no serious damage, though it did knock three spires off Washington, DC's National Cathedral.

They generally are not aggressive, and often will pose for photographs. They can be unpredictable, though, so don't startle them. During mating season (September), the males can become belligerent, so keep your distance.

Black Bear

Despite a decline in numbers, black bears prowl most parts of the region, especially in the Adirondacks, the Great Smoky Mountains and the Midwest's north woods. Males can stand 7ft tall and weigh 550lb – but that depends on when you encounter them. In autumn they weigh up to 30% more than when they emerge from hibernation in the spring. Although they enjoy an occasional meaty snack, black bears usually fill their bellies with berries and other vegetation. They're opportunistic, adaptable and curious animals, and can survive on very small home ranges. As their forests diminish, they're occasionally seen traipsing through nearby populated areas.

Panther

A remnant population of panthers licks its chops in Everglades National Park, Florida. Before European contact, perhaps 1500 roamed the state. The first panther bounty ($5 a scalp) was passed in 1832, and over the next 130 years they were hunted relentlessly. Though hunting was stopped in 1958, it was too late for panthers to survive on their own. Without a captive breeding program, begun in 1991, the Florida panther would now be extinct, and with only some 120 known to exist, they're not out of the swamp yet.

Best Wildlife Watching

» **Moose** Baxter State Park, Maine

» **Whales** Provincetown, Massachusetts

» **Alligators, crocodiles, manatees & sea turtles** Florida Everglades

» **Eagles** Wabasha, Minnesota

Wolf & Coyote

Wolves are rare in the Eastern USA. Those that are here wander mostly in northern Minnesota, particularly the Boundary Waters. The area's cold, boreal forest is prime territory, as well as home to the International Wolf Center (www.wolfcenter.org) in Ely, MN, (Minnesota). Another small pack lives in Michigan's Isle Royale National Park. The wolf can be every bit as fierce and cunning as is portrayed in fairy tales, although it rarely attacks humans. If you're out in the wilderness, you may hear them howling at the moon.

The coyote looks similar to the wolf but is about half the size, ranging from 15lb to 45lb. An icon of the Southwest, coyotes are found all over the Eastern region too, even in cities (Chicago had one recently that loped into a sandwich shop during the lunchtime rush).

The Eastern USA holds 12 national parks, three national preserves (like national parks but with hunting and mining permitted) and 27 historic parks (extended areas of national historic significance). The National Park Service (www.nps.gov) has the lowdown.

Deer

The white-tailed deer can be found everywhere, from top to bottom in the region. Endemic to the Florida Keys are Key deer, a Honey-I-Shrunk-the-Ungulate subspecies: less than 3ft tall and lighter than a 10-year-old boy, they live mostly on Big Pine Key.

Reptiles

Alligator & Crocodile

American alligators slither throughout the southeast's wetlands, mostly in Florida and Louisiana. With snout, eyeballs and pebbled back so still they hardly ripple the water's surface, alligators have watched over the swamps for more than 200 million years.

Louisiana has close to two million gators, and Florida counts 1.5 million among the state's lakes, rivers and golf courses, mostly in the central and southern zones. The Everglades are perhaps the best place to find them lurking. Alligators are alpha predators who keep the rest of the food chain in check, and their 'gator holes' become vital water cups in the dry season and during droughts, aiding the entire wetlands ecosystem. They live about 30 years, can grow up to 14ft long and weigh 1000lb. No longer officially endangered, alligators remain protected because they resemble the still-endangered American crocodile.

Speaking of which: south Florida is also home to the only North American population of American crocodile. Florida's crocs number around 1500; they prefer saltwater, and to distinguish them from gators, check their smile – a croc's snout is more tapered and its teeth stick out.

Best Landscapes off the Beaten Path

» Congaree National Park, SC: swamplands

» Ouachita National Forest, AK: spring-fed mountains

» Cape Henlopen State Park, DE: dunes, wetlands

» Monongahela National Forest, WV: rivers

Sea Turtles

Florida is the hot spot for sea turtle nesting in the continental US. Three main species create over 80,000 nests annually, mostly on southern Atlantic Coast beaches, but extending to all Gulf Coast beaches, too. Loggerheads comprise the vast majority, followed by green and leatherback turtles, and historically hawksbill and Kemp's ridley as well; all five species are endangered or threatened. The leatherback is the largest, bulking up to 10ft and 2000lb.

During the May-to-October nesting season, sea turtles deposit from 80 to 120 eggs in each nest. The eggs incubate for about two months, and then the hatchlings emerge all at once and make for the ocean. Contrary to myth, hatchlings don't need the moon to find their way.

Snakes

First, here's the bad news: there are four species of rattlesnake that are located east of the Mississippi – the diamondback, pygmy, canebrake and timber. At 7ft long, the diamondback is the biggest and the most aggressive. Copperheads, cottonmouths and coral snakes are other poisonous types in the region. All of them hiss primarily in the mid-Atlantic and South.

Now the good news: running into a poisonous snake is uncommon. Need proof? Great Smoky Mountain National Park, with 10 million visitors per year, has never recorded a snakebite fatality in its 70-plus-year history.

Marine Mammals & Fish

For stunning coral reefs and vibrant tropical fish, the Florida Keys are place to go.

Whales & Dolphins

The Eastern USA's top spot to whale-watch is off Massachusetts' coast at Stellwagen Bank National Marine Sanctuary, a summer feeding ground for humpbacks. These awesome creatures average 49ft and 36 tons – serious heft to be launching up and out of the water for their playful breaching. They also come surprisingly close to boats, offering great photo ops. Many of the 300 remaining North Atlantic right whales, the world's most endangered leviathan, frequent the same waters. Cruises depart from Boston, Plymouth and Provincetown, and Gloucester, Massachusetts.

The waters off the coast of Florida are home to several dolphin species. By far the most common species is the bottlenose dolphin, which is highly social, extremely intelligent and frequently encountered around the entire peninsula. Bottlenose dolphins are the species most often seen in captivity.

Manatees

Florida's coast is home to the unusual, gentle manatee, which moves between freshwater rivers and the ocean. Around 10ft long and weighing on average 1000lb, these agile, expressive creatures don't do much, spending most of each day resting and eating 10% of their body weight. In winter they seek out Florida's warm-water springs and power plant discharge canals. In summer they migrate back to the ocean and can be spotted in the coastal waters of Alabama, Georgia and South Carolina, in addition to Florida.

Manatees have been under some form of protection since 1893, and they were included in the first federal endangered species list in 1967. Once hunted for their delicious meat – finer than filet mignon, it's said – manatee collisions with boats are now a leading cause of death, accounting for over 20% annually. Manatees number over 3800 today.

Birds

The bald eagle, the USA's symbol since 1782, is the only eagle unique to North America. Its wingspan can reach more than 6.5ft. Good wintertime viewing sites are along the Mississippi River in Minnesota, Wisconsin and Illinois; in summer, eagles are common throughout Florida, wherever there's fish-rich water for chowing alongside tall trees for nesting. The eagle has come off the endangered species list, having made a remarkable comeback from a low of 417 breeding pairs in 1963 to more than 9750 pairs today (that's in the lower 48; another 30,000-plus live in Alaska).

Does it or does it not exist? *Stalking the Ghost Bird: The Elusive Ivory-Billed Woodpecker in Louisiana* (2008), by Mike Steinberg, tells what happens when kayakers claim to have sighted the 'extinct' bird, igniting a frenzy in the bayou.

White pelicans, which are among the region's largest birds, arrive in winter (October to April), while brown pelicans, the only kind to dive for their food, live here year-round. They're found around the Gulf Coast and throughout Florida.

Plants & Trees

Spring wildflower, and colorful autumn foliage, displays are a New England specialty. Great Smoky Mountains National Park contains all five eastern-forest types – spruce fir, hemlock, pine-oak, and northern and cove hardwood – which support over 100 native species of trees.

In Florida, the Everglades is the last subtropical wilderness in the US. This vital, endangered habitat is a fresh- and saltwater world of marshes, sloughs and coastal prairies that support mangroves, cypresses, sea grasses, tropical plants, pines and hardwoods.

Survival Guide

Directory A–Z

Accommodations

Exceptional picks in this book are marked with a icon, but every property recommended meets a certain baseline standard for quality within its class. Accommodations are listed in order of author recommendation.

For all but the cheapest places and the slowest seasons, reservations are advised.

Seasons

» Peak season is summer, generally May to September, when prices are highest.

» Exceptions include Florida and the northern ski areas, when winter is the busiest and costliest time to visit.

Amenities

» Most properties offer in-room wi-fi. It's typically free in budget and midrange lodgings, while top-end hotels often charge a fee.

» Many smaller properties, especially B&Bs, ban smoking. Marriott and Westin brand hotels are 100% smoke free. All other properties have rooms set aside for nonsmokers. In this book, we have used the nonsmoking icon ( ) to mean that *all* rooms within a property are nonsmoking.

» Air-conditioning is standard at most places.

Discounts

Check the hotel websites listed throughout this book for special online rates. The usual suspects also offer discounted room prices:

Expedia (www.expedia.com)

Hotels.com (www.hotels. com)

Hotwire (www.hotwire.com)

Priceline (www.priceline.com)

Travelocity (www.travelocity. com)

B&Bs & Inns

These accommodations vary from small, comfy houses with shared bathrooms (least expensive) to romantic, antique-filled historic homes and mansions with private baths (most expensive). Those focusing on upscale romance may discourage children. Also, inns and B&Bs often require a minimum stay of two or three days on weekends, and reservations are essential. Always call ahead to confirm policies (regarding kids, pets, smoking) and bathroom arrangements.

B&B agencies are sprinkled throughout this guide. Also check:

Bed & Breakfast Inns Online (www.bbonline.com)

BedandBreakfast.com (www.bedandbreakfast.com)

BnB Finder (www.bnbfinder. com)

Pamela Lanier's Bed & Breakfast Inns (www. lanierbb.com)

Select Registry (www. selectregistry.com)

Camping

Campsites at national and state parks typically come in three types:

» **Primitive** Free to $10 per night, no facilities

» **Basic** $10 to $20, with toilets, drinking water, fire pits and picnic tables

» **Developed** $20 and up, with more amenities such as showers, barbecue grills, RV sites with hookups etc.

Make reservations for national parks and other federal lands through Recreation.gov (518-885-3639, 877-444-6777; www.recreation.gov). Camping is usually limited to 14 days and can be reserved up to six months in advance. For some state park campgrounds, you can make bookings through ReserveAmerica (www.re serveamerica.com).

Most privately owned campgrounds are geared to RVs (motor homes), but will also have a small section avail-

---

BOOK YOUR STAY ONLINE

For more accommodations reviews by Lonely Planet authors, check out hotels.lonelyplanet.com. You'll find independent reviews, as well as recommendations on the best places to stay. Best of all, you can book online.

able for tent campers. Expect tons of amenities, like swimming pools, laundry facilities, convenience stores and bars. **Kampgrounds of America** (KOA; ☎406-248-7444; www. koa.com) is a national network of private campgrounds; their Kamping Kabins have air-con and kitchens.

Hostels

Hostelling International USA (HI-USA; ☎301-495-1240; www.hiusa.org; annual membership adult/child/senior $28/free/$18) runs several hostels in the Eastern US. Most have gender-segregated dorms, a few private rooms, shared baths and a communal kitchen. Overnight fees for dorm beds range from $21 to $45. You don't have to be a member to stay, but you pay a slightly higher rate. Reservations are accepted.

The region also has many independent hostels not affiliated with HI-USA. Browse listings at:

Hostels.com (www.hostels. com)

Hostelworld.com (www. hostelworld.com)

Hostelz.com (www.hostelz. com)

Hotels

Hotels in all categories typically include in-room phones, cable TV, internet access, private baths and a simple continental breakfast. Many

PRICE GUIDE

Rates listed in this guide are based on double occupancy for high season and do not include taxes, which can add 10% to 15%, or even more. When booking, always ask for the rate including taxes.

Rates are categorized as $ (under $100), $$ ($100 to $200) or $$$ (over $200).

midrange properties provide minibars, microwaves, hairdryers and swimming pools, while top-end hotels add concierge services, fitness and business centers, spas, restaurants and bars.

We've tried to highlight independently owned hotels in this guide, but in some towns, chain hotels are the best, and sometimes the only, option. Common chains:

Best Western (☎800-780-7234; www.bestwestern.com)

Comfort Inn (☎877-424-6423; www.comfortinn.com)

Hampton Inn (☎800-426-7866; www.hamptoninn.com)

Hilton (☎800-445-8667; www.hilton.com)

Holiday Inn (☎888-465-4329; www.holidayinn.com)

Marriott (☎888-236-2427; www.marriott.com)

Super 8 (☎800-800-8000; www.super8.com)

Motels

Motels – distinguishable from hotels by having rooms that open onto a parking lot – tend to cluster around interstate exits and along main routes into town. Many are inexpensive 'mom-and-pop' operations; breakfast is rarely included; and amenities might top out at a phone and TV (maybe with cable). Although most motel rooms won't win any style awards,

PRACTICALITIES

Newspapers & Magazines
Regional newspapers *Washington Post, Boston Globe, Miami Herald, Chicago Tribune*
National newspapers *New York Times, Wall Street Journal, USA Today*
Mainstream news magazines *Time, Newsweek, US News & World Report*

Radio & TV
Radio news National Public Radio (NPR), lower end of FM dial
Broadcast TV ABC, CBS, NBC, FOX, PBS (public broadcasting)
Major cable channels &CNN (news), ESPN (sports), HBO (movies), Weather Channel

Video Systems
» NTSC standard (incompatible with PAL or SECAM)
» DVDs coded for Region 1 (US and Canada only)

Weights & Measures
Weight ounces (oz), pounds (lb), tons
Liquid ounces (oz), pints, quarts, gallons
Distance feet (ft), yards (yd), miles (mi)

Smoking
As of 2011, about half the Eastern states, the District of Columbia and many municipalities across the region were entirely smoke-free in restaurants, bars and workplaces.

Currency
US dollar ($)

they can be clean and comfortable and offer good value. Ask to see a room first if you're unsure.

Resorts

Florida, in particular, has behemoth resorts. Facilities can include all manner of fitness and sports, pools, spas, restaurants and bars, and so on. Many also have on-site babysitting services. However, some also tack an extra 'resort fee' onto rates, so always ask.

Activities

Hiking, biking, kayaking, rafting and surfing – the Eastern USA has sweet spots for all, detailed in the regional chapters. Additional resources:

American Canoe Association (www.americancanoe. org) Canoeing and kayaking organization publishes *Paddler* magazine (www. paddlermagazine.com), has a water trails database and offers courses.

(www.americanhiking.org) Links to local hiking clubs and 'volunteer vacations' building trails.

American Whitewater (www.americanwhitewater.org) Group that works to preserve America's wild rivers; has links to local paddling clubs.

Appalachian Trail Conservancy (www.appalachian trail.org) Details on how to hike the famed footpath.

Backpacker (www.back packer.com) Premier national magazine for backpackers, from novices to experts.

Fish & Wildlife Management Offices (www.fws.gov/offices/statelinks.html) Links to each state's fish and wildlife agency, for the lowdown on local fishing regulations and licenses.

National Park Service (www.nps.gov) Info and maps for activities in parks across the land.

Ski Resorts Guide (www. skiresortsguide.com) Comprehensive guide to resorts, with downloadable trail maps, lodging info and more.

Surfer (www.surfermag. com) Travel reports cover the Eastern seaboard and just about every break in the USA.

Business Hours

Reviews won't list operating hours unless they deviate from the following normal opening times:

Banks 8:30am-4:30pm Monday to Thursday, to 5:30pm Friday (and possibly 9am-noon Saturday)

Bars 5pm-midnight Sun-Thu, to 2am Friday and Saturday

Nightclubs 10pm-2am Thursday to Saturday

Post offices 9am-5pm Monday to Friday

Shopping malls 9am-9pm

Stores 10am-6pm Mon-Sat, noon-5pm Sunday

Supermarkets 8am-8pm, some open 24 hours

Customs Regulations

For a complete list of US customs regulations, visit the official portal for **US Customs and Border Protection** (www.cbp.gov).

Duty-free allowance per person is as follows:

» 1L of liquor (provided you are at least 21 years old)

» 100 cigars and 200 cigarettes (if you are at least 18)

» $100 worth of gifts and purchases ($800 if a returning US citizen)

» If you arrive with $10,000 or more in US or foreign currency, it must be declared.

There are heavy penalties for attempting to import illegal drugs. Fruit, vegetables and other food must be declared

(whereby you'll undergo a time-consuming search) or left in the bins in the arrival area.

Discount Cards

The following cards can net savings (usually about 10%) on museums, accommodations and some transport (including Amtrak):

American Association of Retired Persons (AARP; www.aarp.org) For US travelers age 50 and older.

American Automobile Association (AAA; www.aaa. com) For members of AAA or reciprocal clubs in Europe and Australia.

International Student Identity Card (ISIC; www. isic.org) For students any age. For nonstudents under 26 years of age, an **International Youth Travel Card** (IYTC; $22) grants similar benefits.

Student Advantage Card (www.studentadvantage.com) For US and foreign travelers.

Electricity

120V/60Hz

120V/60Hz

Embassies & Consulates

In addition to the following embassies in Washington, DC (see www.embassy.org for a complete list), most countries have an embassy for the UN in New York City. Some countries have consulates in other large cities.

Australia (☏202-797-3000; www.usa.embassy.gov.au; 1601 Massachusetts Ave NW)

Canada (☏202-682-1740; www.canadainternational.gc.ca; 501 Pennsylvania Ave NW)

France (☏202-644-6000; www.info-france-usa.org; 4101 Reservoir Rd NW)

Germany (☏202-298-4000; www.germany.info; 2300 M St NW)

Ireland (☏202-462-3939; www.embassyofireland.org; 2234 Massachusetts Ave NW)

Mexico (☏202-728-1600; http://embamex.sre.gob.mx/eua; 1911 Pennsylvania Ave NW)

Netherlands (☏877-388-2443; http://dc.the-netherlands.org; 4200 Linnean Ave NW)

New Zealand (☏202-328-4800; www.nzembassy.com/usa; 37 Observatory Circle NW)

UK (☏202-588-6500; http://ukinusa.fco.gov.uk; 3100 Massachusetts Ave NW)

Food

Top choices are marked with a 🏆 icon, and restaurants are listed in order of author recommendation. In this book, restaurant prices usually refer to an average main course at dinner and are categorized as $ (under $10), $$ ($10 to $20) or $$$ (over $20). These prices don't include drinks, appetizers, desserts, taxes or tip.

For more on eating and drinking in the East, see p608.

Gay & Lesbian Travelers

In general, the Northeast is the most tolerant region in the Eastern USA and the South the least so, though big cities in all the regions have long-standing gay-friendly communities.

Hot Spots

Manhattan is too crowded and cosmopolitan to worry about who's holding hands, while Fire Island is the sandy gay mecca on Long Island. Other East Coast cities that flaunt it are Boston, Philadelphia, Washington, DC, Massachusetts' Provincetown and Delaware's Rehoboth Beach. Even Maine brags a gay beach destination: Ogunquit.

In the South, there's always steamy 'Hotlanta'. In Florida, Miami and the 'Conch Republic' of Key West support thriving gay communities, though Fort Lauderdale attracts bronzed boys and girls, too. Of course, everyone gets their freak on in New Orleans. In the Midwest, seek out Chicago and Minneapolis.

Attitudes

Most major US cities have a visible and open GLBT community that is easy to connect with. In this guide, many cities include a boxed text or section that describes the city's best GLBT offerings.

The level of acceptance varies nationwide. In some places, there is absolutely no tolerance whatsoever, and in others acceptance is predicated on GLBT people not 'flaunting' their sexual preference or identity. Sadly, bigotry still exists. In rural areas and extremely conservative enclaves, it's unwise to be openly out, as violence and verbal abuse can sometimes occur. When in doubt, assume locals follow a 'don't ask, don't tell' policy. Same-sex marriage, a hotly debated topic, is now legal in a handful of states (of which most are in the Northeast).

Resources

Advocate (www.advocate.com) Gay-oriented news website reports on business, politics, arts, entertainment and travel.

Damron (www.damron.com) Publishes the classic gay travel guides, but they're advertiser-driven and sometimes outdated.

Gay Travel (www.gaytravel.com) Has online guides to dozens of US destinations.

Gay Yellow Network (www.gayyellow.com) Yellow-page listings for over 30 US cities. Also available as smartphone app (GLYP).

OutTraveler (www.outtraveler.com) Has useful online city guides and travel articles to various US and foreign destinations.

Purple Roofs (www.purpleroofs.com) Lists gay-owned and gay-friendly B&Bs and hotels nationwide.

Health

The Eastern region, like the rest of the USA, has a high level of hygiene, so infectious diseases are not a significant problem. There are no required vaccines, and tap water is safe to drink.

Bring any medications you may need in their original containers, clearly labeled. A signed, dated letter from your physician that describes all of your medical conditions and medications (including generic names) is also a good idea.

Health Insurance

The United States offers possibly the finest health care in the world. The problem is that it can be prohibitively expensive. It's essential to purchase travel health insurance if your home policy doesn't cover you for medical expenses abroad. Check the Insurance section of the **Lonely Planet website** (www.lonelyplanet.com) for more information.

Find out in advance if your insurance plan will make payments directly to providers or reimburse you later for overseas health expenditures.

Health Care Availability

» If you have a medical emergency, go to the emergency room of the nearest hospital.

» If the problem isn't urgent, call a nearby hospital and ask for a referral to a local physician; this is usually cheaper than a trip to the emergency room.

» Stand-alone, for-profit urgent-care centers provide good service, but can be the most expensive option.

» Pharmacies are abundantly supplied. However, some medications that are available over the counter in other countries require a prescription in the US.

» If you don't have insurance to cover the cost of prescriptions, these can be shockingly expensive.

Infectious Diseases

Most infectious diseases are acquired by mosquito or tick bites or through environmental exposure. The **Centers for Disease Control** (www.cdc.gov) has further details.

Giardiasis Intestinal infection. Avoid drinking directly from lakes, ponds, streams and rivers.

Lyme Disease Occurs mostly in the Northeast. Transmitted by deer ticks in late spring and summer. Perform a tick check after you've been outdoors.

West Nile Virus Mosquito-transmitted in late summer and early fall. Prevent by keeping covered (wear long sleeves, long pants, hats and shoes rather than sandals) and apply a good insect repellent, preferably one containing DEET, to exposed skin and clothing.

Environmental Hazards

Cold exposure This can be a problem, especially in the northern regions. Keep all body surfaces covered, including the head and neck. Watch out for the 'Umbles' – stumbles, mumbles, fumbles and grumbles – which are signs of impending hypothermia.

Heat exhaustion Dehydration is the main contributor. Symptoms include feeling weak, headache, nausea and sweaty skin. Lay the victim flat with their legs raised, apply cool, wet cloths to the skin, and rehydrate.

Insurance

It's expensive to get sick, crash a car or have things stolen from you in the US. Make sure to have adequate coverage before arriving. For car insurance, see p636. For health insurance, see above left. To insure yourself for items that may be stolen from your car, consult your homeowner's (or renter's) insurance policy or consider investing in travel insurance.

Worldwide travel insurance is available at the Insurance section of the **Lonely Planet website** (www.lonelyplanet.com). You can buy, extend and claim online at any time – even if you're already on the road.

Internet Access

» The Eastern USA is wired-up. Nearly every lodging and many restaurants and businesses offer high-speed internet access. This guide uses an @ to indicate a place has a net-connected computer for public use and a 🛜 when it offers wireless internet access, whether free or fee-based.

» Most cafes offer inexpensive internet access.

» Most libraries have public terminals (though they have time limits) and wi-fi. Occasionally out-of-state residents are charged a small fee.

» For a list of wi-fi hotspots (plus tech and access info), visit (www.wi-fi.org) and Wi-Fi Free Spot (www.wififreespot.com).

» If you bring a laptop from outside the USA, invest in a universal AC and plug adapter. Also confirm that your modem card will work.

Legal Matters

In everyday matters, if you are stopped by the police, note that there is no system of paying traffic tickets or other fines on the spot. The patrol officer will explain your options to you; there is usually a 30-day period to pay fines by mail.

If you are arrested, you are allowed to remain silent, though never walk away from an officer; you are entitled to have access to an attorney. The legal system presumes you're innocent until proven guilty. All persons who are arrested have the right to make one phone call. If you don't have a lawyer or family member to help you, call your embassy or consulate. The police will give you the number on request.

Drugs & Alcohol

» In most places it's illegal to walk with an open alcoholic drink on the street. New Orleans and Memphis' Beale St are notable exceptions.

» Being 'carded' (ie asked to show photo ID to prove you're of legal drinking age) is standard practice everywhere.

» Some states, especially in the South, have 'dry' counties where liquor sales are banned altogether.

» In all states, the blood alcohol limit is 0.08%. Driving under the influence of alcohol or drugs is a serious offense, subject to stiff fines and even imprisonment.

» Possession of any illicit drug, including cocaine, ecstasy, LSD, heroin, hashish or more than an ounce of pot, is a felony potentially punishable by lengthy jail sentences.

Money

See p19 for exchange rates and costs.

Most locals do not carry large amounts of cash for everyday use, relying instead on credit cards, debit cards and ATMs. Don't, however, plan to rely exclusively on credit cards, as some machines (notably at many gas stations) won't accept foreign cards. Smaller businesses may refuse to accept bills over $20.

ATMs

» ATMs are available 24/7 at most banks and in shopping centers, airports, grocery stores and convenience shops.

» Most ATMs charge a service fee of $2.50 or more per transaction and your home

bank may impose additional charges.

» For foreign visitors, ask your bank for exact information about using its cards in stateside ATMs. The exchange rate is usually as good as you'll get anywhere.

Credit Cards

Major credit cards are almost universally accepted. In fact, it's next to impossible to rent a car or make phone reservations without one. Visa and MasterCard are the most widely accepted. Contact the issuing company for lost or stolen cards:

American Express (☑800-528-4800; www.american express.com)

MasterCard (☑800-627-8372; www.mastercard.com)

Visa (☑800-847-2911; www.visa.com)

Currency Exchange

» Banks are usually the best places to exchange foreign currencies. Most large city banks offer the service, but banks in rural areas may not.

» Currency-exchange counters at the airport and in tourist centers typically have the worst rates; ask about fees and surcharges first.

» **Travelex** (☑877-414-6359; www.travelex.com) is a major currency-exchange company, but **American Express** (☑800-528-4800; www.ameri canexpress.com) travel offices may offer better rates.

Taxes

» Sales tax varies by state and county; see each state's 'Facts' boxed text in the regional chapters for specifics.

» Hotel taxes vary by city and these are listed under cities' Sleeping sections.

Tipping

Tipping is *not* optional; only withhold tips in cases of outrageously bad service.

Airport skycaps and hotel bellhops $2 per bag, minimum $5 per cart

Bartenders 10% to 15% per round, minimum $1 per drink

Concierges Nothing for simple information, up to $20 for securing last-minute restaurant reservations, sold-out show tickets etc

Housekeeping staff $2 to $4 daily, left under the card provided

Parking valets At least $2 when handed back your car keys

Restaurant staff and room service 15% to 20%, unless a gratuity is already charged on the bill

Taxi drivers 10% to 15% of metered fare, rounded up to the next dollar

Photography

Print film can be found in drugstores and at specialty camera shops. Digital camera memory cards are widely available at chain retailers such as Best Buy and Target.

When photographing people, politeness is usually all that's needed (though street performers appreciate a tip). In Amish communities, photographing farms and buggies is usually OK (ask first), but photographing people is not.

For a primer on taking good shots, consult Lonely Planet's *Travel Photography*.

Post

The **US Postal Service** (USPS; ☑800-275-8777; www.usps.com) is reliable and inexpensive. For 1st-class mail sent and delivered within the USA, postage rates are 44¢ for letters up to 1oz (20¢ for each additional ounce) and 29¢ for standard-size postcards. International airmail rates for postcards and letters up to 1oz are 80¢ to Canada and Mexico and 98¢ to other countries.

Public Holidays

On the following national public holidays, banks, schools and government offices (including post offices) are closed, and transportation, museums and other services operate on a Sunday schedule. Holidays falling on a weekend are usually observed the following Monday.

New Year's Day January 1

Martin Luther King Jr Day Third Monday in January

Presidents' Day Third Monday in February

Easter March or April

Memorial Day Last Monday in May

Independence Day July 4

Labor Day First Monday in September

Columbus Day Second Monday in October

Veterans' Day November 11

Thanksgiving Fourth Thursday in November

Christmas Day December 25

Safe Travel

Hurricane season along the Atlantic seaboard and Gulf of Mexico extends from June through November, but the peak season is late August through October. Relatively speaking, very few storms become East Coast hurricanes, but the devastation they wreak when they do can be enormous. Travelers should take all hurricane

---

GOVERNMENT TRAVEL ADVICE

Australia (www.smart raveller.gov.au)

Canada (www.voyage. gc.ca)

New Zealand (www. safetravel.govt.nz)

UK (www.fco.gov.uk)

---

alerts, warnings and evacuation orders seriously.

Inland in the Midwest and South, tornado season is roughly from March to July. Again, the chances you'll encounter one are slim.

When natural disasters do threaten, listen to radio and TV news reports. For more information on storms and preparedness, contact the **National Weather Service** (www.nws.noaa.gov).

Telephone

The US phone system mixes regional service providers, competing long-distance carriers and several cell-phone companies. Overall, the system is efficient. Calls from a regular landline or cell phone are usually cheaper than a hotel phone or pay phone.

Cell Phones

Most of the USA's mobile-phone systems are incompatible with the GSM 900/1800 standard used throughout Europe and Asia (though some convertible phones will work). G3 phones such as iPhones will work fine – but beware of roaming costs, especially for data. Check with your service provider about using your phone here.

It might be cheaper to buy a prepaid SIM card for the USA, like those sold by AT&T, which you can insert into your international mobile phone to get a local phone number and voicemail. **Planet Omni** (www.planetomni.com) and **Telestial** (www.telestial.com) offer these services, as well as cell-phone rentals.

You can also buy inexpensive, no-contract (pre-paid) phones with a local number and a set number of minutes, which can be topped up at will. Virgin Mobile, T-Mobile, AT&T and other providers offer phones starting at $20, with a package of minutes starting at around $40 for 400 minutes. Electronics store chain **Best Buy**

(www.bestbuy.com) sells these phones, as well as international SIM cards.

Rural swathes of the East, especially in the mountains and various national parklands, don't pick up a signal. Check your provider's coverage map.

Dialing Codes

All phone numbers within the USA consist of a three-digit area code followed by a seven-digit local number. Typically, if you are calling a number within the same area code, you only have to dial the seven-digit number; however, some places now require you to dial the entire 10-digit number even for a local call. If dialing the seven-digit number doesn't work, try all 10.

» Always dial 🗹1 before domestic long-distance numbers and before toll-free numbers (800, 888, 877, 866). Some toll-free numbers only work within the US.

» Dial the international country code for the USA (🎧1) if calling from abroad (the same as Canada, but international rates apply between the two countries).

» To make an international call from the USA, dial 🗹011 followed by the country code, area code and phone number; Canada is the exception, where you just dial 🗹1 plus the area code and number.

» Dial 🗹00 for assistance making international calls.

» Dial 🗹411 for directory assistance nationwide.

» Dial 🗹800-555-1212 for directory assistance for toll-free numbers.

Pay Phones & Phone Cards

» Pay phones are readily found in major cities, but are becoming rarer.

» Local calls cost 50¢.

» Private prepaid phone cards are available from

convenience stores, super-markets and pharmacies.

» AT&T sells a reliable phone card that is widely available in the USA.

Internet Calls

Services such as Skype (www.skype.com) and Google Voice (www.google.com/voice) can make calling, especially internationally, quite cheap. Check the websites for details.

Time

The Eastern region is split between the Eastern and Central time zones, which are an hour apart. The de-marcation line slices through Indiana, Kentucky, Tennessee and Florida. When it's noon Eastern time, it is 11am Central time (and 5pm Greenwich Mean Time).

The region, as well as most of the country, observes Daylight Saving Time (DST). On the second Sunday in March, clocks are set one hour ahead ('spring ahead'). Then, on the first Sunday of November, clocks are turned back one hour ('fall back').

And FYI: the US date sys-tem is written as month/day/year. Thus, the 8th of June, 2008, becomes 6/8/08.

Tourist Information

Visit the federal govern-ment's 'Tour the US' por-tal (www.usa.gov/visitors/travel.shtml), and you'll find links to every Eastern USA state tourism website, plus links to indoor and outdoor recreation, from museums and historical landmarks to scenic byways and national parks.

Most cities and towns have some sort of tourist center that provides local information. The convention and visitor bureau (CVB) or chamber of commerce typically operates it. These

entities tend to list only the businesses that are bureau/chamber members, so not all of the town's hotels and restaurants receive coverage; keep in mind good, indepen-dent options may be missing.

This book provides tour-ism office and visitor-center information throughout the regional chapters. A couple of websites to get you started:

New York State Tourism (www.iloveny.com)

Visit Florida (www.visit florida.com)

Washington, DC (www.washington.org)

Travelers with Disabilities

Travel in the region is rela-tively accommodating. Most public buildings are wheel-chair accessible and have appropriate restroom facili-ties. Transportation services are generally accessible to all, and telephone companies provide relay operators for the hearing impaired. Many banks provide ATM instruc-tions in Braille, curb ramps are common and many busy intersections have audible crossing signals. Most chain hotels have suites for dis-abled guests. Even so, it's best to call ahead to see what's available.

Many national and some state parks and recreation areas have wheelchair-accessible paved, graded dirt or boardwalk trails.

A number of organizations specialize in the needs of disabled travelers:

Access-Able Travel Source (www.access-able.com) General travel website with useful tips and links.

Flying Wheels Travel (☎507-451-5005; http://flyingwheelstravel.com) A full-service travel agency spe-cializing in disabled travel.

Mobility International USA (www.miusa.org) Ad-vises disabled travelers on mobility issues and runs

an educational exchange program.

Travelin' Talk Network (www.travelintalk.net) Run by the same people as Access-Able Travel Source; a global network of service providers.

Wheelchair Getaways (☎800-642-2042; www.wheel chairgetaways.com) Rents accessible vans throughout the USA.

Visas

Admission requirements are subject to rapid change. The US State Department (www.travel.state.gov/visa) has the latest information or check with a US consulate in your home country.

Visa Waiver Program & ESTA

Under the US visa-waiver program, visas are not required for citizens of 36 countries – including most EU members, Japan, Austra-lia, New Zealand and the UK – for visits of up to 90 days (no extensions allowed), as long as you can present a machine-readable passport and are approved under the Electronic System for Travel Authorization (ESTA; www.cbp.gov/esta). Note you must register at least 72 hours before arrival and there's a $14 fee for process-ing and authorization.

In essence, ESTA requires that you register specific information online (name, address, passport info, etc) prior to entering the US. You will receive one of three responses: 'Authorization Approved' (this usually comes within minutes; most applicants can expect to receive this response); 'Authorization Pending,' in which case you can go back online to check the status within roughly 72 hours; or 'Travel not Authorized,' meaning your application is not approved and you will need to apply for a visa.

Once approved, registration is valid for two years, but note that if you renew your passport or change your name, you will need to re-register. The entire process is stored electronically and linked to your passport, but it is recommended that you bring a printout of the ESTA approval just to be safe.

Canadians are exempt from the process. They do not need visas, though they do need a passport or document approved by the **Western Hemisphere Travel Initiative** (www.getyouhome. gov).

Those who need a visa should apply at the US consulate in their home country.

Visiting Canada

It's temptingly easy to make trips across the border to Canada from the Eastern USA, but upon return, non-Americans will be subject to the full immigration procedure. Always take your passport when you cross the border.

Citizens of most Western countries will not need a visa to visit Canada, so it's really not a problem to cross to the Canadian side of Niagara Falls or detour up to Québec. Travelers entering the USA by bus from Canada may be closely scrutinized. For more information, see Border Crossings, p633.

Volunteering

Volunteering opportunities abound in the Eastern USA, providing a memorable chance to interact with locals and the land in ways you never would when just passing through.

Casual, drop-in volunteer work is plentiful in the big cities. Check weekly alternative newspapers for calendar listings or browse the free classified ads online at Craigslist (www.craigslist. org). The public website

Serve.gov (www.serve.gov) and private websites **Idealist.org** (www.idealist.org) and **VolunteerMatch** (www. volunteermatch.org) offer free searchable databases of short- and long-term volunteer opportunities nationwide.

More formal volunteer programs, especially those designed for international travelers, typically charge a fee of $250 to $1000, depending on the length of the program and what amenities are included (eg housing, meals). None cover travel expenses.

Recommended volunteer organizations:

Green Project (☎504-945-0240; www.thegreenproject. org) Working to rebuild New Orleans post-Katrina in sustainable, green ways.

Habitat for Humanity (☎800-422-4828; www.habitat .org) Focuses on building affordable housing for those in need; it does lots of work in the South.

Sierra Club (☎415-977-5500; www.sierraclub.org) 'Volunteer vacations' restore wilderness areas and maintain trails, including in national parks and nature preserves.

Volunteers for Peace (☎802-540-3060; www.vfp. org) Grassroots, multiweek volunteer projects emphasize manual labor and international exchange.

Wilderness Volunteers (☎928-556-0038; www.wilder nessvolunteers.org) Weeklong trips helping maintain national parklands and outdoor recreation areas. Eastern destinations include Minnesota, Vermont, Maine and Arkansas.

World Wide Opportunities on Organic Farms, USA (☎949-715-9500; www. wwoofusa.org) Represents more than 1000 organic farms in all 50 states that host volunteer workers in exchange for meals and accommodation, with

opportunities for both short- and long-term stays.

Women Travelers

Women traveling by themselves or in a group should encounter no particular problems unique to the Eastern USA. Indeed, there are a number of excellent resources to help traveling women.

The community website www.journeywoman.com facilitates women exchanging travel tips, with links to resources. The Canadian government (www.voyage.gc.ca) also publishes the useful, free, downloadable booklet 'Her Own Way'; online, look under 'Publications.'

These two national advocacy groups might also be helpful:

National Organization for Women (NOW; ☎202-628-8669; www.now.org)

Planned Parenthood (☎800-230-7526; www. plannedparenthood.org) Offers referrals to medical clinics throughout the country.

In terms of safety issues, single women need to exhibit the same street smarts as any solo traveler, but they are sometimes more often the target of unwanted attention or harassment.

If you are assaulted, consider calling a rape-crisis hotline before calling the **police** (☎911); telephone books have listings of local rape-crisis centers or contact the 24-hour **National Sexual Assault Hotline** (☎800-656-4673; www. rainn.org). Alternatively, go straight to a hospital emergency room. Police can sometimes be insensitive with assault victims, while a rape-crisis center or hospital will advocate on behalf of survivors and act as a link to other community services, including the police.

Work

Seasonal service jobs in tourist beach towns, theme parks and ski areas are common and often easy to get, if low-paying.

If you are a foreigner in the USA with a standard nonimmigrant visitors visa, you are expressly forbidden to take paid work in the USA and will be deported if you're caught working illegally. In addition, employers are required to establish the bona fides of their employees or face fines. In particular, South Florida is notorious for large numbers of foreigners working illegally, and immigration officers are vigilant.

To work legally, foreigners need to apply for a work visa before leaving home. Student exchange visitors need a J1 visa, which the following organizations will help arrange:

American Institute for Foreign Study (AIFS; ☑866-906-2437; www.aifs.com)

BUNAC (☑020-7251-3472; www.bunac.org)

Camp America (☑020-7581-7373; www.campamerica.co.uk)

Council on International Educational Exchange (CIEE; ☑800-407-8839; www.ciee.org)

InterExchange (☑212-924-0446; www.interexchange.org) Camp and au-pair programs.

International Exchange Programs (IEP) Australia (☑1300-300-912; www.iep.org.au); New Zealand (☑0800-443-769; www.iep.org.nz)

For nonstudent jobs, temporary or permanent, you need to be sponsored by a US employer (who will arrange an H-category visa). These are not easy to obtain.

Transportation

GETTING THERE & AWAY

Flights, tours and rental cars can be booked online at www.lonelyplanet.com/bookings.

Entering the Country

Entering the USA is pretty straightforward:

» If you are flying, the first airport that you land in is where you must go through immigration and customs, even if you are continuing on the flight to another destination.

» If you have a non–US passport, you must complete an arrival/departure record (form I-94) before you reach the immigration desk. It's usually handed out on the plane or train along with the customs declaration.

» The immigration officer will look at your passport and forms and have you register with the Department of Homeland Security's US-VISIT (www.dhs.gov/us-visit) program. For most visitors (excluding, for now, most Canadian and some Mexican citizens), registration consists of having a digital photo and electronic (inkless) fingerprints taken; the process takes less than a minute.

» Once you go through immigration, you collect your baggage and pass through customs. If you have nothing to declare, you'll probably clear customs without a baggage search, but don't assume this.

» For information on visa requirements for visiting the USA, including the Electronic System for Travel Authorization (ESTA) now required before arrival for citizens of Visa Waiver Program (VWP) countries, see p629.

» Remember: your passport should be valid for at least six months longer than your intended stay in the US.

Air

Airports

The main international gateway airports in the Eastern USA:

Atlanta Hartsfield-Jackson International (ATL; www.atlanta-airport.com)

Boston Logan International (BOS; www.massport.com/logan)

Chicago O'Hare International (ORD; www.flychicago.com)

Charlotte Douglas International (CLT; www.charlotteairport.com)

Miami Miami International (MIA; www.miami-airport.com)

Minneapolis-St Paul Minneapolis-St Paul International (MSP; www.mspairport.com)

New York John F Kennedy International (JFK; www.panynj.gov)

CLIMATE CHANGE & TRAVEL

Every form of transport that relies on carbon-based fuel generates CO_2, the main cause of human-induced climate change. Modern travel is dependent on aeroplanes, which might use less fuel per kilometer per person than most cars but travel much greater distances. The altitude at which aircraft emit gases (including CO_2) and particles also contributes to their climate change impact. Many websites offer 'carbon calculators' that allow people to estimate the carbon emissions generated by their journey and, for those who wish to do so, to offset the impact of the greenhouse gases emitted with contributions to portfolios of climate-friendly initiatives throughout the world. Lonely Planet offsets the carbon footprint of all staff and author travel.

Newark Liberty International (EWR; www.panynj.gov)

Orlando Orlando International (MCO; www.orlando airports.net)

Washington, DC Dulles International (IAD; www.metwashairports.com/dulles)

Tickets

Flying midweek (especially Tuesday and Wednesday) is typically less expensive. Also, keep in mind your entire itinerary when booking. Some deals for travel within the USA can only be purchased overseas in conjunction with an international air ticket, or you may get discounts for booking flights and car rental together.

Land

Border Crossings

The Eastern USA has more than 30 border crossings with Canada, accessed via Maine, New Hampshire, Vermont, New York, Michigan and Minnesota. It is relatively easy crossing into Canada; it's crossing *back* that can pose problems if you haven't brought all your documents (see boxed text p634). **US Customs and Border Protection** (http://apps.cbp.gov/bwt) tracks current wait times at the main border crossings. Some borders are open 24 hours, but most are not.

In general, waits rarely exceed 30 minutes, except during peak times (ie weekends and holidays, more so in summer). Some entry points are especially busy:

» Detroit, MI, to Windsor, ON

» Buffalo, NY, to Niagara Falls, ON

» Calais, ME, to St Stephen, NB

As always, have your papers in order, act polite and don't make jokes or casual conversation with US border officials.

GREYHOUND INTERNATIONAL BUS ROUTES & FARES

ROUTE	APPROX FARE ($)	DURATION (HR)	FREQUENCY (PER DAY)
Boston-Montréal	80–120	7–9½	up to 8
Detroit-Toronto	60–90	5–6	up to 5
New York-Montréal	75–105	8–9	up to 2

Bus

Greyhound (www.greyhound.com) and its Canadian equivalent, **Greyhound Canada** (www.greyhound.ca), operate the largest bus network in North America. There are direct connections between main cities in the USA and Canada, but you usually have to transfer to a different bus at the border (where it takes a good hour for all passengers to clear customs and immigration). Most international buses have free wi-fi on board.

Megabus (www.megabus.com) also has international routes (between Toronto and New York City, and Toronto and Philadelphia), and they are often cheaper than Greyhound. Tickets can only be purchased online.

Car & Motorcycle

» To drive across the US–Canadian border, you'll need the vehicle's registration papers, proof of liability insurance and your home driver's license.

» Rental cars can usually be driven across the border either way, but make sure your rental agreement says so in case you are questioned by border officials.

» If your papers are in order, border crossing is usually fast and easy, but occasionally the authorities of either country decide to search a car *thoroughly*.

Train

Amtrak (www.amtrak.com) and **VIA Rail Canada** (www.viarail.ca) run daily services between Montreal and New York (11 hours), and Toronto and New York via Niagara Falls (14 hours total). Customs inspections happen at the border, not upon boarding.

Sea

Several cities on the East Coast are cruise ships hubs, including New York City, Boston, New Orleans and Charleston, SC. Florida's ports harbor the most ships of all, particularly Miami, followed by Port Canaveral and Port Everglades (Fort Lauderdale).

You can also travel to and from the Eastern USA on a freighter. These vessels usually carry between three and 12 passengers and, though considerably less luxurious than cruise ships, give a salty taste of life at sea.

For more information on the ever-changing routes:

Cruise & Freighter Travel Association (www.travltips.com)

Freighter World Cruises (www.freighterworld.com)

GETTING AROUND

Air

Flying is usually more expensive than traveling by bus, train or car, but it's the way to go when you're in a hurry.

Airlines in the Eastern USA

Overall, air travel in the USA is very safe (much safer than

TRAVELING TO CANADA

It's easy to journey across the border to Canada from the Eastern USA and quite common to do so, especially at Niagara Falls. Here are a few things to keep in mind:

» You will have to show your passport. The exception is US citizens at land and sea borders, who have other options besides using a passport, such as an enhanced driver's license or passport card. See the **Western Hemisphere Travel Initiative** (www.getyouhome.gov) for approved identification documents.

» Citizens of the USA, most Western European nations, Australia, New Zealand and Japan do not need a visa to enter Canada for stays of up to 180 days, but some nationalities do. **Citizenship and Immigration Canada** (CIC; www.cic.gc.ca) has the details.

» Upon return to the USA, non-Americans will be subject to the full immigration procedure. For US visa information, see p629.

» For details on sleeping and eating options on the Canadian side of Niagara Falls, see the boxed text, p120.

» For the lowdown on where to go, what to do and all things north of the border, check out Lonely Planet's *Canada* or *Discover Canada* guides.

driving out on the nation's highways). For comprehensive details by carrier, check out **Airsafe.com** (www.airsafe.com).

The main domestic carriers:

AirTran Airways (☎800-247-8726; www.airtran.com) Atlanta-based airline; primarily serves the South, Midwest and eastern US.

American Airlines (☎800-433-7300; www.aa.com) Nationwide service.

Continental Airlines (☎800-523-3273; www.continental.com) Nationwide service.

Delta Air Lines (☎800-221-1212; www.delta.com) Nationwide service.

Frontier Airlines (☎800-432-1359; www.frontierairlines.com) Denver-based airline with nationwide service.

JetBlue Airways (☎800-538-2583; www.jetblue.com) Nonstop connections between eastern and western US cities, plus Florida and New Orleans.

Southwest Airlines (☎800-435-9792; www.southwest.com) Service across the continental USA.

Spirit Airlines (☎800-772-7117; www.spiritair.com) Florida-based airline; serves many US gateway cities.

United Airlines (☎800-864-8331; www.united.com) Nationwide service.

US Airways (☎800-428-4322; www.usairways.com) Nationwide service.

Virgin America (☎877-359-8474; www.virginamerica.com) Flights between East and West Coast cities and Las Vegas.

There are also smaller regional services:

Cape Air (☎866-227-3247; www.flycapeair.com) Flights to several New England destinations, including Cape Cod, Martha's Vineyard and Nantucket; also a popular Florida route between Fort Myers and Key West.

Nantucket Air (☎800-635-8787; www.nantucketairlines.com) Flights from Cape Cod to Nantucket.

New England Airlines (☎800-243-2460; www.block-island.com/nea) Flights to Block Island from Westerly, RI.

Royale Air Service (☎877-359-4753; www.royaleairservice.com) Flights to Rock Harbor in Isle Royale National Park from Houghton County Airport in Michigan's Upper Peninsula.

Air Passes

International travelers who plan on doing a lot of flying might consider buying a North American air pass. Passes are normally available only to non–North American citizens, and they must be purchased in conjunction with an international ticket. Conditions and cost structures can be complicated, but all passes include a certain number of domestic flights (from two to 10) that typically must be used within a 60-day period. Two of the biggest airline networks offering air passes are **Star Alliance** (www.staralliance.com) and **One World** (www.oneworld.com).

Bicycle

Regional bicycle touring is popular. Winding back roads and scenic coastlines make for great itineraries. Many cities (including New York City, Chicago, Minneapolis and Boston) also have designated bike routes. Renting a bicycle is easy throughout the Eastern USA; see destination chapters for details. Other things to keep in mind:

» Cyclists must follow the same rules of the road as vehicles, but don't expect drivers to always respect your right of way.

» Helmets are mandatory for cyclists in some states and towns (though there is no federal law that requires it). It usually applies to children under age 18. The **Bicycle Helmet Safety Institute** (www.bhsi.org/mandator.htm) has a thorough, state-by-state list of local rules.

» The **Better World Club** (☎866-238-1137; www.betterworldclub.com) provides emergency roadside assistance for cyclists. Membership costs $40 per year, plus a $12 enrollment fee, and entitles you to two free pick-ups.

» The **League of American Bicyclists** (www.bikeleague.org) offers general tips, plus lists of local bike clubs and repair shops.

Transportation

If you're bringing your own wheels, check the **International Bicycle Fund** (www.ibike.org) for bike regulations by airline and other advice. Bikes are considered checked luggage on airplanes, but often must be boxed and fees can be high (over $200). Amtrak trains and Greyhound buses will transport bikes within the USA, typically for much less.

Rental

Outfitters renting bicycles exist in most tourist towns; many are listed throughout this book. Rentals typically cost between $20 and $30 per day, including a helmet and lock. Most companies require a credit card security deposit of $200 or so.

Purchase

Buying a bike is easy, as is reselling it before you leave. Specialist bike shops have the best selection and advice for new bikes, but general sporting-goods stores and big-box retailers may have lower prices. Better yet, buy a used bike. To sniff out the best bargains, scour flea markets, garage sales and thrift shops, or browse the free classified ads at **Craigslist** (www.craigslist.org).

Boat

Several ferry services provide efficient, scenic links in the East. Most ferries transport cars, but you must make reservations well in advance. For costs and other details, see the regional chapters. Popular services across the region:

Northeast

Bay State Cruise Company (☎877-783-3779; www.baystatecruises.com) Ferries between Boston and Provincetown.

Block Island Ferry (☎866-783-7996; www.blockislandferry.com) Ferries to Block Island from Narragansett and Newport, RI.

Lake Champlain Ferries (☎802-864-9804; www.ferries.com) Ferries between Burlington, VT, and Port Kent, NY.

Staten Island Ferry (☎718-876-8441; www.siferry.com) Commuter boats between Staten Island and Manhattan, NY.

Steamship Authority (☎508-477-8600; www.steamshipauthority.com) Ferries to Martha's Vineyard and Nantucket from Cape Cod, MA.

Great Lakes

To reach Mackinac Island, MI, three passenger ferry companies – **Arnold Line** (☎800-542-8528; www.arnoldline.com), **Shepler's** (☎800-828-6157; www.sheplersferry.com) and **Star Line** (☎800-638-9892; www.mackinacferry.com) – operate out of both Mackinaw City and St Ignace, MI.

Lake Express (www.lake-express.com) Crosses Lake Michigan between Milwaukee, WI, and Muskegon, MI.

SS Badger (www.ssbadger.com) Crosses Lake Michigan between Manitowoc, WI, and Ludington, MI.

South

North Carolina Ferry System (☎800-293-3779; www.outer-banks.com/ferry) Ferries throughout the Outer Banks.

Bus

Greyhound (☎800-231-2222; www.greyhound.com) is the major long-distance carrier, plowing along an extensive network throughout the USA, as well as to/from Canada. As a rule, buses are reliable, cleanish and comfortable, with air-conditioning, barely reclining seats, onboard lavatories and a no-smoking policy. Several buses have wi-fi. While some shorter-route buses run express, most stop every 50 to 100 miles to pick up passengers, and long-distance buses stop for meal breaks and driver changes.

Other carriers:

Bolt Bus (☎877-265-8287; www.boltbus.com) Fast, cheap routes between major northeast cities, including NYC, Boston, Philadelphia, Baltimore, Newark and Washington, DC; wi-fi on board.

Megabus (☎877-462-6342; www.megabus.com) Bolt Bus' main competitor, with routes between main cities in the Northeast and also the Midwest, radiating from hubs in NYC or Chicago. Fares can be quite low; tickets booked online only.

Peter Pan Buslines (☎800-343-9999; www.peterpanbus.com) Serves 54 destinations in the northeast, as far north as Concord, NH, and as far south as Washington, DC.

Trailways (☎703-691-3052; www.trailways.com) Mostly in the Midwest and Mid-Atlantic states; may not be as useful as Greyhound for long trips, but fares can be competitive on shorter routes.

Bus Passes

Greyhound's **Discovery Pass** (www.discoverypass.com), which is available to both domestic and international travelers, allows unlimited, unrestricted travel for periods of seven ($246), 15 ($356), 30 ($456) or 60 ($556) consecutive days in both the USA and Canada. You can buy passes at select Greyhound terminals up to two hours before departure, or purchase them online at least 14 days in advance.

Costs

» In general, the earlier you book, the lower the fare.

» On Bolt Bus and Megabus, the first tickets sold for a route cost $1.

» For lower fares on Greyhound, purchase tickets at least seven days in advance (purchasing 14 days in advance will save even more).

» If you're traveling with family or friends, Greyhound's companion fares let up to three additional travelers get 50% off with a minimum three-day advance purchase.

Reservations

Greyhound and Bolt Bus tickets can be bought over the phone or online, as well as at terminals. Megabus tickets can only be purchased online in advance. Seating is normally first-come, first-served. Greyhound recommends arriving an hour before departure to get a seat.

Car & Motorcycle

For maximum flexibility and convenience, and to explore outside of the cities, a car is essential.

Automobile Associations

» The **American Automobile Association** (AAA; ☎800-874-7532; www.aaa.com) has reciprocal membership agreements with several international auto clubs

GREYHOUND DOMESTIC BUS ROUTES & FARES

ROUTE	APPROX FARE ($)	DURATION (HR)	FREQUENCY (PER DAY)
Boston-Philadelphia	30-55	7-10	9
Chicago-New Orleans	120-155	25½-27	3
New York-Chicago	85-125	18-22½	5
Washington, DC-Miami	135-170	27-29	5

(check with AAA and bring your membership card from home). For its members, AAA offers travel insurance, tour books, diagnostic centers for used-car buyers and a wide-ranging network of regional offices. AAA advocates politically for the auto industry.

» A more ecofriendly alternative, the **Better World Club** (☎866-238-1137; www.betterworldclub.com) donates 1% of revenue to assist environmental cleanup, offers ecologically sensitive choices for every service it provides and advocates politically for environmental causes.

» In either organization, the primary member benefit is 24-hour emergency roadside assistance anywhere in the USA. Both also offer trip planning, free travel maps, travel agency services, car insurance and a range of travel discounts (eg on hotels, car rentals and attractions).

Bring Your Own Vehicle

For details on driving your own car over the border, see p633. Unless you're moving to the USA, don't even think about freighting your car.

Driver's License

Foreign visitors can legally drive a car in the USA for up to 12 months using their home driver's license. However, an International Driving Permit (IDP) will have more credibility with US traffic police, especially if your home license doesn't have a photo or isn't in English. Your automobile association at home can issue an IDP, valid for one year, for a small fee. Always carry your home license together with the IDP.

To drive a motorcycle in the USA, you will need either a valid US state motorcycle license or an IDP specially endorsed for motorcycles.

Fuel

Gas stations are ubiquitous and many are open 24 hours a day. Small-town stations may be open only from 7am to 8pm or 9pm. Plan on spending roughly $3 to $4 per US gallon. At many stations, you must pay before you pump.

Insurance

Insurance is legally required. Without it, you risk legal consequences and possible financial ruin if there's an accident.

» Car-rental agencies offer liability insurance, which covers other people and property involved in an accident.

» Collision Damage Waivers (CDW) reduce or eliminate the amount you'll have to reimburse the rental company if there's damage to the car itself.

» Paying extra for all of this insurance increases the cost of a rental car by as much as $10 to $30 a day.

» Some credit cards cover CDW for a certain rental

period (usually less than 15 days), if you use the card to pay for the rental, and decline the policy offered by the rental company. Always check with your card issuer to see what coverage they offer in the USA.

Rental

CAR

To rent a car in the USA you generally need to be at least 25 years old, hold a valid driver's license (see p636) and have a major credit card.

Some companies will rent to drivers between the ages of 21 and 24 for an additional charge.

You should be able to get an economy-sized vehicle for about $30 to $75 per day. Child safety seats are compulsory (reserve them when you book) and cost about $12 per day.

Some national companies, including Avis, Budget and Hertz, offer 'green' fleets of hybrid rental cars (eg Toyota Priuses, Honda Civics), although you'll usually have to pay a lot extra to rent a more fuel-efficient vehicle.

Good independent agencies are listed in this guide. Online, Car Rental Express (www.carrentalexpress.com) rates and compares independent agencies in US cities; it's particularly useful for searching out cheaper long-term rentals.

Major national car-rental companies:

Alamo (☏877-222-9075; www.alamo.com)

Avis (☏800-230-4898; www.avis.com)

Budget (☏800-527-0700; www.budget.com)

Dollar (☏800-800-3665; www.dollar.com)

Enterprise (☏800-261-7331; www.enterprise.com)

Hertz (☏800-654-3131; www.hertz.com)

National (☏877-222-9058; www.nationalcar.com)

Rent-a-Wreck (☏877-877-0700; www.rentawreck.com)

ROAD DISTANCES (MILES)

	Atlanta	Boston	Chicago	New Orleans	New York City	Orlando	Philadelphia	Savannah
Boston	1110							
Chicago	720	985						
New Orleans	470	1530	930					
New York City	915	215	790	1370				
Orlando	440	1320	1160	650	1110			
Philadelphia	800	310	760	1230	95	995		
Savannah	250	1040	960	630	830	280	730	
Washington, DC	685	440	700	1140	230	880	140	600

Thrifty (☏800-847-4389; www.thrifty.com)

MOTORCYCLE & RECREATIONAL VEHICLE (RV)

If you dream of riding a Harley, **EagleRider** (☏888-900-9901; www.eaglerider.com) has offices in major cities nationwide and rents other kinds of adventure vehicles, too. Beware that motorcycle rental and insurance are expensive.

Companies specializing in RV and camper rentals:

Adventures on Wheels (☏866-787-3682; www.wheels9.com)

Cruise America (☏800-671-8042; www.cruiseamerica.com)

Recreational Vehicle Rental Association (www.rvra.org) Good resource for RV information and advice, and helps find rental locations.

Road Conditions & Hazards

Road conditions are generally very good, but keep in mind:

» Winter travel in general can be hazardous due to heavy snow and ice, which may cause roads and bridges to close periodically. The **Federal Highway Administration** (www.fhwa.dot.gov/trafficinfo/index.htm) provides links to road conditions and construction zones for each state.

» If you're driving in winter or in remote areas, make sure your vehicle is equipped with four-seasonal radial or snow tires, and emergency supplies in case you're stranded.

» Where deer and other wild animals frequently appear roadside, you'll see signs with the silhouette of a leaping deer. Take these signs seriously, particularly at night.

Road Rules

If you're new to US roads, here are some basics:

» Drive on the right-hand side of the road. On highways, pass in the left-hand lane.

» The maximum speed limit on most interstates is 65mph or 70mph; a couple of Eastern states go up to 75mph. It then drops to around 55mph in urban areas. Pay attention to the posted signs. City street speed limits vary between 15mph and 45mph.

» The use of seat belts and child safety seats is required in every state. In some states, motorcyclists are required to wear helmets.

» Unless signs prohibit it, you may turn right at a red light after first coming to a full stop (note that NYC is an exception, where it's illegal to turn right on a red).

» At four-way stop signs, the car that reaches the intersection first has right of way. In a tie, the car on the right has right of way.

» When emergency vehicles (ie police, fire or ambulance) approach from either direction, pull over safely and get out of the way.

» In an increasing number of states, it is illegal to talk on a handheld cell phone while driving; use a hands-free device or pull over to take your call.

» The blood-alcohol limit for drivers is 0.08%. Penalties are very severe for 'DUI' – driving under the influence of alcohol and/or drugs.

» In some states it is illegal to carry 'open containers' of alcohol in a vehicle, even if they are empty.

Hitchhiking

Hitchhiking in the USA is potentially dangerous and definitely not recommended. Indeed, drivers have heard so many lurid reports they tend to be just as afraid of those with their thumbs out. Hitchhiking on freeways is prohibited.

Local Transportation

Except in large cities, public transportation is rarely the most convenient option for travelers. However, it is usually cheap, safe and reliable. For fares and other details, see Getting Around sections under city and town listings throughout this book. In addition, more than half the states in the nation have adopted ☎511 as an all-purpose local-transportation help line.

Bicycle

Some cities are more amenable to bicycles than others, but most have at least a few dedicated bike lanes and paths, and bikes can usually be carried on public transportation. See p634 for more on bicycling in the region, including rentals.

Bus

Most cities and larger towns have dependable local bus systems, though they are often designed for commuters and provide limited service in the evening and on weekends. Costs range from free to between $1 and $3 per ride.

Subway & Train

The largest systems are in New York, Chicago, Boston, Philadelphia, Washington, DC, and Chicago. Other cities may have small, one- or two-line rail systems that mainly serve downtown.

Taxi

Taxis are metered, with flagfall charges of around $2.50, plus $1.50 to $2 per mile. They charge extra for waiting and handling baggage, and drivers expect a 10% to 15% tip. Taxis cruise the busiest areas in large cities; otherwise, it's easiest to phone and order one.

Tours

Hundreds of companies offer all kinds of organized tours of the USA; most focus on either cities or regions. See Tours in the city sections throughout this book for more recommendations.

Reputable tour companies:

American Holidays (☎01-673-3840; www.americanholidays.com) Ireland-based company specializes in tours to North America.

Backroads (☎510-527-1555, 800-462-2848; www.backroads.com) Designs a range of active, multisport and outdoor-oriented trips for all abilities and ages.

Contiki (☎866-266-8454; www.contiki.com) Party-hardy sightseeing tour-bus vacations for 18- to 35-year-olds.

Gray Line (☎800-966-8125; www.grayline.com) For those short on time, Gray Line offers a comprehensive range of standard sightseeing tours across the country.

Green Tortoise (☎415-956-7500, 800-867-8647; www.greentortoise.com) Offering budget adventures for independent travelers, Green Tortoise is famous for its sleeping-bunk buses. Most trips traipse around the West, though there are cross-country tours that cover destinations throughout the East.

North America Travel Service (☎020-7569-6710; www.northamericatravelservice.co.uk) UK-based tour operator arranges luxury US trips.

Road Scholar (☎800-454-5768; www.roadscholar.org) For those aged 55 and older, this venerable nonprofit offers 'learning adventures' in all 50 states.

Trek America (☎in North America 800-873-5872, in the UK 0844-576-1400; www.trekamerica.com) For active outdoor adventurers aged 18 to 38; group sizes are kept small.

Train

Amtrak (☎800-872-7245; www.amtrak.com) has an extensive rail system throughout the USA, with several long-distance lines traversing the nation east to west, and even more running north to south. These link all of America's biggest cities and many of its smaller ones. In some places, Amtrak's Thruway buses provide connections to and from the rail network.

» Compared with other modes of travel, trains are rarely the quickest, cheapest or most convenient option, but they turn the journey into a relaxing, social and scenic all-American experience.

» Rail services are busiest in the northeast corridor, where high-speed Acela Express trains run from Boston, MA, to Washington, DC (via New York City, Philadelphia and Baltimore).

» Other busy routes include NYC to Niagara Falls, Chicago to Milwaukee and Chicago to St Louis.

» Free wi-fi is not available on trains, except the Acela Express.

» Smoking is prohibited on all trains.

» Many big cities, such as NYC, Chicago and Miami, also have their own commuter rail networks. These trains provide faster, more frequent services on shorter routes.

Classes

» Coach Class buys you a basic, if indeed quite comfortable, reclining seat with a headrest. On some routes you can reserve seats.

» Business Class is available on many trains, especially on shorter routes in the northeast. Seats are more spacious and have outlets for plugging in laptops. You also get reserved seating and access to quiet cars (no cell phones etc).

» First Class is available on Acela Express trains only, and adds an at-seat meal to the mix.

» Sleeper Class is available on overnight routes. Sleeping cars include simple bunks (called 'roomettes'), bedrooms with en-suite facilities and suites sleeping four with two bathrooms. Sleeping-car rates include meals in the dining car, which offers everyone sit-down meal service (pricey if not included).

AMTRAK SAMPLE FARES

ROUTE	ONE-WAY FARE ($)	DURATION (HR)	FREQUENCY (PER DAY)
Chicago-New Orleans	115	19½	1
New York-Chicago	120	20½	1
Washington, DC-Miami	163	24	2
Boston-New York	68	3½-4	11-19

» Food service on commuter lines, when it exists, consists of sandwich and snack bars. Also bringing your own food and drink is recommended on all trains.

Costs

Various one-way, round-trip and touring fares are available from Amtrak, with the usual discounts available to seniors (15%), students ($20 or so) and children (50% when accompanied by a paying adult). AAA members get 10% off. Web-only 'Weekly Specials' offer good discounts on certain under-sold routes.

Generally, the earlier you book, the lower the price. To get many of the standard discounts, you need to reserve at least three days in advance.

Amtrak Vacations (☎800-268-7252; www.amtrak vacations.com) offers vacation packages that include rental cars, hotels, tours and attractions. Air and Rail packages let you travel by train in one direction, then return by plane in the other.

Reservations

Reservations can be made any time from 11 months in advance up to the day of departure. Space on many trains is limited, and certain routes can be crowded, especially during summer and holiday periods, so it's a good idea to book as far in advance as you can; this also gives you the best chance of fare discounts.

Train Passes

» Amtrak's USA Rail Pass offers coach-class travel for 15 ($389), 30 ($579) or 45 ($749) days, with travel limited to eight, 12 or 18 one-way 'segments,' respectively.

» A segment is not the same as a one-way trip. If reaching your destination requires riding more than one train (for example, getting from New York to Miami with a transfer in Washington, DC) that one-way trip will actually use two segments of your pass.

» Reservations should be made by phone (call ☎800-872-7245 or ☎215-856-7953 from outside the USA) as far in advance as possible. Each segment of the journey must be booked.

» Present your pass at an Amtrak office to pick up your ticket(s) for each trip.

» All travel must be completed within 180 days of purchasing your pass.

» Passes are not valid on the Acela Express, Auto Train, Thruway motorcoach connections or the Canadian portion of Amtrak routes operated jointly with Via Rail Canada.

behind the scenes

SEND US YOUR FEEDBACK

We love to hear from travelers – your comments keep us on our toes and help make our books better. Our well-traveled team reads every word on what you loved or loathed about this book. Although we cannot reply individually to postal submissions, we always guarantee that your feedback goes straight to the appropriate authors, in time for the next edition. Each person who sends us information is thanked in the next edition – and the most useful submissions are rewarded with a free book.

Visit **lonelyplanet.com/contact** to submit your updates and suggestions or to ask for help. Our award-winning website also features inspirational travel stories, news and discussions.

Note: We may edit, reproduce and incorporate your comments in Lonely Planet products such as guidebooks, websites and digital products, so let us know if you don't want your comments reproduced or your name acknowledged. For a copy of our privacy policy visit lonelyplanet.com/privacy.

AUTHOR THANKS

Karla Zimmerman

Many thanks to Denis Agar, Lisa Beran, Marie Bradshaw, Sarah Chandler, Sasha Chang, Lisa DiChiera, Jim DuFresne, Ruggero Fatica, Jill Hurwitz, Joe Kelley, Julie Lange, Katie Law, Kari Lydersen, the McCabe clan, Amanda Powell, Kristin Reither, Betsy Riley, Tamara B Robinson, Jim and Susan Stephan, and the Chicago and Cleveland CVBs. Thanks most to Eric Markowitz, the world's best partner-for-life, who indulges all my hare-brained, pie-filled road trips.

Jeff Campbell

First, Regis and Suki, you made this easy. For their Florida tips, thanks to Anne Higgins, Ali DeLargy, Kathleen Ogle, Michelle Kratochvil (and Judi!), Ed in St Pete, and Bruce in Tampa. To Darby's own, James, Karen and son William: thanks for your companionship to Cayo Costa and great advice. As always, endless thanks to my children, Jackson and Miranda, and my wife, Deanna, for all their love and support, and for not minding my tan.

Ned Friary & Glenda Bendure

We'd like to thank everyone who shared their tips with us and chimed in on their favorite spots, especially Gretchen Grozier, Bob Prescott, Steve Howance, Julie Lipkin, Ken Merrill, Bill O'Neill and Bryan Lantz. And of course thanks to the many travelers we met along the way.

Michael Grosberg

To Rebecca Tessler who is always in my heart. Special thanks to Carly Neidorf for her presence and support, on the road and off, and her navigational abilities. Radie Kaighin-Shields and Annie Humphrey for help on Pittsburgh; to Caitlin Larussa and Olwyn Conway for West Philly tips and my parents for their Philly suggestions; and to all my NYC friends who joined me for research meals and drinks.

Emily Matchar

Thanks to Suki Gear and the rest of the Lonely Planet team. Thanks to Kerry Crawford for sharing her copious Memphis knowledge, to Julie Montgomery for her spot-on Charleston recommendations, to Meg, Maggie, Daniel and every other friend and/or fellow Twitterer for their excellent steers. Special thanks to Leslie Jamison for helping me brave Memphis discos at midnight, and to Jamin Asay, my partner in travel and in life, for his tireless map-reading and, well, everything else.

Kevin Raub

Special thanks to my wife, Adriana Schmidt Raub, whose second opinion in Georgia and New Orleans proved invaluable. Along the way, Jason and Jennifer Hatfield, Dave and Aynsley Corbett, Jeff Fenn, Adam Skolnick, Tracy and Jeff Knapp, Fran Raub, Americas Coffee Shop in Lafayette, Leah Simon, JR and Pam Rivera, Shack Up Inn, Liz Carroll, Marika Cackett, Heidi Flynn Barnett, Vickie Ashford, Rachel Rosenberg, Kelly Norris, Wendy James, Erica Backus, Jason and Bianca Raub, Tom McDermott and Grace Wilson.

Regis St Louis

Thanks go to Suki and my co-authors who did such a stellar job bringing America to life. Thanks to Eve and friends for top tips in Washington and to the Krishna friends at New Vrindaban for a magical visit. Big hugs to Cassandra, Magdalena and Genevieve

for joining on the southern road trip. Lastly, thank you the Kaufman gang for letting us join in the Wrightsville Beach holiday.

ACKNOWLEDGMENTS

Climate map data adapted from Peel MC, Finlayson BL & McMahon TA (2007) 'Updated World Map of the Köppen-Geiger Climate Classification', Hydrology and Earth System Sciences, 11, 163344.ddd. Photograph p8, top: Crown Fountain © Jaume Plensa. Cover photograph: Lincoln Memorial, Washington, DC; Dennis Johnson/LPI. Many of the images in this guide are available for licensing from Lonely Planet Images: www.lonelyplanet images.com.

BEHIND THE SCENES

THIS BOOK

This 1st edition of Eastern USA was written by Karla Zimmerman. The content was researched and written by Karla, along with Glenda Bendure, Jeff Campbell, Ned Friary, Michael Grosberg, Emily Matchar, Kevin Raub and Regis St Louis. This guidebook was commissioned in Lonely Planet's Oakland office, and produced by the following:
Commissioning Editor
Jennye Garibaldi

Coordinating Editors Pete Cruttenden, Alison Ridgway
Coordinating Cartographer Mark Griffiths
Coordinating Layout Designer Lauren Egan
Managing Editors Anna Metcalfe, Martine Power, Angela Tinson
Managing Cartographer Alison Lyall
Managing Layout Designers Chris Girdler, Jane Hart

Assisting Editors Paul Harding, Alan Murphy, Saralinda Turner
Assisting Layout Designers Frank Deim, Jacqui Saunders
Cover Research Naomi Parker
Internal Image Research Sabrina Dalbesio
Thanks to Ryan Evans, Justin Flynn, Gina Tsarouhas

NOTES

644

index

000 Map pages
000 Photo pages

how to use this book

These symbols will help you find the listings you want:

◉	Sights	☞	Tours	🍷	Drinking
🏄	Beaches	✸	Festivals & Events	☆	Entertainment
🏃	Activities	🛏	Sleeping	🔒	Shopping
🎓	Courses	✗	Eating	ℹ	Information/Transport

These symbols give you the vital information for each listing:

☏	Telephone Numbers	🔊	Wi-Fi Access	🚍	Bus
⊙	Opening Hours	🏊	Swimming Pool	⛴	Ferry
Ⓟ	Parking	🥗	Vegetarian Selection	Ⓜ	Metro
⊖	Nonsmoking	🗺	English-Language Menu	Ⓢ	Subway
✳	Air-Conditioning	👪	Family-Friendly	🚊	Tram
@	Internet Access	🐾	Pet-Friendly	🚆	Train

Reviews are organised by author preference.

Look out for these icons:

TOP CHOICE	Our author's recommendation
FREE	No payment required
🌿	A green or sustainable option

Our authors have nominated these places as demonstrating a strong commitment to sustainability – for example by supporting local communities and producers, operating in an environmentally friendly way, or supporting conservation projects.

Map Legend

Sights
- 🏖 Beach
- 🕌 Buddhist
- 🏰 Castle
- ✝ Christian
- 🕉 Hindu
- ☪ Islamic
- ✡ Jewish
- ⬥ Monument
- 🏛 Museum/Gallery
- 🏚 Ruin
- 🍇 Winery/Vineyard
- 🐾 Zoo
- ⊙ Other Sight

Activities, Courses & Tours
- 🤿 Diving/Snorkelling
- 🛶 Canoeing/Kayaking
- ⛷ Skiing
- 🏄 Surfing
- 🏊 Swimming/Pool
- 🚶 Walking
- 🏄 Windsurfing
- ⊕ Other Activity/Course/Tour

Sleeping
- 🛏 Sleeping
- ⛺ Camping

Drinking
- ☕ Drinking
- ☕ Cafe

Entertainment
- 🎭 Entertainment

Shopping
- 🔒 Shopping

Information
- ✉ Post Office
- ℹ Tourist Information

Transport
- ✈ Airport
- ⊗ Border Crossing
- 🚍 Bus
- ⊕⊶ Cable Car/Funicular
- 🚲 Cycling
- ⛴ Ferry
- 🚝 Monorail
- Ⓟ Parking
- Ⓢ Subway
- 🚕 Taxi
- 🚆 Train/Railway
- 🚊 Tram
- ⊖ Tube Station
- Ⓤ U-Bahn
- Ⓜ Underground Train Station/Muni & BART
- • Other Transport

Routes
- ▨ Tollway
- ▨ Freeway
- ▨ Primary
- ▨ Secondary
- ── Tertiary
- ── Lane
- ── Unsealed Road
- ▨ Plaza/Mall
- ▥ Steps
- ⫽ Tunnel
- ── Pedestrian Overpass
- ▨ Walking Tour
- ▨ Walking Tour Detour
- ── Path

Boundaries
- ─── International
- ─── State/Province
- ─── Disputed
- ─── Regional/Suburb
- ── Marine Park
- ⌐ Cliff
- ── Wall

Population
- ⊙ Capital (National)
- ⊙ Capital (State/Province)
- ⊙ City/Large Town
- ⊙ Town/Village

Geographic
- 🛖 Hut/Shelter
- 🗼 Lighthouse
- 👁 Lookout
- ▲ Mountain/Volcano
- ❂ Oasis
- ❂ Park
-)(Pass
- ☂ Picnic Area
- 💧 Waterfall

Hydrography
- ～ River/Creek
- ～ Intermittent River
- Swamp/Mangrove
- Reef
- ～ Canal
- Water
- Dry/Salt/Intermittent Lake
- Glacier

Areas
- Beach/Desert
- + + + Cemetery (Christian)
- × × × Cemetery (Other)
- Park/Forest
- Sportsground
- Sight (Building)
- Top Sight (Building)

Michael Grosberg

New York, New Jersey & Pennsylvania Growing up Michael spent family holidays crisscrossing New York, New Jersey & Pennsylvania, and with his large New York City family he grew to know their neighborhoods as if they were his own. After several long overseas trips and many careers, some abroad, Michael returned to New York City for graduate school and then taught literature in NYC colleges. He's lived in three of the five boroughs and takes every opportunity to hit the road and explore these diverse states.

Emily Matchar

The South A native Tarheel, Emily lives and works in Chapel Hill, North Carolina (when she's not bopping around the globe, that is). Though she doesn't have a Southern accent, she does know how to smoke a hog, hotwire a pickup truck and bake a mean coconut cake. She writes about culture, food and travel for a variety of national magazines and newspapers, and has contributed to a dozen Lonely Planet guides.

Kevin Raub

The South Though Indiana born, Kevin Raub grew up in Atlanta and started his career as a music journalist in New York, working for *Men's Journal* and *Rolling Stone* magazines. The rock 'n' roll lifestyle took its toll, so he needed an extended vacation and took up travel writing while ditching the States for Brazil. This homecoming, covering Georgia, Alabama, Mississippi, Arkansas and Louisiana, only reaffirmed a bumper sticker he has contemplated for years: 'Hoosier by Birth, Southern by the Grace of God'! You can find Kevin at www.kevinraub.net.

Regis St Louis

Washington, DC & the Capital Region A Hoosier by birth, Regis grew up in a sleepy riverside town where he dreamed of big-city intrigue. In 2001 he settled in New York, which had all that and more. He has also lived in San Francisco and Los Angeles and has crossed the country by train, bus and car while visiting remote corners of America. Favorite memories from his most recent trip include chasing the bluegrass scene across southern Virginia, chanting with Krishna devotees in West Virginia and crab feasting all over Maryland. Regis has contributed to more than 30 Lonely Planet titles, including *Washington, DC* and *New York City*.

OUR STORY

A beat-up old car, a few dollars in the pocket and a sense of adventure. In 1972 that's all Tony and Maureen Wheeler needed for the trip of a lifetime – across Europe and Asia overland to Australia. It took several months, and at the end – broke but inspired – they sat at their kitchen table writing and stapling together their first travel guide, *Across Asia on the Cheap*. Within a week they'd sold 1500 copies. Lonely Planet was born.

Today, Lonely Planet has offices in Melbourne, London and Oakland, with more than 600 staff and writers. We share Tony's belief that 'a great guidebook should do three things: inform, educate and amuse'.

OUR WRITERS

Karla Zimmerman

Coordinating Author, Great Lakes Karla has always lived east of the Mississippi River, where the ballparks, breweries and pie shops reign supreme. When she's not home in Chicago watching the Cubs – er, writing for magazines, books and websites – she's out exploring. For this gig, she curled in Minnesota, caught a wave in Michigan, heard the curds squeak in Wisconsin and drank an embarrassing number of milkshakes in Ohio. Karla has written for several Lonely Planet guidebooks covering the USA, Canada, Caribbean and Europe. She blogs about her travels at www.mykindoftownandaround.blogspot.com.

Jeff Campbell

Florida Jeff Campbell is the great-grandson of Florida pioneers who cleared the pines, mined the phosphate and paved the roads in central Florida. As a child, he remembers searching for alligators in the local lake, and riding Space Mountain the year it opened. As an adult, he's been a travel writer for Lonely Planet since 2000. He was the coordinating author of *Florida*, as well as three editions of *USA*, among other US titles.

Ned Friary & Glenda Bendure

New England Ned and Glenda hail from Cape Cod, their home since the 1980s. Ocean swims, long bike rides and road trips around New England are favorite pastimes. The highlight of their latest trip was a climb to the summit of Acadia Mountain in Acadia National Park, where the jaw-dropping views reminded them just how wildly diverse New England is. They've written extensively on the region and are co-authors of Lonely Planet's *New England* and *Discover USA's Best National Parks* guides.

> OVER PAGE | MORE WRITERS

Published by Lonely Planet Publications Pty Ltd
ABN 36 005 607 983
1st edition – April 2012
ISBN 978 1 74220 592 2
© Lonely Planet 2012 Photographs © as indicated 2012
10 9 8 7 6 5 4 3 2 1
Printed in Singapore